Tom Wolfe

TWO COMPLETE BOOKS

THE BONFIRE OF THE VANITIES

THE RIGHT STUFF

WINGS BOOKS
New York • Avenel, New Jersey

This omnibus was originally published by Farrar, Straus and Giroux, Inc. in
separate volumes under the titles:

The Bonfire of the Vanities, copyright © 1987 by Tom Wolfe
The Right Stuff, copyright © 1979, 1983 by Tom Wolfe

A four-part article on the astronauts by Tom Wolfe appeared in *Rolling Stone*,
copyright © 1973 by Tom Wolfe.

This edition contains the complete and unabridged texts of the original
editions. They have been completely reset for this volume.

This 1994 edition is published by Wings Books,
distributed by Random House Value Publishing, Inc.,
40 Engelhard Avenue, Avenel, New Jersey 07001,
by arrangement with Farrar, Straus and Giroux, Inc.

Random House
New York • Toronto • London • Sydney • Auckland

Printed and bound in the United States of America

Library of Congress Cataloging-in-Publication Data

Wolfe, Tom.
    Two complete books : The bonfire of the vanities ; The right stuff / Tom
Wolfe.
      p.   cm.
    ISBN 0-517-11998-6
    1. City and town life—New York (N.Y.)—Fiction.   2. Traffic accidents—
New York (N.Y.)—Fiction.   3. Bankers—New York (N.Y.)—Fiction.
4. Astronautics—United States.   5. Astronauts—United States.   I. Title.
II. Title: Bonfire of the vanities. III. Title: Right stuff.
PS3573.0526A6   1994
813'.54—dc20
                                   94-11788
                                      CIP

8   7   6   5   4   3   2   1

CONTENTS

═══

THE BONFIRE
OF
THE VANITIES

THE
RIGHT STUFF

shows how a scientific program was exploited for political advantage; it provides a revealing character study of seven exceptional Americans."

—*Saturday Review*

"ROMANTIC AND THRILLING . . . One of the most romantic and thrilling books ever written about men who put themselves in peril."

—*Boston Globe*

"CRAMMED with inside poop and racy incident . . . fast cars, booze, astro groupies, the envies and injuries of the military caste system . . . Wolfe lays it all out in brilliantly staged Op Lit scenes."

—*Time*

"IT GIVES YOU the scary feeling that the man's done the impossible. He—Yes! —understands America!"

—*Houston Chronicle*

"IMPROBABLE as some of Tom's tales seem, I know he's telling it like it was."

—*Former astronaut Michael Collins*

Tom Wolfe

TWO COMPLETE BOOKS

THE BONFIRE
OF
THE VANITIES

Grateful acknowledgment is made of the daring of **JANN WENNER**, who published an early version of this book serially, chapter by chapter, as it was being written, without a safety net, in **ROLLING STONE** magazine

Doffing his hat,

the author dedicates this book to

COUNSELOR EDDIE HAYES

who walked among the flames,

pointing at the lurid lights.

And he wishes to express

his deep appreciation to

BURT ROBERTS

who first showed the way

CONTENTS

THE BONFIRE
OF
THE VANITIES

Prologue
===

MUTT ON FIRE

"And then say what? Say, 'Forget you're hungry, forget you got shot inna back by some racist cop—Chuck was here? Chuck come up to Harlem—' "

"No, I'll *tell* you what—"

" 'Chuck come up to Harlem and—' "

"I'll *tell* you what—"

"Say, 'Chuck come up to Harlem and gonna take care a business for the black community'?"

That does it.

Heh-heggggggggggggggggggggghhhhhhhhhhhhhhh!

It's one of those ungodly contralto cackles somewhere out there in the audience. It's a sound from down so deep, from under so many lavish layers, he knows exactly what she must look like. Two hundred pounds, if she's an ounce! Built like an oil burner! The cackle sets off the men. They erupt with those belly sounds he hates so much.

They go, "Hehhehheh . . . *unnnmhhhh-hunhhh* . . . *That's right* . . . *Tell 'im, bro . . . Yo . . ."*

Chuck! The insolent—he's right there, right there in the front—he just called him a Charlie! Chuck is short for Charlie, and Charlie is the old code name for a down-home white bigot. The insolence of it! The impudence! The heat and glare are terrific. It makes the Mayor squint. It's the TV lights. He's inside a blinding haze. He can barely make out the heckler's face. He sees a tall silhouette and the fantastic bony angles the man's elbows make when he throws his hands up in the air. And an earring. The man has a big gold earring in one ear.

The Mayor leans into the microphone and says, "No, I'll *tell* you what. Okay? I'll give you the actual figures. Okay?"

"We don't want your figures, man!"

Man, he says! The insolence! "You brought it up, my friend. So you're gonna get the actual figures. *Okay?*"

"Don't you shine us up with no more your figures!"

Another eruption in the crowd, louder this time: *"Unnnnhunnnnh-unnnh
. . . Tell 'im, bro . . . Y'on the case . . . Yo, Gober!"*

"In this administration—and it's a matter of public record—the percentage of
the total annual budget for New York City—"

"Aw, maaaan," yells the heckler, "don't you stand there and shine us up with
no more your figures and your bureaucratic rhetoric!"

They love it. The insolence! The insolence sets off another eruption. He
peers through the scalding glare of the television lights. He keeps squinting. He's
aware of a great mass of silhouettes out in front of him. The crowd swells up. The
ceiling presses down. It's covered in beige tiles. The tiles have curly incisions all
over them. They're crumbling around the edges. Asbestos! He knows it when he
sees it! The faces—they're waiting for the beano, for the rock fight. Bloody noses!
—that's the idea. The next instant means everything. He can handle it! He can
handle hecklers! Only five-seven, but he's even better at it than Koch used to be!
He's the mayor of the greatest city on earth—New York! Him!

"All right! You've had your fun, and now you're gonna *shut up* for a minute!"

That startles the heckler. He freezes. That's all the Mayor needs. He knows
how to do it.

"Youuuu asked *meeeee* a question, didn't you, and you got a *bigggg* laugh from
your claque. And so now *youuuuu're* gonna keep *quiiiiet* and *lissssten* to the answer. *Okay?"*

"Say, claque?" The man has had his wind knocked out, but he's still standing
up.

"Okay? Now here are the statistics for *yourrr* community, right here, Harlem."

"Say, claque?" The bastard has hold of this word *claque* like a bone. "Ain'
nobody can eat statistics, man!"

"Tell 'im, bro . . . Yo . . . Yo, Gober!"

"Let me finish. Do *youuuuu* think—"

"Don't percentage no annual budget with us, man! We want *jobs!"*

The crowd erupts again. It's worse than before. Much of it he can't make out
—interjections from deep in the bread basket. But there's this *Yo* business. There's
some loudmouth way in back with a voice that cuts through everything.

"Yo, Gober! Yo, Gober! Yo, Gober!"

But he isn't saying *Gober.* He's saying *Goldberg.*

"Yo, Goldberg! Yo, Goldberg! Yo, Goldberg!"

It stuns him. In this place, in Harlem! Goldberg is the Harlem cognomen for
Jew. It's insolent!—outrageous!—that anyone throws this vileness in the face of
the Mayor of New York City!

Boos, hisses, grunts, belly laughs, shouts. They want to see some loose teeth.
It's out of control.

"Do you—"

It's no use. He can't make himself heard even with the microphone. The hate
in their faces! Pure poison! It's mesmerizing.

"Yo, Goldberg! Yo, Goldberg! Yo, Hymie!"

Hymie! That business! There's one of them yelling Goldberg and another one
yelling Hymie. Then it dawns on him. Reverend Bacon! They're Bacon's people.
He's sure of it. The civic-minded people who come to public meetings in Harlem
—the people Sheldon was supposed to make sure filled up this hall—they

wouldn't be out there yelling these outrageous things. Bacon did this! Sheldon fucked up! Bacon got his people in here!

A wave of the purest self-pity rolls over the Mayor. Out of the corner of his eye he can see the television crews squirming around in the haze of light. Their cameras are coming out of their heads like horns. They're swiveling around this way and that. They're eating it up! They're here for the brawl! They wouldn't lift a finger. They're cowards! Parasites! The lice of public life!

In the next moment he has a terrible realization: "It's over. I can't believe it. I've lost."

"No more your . . . Outta here . . . Boooo . . . Don' wanna . . . Yo, Goldberg!"

Guliaggi, the head of the Mayor's plainclothes security detail, is coming toward him from the side of the stage. The Mayor motions him back with a low flap of his hand, without looking at him directly. What could he do, anyway? He brought only four officers with him. He didn't want to come up here with an army. The whole point was to show that he could go to Harlem and hold a town-hall meeting, just the way he could in Riverdale or Park Slope.

In the front row, through the haze, he catches the eye of Mrs. Langhorn, the woman with the shingle hairdo, the head of the community board, the woman who introduced him just—what?—minutes ago. She purses her lips and cocks her head and starts shaking it. This look is supposed to say, "I wish I could help you, but what can I do? Behold the wrath of the people!" Oh, she's afraid like all the rest! She knows she should stand up against this element! They'll go after black people like her next! They'll be happy to do it. She knows that. But the good people are intimidated! They don't dare do a thing! Back to blood! Them and us!

"Go on home! . . . Booooo . . . Ycgggghhh . . . Yo!"

He tries the microphone again. "Is this what—*is this what*—"

Hopeless. Like yelling at the surf. He wants to spit in their eyes. He wants to tell them he's not afraid. You're not making *me* look bad! You're letting a handful of hustlers in this hall make all of Harlem look bad! You let a couple of loudmouths call me Goldberg and Hymie, and you don't shout *them* down—you shout *me* down! It's unbelievable! Do you—you hardworking, respectable, God-fearing people of Harlem, you Mrs. Langhorns, you civic-minded people—do you really think they're your *brothers*! Who have your friends been all these years? The Jews! And you let these hustlers call me a *Charlie*! They call me these things, and you say *nothing*?

The whole hall appears to be jumping up and down. They're waving their fists. Their mouths are open. They're screaming. If they jump any higher, they'll bounce off the ceiling.

It'll be on TV. The whole city will see it. They'll love it. Harlem rises up! What a show! Not the hustlers and the operators and the players rise up—but *Harlem* rises up! All of black New York rises up! He's only mayor for *some* of the people! He's the mayor of White New York! Set fire to the mutt! The Italians will watch this on TV, and they'll love it. And the Irish. Even the Wasps. They won't know what they're looking at. They'll sit in their co-ops on Park and Fifth and East Seventy-second Street and Sutton Place, and they'll shiver with the violence of it and enjoy the show. Cattle! Birdbrains! Rosebuds! *Goyim!* You don't even know, do you? Do you really think this is *your* city any longer? Open your eyes! The greatest city of the twentieth century! Do you think *money* will keep it yours?

Come down from your swell co-ops, you general partners and merger lawyers! It's the Third World down there! Puerto Ricans, West Indians, Haitians, Dominicans, Cubans, Colombians, Hondurans, Koreans, Chinese, Thais, Vietnamese, Ecuadorians, Panamanians, Filipinos, Albanians, Senegalese, and Afro-Americans! Go visit the frontiers, you gutless wonders! Morningside Heights, St. Nicholas Park, Washington Heights, Fort Tryon —*por qué pagar más!* The Bronx—the Bronx is finished for you! Riverdale is just a little freeport up there! Pelham Parkway—keep the corridor open to Westchester! Brooklyn —*your* Brooklyn is no more! Brooklyn Heights, Park Slope—little Hong Kongs, that's all! And Queens! Jackson Heights, Elmhurst, Hollis, Jamaica, Ozone Park—whose is it? Do you know? And where does that leave Ridgewood, Bayside, and Forest Hills? Have you ever thought about that! And Staten Island! Do you Saturday do-it-yourselfers really think you're snug in your little rug? You don't think the future knows how to cross a *bridge?* And you, you Wasp charity-ballers sitting on your mounds of inherited money up in your co-ops with the twelve-foot ceilings and the two wings, one for you and one for the help, do you really think you're impregnable? And you German-Jewish financiers who have finally made it into the same buildings, the better to insulate yourselves from the *shtetl* hordes, do you really think you're insulated from the *Third World?*

You poor fatties! You marshmallows! Hens! Cows! You wait'll you have a Reverend Bacon for a mayor, and a City Council and a Board of Estimate with a bunch of Reverend Bacons from one end of the chamber to the other! You'll get to know them then, all right! They'll come see you! They'll come see you at 60 Wall and Number One Chase Manhattan Plaza! They'll sit on your desks and drum their fingers! They'll dust out your safe-deposit boxes for you, free of charge—

Completely crazy, these things roaring through his head! Absolutely paranoid! Nobody's going to elect Bacon to anything. Nobody's going to march downtown. He knows that. But he feels so alone! Abandoned! Misunderstood! *Me!* You wait'll you don't have *me* any longer! See how you like it then! And you let me stand here alone at this lectern with a goddamned asbestos ceiling coming down on my head—

"*Boooo! . . . Yegggghhh! . . . Yaaaggghhh! . . . Yo! . . . Goldberg!*"

There's a terrific commotion on one side of the stage. The TV lights are right in his face. A whole lot of pushing and shoving —he sees a cameraman go down. Some of the bastards are heading for the stairs to the stage, and the television crews are in the way. So they're going over them. Shoving—shoving somebody back down the stairs—his men, the plainclothes detail, the big one, Norrejo— Norrejo's shoving somebody back down the stairs. Something hits the Mayor on the shoulder. It hurts like hell! There on the floor—a jar of mayonnaise, an eight-ounce jar of Hellman's mayonnaise. Half full! Half consumed! Somebody has thrown a half-eaten jar of Hellman's mayonnaise at him! In that instant the most insignificant thing takes over his mind. Who in the name of God would bring a half-eaten eight-ounce jar of Hellman's mayonnaise to a public meeting?

The goddamned lights! People are up on the stage . . . a lot of thrashing about . . . a regular melee . . . Norrejo grabs some big devil around the waist and sticks his leg behind him and throws him to the floor. The other two detectives, Holt and Danforth, have their backs to the Mayor. They're crouched like blocking backs protecting a passer. Guliaggi is right beside him.

"Get behind me," says Guliaggi. "We're going through that door."

Is he smiling? Guliaggi seems to have this little smile on his face. He motions his head toward a door at the rear of the stage. He's short, he has a small head, a low forehead, small narrow eyes, a flat nose, a wide mean mouth with a narrow mustache. The Mayor keeps staring at his mouth. Is that a smile? It can't be, but maybe it is. This strange mean twist to his lips seems to be saying: "It's been your show up to now, but now it's mine."

Somehow the smile decides the issue. The Mayor gives up his Custer's command post at the lectern. He gives himself over to this little rock. Now the others are closed in around him, too, Norrejo, Holt, Danforth. They're around him like the four corners of a pen. People are all over the stage. Guliaggi and Norrejo are muscling their way through the mob. The Mayor is right on their heels. Snarling faces are all around him. There's some character barely two feet from him who keeps jumping up and yelling, "You little white-haired pussy! You little white-haired pussy!"

Every time the bastard jumps up, the Mayor can see his bulging ivory eyes and his enormous Adam's apple. It's the size of a sweet potato.

"You little white-haired pussy!" He keeps saying it. "You little white-haired pussy!"

Right in front of him—the big heckler himself! The one with the elbows and the gold earring! Guliaggi is between the Mayor and the heckler, but the heckler towers over Guliaggi. He must be six five. He screams at the Mayor, right in his face:

"Go on back—*oof!*"

All at once the big son of a bitch is sinking, with his mouth open and his eyes bugged out. Guliaggi has driven his elbow and forearm into the man's solar plexus.

Guliaggi reaches the door and opens it. The Mayor follows. He feels the other detectives pushing him through from behind. He sprawls against Guliaggi's back. The guy's a piece of stone!

They're going down a stairway. They're clattering on some metal strips. He's in one piece. The mob isn't even on his heels. He's safe—his heart sinks. They're not even trying to follow him. They never really tried to touch him. And in that moment . . . he *knows*. He knows even before his mind can put it all together.

"I did the wrong thing. I gave in to that little smile. I panicked. I've lost it all."

1

THE MASTER OF THE UNIVERSE

A̲T THAT VERY MOMENT, in the very sort of Park Avenue co-op apartment that so obsessed the Mayor . . . twelve-foot ceilings . . . two wings, one for the white Anglo-Saxon Protestants who own the place and one for the help . . . Sherman McCoy was kneeling in his front hall trying to put a leash on a dachshund. The floor was a deep green marble, and it went on and on. It led to a five-foot-wide walnut staircase that swept up in a sumptuous curve to the floor above. It was the sort of apartment the mere thought of which ignites flames of greed and covetousness under people all over New York and, for that matter, all over the world. But Sherman burned only with the urge to get out of this fabulous spread of his for thirty minutes.

So here he was, down on both knees, struggling with a dog. The dachshund, he figured, was his exit visa.

Looking at Sherman McCoy, hunched over like that and dressed the way he was, in his checked shirt, khaki pants, and leather boating moccasins, you would have never guessed what an imposing figure he usually cut. Still young . . . thirty-eight years old . . . tall . . . almost six-one . . . terrific posture . . . terrific to the point of imperious . . . as imperious as his daddy, the Lion of Dunning Sponget . . . a full head of sandy-brown hair . . . a long nose . . . a prominent chin . . . He was proud of his chin. The McCoy chin; the Lion had it, too. It was a manly chin, a big round chin such as Yale men used to have in those drawings by Gibson and Leyendecker, an aristocratic chin, if you want to know what Sherman thought. He was a Yale man himself.

But at this moment his entire appearance was supposed to say: "I'm only going out to walk the dog."

The dachshund seemed to know what was ahead. He kept ducking away from the leash. The beast's stunted legs were deceiving. If you tried to lay hands on him, he turned into a two-foot tube packed with muscle. In grappling with him, Sherman had to lunge. And when he lunged, his kneecap hit the marble floor, and the pain made him angry.

"C'mon, Marshall," he kept muttering. "Hold still, damn it."

The beast ducked again, and he hurt his knee again, and now he resented not only the beast but his wife, too. It was his wife's delusions of a career as an interior decorator that had led to this ostentatious spread of marble in the first place. The tiny black grosgrain cap on the toe of a woman's shoe—

—she was standing there.

"You're having a time, Sherman. What on earth are you doing?"

Without looking up: "I'm taking Marshall for a wa-a-a-a-a-alk."

Walk came out as a groan, because the dachshund attempted a fishtail maneuver and Sherman had to wrap his arm around the dog's midsection.

"Did you know it was raining?"

Still not looking up: "Yes, I know." Finally he managed to snap the leash on the animal's collar.

"You're certainly being nice to Marshall all of a sudden."

Wait a minute. Was this irony? Did she suspect something? He looked up.

But the smile on her face was obviously genuine, altogether pleasant . . . a lovely smile, in fact . . . *Still a very good-looking woman, my wife* . . . with her fine thin features, her big clear blue eyes, her rich brown hair . . . *But she's forty years old!* . . . No getting around it . . . Today *good-looking* . . . Tomorrow they'll be talking about what a *handsome* woman she is . . . Not her fault . . . *But not mine, either!*

"I have an idea," she said. "Why don't you let *me* walk Marshall? Or I'll get Eddie to do it. You go upstairs and read Campbell a story before she goes to sleep. She'd love it. You're not home this early very often. Why don't you do that?"

He stared at her. It wasn't a trick! She was sincere! And yet *zip zip zip zip zip zip zip* with a few swift strokes, a few little sentences, she had . . . *tied him in knots!—thongs of guilt and logic!* Without even trying!

The fact that Campbell might be lying in her little bed—*my only child!*—the *utter innocence of a six-year-old!*—wishing that he would read her a bedtime story . . . while he was . . . doing whatever it was he was now doing . . . *Guilt!* . . . The fact that he usually got home too late to see her at all . . . *Guilt on top of guilt!* . . . He doted on Campbell.—loved her more than anything in the world! . . . To make matters worse—*the logic of it!* The sweet wifely face he was now staring at had just made a considerate and thoughtful suggestion, a logical suggestion . . . so logical he was speechless! There weren't enough white lies in the world to get around such logic! And she was only trying to be nice!

"Go ahead," she said. "Campbell will be so pleased. I'll tend to Marshall."

The world was upside down. What was he, a Master of the Universe, doing down here on the floor, reduced to ransacking his brain for white lies to circumvent the sweet logic of his wife? The Masters of the Universe were a set of lurid, rapacious plastic dolls that his otherwise perfect daughter liked to play with. They looked like Norse gods who lifted weights, and they had names such as Dracon, Ahor, Mangelred, and Blutong. They were unusually vulgar, even for plastic toys. Yet one fine day, in a fit of euphoria, after he had picked up the telephone and taken an order for zero-coupon bonds that had brought him a $50,000 commission, *just like that,* this very phrase had bubbled up into his brain. On Wall Street he and a few others—how many?—three hundred, four hundred, five hundred?— had become precisely that . . . Masters of the Universe. There was . . . no limit whatsoever! Naturally he had never so much as whispered this phrase to a living soul. He was no fool. Yet he couldn't get it out of his head. And here was the Master of the Universe, on the floor with a dog, hog-tied by sweetness, guilt, and logic . . . Why couldn't he (being a Master of the Universe) simply *explain* it to her? Look, Judy, I still love you and I love our daughter and I love our home and I love our life, and I don't want to change any of it—it's just that I, a Master of the Universe, a young man still in the season of the rising sap, deserve *more* from time to time, when the spirit moves me—

—but he knew he could never put any such thought into words. So resentment began to bubble up into his brain . . . In a way she brought it on herself, didn't she . . . Those women whose company she now seems to prize . . . those . . . those . . . The phrase pops into his head at that very instant: *social X rays* . . . They keep themselves so thin, they look like X-ray pictures . . . You can see lamplight through their bones . . . while they're chattering about *interiors* and *landscape gardening* . . . and encasing their scrawny shanks in metallic Lycra tubular tights for their Sports Training classes . . . And it hasn't helped any, has it! . . . See how drawn her face and neck look . . . He concentrated on her face and neck . . . *drawn* . . . No doubt about it . . . Sports Training . . . turning into *one of them*—

He managed to manufacture just enough resentment to ignite the famous McCoy temper.

He could feel his face grow hot. He put his head down and said, "Juuuuuudy . . ." It was a shout stifled by teeth. He pressed the thumb and the first two fingers of his left hand together and held them in front of his clamped jaws and blazing eyes, and he said:

"Look . . . I'm all—set—to—walk—the—dog . . . So I'm—going—out—to—walk—the—dog . . . *Okay?*"

Halfway through it, he knew it was totally out of proportion to . . . to . . . but he couldn't hold back. That, after all, was the secret of the McCoy temper . . . on Wall Street . . . wherever . . . the imperious excess.

Judy's lips tightened. She shook her head.

"Please do what you want," she said tonelessly. Then she turned away and walked across the marble hall and ascended the sumptuous stairs.

Still on his knees, he looked at her, but she didn't look back. *Please do what you want.* He had run right over her. Nothing to it. But it was a hollow victory.

Another spasm of guilt—

The Master of the Universe stood up and managed to hold on to the leash and struggle into his raincoat. It was a worn but formidable rubberized British riding mac, full of flaps, straps, and buckles. He had bought it at Knoud on Madison Avenue. Once, he had considered its aged look as just the thing, after the fashion of the Boston Cracked Shoe look. Now he wondered. He yanked the dachshund along on the leash and went from the entry gallery out into the elevator vestibule and pushed the button.

Rather than continue to pay around-the-clock shifts of Irishmen from Queens and Puerto Ricans from the Bronx $200,000 a year to run the elevators, the apartment owners had decided two years ago to convert the elevators to automatic. Tonight that suited Sherman fine. In this outfit, with this squirming dog in tow, he didn't feel like standing in an elevator with an elevator man dressed up like an 1870 Austrian army colonel. The elevator descended—and came to a stop two floors below. *Browning*. The door opened, and the smooth-jowled bulk of Pollard Browning stepped on. Browning looked Sherman and his country outfit and the dog up and down and said, without a trace of a smile, "Hello, Sherman."

"Hello, Sherman" was on the end of a ten-foot pole and in a mere four syllables conveyed the message: "You and your clothes and your animal are letting down our new mahogany-paneled elevator."

Sherman was furious but nevertheless found himself leaning over and picking the dog up off the floor. Browning was the president of the building's co-op board. He was a New York boy who had emerged from his mother's loins as a fifty-year-old partner in Davis Polk and president of the Downtown Association. He was only forty but had looked fifty for the past twenty years. His hair was combed back smoothly over his round skull. He wore an immaculate navy suit, a white shirt, a shepherd's check necktie, and no raincoat. He faced the elevator door, then turned his head, took another look at Sherman, said nothing, and turned back.

Sherman had known him ever since they were boys at the Buckley School. Browning had been a fat, hearty, overbearing junior snob who at the age of nine knew how to get across the astonishing news that McCoy was a hick name (and a hick family), as in Hatfields and McCoys, whereas he, Browning, was a true Knickerbocker. He used to call Sherman "Sherman McCoy the Mountain Boy."

When they reached the ground floor, Browning said, "You know it's raining, don't you?"

"Yes."

Browning looked at the dachshund and shook his head. "Sherman McCoy. Friend to man's best friend."

Sherman felt his face getting hot again. He said, "That's it?"

"What's it?"

"You had from the eighth floor to here to think up something bright, and that's it?" It was supposed to sound like amiable sarcasm, but he knew his anger had slipped out around the edges.

"I don't know what you're talking about," said Browning, and he walked on ahead. The doorman smiled and nodded and held the door open for him. Browning walked out under the awning to his car. His chauffeur held the car door open for him. Not a drop of rain touched his glossy form, and he was off, smoothly, immaculately, into the swarm of red taillights heading down Park Avenue. No ratty riding mac encumbered the sleek fat back of Pollard Browning.

In fact, it was raining only lightly, and there was no wind, but the dachshund was having none of it. He was beginning to struggle in Sherman's arms. The power of the little bastard! He put the dog down on the runner under the awning and then stepped out into the rain with the leash. In the darkness the apartment buildings on the other side of the avenue were a serene black wall holding back the city's sky, which was a steaming purple. It glowed, as if inflamed by a fever.

Hell, it wasn't so bad out here. Sherman pulled, but the dog dug into the runner with his toenails.

"Come on, Marshall."

The doorman was standing outside the door, watching him.

"I don't think he's too happy about it, Mr. McCoy."

"I'm not, either, Eddie." And never mind the commentary, thought Sherman. "C'mon, c'mon, c'mon, Marhsall."

By now Sherman was out in the rain giving the leash a pretty good pull, but the dachshund wasn't budging. So he picked him up and took him off the rubber runner and set him down on the sidewalk. The dog tried to bolt for the door. Sherman couldn't give him any more slack on the leash or else he was going to be right back where he started. So now he was leaning one way and the dog was leaning the other, with the leash taut between them. It was a tug-of-war between a man and a dog . . . on Park Avenue. Why the hell didn't the doorman get back in the building where he belonged?

Sherman gave the leash a real jerk. The dachshund skidded forward a few inches on the sidewalk. You could hear his toenails scraping. Well, maybe if he dragged him hard enough, he would give up and start walking just to keep from being dragged.

"C'mon, Marshall! We're only going around the corner!"

He gave the leash another jerk and then kept pulling for all he was worth. The dog slid forward a couple of feet. He slid! He wouldn't walk. He wouldn't give up. The beast's center of gravity seemed to be at the middle of the earth. It was like trying to drag a sled with a pile of bricks on it. Christ, if he could only get around the corner. That was all he wanted. Why was it that *the simplest things*—he gave the leash another jerk and then he kept the pressure on. He was leaning like a sailor into the wind. He was getting hot inside his rubberized riding mac. The rain was running down his face. The dachshund had his feet splayed out on the sidewalk. His shoulder muscles were bulging. He was thrashing from side to side. His neck was stretched out. Thank God, he wasn't barking, at least! He *slid*. Christ, you could hear it! You could hear his toenails scraping along the sidewalk. He wouldn't give an inch. Sherman had his head down, his shoulders hunched over, dragging this animal through the darkness and the rain on Park Avenue. He could feel the rain on the back of his neck.

He squatted down and picked up the dachshund, catching a glimpse of Eddie, the doorman, as he did. Still watching! The dog began bucking and thrashing. Sherman stumbled. He looked down. The leash had gotten wrapped around his legs. He began gimping along the sidewalk. Finally he made it around the corner to the pay telephone. He put the dog down on the sidewalk.

Christ! Almost got away! He grabs the leash just in time. He's sweating. His head is soaked with rain. His heart is pounding. He sticks one arm through the loop in the leash. The dog keeps struggling. The leash is wrapped around Sherman's legs again. He picks up the telephone and cradles it between his shoulder and his ear and fishes around in his pocket for a quarter and drops it in the slot and dials.

Three rings, and a woman's voice: "Hello?"

But it was not Maria's voice. He figured it must be her friend Germaine, the one she sublet the apartment from. So he said: "May I speak to Maria, please?"

The woman said: "Sherman? Is that you?"

Christ! It's Judy! He's dialed his own apartment! He's aghast—paralyzed! "Sherman?"

He hangs up. Oh Jesus. What can he do? He'll bluff it out. When she asks him, he'll say he doesn't know what she's talking about. After all, he said only five or six words. How can she be sure?

But it was no use. She'd be sure, all right. Besides, he was no good at bluffing. She'd see right through him. Still, what else could he do?

He stood there in the rain, in the dark, by the telephone. The water had worked its way down inside his shirt collar. He was breathing heavily. He was trying to figure out how bad it was going to be. What would she do? What would she say? How angry would she be? This time she'd have something she could really work on. She deserved her scene if she wanted it. He had been truly stupid. How could he have done such a thing? He berated himself. He was no longer angry at Judy at all. Could he bluff it out, or had he really done it now? Had he really hurt her?

All at once Sherman was aware of a figure approaching him on the sidewalk, in the wet black shadows of the town houses and the trees. Even from fifty feet away, in the darkness, he could tell. It was that deep worry that lives in the base of the skull of every resident of Park Avenue south of Ninety-sixth Street—a black youth, tall, rangy, wearing white sneakers. Now he was forty feet away, thirty-five. Sherman stared at him. Well, let him come! I'm not budging! It's my territory! I'm not giving way for any street punks!

The black youth suddenly made a ninety-degree turn and cut straight across the street to the sidewalk on the other side. The feeble yellow of a sodium-vapor streetlight reflected for an instant on his face as he checked Sherman out.

He had crossed over! What a stroke of luck

Not once did it dawn on Sherman McCoy that what the boy had seen was a thirty-eight-year-old white man, soaking wet, dressed in some sort of military-looking raincoat full of straps and buckles, holding a violently lurching animal in his arms, staring, bug-eyed, and talking to himself.

Sherman stood by the telephone, breathing rapidly, almost panting. What was he to do now? He felt so defeated, he might as well go back home. But if he went back immediately, it would be pretty obvious, wouldn't it? He hadn't gone out to walk the dog but to make a telephone call. Besides, whatever Judy was going to say, he wasn't ready for it. He needed to think. He needed advice. He needed to get this intractable beast out of the rain.

So he dug out another quarter and summoned up Maria's number into his brain. He concentrated on it. He nailed it down. Then he dialed it with a plodding deliberation, as if he were using this particular invention, the telephone, for the first time.

"Hello?"

"Maria?"

"Yes?"

Taking no chances: "It's me."

"Sherman?" It came out Shuhhh-mun. Sherman was reassured. That was Maria, all right. She had the variety of Southern accent in which half the vowels are pronounced like *u*'s and the other half like short *i*'s. Birds were *buds*, pens were *pins*, bombs were *bums*, and envelopes were *invilups*.

"Listen," he said, "I'll be right over. I'm at a telephone booth. I'm only a couple of blocks away."

There was a pause, which he took to mean she was irritated. Finally: "Where on earth have you been?" *Where un uth have you bin?*

Sherman laughed morosely. "Look, I'll be right over."

The staircase of the town house sagged and groaned as Sherman walked up. On each floor a single bare 22-watt circular flucrescent tube, known as the Land-lord's Halo, radiated a feeble tubercular-blue glow upon the walls, which were

Rental Unit Green. Sherman passed apartment doors with innumerable locks, one above the other in drunken columns. There were anti-pliers covers over the locks and anti-jimmy irons over the jambs and anti-push-in screens over the door panels.

In blithe moments, when King Priapus reigned, with no crises in his domain, Sherman made this climb up to Maria's with a romantic relish. How bohemian! How . . . *real* this place was! How absolutely *right* for these moments when the Master of the Universe stripped away the long-faced proprieties of Park Avenue and Wall Street and let his rogue hormones out for a romp! Maria's one room, with its closet for a kitchen and another closet for a bathroom, this so-called apartment of hers, fourth floor rear, which she sublet from her friend Germaine— well, it was perfect. Germaine was something else again. Sherman had met her twice. She was built like a fire hydrant. She had a ferocious hedge of hair on her upper lip, practically a mustache. Sherman was convinced she was a lesbian. But so what? It was all real! Squalid! New York! A rush of fire in the loins!

But tonight Priapus did not rule. Tonight the grimness of the old brownstone weighed on the Master of the Universe.

Only the dachshund was happy. He was hauling his belly up the stairs at a merry clip. It was warm and dry in here, and familiar.

When Sherman reached Maria's door, he was surprised to find himself out of breath. He was perspiring. His body was positively abloom beneath the riding mac, his checked shirt, and his T-shirt.

Before he could knock on the door, it opened about a foot, and there she was. She didn't open it any farther. She stood there, looking Sherman up and down, as if she were angry. Her eyes gleamed above those remarkable high cheekbones of hers. Her bobbed hair was like a black hood. Her lips were drawn up into an O. All at once she broke into a smile and began chuckling with little sniffs through her nose.

"Well, come on," said Sherman, "let me in! Wait'll I tell you what happened."

Now Maria pushed the door all the way open, but instead of ushering him inside, she leaned up against the doorjamb and crossed her legs and folded her arms underneath her breasts and kept staring at him and chuckling. She was wearing high-heeled pumps with a black-and-white checkerboard pattern worked into the leather. Sherman knew little about shoe designs, but it registered on him that this one was of the moment. She wore a tailored white gabardine skirt, very short, a good four inches above the knees, revealing her legs, which to Sherman's eyes were like a dancer's, and emphasizing her tiny waist. She wore a white silk blouse, open down to the top of her breasts. The light in the tiny entryway was such that it threw her entire ensemble into high relief: her dark hair, those cheekbones, the fine features of her face, the swollen curve of her lips, her creamy blouse, those creamy flan breasts, her shimmering shanks, so insouciantly crossed.

"Sherman . . ." Shuhhh-mun. "You know what? You're cute. You're just like my little brother."

The Master of the Universe was mildly annoyed, but he walked on in, passing her and saying: "Oh boy. Wait'll I tell you what happened."

Without altering her pose in the doorway, Maria looked down at the dog, who was sniffing at the carpet. "Hello, Marshall!" Muhshull. "You're a wet little piece a salami, Marshall."

"Wait'll I tell you—"

Maria started to laugh and then shut the door. "Sherman . . . you look like somebody just . . . *balled you up*"—she balled up an imaginary piece of paper—"and threw you down."

"That's what I feel like. Let me tell you what happened."

"Just like my little brother. Every day he came home from school, and his belly button was showing."

Sherman looked down. It was true. His checked shirt was pulled out of his pants, and his belly button was showing. He shoved the shirt back in, but he didn't take off the riding mac. He couldn't settle in here. He couldn't stay too long. He didn't know quite how to get that across to Maria.

"Every day my little brother got in a fight at school . . ."

Sherman stopped listening. He was tired of Maria's little brother, not so much because the thrust of it was that he, Sherman, was childish, but because she insisted on going on about it. At first glance, Maria had never struck Sherman as anybody's idea of a Southern girl. She looked Italian or Greek. But she talked like a Southern girl. The chatter just poured out. She was still talking when Sherman said:

"You know, I just called you from a telephone booth. You want to know what happened?"

Maria turned her back and walked out into the middle of the apartment, then wheeled about and struck a pose, with her head cocked to one side and her hands on her hips and one high-heeled foot slewed out in a carefree manner and her shoulders thrown back and her back slightly arched, pushing her breasts forward, and she said:

"Do you see anything new?"

What the hell was she talking about? Sherman wasn't in a mood for anything new. But he looked her over dutifully. Did she have a new hairdo? A new piece of jewelry? Christ, her husband loaded her with so much jewelry, who could keep track? No, it must be something in the room. His eyes jumped around. It had probably been built as a child's bedroom a hundred years ago. There was a little bay with three leaded casement windows and a window seat all the way around. He surveyed the furniture . . . the same old three bentwood chairs, the same old ungainly oak pedestal table, the same old mattress-and-box-spring set with a corduroy cover and three or four paisley cushions strewn on top in an attempt to make it look like a divan. The whole place shrieked: Make Do. In any event, it hadn't changed.

Sherman shook his head.

"You really don't?" Maria motioned with her head in the direction of the bed.

Sherman now noticed, over the bed, a small painting with a simple frame of blond wood. He took a couple of steps closer. It was a picture of a nude man, seen from the rear, outlined in crude black brushstrokes, the way an eight-year-old might do it, assuming an eight-year-old had a notion to paint a nude man. The man appeared to be taking a shower, or at least there was what looked like a nozzle over his head, and some slapdash black lines were coming out of the nozzle. He seemed to be taking a shower in fuel oil. The man's flesh was tan with sickly lavender-pink smears on it, as if he were a burn case. What a piece of garbage . . . It was sick . . . But it gave off the sanctified odor of serious art, and so Sherman hesitated to be candid.

"Where'd you get that?"

"You like it? You know his work?"

"Whose work?"

"Filippo Chirazzi."

"No, I don't know his work."

She was smiling. "There was a whole article about him, in the *Times*."

Not wanting to play the Wall Street philistine, Sherman resumed his study of this masterpiece.

"Well, it has a certain . . . how can I say it? . . . directness." He fought the urge to be ironic. "Where did you get it?"

"Filippo gave it to me." Very cheery.

"That was generous."

"Arthur's *bought* four of his paintings, great big ones."

"But he didn't give it to Arthur, he gave it to you."

"I wanted one for myself. The big ones are Arthur's. Besides, Arthur wouldn't know Filippo from . . . from I don't know what, if I hadn't told him."

"Ah."

"You don't like it, do you."

"I *like* it. To tell you the truth, I'm rattled. I just did something so goddamned stupid."

Maria gave up her pose and sat down on the edge of the bed, the would-be divan, as if to say, "Okay, I'm ready to listen." She crossed her legs. Her skirt was now halfway up her thighs. Even though those legs, those exquisite shanks and flanks of hers, were beside the point right now, Sherman couldn't keep his eyes off them. Her stockings made them shiny. They glistened. Every time she moved, the highlights shimmered.

Sherman remained standing. He didn't have much time, as he was about to explain.

"I took Marshall out for a walk." Marshall was now stretched out on the rug. "And it's raining. And he starts giving me a very hard time."

When he got to the part about the telephone call itself, he became highly agitated even in the description of it. He noticed that Maria was containing her concern, if any, quite successfully, but he couldn't calm down. He plunged on into the emotional heart of the matter, the things he felt immediately after he hung up—and Maria cut him off with a shrug and a little flick in the air with the back of her hand.

"Oh, that's nothing, Sherman." That's nuthun, Shuhmun.

He stared at her.

"All you did was make a telephone call. I don't know why you just didn't say, 'Oh, I'm sorry. I was calling my friend Maria Ruskin.' That's what I woulda done. I never bother lying to Arthur. I don't tell him every little thing, but I don't lie to him."

Could he possibly have used such a brazen strategy? He ran it through his mind. "Uhmmmmmmmm." It ended up as a groan. "I don't know how I can go out at 9:30 at night and say I'm walking the dog and then call up and say, 'Oh, I'm sorry, I'm really out here calling Maria Ruskin.'"

"You know the difference between you and me, Sherman? You feel sorry for your wife, and I don't feel sorry for Arthur. Arthur's gonna be seventy-two in August. He knew I had my own friends when he married me, and he knew he didn't like them, and he had his own friends, and he knew I didn't like *them*. I can't stand them. All those old Yids . . . Don't look at me as if I've said something awful! That's the way Arthur talks. 'The Yiddim.' And the *goyim*, and I'm a *shiksa*. I never heard of all that stuff before I met Arthur. I'm the one who happens to be married to a Jew, not you, and I've had to swallow enough of this Jewish business over the past five years to be able to use a little of it if I feel like it."

"Have you told him you have your own apartment here?"

"Of course not. I told you, I don't lie to him, but I don't tell him every little thing."

"Is this a little thing?"

"It's not as big a thing as *you* think it is. It's a pain in the neck. The landlord's got himself in an uproar again."

Maria stood up and went to the table and picked up a sheet of paper and handed it to Sherman and returned to the edge of the bed. It was a letter from the law firm of Golan, Shander, Morgan, and Greenbaum to Ms. Germaine Boll concerning her status as the tenant of a rent-controlled apartment owned by Winter Real Properties, Inc. Sherman couldn't concentrate on it. He didn't want to think about it. It was getting late. Maria kept going off on tangents. It was *getting late*.

"I don't know, Maria. This is something Germaine has to respond to."

"Sherman?"

She was smiling with her lips parted. She stood up.

"Sherman, come here."

He took a couple of steps toward her, but he resisted going very close. The look on her face said she had very close in mind.

"You think you're in trouble with your wife, and all you've done is make a phone call."

"Hah. I don't think I'm in trouble, I know I'm in trouble."

"Well, if you're already in trouble, and you haven't even done anything, then you might as well do something, since it's all the same difference."

Then she touched him.

King Priapus, he who had been scared to death, now rose up from the dead.

Sprawled on the bed, Sherman caught a glimpse of the dachshund. The beast had gotten up off the rug and had walked over to the bed and was looking up at them and switching his tail.

Christ! Was there by any chance some way a dog could indicate . . . Was there anything dogs did that showed they had seen . . . Judy knew about animals. She clucked and fussed over Marshall's every mood, until it was revolting. Was there something dachshunds did after observing . . . But then his nervous system began to dissolve, and he no longer cared.

His Majesty, the most ancient king, Priapus, Master of the Universe, had no conscience.

Sherman let himself into the apartment and made a point of amplifying the usual cozy sounds.

"Attaboy, Marshall, okay, okay."

He took off his riding mac with a lot of rustling of the rubberized material and clinking of the buckles and a few *whews*.

No sign of Judy.

The dining room, the living room, and a small library led off the marble entry gallery. Each had its familiar glints and glows of carved wood, cut glass, ecru silk shades, glazed lacquer, and the rest of the breathtakingly expensive touches of his wife, the aspiring decorator. Then he noticed. The big leather wing chair that usually faced the doorway in the library was turned around. He could just see the top of Judy's head, from behind. There was a lamp beside the chair. She appeared to be reading a book.

He went to the doorway.

"Well! We're back!"

No response.

"You were right. I got soaking wet, and Marshall wasn't happy."

She didn't look around. There was just her voice, coming from out of the wing chair:

"Sherman, if you want to talk to someone named Maria, why do you call me instead?"

Sherman took a step inside the room.

"What do you mean? If I want to talk to *who?*"

The voice: "Oh, for God's sake. Please don't bother lying."

"Lying—about *what?*"

Then Judy stuck her head around one side of the wing chair. The look she gave him!

With a sinking heart Sherman walked over to the chair. Within her corona of soft brown hair his wife's face was pure agony.

"What are you *talk*ing about, Judy?"

She was so upset she couldn't get the words out at first. "I wish you could see the cheap look on your face."

"I don't know what you're *talk*ing about!"

The shrillness in his voice made her laugh.

"All right, Sherman, you're going to stand there and tell me you didn't call here and ask to speak to someone named Maria?"

"To *who?*"

"Some little hooker, if I had to guess, named Maria."

"Judy, I swear to God, I don't know what you're talking about! I've been out walking Marshall! I don't even *know* anybody named Maria! Somebody called here asking for somebody named Maria?"

"Uhhh!" It was a short, unbelieving groan. She stood up and looked at him square in the eyes. "You *stand* there! You think I don't know your voice on the phone?"

"Maybe you do, but you haven't heard it tonight. I swear to God."

"You're lying!" She gave him a hideous smile. "And you're a rotten liar. And you're a rotten person. You think you're so swell, and you're so cheap. You're lying, aren't you?"

"I'm *not* lying. I swear to God, I took Marshall for a walk, and I come back in here, and *wham*—I mean, I hardly know what to say, because I truly don't know what you're talking about. You're asking me to prove a negative proposition."

"Negative proposition." Disgust dripped from the fancy phrase. "You were gone long enough. Did you go kiss her good night and tuck her in, too?"

"Judy—"

"Did you?"

Sherman rolled his head away from her blazing gaze and turned his palms upward and sighed.

"Listen, Judy, you're totally . . . totally . . . utterly wrong. I swear to God."

She stared at him. All at once there were tears in her eyes. "Oh, you swear to God. Oh, Sherman." Now she was beginning to snuffle back the tears. "I'm not gonna—I'm going upstairs. There's the telephone. Why don't you call her from here?" She was forcing the words out through her tears. "I don't care. I really don't care."

Then she walked out of the room. He could hear her shoes clicking across the marble toward the staircase.

Sherman went over to the desk and sat down in his Hepple-white swivel chair. He slumped back. His eyes lit on the frieze that ran around the ceiling of the little room. It was carved of Indian redwood, in high relief, in the form of figures hurrying along a city sidewalk. Judy had had it done in Hong Kong for an astonishing amount . . . *of my money*. Then he leaned forward. *Goddamn her*. Desperately he tried to relight the fires of righteous indignation. His parents had been right, hadn't they? He deserved better. She was two years older than he was, and his mother had said such things *could* matter—which, the way she said it, meant it *would* matter, and had he listened? Ohhhhh no. His father, supposedly referring to Cowles Wilton, who had a short messy marriage to some obscure little Jewish girl, had said, "Isn't it just as easy to fall in love with a rich girl from a good family?" And had he listened? Ohhhhhh no. And all these years, Judy, as the daughter of a Midwestern history professor—*a Midwestern history professor!*—had acted as if she was an intellectual aristocrat—but she hadn't minded using his money and his family to get in with this new social crowd of hers and start her decorating business and smear their names and their apartment across the pages of these vulgar publications, *W* and *Architectural Digest* and the rest of them, had she? Ohhhhhhhhh no, not for a minute! And what was he left with? A forty-year-old bolting off to her Sports Training classes—

—and all at once, he sees her as he first saw her that night fourteen years ago in the Village at Hal Thorndike's apartment with the chocolate-brown walls and the huge table covered with obelisks and the crowd that went considerably beyond bohemian, if he understood bohemian—and the girl with the light brown hair and the fine, fine features and the wild short skimpy dress that revealed so much of her perfect little body. And all at once he *feels* the ineffable way they closed themselves up in the perfect cocoon, in his little apartment on Charles Street and her little apartment on West Nineteenth, immune to all that his parents and Buckley and St. Paul's and Yale had ever imposed on him—and he *remembers* how he told her—in *practically these words!*—that their love would transcend . . . *everything*—

—and now she, forty years old, starved and Sports Trained to near-perfection, goes crying off to bed.

He slumped back in the swivel chair once more. Like many a man before him, he was no match, at last, for a woman's tears. He hung his noble chin over his collarbone. He folded.

Absentmindedly he pressed a button on the desktop. The tambour door of a *faux*-Sheraton cabinet rolled back, revealing the screen of a television set.

Another of his dear weeping decorator's touches. He opened the desk drawer and took out the remote-control gadget and clicked the set to life. The news. The Mayor of New York. A stage. An angry crowd of black people. Harlem. A lot of thrashing about. A riot. The Mayor takes cover. Shouts . . . chaos . . . a real rhubarb. Absolutely pointless. To Sherman it had no more meaning than a gust of wind. He couldn't concentrate on it. He clicked it off.

She was right. The Master of the Universe was cheap, and he was rotten, and he was a liar.

2

GIBRALTAR

THE NEXT MORNING, to Lawrence Kramer, she appears, from out of a feeble gray dawn, the girl with brown lipstick. She stands right beside him. He can't make out her face, but he knows she's the girl with brown lipstick. He can't make out any of the words, either, the words that tumble like tiny pearls from between those lips with brown lipstick, and yet he knows what she's saying. *Stay with me, Larry. Lie down with me, Larry.* He wants to! He wants to! He wants nothing more in this world! Then why doesn't he? What holds him back from pressing his lips upon those lips with brown lipstick? His wife, that's what. His wife, his wife, his wife, his wife, his wife—

He woke up to the pitch and roll of his wife crawling down to the foot of the bed. What a flabby, clumsy spectacle . . . The problem was that the bed, a queen-size resting on a plywood platform, was nearly the width of the room. So you had to crawl down or otherwise traverse the length of the mattress to reach the floor.

Now she was standing on the floor and bending over a chair to pick up her bathrobe. The way her flannel nightgown came down over her hips, she looked a mile wide. He immediately regretted thinking any such thought. He tingled with sentiment. My Rhoda! After all, she had given birth just three weeks ago. He was looking at the loins that had brought forth his first child. A son! She didn't have her old shape back yet. He had to allow for that.

Still, that didn't make the view any better.

He watched her wiggle into the bathrobe. She turned toward the doorway. A light came from the living room. No doubt the baby nurse, who was from England, Miss Efficiency, was already up and waxing efficient. In the light he could see his wife's pale, puffy, undecorated face in profile.

Only twenty-nine, and already she looked just like her mother.

She was the same person all over again. She *was* her mother! No two ways about it! It was only a matter of time! She had the same reddish hair, the same freckles, the same chubby peasant nose and cheeks, even the beginning of her mother's double chin. A *yenta* in embryo! Little Gretel of the *shtetl*! Young and yitzy on the Upper West Side!

He narrowed his eyelids to slits so that she wouldn't know he was awake. Then she left the room. He could hear her saying something to the baby nurse and to the baby. She had a way of saying "Jo-shu-a" in baby cadence. That was a name he was already beginning to regret. If you wanted a Jewish name, what was wrong with Daniel or David or Jonathan? He pulled the covers back up over his shoulders. He would return to the sublime narcosis of sleep for another five or ten minutes. He would return to the girl with brown lipstick. He closed his eyes . . . It was no use. He couldn't get her back. All he could think of was what the rush to the subway would be like if he didn't get up now.

So he got up. He walked down the mattress. It was like trying to walk along the bottom of a rowboat, but he didn't want to crawl. So flabby and clumsy . . . He was wearing a T-shirt and B.V.D. shorts. He became aware that he had that common affliction of young men, a morning erection. He went to the chair and put on his old plaid bathrobe. Both he and his wife had started wearing bathrobes since the English baby nurse had come into their lives. One of the apartment's many tragic flaws was that there was no way of getting from the bedroom to the bathroom without going through the living room, where the nurse slept on the convertible couch and the baby resided in a crib beneath a music-box mobile hung with tiny stuffed clowns. He could hear it now. The music box played the tune "Send in the Clowns." It played it over and over again. Plink plink plinkplink, plink plink plinkplink, plink PLINK plinkplink.

He looked down. The bathrobe did not do the trick. It looked as if there was a tent pole underneath it. But if he bent over, like this, it wasn't noticeable. So he could walk through the living room and let the baby nurse see the tent pole, or he could walk through hunched over as if he had a back spasm. So he just stood where he was, in the gloom.

The gloom was right. The presence of the baby nurse had made him and Rhoda acutely aware of what a dump they lived in. This entire apartment, known as a 3½-room in New York real-estate parlance, had been created out of what had once been a pleasant but by no means huge bedroom on the third floor of a town house, with three windows overlooking the street. The so-called room he now stood in was really nothing more than a slot that had been created by inserting a plasterboard wall. The slot had one of the windows. What was left of the original room was now called a living room, and it had the other two windows. Back by the door to the hallway were two more slots, one for a kitchen two people couldn't pass each other in, and the other for a bathroom. Neither had a window. The place was like one of those little ant colonies you can buy, but it cost them $888 a month, rent-stabilized. If it hadn't been for the rent-stabilization law, it would have cost probably $1,500, which would be out of the question. And they had been happy to find it! My God, there were college graduates his age, thirty-two, all over New York who were dying to find an apartment like this, a 3½, with a view, in a town house, with high ceilings, rent-stabilized, in the West Seventies! Truly pathetic, wasn't it? They could barely afford it when they were both working and their combined salaries had been $56,000 a year, $41,000 after deductions. The plan had been that Rhoda's mother would give them the money as a sort of baby present to hire a baby nurse for four weeks, while Rhoda got back on her feet and went back to work. In the meantime, they would find an *au pair* girl to live in and look after the baby in return for room and board. Rhoda's mother had come through with her part of the plan, but it was already obvious that this *au pair* girl who was willing to sleep on a convertible couch in the living room in an ant colony on the West Side did not exist. Rhoda would not be able to go back to work. They were going to have to get by on his $25,000-after-taxes, and the yearly rent here in this dump, even with the help of rent stabilization, was $10,656.

Well, at least these morbid considerations had restored his bathrobe to a decent shape. So he emerged from the bedroom.

"Good morning, Glenda," he said.

"Oh, good morning, Mr. Kramer," said the baby nurse.

Very cool and British, this voice of hers. Kramer was convinced he really couldn't care less about British accents or the Brits themselves. In fact, they intimidated him, the Brits and their accents. In the baby nurse's *oh*, a mere *oh*, he detected a whiff of *Finally getting up, are you?*

A plump, fiftyish woman, she was already efficiently turned out in her white uniform. Her hair was pulled back into a perfect bun. She had already closed up the convertible couch and put the cushions back in place, so that it had resumed its daytime mode as a dingy yellow, synthetic-linen-covered piece of parlor furniture. She sat on the edge of the thing, her back perfectly straight, drinking a cup of tea. The baby was lying on his back in his crib, perfectly content. Perfectly was the woman's middle name. They had found her through the Gough Agency, which an article in the Home section of the *Times* had listed as one of the best and most fashionable. So they were paying the fashionable price of $525 a week for an English baby nurse. From time to time she mentioned other places where she had worked. Always it was Park Avenue, Fifth Avenue, Sutton Place . . . Well, too bad! Now you're getting an eyeful of a jack-legged walkup on the West Side! They called her Glenda. She called them Mr. Kramer and Mrs. Kramer, instead of Larry and Rhoda. Everything was upside down. Glenda was the very picture of gentility, having tea, while Mr. Kramer, lord of the ant colony, came tramping through to the bathroom barefooted, bare-legged, tousle-headed, wearing a tattered old plaid bathrobe. Over in the corner, under an extremely dusty *Dracaena fragrans* plant, the TV set was on. A commercial flared to an end, and some smiling heads began talking on the *Today* show. But the sound was not on. She wouldn't be so imperfect as to have the TV blaring. What on earth was she really thinking, this British arbiter sitting in judgment (on an appalling fold-out sofa) upon the squalor of *chez* Kramer?

As for the mistress of the household, Mrs. Kramer, she was just emerging from the bathroom, still in her bathrobe and slippers.

"Larry," she said, "look at my fuh-head. I think theh's something theh, like a rash. I sawr it in the mirror."

Still foggy, Kramer tried to look at her fuh-head.

"It's nothing, Rhoda. It's like the beginning of a pimple."

That was another thing. Since the baby nurse had arrived, Kramer had also become acutely aware of the way his wife talked. He had never noticed it before, or hardly. She was a graduate of New York University. For the past four years she had been an editor at Waverly Place Books. She was an intellectual, or at least she seemed to be reading a lot of the poetry of John Ashbery and Gary Snyder when he first met her, and she had a lot to say about South Africa and Nicaragua.

Nevertheless, a forehead was a fuh-head, and *there* had no r at the end, but *saw* did.

That was like her mother, too.

Rhoda padded on by, and Kramer entered the bathroom slot. The bathroom was pure Tenement Life. There was laundry hanging all along the shower curtain rod. There was more laundry on a line that ran diagonally across the room, a baby's zip-up suit, two baby bibs, some bikini panties, several pairs of panty hose, and God knew what else, none of it the baby nurse's, of course. Kramer had to duck down to get to the toilet. A wet pair of panty hose slithered over his ear. It was revolting. There was a wet towel on the toilet seat. He looked around for some place to hang it. There was no place. He threw it on the floor.

After urinating, he moved twelve or fourteen inches to the sink and took off his bathrobe and his T-shirt and draped them over the toilet seat. Kramer liked to survey his face and his build in the mornings. What with his wide, flat features, his blunt nose, his big neck, nobody ever took him for Jewish at first. He might be Greek, Slavic, Italian, even Irish—in any event, something tough. He wasn't happy that he was balding on top, but in a way that made him look tough, too. He was balding the way a lot of professional football players were balding. And his build . . . But this morning he lost heart. Those powerful deltoids, those massive sloping trapezii, those tightly bunched pectorals, those curving slabs of meat, his biceps—they looked deflated. He was fucking *atrophying!* He hadn't been able to work out since the baby and the baby nurse arrived. He kept his weights in a carton behind the tub that held the dracaena plant, and he worked out between the plant and the couch—and there was no way in the world he could work out, could grunt and groan and strain and ventilate and take appreciative looks at himself in the mirror in front of the English baby nurse . . . or the mythical *au pair* girl of the future, for that matter . . . Let's face it! It's time to give up those childish dreams! You're an American workadaddy now! Nothing more.

When he left the bathroom, he found Rhoda sitting on the couch next to the English baby nurse, and both of them had their eyes pinned on the TV set, and the sound was up. It was the news segment of the *Today* show.

Rhoda looked up and said excitedly: "Look at this, Larry! It's the Mayor! There was a riot in Harlem last night. Someone threw a bottle at him!"

Kramer only barely noticed that she said *meh-uh* for *mayor* and *boh-uhl* for *bottle*. Astonishing things were happening on the screen. A stage—a melee—heaving bodies—and then a huge hand filled the screen and blotted out everything for an instant. More screams and grimaces and thrashing about, and then pure vertigo. To Kramer and Rhoda and the baby nurse it was as if the rioters were breaking through the screen and jumping onto the floor right beside little Joshua's crib. And this was the *Today* show, not the local news. This was what America was having for breakfast this morning, a snootful of the people of Harlem rising up in their righteous wrath and driving the white Mayor off the stage in a public hall. There goes the back of his head right there, burrowing for cover. Once he was the Mayor of New York City. Now he is the Mayor of White New York.

When it was over, the three of them looked at one another, and Glenda, the English baby nurse, spoke up, with considerable agitation.

"Well, I think that's perfectly disgusting. The colored don't know how good they've got it in this country, I can tell you that much. In Britain there's not so much as a colored in a police uniform, much less an important public official, the way they have here. Why, there was an article just the other day. There's more than two hundred coloreds who are mayors in this country. And they want to bash the Mayor of New York about. Some people don't know how well off they are, if you ask me."

She shook her head angrily.

Kramer and his wife looked at each other. He could tell she was thinking the same thing he was.

Thank God in heaven! What a relief! They could let their breaths out now. Miss Efficiency was a bigot. These days the thing about bigotry was, it was undignified. It was a sign of Low Rent origins, of inferior social status, of poor taste. So they were the superiors of their English baby nurse, after all. What a fucking relief.

The rain had just about stopped when Kramer started walking to the subway. He was wearing an old raincoat over his usual gray suit, button-down shirt, and necktie. He had on a pair of Nike running shoes, white with stripes on the sides. He carried his brown leather dress shoes in a shopping bag, one of those slippery white plastic bags you get at the A&P.

The subway stop where he could catch the D train to the Bronx was at Eighty-first Street and Central Park West. He liked to walk across to Central Park West on Seventy-seventh Street and then walk up to Eighty-first, because that took him past the Museum of Natural History. It was a beautiful block, the most beautiful block on the West Side, to Kramer's way of thinking, like a street scene in Paris; not that he had ever been to Paris. Seventy-seventh Street was very wide at that point. On one side was the museum, a marvelous Romanesque Revival creation in an old reddish stone. It was set back in a little park with trees. Even on a cloudy day like this the young spring leaves seemed to glow. *Verdant* was the word that crossed his mind. On this side of the street, where he was walking, was a cliff of elegant apartment houses overlooking the museum. There were doormen. He got glimpses of marbled halls. And then he thought of the girl with brown lipstick . . . He could see her very clearly now, much more clearly than in the dream. He clenched his fist. Damn it! He was going to do it! *He was going to call her.* He was going to make that telephone call. He'd have to wait until the end of the trial, of course. But he was going to do it. He was tired of watching *other people* lead . . . The Life. The girl with brown lipstick!—the two of them, looking into each other's eyes across a table in one of those restaurants with blond wood and exposed brick and hanging plants and brass and etched glass and menus with crayfish Natchez and veal and plantains mesquite and cornbread with cayenne pepper!

Kramer had that vision comfortably in place when just up ahead, from the swell-looking doorway of 44 West Seventy-seventh Street emerged a figure that startled him.

It was a young man, almost babyish in appearance, with a round face and dark hair, neatly combed back. He was wearing a covert-cloth Chesterfield topcoat with a golden brown velvet collar and carrying one of those burgundy leather attaché cases that come from Mädler or T. Anthony on Park Avenue and have a buttery smoothness that announces: "I cost $500." You could see part of the uniformed arm that held the door open for him. He was walking with brisk little steps under the canopy, across the sidewalk, toward an Audi sedan. There was a driver in the front seat. There was a number—271—in the rear side window; a private car service. And now the doorman was hurrying out, and the young man paused to let him catch up and open the sedan's rear door.

And this young man was . . . Andy Heller! No doubt about it whatsoever. He had been in Kramer's class at Columbia Law School—and how superior Kramer had felt when Andy, chubby bright little Andy, had done the usual thing, namely, gone to work Downtown, for Angstrom & Molner. Andy and hundreds like him would spend the next five or ten years humped over their desks checking commas, document citations, and block phrases to zip up and fortify the greed of mortgage brokers, health-and-beauty-aid manufacturers, merger-and-acquisition arbitragers, and re-insurance discounters—while he, Kramer, would embrace life and wade up to his hips into the lives of the miserable and the damned and stand up on his feet in the courtrooms and fight, *mano a mano* before the bar of justice.

And that was the way it had, in fact, turned out. Why, then, did Kramer now hold back? Why didn't he march right up and sing out, "Hi, Andy"? He was no more than twenty feet from his old classmate. Instead, he stopped and turned his head toward the front of the building and put his hand to his face, as if he had something in his eye. He was damned if he felt like having Andy Heller—while his doorman held his car door open for him and his driver waited for the signal to depart—he was damned if he felt like having Andy Heller look him in the face and say, "Larry Kramer, how you doing!" and then, "What you doing?" And he would have to say, "Well, I'm an assistant district attorney up in the Bronx." He wouldn't even have to add, "Making $36,600 a year." That was common knowledge. All the while, Andy Heller would be scanning his dirty raincoat, his old gray suit, which was too short in the pants, his Nike sneakers, his A&P shopping bag . . . Fuck that . . . Kramer stood there with his head turned, faking a piece of grit in his eye, until he heard the door of the Audi shut. It sounded like a safe closing. He turned around just in time to catch a nice fluffy little cloud of German-luxury-auto fumes in his face as Andy Heller departed for his office. Kramer didn't even want to think about what the goddamned place probably looked like.

On the subway, the D train, heading for the Bronx, Kramer stood in the aisle holding on to a stainless-steel pole while the car bucked and lurched and screamed. On the plastic bench across from him sat a bony old man who seemed to be growing like a fungus out of a backdrop of graffiti. He was reading a newspaper. The headline on the newspaper said HARLEM MOB CHASES MAYOR. The words were so big, they took up the entire page. Up above, in smaller letters, it said *"Go Back Down to Hymietown!"* The old man was wearing a pair of purple-and-white-striped running sneakers. They looked weird on such an old man, but there was nothing really odd about them, not on the D train. Kramer scanned the floor. Half the people in the car were wearing sneakers with splashy designs on them and molded soles that looked like gravy boats. Young people were wearing them, old men were wearing them, mothers with children on their laps were wearing them, and for that matter, the children were wearing them. This was not for reasons of Young Fit & Firm Chic, the way it was downtown, where you saw a lot of well-dressed young white people going off to work in the morning wearing these sneakers. No, on the D train the reason was, they were cheap. On the D train these sneakers were like a sign around the neck reading SLUM or EL BARRIO.

Kramer resisted admitting to himself why *he* wore them. He let his eyes drift up. There were a few people looking at the tabloids with the headlines about the riot, but the D train to the Bronx was not a readers' train . . . No . . . Whatever happened in Harlem would have exactly no effect in the Bronx. Everybody in the car was looking at the world with the usual stroked-out look, avoiding eye contact.

Just then there was one of those drops in sound, one of those holes in the roar you get when a door opens between subway cars. Into the car came three boys, black, fifteen or sixteen years old, wearing big sneakers with enormous laces, untied but looped precisely in parallel lines, and black thermal jackets. Kramer braced and made a point of looking tough and bored. He tensed his sternocleido-mastoid muscles to make his neck fan out like a wrestler's. One on one . . . he could tear any one of them apart . . . But it was never one on one . . . He saw boys like this every day in court . . . Now the three of them were moving through the aisle . . . They walked with a pumping gait known as the Pimp Roll . . . He saw the Pimp Roll in the courtroom every day, too . . . On warm days in the Bronx there were so many boys out strutting around with the Pimp Roll, whole streets seemed to be bobbing up and down . . . They drew closer, with the invariable cool blank look . . . Well, what could they possibly do? . . . They passed on by, on either side of him . . . and nothing happened . . . Well, of course nothing happened . . . An ox, a stud like him . . . he'd be the last person in the world they'd choose to tangle with . . . Just the same, he was always glad when the train pulled into the 161st Street station.

Kramer climbed the stairs and came out onto 161st Street. The sky was clearing. Before him, right there, rose the great bowl of Yankee Stadium. Beyond the stadium were the corroding hulks of the Bronx. Ten or fifteen years ago they had renovated the stadium. They had spent a hundred million dollars on it. That was supposed to lead to "the revitalization of the heart of the Bronx." What a grim joke! Since then, this precinct, the 44th, these very streets, had become the worst in the Bronx for crime. Kramer saw that every day, too.

He started walking up the hill, up 161st Street, in his sneakers, carrying his A&P bag with his shoes inside. The people of these sad streets were standing outside the stores and short-order counters along 161st.

He looked up—and for an instant he could see the old Bronx in all its glory. At the top of the hill, where 161st Street crossed the Grand Concourse, the sun had broken through and had lit up the limestone face of the Concourse Plaza Hotel. From this distance it could still pass for a European resort hotel from the 1920s. The Yankee ballplayers used to live there during the season, the ones who could afford it, the stars. He always pictured them living in big suites. Joe DiMaggio, Babe Ruth, Lou Gehrig . . . Those were the only names he could remember, although his father used to talk about a lot more. O golden Jewish hills of long ago! Up there at the top of the hill, 161st Street and the Grand Concourse had been the summit of the Jewish dream, of the new Canaan, the new Jewish borough of New York, the Bronx! Kramer's father had grown up seventeen blocks from here, on 178th Street—and he had dreamed of nothing in this world more glorious than having an apartment . . . someday . . . in one of these grand buildings on the summit, on the Grand Concourse. They had created the Grand Concourse as the Park Avenue of the Bronx, except the new land of Canaan was going to do it better. The Concourse was wider than Park Avenue, and it had been more lushly landscaped—and there you had another grim joke. Did you want an apartment on the Concourse? Today you could have your pick. The Grand Hotel of the Jewish dream was now a welfare hotel, and the Bronx, the Promised Land, was 70 percent black and Puerto Rican.

The poor sad Jewish Bronx! When he was twenty-two, just entering law school, Kramer had begun to think of his father as a little Jew who over the course of a lifetime had finally made the great Diasporic migration from the Bronx to Oceanside, Long Island, all of twenty miles away, and who still trundled back and forth every day to a paper-carton warehouse in the West Twenties, in Manhattan, where he was "comptroller." He, Kramer, would be the lawyer . . . the cosmopolitan . . . And now, ten years later, what had happened? He was living in an ant colony that made the old man's Tract Colonial three-bedroom in Oceanside look like San Simeon and taking the D train—the *D train!*—to work every day in . . . *the Bronx!*

Right before Kramer's eyes the sun began to light up the other great building at the top of the hill, the building where he worked, the Bronx County Building. The building was a prodigious limestone parthenon done in the early thirties in the Civic Moderne style. It was nine stories high and covered three city blocks, from 161st Street to 158th Street. Such open-faced optimism they had, whoever dreamed up that building back then!

Despite everything, the courthouse stirred his soul. Its four great façades were absolute jubilations of sculpture and bas-relief. There were groups of classical figures at every corner. Agriculture, Commerce, Industry, Religion, and the Arts, Justice, Government, Law and Order, and the Rights of Man—noble Romans wearing togas in the Bronx! Such a golden dream of an Apollonian future!

Today, if one of those lovely classical lads ever came down from up there, he wouldn't survive long enough to make it to 162nd Street to get a Choc-o-pop or a blue Shark. They'd whack him out just to get his toga. It was no joke, this precinct, the 44th. On the 158th Street side the courthouse overlooked Franz Sigel Park, which from a sixth-floor window was a beautiful swath of English-style landscaping, a romance of trees, bushes, grass, and rock outcroppings that stretched down the south side of the hill. Practically nobody but him knew the name of Franz Sigel Park anymore, however, because nobody with half a brain in his head would ever go far enough into the park to reach the plaque that bore the name. Just last week some poor devil was stabbed to death at 10:00 a.m. on one of the concrete benches that had been placed in the park in 1971 in the campaign to "provide urban amenities to revitalize Franz Sigel Park and reclaim it for the community." The bench was ten feet inside the park. Somebody killed the man for his portable radio, one of the big ones known in the District Attorney's Office as Bronx attaché cases. Nobody from the District Attorney's Office went out into the park on a sunny day in May to have lunch, not even somebody who could bench-press two hundred pounds, the way he could. Not even a court officer, who had a uniform and legally carried a .38, ever did such a thing. They stayed inside the building, this island fortress of the Power, of the white people, like himself, this Gibraltar in the poor sad Sargasso Sea of the Bronx.

On the street he was about to cross, Walton Avenue, three orange-and-blue

Corrections Department vans were lined up, waiting to get into the building's service bay. The vans brought prisoners from the Bronx House of Detention, Rikers Island, and the Bronx Criminal Court, a block away, for appearances at Bronx County Supreme Court, the court that handled serious felonies. The courtrooms were on the upper floors, and the prisoners were brought into the service bay. Elevators took them up to holding pens on the courtroom floors.

You couldn't see inside the vans, because their windows were covered by a heavy wire mesh. Kramer didn't have to look. Inside those vans would be the usual job lots of blacks and Latins, plus an occasional young Italian from the Arthur Avenue neighborhood and once in a while an Irish kid from up in Woodlawn or some stray who had the miserable luck to pick the Bronx to get in trouble in.

"The chow," Kramer said to himself. Anybody looking at him would have actually seen his lips move as he said it.

In about forty-five seconds he would learn that somebody was, in fact, looking at him. But at that moment it was nothing more than the usual, the blue-and-orange vans and him saying to himself, "The chow."

Kramer had reached that low point in the life of an assistant district attorney in the Bronx when he is assailed by Doubts. Every year forty thousand people, forty thousand incompetents, dimwits, alcoholics, psychopaths, knockabouts, good souls driven to some terrible terminal anger, and people who could only be described as stone evil, were arrested in the Bronx. Seven thousand of them were indicted and arraigned, and then they entered the maw of the criminal justice system—right here—through the gateway into Gibraltar, where the vans were lined up. That was about 150 new cases, 150 more pumping hearts and morose glares, every week that the courts and the Bronx County District Attorney's Office were open. And to what end? The same stupid, dismal, pathetic, horrifying crimes were committed day in and day out, all the same. What was accomplished by assistant D.A.'s, by any of them, through all this relentless stirring of the muck? The Bronx crumbled and decayed a little more, and a little more blood dried in the cracks. The Doubts! One thing was accomplished for sure. The system was fed, and those vans brought in the chow. Fifty judges, thirty-five law clerks, 245 assistant district attorneys, one D.A.—the thought of which made Kramer twist his lips in a smile, because no doubt Weiss was up there on the sixth floor right now screaming at Channel 4 or 7 or 2 or 5 about the television coverage he didn't get yesterday and wants today—and Christ knew how many criminal lawyers, Legal Aid lawyers, court reporters, court clerks, court officers, correction officers, probation officers, social workers, bail bondsmen, special investigators, case clerks, court psychiatrists—what a vast swarm had to be fed! And every morning the chow came in, the chow and the Doubts.

Kramer had just set foot on the street when a big white Pontiac Bonneville came barreling by, a real boat, with prodigious overhangs, front and back, the kind of twenty-foot frigate they stopped making about 1980. It came screeching and nose-diving to a stop on the far corner. The Bonneville's door, a gigantic expanse of molded sheet metal, about five feet wide, opened with a sad torque pop, and a judge named Myron Kovitsky climbed out. He was about sixty, short, thin, bald, wiry, with a sharp nose, hollow eyes, and a grim set to his mouth. Through the back window of the Bonneville, Kramer could see a silhouette sliding over into the driver's seat vacated by the judge. That would be his wife.

The sound of the enormous old car door opening and the sight of this little figure getting out were depressing. The judge, Mike Kovitsky, comes to work in a greaser yacht practically ten years old. As a Supreme Court judge, he made $65,100. Kramer knew the figures by heart. He had maybe $45,000 left after taxes. For a sixty-year-old man in the upper reaches of the legal profession, that was pathetic. Downtown . . . in the world of Andy Heller . . . they were paying people right out of law school that much to start. And this man whose car goes *thwop* every time he opens the door is at the top of the hierarchy here in the island fortress. He, Kramer, occupied some uncertain position in the middle. If he played his cards right and managed to ingratiate himself with the Bronx Democratic organization, this—*thwop!*—was the eminence to which he might aspire three decades from now.

Kramer was halfway across the street when it began:

"Yo! Kramer!"

It was a huge voice. Kramer couldn't tell where it was coming from.

"You cocksucker!"

Whuh? It stopped him in his tracks. A sensation—a sound—like rushing steam—filled his skull.

"Hey, Kramer, you piece a shit!"

It was another voice. They—

"Yo! Fuckhead!"

They were coming from the back of the van, the blue-and-orange van, the one closest to him, no more than thirty feet away. He couldn't see them. He couldn't make them out through the mesh over the windows.

"Yo! Kramer! You Hymie asshole!"

Hymie! How did they even know he was Jewish! He didn't look—Kramer wasn't a—why would they—it rocked him!

"Yo! Kramer! You faggot! Kiss my ass!"

"Aaayyyyyyy, maaaaan, you steeeck uppy yass! You steeeck uppy yass!"

A Latin voice—the very barbarism of the pronunciation twisted the knife in a little farther.

"Yo! Shitface!"

"Aaaayyyyyy! You keesa sol! You keeeesa sol!"

"Yo! Kramer! Eatcho muvva!"

"Aaaaaaayy! Maaaan! Fokky you! Fokky you!"

It was a chorus! A rain of garbage! A *Rigoletto* from the sewer, from the rancid gullet of the Bronx!

Kramer was still out in the middle of the street. What should he do? He stared at the van. He couldn't make out a thing. Which ones? . . . Which of them . . . from out of that endless procession of baleful blacks and Latins . . . But no! Don't look! He looked away. Who was watching? Did he just take this unbelievable abuse and keep walking to the Walton Avenue entrance, while they poured more of it all over him, or did he confront them? . . . Confront them? *How?* . . . No! He'd pretend it wasn't him they were yelling at . . . Who was to know the difference! . . . He'd keep walking up 161st Street and go around to the main entrance! No one had to know it was him! He scanned the sidewalk by the Walton Avenue entrance, which was close to the vans . . . Nothing but the usual poor sad citizens . . . They had stopped in their tracks. They were staring at the van . . . The guard! The guard at the Walton Avenue entrance knew him! The guard would know he was trying to get away and finesse the whole thing! But the guard wasn't there . . . He'd probably ducked inside the doorway so he wouldn't have to do anything himself. Then Kramer saw Kovitsky. The judge was on the sidewalk about fifteen feet from the entrance. He was standing there, staring at the van. Then he locked right at Kramer. Shit! He knows me! He knows they're yelling at *me!* This little figure, who had just emerged—*thwop!*—from his Bonneville, stood between Kramer and his orderly retreat.

"Yo! Kramer! You yellow shitbird!"

"Hey! You bald-headed worm!"

"Aaaaaayyyy! You steecka balda ed uppas sol! Steeecka balda ed uppas sol!"

Bald? Why bald? He wasn't bald. He was losing a little hair, you bastards, but he was a long way from being bald! Wait a minute! Not him at all—they'd spotted the judge, Kovitsky. Now they had two targets.

"Yo! Kramer! What you got inna bag, man?"

"Hey, you bald-headed old fart!"

"You shiny ol' shitfa brains!"

"Gotcho balls inna bag, Kramer?"

They were in it together, him and Kovitsky. Now he couldn't make his end run to the 161st Street entrance. So he kept walking across the street. He felt as if he were underwater. He cut a glance at Kovitsky. But Kovitsky was no longer looking at him. He was walking straight toward the van. His head was lowered. He was glaring. You could see the whites of his eyes. His pupils were like two death rays burning just beneath his upper eyelids. Kramer had seen him in court like this . . . with his head lowered and his eyes ablaze.

The voices inside the van tried to drive him back.

"What you looking at, you shriveled little pecker?"

"Yaaaaggghh, come on! Come on, wormdick!"

But the chorus was losing its rhythm. They didn't know what to make of this wiry little fury.

Kovitsky walked right up to the van and tried to stare through the mesh. He put his hands on his hips.

"Yeah! What you think you looking at?"

"Sheeeeuh! Gon' give you something to look at, bro'!"

But they were losing steam. Now Kovitsky walked to the front of the van. He turned those blazing eyes on the driver.

"Do . . . you . . . hear . . . that?" said the little judge, pointing toward the rear of the van.

"Whuh?" says the driver. "Whaddaya?" He didn't know what to say.

"Are you fucking deaf?" said Kovitsky. "Your prisoners . . . *your* . . . pris-oners . . . You're an officer of the Department of Corrections . . ."

He started jabbing his finger toward the man.

"*Your . . . prisoners . . . You let your prisoners* pull . . . this *shit* . . . on the citizens of this community and on the officers of *this court?*"

The driver was a swarthy fat man, pudgy, around fifty, or some gray-lard middle age, a civil-service lifer . . . and all at once his eyes and his mouth opened up, without a sound coming out, and he lifted his shoulders, and he turned his palms up and the corners of his mouth down.

It was the primordial shrug of the New York streets, the look that said,

"Egggh, whaddaya? Whaddaya want from me?" And in this specific instance: "Whaddaya want me to do, crawl back in that cage with that lot?"

It was the age-old New York cry for mercy, unanswerable and undeniable.

Kovitsky stared at the man and shook his head the way you do when you've just seen a hopeless case. Then he turned and walked back to the rear of the van.

"Here come Hymie!"

"Unnh! Unnnh! Unnnhh!"

"Chew my willie, Yo' Honor."

Kovitsky stared at the window, still trying to make out his enemy through the heavy mesh. Then he took a deep breath, and there was a tremendous snuffling sound in his nose and a deep rumbling in his chest and throat. It seemed incredible that such a volcanic sound could come from out of such a small thin body. And then he *spit*. He propelled a prodigious gob of spit toward the window of the van. It hit the wire mesh and hung there, a huge runny yellow oyster, part of which began to sag like some hideous virulent strand of gum or taffy with a glob on the bottom of it. And there it remained, gleaming in the sun for those inside, whoever they might be, to contemplate at their leisure.

It stunned them. The whole chorus stopped. For one strange feverish moment there was nothing in the world, in the solar system, in the universe, in all of astronomy, but the cage and this one gleaming, oozing, pendulous sunlit gob of spit.

Then, keeping his right hand close to his chest so that no one on the sidewalk could see it, the judge shot them a finger and turned on his heels and walked toward the entrance to the building.

He was halfway to the door before they got their breath back.

"Yeggghhh, fuck you, too, man!"

"You wanna . . . sheeeeuh . . . you try that . . ."

But their hearts weren't in it anymore. The grisly esprit of the prison-van uprising had fizzled in the face of this furious blazing little steel rod of a man.

Kramer hurried after Kovitsky and caught up with him as he was going in the Walton Street entrance. He *had* to catch up with him. He had to show him that he was with him all along. It was the two of them out there taking that insidious abuse.

The guard had reappeared at the door. "Good morning, Judge," he said, as if it were just another day at the island fortress of Gibraltar.

Kovitsky barely looked at him. He was preoccupied. His head was down.

Kramer touched his shoulder. "Hey, Judge, you're too much!" Kramer beamed, as if the two of them had just been through a great battle, shoulder to shoulder. "They shut up! I couldn't believe it! They *shut up!*"

Kovitsky stopped and looked Kramer up and down, as if looking at someone he had never seen before.

"Fucking useless," said the judge.

He's blaming me for doing nothing, for not helping him—but in the next instant Kramer realized that Kovitsky was in fact talking about the driver of the van.

"Well, the poor sonofabitch," said Kovitsky, "he's terrified. I'd be ashamed to have a job like that if I was that fucking terrified."

He seemed to be talking more to himself than to Kramer. He kept on talking about this fucking whatever and that fucking whatever. The profanity scarcely even registered on Kramer. The courthouse was like the army. From the judges on down to the guards there was one all-purpose adjective or participle or whatever it should be called, and after a while it was as natural as breathing. No, Kramer's mind was racing ahead. He was afraid the next words out of Kovitsky's mouth were going to be "Why did you just fucking stand there, doing nothing?" He was already inventing excuses. "I couldn't tell where it was coming from . . . I didn't know if it was from the van or . . ."

The fluorescent lighting gave the hallway the dim toxic haze of an X-ray clinic.

". . . this Hymie business," Kovitsky was saying. Then he gave Kramer a look that clearly required a response.

Kramer didn't know what the hell he had been talking about.

"Hymie?"

"Yeah, 'Here comes Hymie,' " said Kovitsky. " ' Wormdick.' What difference does that make, 'wormdick.' " He laughed, genuinely amused by the thought. " 'Wormdick' . . . But 'Hymie.' That's fucking poison. That's *hate!* That's anti-Semitic. And for *what?* Without the Yiddishe, they'd still be laying asphalt and looking up shotgun barrels in South Carolina, is what the fuck they'd be doing, the poor bastards."

An alarm went off. A frantic ring filled the hall. It pounded Kramer's ears in waves. Judge Kovitsky had to raise his voice to be heard, but he didn't even look around. Kramer didn't bat an eye. The alarm meant a prisoner had escaped or some skinny little thug's brother had pulled out a revolver in a courtroom, or some gargantuan tenant had grabbed a 130-pound hearing officer in a hammer-lock. Or maybe it was only a fire. The first few times Kramer heard the alarm on the island fortress of Gibraltar, his eyes jumped around and he braced himself for the clatter of a herd of guards wearing military-box-toed leather shoes and waving .38s, running along the marble floors trying to catch some nutball in supergraphic sneakers who, jacked up by fear, does the hundred in 8.4. But after a while he ignored it. It was the normal state of red alert, panic, and disarray in the Bronx County Building. All around Kramer and the judge, people were swiveling their heads in every direction. Such sad faces . . . They were entering Gibraltar for the first time, on Christ knows what sad missions.

All at once Kovitsky was motioning toward the floor and saying, ". . . is this, Kramer?"

"This?" said Kramer, desperately trying to figure out what the judge was talking about.

"These fucking shoes," said Kovitsky.

"Ah! Shoes," said Kramer. "They're running shoes, Judge."

"Is that something Weiss thought up?"

"Noooo," said Kramer, chuckling as if moved by the judge's wit.

"Jogging for Justice? Is that what Abe has you guys doing, jogging for Justice?"

"No, no, no, no." More chuckles and a big grin, since Kovitsky obviously loved this line, jogging for Justice.

"Christ, every kid who sticks up a Red Apple's in my courtroom wearing these goddamned things, and now you guys?"

"Nooo-ho-ho."

"You think you're gonna come in my part looking like this?"

"Nooooooo-ho-ho-ho! Wouldn't think of it, Judge."

The alarm kept ringing. The new people, the new sad faces who had never been inside this citadel before, looked all about with their eyes wide and their mouths open, and they saw a bald-headed old white man in a gray suit and a white shirt and a necktie and a balding young white man in a gray suit and a white shirt and a necktie just standing there talking, smiling, yakking, shooting the breeze, and so if these two white people, so obviously a part of the Power, were just standing there, without so much as lifting an eyebrow, how bad could it be?

As the alarm rang in his head, Kramer grew still more depressed.

Right then and there he made up his mind. He was going to do something— something startling, something rash, something desperate, whatever it took. He was going to break out of here. He was going to rise up from this muck. He was going to light up the sky, seize The Life for himself—

He could see the girl with brown lipstick again, just as surely as if she was standing right next to him in this sad grim place.

3

FROM THE FIFTIETH FLOOR

SHERMAN McCOY walked out of his apartment building holding his daughter Campbell's hand. Misty days like this created a peculiar ashy-blue light on Park Avenue. But once they stepped out from under the awning over the entrance . . . such radiance! The median strip on Park was a swath of yellow tulips. There were thousands of them, thanks to the dues apartment owners like Sherman paid to the Park Avenue Association and the thousands of dollars the association paid to a gardening service called Wiltshire Country Gardens, run by three Koreans from Maspeth, Long Island. There was something heavenly about the yellow glow of all the tulips. That was appropriate. So long as Sherman held his daughter's hand in his and walked her to her bus stop, he felt himself a part of God's grace. A sublime state, it was, and it didn't cost much. The bus stop was only across the street. There was scarcely a chance for his impatience over Campbell's tiny step to spoil this refreshing nip of fatherhood he took each morning.

Campbell was in the first grade at Taliaferro, which, as everybody, *tout le monde*, knew, was pronounced Toliver. Each morning the Taliaferro school dispatched its own bus, bus driver, and children's chaperone up Park Avenue. Few, indeed, were the girls at Taliaferro who did not live within walking distance of that bus route.

To Sherman, as he headed out onto the sidewalk holding Campbell's hand, she was a vision. She was a vision anew each morning. Her hair was a luxuriance of soft waves like her mother's, but lighter and more golden. Her little face—perfection! Not even the gawky years of adolescence would alter it. He was sure of that. In her burgundy school jumper, her white blouse with its buttercup collar, her little nylon backpack, her white knee-high socks, she was an angel. Sherman found the very sight touching beyond belief.

The morning-shift doorman was an old Irishman named Tony. After opening the door for them, he stepped outside under the awning and watched them depart. That was fine . . . fine! Sherman liked to have his fatherhood observed. This morning he was a serious individual, representing Park Avenue and Wall

Street. He wore a blue-gray nailhead worsted suit, custom-tailored in England for $1,800, two-button, single-breasted, with ordinary notched lapels. On Wall Street double-breasted suits and peaked lapels were considered a bit sharp, a bit too Garment District. His thick brown hair was combed straight back. He squared his shoulders and carried his long nose and wonderful chin up high.

"Sweetheart, let me button your sweater. It's a little chilly."

"No way, José," said Campbell.

"Come on, sweetie, I don't want you to catch cold."

"N O, Séjo, N O." She jerked her shoulders away from him. Séjo was José backward. "N-n-n-n Ohhhhh." So Sherman sighed and abandoned his plan to save his daughter from the elements. They walked on a bit.

"Daddy?"

"Yes, sweetheart?"

"Daddy, what if there isn't any God?"

Sherman was startled, bowled over. Campbell was looking up at him with a perfectly ordinary expression, as if she had just asked what those yellow flowers were called.

"Who said there isn't any God?"

"But what if there *isn't?*"

"What makes you think—did somebody tell you there wasn't any God?"

What insidious little troublemaker in her class had been spreading this poison? So far as Sherman knew, Campbell still believed in Santa Claus, and here she was, beginning to question the existence of God! And yet . . . it was a precocious question for a six-year-old, wasn't it? No two ways about that. To think that such a speculation—

"But what if there *isn't!*" She was annoyed. Asking her about the history of the question was no answer.

"But there *is* a God, sweetie. So I can't tell you about 'if there isn't.'" Sherman tried never to lie to her. But this time he felt it the prudent course. He had hoped he would never have to discuss religion with her. They had begun sending her to Sunday school at St. James' Episcopal Church, at Madison and Seventy-first. That was the way you took care of religion. You enrolled them at St. James', and you avoided talking or thinking about religion again.

"Oh," said Campbell. She stared out into the distance. Sherman felt guilty. She had brought up a difficult question, and he had ducked it. And here she was, at the age of six, trying to piece together the greatest puzzle of life.

"Daddy?"

"Yes, darling?" He held his breath.

"You know Mrs. Winston's bicycle?"

Mrs. Winston's bicycle? Then he remembered. Two years ago, at Campbell's nursery school, there had been a teacher named Mrs. Winston who braved the traffic and rode a bicycle to school every day. All the children had thought this was wonderful, a teacher who rode a bicycle to school. He had never heard Campbell mention the woman since then.

"Oh yes, I remember." An anxious pause.

"MacKenzie has one just like it."

MacKenzie? MacKenzie Reed was a little girl in Campbell's class.

"She does?"

"Yes. Only it's smaller."

Sherman waited . . . for the leap of logic . . . but it never came. That was it. God lives! God is dead! Mrs. Winston's bicycle! No way, José! N O, Séjo! They all came out of the same heap in the toy box. Sherman was relieved for a moment, but then he felt cheated. The thought that his daughter might actually have questioned the existence of God at the age of six—this he had taken as a sign of superior intelligence. Over the past ten years, on the Upper East Side, for the first time, intelligence had become socially correct for girls.

Several little girls in burgundy jumpers, and their parents or nannies, were assembled at the Taliaferro bus stop, on the other side of Park Avenue. As soon as Campbell saw them, she tried to remove her hand from Sherman's. She had reached that age. But he wouldn't let her. He held her hand tightly and led her across the street. He was her protector. He glowered at a taxi as it came to a noisy stop at the light. He would gladly throw himself in front of it, if that was what it would take to save Campbell's life. As they crossed Park Avenue, he had a mental picture of what an ideal pair they made. Campbell, the perfect angel in a private-school uniform; himself, with his noble head, his Yale chin, his big frame, and his $1,800 British suit, the angel's father, a man of parts; he visualized the admiring stares, the envious stares, of the drivers, the pedestrians, of one and all.

As soon as they reached the bus stop, Campbell pulled free. The parents who brought their girls to the Taliaferro bus stop in the morning were a cheery bunch. What a chipper mood they were always in! Sherman began saying his good mornings. Edith Tompkins, John Channing, MacKenzie Reed's mother, Kirby Coleman's nanny, Leonard Schorske, Mrs. Lueger. When he got to Mrs. Lueger— he had never known her first name—he did a double take. She was a thin pale blond woman who never wore makeup. This morning she must have rushed down to the bus stop with her daughter at the last minute. She was wearing a man's blue button-down shirt with the top two buttons unbuttoned. She had on a pair of old blue jeans and some ballet slippers. The jeans were very tight. She had a terrific little body. He had never noticed that before. Really quite terrific! She looked so . . . . pale and half-awake and vulnerable. You know, what you need is a cup of coffee, Mrs. Lueger. Come on, I'm going over to that coffee shop on Lexington. Oh, that's silly, Mr. McCoy. Come on up to the apartment. I have some coffee already made. He stared at her for a good two seconds longer than he should have, and then . . . *pop* . . . the bus arrived, a big solid Greyhound-size vehicle, and the children bounded up the steps.

Sherman turned away, then looked back at Mrs. Lueger. But she wasn't look-ing at him. She was walking toward her apartment building. The back seam of her jeans practically clove her in two. There were whitish spots on either side of the seat. They were like highlights for the flesh that welled up underneath. What a marvelous bottom she had! And he had always thought of these women as moms. Who knew what hot little fires burned within these moms?

Sherman started walking east, toward the taxi stand at First Avenue and Seventy-ninth Street. He felt buoyant. Just why, he couldn't have explained. The discovery of the lovely little Mrs. Lueger . . . yes, but in fact he always left the bus stop in a good mood. The Best School, the Best Girls, the Best Families, the Best Section of the capital of the Western world in the late twentieth century— but the only part that stuck in his mind was the sensation of Campbell's little hand holding his. That was why he felt so good. The touch of her trusting, utterly dependent little hand was life itself!

Then his spirits sank. He was walking along at a good clip, his eyes idly panning the façades of the brownstone houses. On this gray morning they looked old and depressing. Shapeless polyethylene bags of trash, in shades of Dogshit Brown and Turd Green, were deposited in front of them, out by the curbs. The bags had a slimy-looking surface. How could people live this way? Just two blocks away was Maria's apartment . . . Ralston Thorpe's was around here somewhere . . . Sherman and Rawlie had gone to Buckley, St. Paul's, and Yale together, and now they both worked at Pierce & Pierce. Rawlie had moved from a sixteen-room apartment on Fifth Avenue to the top two floors of a brownstone somewhere along here after his divorce. Very depressing. Sherman had taken a nice big step toward a divorce last night, hadn't he? Not only had Judy caught him, *in flagrante telephone*, as it were, but then he, abject creature of lust that he was, had gone ahead and gotten laid—right! nothing more than that!—*laid!*—and not returned home for forty-five minutes . . . What would it do to Campbell if he and Judy ever broke up? He couldn't imagine his life after such a thing. Weekend visitation rights with his own daughter? What was that phrase they used? "Quality time"? So tawdry, so tawdry . . . Campbell's soul hardening, month by month, into a brittle little shell . . .

By the time he had gone half a block, he hated himself. He felt like turning around and heading back to the apartment and begging forgiveness and swearing *never again*. He felt like it, but he knew he wouldn't do it. That would make him late getting to the office, which was much frowned upon at Pierce & Pierce. No one ever said anything openly, but you were supposed to get there early and start making money . . . and master the universe. A surge of adrenaline—the Giscard! He was closing in on the biggest deal of his life, the Giscard, the gold-backed bond—Master of the Universe!—then he sank again. Judy had slept on the daybed in the dressing room of their bedroom suite. She was still asleep, or pretending to be, when he got up. Well, thank God for that. He hadn't relished another round with her this morning, especially with Campbell or Bonita listening in. Bonita was one of those South American servants with perfectly pleasant but nonetheless formal demeanors. To display temper or anguish in front of her would be a gaffe. No wonder marriages used to hold up better. Sherman's parents and their friends had all had plenty of servants, and the servants had worked long hours and lived in. If you were unwilling to argue in front of the servants, then there wasn't much opportunity to argue at all.

So in the best McCoy manner, just as his father would have done it—except that he couldn't imagine his father ever being in such a jam—Sherman had kept up appearances. He had breakfast in the kitchen with Campbell, while Bonita got her through breakfast and ready for school. Bonita had a portable television set in the kitchen, and she kept turning toward it to watch the news report of the riot in Harlem. It was hot stuff, but Sherman hadn't paid attention to it. It had all seemed so remote . . . the sort of thing that happened out there . . . among those people . . . He had been busy trying to pump out charm and cheeriness so that Bonita and Campbell wouldn't sense the poisonous atmosphere that enveloped the household.

By now Sherman had walked as far as Lexington Avenue. He always stopped at a candy store near the corner and bought the *Times*. As he turned the corner, a girl was heading toward him, a tall girl with a lot of blond hair. A large handbag hung from her shoulder by a strap. She was walking rapidly, as if heading for the subway at Seventy-seventh Street. She had on a long sweater that was wide open down the front, revealing a polo shirt with a little embroidered emblem over the left breast. She wore some sort of go-to-hell white pants that were very loose and floppy in the legs but exceptionally tight in the crotch. *Exceptionally!* There was an astonishing crevice. Sherman stared and then looked at her face. She stared right back. She looked him right in the eye and smiled. She didn't slow down or give him a provocative look. It was a confident, optimistic look that as much as said, "Hi! We're a couple of good-looking animals, aren't we!" So frank! So unabashed! So eagerly immodest!

In the candy store, after paying for the *Times*, Sherman turned to go out the door and his eyes swept across a magazine rack. The salmon flesh jumped out at him . . . girls . . . boys . . . girls with girls . . . boys with boys . . . girls with boys . . . girls with bare breasts, girls with bare bottoms . . . girls with paraphernalia . . . a happy grinning riot of pornography, a rout, an orgy, a hog wallow . . . On the cover of one magazine is a girl wearing only a pair of high-heeled shoes and a loincloth . . . Except that it isn't a loincloth, it's a snake . . . Somehow it's wedged in her groin and looking right at Sherman . . . She's looking right at him, too . . . On her face is the sunniest, most unaffected smile imaginable . . . It's the face of the girl who serves you a chocolate-chip ice-cream cone at the Baskin-Robbins . . .

Sherman resumed his walk toward First Avenue in a state of agitation. It was in the air! It was a wave! Everywhere! Inescapable! . . . Sex! . . . There for the taking! . . . It walked down the street, as bold as you please! . . . It was splashed all over the shops! If you were a young man and halfway alive, what chance did you have? . . . Technically, he had been unfaithful to his wife. Well, sure . . . but who could remain monogamous with this, this, this *tidal wave* of concupiscence rolling across the world? Christ almighty! A Master of the Universe couldn't be a saint, after all . . . It was unavoidable. For Christ's sake, you can't dodge snowflakes, and this was a blizzard! He had merely been caught at it, that was all, or halfway caught at it. It meant nothing. It had no moral dimension. It was nothing more than getting soaking wet. By the time he reached the cab-stand at First and Seventy-ninth, he had just about worked it out in his mind.

At Seventy-ninth Street and First Avenue the taxis lined up every day to take the young Masters of the Universe down to Wall Street. According to the regulations, every cabdriver was supposed to take you anywhere you wanted to go, but the drivers in the line at Seventy-ninth and First wouldn't budge unless you were going down to Wall Street or close to it. From the cabstand they swung two blocks east and then went down along the East River on the highway, the FDR, the Franklin Delano Roosevelt Drive.

It was a ten-dollar ride each morning, but what was that to a Master of the Universe? Sherman's father had always taken the subway to Wall Street, even when he was the chief executive officer of Dunning Sponget & Leach. Even now, at the age of seventy-one, when he took his daily excursions to Dunning Sponget to breathe the same air as his lawyer cronies for three or four hours, he went by subway. It was a matter of principle. The more grim the subways became, the more graffiti those people scrawled on the cars, the more gold chains they snatched off girls' necks, the more old men they mugged, the more women they pushed in front of the trains, the more determined was John Campbell McCoy that they weren't going to drive him off the New York City subways. But to the new breed, the young breed, the masterful breed, Sherman's breed, there was no such principle. *Insulation!* That was the ticket. That was the term Rawlie Thorpe used. "If you want to live in New York," he once told Sherman, "you've got to insulate, insulate, insulate," meaning insulate yourself from those people. The cynicism and smugness of the idea struck Sherman as very *au courant*. If you could go breezing down the FDR Drive in a taxi, then why file into the trenches of the urban wars?

The driver was . . . a Turk? An Armenian? Sherman tried to make out his name on the card in the frame on the dashboard. Once the taxi reached the drive, he settled back to read the *Times*. There was a picture on the front page of a mob of people on a stage and the Mayor standing near a podium, staring at them. The riot, no doubt. He began to read the story, but his mind wandered. The sun was beginning to break through the clouds. He could see it on the river, off to his left. At this moment the poor filthy river sparkled. It was a sunny day in May, after all. Up ahead, the towers of New York Hospital rose straight up from the edge of the highway. There was a sign for the East Seventy-first Street exit, the one his father had always taken when they drove back from Southampton on Sunday evenings. The very sight of the hospital and the exit made Sherman think of—no, not so much think of as *feel* the house on Seventy-third Street with its Knickerbocker-green rooms. He had grown up in those pale grayish-green rooms and trudged up and down those four flights of narrow stairs believing that he was living in the height of elegance in the household of the mighty John Campbell McCoy, the Lion of Dunning Sponget & Leach. Only recently had it dawned on him that back in 1948, when his parents had bought and renovated that house, they had been a mildly adventurous young couple, tackling what at the time was an old wreck in a down-at-the-heels block, keeping a stern eye on costs every step of the way, and taking pride in what a proper house they had created for a relatively modest amount. Christ! If his father ever found out how much he had paid for his apartment and how he had financed it, he'd have a stroke! Two million six hundred thousand dollars, with $1,800,000 of it borrowed . . . $21,000 a month in principal and interest with a million-dollar balloon payment due in two years . . . The Lion of Dunning Sponget would be appalled . . . and, worse than appalled, wounded . . . wounded at the thought of how his endlessly repeated lessons concerning duty, debt, ostentation, and proportion had whistled straight through his son's skull . . .

Had his father ever played around? It wasn't out of the question. He was a handsome man. He had the Chin. Yet Sherman couldn't imagine it.

And by the time he saw the Brooklyn Bridge up ahead, he stopped trying to. In a few minutes he would be on Wall Street.

The investment-banking firm of Pierce & Pierce occupied the fiftieth, fifty-first, fifty-second, fifty-third, and fifty-fourth floors of a glass tower that rose up sixty stories from out of the gloomy groin of Wall Street. The bond trading room, where Sherman worked, was on the fiftieth. Every day he stepped out of an aluminum-walled elevator into what looked like the reception area of one of those new London hotels catering to the Yanks. Near the elevator door was a fake fireplace and an antique mahogany mantelpiece with great bunches of fruit carved on each corner. Out in front of the fake fireplace was a brass fence or fender, as they called it in country homes in the west of England. In the appropriate months a fake fire glowed within, casting flickering lights upon a prodigious pair of brass andirons. The wall surrounding it was covered in more mahogany, rich and reddish, done in linen-fold panels carved so deep, you could *feel* the expense in the tips of your fingers by just looking at them.

All of this reflected the passion of Pierce & Pierce's chief executive officer, Eugene Lopwitz, for things British. Things British—library ladders, bow-front consoles, Sheraton legs, Chippendale backs, cigar cutters, tufted club chairs, Wilton-weave carpet—were multiplying on the fiftieth floor at Pierce & Pierce day by day. Alas, there wasn't much Eugene Lopwitz could do about the ceiling, which was barely eight feet above the floor. The floor had been raised one foot. Beneath it ran enough cables and wires to electrify Guatemala. The wires provided the power for the computer terminals and telephones of the bond trading room. The ceiling had been lowered one foot, to make room for light housings and air-conditioning ducts and a few more miles of wire. The floor had risen; the ceiling had descended; it was as if you were in an English mansion that had been squashed.

No sooner did you pass the fake fireplace than you heard an ungodly roar, like the roar of a mob. It came from somewhere around the corner. You couldn't miss it. Sherman McCoy headed straight for it, with relish. On this particular morning, as on every morning, it resonated with his very gizzard.

He turned the corner, and there it was: the bond trading room of Pierce & Pierce. It was a vast space, perhaps sixty by eighty feet, but with the same eight-foot ceiling bearing down on your head. It was an oppressive space with a ferocious glare, writhing silhouettes, and the roar. The glare came from a wall of plate glass that faced south, looking out over New York Harbor, the Statue of Liberty, Staten Island, and the Brooklyn and New Jersey shores. The writhing silhouettes were the arms and torsos of young men, few of them older than forty. They had their suit jackets off. They were moving about in an agitated manner and sweating early in the morning and shouting, which created the roar. It was the sound of well-educated young white men baying for money on the bond market.

"Pick up the fucking phone, please!" a chubby, pink-faced member of the Harvard Class of 1976 screamed at someone two rows of desks away. The room was like a newspaper city room in that there were no partitions and no signs of visible rank. Everyone sat at light gray metal desks in front of veal-colored computer terminals with black screens. Rows of green-diode letters and numbers came skidding across.

"I said please pick up the fucking phone! I mean holy shit!" There were dark half-moons in the armpits of his shirt, and the day had just begun.

A member of the Yale Class of 1973 with a neck that seemed to protrude twelve inches out of his shirt stared at a screen and screamed over the telephone at a broker in Paris: "If you can't see the fucking screen . . . Oh, for Christ's sake, Jean-Pierre, that's the *buyer's* five million! The *buyer's!* Nothing further's coming in!"

Then he covered the telephone with his hand and looked straight up at the ceiling and said out loud to no one, except Mammon, "The frogs! The fucking frogs!"

Four desks away, a member of the Stanford Class of 1979 was sitting down, staring at a sheet of paper on his desk and holding a telephone to his ear. His right foot was up on the stirrup of a portable shoeshine stand, and a black man named Felix, who was about fifty—or was he about sixty?—was humped over his foot, stropping his shoe with a high-shine rag. All day long Felix moved from desk to desk, shining the shoes of young bond traders and salesmen as they worked, at three dollars per, counting the tip. Seldom was a word exchanged; Felix scarcely registered on their maculae. Just then Stanford '79 rose from his chair, his eyes still fastened on the sheet of paper, the telephone still at his ear—and his right foot still on the shoeshine stirrup—and he shouted: "Well then, why do you think everybody's stripping the fucking twenty-years?"

Never took his foot off the shoeshine stand! What powerful legs he must have! thought Sherman. Sherman sat down before his own telephone and computer terminals. The shouts, the imprecations, the gesticulations, the fucking fear and greed, enveloped him, and he loved it. He was the number one bond salesman, "the biggest producer," as the phrase went, in the bond trading room of Pierce & Pierce on the fiftieth floor, and he loved the very roar of the storm.

"This Goldman order really fucked things up good!"

"—step up to the fucking plate and—"

"—bid 8¹/₂—"

"I'm away by two thirty-seconds!"

"Somebody's painting you a fucking picture! Can't you see that?"

"I'll take an order and buy 'em at 6-plus!"

"Hit the five-year!"

"Sell five!"

"You couldn't do ten?"

"You think this thing continues up?"

"Strip fever in the twenty-year! That's all these jerks keep talking about!"

"—a hundred million July-nineties at the buck—"

"—naked short—"

"Jesus Christ, what's going on?"

"I don't fucking believe this!"

"Holy fucking shit!" shouted the Yale men and the Harvard men and the Stanford men. "Ho-lee fuc-king shit."

How these sons of the great universities, these legatees of Jefferson, Emerson, Thoreau, William James, Frederick Jackson Turner, William Lyons Phelps, Samuel Flagg Bemis, and the other three-name giants of American scholarship—how these inheritors of the *lux* and the *veritas* now flocked to Wall Street and to the bond trading room of Pierce & Pierce! How the stories circulated on every campus! If you weren't making $250,000 a year within five years, then you were either grossly stupid or grossly lazy. That was the word. By age thirty, $500,000—and that sum had the taint of the mediocre. By age forty you were either making a million a year or you were timid and incompetent. *Make it now!* That motto burned in every heart, like myocarditis. Boys on Wall Street, mere boys, with smooth jawlines and clean arteries, boys still able to blush, were buying three-million-dollar apartments on Park and Fifth. (Why wait?) They were buying thirty-room, four-acre summer places in Southampton, places built in the 1920s and written off in the 1950s as white elephants, places with decaying servants' wings, and they were doing over the servants' wings, too, and even adding on. (Why not? We've got the servants.) They had carnival rides trucked in and installed on the great green lawns for their children's birthday parties, complete with teams of carnival workers to operate them. (A thriving little industry.)

And where did all of this astonishing new money come from? Sherman had heard Gene Lopwitz discourse on that subject. In the Lopwitz analysis, they had Lyndon Johnson to thank. Ever so quietly, the U.S. had started printing money by the billions to finance the war in Vietnam. Before anyone, even Johnson, knew what was happening, a worldwide inflation had begun. Everyone woke up to it when the Arabs suddenly jacked up oil prices in the early 1970s. In no time, markets of all sorts became heaving crapshoots: gold, silver, copper, currencies, bank certificates, corporate notes—even bonds. For decades the bond business had been the bedridden giant of Wall Street. At firms such as Salomon Brothers, Morgan Stanley, Goldman Sachs, and Pierce & Pierce, twice as much money had always changed hands on the bond market as on the stock market. But prices had budged by only pennies at a time, and mostly they went down. As Lopwitz put it, "The bond market has been going down ever since the Battle of Midway." The Battle of Midway (Sherman had to look it up) was in the Second World War. The Pierce & Pierce bond department had consisted of only twenty souls, twenty rather dull souls known as the Bond Bores. The less promising members of the firm were steered into bonds, where they could do no harm.

Sherman resisted the thought that it had been even thus when he entered the bond department. Well, there was no more talk about Bond Bores these days . . . Oh no! Not at all! The bond market had caught fire, and experienced salesmen such as himself were all at once much in demand. All of a sudden, in investment houses all over Wall Street, the erstwhile Bond Bores were making so much money they took to congregating after work in a bar on Hanover Square called Harry's, to tell war stories . . . and assure one another this wasn't dumb luck but, rather, a surge of collective talent. Bonds now represented four-fifths of Pierce & Pierce's business, and the young hotshots, the Yalies, Harvards, and Stanfords, were desperate to get to the bond trading room of Pierce & Pierce, and at this very moment their voices ricocheted off Eugene Lopwitz's linen-fold mahogany walls.

Masters of the Universe! The roar filled Sherman's soul with hope, confidence, esprit de corps, and righteousness. Yes, righteousness! Judy understood none of this, did she? None of it. Oh, he noticed her eyes glazing over when he talked about it. Moving the lever that moves the world was what he was doing—and all she wanted to know was why he never made it home for dinner. When he did make it home for dinner, what did she want to talk about? Her precious interior-decorating business and how she had gotten their apartment into *Architectural Digest*, which, frankly, to a true Wall Streeter was a fucking embarrassment. Did she commend him for the hundreds of thousands of dollars that made her decorating and her lunches and whatever the hell else she did possible? No, she did not. She took it for granted . . .

. . . and so forth and so on. Within ninety seconds, emboldened by the mighty roar of the bond trading room of Pierce & Pierce, Sherman managed to work up a good righteous head of resentment against this woman who had dared make him feel guilty.

He picked up the telephone and was ready to resume work on the greatest coup of his young career, the Giscard, when he spotted something out of the corner of his eye. He *detected* it—righteously!—amid that great bondscape of writhing limbs and torsos. *Arguello was reading a newspaper.*

Ferdinand Arguello was a junior bond salesman, twenty-five or -six years old, from Argentina. He was leaning back in his chair nonchalantly reading a newspaper, and even from here Sherman could see what it was: *The Racing Form. The Racing Form!* The young man looked like a caricature of a South American polo player. He was slender and handsome; he had thick wavy black hair, combed straight back. He was wearing a pair of red silk moiré suspenders. *Silk moiré.* The bond department of Pierce & Pierce was like an Air Force fighter squadron. Sherman knew it even if this young South American didn't. As the number one bond salesman, Sherman had no official rank. Nevertheless, he occupied a moral eminence. You were either capable of doing the job and willing to devote 100 percent to the job, or you got out. The eighty members of the department received a base salary, a safety net, of $120,000 a year each. This was regarded as a laughably small sum. The rest of their income came from commissions and profit-sharing. Sixty-five percent of the department's profits went to Pierce & Pierce. But 35 percent was split among the eighty bond salesmen and traders themselves. All for one and one for all, and lots for oneself! And therefore . . . no slackers allowed! no deadwood! no lightweights! no loafers! You headed straight for your desk, your telephone, and your computer terminal in the morning. The day didn't start with small talk and coffee and perusals of *The Wall Street Journal* and the financial pages of the *Times*, much less *The Racing Form*. You were expected to get on the telephone and start making money. If you left the office, even for lunch, you were expected to give your destination and a telephone number to one of the "sales assistants," who were really secretaries, so that you could be summoned immediately if a new issue of bonds came in (and had to be sold fast). If you went out for lunch, it better have something directly to do with selling bonds for Pierce & Pierce. Otherwise—sit here by the telephone and order in from the deli like the rest of the squadron.

Sherman walked to Arguello's desk and stood over him. "What are you doing, Ferdi?"

From the moment the young man looked up, Sherman could tell he knew what the question meant and that he knew he was wrong. But if there was one thing an Argentine aristocrat knew, it was how to brazen it out.

Arguello locked a level gaze onto Sherman's eyes and said, in a voice just slightly louder than necessary: "I'm reading *The Racing Form.*"

"What for?"

"What for? Because four of our horses are racing at Lafayette today. That's a track outside of Chicago."

With this he resumed reading the newspaper.

It was the *our* that did it. *Our* was supposed to remind you that you were in the presence of the House of Arguello, lords of the pampas. Besides that, the little shit was wearing a pair of red silk moiré suspenders.

"Look . . . sport," said Sherman, "I want you to put that sheet away."

Challengingly: "What did you say?"

"You heard me. I said put that fucking sheet away!" It was supposed to come out calmly and firmly, but it came out furiously. It came out furiously enough to finish off Judy, Pollard Browning, the doorman, and a would-be mugger.

The young man was speechless.

"If I ever see you with a *Racing Form* in here again, you can go sit outside Chicago and make your money! You can sit on the clubhouse turn and bet perfectas! This is Pierce & Pierce, not OTB!"

Arguello was crimson. He was paralyzed with anger. All he could do was beam a ray of pure hatred at Sherman. Sherman, the righteous wrathful one, turned away, and as he did, he noticed with satisfaction that the young man was slowly closing the open expanse of *The Racing Form*.

Wrathful! Righteous! Sherman was elated. People were staring. Good! Idleness was a sin not against the self or against God but against Mammon and Pierce & Pierce. If he had to be the one to call this greaseball to accounts, then—but he regretted the *greaseball*, even in his thoughts. He considered himself as part of the new era and the new breed, a Wall Street egalitarian, a Master of the Universe who was a respecter only of performance. No longer did Wall Street or Pierce & Pierce mean Protestant Good Family. There were plenty of prominent Jewish investment bankers. Lopwitz himself was Jewish. There were plenty of Irishmen, Greeks, and Slavs. The fact that not one of the eighty members of the bond department was black or female didn't bother him. Why should it? It didn't bother Lopwitz, who took the position that the bond trading room at Pierce & Pierce was no place for symbolic gestures.

"Hey, Sherman."

He happened to be passing Rawlie Thorpe's desk. Rawlie was bald, except for a fringe of hair around the back of his head, and yet he still looked youthful. He was a great wearer of button-down shirts and Shep Miller suspenders. The button-down collars had a flawless roll.

"What was that all about?" he asked Sherman.

"I couldn't believe it," said Sherman. "He's over there with *The Racing Form*, working on fucking horse charts." He felt compelled to embellish the offense a bit.

Rawlie started laughing. "Well, he's young. He's probably had it with electric doughnuts."

"Had it with what?"

Rawlie picked up his telephone and pointed to the mouthpiece. "See that? That's an electric doughnut."

Sherman stared. It did look sort of like a doughnut, with a lot of little holes instead of one big one.

"It just dawned on me today," said Rawlie. "All I do all day is talk to other electric doughnuts. I just hung up from talking to a guy over at Drexel. I sold him a million and a half Joshua Tree bonds." On Wall Street you didn't say *a million and a half dollars' worth of bonds*. You said *a million and a half bonds*. "That's some goddamned outfit in Arizona. His name is Earl. I don't even know his last name. Over the past two years I bet I've done a couple dozen transactions with him, fifty, sixty million bonds, and I don't even know his last name, and I've never met him, and I probably never will. He's an electric doughnut."

Sherman didn't find this amusing. In some way it was a repudiation of his triumph over the shiftless young Argentinian. It was a cynical denial of his very righteousness itself. Rawlie was a very amusing man, but he hadn't been himself since his divorce. Maybe he was no longer such a great squadron warrior, either.

"Yeah," said Sherman, managing a half smile for his old friend. "Well, I gotta go call some a *my* doughnuts."

Back at his desk Sherman settled down to the work at hand. He stared at the little green symbols trucking across the computer screen in front of him. He picked up the telephone. The French gold-backed bond . . . A weird, very promising situation, and he had discovered it when one of the fellows, quite casually, mentioned the bond, in passing, one evening at Harry's.

Back in the innocent year 1973, on the eve of the heaving crapshoot, the French government had issued a bond known as the Giscard, after the French President, Giscard d'Estaing, with a face value of $6.5 billion. The Giscard had an interesting feature: it was backed by gold. So as the price of gold went up and down, so did the price of the Giscard. Since then the price of both gold and the French franc had shot up and down so crazily, American investors had long since lost interest in the Giscard. But lately, with gold holding firm in the $400 range, Sherman had discovered that an American buying Giscards stood to make two to three times the interest he could make on any U.S. government bond, plus a 30 percent profit when the Giscard matured. It was a sleeping beauty. The big danger would be a drop in the value of the franc. Sherman had neutralized that with a scheme for selling francs short as a hedge.

The only real problem was the complexity of the whole thing. It took big, sophisticated investors to understand it. Big, sophisticated, *trusting* investors; no newcomer could talk anybody into putting millions into the Giscard. You had to have a track record. You had to have talent—genius!—mastery of the universe!—like Sherman McCoy, biggest producer at Pierce & Pierce. He had convinced Gene Lopwitz to put up $600 million of Pierce & Pierce's money to buy the Giscard. Gingerly, stealthily, he had bought the bonds from their various European owners without revealing the mighty hand of Pierce & Pierce, by using various "blind" brokers. Now came the big test for a Master of the Universe. There were only about a dozen players who were likely buyers of anything as esoteric as the Giscard. Of these Sherman had managed to start negotiations with five: two trust banks, Traders' Trust Co. (known as Trader T) and Metroland; two money managers; and one of his best private clients, Oscar Suder of Cleveland, who had indicated he would buy $10 million. But by far the most important was Trader T, which was considering taking half the entire lot, $300 million.

The deal would bring Pierce & Pierce a 1 percent commission up front—$6 million—for conceiving of the idea and risking its capital. Sherman's share, including commissions, bonuses, profit-sharing, and resale fees, would come to about $1.75 million. With that he intended to pay off the horrendous $1.8 million personal loan he had taken out to buy the apartment.

So the first order of business today was a call to Bernard Levy, a Frenchman who was handling the deal at Trader T; a relaxed, friendly call, the call of a biggest-producing salesman (Master of the Universe), to remind Levy that although both gold and the franc had fallen in value yesterday and this morning (on the European exchanges), it meant nothing; all was well, very well indeed. It was true that he had met Bernard Levy only once, when he made the original presentation. They had been conferring on the telephone for months . . . but *electric doughnut?* Cynicism was such a cowardly form of superiority. That was Rawlie's great weakness. Rawlie cashed his checks. He wasn't too cynical to do that. If he wanted to belly up because he couldn't deal with his wife, that was his sad problem.

As Sherman dialed and waited for Bernard Levy to come on the line, the rousing sound of the greed storm closed in about him once again. From the desk right in front of his, a tall bug-eyed fellow (Yale '77): "Thirty-one bid January eighty-eights—"

From a desk somewhere behind him: "I'm short seventy million ten-year!"

From he knew not where: "They got their fucking buying shoes on!"

"I'm in the box!"

"—long 125—"

"—a million four-years from Midland—"

"Who's fucking around with the W-Is?"

"I tell you, I'm in the box!"

"—bid 80½—"

"—buy 'em at 6-plus—"

"—pick up 2½ basis points—"

"Forget it! It's nut-cutting time!"

At ten o'clock, Sherman, Rawlie, and five others convened in the conference room of Eugene Lopwitz's suite of offices to decide on Pierce & Pierce's strategy for the main event of the day in the bond markets, which was a U.S. Treasury auction of 10 billion bonds maturing in twenty years. It was a measure of the importance of the bond business to Pierce & Pierce that Lopwitz's offices opened right out into the bond trading room.

The conference room had no conference table. It looked like the lounge in the English hotel for the Yanks where they serve tea. It was full of small antique tables and cabinets. They were so old, brittle, and highly polished, you got the feeling that if you flicked one of them hard with your middle finger, it would shatter. At the same time, a wall of plate glass shoved a view of the Hudson River and the rotting piers of New Jersey into your face.

Sherman sat in a George II armchair. Rawlie sat next to him, in an old chair with a back shaped like a shield. In other antique or antiqued chairs, with Shera-ton and Chippendale side tables beside them, were the head government trader, George Connor, who was two years younger than Sherman; his deputy, Vic Scaasi, who was only twenty-eight; the chief market analyst, Paul Feiffer; and Arnold Parch, the executive vice president, who was Lopwitz's first lieutenant.

Everyone in the room sat in a classic chair and stared at a small brown plastic speaker on top of a cabinet. The cabinet was a 220-year-old Adam bowfront, from the period when the brothers Adam liked to paint pictures and ornate borders on wooden furniture. On the center panel was an oval-shaped painting of a Greek maiden sitting in a dell or grotto in which lacy leaves receded fuzzily in deepening shades of green into a dusky teal sky. The thing had cost an astonishing amount of money. The plastic speaker was the size of a bedside clock radio. Everyone stared at it, waiting for the voice of Gene Lopwitz. Lopwitz was in London, where it was now 4:00 p.m. He would preside over this meeting by telephone.

An indistinct noise came out of the speaker. It might have been a voice and it might have been an airplane. Arnold Parch rose from his armchair and ap-proached the Adam cabinet and looked at the plastic speaker and said, "Gene, can you hear me all right?"

He looked imploringly at the plastic speaker, without taking his eyes off it, as if in fact it *were* Gene Lopwitz, transformed, the way princes are transformed into frogs in fairy tales. For a moment the plastic frog said nothing. Then it spoke.

"Yeah, I can hear you, Arnie. There was a lotta cheering going on." Lopwitz's voice sounded as if it were coming from out of a storm drain, but you could hear it.

"Where are you, Gene?" asked Parch.

"I'm at a cricket match." Then less clearly: "What's the name a this place again?" He was evidently with some other people. "Tottenham Park, Arnie. I'm on a kind of a terrace."

"Who's playing?" Parch smiled, as if to show the plastic frog that this wasn't a serious question.

"Don't get technical on me, Arnie. A lot of very nice young gentlemen in cable-knit sweaters and white flannel pants, is the best I can tell you."

Appreciative laughter broke out in the room, and Sherman felt his own lips bending into the somehow obligatory smile. He glanced about the room. Everyone was smiling and chuckling at the brown plastic speaker except for Rawlie, who had his eyes rolled up in the Oh Brother mode.

Then Rawlie leaned over toward Sherman and said, in a noisy whisper: "Look at all these idiots grinning. They think the plastic box has eyes."

This didn't strike Sherman as very funny, since he himself had been grinning. He was also afraid that Lopwitz's loyal aide, Parch, would think he was Rawlie's confederate in making sport of the maximum leader.

"Well, everybody's here, Gene," Parch said to the box, "and so I'm gonna get George to fill you in on where we stand on the auction as of now."

Parch looked at George Connor and nodded and walked back to his chair, and Connor got up from his and walked over to the Adam cabinet and stared at the brown plastic box and said: "Gene? This is George."

"Yeah, hi, George," said the frog. "Go ahead."

"Here's the thing, Gene," said Connor, standing in front of the Adam commode, unable to take his eyes off the plastic box, "it feels pretty good. The old twenties are trading at 8 percent. The traders are telling us they'll come in on the new ones at 8.05, but we think they're playing games with us. We think we're gonna get action right down to 8. So here's what I figure. We'll scale in at 8.01, 8.02, 8.03, with the balance at 8.04. I'm ready to go 60 percent of the issue."

Which, translated, meant: he was proposing to buy $6 billion of the $10 billion in bonds offered in the auction, with the expectation of a profit of two thirty-seconds of a dollar—$6\frac{1}{4}$¢—on every one hundred dollars put up. This was known as "two ticks."

Sherman couldn't resist another look at Rawlie. He had a small, unpleasant smile on his face, and his gaze seemed to pass several degrees to the right of the Adam commode, toward the Hoboken docks. Rawlie's presence was like a glass of ice water in the face. Sherman resented him all over again. He knew what was on his mind. Here was this outrageous arriviste, Lopwitz—Sherman knew Rawlie thought of him that way—trying to play the nob on the terrace of some British cricket club and at the same time conduct a meeting in New York to decide whether Pierce & Pierce was going to stake two billion, four billion, or six billion on a single government bond issue three hours from now. No doubt Lopwitz had his own audience on hand at the cricket club to watch this performance, as his great words bounced off a communications satellite somewhere up in the empyrean and hit Wall Street. Well, it wasn't hard to find something laughable in it, but Lopwitz was, in truth, a Master of the Universe. Lopwitz was about forty-five years old. Sherman wanted nothing less seven years down the line, when he was forty-five. To be astride the Atlantic . . . with billions at stake! Rawlie could snigger . . . and sink into his kneecaps . . . but to think what Lopwitz now had in his grasp, to think what he made each year, just from Pierce & Pierce, which was at least $25 million, to think of the kind of life he led—and what Sherman thought of first was Lopwitz's young wife, Snow White. That was what Rawlie called her. Hair as dark as ebony, lips as red as blood, skin as white as snow . . . She was Lopwitz's fourth wife, French, a countess, apparently, no more than twenty-five or twenty-six, with an accent like Catherine Deneuve doing a bath-oil commercial. She was something . . . Sherman had met her at a party at the Petersons'. She had put her hand on his forearm, just to make a point in conversation—but the way she kept the pressure on his arm and stared at him from about eight inches away! She was a young and frisky animal. Lopwitz had taken what he wanted. He had wanted a young and frisky animal with lips as red as blood and skin as white as snow, and that was what he had taken. What had ever happened to the other three Mrs. Eugene Lopwitzes was a question Sherman had never heard brought up. When you had reached Lopwitz's level, it didn't even matter.

"Yeah, well, that sounds all right, George," said the plastic frog. "What about Sherman? Are you there, Sherman?"

"Hi, Gene!" said Sherman, rising from the George II armchair. His own voice sounded very odd to him, now that he was talking to a plastic box, and he didn't dare even take a quick glance at Rawlie as he walked over to the Adam commode and took his stance and stared, rapt, at the machine on top.

"Gene, all my customers are taking 8.05. My gut feeling, though, is that they're on our side. The market has a good tone. I think we can bid ahead of the customer interest."

"Okay," said the voice in the box, "but just make sure you and George stay on top a the trading accounts. I don't wanna hear about Salomon or anybody horsing around with shorts."

Sherman found himself marveling at the frog's wisdom.

Some sort of throttled roar came over the speaker. Everybody stared at it.

Lopwitz's voice returned. "Somebody just hit the hell outta the ball," he said. "The ball's kinda dead, though. Well, you kinda hadda be there." It wasn't clear what he meant by that. "Well, look, George. Can you hear me, George?"

Connor hopped to it, rose from his chair, hustled over to the Adam commode.

"I can hear you, Gene."

"I was just gonna say, if you feel like stepping up to the plate and taking a good whack at it today, go ahead. It sounds okay.'

And that was that.

At forty-five seconds before the auction deadline of 1:00 p.m., George Connor, at a telephone in the middle of the bond trading room, read off his final scaled-in bids to a Pierce & Pierce functionary sitting at a telephone at the Federal Building, which was the physical site of the auction. The bids averaged $99.62643 per $100 worth of bonds. Within a few seconds after 1:00 p.m., Pierce & Pierce now owned, as planned, $6 billion worth of the twenty-year bond. The bond department had four hours in which to create a favorable market. Vic Scaasi led the charge on the bond trading desk, reselling the bonds mainly to the brokerage houses—by telephone. Sherman and Rawlie led the bond salesmen, reselling the bonds mainly to insurance companies and trust banks—by telephone. By 2:00 p.m., the roar in the bond trading room, fueled more by fear than greed, was unearthly. They all shouted and sweated and swore and devoured their electric doughnuts.

By 5:00 p.m. they had sold 40 percent—$2.4 billion—of the $6 billion at an average price of $99.75062 per $100 worth of bonds, for a profit of not two but four ticks! *Four ticks!* That was a profit of twelve and a half cents per one hundred dollars. *Four ticks!* To the eventual retail buyer of these bonds, whether an individual, a corporation or an institution, this spread was invisible. But—*four ticks!* To Pierce & Pierce it meant a profit of almost $3 million for an afternoon's work. And it wouldn't stop there. The market was holding firm and edging up. Within the next week they might easily make an additional $5 to $10 million on the 3.6 billion bonds remaining. *Four ticks!*

By five o'clock Sherman was soaring on adrenaline. He was part of the pulverizing might of Pierce & Pierce, Masters of the Universe. The audacity of it all was breathtaking. To risk $6 billion in one afternoon to make *two ticks*—six and a quarter cents per one hundred dollars—and then to make four ticks—*four ticks!*—the audacity!—the audacity! Was there any more exciting power on the face of the earth? Let Lopwitz watch all the cricket matches he wants to! Let him play the plastic frog! Master of the Universe—the audacity!

The audacity of it flowed through Sherman's limbs and lymph channels and loins. Pierce & Pierce was the power, and he was wired into the power, and the power hummed and surged in his very innards.

Judy . . . He hadn't thought of her for hours. What was a single, albeit boneheaded, telephone call . . . on the stupendous ledger kept by Pierce & Pierce? The fiftieth floor was for people who weren't afraid to take what they wanted. And, Christ, he didn't want much, compared to what he, a Master of the Universe, should rightfully have. All he wanted was to be able to kick the gong around when he pleased, to have the simple pleasures due all mighty warriors.

Where did she get off, giving him such a hard time?

If Middle Age wishes the continued support and escort of a Master of the Universe, then she must allow him the precious currency he has earned, which is youth and beauty and juicy jugs and loamy loins—

It made no sense! Somehow, for no explicable reason, Judy had always had his number. She looked down on him—from a wholly fictive elevation; nevertheless, she looked down on him. Still the daughter of Professor Miller, E. (for Egbord!) Ronald Miller of DesPortes University, Terwilliger, Wisconsin, poor stodgy Professor Miller, in his rotting tweeds, whose one claim to fame was a rather mealy-mouthed attack (Sherman had once plowed through it) on his fellow Wisconsinite, Senator Joseph McCarthy, in the magazine *Aspects* in 1955. Yet, back there in the cocoon of their early days together in the Village, Sherman had validated her claim. He had *enjoyed* telling Judy that while he worked *on* Wall Street, he was not *of* Wall Street and was only *using* Wall Street. He had been *pleased* when she condescended to admire him for the enlightenment that was stirring in his soul. Somehow she was assuring him that his own father, John Campbell McCoy, the Lion of Dunning Sponget, was a rather pedestrian figure, after all, a high-class security guard for other people's capital. As to why that might be important to him, Sherman didn't even know how to speculate. His interest in psychoanalytical theory, never lively, had ended one day at Yale when Rawlie Thorpe had referred to it as "a Jewish science" (precisely the attitude that had most troubled and infuriated Freud seventy-five years earlier).

But that was all part of the past, of his childhood, his childhood on East Seventy-third Street and his childhood in the Village. This was a new era! This was a new Wall Street—and Judy was . . . an article left over from his childhood . . . and yet she lived on and grew older, thinner . . . *handsome* . . .

Sherman leaned back in his chair and surveyed the bond trading room. The processions of phosphorescent green characters still skidded across the faces of the computer terminals, but the roar had subsided to something more like locker-room laughter. George Connor stood beside Vic Scaasi's chair with his hands in his pockets, just chatting. Vic arched his back and rolled his shoulders and seemed about to yawn. There was Rawlie, reared back in his chair, talking on the telephone, grinning and running his hand over his bald pate. Victorious warriors after the fray . . . Masters of the Universe . . .

And she has the gall to cause him grief over a *telephone call!*

4

KING OF THE JUNGLE

*T*humpathumpathumpathumpathumpathumpathumpa—the noise of the airliners taking off pounded down so hard, he could feel it. The air was full of jet fumes. The stench cut straight through to his stomach. Cars kept popping up from out of the mouth of a ramp and threading their way through the swarms of people who were roaming about on the roof in the dusk looking for the elevators or their cars or other people's cars—steal! steal! steal!—and his would be the leading candidate, wouldn't it? Sherman stood with one hand resting on the door, wondering if he dared leave it here. The car was a black Mercedes two-seat sports roadster that had cost $48,000—or $120,000, according to how you wanted to look at it. In a Master of the Universe tax bracket, with federal, New York State, and New York City taxes to pay, Sherman had to make $120,000 in order to have $48,000 left to spend on a two-seat sports roadster. How would he explain it to Judy if the thing were stolen from up here on the roof of a terminal at Kennedy Airport?

Well—why would he even owe her an explanation? For a solid week he had had dinner at home every night. It must have been the first time he had managed that since he started working for Pierce & Pierce. He had been attentive to Campbell, spending upward of forty-five minutes with her one evening, which was unusual, although he would have been suprised and offended if anybody had ever pointed that out. He had rewired a floor lamp in the library without any undue fuming and sighing. After three days of his model performance, Judy had given up the daybed in the dressing room and come back to the bedroom. True, the Berlin Wall now ran down the center of the bed, and she wouldn't give him an inch of small talk. But she was always civil to him when Campbell was around. That was the most important thing.

Two hours ago when he had called Judy to say he would be working late, she had taken it in stride. Well—he deserved it! He took one last look at the Mercedes and headed for the international arrivals area.

It was down in the bowels of the building, in what must have been designed as a baggage area originally. Strips of fluorescent lights struggled against the gloominess of the space. People were jammed behind a metal fence, waiting for passengers coming in from abroad to emerge from Customs. Suppose there was someone here who knew him and Judy? He surveyed the crowd. Shorts, sneakers, jeans, football jerseys—Christ, who were these people? One by one the travelers were straggling out of Customs. Sweat suits, T-shirts, windbreakers, tube socks, overalls, warm-up jackets, baseball caps, and tank tops; just in from Rome, Milan, Paris, Brussels, Munich, and London; the world travelers; the cosmopolites; Sherman lifted his Yale chin against the tide.

When Maria finally appeared, she wasn't hard to spot. In this mob she looked like something from another galaxy. She was wearing a skirt and a big-shouldered jacket of a royal blue that was fashionable in France, a blue-and-white-striped silk blouse, and electric-blue lizard pumps with white calf caps on the toes. The price of the blouse and the shoes alone would have paid for the clothes on the backs of any twenty women on the floor. She walked with a nose-up sprocket-hipped model-girl gait calculated to provoke maximum envy and resentment. People were staring. Beside her marched a porter with an aluminum dolly cart heaped with luggage, a prodigious amount of it, a matched set, cream-colored leather with chocolate leather trim on the edges. Vulgar, but not as vulgar as Louis Vuitton, thought Sherman. She had only gone to Italy for a week, to find a house on Lake Como for the summer. He couldn't imagine why she had taken so many bags. (Unconsciously he associated such things with a slack upbringing.) He wondered how he was going to get it all in the Mercedes.

He made his way around the fence and strode toward her. He squared his shoulders.

"Hello, babe," he said.

"*Babe?*" said Maria. She added a smile, as if she weren't really annoyed, but obviously she was. It was true that he had never called her babe before. He had wanted to sound confident but casual, like a Master of the Universe meeting his girlfriend in an airport.

He took her arm and fell in step with her and decided to try again. "How was the flight?"

"It was great," said Maria, "if you don't mind being bowed by some Brit for six hours." It was a couple of beats before Sherman realized she was saying *bored.* She gazed into the distance, as if reflecting upon her ordeal.

Up on the roof, the Mercedes had survived the thieving multitudes. The skycap couldn't get much of the luggage into the car's sporty little trunk. He had to stack half of it up on the back seat, which wasn't much more than an upholstered ledge. Terrific, thought Sherman. If I have to stop short, I'll get hit in the base of the skull by matched flying cream-colored vanity cases with chocolate-brown trim.

By the time they got out of the airport and went onto the Van Wyck Expressway toward Manhattan, only the last low dull glow of daylight was visible behind the buildings and the trees of South Ozone Park. It was that hour of dusk when the streetlights and headlights come on but make little difference. A stream of red taillights rolled on ahead of them. Over on the side of the expressway, just past Rockaway Boulevard, he saw an enormous two-door sedan, the sort of car they used to make in the 1970s, up against a stone retaining wall. A man . . . spread-eagled on the highway! . . . No, as they drew closer, he could see it wasn't a man at all. It was the hood of the car. The entire hood had been pulled off and was lying on the pavement. The wheels, seats, and steering wheel were gone . . . This huge derelict machine was now part of the landscape . . . Sherman, Maria, the luggage, and the Mercedes rolled on.

He tried once more. "Well, how was Milan? What's going on at Lake Como?"

"Sherman, who's Christopher Marlowe?" Shuhmun, who's Christuphuh Muhlowe?

Christopher Marlowe? "I don't know. Do I know him?"

"The one I'm talking about was a writer."

"You don't mean the playwright?"

"I guess so. Who was he?" Maria continued to look straight ahead. She sounded as if her last friend had died.

"Christopher Marlowe . . . He was a British playwright, about the time of Shakespeare, I think. Maybe a little before Shakespeare. Why?"

"Which was when?" She couldn't have sounded more miserable.

"Let's see. I don't know . . . The sixteenth century—15-something. Why?"

"What did he write?"

"God . . . beats me. Listen, I thought I was doing well just to remember who he was. Why?"

"Yes, but you do know who he was."

"Barely. Why?"

"What about Dr. Faustus?"

"Dr. Faustus?"

"Did he write something about Dr. Faustus?"

"Mmmmmmmm." A tiny flash of memory; but it slipped away. "Could be. Dr. Faustus . . . *The Jew of Malta!* He wrote a play called *The Jew of Malta.* I'm pretty sure of that. *The Jew of Malta.* I don't even know how I remember *The Jew of Malta.* I'm sure I never read it."

"But you do know who he was. That's one of the things you're supposed to know, isn't it?"

And there she had put her finger on it. The only thing that had truly stuck in Sherman's mind about Christopher Marlowe, after nine years at Buckley, four years at St. Paul's, and four years at Yale, was that you were, in fact, supposed to know who Christopher Marlowe was. But he wasn't about to say that.

Instead, he asked: "Who's supposed to?"

"Anybody," Maria mumbled. "Me."

It was getting darker. The Mercedes's spiffy dials and gauges were now lit up like a fighter plane's. They were nearing the Atlantic Avenue overpass. There was another abandoned car by the side of the road. The wheels were gone, the hood was up, and two figures, one holding a flashlight, were jackknifed over the engine well.

Maria continued to look straight ahead as they merged with the traffic on Grand Central Parkway. A galaxy of streaming headlights and taillights filled their field of vision, as if the energy of the city were now transformed into millions of globes of light orbiting in the darkness. Here, inside the Mercedes, with the windows rolled up, the entire stupendous show came gliding by without a sound.

"You know something, Sherman?" You know somethun, Shuhmun? "I hate the Brits. I *hate* 'um."

"You hate Christopher Marlowe?"

"Thank you, smartie," said Maria. "You sound just like the sonofabitch I sat next to."

Now she was looking at Sherman and smiling. It was the kind of smile you bring up bravely through great pain. Her eyes looked as if they might be about to spring tears.

"Which sonofabitch?" he said.

"On the plane. This *Brit*." Synonymous with worm. "He started talking to me. I was looking at the catalogue from the Reiner Fetting show I saw in Milano" —it annoyed Sherman that she used the Italian, Milano, instead of the English, Milan, especially since he had never heard of Reiner Fetting— "and he starts talking about Reiner Fetting. He had one a those gold Rolexes, those huge things? It's a wonder you can lift your arm?" She had the Southern Girl habit of turning declarative sentences into questions.

"You think he was making a play?"

Maria smiled, this time with pleasure. "Of course he was!"

The smile brought Sherman great relief. The spell was broken. Just why, he didn't know. He didn't realize that there were women who thought about sexual attractiveness the way he thought about the bond market. He only knew that the spell had been broken and that the weight had been lifted. It didn't really matter what she chattered on about now. And she did chatter on. She headed deep into the indignity she had suffered.

"He couldn't wait to tell me he was a movie producer. He was making a movie based on this play, *Doctor Faustus*, by Christopher Marlowe, or just Marlowe, I think that was all he said, just Marlowe, and I don't even know why I said anything, but I thought somebody named Marlowe wrote for the movies. Actually, what I think I was thinking about was, there was this movie with a *character* named Marlowe. Robert Mitchum was in it."

"That's right. It was a Raymond Chandler story."

Maria looked at him with utter blankness. He dropped Raymond Chandler. "So what did you say to him?"

"I said, 'Oh, Christopher Marlowe. Didn't he write a movie?" And you know what this . . . bastard . . . says to me? He says, 'I shouldn't think so. He died in 1593.' *I shouldn't think so.*"

Her eyes were blazing with the recollection. Sherman waited a moment. "That's it?"

"That's *it*? I wanted to strangle him. It was . . . humiliating. *I shouldn't think so.* I couldn't be*lieve* the . . . snottiness."

"What did you say to him?"

"Nothing. I turned red. I couldn't say a word."

"And that's what accounts for this mood of yours?"

"Sherman, tell me the honest truth. If you don't know who Christopher Marlowe is, does that make you stupid?"

"Oh, for God's sake, Maria. I can't believe that's what put you in such a mood."

"What mood?"

"This black cloud you landed in."

"You didn't answer me, Sherman. Does that make you stupid?"

"Don't be ridiculous. I could barely think of who he was, and I probably had him in a course or something."

"Well, that's just the point. At least you had him in a course. I didn't have him in any course. That's what makes me feel so—you don't even understand what I'm talking about, do you?"

"I sure don't." He smiled at her, and she smiled back.

By now they were passing La Guardia Airport, which was lit up by hundreds of sodium vapor lights. It didn't look like a great gateway to the sky. It looked like a factory. Sherman swung to the outside and hit the accelerator and sent the Mercedes barreling under the Thirty-first Street overpass and up the ramp onto the Triborough Bridge. The cloud had passed. He was feeling pleased with himself once again. He had jollied her out of it.

Now he had to slow down. All four lanes were heavy with traffic. As the Mercedes ascended the bridge's great arc, he could see the island of Manhattan off to the left. The towers were jammed together so tightly, he could feel the mass and stupendous weight. Just think of the millions, from all over the globe, who yearned to be on that island, in those towers, in those narrow streets! There it was, the Rome, the Paris, the London of the twentieth century, the city of ambition, the dense magnetic rock, the irresistible destination of all those who insist on being *where things are happening*—and he was among the victors! He lived on Park Avenue, the street of dreams! He worked on Wall Street, fifty floors up, for the legendary Pierce & Pierce, overlooking the world! He was at the wheel of a $48,000 roadster with one of the most beautiful women in New York—no Comp. Lit. scholar, perhaps, but gorgeous—beside him! A frisky young animal! He was of that breed whose natural destiny it was . . . to have what they wanted!

He took one hand off the wheel and made a grand gesture toward the mighty island.

"There it is, babe!"

"We're back to babe again?"

"I just feel like calling you babe, babe. New York City. There it is."

"Do you really think I'm the babe type?"

"You're as babe as they come, Maria. Where do you want to have dinner? It's all yours. New York City."

"Sherman! Aren't you supposed to turn there?"

He looked to the right. It was true. He was two lanes to the left of the lanes that led to the off-ramp to Manhattan, and there was no way he could cut across. By now this lane—the next lane—the next lane—every lane—was a train of cars and trucks, bumper to bumper, inching toward a toll plaza a hundred yards ahead. Above the plaza was a huge green sign, lit up by yellow lamps, saying BRONX UPSTATE N.Y. NEW ENGLAND.

"Sherman, I'm sure that's the turnoff to Manhattan."

"You're right, sweetheart, but there's no way I can get over there now."

"Where does this go?"

"The Bronx."

The trains of vehicles inched forward in a cloud of carbon and sulphur particles toward the toll gates.

The Mercedes was so low-slung, Sherman had to reach way up to surrender two dollar bills at the booth. A tired-looking black man stared down at him from the window of a very high perch. Something had made a long gash in the side of the booth. The gully was corroding.

A vague smoky abysmal uneasiness was seeping into Sherman's skull. The Bronx . . . He had been born and raised in New York and took a manly pride in knowing the city. *I know the city.* But in fact his familiarity with the Bronx, over the course of his thirty-eight years, was derived from five or six trips to the Bronx Zoo, two to the Botanical Gardens, and perhaps a dozen trips to Yankee Stadium, the last one in 1977 for a World Series game. He did know that the Bronx had numbered streets, which were a continuation of Manhattan's. What he would do would be—well, he would get on a cross street and take that west until he reached one of the avenues that take you back down into Manhattan. How bad could it be?

The tide of red taillights flowed on ahead of them, and now they bothered him. In the darkness, amid this red swarm, he couldn't get his bearings. His sense of direction was slipping away. He must be heading north still. The down side of the bridge hadn't curved a great deal. But now there were only signs to go by. His entire stock of landmarks was gone, left behind. At the end of the bridge the expressway split into a Y. MAJOR DEEGAN GEO. WASHINGTON BRIDGE . . . BRUCKNER NEW ENGLAND . . . Major Deegan went upstate . . . No! . . . Veer right . . . Suddenly another Y . . . EAST BRONX NEW ENGLAND . . . EAST 138TH BRUCKNER BOULEVARD . . . Choose one, you ninny! . . . Acey-deucey . . . one finger, two fingers . . . He veered right again . . . EAST 138TH . . . a ramp . . . All at once there was no more ramp, no more clean cordoned expressway. He was at ground level. It was as if he had fallen into a junkyard. He seemed to be underneath the expressway. In the blackness he could make out a cyclone fence over on the left . . . something caught in it . . . A woman's head! . . . No, it was a chair with three legs and a burnt seat with the charred stuffing hanging out in great wads, rammed halfway through a cyclone fence . . . Who on earth would jam a chair into the mesh of a cyclone fence? And why?

"Where are we, Sherman?"

He could tell by the tone of her voice that there weren't going to be any more discussions of Christopher Marlowe or where to have dinner.

"We're in the Bronx."

"You know how to get outta here?"

"Sure. If I can just find a cross street . . . Let's see, let's see, let's see . . . 138th Street . . ."

They were traveling north underneath the expressway. But what expressway? Two lanes, both heading north . . . To the left a retaining wall and cyclone fencing and concrete columns supporting the expressway . . . Should head west to find a street back to Manhattan . . . turn left . . . but he can't turn left because of the wall . . . Let's see, let's see . . . 138th Street . . . Where is it? . . . There! The sign—138th Street . . . He keeps to the left, to make the turn . . . A big opening in the wall . . . 138th Street . . . But he can't turn left! To his left are four or five lanes of traffic, down here underneath the expressway, two going north, two going south, and another one beyond them, cars and trucks barreling in both directions—there's no way he can cut across that traffic . . . So he keeps going . . . into the Bronx . . . Another opening in the wall coming up . . . He hugs the left lane . . . Same situation! . . . No way to turn left! . . . He begins to feel trapped here in the gloom beneath the expressway . . . But how bad could it be? . . . Plenty of traffic . . .

"What are we doing, Sherman?"

"I'm trying to turn left, but there's no way you can turn left off of this goddamned road. I'm going to have to turn right somewhere up here and make a U-turn or something and come back across."

Maria had no comment. Sherman glanced at her. She was looking straight ahead, grimly. Off to the right, above some low decrepit buildings, he could see a billboard that said

TOPS IN THE BRONX
MEAT WAREHOUSE

Meat warehouse . . . deep in the Bronx . . . Another opening in the wall up ahead . . . He starts bearing to the right this time—a tremendous horn!—a truck passing him on the right . . . He swerves left—

"Sherman!"

"Sorry, babe."

—too late to make the right turn . . . He keeps going, hugs the right side of the right lane, ready for the turn . . . Another opening . . . turns right . . . a wide street . . . What a lot of people all of a sudden . . . Half of them seem to be out in the street . . . dark, but they look Latin . . . Puerto Ricans? . . . Over there a long low building with scalloped dormer windows . . . like something from a storybook Swiss chalet . . . but terribly blackened . . . Over here a bar—he stares—half covered in metal shutters . . . So many people in the street . . . He slows down . . . Low apartment buildings with windows missing . . . entire sashes gone . . . A red light. He stops. He can see Maria's head panning this way and that . . . "Ooooooaaaggggh!" A tremendous scream off to the left . . . A young man with a wispy mustache and a sport shirt is sauntering across the street. A girl runs after him screaming. "Ooooooaggggh!" . . . Dark face, frizzy blond hair . . . She throws her arm around his neck, but in slow motion, as if she's drunk. "Ooooooaaggggh!" Trying to strangle him! He doesn't even look at her. He just rams his elbow back into her stomach. She slides off his body. She's down on the street on all fours. He keeps walking. Never looks back. She gets up. She lunges toward him again. "Ooooaagggh!" Now they're right in front of the car. Sherman and Maria are sitting in their tan leather bucket seats staring right at them. The girl—she has her man by the neck again. He gives her another whack in the midsection with his elbow. The light changes, but Sherman can't budge. People have come out into the street from both sides to watch the imbroglio. They're laughing. They're cheering. She's pulling his hair. He's grimacing and whacking her backward with both elbows. People all over the place. Sherman looks at Maria. Neither has to say a word. Two white people, one of them a young woman decked out in a royal-blue Avenue Foch jacket with shoulders out to here . . . enough matched luggage in the back seat for a trip to China . . . a $48,000 Mercedes roadster . . . in the middle of the South Bronx . . . Miraculous! No one pays any attention to them. Just another car at the light. The two combatants gradually edge off to the other side of the street. Now they're grappling like Sumo wrestlers, face to face. They're staggering, weaving. They're worn out. They're gasping for breath. They've had it. They might as well be dancing. The crowd's losing interest, drifting away.

Sherman says to Maria, "True love, babe." Wants to make her think he's not worried.

Now there's no one in front of the car, but the light has turned red again. He waits it out, then heads down the street. Not so many people now . . . a wide street. He makes a U-turn, heads back the way they came . . .

"What are you gonna do now, Sherman?"

"I think we're okay. This is a main cross street. We're heading in the right direction. We're heading west."

But when they crossed the big thoroughfare under the expressway, they found themselves in a chaotic intersection. Streets converged from odd angles . . . People were crossing the street in every direction . . . Dark faces . . . Over this way a subway entrance . . . Over there low buildings, shops . . . Great Taste Chinese Takeout . . . He couldn't tell which street went due west . . . *That* one—the likeliest—he turned that way . . . a wide street . . . cars parked on both sides . . . up ahead, double-parked . . . triple-parked . . . a crowd . . . Could he even get through? . . . So he turned . . . *that way* . . . There was a street sign, but the names of the streets were no longer parallel to the streets themselves. East Something seemed to be . . . in that direction . . . So he took that street, but it quickly merged with a narrow side street and ran between some low buildings. The buildings appeared to be abandoned. At the next corner he turned—west, he figured—and followed that street a few blocks. There were more low buildings. They might have been garages and they might have been sheds. There were fences with spirals of razor wire on top. The streets were deserted, which was okay, he told himself, and yet he could feel his heart beating with a nervous twang. Then he turned again. A narrow street lined with seven- or eight-story apartment buildings; no sign of people; not a light in a window. The next block, the same. He turned again, and as he rounded the corner—

—*astonishing.* Utterly empty, a vast open terrain. Block after block—how many?—six? eight? a dozen?—entire blocks of the city without a building left standing. There were streets and curbing and sidewalks and light poles and nothing else. The eerie grid of a city was spread out before him, lit by the chemical yellow of the street lamps. Here and there were traces of rubble and slag. The earth looked like concrete, except that it rolled down this way . . . and up that way . . . the hills and dales of the Bronx . . . reduced to asphalt, concrete, and cinders . . . in a ghastly yellow gloaming.

He had to look twice to make sure he was in fact still driving on a New York street. The street led up a long slope . . . Two blocks away . . . three blocks away . . . it was hard to tell on this enormous vacant lot . . . There was a lone building, the last one . . . It was on the corner . . . three or four stories high . . . It looked as if it were ready to keel over at any moment . . . It was lit up at the ground level, as if there was a store or a bar . . . Three or four people were out on the sidewalk. Sherman could see them under the streetlight on the corner.

"What is this, Sherman?" Maria was staring right at him.

"The southeast Bronx, I guess."

"You mean you don't know where we are?"

"I know *about* where we are. As long as we keep heading west we'll be all right."

"What makes you think we're heading west?"

"Oh, don't worry, we're heading west. It's just, uh . . . ."

"It's just what?"

"If you see a street sign . . . I'm looking for a numbered street."

The truth was, Sherman could no longer tell which way he was heading. As they drew near the building, he could hear *thung thung thung thung thung thung*. He could hear it even though the windows of the cars were up . . . A bass violin . . . An electrical cord looped down from the light pole on the corner through the open door. Out on the sidewalk was a woman wearing what looked like a basketball jersey and shorts, and two men in short-sleeved sport shirts. The woman was leaning over with her hands on her knees, laughing and swinging her head around in a big circle. The two men were laughing at her. Were they Puerto Rican? There was no telling. Inside the doorway, the doorway where the electrical cord went, Sherman could see a low light and silhouettes. *Thung thung thung thung thung* . . . the bass . . . then the tops of some trumpet notes . . . Latin music? . . . The woman's head went around and around.

He glanced at Maria. She sat there in her terrific royal-blue jacket. Her thick dark bobbed hair framed a face that was as frozen as a photograph. Sherman sped up and left the eerie outpost in the wasteland.

He turned toward some buildings . . . over there . . . He passed houses with no sashes in the windows . . .

They came upon a little park with an iron railing around it. You had to turn either left or right. The streets went off at odd angles. Sherman had lost track of the grid pattern altogether. It no longer looked like New York. It looked like some small decaying New England city. He turned left.

"Sherman, I'm beginning not to like this."

"Don't worry, kid."

"It's kid now?"

"You didn't like babe." He wanted to sound nonchalant.

Now there were cars parked along the street . . . Three youths stood beneath a streetlight; three dark faces. They wore quilted jackets. They stared at the Mercedes. Sherman turned again.

Up ahead he could see the fuzzy yellow glow of what seemed to be a wider, more brightly lit street. The closer they came to it, the more people . . . on the sidewalks, in doorways, out in the street . . . What a lot of dark faces . . . Up ahead, something in the street. His headlights were soaked up by the darkness. Then he could make it out. A car parked out in the middle of the street, nowhere near the curb . . . a group of boys standing around it . . . More dark faces . . . Could he even get around them? He pushed the button that locked the doors. The electronic click startled him, as if it were the beat of a snare drum. He eased by. The boys stooped down and stared in the windows of the Mercedes.

Out of the corner of his eye he could see one of them smiling. But he said nothing. He just stared and grinned. Thank God, there was enough room. Sherman kept easing on by. Suppose he had a flat tire? Or the engine flooded? That would be a pretty fix. But he didn't feel rattled. He was still on top of it. Just keep rolling. That's the main thing. A $48,000 Mercedes. Come on, you Krauts, you Panzer heads, you steely-brained machinists . . . Do it right . . . He made it past the car. Up ahead, a thoroughfare . . . Traffic was going across the intersection at a good clip in both directions. He let his breath out. He'd take it! To the right! To the left! It didn't matter. He reached the intersection. The light was red. Well, the hell with that. He started through.

"Sherman, you're going through a red light!"

"Good. Maybe the cops'll come. That wouldn't upset me too much."

Maria wasn't saying a word. The concerns of her luxurious life were now tightly focused. Human existence had but one purpose: to get out of the Bronx.

Up ahead the vaporous mustard glow of the streetlights was brighter and more spread out . . . Some sort of major intersection . . . Wait a second . . . Up there, a subway entrance . . . Over here, shops, cheap food joints . . . Texas Fried Chicken . . . Great Taste Chinese Takeout . . . *Great Taste Chinese Takeout!*

Maria was thinking the same thing. "Jesus Christ, Sherman, we're back where we started! You been around in a circle!"

"I know it. I know it. Just hold on a second. I tell you what. I'm gonna take a right. I'm gonna head back down under the expressway. I'm gonna—"

"Don't get under that thing again, Sherman."

The expressway was right up above. The light was green. Sherman didn't know what to do. Someone was blowing a horn behind him.

"Sherman! Look over there! It says George Washington Bridge!"

Where? The horn kept blowing. Then he saw it. It was on the far side, beneath the expressway, in the decrepit gray gloaming, a sign on a concrete support . . . 95. 895 EAST. GEO. WASH. BRIDGE . . . Must be a ramp . . .

"But we don't want to go in that direction! That's north!"

"So what, Sherman? At least you know what it is! At least it's civilization! Let's get outta here!"

The horn blared. Somebody was back there yelling. Sherman gunned it, while he still had the light. He drove across the five lanes toward the little sign. He was back under the expressway.

"It's right over there, Sherman!"

"Okay, okay, I see it."

The ramp looked like a black chute stuck up between the concrete supports. The Mercedes took a hard bounce from a pothole.

"Christ," said Sherman, "I didn't even see that."

He leaned forward over the steering wheel. The headlights shot across the concrete columns in a delirium. He shifted into second gear. He turned left around an abutment and gunned it up the ramp. Bodies! . . . Bodies in the road! . . . Two of them curled up! . . . No, not bodies . . . ridges in the side . . . molds . . . No, containers, some kind of containers . . . Trash cans . . . He'd have to squeeze to the left to get around them . . . He shifted down into first gear and turned to the left . . . A blur in his headlights . . . For an instant he thought someone had jumped off the guardrail of the ramp . . . Not big enough . . . It was an animal . . . It was lying in the road, blocking the way . . . Sherman jammed down on the brake . . . A piece of luggage hit him in the back of his head . . . two pieces . . .

A shriek from Maria. A suitcase was on top of her headrest. The car had stalled. Sherman set the brake and pulled the suitcase off her and shoved it back.

"You okay?"

She wasn't looking at him. She was staring through the windshield. "What is that?"

Blocking the road—it wasn't an animal . . . Treads . . . It was a wheel . . . His first thought was that a wheel had come off a car up on the expressway and it had bounced down here onto the ramp. All at once the car was dead quiet, because the engine had stalled out. Sherman started the engine up again. He tested the brake to make sure it was secure. Then he opened the door.

"What are you doing, Sherman?"

"I'm gonna push it out of the way."

"Be careful. What if a car's coming?"

"Well." He shrugged and got out.

He felt strange from the moment he set foot on the ramp. From overhead the tremendous clanging noise of vehicles going over some sort of metal joint or plate in the expressway. He was staring up at the expressway's black underbelly. He couldn't see the cars. He could only hear them pounding the road, apparently at great speed, making the clanging noise and creating a field of vibration. The vibration enveloped the great corroded black structure with a hum. But at the same time he could hear his shoes, his $650 New & Lingwood shoes, New & Lingwood of Jermyn Street, London, with their English leather soles and heels, making tiny gritty scraping sounds as he walked up the incline toward the wheel. The tiny gritty scraping sound of his shoes was as sharp as any sound he had ever heard. He leaned over. It wasn't a wheel, after all, only a tire. Imagine a car losing a tire. He picked it up.

"Sherman!"

He turned around, toward the Mercedes. Two figures! . . . Two young men —black—on the ramp, coming up behind him . . . *Boston Celtics!* . . . The one nearest him had on a silvery basketball warm-up jacket with CELTICS written across the chest . . . He was no more than four or five steps away . . . powerfully built . . . His jacket was open . . . a white T-shirt . . . tremendous chest muscles . . . a square face . . . wide jaws . . . a wide mouth . . . What was that look? . . . Hunter! Predator! . . . The youth stared Sherman right in the eye . . . walking slowly . . . The other one was tall but skinny, with a long neck, a narrow face . . . a delicate face . . . eyes wide open . . . startled . . . He looked terrified . . . He wore a big loose sweater . . . He was a step or two behind the big one . . .

"Yo!" said the big one. "Need some help?"

Sherman stood there, holding the tire and staring.

"What happen, man? Need some help?"

It was a neighborly voice. *Setting me up! One hand inside his jacket pocket!* But he sounds sincere. *It's a setup, you idiot!* But suppose he merely wants to help? *What are they doing on this ramp!* Haven't done anything—haven't threatened. *But they will!* Just be nice. *Are you insane? Do something! Act!* A sound filled his skull, the sound of rushing steam. He held the tire up in front of his chest. *Now!* Bango —he charged at the big one and shoved the tire at him. It was coming right back at him! The tire was coming right back at him! He threw his arms up. It bounced off his arms. A sprawl—the brute fell over the tire. Silvery CELTICS jacket—on the pavement. Sherman's own momentum carried him forward. He skidded on the New & Lingwood party shoes. He pivoted.

"Sherman!"

Maria was behind the wheel of the car. The engine was roaring. The door on the passenger side was open.

"Get in!"

The other one, the skinny one, was between him and the car . . . a terrified look on his mug . . . eyes wide open . . . Sherman was pure frenzy . . . Had to get to the car! . . . He ran for it. He lowered his head. He crashed into him. The boy went spinning back and hit the rear fender of the car but didn't fall down.

"Henry!"

The big one was getting up. Sherman threw himself into the car.

Maria's ghastly stricken face: "Get in! Get in!"

The roaring engine . . . the Panzer-head Mercedes dials . . . A blur outside the car . . . Sherman grabbed the door pull and with a tremendous adrenal burst banged it shut. Out of the corner of his eye, the big one—almost to the door on Maria's side. Sherman hit the lock mechanism. *Rap!* He was yanking on the door handle—CELTICS inches from Maria's head with only the glass in between. Maria shoved the Mercedes into first gear and squealed forward. The youth leaped to one side. The car was heading straight for the trash cans. Maria hit the brakes. Sherman was thrown against the dash. A vanity case landed on top of the gearshift. Sherman pulled it off. Now it was on his lap. Maria threw the car into reverse. It shot backward. He glanced to his right. The skinny one . . . The skinny boy was standing there staring at him . . . pure fear on his delicate face . . . Maria shoved it into first gear again . . . She was breathing in huge gulps, as if she were drowning . . .

Sherman yelled, "Look out!"

The big one was coming toward the car. He had the tire up over his head. Maria squealed the car forward, right at him. He lurched out of the way . . . a blur . . . a terrific jolt . . . The tire hit the windshield and bounced off, without breaking the glass . . . The Krauts! . . . Maria cut the wheel to the left, to keep from hitting the cans . . . The skinny one standing right there . . . The rear end fishtailed . . . *thok!* . . . The skinny boy was no longer standing . . . Maria fought the steering wheel . . . A clear shot between the guardrail and the trash cans . . . She floored it . . . A furious squeal . . . The Mercedes shot up the ramp . . . The road rose beneath him . . . Sherman hung on . . . The huge tongue of the expressway . . . Lights rocketing by . . . Maria braked the car . . . Sherman and the vanity case were thrown up against the dashboard . . . *Hahhh hahhhhh hahhhhh hahhhhh* . . . At first he thought she was laughing. She was only trying to get her breath.

"You okay?"

She gunned the car forward. The blare of a horn—

"For Christ's sake, Maria!"

The blaring horn swerved and hurtled past, and they were out on the expressway.

His eyes were stinging with perspiration. He took one hand off the vanity case to rub his eyes, but it started shaking so badly he put it back on the case. He could feel his heart beating in his throat. He was soaking wet. His jacket was coming apart. He could feel it. It was ripped in the back seams. His lungs were struggling for more oxygen.

They were barreling along the expressway, much too fast.

"Slow down, Maria! Jesus Christ!"

"Where's it go, Sherman? Where's it go?"

"Just follow the signs that say George Washington Bridge, and for Christ's sake, slow down."

Maria took one hand off the steering wheel to push back her hair from her forehead. Her entire arm, as well as her hand, was shaking. Sherman wondered if she could control the car, but he didn't want to break her concentration. His heart was racing along with hollow thuds, as if it had broken loose inside his rib cage.

"Aw shit, my arms are shaking!" said Maria. Aw shit, muh uhms uh shakin'. He had never heard her use the word *shit* before.

"Just take it easy," said Sherman. "We're okay now, we're okay."

"But where's it go!"

"Just take it easy! Just follow the signs. George Washington Bridge."

"Aw shit, Sherman, that's what we did before!"

"Take it *easy*, for Christ's sake. I'll tell you where."

"Don't fuck up this time, Sherman."

Sherman found his hands gripping the vanity case in his lap as if it were a second wheel. He tried to concentrate on the road ahead. Then he stared at a sign over the highway up ahead: CROSS BRONX GEO. WASH. BRIDGE.

"Cross Bronx! What's that?"

"Just take it!"

"Shit, Sherman!"

"Stay on the highway. We're okay." The navigator.

He stared at the white line on the roadbed. He stared so hard, they began separating on him . . . the lines . . . the signs . . . the taillights . . . He couldn't figure out the pattern any longer . . . He was concentrating on . . . fragments! . . . molecules! . . . atoms! . . . Jesus Christ! . . . *I've lost the power to reason!* . . . His heart went into palpitations . . . and then a big . . . snap! . . . it went back into a regular rhythm . . .

Then, overhead: MAJOR DEEGAN TRIBORO BRIDGE.

"See that, Maria? Triborough Bridge! Take that!"

"Jesus Christ, Sherman, George Washington Bridge!"

"No! We want the Triborough, Maria! That'll take us right back into Manhattan!"

So they took that expressway. Presently, overhead: WILLIS AVE.

"What's Willis Avenue?"

"I think it's the Bronx," said Sherman.

"Shit!"

"Just stay to your left! We're okay!"

"Shit, Sherman!"

Over the highway a big sign: TRIBORO.

"There it is, Maria! You see that!"

"Yeah."

"Bear to your right up there. You exit to the right!" Now Sherman was gripping the vanity case and giving it the body English for a right turn. He was holding a vanity case and giving it body English. Maria had on an Avenue Foch royal-blue jacket with shoulder pads . . . out to *here* . . . a tense little animal writhing under royal-blue shoulder pads from Paris . . . the two of them in a $48,000 Mercedes with spiffy airplane dials . . . desperate to escape the Bronx . . .

They reached the exit. He held on for dear life, as if a tornado were going to rise up at any moment and blow them out of the proper groove and—*back to the Bronx!*

They made it. Now they were on the long incline that led to the bridge and to Manhattan.

Hahhhhh hahhhhhh hahhhhhh hahhhhh "Sherman!"

He stared at her. She was sighing and taking in huge gulps of air.

"It's okay, sweetheart."

"Sherman, he threw it . . . right at me!"

"Threw what?"

"That . . . wheel, Sherman!"

The tire had hit the windshield right in front of her eyes. But something else flashed into Sherman's mind . . . *thok!* . . . the sound of the rear fender hitting something and the skinny boy disappearing from view . . . Maria let out a sob.

"Get a grip on yourself! We've only got a little farther!"

She snuffled back her tears. "God . . ."

Sherman reached over and massaged the back of her neck with his left hand.

"You're okay, honey. You're doing swell."

"Oh, Sherman."

The odd thing was—and it struck him as odd in that very moment—he wanted to smile. I saved her! I am her protector! He kept rubbing her neck.

"It was only a tire," said the protector, savoring the luxury of calming the weak. "Otherwise it would've broken the windshield."

"He threw it . . . right . . . at me."

"I know, I know. It's okay. It's all over."

But he could hear it again. The little *thok*. And the skinny boy was gone.

"Maria, I think you—I think we hit one of them."

You—we—already a deep instinct was summoning up the clammy patriarch, blame.

Maria didn't say anything.

"You know when we skidded. There was this kind of a . . . this kind of a . . . little sound, a little *thok*."

Maria remained silent. Sherman was staring at her. Finally she said, "Yeah—I —I don't know. I don't give a shit, Sherman. All I care is, we got outta there."

"Well, that's the main thing, but—"

"Oh, God, Sherman, like—the worst nightmare!" She started choking back sobs, all the while hunched forward and staring straight ahead, through the windshield, concentrating on the traffic.

"It's okay, sweetheart. We're okay now." He rubbed her neck some more. The skinny boy was standing there. *Thok*. He wasn't standing there anymore.

The traffic was getting heavier. The tide of red taillights ahead of them ran under an overpass and turned up an incline. They weren't far from the bridge. Maria slowed down. In the darkness, the toll plaza was a great smear of concrete turned yellowish by the lights above. Out front, the red lights became a swarm closing in on the tollbooths. In the distance Sherman could see the dense black of Manhattan.

Such gravity . . . so many lights . . . so many people . . . so many souls sharing this yellow smear of concrete with him . . . and all of them oblivious of what he had just been through!

* * *

Sherman waited until they were rolling down the FDR Drive, along the East River, back in White Manhattan and Maria was calmer, before he brought the subject up again.

"Well, what do you think, Maria? I guess we ought to report this to the police."

She didn't say anything. He looked at her. She stared grimly at the roadway.

"What do you think?"

"What for?"

"Well, I just think—"

"Sherman, shut up." She said it softly, gently. "Just let me drive this goddamn car."

The familiar 1920s Gothic palisades of New York Hospital were just up ahead. White Manhattan! They took the Seventy-first Street exit off the drive.

Maria parked across the street from the town house and her fourth-floor hideaway. Sherman got out and immediately scrutinized the right rear fender. To his great relief—no dent; no sign of anything, at least not here in the dark. Since Maria had told her husband she wouldn't be returning from Italy until the next day, she wanted to take the luggage up to the little apartment, too. Three times Sherman climbed up the creaking staircase, in the miserable gloaming of the Landlord's Halos, hauling up the luggage.

Maria took off her royal-blue jacket with the Paris shoulders and put it on the bed. Sherman took off his jacket. It was badly ripped in the back, in the side seams. Huntsman, Savile Row, London. Cost a goddamned fortune. He threw it on the bed. His shirt was wringing wet. Maria kicked off her shoes and sat down in one of the bentwood chairs by the oak pedestal table and put one elbow on the table and let her head keel over against her forearm. The old table sagged in its sad way. Then she straightened up and looked at Sherman.

"I want a drink," she said. "You want one?"

"Yeah. You want me to fix them?"

"Unh-hunh. I want a lot of vodka and a little orange juice and some ice. The vodka's up in the cabinet."

He went in the mean little kitchen and turned on the light. A cockroach was sitting on the rim of a dirty frying pan on the stove. Well, the hell with it. He made Maria her vodka-and-orange juice and then poured himself an Old Fashioned glass full of scotch and put in some ice and a little water. He sat in one of the bentwood chairs across the table from her. He found that he wanted the drink very badly. He longed for each ice-cold burning jolt in his stomach. The car fishtailed. *Thok.* The tall delicate one wasn't standing there any longer.

Maria had already drunk half the big tumbler he had brought her. She closed her eyes and threw her head back and then looked at Sherman and smiled in a tired fashion. "I swear," she said, "I thought that was gonna be . . . it."

"Well, what do we do now?" said Sherman.

"What do you mean?"

"I guess we oughta—I guess we oughta report it to the police."

"That's what you said. Okay. Tell me what for."

"Well, they tried to rob us—and I think maybe you—I think it's possible you hit one of them."

She just looked at him.

"It was when you really gunned it, and we skidded."

"Well, you wanna know something? I hope I did. But if I did, I sure didn't hit him very hard. I just barely heard something."

"It was just a little *thok*. And then he wasn't standing there anymore."

Maria shrugged her shoulders.

"Well—I'm just thinking out loud," said Sherman. "I think we ought to report it. That way we protect ourselves."

Maria expelled air through her lips, the way you do when you're at your wit's end, and looked away.

"Well, just suppose the guy is hurt."

She looked at him and laughed softly. "Frankly, I couldn't care less."

"But just suppose—"

"Look, we got outta there. How we did it doesn't matter."

"But suppose—"

"Suppose *bullshit*, Sherman. Where you gonna go to *tell the police?* What are you gonna say?"

"I don't know. I'll just tell them what happened."

"Sherman, I'm gonna tell *you* what happened. I'm from South Carolina, and I'm gonna tell you in plain English. Two niggers tried to kill us, and we got away. Two niggers tried to kill us in the jungle, and we got outta the jungle, and we're still breathing, and that's that."

"Yeah, but suppose—"

"*You* suppose! Suppose you go to the police. What are you gonna say? What are you gonna say we were doing in the Bronx? You say you're just gonna tell them what happened. Well, you tell *me*, Sherman. What happened?"

So that was what she was actually saying. Do you tell the police that Mrs. Arthur Ruskin of Fifth Avenue and Mr. Sherman McCoy of Park Avenue happened to be having a nocturnal *tête-à-tête* when they missed the Manhattan off-ramp from the Triborough Bridge and got into a little scrape in the Bronx? He ran that through his mind. Well, he could just tell Judy—no, there was no way he could *just tell Judy* about a little ride with a woman named Maria. But if they—if Maria had hit the boy, then it was better to grit his teeth and just tell what happened. Which was what? Well . . . two boys had tried to rob them. They blocked the roadway. They approached him. They said . . . A little shock went through his solar plexus. *Yo! You need some help?* That was all the big one had said. He hadn't produced a weapon. Neither of them had made a threatening gesture until after he had thrown the tire. Could it be—now, wait a minute. That's crazy. What else were they doing out on a ramp to an expressway beside a blockade, in the dark—except to—Maria would back up his interpretation—*interpretation!*—a frisky wild animal—all of a sudden he realized that he barely knew her.

"I don't know," he said. "Maybe you're right. Let's think about it. I'm only thinking out loud."

"I don't have to think about it, Sherman. Some things I understand better than you do. Not many things, but some things. They'd love to get their hands on you and me."

"Who would?"

"The police. And what good would it do, anyway? They'll never catch those boys."

"What do you mean, get their hands on us?"

"Please, forget the police."

"What are you talking about?"

"You, for a start. You're a socialite."

"I am *not* a socialite." Masters of the Universe existed on a plateau far above socialites.

"Oh no? Your apartment was in *Architectural Digest*. Your picture's been in *W*. Your father was—is—well, whatever he is. You know."

"My *wife* put the apartment in the magazine!"

"Well, you can explain that to the police, Sherman. I'm sure they'll appreciate the distinction."

Sherman was speechless. It was a hateful thought.

"And they won't half mind getting holda me, either, as far as that goes. I'm just a little girl from South Carolina, but my husband has a hundred million dollars and an apartment on Fifth Avenue."

"All right, I'm just trying to figure out the sequence, the things that might come up, that's all. What if you did hit the boy—what if he's injured?"

"Did you see him get hit?"

"No."

"Neither did I. As far as I'm concerned, I didn't hit anybody. I hope to God I did, but as far as I'm concerned, and as far as you're concerned, I didn't hit anybody. Okay?"

"Well, I guess you're right. I didn't see anything. But I heard something, and I felt something."

"Sherman, it all happened so fast, you don't know *what* happened, and neither do I. Those boys aren't going to the police. You can be goddamned sure a that. And if you go to the police, they won't find them, either. They'll just have a good time with your story—and you don't know what happened, do you?"

"I guess I don't."

"I guess you don't, either. If the question ever comes up, all that happened was, two boys blocked the road and tried to rob us, and we got away from them. Period. That's all we know."

"And why didn't we report it?"

"Because it was pointless. We weren't hurt, and we figured they'd never find those boys, anyway. And you know something, Sherman?"

"What?"

"That happens to be the whole truth. You can imagine anything you want, but that happens to be all you know and all I know."

"Yeah. You're right. I don't know, I'd just feel better if—"

"You don't have to feel better, Sherman. I was the one who was driving. If I hit the sonofabitch, then it was me who hit him—and I'm saying I didn't hit anybody, and I'm not reporting anything to the police. So just don't you worry about it."

"I'm not *worrying* about it, it's just that—"

"Good."

Sherman hesitated. Well, that was true, wasn't it? *She* was driving. It was his car, but *she* took it upon herself to drive it, and if the question ever came up, whatever happened was her responsibility. *She* was driving . . . and so if there was anything to report, that was her responsibility, too. Naturally, he would stick by her . . . but already a great weight was sliding off his back.

"You're right, Maria. It was like something in the jungle." He nodded several times, to indicate that the truth had finally dawned on him.

Maria said, "We coulda been killed, right there, just as easy as not."

"You know something, Maria? We fought."

"Fought?"

"We were in the goddamned jungle . . . and we were attacked . . . and we fought our way out." Now he sounded as if the dawn were breaking wider and wider. "Christ, I don't know when the last time was I was in a fight, an actual fight. Maybe I was twelve, thirteen. You know something, babe? You were great. You were fantastic. You really were. When I saw you behind the wheel—I didn't even know if you could drive the car!" He was elated. *She* was driving. "But you drove the hell out of it! You were great!" Oh, the dawn had broken. The world glowed with its radiance.

"I don't even remember what I did," said Maria. "It was just a—a—everything happened at once. The worst part was getting over into the seat. I don't know why they put that gearshift thing in the middle there. I caught my skirt on it."

"When I saw you there, I couldn't believe it! If you hadn't done that"—he shook his head—"we'd've never made it."

Now that they were into the exultation of the war story, Sherman couldn't resist giving himself an opening for a little praise.

Maria said, "Well, I just did it on—I don't know—instinct." Typical of her; she didn't notice the opening.

"Yeah," said Sherman, "well, it was a damned good instinct. I kind of had my hands full at that point!" An opening big enough for a truck.

This one even she noticed. "Oh, Sherman—I know you did. When you threw that wheel, that tire, at that boy—oh, God, I thought—I just about—you beat them both. Sherman! You beat them both!"

I beat them both. Never had there been such music in the ears of the Master of the Universe. Play on! Never stop!

"I couldn't figure out what was happening!" said Sherman. Now he was smiling with excitement and not even trying to hold back the smile. "I threw the tire, and all of a sudden it was coming back in my face!"

"That was because he put up his hands to block it, and it bounced off, and—"

They plunged into the thick adrenal details of the adventure.

Their voices rose, and their spirits rose, and they laughed, supposedly over the bizarre details of the battle but actually with sheer joy, spontaneous exultation over *the miracle*. Together they had faced the worst nightmare of New York, and they had triumphed.

Maria sat up straight and began looking at Sherman with her eyes extra wide and her lips parted in the suggestion of a smile. He had a delicious premonition. Without a word she stood up and took off her blouse. She wore nothing underneath it. He stared at her breasts, which were glorious. The fair white flesh was gorged with concupiscence and glistening with perspiration. She walked over to him and stood between his legs as he sat in the chair and began untying his tie. He put his arms around her waist and pulled her so hard she lost her balance. They rolled down onto the rug. What a happy, awkward time they had wriggling out of their clothes!

Now they were stretched out on the floor, on the rug, which was filthy, amid the dust balls, and who cared about the dirt and the dust balls? They were both hot and wet with perspiration, and who cared about that, either? It was better that way. They had been through the wall of fire together. They had fought in the jungle together, hadn't they? They were lying side by side, and their bodies were still hot from the fray. Sherman kissed her on the lips, and they lay like that for a long time, just kissing, with their bodies pressed together. Then he ran his fingers over her back and the perfect curve of her hip and the perfect curve of her thigh and the perfect inside of her thigh—and never before such excitement! The rush ran straight from his fingertips to his groin and then throughout his nervous system to a billion explosive synaptic cells. He wanted to *have* this woman literally, to enclose her in his very hide, to subsume this hot fair white body of hers, in the prime of youth's sweet rude firm animal health, and make it his forever. Perfect love! Pure bliss! Priapus, king and master! Master of the Universe! King of the Jungle!

Sherman kept both his cars, the Mercedes and a big Mercury station wagon, in an underground garage two blocks from his apartment house. At the bottom of the ramp he stopped, as always, beside the wooden cashier's hut. A chubby little man in a short-sleeved sport shirt and baggy gray twill pants came out the door. It was the one he disliked, Dan, the redheaded one. He got out of the car and quickly rolled up his jacket, hoping the little attendant wouldn't see it was torn.

"Hey, Sherm! Howya doin'?"

That was what Sherman truly detested. It was bad enough that this man insisted on calling him by his first name. But to shorten it to *Sherm*, which no one had ever called him—that was escalating presumptuousness into obnoxiousness. Sherman could think of nothing he had ever said, no gesture he had ever made, that had given him the invitation or even the opening to become familiar. Gratuitous familiarity was not the sort of thing you were supposed to mind these days, but Sherman minded it. It was a form of aggression. *You think I am your inferior, you Wall Street Wasp with the Yale chin, but I will show you.* Many times he had tried to think of some polite but cold and cutting response to these hearty pseudo-friendly greetings, and he had come up with nothing.

"Sherm, howawya?" Dan was right beside him. He wouldn't let up.

"Fine," Mr. McCoy said frostily . . . but also lamely. One of the unwritten rules of status conduct is that when an inferior greets you with a how-are-you, you do not answer the question. Sherman turned to walk away.

"Sherm!"

He stopped. Dan was standing beside the Mercedes with his hands on his chubby hips. He had hips like an old woman's.

"You know your coat is ripped?"

The block of ice, his Yale chin jutting out, said nothing.

"Right there," said Dan with considerable satisfaction. "You can see the lining. How'd you do that?"

Sherman could hear it—*thok*—and he could feel the rear end of the car fishtailing, and the tall skinny boy was no longer standing there. *Not a word about that*—and yet he had a terrific urge to tell this odious little man. Now that he had been through the wall of fire and survived, he was experiencing one of man's keenest but least understood drives: information compulsion. He wanted to tell his war story.

But caution triumphed, caution bolstered by snobbery. He probably should talk to no one about what had happened; and to this man least of all.

"I have no idea," he said.

"You didn't notice it?"

The frosty snowman with the Yale chin, Mr. Sherman McCoy, motioned toward the Mercedes. "I won't be taking it out again until the weekend." Then he did an about-face and left.

As he reached the sidewalk, a puff of wind swept the street. He could feel how damp his shirt was. His pants were still damp behind the knees. His ripped jacket was draped over the crook of his arm. His hair felt like a bird's nest. He was a mess. His heart was beating a little too fast. *I have something to hide.* But what was he worrying about? He wasn't driving the car when it happened—if it happened. Right! *If* it happened. He hadn't *seen* the boy get hit, and she hadn't, either, and besides, it was in the heat of a fight for their very lives—and she was driving, in any case. If she didn't want to report it, that was her business.

He stopped and took a breath and looked around. Yes; White Manhattan, the sanctuary of the East Seventies. Across the street a doorman stood under the canopy of an apartment house, smoking a cigarette. A boy in a dark business suit and a pretty girl in a white dress were strolling toward him. The fellow was talking to her a mile a minute. So young, and dressed like an old man in a Brooks Brothers or Chipp or J. Press suit, just the way he had looked when he first went to work at Pierce & Pierce.

All at once a wonderful feeling swept over Sherman. For Christ's sake, what was he worried about? He stood there on the sidewalk, stock-still, with his chin up and big grin on his face. The boy and girl probably thought he was a lunatic. In fact—he was a man. Tonight, with nothing but his hands and his nerve he had fought the elemental enemy, the hunter, the predator, and he had prevailed. He had fought his way out of an ambush on the nightmare terrain, and he had prevailed. He had saved a woman. The time had come to act like a man, and he had acted and prevailed. He was not merely a Master of the Universe; he was more; he was a man. Grinning and humming, "Show me but ten who are stout-hearted men," the stouthearted man, still damp from the fray, walked the two blocks to his duplex apartment overlooking the street of dreams.

5

THE GIRL WITH BROWN LIPSTICK

On the mezzanine of the sixth floor of the Bronx County Building, near the elevators, was a wide entryway framed in two or three tons of mahogany and marble and blocked by a counter and a gate. Behind the counter sat a guard with a .38-caliber revolver in a holster on his hip. The guard served as a receptionist. The revolver, which looked big enough to stop a florist's van, was supposed to serve as a deterrent to the random berserk vengeful felons of the Bronx.

Over this entryway were some large Roman-style capital letters that had been fabricated in brass at considerable expense to the taxpayers of New York and cemented to the marble facing with epoxy glue. Once a week a handyman got up on a ladder and rubbed Simichrome polish across the letters, so that the legend RICHARD A. WEISS, DISTRICT ATTORNEY, BRONX COUNTY blazed away more brightly than anything the building's architects, Joseph H. Freedlander and Max Hausle, had the nerve to put even on the outside of the building in its golden dawn half a century ago.

As Larry Kramer got off the elevator and walked toward this brassy gleam, the right side of his lips twisted subversively. The A stood for Abraham. Weiss was known to his friends and his political cronies and the newspaper reporters and Channels 1, 2, 4, 5, 7, and 11 and his constituents, most prominently the Jews and Italians up around Riverdale and the Pelham Parkway and Co-op City, as Abe Weiss. He hated the nickname Abe, which he had been stuck with when he was growing up in Brooklyn. A few years back he had let it be known that he preferred to be called Dick, and he had practically been laughed out of the Bronx Democratic organization. That was the last time Abe Weiss ever mentioned Dick Weiss. To Abe Weiss, being laughed out of the Bronx Democratic organization, being separated from it in any fashion whatsoever, for that matter, would have been like being thrown over the railing of a Christmas cruise ship in the middle of the Caribbean Sea. So he was Richard A. Weiss only in *The New York Times* and over this doorway.

The guard buzzed Kramer through the gate, and Kramer's running shoes squeaked on the marble floor. The guard gave them a dubious once-over. As usual, Kramer was carrying his leather shoes in an A&P shopping bag.

Beyond the entryway, the level of grandeur in the District Attorney's Office went up and down. The office of Weiss himself was bigger and showier, thanks to its paneled walls, than the Mayor of New York's. The bureau chiefs, for Homicide, Investigations, Major Offenses, Supreme Court, Criminal Court, and Appeals, had their share of the paneling and the leather or school-of-leather couches and the Contract Sheraton armchairs. But by the time you got down to an assistant district attorney, like Larry Kramer, you were looking at Good Enough for Government Work when it came to interior decoration.

The two assistant district attorneys who shared the office with him, Ray Andriutti and Jimmy Caughey, were sitting sprawled back in the swivel chairs. There was just enough floor space in the room for three metal desks, three swivel chairs, four filing cabinets, an old coat stand with six savage hooks sticking out from it, and a table bearing a Mr. Coffee machine and a promiscuous heap of plastic cups and spoons and a gummy collage of paper napkins and white sugar envelopes and pink saccharine envelopes stuck to a maroon plastic tray with a high sweet-smelling paste composed of spilled coffee and Cremora powder. Both Andriutti and Caughey were sitting with their legs crossed in the same fashion. The left ankle was resting on top of the right knee, as if they were such studs, they couldn't have crossed their legs any farther if they had wanted to. This was the accepted sitting posture of Homicide, the most manly of the six bureaus of the District Attorney's Office.

Both had their jackets off and hung with the perfect give-a-shit carelessness on the coatrack. Their shirt collars were unbuttoned, and their necktie knots were pulled down an inch or so. Andriutti was rubbing the back of his left arm with his right hand, as if it itched. In fact, he was feeling and admiring his triceps, which he pumped up at least three times a week by doing sets of French curls with dumbbells at the New York Athletic Club. Andriutti could afford to work out at the Athletic Club, instead of on a carpet between a *Dracaena fragrans* tub and a convertible couch, because he didn't have a wife and a child to support in an $888-a-month ant colony in the West Seventies. He didn't have to worry about his triceps and his deltoids and his lats deflating. Andriutti liked the fact that when he reached around behind one of his mighty arms with the other hand, it made the widest muscles of his back, the lats, the latissima dorsae, fan out until they practically split his shirt, and his pectorals hardened into a couple of mountains of pure muscle. Kramer and Andriutti were of the new generation, in which the terms *triceps*, *deltoids*, *latissima dorsae*, and *pectoralis major* were better known than the names of the major planets. Andriutti rubbed his triceps a hundred and twenty times a day, on the average.

Still rubbing them, Andriutti looked at Kramer as he walked in and said: "Jesus Christ, here comes the bag lady. What the hell is this fucking A&P bag, Larry? You been coming in here with this fucking bag every day this week." Then he turned to Jimmy Caughey and said, "Looks like a fucking bag lady."

Caughey was also a jock, but more the Triathlon type, with a narrow face and a long chin. He just smiled at Kramer, as much as to say, "Well, what do you say to that?"

Kramer said, "Your arm itch, Ray?" Then he looked at Caughey and said,

"Ray's got this fucking allergy. It's called weight lifter's disease." Then he turned back to Andriutti. "Itches like a sonofabitch, don't it?"

Andriutti let his hand drop off his triceps. "And what are these *jogging* shoes?" he said to Kramer. "Looks like those girls walking to work at Merrill Lynch. All dressed up, and they got these fucking rubber gunboats on their feet."

"What the hell *is* in the bag?" said Caughey.

"My high heels," said Kramer. He took off his jacket and jammed it down, give-a-shit, on a coatrack hook in the accepted fashion and pulled down his necktie and unbuttoned his shirt and sat down in his swivel chair and opened up the shopping bag and fished out his Johnston & Murphy brown leather shoes and started taking off the Nikes.

"Jimmy," Andriutti said to Caughey, "did you know that Jewish guys—Larry, I don't want you to take this personally—did you know that Jewish guys, even if they're real stand-up guys, all have one faggot gene? That's a well-known fact. They can't stand going out in the rain without an umbrella or they have all this modern shit in their apartment or they don't like to go hunting or they're for the fucking nuclear freeze and affirmative action or they wear jogging shoes to work or some goddamn thing. You know?"

"Gee," said Kramer, "I don't know why you thought I'd take it personally."

"Come on, Larry," said Andriutti, "tell the truth. Deep down, don't you wish you were Italian or Irish?"

"Yeah," said Kramer, "that way I wouldn't know what the fuck was going on in this fucking place."

Caughey started laughing. "Well, don't let Ahab see those shoes, Larry. He'll have Jeanette issue a fucking memorandum."

"No, he'll call a fucking press conference," said Andriutti.

"That's always a safe fucking bet."

And so another fucking day in the fucking Homicide Bureau of the Bronx Fucking District Attorney's Office was off to a fucking start.

An assistant D.A. in Major Offenses had started calling Abe Weiss "Captain Ahab," and now they all did. Weiss was notorious in his obsession for publicity, even among a breed, the district attorney, that was publicity-mad by nature. Unlike the great D.A.s of yore, such as Frank Hogan, Burt Roberts, or Mario Merola, Weiss never went near a courtroom. He didn't have time. There were only so many hours in the day for him to stay in touch with Channels 1, 2, 4, 5, 7, and 11 and the New York *Daily News*, the *Post*, *The City Light*, and the *Times*.

Jimmy Caughey said, "I was just in seeing the captain. You shoulda—"

"You were? What for?" asked Kramer with just a shade too much curiosity and incipient envy in his voice.

"Me and Bernie," said Caughey. "He wanted to know about the Moore case."

"Any good?"

"Piece a shit," said Caughey. "This fucking guy Moore, he has a big house in Riverdale, and his wife's mother lives there with 'em, and she's been giving him a hard time for about thirty-seven fucking years, right? So this guy, he loses his job. He's working for one a these reinsurance companies, and he's making $200,000 or $300,000 a year, and now he's out a work for eight or nine months, and nobody'll hire him, and he don't know what the hell to do, right? So one day he's puttering around out in the garden, and the mother-in-law comes out and says, 'Well, water seeks its own level.' That's a verbatim quote. 'Water seeks its own level. You oughta get a job as a gardener.' So this guy, he's out of his fucking mind, he's so mad. He goes in and tells his wife, 'I've had it with your mother. I'm gonna get my shotgun and scare her.' So he goes up to his bedroom, where he keeps this 12-gauge shotgun, and he comes downstairs and heads for the mother-in-law, and he's gonna scare the shit out of her, and he says, 'Okay, Gladys,' and he trips on the rug, and the gun goes off and kills her, and—ba-bing!—Murder Two."

"Why was Weiss interested?"

"Well, the guy's white, he's got some money, he lives in a big house in Riverdale. It looks at first like maybe he's gonna fake an accidental shooting."

"Is that possible?"

"Naw. Fucking guy's one a my boys. He's your basic Irish who made good, but he's still a Harp. He's drowning in remorse. You'd think he'd shot his own mother, he feels so fucking guilty. Right now he'd confess to anything. Bernie could sit him in front of the videocamera and clean up every homicide in the Bronx for the past five years. Naw, it's a piece a shit, but it looked good at first."

Kramer and Andriutti contemplated this piece a shit without needing any amplification. Every assistant D.A. in the Bronx, from the youngest Italian just out of St. John's Law School to the oldest Irish bureau chief, who would be somebody like Bernie Fitzgibbon, who was forty-two, shared Captain Ahab's mania for the Great White Defendant. For a start, it was not pleasant to go through life telling yourself, "What I do for a living is, I pack blacks and Latins off to jail." Kramer had been raised as a liberal. In Jewish families like his, liberalism came with the Similac and the Mott's apple juice and the Instamatic and Daddy's grins in the evening. And even the Italians, like Ray Andriutti, and the Irish, like Jimmy Caughey, who were not exactly burdened with liberalism by their parents, couldn't help but be affected by the mental atmosphere of the law schools, where, for one thing, there were so many Jewish faculty members. By the time you finished law school in the New York area, it was, well . . . *impolite!* . . . on the ordinary social level . . . to go around making jokes about the *yoms*. It wasn't that it was morally wrong . . . It was that it was in *bad taste*. So it made the boys uneasy, this eternal prosecution of the blacks and Latins.

Not that they weren't guilty. One thing Kramer had learned within two weeks as an assistant D.A. in the Bronx was that 95 percent of the defendants who got as far as the indictment stage, perhaps 98 percent, were truly guilty. The caseload was so overwhelming, you didn't waste time trying to bring the marginal cases forward, unless the press was on your back. They hauled in guilt by the ton, those blue-and-orange vans out there on Walton Avenue. But the poor bastards behind the wire mesh barely deserved the term *criminal*, if by criminal you had in mind the romantic notion of someone who has a goal and seeks to achieve it through some desperate way outside the law. No, they were simpleminded incompetents, most of them, and they did unbelievably stupid, vile things.

Kramer looked at Andriutti and Caughey, sitting there with their mighty thighs akimbo. He felt superior to them. He was a graduate of the Columbia Law School, and they were both graduates of St. John's, widely known as the law school for the also-rans of college academic competition. And he was Jewish. Very early in life he had picked up the knowledge that the Italians and the Irish were animals. The Italians were pigs, and the Irish were mules or goats. He couldn't remember if his parents had actually used any such terms or not, but they got the idea across very clearly. To his parents, New York City—New York? hell, the whole U.S., the whole world!—was a drama called *The Jews Confront the Goyim*, and the *goyim* were animals. And so what was he doing here with these animals? A Jew in the Homicide Bureau was a rare thing. The Homicide Bureau was the elite corps of the District Attorney's Office, the D.A.'s Marines, because homicide was the most serious of all crimes. An assistant D.A. in Homicide had to be able to go out on the street to the crime scenes at all hours, night and day, and be a real commando and rub shoulders with the police and know how to confront defendants and witnesses and intimidate them when the time came, and these were likely to be the lowest, grimmest, scurviest defendants and witnesses in the history of criminal justice. For fifty years, at least, maybe longer, Homicide had been an Irish enclave, although recently the Italians had made their way into it. The Irish had given Homicide their stamp. The Irish were stone courageous. Even when it was insane not to, they never stepped back. Andriutti had been right, or half right. Kramer didn't want to be Italian, but he did want to be Irish, and so did Ray Andriutti, the dumb fuck. Yes, they were animals! The *goyim* were animals, and Kramer was proud to be among the animals, in the Homicide Bureau.

Anyway, here they were, the three of them, sitting in this Good Enough for Government Work office at $36,000 to $42,000 a year instead of down at Cravath, Swaine & Moore or some such place at $136,000 to $142,000. They had been born a million miles from Wall Street, meaning the outer boroughs, Brooklyn, Queens, and the Bronx. To their families, their going to college and becoming lawyers had been the greatest thing since Franklin D. Roosevelt. And so they sat around in the Homicide Bureau talking about this fucking thing and that fucking thing and using *don'ts* for *doesn'ts* and *naws* for *no's*, as if they didn't know any better.

Here they were . . . and here he was, and where was he going? What were these cases he was handling? Pieces of shit! Garbage collection . . . Arthur Rivera. Arthur Rivera and another drug dealer get into an argument over an order of pizza at a social club and pull knives, and Arthur says, "Let's put the weapons down and fight man to man." And they do, whereupon Arthur pulls out a second knife and stabs the other fellow in the chest and kills him . . . Jimmy Dollard. Jimmy Dollard and his closest pal, Otis Blakemore, and three other black guys are drinking and taking cocaine and playing a game called the dozens, in which the idea is to see how outrageously you can insult the other fellow, and Blakemore is doing an inspired number on Jimmy, and Jimmy pulls out a revolver and shoots him through the heart and then collapses on the table, sobbing and saying, "My man! My man Stan! I shot my man Stan!" . . . And the case of Herbert 92X—

For an instant the thought of Herbert's case triggered a vision of the girl with brown lipstick—

The press couldn't even *see* these cases. It was just poor people killing poor people. To prosecute such cases was to be part of the garbage-collection service, necessary and honorable, plodding and anonymous.

Captain Ahab wasn't so ridiculous, after all. Press coverage! Ray and Jimmy could laugh all they wanted, but Weiss had made sure the entire city knew his name. Weiss had an election coming up, and the Bronx was 70 percent black and Latin, and he was going to make sure the name Abe Weiss was pumped out to them on every channel that existed. He might not do much else, but he was going to do that.

A telephone rang: Ray's. "Homicide," he said. "Andriutti . . . Bernie's not here. I think he's in court . . . What? . . . Go over that again?" Long pause. "Well, was he hit by a car or wasn't he? . . . Unnh-hunnh . . . Well, shit, I don't know. You better talk it over with Bernie. Okay? . . . Okay." He hung up and shook his head and looked at Jimmy Caughey. "That was some detective who's over at Lincoln Hospital. Says they got a likely-to-die, some kid who comes into the emergency room and don't know whether he slipped in the bathtub and broke his wrist or got hit by a Mercedes-Benz. Or some such shit. Wants to talk to Bernie. So let him fucking talk to Bernie."

Ray shook his head some more, and Kramer and Caughey nodded sympathetically. The eternal pieces a shit in the Bronx.

Kramer looked at his watch and stood up.

"Well," he said, "you guys can sit here and fuck-all, if you want, but I gotta go fucking listen to that renowned Middle Eastern scholar Herbert 92X read from the Koran."

There were thirty-five courtrooms in the Bronx County Building devoted to criminal cases, and each one was known as a "part." They had been built at a time, the early 1930s, when it was still assumed that the very look of a courtroom should proclaim the gravity and omnipotence of the rule of law. The ceilings were a good fifteen feet high. The walls were paneled throughout in a dark wood. The judge's bench was a stage with a vast desk. The desk had enough cornices, moldings, panels, pilasters, inlays, and sheer hardwood mass to make you believe that Solomon himself, who was a king, would have found it imposing. The seats in the spectators' section were separated from the judge's bench, the jury box, and the tables of the prosecutor, the defendant, and the clerk of the court by a wooden balustrade with an enormous carved top rail, the so-called Bar of Justice. In short, there was nothing whatsoever in the look of the premises to tip off the unwary to the helter-skelter of a criminal court judge's daily task.

The moment Kramer walked in, he could tell that the day had gotten off to a bad start in Part 60. He had only to look at the judge. Kovitsky was up on the bench, in his black robes, leaning forward with both forearms on his desktop. His chin was down so low it seemed about to touch it. His bony skull and his sharp beak jutted out of the robe at such a low angle he looked like a buzzard. Kramer could see his irises floating and bobbing on the whites of his eyes as he scanned the room and its raggedy collection of humanity. He looked as if he were about to flap his wings and strike. Kramer felt ambivalent about Kovitsky. On one hand, he resented his courtroom tirades, which were often personal and designed to humiliate. On the other hand, Kovitsky was a Jewish warrior, a son of the Masada. Only Kovitsky could have stopped the loudmouths in the prison vans with a gob of spit.

"Where's Mr. Sonnenberg?" said Kovitsky. There was no response.

So he said it again, this time in an amazing baritone that nailed every syllable into the back wall and startled all newcomers to the courtroom of Judge Myron Kovitsky: "WHERE IS MIS-TER SON-NEN-BERG!"

Except for two little boys and a little girl, who were running between the benches and playing tag, the spectators froze. One by one they congratulated themselves. No matter how miserable their fates, at least they had not fallen so low as to be Mr. Sonnenberg, that miserable insect, whoever he was.

That miserable insect was a lawyer, and Kramer knew the nature of his offense, which was that his absence was impeding the shoveling of the chow into the gullet of the criminal justice system, Part 60. In each part, the day began with the so-called calendar session, during which the judge dealt with motions and pleas in a variety of cases, perhaps as many as a dozen in a morning. Kramer had to laugh every time he saw a television show with a courtroom scene. They always showed a trial in progress. A trial! Who the hell dreamed up these goddamned shows? Every year there were 7,000 felony indictments in the Bronx and the capacity for 650 trials, at the most. The judges had to dispose of the other 6,350 cases in either of two ways. They could dismiss a case or they could let the defendant plead guilty to a reduced charge in return for not forcing the court to go through a trial. Dismissing cases was a hazardous way to go about reducing the backlog, even for a grotesque cynic. Every time a felony case was thrown out, somebody, such as the victim or his family, was likely to yell, and the press was only too happy to attack judges who let the malefactors go free. That left the plea bargains, which were the business of the calendar sessions. So the calendar sessions were the very alimentary canal of the criminal justice system in the Bronx.

Every week the clerk of each part turned in a scorecard to Louis Mastroiani, chief administrative judge for the criminal division, Supreme Court, Bronx County. The scorecard showed how many cases the judge in that part had on his docket and how many he had disposed of that week, through plea bargains, dismissals, and trials. On the wall of the courtroom, over the judge's head, it said IN GOD WE TRUST. On the scorecard, however, it said CASE BACKLOG ANALYSIS, and a judge's effectiveness was rated almost entirely according to CASE BACKLOG ANALYSIS.

Practically all cases were called for 9:30 a.m. If the clerk called a case, and the defendant was not present or his lawyer was not present or if any of a dozen other things occurred to make it impossible to shove this case a little farther through the funnel, the principals in the next case would be on hand, presumably, ready to step forward. So the spectators' section was dotted with little clumps of people, none of them spectators in any sporting sense. There were defendants and their lawyers, defendants and their pals, defendants and their families. The three small children came slithering out from between two benches, ran toward the back of the courtroom, giggling, and disappeared behind the last bench. A woman turned her head and scowled at them and didn't bother to go fetch them. Now Kramer recognized the trio. They were Herbert 92X's children. Not that he found this at all remarkable; there were children in the courtrooms every day. The courts were a form of day-care center in the Bronx. Playing tag in Part 60 during Daddy's motions, pleas, trials, and sentencings was just a part of growing up.

Kovitsky turned toward the clerk of the court, who sat at a table below the judge's bench and off to the side. The clerk was a bull-necked Italian named Charles Bruzzielli. He had his jacket off. He wore a short-sleeved dress shirt with the collar open and his necktie at half-mast. You could see the top of his T-shirt. The tie had a huge Windsor knot.

"Is that Mr. . . ." Kovitsky looked down at a piece of paper on his desk, then at Bruzzielli. ". . . Lockwood?"

Bruzzielli nodded yes, and Kovitsky looked straight ahead at a slender figure who had walked from the spectators' benches up to the bar.

"Mr. Lockwood," said Kovitsky, "where's your attorney? Where's Mr. Sonnenberg?"

"I 'unno," said the figure.

He was barely audible. He was no more than nineteen or twenty. He had dark skin. He was so thin there was no sign of shoulders under his black thermal jacket. He wore black stovepipe jeans and a pair of huge white sneakers that closed with Velcro tabs rather than shoelaces.

Kovitsky stared at him a moment, then said, "All right, Mr. Lockwood, you take a seat. If and when Mr. Sonnenberg deigns to favor us with his presence, we'll call your case again."

Lockwood turned around and began walking back to the spectators' benches. He had the same pumping swagger that practically every young defendant in the Bronx affected, the Pimp Roll. Such stupid self-destructive macho egos, thought Kramer. They never failed to show up with the black jackets and the sneakers and the Pimp Roll. They never failed to look every inch the young felon before judges, juries, probation officers, court psychiatrists, before every single soul who had any say in whether or not they went to prison or for how long. Lockwood pimp-rolled to a bench in the rear of the spectators' section and sat down next to two more boys in black thermal jackets. These were no doubt his buddies, his comrades. The defendant's comrades always arrived in court in *their* shiny black thermal jackets and go-to-hell sneakers. That was very bright, too. That immediately established the fact that the defendant was not a poor defenseless victim of life in the ghetto but part of a pack of remorseless young felons of the sort who liked to knock down old ladies with Lucite canes on the Grand Concourse and steal their handbags. The whole pack entered the courtroom full of juice, bulging with steel muscles and hard-jawed defiance, ready to defend the honor and, if necessary, the hides of their buddies against the System. But soon a stupefying tide of tedium and confusion rolled over them all. They were primed for action. They were not primed for what the day required, which was waiting while something they never heard of, a calendar session, swamped them in a lot of shine-on language, such as "deigns to favor us with his presence."

Kramer walked past the bar and headed over to the clerk's table. Three other assistant D.A.'s stood there, looking on and waiting their turns before the judge.

The clerk said, "The People versus Albert and Marilyn Krin—"

He hesitated and looked down at the papers before him. He looked at a young woman standing three or four feet away, an assistant district attorney named Patti Stullieri, and he said in a stage whisper, "What the hell is this?"

Kramer looked over his shoulder. The document said, "Albert and Marilyn Krnkka."

"Kri-nick-a," said Patti Stullieri.

"Albert and Marilyn Kri-nick-a!" he declaimed. "Indictment number 3-2-8-1." Then to Patti Stullieri: "Jesus, what the hell kind of name is that?"

"It's Yugoslav."

"Yugoslav. It looks like somebody's fingers got caught in a fucking typewriter."

From the rear of the spectators' section, a couple came marching up to the great railing and leaned forward. The man, Albert Krnkka, smiled in a bright-eyed fashion and seemed to want to engage the attention of Judge Kovitsky. Albert Krnkka was a tall, gangling man with a five-inch goatee but no mustache at all and long blond hair like an old-fashioned rock musician's. He had a bony nose, a long neck, and an Adam's apple that seemed to move up and down a foot when he swallowed. He wore a teal-green shirt with an outsized collar and, in place of buttons, a zipper that ran diagonally from his left shoulder to the right side of his waist. Beside him was his wife. Marilyn Krnkka was a black-haired woman with a thin, delicate face. Her eyes were two slits. She kept compressing her lips and grimacing.

Everyone, Judge Kovitsky, the clerk, Patti Stullieri, even Kramer himself, looked toward the Krnkkas, expecting their lawyer to come forward or come in through the side door or materialize in some fashion. But there was no lawyer.

Furious, Kovitsky turned toward Bruzzielli and said, "Who's representing these people?"

"I think Marvin Sunshine," said Bruzzielli.

"Well, where is he? I saw him back there a few minutes ago. What's gotten into all these characters?"

Bruzzielli gave him the Primordial Shrug and rolled his eyes, as if the whole thing pained him tremendously but there was nothing he could do about it.

Kovitsky's head was now down very low. His irises were floating like destroyers on a lake of white. But before he could launch into a blistering discourse on delinquent lawyers, a voice spoke up from the bar.

"Your Honor! Your Honor! Hey, Judge!"

It was Albert Krnkka. He was waving his right hand, trying to get Kovitsky's attention. His arms were thin, but his wrists and his hands were huge. His mouth hung open in a half smile that was supposed to convince the judge that he was a reasonable man. In fact, he looked, every inch of him, like one of those wild tall raw-boned men whose metabolisms operate at triple speed and who, more than any other people on earth, are prone to explosions.

"Hey, Judge! Look."

Kovitsky stared, amazed by this performance. "Hey, Judge! Look. Two weeks ago she told us two to six, right?"

When Albert Krnkka said "two to six," he raised both hands up in the air and stuck out two fingers on each hand, like a *v* for victory or a peace sign, and flailed them in the air, as if he were beating a pair of invisible aerial drums in time to the phrase "two to six."

"Mr. Krnkka," said Kovitsky, rather softly for him.

"And now she's coming in 'ere wit' three to nine," said Albert Krnkka. "We awready said, 'Okay, two to six' "—once again he raised his hands and the pair of *v*'s and beat the air in time to "two to six"— "and she's coming in 'ere wit' three to nine. Two to six"—he beat the air— "two to six—"

"MIS-TER KRI-NICK-A, IF YOU—"

But Albert Krnkka was unbowed by Judge Kovitsky's hammering voice.

"Two to six"—*blam, blam, blam*—"you got it!"

"MIS-TER KRI-NICK-A. If you want to petition the court, you must do so through your attorney."

"Hey, Judge, you ask *her!*" He stabbed his left forefinger toward Patti Stullieri. His arm seemed a mile long. "She's the one. She offered two to six, Judge. Now she come in here wit'—"

"Mister Krnkka—"

"Two to six, Judge, two to six!" Realizing that his time at the bar was growing short, Albert Krnkka now compressed his message into its key phrase, all the while beating the air with his huge hands.

"Two to six! You got it! Two to six! You got it!"

—

"Mister Krnkka . . . SIDDOWN! Wait for your attorney."

Albert Krnkka and his wife began backing away from the bar, looking at Kovitsky the whole time, as if leaving a throne room. Albert kept mouthing the words "two to six" and waving his v fingers.

Larry Kramer moved over to where Patti Stullieri was standing and said, "What did *they* do?"

Patti Stullieri said, "The wife held a knife to a girl's throat while the husband raped her."

"Jesus," said Kramer, in spite of himself.

Patti Stullieri smiled in a world-weary fashion. She was twenty-eight or twenty-nine years old. Kramer wondered if she was worth making a play for. She was not a looker, but her Hard Number pose turned him on somehow. Kramer wondered what she had been like in high school. He wondered if she had been one of those thin nervous skanks who were always irritable and difficult and lacking in femininity without being strong. On the other hand, she had the olive skin, the thick black hair, the big dark eyes, the Cleopatra lips that in Kramer's mind added up to the Italian Dirty Girl look. In high school—Jesus, those Italian Dirty Girls!—Kramer had always found them gross, stupid beyond belief, anti-intellectual, unapproachable, and intensely desirable.

The door to the courtroom swung open, and in walked an old man with a large, florid, rather lordly head. *Debonair*, that was the word. Or at least he was debonair by the standards of Gibraltar. He wore a navy-blue double-breasted pinstripe suit, a white shirt with a starched collar, and a dark red necktie. His black hair, which was thin and had the irky dullness of a dye job, was combed straight back and plastered down on his skull. He had an old-fashioned pencil mustache, creating a sharp black line on either side of the gully under his nose.

Larry Kramer, who was standing near the clerk's desk, looked up and stared. He knew the man. There was something charming—no, brave—about his style. At the same time, it made you shiver. This man had once been, as Kramer was now, an assistant district attorney. *Bing! Bing! Bing.* Thirty years had gone by, and here he was finishing out his career in private practice, representing these poor incompetents, including the 18-b's, the ones who couldn't afford lawyers. *Bing! Bing! Bing!* Not a very long time, thirty years!

Larry Kramer wasn't the only one who stopped and stared. The man's entrance was an event. His chin was the shape of a melon. He held it cocked up at a self-satisfied angle, as if he were a *boulevardier*, as if the Grand Concourse could still be called a boulevard.

"MIS-TER SONNENBERG!"

The old lawyer looked toward Kovitsky. He seemed pleasantly surprised that his arrival should occasion such a hearty greeting.

"We called your case five minutes ago!"

"I apologize, Your Honor," said Sonnenberg, sauntering up to the defendant's desk. He swung his great chin upward in an elegant arc toward the judge. "I was held over in Part 62 by Judge Meldnick."

"Whaddaya doing with a case in Part 62 when you knew this court was putting you at the top of the calendar as a personal accommodation? Your client Mr. Lockwood has a job, as I recall."

"That's correct, Your Honor, but I was assured—"

"Your client is here."

"I know."

"He's waiting for you."

"I'm aware of that, Your Honor, but I had no idea that Judge Meldnick—"

"All right, Mr. Sonnenberg, are you ready to proceed now?"

"Yes, Your Honor."

Kovitsky had the clerk, Bruzzielli, recall the case. The black youth, Lockwood, got up from the spectators' section and came pimp-rolling up to the defendant's desk, beside Sonnenberg. It soon became apparent that the purpose of this hearing was to allow Lockwood to plead guilty to the charge, which was armed robbery, in return for a light sentence, two to six years, offered by the District Attorney's Office. But Lockwood wasn't going for it. All that Sonnenberg could do was reiterate his client's plea of not guilty.

Kovitsky said, "Mr. Sonnenberg, would you approach the bench, please? And Mr. Torres?"

Torres was the assistant district attorney on the case. He was short and quite fat, even though he was barely thirty years old. He had the sort of mustache that young lawyers and doctors wear to try to look older and graver.

As Sonnenberg drew near, Kovitsky said, in an amiable, conversational tone, "You look just like David Niven today, Mr. Sonnenberg."

"Oh no, Judge," said Sonnenberg, "David Niven I'm not. William Powell maybe, but not David Niven."

"William Powell? You're dating yourself, Mr. Sonnenberg. You're not that old, are you?" Kovitsky turned to Torres and said, "The next thing we know, Mr. Sonnenberg's gonna be leaving us for the Sun Belt. He's gonna be down there in a condominium, and all he'll have to worry about is getting to the shopping mall in time for the Early Bird special at Denny's. He won't even have to think about getting up in the morning and making pleas in Part 60 in the Bronx."

"Listen, Judge, I swear—"

"Mr. Sonnenberg, do you know Mr. Torres?"

"Oh yes."

"Well, Mr. Torres understands about condominiums and Early Bird specials. He's half a Yiddeleh himself."

"Yeah?" Sonnenberg didn't know whether he was supposed to appear pleased or what.

"Yeah, he's half a Puerto Rican and half a Yiddeleh. Right, Mr. Torres?"

Torres smiled and shrugged, trying to appear appropriately amused.

"So he used his Yiddisheh *kop* and applied for a minority scholarship to law school," said Kovitsky. "His Yiddisheh half applied for a minority scholarship for his Puerto Rican half! Is that One World or isn't it? It's using your fucking *kop*, anyway."

Kovitsky looked at Sonnenberg until he smiled, and then he looked at Torres until he smiled, and then Kovitsky beamed at both of them. Why had he turned so jolly all of a sudden? Kramer looked over at the defendant, Lockwood. He was standing at the defendant's table and staring at this jolly threesome. What must be going through his mind? His fingertips rested on the table, and his chest seemed to have caved in. His eyes! His eyes were the eyes of the hunted in the night. He stared at the spectacle of his lawyer grinning and chuckling with the judge and the prosecutor. There he was, his white lawyer smiling and jabbering with the white judge and the fat white prick who was trying to put him away.

Sonnenberg and Torres were both standing at the bench, looking up at Kovitsky. Now Kovitsky got down to work.

"What have you offered him, Mr. Torres?"

"Two to six, Judge."

"What's your client say, Mr. Sonnenberg?"

"He won't take it, Judge. I talked to him last week, and I talked to him this morning. He wants to go to trial."

"Why?" asked Kovitsky. "Did you explain to him that he'll be eligible for work release in a year? It's not a bad deal."

"Well," said Sonnenberg, "the problem is, as Mr. Torres knows, my client's a Y.O. That one was for the same thing, armed robbery, and if he pleads guilty to this one, then he's gotta serve time for that one, too."

"Ah," said Kovitsky. "Well, what *will* he take?"

"He'll take one and a half to four and a half, with the sentence for the first one subsumed under this one."

"What about it, Mr. Torres?"

The young assistant district attorney sucked in his breath and lowered his eyes and shook his head. "I can't do it, Judge. We're talking about armed robbery!"

"Yeah, I know," said Kovitsky, "but was he the one with the gun?"

"No," said Torres.

Kovitsky lifted his eyes from the faces of Sonnenberg and Torres and looked out at Lockwood.

"He doesn't look like a bad kid," said Kovitsky, for Torres's benefit. "In fact, he looks like a baby. I see these kids in here every day. They're easily led. They live in some kinda shithook neighborhood, and they end up doing stupid things. What's he like, Mr. Sonnenberg?"

"That's about the size of it, Judge," said Sonnenberg. "The kid's a follower. He's no brain surgeon, but he's no hard case, either. Not in my opinion."

This personality profile was evidently supposed to wear Torres down into offering Lockwood a sentence of only one and a third to four years, with his Y.O. conviction in effect forgotten. Y.O. stood for "youthful offender."

"Look, Judge, it's no use," Torres said. "I can't do it. Two to six is as low as I can go. My office—"

"Why don't you call Frank?" asked Kovitsky.

"It's no use, Judge. We're talking about armed robbery! He may not've held a gun on the victim, but that was because he was going through his pockets with both hands! A sixty-nine-year-old man with a stroke. Walks like this."

Torres did a shuffle in front of the bench, gimping along like an old man with a stroke.

Kovitsky smiled. "That's the Yiddeleh coming out! Mr. Torres has some of Ted Lewis's chromosomes and doesn't even know it."

"Ted Lewis was Jewish?" asked Sonnenberg.

"Why not?" said Kovitsky. "He was a comedian, wasn't he? Okay, Mr. Torres, calm down."

Torres came back to the bench. "The victim, Mr. Borsalino, says he broke a rib. We're not even charging him with that, because the old man never went to see a doctor about the rib. No, two to six is it."

Kovitsky thought that over. "Did you explain that to your client?"

"Sure I did," said Sonnenberg. He shrugged and made a face, as if to say his client wouldn't listen to reason. "He's willing to take his chances."

"Take his chances?" said Kovitsky. "But he signed a confession."

Sonnenberg made the face again and arched his eyebrows.

Kovitsky said, "Let me talk to him."

Sonnenberg screwed up his lips and rolled his eyes, as if to say, "Good luck."

Kovitsky looked up again and stared at Lockwood and stuck his chin up in the air and said, "Son . . . come here."

The boy stood at the table, frozen, not altogether sure the judge was talking to him and not somebody else. So Kovitsky put on a smile, the smile of the benevolent leader, He Who Is Willing to Be Patient, and he beckoned with his right hand and said, "Come on up here, son. I want to talk to you."

The boy, Lockwood, started walking, slowly, warily, up to where Sonnenberg and Torres were standing and looked at Kovitsky. The look he gave him was completely empty. Kovitsky stared back. It was like looking at a small empty house at night with all the lights out.

"Son," said Kovitsky, "you don't look like a bad sort to me. You look like a nice young man. Now, I want you to give yourself a chance. I'll give you a chance, but first you've got to give yourself a chance."

Then Kovitsky stared into Lockwood's eyes as if what he was about to say were one of the most important things he was likely to hear in his lifetime.

"Son," he said, "whaddaya wanna get involved in all these fucking robberies for?"

Lockwood's lips moved, but he fought the impulse to say anything, perhaps for fear he might incriminate himself.

"What does your mother say? You live with your mother?"

Lockwood nodded yes.

"What does your mother say? She ever hit you upside the head?"

"Naw," said Lockwood. His eyes appeared misty. Kovitsky took this as a sign that he was making progress.

"Now, son," he said, "do you have a job?"

Lockwood nodded yes.

"Whaddaya do?"

"Security guard."

"Security guard," said Kovitsky. He stared off at a blank spot on the wall, as if pondering the implication for society of that answer, and then decided to stick to the issue at hand.

"See?" said Kovitsky. "You've got a job, you've got a home, you're young, you're a nice-looking, bright young man. You've got a lot going for you. You've got more than most people. But you've got one big problem to overcome. YOU BEEN INVOLVED IN THESE FUCKING ROBBERIES! Now, the district attorney has made you an offer of two to six years. If you take that offer and you behave yourself, this will all be behind you, in no time, and you'll still be a young man with your whole life ahead of you. If you go to trial and you're convicted, you could get eight to twenty-five. Now think about that. The district attorney has made you an offer."

Lockwood said nothing.

"Why don't you take it?" asked Kovitsky.

"No reason."

"No reason?"

Lockwood looked away. He wasn't going to parry words. He was just going to hold tight.

"Look, son," said Kovitsky, "I'm trying to help you. This thing won't go away. You can't just close your eyes and hope it's all gonna disappear. Do you understand what I'm saying?"

Lockwood kept looking down or to the side, always a few inches away from eye contact with the judge. Kovitsky kept moving his head as if to intercept him, like a hockey goalie.

"Look at me, son. Do you understand?"

Lockwood gave in and looked at him. It was the sort of look a firing squad might expect to see.

"Now, son, think of it this way. It's like having cancer. You know about cancer."

There wasn't a glimmer of comprehension of cancer or anything else.

"Cancer doesn't just go away, either. You have to do something about it. If you catch it early, while it's small, before it spreads through your whole body and takes over your whole life—and ruins your life—and *ends* your life—you understand?—*ends* your life—if you do something about it while it's a small problem, if you have the *small* operation you need, then that's it!" Kovitsky threw his hands up in the air and lifted his chin and smiled, as if he were the very personification of buoyancy. "Now, it's the same way with the problem you have now. Right now it's a small problem. If you plead guilty and receive a sentence of two to six years and you behave yourself, you'll be eligible for a work-release program after one year and full parole after two years. And it'll all be behind you. But if you go to trial and you're found guilty, then your minimum sentence will be eight years. Eight and a third to twenty-five. *Eight*—you're only nineteen now. Eight years, that's almost half as long as you've been on this earth. You wanna spend your whole fucking youth in jail?"

Lockwood averted his eyes. He didn't say one thing or the other.

"So how about it?" asked Kovitsky.

Without looking up, Lockwood shook his head no.

"All right, if you're innocent, I don't want you to plead guilty, no matter what anybody offers you. But you signed a confession! The district attorney has a videotape of you making that confession! Whaddaya gonna do about that?"

"I 'unno," said Lockwood.

"What does your attorney say?"

"I 'unno."

"Come on, son. Of course you know. You have an excellent attorney. He's one of the best, Mr. Sonnenberg is. He has a lot of experience. You listen to him. He'll tell you I'm right. This thing isn't gonna go away, any more than cancer's gonna go away."

Lockwood kept looking down. Whatever his lawyer and the judge and the D.A. had cooked up, he wasn't buying it.

"Look, son," said Kovitsky, "talk it over some more with your attorney. Talk it over with your mother. What does your mother say?"

Lockwood looked up with live hatred. Tears began to form in his eyes. It was very touchy business, talking to these boys about their mothers. But Kovitsky stared right at him.

"All right, Counselor!" said Kovitsky, raising his voice and looking over toward Sonnenberg. "And, Mr. Torres. I'm postponing this until two weeks from today. And, son," he said to Lockwood, "you think over what I told you, and you confer with Mr. Sonnenberg, and you make up your mind. Okay?"

Lockwood gave Kovitsky one last flicker of a glance and nodded yes and walked away from the bench toward the spectators' section. Sonnenberg walked with him and said something, but Lockwood made no response. When he passed the railing and saw his buddies getting up from the last bench, Lockwood began pimp-rolling. Outta here! Back to . . . the Life! The three of them pimp-rolled out of the courtroom, with Sonnenberg sauntering behind, his chin cocked up at a thirty-degree angle.

The morning was grinding on, and so far Kovitsky hadn't disposed of a single case.

It was late in the morning when Kovitsky finally worked his way through the calendar and reached the trial of Herbert 92X, which was now in its fourth day. Kramer was standing by the prosecution table. The court officers were rotating their shoulder sockets and stretching and otherwise readying themselves for the arrival of Herbert 92X, whom they considered enough of a maniac to do something stupid and violent in the courtroom. Herbert 92X's lawyer, Albert Teskowitz, appointed by the court, walked over from the defense table. He was a scrawny stooped man with a pale blue plaid jacket that rode three or four inches off his neck and a pair of brown slacks that had never been introduced to the jacket. His thinning gray hair was the color of dry ice. He flashed Kramer a screwy little smile that as much as declared, "The charade is about to begin."

"Well, Larry," he said, "are you ready for the wisdom of Allah?"

"Let me ask you something," said Kramer. "Does Herbert select this stuff every day with the idea that it makes some kind of comment on what's going on in the case, or does he just open the book? I can't tell."

"I don't know," said Teskowitz. "I stay off the subject, to tell you the truth. Just mention it, and it's an hour out of your life. You ever talk to a logical lunatic before? They're much worse than a plain lunatic."

Teskowitz was such a bad lawyer, Kramer felt sorry for Herbert. But, then, he felt sorry for him, anyway. Herbert 92X's legal name was Herbert Cantrell; 92X was his Muslim name. He was a driver for a liquor distributor. That was one of a number of things that made Kramer believe he wasn't a real Muslim. A real Muslim wouldn't have anything to do with liquor. In any case, one day Herbert's truck was hijacked on Willis Avenue by three Italians from Brooklyn who had done little else for the past decade but hijack trucks for whoever was paying for hijacking trucks. They pulled guns on Herbert, tied him up, gave him a punch in the face, threw him into a dumpster on a side street, and warned him not to move for an hour. Then the three Italians drove the liquor truck to the warehouse of their employer of the moment, a wiseguy liquor distributor who routinely cut costs by hijacking merchandise. They drove up with the hijacked truck, and the loading-dock foreman said, "Holy shit! You guys are in a lotta trouble! That's one a our trucks!"

"Whaddaya mean?"

"That's one a our trucks! I just loaded it two hours ago! You're boosting stuff we just got through boosting! You just worked over one a our guys! You're in a lotta trouble!"

So the three Italians jumped into the truck and sped to the dumpster to give Herbert 92X back his truck. But Herbert had managed to get out. They started driving up and down the streets in the truck, looking for him. They finally found him in a bar where he had gone to steady his nerves. This was definitely not the Muslim way. They came walking in to tell him they were sorry and that he could have his truck back, but Herbert thought they were coming after him because he had ignored their warning to stay in the dumpster. So he pulled a .38-caliber revolver out from under his thermal jacket—it had been there all along, but these hard cases had gotten the drop on him—and he fired two shots. He missed the three Italians but hit and killed a man named Nestor Cabrillo, who had come in to make a telephone call. The firearm was perhaps a necessary item of defense in what was obviously a hazardous occupation. But he was not licensed to carry it, and Nestor Cabrillo was an upstanding citizen with five children. So Herbert was charged with manslaughter and criminal possession of a weapon, and the case had to be prosecuted, and Kramer was stuck with that task. The case was a study in stupidity, incompetence, and uselessness; in short, a piece a shit. Herbert 92X refused to accept a plea bargain, since he regarded what had happened as an accident. He was only sorry that the .38 had jerked his hand around so. So this piece a shit had now gone to trial.

A door off to the side of the judge's bench opened, and out came Herbert 92X and two corrections officers. The Corrections Department ran the detention pens, which were some windowless cages half a floor above the courtroom. Herbert 92X was a tall man. His eyes shone out of the shadow of a checked Yasir Arafat-style headgear that hung over his forehead. He wore a brown gown that came down to his calves. Below the gown you could see cream-colored pants, whose lapped side seams had contrasting stitching, and a pair of brown Tuczek-toed shoes. His hands were behind his back. When the corrections officers turned him around to unlock his handcuffs, Kramer could see that he was holding the Koran.

"Yo, Herbert!" The voice of a cheery little boy. It was one of the children, up by the bar. The court officers glowered at him. A woman back in the spectator benches yelled out, "You come here!" The little boy laughed and ran back to where she was sitting. Herbert stopped and turned toward the boy. His furious visage dissolved. He gave the boy a wide-eyed smile of such warmth and love, it caused Kramer to swallow—and to have another small spasm of the Doubts. Then Herbert sat down at the defense table.

The clerk, Bruzzielli, said, "The People versus Herbert Cantrell, Indictment Number 2-7-7-7."

Herbert 92X was on his feet with his hand in the air. "He called me out of my name again!"

Kovitsky leaned forward over his desk and said patiently, "Mr. 92X, I explained this to you yesterday and the day before yesterday and the day before that."

"He called me out of my name!"

"I explained this to you, Mr. 92X. The clerk is bound by a legal requirement. But in view of your evident intention to change your name, which is your right, and for which legal process exists, the court is content to refer to you as Herbert 92X for the purpose of these proceedings. That okay with you?"

"Thank you, Your Honor," said Herbert 92X, still standing. He opened the Koran and began riffling through the pages. "This morning, Your Honor—"

"Can we proceed?"

"Yes, Judge. This morning—"

"Then sid-down!"

Herbert 92X stared at Kovitsky for a moment, then sank down into his seat, still holding the Koran open. Somewhat sulkily he said: "You gonna let me read?"

Kovitsky looked at his wristwatch and nodded yes and then swiveled away about forty-five degrees and gazed at the wall above the empty jury box.

Seated, Herbert 92X placed the Koran on the defense table and said: "This morning, Your Honor, I shall read from Chapter 41, entitled 'Are Distinctly Explained, Revealed at Mecca' . . . in the name of the Most Merciful God . . . This is a revelation from the Most Merciful . . . Warn them of the day on which the enemies of God shall be gathered together unto hellfire and shall march in distinct bands until, when they shall arrive thereat, their ears and their eyes and their skins shall bear witness against them . . ."

The court officers were rolling their eyes up in their heads. One of them, Kaminsky, a real porker whose white uniform shirt barely contained the roll of fat that rode on his gunbelt, let out an audible sigh and spun 180 degrees on the soles of his big black leather cop shoes. The prosecutors and defense lawyers regarded Kovitsky as a holy terror. But the court officers were basic working-class line troops from the civil service, and they regarded Kovitsky, like practically every other judge, as outrageously and cravenly soft on criminals . . . letting this maniac sit there and read from the Koran while his children ran around the courtroom yelling, "Yo, Herbert!" Kovitsky's reasoning seemed to be that since Herbert 92X was a hothead, and since reading from the Koran cooled him off, he was saving time in the long run.

". . . turn away evil with that which is better, and behold, the man between whom and thyself there was enmity shall become, as it were, thy warmest friend, but none shall attain to . . ." In Herbert's doleful orotund reading, the words descended upon the room like a drizzle . . . Kramer's mind wandered . . . The girl with brown lipstick . . . Soon she would be coming out . . . The very thought made him straighten himself up in his chair . . . He wished he had taken a look at himself before he came into the courtroom . . . at his hair, his tie . . . He tensed his neck and threw his head back . . . He was convinced that women were impressed by men with huge sternocleidomastoid muscles . . . He closed his eyes . . .

Herbert was still reading away, when Kovitsky broke in: "Thank you, Mr. 92X, that concludes the reading from the Koran."

"Say what? I'm not finished!"

"I said that concludes the reading from the Koran, Mr. 92X. DO I MAKE MYSELF CLEAR?"

Kovitsky's voice was suddenly so loud, people in the spectators' section gasped.

Herbert jumped to his feet. "You're violating my rights!" His chin was jutted toward Kovitsky, and his eyes were on fire. He looked like a rocket about to take off.

"Sid-down!"

"You're violating my freedom of religion!"

"SID-DOWN, MR. 92X!"

"Mistrial!" shouted Herbert. "Mistrial!" Then he turned his fury on

Teskowitz, who was still seated beside him. "Get up on your *feet*, man! This is a mistrial!"

Startled and a bit frightened, Teskowitz got up.

"Your Honor, my client—"

"I SAID SID-DOWN! BOTH A YOU!"

Both sat down.

"Now, Mr. 92X, this court has been very indulgent with you. Nobody is violating your freedom of religion. The hour grows late, and we've got a jury out there in a jury room that hasn't been painted in twenty-five years, and the time has come to conclude the reading of the Koran."

"Say, con*clude?* You mean for*bid!* You're violating my religious rights!"

"The defendant will SHUDDUP! You don't have the right to read the Koran or the Talmud or the Bible or the words of the Angel Moroni, who wrote the Book of Mormon, or any other spiritual tome, no matter how divine—you don't have the right to read it in this courtroom. Let me remind you, sir, that this is not the Nation of Islam. We happen to live in a republic, and in this republic there is a separation of church and state. Do you understand? And this court is governed by the laws of that republic, which are embodied in the Constitution of the United States."

"That's not true!"

"What's not true, Mr. 92X?"

"The separation of church and state. And I can prove it."

"Whaddaya talking about, Mr. 92X?"

"Turn around! Look up on the wall!" Herbert was on his feet again, pointing at the wall up above Kovitsky's head. Kovitsky swiveled about in his chair and looked up. Sure enough, incised in the wood paneling were the words IN GOD WE TRUST.

"Church and state!" Herbert cried triumphantly. "You got it carved in the wall over your head!"

Heh heh heggggh! A woman in the spectators' section started laughing. One of the court officers guffawed but turned his head before Kovitsky could spot him. The clerk, Bruzzielli, couldn't keep the grin off his face. Patti Stullieri had her hand over her mouth. Kramer looked at Mike Kovitsky, waiting for the explosion.

Instead, Kovitsky put a broad smile on his face. But his head was lowered, and his irises were once again floating, bobbing on a turbulent white sea.

"I can see you're very observant, Mr. 92X, and I commend you for that. And since you are so observant, you will also observe that I do not have eyes in the back of my head. But I do have eyes in the front of my head, and what they are looking at is a defendant who is on trial on serious charges and faces the prospect of a prison term of twelve and a half to twenty-five years, should he be found guilty by a jury of his peers, and I want that jury to have the time to tend the scales of justice . . . with CARE and FAIRNESS! . . . in determining the guilt or innocence of that defendant. It's a free country, Mr. 92X, and nobody can stop you from believing in any deity you want. But as long as you're in this courtroom, you better believe in THE GOSPEL ACCORDING TO MIKE!"

Kovitsky said it with such ferocity that Herbert sat back down in his chair. He didn't say a word. Instead, he looked at Teskowitz. Teskowitz merely shrugged and shook his head, as if to say, "That's about the size of it, Herbert."

"Bring in the jury," said Kovitsky.

A court officer opened the door that led to the jury room. Kramer sat up straight in his chair at the prosecution table. He threw his head back to bring out that powerful neck. The jurors began filing in . . . three blacks, six Puerto Ricans . . . Where was she? . . . There she was, just coming through the door! . . . Kramer didn't even try to be subtle about it. He stared right at her. That long lustrous dark brown hair, thick enough to bury your head in, parted in the middle and pulled back to reveal that perfect pure white forehead, those big eyes and luxurious lashes, and those perfectly curved lips . . . with brown lipstick! Yes! She had it on again! The brown lipstick, the color of caramel, hellish, rebellious, perfectly elegant—

Kramer quickly surveyed the competition. The big clerk, Bruzzielli, had his eyes pinned on her. The three court officers were staring at her so hard Herbert could have taken a walk and they would have never noticed. But Herbert himself was checking her out. Teskowitz was looking at her. Sullivan, the court stenographer, sitting at the stenotype machine, was looking at her. And Kovitsky! Him, too! Kramer had heard stories about Kovitsky. He didn't seem to be the type—but you never knew.

To get to the jury box she had to file right past the prosecution table. She had on a peach-colored sweater, fluffy, angora or mohair, open up the front, and a ribbon-silk blouse with pink-and-yellow stripes, beneath which Kramer could detect, or thought he could detect, the voluptuous swell of her breasts. She wore a cream-colored gabardine skirt, tight enough to bring out the curve of her thighs.

The hell of it was, practically every man on this side of the Bar of Justice had a fighting chance. Well, not Herbert, but his wispy little lawyer, Teskowitz, did. Even that fat court officer over there, that tub Kaminsky. The number of court officers, defense lawyers, court clerks, assistant district attorneys (oh yes!) and even judges (don't rule them out!) who have humped (that's the word!) juicy little jurors in criminal cases—God! if the press ever got hold of that story—but the press never showed up in the courthouse in the Bronx.

First-time jurors in the criminal courts had a way of becoming intoxicated by the romance, the raw voltage, of the evil world they were now getting a box-seat look at, and the young women became the tipsiest of all. To them the defendants were not chow; anything but. They were desperadoes. And these cases were not pieces a shit. They were stark dramas of the billion-footed city. And those with the courage to deal with the desperadoes, wrestle with them, bridle them, were . . . real men . . . even a court officer with a four-inch tube of fat riding up over his gunbelt. But who was more manly than a young prosecutor, he who stood not ten feet from the accused, with nothing between the two of them but thin air, and hurled the charges of the People in his teeth?

Now she was in front of Kramer. She looked right back at him. Her expression said nothing, but the look was so frank and forthright! And she wore brown lipstick!

And then she was past him and going through the little gate into the jury box. He couldn't very well *turn around* and stare at her, but he was tempted. How many of them had gone to the clerk, Bruzzielli, and looked up her address and telephone numbers, at home and at work—as he had? The clerk kept the slips with this information, the so-called ballots, in a box on his desk in the courtroom, so that the court could get hold of jurors quickly to inform them of changes in schedule or whatever. As the prosecutor in the case, he, Kramer, could approach

Bruzzielli and ask to see the ballot for the girl with brown lipstick or any other juror with a straight face. So could the defense attorney, Teskowitz. Kovitsky could do it with a reasonably straight face, and of course Bruzzielli himself could take a look anytime he felt like it. As for a court officer like Kaminsky, for him to ask to take a look fell under the category of . . . a wink and a favor. But hadn't Kramer already seen Kaminsky huddled with Bruzzielli over by Bruzzielli's desk, deep in conversation over . . . something? The thought that even such creatures as the fat Kaminsky were after this . . . this *flower* . . . made Kramer more determined than ever. (He would save her from the others.)

Miss Shelly Thomas of Riverdale.

She was from the very best part of Riverdale, a leafy suburb that was geographically part of Westchester County but politically part of the Bronx. There were still plenty of nice places to live in the North Bronx. People in Riverdale generally had money, and they also had their ways of getting off jury duty. They would pull every string that existed before submitting to the prospect of coming down to the South Bronx, to the 44th Precinct, to the island fortress of Gibraltar. The typical Bronx jury was Puerto Rican and black, with a sprinkling of Jews and Italians.

But every now and then a rare flower like Miss Shelly Thomas of Riverdale landed in a jury box. What kind of name was that? Thomas was a Waspy name. But there was Danny Thomas, and he was an Arab, a Lebanese or something. Wasps were rare in the Bronx, except for those society types who came up from Manhattan from time to time, in cars with drivers, to do good deeds for the Ghetto Youth. The Big Brother organization, the Episcopal Youth Service, the Daedalus Foundation—these people showed up in Family Court, which was the court for criminals under the age of seventeen. They had these *names* . . . Farnsworth, Fiske, Phipps, Simpson, Thornton, Frost . . . and spotless intentions.

No, the chances that Miss Shelly Thomas might be a Wasp were remote. But what was she? During jury selection he had elicited from her the information that she was an art director, which apparently meant some kind of designer, for the Prischker & Bolka advertising agency in Manhattan. To Kramer that suggested an inexpressibly glamorous life. Beautiful creatures scampering back and forth to taped New Wave music in an office with smooth white walls and glass brick . . . a sort of MTV office . . . terrific lunches and dinners in restaurants with blond wood, brass, indirect lighting, and frosted glass with chevron patterns on it . . . baked quail with chanterelles on a bed of sweet potato and a ruff of braised dandelion leaves . . . He could see it all. She was part of *that life,* those places where the girls with brown lipstick go! . . . He had both of her telephone numbers, at Prischker & Bolka and at home. Naturally he couldn't do a thing while the trial was in progress. But afterward . . . Miss Thomas? This is Lawrence Kramer. I'm—oh! you remember! That's terrific! Miss Thomas, I'm calling because every so often, after one of these major cases is completed, I like to ascertain what it is exactly that convinced the jury—a sudden stab of doubt . . . Suppose all that happened was that she lost the case for him? Bronx juries were difficult enough for a prosecutor as it was. They were drawn from the ranks of those who know that in fact the police are capable of lying. Bronx juries entertained a lot of doubts, both reasonable and unreasonable, and black and Puerto Rican defendants who were stone guilty guilty as sin, did walk out of the fortress free as birds. Fortunately, Herbert 92X had shot a good man, a poor man, a family man from the ghetto. Thank God for that! No juror who lived in the South Bronx was likely to have sympathy for a foul-tempered nut case like Herbert. Only a wild card like Miss Shelly Thomas of Riverdale was likely to have sympathy! A well-educated young white woman, well-to-do, the artistic type, possibly Jewish . . . She was just the type to turn idealistic on him and refuse to convict Herbert on the grounds that he was black, romantic, and already put upon by Fate. But he had to take that chance. He didn't intend to let her slip by. He needed her. He needed this particular triumph. In this courtroom he was in the center of the arena. Her eyes had never left him. He knew that. He could feel it. There was already something between them . . . Larry Kramer and the girl with brown lipstick.

The regulars were amazed that day by the zeal and aggressiveness of Assistant District Attorney Kramer in this nickel-and-dime Bronx manslaughter case.

He started tearing into Herbert's alibi witnesses.

"Isn't it true, Mr. Williams, that this 'testimony' of yours is part of a cash transaction between you and the defendant?"

What the hell had gotten into Kramer? Teskowitz was beginning to get furious. This sonofabitch Kramer was making him look bad! He was tearing up the courtroom as if this piece a shit were the trial of the century.

Kramer was oblivious of the wounded feelings of Teskowitz or Herbert 92X or any of the rest of them. There were only two people in that cavernous mahogany hall, and they were Larry Kramer and the girl with brown lipstick.

During the lunch recess Kramer went back to the office, as did Ray Andriutti and Jimmy Caughey. An assistant district attorney who had a trial going was entitled to lunch for himself and his witnesses courtesy of the State of New York. In practice what this meant was that everybody in the office stood to get a free lunch, and Andriutti and Caughey were first in line. This pathetic little perk of the office was taken very seriously. Bernie Fitzgibbon's secretary, Gloria Dawson, ordered sandwiches in from the deli. She got one, too. Kramer had a roast-beef sandwich on an onion roll with mustard. The mustard came in a gelatinous sealed plastic envelope that he had to open with his teeth. Ray Andriutti was having a pepperoni hero with everything you could throw into it thrown in, except for two enormous slices of dill pickle that were lying on a piece of waxed paper on his desk. The smell of dill brine filled the room. Kramer watched with disgusted fascination as Andriutti lunged forward, over his desk, so that the pieces and the juices that squirted overboard from the hero would fall on the desk instead of his necktie. He did that with every bite; he lunged over the desk, and bits of food and juice spilled from his maw, as if he were a whale or a tuna. With each lunge his jaw shot past a plastic cup of coffee which was on the desk. The coffee came from the Mr. Coffee. The cup was so full, the coffee bulged with surface tension. All at once, it began to overflow. A viscous yellow creek, no wider than a string, began running down the side of the cup. Andriutti didn't even notice. When the filthy yellow flow reached the desktop, it created a pool about the size of a Kennedy half-dollar. In no time, it was the size and color of a dollar pancake. Soon the corners of two empty sugar packets were submerged in the muck. Andriutti always loaded his coffee with Cremora powder and sugar until it turned into a heavy sweet sick high-yellow bile. His gaping jaws, with the pepperoni hero stuffed in, kept lunging in front of the cup. The high point of the day! A free lunch!

And it doesn't get any better, thought Kramer. It was not just young assistant D.A.'s like him and Andriutti and Jimmy Caughey. All over Gibraltar, at this moment, from the lowest to the highest, the representatives of the Power in the Bronx were holed up in their offices, shell-backed, hunched over deli sandwiches, ordered in. Around the big conference table in Abe Weiss's office they were hunched over their deli sandwiches, they being whomever Weiss thought he needed and could get hold of that day in his crusade for publicity. Around the big conference table in the office of the chief administrative judge for the Criminal Division, Louis Mastroiani, they were hunched over their deli sandwiches. Even when this worthy jurist happened to have a great luminary in to visit, even when a United States senator came by, they sat there hunched over their deli sandwiches, the luminary, too. You could ascend to the very top of the criminal justice system in the Bronx and eat deli sandwiches for lunch until the day you retired or died.

And why? Because they, the Power, the Power that ran the Bronx, were terrified! They were terrified to go out into the heart of the Bronx at high noon and have lunch in a restaurant! Terrified! And they ran the place, the Bronx, a borough of 1.1 million souls! The heart of the Bronx was now such a slum there was no longer anything even resembling a businessman's sit-down restaurant. But even if there were, what judge or D.A. or assistant D.A., what court officer, even packing a .38, would leave Gibraltar at lunchtime to get to it? First there was plain fear. You walked from the Bronx County Building across the Grand Concourse and down the slope of 161st Street to the Criminal Courts Building, a distance of a block and a half, when you had to, but the prudent bearer of the Power kept his wits about him. There were holdups on the crest of the Grand Concourse, this great ornament of the Bronx, at 11:00 a.m. on nice sunny days. And why not? More wallets and handbags were out on foot in the middle of nice sunny days. You didn't go beyond the Criminal Courts Building at all. There were assistant D.A.'s who had worked in Gibraltar for ten years who couldn't tell you, on a bet, what was on 162nd Street or 163rd Street, a block off the Grand Concourse. They had never even been to the Bronx Museum of Art on 164th. But suppose you were fearless in that sense. There remained another, subtler fear. You were an alien on the streets of the 44th Precinct, and you knew that at once, every time Fate led you into *their* territory. The locks! The looks! The deadly mistrust! You were not wanted. You were not welcome. Gibraltar and the Power belonged to the Bronx Democratic Party, to the Jews and Italians, specifically, but the streets belonged to the Lockwoods and the Arthur Riveras and the Jimmy Dollards and Otis Blakemores and the Herbert 92X's.

The thought depressed Kramer. Here they were, himself and Andriutti, the Jew and the Italian, wolfing down their sandwiches, ordered in, inside the fortress, inside the limestone rock. And for what? What did they have to look forward to? How could this setup survive long enough for them to reach the top of the pyramid, even assuming it was worth reaching? Sooner or later the Puerto Ricans and the blacks would pull themselves together politically, and they would seize even Gibraltar and everything in it. And meantime, what would he be doing? He'd be stirring the muck . . . stirring the muck . . . until they took the stick away from him.

Just then the telephone rang.

"Hello?"

"Bernie?"

"You got the wrong extension," said Kramer, "but I don't think he's here anyway."

"Who is this?"

"Kramer."

"Oh yeah, I remember you. This is Detective Martin."

Kramer didn't really remember Martin, but the name and the voice triggered a vaguely unpleasant recollection.

"What can I do for you?"

"Well, I'm over here at Lincoln Hospital with my partner, Goldberg, and we got this half-a-homicide case, and I thought we ought to tell Bernie about it."

"Did you talk to somebody here a couple hours ago? Ray Andriutti?"

"Yeah."

Kramer sighed. "Well, Bernie's still not back. I don't know where he is."

A pause. "Shit. Maybe you can pass this along to him."

Another sigh. "Okay."

"There's this kid, Henry Lamb, L-A-M-B, eighteen years old, and he's in the intensive-care unit. He came in here last night with a broken wrist. Okay? When he came in here, at least from what's on this sheet of paper, he didn't say nothing about getting hit by a car. It just says he fell. Okay? So they fixed up the broken wrist in the emergency room, and they sent him home. This morning the kid's mother, she brings him back in here, and he's got a concussion, and he goes into a coma, and now they classify him as a likely-to-die. Okay?"

"Yeah."

"The kid was in the coma by the time they called us, but there's this nurse here that says he told his mother he was hit by a car, a Mercedes, and the car left the scene, and he got a partial license number."

"Any witnesses?"

"No. This is all from the nurse. We can't even find the mother."

"Is this supposed to be two accidents or one accident? You said a broken wrist and a concussion?"

"One, according to this nurse, who's all excited and breaking my balls about a hit-and-run. It's all fucked-up, but I just thought I'd tell Bernie, in case he wants to do anything about it."

"Well, I'll tell him, but I don't see what it's got to do with us. There's no witness, no driver—the guy is in a coma—but I'll tell him."

"Yeah, I know. If we find the mother and get anything, tell Bernie I'll call him."

"Okay."

After he hung up, Kramer scribbled a note to Bernie Fitzgibbon. The victim neglected to mention he was hit by a car. A typical Bronx case. Another piece a shit.

6

A LEADER OF THE PEOPLE

THE NEXT MORNING Sherman McCoy experienced something that was new to him in the eight years he had been at Pierce & Pierce. He was unable to concentrate. Ordinarily, as soon as he entered the bond trading room and the glare from the plate glass hit him and the roar of a legion of young men crazed by greed and ambition engulfed him, everything else in his life fell away and the world became the little green symbols that slid across the black screens of the computer terminals. Even on the morning after the most stupid telephone call he had ever made, the morning he woke up wondering if his wife was going to leave him and take the most precious thing in his life with her, namely, Campbell—even on that morning he had walked into the bond trading room and, *just like that*, human existence had narrowed down to French goldbacked bonds and U.S. government twenty-years. But now it was as if he had a two-track tape in his skull and the mechanism kept jumping from one track to the other without his having any control over it. On the screen:

"U Frag 10.1 '96 102." Down a whole point! The United Fragrance thirteen-year bonds, maturing in 1996, had slipped from 103 to 102.5 yesterday. Now, at 102, the yield would be 9.75 percent—and the question he asked himself was:

Did it have to be a *person* that the car hit when she backed up? Why couldn't it have been the tire or a trash can or something else entirely? He tried to feel the jolt again in his central nervous system It was a . . . *thok* . . . a little tap. It really hadn't been much. It could have been almost anything. But then he lost heart. What else could it have been but that tall skinny boy?—and then he could see that dark delicate face, the mouth hanging open with fear . . . It wasn't too late to go to the police! Thirty-six hours—forty by now—how would he put it? I think that we—that is, my friend Mrs. Ruskin and I—may have—for God's sake, man, get hold of yourself! After forty hours it wouldn't be reporting an accident, it would be a confession! You're a Master of the Universe. You aren't on the fiftieth floor at Pierce & Pierce because you cave in under pressure. This happy thought steeled him for the task at hand, and he focused again on the screen.

The numbers were sliding across in lines, as if a radium-green brush were painting them, and they had been sliding across and changing right before his eyes but without registering in his mind. That startled him. United Fragrance was down to 101⅞, meaning the yield was up to almost 10 percent. Was something wrong? But just yesterday he had run it by Research, and United Fragrance was in good shape, a solid AA. Right now all he needed to know was:

Was there anything in *The City Light?* It sizzled on the floor at his feet. There had been nothing in the *Times,* the *Post,* and the *Daily News,* which he had gone through in the taxi on the way down. The first edition of *The City Light,* an afternoon newspaper, didn't come out until after 10 a.m. So twenty minutes ago he had given Felix, the shoeshine man, five dollars to go downstairs and bring *The City Light* to him. But how could he possibly read it? He couldn't even let himself be seen with it on top of his desk. Not him; not after the tongue-lashing he had given young Señor Arguello. So it was under the desk, on the floor, sizzling at his feet. It sizzled, and he was on fire. He burned with a desire to pick it up and go through it . . . *right now* . . . and the hell with what it looked like . . . But of course that was irrational. Besides, what difference would it make whether he read it now or six hours from now? What could it possibly change? Not very much, not very much. And then he burned some more, until he thought he couldn't stand it.

Shit! Something was happening with the United Fragrance thirteen-years! They were back up to 102! Other buyers were spotting the bargain! Act fast! He dialed Oscar Suder's number in Cleveland, got his aide-de-camp, Frank . . . Frank . . . What was his last name? . . . Frank . . . Frank the doughnut . . . "Frank? Sherman McCoy at Pierce & Pierce. Tell Oscar I can get him United Fragrance ten-tens of '96 yielding 9.75, if he's interested. But they're moving up."

"Hold on." In no time the doughnut was back. "Oscar'll take three."

"Okay. Fine. Three million United Fragrance ten-point-tens of '96."

"Right."

"Thanks, Frank, and best to Oscar. Oh, and tell him I'll be back to him before long about the Giscard. The franc is down a bit, but that's easy to hedge. Anyway, I'll talk to him."

"I'll tell him," said the doughnut in Cleveland—

—and even before he finished writing out the order chit and handed it to Muriel, the sales assistant, he was thinking: Maybe I should see a lawyer. I should call Freddy Button. But he knew Freddy too well. Freddy was at Dunning Sponget, after all. His father had steered him to Freddy in the first place—and suppose he said something to the Lion? He wouldn't—or would he? Freddy regarded himself as a family friend. He knew Judy, and he asked about Campbell whenever they chatted, even though Freddy was probably homosexual. Well, homosexuals could care about children, couldn't they? Freddy had children of his own. That didn't mean he wasn't a homosexual, however—Christ! what the hell did it matter, Freddy Button's sex life? It was crazy to let his mind wander like this. Freddy Button. He would feel like a fool if he told this whole story to Freddy Button and it turned out to be a false alarm . . . which it probably was. Two young thugs had tried to rob him and Maria, and they had gotten what was coming to them. A fracas in the jungle, by the rules of the jungle; that was all that had occurred. For a moment he felt good about himself all over again. The law of the jungle! The Master of the Universe!

Then the bottom dropped out. They had never overtly threatened him. *Yo! Need some help?* And Maria had probably hit him with the car. Yes, it was Maria. *I wasn't driving. She was driving.* But did that absolve him of responsibility in the eyes of the law? And did—

What was that? On the screen, United Fragrance ten-point-tens of '96 blipped up to 102⅛. Ah! That meant he'd just gained a quarter of a percentage point on three million bonds for Oscar Suder by acting fast. He'd let him know that tomorrow. Would help ice the Giscard—but if anything happens with the . . . *thok* . . . the tall delicate boy . . . The little green symbols glowed radioactively on the screen. They hadn't budged for at least a minute. He couldn't stand it any longer. He would go to the bathroom. There was no law against that. He took a big manila envelope off his desk. The flap had a string that you wrapped around a paper disk in order to close the envelope. It was the sort of envelope that was used to relay documents from one office to another. He panned across the bond trading room to see if the coast was clear, then put his head under the desk and stuffed *The City Light* into the envelope and headed for the bathroom.

There were four cubicles, two urinals, and a large sink. In the cubicle he was dreadfully aware of the rustle of the newspaper as he took it out of the envelope. How could he possibly turn the pages? Every rustling crinkling crackling turn of the page would be a thunderous announcement that some slacker was in here goofing on a newspaper. He pulled his feet in toward the china base of the toilet bowl. That way no one could get a glimpse under the cubicle door of his half-brogued New & Lingwood shoes with the close soles and the beveled insteps and conclude, "Aha! McCoy."

Hidden behind the toilet door, the Master of the Universe began ransacking the newspaper at a furious clip, page by filthy page.

There was nothing, no mention of a boy struck down on a highway ramp in the Bronx. He felt vastly relieved. Almost two full days had now passed—and nothing. Christ, it was hot in here. He was perspiring terribly. How could he let himself get carried away like this? Maria was right. The brutes had attacked, and he had beaten the brutes, and they had escaped, and that was that. With his bare hands he had triumphed!

Or was it that the boy had been hit and the police were looking for the car, but the newspapers didn't regard it as important enough to rate a story?

The fever began to rise again. Suppose something *did* get in the papers . . . even a hint . . . How could he ever put the Giscard deal together under a cloud like that? . . . He'd be finished! . . . *finished!* . . . And even as he quaked with fear of such a catastrophe, he knew he was letting himself wallow in it for a superstitious reason. If you consciously envisioned something that dreadful, then it couldn't possibly take place, could it . . . God or Fate would refuse to be anticipated by a mere mortal, wouldn't He . . . He always insisted on giving His disasters the purity of surprise, didn't He . . . And yet—and yet—some forms of doom are so obvious you can't avoid them that way, can you! *One breath of scandal—*

—his spirits plunged even lower. One breath of scandal, and not only would the Giscard scheme collapse but *his very career* would be finished! And what would he do then? *I'm already going broke on a million dollars a year!* The appalling figures came popping up into his brain. Last year his income had been $980,000. But he had to pay out $21,000 a month for the $1.8 million loan he had taken out to buy the apartment. What was $21,000 a month to someone making a million a year? That was the way he had thought of it at the time—and in fact, it was merely a *crushing, grinding burden*—that was all! It came to $252,000 a year, none of it deductible, because it was a personal loan, not a mortgage. (The cooperative boards in Good Park Avenue Buildings like his didn't allow you to take out a mortgage on your apartment.) So, considering the taxes, it required $420,000 in income to pay the $252,000. Of the $560,000 remaining of his income last year, $44,400 was required for the apartment's monthly maintenance fees; $116,000 for the house on Old Drover's Mooring Lane in Southampton ($84,000 for mortgage payment and interest, $18,000 for heat, utilities, insurance, and repairs, $6,000 for lawn and hedge cutting, $8,000 for taxes). Entertaining at home and in restaurants had come to $37,000. This was a modest sum compared to what other people spent; for example, Campbell's birthday party in Southampton had had only one carnival ride (plus, of course, the obligatory ponies and the magician) and had cost less than $4,000. The Taliaferro School, including the bus service, cost $9,400 for the year. The tab for furniture and clothes had come to about $65,000; and there was little hope of reducing that, since Judy was, after all, a decorator and had to keep things up to par. The servants (Bonita, Miss Lyons, Lucille the cleaning woman, and Hobie the handyman in Southampton) came to $62,000 a year. That left only $226,200, or $18,850 a month, for additional taxes and this and that, including insurance payments (nearly a thousand a month, if averaged out), garage rent for two cars ($840 a month), household food ($1,500 a month), club dues (about $250 a month)—the abysmal truth was that he had spent *more* than $980,000 last year. Well, obviously he could cut down here and there—but not nearly enough—*if the worst happened!* There was no getting out from under the $1.8 million loan, the crushing $21,000-a-month nut, without paying it off or selling the apartment and moving into one far smaller and more modest—an *impossibility!* There was no turning back! Once you had lived in a $2.6 million apartment on Park Avenue—it was impossible to live in a $1 million apartment! Naturally, there was no way to explain this to a living soul. Unless you were a complete fool, you couldn't even make the words come out of your mouth. Nevertheless—*it was so!* It was . . . *an impossibility!* Why, his building was one of the great ones built just before the First World War! Back then it was still not entirely proper for a good family to live in an apartment (instead of a house). So the apartments were built like mansions, with eleven-, twelve-, thirteen-foot ceilings, vast entry galleries, staircases, servants' wings, herringbone-parquet floors, interior walls a foot thick, exterior walls as thick as a fort's, and fireplaces, fireplaces, fireplaces, even though the buildings were all built with central heating. A mansion!—except that you arrived at the front door via an elevator (opening upon your own private vestibule) instead of the street. That was what you got for $2.6 million, and anyone who put one foot in the entry gallery of the McCoy duplex on the tenth floor knew he was in . . . *one of those fabled apartments that the world,* le monde, *died for!* And what did a million get you today? At most, at most, at *most*: a three-bedroom apartment—no servants' rooms, no guest rooms, let alone dressing rooms and a sunroom—in a white-brick high-rise built east of Park Avenue in the 1960s with 8½-foot ceilings, a dining room but no library, an entry gallery the size of a closet, no fireplace, skimpy lumberyard moldings, if any, plasterboard walls that transmit whispers, and no private elevator stop. Oh no; instead, a mean windowless elevator hall with at least five pathetically plain bile-beige metal-sheathed doors, each protected by two or more ugly drop locks, opening upon it, one of these morbid portals being *yours*.

Patently . . . *an impossibility!*

He sat with his $650 New & Lingwood shoes pulled up against the cold white bowl of the toilet and the newspaper rustling in his trembling hands, envisioning Campbell, her eyes brimming with tears, leaving the marbled entry hall on the tenth floor for the last time, commencing her descent into the lower depths.

Since I've foreseen it, God, you can't let it happen, can you?

The Giscard! . . . Had to move fast! Had to have a print! . . . This phrase suddenly possessed his mind, *have a print*. When a big deal such as the Giscard was completed, closed, once and for all, it was set down in the form of a contract that was actually printed by a printing company, on a press. *Have a print! Have a print!*

He sat there, riding a white china toilet bowl, beseeching the Almighty for a print.

Two young white men sat in a mansion in Harlem staring at a middle-aged black man. The younger one, the one doing the talking, was rattled by what he saw. He felt as if he had been removed from his own body by astral projection and was listening like a spectator to his own words as they came out of his mouth.

"So I don't know exactly how to put it, Reverend Bacon, but the thing is, we —I mean the diocese—the Episcopal Church—we've given you $350,000 as seed money for the Little Shepherd Day Care Center, and we received a telephone call yesterday from a newspaper reporter, and he said the Human Resources Administration turned down your license application *nine weeks* ago, and I mean, well, we just couldn't believe it. It was the first thing we'd even heard about it, and so . . ."

The words continued to come out of his mouth, but the young man, whose name was Edward Fiske III, was no longer thinking about them. His voice was on automatic, while his mind tried to make sense out of the situation he was in. The room was a vast Beaux Arts salon full of high-grained oak architraves and cornices and plaster rosettes and swags with gilt highlights and fluted corner beads and ogeed baseboards, all of it carefully restored to the original turn-of-the-century style. It was the sort of mansion the dry-goods barons used to erect in New York before the First World War. But now the baron of these premises, seated behind a huge mahogany desk, was a black man.

His high-backed swivel chair was upholstered in a rich oxblood-colored leather. There wasn't a trace of emotion on his face. He was one of those thin, rawboned men who look powerful without being muscular. His receding black hair was combed straight back for about two inches before it broke into ruffles of small curls. He wore a black double-breasted suit with peaked lapels, a white shirt with a high starched spread collar, and a black necktie with broad white diagonal stripes. On his left wrist was a watch with enough gold to read a meter by.

Fiske became unnaturally aware of the sound of his own voice: ". . . and then we made—actually, I made—a telephone call to the HRA, and I spoke to a Mr. Lubidoff, and he told me—and I'm only repeating to you what he said—he said that several—actually, he said seven—he said seven of the nine directors of the Little Shepherd Day Care Center have prison records, and three are on parole, which means that technically, legally"—he glanced at his young colleague, Moody, who was a lawyer— "they are considered or accorded or, I should say, burdened with the status of an inmate."

Fiske stared at Reverend Bacon and opened his eyes wide and arched his eyebrows. It was a desperate attempt to coax the baron into the conversational vacuum. He didn't dare try to *question* him, *interrogate* him. The best he could hope for was to lay down certain facts that would compel him, through the logic of the situation, to respond.

But Reverend Bacon didn't even change his expression. He just stared at the young man as if he were looking at a gerbil on a treadmill in a cage. The narrow mustache that outlined his upper lip didn't budge. Then he began drumming the first two fingers of his left hand on his desk, as if to say, "And therefore?"

It wasn't Reverend Bacon but Fiske himself who couldn't bear the vacuum and plunged in.

"And therefore—well, I mean, in the eyes of the HRA—the way they look at it—and they're the licensing authority for day-care centers—and you're aware of all the furor—how sensitive they are about day-care centers—it's a big political issue—that three directors of the Little Shepherd Day Care Center, the ones still on parole, they are *still in prison*, because people on parole are still serving a prison sentence and are still subject to all the . . . all the . . . well, whatever . . . and the other four also have records, which by itself is enough to . . . to . . . Well, the regulations don't allow it—"

The words were gushing out in awkward spurts, while his mind rushed all over the room, trying to find an exit. Fiske was one of those superbly healthy white people who retain the peachy complexion of a thirteen-year-old until well into their late twenties. Just now his fine fair face was beginning to redden. He was embarrassed. No, he was scared. In a few moments he was going to have to get to the part about the $350,000, unless his sidekick over here, Moody, the lawyer, did it for him. God almighty, how had it come to this? After leaving Yale, Fiske had gone to the Wharton School of Business, where he had written a master's thesis entitled "Quantitative Aspects of Ethical Behavior in a Capital-Intensive Corporation." For the past three years he had been Community Outreach Director of the Episcopal Diocese of New York, a position that involved him in the diocese's heavy moral and financial support of Reverend Bacon and his works. But even in the auspicious heart-warming early days, two years ago, he had been uneasy about these trips to this big old town house in Harlem. From the beginning, a thousand little things had snapped away at the ankles of his profound intellectual liberalism, starting with this business of "Reverend Bacon." Every Yale man, or certainly every Episcopalian among them, knew that *Reverend* was an adjective, not a noun. It was like *Honorable* before the name of a legislator or a judge. You might refer to "the Honorable William Rehnquist," but you wouldn't call him "Honorable Rehnquist." In the same way, you could refer to "the Reverend Reginald Bacon" or "the Reverend Mr. Bacon," but you wouldn't say "Reverend Bacon"— except in this house and in this part of New York, where you called him whatever he wanted to be called, and you forgot about Yale. The truth was, Fiske had found Reverend Bacon forbidding even in those early days when he had been all smiles. They agreed on practically all philosophical and political issues. Yet they were *in no way similar people*. And these were not the early days. These were what you might call the last days.

". . . And so, obviously we have a problem, Reverend Bacon. Until we can get this straightened out about the license—and I wish we had known about it nine weeks ago, when it happened—well, I don't see that there's any way the project can go forward until we resolve it. Not that it can't be resolved, of course —but you've got to—well, the first thing we've got to do, it seems to me, we've got to be very realistic about the $350,000. Naturally, this board—I mean, your present board—this board can't spend any of those moneys on the day-care center, because the board will have to be reorganized, it seems to me, which, when you get right down to it, means a reorganization of the corporation, and that will take some time. Not a lot of time, perhaps, but it will take some time, and . . ."

As his voice struggled on, Fiske cut his eyes toward his colleague. This fellow Moody didn't seemed fazed at all. He sat there in an armchair, with his head cocked to one side, very coolly, as if he had Reverend Bacon's number. This was his first trip up to the House of Bacon, and he seemed to regard it as a bit of a lark. He was the latest junior member whom the firm of Dunning Sponget & Leach had fobbed off on the diocese, an account they regarded as prestigious but "soft." On the way up in the car, the young lawyer had told Fiske that he, too, had gone to Yale. He had been a line-backer on the football team. He managed to mention that about five different times. He had come walking into Reverend Bacon's headquarters as if he had a keg of Dortmunder Light between his legs. He had sat down in the chair and leaned back, gloriously relaxed. But he said nothing . . . "So in the meantime, Reverend Bacon," said Ed Fiske, "we thought the prudent thing would be—we talked this over at the diocese—this was everybody's thought on the thing, not just mine—we thought the wise thing—I mean, all we're concerned about here is the future of the project, of the Little Shepherd Day Care Center—because we're still a hundred percent behind the project— that hasn't changed a bit—we thought the prudent thing would be to place the $350,000—not counting the money that's already gone toward leasing the building on West 129th Street, of course—we ought to put the other—what?— $340,000, or whatever it is, into an escrow account, and then when you've gotten the business of the board of directors straightened out, and you've gotten the licensing from the HRA, and there's no more red tape to worry about, those moneys will be turned over to you and your new board, and, well, that's . . . sort of it!"

Fiske opened his eyes wide again and arched his eyebrows and even attempted a little friendly smile, as if to say, "Hey! We're all in the same boat here, aren't we!" He looked at Moody, who continued to stare at Reverend Bacon in his cool fashion. Reverend Bacon didn't even so much as blink, and something about that implacable gaze made Fiske decide that it was unwise to continue looking into his eyes. He looked at Reverend Bacon's fingers as they did their paradiddle on the desk. Not a word. So he scanned the top of the desk. There was a large handsome leather-bound desk blotter, a gold Dunhill pen-and-pencil set mounted on an onyx pedestal, a collection of paperweights and medals imbedded in Lucite, several of which had been inscribed to Reverend Reginald Bacon by civic organizations, a stack of papers held down by a paperweight consisting mainly of the letters WNBC-TV in thick brass, an intercom with a row of buttons, and a large box-shaped ashtray with leather sides framed in brass and a brass grillwork over the top . . .

Fiske kept his eyes lowered. Into the vacuum came the sounds of the building.

On the floor above, heavily muffled by the building's thick floors and walls, the faint sound of a piano . . . Moody, sitting right next to him, probably didn't even notice. But Fiske, in his mind, could sing right along with those rich crashing chords.

"The mil-len-ni-al rei-eign . . .

"Is going . . . to be . . ."

Huge chords.

"One thousand years of . . . e-ter-*ni*-tee . . .

"Lord of lo-ords . . .

"Ho-ost of hosts . . ."

More chords. A whole ocean of chords. She was up there right now. When this thing first started, this business of the diocese and Reverend Bacon, Fiske used to play Reverend Bacon's mother's records in his apartment at night and sing along, at the top of his lungs, with ecstatic abandon—"The mil-len-ni-al rei-eiggn!"—a song made famous by Shirley Caeser . . . oh, he knew his gospel singers—him!—Edward Fiske III, Yale '80!—who now had legitimate entry into that rich black world . . . The name Adela Bacon still appeared on the gospel music charts from time to time. Of all the organizations listed in the mansion's entry hall down below, ALL PEOPLE'S SOLIDARITY, THE GATES OF THE KINGDOM CHURCH, THE OPEN GATES EMPLOYMENT COALITION, MOTHERHOOD ALERT, THE LITTLE CHILDREN'S ANTI-DRUG CRUSADE, THE THIRD WORLD ANTI-DEFAMATION LEAGUE, THE LITTLE SHEPHERD DAY CARE CENTER, and the rest of them, only Adela Bacon's MILLENNIAL REIGN MUSIC CORPORATION was a conventional business organization. He regretted that he had never really come to know her. She had founded the Gates of the Kingdom Church, which was supposedly Reverend Bacon's church but which in reality scarcely existed any longer. She had run it; she had conducted the services; she had uplifted the church's Pentecostal flock with her amazing contralto voice and the cresting waves of her oceans of chords—and she and she alone had been the church body that had ordained her son Reggie as the Reverend Reginald Bacon. At first Fiske had been shocked to learn this. Then a great sociological truth dawned upon him. *All* religious credentials are arbitrary, self-proclaimed. Who originated the articles of faith under which his own boss, the Episcopal Bishop of New York, had been ordained? Did Moses bring them down in stone from the mountaintop? No, some Englishman dreamed them up a few centuries ago, and a lot of people with long white faces agreed to call them rigorous and sacred. The Episcopal faith was merely older, more ossified, and more respectable than the Baconian in white society.

But it was long past time to worry about theology and church history. It was time to retrieve $350,000.

Now he could hear water running and a refrigerator door opening and one of those hair-trigger coffee machines coming to a boil. That meant the door to the little service kitchen was open. A tall black man was peering out. He wore a blue work shirt. He had a long powerful neck and wore a single large gold earring, like a storybook pirate. That was one of the things about this place . . . the way these . . . these . . . these . . . *heavies* were always around. They no longer seemed like romantic revolutionaries to Fiske . . . They seemed like . . . The thought of what they might be caused Fiske to avert his eyes . . . Now he looked past Bacon, out the bay window behind him. The window looked out on a back yard. It was early afternoon, but the yard received only a gloomy greenish light because of the buildings that had gone up on the streets behind it. Fiske could see the trunks of three huge old sycamores. That was all that remained of what must have been quite a little piece of scenery, by New York standards, in its day.

The muffled chords. In his mind, Fiske could hear the beautiful voice of Adela Bacon:

"Oh, *what* . . . shall I *say*, Lord?"

"And it *came* . . . to *pass* . . ."

Waves of muffled chords.

"A voice . . . from on high said . . .

" 'All *flesh* . . . is *grass* . . .' "

A whole ocean of chords.

Reverend Bacon stopped drumming his fingers. He placed the tips of the fingers of both hands on the edge of the desk. He lifted his chin slightly and he said:

"This is Harlem."

He said it slowly and softly. He was as calm as Fiske was nervous. Fiske had never known the man to raise his voice. Reverend Bacon froze the look on his face and the position of his hands, in order to let his words sink in completely.

"This," he said once more, "is Harlem . . . see . . ."

He paused.

"You come up here now, after all this time, and you tell *me* there are people *with prison records* on the board of directors of the Little Shepherd Day Care Center. You inform me of that fact."

"*I'm* not telling you, Reverend Bacon," said Fiske. "That's what the Human Resources Administration is telling us both."

"I want to tell *you* something. I want to re*mind* you of something *you* told *me*. Who do we *want* to run the Little Shepherd Day Care Center? Do you remember? Do we want your Wellesley girls and your Vassar girls coming up here to take care of the children of Harlem? Do we want your social benefactors? Do we want your licensed civil-service bureaucrats? Your lifers from City Hall? Is that what we want? Is *that* what we want?"

Fiske felt compelled to answer. Obediently as a first-grader, he said, "No."

"No," said Reverend Bacon approvingly, "that is not what we want. What *do* we want? We want the people of Harlem looking after the children of Harlem. We're going to draw our strength . . . our *strength* . . . from our people and our own streets. I told you that a long time ago, in the earliest days. Do you remember? Do you remember *that*?"

"Yes," said Fiske, feeling more juvenile by the minute, and more helpless in the face of that steady gaze.

"Yes. Our own streets. Now, a young man grows up on the streets of Harlem, the chances are the police have a sheet on that young man. You understand? They have a sheet on that young man. I'm talking about a police record. So if you're saying to everybody who's ever been in jail and everybody coming *out* of jail and everybody *on parole*, if you're saying, 'You can't participate in the rebirth of Harlem, because we gave up on you soon as you got a record' . . . see . . . then you are not talking about the rebirth of Harlem. You're talking about some make-believe place, some magic kingdom. You're fooling yourself. You're not looking for a radical solution. You're wanting to play the same old game, you're wanting to see the same old faces. You're wanting to practice the same old colonialism. You understand? You understand what I'm saying?"

Fiske was about to nod yes, when all at once Moody spoke up: "Look, Reverend Bacon, we know all about that, but that's not the problem. We've got an immediate, specific, technical, legal problem. By law, the HRA is forbidden to issue a license under these circumstances, and that's all there is to that. So let's take care of that problem, and let's see about the $350,000, and then we'll be in a position to solve the larger problems."

Fiske couldn't believe what he was hearing. Involuntarily he slid down in his seat and took a wary glance at Reverend Bacon. Reverend Bacon stared at Moody without any expression at all. He stared at him long enough for the silence to envelop him. Then, without parting his lips, he stuck his tongue into his cheek until his cheek popped out the size of a golf ball. He turned to Fiske and said softly:

"How'd you get up here?"

"Uh . . . we drove," said Fiske.

"Where's your car? What's it look like?"

Fiske hesitated. Then he told him.

"You should've told me sooner," said Reverend Bacon. "There's a bad element around here." He called out, "Hey, Buck!"

Out of the kitchen came the tall man with the gold earring. The sleeves of his work shirt were rolled up. He had tremendous elbows. Reverend Bacon motioned to him, and he came over and bent down and put his hands on his hips, and Reverend Bacon said something in a low voice. The man's arms created terrific angles where they bent at the elbows. The man stood up and looked very seriously at Reverend Bacon and nodded and started to leave the room.

"Oh, Buck," said Reverend Bacon.

Buck stopped and looked around.

"And you keep your eye on that car."

Buck nodded again and walked out.

Reverend Bacon looked at Fiske. "I hope none of those trifling boys—anyway, they won't fool with Buck. Now, what was I saying?" All of this was to Fiske. It was as if Moody were no longer in the room.

"Reverend Bacon," said Fiske, "I think—"

Reverend Bacon's intercom buzzed.

"Yes?"

A woman's voice said: "Irv Stone from Channel 1, on 4-7."

Reverend Bacon turned to a telephone on a little cabinet near his chair. "Hello, Irv . . . Fine, fine . . . No, no. Mostly the APS, All People's Solidarity. We've got a mayor to defeat in November . . . Not this time, Irv, not this time. This man, all he needs is a shove. But that's not what I called you about. I called you about the Open Gates Employment Coalition . . . I said the Open Gates Employment Coalition . . . How long? A long time, a long time. Don't you read the newspapers? . . . Well, that's okay. That's what I called you about. You know those restaurants downtown, down in the East Fifties and the East Sixties, those restaurants where the people, they spend a hundred dollars for lunch, and they spend two hundred dollars for dinner, and they don't even think twice about it? . . . What? Don't kid me, Irv. I know about you TV people. You know that place you have lunch every day. La Boue d'Argent?" Fiske noticed that

Reverend Bacon had no trouble at all pronouncing the name of one of the most expensive and fashionable restaurants in New York. "Heh, heh, well, that's what they told me. Or is it Leicester's?" He got that one right, too. Leicester's was pronounced *Lester's*, in the British fashion. Reverend Bacon was chuckling and smiling now. Evidently he was having his joke. Fiske was glad to see him smile— over anything. "Well, what I'm saying is, in any a those places, did you ever see *a black waiter?* Did you? Did you *ever* see a black waiter? . . . That's right, you never did. You never did. In *any* of them. And why? . . . That's right. The unions, too. You understand what I'm saying? . . . That's right. Well, that's what has to change . . . see . . . has to change. Next Tuesday, starting at noon, the coalition's going to demonstrate at Leicester's restaurant, and when we get through with that one, we're going to La Boue d'Argent and the Macaque and La Grise and the Three Ortolans and all those places . . . How? By any means necessary. You're always talking about footage, Irv. Well, I can promise you one thing. You'll have *footage*. Do you follow me? . . . Call Leicester's? Sure. Go ahead . . . No, indeed. I don't mind."

When he hung up, he said, as if talking to himself, "I hope they do call 'em up."

Then he looked at the two young men. "Now!" he said, as if the time had come to wrap things up and send everyone on his way. "You fellows see what I got to deal with here. I've got the fight of my life. The fight . . . of . . . my . . . life. The APS, All People's Solidarity, in November we got to defeat the most racist mayor in the history of the United States. The Open Gates Employment Coalition, we got to break down the walls of apartheid in the job market. And the Third World Anti-Defamation League, we're negotiating with a bunch of exploiters making a stone racist movie called *Harlem's Angels*. Gangs and drug dealers and addicts and winos, that's all. Racial stereotypes. They think because they got this black man who leads a young gang to Jesus, they are not racist. But they are stone racist, and they must be suitably apprised of that reality. So the day is coming in New York. The hour is drawing nigh. The final battle, you might say. Gideon's Army . . . and *you!* . . . you come up here and lay some chickensh —some trifling thing on me about the board of directors of the Little Shepherd Day Care Center!"

A fury had crept into the baron's voice. He had come close to uttering the word *chickenshit*, and Fiske had never known him to say so much as a single foul word, not even a *damn*, in all the time he had known him. Fiske was torn between the desire to depart this house before the final battle began and the hellfire rained down and the desire to save his job, such as it was. He was the one who had dispatched the $350,000 to Reverend Bacon in the first place. Now he had to retrieve it.

"Well," he said, testing a middle ground, "you may be right, Reverend Bacon. And we—the diocese—we are not here to complicate things. Frankly, we want to protect you, and we want to protect our investment in you. We gave you $350,000 contingent on the licensing of the day-care center. So if you'll turn over the $350,000 or the $340,000, whatever the exact balance is, and let us put it into an escrow account, then we'll help you. We'll go to bat for you."

Reverend Bacon looked at him distractedly, as if pondering a great decision. "It is not that simple," he said.

"Well—why not?"

"That money is mostly . . . committed."

"Committed?"

"To the contractors."

"The contractors? What contractors?"

"*What* contractors? Good Lord, man, the equipment, the furniture, the computers, the telephones, the carpet, the air conditioning, the ventilation—very important with children, the ventilation—the safety toys. It's hard to remember all the things."

"But, Reverend Bacon," said Fiske, his voice rising, "all you've got so far is an old empty warehouse! I was just by there! There's nothing in there! You haven't hired an architect! You don't even have any plans!"

"That's the least of it. Coordination is the main thing in a project of this kind. Coordination."

"Coordination? I don't see—well, that may be, but if you've made commitments to contractors, then it seems to me you've just got to explain to them that there's going to be an unavoidable delay." Fiske was all at once afraid that he was taking too stern a tone. "If you don't mind, how much of the money remains in your hands, Reverend Bacon, whether committed or not?"

"None of it," said Reverend Bacon.

"*None* of it? How can that be?"

"This was seed money. We had to sow the seed. Some of it fell on fallow ground."

"Sow the seed? Reverend Bacon, surely you didn't advance these people their money before they did the work!"

"These are minority firms. People from the community. That was what we wanted. Am I not correct?"

"Yes. But surely you have not advanced—"

"These are not firms with your 'lines of credit,' your 'computerized inventories,' your 'pre-staggered cash flows,' your 'convertible asset management,' your 'capital-sensitive liquidity ratios,' and all that. These are not firms with factors to go to, like they have in the garment industry, when bad luck knocks on the door with your 'unavoidable delays' . . . see . . . These are firms founded by people in the community. These are the tender shoots that sprout up from the seeds we sow—you, me, the Episcopal Church, the Gates of the Kingdom Church. Tender shoots . . . and you say, 'unavoidable delay.' That's not just a *term,* that's not just your *red tape*—that's a sentence of death. A sentence of death. That's saying 'Kindly drop dead.' So don't tell me I can just *explain* it to them. *Unavoidable delay* . . . Say, *unavoidable death.*"

"But, Reverend Bacon—we're talking about $350,000! Surely—"

Fiske looked at Moody. Moody was sitting up straight. He no longer looked very cool, and he wasn't saying a word.

"The diocese will—there'll have to be an audit," said Fiske. "Right away."

"Oh yes," said Reverend Bacon. "There'll be an audit. I'll give you an audit . . . right away. I'm gonna tell you something. I'm gonna tell you something about capitalism north of Ninety-sixth Street. Why do you people think you're investing all this money, your $350,000, in a day-care center in Harlem? Why are you?"

Fiske said nothing. Reverend Bacon's Socratic dialogues made him feel childish and helpless.

But Bacon insisted. "Now, you go ahead and tell me. I want to hear it from *you*. Like you say, we're going to have an audit. An *audit*. I want to hear it from you in your own words. Why are you people investing all this money in a day-care center in Harlem? Why."

Fiske couldn't hold out any longer. "Because day-care centers are desperately needed in Harlem," he said, feeling about six years old.

"No, my friend," said Bacon softly, "that is not why. If you people were that worried about the children, you would build the day-care center yourself and hire the best professional people to work in it, people with experience. You wouldn't even talk about hiring the people of the streets. What do the people of the streets know about running a day-care center? No, my friend, you're investing in something else. You're investing in steam control. And you're getting value for money. *Value for money*."

"Steam control?"

"*Steam* control. It's a capital investment. It's a very good one. You know what capital is? You think it's something you own, don't you. You think it's factories and machines and buildings and land and things you can sell and stocks and money and banks and corporations. You think it's something you own, because you always owned it. You owned all this land." He waved his arm back toward the bay window and the gloomy back yard and the three sycamore trees. "You owned all the land, and out there, out there in . . . Kansas . . . and . . . Oklahoma . . . everybody just lined up, and they said, 'On the mark, get set, go!' and a whole lot of white people started running, and there was all this land, and all they had to do was get to it and stand on it, and they owned it, and their white skin was their deed of property . . . see . . . The red man, he was in the way, and he was eliminated. The yellow man, he could lay rails across it, but then he was shut up in Chinatown. And the black man, he was in chains the whole time anyway. And so you owned it all, and you still own it, and so you think capital is owning things. But you are mistaken. Capital is controlling things. Controlling things. You want land in Kansas? You want to exercise your white deed of property? First you got to control Kansas . . . see . . . Controlling things. I don't suppose you ever worked in a boiler room. I worked in a boiler room. People *own* the boilers, but that don't do 'em a bit of good unless they know how to control the *steam* . . . see . . . If you can't control . . . the steam, then it's Powder Valley for you and your whole gang. If you ever see a steam boiler go out of control, then you see a whole lot of people running for their lives. And those people, they are not thinking about that boiler as a capital asset, they are not thinking about the return on their investment, they are not thinking about the escrow accounts and the audits and the prudent thing . . . see . . . They are saying, 'Great God almighty, I lost control,' and they are running for their lives. They're trying to save their very hides. You see this house?" He gestured vaguely toward the ceiling. "This house was built in the year nineteen hundred and six by a man named Stanley Lightfoot Bowman. Lightfoot. Turkish towels and damask tablecloths, wholesale, Stanley Lightfoot Bowman. He sold those Turkish towels and damask tablecloths in job lots. He spent almost a half a million dollars on this house in nineteen hundred and six . . . see . . . The man's initials, S.L.B., they're down there made of bronze, going all the way up the stairs, instead a spindles. This was the place to be in nineteen hundred and six. They built these big houses all the way up the West Side, starting at Seventy-second Street, all the way up here. Yeah, and I bought this house from a—from a Jewish fellow—in nineteen hundred and seventy-eight for sixty-two thousand dollars, and that fellow was happy to get that money. He was licking his chops and saying, 'I got some —some fool to give me sixty-two thousand dollars for that place.' Well, what happened to all those Stanley Lightfoot Bowmans? Did they lose their money? No, they lost con*trol* . . . see . . . They lost control north of Ninety-sixth Street, and when they lost con*trol*, they lost the *capital*. You understand? All that capital, it vanished off the face of the earth. The house was still there, but the capital, it *vanished* . . . see . . . So what I'm telling you is, you best be waking up. You're practicing the capitalism of the future, and you don't even know it. You're not investing in a day-care center for the children of Harlem. You're investing in the souls . . . the *souls* . . . of the people who've been in Harlem too long to look at it like children any longer, people who've grown up with a righteous anger in their hearts and a righteous *steam* building up in their souls, ready to blow. A *righteous* steam. When you people come up here and talk about 'minority contractors' and 'minority hiring' and day-care centers for the street people, of the street people, and by the street people, you're humming the right tune, but you don't want to sing the right words. You don't want to come right out and say it: 'Please, dear Lord, God almighty, let'm do what they want with the money, just so long's it con*trols the steam* . . . before it's too late . . . Well, you go ahead and have your audit and talk to your HRA and reorganize your boards and cross all the *t*'s and dot all the *i*'s. Meantime, I've done your investing for you, and thanks to me, you're already ahead of the game . . . Oh, *conduct your audit!* . . . But the time is coming when you will say: 'Thank God. Thank God! Thank God we entered the money on the books Reverend Bacon's way!' Because I'm the conservative, whether you know it or not. You don't know who's *out there* on those wild and hungry streets. I am your prudent broker on Judgment Day. Harlem, the Bronx, and Brooklyn, they're gonna *blow*, my friend, and on that day, how grateful you will be for your prudent broker . . . your prudent broker . . . who can control the steam. Oh yes. On that day, the owners of capital, how happy they will be to exchange what they own, how happy they will be to give up their very *birth*rights, just to control that wild and hungry steam. No, you go on back down, and you say, 'Bishop, I've been uptown, and I'm here to tell you we made a good investment. We found a prudent broker. We're gonna occupy the high ground when it all comes down."

Just then the intercom buzzer sounded again, and the secretary's voice said: "There's a Mr. Simpson on the phone, from the Citizens Mutual Insurance Company. He wants to talk to the president of Urban Guaranty Investments."

Reverend Bacon picked up the telephone. "This is Reginald Bacon . . . That's right, president and chief executive officer . . . That's right, that's right . . . Yes, well, I appreciate your interest, Mr. Simpson, but we already brought that issue to market . . . That's right, the entire issue . . . Oh, absolutely, Mr. Simpson, those school bonds are very popular. Of course, it helps to know that particular market, and that's what Urban Guaranty Investment is here for. We want to put Harlem in the market . . . That's right, that's right, Harlem's always been *on* the market . . . see . . . Now Harlem's gonna be *in* the market . . . Thank you, thank you . . . Well, why don't you try one of our associates downtown. Are you familiar with the firm of Pierce & Pierce? . . . That's right . . .

They brought a very large block of that issue to market, a *very* large block. I'm sure they'll be happy to do business with you."

Urban Guaranty Investments? Pierce & Pierce? Pierce & Pierce was one of the biggest and hottest investment banking houses on Wall Street. A terrible suspicion invaded Fiske's ordinarily charitable heart. He cut a glance at Moody, and Moody was looking at him, and, it was obvious, wondering the same thing. Had Bacon shifted $350,000 into this securities operation, whatever in the name of God it actually was? If the money had entered the securities market, then by now it could have vanished without a trace.

As soon as Reverend Bacon hung up, Fiske said: "I didn't know you had—I'd never heard of—well, perhaps you—but I don't think so—what is—I couldn't help but hear you mention—what is Urban Guaranty Investments?"

"Oh," said Reverend Bacon, "we do a little underwriting, whenever we can help out. No reason why Harlem should always buy retail and sell wholesale . . . see . . . Why not make Harlem the broker?"

To Fiske this was pure gibberish. "But where do you get—how are you able to finance—I mean something like that—" He could think of no way to put this particular lit firecracker into words. The necessary euphemisms eluded him. To his surprise, Moody spoke up again.

"I know a little about securities firms, Reverend Bacon, and I know they require a lot of capital." He paused, and Fiske could tell that Moody was thrashing about in the swollen seas of circumlocution, too. "Well, what I mean is, ordinary capital, capital in the ordinary sense. You've—we've just been talking about capital north of Ninety-sixth Street and controlling . . . uh, the steam, as you mentioned . . . but this sounds like straight capitalism, basic capitalism, if you see what I mean."

Reverend Bacon looked at him balefully, then chuckled in his throat and smiled, not with kindness.

"It don't require capital. We're underwriters. We bring the issues to market, so long as they're for the good of the community . . . see . . . schools, hospitals—"

"Yes, but—"

"As Paul knew, there are many roads to Damascus, my friend. Many roads." *Many roads* hung in the air, humid with meaning.

"Yes, I know, but—"

"If I were you," said Reverend Bacon, "I wouldn't worry about Urban Guaranty Investments. If I were you, I'd do like the old folks say. I'd stick to my knitting."

"That's what I'm trying to do, Reverend Bacon," said Moody. "My knitting is —well, it amounts to three hundred and fifty thousand dollars."

Fiske slumped down in his seat again. Moody had regained his fool's courage. Fiske cut a glance at the fool killer behind the desk. Just then the intercom buzzed again.

The secretary's voice said: "I got Annie Lamb on the line. Says she's got to talk to you."

"Annie Lamb?"

"That's right, Reverend."

A big sigh. "All right, I'll take it." He picked up the telephone. "Annie? . . . Annie, wait a minute. Slow down . . . Say what? Henry? . . . That's terrible,

Annie. How bad is it? . . . Aw, Annie, I'm sorry . . . He did?" A long pause, as Reverend Bacon listened, eyes cast down. "What do the police say? . . . *Park*ing tickets? That don't— . . . That don't— . . . I say, that don't— . . . Okay, Annie, look here. You come on over here and you tell me the whole thing . . . Meantime, I'm calling the hospital. They didn't do the right thing, Annie. That's what it sounds like to me. They did not do the right thing . . . What? . . . You are absolutely right. You're right as rainwater. They did not do the right thing, and they're going to hear from me . . . Don't worry. You come right on over here."

Reverend Bacon hung up the telephone and swiveled back toward Fiske and Moody and narrowed his eyes and looked at them gravely. "Gentlemen, I've got an emergency here. One of my most loyal workers, one of my community leaders, her son's been struck down by a hit-and-run driver . . . in a Mercedes-Benz. A Mercedes-Benz . . . He's at death's door, and this good woman is afraid to go to the police, and do you know why? *Park*ing tickets. They've got a warrant out for her arrest for *park*ing tickets. This lady *works*. She works downtown at City Hall, and she *needs* that car, and they've got a warrant out for . . . *park*ing tickets. That wouldn't stop you if it was your son, but you've never lived in the ghetto. If it was your son, they wouldn't do what they did. They wouldn't wrap up his wrist and send him packing when what he's got is a concussion and he's at death's door . . . see . . . But that's the story of the ghetto. Gross negligence. That's what the ghetto is . . . gross negligence . . . Gentlemen, our conference is adjourned. I've got some serious business to tend to now."

On the drive back downtown the two young Yale men didn't say much until they were almost at Ninety-sixth Street. Fiske was happy enough to have found the car where he had left it, with the tires still inflated and the windshield in one piece. As for Moody—twenty blocks had gone by and Fiske hadn't heard a peep out of Moody about being a linebacker at Yale.

Finally, Moody said, "Well, you want to have dinner at Leicester's? I know the maître d', a big tall black fellow with a gold earring."

Fiske smiled faintly but said nothing. Moody's little joke made Fiske feel superior. Part of the presumed humor was the implausibility of the notion that either of them would be dining at Leicester's, which was this year's most fashionable restaurant of the century. Well, it just so happened that Fiske was going to Leicester's this very evening. Moody also didn't realize that Leicester's, although fashionable, was not a formal restaurant featuring a starched regiment of maître d's and captains. It was more the British bistro-out-Fulham-Road sort of thing. Leicester's was the favorite hangout of the British colony in New York, and Fiske had gotten to know quite a few of them—and, well, it was the kind of thing he could never explain to a fellow like Moody, but the British understood the art of conversation. Fiske considered himself essentially British, British in ancestry and British in . . . well, in a certain innately aristocratic comprehension of how one conducted one's life, aristocratic in the sense not of the richest but of *the best*. He was like the great Lord Philbank, wasn't he?—Philbank, a pillar of the Church of England who had used his social connections and his knowledge of the financial markets to help the poor of London's East End.

"Come to think of it," said Moody, "I never *have* seen a black waiter in a restaurant in New York, except for lunch counters. You really think Bacon is going to get anywhere?"

"Depends on what you mean by that."

"Well, what *will* happen?"

"I don't know," said Fiske, "but they want to be waiters at Leicester's about as much as you and I do. I kind of think they just might settle for a contribution to the Reverend Mr. Bacon's good works in Harlem, and then they'll move on to the next restaurant."

"Then it's just a payoff," said Moody.

"Well, that's the funny thing," said Fiske. "Things do change. I'm not sure he cares whether they change or not, but they change. Places he never heard of, and wouldn't care about if he had, they'll start hiring black waiters rather than wait for Buck and all those characters to turn up."

"The steam," said Moody.

"I suppose," said Fiske. "Didn't you just love all that about the boiler room? He's never worked in any boiler room. But he's discovered a new resource, I guess you could call it. Maybe it's even a form of capital, if you define capital as anything you can use to create more wealth. I don't know, maybe Bacon is no different from Rockefeller or Carnegie. You discover a new resource and you take your money while you're young, and when you're old they give you awards and name things after you, and you're remembered as a leader of the people."

"All right, then what about Urban Guaranty Investments? That doesn't sound like any new resource."

"I wouldn't be too sure. I don't know what it is, but I'm going to find out. I'm willing to bet you one thing. Whatever it is, it's going to have some kind of weird angle, and it's going to drive me a little bit farther around the fucking bend."

Then Fiske bit his lip, because he was in truth a devout Episcopalian and seldom swore and regarded foul language not only as wrong but as common. This was one of quite a few points on which, even at this late date, he happened to agree with Reginald Bacon.

By the time they reached Seventy-ninth Street, securely in White Manhattan, Fiske knew that Bacon was right once more. They weren't investing in a day-care center, were they . . . They were trying to buy souls. They were trying to tranquilize the righteously angry soul of Harlem.

Let's face facts!

Then he snapped out of it. *Fiske . . . you idiot . . .* If he didn't manage to retrieve the $350,000, or most of it, he was going to look like a most righteous fool.

7

CATCHING THE FISH

THE TELEPHONE BLASTED Peter Fallow awake inside an egg with the shell peeled away and only the membranous sac holding it intact. Ah! The membranous sac was his head, and the right side of his head was on the pillow, and the yolk was as heavy as mercury, and it rolled like mercury, and it was pressing down on his right temple and his right eye and his right ear. If he tried to get up to answer the telephone, the yolk, the mercury, the poisoned mass, would shift and roll and rupture the sac, and his brains would fall out.

The telephone was on the floor, in the corner, near the window, on the brown carpet. The carpet was disgusting. Synthetic; the Americans manufactured filthy carpet; Metalon, Streptolon, deep, shaggy, with a feel that made his flesh crawl. Another explosion; he was looking straight at it, a white telephone and a slimy white cord lying there in a filthy shaggy brown nest of Streptolon. Behind the Venetian blinds the sun was so bright it hurt his eyes. The room got light only between one and two in the afternoon, when the sun moved between two buildings on its trip across the southern sky. The other rooms, the bathroom, the kitchen, and the living room, never got any sun at all. The kitchen and the bathroom didn't even have windows. When one turned on the light in the bathroom, which had a plastic tub-and-shower-stall module—*module!*—a single molded unit that deflected slightly when he stepped into the tub—when one turned on the light in the bathroom, a ceiling fan went on up above a metal grille in the ceiling to provide ventilation. The fan created a grinding din and a tremendous vibration. So when he first got up, he no longer turned on the light in the bathroom. He depended solely on the sickly blue dawn provided by the overhead fluorescent light in the passageway outside. More than once he had gone to work without shaving.

His head still on the pillow, Fallow kept staring at the telephone, which continued to explode. He really had to get a table to put by the bed, if one could call a mattress and springs on one of those American adjustable metal frames, good for cutting off knuckles and fingers mainly when one tried to adjust them—

if one could call this a bed. The telephone looked slimy and filthy lying there on the filthy carpet. But he never invited anybody up here, except for girls, and that was always late in the evening when he had been through two or three bottles of wine and didn't give a damn. That wasn't really true, was it? When he brought a girl up here, he always saw this pathetic hole through her eyes, at least for a moment. The thought of wine and a girl tripped a wire in his brain, and a shudder of remorse went through his nervous system. Something had happened last night. These days he often woke up like this, poisonously hung over, afraid to move an inch and filled with an abstract feeling of despair and shame. Whatever he had done was submerged like a monster at the bottom of a cold dark lake. His memory had drowned in the night, and he could feel only the icy despair. He had to look for the monster deductively, fathom by fathom. Sometimes he knew that whatever it had been, he couldn't face it, and he would decide to turn away from it forever, and just then something, some stray detail, would send out a signal, and the beast would come popping to the surface on its own and show him its filthy snout.

He did remember how it started, namely, at Leicester's, where, like many of the Englishmen who frequented the place, he managed to insinuate himself at the table of an American who could be counted on to pick up the bill without pouting over it, in this case a fat fellow named Aaron Gutwillig, who had recently sold a simulator-leasing company for twelve million dollars and liked to be invited to parties given by the English colony and the Italian colony in New York. Another Yank, a crude but amusing little man named Benny Grillo, who produced so-called news documentaries for television, had a head on and wanted to go downtown to the Limelight, a discotheque set up in what used to be an Episcopal church. Grillo was good for the bill at the Limelight, and so he had gone down there with Grillo and two American model girls and Franco di Nodini, who was an Italian journalist, and Tony Moss, whom he had known at the University of Kent, and Caroline Heftshank, who had just arrived from London and was absolutely petrified with fear of street crime in New York, which she read about every day in London, and she jumped at every shadow, which was funny at first. The two model girls had ordered roast-beef sandwiches at Leicester's, and they pulled the meat out and dangled it above their mouths and ate it out of their fingers. Caroline Heftshank jumped a lot when they got out of the taxi in front of the Limelight. The place was practically ringed by black youths wearing enormous sneakers and perching on the old iron church fence, eyeing the drunks and heads going in and out of the door. Inside, the Limelight looked unusually grotesque, and Fallow felt unusually witty, drunk, and charming. So many transvestities! So many supremely repulsive punkers! So many pasty-faced little American girls with ortho-perfect teeth and silver lipstick and wet-night eye makeup! Such loud seamless endless metallic music and such foggy grainy videotapes up on the screens full of morose skinny boys and smoke bombs! Deeper and deeper into the lake it had all gone. They were in a taxi going back and forth across streets in the West Fifties looking for a place with a galvanized-metal door, called the Cup. A black studded rubber floor, and some loathsome Irish boys with no shirts on, or they looked Irish, spraying beer out of cans over everybody; and then some girls with no shirts on. Ah. Something had happened in front of some people in a room. Insofar as he had a true memory of it, he did remember that . . . Why did he do these things? . . . The house in Canterbury

. . . the locker room at Cross Keys . . . He could see himself as he looked back then . . . his Victorian-picture-book blond hair, of which he had been so proud . . . his long pointed nose, his long slender jaw, his spindly body, always too thin for his great height, of which he had also been so proud . . . his spindly body . . . A *ripple* . . . The monster was heading up from the bottom of the lake! In a moment . . . *its filthy snout!*

Can't face it—

The telephone exploded again. He opened his eyes and squinted at the sun-drenched modern squalor, and with his eyes open it was even worse. With his eyes open—the immediate future. Such hopelessness! Such icy despair! He squinted and shuddered and closed his eyes again. *The snout!*

He opened them immediately. This thing he had done when he was very drunk—in addition to despair and remorse, he now felt fear.

The ringing telephone began to alarm him. Suppose it was *The City Light*. After the Dead Mouse's last lecture, he had sworn to himself to be at the office by ten o'clock every morning, and it was now after one. In that case—he'd better not answer it. No—if he didn't answer the telephone, he would sink to the bottom forever, along with the monster. He rolled out of the bed and put his feet on the floor, and the horrible yolk shifted. He was thrown into a violent headache. He wanted to vomit, but he knew it would hurt his head too much for him to possibly allow it to happen. He started toward the telephone. He sank to his knees and then to all fours. He crawled to the telephone, picked up the receiver, and then lay down on the carpet, hoping the yolk would settle again.

"Hello," he said.

"Peter?" *Pee-tuh?* Thank God, it was an English voice.

"Yes?"

"Peter, you're gurgling. I woke you up, didn't I. This is Tony."

"No, no, no, no, no. I'm—I was, I was in the other room. I'm working at home today." He realized that his voice had sunk to a furtive baritone.

"Well, you do a very good imitation of having just woke up."

"You don't believe me, do you?" Thank God it was Tony. Tony was an Englishman who had come to work on *The City Light* at the same time he had. They were fellow commandos in this gross country.

"Of course I believe you. But that puts me in the minority just now. If I were you, I'd come down here as soon as I could."

"Ummmmmm. Yes."

"The Mouse just came over and asked me where you were. Not out of curiosity, either. He acted extremely pissed."

"What did you tell him?"

"I told him you were at the Surrogate's Court."

"Ummmm. Not to pry, but what am I doing there?"

"Great Christ, Peter, I really did get you out of bed, didn't I? That Lacey Putney business."

"Ummmmmmm. Lacey Putney." Pain, nausea, and sleep rolled through Fallow's head like a Hawaiian wave. His head was flat on the carpet. The poisonous yolk sloshed about terribly. "Ummmmmmmmmmm."

"Don't fade out on me, Peter. I'm not joking. I think you should come down here and put in an appearance."

"I know, I know I know I know I know. Thanks, Tony. You're absolutely right."

"Are you coming?"

"Yes." Even as he said it, he knew what it was going to feel like to try to stand up.

"And do me a favor."

"Anything."

"Try to remember that you were at the Surrogate's Court. The Lacey Putney estate. Not that the Mouse necessarily believed me. But, you know."

"Yes. Lacey Putney. Thanks, Tony."

Fallow hung up, got up off the floor, staggered into the Venetian blinds, and cut his lip. The slats were the narrow metal ones the Yanks liked. They were like blades. He wiped the blood off his lip with the back of his index finger. He couldn't hold his head up straight. The mercury yolk ruined his sense of balance. He lurched to the bathroom and entered by the tubercular blue dawn of the fluorescent light in the passageway outside. In the mirror on the medicine cabinet door, in this diseased light, the blood on his lip looked purple. That was all right. He could live with purple blood. But if he turned on the light in the bathroom, he was finished.

Rows of diode-light computer terminals in putty-gray 2001 sci-fi casings lent the city room of *The City Light* a gloss of order and modernity. It never survived a second glance. The desks were covered in the usual litter of paper, plastic cups, books, manuals, almanacs, magazines, and sooty ashtrays. The usual shell-backed young men and women sat at the keyboards. A numb dull clattering—*thuk thuk thuk thuk thuk thuk thuk thuk thuk thuk thuk thuk thuk*—rose from the keyboards, as if an immense mah-jongg tournament was in progress. The reporters, rewrite men, and copy editors were hunched over in the age-old way of journalists. Every few seconds a head would straighten up, as if coming up for air, and yell out something about slugs, headline counts, or story lengths. But not even the excitement of deadline pressure could survive for long. A rear door opened, and a Greek wearing a white uniform came staggering in carrying a prodigious tray full of coffee and soda containers, boxes of doughnuts, cheese Danishes, onion rolls, crullers, every variety of muck and lard known to the takeout food business, and half the room deserted the computer consoles and descended upon him, rooting about the tray like starving weevils.

Fallow took advantage of this hiatus to make his way across the room toward his cubicle. Out in the middle of the field of computer terminals, he stopped and, with an air of professional scrutiny, picked up a copy of the second edition, which had just been brought upstairs. Below the logo—THE CITY LIGHT—the front page consisted of enormous capital letters running down the right side—

SCALP
GRANDMA,
THEN
ROB HER

—and a photograph running down the left. The photograph was a cropped blowup of the sort of smiling lineless portrait that studios produce. It was a picture of a woman named Carolina Pérez, fifty-five years old and not particularly grand-motherly, with a luxuriant head of black hair pulled up behind in the old-fashioned Lady of Spain style.

Christ God! Scalping her must have been an undertaking! Had he been feeling better, Fallow would have paid a silent tribute to the extraordinary *esthé-tique de l'abattoir* that enabled these shameless devils, his employers, his compatri-ots, his fellow Englishmen, his fellow progeny of Shakespeare and Milton, to come up with things like this day after day. Just think of the fine sense of gutter syntax that inspired them to create a headline that was all verbs and objects, with the subject missing, the better to make you claw your way inside these smeary black pages to find out what children of evil were fiendish enough to complete the sentence! Just think of the maggot's perseverance that enabled some reporter to invade *chez* Pérez and extract a picture of Granny that made you feel the bloody act in your fingertips—in your very shoulder joints! Just think of the anticlimax of "*scalp* Grandma" . . . "then *rob* her." The pointless *brilliant* anti-climax! Christ, if they'd had more room, they would have added, "then leave all the lights on in her kitchen."

At the moment, however, he was too poisonously ill to enjoy it. No, he stood there staring at this latest bit of tabloid genius only to establish the fact, for all to see—and most especially, he hoped, the Dead Mouse himself—that he was on the premises and interested in little else in the world other than the New York *City Light*.

Holding the newspaper in his hands and staring at the front page, as if trans-fixed by the virtuosity of it, he walked the rest of the way across the room and entered his cubicle. It consisted of four-foot-high walls of particleboard in a sickly salmon color, a so-called work station with little high-tech curves at the corners, fencing in a gray metal desk, the ubiquitous computer terminal and keyboard, a plastic desk chair molded in an unpleasant orthopedic fashion and a modular plastic coatrack, which snapped ingeniously onto the modular wall. It was already cracked in the stem. On the rack hung a single drab garment, Peter Fallow's raincoat, which never left the cubicle.

Just by the coatrack was a window, and he could see his reflection. Head on, he looked a young and handsome thirty-six rather than fortyish and gone to seed. Head on, his widow's peak and the longish wavy blond hair that flowed back from it still looked . . . well, *Byronic* . . . rather than a bit lonely on the dome of his skull. Yes, at this head-on angle . . . it was going to be all right! His long thin nose looked patrician from top to bottom rather than too bulbous in the tip. His big cleft chin did not look overly compromised by the jowls that were forming on either side. His navy blazer, which had been made by Blades eight—no, *ten!*—years ago was getting a little . . . *shiny* . . . on the lapels . . . but he could probably raise the nap with one of those wire brushes . . . He had the begin-nings of a belly and was getting too fleshy in the hips and thighs. But this would be no problem now that he was finished with drinking. Never again. He would begin an exercise regimen tonight. Or tomorrow, in any case; he felt too bilious to think about tonight. It wouldn't be this pathetic American business of jogging, either. It would be something clean, crisp, brisk, strenuous . . . English. He thought of medicine balls and exercise ladders and leather horses and Indian clubs and pulley weights and parallel bars and stout ropes with leather bindings on the end, and then he realized that these were the apparatus of the gymnasium at Cross Keys, the school he had attended prior to the University of Kent. Dear God . . . twenty years ago. But he was still only thirty-six, and he was six-foot-two, and he had a perfectly sound physique, fundamentally.

He pulled in his stomach and drew a deep breath. It made him feel woozy. He picked up the telephone and put the receiver to his ear. Look busy! That was the main idea. He found the dial tone soothing. He wished he could crawl inside the receiver and float on his back in the dial tone and let the hum of it wash over his nerve endings. How easy it would be to put his head down on the desk and close his eyes and catch forty winks. Perhaps he could get away with it if he put one side of his face down on the desk, with the back of his head to the city room, and kept the telephone over his other ear as if he were talking. No, it would still look strange. Perhaps . . .

Oh, Christ God. An American named Robert Goldman, one of the reporters, was heading for the cubicle. Goldman had on a necktie with vivid red, yellow, black, and sky-blue diagonal stripes. The Yanks called these bogus regimental ties "rep" ties. The Yanks always wore neckties that leapt out in front of their shirts, as if to announce the awkwardness to follow. Two weeks ago he had borrowed a hundred dollars from Goldman. He had told him he had to repay a gambling debt by nightfall—backgammon—the Bracers' Club—fast European crowd. The Yanks had very big eyes for stories of Rakes and Aristocrats. Since then, the little shit had already pestered him three times for the money, as if his future on this earth turned on a hundred dollars. The receiver still at his ear, Fallow glanced at the approaching figure, and the blazing tie that heralded him, with contempt. Like more than one Englishman in New York, he looked upon Americans as hopeless children whom Providence had perversely provided with this great swollen fat fowl of a continent. Any way one chose to relieve them of their riches, short of violence, was sporting, if not morally justifiable, since they would only squander it in some tasteless and useless fashion, in any event.

Fallow began talking into the receiver, as if deep in conversation. He searched his poisoned brain for the sort of one-sided dialogue playwrights have to come up with for telephone scenes.

"What's that? . . . You say the surrogate refuses to allow the stenographer to give us a transcript? Well, you tell him . . . Right, right . . . Of course . . . It's an absolute violation . . . No, no . . . Now listen carefully . . ."

The necktie—and Goldman—were standing right beside him. Peter Fallow kept his eyes down and lifted one hand, as if to say, "Please! This call cannot be interrupted."

"Hello, Pete," said Goldman.

Pete! he said, and not very cheerily, either. *Pete!* The very sound set Fallow's teeth on edge. This . . . appalling . . . Yank . . . familiarity! And cuteness! The Yanks!—with their Arnies and Buddies and Hanks and . . . *Petes!* And this lubberly gauche lout with his screaming necktie has the gall to walk into one's office while one is on the telephone, because he's a nervous wreck over his pathetic hundred dollars!—and call one *Pete!*

Fallow screwed his face into a look of great intensity and began talking a mile a minute.

"So! . . . You tell the surrogate *and* the stenographer that we want the transcript by noon tomorrow! . . . Of course! . . . It's obvious! . . . This is something her barrister has cooked up! They're all thick as thieves over there!"

"It's 'judge,' " said Goldman tonelessly.

Fallow flicked his eyes up toward the American with a furious black look.

Goldman stared back with a faintly ironic twist to his lips.

"They don't say 'stenographer,' they say 'court reporter.' And they don't say 'barrister,' although they'll know what you mean."

Fallow closed his eyes and his lips into three tight lines and shook his head and flapped his hand, as if confronted by an intolerable display of impudence.

But when he opened his eyes, Goldman was still there. Goldman looked down at him and put a look of mock excitement on his face and raised both hands and lifted his ten fingers straight up in front of Fallow and then made two fists and popped the ten fingers straight up again and repeated this gesture ten times—and said, "One hundred big ones, Pete," and turned and walked back out into the city room.

The impudence! The impudence! Once it was clear the impudent little wet smack wasn't returning, Fallow put down the receiver and stood up and went over to the coatrack. He had vowed—but Christ God! What he had just been subjected to *was . . . just . . . a . . . bit . . . much.* Without removing it from the hook, he opened the raincoat and put his head inside it, as if he were inspecting the seams. Then he brought the raincoat around his shoulders so that the upper half of his body disappeared from view. It was the kind of raincoat that has slash pockets with openings on the inside as well as the outside, so that in the rain you can get to your jacket or pants without unbuttoning the coat in front. Beneath his poplin tent, Fallow felt around for the inside opening of the left-hand pocket. From the pocket he withdrew a pint-sized camping canteen.

He unscrewed the top, put the opening to his lips, and took two long gulps of vodka and waited for the jolt in his stomach. It hit and then bounced up through his body and his head like a heat wave. He screwed the top back on and slipped the canteen back in the pocket and emerged from the raincoat. His face was on fire. There were tears in his eyes. He took a wary look toward the city room, and—

Oh shit.

—the Dead Mouse was looking straight at him. Fallow didn't dare so much as blink, much less smile. He wanted to provoke no response in the Mouse whatsoever. He turned away as if he hadn't seen him. Was vodka truly odorless? He devoutly hoped so. He sat down at the desk and picked up the telephone again and moved his lips. The dial tone hummed, but he was too nervous to surrender himself to it. Had the Mouse seen him under the raincoat? And if he had, would he guess anything? Oh, how different that little nip had been from those glorious toasts of six months ago! Oh, what glorious prospects he had pissed away! He could see the scene . . . the dinner at the Mouse's grotesque flat on Park Avenue . . . the pompous, overformal invitation cards with the raised script: *Sir Gerald Steiner and Lady Steiner request the pleasure of your company at dinner in honour of Mr. Peter Fallow* (dinner and *Mr. Peter Fallow* written in by hand) . . . the ludicrous museum of Bourbon Louis furniture and threadbare Aubusson rugs the Dead Mouse and Lady Mouse had put together on Park Avenue. Nevertheless, what a heady evening that had been! Everyone at the table had been English. There were only three or four Americans in the upper echelons of *The City Light* anyway, and none was invited. There were dinners like this all over the East Side of Manhattan every night, he had soon discovered, lavish parties that were all English or all French or all Italian or all European; no Americans, in any case. One had the sense of a very rich and very suave secret legion that had insinuated itself into the cooperative apartment houses of Park Avenue and Fifth Avenue, from there to pounce at will upon the Yanks' fat fowl, to devour at leisure the last plump white meat on the bones of capitalism.

In England, Fallow had always thought of Gerald Steiner as "that Jew Steiner," but on this night all base snobberies had vanished. They were comrades-in-arms in the secret legion, in the service of Great Britain's wounded chauvinism. Steiner had told the table what a genius Fallow was. Steiner had been swept off his feet by a series on country life among the rich that Fallow had done for the *Dispatch*. It had been full of names and titles and helicopters and perplexing perversions ("that thing with the cup") and costly diseases, and all of it was so artfully contrived as to be fireproof in terms of libel. It had been Fallow's greatest triumph as a journalist (his only one, in point of fact), and Steiner couldn't imagine how he had pulled it off. Fallow knew exactly how, but he managed to hide the memory of it with the embroideries of vanity. Every spicy morsel in the series came from a girl he was seeing at that time, a resentful little girl named Jeannie Brokenborough, a rare-book dealer's daughter who ran with the Country Set as the social runt in the stable. When little Miss Brokenborough moved on, Fallow's daily magic vanished with her.

Steiner's invitation to New York had arrived just in time, although Fallow did not see it that way. Like every writer before him who has ever scored a triumph, even on the level of the London *Dispatch*, Fallow was willing to give no credit to luck. Would he have any trouble repeating his triumph in a city he knew nothing about, in a country he looked upon as a stupendous joke? Well . . . why should he? His genius had only begun to flower. This was only journalism, after all, a cup of tea on the way to his eventual triumph as a novelist. Fallow's father, Ambrose Fallow, was a novelist, a decidedly minor novelist, it had turned out. His father and his mother were from East Anglia and had been the sort of highly educated young people of good blood and good bone who after the Second World War had been susceptible to the notion that literary sensitivity could make one an aristocrat. The notion of being aristocratic was never far from their minds, nor from Fallow's. Fallow had tried to make up for his lack of money by being a wit and a rake. These aristocratic accomplishments had gained him nothing more than an insecure place in the tail of the comet of the smart crowd in London.

Now, as part of the Steiner brigade in New York, Fallow was also going to make his fortune in the fat white-meat New World.

People wondered why Steiner, who had no background in journalism, had come to the United States and undertaken the extremely costly business of setting up a tabloid newspaper. The smart explanation was that *The City Light* had been created as the weapon of attack or reprisal for Steiner's much more important financial investments in the United States, where he was already known as "the Dread Brit." But Fallow knew it was the other way around. The "serious" investments existed at the service of *The City Light*. Steiner had been reared, schooled, drilled, and handed a fortune by Old Steiner, a loud and pompous self-made financier who wanted to turn his son into a proper British peer, not just a rich Jewish boy. Steiner *fils* had become the well-mannered, well-educated, well-dressed, proper mouse his father required. He had never found the courage to rebel. Now, late in life, he had discovered the world of the tabloids. His daily dive

into the mud—SCALP GRANDMA, THEN ROB HER—brought him inexpressible joy.
Uhuru! Free at last! Every day he rolled up his sleeves and plunged into the life of
the city room. Some days he wrote headlines himself. It was possible that he had
written SCALP GRANDMA, although that had the inimitable touch of his managing
editor, a Liverpool prole named Brian Highridge. Despite the many victories of
his career, however, he had never been a social success. This was largely due to
his personality, but anti-Jewish sentiment was not dead, either, and he could not
discount it altogether. In any case, he looked with genuine relish upon the prospect of Peter Fallow building a nice toasty bonfire under all the nobs who looked
down on him. And so he waited . . .

And waited. At first, Fallow's expense account, which was far larger than any
other *City Light* writer's (not counting the rare foreign assignment), caused no
concern. After all, to penetrate the high life one had to live it, to some extent.
The staggering lunch bills, dinner bills, and bar bills were followed by amusing
reports of the swath Mr. Peter Fallow was cutting as a jolly Brit giant in fashionable low dives. After a while they were not amusing anymore. No great coup in
the chronicling of the high life was forthcoming from this particular soldier of
fortune. More than once, Fallow had turned in stories only to find them reduced
to unsigned column items the following day. Steiner had called him in for several
progress reports. These chats had become chillier and chillier. His pride wounded,
Fallow had begun entertaining his colleagues by referring to Steiner, the renowned "Dread Brit," as the Dead Mouse. Everyone seemed to enjoy this enormously. After all, Steiner *did* have a long pointed nose like a mouse and no chin
and a crumpled little mouth and large ears and tiny hands and feet and eyes in
which the light seemed to have gone out and a tired little voice. Recently,
however, Steiner had become downright cold and abrupt, and Fallow began to
wonder if in fact he somehow had learned of the Dead Mouse crack.

He looked up . . . there was Steiner, six feet away in the doorway to the
cubicle, looking straight at him, one hand resting on a modular wall.

"Nice of you to pay us a visit, Fallow."

Fallow! It was the most contemptuous sort of school-proctor stuff! Fallow was
speechless.

"Well," said Steiner, "what do you have for me?"

Fallow opened his mouth. He ransacked his poisoned brain in search of the
facile conversation for which he was renowned and came up gasping and sputtering.

"Well!—you'll remember—the Lacey Putney estate—I mentioned that—if
I'm not mistaken—they've tried to give us a very hard time at the Surrogate's
Court, the—the—" Damn! Was it stenographers or something about reporters?
What had Goldman said? "Well!—I hardly—but I've really got the whole thing
now! It's just a matter of—I can tell you—this is really going to break open . . ."

Steiner didn't even wait for him to finish.

"I sincerely hope so, Fallow," he said quite ominously. "I sincerely hope so."
Then he left and plunged back into his beloved tabloid city room.

Fallow sank down into his chair. He managed to wait almost a full minute
before he got up and disappeared into his raincoat.

Albert Teskowitz was not what Kramer or any other prosecutor would call a
threat when it came to swaying a jury with the magic of his summations.

Emotional crescendos were beyond him, and even what rhetorical momentum he could manage was quickly undercut by his appearance. His posture was so bad that every woman on a jury, or every good mother, in any case, was aching to cry out, "Hold your shoulders back!" As for his delivery, it wasn't that he didn't prepare his summations, it was that he obviously prepared them on a yellow legal pad, which lay on top of the defense table.

"Ladies and gentlemen, the defendant has three children, ages six, seven, and nine," Teskowitz was saying, "and they are in the courtroom at this moment, awaiting the outcome of this trial." Teskowitz avoided calling his client by name. If he could have said Herbert Cantrell, Mr Cantrell, or even Herbert, it would have been all right, but Herbert wouldn't put up even with Herbert. "My name is not Herbert," he told Teskowitz when he first took the case. "I am not your limo driver. My name is Herbert 92X."

"It was not some criminal sitting in the Doubleheader Grill that afternoon," Teskowitz continued, "but a workingman with a job and a family." He hesitated and turned his face upward with the far, far, far-off expression of someone about to have an epileptic seizure. "A job and a family," he repeated dreamily, a thousand miles away. Then he turned on his heels and went to the defense table and bent his already stooped torso at the waist and stared at his yellow legal pad with his head cocked to one side, like a bird eyeing a wormhole. He held that pose for what seemed like an eternity and then walked back to the jury box and said, "He was not an aggressor. He was not attempting to settle a score or make a score or get even with anybody. He was a workingman with a job and a family who was concerned with only one thing, and that he had every right to, which was his life was in danger." The little lawyer's eyes opened up like a time exposure again, and he did an about-face and walked back to the defense table and stared at the yellow pad some more. Bent over the way he was, he had a silhouette like a slop-sink spigot . . . A slop-sink spigot . . . a dog with the chuck horrors . . . Rogue images began to seep into the jurors' minds. They began to be aware of things such as the film of dust on the huge courtroom windows and the way the dying afternoon sun lit up the dust, as if it were that kind of plastic they make toys out of, the kind that picks up light, and every housekeeper on the jury, even the bad ones, wondered why somebody didn't wash those windows. They wondered about many things and about almost anything other than what Albert Teskowitz was saying about Herbert 92X, and above all they wondered about the yellow legal pad, which seemed to have Teskowitz's poor bent scrawny neck on a leash.

". . . and find this defendant . . . not guilty." When Teskowitz finally completed his summation, they weren't even sure he had finished. Their eyes were pinned on the yellow legal pad. They expected it to jerk him back to the table once more. Even Herbert 92X, who hadn't missed a beat, looked puzzled.

Just then a low chant began in the courtroom.

"Yo-ohhhhhhh . . ." It came from over here.

"Yo-ohhhhhhhhhhhhhhh . . ." It came from over there.

Kaminsky, the fat officer, started it, and then Bruzzielli, the clerk, picked it up, and even Sullivan, the court reporter, who was sitting at his stenotype machine just below the brow of Kovitsky's bench, joined in with his own low discreet version. "Yo-ohhh."

Without batting an eye Kovitsky tapped his gavel and declared a thirty-minute recess.

Kramer didn't think twice about it. It was wagon-train time at the fortress, that was all. Wagon-training was standard practice. If a trial was likely to run past sundown, then you had to wagon-train. Everybody knew that. This trial was going to have to continue past sundown, because the defense had just completed its summation, and the judge couldn't adjourn for the night without letting the prosecution make its summation. So it was time to wagon-train.

During a wagon-train recess, all employees who had driven to work and who had to stay on at the courthouse after dark because of the trial got up and went outside and headed for their cars in the parking lots. The judge, Kovitsky, was no exception. Today he had driven himself to work, and he went to his robing room, which was through a door to one side of the bench, where he took off his black robe and headed for the parking lot, like everybody else.

Kramer had no car, and he couldn't afford to pay eight or ten dollars to take a gypsy cab home. The gypsies—many of them driven by recent African immigrants, from places like Nigeria and Senegal—were the only cabs that came near the courthouse day or night, except for the taxis that brought fares from Manhattan to the Bronx County Building. The drivers switched on the OFF DUTY sign even before the brake pedal took its first bite of friction out of the drum, dropped off their fares, and then sped off. No, with a slight chill around the heart, Kramer realized that this was one of those nights when he would have to walk three blocks to the 161st Street subway station in the dark and stand there and wait on what was rated as one of the ten most dangerous subway platforms in the city, in terms of crime, and hope there was a car full enough of people so that he wouldn't be picked off by the wolf packs like some stray calf from the herd. He figured the Nike running shoes gave him at least half a fighting chance. For a start, they were camouflage. On the subway in the Bronx, a pair of Johnston & Murphy leather business shoes labeled you as a prime target right off the bat. It was like wearing a sign around your neck saying ROB ME. The Nikes and the A&P shopping bag would at least make them think twice. They might take him for a plainclothes cop on the way home. There no longer existed a plainclothes cop in the Bronx who didn't wear sneakers. The other thing was, if the evil shit ever did rain down, with the Nikes he could at least run for it or dig in and fight. He wasn't about to mention any of this to Andriutti and Caughey. Andriutti he didn't really give a damn about, but Caughey's contempt he knew he couldn't stand. Caughey was Irish and would have sooner taken a bullet in the face than wear fucking camouflage on the subway.

As the jurors headed back to the jury room, Kramer stared at Miss Shelly Thomas until he could *feel* the smoothness of her brown lipstick as she walked past, and she looked at him for an instant—*with just a trace of a smile!*—and he began to agonize over how she would get home, and there was nothing he could do about it, since of course he couldn't go near her and convey any sort of message to her. Even with all this *yo-ohhhhhing* no one ever informed the jury or the witnesses about wagon-training, not that a juror would be allowed to go to a parking lot during a trial recess, in any case.

Kramer went downstairs to the Walton Avenue entrance, to stretch his legs, get some air, and watch the parade. Out on the sidewalk one group, including Kovitsky and his law clerk, Mel Herskowitz, had already formed. The court officers were with them, standing around like troop leaders. The big tub, Kaminsky, was on his tiptoes, craning around, to see if there was anybody else who wanted to come along. The parking lot favored by the courthouse regulars was just over the crest of the Grand Concourse and down the slope, on 161st Street, in an enormous dirt pit across from the Criminal Courts Building. The pit, which occupied an entire city block, had been dug as the excavation for a building project that never went up.

The group assembled with Kaminsky in the lead and another court officer bringing up the rear. The court officers had their .38s plainly visible on their hips. The little contingent headed off bravely into Indian country. It was about 5:45. Walton Avenue was quiet. There wasn't much of a rush hour in the Bronx. The parking spaces on Walton Avenue next to the fortress were at a 90-degree angle to the curb. Only a handful of cars remained. There were ten reserved spaces near the entrance, for Abe Weiss, Louis Mastroiani, and other supreme bearers of the Power in the Bronx. The guard at the door put Day-Glo-red plastic traffic cones in the spaces when the appointed users were away. Kramer noticed that Abe Weiss's car was still there. There was one other, which he didn't recognize, but the other spaces were vacant. Kramer walked back and forth on the sidewalk near the entrance with his head down and his hands in his pockets, concentrating on his summation. He was here to speak for the one principal in this case who could not speak for himself, namely, the victim, the deceased, Nestor Cabrillo, a good father and a good citizen of the Bronx. It all fell into place very easily. Brick-wall arguments wouldn't be enough, however; not for what he had to achieve. This summation had to *move* her, move her to tears or awe or, at the very least, to utter inebriation from a crime-high in the Bronx, featuring a tough young assistant D.A. with a golden tongue and a fearless delivery, not to mention a hell of a powerful neck. So he walked up and down the sidewalk outside the Walton Avenue entrance to the fortress, cooking Herbert 92X's goose and tensing his sternocleidomastoid muscles while a vision of the girl with brown lipstick danced in his head.

Pretty soon the first of the cars arrived. Here came Kovitsky in his huge ancient white boat, the Pontiac Bonneville. He nosed into one of the reserved spaces near the door. *Thwop!* The huge door torqued, and he got out, an inconspicuous-looking little bald man in a very ordinary gray suit. And then here came Bruzzielli in some little Japanese sports car that he seemed about to burst out of. Then Mel Herskowitz and Sullivan, the court reporter. Then Teskowitz in a new Buick Regal. Shit, thought Kramer. Even Al Teskowitz can afford a car. Even him, an 18b lawyer, and I'm going home on the subway! Pretty soon practically every space on the Walton Avenue side of the building was filled by the regulars. The last car to pull in was Kaminsky's own. He had given the other court officer a lift back. The two of them got out, and Kaminsky spotted Kramer and broke into a good-natured grin and sang out, "Yo-ohhhhhhhhhhhhhhhhhh!"

"Yo ho ho," said Kramer.

The wagon train. "Yo-ohhhhhhh" was the cry of John Wayne, the hero and chief scout, signaling the pioneers to move the wagons. This was Indian country and bandit country, and it was time to put the wagons in a circle for the night. Anybody who thought he was going to be able to walk two blocks from Gibraltar to the parking lot after dark in the Four-four and drive peacefully home to Mom and Buddy and Sis was playing the game of life with half a deck.

* * *

Late in the day, Sherman got a call from Arnold Parch's secretary saying
Parch wanted to see him. Parch had the title executive vice president, but he was
not the sort who very often summoned people from the trading floor into his
office.

Parch's office was, naturally, smaller than Lopwitz's, but it had the same
terrific view to the west, out over the Hudson River and New Jersey. In contrast
to Lopwitz's office, with its antiques, Parch's was done with modern furniture and
large modern paintings of the sort that Maria and her husband liked.

Parch, who was a great smiler, smiled and motioned to a gray upholstered
chair that was so sleek and close to the floor it looked like a submarine surfacing.
Sherman sank down until he had the sensation of being below floor level. Parch
sat down in an identical chair across from him. Sherman was conscious mainly of
legs, his and Parch's. In Sherman's line of vision, Parch's chin barely cleared the
tops of his knees.

"Sherman," said the smiling face behind the kneetops, "I just received a call
from Oscar Suder in Columbus, Ohio, and he is really pissed off about these
United Fragrance bonds."

Sherman was astounded. He wanted to lift his head up higher, but he
couldn't. "He is? And he called *you?* What did he say?"

"He said you called him and sold him three million bonds at 102. He also said
you told him to buy them fast, because they were heading up. This morning
they're down to 100."

"Par! I don't believe it!"

"Well, it's a fact, and they're going lower, if they're going anywhere. Standard
& Poor's just knocked them down from double A to triple B."

"I don't . . . *believe* it, Arnold! I saw them go from 103 to 102.5 day before
yesterday, and I checked with Research, and everything was okay. Then yesterday
they went down to 102, then 101⅞, and then they came back up to 102. So I
figured other traders were spotting it, and that's when I called Oscar. They were
heading back up. It was a damned good bargain at 102. Oscar had been looking
for something over 9, and here was 9.75, almost 10, double A."

"But did you check with Research yesterday, before you got them for Oscar?"

"No, but they went up another eighth after I bought them. They were going
up. I'm bowled over by all this. *Par!* It's unbelievable."

"Well, golly, Sherman," said Parch, who was no longer smiling, "can't you see
what was happening? Somebody at Salomon was painting you a picture. They
were loaded with U Frags, and they knew the S&P report was on the way, and so
they painted a picture. They lowered the price two days ago, looking for nibbles.
Then they brought it back up to make it look like there was some trading going
on. Then they lowered it again yesterday and they pulled it up. Then when they
got your nibble—quite a nice little nibble—they raised the price again, to see if
you'd nibble again at 102⅛. You and Solly were the whole market, Sherman!
Nobody else was touching it. They painted you a picture. Now Oscar's out
$60,000 and he's got three million triple B's he doesn't want."

A terrible clear light. Of course it was true. He had let himself be suckered in
the most amateurish fashion. And Oscar Suder, of all people! Oscar, whom he
was counting on as part of the Giscard package . . . only $10 million out of
$600 million, but that was $10 million he'd have to find somewhere else . . .

"I don't know what to say," said Sherman. "You're absolutely right. I goofed." He realized *goofed* sounded as if he were letting himself off easy. "It was a stupid blunder, Arnold. I should've seen it coming." He shook his head. "Boy. Oscar, of all people. I wonder if I should call him myself?"

"I wouldn't just yet. He's really pissed off. He wanted to know if you or anybody else here knew the S&P report was coming. I said no, because I knew you wouldn't pull anything on Oscar. But in fact Research did know about it. You should've checked with 'em, Sherman. After all, three million bonds . . ."

Parch smiled the smile of no-hard-feelings. He obviously didn't like sessions like this himself. "It's okay. It happens; it happens. But you're our number one man out there, Sherman." He lifted his eyebrows and kept them way up on his forehead, as if to say, "You get the picture?"

He hauled himself up from out of his chair. Likewise, Sherman. With considerable embarrassment Parch extended his hand, and Sherman shook it.

"Okay, go get 'em," Parch said with a large but flat smile.

The distance from where Kramer stood at the prosecution table to where Herbert 92X sat at the defense table was no more than twenty feet to begin with. Kramer took a couple of steps closer, narrowing the gap until everybody in the courtroom could tell that something odd was taking place without being able to tell exactly what. He had reached the part where it was time to demolish whatever pity for Herbert that Teskowitz might have managed to create.

"Now, I know we've heard certain things about the personal history of Herbert 92X," said Kramer, facing the jury, "and here Herbert 92X sits today, in this courtroom." Unlike Teskowitz, Kramer threw the name Herbert 92X into almost every sentence, until he began to sound like a sci-fi movie robot. Then he pivoted and lowered his head and stared Herbert in the face and said, "Yes, here is Herbert 92X . . . in *perfect health!* . . . full of *energy!* . . . ready to return to the streets and *resume* his life, in the Herbert 92X style which involves carrying *a concealed unlicensed illegal .38-caliber revolver!*"

Kramer looked Herbert 92X in the eye. He was now barely ten feet away from him, and he hurled *health, energy,* and *resume* in his teeth, as if he personally was ready to remove the man's health, energy, and potential for the resumption of a workaday life or life of any sort, for that matter, with his bare hands. Herbert was not one to shrink from a challenge. He contemplated Kramer with a cool smile on his face that as much as said, "Just keep on talking, sucker, because I'm going to count to ten and then . . . *squash* you." To the jurors—to her—Herbert must have looked as if he was close enough to reach out and throttle him and, on top of that, eager to throttle him. That didn't worry Kramer. He was backed up by three court officers who were already in high spirits from the thought of the overtime pay they would be getting for the evening's work. So let Herbert sit there in his Arab outfit and look as tough as he wants! The tougher Herbert looked in the eyes of the jury, the better it was for Kramer's case. And the more dangerous he looked in the eyes of Miss Shelly Thomas—the more heroic the aura of the fearless young prosecutor!

The truly incredulous person was Teskowitz. His head was going back and forth slowly, like a lawn sprinkler. He couldn't believe the performance he was witnessing. If Kramer was going after Herbert this way in this piece a shit, what the hell would he do if he had a real killer on his hands?

"Well, ladies and gentlemen," said Kramer, turning back toward the jury but remaining just as close to Herbert, "it is my duty to speak for someone who is not sitting before us in this courtroom, because he was struck down and killed by a bullet from a revolver in the possession of a man he had never seen before in his life, Herbert 92X. I would remind you that the issue in this trial is not the life of Herbert 92X but the death of Nestor Cabrillo, a good man, a good citizen of the Bronx, a good husband, a good father . . . of *five children* . . . cut down in the prime of his life because of Herbert 92X's *arrogant belief* . . . that he is entitled to conduct his business with a concealed, unlicensed, illegal .38-caliber revolver in his possession . . ."

Kramer let his eyes grace each juror, one by one. But at the end of each orotund period they came to rest upon *her*. She was sitting next to the end on the left side in the second row, and so it was a little awkward, perhaps even a little obvious. But life is short! And, my God!—such a flawless white face!—such a luxurious corona of hair!—such perfect lips with brown lipstick! And such an admiring gleam did he now detect in those big brown eyes! Miss Shelly Thomas was roaring drunk, high on crime in the Bronx.

Out on the sidewalk, Peter Fallow could see the cars and taxis speeding uptown on West Street. Christ God, how he longed to be able to crawl into a taxi and go to sleep until he reached Leicester's. *No!* What was he thinking? No Leicester's tonight; not a drop of alcohol in any form. Tonight he was going straight home. It was getting dark. He'd give anything for a taxi . . . to curl up in a taxi and go to sleep and head straight home . . . But the ride would be nine or ten dollars, and he had less than seventy-five dollars to last him until payday, which was next week, and in New York seventy-five dollars was nothing, a mere sigh, a deep breath, a passing thought, a whim, a snap of the fingers. He kept looking at the front entrance to the *City Light* building, which was a dingy Moderne tower from the 1920s, hoping to spot some American from the newspaper with whom he could share a taxi. The trick was to find out where the American was heading and then to pick out some destination four or five blocks short of there and announce that as one's own destination. No American had the nerve to ask one to share the cost of the ride under those circumstances.

After a bit there emerged an American named Ken Goodrich, the *City Light*'s director of marketing, whatever in God's name *marketing* was. Did he dare once more? He had already hitched rides with Goodrich twice in the past two months, and the second time Goodrich's delight over the opportunity to converse with an Englishman on the ride uptown had been considerably less intense; considerably. No, he did not dare. So he girded his loins for the eight-block walk to City Hall, where he could catch the Lexington Avenue subway.

This old part of lower Manhattan emptied out quickly in the evenings, and as Fallow trudged along in the gloaming he felt increasingly sorry for himself. He searched his jacket pocket to see if he had a subway token. He did, and this provoked a depressing recollection. Two nights ago at Leicester's he had reached into his pocket to give Tony Moss a quarter for a telephone call—he wanted to be big about the quarter, because he was beginning to get a reputation as a cadger even among his fellow countrymen—and he produced a handful of change, and right there, among the dimes, quarters, nickels, and pence, were two subway tokens. He felt as if the entire table was staring at them. Certainly Tony Moss saw them.

Fallow had no physical fear of riding the New York subways. He fancied himself a rugged fellow, and in any case, nothing untoward had ever befallen him in the Underground. No, what he feared—and it amounted to a true fear—was the squalor. Heading down the stairs of the City Hall subway station with all these dark shabby people was like descending, voluntarily, into a dungeon, a very dirty and noisy dungeon. Grimy concrete and black bars were everywhere, cage after cage, level upon level, a delirium seen through black bars in every direction. Every time a train entered or left the station there was an agonized squeal of metal, as if some huge steel skeleton were being pried apart by a lever of incomprehensible power. Why was it that in this gross fat country, with its obscene heaps of wealth and its even more obscene obsession with creature comforts, they were unable to create an Underground as quiet, orderly, presentable, and—well—decent as London's? Because they were childish. So long as it was underground, out of sight, it didn't matter what it was like.

Fallow was able to get a seat at this hour, if a space on a narrow plastic bench could be called a seat. Before him were spread the usual grim riot of graffiti, the usual dark shabby people with their gray and brown clothes and their sneakers—except for a pair just across from him, a man and a boy. The man, who was probably in his forties, was short and plump. He was wearing a tasteful and expensive-looking gray chalk-stripe suit, a crisp white shirt, and, for an American, a discreet necktie. He also wore a pair of trim, well-made, well-shined black shoes. American men usually destroyed otherwise presentable ensembles by wearing bulky, big-soled, badly kept shoes. (They seldom saw their own feet, and so, being childish, scarcely bothered about what was on them.) Between his feet was an obviously expensive dark leather attaché case. He was leaning over to talk into the ear of the boy, who appeared to be eight or nine years old. The boy wore a navy school blazer, a white button-down shirt, and a striped necktie. Still talking to the boy, the man cast his eyes here and there and gestured with his right hand. Fallow figured that here was a man who worked on Wall Street who had had his son down to his office for a visit and was now giving him a ride on the subway and was pointing out the arcana of this rolling dungeon.

Absentmindedly he watched the two of them, as the train picked up speed and settled into the rocking lurching roaring momentum of the trip uptown. Fallow could see his own father. A poor little weed, a sad little fellow, was all he had turned out to be, a poor little weed who had had a son named Peter, a poor little failure who sat there amid his bohemian props in a tumbledown house in Canterbury . . . And what am I, thought Fallow, sitting in this rolling dungeon in this insane city in this lunatic country? Longing for a drink, longing for a drink . . . Another swell of despair rolled over him . . . He looked down at his lapels. He could see them shining even in this miserable light. He had slid . . . below bohemian . . . The dread word popped into his head: seedy.

The subway stop at Lexington Avenue and Seventy-seventh Street was dangerously close to Leicester's. But that was no problem. Peter Fallow was no longer going to play that game. As he reached the top of the stairs and stepped onto the sidewalk in the twilight, he summoned the scene up into his mind, merely for the purpose of proving to himself his resolve and rejecting it. The old wood, the frosted-glass lamps, the lights from the well behind the bar and the way it lit up

the rows of bottles, the pubby crush of people, the roaring hearth of their voices
—their voices—*English voices* . . . Perhaps if he just had an orange juice and
ginger ale and fifteen minutes of English voices . . . *No!* He would be firm.

Now he was in front of Leicester's, which to the innocent passerby no doubt
looked like just another cozy East Side bistro or trattoria. Between the old-fashioned mullions of the panes he could see all the cozy faces clustered at the tables
by the windows, cozy happy white faces lit up by rosy amber lamps. That did it.
He needed solace and an orange juice and ginger ale and English voices.

As one enters Leicester's, from Lexington Avenue, one finds himself in a
room full of tables with red-checked cloths, in the bistro fashion. Along one wall
runs a big saloon bar with a brass foot rail. Off to one side is a smaller dining
room. In this room, under the window that looks out on Lexington Avenue, is a
table around which eight or ten people can be crammed, assuming they are
convivial. By unspoken custom this has become the English table, a kind of club
table where, in the afternoon and early evening, the Brits—members of the
London *bon ton* now living in New York—come and go, to have a few . . . and
hear English voices.

The voices! The hearth was already roaring as Fallow walked in.

"Hello, Peter!"

It was Grillo, the American, standing among the crowd at the bar. He was an
amusing fellow, and friendly, but Fallow had had enough of America for one day.
He smiled and sang out "Hello, Benny!" and headed straight for the side room.

Tony Moss was at the Table; and Caroline Heftshank; and Alex Britt-Withers, who owned Leicester's; and St. John Thomas, the museum director and (on
the QT) art dealer; and St. John's boyfriend, Billy Cortez, a Venezuelan who had
gone to Oxford and might as well have been English; and Rachel Lampwick, one
of Lord Lampwick's two remittance daughters in New York; and Nick Stopping,
the Marxist journalist—Stalinist was more like it—who lived chiefly on articles
flattering the rich in *House & Garden*, *Art & Antiques*, and *Connoisseur*. Judging
by the glasses and bottles, the Table had been in session for some time, and pretty
soon they would be looking for a fish, unless Alex Britt-Withers, the owner—but
no, Alex never forgave the tab.

Fallow sat down and announced that he was turning over a new leaf and
wanted only an orange juice with ginger ale. Tony Moss wanted to know if this
meant he had stopped drinking or stopped paying. Fallow didn't mind that, since
it came from Tony, whom he liked, and so he laughed and said that in fact
nobody's money was any good this evening since their generous host, Alex, was at
the Table. And Alex said, "Least of all yours, I suspect." Caroline Heftshank said
Alex had hurt Fallow's feelings, and Fallow said that was true and that under the
circumstances he was forced to change his mind. He told the waiter to bring him
a "vodka Southside." Everybody laughed, because this was an allusion to Asher
Herzfeld, an American, heir to the Herzfeld glass fortune, who had gotten into a
furious row with Alex last night because he couldn't get a table. Herzfeld had
always driven the waiters and the bartenders crazy by ordering the noxious American drink, the vodka Southside, which was made with mint, and then complaining that the mint wasn't fresh. That got the Table to telling Herzfeld stories.
St. John Thomas, in his flutiest voice, told how he had been to dinner at
Herzfeld's apartment on Fifth Avenue, and Herzfeld had insisted on introducing
the guests to his staff of four, which embarrassed the servants and annoyed the

guests. He was sure he had heard the young South American houseboy say, "Well, then, why don't we all go have dinner at my place," which probably would have made for a more amusing evening, in St. John's opinion. "Well, would it or wouldn't it?" asked Billy Cortez, with a hint of genuine reproach. "I'm sure you've taken him up on it since then. A pimply little Puerto Rican, by the way." "Not Puerto Rican," said St. John, "Peruvian. And not pimply." Now the Table settled in for the staple topic, which was the domestic manners of the Americans. The Americans, with their perverted sense of guilt, were forever introducing guests to servants, especially "people like Herzfeld," said Rachel Lampwick. Then they talked about the wives, the American wives, who exercised tyrannical control over their husbands. Nick Stopping said he had discovered why American businessmen in New York took such long lunch hours. It was the only time they could get away from their wives to have sex. He was going to do a piece called "Sex at Noon" for *Vanity Fair*. Sure enough, the waiter brought Fallow a vodka Southside, and, amid much gaiety and toasting and complaining to Alex about the condition of the mint, he drank it and ordered another. It was actually very tasty. Alex left the Table to see how things were going in the big room, and Johnny Robertson, the art critic, arrived and told a funny story about an American who insisted on calling the Italian foreign minister and his wife by their first names at the opening of the Tiepolo show last night, and Rachel Lampwick told about the American who was introduced to her father— "This is Lord Lampwick"—and said, "Hiya, Lloyd." But American university professors are all terribly hurt if one doesn't remember to call them Doctor, said St. John, and Caroline Heftshank wanted to know why Americans insist on putting return addresses on the face of the envelope, and Fallow ordered another vodka Southside, and Tony and Caroline said why didn't they order another bottle of wine. Fallow said he didn't mind the Yanks calling him by his first name, if only they wouldn't insist on condensing it to Pete. All the Yanks at *The City Light* called him Pete, and they called Nigel Stringfellow Nige, and they also wore bogus regimental neckties that leaped out in front of their shirts, so that every time he saw one of these screaming neckties it set up a stimulus-response bond and he cringed and braced himself for *Pete*. Nick Stopping said he had dinner the other night at the home of Stropp, the investment banker, on Park Avenue, and Stropp's four-year-old daughter, by his second wife, came into the dining room pulling a toy wagon, upon which was a fresh human turd—yes, a turd!—her own, one hoped, and she circled the table three times, and neither Stropp nor his wife did a thing but shake their heads and smile. This required no extended comment, since the Yanks' treacly indulgence of their children was well known, and Fallow ordered another vodka Southside and toasted the absent Asher Herzfeld, and they ordered drinks all around.

Now it began to dawn on Fallow that he had ordered twenty dollars' worth of drinks, which he was not about to pay for. As if bound together by Jung's collective unconscious, Fallow and St. John and Nick and Tony were aware that the hour of the fish had arrived. But which fish?

It was Tony, finally, who sang out: "Hello, Ed!" With the heartiest possible grin on his face, he began beckoning a tall figure toward the Table. He was an American, well dressed, quite handsome really, with aristocratic features and a face as fair, pink, lineless, and downy as a peach.

"Ed, I want you to meet Caroline Heftshank. Caroline, this is my good friend Ed Fiske."

Howjados all around, as Tony introduced the young American to the Table. Then Tony announced: "Ed is the Prince of Harlem."

"Oh, come on," said Mr. Ed Fiske.

"It's true!" said Tony. "Ed is the only person I know who can walk the length, the breadth, the width, the highways, the byways, the high life, the low dives, of Harlem whenever he wants, wherever he wants, any time, day or night, and be absolutely welcome."

"Tony, that's a terrible exaggeration," said Mr. Ed Fiske, blushing but also smiling in a way that indicated it wasn't an *outrageous* exaggeration. He sat down and was encouraged to order a drink, which he did.

"What *is* going on in Harlem, Ed?"

Blushing some more, Mr. Ed Fiske confessed to having been in Harlem that very afternoon. Mentioning no names, he told of an encounter with an individual from whom it was his delicate mission to insist upon the return of quite a lot of money, three hundred and fifty thousand dollars. He told the story haltingly and a bit incoherently, since he was careful not to stress the factor of color or to explain why so much money was involved—but the Brits hung on every word with rapt and beaming faces, as if he were the most brilliant raconteur they had come across in the New World. They chuckled, they laughed, they repeated the tag ends of his sentences, like a Gilbert and Sullivan chorus. Mr. Ed Fiske kept talking, gaining steadily in confidence and fluency. The drink had hit the spot. He unfurled his fanciest and choicest Harlem lore. What admiring British faces all around him! How they beamed! They did indeed appreciate the art of conversation! With casual largesse he ordered a round of drinks for the Table, and Fallow had another vodka Southside, and Mr. Ed Fiske told about a tall menacing man nicknamed Buck who wore a large gold earring, like a pirate.

The Brits had their drinks, and then one by one they slipped away, first Tony, then Caroline, then Rachel, then Johnny Robertson, then Nick Stopping. When Fallow said, softly, "Excuse me a moment," and got up, only St. John Thomas and Billy Cortez were left, and Billy was tugging on St. John's sleeve, because he now detected more than a little sincerity in the rapt look St. John was beaming toward this beautiful and apparently rich boy with the peach complexion.

Outside, on Lexington Avenue, Fallow wondered about the size of the bill that would be handed shortly to young Mr. Fiske. He grinned in the darkness, being blissfully high. It was bound to be close to two hundred dollars. He would no doubt pay it without a murmur, the poor fish.

The Yanks. Dear God.

Only the problem of dinner remained to be solved. Dinner at Leicester's, even without wine, was at least forty dollars per person. Fallow headed for the coin telephone on the corner. There was this Bob Bowles, the American magazine editor . . . It should work out . . . The skinny woman he lived with, Mona something, was very nearly unbearable, even when she wasn't talking. But everything in life had its price, didn't it?

He entered the booth and dropped a quarter in the slot. With luck he would be back inside of Leicester's within the hour, eating his favorite dish, the chicken paillard, which tasted especially good with red wine. He liked Vieux Galouches, a French wine that came in a bottle with an eccentric neck, the best.

8

THE CASE

Martin, the Irish detective, was at the wheel, and his partner, Goldberg, the Jewish detective, was in the passenger seat, and Kramer was in the back seat, sitting at just the right angle, it so happened, to see the speedometer. They were driving down the Major Deegan Expressway at a good Irish sixty-five miles an hour, heading for Harlem.

Martin's being Irish was very much on Kramer's mind at this moment. He had just figured out where he had first seen the man. It was soon after he joined the Homicide Bureau. He had been sent out to East 152nd Street, where a man had been shot to death in the back of an automobile. The automobile was a Cadillac Sedan DeVille. One of the rear doors was open, and there was a detective standing by it, a little fellow, no more than 150 pounds, with a thin neck, a skinny, slightly lopsided face, and the eyes of a Doberman pinscher. Detective Martin. Detective Martin gestured toward the open door with a sweep of his hand, like a headwaiter. Kramer looked in, and what he saw was horrible beyond anything the phrase "shot to death in the back of an automobile" had even begun to suggest to him. The victim was a fat man in a loud, checked jacket. He was sitting on the back seat with his hands on his legs, just above his knees, as if he were about to hitch up his pants to keep them from being stretched by his kneecaps. He appeared to be wearing a bright scarlet bib. Two-thirds of his head was gone. The rear window of the Cadillac looked as if someone had thrown a pizza up against it. The red bib was arterial blood, which had pumped out of the stalk of his head like a fountain. Kramer backed out of the car. "Shit!" he said. "Did you see that? How did they—I mean, *shit!*—it's all over the car!" To which Martin had said, "Yeah, musta ruined his whole fucking day." At first Kramer had taken this as a rebuke for his becoming unglued by the sight, but later he figured Martin wouldn't have had it any other way. What was the fun of introducing people to vintage Bronx mayhem if they didn't become unglued? After that, Kramer made a point of being as Irish as they come at the crime scenes.

Martin's partner, Goldberg, was twice his size, a real side of beef, with thick curly hair, a mustache that drooped slightly at the corners of the mouth, and a fat neck. There were Irishmen named Martin and Jews named Martin. There were Germans named Kramer and Jews named Kramer. But every Goldberg in the history of the world was a Jew, with the possible exception of this one. By now, being Martin's partner, he had probably turned Irish, too.

Martin, in the driver's seat, turned his head slightly to talk to Kramer in the back seat. "I can't believe I'm actually driving to Harlem to listen to this asshole. If it was a wiretap, that I could believe. How the hell did he get to Weiss?"

"I don't know," said Kramer. He said it wearily, just to show that he was a good knockabout fellow who realized this mission was a jerk-off. In fact, he was still sailing on the verdict that had come in last night. Herbert 92X had gone down. Shelly Thomas had popped up, glorious as the sun. "Apparently Bacon called Joseph Leonard. You know Leonard? The black assemblyman?"

Kramer's radar told him that *black* was too delicate, too refined, too trendy-liberal a designation for a conversation with Martin and Goldberg, but he didn't want to try out anything else.

"Yeah, I know him," said Martin. "He's a piece a work, too."

"Well, I'm only guessing," said Kramer, "but Weiss has an election coming up in November, and if Leonard wants a favor, Weiss'll do him a favor. He thinks he needs black support. This Puerto Rican, Santiago, is running against him in the primary."

Goldberg snorted. "I love the word they use, *support*. Like they think there's some organization out there. That's a fucking laugh. In the Bronx they couldn't organize a cup a coffee. Bedford-Stuyvesant, the same thing. I've worked the Bronx, Bedford-Stuyvesant, and Harlem. In Harlem they're more sophisticated. In Harlem if you bring some asshole in and you tell him, 'Look, there's two ways we can do this, the easy way and the hard way, it's up to you,' at least they know what you're talking about. In the Bronx or Bed-Stuy, fuhgedaboudit. Bed-Stuy's the worst. In Bed-Stuy you just might as well start rolling in the dirt from the git-go. Right, Marty?"

"Yeah," said Martin, without enthusiasm. Goldberg had used no designation at all, other than *they*. Martin didn't seem to want to get into a discussion of cop philosophy in the first place. "So Bacon calls Leonard, and Leonard calls Weiss," said Martin. "And then what?"

"This kid Lamb, his mother works for Bacon, or she used to work for Bacon," said Kramer. "She claims she has some information about what happened to her son, but she has a whole buncha parking tickets, and there's a scofflaw warrant out for her, and she's afraid to go to the police. So the deal is, Weiss quashes the warrant and works out a schedule whereby she can pay off the tickets, and she gives us the information, but it has to be in Bacon's presence."

"And Weiss agrees to this."

"Yep."

"Beautiful."

"Well, you know Weiss," said Kramer. "All he cares about is, he's Jewish and he's running for re-election in a county that's 70 percent black and Puerto Rican."

Goldberg said, "You ever run into Bacon before?"

"No."

"You better take off your watch before you go in there. Fucking guy don't lift a finger except to steal."

Martin said, "I was thinking about that, Davey. I can't see where's there's any money in this thing, but you can bet it's there somewhere." Then to Kramer: "You ever hear a the Open Gates Employment Coalition?"

"Sure."

"That's one a Bacon's operations. You know how they turn up at restaurants demanding jobs for minorities? You shoulda been at that fucking brawl up on Gun Hill Road. There wasn't a fucking white face working up there. So I don't know what kinda minorities they're talking about, unless a buncha bongos carrying lengths a pipe, you call that a minority."

Kramer wondered whether or not *bongos* could be interpreted as a racial epithet. He didn't want to be that Irish. "Well then, what's in it for them?"

"Money," said Martin. "If the manager said, 'Oh yeah, we need some extra hands, you can all have jobs,' they'd look at him like he had bugs on his eyeballs. They just take money to stay away. It's the same way with the Third World Anti-Defamation League. They're the ones that go downtown to Broadway and raise hell. That's one a Bacon's operations, too. He's a sweetheart."

"But the Open Gates Employment Coalition," said Kramer, "they actually get in fights."

"Pitched fucking battles," said Goldberg.

"If it's a scam, why would they do that? They could get killed."

"You have to see 'em," said Martin. "Those crazy fucks'll go brawling all day for nothing. So why wouldn't they do it if somebody pays 'em a few dollars?"

"Remember that one that swung on you with the pipe, Marty?"

"Remember him? I saw him in my fucking sleep. A big tall asshole with a gold earring hanging off his head, like this." Martin made a big O with his thumb and forefinger and put it under his right ear.

Kramer didn't know how much of this to believe. He had once read an article in *The Village Voice* describing Bacon as a "street socialist," a black political activist who had arrived at his own theories about the shackles of capitalism and the strategies required to give black people their due. Kramer had no interest in left-wing politics, and neither did his father. Yet in their house, when he was growing up, the word *socialist* had religious overtones. It was like *Zealot* and *Masada*. There was something Jewish about it. No matter how wrongheaded a socialist might be, no matter how cruel and vindictive, he possessed somewhere in his soul a spark of the light of God, of Yahweh. Maybe Bacon's operation was extortion, and maybe it wasn't. Looked at one way, the entire history of the labor movement was extortion. What was a strike but extortion backed up by real or implied threat of violence? The labor movement had a religious aura in Kramer's house, too. The unions were a Masada uprising against the worst of the *goyim*. His father was a would-be capitalist, a servant of capitalists in actual fact, who had never belonged to a labor union in his life and felt infinitely superior to those who did. Yet one night Senator Barry Goldwater had been on TV promoting a right-to-work bill, and his father had started growling and cursing in a way that would have made Joe Hill and the Wobblies look like labor mediators. Yes, the labor movement was truly religious, like Judaism itself. It was one of those things you believed in for all mankind and didn't care about for a second in your own life. It was funny about religion . . . His father wrapped it around himself like a cape

. . . This guy Bacon wrapped it around himself . . . Herbert wrapped it around himself . . . Herbert . . . All at once Kramer saw a way to talk about his triumph.

"It's funny about these guys and religion," he said to the two cops in the front seat. "I just got off a case, a guy called Herbert 92X." He didn't say, "I just won a case." He would work that in. "This guy . . ."

Martin and Goldberg probably didn't give a damn, either. But at least they would . . . comprehend . . .

He remained an animated raconteur all the way to Harlem.

Not a soul was in Reverend Bacon's great parlor office when the secretary led Kramer, Martin, and Goldberg in. Most conspicuously absent was Reverend Bacon himself. His big swivel chair rose up in suspenseful emptiness behind the desk.

The secretary showed the three of them to armchairs facing the desk, and then she left. Kramer looked out the bay window behind the swivel chair at the gloomy tree trunks in the garden. The trunks were mottled in patches of swamp yellow and rotting green. Then he looked at the ceiling coving and the plaster dental moldings and all the other architectural details that had proclaimed Millionaire eighty years ago. Martin and Goldberg were doing the same thing. Martin looked at Goldberg and twisted his lips upward on one side with the look that says, "This is a shuck."

A door opened, and a tall black man entered the room, looking like ten million dollars. He wore a black suit, tailored in a way that brought out the width of his shoulders and the trimness of his waist. The jacket had a two-button roll that revealed a gorgeous acre of white shirtfront. The starched collar was immaculate against the man's dark skin. He wore a white necktie with a black crisscross pattern, the sort of necktie that Anwar Sadat used to wear. Kramer felt rumpled just looking at him.

For an instant he debated whether or not he should rise from his chair, knowing what Martin and Goldberg would think of any gesture of respect. But he couldn't think of any way out of it. So he stood up. Martin waited a couple of moments, but then he stood up, too, and Goldberg followed suit. They looked at each other, and both of them shrugged their lips this time. Since Kramer was up first, the man walked toward him and held out his hand and said, "Reginald Bacon."

Kramer shook hands and said, "Lawrence Kramer, Bronx District Attorney's Office. Detective Martin. Detective Goldberg."

From the way Martin looked at Reverend Bacon's hand with his Doberman pinscher eyes, Kramer didn't know whether he was going to shake it or chew it. He finally shook it. He shook it for at least a fourth of a second, as if he had just picked up a chunk of creosote. Goldberg followed suit.

"Get you gentlemen some coffee?"

"No, thanks," said Kramer.

Martin gave Reverend Bacon a frozen stare and then shook his head from side to side twice, ve-ry slow-ly, successfully conveying the message "Not even if I was dying of thirst." Goldberg, the Jewish Shamrock, followed suit.

Reverend Bacon walked around behind the desk to his great chair, and they all sat down. He leaned back in the chair and looked at Kramer with an impassive expression for what seemed like a very long time and then said in a soft, low voice. "The district attorney explained to you Mrs. Lamb's situation?"

"My bureau chief did, yes."

"Your bureau chief?"

"Bernie Fitzgibbon. He's the chief of the Homicide Bureau."

"You're from the Homicide Bureau?"

"When a case is listed likely-to-die, they turn it over to the Homicide Bureau. Not always, but a lot of the time."

"You don't need to tell Mrs Lamb you're from the Homicide Bureau."

"I understand," said Kramer.

"I'd appreciate that."

"Where is Mrs. Lamb?"

"She's here. She's coming in a minute. But I want to tell you something before she comes in here. She is very upset. Her son is dying, and she knows that, and she don't know that . . . see . . . It's something she knows and something she don't want to know. You understand? And all this time, here she is, she's in trouble over a lot of parking tickets. She says to herself, 'I have got to be with my son, and suppose they arrest me over a lot of parking tickets' . . . See?"

"Well, she—she don't have to worry about that," said Kramer. In a room with three people who said *She don't*, he couldn't get a *doesn't* out of his mouth. "The district attorney is quashing the warrant. She's still gonna have to pay the tickets, but nobody's gonna arrest her."

"I told her that, but it's gonna help if you tell her."

"Oh, we're here to help, but I thought she had something to tell us." This was for the benefit of Martin and Goldberg, so they wouldn't think he was being a pushover.

Reverend Bacon paused again and stared at Kramer, then resumed, softly, as before. "That is true. She has something to tell you. But you ought to know about her and her son, Henry. Henry is . . . was . . . *was* . . . Lord, this is a tragedy. Henry is a fine young man . . . a fine young man, fine as you wanna meet . . . see . . . Goes to church, never been in trouble, about to graduate from high school, getting ready to go to college . . . a fine young man. And he already graduated from something tougher than Harvard University. He grew up in the projects, and he made it. He survived. He came out of it a fine young man. Henry Lamb is . . . *was!* . . . *the hope!* . . . see . . . the hope. And now somebody just come along and"—Whop! He slapped his hand down on the desktop—"run him down and don't even stop."

Because Martin and Goldberg were there, Kramer felt the need to quench the histrionics.

"That may well be, Reverend Bacon," he said, "but so far we don't have any evidence of a hit-and-run."

Reverend Bacon gave him his level gaze and then, for the first time, smiled. "You're going to have all the evidence you need. You're going to mee Henry Lamb's mother. I know her very well . . . see . . . and you can believe what she says. She's a member of my church. She's a hardworking woman, a good woman . . . see . . . a good woman. She's got a good job, down at the Municipal Building, in the Marriage Bureau. Don't take a nickel of welfare. A good woman with a good son." Then he pressed a button on his desk and leaned forward and said, "Miss Hadley, show Mrs Lamb in. Oh, one more thing. Her husband, Henry's father, was killed six years ago, shot to death, coming home one night, outside the project. Tried to resist a robber." Reverend Bacon looked at each of the three of them, nodding the whole time.

With this, Martin stood up and stared out the bay window. He stared so intently Kramer thought he must have spotted a burglary in progress, at the very least. Reverend Bacon looked at him, puzzled.

"What kind of trees are they?" Martin asked.

"Which ones, Marty?" asked Goldberg, and he stood up, too.

"Right there," said Martin, pointing.

Reverend Bacon swiveled around in his chair and looked out the window himself. "Those are sycamore trees," he said.

"Sycamores," said Martin, in the contemplative tone of a young naturalist in an arboriculture program. "Look at those trunks. They must go up fifty feet."

"Trying to reach the light," said Reverend Bacon, "trying to find the sun."

Behind Kramer a pair of huge oak doors opened, and the secretary, Miss Hadley, ushered in a trim black woman, no more than forty, perhaps younger. She wore a businesslike blue skirt and jacket and a white blouse. Her black hair was done in soft waves. She had a thin, almost delicate face and large eyes and the self-possessed look of a teacher or someone else used to meeting the public.

Reverend Bacon stood up and walked around the desk to meet her. Kramer stood up also—and understood Martin's and the Jewish Shamrock's sudden interest in the arboreal species. They didn't want to get trapped into having to stand when the woman came into the room. It had been bad enough having to get up for a hustler like Bacon. Doing it again for some woman from the projects who was part of his setup was taking this thing too far. This way they were already on their feet, studying the sycamore trees, when she came in the room.

"Gentlemen," said Reverend Bacon, "this is Mrs. Annie Lamb. This is the gentleman from the District Attorney's Office in the Bronx, Mr. Kramer. And, uh—"

"Detective Martin, and Detective Goldberg," said Kramer. "They're in charge of the investigation of your son's case."

Mrs. Lamb didn't step forward to shake hands and she didn't smile. She nodded ever so slightly. She seemed to be withholding judgment on the three of them.

Very much the shepherd, Reverend Bacon pulled up an armchair for her. Instead of returning to his big swivel chair, he sat on the edge of the desk with an athletic casualness.

Reverend Bacon said to Mrs. Lamb, "I was talking to Mr. Kramer here, and the parking tickets, they're taken care of." He looked at Kramer.

"Well, the warrant's been quashed," said Kramer. "There's no more warrant. Now there's just the tickets, and as far as we're concerned, we're not interested in the tickets, anyway."

Reverend Bacon looked at Mrs. Lamb and smiled and nodded his head a few times, as if to say, "Reverend Bacon delivers." She just looked at him and pursed her lips.

"Well, Mrs. Lamb," said Kramer, "Reverend Bacon tells us you have some information for us about what happened to your son."

Mrs. Lamb looked at Reverend Bacon. He nodded yes and said, "Go ahead. Tell Mr. Kramer what you told me."

She said, "My son was hit by a car, and the car didn't stop. It was a hit-and-run. But he got the license number, or he got part of it."

Her voice was businesslike.

"Wait a minute, Mrs. Lamb," said Kramer. "If you don't mind, start at the beginning. When did you first learn about this? When did you first know your son had been injured?"

"When he came home from the hospital with his wrist in this—uh—I don't know what you call it."

"A cast?"

"No, it wasn't a cast. It was more like a splint, only it looked like a big canvas glove."

"Well, anyway, he came home from the hospital with this wrist injury. When was that?"

"That was . . . three nights ago."

"What did he say had happened?"

"He didn't say much. He was in a lot of pain, and he wanted to go to bed. He said something about a car, but I thought he was riding in a car and they had an accident. Like I say, he didn't want to talk. I think they gave him something at the hospital, for the pain. He just wanted to go to bed. So I told him to go to bed."

"Did he say who he was with when it happened?"

"No. He wasn't with anybody. He was by himself."

"Then he wasn't in a car."

"No, he was walking."

"All right, go ahead. What happened next?"

"The next morning he felt real bad. He tried to lift his head, and he nearly passed out. He felt so bad I didn't go to work. I called in—I stayed home. That was when he told me a car hit him."

"How did he say it happened?"

"He was walking across Bruckner Boulevard, and this car hit him, and he fell on his wrist, and he must have hit his head, too, because he has a terrible concussion." At this point her composure broke. She closed her eyes, and they were full of tears when she opened them.

Kramer waited a moment. "Where on Bruckner Boulevard was this?"

"I don't know. When he tried to talk, it was too painful for him. He'd open his eyes and shut his eyes. He couldn't even sit up."

"But he was by himself, you said. What was he doing on Bruckner Boulevard?"

"I don't know. There's a takeout place up there, at 161st Street, the Texas Fried Chicken, and Henry, he likes these things they have there, the chicken nuggets, and so maybe he was going there, but I don't know."

"Where did the car hit him? Where on his body?"

"I don't know that, either. The hospital, maybe they can tell you that."

Reverend Bacon broke in: "The hospital, they fell down on the job. They didn't X-ray that young man's head. They didn't give him the CAT scan or the nuclear magnetic resonance or any of those other things. That young man comes in with a very serious injury to his head, and they treat his *wrist* and send him home."

"Well," said Kramer, "apparently they didn't know he'd been hit by a car." He turned to Martin. " 'S'at right?"

"The emergency-room report don't mention an automobile," said Martin.

"The boy had a serious injury to his head!" said Reverend Bacon. "He probably didn't know half of what he was saying. They're supposed to figure out those things."

"Well, let's don't get sidetracked on that," said Kramer.

"He got part of the license plate," said Mrs. Lamb.

"What'd he tell you?"

"He said it started with R. That was the first letter. The second letter was E or F or P or B or some letter like that. That was what it looked like."

"What state? New York?"

"What state? I don't know. I guess New York. He didn't say it was something else. And he told me the make."

"What was it?"

"A Mercedes."

"I see. What color?"

"I don't know. He didn't say."

"Four-door? Two-door?"

"I don't know."

"Did he say what the driver looked like?"

"He said there was a man and a woman in the car."

"A man was driving?"

"I guess so. I don't know."

"Any description of the man or the woman?"

"They were white."

"He said they were white? Anything else?"

"No, he just said they were white."

"That's all? He didn't say anything else about them or about the car?"

"No. He could hardly talk."

"How did he get to the hospital?"

"I don't know. He didn't tell me."

Kramer asked Martin, "Did they say at the hospital?"

"He was a walk-in."

"He couldn'ta walked from Bruckner Boulevard to Lincoln Hospital with a broken wrist."

"Walk-in don't mean he walked all the way there. It just means he walked in the emergency room. He wasn't carried in. The EMS didn't bring him. He didn't come in an ambulance."

Kramer's mind was already jumping ahead to trial preparation. All he could see were dead ends. He paused and then shook his head and said, to no one in particular: "That don't give us very much."

"Whaddaya mean?" said Bacon. For the first time there was a sharp tone in his voice. "You got the first letter on the license plate, and you got a line on the second letter, and you got the make of the car—how many Mercedeses with a license plate beginning with RE, RF, RB, or RP you think you gonna find?"

"There's no telling," said Kramer. "Detective Martin and Detective Goldberg will run that down. But what we need is a witness. Without a witness there's no case here yet."

"No case?" said Reverend Bacon. "You got a case and a half seems to me. You got a young man, an outstanding young man, at death's door. You got a car and a license plate. How much case you need?"

"Look," said Kramer, hoping that an ultra-patient, slightly condescending tone would take care of the implied rebuke. "Let me explain something to you. Let's assume we identify the car tomorrow. Okay? Let's assume the car is registered in the state of New York, and there's only one Mercedes with a license number that begins with R. Now we've got a car. But we got no driver."

"Yeah, but you can—"

"Just because somebody owns a car doesn't mean"—as soon as it slipped out, Kramer hoped the *doesn't* would blow by undetected—"he was driving it at a particular time."

"But you can question that man."

"That's true, and we would. But unless he says, 'Sure, I was involved in such-and-such a hit-and-run accident,' we're back where we started."

Reverend Bacon shook his head. "I don't see that."

"The problem is, we don't have a witness. We not only don't have anybody to tell us where this thing happened, we don't even have anybody who can tell us he was hit by any car at all."

"You got Henry Lamb himself!"

Kramer raised his hands from his lap and shrugged gently, so as not to over-emphasize the fact that Mrs. Lamb's son would probably never be able to bear witness to anything again.

"You got what he told his mother. He told her himself."

"It gives us a lead, but it's hearsay."

"It's what he told his *mother*."

"You may accept it as the truth, and I may accept it as the truth, but it's not admissible in a court of law."

"That don't make sense to me."

"Well, that's the law. But in all candor I ought to bring out something else. Apparently when he came into the emergency room three nights ago, he didn't say anything about being hit by a car. That don't help matters any." *Don't*. He got it right that time.

"He had a concussion . . . and a broken wrist . . . Probably a lot of things he didn't say."

"Well, was he thinking any more clearly the next morning? You could make that argument, too."

"*Who's* making that argument?" said Reverend Bacon. "*You're* making that argument?"

"I'm not making any argument. I'm just trying to show you that without a witness there's a lot of problems."

"Well, you can find the car, can't you? You can interrogate the owner. You can check that car for evidence, can't you?"

"Sure," said Kramer. "As I told you, they're gonna run that down." He nodded toward Martin and Goldberg. "They'll try to find witnesses, too. But I don't think a car would yield much evidence. If a car hit him, it must've grazed him. He has some bruises, but he don't have the kind of bodily injuries you'd have from being really *hit* by a car."

"Say *if* a car hit him?"

"This case is fulla ifs, Reverend Bacon. If we find a car and an owner, and if the owner says, 'Yeah, I hit this young man the other night, and I didn't stop, and I didn't report it,' then we got a case. Otherwise, we got a lot of problems."

"Unh-hunh," said Reverend Bacon. "So it might be you can't spend a whole lot a time on this case, being as it has so many problems?"

"That's not true. This case will get as much attention as any other case."

"You say be candid. Well, I'm going to be candid. Henry Lamb is not a prominent citizen, and he's not the son of a prominent citizen, but he's a fine young man all the same . . . see . . . He's about to graduate from high school. He didn't drop out. He was—he's thinking about going to college. Never been in trouble. But he's from the Edgar Allan Poe projects. The Edgar Allan Poe projects. He's a young black man from the projects. Now, let's turn this thing around for a minute. Suppose Henry Lamb was a young white man and he lived on Park Avenue, and he was about to go to Yale, and he was struck down on Park Avenue by a black man and a black woman in a . . . a . . . Pontiac Firebird instead of a Mercedes . . . see . . . And that boy told his mother what Henry Lamb told his mother. You mean to tell me you wouldn't *have a case?* Instead of talking about problems, you'd be turning that information inside out and counting the stitches."

Martin came rumbling to life. "We'd do the same thing we're doing right now. We been trying to find Mrs. Lamb here for two days. When did we find out about a license number? You heard it. I've worked Park Avenue and I've worked Bruckner Boulevard. It don't make any difference."

Martin's voice was so calm and definite, and his stare was so implacable, so mule-like, so stone Irish, it seemed to jolt Reverend Bacon for a moment. He tried to outstare the little Irishman, without success. Then he smiled slightly and said, "You can tell me that, because I'm a minister, and I want to believe that justice is blind . . . see . . . I want to believe it. But you best not be going out on the streets of Harlem and the Bronx trying to tell people that. You best not be informing them about these blessings, because they already know the truth. They discover it the hard way."

"I'm on the streets of the Bronx every day," said Martin, "and I'll tell anybody who wants to know."

"Unh-hunh," said Reverend Bacon. "We have an organization, All People's Solidarity. We survey the communities, and the people come to us, and I can tell you that the people are not getting your message. They are getting another message."

"I been in one a your surveys," said Martin.

"You been in what?"

"One a your surveys. Up on Gun Hill Road."

"Yeah, well, I don't know what you're talking about."

"It was on the streets of the Bronx," said Martin.

"Anyway," said Kramer, looking at Mrs. Lamb, "thank you for your information. And I hope you'll have some good news about your son. We'll check out that license number. In the meantime, if you hear about anyone who was with your son the other night, or saw anything, you let us know, okay?"

"Unh-hunh," she said, striking the same dubious note as she had at the outset. "Thank you."

Martin was still staring at Reverend Bacon with his Doberman pinscher eyes.

So Kramer turned to Goldberg and said, "You have a card you can give Mrs. Lamb, with a telephone number?"

Goldberg fished around in an inside pocket and handed her a card. She took it without looking at it.

Reverend Bacon stood up. "You don't have to give me your card," he said to Goldberg. "I know you . . . see . . . I'm going to *call* you. I'm going to be *on* your case. I want to see something done. All People's Solidarity wants to see something done. And something *will* be done . . . see . . . So one thing you can count on: you will hear from *me*."

"Anytime," said Martin. "Anytime you like."

His lips were parted ever so slightly, with the suggestion of a smile at the corners. It reminded Kramer of the expression, the Smirking Fang, that boys wore at the beginning of a playground brawl.

Kramer started walking out, saying his goodbyes over his shoulder as he went, hoping that would coax Battling Martin and the Jewish Shamrock out of the room.

On the drive back up to the fortress, Martin said, "Christ, now I know why they send you guys to law school, Kramer. So you can learn how to keep a straight face." He said it good-naturedly, however.

"Well, hell, Marty," said Kramer, figuring that, having been a fellow soldier with him in the bullshit skirmish at Reverend Bacon's, he could go on a nick-name basis with the dauntless little Irish Donkey, "the kid's mother was sitting right there. Besides, maybe the license number will turn up something."

"You wanna bet on it?"

"It's a possibility."

"My ass, it's a possibility. You get hit by a fucking car, and you go to the hospital and you don't happen to mention that to them? And then you go home and you don't happen to mention it to your mother? And the next morning you're not feeling so hot, so you say, 'Oh, by the way, I got hit by a car'? Gedoudahere. That poor bastard took a beating, but it wasn't from anything he wanted to tell anybody about."

"Oh, I don't doubt that. See if there's a sheet on him, will you?"

"You know," said Goldberg, "I feel sorry for those people. They sit there saying the kid don't have a record, like that's a real fucking accomplishment. And in the projects, that's what it is. Just not having a record! That's something special. I feel sorry for her."

And a little of the Jew oozes out of the Jewish Shamrock, thought Kramer.

But then Martin took up the refrain. "A woman like that, she shouldn't even be living in the project, f'r Chrissake. She was all right. She was straight. Now I remember that case when her husband got killed. The guy was a working stiff who had heart. Stood up to some lowlife, and the fucking guy shot him right in the mouth. She works, don't take welfare, sends the kid to church, keeps him in school—she's all right. No telling what the kid got himself involved in, but she's all right. Halfa these people, you know, something happens, and you talk to them, and they spend so much time blaming the fucking world for what happened, you can't halfway find out what the fuck happened in the first place. But this one, she was straight. Too bad she's stuck in the fucking project, but you know"—he looked at Kramer when he said this— "there's a lotta decent people in the projects, people that show up for work."

Goldberg nodded sagely and said, "You'd never know it now, but that's what the fucking places were built for, working people. That was the whole idea, low-cost housing for working people. And now you find somebody in'eh who goes to work and tries to do the right thing, it breaks your fucking heart."

Then it dawned on Kramer. The cops weren't all that much different from the assistant D.A.'s. It was the muck factor. The cops got tired of packing blacks and Latins off to jail all day, too. It was even worse for them, because they had to dive deeper into the muck to do it. The only thing that made it *constructive* was the idea that they were doing it *for* somebody—for *the decent people*. So they opened their eyes, and now they were attuned to all the good people with colored skin . . . who rose to the top . . . during all this relentless stirring of the muck . . .

You couldn't exactly call it enlightenment, thought Kramer, but it was a fucking start.

9

SOME BRIT NAMED FALLOW

THIS TIME the explosion of the telephone threw his heart into tachycardia, and each contraction forced the blood through his head with such pressure—a stroke! —he was going to have a stroke!—lying here alone in his high-rise American hovel!—a stroke! The panic roused the beast. The beast came straight to the surface and showed its snout.

Fallow opened one eye and saw the telephone lying in a brown Streptolon nest. He was dizzy, and he hadn't even lifted his head. Great curds of eye trash swam in front of his face. The pounding blood was breaking up the mercury yolk into curds, and the curds were coming out of his eye. The telephone exploded again. He closed his eye. The snout of the beast was right behind his eyelid. That *pedophile* business—

And last night had started off as such an ordinary evening!

Having less than forty dollars to get him through the next three days, he had done the usual. He had called up a Yank. He had called up Gil Archer, the literary agent, who was married to a woman whose name Fallow could never remember. He had suggested that they meet for dinner at Leicester's, leaving the impression he would be bringing a girl along himself. Archer arrived with his wife, whereas he arrived alone. Naturally, under the circumstances, Archer, ever the bland polite Yank, picked up the bill. Such a quiet evening; such an early evening; such a routine evening for an Englishman in New York, a dull dinner paid for by a Yank; he really was thinking about getting up and going home. And then Caroline Heftshank and this artist friend of hers, an Italian, Filippo Chirazzi, came in, and they stopped by the table and sat down, and Archer asked them if they would like something to drink, and he said why didn't they get another bottle of wine, and so Archer ordered another bottle of wine, and they drank that, and then they drank another one and another one, and now Leicester's was packed and roaring with all the usual faces, and Alex Britt-Withers sent over one of his waiters to offer a round of drinks on the house, which made Archer feel socially successful, recognized-by-the-owner sort of thing—the Yanks were very keen on that—and Caroline Heftshank kept hugging her handsome young Italian, Chirazzi, who was posing with his pretty profile up in the air, as if one were to feel privileged just to be breathing the same air as himself. St. John came over from another table to admire young Signor Chirazzi, much to Billy Cortez's displeasure, and Signor Chirazzi told St. John it was necessary for a painter to paint with "the eyes of a child," and St. John said that he himself tried to view the world with the eyes of a child, to which Billy Cortez said, "He said child, St. John, not pedophile." Signor Chirazzi posed some more, with his long neck and Valentino nose rising up from out of a ridiculous electric-blue Punk shirt with a three-quarter-inch collar and a pink glitter necktie, and so Fallow said it was more Post-modern for a painter to have the eyes of a pedophile than the eyes of a child, and what did Signor Chirazzi think? Caroline, who was quite drunk, told him not to be stupid, said it quite sharply, and Fallow reared back, meaning only to strike a pose mocking the young painter, but lost his balance and fell on the floor. Much laughter. When he got up, he was dizzy, and he held on to Caroline, just to steady himself, but young Signor Chirazzi took offense, from the depths of his Italian manly honor, and tried to shove Fallow, and both Fallow and Caroline now went down, and Chirazzi tried to jump on Fallow, and St. John, for whatever reason, now jumped on the pretty Italian, and Billy Cortez was screaming, and Fallow struggled up, carrying an enormous weight, and Britt-Withers was over him, yelling, "For God's sake!" and then a whole bunch of people were on top of him, and they all went crashing out the front door onto the sidewalk on Lexington Avenue—

The telephone exploded again, and Fallow was terrified at what he might hear if he picked up the receiver. He could remember nothing from the time they all went crashing out onto the sidewalk until this moment. He swung his feet out of the bed, and they were all still roaring and boiling inside his skull, and his whole body felt sore. He crawled across the carpet to the exploding telephone and lay down beside it. The carpet felt dry, metallic, dusty, filthy against his cheek.

"Hello?"

"Aaaayyy, Pete! How wahya!"

It was a cheery voice, a Yank voice, a New York voice, a particularly crude sort of New York voice. Fallow found this Yank voice even more jarring than the Pete. Well, at least it wasn't The City Light. Nobody at The City Light would be calling him with such a cheery voice.

"Who is it?" said Fallow. His own voice was an animal in a hole.

"Jeezus, Pete, you sound terrific. Any pulse? Hey. This is Al Vogel."

The news made him close his eyes again. Vogel was one of those typical Yank celebrities who, to an Englishman reading about them in London, seemed so colorful, irrepressible, and morally admirable. In person, in New York, they always turned out the same way. They were Yanks; which is to say, crude bores. Vogel was well known in England as an American lawyer whose specialty was unpopular political causes. He defended radicals and pacifists, much the way Charles Garry, William Kunstler, and Mark Lane had. Unpopular, of course, merely meant unpopular with ordinary people. Vogel's defendants were certainly popular enough with the press and intellectuals in the 1960s and 1970s, especially in Europe, where anyone defended by Albert Vogel grew wings, a halo, a toga, and a torch. Few of these latter-day saints had any money, however, and Fallow often wondered how Vogel made a living, especially since the 1980s had not been kind to him. In the 1980s not even the press and intellectuals had any patience for the sort of irascible, seething, foul-humored, misery-loving, popped-vein clientele he specialized in. Lately Fallow had been running into the great defender at the most extraordinary parties. Vogel would go to the opening of a parking lot (and Fallow would say hello to him there).

"Oh, hi-i-i-i," said Fallow in what ended up as a moan.

"I called your office first, Pete, and they said they hadn't seen you."

Not good, thought Fallow. He wondered when, if, why, where he had given Vogel his home telephone number.

"You still there, Pete?"

"Ummmmmmmm." Fallow had his eyes closed. He had no sense of up or down. "It's all right. I'm working at home today."

"I've got something I want to talk to you about, Pete. I think there's a hell of a story in it."

"Ummmm."

"Yeah, only I'd just as soon not go into it over the telephone. I tell you what. Whyn't you come have lunch with me. I'll meet you at the Regent's Park at one o'clock."

"Ummmm. I don't know, Al. The Regent's Park. Where is that?"

"On Central Park South, near the New York Athletic Club."

"Ummmmm."

Fallow was torn between two profound instincts. On the one hand, the thought of getting off the floor, of shifting the mercury yolk for a second time, for no other reason than to listen to an American bore and has-been for an hour or two . . . On the other hand, a free meal at a restaurant. The pterodactyl and the brontosaurus were locked in mortal combat on the cliff over the Lost Continent.

The free meal won, as it had so often in the past.

"All right, Al, I'll see you at one o'clock. Where is this place again?"

"On Central Park South, Pete, right near the New York A.C. It's a nice place. You can look at the park. You can look at a statue of José Martí on a horse."

Fallow said goodbye and struggled to his feet, and the yolk was yawing this way and that way, and he stubbed his toe on the metal frame of the bed. The pain was terrific, but it focused his central nervous system. He took a shower in the dark. The plastic shower curtain was suffocating. When he closed his eyes he had the feeling he was keeling over. From time to time he had to hold on to the shower head.

The Regent's Park was the sort of New York restaurant favored by married men having affairs with young women. It was grand, glossy, and solemn, with a great deal of marble inside and out, a colossal stiff neck whose *hauteur* appealed mainly to people staying at the nearby Ritz-Carlton, Park Lane, St. Moritz, and Plaza Hotels. In the history of New York no conversation had ever begun with: "I was having lunch at the Regent's Park the other day and . . ."

True to his word, Albert Vogel had secured a table beside the great window. This was not a hard ticket at the Regent's Park. Nevertheless, there it was, the park, in its springtime glory. And there was the statue of José Martí, which Vogel had also promised. Martí's horse was rearing up, and the great Cuban revolutionary was leaning perilously to the right in his saddle. Fallow averted his eyes. An unsteady park statue was too much to contend with.

Vogel was in his usual hearty mood. Fallow watched his lips move without hearing a word. The blood drained from Fallow's face, and then his chest and arms. His hide turned cold. Then a million little scalding hot minnows tried to escape from his arteries and reach the surface. Perspiration broke out on his forehead. He wondered if he was dying. This was the way heart attacks began. He had read that. He wondered if Vogel knew about coronary resuscitation. Vogel looked like someone's grandmother. His hair was white, not a gray-white, but a silky pure white. He was short and pudgy. In his palmy days he had been pudgy, too, but he had looked "scrappy," as the Yanks liked to say. Now his skin was pinkish and delicate. His hands were tiny and had ropy old veins leading up to the knuckles. A cheery old woman.

"Pete," said Vogel, "what'll you have to drink?"

"Not a thing," said Fallow, rather overemphatically. Then to the waiter: "Could I have some water."

"I want a margarita on the rocks," said Vogel. "Sure you won't change your mind, Pete?"

Fallow shook his head. That was a mistake. A poisonous hammering began inside his skull.

"Just one to turn the motor over?"

"No, no."

Vogel put his elbows on the table and leaned forward and began scanning the room, and then his eyes fastened on a table slightly behind him. At the table were a man in a gray business suit and a girl in her late teens with long, straight, very showy blond hair.

"You see that girl?" said Vogel. "I could swear that girl was on this committee, whatever they call it, at the University of Michigan."

"What committee?"

"This student group. They run the lecture program. I gave a lecture at the University of Michigan two nights ago."

So what? thought Fallow. Vogel looked over his shoulder again.

"No, it's not her. But, Christ, it sure looks like her. These goddamned girls at these colleges—you wanna know why people go out on the lecture circuit in this country?"

No, thought Fallow.

"Okay, for the money. But not counting that. You wanna know why?"

The Yanks constantly repeated introductory questions.

"These goddamned girls." Vogel shook his head and stared off distractedly for a moment, as if stunned by the very thought. "I swear to God, Pete, you have to hold yourself back. Otherwise, you'd feel so fucking guilty. These girls—today—well, when I was growing up, the big deal was that when you went to college, you could drink when you felt like it. Okay? These girls, they go to college so they can get laid when they feel like it. And who do they want? This is the part that's really pathetic. Do they want nice-looking healthy boys their own age? No. You wanna know who? They want . . . Authority . . . Power . . . Fame . . . Prestige . . . They wanna get laid by the teachers! The teachers go crazy at these places now. You know, when the Movement was going strong, one of the things we tried to do on the campuses was to break down that wall of formality between the faculty and the students, because it was nothing but an instrument of control. But now, Jesus Christ, I wonder. I guess they all want to get laid by their fathers, if you believe Freud, which I don't. You know, this is one thing the women's movement has made no headway with. When a woman reaches forty, her problems are just as big now as they ever were—and a guy like me has never had it so good. I'm not so old, but, f'r Chrissake, I've got gray hair—"

White, thought Fallow, like an old woman's.

"—and it doesn't make any difference whatsoever. A little touch of celebrity and they fall over. They just *fall over.* I'm not bragging, because it's so pathetic. And these goddamned girls, each one is more of a knockout than the last one. I'd like to give them a lecture on *that* subject, but they probably wouldn't know what I was talking about. They have no frame of reference, about anything. The lecture I gave the night before last was on student commitment in the 1980s."

"I was dying to know," said Fallow in the back of his throat, without moving his lips.

"Pardon?"

The Yanks said *pardon?* instead of *what?*

"Nothing."

"I told them what it was like on the campuses fifteen years ago." His face clouded over. "But I don't know . . . fifteen years ago, fifty years ago, a hundred years ago . . . they have no frame of reference. It's all so remote to them. Ten years ago . . . *five* years ago . . . Five years ago was before Walkman earphones. They can't imagine that."

Fallow stopped listening. There was no way Vogel could be deflected from his course. He was irony-proof. Fallow glanced at the girl with the long yellow hair. Thrashing through the restaurant. Caroline Heftshank and the frightened look on her face. Had he done something just before they all went crashing out the door? Whatever—she deserved it—but what was it? Vogel's lips were moving. He was going through his entire lecture. Fallow's eyelids dropped shut. The beast broke the surface and thrashed about and eyed him. He eyed him straight down his filthy snout. Now the beast had him. He couldn't move.

". . . Managua?" asked Vogel.

"What?"

"You ever been there?" asked Vogel.

Fallow shook his head. The yawing motion made him nauseous.

"You oughta go. Every journalist oughta go. It's about the size of . . . oh, I don't know, East Hampton. If it's that big. Would you like to go there? It would be easy enough to set it up for you."

Fallow didn't want to shake his head again. "Is that the story you wanted to tell me about?"

Vogel paused a moment, as if weighing the remark for sarcastic content.

"No," he said, "but it's not a bad idea. About one-fiftieth of everything that oughta be said about Nicaragua gets printed in this country. No, what I was talking about is something that happened in the Bronx four days ago. It might as well be Nicaragua, if you happen to live there. Anyway, you know who Reverend Bacon is, don't you?"

"Yes. I think so."

"He's a—well, he's a—you've read about him or seen him on TV, haven't you?"

"Yes."

Vogel laughed. "You wanna know where I first met him? In this gigantic duplex apartment on Park Avenue, Peggy Fryskamp's apartment, back when she was interested in the Geronimo Brotherhood. She gave a fund-raising party there. This must've been the late sixties, early seventies. There was this guy Flying Deer. He gave the soul talk, we used to call it. There was always the soul talk and the money talk. Anyway, he gave the soul talk, the spiritual talk. She didn't know the sonofabitch was loaded. She just thought it was Indian talk, the crazy way he sounded. Fifteen minutes later he threw up all over this eighty-thousand-dollar Duncan Phyfe piano Peggy had, all over the keys and the strings and the hammers and everything. You know those little felt hammers? Oh, it was outrageous. She never got over it. That jerk blew a good deal that night. And you wanna know who really gave him hell? Reverend Bacon. Yeah. He was getting ready to ask Peggy to support some of the things he had going, and when this Flying Deer threw his cookies all over the Duncan Phyfe, he knew he could say goodbye to Peggy Fryskamp. He started calling him Flying Beer. 'Flying *Deer*? Flying *Beer*, if I know anything about it!' Jesus, it was funny. But he wasn't trying to be funny. Bacon never tries to be funny. Anyway, he has this woman who works for him sometimes, Annie Lamb, from the Bronx. Annie Lamb lives in the Edgar Allan Poe project with this one son she has, Henry."

"She's black?" asked Fallow.

"Yeah, she's black. Practically everybody in the Poe projects is black or Puerto Rican. By law, incidentally, all these projects are supposed to be integrated." Vogel shrugged his eyebrows. "Anyway, this Annie Lamb is an unusual woman." Vogel recounted the history of Annie Lamb and her family, culminating in the hit-and-run Mercedes-Benz that had left her promising son, Henry, at death's door.

Unfortunate, thought Fallow, but where's the story?

As if anticipating that objection, Vogel said: "Now, there's two sides to this thing, and both of them have to do with what happens to a good kid like this if he has the misfortune of being black and growing up in the Bronx. I mean, here's a kid who did everything right. You talk about Henry Lamb, you're talking about the one percent who do exactly what the system tells them they're supposed to do. Okay? So what happens? First, the hospital treats the kid for . . . *a broken wrist!* If this had been a middle-class white kid, they'd've gone over him with the X-ray, the CAT scan, the nuclear magnetic resonance, everything there is. Second, the police and the D.A. won't move on the case. This is what really infuriates the kid's mother. Here's a hit-and-run, they've got part of the license number and the make of the car, and they're doing zip about it."

"Why?"

"Well, basically, it's just some kid in the South Bronx who gets hit by a car, as far as they're concerned. They can't be bothered. But what they're saying is, there were no witnesses, except for the victim himself, and he's in a terminal coma, and so they wouldn't have a case even if they found the car and the driver. Now, suppose this were your son. He's provided the information, but they're not going to use it because technically it's hearsay."

The whole thing made Fallow's head hurt. He couldn't imaging having a son, and certainly not in some council flats in the Bronx section of New York City in America.

"It's an unfortunate situation," said Fallow, "but I'm not altogether sure there's a story in it."

"Well, there's gonna be a story in it very shortly for *somebody*, Pete," said Vogel. "The community is up in arms. They're about to explode. Reverend Bacon is organizing a protest demonstration."

"What exactly are they exploding over?"

"They're tired of being treated as if human life in the South Bronx means nothing! And I'm telling you, when Bacon gets hold of something, things happen. He's not Martin Luther King or Bishop Tutu. Okay? He's not gonna win any Nobel Prize. He's got his own way of doing things, and sometimes it might not stand close scrutiny. But that's one reason he's effective. He's what Hobsbawm called a primitive revolutionary. Hobsbawm was a Brit, right?"

"He still is."

"I thought he was. He had this theory about primitive revolutionaries. There are certain natural leaders of the underclasses, and the power structure interprets what they do as crime—they may even sincerely interpret it that way—but what that person is, is a revolutionary. And that's what Bacon is. I admire him. And I feel sorry for these people. Anyway, I think there's a hell of a story here, quite aside from the philosophical considerations."

Fallow closed his eyes. He saw the snout of the beast, lit up by soft bistro lights. Then the icy chill. He opened his eyes. Vogel was staring at him with his cheery old pink nanny's grin. This ridiculous country.

"Look, Pete, the worst you'll get out of this is a good human-interest story. And if things break right, you'll be on to something big. I can get you an interview with Annie Lamb. I can get you an interview with Reverend Bacon. I can take you right into the intensive-care unit, where the kid is. I mean, he's in a coma, but you can see him."

Fallow tried to conceive of transferring the mercury egg and his bilious innards to the Bronx. He could scarcely imagine surviving the trip. From his viewpoint the Bronx was like the Arctic. It was somewhere to the north, and people didn't go there.

"I don't know, Al. My specialty is supposed to be the high life." He attempted a smile.

"Supposed to be, Peter, supposed to be. They won't fire you if you come in with a hell of a good story from the low life."

The word *fire* was what did it. He closed his eyes. The snout was not there. Instead, he saw the Dead Mouse's face. He could see the Mouse looking toward his cubicle in the city room at this moment and finding it empty. Fear suffused his every cell, and he put his napkin to his forehead.

"Do you mind if I ask you something, Al?"

"Go ahead."

"What's your interest in all this?"

"None, if you're talking about material interest. Reverend Bacon called me and asked my advice, and I told him I'd try to help him out, that's all. I like him. I like what he's trying to do. I like the way he shakes up this fucking city. I'm on his side. I told him he should try to get this thing into the newspapers before he has the protest demonstration. That way he's gonna get more television coverage and everything else. I'm telling you the plain truth now. I thought of you because I figured maybe you could use an opportunity like this. This could be to your advantage and to the advantage of a lot of decent people who never get a fucking break in this city."

Fallow shuddered. Just what had Vogel heard about his situation? He didn't really want to know. He knew he was being used. At the same time, here was a piece of meat to throw to the Mouse.

"Well, maybe you're right."

"I know I'm right, Pete. This is gonna be a big story one way or the other. You might as well be the one to break it."

"You can take me to see these people?"

"Oh, sure. Don't worry about that. The only thing is, you can't sit on the story. Bacon is ready to go."

"Ummmm. Let me take down some of these names." Fallow reached into the side pocket of his jacket. Christ, he hadn't even picked up a notebook or a piece of paper before he left. From out of the pocket he brought a notice from Con Edison warning him that his gas and electricity were about to be cut off. He couldn't even write on it. It had print on both sides. Vogel watched all this and, without comment, produced a memorandum pad and handed it to him. Then he handed him a silver ballpoint pen. He repeated the names and details.

"I tell you what," said Fallow. "I'm going to call the city desk straightaway."

He got up and caromed off a chair at the next table, where an old woman in a Chanel-style suit was trying to lift a spoonful of sorrel soup to her mouth. She glared at him.

"Whaddaya want to eat?" said Vogel. "I'll order for you."

"Nothing. A bowl of tomato soup. Some chicken paillard."

"Some wine?"

"No. Well. Just a glass."

The coin telephone was in a vestibule across from the hatcheck room, where a pretty girl sat on a high stool reading a book. Her eyes peeked out from a sinister black ellipse carefully drawn around her eyelids. Fallow rang up Frank de Pietro, the city editor of *The City Light*. De Pietro was one of the few Americans in an important editorial position on the newspaper. They needed someone from New York as city editor. The other Englishmen who worked there, like Fallow himself, were acquainted with a single stretch of Manhattan from the trendy restaurants in TriBeCa on the south to the trendy restaurants in Yorkville, near Eighty-sixth Street, on the north. The rest of New York might as well have been Damascus.

"Yeah?" The voice of Frank de Pietro. His enthusiasm over having a call from Peter Fallow at a busy time of the day was imperceptible.

"Frank," said Fallow, "are you familiar with a place called the Edgar Allan Poe projects?"

"Yeah. Are you?"

Fallow didn't know which was more unpleasant, this Yank habit of saying *yeah* for *yes*, or the incredulity in the man's voice. Nevertheless, he plowed on, telling Albert Vogel's story with embellishments, where needed, and with no mention of Albert Vogel. He left the impression that he had already been in touch with Reverend Bacon and the victim's mother, and that his imminent appearance in the Bronx was awaited by one and all. De Pietro told him to go ahead and check it out. This he did with no particular enthusiasm, either. And yet Fallow felt his heart fill with a quite unexpected joy.

When he returned to the table, Vogel said, "Hey, how'd it go? Your soup's getting cold." The words barely made it out of his mouth, which was crammed full of food.

A large bowl of tomato soup and a glass of white wine were at Fallow's place. Vogel was busy working on a hideous-looking joint of veal.

"They like it, hunh?"

"Ummmmmm." Well, they don't despise it, thought Fallow. His nausea began withdrawing. The yolk grew smaller. A crisp exhilaration, not unlike that of an athlete entering the fray, stole into his nervous system. He felt . . . almost clean. It was the emotion, never commented upon by the poets, enjoyed by those who feel that, for once, they are earning their pay.

It was Kramer's turn to wear the beeper on his waistband for twelve hours. In the Homicide Bureau of the Bronx District Attorney's Office, somebody, some assistant district attorney, was on call at all times. The purpose was to have someone to go to crime scenes immediately, to interview witnesses before they vanished or lost the urge to talk about the mayhem. For those twelve hours an assistant D.A. was likely to get stuck with every piece a shit in the Bronx that involved a homicide, and it was a classic Bronx piece a shit that had brought Kramer here to this precinct house. A black detective sergeant named Gordon was standing near the booking desk giving him the details.

"They call the guy Pimp," said Gordon, "but he's not a pimp. He's a gambler, mainly, and he probably does some dealing in drugs, but he dresses like a pimp. You'll see him in a minute. He's back there in the locker room wearing some kind of trick suit with a double-breasted vest." Gordon shook his head. "He's sitting on the edge of a chair eating ribs, holding them like this"—he leaned forward and raised his hand in a dainty gesture—"so the sauce won't get on the suit. He had about forty suits, and when he tells you about those fucking suits, you'll think it was his fucking child that's missing."

The whole thing had happened because someone had stolen the forty suits. Oh, this was a real piece a shit. Waves and waves of childishness and pointless violence, and Kramer hadn't even heard the whole story yet.

The main room of the precinct was saturated with the dank and oddly sweet smell of rotting wood, caused by decades of steam radiators leaking onto the floors. Most of the floor had been replaced with concrete. The walls were painted Government Work Green except for an old battered tongue-and-groove wainscoting, three feet high, around the bottom. The building had thick walls and high ceilings, now overgrown with trays of fluorescent lights. Across the way Kramer could see the backs of the two patrolmen. Their hips were enormous with weaponry and paraphernalia, including flashlights, summons books, walkie-talkies, and handcuffs. One of them kept lifting his hands in explanatory gestures to two women and a man, local residents, whose faces said they didn't believe a word of it.

Gordon was telling Kramer: "So he's in this apartment, and there's four guys in there, and one of them is this André Potts, who he figures knows who took the suits, only André says he don't know nothing from nothing, and they're going back and forth, and finally André's had enough of this, and he gets up and walks out of the room. And so what would you do if some disrespectful sucker got up and turned his back on you while you're inquiring about your fucking forty suits? You'd shoot him in the back, right? So that's what Pimp did. He shot Mr. André Potts in the back three times with a .38."

"You got witnesses?" asked Kramer.

"Oh, we got 'em stacked up."

At that moment the beeper went off on Kramer's waistband.

"Can I use your phone?"

Gordon motioned toward an open door that led into the Detective Bureau, which was an office off the main room. Inside were three dismal Government Work Gray metal desks. At each desk sat a black man in his thirties or forties. Each had on Bronx street garb a bit too funky to be true. Kramer thought of how unusual it was to come across an entire bureau made up of black detectives. The one at the desk nearest the door wore a black thermal vest and a sleeveless black T-shirt that showed off his powerful arms.

Kramer reached toward the telephone on his desk and said, "Use your phone?"

"Hey, what the fuck, man!"

Kramer pulled his hand back.

"How long I gotta sit here chained up like a fucking animal?"

With that, the man raised his powerful left arm with a terrific clattering. There was a manacle on his wrist, and from the manacle a chain. The other end of the chain was manacled to the leg of the desk. Now the other two, at the other desks, had their arms up in the air, clattering and yammering. All three of them were chained to the desks.

"All I did was *see* the motherfucker whack that sucker, and he was the motherfucker that *whacked* that sucker, and I'm the one you got chained up like a fucking animal, and that motherfucker"—another terrific clatter as he gestured toward a room in the rear with his left hand—"he's sitting back there watching fucking TV and eating ribs."

Kramer looked to the back of the room, and sure enough, back there in a locker room was a figure sitting on the edge of a chair lit by the hectic flush of the television set and eating a length of barbecued rib of pork. And he was indeed leaning forward daintily. The sleeve of his jacket was tailored to show a lot of white cuff and gleaming cuff link.

Now all three were yammering. *Fucking ribs* . . . *fucking chains!* . . . *fucking TV!*

But of course! The witnesses. Once Kramer realized that, everything, chains and all, fell into place.

"Yeah, okay, okay," he said to the man in an impatient fashion, "I'll take care a you in a minute. I gotta make a phone call."

Fucking ribs! . . . *shee-uh!* . . . *fucking chains!*

Kramer called the office, and Gloria, Bernie Fitzgibbon's secretary, said Milt Lubell wanted to talk to him. Lubell was Abe Weiss's press secretary. Kramer barely knew Lubell; he couldn't remember talking to him more than four or five times. Gloria gave him Lubell's number.

Milt Lubell had worked on the old New York *Mirror* back when Walter Winchell still had his column. He had known the great man ever so slightly and had carried his breathless snap-brim way of talking onward into the last days of the twentieth century.

"Kramer," he said, "Kramer, Kramer, lemme see, Kramer. Yeah, yeah, yeah, okay, I got it. The case of Henry Lamb. Likely to die. What's it amount to?"

"It's a piece a shit," said Kramer.

"Well, I got a query from *The City Light*, some Brit named Fallow. Guy's got this accent. I thought I was listening to Channel 13. Anyway, he's reading me a statement from Reverend Bacon about the case of Henry Lamb. That's all I need. The words of Reverend Reginald Bacon in a British accent. You know Bacon?"

"Yeah," said Kramer. "I interviewed Henry Lamb's mother in Bacon's office."

"This guy has something from her, too, but mainly it's Bacon. Lemme see, lemme see, lemme see. It says, uh . . . blah blah blah, blah blah blah . . . human life in the Bronx . . . malfeasance . . . white middle class . . . blah blah blah . . . nuclear magnetic resonance . . . Goes on about the nuclear magnetic resonance. There's maybe two a the fucking machines in the whole country, I think . . . blah blah blah . . . Lemme see, here it is. He accuses the district attorney of dragging his feet. We won't go to the trouble of proceeding with the case because the kid is a black youth from the Poe projects and it's too much trouble."

"That's bullshit."

"Well, I know that, and you know that, but I gotta call this Brit back and tell him something."

A tremendous clatter. "How long I gotta sit here in these chains, man!" The man with the big arms was erupting again. "This is against the law!"

"Hey!" said Kramer, genuinely annoyed. "You wanna get outta here, you'll knock it off. I can't fucking hear myself talk." Then to Lubell: "Sorry, I'm over at the precinct." He wrapped his hand around his mouth and the mouthpiece of the telephone and said in a low voice: "They got three homicide witnesses over here chained to the fucking desk legs in the Detective Bureau, and they're going bananas." He enjoyed the low-level macho jolt of trotting out this little war story for Lubell, even though he didn't even know the man.

"The desk legs!" said Lubell, with an appreciative note. "Jesus Christ, that I never heard of."

"Anyway," said Kramer, "where was I? Okay, we got a Mercedes-Benz with a license plate beginning with R. For a start, we don't even know if we're talking about a New York State license plate. Okay? That's for a start. But let's suppose we are. There's 2,500 Mercedes registered in New York State with license plates starting with R. Okay, now, the second letter supposedly looks like an E or an F, or maybe a P or a B or an R, some letter with a vertical on the left and some horizontals going off of it. Suppose we go with that. We're still talking about almost five hundred cars. So whaddaya do? Go after five hundred cars? If you have a witness who can tell you the boy was hit by such a car, maybe you do. But there's no witness, except for the kid, and he's in a coma and isn't coming out. We got no information about a driver. All we have is two people in a car, two white people, a man and a woman, and on top of that the kid's story don't add up in the first place."

"Well, whadda I say? The investigation is continuing?"

"Yeah. The investigation *is* continuing. But unless Martin finds a witness, there's no case here. Even if the kid was hit by a car, it probably wasn't the kind of collision that would yield forensic evidence from the car, because the kid don't have the bodily injuries that are consistent with such a collision—I mean, f'r Chrissake, there are so many fucking ifs in this cockamamie story. If you ask me, it's a piece a shit. The kid seems like a decent sort, and so does his mother, but between you and me, I think he got in some kind of scrape and made up this bullshit story to tell his mother."

"Well then, why would he dream up part of a license plate? Why wouldn't he say he didn't get the number?"

"How do I know? Why does anybody do anything that they do in this country? You think this guy, this reporter, is actually gonna write something?"

"I don't know. I'm just gonna say that naturally we're following the thing closely."

"Anybody else called you about it?"

"Naw. It sounds like Bacon reached this guy some way."

"What does Bacon get out of it?"

"Oh, this is one of the hobby horses he rides. The double standard, white justice, blah blah blah. He's always out to embarrass the Mayor."

"Well," said Kramer, "if he can make something out of this piece a shit, then he's a magician."

By the time Kramer hung up, the three shackled witnesses were clattering and complaining again. With a heavy heart he realized he was actually going to have to sit down and talk to these three germs and get something coherent out of them about a man named Pimp who shot a man who knew a man who may or may not have known the whereabouts of forty suits. His entire Friday night was going to get shot in the ass, and he would have to shoot dice with Fate and ride the subway back down to Manhattan. He looked back into the locker room once more. That very vision himself, that *Gentleman's Quarterly* cover boy, the man named Pimp, was still back there, eating ribs and hugely enjoying something on the TV, which lit up his face in tones of first-degree-burn pink and cobalt-therapy blue.

Kramer stepped outside the Detective Bureau and said to Gordon: "Your witnesses are getting kinda restless in there. That one guy wants to wrap his chain around my throat."

"I had to put the chain on him."

"I know that. But lemme ask you something. This fellow Pimp, he's just sitting back there eating ribs. He's not chained to anything."

"Oh, I'm not worried about Pimp. He's not going anywhere. He's cooling out. He's contented. This crummy neighborhood is all he knows. I bet he don't know New York is on the Atlantic Ocean. He's a home boy. No, he's not going anywhere. He's only the perpetrator. But a *witness*—hey, baby, if I didn't put the chain on the witness, you wouldn't have no-o-o-o-o-body to interview. You'd never see his ass again. A fucking witness'll cut out for Santo Domingo faster'n you can say off-peak fare."

Kramer headed back to the Detective Bureau to do his duty and interview the three irate citizens in chains and try to find some order in this latest piece a shit.

Since *The City Light* published no Sunday newspaper, there was only a skeleton crew in the city room on Saturday afternoons. Most of them were wire-copy editors, scavenging through the material that continued to come stuttering and shuddering out of the Associated Press and United Press International machines for items that might be of use for Monday's edition. There were three reporters in the city room, plus one down at Manhattan Central Police Headquarters, in case there occurred some catastrophe or piece of mayhem so gory that *The City Light*'s readers would still want to lap it up on Monday. There was a lone assistant city editor, who spent most of the afternoon on the telephone, making sales calls on the *City Light*'s WATS line, for a sideline of his, which was selling college fraternity jewelry, wholesale, to fraternity house managers, who sold the stuff, the tie tacks and rings and pledge pins and whatnot, to the brothers at retail and kept the difference for themselves. The boredom and lassitude of these sentinels of the press could scarcely be exaggerated.

And on this particular Saturday afternoon there was also Peter Fallow.

Fallow, by contrast, was fervor personified. Of the various cubicles around the edges of the city room, his was the only one in use. He was perched on the edge of his chair with the telephone at his ear and a Biro in his hand. He was so keyed up, his excitement cut through today's hangover with something approaching clarity.

On his desk was a telephone directory for Nassau County, which was on Long Island. A great hefty thing, it was, this directory. He had never heard of Nassau County, although he now reckoned he must have passed through it during the weekend when he had managed to inspire St. John's superior at the museum, Virgil Gooch III—the Yanks loved to string Roman numerals after their sons' names—to invite him to his ludicrously grand house by the ocean in East Hampton, Long Island. There was no second invitation, but . . . ah, well, ah, well . . . As for the town of Hewlett, which was in the county of Nassau, its existence on the face of the earth was news to him, but somewhere in the town of Hewlett a telephone was ringing, and he desperately wanted it to be answered. Finally, after seven rings, it was.

"Hello?" Out of breath.

"Mr. Rifkind?"

"Yes . . ." Out of breath and wary.

"This is Peter Fallow of the New York *City Light*."

"Don't want any."

"Excuse me? I do hope you'll forgive me for ringing you up on a Saturday afternoon."

"You hope wrong. I subscribed to the *Times* once. Actually got it about once a week."

"No, no, no, I'm not—"

"Either somebody swiped it from the front door before I left the house or it was soaking wet or it was never delivered."

"No, I'm a journalist, Mr. Rifkind. I *write* for The *City Light*."

He finally managed to establish this fact to Mr. Rifkind's satisfaction.

"Well, okay," said Mr. Rifkind, "go ahead. I was just out in the driveway having a few beers and making a FOR SALE sign to put up in the window of my car. You're not by any chance in the market for a 198⸱ Thunderbird."

"I'm afraid not," said Fallow with a chortle, as if Mr. Rifkind were one of the great Saturday-afternoon wits of his experience. "Actually, I'm calling to inquire about one of your students, a young Mr. Henry Lamb."

"Henry Lamb. Doesn't ring a bell. What's he done?"

"Oh, he hasn't *done* anything. He's been seriously injured." He proceeded to lay out the facts of the case, stacking them rather heavily toward the Albert Vogel–Reverend Bacon theory of the incident. "I was told he was a student in your English class."

"Who told you that?"

"His mother. I had quite a long talk with her. She's a very nice woman and very upset, as you can imagine."

"Henry Lamb . . . Oh yes, I know who you mean. Well, that's too bad."

"What I would like to find out, Mr. Rifkind, is what kind of student Henry Lamb is."

"What *kind?*"

"Well, would you say he was an *outstanding* student?"

"Where are you from, Mr.—I'm sorry, tell me your name again?"

"Fallow."

"Mr. Fallow. I gather you're not from New York."

"That's true."

"Then there's no reason why you should know anything about Colonel Jacob Ruppert High School in the Bronx. At Ruppert we use comparative terms, but *outstanding* isn't one of them. The range runs more from cooperative to life-threatening." Mr. Rifkind began to chuckle. "F'r Chrissake, don't say I said that."

"Well, how would you describe Henry Lamb?"

"Cooperative. He's a nice fellow. Never gives *me* any trouble."

"Would you describe him as a good student?"

"*Good* doesn't work too well at Ruppert, either. It's more 'Does he attend class or doesn't he?' "

"Did Henry Lamb attend class?"

"As I recall, yes. He's usually there. He's very dependable. He's a nice kid, as nice as they come."

"Was there any part of the curriculum he was particularly good—or, let me say, adept at, anything he did better than anything else?"

"Not particularly."

"No?"

"It's difficult to explain, Mr. Fallow. As the saying goes, '*Ex nihilo nihil fit.*' There's not a great range of activities in these classes, and so it's hard to compare performances. These boys and girls—sometimes their minds are in the classroom, and sometimes they're not."

"What about Henry Lamb?"

"He's a nice fellow. He's polite, he pays attention, he doesn't give me any trouble. He tries to learn."

"Well, he must have some abilities. His mother told me he was considering going to college."

"That may well be. She's probably talking about C.C.N.Y. That's the City College of New York."

"I believe Mrs. Lamb did mention that."

"City College has an open-admissions policy. If you live in New York City and you're a high-school graduate and you want to go to City College, you can go."

"Will Henry Lamb graduate, or would he have?"

"As far as I know. As I say, he has a very good attendance record."

"How do you think he would have fared as a college student?"

A sigh. "I don't know. I can't imagine what happens with these kids when they enter City College."

"Well, Mr. Rifkind, can you tell me anything at *all* about Henry Lamb's performance or his aptitude, anything at *all?*"

"You have to understand that they give me about sixty-five students in each class when the year starts, because they know it'll be down to forty by mid-year and thirty by the end of the year. Even thirty's too many, but that's what I get. It's not exactly what you'd call a tutorial system. Henry Lamb's a nice young man who applies himself and wants an education. What more can I tell you?"

"Let me ask you this. How does he do on his written work?"

Mr. Rifkind let out a whoop. "Written work? There hasn't been any written work at Ruppert High for fifteen years! Maybe twenty! They take multiple-choice tests. Reading comprehension, that's the big thing. That's all the Board of Education cares about."

"How was Henry Lamb's reading comprehension?"

"I'd have to look it up. Not bad, if I had to guess."

"Better than most? Or about average? Or what would you say?"

"Well . . . I know it must be difficult for you to understand, Mr. Fallow, being from England. Am I right? You're British?"

"Yes, I am."

"Naturally—or I guess it's natural—you're used to levels of excellence and so forth. But these kids haven't reached the level where it's worth emphasizing the kind of comparisons you're talking about. We're just trying to get them up to a certain level and then keep them from falling back. You're thinking about 'honor students' and 'higher achievers' and all that, and that's natural enough, as I say. But at Colonel Jacob Ruppert High School, an honor student is somebody who attends class, isn't disruptive, tries to learn, and does all right at reading and arithmetic."

"Well, let's use that standard. By that standard, is Henry Lamb an honor student?"

"By that standard, yes."

"Thank you very much, Mr. Rifkind."

"That's okay. I'm sorry to hear about all this. Seems like a nice boy. We're not supposed to call them boys, but that's what they are, poor sad confused boys with a whole lotta problems. Don't quote me, for Christ's sake, or I'll have a whole lotta problems. Hey, listen. You sure you couldn't use a 1981 Thunderbird?"

10

SATURDAY'S SATURNINE LUNCHTIME

AT THAT MOMENT, also on Long Island, but sixty miles to the east, on the south shore, the beach club had just opened for the season. The club owned a low, rambling stucco building athwart the dunes and about a hundred yards of beach-front, bounded by two dock ropes threaded through metal stanchions. The club facilities were spacious and comfortable but were maintained, devoutly, in the Brahmin Ascetic or Boarding School Scrubbed Wood mode that had been fashionable in the 1920s and 1930s. So it was that Sherman McCoy now sat on the deck at a perfectly plain wooden table under a large faded umbrella. With him were his father, his mother, Judy, and, intermittently, Campbell.

You could step or, in Campbell's case, run directly from the deck onto the sand that lay between the two ropes, and Campbell was just now somewhere out there with Rawlie Thorpe's little girl, Eliza, and Garland Reed's little girl, Mac-Kenzie. Sherman was attentively not listening to his father tell Judy how Talbot, the club's bartender, had made his martini, which was the color of pale tea.

". . . know why, but I've always preferred a martini made with sweet vermouth. Shaken until it foams. Talbot always gives me an argument . . ."

His father's thin lips were opening and closing, and his noble chin was going up and down, and his charming raconteur's smile was wrinkling his cheeks. Once, when Sherman was Campbell's age, his father and mother had taken him for a picnic out on the sand beyond the ropes. There was a spirit of adventure about this excursion. They were roughing it. The strangers out there on the sand, the handful who remained in the late afternoon, turned out to be harmless.

Now Sherman let his eyes slide off his father's face to explore the sand beyond the ropes again. It made him squint, because where the cluster of tables and umbrellas ended, the beach was sheer dazzling light. So he shortened his range and found himself focusing on a head at the table just behind his father. It was the unmistakable round head of Pollard Browning. Pollard was sitting there with Lewis Sanderson the elder, who had always been Ambassador Sanderson when Sherman was growing up, and Mrs. Sanderson and Coker Channing and his wife.

How Channing had ever become a member was beyond Sherman, except that he made a career of ingratiating himself with people like Pollard. Pollard was president of the club. Christ, he was president of Sherman's co-op board, too. That dense, round head . . . But given his current frame of mind, Sherman was reassured by the sight of it . . . dense as a rock, solid as a rock, rich as Croesus, immovable.

His father's lips stopped moving for an instant, and he heard his mother say, "Dear, don't bore Judy with martinis. It makes you sound so old. Nobody but you drinks them any longer."

"Here at the beach they do. If you don't believe me—"

"It's like talking about flappers or rumble seats or dining cars or—"

"If you don't believe me—"

"—K rations or the Hit Parade."

"If you don't believe me—"

"Did you ever hear of a singer named Bonnie Baker?" She directed this at Judy, ignoring Sherman's father. "Bonnie Baker was the star of the Hit Parade, on the radio. Wee Bonnie Baker she was called. The entire country used to listen to her. Totally forgotten now, I expect."

Sixty-five years old and still beautiful, thought Sherman. Tall, lean, erect, thick white hair—refuses to color it—an aristocrat, much more of one than his father, with all his dedication to being one—and still chipping away at the base of the statue of the great Lion of Dunning Sponget.

"Oh, you don't have to go back that far," said Judy. "I was talking to Garland's son, Landrum. He's a junior, I think he said, at Brown—"

"Garland Reed has a son in college?"

"Sally's son."

"Oh dear. I'd totally forgotten about Sally. Isn't that awful?"

"Not awful. Up-to-date," said Judy, without much of a smile.

"If you don't believe me, ask Talbot," said Sherman's father.

"Up-to-date!" said his mother, laughing and ignoring the Lion and his martinis and his Talbot.

"Anyway," said Judy, "I happened to say something to him about hippies, and he just stared at me. Never heard of them. Ancient history."

"Here at the beach—"

"Like martinis," Sherman's mother said to Judy.

"Here at the beach you're still permitted to enjoy life's simple pleasures," said Sherman's father, "or you were until a moment ago."

"Daddy and I went to that little restaurant in Wainscott last night, Sherman, the one Daddy likes so much, with Inez and Herbert Clark, and do you know what the owner said to me—you know the pretty little woman who owns it?"

Sherman nodded yes.

"I find her very jolly," said his mother. "As we were leaving, she said to me—well, first I must mention that Inez and Herbert had two gin-and-tonics apiece, Daddy had his three martinis, *and* there was wine, and she said to me—"

"Celeste, your nose is growing. I had *one*."

"Well, perhaps not three. Two."

"Celeste."

"Well, she thought it was a lot, the owner did. She said to me, 'I like my older customers best of all. They're the only ones who drink anymore.' 'My *older customers*'! I can't imagine how she thought that was supposed to sound to me."

"She thought you were twenty-five," said Sherman's father. Then to Judy: "All of a sudden I'm married to a White Ribbon."

"A white ribbon?"

"More ancient history," he muttered. "Or else I'm married to Miss Trendy. You always have been up-to-date, Celeste."

"Only compared to you, darling." She smiled and put her hand on his forearm. "I wouldn't take away your martinis for the world. Talbot's, either."

"I'm not worried about Talbot," said the Lion.

Sherman had heard his father talk about how he liked his martinis mixed at least a hundred times, and Judy must have heard it twenty, but that was all right. It got on his mother's nerves, not his. It was comfortable; everything was the same as always. That was the way he wanted things this weekend; the same, the same, the same, and neatly bounded by the two ropes.

Just getting out of the apartment, where *May I speak to Maria* still poisoned the air, had helped considerably. Judy had driven out early yesterday afternoon in the station wagon with Campbell, Bonita, and Miss Lyons, the nanny. He had driven out last night in the Mercedes. This morning, in the driveway outside the garage behind their big old house on Old Drover's Mooring Lane, he had gone over the car in the sunlight. No evidence at all, that he could detect, of the fracas . . . Everything was brighter this morning, including Judy. She had chatted quite amiably at the breakfast table. Just now she was smiling at his father and mother. She looked relaxed . . . and really rather pretty, rather chic . . . in her polo shirt and pale yellow Shetland sweater and white slacks . . . She wasn't young, but she did have the kind of fine features that would age well . . . Lovely hair . . . The dieting and the abominable Sports Training . . . and age . . . had taken their toll on her breasts, but she still had a trim little body . . . firm . . . He felt a mild tingle . . . Perhaps tonight . . . or the middle of the afternoon! . . . Why not? . . . That might give the thaw, the rebirth of spring, the return of the sun . . . a more solid foundation . . . If she would agree, then the . . . ugly business . . . would be over . . . Perhaps *all* the ugly business would be over. Four days had now passed and there had not been a shred of news about anything dreadful happening to a tall skinny boy on an expressway ramp in the Bronx. No one had come knocking at his door. Besides, *she* was driving. She had put it that way herself. And whatever happened, he was *morally correct*. (Nothing to fear from God.) He had been fighting for his life and for hers . . .

Maybe the whole thing was one of God's warnings. Why didn't he and Judy and Campbell get out of the madness of New York . . . and the megalomania of Wall Street? Who but an arrogant fool would want to be a Master of the Universe —and take the insane chances he had been taking? A close call! . . . Dear God, I swear to you that from now on . . . Why didn't they sell the apartment and move out here to Southampton year round—or to Tennessee . . . Tennessee . . . His grandfather William Sherman McCoy had come to New York from Knoxville when he was thirty-one . . . a hick in the eyes of the Brownings . . . Well, what was so wrong with good American hicks! . . . Sherman's father had taken him to Knoxville. He had seen the perfectly adequate house where his grandfather had grown up . . . A lovely little city, a sober, reasonable little city, Knoxville . . . Why didn't he go there and get a job in a brokerage house, a regular job, a sane, responsible job, not trying to spin the world on its head, a nine-to-five job, or whenever it is they work in places like Knoxville; $90,000 or $100,000 a year, a tenth or less of what he so foolishly thought he needed now, and it would be plenty . . . a Georgian house with a screen porch at one end . . . an acre or two of good green lawn, a Snapper lawn mower that he might operate himself occasionally, a garage with a door that opens with a Genie that you keep clipped onto the visor of your car, a kitchen with a magnetic bulletin board where you leave messages for each other, a cozy life, a loving life, Our Town . . .

Judy was now smiling at something his father had said, and the Lion was smiling in pleasure at her appreciation of his wit, and his mother was smiling at both of them, and at the tables beyond, Pollard was smiling and Rawlie was smiling and Ambassador Sanderson, his lanky old legs and all, was smiling, and the sweet sun of early June by the sea warmed Sherman's bones, and he relaxed for the first time in two weeks, and he smiled at Judy and his father and his mother, as if he had actually been paying attention to their banter.

"Daddy!"

Campbell came running toward him, from out of the sand and the dazzling light, onto the deck, between the tables.

"Daddy!"

She looked absolutely glorious. Now almost seven years old, she had lost her babyish features and was a little girl with slender arms and legs and firm muscles and not a blemish anywhere. She was wearing a pink bathing suit with the letters of the alphabet printed on it in black and white. Her skin glowed with sun and exercise. The very sight of her, of this . . . vision . . . brought smiles to the faces of his father and his mother and Judy. He pivoted his legs out from under the table and opened his arms. He wanted her to run straight into his embrace.

But she stopped short. She hadn't come for affection. "Daddy." She was breathing hard. She had an important question. "Daddy."

"Yes, darling!"

"Daddy." She could scarcely get her breath.

"Take it easy, sweetheart. What is it?"

"Daddy . . . what do you do?"

What did he do?

"Do? What do you mean, sweetheart?"

"Well, MacKenzie's daddy makes books, and he has eighty people working for him."

"That's what MacKenzie told you?"

"Yes."

"Oh ho! Eighty people!" said Sherman's father, in the voice he used for small children. "My, my, my!"

Sherman could imagine what the Lion thought of Garland Reed. Garland had inherited his father's printing business and for ten years had done nothing with it but keep it alive. The "books" he "made" were printing jobs given him by the actual publishers, and the products were as likely to be manuals, club rosters, corporate contracts, and annual reports as anything even remotely literary. As for the eighty people—eighty ink-stained wretches was more like it, typesetters, pressmen, and so forth. At the height of his career the Lion had had *two hundred Wall Street lawyers* under his whip, most of them Ivy League.

"But what do you *do?*" asked Campbell, now growing impatient. She wanted to get back to MacKenzie to give her report, and something impressive was clearly called for.

"Well, Sherman, how about it?" said his father with a big grin. "I want to hear the answer to this myself. I've often asked myself what it is you fellows do exactly. Campbell, that's an *excellent* question."

Campbell smiled, taking her grandfather's praise at face value.

More irony; and not so welcome this time. The Lion had always resented his going into the bond business instead of the law, and the fact that he had prospered at it only made things worse. Sherman began to feel angry. He couldn't sit here and present a picture of himself as a Master of the Universe, not with his father and mother and Judy hanging on every word. At the same time, he couldn't give Campbell some modest depiction of himself as a salesman, one among many, or even as the chief bond salesman, which would sound pompous without sounding impressive and wouldn't mean anything to Campbell in any case—Campbell, who stood there panting, primed to race back to her little friend, who had a daddy who *made books* and had *eighty people* working for him.

"Well, I deal in *bonds*, sweetheart. I buy them, I sell them, I—"

"What are bonds? What is deal?"

Now his mother began laughing. "You've got to do better than that, Sherman!"

"Well, honey, bonds are—a bond is—well, let me see, what's the best way to explain it to you."

"Explain it to me, too, Sherman," said his father. "I must have done five thousand leveraged purchase contracts, and I always fell asleep before I could figure out why anyone wanted the bonds."

That's because you and your two hundred Wall Street lawyers were nothing but functionaries for the Masters of the Universe, thought Sherman, getting more annoyed by the second. He saw Campbell looking at her grandfather in consternation.

"Your grandfather's only joking, honey." He shot his father a sharp look. "A bond is a way of loaning people money. Let's say you want to build a road, and it's not a little road but a big highway, like the highway we took up to Maine last summer. Or you want to build a big hospital. Well, that requires a lot of money, more money than you could ever get by just going to a bank. So what you do is, you issue what are called bonds."

"You build roads and hospitals, Daddy? That's what you do?"

Now both his father and his mother started laughing. He gave them openly reproachful looks, which only made them merrier. Judy was smiling with what appeared to be a sympathetic twinkle.

"No, I don't actually build them, sweetheart. I handle the bonds, and the bonds are what make it possible—"

"You *help* build them."

"Well, in a way."

"Which ones?"

"Which *ones?*"

"You said roads and hospitals."

"Well, not any one specifically."

"The road to Maine?"

Now both his father and mother were giggling the infuriating giggle of people who are trying their best not to laugh right in your face.

"No, not the—"

"I think you're in over your head, Sherman!" said his mother. *Head* came close to soaring into a whoop.

"Not the road to Maine," said Sherman, ignoring the comment. "Let me try to put it another way."

Judy broke in. "Let me try."

"Well . . . all right."

"Darling," said Judy, "Daddy doesn't build roads or hospitals, and he doesn't help build them, but he does handle the *bonds* for the people who raise the money."

"Bonds?"

"Yes. Just imagine that a bond is a slice of cake and you didn't bake the cake, but every time you hand somebody a slice of the cake a tiny little bit comes, off, like a little crumb, and you can keep that."

Judy was smiling, and so was Campbell, who seemed to realize that this was a joke, a kind of fairy tale based on what her daddy did.

"Little crumbs?" she said encouragingly.

"Yes," said Judy. "Or you have to imagine little crumbs, but a *lot* of little crumbs. If you pass around enough slices of cake, then pretty soon you have enough crumbs to make a *gigantic* cake."

"For real life?" asked Campbell.

"No, not for real life. You just have to imagine that." Judy looked to Sherman's father and mother for approval of this witty description of the bond business. They smiled, but uncertainly.

"I'm not sure you're making it any clearer for Campbell," said Sherman. "My goodness . . . *crumbs.*" He smiled to show he knew this was only lunch-table banter. In fact . . . he was used to Judy's supercilious attitude toward Wall Street, but he was not happy about . . . *crumbs.*

"I don't think it's such a bad metaphor," said Judy, also smiling. Then she turned to his father. "Let me give you an actual example, John, and you be the judge."

John. Even though there was something . . . off . . . about *crumbs,* this was the first real indication that things might be going over the edge. *John.* His father and mother had encouraged Judy to call them John and Celeste, but it made her uncomfortable. So she avoided calling them anything. This casual, confident *John* was not like her. Even his father appeared a bit on guard.

Judy launched into a description of his Giscard scheme. Then she said to his father, "Pierce & Pierce doesn't issue them for the French government and doesn't buy them from the French government but from whoever's already bought them from the French government. So Pierce & Pierce's transactions have nothing to do with anything France hopes to build or develop or . . . achieve. It's all been done long before Pierce & Pierce enters the picture. So they're just sort of . . . slices of cake. Golden cake. And Pierce & Pierce collects millions of marvelous"—she shrugged—"golden crumbs."

"You can call them crumbs if you want," said Sherman, trying not to sound testy, and failing.

"Well, that's the best I can do," Judy said brightly. Then to his father and mother: "Investment banking is an unusual field. I don't know if there *is* any way you can explain it to anyone under twenty. Or perhaps under *thirty*."

Sherman now noticed that Campbell was standing by with a distressed look on her face. "Campbell," he said, "you know what? I think Mommy wants me to change professions." He grinned, as if this were one of the funniest discussions in years.

"Not at all," said Judy, laughing. "I'm not complaining about your golden crumbs!"

Crumbs—*enough!* He could feel his anger rising. But he kept on smiling. "Perhaps I ought to try decorating. Excuse me, interior designing."

"I don't think you're cut out for it."

"Oh, I don't know. It must be fun getting pouffe curtains and polished chintz for—who were those people?—those Italians you did that apartment for?—the di Duccis?"

"I don't know that it's fun particularly."

"Well, then it's *creative*. Right?"

"Well . . . at least you're able to point to something you've *done*, something tangible, something clear-cut—"

"For the di Duccis."

"Even if it's for people who are shallow and vain, it's something *real*, something describable, something contributing to simple human satisfaction, no matter how meretricious and temporary, something you can at least explain to your children. I mean, at Pierce & Pierce, what on earth do you tell *each other* you do every day?"

All at once, a wail. Campbell. Tears were coming down her face. Sherman put his arms around her, but her body was rigid.

"It's all right, sweetie!"

Judy got up and came over and put her arms around her, too. "Oh, Campbell, Campbell, Campbell, sweetie pie! Daddy and I were only teasing each other."

Pollard Browning was looking their way. So was Rawlie. Faces at tables all around, staring at the wounded child.

Because they were both trying to embrace Campbell, Sherman found his face close to Judy's. He wanted to strangle her. He glanced at his parents. They were aghast.

His father stood up. "I'm going to get a martini," he said. "You're all too up-to-date for me."

Saturday! In SoHo! After a wait of less than twenty minutes, Larry Kramer and his wife, Rhoda, and Greg Rosenwald and his live-in girlfriend, Mary Lou Love-Greg, and Herman Rappaport and his wife, Susan, now occupied a window table at the Haiphong Harbor restaurant. Outside, on West Broadway, it was such a clear sparkling late-spring day that not even the grime of SoHo could obscure it. Not even Kramer's envy of Greg Rosenwald could obscure it. He and Greg and Herman had been classmates at New York University. They had worked on the Student Activities Board together. Herman was now an editor, one among many, at Putnam, the publishing house, and it was largely thanks to him that Rhoda had gotten her job at Waverly Place Books. Kramer was an assistant district attorney, one among 245, in the Bronx. But Greg, Greg with his Downtown clothes on and the lovely Mary Lou Blonde at his side, was a writer for *The Village Voice*. So far

Greg was the only star that had risen from their little group of campus hotshots. That had been apparent from the moment they sat down. Any time the others had a comment to make, they looked at Greg when they made it.

Herman was looking at Greg when he said, "Have you been in this place Dean and DeLuca? Have you checked out the prices? Smoked . . . Scottish . . . salmon . . . thirty-three dollars a pound? Susan and I were just in there."

Greg smiled knowingly. "That's for the Short Hills Seville set."

"The Short Hills Seville set?" asked Rhoda. My wife, the perfect foil. Not only that, she had the kind of grin on her face that you put on when you just *know* you're going to get a witty reply.

"Yeah," said Greg, "take a look out there." *Take a look oudeh.* His accent was as atrocious as Rhoda's. "Every other car"—*evvy udda kah*— "is a Cadillac Seville with Jersey license plates. And take a look at what they *wear.*" *Take a lookad whuddeh weh.* Not only did he have an atrocious accent, he had the 300-watt animation of David Brenner, the comedian. "They roll out of these six-bedroom Georgians in Short Hills with their bomber jackets and blue jeans, and they get in their Cadillac Sevilles and they drive to SoHo every Saturday."

Evvy Saddy. But Rhoda and Herman and Susan beamed and chuckled in appreciation. They thought this was rich stuff. Only Mary Lou Blonde Headlights looked less than swept away by this priceless urbanity. Kramer decided that if he got a word in edgewise, he would direct it toward her.

Greg was off on a disquisition on all the bourgeois elements who were now attracted to the artists' quarter. Why didn't he start with himself? Look at him. A wavy red beard as big as the King of Hearts's hiding his receding chin . . . a blackish-green tweed jacket with enormous shoulders and lapels with notches down around his ribs . . . a black T-shirt with the logo of the Pus Casserole, the band, across the chest . . . black pegged pants . . . the Greasy Black look that was so . . . so Post-Punk, so Downtown, so . . . of the moment . . . And in fact he was a nice little Jewish boy from Riverdale, which was the Short Hills of the New York City limits, and his parents had a nice big Colonial house, or Tudor, or whatever it was . . . A middle-class twerp . . . a writer for *The Village Voice,* a know-it-all, possessor of Mary Lou Downy Shanks . . . Greg had started living with Mary Lou when she enrolled in the Investigative Journalism seminar he was teaching at N.Y.U. two years ago. She had a fantastic body, *outstanding* breasts, and classic Wasp looks. She stood out on the N.Y.U. campus like somebody from another planet. Kramer called her Mary Lou Love-Greg, which was a way of saying she had given up her actual identity to live with Greg. She bothered them. She bothered Kramer most of all. He found her dense, distant —intensely desirable. She reminded him of the girl with brown lipstick. And for this he envied Greg most of all. He had taken this gorgeous creature and possessed her, without assuming any obligations, without getting stuck in an ant colony on the West Side, without having an English nanny sitting on his neck, without having a wife he had to watch turning into her *shtetl* mama . . . Kramer cut a look at Rhoda and her beaming puffy face and immediately felt guilty. He *loved* his new son, he was *bound* to Rhoda, forever, in a sacred way . . . and yet . . . *This is New York! And I'm young!*

Greg's words flowed past him. His eyes wandered. For a moment they met Mary Lou's. She held them. *Could it be*— But he couldn't look at her forever. He looked out the window at the people walking along West Broadway. Most were young or youngish—so smartly turned out!—so Downtown!—sparkling, even in Greasy Black, on a perfect Saturday in late spring.

Then and there, sitting at a table in the Haiphong Harbor, Kramer vowed that he would be *part of it*. The girl with brown lipstick—

—had held his eyes, and he had held hers, when the verdict came. He had won. He had carried the jury and sunk Herbert, who would get a sentence of three to six, at the very least, since he already had a felony conviction on his record. He had been tough, fearless, shrewd—and he had won. He had won *her*. When the foreman, a black man named Forester, had announced the verdict, he had looked into her eyes and she had looked into his, and they had stayed that way for what seemed like a very long time. There was no question about it.

Kramer tried to catch Mary Lou's eyes again but missed. Rhoda was looking at the menu. He heard her ask Susan Rappaport, "Jeet foya came down heh?" Which meant, "Did you eat before you came down here?"

Susan said, "No, ju?" No, did you?

"No, I couldn't waida get oudada house. I won't be able a do'is again for sixteen years."

"Do what?"

"Oh, just go to SoHo because I feel like going to SoHo. Go anywhere. The baby nurse is leaving on Wednesday."

"Whyn't you get somebody else?"

"Are you kidding? You wanna know how much we're paying her?"

"How much?"

"Five hundred and twenty-five dollars a week. My mother's been paying for it, for four weeks."

Thanks a lot. Go ahead. Tell all these yentas your husband can't even afford the goddamned baby nurse. He noticed that Susan's eyes left Rhoda's face and looked up. On the sidewalk, just on the other side of the plate glass, stood a young man trying to peer in. If it hadn't been for the quarter inch of plate glass, he would have been leaning right across their table. He kept peering, peering, peering, until the tip of his nose was almost pressed against the glass. Now all six of them were looking at the fellow, but he apparently couldn't see them. He had a lean, lineless, fair young face and soft curly light brown hair. In his open-neck shirt, with the collar of his navy warm-up jacket turned up, he looked like a young aviator from long ago.

Mary Lou Caress turned toward Susan with a mischievous look on her face. "I think we ought to ask him if he's had lunch."

"Ummmmm," said Susan, who, like Rhoda, had already laid on her first subcutaneous layer of Matron.

"He looks hungry to me," said Mary Lou.

"Looks retarded to me," said Greg. Greg was scarcely a foot away from the young man, and the contrast between Greg's unhealthy Greasy Black Downtown hip weasel appearance and the young man's rosy good looks was overwhelming. Kramer wondered if the others noticed. Mary Lou must have noticed. This redbearded Riverdale twerp didn't deserve her.

Kramer caught her eye again for a moment, but she watched the young man, who, baffled by the reflections, now turned away from the window and began walking up West Broadway. On the back of his jacket was embroidered a golden thunderbolt and, above it, the words RADARTRONIC SECURITY.

"Radartronic Security," said Greg in a way that indicated what a cipher, a nullity, was this character Mary Lou had decided to go gaga over.

"You can be sure he doesn't work for any security company," said Kramer. He was determined to capture Mary Lou's attention.

"Why not?" said Greg.

"Because I happen to know who does. I see them every day. I wouldn't hire a security guard in this city if my life depended on it—especially if my life depended on it. They're all predicate violent felons."

"They're what?" asked Mary Lou.

"Predicate violent felons. They already have a least one conviction for a felony involving violence against a person."

"Oh, come on," said Herman. "That can't be true." He had their attention now. He was playing his one strong suit, Macho Insider from the Bronx.

"Well, not all, but I bet 60 percent. You ought to sit in on the plea-bargaining sessions some morning up on the Grand Concourse. One of the ways you justify a plea bargain is, the judge asks the defendant if he has a job, and if he does, that's supposed to show he has roots in the community, and so on. So the judge'll ask these kids if they have a job, and I mean these kids are being held for armed robbery, muggings, assaults, manslaughter, attempted murder, you name it, and every one of them, if they have any job at all, they'll say, 'Yeah, security guard.' I mean, who do you think takes these jobs? They pay minimum wage, they're boring, and when they're not boring, they're unpleasant."

"Maybe they're good at it," said Greg. "They like to mix it up. They know how to handle weapons."

Rhoda and Susan laughed. Such a wit, such a wit.

Mary Lou didn't laugh. She kept looking at Kramer.

"No doubt they do," he said. He didn't want to lose control of the conversation and those big-breasted blue eyes. "Everybody in the Bronx carries weapons. Let me tell you about a case I just finished." Ahhhhhhh! This was his chance to tell about the triumph of the People over that desperado Herbert 92X, and he plunged into the story with relish. But from the first Greg caused problems. As soon as he heard the name Herbert 92X, he butted in with some story he had done on prisons for *The Village Voice*.

"If it weren't for the Muslims, the prisons in this city would *really* be out of control."

That was bullshit, but Kramer didn't want the discussion to get onto the Muslims and Greg's goddamned story. So he said, "Herbert's not really a Muslim. I mean, Muslims don't go to bars."

It was slow going. Greg knew it all. He knew all about Muslims, prisons, crime, street life in the billion-footed city. He began to turn the story against Kramer. Why were they so anxious to prosecute a man who had done nothing but follow the natural instinct to protect your own life?

"But he *killed* a man, Greg!—with an unlicensed gun that he carried every day, as a routine thing."

"Yeah, but look at the job he had! It's obviously a dangerous occupation. You said yourself everybody carries weapons up there."

"Look at his *job*? Okay, let's look at it. He works for a goddamned *boot*legger!"

"Whaddaya want him to do, work for IBM?"

"You talk like that's out of the question. I bet IBM has plenty of programs for minorities, but Herbert wouldn't want one a their jobs if they gave it to him. Herbert is a player. He's a hustler who tries to cover himself with this religious mantle, and he just goes on being childish, egocentric, irresponsible, shiftless—"

Suddenly it dawned on Kramer that they were all looking at him in a funny way, all of them. Rhoda . . . Mary Lou . . . They were giving him the look you give someone who turns out to be a covert reactionary. He was too far gone in this criminal-justice scam . . . He was humming with the System's reactionary overtones . . . This was like one of the bull sessions the gang used to have when they were all back at N.Y.U., except that now they were in their early thirties and they were looking at him as if he had become something awful. And he knew in an instant there was no way he could explain to them what he had seen over the past six years. They wouldn't understand, least of all Greg, who was taking his triumph over Herbert 92X and stuffing it down his throat.

It was going so badly that Rhoda felt compelled to come to the rescue.

"You don't understand, Greg," she said. "You have no idea, the caseload Larry has. There are seven thousand criminal indictments every year in the Bronx, and they only have the capacity"—the kehpehsity— "for five hundred trials. There's no way they can study every aspect of every case and take all these different things into consideration."

"I can just imagine somebody trying to tell that to this fellow Herbert 92X."

Kramer looked up at the ceiling of the Haiphong Harbor. It had been painted matte black, along with all sorts of ducts, pipes, and lighting fixtures. Looked like intestines. His own wife. Her idea of coming to his defense was to say, "Larry's got so many colored people to put away, he hasn't got time to treat them as individuals. So you mustn't be hard on him." He had broken his hump on the Herbert 92X case, handled it brilliantly, looked Herbert himself right in the eye, avenged the father of five, Nestor Cabrillo—and what did he get for it? Now he had to defend *himself* against a bunch of intellectual trendies in a trendy bistro in trendy fucking SoHo.

He scanned the table. Even Mary Lou was giving him the fishy look. The big beautiful whitebread airhead had become as trendy as the rest of them.

Well, there was one person who understood the Herbert 92X case, who understood how brilliant he had been, who understood the righteousness of the justice he had wrought, and she made Mary Lou Jugs look like . . . like . . . nothing.

For a moment he caught Mary Lou's eyes again, but the light had gone out.

11

THE WORDS ON THE FLOOR

THE PARIS STOCK EXCHANGE, the Bourse, was open for trading only two hours a day, 1 to 3 p.m., which was 7 to 9 a.m., New York time. So on Monday, Sherman arrived at the bond trading room of Pierce & Pierce at 6:30. By now it was 7:30, and he was at his desk with his telephone at his left ear and his right foot up on Felix's portable shoeshine stand.

The sound of young men baying for money on the bond market had already risen in the room, for the market was now an international affair. Across the way was the young lord of the pampas, Arguello, with his telephone at his right ear and his left hand over his left ear, talking to Tokyo in all probability. He had been in the office for at least twelve hours when Sherman arrived, working on a huge sale of U.S. Treasuries to the Japanese postal service. How this kid had ever even gotten his finger into such a deal, Sherman couldn't imagine, but there he was. The Tokyo exchange was open from 7:30 p.m. to 4 a.m., New York time. Arguello was wearing some kind of go-to-hell suspenders with pictures of Tweety Pie, the cartoon character, on them, but that was all right. He was working, and Sherman was at peace.

Felix, the shoeshine man, was humped over, stropping Sherman's right shoe, a New & Lingwood half-brogue, with his highshine rag. Sherman liked the way the elevation of his foot flexed his leg and sprung it out and put pressure on the inside of his thigh. It made him feel athletic. He liked the way Felix humped over, shell-backed, as if enveloping the shoe with his body and soul. He could see the top of the black man's head, which was no more than twenty inches below his eye level. Felix had a perfectly round caramel-brown bald spot on the crown of his skull, which was odd, since the hair surrounding it was quite thick. Sherman liked this perfect round bald spot. Felix was dependable and droll, not young, resentful, and sharp.

Felix had a copy of *The City Light* on the floor beside his stand, reading it while he worked. It was open to the second page and folded over in the middle. Page 2 contained most of *The City Light*'s international news. The headline at the top said: BABY PLUNGES 200 FEET—AND LIVES. The dateline was Elaiochori, Greece. But that was all right. The tabloids no longer held any terrors for Sherman. Five days had now passed and there had not been a word in any of the newspapers about some dreadful incident on an expressway ramp in the Bronx. It was just as Maria had said. They had been drawn into a fight in the jungle, and they had fought and won, and the jungle did not scream about its wounded. This morning Sherman had bought only the *Times* at the little shop on Lexington. He had actually read about the Soviets and the Sri Lankans and the internecine strife at the Federal Reserve on the taxi ride downtown, instead of turning at once to Section B, Metropolitan News.

After a solid week of fear, he could now concentrate on the radium-green numbers sliding across the black screens. He could concentrate on the business at hand . . . the Giscard . . .

Bernard Levy, the Frenchman he dealt with at Traders' Trust Co., was now in France doing a last bit of research on the Giscard before Trader T committed their $300 million and they closed the deal and had a print . . . *the crumbs* . . . Judy's contemptuous phrase slipped into his mind and right out again . . . crumbs . . . So what? . . . They were crumbs of gold . . . He concentrated on Levy's voice on the other end of the satellite carom:

"So look, Sherman, here's the problem. The debt figures the government has just released have everybody on edge here. The franc is falling, and it's bound to fall further, and at the same time, as you know, gold is falling, even though it's for different reasons. The question is where the floor's going to be, and . . ."

Sherman just let him talk. It wasn't unusual for people to get a little squirrelly on the verge of committing a sum like $300 million. He had spoken to Bernard— he called him by his first name—almost every day for six weeks now, and he could barely remember what he looked like. *My French doughnut*, he thought—and immediately realized this was Rawlie Thorpe's crack, Rawlie's cynicism, sarcasm, pessimism, nihilism, which were all ways of saying Rawlie's *weakness*, and so he banished *doughnut* as well as *crumbs* from his mind. This morning he was once more on the side of strength and Destiny. He was almost ready to entertain, once again, the notion of . . . mastery of the universe . . . The baying of the young titans sounded all around him—

"I'm sixteen, seventeen. What does he want to do?"

"Bid me twenty-five of the ten-year!"

"I want out!"

—and once more it was music. Felix was stropping the highshine rag back and forth. Sherman enjoyed the pressure of the rag on his metatarsal bones. It was a tiny massage of the ego, when you got right down to it—this great strapping brown man with the bald spot in his crown down there at his feet, stropping, oblivious of the levers with which Sherman could move another nation, another continent, merely by bouncing a few words off a satellite.

"The franc is no problem," he said to Bernard. "We can hedge that to next January or to term or both."

He felt Felix tapping the bottom of his right shoe. He lifted his foot off the stand, and Felix picked it up and moved it around to the other side of his chair, and Sherman hoisted his mighty athletic left leg and put his left shoe on the metal shoeshine stirrup. Felix turned the newspaper over and folded it down the middle and put it on the floor beside the stand and begun to work on the left New & Lingwood half-brogue.

"Yes, but you have to pay for a hedge," said Bernard, "and we've been talking all along about operating under very blue skies, and . . ."

Sherman tried to imagine his doughnut, Bernard, sitting in an office in one of those dinky modern buildings the French build, with hundreds of tiny cars buzzing by and tooting their toy horns on the street down below . . . below . . . and his eye happened to drift down to the newspaper on the floor below . . .

The hair on his arms stood on end. At the top of the page, the third page of *The City Light*, was a headline saying:

HONOR STUDENT'S MOM:
COPS SIT ON HIT'N'RUN

Above it in smaller white letters on a black bar it said: *While he lies near death.* Below was another black bar saying, A CITY LIGHT *Exclusive.* And below that: *By Peter Fallow.* And below that, set into a column of type, was a picture, head and shoulders, of a smiling black youth, neatly dressed in a dark jacket, a white shirt, and a striped necktie. His slender delicate face was smiling.

"I think the only sensible thing is to find out where this thing bottoms out," said Bernard.

"Well . . . I think you're exaggerating the, uh . . . the, uh . . ." *That face!* ". . . the, uh . . ." *That slender delicate face, now with a shirt and tie! A young gentleman!* ". . . the, uh, problem."

"I hope so," said Bernard. "But either way, it won't hurt to wait."

"Wait?" *Yo! You need any help! That frightened delicate face! A good person!* Did Bernard say "Wait"? "I don't get it, Bernard. Everything's in *place!*" He hadn't meant to sound so emphatic, so urgent, but his eyes were fastened on the words lying on the floor below.

> Fighting back tears, a Bronx widow told *The City Light* yesterday how her honor-student son was run down by a speeding luxury sedan—and accused police and the Bronx District Attorney's Office of sitting on the case.
>
> Mrs. Annie Lamb, a clerk at the city Marriage Bureau, said her son, Henry, 18, due to graduate with honors from Colonel Jacob Ruppert High School next week, gave her part of the license number of the car—a Mercedes-Benz—before he slipped into a coma.
>
> "But the man from the District Attorney's Office called the information useless," she said, on the grounds that the victim himself was the only known witness.
>
> Doctors at Lincoln Hospital termed the coma "probably irreversible" and said Lamb's condition was "grave."
>
> Lamb and his mother live in Edgar Allan Poe Towers, a Bronx housing project. Described by neighbors and teachers as "an exemplary young man," he was slated to enter college in the fall.
>
> The teacher of Lamb's advanced literature and composition class at Ruppert, Zane J. Rifkind, told *The City Light*: "This is a tragic situation. Henry is among that remarkable fraction of students who

are able to overcome the many obstacles that life in the South Bronx places in their paths and concentrate on their studies and their potential and their futures. One can only wonder what he might have achieved in college."

Mrs. Lamb said her son had left their apartment early last Tuesday evening, apparently to buy food. While crossing Bruckner Boulevard, she said, he was struck by a Mercedes-Benz carrying a man and a woman, both white. The car did not stop. The neighborhood is predominantly black and Hispanic.

Lamb managed to make his way to the hospital, where he was treated for a broken wrist and released. The next morning he complained of a severe headache and dizziness. He fell unconscious in the emergency room. It was determined that he had suffered a subdural concussion.

Milton Lubell, spokesman for Bronx District Attorney Abe Weiss, said detectives and an assistant district attorney had interviewed Mrs. Lamb and that "an investigation is underway," but that 2,500 Mercedes-Benzes are registered in New York State with license plates beginning with R, the letter provided by Mrs. Lamb. She said her son thought the second letter was E, F, B, P, or R. "Even assuming one of those is the second letter," said Lubell, "we're talking about almost 500 cars—

RF—Mercedes-Benz—the data on the pages of a million newspapers—went through Sherman's solar plexus like a tremendous vibration. His license plate began: RFH. With a horrifying hunger for the news of his own doom, he read on:

—and we have no description of a driver and no witnesses and

That was as much as he could read. Felix had folded the newspaper at that point. The rest was on the lower half of the page. His brain was on fire. He was dying to reach down and turn the newspaper over—and dying never to have to know what it would reveal. Meantime, the voice of Bernard Levy droned on from across the ocean, bouncing off an AT&T communications satellite.

". . . talking ninety-six, if that's what you mean by 'in place.' But that's beginning to look rather pricey, because . . ."

Pricey? Ninety-six? *No mention of a second boy! No mention of a ramp, a barricade, an attempted robbery!* The price had always been set! How could he bring that up now? *Could it be—not a robbery attempt, after all!* He'd paid an average of ninety-four for them. Only a two-point spread! Couldn't lower it! *This nice-looking lad dying! My car!* Must focus on it . . . the Giscard! Couldn't fail, not after all this time—and the tabloid sizzled on the floor.

"Bernard . . ." His mouth had gone dry. "Listen . . . Bernard . . ."

"Yes?"

But perhaps if he took his foot off the shoeshine stand—

"Felix? Felix?" Felix didn't seem to hear him. The perfect caramel-brown bald spot on the crown of his head continued to go back and forth as he worked on the New & Lingwood half-brogue.

"Felix!"

"Hello, Sherman! What did you say?" In his ear, the voice of the French doughnut, sitting on top of 300 million gold-backed bonds—in his eyes, the top of the head of a black man sitting on top of a shoeshine stand and engulfing his left foot.

"Excuse me, Bernard! . . . Just a moment . . . Felix?"

"You say Felix?"

"No, Bernard! I mean just a minute . . . Felix!"

Felix stopped working on the shoe and looked up.

"Sorry, Felix, I've got to stretch my leg a second."

The French doughnut: "Hello, Sherman, I can't understand you!"

Sherman took his foot off the stand and made a great show of extending it, as if it felt stiff.

"Sherman, are you there?"

"Yes! Excuse me a second, Bernard."

As he hoped, Felix took this opportunity to turn *The City Light* over in order to read the lower half of the page. Sherman put his foot back on the stand, and Felix hunched over the shoe again, and Sherman put his head down, trying to focus on the words lying on the floor. He bent his head down so close to Felix's that the black man looked up. Sherman pulled his head back and smiled weakly.

"Sorry!" he said.

"You say 'Sorry'?" asked the French doughnut.

"Sorry, Bernard, I was talking to someone else."

Felix shook his head reprovingly, then lowered it and went to work again.

" 'Sorry'?" repeated the French doughnut, still baffled.

"Never mind, Bernard. I was talking to someone else." Slowly Sherman lowered his head again and fixed his eyes upon the print way down below.

> —no one who can tell us what happened, not even the young man himself."

"Sherman, are you there? Sherman—"

"Yes, Bernard. Sorry. Uh . . . tell me again what you were saying about price? Because, really, Bernard, we're all set on that. We've been all set for *weeks!*"

"Again?"

"If you don't mind. I was interrupted here."

A big sigh, from Europe, by satellite. "I was saying that we've moved from a stable to an unstable mix here. We can no longer extrapolate from the figures we were talking about when you made your presentation . . ."

Sherman tried to pay attention to both things at once, but the Frenchman's words quickly became a drizzle, a drizzle by satellite, as he devoured the print visible below the skull of the shoeshine man:

> But the Rev. Reginald Bacon, chairman of the Harlem-based All People's Solidarity, called this "the same old story. Human life, if it's black human life or Hispanic human life, is not worth much to the power structure. If this had been a white honor student struck down on Park Avenue by a black driver, they wouldn't be trifling with statistics and legal obstacles."

He called the hospital's failure to diagnose Lamb's concussion immediately "outrageous" and demanded an investigation.

Meantime, neighbors came by Mrs. Lamb's small, neatly kept apartment in the Poe Towers to comfort her as she reflected upon this latest development in her family's tragic history.

"Henry's father was killed right out there six years ago," she told *The City Light*, pointing toward a window overlooking the project's entry. Monroe Lamb, then 36, was shot to death by a mugger one night as he returned from his job as an air-conditioning mechanic.

"If I lose Henry, that will be the end of me, too, and nobody will care about that either," she said. "The police never found out who killed my husband, and they don't even want to look for who did this to Henry."

But Rev. Bacon vowed to put pressure on the authorities until something is done: "If the power structure is telling us it doesn't even matter what happens to our very best young people, the very hope of these mean streets, then it's time we had a message for the power structure: 'Your names are not engraved on tablets that came down from the mountain. There's an election coming up, and you can be replaced.' "

Abe Weiss, Bronx District Attorney, faces a stiff challenge in September's Democratic primary. State Assemblyman Robert Santiago has the backing of Bacon, Assemblyman Joseph Leonard, and other black leaders, as well as the leadership of the heavily Puerto Rican southern and central Bronx.

". . . and so I say we let it sit for a few weeks, let the particles settle. By then we'll know where bottom is. We'll know if we're talking about realistic prices. We'll know . . ."

It suddenly dawned on Sherman what the frightened doughnut Frog was saying. But he *couldn't wait*—not with *this thing* closing in on him—had to have a print—*now!*

"Bernard, now you listen. We *can't* wait. We've spent all this time getting everything in place. It doesn't have to sit and settle. It's *settled*. We've got to *move now!* You're raising phantom issues. We've got to pull ourselves together and *do it!* We've thrashed out all these things a long time ago! It doesn't *matter* what happens to gold and francs on a day-to-day basis!"

Even as he spoke, he recognized the fatal urgency in his voice. On Wall Street, a frantic salesman was a dead salesman. He knew that! But he couldn't hold back—

"I can't very well just close my eyes, Sherman."

"Nobody's asking you to." *Thok*. A *little tap*. A tall delicate boy, an honor student! The terrible thought possessed his entire consciousness: *They really were only two well-meaning boys who wanted to help* . . . Yo! . . . The ramp, the darkness . . . But what about him—the big one? No mention of a second boy at all . . . No mention of a ramp . . . It made no sense . . . *Only a coincidence perhaps!—another Mercedes!—R—2,500 of them—*

But in the Bronx on that very same evening?

The horror of the situation smothered him all over again.

"I'm sorry, but we can't do this one by Zen archery, Sherman. We're going to have to sit on the eggs for a while."

"What are you talking about? How long is 'a while,' for God's sake?" *Could they conceivably check out 2,500 automobiles?*

"Well, next week or the week after. I'd say three weeks at the outside."

"Three weeks!"

"We have a whole series of big presentations coming up. There's nothing we can do about that."

"I can't wait three weeks, Bernard! Now look, you've let a few minor problems—hell, they're not even *problems*. I've covered every one of those eventualities twenty goddamned times! You've *got to* do it now! Three weeks won't help a thing!"

On Wall Street, salesmen didn't say *got to*, either.

A pause. Then the doughnut's soft patient voice from Paris, by satellite: "Sherman. Please. For 300 million bonds nobody's *got to* do anything on hot flashes."

"Of course not, of course not. It's just that I know I've explained . . . I know I've . . . I know . . ."

He knew he had to talk himself down from this giddy urgent plateau as quickly as possible, become the smooth calm figure from the fiftieth floor at Pierce & Pierce that the Trader T doughnut had always known, a figure of confidence and unshakable *puissance*, but . . . it was *bound to be his car. No way out of it! Mercedes, RF, a white man and woman!*

The fire raged inside his skull. The black man stropped away on his shoe. The sounds of the bond trading room closed in on him like the roar of beasts:

"He's seeing them at six! Your offering is five!"

"Bid out! The Feds are doing reverses!"

"Feds buying all coupons! Market subject!"

"Holy fucking shit! I want out!"

All was confusion in Part 62, Judge Jerome Meldnick presiding. From behind the clerk's table, Kramer gazed upon Meldnick's bewilderment with amused contempt. Up on the bench, Meldnick's large pale head resembled a Gouda cheese. It was bent over next to that of his law secretary, Jonathan Steadman. Insofar as the judgeship of Jerome Meldnick had any usable legal background, it was lodged in the skull of Steadman. Meldnick had been executive secretary of the teachers' union, one of the largest and most solidly Democratic unions in the state, when the governor appointed him as a judge in the criminal division of the State Supreme Court in recognition of his jurisprudential potential and his decades of dog's work for the party. He had not practiced law since the days when he ran errands, shortly after passing the bar, for his uncle, who was a lawyer who handled wills and real-estate contracts and sold title insurance out of a two-story taxpayer on Queens Boulevard.

Irving Bietelberg, the lawyer for a felon named Willie Francisco, was on tiptoes on the other side of the bench, peering over and trying to get a word in. The defendant himself, Francisco, fat, twenty-two, wearing a wispy mustache and a red-and-white-striped sport shirt, was on his feet yelling at Bietelberg: "Yo! Hey! Yo!" Three court officers were positioned to the sides and rear of Willie, in case he got too excited. They would have been happy to blow his head off, since he had killed a cop without batting an eye. The cop had apprehended him when he came running out of an optician's with a pair of Porsche sunglasses in his hand. Porsche sunglasses were much admired in the Morrisania section of the Bronx, because they cost $250 a pair and had the name *Porsche* etched in white on the upper rim of the left lens. Willie had gone into the optician's with a forged Medicaid prescription for glasses and announced he wanted the Porsches. The clerk said he couldn't have them, because Medicaid wouldn't reimburse the store for glasses that cost that much. So Willie grabbed the Porsches and ran out and shot the cop.

It was a true piece a shit, this case, and an open-and-shut piece a shit, and Jimmy Caughey hadn't even had to breathe hard to win it. But then this weird thing had happened. The jury had gone out yesterday afternoon and after six hours had returned without reaching a verdict. This morning Meldnick was plowing through his calendar session when the jury sent in word they had reached a verdict. They came filing in, and the verdict was guilty. Bietelberg, just doing the usual, asked that the jury be polled. "Guilty," "Guilty," "Guilty," said one and all until the clerk got to an obese old white man, Lester McGuigan, who also said "Guilty" but then looked into the Porscheless eyes of Willie Francisco and said: "I don't feel absolutely right about it, but I guess I have to cast a vote, and that's the way I cast it."

Willie Francisco jumped up and yelled "Mistrial!" even before Bietelberg could yell it—and after that all was confusion. Meldnick wrapped his forearms around his head and summoned Steadman, and that was where things stood. Jimmy Caughey couldn't believe it. Bronx juries were notoriously unpredictable, but Caughey had figured McGuigan was one of his solid rocks. Not only was he white, he was Irish, a lifetime Bronx Irishman who would certainly know that anyone named Jimmy Caughey was a worthy young Irishman himself. But McGuigan had turned out to be an old man with time on his hands who thought too much and waxed too philosophical about things, even the likes of Willie Francisco.

Kramer was amused by Meldnick's confusion but not Jimmy Caughey's. For Jimmy he had only commiseration. Kramer was in Part 62 with a similar piece a shit and had similar ridiculous catastrophes to fear. Kramer was on hand to hear a motion for an evidentiary hearing from the lawyer, Gerard Scalio, in the case of Jorge and Juan Terzio, two brothers who were "a couple of real dummies." They had tried to hold up a Korean grocery store on Fordham Road but couldn't figure out which buttons to hit on the cash register and settled for pulling two rings off the fingers of a female customer. This so angers another customer, Charlie Esposito, that he runs after them, catches up with Jorge, tackles him, pins him to the ground, and says to him, "You know something? You're a couple of real dummies." Jorge reaches inside his shirt, pulls out his gun, and shoots him right in the face, killing him.

A true piece a shit.

As the shitstorm grew louder and Jimmy Caughey rolled his eyes in ever more hopeless arcs, Kramer thought of a brighter future. Tonight he would meet her at last . . . the Girl with Brown Lipstick.

Muldowny's, that restaurant on the East Side, Third Avenue at Seventy-eighth Street . . . exposed brick walls, blond wood, brass, etched glass, hanging plants . . . aspiring actresses who waited on tables . . . celebrities . . . but informal and not very expensive, or that's what he heard . . . the electric burble of young people in Manhattan leading . . . the Life . . . a table for two . . . He's looking into the incomparable face of Miss Shelly Thomas . . .

A small timid voice told him he shouldn't do it, or not yet. The case was over, so far as the trial went, and Herbert 92X had been duly convicted, and the jury had been dismissed. So what was the harm in his meeting a juror and asking her about the nature of the deliberations in this case? Nothing . . . except that the sentence had not been handed down yet, so that technically the case was not over. The prudent thing would be to wait. But in the meantime Miss Shelly Thomas might . . . decompress . . . come down from her crime high . . . no longer be enthralled by the magic of the fearless young assistant district attorney with the golden tongue and the powerful sternocleidomastoid muscles . . .

A strong manly voice asked him if he was going to play it safe and small-time the rest of his life. He squared his shoulders. He would keep the date. Damned right! The excitement in her voice! It was almost as if she had been *expecting* him to call. She was there in that glass-brick and white-pipe-railing MTV office at Prischker & Bolka, in the heart of the Life, still pulsing to the rogue beat of life in the raw in the Bronx, still thrilling to the strength of those who were manly enough to deal with the predators . . . He could see her, he could see her . . . He closed his eyes tightly . . . Her thick brown hair, her alabaster face, her lipstick . . .

"Hey, Kramer!" He opened his eyes. It was the clerk. "You got a phone call."

He picked up the telephone, which was on the clerk's desk. Up on the bench, Meldnick, in thick Gouda consternation, was still huddled with Steadman. Willie Francisco was still yelling, "Yo! Hey! Yo!"

"Kramer," said Kramer.

"Larry, this is Bernie. Have you seen *The City Light* today?"

"No."

"There's a big article on page 3 about this Henry Lamb case. Claims the cops are dragging their feet. Claims we are, too. Says you told this Mrs. Lamb the information she gave you was useless. It's a big article."

"What!"

"Don't mention you by name. Just says 'the man from the District Attorney's Office.' "

"That's absolute total bullshit, Bernie! I told her the fucking opposite! I said it was a good lead she gave us! It was just that it wasn't enough to build a case out of."

"Well, Weiss is going bananas. He's ricocheting off the walls. Milt Lubell's coming down here every three minutes. What are you doing right now?"

"I'm waiting for an evidentiary hearing in this Terzio brothers case, the two dummies. The Lamb case! Jesus Christ. Milt said the other day there was some guy, some fucking Englishman, calling up from *The City Light*—but Jesus Christ, this is outrageous. This case is fucking fulla holes. I hope you realize that, Bernie."

"Yeah, well, listen, get a postponement on the two dummies and come on down here."

"I can't. For a change, Meldnick is up on the bench holding his head. Some juror just recanted his guilty vote in the Willie Francisco case. Jimmy's up here with smoke coming out of his ears. Nothing's gonna happen here until Meldnick can find someone to tell him what to do."

"Francisco? Oh, f'r Chrissake. Who's the clerk there, Eisenberg?"

"Yeah."

"Lemme talk to him."

"Hey, Phil," said Kramer. "Bernie Fitzgibbon wants to talk to you."

While Bernie Fitzgibbon talked to Phil Eisenberg on the telephone, Kramer went around the other side of the clerk's table to gather up his papers on the Terzio brothers. He couldn't believe it. The poor widow Lamb, the woman even Martin and Goldberg had such pity for—she turns out to be a snake! Where was a newspaper? He was dying to get his hands on it. He found himself near the court stenographer, or court reporter, as the breed was actually called, the tall Irishman, Sullivan. Sullivan had stood up from his stenotype machine, just below the brow of the judge's bench, and was stretching. Sullivan was a good-looking, thatchy-haired man in his early forties, famous, or notorious, on Gibraltar for his dapper dress. At the moment he was wearing a tweed jacket that was so soft and luxurious, so full of heather glints from the Highlands, Kramer knew he couldn't have afforded it in a million years. From behind Kramer came an old courthouse regular named Joe Hyman, the supervisor of court reporters. He walked up to Sullivan and said, "There's a murder coming into this part. It'll go daily. How about it?"

Sullivan said, "What? C'mon, Joe. I just got through a murder. Whadda I want wit' another murder? I'll have to wagon-train. I got theater tickets. Cost me thirty-five dollars apiece."

Hyman said, "Awright, awright. What about the rape? There's a rape that's gotta be covered."

"Well, shit, Joe," said Sullivan, "a rape—that's a wagon train, too. Why me? Why do I always have to be the one? Sheila Polsky hasn't stayed with a jury for months. What about her?"

"She has a bad back. She can't sit that long."

"A bad back?" said Sullivan. "She's twenty-eight years old, f'r Chrissake. She's a goldbrick. That's all 'at'sa matter wit' her."

"All the same—"

"Look, we gotta have a meeting. I'm tired of always being the one. We gotta talk about the assignments. We gotta confront the goof-offs."

"Awright," said Hyman. "I'll tell you what. You take the rape and I'll put you in a half-a-day calendar part next week. Okay?"

"I don't know," said Sullivan. He wrapped his eyebrows around his nose, as if facing one of the agonizing decisions of a lifetime. "You think there'll be daily copy on the rape?"

"I don't know. Probably."

Daily copy. Now Kramer knew why he resented Sullivan and his fancy clothes. After fourteen years as a court reporter, Sullivan had achieved the civil-service ceiling of $51,000 a year—$14,500 more than Kramer made—and that was just the base. On top of that, the court reporters *sold* the transcripts page by page, at a minimum of $4.50 a page. "Daily copy" meant that each defense lawyer and the assistant D.A., plus the court, meaning the judge, wanted transcripts of each day's proceedings, a rush order that entitled Sullivan to a premium of $6 or more. If there were "multiple defendants"—and in rape cases there often were—it might go up to $14 or $15 a page. The word was that last year, in a murder trial involving a gang of Albanian drug dealers, Sullivan and another reporter had split $30,000 for two and a half weeks' work. It was nothing for these characters to make $75,000 a year, $10,000 more than the judge and *twice* as much as himself. A court reporter! An automaton at the stenotype machine! He who can't even open his mouth in a courtroom except to ask the judge to have someone repeat a word or a sentence!

And here was himself, Larry Kramer, a graduate of Columbia Law, an assistant D.A.—wondering if he was really going to be able to afford to take a girl with brown lipstick to a restaurant on the Upper East Side!

"Hey, Kramer." It was Eisenberg, the clerk, lifting the telephone toward him. "Yeah, Bernie?"

"I straightened it out with Eisenberg, Larry. He's gonna put the Terzio brothers at the bottom of the calendar. Come on down here. We gotta get something going on this fucking Lamb case."

"The way the Yanks build their council flats, the lifts stop only on every other floor," said Fallow, "and they smell like piss. The lifts, I mean. As soon as one enters—great fluffy fumes of human piss."

"Why every other floor?" asked Sir Gerald Steiner, devouring this tale of the lower depths. His managing editor, Brian Highridge, stood beside him, similarly rapt. In the corner of the cubicle Fallow's dirty raincoat still hung on the plastic coatrack, and the canteen of vodka was still cached in the slash pocket. But he had attention, praise, and exhilaration to deal with this morning's hangover.

"To save money in the construction. I should imagine," he said. "Or to remind the poor devils they're on the dole. It's all well and good for the ones who have flats on the floor where the lift stops, but the other half have to take it to the floor above and walk down. In a council flat in the Bronx it seems that's a hazardous arrangement. The boy's mother, this Mrs. Lamb, told me she lost half her furniture when she moved in." The recollection brought a smile to Fallow's lips, the sort of wry smile that says that this is a sad story and yet one has to admit it's funny. "She brought the furniture up on the lift to the floor above their flat. They had to carry each piece down the stairs, and each time they returned to the floor above, something would be missing. It's a custom! When new people move into an off-floor, the natives nip their belongs from beside the lift!"

The Dead Mouse and Highridge tried to choke back their laughter, since after all it was a lot of unfortunate poor people they were talking about. The Dead Mouse sat down on the edge of Fallow's desk, which indicated that he was pleased enough with all this to settle in for a moment. Fallow's soul expanded. What he saw before him was no longer . . . the Dead Mouse . . . but Sir Gerald Steiner, the enlightened baron of British publishing who had summoned him to the New World.

"Apparently it's worth your life just to go down the stairs at all," he continued. "Mrs. Lamb told me I shouldn't use them under any circumstances."

"Why not?" asked Steiner.

"It seems the staircases are the back streets of the council flats, so to speak. The flats are stacked up in these great towers, you see, and the towers are set this way and that"—he motioned with his hands to indicate the irregular arrangement—"in what are intended to be parks. Of course not a blade of grass survives, but in any case there are no streets or alleys or byways or pubs or whatever between the buildings, just these open blasted heaths. There's no place for the natives to *sin*. So they use the landings of the stairways. They do . . . *everything* . . . on the landings of the stairways."

The wide eyes of Sir Gerald and his managing editor were too much for Fallow. They sent a surge of poetic license up his brain stem.

"I must confess, I couldn't resist a look. So I decided to retrace the route Mrs. Lamb and her son had taken when they first moved into the Edgar Allan Poe Towers."

In fact, after the warning, Fallow hadn't dared go near the stairway. But now lies, graphic lies, bubbled up into his brain at an intoxicating rate. In his intrepid trip down the stairs he encountered every sort of vice: fornication, crack smoking, heroin injection, dice games and three-card monte, and more fornication.

Steiner and Highridge stared, agape and bug-eyed.

"Are you serious?" said Highridge. "What did they do when they saw you?"

"Nothing but slog away. In their sublime state, what was a mere passing journalist?"

"It's bloody Hogarth," said Steiner. "Gin Lane. Except that it's vertical."

Fallow and Highridge both laughed with enthusiastic appreciation of this comparison.

"The Vertical Gin Lane," said Highridge. "You know, Jerry, that wouldn't make a bad two-part series. Life-in-a-subsidized-slum sort of thing."

"Hogarth Up and Down," said Steiner, wallowing a bit in his new role as phrasemaker. "Or will the Americans have the faintest familiarity with Hogarth and Gin Lane?"

"Oh, I don't think that's any great problem," said Highridge. "You remember our story on the Bluebeard of Howard Beach. I'm sure they didn't have a ghost of an idea who Bluebeard was, but it can be explained in a paragraph, and then they're pleased about what they've just learned. And Peter here can be our Hogarth."

Fallow felt a slight stirring of alarm.

"On second thought," said Steiner, "I'm not sure it's such a good idea."

Fallow felt greatly relieved.

"Why not, Jerry?" asked Highridge. "I think you've really hit on something."

"Oh, I think it's intrinsically an important story. But, you know, they're very sensitive about this sort of thing. If we did a story about life in the white council flats, that would be all right, but I don't think there are any white council flats in New York. This is a very delicate area and one that's causing me some concern just now. We're already getting some rumblings from these organizations, accusing *The City Light* of being anti-minority, to use their term. Now, it's all right to *be* a white newspaper—what could be more pure white than the *Times?*—but it's quite another thing to pick up that reputation. That makes a great many influential people uneasy, including, I might say, advertisers. I received a dreadful letter the other day from some outfit calling itself the Third World Anti-Defamation League." He dragged out the term *Anti-Defamation* as if it were the most ludicrous concoction imaginable. "What was that all about, Brian?"

"The Laughing Vandals," said Highridge. "We had a picture on page one last week of three black boys in a police station, laughing. They'd been arrested for destroying the physical-therapy facilities in a school for handicapped children. Sprayed petrol and lit matches. Lovely fellows. The police said they were laughing about it after they brought them in, and so I sent one of our photographers,

Silverstein—he's an American—brazen little man—to go get a picture of them laughing." He shrugged, as if it had been a routine journalistic decision.

"The police were very cooperative. They brought them out of the lockup, out by the front desk, so our man could get a picture of them laughing, but when they saw Silverstein with his camera, they wouldn't laugh. So Silverstein told them a smutty joke. A *smutty joke!*" Highridge began laughing before he could finish. "It was about a Jewish woman who goes on a safari to Africa, and she's kidnapped by a gorilla, and he takes her up in a tree and rapes her, and he keeps her there for a month, raping her day and night, and finally she escapes, and she makes her way back to the United States, and she's relating all this to another woman, her best friend, and she breaks into tears. And the friend says, 'There, there, there, you're all right now.' And the woman says, 'That's easy for you to say. You don't know how I feel. He doesn't *write* . . . he doesn't *call* . . .' And the three boys start laughing, probably out of embarrassment at this terrible joke, and Silverstein takes their picture, and we ran it. 'The Laughing Vandals.'"

Steiner exploded. "Oh, that's rich! I shouldn't laugh. Oh my God! What did you say the chap's name was? Silverstein?'

"Silverstein," said Highridge. "You can't miss him. Always goes about with cuts on his face. He puts scraps of *toilet paper* on the cuts to stop the bleeding. Always has toilet paper stuck to his face."

"Cuts? What sort of cuts?"

"From a razor. Seems his father left him his straight razor when he died. He insists on using it. Can't get the hang of it. Cuts himself to pieces every day. Fortunately, he *can* take pictures."

Steiner was breathless with mirth "The Yanks! Dear God, I love them! Tells them a joke. Dear God, dear God . . . I do like a fellow with sand. Make a note of this, Brian. Give him a rise in pay. Twenty-five dollars a week. But for God's sake don't tell him or anyone else what for. Tells them a *joke!* Raped by a *gorilla!*"

Steiner's love of yellow journalism, his awe of the "sand" that gave journalists the courage to try such stunts, was so genuine, Fallow and Highridge couldn't help but laugh along with him. Steiner's little face was far from that of a Dead Mouse at this moment. The outrageous zest of this American photographer, Silverstein, lent him life, even radiance.

"All the same," said Steiner, sobering up, "we've got this problem."

"I think we were perfectly justified," said Highridge. "The police assured us they had been laughing about it. It was their lawyer, one of these Legal Aid people, I think they call them, who made a fuss, and he probably got hold of this Anti-Defamation whatever-it-is."

"The facts aren't what matters, unfortunately," Steiner said. "We have to alter some perceptions, and I think this hit-and-run case is a good place to start. Let's see what we can do for this family, these poor Lamb people. They already seem to have some support. This man Bacon."

"The poor Lambs," said Brian Highridge. "Yes." Steiner looked puzzled; his turn of phrase had been inadvertent.

"Now, let me ask you, Peter," said Steiner, "does the mother, this Mrs. Lamb, strike you as a credible person?"

"Oh yes," said Fallow. "She makes a good appearance, she's well-spoken, very sincere. She has a job, she seems very neat in her habits—I mean, these council flats are squalid little places, but hers is very orderly . . . pictures on the walls

. . . sofa-with-end-tables sort of thing . . . even a little-table-inside-the-front-door sort of thing."

"And the boy—he's not going to blow up in our faces, is he? I believe he's some sort of honor student?"

"By the standards of his school. I'm not sure how he would fare at Holland Park Comprehensive." Fallow smiled. This was a school in London. "He's never been in trouble with the police. That's so unusual in these council flats, they talk about it as if one's bound to be impressed by this remarkable fact."

"What do the neighbors say about him?"

"Oh . . . that he's a pleasant . . . well-behaved sort of boy," said Fallow. In fact, Fallow had gone straight to Annie Lamb's apartment with Albert Vogel and one of Reverend Bacon's people, a tall man with a gold ring in one ear, and had interviewed Annie Lamb and departed. But by now his status as an intrepid explorer of the lower depths, Bronx version, was so exalted in the eyes of his noble employer, he didn't care to back off just yet.

"Very well," said Steiner. "What do we have as a follow-up?"

"Reverend Bacon—that's what everybody calls him, Reverend Bacon—Reverend Bacon is organizing a large demonstration for tomorrow. It's to protest—"

Just then Fallow's telephone rang.

"Hello?"

"Ayyyy, Pete!" It was the unmistakable voice of Albert Vogel. "Things are poppin'. Some kid just called Bacon, some kid down at the Motor Vehicle Bureau." Fallow began making notes. "This kid, he read your story, and he took it upon himself to get on the computer down there, and he claims he's got it narrowed down to 124 cars."

"A hundred and twenty-four? Can the police handle that?"

"Nothing to it—if they want to. They can check 'em out in a few days, if they want to put the men on it."

"Who is this . . . fellow?" Fallow detested the American habit of using the word *kid*, which properly referred only to goats, to mean "young person."

"Just some kid who works there, some kid who figures the Lambs are getting the usual raw deal. I told you that's what I like about Bacon. He galvanizes people who want to challenge the power structure."

"How do I get in touch with this . . . fellow?"

Vogel gave him all the details, then said: "Now, Pete, listen to me a second. Bacon just read your story and he liked it very much. Every newspaper and TV station in town has been calling him, but he's saving this Motor Vehicle Bureau angle for you. It's yours, exclusive. Okay? But you gotta push it. You gotta run with the goddamned ball. You understand what I'm saying?"

"I understand."

After he hung up, Fallow smiled at Steiner and Highridge, who were all eyes, nodded knowingly, and said: "Yesssss . . . I think we're rolling. That was a tipster at the Motor Vehicle Bureau, where they keep records of all the license plates."

It was just the way he had dreamed it would be. It was precisely that way, it made him want to hold his breath for fear something would break the spell. She was looking into his eyes from just a tiny table's width away. She was absorbed in his words, drawn into his magnetic field, so far into it that he had the urge to slide his hands across the table and slip his fingertips under hers—already!—just twenty minutes after he's met her—such electricity! But he mustn't rush it, mustn't destroy the exquisite poise of this moment.

In the background were the exposed brick, the mellow highlights of the brass, the pubby carved cataracts of the etched glass, the aerobic voices of the young and swell. In the foreground, her great mane of dark hair, the Berkshire autumn glow of her cheeks—in point of fact, he realized, even in the midst of the magic, the autumnal glow was probably makeup. Certainly the mauve-and-purple rainbows on her upper eyelids and occipital orbits were makeup—but such was the nature of contemporary perfection. From her lips, swollen with desire, glistening with brown lipstick, came the words:

"But you were so *close* to him and practically *yelling* at him, and he was giving you such *murderous* looks—I mean, weren't you afraid he was just going to *jump up* and—I don't know—I mean, he did not look like a nice person!"

"Ayyyyyyyyy," said Kramer, dismissing mortal danger with a shrug of his shoulders and a distention of his mighty sternocleidomastoid muscles. "These characters are 90 percent show, although it's a good idea to keep your eye out for the other 10 percent. Hah hah, yes. The main thing was, somehow I had to bring out Herbert's violent side, so everybody could see it. His lawyer, Al Teskowitz— well, I don't have to tell you, he's not the greatest orator in the world, but that don't—doesn't"—it was time to shift gears in the third person singular—"necessarily make any difference in a criminal trial. Criminal law is a thing unto itself, because the stakes are not money but human life and human freedom, and I tell you, that sets off a lot of crazy emotions. Teskowitz, believe it or not, can be a genius at messing up the minds—manipulating a jury. He looks so woebegone himself—and it's *calculated*—oh, sure. He knows how to work up pity for a client. Half of it is—what's the term?—body language, I guess you'd call it. Maybe just ham *acting* is what it is, but he knows how to do that one thing very well, and I couldn't let this idea that Herbert is a nice family man—a *family* man!—just hang there in the air like some kind of pretty balloon, you know. So what I figured was—"

The words were just gushing out, in torrents, all the marvelous things about his bravery and talent for the fray that he had no one to tell about. He couldn't go on like this to Jimmy Caughey or Ray Andriutti or, any longer, to his wife, whose threshold for crime highs was by now a stone wall. But Miss Shelly Thomas —I must keep you high! She drank it all in. Those eyes! Those glistening brown lips! Her thirst for his words was bottomless, which was a good thing, because she wasn't drinking anything but designer water. Kramer had a glass of house white wine and was trying to keep from gulping it, because he could already tell this place was not as inexpensive as he had thought. Christ! His goddamned mind was double-tracking a mile a minute! It was like a two-track tape. On one track he was gushing out this speech about how he handled the trial—

"—out of the corner of my eye I could see he was about to snap. The string was pulled tight! I didn't even know if I'd make it to the end of my summation, but I was willing—"

—and on the second track he was thinking about *her*, the bill (and they hadn't even ordered dinner yet), and where he could possibly take her (if!), and the crowd here at Muldowny's. Jesus! Wasn't that John Rector, the anchorman of Channel 9 news, over there at that table up near the front, by the exposed-brick wall? But no! He wouldn't point that out. Only space for one celebrity here—himself—victor over the violent Herbert 92X and the clever Al Teskowitz. A young crowd, a swell-looking crowd in here—the place was packed—perfect—couldn't be better. Shelly Thomas had turned out to be Greek. Bit of a disappointment. He had wanted—didn't know what. Thomas was her stepfather's name; he manufactured plastic containers in Long Island City. Her own father was named Choudras. She lived in Riverdale with her stepfather and her mother, worked for Prischker & Bolka, couldn't afford an apartment in Manhattan, wanted one badly—no longer could you find "some little place in Manhattan" (didn't have to tell him)—

"—thing is, juries in the Bronx are very unpredictable. I could tell you what happened to one of the fellows in my office in court this morning!—but you probably noticed what I'm talking about. I mean, you get people who come into the jury box with their minds—how should I say it?—set in a certain way. There's a lot of Us versus Them, Them being the police and prosecutors—but you probably picked up some of that."

"No, actually I didn't. Everybody was very sensible, and they seemed to want to do the right thing. I didn't know what to expect, but I was very pleasantly surprised."

Does she think I'm prejudiced? "No, I don't mean—there are plenty of good people in the Bronx, it's just that some people have a chip on their shoulder, and some very weird things happen." Let's move off this terrain. "As long as we're being candid, do you mind if I tell you something? I was worried about *you* as a juror."

"Me!" She smiled and seemed to blush clear through the makeup glow, tickled pink to have been a factor in strategic thinking in Supreme Court, the Bronx.

"Yes! It's the truth! You see, in a criminal trial you learn to look at things from a different perspective. It may be a warped perspective, but it's the nature of the beast. In a case like this one—you're—well, you added up as *too* bright, *too* well educated, *too removed* from the world of a character like Herbert 92X, and therefore—and this is the irony of it—too capable of understanding his problems, and like the French say, 'To understand all is to forgive all.' "

"Well, actually—"

"I'm not saying that's fair or accurate, but that's the way you learn to look at things in these cases. Not you—but someone like you—can be *too sensitive.*"

"But you didn't challenge me. Is that the term?"

"Yeah. No, I didn't. Well, for one thing, I don't think it's right to challenge a juror just because he's—she's intelligent and well educated. I mean, I'm sure you noticed there was nobody else from Riverdale on your jury. There wasn't even anybody else from Riverdale on your panel during the *voir dire.* Everybody is always moaning over the fact that we don't get more educated jurors in the Bronx, and then when we get one—well, it's almost like wasting a resource or something to challenge one just because you think she might be *sensitive.* Besides . . ." Did he dare try it? He *dared.* ". . . I just . . . to be honest about it . . . I just wanted you on that jury."

He looked as deeply into those big mauve-rainbow eyes as he could and put as honest and open a look on his face as he knew how and lifted his chin, so she could see the fullness of his sternocleidomastoids.

She lowered her eyes and blushed clear through autumn in the Berkshires again. Then she raised her eyes and looked deeply into his.

"I did sort of notice you looking at me a lot."

Me 'n' every other regular in the courtroom!—but it wouldn't do to let her know about that.

"You did? I was hoping it wasn't that obvious! God, I hope other people didn't notice it."

"Hah hah! I think they did. You know the lady who was sitting next to me, the black lady? She was a very nice person. She works for a gynecologist, and she's very sweet, very intelligent. I asked her for her telephone number, and I told her I'd call her. Anyway, you want to know what she said to me?"

"What?"

"She said, 'I think that district attorney kind of likes you, Shelly.' She called me Shelly. We hit it off very well. 'He can't take his eyes off you.' "

"She said that?" He broke into a smile.

"Yes."

"Did she resent it? I mean, oh my God. I didn't think it was *that* obvious!"

"No, she thought it was cute. Women like things like that."

"It was that obvious, hunh?"

"It was to her!"

Kramer shook his head, as if in embarrassment, all the while pouring his eyes into hers, and she was pouring hers right back into his. They had already jumped over the moat, and rather effortlessly, too. He knew—he *knew!*—he could slide his hands across the table and take her fingertips in his, and she would let him, and it would all happen without their eyes leaving one another's, but he held back. It was too perfect and going too well to take the slightest risk.

He kept shaking his head and smiling . . . ever more significantly . . . In fact, he was embarrassed, although not over the fact that others had noticed how possessed with her he had been in the courtroom. Where to *go*—that was what he was embarrassed about. She didn't have an apartment, and of course there was no way in God's world he could take her to his ant colony. A hotel?—far too gross, and besides, how the hell could he afford it? Even a second-rate hotel was almost a hundred dollars a room. God only knew what this meal was going to cost. The menu had an artless hand-lettered look that set off an alarm in Kramer's central nervous system: *money.* Somehow he knew, based on very little experience, that this *faux*-casual shit spelled *money.*

Just then the waitress returned. "Have you had a chance to decide?"

She was a perfect confection, too. Young, blond, curly-haired, brilliant blue eyes, the perfect aspiring-actress type, with dimples and a smile that said: "Well! I can see that you two have decided *something!*" Or did it say, "I'm young, pretty, and charming, and I expect a big tip when you pay your big bill"?

Kramer looked into her twinkling face, and then he looked into Miss Shelly Thomas's. He was consumed by feelings of lust and poverty.

"Well, Shelly," he said, "you know what you'd like?"

It was the first time he had called her by her first name.

Sherman sat on the edge of one of the bentwood chairs. He was leaning forward with his hands clasped between his knees and his head down. The noxious, incriminating copy of *The City Light* lay on top of the oak pedestal table like something radioactive. Maria sat in the other chair, more composed but not exactly her old insouciant self, either.

"I knew it," said Sherman, without looking at her, "I knew it at the time. We should have reported it immediately. I can't believe I'm—I can't believe we're in this situation."

"Well, it's too late now, Sherman. That's spilt milk."

He sat up straight and looked at her. "Maybe it's not too late. What you say is, you say you didn't know until you read this newspaper that you'd hit anyone."

"Oh, sure," said Maria. "Then how do I say it happened, this thing I didn't even know happened in the first place?"

"Just . . . tell what actually happened."

"That'll sound *wonderful*. Two boys stopped us and tried to rob us, but you threw a tire at one of them, and I drove outta there like a . . . a . . . *hot-rodder*, but I didn't know I hit anybody."

"Well, that's exactly what happened, Maria."

"And who's gonna believe it? You read that story. They're calling that boy some kinda *honor* student, some kinda saint. They don't say anything about the other one. They don't even say anything about a ramp. They're talking about a little saint who went to get food for his family."

The terrible possibility flared up once more. What if the two boys *were* only trying to help?

There sat Maria in a turtleneck jersey that brought out her perfect breasts even at this moment. She wore a short checked skirt, and her glistening legs were crossed, and one of her pair of pumps dangled off the tip of her foot.

Beyond her was the make-do bed, and above the bed there was now a second small oil painting, of a nude woman holding a small animal. The brushwork was so atrociously crude, he couldn't tell what kind of animal it was. It could be a rat as easily as a dog. His misery made his eye hang on it for a moment.

"You noticed it," said Maria, attempting a smile. "You're getting better. Filippo gave it to me."

"Terrific." The question of why some greaseball artist might feel so generous toward Maria no longer interested Sherman in the slightest. The world had shrunk. "So what do you think we ought to do?"

"I think we ought to take ten deep breaths and relax. That's what I think."

"And then what?"

"And then maybe nothing." 'N thin mibby nuthun. "Sherman, if we tell 'em the truth, they're gonna *kill* us. You understand that? They're gonna cut us up in little pieces. Right now they don't know whose car it was, they don't know who was driving, they don't have any witnesses, and the boy himself is in a coma and it doesn't look like he's . . . he's ever gonna come to."

You were driving, thought Sherman. Don't forget that part. It reassured him to hear her say it. Then a jolt of fear: suppose she denied it and said he was driving? But the other boy knew, wherever he might be.

All he said, however, was: "What about the other boy? Suppose he shows up."

"If he was gonna show up, he woulda showed up by now. He's not gonna show up, because he's a criminal."

Sherman leaned forward and put his head down again. He found himself staring at the shiny tops of his New & Lingwood half-brogues. The colossal vanity of his bench-made English shoes sickened him. What availeth a man . . . He couldn't remember the quotation. He could see the pitiful brown moon on the crown of Felix's skull . . . Knoxville . . Why hadn't he moved to Knoxville long ago? . . . a simple Georgian house with a screen porch at one end . . .

"I don't know, Maria," he said, without looking up. "I don't think we can outguess them. I think maybe we ought to get in touch with a lawyer"—*two* lawyers, said a small voice in the back of his skull, since I don't know this woman and we may not be on the same side forever— "and . . . come forward with what we know."

"And stick our heads in the tiger's mouth is what you mean." 'N stick uh hids in thuh tiguh's mouth. Maria's Southernism was beginning to get on Sherman's nerves. "I'm the one who was driving the car, Sherman,'and so I think it's up to me to decide."

I'm the one who was driving the car! She had said it herself. His spirits lifted a bit. "I'm not trying to talk you into anything," he said. "I'm just thinking out loud."

Maria's expression grew softer. She smiled at him in a warm, almost motherly fashion. "Sherman, let me tell you something. There's two kinds of jungles. Wall Street is a jungle. You've heard that, haven't you? You know how to handle yourself in that jungle." The Southern breeze was blowing past his ears—but it was true, wasn't it? His spirits rose a bit more. "And then there's the other jungle. That's the one we got lost in the other night, in the Bronx. And you *fought*, Sherman! You were wonderful!" He had to resist congratulating himself with a smile. "But you don't live in that jungle, Sherman, and you never have. You know what's in that jungle? People who are all the time crossing back and forth, back and forth, back and forth, from this side of the law to the other side, from this side to the other side. You don't know what that's like. You had a *good* upbringing. Laws weren't any kind of a threat to you. They were *your laws*, Sherman, people like you and your family's. Well, I didn't grow up that way. We were always staggering back and forth across the line, like a buncha drunks, and so I know and it doesn't frighten me. And let me tell you something else. Right there on the line everybody's an animal—the police, the judges, the criminals, everybody."

She continued to smile warmly at him, like a mother who has let a child in on a great truth. He wondered if she really knew what she was talking about or whether she was just indulging in a little sentimental reverse snobbery.

"So what are you saying?" he asked.

"I'm saying I think you ought to trust my instincts."

Just then there was a knock on the door.

"Who's that?" said Sherman, going on red alert.

"Don't worry," said Maria. "It's Germaine. I told her you'd be here." She got up to go to the door.

"You didn't tell her what happened . . ."

"Of course not."

She opened the door. But it wasn't Germaine. It was a gigantic man in an outlandish black outfit. He came walking in as if he owned the place, took a quick look around the room, at Sherman, the walls, the ceiling, the floor, and then at Maria.

"You Germaine Boll?"—he was gasping for breath, apparently because he had just walked up the stairs—"or Bowl?"

Maria was speechless. So was Sherman. The giant was young, white, with a big crinkly black beard, a huge apoplectic-red face glistening with perspiration, a black homburg with an absolutely flat brim, a too-small black homburg perched way up on his huge head like a toy, a rumpled white shirt buttoned at the throat, but no tie, and a shiny black double-breasted suit with the right side of the jacket overlapping the left, the way a woman's jacket is usually made. A Hasidic Jew. Sherman had often seen Hasidic Jews in the Diamond District, which was on Forty-sixth and Forty-seventh Streets between Fifth and Sixth Avenues, but he had never seen one so enormous. He was probably six feet five, well over 250 pounds, grossly fat but powerfully built, bulging out of his liverish skin like a length of bratwurst. He took off his homburg. His hair was pasted down on his skull with perspiration. He hit the side of his great head with the heel of his hand, as if he were tamping it back into shape. Then he put his hat back on his head. It was perched up so high, it looked as if it might fall off at any moment. Perspiration rolled down the giant's forehead.

"Germaine Boll? Bowl? Bull?"

"No, I'm not," said Maria. She had recovered. She was testy, already on the attack. "She's not here. What do you want?"

"You live here?" For such a big man, he had an oddly high-pitched voice.

"Miss Boll isn't here now," said Maria, ignoring the question.

"You live here or she live here?"

"Look, we're kinda busy." Exaggerated patience. "Why don't you try later?" Challengingly: "How'd you get in this building?"

The giant reached into the right-hand pocket of his jacket and pulled out an enormous ring of keys. There appeared to be scores of them. He ran a great fat forefinger around the ruff of keys and stopped at one of them and delicately lifted it with his forefinger and thumb.

"With this. Winter Real Estate." Wid dis. Wint-tuh Reelastate. He had a slightly Yiddish accent.

"Well, you'll have to come back later and talk to Miss Boll."

The giant didn't budge. He looked around the apartment again. "You don't live here?"

"Now, listen—"

"It's okay, it's okay. We gonna paint in here." With that the giant stretched both his arms out, like wings, as if he were about to do a swan dive, and walked over to a wall and faced it. Then he pressed his left hand against the wall and sidled over and lifted his left hand and pressed his right hand down on that spot and shuffled over to his left until he was spread out in the swan-dive position again.

Maria looked at Sherman. He knew he was going to have to do something, but he couldn't imagine what. He walked over to the giant. In as frosty and commanding a tone as he could create, just as the Lion of Dunning Sponget would have done it, he said: "Just a minute. What are you doing?"

"Measuring," said the giant, still doing his swan-dive shuffle around the wall. "Got to paint in here."

"Well, I'm very sorry, but we don't have time for that now. You'll have to make your arrangements some other time."

The enormous young man turned around slowly and put his hands on his hips. He took a deep breath, so that he looked puffed up to about five hundred pounds.

On his face was the look of someone forced to deal with a pest. Sherman had the sinking feeling that this monster was used to such confrontations and, in fact, relished them. But the male battle was now on.

"*You* live here?" asked the giant.

"I said we don't have time for this," said Sherman, trying to maintain the Lion's tone of cool command. "Now, be a good fellow and leave and come back and do your painting some other time."

"You *live* here?"

"In point of fact, I *don't* live here, but I'm a guest here, and I don't—"

"*You* don't live here and *she* don't live here. What you doing here?"

"That's not your concern!" said Sherman, unable to control his anger but feeling more helpless by the second. He pointed toward the door. "Now, be a good fellow and leave!"

"You don't belong here. Okay? We got a real problem." *We gottuh reel problem.* "We gottuh wrong people living in this building. This a rent-control building, and the people, they turn around"—*zuhn arount*—"and they rent the apartments to other people for a thousand, two thousand dollars a month. The rent in this apartment here, it's only $331 a month. See? Germaine Boll—but we never see huh here. How much you pay huh?"

Such insolence! The male battle! What could he do? In most situations Sherman felt like a big man, physically. Next to this outlandish creature . . . He couldn't possibly touch him. He couldn't intimidate him. The Lion's cool commands had no effect. And beneath it all the very foundations were rotten. He was at a complete moral disadvantage. He *didn't* belong here—and he had everything in the world to hide. And what if this incredible monster was not actually from the Winter Real Estate Company? Suppose—

Fortunately Maria intervened. "It so happens Miss Boll's gonna be here very shortly. In the meantime—"

"Okay! Good! I wait fuh huh."

The giant began walking across the room like a rocking druid. He stopped at the oak pedestal table, and with glorious casualness, he lowered his tremendous heft into one of the bentwood chairs.

"All right!" said Maria. "That's about enough!"

The giant's response to that was to fold his arms and close his eyes and lean back, as if to settle in for the duration. In that instant Sherman realized he would truly have to do something, no matter what, or else be stripped of all manhood. The male battle! He started to step forward.

Craaaacccckkkk! All at once the monster was on the floor, on his back, and the stiff brim of his homburg was cartwheeling crazily along the rug. One leg of the chair was cracked almost in two, near the seat, with the light wood underneath the exterior stain showing. The chair had collapsed under his weight.

Maria was screaming. "Now look what you've done, you peckerwood! You brood sow! You tub a lard!"

With much huffing and puffing, the giant righted himself and began hoisting himself to his feet. His insolent pose was shattered. He was red in the face, and the perspiration was pouring down again. He leaned over to pick up his hat and almost lost his balance.

Maria continued on the attack. She pointed at the remains of the chair. "I hope you realize you're gonna have to pay for that!"

"Whaddaya whaddaya," said the giant. "It don't belong to you!" But he was retreating. Maria's reproaches and his own embarrassment were too much for him.

"That's gonna cost you five hundred dollars and a—and a lawsuit!" said Maria. "That's breaking and entering and entering and breaking!"

The giant paused by the door and glowered, but it was all too much for him. He went rocking out the door in great disarray.

As soon as she heard him clumping down the stairs, Maria closed the door and locked it. She turned around and looked at Sherman and gave a great whoop of laughter.

"Did . . . you . . . see . . . him . . . on . . . the . . . floor!" She was laughing so hard, she could scarcely get the words out.

Sherman stared at her. It was true—she was right. They were different animals. Maria had the stomach for . . . for whatever was happening to them. She fought—with relish! Life was a fight on the line she was talking about—and so what? He *wanted* to laugh. He wanted to share her animal joy in the ludicrous scene they had just witnessed. But he couldn't. He couldn't even manage a smile. He felt as if the very insulation of his position in the world was unraveling. These . . . unbelievable people . . . could now walk into his life.

"Craaaaasssssssh!" said Maria, weeping with laughter. "Oh God, I wish I had a videotape a that!" Then she caught the look on Sherman's face. "What's the matter?"

"What do you think that was all about?"

"What do you mean, 'all about'?"

"What do you think he was doing here?"

"The *land*lord sent him. You remember that letter I showed you."

"But isn't it kind of odd that—"

"Germaine pays only $331 a month, and I pay her $750. It's rent-controlled. They'd love to get her out of here."

"It doesn't strike you as odd that they'd decide to barge in here—right now?"

"Right now?"

"Well, maybe I'm crazy, but today—after this thing is in the paper?"

"In the *paper*?" Then it dawned on her what he was saying, and she broke into a smile. "Sherman, you *are* crazy. You're paranoid. You know that?"

"Maybe I am. It just seems like a very odd coincidence."

"Who do you think sent him in here, if the landlord didn't? The police?"

"Well . . ." Realizing it did sound rather paranoid, he smiled faintly.

"The police are gonna send a colossal great Hasidic piece-a-blubber moron lunatic to *spy* on you?"

Sherman hung his mighty Yale chin down over his collarbone. "You're right."

Maria walked over and lifted his chin with her forefinger and looked into his eyes and smiled the most loving smile he had ever seen.

"Sherman." Shuhmun. "The entire world isn't standing still thinking about you. The entire world isn't out to *get* you. Only I am."

She took his face in both hands and kissed him. They ended up on the bed, but this time it took some doing on his part. It wasn't the same when you were scared half to death.

12

THE LAST OF THE GREAT SMOKERS

AFTER A FITFUL SLEEP, Sherman reached Pierce & Pierce at eight o'clock. He was exhausted, and the day hadn't begun. The bond trading room had an hallucinatory quality. The appalling glare on the harbor side . . . the writhing silhouettes . . . the radium-green numbers skidding across the faces of an infinite number of terminals . . . the young Masters of the Universe, so utterly unknowing, bawling at the electric doughnuts:

"I'll pay two!"

"Yeah, but what about the when-issued?"

"Down two ticks!"

"Bullshit! You can't turn off a fuse!"

Even Rawlie, poor dispirited Rawlie, was on his feet, his telephone at his ear, his lips moving a mile a minute, drumming his desktop with a pencil. Young Arguello, lord of the pampas, was rocked back in his chair with his thighs akimbo, the telephone at his ear, his moiré suspenders blazing away, and a big grin on his young gigolo face. He had scored a smashing coup yesterday in Japan with the Treasuries. The whole trading room was talking about it. Grinning grinning grinning grinning, the greaseball lounged in triumph.

Sherman had a craving to go to the Yale Club and take a steam bath and lie down on one of those leather-top tables and get a good hot hammering massage and go to sleep.

On his desk was a message, marked urgent, to call Bernard Levy in Paris.

Four computer terminals away, Felix was working on the right shoe of a gangling, obnoxious young whiz named Ahlstrom, just two years out of Wharton. Ahlstrom was on the telephone. Gobble, gobble, gobble, eh, Mr. Ahlstrom? Felix —*The City Light*. It would be on the stands by now. He wanted to see it, and he dreaded seeing it.

Scarcely even aware what he was doing, Sherman put the telephone to his ear and dialed the Trader T number in Paris. He leaned over the desk and supported himself with both elbows. As soon as Felix was through with the hot young

Ahlstrom, he would call him over. Some part of his mind was listening when the French doughnut, Bernard Levy, said:

"Sherman, after we spoke yesterday, I talked it over with New York, and everyone agrees you're right. There's no point waiting."

Thank God.

"But," Bernard continued, "we can't go ninety-six."

"Can't go ninety-six?"

He was hearing portentous words . . . and yet he couldn't concentrate . . . The morning newspapers, the *Times*, the *Post*, the *News*, which he had read in the taxi on the way downtown, contained rehashes of the *City Light* story, plus more statements from this black man, Reverend Bacon. Ferocious denunciations of the hospital where the boy still lay in a coma. For a moment Sherman had taken heart. *They were blaming it all on the hospital!* Then he realized this was wishful thinking. They would blame . . . *She* was driving. If they closed in, finally, if all else failed, *she* was driving. It was *her*. He clung to that.

"No, ninety-six is no longer on the table," said Bernard. "But we're ready at ninety-three."

"Ninety-three!"

Sherman sat up straight. This could not be true. Certainly in the next moment Bernard would tell him he'd made a slip. He'd say ninety-five at the worst. Sherman had paid ninety-four. Six hundred million bonds at ninety-four! At ninety-three Pierce & Pierce would lose six million dollars.

"Surely you didn't say ninety-three!"

"Ninety-three, Sherman. We think it's a very fair price. In any event, that's the offer."

"Christ almighty . . . I've got to think for a second. Listen, I'll call you back. Will you be there?"

"Of course."

"All right. I'll call you right back."

He hung up and rubbed his eyes. Christ! There must be a way to pull this out. He had let himself get rattled with Bernard yesterday. Fatal! Bernard had detected panic in his voice and had pulled back. Get yourself together! Regroup! Think this thing out! There's no way you can let it collapse after all this! Call him back and be yourself, best producer of Pierce & Pierce!—Master of the . . . He lost heart. The more he urged himself on, the more nervous he became. He looked at his watch. He looked at Felix. Felix was just rising from the shoe of the hot child, Ahlstrom. He waved him over. He took his money clip out of his pants pocket, sat down, put it between his knees to hide it, withdrew a five-dollar bill and slipped it into an interoffice envelope, then stood up as Felix walked over.

"Felix, there's five dollars in there. Go downstairs and get me a *City Light*, will you? The change is yours."

Felix looked at him and then gave him a funny smile and said, "Yeah, okay, but you know, last time they keep me waiting down there at the stand, and the elevator don't come, and I lose a lotta time. It's fifty floors down there. Cost me a lotta time." He didn't budge.

It was outrageous! He was claiming that five dollars to go fetch a thirty-five-cent newspaper was cutting into his profit margin as a shoeshine man! He had the nerve to gouge him—ahhhhhhhh . . . that was it. Some kind of street radar

told him that if he was hiding the newspaper in an envelope, then it was contra-
band. It was smuggling. It was desperation, and desperate people pay money.

Scarcely able to contain his fury, Sherman dug into his pocket and came up
with another five dollars and thrust it at the black man, who took it, gave him a
fastidiously bored look, and went off with the envelope.

He dialed Paris again.

"Bernard?"

"Yes?"

"Sherman. I'm still working on it. Give me another fifteen or twenty minutes."

A pause. "All right."

Sherman hung up and looked toward the great rear window. The silhouettes
bobbed and jerked about in insane patterns. If he was willing to come up to
ninety-five . . . In no time the black man was back. He handed him the envelope without a word or a fathomable expression.

The envelope was fat with the tabloid. It was as if there were something alive
in there. He put it under his desk, where it gnashed and thrashed about.

If he threw part of his own profit into it . . . He began jotting down the
figures on a piece of paper. The sight of them—meaningless! Attached to nothing! He could hear himself breathing. He picked up the envelope and headed for
the men's room.

Inside the cubicle, the pants of his two-thousand-dollar Savile Row suit grac-
ing the bare toilet seat, his New & Lingwood cap-toed shoes pulled back up
against the china toilet bowl, Sherman opened up the envelope and withdrew the
newspaper. Every crackle of the paper accused him. The front page . . . CHINA-
TOWN GHOST VOTER SCANDAL . . . of no earthly interest . . . He opened it up
. . . Page 2 . . . Page 3 . . . a picture of a Chinese restaurant owner . . . It
was at the bottom of the page:

SECRET PRINTOUT
IN BRONX HIT'N'RUN

Above the headline, in smaller white letters upon a black bar: *New Bombshell in
Lamb Case*. Below the headline, on another black bar, it said: A CITY LIGHT
Exclusive. The story was by the same Peter Fallow:

> Declaring "I'm fed up with the foot-dragging," a source within the
> Division of Motor Vehicles yesterday provided *The City Light* with a
> computer printout narrowing down to 124 the number of vehicles that
> might have been involved in last week's hit-and-run maiming of
> Bronx honor student Henry Lamb.
>
> The source, who has worked with police on similar cases in the
> past, said: "They can check out 124 vehicles in a few days. But first
> they have to want to commit the manpower. When the victim is from
> the projects, they don't always want to."
>
> Lamb, who lives with his widowed mother in the Edgar Allan Poe
> Towers, a Bronx housing project, lies in an apparently irreversible
> coma. Before losing consciousness, he was able to give his mother the
> first letter—R—and five possibilities for the second letter—E, F, B, R,

P—of the license plate of the luxurious Mercedes-Benz that ran him down on Bruckner Boulevard and sped off.

Police and the Bronx District Attorney's Office have objected that almost 500 Mercedes-Benzes registered in New York State have plates beginning with those letters, too many to justify a vehicle-by-vehicle check in a case where the only known witness, Lamb himself, may never regain consciousness.

But *The City Light*'s DMV source said: "Sure, there are 500 possibilities, but only 124 that are likely. Bruckner Boulevard, where this young man was run down, is not exactly a tourist attraction. It stands to reason that the vehicle belongs to someone in New York City or Westchester. If you go on that assumption—and I've seen the cops do it in other cases—that narrows it down to 124."

The revelation prompted new demands by a black leader, Rev. Reginald Bacon, for a full-scale investigation of the incident.

"If the police and the District Attorney won't do it, we'll do it ourselves," he said. "The power structure lets this brilliant young man's life be destroyed and then just yawns. But we're not going to stand for that. We've got the printout now, and we'll track down those cars ourselves if we have to."

Sherman's heart jumped inside his chest.

Lamb's South Bronx neighborhood was described as "up in arms" and "seething with fury" over the handling of his injuries and the alleged reluctance of authorities to move on the case.

A spokesman for the Health and Hospital Administration said an "internal investigation" was under way. Police and the office of Bronx District Attorney Abe Weiss said their investigations were "continuing." They refused comment on the narrowing down of the number of vehicles, but a DMV spokesman, Ruth Berkowitz, referring to the material obtained by *The City Light*, said: "The unauthorized release of ownership data in a sensitive case such as this is a serious and very irresponsible breach of departmental policy."

That was it. Sherman sat on the toilet seat staring at the block of type. Closing the noose! But the police weren't paying any attention to it . . . Yes, but suppose this . . . this *Bacon* . . . and a bunch of seething black people, up in arms, started checking the cars themselves . . . He tried to picture it . . . Too gross for his imagination . . . He looked up at the gray-beige door of the toilet cubicle . . . The air hinge of the door to the men's room was opening. Then a door opened just a couple of cubicles away. Slowly Sherman closed the newspaper and folded it over and slipped it back inside the interoffice envelope. Ever so slowly he rose from the toilet seat; ever so quietly he opened the cubicle door; ever so stealthily he stole across the men's-room floor, while his heart raced on ahead.

Once more in the bond trading room, he picked up the telephone. Must call Bernard. *Must call Maria.* He tried to put a businesslike expression on his fa‑ Personal calls from the bond trading room of Pierce & Pierce were much ‑

upon. He dialed her apartment on Fifth. A woman with a Spanish accent answered. Mrs. Ruskin not at home. He called the hideaway, dialing the numbers with great deliberation. No answer. He rocked back in his chair. His eyes focused in the distance . . . the glare, the flailing silhouettes, the roar . . .

The sound of someone's fingers snapping over his head . . . He looked up. It was Rawlie, snapping his fingers.

"Wake up. Thinking's not allowed around here."

"I was just . . ." He didn't bother to finish, because Rawlie had already passed by.

He hunched over his desk and looked at the radium-green numbers trucking across the screens.

Just like that he decided to go see Freddy Button.

What would he tell Muriel, the sales assistant? He would tell her he was going to see Mel Troutman at Polsek & Fragner about the Medicart Fleet issue . . . That was what he would tell her . . . and the notion sickened him. One of the Lion's maxims was "A lie may fool someone else, but it tells you the truth: you're weak."

He couldn't remember Freddy Button's telephone number. It had been that long since he had called him. He looked it up in his address book.

"This is Sherman McCoy. I'd like to speak to Mr. Button."

"I'm sorry, Mr. McCoy, he's with a client. Can he call you back?"

Sherman paused. "Tell him it's urgent."

The secretary paused. "Hold on."

Sherman was hunched over his desk. He looked down at his feet . . . the envelope with the newspaper . . . No! Suppose she called in to Freddy over an intercom, and another lawyer, someone who knew his father, heard her say it . . . "Sherman McCoy, urgent" . . .

"Excuse me! Wait a second! Never mind—are you there?" He was yelling into the telephone. She was gone.

He stared down at the envelope. He scribbled some figures on a piece of paper, so as to look busy and businesslike. The next thing he heard was the ever-suave, ever-nasal voice of Freddy Button.

"Sherman. How are you? What's up?"

On the way out, Sherman told his lie to Muriel and felt cheap, sordid, and weak.

Like a lot of other old-line, well-fixed Protestant families in Manhattan, the McCoys had always made sure that only other Protestants ministered to their private affairs and their bodies. By now, this took some doing. Protestant dentists and accountants were rare creatures, and Protestant doctors weren't easy to find.

Protestant lawyers were still plentiful, however, at least on Wall Street, and Sherman had become a client of Freddy Button the same way he had joined the Knickerbocker Greys, the kiddie cadet corps, as a boy. His father had arranged it. When Sherman was a senior at Yale, the Lion thought it was time he made out a will, as an orderly and prudent part of growing up. So he passed him along to Freddy, who was then a young and newly made partner at Dunning Sponget. Sherman had never had to worry about whether Freddy was a good lawyer or not. He had gone to him to be tidy: for wills, redrafted when he married Judy and when Campbell was born, for contracts when he bought the apartment on Park

Avenue and the house in Southampton. The purchase of the apartment had made Sherman think twice. Freddy knew he had borrowed $1.8 million to buy it, and that was more than he wanted his father (technically Freddy's partner) to know. Freddy had kept his counsel. But in an obscene business like this, with the newspapers screaming, was there some reason why—some procedure—some practice of the firm—something that would cause the matter to be circulated to other partners—to the aging Lion himself?

Dunning Sponget & Leach occupied four floors of a skyscraper on Wall Street, three blocks from Pierce & Pierce. When it was built, it had been the very latest in the 1920s Moderne style, but now it had the grimy gloom that was typical of Wall Street. The Dunning Sponget offices resembled Pierce & Pierce's. In both cases modern interiors had been caked with eighteenth-century English paneling and stocked with eighteenth-century English furniture. This was lost on Sherman, however. To him, everything about Dunning Sponget was as venerable as his father.

To his relief, the receptionist didn't recognize him or his name. Of course, by now the Lion was nothing more than one of the wrinkled old partners who infested the corridors for a few hours each day. Sherman had just taken a seat in an armchair when Freddy Button's secretary, Miss Zilitsky, appeared. She was one of those women who look fiftyish and loyal. She led him down a silent hall.

Freddy, tall, lank, elegant, charming, smoking away, stood waiting for him at the door of his office.

"Hel-lo, Sherman!" A plume of cigarette smoke, a magnificent smile, a warm handshake, a charming display of pleasure at the very sight of Sherman McCoy. "My goodness, my goodness, how are you? Have a seat. How about some coffee? Miss Zilitsky!"

"No, thanks. Not for me."

"How's Judy?"

"Fine."

"And Campbell?" He always remembered Campbell's name, which Sherman appreciated even in his present state.

"Oh, she's thriving."

"She's at Taliaferro now, isn't she?"

"Yes. How did you know that? Did my father mention it?"

"No, my daughter Sally. She graduated from Taliaferro two years ago. Absolutely loved it. Keeps up with everything. She's at Brown now."

"How does she like Brown?" Jesus Christ, why am I even bothering to ask? But he knew why. Freddy's thick, fast, meaningless current of charm swept you up. Helpless, you said the usual.

It was a mistake. Freddy was immediately off on an anecdote about Brown and coed dorms. Sherman didn't bother listening. To make a point, Freddy flipped his long hands upward in a languid, effeminate gesture. He was always talking about families, his family, your family, other people's families, and he was a homosexual. No doubt about it. Freddy was about fifty years old, six feet four or more, slender, awkwardly put together but elegantly dressed in the English "drape" style. His limp blond hair, now dulled by a rising tide of gray, was slicked back in the 1930s fashion. Languidly he settled into his chair, across the desk from Sherman, talking as he did so, and smoking. He took a deep draft of the cigarette and let the smoke curl out of his mouth and drained it up into his nostrils in two thick columns.

This was once known as French inhaling and was so known to Freddy Button, the last of the Great Smokers. He blew smoke rings. He French-inhaled and blew large smoke rings and then blew speedy little smoke rings through the large ones. From time to time he held his cigarette not between his first two fingers but between his thumb and forefinger, upright, like a candle. Why was it that homosexuals smoked so much? Perhaps because they were self-destructive. But the word *self-destructive* was the outer limit of Sherman's familiarity with psychoanalytical thought, and so his eyes began to drift. Freddy's office was *done*, the way Judy talked about *doing* apartments. It looked like something from one of those abominable magazines . . . burgundy velvet, oxblood leather, burled wood, brass and silver bibelots . . . All at once Freddy and his charm and his taste were supremely annoying.

Freddy must have sensed his irritation, because he broke off his story and said, "Well—you said something happened with you and your car."

"Unfortunately, you can read about it, Freddy." Sherman opened his attaché case and took out the Pierce & Pierce interoffice envelope and withdrew the copy of *The City Light* and folded it back to page 3 and handed it across the desk. "The piece at the bottom of the page."

Freddy took the newspaper with his left hand, and with his right he put the cigarette out in a Lalique ashtray with a lion's head sculpted on the rim. He reached toward a white silk handkerchief that debouched carelessly, voluptuously, from the breast pocket of his jacket and withdrew a pair of horn-rimmed glasses. Then he put the newspaper down and put the glasses on with both hands. From his inside breast pocket he took out a silver-and-ivory cigarette case, opened it, and removed a cigarette from under a silver clip. He tamped it on the outside of the case, lit it with a slender fluted silver lighter, then picked up the newspaper and commenced reading; or reading and smoking. With his eyes fixed on the newspaper, he brought the cigarette to his lips in the candle position, between his thumb and forefinger, took a deep drag, twirled his fingers and—bingo!—the cigarette popped out between the knuckles of his forefinger and middle finger. Sherman was amazed. How had he done it? Then he was furious. He turns into a tobacco acrobat—*in the middle of my crisis!*

Freddy finished the article and laid the cigarette in the Lalique ashtray with great care and took off his glasses and tucked them back beneath the lustrous silk handkerchief and picked up the cigarette again and took another profound drag on it.

Sherman, spitting the words out: "That's my car you just read about."

The anger in his voice startled Freddy. Gingerly, as if tiptoeing, he said: "You have a Mercedes with a license number that starts with R? R-something?"

"Exactly." With a hiss.

Freddy, befuddled: "Well . . . why don't you tell me what happened?"

Not until Freddy said those words did Sherman realize that . . . he was dying to! He was dying to confess—to someone! Anyone! Even this nicotine *Turnvereiner*, this homosexual fop who was a partner of his father! He had never looked at Freddy with such clarity before. He could *see* him. Freddy was the sort of willowy wand of charm into whose office a Wall Street firm of the Dunning Sponget magnitude shunted all the widows and legacies, such as himself, who were presumed to have more money than problems. Yet he was the only confessor available.

"I have a friend named Maria Ruskin," he said. "She's the wife of a man named Arthur Ruskin, who's made a lot of money doing God knows what."

"I've heard of him," said Freddy, nodding.

"I've—" Sherman stopped. He didn't know quite how to word it. "I've been seeing a bit of Mrs. Ruskin." He pursed his lips and stared at Freddy. The unspoken message was "Yes; precisely; it's the usual sordid case of cheap lust."

Freddy nodded.

Sherman hesitated again, then plunged on into the details of the automobile ride into the Bronx. He studied Freddy's face for signs of disapproval or—worse! —enjoyment! He detected nothing but a friendly concern punctuated by smoke rings. Sherman no longer resented him, however. Such relief! The vile poison was gushing out! My confessor!

As he told his tale, he was aware of something else: an irrational joy. He was the main character in an exciting story. All over again he took pride—stupid pride!—in having fought in the jungle and triumphed. He was on stage. He was the star! Freddy's expression had progressed from friendly and concerned . . . to entranced . . .

"And so here I am," Sherman said, finally. "I can't figure out what to do. I wish I'd gone straight to the police when it happened."

Freddy leaned back in his chair and looked away and took a drag on his cigarette, then turned back and gave Sherman a reassuring smile.

"Well, from what you've told me, you're not responsible for the injury to the young man." As he spoke, inhaled smoke came out of his mouth in faint jets. Sherman hadn't seen anyone do that for years. "You may have some obligation, as the owner of the vehicle, to report the incident, and there may be the question of leaving the scene of the accident. I'd have to look up the statute. I suppose they could develop an assault charge, for throwing the tire, but I don't think it would hold up, since you clearly had reason to believe your life was in danger. In fact, this really isn't as unusual a circumstance as you might think. Do you know Clinton Danforth?"

"No."

"He's the chairman of the board of Danco. I represented him in a suit against the Triple A. The Automobile Club of New York was the actual entity, I believe. He and his wife—you've never seen Clinton?"

Seen him? "No."

"Very proper. Looks like one of those capitalists the cartoonists used to draw, with the silk topper. Anyway, one night Clinton and his wife were driving home—" Now he was off on some story about the car of this illustrious client of his breaking down in Ozone Park, Queens. Sherman sifted the words for some little nugget of hope. Then it dawned on him that this was merely Freddy's charm reflex at work. The essence of the social charmer was having a story, preferably with Fat Names in it, to fit every subject. In a quarter century of law practice, this was probably the only case Freddy ever handled that even touched the streets of New York.

". . . a black man with a police dog on a leash—"

"Freddy." Sherman, hissing again. "I don't care about your fat friend Danforth."

"What?" Freddy, befuddled and shocked.

"I haven't got time for it. I have a problem."

"Oh, listen. Please. Forgive me." Freddy spoke softly, warily; also sadly, the way you might talk to a lunatic who was heating up. "Really, I was only trying to show you—"

"Never mind showing me. Put out that cigarette and tell me what you think."

Without taking his eyes off Sherman's face, Freddy put out the cigarette in the Lalique ashtray. "All right, I'll tell you exactly what I think."

"I don't mean to be abrupt, Freddy, but Jesus Christ."

"I know, Sherman."

"Please smoke if you want to, but let's stick to the point."

The hands fluttered up to indicate that smoking wasn't important.

"All right," said Freddy, "here's what I see. I think you're in the clear on the major issue here, which is the personal injury. You might conceivably be at risk of a felony charge for leaving the scene and not notifying the police. As I say, I'll research that. But I think that's not too serious a proposition, assuming we can establish the sequence of events as you've outlined them to me."

"What do you mean, 'establish'?"

"Well, the thing that worries me about this newspaper story is that it's so far off from the facts as you've given them to me."

"Oh, I know it!" said Sherman. "There's no mention of the other—the other fellow, the one who first approached me. There's not one word about the barricade or even the ramp. They're saying it happened on Bruckner Boulevard. It didn't happen on Bruckner Boulevard or any other boulevard. They're making out that this boy, this . . . *honor* student . . . this black saint . . . was walking across the street, minding his own business, and some white bigot in a 'luxury car' comes along and runs him down and keeps going. It's lunacy! They keep calling it a 'luxury car,' and all it is, is a Mercedes. Christ, a Mercedes is like a Buick used to be."

Freddy's arch of the eyebrows said, "Not precisely." But Sherman pressed on.

"Let me ask you this, Freddy. Does the fact that"—he started to say "Maria Ruskin" but didn't want to appear to be anxious to lay off blame—"the fact that I wasn't driving when the boy was hit, does that put me in the clear legally?"

"So far as the injury to the young man is concerned, it seems to me. Again, I'd want to review the statutes. But let me ask you something. What is your friend Mrs. Ruskin's version of what happened?"

"Her version?"

"Yes. How does she say this fellow got hit? Does she say she was driving?"

"Does she *say* she was driving? She *was driving*."

"Yes, but let's suppose she sees some possibility of a felony charge if she says she was driving."

Sherman was speechless for a moment. "Well, I can't imagine she would . . ." *Lie* was the word he meant to say but didn't, for in fact it was not utterly beyond the realm of the imagination. The notion shocked him. "Well . . . all I can tell you is that every time we've talked about it, she's said the same thing. She's always used the expression 'After all, I was the one who was driving.' When I first suggested going to the police, right after it happened, that was what she said. 'I was the one who was driving. So it's up to me to decide.' I mean, I guess anything can happen, but . . . God almighty."

"I'm not trying to sow doubt, Sherman. I just want to make sure you know that she may be the only person who can corroborate your version of this thing—and at some risk to herself."

Sherman sank back in his chair. The voluptuous warrior who had fought beside him in the jungle and then, glistening, made love to him on the floor . . .

"So if I go to the police now," he said, "and I tell them what happened, and she doesn't back me up, then I'm worse off than I am now."

"It's a possibility. Look, I'm not suggesting she won't back you up. I just want you to be aware of . . . where you stand."

"What do you think I should do, Freddy?"

"Who have you talked to about this?"

"No one. Just you."

"How about Judy?"

"No. Least of all Judy, if you want to know the truth."

"Well, for the time being you shouldn't talk to anybody about it, probably not even Judy, unless you feel compelled to. Even then, you should impress upon her the need to keep absolutely quiet about it. You'd be amazed at how the things you say can be picked up and turned against you, if someone wants to do it. I've seen it happen too many times."

Sherman doubted that, but he merely nodded.

"In the meantime, with your permission, I'm going to talk this situation over with another lawyer I know, a fellow who works in this area all the time."

"Not somebody here at Dunning Sponget—"

"No."

"Because I'd hate to have this thing kicking around the halls here at this goddamned place."

"Don't worry, it's another firm entirely."

"What firm?"

"It's called Dershkin, Bellavita, Fishbein & Schlossel."

The torrent of syllables was like a bad smell.

"What kind of firm is that?"

"Oh, they have a general practice, but they're best known for their work in criminal law."

"*Criminal* law?"

Freddy smiled faintly. "Don't worry. Criminal lawyers help people who aren't criminals, too. We've used this fellow before. His name is Thomas Killian. He's very bright. He's about your age. He went to Yale, as a matter of fact, or at least he went to the law school. He's the only Irishman who ever graduated from the Yale Law School, and he's the only graduate of the Yale Law School who ever practiced criminal law. I'm exaggerating, of course."

Sherman sank back into the chair again and tried to let the term *criminal law* sink in. Seeing that he was once more The Lawyer with the upper hand, Freddy took out the silver-and-ivory case, eased a Senior Service from under the silver clip, tamped it, lit up, and inhaled with profound satisfaction.

"I want to see what he thinks," said Freddy, "particularly since, judging by this newspaper story, this case is taking on political overtones. Tommy Killian can give us a much better reading on that than I can."

"Dershkin, Something & Schloffel?"

"Dershkin, Bellavita, Fishbein & Schlossel," said Freddy. "Three Jews and an Italian, and Tommy Killian is an Irishman. Let me tell you something, Sherman.

The practice of law gets very specialized in New York. It's as if there are a lot of little . . . *clans* . . . of *trolls* . . . I'll give you an example. If I was being sued in an automobile negligence case, I wouldn't want anybody at Dunning Sponget representing me. I'd go to one of these lawyers on lower Broadway who don't do anything else. They're the absolute bottom of the barrel of the legal profession. They're all Bellavitas and Schlossels. They're crude, coarse, sleazy, unappetizing—you can't even imagine what they're like. But that's who I'd go to. They know all the judges, all the clerks, the other lawyers—they know how to make the deals. If somebody named Bradshaw or Farnsworth showed up from Dunning Sponget & Leach, they'd freeze him out. They'd sabotage him. It's the same way with criminal law. The criminal lawyers aren't exactly the *bout en train*, either, but in certain cases you've got to use them. Given that situation, Tommy Killian is a very good choice."

"Jesus Christ," said Sherman. Of all the things Freddy had said, only the words *criminal law* had stuck.

"Don't look so gloomy, Sherman!"

Criminal law.

When he returned to the bond trading floor at Pierce & Pierce, the sales assistant, Muriel, gave him a dour look.

"Where were you, Sherman? I've been trying to reach you."

"I was—" He started to repeat the lie, with improvements, but the look on her face told him it would only make things worse. "Okay, what's wrong?"

"An issue came in just after you left, 200 million Fidelity Mutuals. So I called over to Polsek and Fragner, but you weren't there, and they said they weren't even expecting you. Arnold's not happy, Sherman. He wants to see you."

"I'll go see him." He turned away and started toward the desk.

"Wait a second," said Muriel. "This fellow in Paris has been trying to get you, too. He's called about four times. Mr. Levy. Said you were supposed to call him back. Said to tell you ninety-three is it. 'Final,' he said. He said you'd know what he meant."

13

THE DAY-GLO EEL

Kramer and the two detectives, Martin and Goldberg, arrived at the Edgar Allan Poe Towers in an unmarked Dodge sedan about 4:15. The demonstration was scheduled for five o'clock. The housing project had been designed during the Green Grass era of slum eradication. The idea had been to build apartment towers upon a grassy landscape where the young might gambol and the old might sit beneath shade trees, along sinuous footpaths. In fact, the gamboling youth broke off, cut down, or uprooted the shade-tree seedlings during the first month, and any old person fool enough to sit along the sinuous footpaths was in for the same treatment. The project was now a huge cluster of grimy brick towers set on a slab of cinders and stomped dirt. With the green wooden slats long gone, the concrete supports of the benches looked like ancient ruins. The ebb and flow of the city, caused by the tides of human labor, didn't cause a ripple at the Edgar Allan Poe Towers, where the unemployment rate was at least 75 percent. The place was no livelier at 4:15 p.m. than it was at noon. Kramer couldn't spy a soul, except for a small pack of male teenagers scurrying past the graffiti at the base of the buildings. The graffiti looked halfhearted. The grimy brick, with all its mortar gulleys, depressed even the spray-can juvies.

Martin slowed the car down to a crawl. They were on the main drag, out in front of Building A, where the demonstration was supposed to be held. The block was empty, except for a gangling teenager out in the middle of the street working on the wheel of a car. The car, a red Camaro, was nosed into a parking space along the curb. The rear end stuck out into the street. The boy wore black jeans, a black T-shirt, and striped sneakers. He was sitting on his haunches with a lug wrench in his hands.

Martin stopped the car barely ten feet from him and shut off the engine. The boy, still on his haunches, stared at the Dodge. Martin and Goldberg were in the front seat, and Kramer was in the back. Martin and Goldberg just sat there, looking straight ahead. Kramer couldn't imagine what they were doing. Then Martin got out. He was wearing a tan windbreaker, a polo shirt, and a pair of cheap-looking gray pants. He walked over to the boy and stood over him and said, "Whaddaya doing?" He didn't say it nicely, either.

Baffled, the boy said, "Nothing. Fixing a hubcap."

"*Fixing* a hubcap?" asked Martin, his voice sopping with insinuation.

"Yehhhhhhh . . ."

"You always park like this, out inna middle a the fucking street?"

The boy stood up. He was well over six feet tall. He had long muscular arms and powerful hands, one of which was holding the lug wrench. His mouth open, he stared down at Martin, who suddenly looked like a dwarf. Martin's narrow shoulders seemed nonexistent under the windbreaker. He wore no badge or any other police insignia. Kramer couldn't believe what he was watching. Here they were in the South Bronx, thirty minutes away from a demonstration protesting the shortcomings of White Justice, and Martin throws down the gauntlet to a black youth twice his size with a lug wrench in his hand.

Martin cocked his head to one side and stared into the boy's incredulous face without so much as a blink. The boy apparently found it exceedingly strange, too, because he didn't move or say anything, either. Now he glanced at the Dodge and found himself staring into the big meaty face of Goldberg, with its slits for eyes and its drooping black mustache. Then he looked at Martin again and put on a brave and angry face.

"Just fixing a hubcap, champ. Got nothing to do with you."

Before he got to the word *you*, he was already moving away from Martin with what was supposed to pass for a saunter. He opened the door of the Camaro and tossed the wrench in the back seat and sauntered around to the driver's side and got in and started up the car and maneuvered it out of the parking place and headed off. The Camaro gave a great throaty roar. Martin returned to the Dodge and got behind the wheel.

"I'm putting you in for a community relations commendation, Marty," said Goldberg.

"Kid's lucky I didn't run a check," said Martin. "Besides, that's the only parking place on the fucking block."

And they wonder why people hate them in the ghetto, thought Kramer. Yet in that very moment he marveled . . . *marveled!* He, Kramer, was big enough and strong enough to have fought the boy with the wrench, and conceivably he might have beaten him. But he would have *had to do that.* If he had confronted the boy, it would have reached the fighting stage immediately. But Martin knew from the beginning that it wouldn't. He knew that something in his eyes would make the boy sense Irish Cop Who Don't Back Off. Of course, it didn't hurt to have Goldberg sitting there looking like the Original Cruel Thug, and it didn't hurt to have a .38 under your jacket. Nevertheless, Kramer knew he couldn't have done what this outrageous little featherweight champion of the breed had done, and for the five hundredth time in his career as an assistant district attorney in the Bronx he paid silent homage to that most mysterious and coveted of male attributes, Irish machismo.

Martin parked the Dodge in the space the boy had vacated, and the three of them sat back and waited.

"Bullshit reigns," said Martin.

"Hey, Marty," said Kramer, proud to be on a first-name basis with this paragon, "you guys find out who gave that printout to *The City Light?*"

Without turning around, Martin said, "One a da *brothers*," giving an Irish rendition of a black accent. He turned his head slightly and twisted his lips to indicate it was about what you would expect and that there was nothing to be done about it.

"You gonna check out all 124 cars or whatever it is?"

"Yeah. Weiss has been on the C.O.'s case all day."

"How long will it take?"

"Three or four days. He's assigned six men. Bullshit reigns."

Goldberg turned around and said to Kramer: "What's with Weiss? Does he really believe this shit he reads in the newspapers or what?"

"That's all he believes," said Kramer. "And anything with a racial angle drives him crazy. Like I told you, he's up for re-election."

"Yeah, but what makes him think we're gonna find witnesses at this demonstration, which is *pure* bullshit?"

"I don't know. But that's what he told Bernie."

Goldberg shook his head. "We don't even have a location where the goddamned thing happened. You realize that? Marty and me been up and down Bruckner Boulevard and I'll be goddamned if we can establish where it happened. That's another thing the kid forgot to tell his mother when he came up with the bullshit license plate, where it's fucking supposeda've happened."

"Speaking of that," said Kramer, "how would a kid in the Poe project even know what a Mercedes looks like?"

"Oh, they know that," said Martin, without turning his head. "The pimps and wiseguys drive the Mercedes."

"Yeah," said Goldberg. "They won't look at a Cadillac anymore. You see these kids with these things, these hood ornaments from the Mercedes, hanging around their necks."

"If a kid up here wants to think up a bullshit car for a bullshit story," said Martin, "the Mercedes is the first one he's gonna think of. Bernie knows that."

"Well, Weiss is all over Bernie's case, too," said Kramer. He looked around some more. The huge project was so quiet it was eerie. "You sure this is the right place, Marty? There's nobody here."

"Don't worry," said Martin. "They'll be here. Bullshit reigns."

Pretty soon a bronze-colored passenger van pulled into the block and stopped up ahead of them. About a dozen men got out. All of them were black. Most of them wore blue work shirts and dungarees. They appeared to be in their twenties or early thirties. One of them stood out because he was so tall. He had an angular profile and a large Adam's apple and wore a gold ring in one ear. He said something to the others, and they began pulling lengths of lumber out of the van. These turned out to be the shafts of picket signs. They stacked the signs on the sidewalk. Half the men leaned up against the van and began talking and smoking cigarettes.

"I've seen that tall asshole somewhere," said Martin.

"I think I seen him, too," said Goldberg. "Oh, shit, yes. He's one a Bacon's assholes, the one they call Buck. He was at that thing on Gun Hill Road."

Martin sat up straight. "You're right, Davey. That's the same asshole." He stared across the street at the man. "I'd really love to . . ." He spoke in a dreamy fashion. "Please, you asshole, please just do one stupid thing, you asshole . . . I'm getting out."

Martin got out of the Dodge and stood on the sidewalk and very ostentatiously began rolling his shoulders and arms about, like a prizefighter loosening up. Then Goldberg got out. So Kramer got out, too. The demonstrators across the street began staring at them.

Now one of them, a powerfully built young man in a blue work shirt and blue jeans, came walking across the street with a cool Pimp Roll and approached Martin.

"Yo!" he said. "You from the TV?"

Martin put his chin down and shook his head no; very slowly, in a way that was pure menace.

The black man measured him with his eyes and said, "Then where you from, Jack?"

"Jump City, Agnes," said Martin.

The young man tried a scowl, and then he tried a smile, and he got nothing with either one but a face full of Irish contempt. He turned around and walked back across the street and said something to the others, and the one named Buck stared at Martin. Martin stared back with a pair of Shamrock lasers. Buck turned his head and gathered four or five of the others around him in a huddle. From time to time they stole glances at Martin.

This Mexican standoff had been going on for a few minutes when another van arrived. Some young white people got out, seven men and three women. They looked like college students, with the exception of one woman with long wavy gray-blond hair.

"Yo, Buck!" she sang out. She went up to the tall man with the gold earring and held out both her hands and smiled broadly. He took her hands, although not all that enthusiastically, and said, "Hey, how you doing, Reva?" The woman pulled him toward her and kissed him on one cheek and then on the other.

"Oh, give me a fucking break," said Goldberg. "That skank."

"You know her?" asked Kramer.

"Know who she is. She's a fucking Communist."

Then the white woman, Reva, turned around and said something, and a white man and a white woman went back to the van and hauled out more placards.

Presently a third van arrived. Nine or ten more white people got out, male and female, most of them young. They hauled a big roll of cloth out of the van and unfurled it. It was a banner. Kramer could make out the words GAY FIST STRIKE FORCE AGAINST RACISM.

"What the hell's that?" he said.

"That's the lesbos and the gaybos," said Goldberg.

"What are they doing here?"

"They're at alla these things. They must like the fresh air. They really get it on."

"But what's their interest in the case?"

"Don't ask me. The unity of the oppressed, they call it. Any of these groups need bodies, they'll show up."

So now there were about two dozen white and a dozen black demonstrators, lolling about, chatting and assembling placards and banners.

Now a car arrived. Two men got out. One of them carried two cameras on straps around his neck and a saddlebag with the printed logo THE CITY LIGHT taped to it. The other was a tall man in his thirties, with a long nose and blond hair that flowed from a narrow widow's peak. His fair complexion was splotched with red. He wore a blue blazer of an unusual and, to Kramer's eyes, foreign cut. For no apparent reason he suddenly lurched to his left. He appeared to be in agony. He stood stock-still on the sidewalk, tucked a spiral notebook under his left arm, closed his eyes, and pressed both hands to his temples, massaged them for a long time, then opened his eyes and winced and blinked and looked all about.

Martin began to laugh. "Look at that face. Looks like a working vat a rye mash. Guy's so hung over, he's bleeding into his squash."

Fallow lurched to his left again. He kept listing to port. Something was seriously wrong with his vestibular system. It was absolutely poisonous, this one, as if his brain were wrapped in membranous strings, like the strings of the membranes of an orange, and each contraction of his heart tightened the strings, and the poison was squeezed into his system. He had had throbbing headaches before, but this was a *toxic* headache, poisonous in the extreme—

Where were the crowds? Had they come to the wrong place? There seemed to be a handful of black people and about twenty white students, just standing about. A huge banner said GAY FIST *Gay Fist?* He had dreaded the thought of the noise and the commotion, but now he was worried about the silence.

On the sidewalk, just ahead of him, was the same tall black man with the gold earring who had driven him and Vogel up here two days ago. Vogel. He closed his eyes. Vogel had taken him to dinner at Leicester's last night as a kind of celebration (payment?) for the article . . . He had a vodka Southside . . . then another one . . . *The snout of the beast!—lit up by a radium-blue flare!* . . . Tony Stalk and Caroline Heftshank came over and sat down, and Fallow tried to apologize for what had happened with her young friend, Chirazzi, the artist, and Caroline gave him a strange smile and said he shouldn't worry about that, and he had another vodka Southside, and Caroline kept drinking Frascati and shrieking to Britt-Withers in a very silly way, and finally he came over, and she unbuttoned his shirt and pulled the hair on his chest so hard he swore, and then Fallow and Caroline were in Britt-Withers's office upstairs, where Britt-Withers had a watery-eyed bull terrier on a chain, and Caroline kept looking at Fallow with her strange smile, and he tried to unbutton her blouse, and she laughed at him and patted him on the bottom, contemptuously, but it made him feel crazy, and—*a ripple!— the beast stirred in the icy depths!*—and she curved her finger and beckoned, and he knew she was mocking him, but he walked across the office anyway, and there was a machine—something about a machine and a radium-blue flare—*thrashing! heading for the surface!*—a rubbery flap—he could almost see it now—*almost!*— and she was mocking him, but he didn't care, and she kept pressing something, and the radium blue flared from inside, and there was a grinding hum, and she reached down and she picked it up—she showed him—he could almost see it— no holding it back—*it broke through the surface and looked at him straight down its filthy snout*—and it was like a woodblock outlined in a radium aura against a black ground, and the beast kept staring at him down its snout, and he wanted to open his eyes to drive it away, but he couldn't, and the bull terrier started growling, and Caroline no longer looked at him, even to show her contempt, and so he touched her on the shoulder, but she was suddenly all business, and the machine kept grinding and humming and grinding and humming and flaring in radium blue, and then she had a stack of pictures in her hand, and she ran down the stairs to the restaurant, and he kept keeling to one side, and then a terrible thought came to him. He ran down the stairs, which were in a tight spiral, and that made him dizzier. On the floor of the restaurant, so many roaring faces and boiling teeth!— and Caroline Heftshank was standing near the bar showing the picture to Cecil Smallwood and Billy Cortez, and then there were pictures all over the place, and he was thrashing through the tables and the people grabbing for the pictures—

He opened his eyes and tried to keep them open. The Bronx, the Bronx, he was in the Bronx. He walked toward the man with the gold earring, Buck. He kept listing to port. He felt dizzy. He wondered if he had suffered a stroke.

"Hello," he said to Buck. He meant it to be cheery, but it came out as a gasp. Buck looked at him without a trace of recognition. So he said: "Peter Fallow, from *The City Light.*"

"Oh, hey, how you doing, bro." The black man's tone was agreeable but not enthusiastic. The author of the brilliant scoops in *The City Light* had expected enthusiasm. The black man resumed his conversation with the woman.

"When does the demonstration begin?" said Fallow.

Buck looked up distractedly. "Soon's Channel 1 gets here." By the time he reached the word *here*, he was once again looking at the woman.

"But where are the people?"

He stared at Fallow and paused, as if trying to figure him out. "They'll be here . . . soon's Channel 1 gets here." He used the sort of voice you use for someone who is blameless but dense.

"I see," said Fallow, who couldn't see at all. "When, uh, as you say, Channel 1 arrives, uh . . . what takes place then?"

"Give the man the release, Reva," said Buck. An intense demented-looking white woman dug down into a big vinyl tote bag on the sidewalk by her feet and handed him two pieces of paper stapled together. The paper, which was Xeroxed —*Xeroxed! Radium-blue! The snout!*—bore the letterhead of the American People's Alliance. A headline, typed in capital letters, said: THE PEOPLE DEMAND ACTION IN THE LAMB CASE.

Fallow started to read it, but the words ran together like goulash in front of his face. Just then a bouncy young white man materialized. He was wearing an appallingly tasteless tweed jacket.

"Neil Flannagan from the *Daily News*," said the bouncy man. "What's going on?"

The woman named Reva dug out another press release. Mr. Neil Flannagan, like Fallow himself, was accompanied by a photographer. The bouncy Mr. Flannagan had nothing to say to Fallow, but the two photographers fell in with one another at once. Fallow could hear them complaining about the assignment. Fallow's photographer, an odious little man who wore a cap, kept using the expression "crock a shit." That was all that American newspaper photographers seemed to talk about with any relish whatsoever, their displeasure at being asked to leave the office and take pictures. The dozen demonstrators, meantime, were clearly unmoved by the presence of representatives of two of the city's tabloids, *The City Light* and the *Daily News*. They continued to lounge about the van, their rage, if any, about the injustices wrought upon Henry Lamb successfully contained.

Fallow tried once more to read the press release 4but soon gave up. He looked about. The Poe Towers remained peaceful; abnormally so, given their size. On the other side of the street stood three white men. There was a little man in a tan windbreaker, a big porcine man with a drooping mustache wearing a warm-up jacket, and a balding man with blunt features wearing a poorly made gray suit and a Yank striped necktie. Fallow wondered who they were. But mainly he wanted to sleep. He wondered if he could sleep standing up, like a horse.

Presently he heard the woman, Reva, say to Buck: "I think that's them." Both of them looked down the street. The demonstrators came to life.

Coming up the street was a large white van. On its side, in huge letters, was the inscription THE LIVE 1. Buck, Reva, and the demonstrators began walking toward it. Mr. Neil Flannagan, the two photographers, and, finally, Fallow himself tagged along behind them. Channel 1 had arrived.

The van came to a stop, and out of the passenger's side of the front seat came a young man with a great fluffy head of dark curly hair and a navy blazer and tan pants.

"Robert Corso," said Reva, reverently.

The side doors of the van slid open, and two young men in jeans and sweaters and running shoes stepped out. The driver stayed at the wheel. Buck hurried forward.

"Yo-o-o-o-o! Robert Corso! How you doing, man!" Suddenly Buck had a smile that lit up the street.

"Okay!" said Robert Corso, trying to sound enthusiastic in return. "Okay." He obviously had no idea who this black man with the gold earring was.

"What you want us to do?" asked Buck.

The bouncy young man broke in: "Hey, Corso, Neil Flannagan, *Daily News.*"

"Oh, hi."

"What you want us to—"

"Where you guys been?"

"What you want us to—"

Robert Corso looked at his watch. "It's only 5:10. We're going on live at 6:00. We got plenty a time."

"Yeah, but I got a seven o'clock deadline."

"What you want us to do?" Buck insisted.

"Well . . . hey!" said Robert Corso. "I don't know. What would you do if I wasn't here?"

Buck and Reva looked at him with funny little grins on, as if he must be joking.

"Where are Reverend Bacon and Mrs. Lamb?" said Robert Corso.

"In Mrs. Lamb's apartment," said Reva. Fallow took it badly. No one had bothered to apprise him of this fact.

"Hey, whenever you say," said Buck.

Robert Corso shook his great fluffy head. He muttered, "Well, hell, I can't run this thing for you." Then, to Buck: "It'll take us a little while to set up. I guess the sidewalk's the best place. I want to get the buildings in the background."

Buck and Reva went to work. They began gesturing and giving instructions to the demonstrators, who now went back toward their van and began picking up the picket signs, which were stacked on the sidewalk. A few people had begun drifting over from the Poe Towers to the scene.

Fallow gave up on Buck and Reva and approached Robert Corso. "Excuse me," he said. "I'm Peter Fallow, from *The City Light* Did I hear you say that Reverend Bacon and Mrs. Lamb are here?"

"Fallow?" said Robert Corso. "You're the one who wrote the stories?" He held out his hand and shook Fallow's with enthusiasm.

"I'm afraid so."

"You're the reason we're up at this goddamned place?" He said it with an appreciative smile.

"Sorry about that." Fallow felt a glow inside. This was the sort of tribute he expected all along, but he hadn't expected to get it from a TV person.

Robert Corso turned serious. "Do you think Bacon is really on the level about this one? Well, obviously you do."

"You don't?" asked Fallow.

"Aw hell, you never know with Bacon. He's fairly outrageous. But when I interviewed Mrs. Lamb, I was impressed, to tell you the truth. She seems like a good person to me—she's bright, she's got a steady job, she has a nice, neat little apartment. I was impressed. I don't know—I believe her. What do you think?"

"You've already interviewed her? I thought you were getting ready to interview her here."

"Well, yeah, but that's just for the wraparound. We'll wrap around live at six o'clock."

"Wrap around live . . . I don't believe I know about wrapping around live."

The irony was lost on the American, however. "Well, what we do is, I came up here with a crew this afternoon, after your story came out. Thanks a lot for that! I really love assignments in the Bronx. Anyway, we interviewed Mrs. Lamb and we interviewed a couple of the neighbors and we got some footage of Bruckner Boulevard and the place where the boy's father was killed and all that stuff, and some stills of the boy. So we've already got most of the story on tape. It'll run for about two minutes, and what we do now is, we got on live during the demonstration, and then we'll roll the tape, and then we'll cut back in live and wrap it up with a live segment. That's wrapping it up live."

"But what will you show? There's no one here but this lot. Most of them are white." Fallow motioned toward Buck and Reva.

"Oh, don't worry. There'll be plenty of people here as soon as our telescope goes up."

"Your telescope."

"Our remote transmitter." Robert Corso looked toward the van. Fallow followed his eyes. He could see the two crewmen in blue jeans inside.

"Your remote transmitter. By the way, where are your competitors?"

"Our competitors?"

"The other television stations."

"Oh, we were promised an exclusive."

"Really? By whom?"

"Bacon, I guess. That's what I don't like about the setup. Bacon's so fucking manipulative. He's got a pipeline to my producer, Irv Stone. You know Irv?"

"I'm afraid I don't."

"You've heard of him."

"Ummm, actually I haven't."

"He's won a lot of awards."

"Ummm."

"Irv's—well, Irv's all right, but he's one of these old bastards who was a campus radical back in the 1960s, when they were having the antiwar demonstrations and everything. He thinks Bacon's this romantic leader of the people. He's a fucking operator, is what I think. But anyway, he promised Irv an exclusive if he'd put it on live at six o'clock."

"That's very cozy. But why would he want to do that? Why wouldn't he want all the stations to be here?"

"Because that way he might get nothing out of it. I bet you every day there's twenty or thirty demonstrations going on in New York, and they're all competing for coverage. This way he knows we'll play it big. If we go to the trouble of sending out the remote van, and if we go live, and if we think we have an exclusive, then it'll go at the top of the news. It'll be live, and it'll be a big deal, and tomorrow 5 and 7 and 2 and the rest of them'll figure they better cover the story, too."

"I see," said Fallow. "Hmmmm . . . But how can he guarantee you, as you say, an exclusive? What will prevent the other, uh, channels from coming here?"

"Nothing, except that he won't tell them the time or the place."

"He wasn't so considerate of me, was he?" said Fallow. "I notice the *Daily News* seems to have the time and the place."

"Yes," said Robert Corso, "but you've had exclusives for two days now. Now he has to let the other newspapers in on it." He paused. His handsome young fluffy-haired American face looked melancholy all of a sudden. "But you do think it's a legitimate story, don't you?"

"Oh, absolutely," Fallow said.

Corso said, "This Henry Lamb is—was—is a nice kid. An honor student, no police record, he's quiet, the neighbors seem to like him—isn't that the way it strikes you?"

"Oh, no question about it," said the creator of the honor student.

Reva approached them. "We're all set. Just say when."

Robert Corso and Fallow looked to the sidewalk, where the three dozen pickets were now lined up informally. They held the shafts of the picket signs on their shoulders, like wooden guns.

Robert Corso said, "Bacon's ready? And Mrs. Lamb?"

Reva said, "Well, you tell me or Buck. Reverend Bacon doesn't want to come down here with Mrs. Lamb and just stand around. But he's ready."

"Okay," said Robert Corso. He turned toward THE LIVE 1 van. "Hey, Frank! You guys ready?"

From inside the van: "Just about!"

A heavy whirring noise began. Out of the top of the van rose a silvery shaft, a cylinder. Attached to the top of the shaft was a Day-Glo-orange banner or bunting. No, it was a cable, a heavily insulated cable, wide but flat, like an electric eel. The screaming orange eel was wrapped around the shaft in a spiral. The silvery shaft and the orange spiral kept rising, rising, rising. The shaft was in sections, like a telescope, and it went up, up, up, and the van whirred and whirred and whirred.

People began emerging from the silent towers of the project, which was silent no longer. A boiling noise, the boiling noise of many voices, rose from the blasted heath. Here they came, men, women, packs of boys, young children, their eyes fastened to the ascending silver-and-orange lance and its Radiation Orange banner.

Now the shaft had risen two and a half stories above the street, with its orange eel wrapped around it. The street and the sidewalk were empty no longer. A huge good-natured crowd gathered around for the beano. A woman yelled out, "Robert Corso!" Channel 1! The fluffy-haired man who would be on TV!

Robert Corso looked toward the pickets, who had formed a lazy oval on the sidewalk and were beginning to march. Buck and Reva stood by. Buck had a bullhorn in his hand. He kept his eyes pinned on Robert Corso. Then Robert Corso looked toward his crewmen. His cameraman stood six feet away. The camera looked very small next to the van and the tremendous shaft, but the crowd was spellbound by its deep, deep cataract eye. The camera wasn't even on, but every time the cameraman turned to talk to the soundman, and the great eye swung about, a ripple went through the crowd, as if the machine had its own invisible kinetic momentum.

Buck looked at Robert Corso and raised one hand, palm up, which asked, "When?" Robert Corso shrugged and then wearily pointed his finger toward Buck. Buck lifted the bullhorn to his mouth and yelled: "Whadda we want?"

"Justice!" chanted the three dozen pickets. Their voices sounded terribly thin against the backdrop of the crowd and the towers of the project and the splendid silver lance of THE LIVE 1.

"WHADDA WE GET?"

"Ra-cism!"

"WHADDA WE WANT?"

"Jus-tice!" They were a little louder, but not much.

"WHADDA WE GET?"

"Ra-cism!"

Six or eight boys in their early teens were shoving and bumping one another and laughing, struggling to get into the camera's line of vision. Fallow stood off to one side of the star, Robert Corso, who was holding his microphone but saying nothing. The man with the high-tech horn moved closer to the oval line of pickets, and the crowd heaved in response. The signs and banners came bobbing by. WEISS JUSTICE IS WHITE JUSTICE . . . LAME: SLAUGHTERED BY INDIFFERENCE . . . LIBERATE JOHANNESBRONX . . . GAY FIST STRIKE FORCE AGAINST RACISM . . . THE PEOPLE CRY OUT: AVENGE HENRY! . . . QUIT STALLING, ABE! . . . GAY AND LESBIAN NEW YORK DEMAND JUSTICE FOR OUR BROTHER HENRY LAMB . . . CAPITALISM + RACISM = LEGALIZED MURDER . . . HIT'N'RUN'N'LIE TO THE PEOPLE! . . . ACTION NOW! . . .

"Whadda we want?"

"Jus-tice!"

Whadda we get?"

"Racism!"

Buck turned the bullhorn toward the crowd. He wanted to get their voices into the act.

"WHADDA WE WANT?"

Nothing came back. In the best of moods, they watched the show.

Buck answered his own question: "JUS-TICE."

"WHADDA WE GET?"

Nothing.

"RA-CISM!"

"OKAY! WHADDA WE WANT?"

Nothing.

"BROTHERS AND SISTERS," said Buck, the red bullhorn in front of his face, "*Our brother, our neighbor, Henry Lamb, he was struck down . . . by a hit-and-run driver . . . and the hospital . . . they don't do nothing for him . . . and the cops and the D.A. . . . they can't be bothered . . . Henry's at death's door . . . and they don't care . . . Henry's an honor student . . . and they say, 'So what?' . . . 'cause he's poor, he's from the project . . . 'cause he's black . . . So why are we here, brothers and sisters? . . . To make Chuck do the right thing!*"

That brought some appreciative laughter from the crowd.

"*To get justice for our brother, Henry Lamb!* " Buck continued. "Okay. SO WHADDA WE WANT?"

"Justice," said voices from the crowd.

"AND WHADDA WE GET?"

Laughter and stares.

The laughter came from six or eight boys in their early teens who were shoving and bumping one another, struggling to occupy a position just behind Buck. That would put them in a direct line with the eye of the camera, whose mesmerizing red light was now on.

"Who's Chuck?" asked Kramer.

"Chuck is Charlie," said Martin, "and Charlie is The Man, and speaking for The Man, I'd like to get my hands on that big shitcake."

"You see those signs?" asked Kramer. "WEISS JUSTICE IS WHITE JUSTICE and QUIT STALLING, ABE!?"

"Yeah."

"If they show that on TV, Weiss's gonna fucking freak out."

" 'S'already freaked out, if you ask me," said Goldberg. "Look at this bullshit."

From where Kramer, Goldberg, and Martin stood, the scene across the street was a curious little theater-in-the-round. The play concerned the Media. Beneath the towering spire of a TV van, three dozen figures, two dozen of them white, marched about in a small oval, carrying signs. Eleven people, two of them black, nine of them white, attended them, in order to bring their thin voices and felt-tip-marker messages to a city of seven million: a man with a bullhorn, a woman with a tote bag, a fluffy-haired TV announcer, a cameraman and a soundman attached to the van by umbilical cords, two technicians visible inside the open sliding doors of the van, the van driver, two newspaper photographers and two newspaper reporters with notebooks in their hands, one of them still lurching to port every now and again. An audience of two or three hundred souls was packed in around them, enjoying the spectacle.

"Okay," said Martin, "time to start talking to witnesses." He started walking across the street, toward the crowd.

"Hey, Marty," said Goldberg. "Be cool. Okay?"

Took the words right out of Kramer's mouth. This was not the ideal setting for trying to demonstrate Irish machismo to the world. He had a horrible vision of Martin taking the bullhorn from the man with the earring and trying to stuff it down his throat before the assembled residents of the Poe Towers.

The three of them, Kramer, Martin, and Goldberg, were halfway across the street when the pickets and the crowd suddenly got religion. They began making a real racket. Buck was bellowing something on the bullhorn. The cameraman's high-tech proboscis was weaving this way and that. From somewhere a tall figure had appeared, a man with a black suit and a terrific stiff white collar and a black necktie with white stripes. With him was a small black woman wearing a dark dress with a luster, like silk or satin. It was Reverend Bacon and Mrs. Lamb.

Sherman was halfway across the marble floor of the entry gallery when he saw Judy, sitting in the library. She was sitting in the wing chair, with a magazine on her lap, watching television. She looked up at him. What was that look? It was surprise, not warmth. If she would give him even a hint of warmth, he would go straight in and—*and tell her!* Oh yes? Tell her what? Tell her . . . about the debacle in the office at least, about the way Arnold Parch had talked to him and, worse, *looked* at him! The others, too! As if . . . He avoided forming in words what they must have thought of him. His disappearance, the collapse of the gold-backed bond scheme—and then tell her the rest, too? Had she by now seen a newspaper article about a Mercedes . . . RF . . . But there was not a hint of warmth. There was only surprise. It was six o'clock. He hadn't been home this early in a long time . . . There was only surprise in that sad thin face with the corona of soft brown hair.

He kept walking toward her. He would go in the library, anyway. He would sit down in the other armchair and watch television, too. That had been silently agreed upon. The two of them could sit together in the library and read or watch television. That way they could go through the frozen motions of being a family, for Campbell's benefit as much as anything else, without having to talk.

"Daddy!"

He turned around. Campbell was coming toward him from the door that led to the kitchen. She had a glorious smile on her face. It nearly broke his heart.

"Hello, sweetheart." He put his hands under her armpits and swept her up off the floor and wrapped his arms around her. She put her arms around his neck and her legs around his waist, and she said, "Daddy! Guess what I made!"

"What?"

"A rabbit."

"You did? A rabbit?"

"I'll show you." She started wriggling, to get down.

"You'll show me?" He didn't want to see her rabbit, not now, but the obligation to seem enthusiastic overwhelmed him. He let her slither to the floor.

"Come on!" She took him by the hand and began pulling with terrific force. She pulled him off balance.

"Hey! Where are we going?"

"Come on! It's in the kitchen!" Towing him toward the kitchen, she now leaned so far over that almost the entire weight of her body hung from his hand, which held hers.

"Hey! Watch it. You're gonna fall down, sweetheart."

"*Come . . . on!*" He lurched behind her, ground between his fears and his love for a six-year-old who wanted to show him a rabbit.

The doorway led into a short hallway, lined with closets, and then into the butler's pantry, lined with glass-front cabinets containing sparkling battalions of crystal, and stainless-steel sinks. The cabinets, with their beadings, muntins, mullions, cornices—he couldn't remember all the terms—had cost thousands . . .

thousands . . . The *passion* Judy had put into these . . . *things* . . . The way they had spent money . . . Hemorrhaging money . . .

And now they were in the kitchen. More cabinets, cornices, stainless steel, tiles, spotlights, the Sub-Zero, the Vulcan—all of it the best Judy's endless research could find, all of it endlessly expensive, hemorrhaging and hemorrhaging . . . Bonita was by the Vulcan stove.

"Hi, Mr. McCoy."

"Hello, Bonita."

Lucille, the maid, was sitting on a stool by a counter, drinking a cup of coffee.

"Mr. McCoy."

"Why, hello, Lucille." Hadn't seen her in ages; hadn't been home early enough. He should have something to say to her, since it had been so long, but he couldn't think of a thing except for how sad it all was. They were proceeding with their routines, secure in their belief that everything was the way it always had been.

"Over here, Daddy." Campbell kept pulling. She didn't want him to get sidetracked talking to Bonita and Lucille.

"Campbell!" said Bonita. "Don't pull your daddy like that!"

Sherman smiled and felt ineffectual. Campbell ignored her. Then she stopped pulling.

"Bonita's gonna bake it for me. So it'll be hard."

There was the rabbit. It was on a white Formica-topped table. Sherman stared. He could scarcely believe it. It was an astonishingly good rabbit, made of clay. It was primitive in execution, but the head was cocked to one side and the ears were set at expressive angles and the legs were spread out in an unconventional pose, as bunnies went, and the massing and proportion of the haunches was excellent. The animal seemed startled.

"Sweetheart! You did this?"

Very proud: "Yes."

"Where?"

"In school."

"All by yourself?"

"Yes. For real life."

"Well, Campbell—this is a beautiful rabbit! I'm very proud of you! You're so talented!"

Very timid: "I know."

All at once he wanted to cry. A startled bunny. To think of what it meant to be able to *wish*, in this world, to make a bunny rabbit and then to *do* it in all innocence, in all confidence that the world would receive it with love and tenderness and admiration—to think of what she *assumed* at the age of six, namely, that this was the nature of the world and that her mommy and daddy—her *daddy!* —made it that way and of course would never let it be any other way.

"Let's show it to Mommy," he said.

"She saw it."

"I bet she loved it."

The very timid voice: "I know."

"Well, let's both show it to her."

"Bonita has to bake it. So it'll be hard."

"Well, I want to go tell Mommy how much *I* like it." With a show of gusto, he swept Campbell up into his arms and threw her over his shoulder. She took this as a great game.

"Daddy!"

"Campbell, you're getting so *big!* Soon I won't be able to carry you like a sack of meal anymore. Low bridge! We're going through the door."

Amid much giggling and wriggling, he carried her across the marble floor, to the library. Judy looked up sharply.

"Campbell, don't make Daddy carry you. You're too big for that."

With just a touch of defiance: "I didn't *make* him."

"We were just playing," said Sherman. 'Did you see Campbell's rabbit? Isn't it beautiful?"

"Yes. It's lovely." She turned her head back toward the television set.

"I'm *really impressed.* I think we've got an extremely talented little girl on our hands."

No reply.

Sherman lowered Campbell from his shoulder down into his arms, as if she were a baby, and then sat in the armchair and settled her on his lap. Campbell moved around to get more comfortable and snuggled up against him, and he put his arms around her. They looked at the television screen.

The news was on. An announcer's voice. A blur of black faces. A picket sign: ACTION—NOW!

"What are they doing, Daddy?"

"It looks like a demonstration, sweetheart."

Another sign: WEISS JUSTICE IS WHITE JUSTICE.

Weiss?

"What's a demonstration?" Campbell sat up in his lap and looked at him when she asked the question, obscuring his view of the screen. He tried to look around her.

"What's a demonstration?"

Distractedly, trying to keep one eye on the screen: "Uh . . . it's a—sometimes when people get angry about something, they make some signs and they march around with them."

HIT'N'RUN'N'LIE TO THE PEOPLE!

Hit and run!

"What do they get angry about?"

"Just a minute, sweetheart."

"What do they get angry about, Daddy?"

"Almost anything." Sherman was now leaning far to the left, in order to see the screen. He had to hold tight to Campbell's waist to keep from spilling her off his lap.

"But what?"

"Well, let's see."

Campbell turned her head toward the screen but immediately turned back. There was only some man talking, some black man, very tall, dressed in a black jacket and a white shirt and a striped tie, standing next to a thin black woman in a dark dress. There was a huge cluster of black faces crowded in behind them. Boys with smirks on their faces kept popping out from behind them and staring into the camera.

"When a young man like Henry Lamb," the man was saying, "an honor student, an outstanding young man, when a young man like Henry Lamb comes into the hospital with acute cerebral concussion and they treat him for a broken wrist . . . see . . . when his mother gives the Police Department and the district attorney a description of the car that struck him down, a description of that car . . . see . . . and they do nothing, they drag their feet—"

"Daddy, let's go back to the kitchen. Bonita's gonna bake my rabbit."

"In a second—"

"—to our people is, 'We don't care. Your young people, your honor students, your hopes don't count, don't matter at all' . . . see . . . That's the message. But we care, and we're not gonna stand still, and we're not gonna be silent. If the power structure don't want to do nothing—"

Campbell slid off Sherman's lap and grabbed his right wrist with both hands and began pulling. "Come on, Daddy."

The face of the thin black woman filled the screen. Tears rolled down her cheeks. A flutty-haired young white man was on the screen with a microphone at his lips. There was a whole universe of black faces behind him and more boys mugging for the camera.

"—that as yet unidentified Mercedes-Benz sedan with a license plate beginning with RE, RF, RB, or RP. And just as Reverend Bacon maintains that a message is coming through to this community from the authorities, these protesters have a message for them: 'If you don't launch a full-scale investigation, we'll do it ourselves.' This is Robert Corso, THE LIVE 1, in the Bronx."

"Daddy!" She was pulling on him so hard the chair began to tip.

"RF?" Judy had turned to look at Sherman. "*Ours* begins with RF, doesn't it?"

Now! Tell her!

"Daddy! Come on! I wanna bake the rabbit!"

There was no concern in Judy's face. She was merely surprised by the coincidence; so surprised, she had initiated a conversation.

Now!

"Daddy, come on!"

See about baking the rabbit.

14

I DON'T KNOW HOW TO LIE

SHERMAN WOKE UP from a dream he couldn't remember, with his heart flailing away at his chest wall. It was the drinker's hour, that hour in the dead of the night when drinkers and insomniacs suddenly wake up and know it's all over, this sleep dodge. He resisted the urge to look at the illuminated clock on the radio on the table beside the bed. He didn't want to know how many hours he would have to lie here fighting with this stranger, his heart, which was desperate to escape to some far far far far far far far far far far Canada.

The windows were open on Park and on the side street. Between the sills and the bottom of the shades was a band of purplish gloom. He heard an automobile, a lone automobile, starting off from a stoplight. Then he heard an airplane. It was not a jet but an airplane with a propeller. The motor stopped. It was going to crash! Then he heard it again, droning and groaning over New York City. How very odd . . .

. . . in the dead of the night. His wife slept, fifteen inches away, on the other side of the Berlin Wall, breathing regularly . . . oblivious . . . She was turned away from him, on her side, her knees bent. How nice it would be to roll toward her and tuck his knees in behind hers and press his chest upon her back. Once they were able . . . once, when they were so close . . . they could do that without waking each other up . . . in the dead of the night.

This couldn't be true! There was no way they could break through these walls to invade his life! The tall skinny boy, the newspapers, police . . . at the drinker's hour.

His dear sweet daughter slept down the hall. Dear Campbell. A happy little girl—oblivious! A mist came to his wide-open eyes.

He stared at the ceiling and tried to trick himself into falling back asleep. He thought of . . . other things . . . That girl he met in the dining room of the hotel in Cleveland that time . . . the businesslike way she undressed in front of him . . . as contrasted with Maria . . . who did this and that, gorged red with

. . . *Lust!* . . . *Lust* had led him into it . . . the bowels of the Bronx, the tall
skinny boy . . . Down he goes—

There were no *other* things. Everything was tied to these things, and he lay
there with them flaring up in his mind in ghastly pictures . . . The ghastly faces
on the television screen, Arnold Parch's dreary face, with its ghastly attempt at
sternness . . . the evasive voice of Bernard Levy . . . the look on Muriel's face,
as if she knew he now bore some terrible taint and was no longer an Olympian at
Pierce & Pierce . . . Hemorrhaging money . . . Surely these were dreams! His
eyes were wide open, staring at the purplish gloom where the Roman shades fell
just short of the windowsill . . . in the dead of the night, dreading the light of
the dawn.

He got up early, walked Campbell to the bus stop, bought the newspapers on
Lexington Avenue, and took a taxi down to Pierce & Pierce. In the *Times* . . .
nothing. In the *Post* . . . nothing. In the *Daily News*, only a picture and a
caption. The picture showed pickets and a crowd. A sign in the foreground said
WEISS JUSTICE IS WHITE JUSTICE. In another two hours . . . *The City Light* would be
on the stands.

It was a quiet day at Pierce & Pierce, at least for him. He made his routine
calls, to Prudential, Morgan Guaranty, Allen & Company . . . *The City Light*
. . . Felix was over on the other side of the room. Even to attempt to use him
again would be too demeaning . . . Not a word from Arnold Parch or anyone
else. *Freezing me out* . . . *The City Light* . . . He would call Freddy and have
him get the newspaper. Freddy could read it to him. So he called Freddy, but he
had left the office for an appointment. He called Maria; nowhere to be found
. . . *The City Light* . . . He couldn't stand it any longer. He would go downstairs and buy the newspaper and read it in the lobby and return. Yesterday he was
AWOL when a bond issue came in. He blew millions—*millions!*—in the gold-
backed bonds. How much worse could one more transgression make it? As coolly
as he could, he began walking across the bond trading room toward the elevators.
No one seemed to notice. (No one any longer cares!)

Downstairs, at the newsstand in the lobby, he looked left and right and then
bought *The City Light*. He walked over behind a big pink marble column. His
heart was pounding away. How grim! how odd!—to live in *personal fear*, every
day, of the newspapers in New York! Nothing on the front page . . . or page 2 or
page 3 . . . It was on page 5, a picture and a story by this person, Peter Fallow.
The picture showed the thin black woman crying, while the tall black man in the
suit comforted her. Bacon. There were picket signs in the background. The story
was not long. He raced through it . . . "fury of the community" . . . "luxury
car" . . . "white driver" . . . No clear indication what the police were doing.
At the end of the article was a box that said "Editorial, page 36." His heart
started racing again. His fingers shook as he rustled forward toward page 36 . . .
There, at the top of the editorial column, the heading HIT-OR-MISS JUSTICE.

On Monday *The City Light*'s Peter Fallow broke the tragic story of
Henry Lamb, the Bronx honor student who was critically injured in a
hit-and-run accident—and abandoned like just another piece of debris
in a littered city.

   True, from a legal standpoint Henry Lamb's is not a tidy case. But
neither has he enjoyed a tidy life. He managed to survive the worst

that growing up in a city housing project could throw his way—including the murder of his father by a mugger—and achieved an outstanding record at Ruppert High School. He was struck down on the threshold of a brilliant future.

Our pity is not enough for Henry Lamb and the many other good people who are determined to beat the odds in the less affluent sections of our city. They need to know that their hopes and dreams are important to the future of all New York. We call for an aggressive investigation of every angle of the Lamb case.

He was rocked. The thing was becoming a crusade. He stared at the newspaper. Should he save it? No; better not to be seen with it. He looked for a trash receptacle or a bench. Nothing. He closed the newspaper up and folded it in two and let it fall on the floor behind the column and hurried back to the elevators.

He had lunch at his desk, a sandwich and orange juice, in the interest of appearing diligent. He was jittery and dreadfully tired. He couldn't finish the sandwich. By early in the afternoon he had an overwhelming desire to close his eyes. His head felt so heavy . . . The beginning of a headache had a tight grip on his forehead. He wondered if he was getting the flu. He ought to call Freddy Button. But he was so tired. Just then a call came in. It was Freddy calling him.

"It's funny, I was just thinking of calling you. There was this goddamned editorial today, Freddy."

"I know. I read it."

"You read it?"

"I read all four papers. Listen, Sherman, I've taken the liberty of calling Tommy Killian. Why don't you go see him? He's on Reade Street. It's not far from where you are, near City Hall. Give him a ring." In his occluded smoker's voice he recited a telephone number.

"I guess it doesn't look so great," said Sherman.

"It's not that. There's nothing in what I read that's of any material significance. It's just that it's taking on more of a political complexion, and Tommy will have a good fix on that."

"Okay. Thanks, Freddy. I'll call him."

Some Irishman on Reade Street named Tommy Killian.

He didn't call him. He had such a headache, he closed his eyes and massaged his temples with the tips of his fingers. At five o'clock sharp, the official end of the day, he left. This was not good form. The end of the trading day was the beginning of the second part of the day for a Master of the Universe.

The end of the trading day was like the end of a battle. After five o'clock the Masters of the Universe took care of all the things people in other businesses spent the entire day doing. They figured out the "net net," which is to say, the actual profit and loss for the day's work. They reviewed the markets, reviewed strategies, discussed personnel problems, researched new issues, and did all the reading of the financial press that was forbidden during the daily battle. They told war stories and beat their breasts and yodeled, if they deserved it. The one thing you *never* did was simply go home to the wife'n'kiddies.

Sherman had Muriel order a car for him from the car service. He studied her face for signs of his fall from grace. A blank.

Out in front of the building the street was four and five deep with car-service cars and white men in business suits threading their way among them, heads lowered, squinting, looking for their numbers. The name of the car service and the number of the car were always posted in a side window. Pierce & Pierce used a company called Tango. All Oldsmobile and Buick sedans. Pierce & Pierce ordered three to four hundred rides a day at an average of $15 per. Some clever devil at Tango, whoever owned it, was probably clearing a million dollars a year on Pierce & Pierce alone. Sherman was looking for Tango 278. He wandered amid the sea of sedans, occasionally caroming off men who looked much like himself, heads lowered, squinting . . . dark gray suits . . . " 'Scuse me" . . . " 'Scuse me" . . . The new rush hour! In the old movies, the Wall Street rush hour was all subways . . . *Subways?* . . . down there with . . . *them?* . . . *Insulate!* . . . Today . . . roaming, roaming . . . amid the sedans . . . squinting, squinting . . . 'Scuse me, 'scuse me . . . Finally he found Tango 278.

Bonita and Lucille were surprised to see him come walking in the apartment at 5:30. He didn't feel well enough to sound pleasant. Judy and Campbell weren't home. Judy had taken her over to a birthday party on the West Side.

Sherman trudged up the great curved staircase. He went into the bedroom and took off his jacket and his tie. Without taking off his shoes, he stretched out on the bed. He closed his eyes. He felt consciousness falling away, falling away. It was unbearably heavy, consciousness.

Mister McCoy. Mister McCoy.

Bonita was standing over him. He couldn't figure out why.

"I no want disturb," she said. "The doorman, he say two men from the police downstairs."

"What?"

"The doorman, he say—"

"Downstairs?"

"Yes. He say from the police."

Sherman propped himself up on one elbow. There were his legs, stretched out on the bed. He couldn't figure out why. It must be morning, but he had his shoes on. Bonita was standing over him. He rubbed his face.

"Well . . . tell them I'm not here."

"The doorman, he already say you here."

"What do they want?"

"Don't know, Mr. McCoy."

A soft dim gloaming. Was it dawn? He was in a hypnagogic state. He felt as if his neural pathways were blocked. No pattern at all. Bonita; the police. The panic set in even before he could focus on the reasons.

"What time is it?"

"Six o'clock."

He looked at his legs again, at his shoes. Must be six o'clock at night. Came home at 5:30. Fell asleep. Still stretched out . . . in front of Bonita. A sense of propriety, as much as anything else, made him swing his legs off the bed and sit on the edge.

"What I tell him, Mr. McCoy?"

She must mean the doorman. He couldn't get it straight. They were downstairs. Two policemen. He was sitting on the edge of his bed, trying to come to. There were two policemen downstairs with the doorman. What should he say?

"Tell him . . . they'll have to wait a minute, Bonita."

He stood up and started walking toward the bathroom. So groggy, so stiff; his head hurt; there was a rushing sound in his ears. The face in the bathroom mirror had the noble chin but was creased and bleary and decrepit. His shirt was wrinkled and pulled out of his pants. He splashed water on his face. A drop of it hung from the tip of his nose. He dried his face with a hand towel. If only he could think. But it was all blocked. It was all fog. If he refused to see them, and they knew he was up here, and they did, then they'd be suspicious, wouldn't they? But if he talked to them, and they asked him—what? He tried to imagine . . . He couldn't focus on it. Whatever they ask . . . he doesn't know . . . No! He can't take a chance! Mustn't see them! But what had he told Bonita? "They'll have to wait"—as if to say, I *will* see them, but they'll have to wait a minute.

"Bonita!" He went back into the bedroom, but she wasn't there. He went out into the hallway. "Bonita!"

"Down here, Mr. McCoy."

From the hallway balcony he could see her standing at the foot of the staircase. "You haven't called down to the doorman yet, have you?"

"Yes, I call. I tell him they have to wait."

Shit. Implied he would see them. Too late to back out. Freddy! He'd call Freddy! He went back to the bedroom, to the telephone by the bed. He called Freddy's office. No answer. He called the main number of Dunning Sponget and asked for him; after what seemed like an interminable wait, was told he had gone. Call him at home. What was the number? In the address book downstairs in the library.

He went running down the staircase—realized Bonita was still in the entry gallery. Mustn't look rattled in front of her. Two policemen downstairs with the doorman. Walked across the marble floor with what perhaps passed for a calm gait.

He kept the address book on a shelf behind the desk. His fingers were shaking as he went through the pages. B. The telephone—it wasn't on the desk. Someone had left it on the side table next to the wing chair. An *outrage*. He hurried around the desk to the chair. Time rolling by. He dialed Freddy's number. A maid answered. Buttons out to dinner. Shit. What now? Time rolling, rolling, rolling. What would the Lion do? The sort of family in which cooperation with the authorities was automatic. There could be only one reason not to cooperate: You did have something to hide. Naturally they would detect that immediately, because you do not cooperate. If only—

He left the library and went back out into the entry gallery. Bonita was still standing there. She looked at him very intently—and that was what did it. Didn't want to look frightened or indecisive in front of the servants. Didn't want to look like someone in trouble.

"All right, Bonita." He tried to sound like someone who was already bored and knew he was in for a further waste of time. "What doorman's on tonight? Eddie?"

"Eddie."

"Tell him to send them on up. Have them wait here. I'll be back down in a minute."

He walked very deliberately up the staircase. When he reached the upstairs hallway, he hurried to the bedroom. What he saw in the mirror was someone very bleary and rumpled. He thrust his chin upward. That helped. He would be strong. He wouldn't lose his head. He would be . . . he allowed himself the phrase . . . a Master of the Universe.

How should he look? Should he put his jacket and tie back on? He had on a white shirt, the pants of a gray nailhead worsted suit and a pair of black cap-toed shoes. With the tie and the jacket on, he would look terribly Wall Street, terribly conservative. They might resent that. He hurried into the other bedroom, which had become his dressing room, and took a tweed jacket with a plaid design from the closet and slipped it on. Time rolling by, rolling by. Much more casual, relaxed; a man in his own home, completely relaxed. But the soft tweed jacket didn't go with the hard-finished pants. Besides . . . a sport jacket . . . a *sport* . . . a young rip who takes wild rides in a sports roadster . . . He took off the tweed jacket and threw it on the daybed and hurried back to the master bedroom. His jacket and tie were strewn across a stuffed chair. He put on the tie and pulled it up into a tight knot. Time rolling by, rolling by. He put on the jacket and buttoned it. He lifted his chin and squared his shoulders. Wall Street. He went into the bathroom and brushed his hair back. He lifted his chin again. Be strong. A Master of the Universe.

He rushed back down the hallway, then slowed down as he neared the stairs. He descended with a slow tread and tried to remember to keep himself erect.

They were standing in the middle of the marble floor, two men and Bonita. How strange it all seemed! The two men stood slightly spread-legged, and Bonita stood seven or eight feet away, as if they were her little flock. His heart was beating at a good clip.

The larger of the two looked like a great slab of meat with clothes on. His suit jacket sat out from his wrestler's gut like cardboard. He had a fat swarthy face, a Mediterranean face, to Sherman's way of thinking. He had a mustache that didn't go with his hair. The mustache curled down each side of his lips, a style that to a Pierce & Pierce bond salesman immediately said Lower Class. This one stared at Sherman as he came down the stairs, but the other one, the smaller one, didn't. He was wearing a sport jacket and the sort of brown pants a wife might choose to go with it. He was taking in the entry gallery, like a tourist . . . the marble, the yew-wood glove chest, the apricot-silk on the walls, the Thomas Hope chairs, Judy's tens of thousands of hemorrhaging dollars' worth of perfect little details . . . The man's nose was big, and his chin and jaw were weak. He held his head cocked at an angle. He looked as if some terrific force had hit him on one side of his head. Then he turned his cockeyed stare toward Sherman. Sherman was aware of his heartbeat and the sound his shoes made as he walked across the marble. He kept his chin up and made himself smile amiably.

"Gentlemen, how can I help you?" He looked at the big one when he said it, but it was the little one, the cockeyed one, who answered.

"Mr. McCoy? I'm Detective Martin, and this is Detective Goldberg."

Should he shake hands? Might as well. He held out his hand, and the small one shook it and then the large one. It seemed to embarrass them. They didn't shake hands very forcefully.

"We're investigating an automobile accident involving a personal injury. Maybe you've read about it or seen something about it on television." He reached inside his jacket and pulled out a piece of paper, folded once down the middle. He handed it to Sherman. On it was a newspaper clipping, the original story from

The City Light. The picture of the tall skinny boy. Parts of the story were under-lined in a yellow marker. Bruckner Boulevard Mercedes-Benz. R. *Would his fingers tremble!* If he held the paper long enough to read the entire story, they would. He looked up at the two detectives.

"We saw something about this on television last night, my wife and I." *Should he say he was surprised? Or what a coincidence?* It dawned on him, in just these words: *I don't know how to lie.* "We thought, Good Lord, we have a Merce-des, and the license number starts with R." He glanced back down at the clipping and quickly returned it to the small one, Martin.

"You and a lotta people," said Martin with a reassuring smile. "We're trying to check 'em all out."

"How many are there?"

"A lot. We got a lotta officers working on this. My partner and me got a list here with about twenty on it ourselves."

Bonita was still standing there, looking on, taking it all in.

"Well, come on in here," Sherman said to the one called Martin. He mo-tioned toward the library. "Bonita, do me a favor. If Mrs. McCoy and Campbell come back, tell them I'll be busy with these gentlemen, in the library."

Bonita nodded and retreated toward the kitchen.

In the library, Sherman went around behind the desk and gestured toward the wing chair and the Sheraton armchair. The little one, Martin, looked all around. Sherman became acutely aware of how much obviously expensive . . . *stuff* . . . was crammed into this one small room . . . the fabulous clutter . . . the knick-knacks . . . and when the little detective's eyes reached the carved frieze, they remained pinned there. He turned toward Sherman with an open, boyish look on his face, as if to say, *Not bad!* Then he sat down in the armchair, and the big one, Goldberg, sat down in the wing chair. Sherman sat down behind the desk.

"Well, let's see," said Martin. "Can you tell us if your car was in use the night this happened?"

"When exactly was it?" *Well—now I'm committed to lying.*

"Tuesday a week ago," said Martin.

"I don't know," said Sherman, "I'd have to try to figure."

"How many people use your car?"

"Me mostly, sometimes my wife."

"You have any children?"

"I have a daughter, but she's only six."

"Anybody else have access to the car?"

"No, I guess not, except for the people at the garage."

"The garage?" asked Martin. "A parking garage?"

"Yes." *Why had he mentioned the garage?*

"You leave the car there, with the keys, and they park it?"

"Yes."

"Where is it, the garage?"

"It's . . . near here." Sherman's mind began spinning at a furious rate. *They suspect the attendants! No, that's crazy. Dan!* He could see the chubby little redheaded troll. *He'll be happy to tell them I took the car out that night! Perhaps he wouldn't remember or wouldn't know what night it was. Oh, he'll know! The way I froze him out—*

"Could we go there and take a look at it?"

Sherman's mouth had gone dry. He could feel his lips contracting.

"The car?"

"Yes."

"When?"

"Soon's we leave here's good a time as any, for us."

"You mean *now?* Well, I don't know . . ." Sherman felt as if the muscles of his lips were being constricted by a purse string.

"There's certain things that's consistent with an incident like this. If a car don't have those things, then we keep on going down the list. At this point we're looking for a car. We don't have a description of a driver. So—that okay with you?"

"Well . . . I don't know . . ." No! Let them look at it! There's nothing for them to find! Or is there? Something I don't know about, never heard of! But if I say no—they'll be suspicious! Say yes! But suppose the little redheaded attendant is on!

"It's the routine. We look at all the cars."

"I know, but, uh, if this, uh, is a routine, then I guess I ought to . . . follow the routine that I—that's appropriate to me, to someone with a car in this situation." His mouth kept tightening. He saw the two men exchange glances.

The small one, Martin, had a look of great disappointment on his face. "You want to cooperate, don't you?"

"Yes, of course."

"Well, this is no big deal. This is part of the routine. We check the cars."

"I know, but if there's a routine—then that's what I should do, too, follow a routine. Or that would be the logical thing, it seems to me."

Sherman was acutely aware of sputtering nonsense, but he hung on to this word *routine* for dear life. If only he could control the muscles around his mouth—

"I'm sorry, I don't get it," said Martin. "What routine?"

"Well, you mentioned a routine, your routine, for investigating a case like this. I don't know how these things work, but there must be a routine for the owner of a car in this situation—I mean, I happen to own a car of a make and a license number—with a license number—and I know there must be a routine. That's what I'm trying to say. I think that's what I need to consider. The routine."

Martin stood up and started looking at the carved frieze again. His eyes followed it halfway around the room. Then he looked at Sherman with his head at the cockeyed angle. There was a small smile on his lips. Impudent! Chilling!

"Awright, the routine is—it ain't nothing complicated. If you wanna cooperate with us, and you don't mind cooperating with us, then you cooperate with us and we look at the car, and we go on our way. Nothing complicated. Okay? If you don't wanna cooperate, if you have your reasons for not cooperating, then you don't cooperate, and then we have to go through channels, and the same thing happens anyway, and so it's up to you."

"Well, it's just that . . ." He didn't know how he was going to end the sentence.

"When's the last time you drove your car, Mr. McCoy?" It was the other one, the big one, Goldberg, who was still sitting in the wing chair. For an instant Sherman was grateful for the change of subject.

"Let me see . . . Over the weekend, I guess, unless . . . let me see, have I driven it since then . . ."

"How many times you driven it over the past two weeks?"

"I don't know exactly . . . Let me see . . ."

He was looking at the great slab of meat in the wing chair, desperately trying to figure out how to lie to these questions—and out of the corner of his eye he could see the smaller one walking toward him, around the side of the desk.

"How often you usually drive it?" asked Goldberg.

"It varies."

"How many times a week?"

"As I say, it varies."

"It varies. You drive it to work?"

Sherman stared at the great slab of meat with the mustache. Something grossly insolent about this interrogation. Time to cut it off, assert himself. But what tone to take? These two were connected by an invisible line to a dangerous . . . Power . . . that he did not comprehend. *What?*—

The small one, Martin, had now come all the way around to his side of the desk. From way down here in his chair, Sherman looked up at Martin, and Martin looked down upon him with his cockeyed expression. At first he looked very sad. Then he smiled a brave smile.

"Look, Mr. McCoy," he said, smiling through his sadness, "I'm sure you wanna cooperate, and I don't wanna see you get hung up on the routine. It's just that we gotta go over everything in this case very carefully, because the victim, this Mr. Lamb, is in very bad shape. The best information we got is, he's gonna die. So we're asking everybody to cooperate, but there's nothing says you have to. If you want to, you can say nothing at all. You have that right. You understand?"

When he said, "You understand?" he cocked his head at an extreme angle and smiled an incredulous smile that indicated Sherman would have to be a terrible ingrate, troublemaker, and callous citizen, indeed, if he did not cooperate.

Then he put both hands on the top of Sherman's desk and leaned forward until his arms supported the weight of his upper body. This brought his face closer to Sherman's, although he was still looking down at him.

"I mean, you know," he said, "you have the right to an *attorney.*"

The way he said *attorney*, it was as if he was trying to think of every crazy and ridiculous choice a man—a smaller and far more devious man than Sherman McCoy—might have. "You understand, don't you?"

Sherman found himself nodding yes in spite of himself. A cold tremor began to spread through his body.

"I mean, for that matter, if you lacked the funds for an attorney"—he said this with such a comradely smile and such great good humor, it was as if he and Sherman had been pals for years and had their little jokes—"and you wanted an attorney, the state would provide you with one free of charge. If there was any reason you wanted one."

Sherman nodded again. He stared at the man's lopsided face. He felt powerless to act or resist. The man's message seemed to be: "I don't need to tell you these things. You're a substantial citizen, and you're above them. But if you aren't . . . then you must be the kind of germ we have to exterminate."

"All I'm saying is, we need your cooperation."

Then he swung about and sat on the edge of the desk and looked straight down into Sherman's face. *He's sitting on the edge of my desk!*

He smiled the warmest smile imaginable and asked softly, "Well, what about it, Mr. McCoy? My partner was asking if you drive your car to work." He kept smiling.

The effrontery! The *threat! Sitting on my desk!* The barbarous insolence!

"Well, do you?" Smiling his lopsided smile. "You drive it to work?"

Fear and outrage welled up together. But fear rose higher. "No . . . I don't."

"Then when do you use it?"

"On the weekends . . . Or—whenever it's convenient . . . during the day or maybe sometimes at night. I mean not much during the day except when my wife uses it, which is to say, I mean, it's hard to say."

"Could your wife a been using it Tuesday night a week ago?"

"No! I mean, I don't think so."

"So it might be you use it any time, but you don't remember."

"It's not that. It's just that—I use the car, I don't make a note of it, I don't keep a record, I don't think that much about it, I guess."

"How often do you use it at night?"

Desperately Sherman tried to calculate the correct answer. If he said *often,* did that make it more likely he was out driving *that night?* But if he said *seldom*—then wouldn't he be more certain about whether he was driving or not that particular night?

"I don't know," he said. "Not a *lot*—but I guess reasonably often, comparatively."

"Not a lot but reasonably often comparatively," said the little detective in a monotone. By the time he reached *comparatively,* he was looking at his partner. He turned back and looked down at Sherman once more from his perch on the edge of the desk.

"Well, let's get back to the car. Why don't we go take a look at it. Whaddaya say?"

"Now?"

"Sure."

"This isn't a good time."

"You got an appointment or something?"

"I'm—waiting for my wife."

"You going out?"

"I—uhhhhhhhhhhh." The first-person singular degenerated into a sigh.

"You going out in the car?" asked Goldberg. "We could take a look at it. Don't take a second."

For an instant Sherman thought of bringing the car from the garage and letting them look at it in front of the building. But suppose they didn't sit still for that? Suppose they came along—and talked to Dan?

"I hear you say your wife's coming home soon?" asked the smaller one. "Maybe we oughta wait and talk to her, too. Maybe she'll remember if anybody was using the car Tuesday night a week ago."

"Well, she—this just isn't a good time, gentlemen."

"When is a good time?" asked the smaller one.

"I don't know. If you can just give me a little time to think about it."

"Think about what? When's a good time? Or if you're gonna cooperate?"

"It's not a question of that. I'm—well, I'm worried about the procedure."

"The procedure?"

"Just how this should be handled. Correctly."

"Is the procedure the same as the routine?" The detective peered down at him with an insulting little smile.

"Procedure . . . routine . . . I'm not familiar with the terminology. I suppose it does come out the same."

"I'm not familiar with it, either, Mr. McCoy, because there ain't no such terminology, ain't no such procedure, ain't no such routine. You either cooperate in an investigation or you don't. I thought you wanted to cooperate."

"I do, but you've narrowed the choices."

"What choices?"

"Well—look. I guess what I should do is, I should . . . I should talk this over with an attorney."

As soon as the words came out of his mouth, he felt he had made a terrible admission.

"As I told you," said the little detective, "that's your right. But why would you wanna talk to an attorney? Why would you wanna go to that trouble and expense?"

"I just want to make sure I proceed"—immediately he was afraid he would be in trouble for uttering the verb form of *procedure*—"correctly."

The fat one, sitting in the wing chair, spoke up. "Let me ask you something, Mr. McCoy. Is there anything you'd like to get off your chest?"

Sherman grew cold. "Get off my chest?"

"Because if there is"—a fatherly smile—*insolence!*—"now is the time to do it, before things go any further and get complicated."

"What would I have to get off my chest?" He meant to sound firm, but it came out . . . bewildered.

"That's what I'm asking you."

Sherman stood up and shook his head. "I don't think there's any use continuing this right now. I'm gonna have to talk—"

The little one, still sitting on the desk, finished the sentence for him: "—to a lawyer?"

"Yes."

The small one shook his head the way you do when somebody you're advising seems determined to stick to a foolish course. "That's your privilege. But if you got anything substantial here to talk to a lawyer about, you're gonna be better off coming out with it right now. And you're gonna *feel* better. Whatever it is, it probably ain't as bad as you think. Everybody makes mistakes."

"I didn't say there was anything substantial. There isn't." He felt trapped. *I'm trying to play their game—when I should be rejecting the game itself!*

"You sure?" asked the fat one with what he obviously thought was a paternal smile on his face. In fact, it was . . . horrible . . . obscene . . . The *impudence!*

Sherman edged past the smaller one, who remained seated on the desk and followed him with his menacing little eyes. Near the door Sherman turned around and looked at them both.

"I'm sorry," he said, "but I don't see any point in going into this—I don't think I should discuss it any further."

Finally the smaller on stood up—*finally removes himself from his insolent perch on my desk!* He shrugged and looked at the fat one, who also stood up.

"Okay, Mr. McCoy," said the smaller one, "we'll see you . . . with your lawyer." The way he said it, it seemed to mean "We'll see you . . . *in court.*"

Sherman opened the door of the library and motioned for them to head out into the entry gallery. It seemed terribly important for him to usher them out and leave the room last—to prove that this was, after all, his household and that he was master of it.

When they reached the door to the elevator vestibule, the smaller one said to the fat one, "Davey, you got a card? Give Mr. McCoy a card."

The fat one took a card from the side pocket of his jacket and handed it to Sherman. The card was wrinkled.

"You change your mind," said the smaller one, "you give us a call."

"Yeah, think it over," said the fat one, with his hideous smile. "Whatever's on your mind, the sooner you tell us, the better it's gonna be for you. That's the way it is. Right now you're still in a position to cooperate. You wait . . . the machinery starts . . ." He turned his palms up, as if to say, "And then you're in a hell of a mess."

Sherman opened the door. The smaller one said, "Think it over."

As they walked out, the fat one gave him a horrible wink.

Sherman closed the door. They were gone. Far from being relieved, he was swept by an overpowering dismay. His entire central nervous system told him he had just suffered a catastrophic defeat—and yet he didn't know what had happened. He couldn't analyze his wounds. He had been outrageously violated—but how had it happened? How had these two . . . insolent . . . Low Rent . . . *animals* . . . invaded his life?

When he turned around, Bonita had emerged from the kitchen and was standing on the edge of the marble floor. He had to say something to her. She knew they were the police.

"They're investigating an automobile accident, Bonita." Too flustered.

"Oh, an *accident.*" Her wide eyes said, "Tell me more."

"Yes . . . I don't know. One of the cars involved had a license plate close to one of ours. Or something." He sighed and made a helpless gesture. "I couldn't figure it all out."

"You don't worry, Mr. McCoy. They know it's not you." The way she said it, he could tell he looked very worried indeed.

Sherman went into the library and closed the door and waited three or four minutes. He knew it was irrational, but he had the feeling that if he didn't wait until the two policemen were out of the building, they would somehow reappear, pop back in, just like that, smirking and winking in the horrible way they had. Then he called Freddy Button's home and left word that he should call whenever he got in.

Maria. Had to talk to her. Did he dare call her? Didn't even know where she would be . . . the hideaway, the apartment on Fifth . . . *Telephone tap!* . . . Could they somehow tap his telephone immediately? Had they left a listening device in the room? . . . Calm down . . . That's crazy . . . But suppose Judy has already come back, and I didn't hear her!

He got up from the chair and walked out into his grand entry gallery . . . No one around . . . He heard a little *clink clink* . . . Marshall's license tags . . . The doleful dachshund came waddling out of the living room . . . The beast's toenails clattered on the marble . . . The little piece of salami that walks . . . the cause of half my problems . . . And what do you care about the police? . . . Food and a walk, food and a walk . . . Then Bonita poked her head in the doorway . . . Don't want to miss anything, hunh? Want to gobble up all the cop stuff, right? . . . Sherman stared at her accusingly.

"Oh, I think Mrs. McCoy come home," she said.

"Don't worry," he said, "when Mrs. McCoy and Campbell come in, you'll hear them." And until then keep your nose out of my affairs.

Picking up the tone of his voice clearly enough, Bonita retreated into the kitchen. Sherman headed back toward the library. I'll risk a call. Just then the door from the elevator vestibule opened.

Judy and Campbell.

Now what? How could he call Maria? Would he have to tell Judy about the police first? If he didn't, Bonita would.

Judy looked at him quizzically. What the hell was she wearing? White flannel pants, a white cashmere sweater, and some sort of black punk jacket with shoulder pads . . . out to . . . here . . . sleeves pushed up almost to her elbow, a collar with a ridiculously wide notch way down . . . here . . . All the while Campbell looked supremely ladylike in her burgundy Taliaferro jumper and blazer and white blouse with a buttercup collar . . . Why was it that these days all the little girls were dressed like ladies and their mothers were dressed like teenage brats?

"Sherman," said Judy, looking concerned, "is something wrong?"

Should he tell her about the police immediately? No! Get out and call Maria!

"Uh, no," he said, "I was just—"

"Daddy!" said Campbell, walking toward him. "See these cards?"

See these cards?

She held up three miniature playing cards toward him, the ace of hearts, the ace of spades, and the ace of diamonds.

"What are they?" she said.

What are they?

"I don't know, sweetheart. Playing cards."

"But what *are* they?"

"Just a minute, sweetie. Judy, I've got to go out for a minute."

"*Daddy!* What *are* they!"

"The magician gave them to her," said Judy. "Tell her what they are." A little nod of the head that said, "Humor her. She wants to show you a trick."

"When I come back," he said to Campbell. "I have to go out for just a second."

"*Daddy!*" She hopped up and down, trying to put the cards right in his face.

"One *second*, sweetheart!"

"You're going out?" said Judy. "Where are you going?"

"I have to go over to—"

"DADDY! TELL—ME—WHAT—THEY—ARE!"

"—Freddy Button's."

"DADDY!"

"Shhhhhhhhhh," said Judy. "Hush up."

"Daddy . . . look!" The three cards were dancing in the air in front of his face.

"Freddy *Button's?* Do you know what time it is? We have to get ready to go out!"

"Tell me what they *are,* Daddy!"

Christ! He'd totally forgotten! They were supposed to go to dinner at these dreadful people's, the Bavardages'! Judy's bunch . . . the social X rays . . . Tonight? Impossible!

"I don't know, Judy. I . . . don't know how long I'll have to be at Freddy's. I'm sorry, I—"

"What do you mean, *you don't know?*"

"DADDY!" Close to tears, in her frustration.

"For God's sake, Sherman, look at the cards."

"Don't say 'God,' Mommy."

"You're absolutely right, Campbell. I shouldn't have said that."

He leaned over and peered at the cards. "Well . . . the ace of hearts . . . the ace of spades . . . and the ace of diamonds."

"You're *sure?*"

"Yes."

Big smile. Triumphant. "I just *wave* them like this." She began fanning the cards about at a furious rate, until they were a blur in the air.

"Sherman, you don't have *time* to go to Freddy Button's." A stern *and-that's-that* look.

"Judy, I have to." Rolling his eyes toward the library, as if to say, "I'll explain it to you in there."

"Bibbidy, bobbidy, boo!" said Campbell. "Now look, Daddy!"

Judy, in a voice under tight rein: "We're going . . . to—that—dinner."

He leaned over again. "The ace of diamonds . . . the ace of hearts . . . the ace of . . . *clubs!* Whuh—Campbell! How did the ace of *clubs* get there?"

Delighted. "It just—*did!*"

"Why—it's *magic!*"

"Sherman—"

"How did you *do* that? I can't believe it!"

"Sherman, did you hear me?"

Campbell, with great modesty: "The magician showed me."

"Ah! The magician. What magician?"

"At MacKenzie's birthday party."

"That's amazing!"

"Sherman, look at me."

He looked at her.

"Daddy! You want to see how I did it?"

"Sherman." More *and-that's-that.*

"Look, Daddy, I'll show you."

Judy, with frantic sweetness: "Campbell, you know who just *loves* magic tricks?"

"Who?"

"Bonita. She's crazy about them. Why don't you go show her before she's busy fixing your dinner. Then you can come back and show Daddy how you did it."

"Oh, all right." She trudged off to the kitchen disconsolately. Sherman felt guilty.

"Come on in the library," he said to Judy in a portentous voice.

They went into the library, and he shut the door and told Judy to sit down. *This will be too much for you to take standing up.* She sat down in the wing chair, and he sat in the armchair.

"Judy, you remember that thing on television last night, about the hit-and-run accident in the Bronx, and they're looking for a Mercedes with a license plate that begins with R?"

"Yes."

"Well, two policemen came by here, just before you and Campbell came home. Two detectives, and they asked me a lot of questions."

"Oh?"

He described the interrogation, wanting it to sound menacing—*I must go see Freddy Button!*—but avoiding his own feelings of inadequacy and fear and guilt.

"So I called Freddy, but he wasn't in, although they're expecting him. So I'm going over to his apartment and leave him this note"—he pressed the breast of his jacket, as if there were a letter in the inside pocket— "and if he's back when I get there, I'll talk to him. So I'd better go."

Judy just looked at him for a moment. "Sherman, that makes no sense whatsoever." She spoke almost warmly, with a little smile, the way you talk to someone who needs to be coaxed back from the edge of the roof. "They're not going to put you in jail because you have half a license number. I saw something in the *Times* about it this morning. Apparently there are 2,500 Mercedeses with license plates that begin with R. I was joking with Kate di Ducci at lunch. We had lunch at La Boue d'Argent. What on earth are you worried about? You certainly weren't out driving that night in the Bronx, whenever it was."

Now! . . . Tell her! . . . Get rid of this horrible weight once and for all! Come clean! With something approaching elation he scaled the last few feet of the great wall of deceit he had erected between himself and his family, and—

"Well . . . I know I wasn't. But they acted as if they didn't believe me."

—and immediately fell back.

"I'm sure you're imagining things, Sherman. That's probably just the way they *are*. For goodness' sake. If you want to talk to Freddy, you'll have plenty of time to talk to him in the morning."

"No! Really! I've got to go over there."

"And have a long talk, if necessary."

"Well, yes, if necessary."

She smiled in a way he didn't like. Then she shook her head. She was still smiling. "Sherman, we accepted this invitation five weeks ago. We're due there in an hour and a half. And I'm going. And *you're* going. If you want to leave the Bavardages' number for Freddy to call you, that's fine. I'm sure Inez and Leon won't mind. But we're going."

She continued to smile warmly . . . at the jumper on the roof . . . *and that's that.*

The calmness . . . the smile . . . the would-be warmth . . . Her face got the point across more firmly than any explanation she could have ever come up with. Words might have given him openings to wriggle through. This look offered no openings at all. Dinner at Inez and Leon Bavardages' was as important to Judy as the Giscard had been to him. The Bavardages were this year's host and hostess of the century, the most busily and noisily arrived of the *arrivistes*. Leon Bavardage was a New Orleans chicory salesman who had gone on to make a fortune in real estate. His wife, Inez, perhaps really was a member of an old Louisiana family, the Belairs. To Sherman (the Knickerbocker) they were ridiculous.

Judy smiled—and she had never been more serious in her life.

But he had to talk to Maria!

He jumped up. "All right, we're going—but I've got to run over to Freddy's! I won't be long!"

"Sherman!"

"I promise you! I'll be right back!"

He all but ran across the dark green marble of the entry gallery. He halfway expected her to run after him and yank him back inside from the elevator vestibule.

Downstairs, Eddie, the doorman, said, "Evening, Mr. McCoy," and stared at him with a look that seemed to say, "And why did the cops come to see you?"

"Hello, Eddie," he said without pausing to look at him. He began walking up Park Avenue.

Once he reached the corner, he rushed to the fateful telephone booth.

Carefully, carefully, he dialed Maria's number. First at the hideaway. No answer. Then he called the apartment on Fifth. A Spanish voice said Mrs. Ruskin couldn't come to the telephone. *Damn!* Should he say it's urgent? Should he leave his name? But the old man, her husband, Arthur, might very well be there. He said he would call back.

Had to kill some time to make it plausible that he went to Freddy Button's building and dropped off a note and came back. He walked over to Madison Avenue . . . the Whitney Museum . . . the Carlyle Hotel . . . Three men came out of the door that led to the Café Carlyle. They were about his age. They were talking and laughing, with their heads thrown back, blissfully boiled . . . All three carried attaché cases, and two of them wore dark suits, white shirts, and pale yellow ties with small print patterns. These pale yellow ties had become the insignia of the worker bees of the business world . . . What the hell did they have to laugh and crow about, other than the alcoholic buzz in their brains, the poor deluded—

He was experiencing the resentment of those who discover that, despite their own grave condition, the world goes on about its business, heartless, without even so much as a long face.

When he returned to the apartment, Judy was upstairs in their bedroom suite.

"Well—see? Didn't take so long," he said. He sounded as if he expected a star, for keeping his word.

Several possible comments had time to run through her head. What she in fact said, finally, was: "We have less than an hour, Sherman. Now, do me a favor. Please wear the navy suit you got last year, the *deep* navy. Midnight blue, I think it is. And a solid tie, not one of those prints. That navy crepe de chine. Or a shepherd's check is all right. You always look nice in those."

A *shepherd's check is all right* . . . He was overcome by despair and guilt. *They* were out there, circling, and he hadn't had the courage to tell her. She thought she could still afford the incalculable luxury of worrying about the correct necktie.

15

THE MASQUE OF THE
RED DEATH

Sherman and Judy arrived at the Bavardages' building on Fifth Avenue in a black Buick sedan, with a white-haired driver, hired for the evening from Mayfair Town Car, Inc. They lived only six blocks from the Bavardages, but walking was out of the question. For a start, there was Judy's dress. It was bare-shouldered but had short puffed sleeves the size of Chinese lampshades covering the upper arms. It had a fitted waist but was puffed up in the skirt to a shape that reminded Sherman of an aerial balloon. The invitation to dinner at the Bavardages' prescribed "informal" dress. But this season, as *tout le monde* knew, women dressed far more extravagantly for informal dinners in fashionable apartments than for formal dances in grand ballrooms. In any event, it was impossible for Judy to walk down the street in this dress. A five-mile-an-hour head wind would have stopped her cold.

But there was a yet more compelling reason for the hired car and driver. It would be perfectly *okay* for the two of them to arrive for dinner at a Good Building (the going term) on Fifth Avenue by taxi, and it would cost less than three dollars. But what would they do *after* the party? How could they walk *out* of the Bavardages' building and have all the world, *tout le monde*, see them standing out in the street, the McCoys, that game couple, their hands up in the air, bravely, desperately, pathetically trying to hail a taxi? The doormen would be no help, because they would be tied up ushering *tout le monde* to their limousines. So he had hired this car and this driver, this white-haired driver, who would drive them six blocks, wait three and a half or four hours, then drive them six blocks and depart. Including a 15 percent tip and the sales tax, the cost would be $197.20 or $246.50, depending on whether they were charged for four or five hours in all.

Hemorrhaging money! Did he even have a job left! Churning fear . . . Lopwitz . . . Surely, Lopwitz wouldn't *sack* him . . . because of three miserable days . . . *and $6 million, you ninny!* . . . Must start cutting back . . . tomorrow . . . Tonight, of course, it was imperative to have a car and driver.

To make matters worse, the driver couldn't pull up to the sidewalk near the entrance, because so many limousines were in the way. He had to double-park. Sherman and Judy had to thread their way between the limousines . . . Envy . . . envy . . . From the license plates Sherman could tell that these limousines were not hired. They were *owned* by those whose sleek hides were hauled here in them. A chauffeur, a good one willing to work long hours and late hours, cost $36,000 a year, minimum; garage space, maintenance, insurance, would cost another $14,000 at least; a total of $50,000, none of it deductible. *I make a million dollars a year—and yet I can't afford that!*

He reached the sidewalk. *Whuh?* Just to the left, in the gloaming. a figure—*a photographer*—right over there—

Sheer terror!

My picture in the paper!

The other boy, the big one, the brute, sees him and goes to the police!

The police! The two detectives! The fat one! The one with the lopsided face! McCoy—goes to parties at the Bavardages', does he! Now they truly smell blood!

Horrified, he stares at the photographer—

—and discovers that it's only a young man walking a dog. He has stopped near the canopy that leads up to the entrance . . . Not even looking at Sherman . . . staring at a couple who are nearing the door . . . an old man in a dark suit and a young woman, a blonde, in a short dress.

Calm down, for God's sake! Don't be crazy! Don't be paranoid!

But a smirking, insulting voice says: *You got something you wanna get off your chest?*

Now Sherman and Judy were under the canopy, only three or four steps behind the old man and the blonde, heading for the entrance. A doorman in a starched white dickie pushed it open. He wore white cotton gloves. The blonde entered first. The old man, who was not much taller than she was, looked sleepy and somber. His thinning gray hair was combed straight back. He had a big nose and heavy eyelids, like a movie Indian. *Wait a minute—I know him* . . . No, he had *seen* him somewhere . . . But where? . . . *Bango!* . . . In a picture, of course . . . It was Baron Hochswald, the German financier.

This was all Sherman needed, on this night of all nights . . . After the catastrophes of the past three days, in this perilous low point of his career on Wall Street, to run into this man, whose success was so complete, so permanent, whose wealth was so vast and unassailable—to have to set eyes upon this immovably secure and ancient German—

Perhaps the baron merely *lived* in this building . . . Please, God, don't let him be going to the same dinner party—

In that very moment he heard the baron say to the doorman in a heavy European accent: "Bavardage." The doorman's white glove gestured toward the rear of the lobby.

Sherman despaired. He despaired of this evening and of this life. Why hadn't he gone to Knoxville six months ago? A little Georgian house, a leaf-blowing machine, a badminton net in the back yard for Campbell . . . But no! He had to tag along behind this walnut-eyed German, heading for the home of some overbearingly vulgar people named Bavardage, a glorified traveling salesman and his wife.

Sherman said to the doorman, "The Bavardages', please." He hit the accented syllable hard, so that no one would think he had paid the slightest attention to the fact that the noble one, Baron Hochswald, had said the same thing. The baron, the blonde, Judy, and Sherman headed for the elevator. The elevator was paneled in old mahogany. It glowed. The grain was showy but rich and mellow. As he entered, Sherman overheard Baron Hochswald saying the name *Bavardage* to the operator. So Sherman repeated it, as before, "The Bavar*dages'* "—lest the baron himself get the impression that he, Sherman, was cognizant of his existence.

Now all four of them knew they were going to the same dinner party, and they had to make a decision. Did you do the decent, congenial, neighborly, and quite American thing—the sort of thing that would have been done without hesitation on an elevator in a similar building on Beacon Hill or Rittenhouse Square—or in a building in New York, for that matter, if the party were being given by someone of good blood and good bone, such as Rawlie or Pollard (in the present company, Pollard suddenly seemed quite okay, quite a commendable old Knickerbocker)—did you do the good-spirited thing and smile and introduce yourselves to one another . . . or did you do the vulgar snobbish thing and stand there and pretend you were unaware of your common destination and stare stiffly at the back of the elevator operator's neck while this mahogany cab rose up its shaft?

Sherman cut an exploratory glance at Hochswald and the blonde. Her dress was a black sheath that ended several inches above her knees and hugged her luscious thighs and the lubricious declivity of her lower abdomen and rose up to a ruff at the top that resembled flower petals. Christ, she was sexy! Her creamy white shoulders and the tops of her breasts swelled up as if she was dying to shed the sheath and run naked through the begonias . . . Her blond hair was swept back to reveal a pair of enormous ruby earrings . . . No more than twenty-five years old . . . A tasty morsel! A panting animal! . . . The old bastard had taken what he wanted, hadn't he! . . . Hochswald wore a black serge suit, a white shirt with a spread collar, and a black silk necktie with a large, almost rakish knot . . . all of it fashioned *just so* . . . Sherman was glad Judy had pressured him into wearing the navy suit and navy tie . . . Nevertheless, the baron's ensemble seemed terribly smart by comparison.

Now he caught the old German flicking his eyes up and down Judy and himself. Their glances engaged for the briefest of instants. Then both stared once more at the piping on the back of the collar of the elevator operator.

So they ascended, an elevator operator and four social mutes, toward some upper floor. The answer was: You did the vulgar snobbish thing.

The elevator stopped, and the four mutes walked out into the Bavardages' elevator vestibule. It was lit by clusters of tiny silk lampshades on either side of a mirror with a gilded frame. There was an open doorway . . . a rich and rosy glow . . . the sound of a hive of excited voices . . .

They went through the doorway, into the apartment's entry gallery. Such voices! Such delight! Such laughter! Sherman faced catastrophe in his career, catastrophe in his marriage—and the police were circling—and yet the hive—the hive!—the hive!—the sonic waves of the hive made his very innards vibrate. Faces full of grinning, glistening, boiling teeth! How fabulous and fortunate we are, we few, to be in these upper rooms together with our radiant and incarnadine glows!

The entry gallery was smaller than Sherman's, but whereas his (decorated by his wife, the interior designer) was grand and solemn, this one was dazzling, effervescent. The walls were covered in a brilliant Chinese-red silk, and the silk was framed by narrow gilded moldings, and the moldings were framed by a broad burnt-umber upholsterer's webbing, and the webbing was framed by more gilded moldings, and the light of a row of brass sconces made the gilt gleam, and the glow of the gilt and the Chinese-red silk made all the grinning faces and lustrous gowns yet more glorious.

He surveyed the crowd and immediately sensed a pattern . . . *presque vu! presque vu!* almost seen! . . . and yet he couldn't have put it into words. That would have been beyond him. All the men and women in this hall were arranged in clusters, conversational bouquets, so to speak. There were no solitary figures, no strays. All faces were white. (Black faces might show up, occasionally, at fashionable charity dinners but not in fashionable private homes.) There were no men under thirty-five and precious few under forty. The women came in two varieties. First, there were women in their late thirties and in their forties and older (women "of a certain age"), all of them skin and bones (starved to near perfection). To compensate for the concupiscence missing from their juiceless ribs and atrophied backsides, they turned to the dress designers. This season no puffs, flounces, pleats, ruffles, bibs, bows, battings, scallops, laces, darts, or shirs on the bias were too extreme. They were the social X rays, to use the phrase that had bubbled up into Sherman's own brain. Second, there were the so-called Lemon Tarts. These were women in their twenties or early thirties, mostly blondes (the Lemon in the Tarts), who were the second, third, and fourth wives or live-in girlfriends of men over forty or fifty or sixty (or seventy), the sort of women men refer to, quite without thinking, as *girls*. This season the Tart was able to flaunt the natural advantages of youth by showing her legs from well above the knee and emphasizing her round bottom (something no X ray had). What was entirely missing from *chez* Bavardage was that manner of woman who is neither very young nor very old, who has laid in a lining of subcutaneous fat, who glows with plumpness and a rosy face that speaks, without a word, of home and hearth and hot food ready at six and stories read aloud at night and conversations while seated on the edge of the bed, just before the Sandman comes. In short, no one ever invited . . . Mother.

Sherman's attention was drawn to a bouquet of ecstatic boiling faces in the immediate foreground. Two men and an impeccably emaciated woman were grinning upon a huge young man with pale blond hair and a cowlick at the top of his forehead . . . *Met him somewhere . . . but who is he? . . . Bango! . . .* Another face from the press . . . The Golden Hillbilly, the Towheaded Tenor . . . That was what they called him . . . His name was Bobby Shaflett. He was the new featured tenor of the Metropolitan Opera, a grossly fat creature who had somehow emerged from the upland hollows of the Appalachians. You could hardly read a magazine or a newspaper without seeing his picture. As Sherman watched, the young man's mouth opened wide. *Haw haw haw haw haw haw haw haw haw*, he broke out into a huge barnyard laugh, and the grinning faces around him became even more radiant, more transported, than before.

Sherman lifted his Yale chin, squared his shoulders, straightened his back, raised himself to his full height, and assumed the Presence, the presence of an older, finer New York, the New York of his father, the Lion of Dunning Sponget.

A butler materialized and asked Judy and Sherman what they wanted to drink. Judy asked for "sparkling water." (To say "Perrier" or any other brand name had become too trite.) Sherman had intended to drink nothing. He had intended to be aloof from everything about these people, these Bavardages, starting with their liquor. But the hive had closed in, and the cowlicked towhead of the Golden Hillbilly boomed away.

"A gin-and-tonic," said Sherman McCoy from the eminence of his chin.

A blazing bony little woman popped out from amid all the clusters in the entry gallery and came toward them. She was an X ray with a teased blond pageboy bob and many tiny grinning teeth. Her emaciated body was inserted into a black-and-red dress with ferocious puffed shoulders, a very narrow waist, and a long skirt. Her face was wide and round—but without an ounce of flesh on it. Her neck was much more drawn than Judy's. Her clavicle stuck out so far Sherman had the feeling he could reach out and pick up the two big bones. He could see lamplight through her rib cage.

"Dear Judy!"

"Inez!" said Judy, and the two of them kissed or, rather, swung their cheeks past one another, first on this side, then on that side, in a European fashion that Sherman, now the son of that staunch Knickerbocker, that Old Family patriarch, that Low Church Episcopal scourge of the fleshpots, John Campbell McCoy, found pretentious and vulgar.

"Inez! I don't think you've met Sherman!" She forced her voice into an exclamation, in order to be heard above the hive. "Sherman, this is Inez Bavardage!"

"Howja do," said the Lion's scion.

"I certainly *feel* like I know you!" said the woman, looking him squarely in the eye and flashing her tiny teeth and thrusting her hand toward him. Overwhelmed, he took it. "You should hear Gene Lopwitz go on about you!" Lopwitz! When? Sherman found himself clutching at this rope of hope. (Perhaps he had built up so many points in the past, the Giscard debacle would not finish him!) "And I know your father, too. Scared to death of him!" With this the woman gripped Sherman's forearm and fastened her eyes onto his and broke into an extraordinary laugh, a hacking laugh, not *hah hah hah* but *hack hack hack hack hack hack hack hack hack*, a laugh of such heartiness and paroxysmal rapture that Sherman found himself grinning foolishly and saying:

"You don't say!"

"Yes!" *Hack hack hack hack hack hack hack.* "I never told you this, Judy!" She reached out and hooked one arm inside Judy's and the other inside Sherman's and pulled the two of them toward her, as if they were the two dearest chums she had ever had. "There was this dreadful man named Derderian who was suing Leon. Kept trying to at*tach* things. Pure harassment. So one weekend we were out on Santa Catalina Island at Angie Civelli's." She dropped the name of the famous comedian without so much as a syncopation. "And we're having dinner, and Leon starts talking about all the trouble he's having with this man Derderian, and Angie says—believe me, he was *absolutely* serious—he says, 'You want me to take care of it?'" With this, Inez Bavardage pushed her nose to one side with her forefinger to indicate the Bent-Nose Crowd. "Well, I mean I'd *heard* about Angie and The Boys, but I didn't believe it—but he was *serious!*" *Hack hack hack hack hack hack hack hack.* She pulled Sherman yet closer and put her eyes right in his face. "When Leon got back to New York, he went to see your father, and he told him what Angie had said, and then he said to your father, 'Maybe that's the simplest way to take care of it.' I'll never forget what your father said. He said, 'No, Mr. Bavardage, you let *me* take care of it. It won't be simple, it won't be fast, and it'll cost you a *lot* of money. But my bill you can pay. The other—no one is rich enough to pay them. They'll keep collecting until the day you die.' "

Inez Bavardage remained close to Sherman's face and gave him a look of bottomless profundity. He felt obliged to say something.

"Well . . . which did your husband do?"

"What your father said, of course. When he spoke—people jumped!" A *hack-hack-hack-hacking* peeeealllll of laughter.

"And what about the bill?" asked Judy, as if delighted to be in on this story about Sherman's incomparable father.

"It was sensational! It was astonishing, that bill!" *Hack hack hack hack hack.* Vesuvius, Krakatoa, and Mauna Loa erupted with laughter, and Sherman felt himself swept up in the explosion, in spite of himself. It was irresistible—Gene Lopwitz loves you!—your incomparable father!—your aristocratic lineage!—what euphoria you arouse in my bony breast!

He knew it was irrational, but he felt warm, aglow, high, in Seventh Heaven. He eased the revolver of his Resentment back into his waistband and told his Snobbery to go lie down by the hearth. Really a very charming woman! Who would have thought it, after all the things one hears about the Bavardages! A social X ray, to be sure, but one can't very well hold that against her! Really very warm—and quite amusing!

Like most men, Sherman was innocent of the routine salutatory techniques of the fashionable hostesses. For at least forty-five seconds every guest was the closest, dearest, jolliest, most wittily conspiratorial friend a girl ever had. Every male guest she touched on the arm (any other part of the body presented problems) and applied a little heartfelt pressure. Every guest, male or female, she looked at with a radar lock upon the eyes, as if captivated (by the brilliance, the wit, the beauty, and the incomparable memories).

The butler returned with the drinks for Judy and Sherman, Sherman took a long deep draught of the gin-and-tonic, and the gin hit bottom, and the sweet juniper rose, and he relaxed and let the happy buzz of the hive surge into his head.

Hack hack hack hack hack hack hack went Inez Bavardage.

Haw haw haw haw haw haw haw haw went Bobby Shaflett.

Hah hah hah hah hah hah hah hah went Judy.

Heh heh heh heh heh heh heh heh went Sherman.

The hive buzzed and buzzed.

In no time Inez Bavardage had steered him and Judy over to the bouquet where the Golden Hillbilly held forth. Nods, hellos, handshakes, under the aegis of Sherman's new best friend, Inez. Before he quite realized what had happened, Inez had steered Judy out of the entry gallery, into some inner salon, and Sherman was left with the celebrated Appalachian fat boy, two men, and an X ray. He looked at each of them, starting with Shaflett. None returned his gaze. The two men and the woman stared, rapt, at the huge pale head of the tenor as he recounted a story of something that had happened on an airplane:

"—so I'm settin'up'eh waitin' fuh Barb'ra—she's supposed to be ridin' back to

New York with me?" He had a way of ending a declarative sentence with a question that reminded Sherman of Maria . . . Maria . . . and the huge Hasidic Jew! The great blond ball of fat before him was like that huge sow from the real-estate company—if that was where he was from. A cold tremor . . . They were out there circling, circling . . . "And I'm in my seat—I got the one by the window? And from back'eh, here come 'is *un*believable, *out*rageous black man." The way he hit the *un* and the *out* and fluttered his hands in the air made Sherman wonder if this hillbilly giant was, in fact, a homosexual. "He's wearin' this'eh ermine overcoat?—down to here?—and 'is'eh matchin' ermine fedora?— and he's got more rings'n Barb'ra's got, and he's got three re*tain*ers with 'im?— right outta *Shaft?*"

The giant bubbled on, and the two men and the woman kept their eyes on his huge round face and their grins fixed; and the giant, for his part, looked only at them, never at Sherman. As the seconds rolled by, he grew increasingly aware that all four of them were acting as if he didn't exist. A giant fairy with a hillbilly accent, thought Sherman, and they were hanging on his every word. Sherman took three deep gulps of his gin-and-tonic.

The story seemed to revolve about the fact that the regal black man, who had sat down next to Shaflett on the airplane, was the cruiser-weight champion of the world, Sam (Assassin Sam) Assinore. Shaflett found the term "cruiser weight" vastly amusing—*haw haw haw haw haw haw haw*—and the two men went into excited screams of laughter. Sherman labeled them homosexual, too. Assassin Sam hadn't known who Shaflett was, and Shaflett hadn't known who Assassin Sam was. The point of the entire story seemed to be that the only two people in the first-class section of the airliner who hadn't known who both these celebrities were . . . were Shaflett and Assinore themselves! *Haw haw haw haw haw haw haw haw—hee hee hee hee hee hee hee*—and—*aha!*—a conversational nugget about Assassin Sam Assinore popped into Sherman's brain. Oscar Suder—*Oscar Suder!* —he winced at the memory but pressed on—Oscar Suder was part of a syndicate of Midwestern investors who backed Assinore and controlled his finances. A nugget! A conversational nugget! A means of entry into this party cluster!

As soon as the laughter had receded, Sherman said to Bobby Shaflett, "Did you know that Assinore's contract, and his ermine coat, for all I know, is owned by a syndicate of businessmen in Ohio, mostly from Cleveland and Columbus?"

The Golden Hillbilly looked at him as if he were a panhandler. "Hmmmmmmmmm," he said. It was the *hmmmmmmmmm* that says, "I understand, but I couldn't care less," whereupon he turned back to the other three and said, "So I asked him if he'd sign my menu. You know, they give you this menu?— and—"

That was all for Sherman McCoy. He pulled the revolver of Resentment back out of his waistband. He wheeled away from the cluster and turned his back on them. Not one of them noticed. The hive raged in his head.

Now what would he do? All at once he was alone in this noisy hive with no place to roost. Alone! He became acutely aware that the entire party was now composed of these bouquets and that not to be in one of them was to be an abject, incompetent social failure. He looked this way and that. Who was that, right there? A tall, handsome, smug-looking man . . . admiring faces looking up at his . . . Ah! . . . It registered . . . an author . . . His name was Nunnally Voyd . . . a novelist . . . he'd seen him on a television talk show . . .

snide, acerbic . . . Look at the way those fools doted on him . . . Didn't dare
try that bouquet . . . Would be a repeat of the Golden Hillbilly, no doubt . . .
Over there, someone he knew . . . No! Another famous face . . . the ballet
dancer . . . Boris Korolev . . . Another circle of adoring faces . . . glistening
with rapture . . . The idiots! Human specks! What is this business of groveling
before dancers, novelists, and gigantic fairy opera singers? They're nothing but
court jesters, nothing but light entertainment for . . . the Masters of the Universe, those who push the levers that move the world . . . and yet these idiots
worship them as if they were pipelines to the godhead . . . They didn't even
want to know who he was . . . and wouldn't even be capable of understanding,
even if they had . . .

He found himself standing by another cluster . . . Well, at least no one
famous in this one, no smirking court jester . . . A fat, reddish man was talking,
in a heavy British accent: "He was lying in the road, you see, with a broken leg
. . ." *The delicate skinny boy! Henry Lamb! He was talking about the story in the
newspaper! But wait a minute—a broken leg—*". . . and he kept saying, 'How very
boring, how very boring.' " *No,* he was talking about some Englishman. *Nothing to
do with me* . . . The others in the cluster were laughing . . . a woman, about
fifty, with pink powder all over her face . . . How grotesque . . . Wait! . . .
He knew that face. The sculptor's daughter, now a stage designer. He couldn't
remember her name . . . But then he did . . . Barbara Cornagglia . . . He
moved on . . . Alone! . . . Despite all, despite the fact that *they* were circling
—the police!—he felt the pressure of social failure . . . What could he do to
make it appear as if he *meant* to be by himself, as if he were moving through the
hive alone by choice? The hive buzzed and buzzed.

Near the doorway through which Judy and Inez Bavardage had disappeared
was an antique console bearing a pair of miniature Chinese easels. Upon each
easel was a burgundy velvet disk the size of a pie, and in slits in the velvet, little
pockets, were stuck name cards. They were models of the seating arrangement for
dinner, so that each guest would know who his dinner partners were going to be.
It struck Sherman, the leonine Yale man, as another piece of vulgarity. Nevertheless, he looked. It was a way of appearing occupied, as if he were alone for no
other reason than to study the seating arrangement.

There were evidently two tables. Presently he saw a card with Mr. McCoy on
it. He would be sitting next to, let's see, a Mrs. Rawthrote, whoever she might be,
and a Mrs. Ruskin. *Ruskin!* His heart bolted. It couldn't be—not Maria!

But of course it could be. This was precisely the sort of event to which she
and her rich but somewhat shadowy husband would be invited. He downed the
rest of his gin-and-tonic and hurried through the doorway into the other room.
Maria! Had to talk to her!—but also had to keep Judy away from her! *Don't need
that on top of everything else!*

He was now in the apartment's living room, or salon, since it was obviously
meant for entertaining. It was enormous, but it appeared to be . . . *stuffed*
. . . with sofas, cushions, fat chairs, and hassocks, all of them braided, tasseled,
banded, bordered and . . . *stuffed* . . . Even the walls; the walls were covered
in some sort of padded fabric with stripes of red, purple, and rose. The windows
overlooking Fifth Avenue were curtained in deep folds of the same material,
which was pulled back to reveal its rose lining and a trim of striped rope braid.
There was not so much as a hint of the twentieth century in the decor, not even

in the lighting. A few table lamps with rosy shades provided all the light, so that the terrain of this gloriously stuffed little planet was thrown into deep shadows and mellow highlights.

The hive buzzed with the sheer ecstasy of being in this mellow rosy stuffed orbit. *Hack hack hack hack hack hack,* the horse laugh of Inez Bavardage rose somewhere. So many bouquets of people . . . grinning faces . . . boiling teeth . . . A butler appeared and asked him if he wanted a drink. He ordered another gin-and-tonic. He stood there. His eyes jumped around the deep stuffed shadows. *Maria.*

She was standing by one of the two corner windows. Bare shoulders . . . a red sheath . . . She caught his eye and smiled. Just that, a smile. He answered with the smallest smile imaginable. Where was Judy?

In Maria's cluster was a woman he didn't recognize, a man he didn't recognize, and a bald-headed man he knew from somewhere, another of the . . . *famous faces* this zoo specialized in . . . a writer of some sort, a Brit . . . He couldn't think of his name. Com*plete*ly bald; not a hair on his long thin head; gaunt; a skull.

Sherman panned the room, desperately searching for Judy. Well, what difference would it make if Judy did meet someone in this room named Maria? It wasn't that unusual a name. But would Maria be discreet? She was no genius, and she had a mischievous streak—and he was supposed to sit next to her!

He could feel his heart kicking up in his chest. Christ! Was it possible that Inez Bavardage knew about the two of them and put them together on purpose? *Wait a minute! That's very paranoid!* She'd never risk having an ugly scene. Still— *Judy.*

There she was, standing over near the fireplace, laughing so hard—*her new party laugh*—*wants to be an Inez Bavardage*—laughing so hard her hair was bouncing. She was making a new sound, *hock hock hock hock hock hock hock.* Not yet Inez Bavardage's *hack hack hack hack,* just an intermediary *hock hock hock hock.* She was listening to a barrel-chested old man with receding gray hair and no neck. The third member of the bouquet, a woman, elegant, slim, and fortyish, was not nearly so amused. She stood like a marble angel. Sherman made his way through the hive, past the knees of some people sitting down on a huge round Oriental hassock, toward the fireplace. He had to push his way through a dense flotilla of puffed gowns and boiling faces . . .

Judy's face was a mask of mirth. She was so enthralled by the conversation of the barrel-chested man she didn't notice Sherman at first. *Then* she saw him. Startled! But of course!—it was a sign of social failure for one spouse to be reduced to joining another in a conversational cluster. *But so what! Keep her away from Maria!* That was the main thing. Judy didn't look at him. Once again she beamed her grinning rapture at the old man.

"—so last week," he was saying, "my wife comes back from Italy and informs me we have a summer place on 'Como.' 'Como,' she says. It's this Lake Como. So all right! We'll have a summer place on 'Como.' It's better than Hammamet. That was two summers ago." He had a rough voice, a brushed-up New York street voice. He was holding a glass of soda water and looking back and forth, from Judy to the marble angel, as he told his story, getting vast effusions of approval from Judy and the occasional wriggle of the upper lip when he looked directly into the angel's face. A wriggle; it could have been the beginning of a polite smile. "At least I know where 'Como' is. I never hearda Hammamet. My wife's gone gaga about Italy. Italian paintings, Italian clothes, and now 'Como.' "

Judy went off into another automatic-weapon burst of laughter, *Hock hock hock hock hock hock*, as if the way the old man pronounced "Como," in mockery of his wife's love of things Italian, was the funniest thing in the world—*Maria*. It came over him, *just like that*. It was Maria he was talking about. This old man was her husband, Arthur Ruskin. Had he mentioned her by name yet, or had he been talking only about "my wife"?

The other woman, marble angel, just stood there. The old man suddenly reached toward her left ear and took her earring between his thumb and forefinger. Appalled, the woman stiffened. She would have jerked her head away, but her ear was now between the thumb and forefinger of this ancient and appalling ursine creature.

"Very nice," said Arthur Ruskin, still holding on to the earring. "Nadina D., right?" Nadina Dulocci was a highly mentionable jewelry designer.

"I believe so!" said the woman in a timorous, European voice. Hurriedly she brought her hands to her ears and unfastened both earrings and handed them to him, most emphatically, as if to say, "There, take them. But be so kind as not to rip my ears off my head."

Unconcerned, Ruskin took them in his hairy paws and inspected them further. "Nadina D., all right. Very nice. Where'd you get 'em?"

"They were a gift." Cold as marble. He returned them to her, and she quickly put them in her purse.

"Very nice, very nice. My wife—"

Suppose he said "Maria"! Sherman broke in. "Judy!" To the others: "Excuse me." To Judy: "I was wondering—"

Judy instantly transformed her startled expression into one of radiance. No wife in all of history had ever been more charmed to see her husband arrive at a conversational bouquet.

"Sherman! Have you met Madame Prudhomme?"

Sherman extended his Yale chin and put on an expression of the most proper Knickerbocker charm to greet the shaken Frenchwoman. "Howja do?"

"And Arthur Ruskin," said Judy. Sherman shook the hairy mitt firmly.

Arthur Ruskin was not a young seventy-one. He had big ears with thick rinds and wire hairs sprouting out. There were curdled wattles under his big jaws. He stood erectly, rocking back on his heels, which brought out his chest and his ponderous gut. His heft was properly swathed in a navy suit, white shirt, and navy tie.

"Forgive me," said Sherman. To Judy, with a charming smile: "Come over here a moment." To Ruskin and the Frenchwoman he flashed a smile of apology and moved off a few feet, Judy in tow. Madame Prudhomme's face fell. She had looked to his arrival in the bouquet as a salvation from Ruskin.

Judy, with a fireproof smile still on her face: "What is it?"

Sherman, a smiling mask of Yale Chin charm: "I want you to . . . uh come meet Baron Hochswald."

"Who?"

"Baron Hochswald. You know, the German—one of the Hochswalds."

Judy, the smile still locked on: "But why?"

"We rode up in the elevator with him."

This obviously made no sense to Judy at all. Urgently: "Well, where is he?" Urgently, because it was bad enough to be caught in a large conversational cluster with your husband. To form a minimal cluster with him, just the two of you—

Sherman, looking around: "Well, he was here just a minute ago."

Judy, the smile gone: "Sherman, what on earth are you doing? What are you talking about, 'Baron Hochswald'?"

Just then the butler arrived with Sherman's gin-and-tonic. He took a big swallow and looked around some more. He felt dizzy. Everywhere . . . social X rays in puffed dresses shimmering in the burnt-apricot glow of the little table lamps . . .

"Well—you two! What are *you* trying to cook up!" *Hack hack hack hack hack hack hack.* Inez Bavardage took them both by their arms. For a moment, before she could get her fireproof grin back onto her face, Judy looked stricken. Not only had she ended up in a minimal cluster with her husband, but New York's reigning hostess, this month's ringmistress of the century, had spotted them and felt compelled to make this ambulance run to save them from social ignominy.

"Sherman was—"

"I was looking for you! I want you to meet Ronald Vine. He's doing over the Vice President's house, in Washington."

Inez Bavardage towed them through the hive of grins and gowns and inserted them in a bouquet dominated by a tall, slender, handsome, youngish man, the aforesaid Ronald Vine. Mr. Vine was saying, ". . . jabots, jabots, jabots. I'm afraid the Vice President's wife has discovered jabots." A weary roll of the eyes. The others in the bouquet, two women and a bald man, laughed and laughed. Judy could barely summon up even a smile . . . Crushed . . . Had to be rescued from social death by the hostess . . .

Such sad irony! Sherman hated himself. He hated himself for all the catastrophes she didn't yet know about.

The Bavardages' dining-room walls had been painted with so many coats of burnt-apricot lacquer, fourteen in all, they had the glassy brilliance of a pond reflecting a campfire at night. The room was a triumph of nocturnal reflections, one of many such victories by Ronald Vine, whose forte was the creation of glitter without the use of mirros. Mirror Indigestion was now regarded as one of the gross sins of the 1970s. So in the early 1980s, from Park Avenue to Fifth, from Sixty-second Street to Ninety-sixth, there had arisen the hideous cracking sound of acres of hellishly expensive plate-glass mirror being pried off the walls of the great apartments. No, in the Bavardages' dining room one's eyes fluttered in a cosmos of glints, twinkles, sparkles, highlights, sheens, shimmering pools, and fiery glows that had been achieved in subtler ways, by using lacquer, glazed tiles in a narrow band just under the ceiling cornices, gilded English Regency furniture, silver candelabra, crystal bowls, School of Tiffany vases, and sculpted silverware that was so heavy the knives weighed on your fingers like saber handles.

The two dozen diners were seated at a pair of round Regency tables. The banquet table, the sort of Sheraton landing field that could seat twenty-four if you inserted all the leaves, had disappeared from the smarter dining rooms. One shouldn't be so formal, so grand. Two small tables were much better. So what if these two small tables were surrounded and bedecked by a buildup of *objets*, fabrics, and *bibelots* so lush it would have made the Sun King blink? Hostesses such as Inez Bavardage prided themselves on their gift for the informal and the intimate.

To underscore the informality of the occasion there had been placed, in the middle of each table, deep within the forest of crystal and silver, a basket woven from hardened vines in a highly rustic Appalachian Handicrafts manner. Wrapped around the vines, on the outside of the basket, was a profusion of wildflowers. In the center of the basket were massed three or four dozen poppies. This *faux-naïf* centerpiece was the trademark of Huck Thigg, the young florist, who would present the Bavardages with a bill for $3,300 for this one dinner party.

Sherman stared at the plaited vines. They looked like something dropped by Gretel or little Heidi of Switzerland at a feast of Lucullus. He sighed. All . . . too much. Maria was sitting next to him, on his right, chattering away at the cadaverous Englishman, whatever his name was, who was on her right. Judy was at the other table—but had a clear view of him and Maria. He had to talk to Maria about the interrogation by the two detectives—but how could he do it with Judy looking right at them? He'd do it with an innocuous party grin on his face. That was it! He'd grin through the whole discussion! She'd never know the difference . . . Or would she? . . . Arthur Ruskin was at Judy's table . . . But thank God, he was four seats away from her . . . wouldn't be chatting with her . . . Judy was sitting between Baron Hochswald and some rather pompous-looking youngish man . . . Inez Bavardage was two seats away from Judy, and Bobby Shaflett was on Inez's right. Judy was grinning an enormous social grin at the pompous man . . . *Hock hock hock hock hock hock hock hock hock hock!* Clear above the buzz of the hive he could hear her laughing her new laugh . . . Inez was talking to Bobby Shaflett but also to the grinning social X ray seated to the Golden Hillbilly's right and to Nunnally Voyd, who was to the right of the X ray. *Haw haw haw haw haw haw haw,* sang the Towheaded Tenor . . . *Hack hack hack hack hack hack,* sang Inez Bavardage . . . *Hock hock hock hock hock hock hock hock hock,* bawled his own wife . . .

Leon Bavardage sat four chairs to Sherman's right, beyond Maria, the cadaverous Englishman, and the woman with the pink powder on her face, Barbara Cornagglia. In contrast to Inez Bavardage, Leon had all the animation of a raindrop. He had a placid, passive, lineless face, wavy blondish hair, which was receding, a long delicate nose, and very pale, almost livid skin. Instead of a 300-watt social grin, he had a shy, demure smile, which he was just now bestowing upon Miss Cornagglia.

Belatedly it occurred to Sherman that he should be talking to the woman on his left. Rawthrote, Mrs. Rawthrote; who in the name of God was she? What could he say to her? He turned to his left—*and she was waiting.* She was staring straight at him, her laser eyes no more than eighteen inches from his face. A real X ray with a huge mane of blond hair and a look of such intensity he thought at first that she must *know* something . . . He opened his mouth . . . he smiled . . . he ransacked his brain for something to say . . . he did the best he could . . . He said to her, "Would you do me a great favor? What is the name of the gentleman to my right, the *thin* gentleman? His face is so familiar, but I can't think of his name for the life of me."

Mrs. Rawthrote leaned still closer, until their faces were barely eight inches apart. She was so close she seemed to have three eyes. "Aubrey Buffing," she said. Her eyes kept burning into his.

"Aubrey Buffing," said Sherman lamely. It was really a question.

"The poet," said Mrs. Rawthrote. "He's on the short list for the Nobel Prize. His father was the Duke of Bray." Her tone said, "How on earth could you not know that?"

"Of course," said Sherman, feeling that in addition to his other sins he was also a philistine. "The poet."

"How do you think he looks?" She had eyes like a cobra's. Her face remained right in his. He wanted to pull back but couldn't. He felt paralyzed.

"Looks?" he asked.

"Lord Buffing," she said. "The state of his health."

"I—can't really say. I don't know him."

"He's being treated at Vanderbilt Hospital. He has AIDS." She pulled back a few inches, the better to see how this zinger hit Sherman.

"That's terrible!" said Sherman. "How do you know that?"

"I know his best boyfriend." She closed her eyes and then opened them, as if to say: "I know such things, but don't ask too many questions." Then she said, "This is *entre nous*." *But I've never met you before!* "Don't tell Leon or Inez," she continued. "He's their house guest—has been for the past two and a half weeks. Never invite an Englishman for a weekend. You can't get them out." She said this without smiling, as if it was the most serious advice she had ever offered free of charge. She continued her myopic study of Sherman's face.

In order to break eye contact, Sherman took a quick glance at the gaunt Englishman, Lord Buffing the Short-List Poet.

"Don't worry," said Mrs. Rawthrote. "You can't get it at the table. If you could, we'd all have it by now. Half the waiters in New York are gay. You show me a happy homosexual, I'll show you a gay corpse." She repeated this *mot farouche* in the same rat-tat-tat voice as everything else, without a trace of a smile.

Just then a good-looking young waiter, Latin in appearance, began serving the first course, which looked like an Easter egg under a heavy white sauce on a plateau of red caviar resting on a bed of Bibb lettuce.

"Not these," said Mrs. Rawthrote, right in front of the young man. "They work full-time for Inez and Leon. Mexicans, from New Orleans. They live in their place in the country and drive in to serve dinner parties." Then, without any preamble, she said, "What do you do, Mr. McCoy?"

Sherman was taken aback. He was speechless. He was as flabbergasted as he had been when Campbell asked the same question. A nonentity, a thirty-five-year-old X ray, and yet . . . *I want to impress her!* The possible answers came thundering through his mind . . . *I'm a senior member of the bond division at Pierce & Pierce* . . . No . . . makes it sound as if he's a replaceable part in a bureaucracy and proud to be one . . . *I'm the number one producer* . . . No . . . sounds like something a vacuum-cleaner salesman would say . . . *There's a group of us who make the major decisions* . . . No . . . not accurate and an utterly gauche observation . . . *I made $980,000 selling bonds last year* . . . That was the true heart of the matter, but there was no way to impart such information without appearing foolish . . . *I'm—a Master of the Universe!* . . . Dream on! —and besides, there's no way to utter it! . . . So he said, "Oh, I try to sell a few bonds for Pierce & Pierce." He smiled ever so slightly, hoping the modesty of the statement would be taken as a sign of confidence to burn, thanks to tremendous and spectacular achievements on Wall Street.

Mrs. Rawthrote lasered in on him again. From six inches away: "Gene Lopwitz is one of our clients."

"Your client?"

"At Benning and Sturtevant."

Where? He stared at her.

"You do know Gene," she said.

"Well, yes, I work with him."

Evidently the woman did not find that convincing. To Sherman's astonishment, she turned ninety degrees, without another word, to her left, where a jolly, florid, red-faced man was talking to the Lemon Tart who had arrived with Baron Hochswald. Sherman now realized who he was . . . a television executive named Rale Brigham. Sherman stared at Mrs. Rawthrote's bony vertebrae, where they popped up from out of her gown . . . Perhaps she had turned away for only a moment and would turn back to resume their conversation . . . But no . . . she had barged in on the conversation of Brigham and the Tart . . . He could hear her rat-tat-tat voice . . . She was leaning in on Brigham . . . lasering in . . . She had devoted all the time she cared to devote . . . to a mere bond salesman!

He was stranded again. To his right, Maria was still deep in conversation with Lord Buffing. He was facing social death once more. He was a man sitting utterly solo at a dinner table. The hive buzzed all around him. Everyone else was in a state of social bliss. Only he was stranded. Only he was a wallflower with no conversational mate, a social light of no wattage whatsoever in the Bavardage Celebrity Zoo . . . *My life is coming apart!*—and yet through everything else in his overloaded central nervous system burned the shame—the shame!—of social incompetence.

He stared at Huck Thigg's hardened vines in the center of the table, as if a student of floral arrangements. Then he put a smirk on his face, as if confidently amused. He took a deep gulp of wine and looked across to the other table, as if he had caught the eye of someone there . . . He smiled . . . He murmured soundlessly toward vacant spots on the wall. He drank some more wine and studied the hardened vines some more. He counted the vertebrae in Mrs. Rawthrote's backbone. He was happy when one of the waiters, one of the *varones* from the country, materialized and refilled his glass of wine.

The main course consisted of slices of pink roast beef brought in on huge china platters, with ruffs of stewed onions, carrots, and potatoes. It was a simple, hearty American main course. Simple Hearty American main courses, insinuated between exotically contrived prologues and epilogues, were *comme il faut,* currently, in keeping with the informal mode. When the Mexican waiter began hoisting the huge platters over the shoulders of the diners, so that they could take what they wanted, that served as the signal to change conversational partners. Lord Buffing, the stricken English poet, *entre nous,* turned toward the powdered Madame Cornagglia. Maria turned toward Sherman. She smiled and looked deeply into his eyes. Too deeply! Suppose Judy should look at them right now! He put on a frozen social grin.

"Whew!" said Maria. She rolled her eyes in the direction of Lord Buffing. Sherman didn't want to talk about Lord Buffing. He wanted to talk about the visit from the two detectives. *But best start off slowly, in case Judy is looking.*

"Ah, that's right!" he said. A great social grin. "I forgot. You don't care for Brits."

"Oh, it's not that," said Maria. "He seems like a nice man. I could hardly understand what he was saying. You never heard such an accent."

Social grin: "What did he talk about?"

"The purpose of life. I'm not kidding."

Social grin: "Did he happen to mention what it is?"

"As a matter of fact, he did. Reproduction."

Social grin: "Reproduction?"

"Yes. He said id'd taken him seventy years to realize that's the sole purpose of life: reproduction. Said, 'Nature is concerned with but one thing: reproduction for the sake of reproduction.'"

Social grin: "That's very interesting, coming from him. You know he's homosexual, don't you?"

"Aw, come on. Who told you that?"

"This one." He gestured toward the back of Mrs. Rawthrote. "Who is she, anyhow? Do you know her?"

"Yeah. Sally Rawthrote. She's a real-estate broker."

Social grin: "A real-estate broker!" Dear God. Who on earth would invite a *real-estate broker* to dinner!

As if reading his mind, Maria said, "You're behind the times, Sherman. Real-estate brokers are very chic now. She goes everywhere with that old red-faced tub over there, Lord Gutt." She nodded toward the other table.

"The fat man with the British accent?"

"Yes."

"Who is he?"

"Some banker or other."

Social grin: "I've got something to tell you, Maria, but—I don't want you to get excited. My wife is at the next table and she's facing us. So please be cool."

"Well, well, well. Why, Mr. McCoy, honey."

Keeping the social grin clamped on his mug the whole time, Sherman gave her a quick account of his confrontation with the two policemen.

Just as he feared, Maria's composure broke. She shook her head and scowled. "Well, why didn't you let 'em see the goddamned car, Sherman! You said it's clean!"

Social grin: "Hey! Calm down! My wife may be looking. I wasn't worried about the car. I just didn't want them to talk to the attendant. It may be the same one who was there that night, when I brought the car back."

"Jesus Christ, Sherman. You talk to me about being *cool*, and you're so uncool. You sure you didn't tell 'em anything?"

Social grin: "Yes, I'm sure."

"For Christ's sake, get that stupid smile off your face. You're allowed to have a serious conversation with a girl at the dinner table, even if your wife is looking. I don't know why you agreed to talk to the goddamned police in the first place."

"It seemed like the right thing to do at the time."

"I *told* you you weren't cut out for this."

Clamping the social grin back on, Sherman glanced at Judy. She was busy grinning toward the Indian face of Baron Hochswald. He turned back to Maria, still grinning.

"Oh, for God's sake," said Maria.

He turned off the grin. "When can I talk to you? When can I see you?"

"Call me tomorrow night."

"Okay. Tomorrow night. Let me ask you something. Have you heard anybody talking about the story in *The City Light?* Anybody here, tonight?"

Maria started laughing. Sherman was glad. If Judy was watching, it would appear they were having an amusing conversation. "Are you serious?" said Maria. "The only thing these people read in *The City Light* is *her* column." She motioned toward a large woman across the table, a woman of a certain age with an outrageous mop of blond hair and false eyelashes so long and thick she could barely lift her upper lids.

Social grin: "Who's that?"

"That's 'The Shadow.' "

Sherman's heart kicked up. "You're joking! They invite a newspaper columnist to dinner?"

"Sure. Don't worry. She id'n interested in you. And she id'n interested in automobile accidents in the Bronx, either. If I shot Arthur, she'd be interested in that. And I'd be glad to oblige her."

Maria launched into a denunciation of her husband. He was consumed with jealousies and resentments. He was making her life hell. He kept calling her a whore. Her face was becoming more and more contorted. Sherman was alarmed —Judy might be looking! He wanted to put his social grin back on, but how could he, in the face of this lamentation? "I mean, he goes around the apartment calling me a *whore*. 'You whore! You whore!—right in front of the servants! How do you think that feels? If he calls me that one more time, I'm gonna hit him over the head with something, I swear to God!"

Out of the corner of his eye, Sherman could see Judy's face turned toward the two of them. Oh Christ!—and him without his grin on! Quickly he retrieved it and clamped it on his face and said to Maria, "That's terrible! It sounds like he's senile."

Maria stared at his pleasant social visage for a moment, then shook her head. "Go to hell, Sherman. You're as bad as he is."

Startled, Sherman kept the grin on and let the sound of the hive engulf him. Such ecstasy on all sides! Such radiant eyes and fireproof grins! So many boiling teeth! *Hack hack hack hack hack hack hack*, Inez Bavardage's laugh rose in social triumph. *Haw haw haw haw haw haw haw haw haw*, the Golden Hillbilly's barnyard bray rose in response. Sherman gulped down another glass of wine.

The dessert was apricot soufflé, prepared individually, for each diner, in a stout little crock of the Normandy sort, with borders *au rustaud* painted by hand near the rim. Rich desserts were back in fashion this season. The sort of dessert that showed you were conscious of calories and cholesterol, all the berries and melon balls with dollops of sherbet, had become just a bit Middle America. On top of that, to be able to serve twenty-four individual soufflés was a *tour de force*. It required quite a kitchen and a staff and a half.

Once the *tour de force* had run its course, Leon Bavardage rose to his feet and tapped on his wineglass—a glass of sauterne of a deep rosy golden hue—heavy dessert wines were also *comme il faut* this season—and was answered by the happy drunken percussion of people at both tables tapping their wineglasses in a risory fashion. *Haw haw haw haw*, Bobby Shaflett's laugh rang out. He was banging his glass for all he was worth. Leon Bavardage's red lips spread across his face, and his eyes crinkled, as if the crystal percussion was a great tribute to the joy the assembled celebrities found in his home.

"You are all such dear and special friends of Inez's and mine that we don't need a *special* occasion to want to have you all around us in our home," he said in a bland, slightly feminine, Gulf Coast drawl. Then he turned toward the other table, where Bobby Shaflett sat. "I mean, sometimes we ask Bobby to come over just so we can listen to his *laugh*. Bobby's laugh is music, far as I'm concerned—besides, we never can get him to sing for us, even when Inez plays the piano!"

Hack hack hack hack hack hack hack hack went Inez Bavardage. *Haw haw haw haw haw haw haw haw*, the Golden Hillbilly drowned her out with a laugh of his own. It was an amazing laugh, this one. *Haw haw haww hawww hawwww hawwwww hawwwwww*, it rose and rose and rose, and then it began to fall in a curious, highly stylized way, and then it broke into a sob. The room froze—dead silence—for that instant it took the diners, or most of them, to realize they had just heard the famous laughing sob of the "Vesti la giubba" aria from *Pagliacci*.

Tremendous applause from both tables, beaming grins, laughter, and cries of "More! More! More!"

"Aw, naw!" said the great blond giant. "I only sing for my supper, an'at's enough for supper right'eh! My *soufflé* wud'n big enough, Leon!"

Storms of laughter, more applause. Leon Bavardage motioned languidly toward one of the Mexican waiters. "More soufflé for Mr. Shaflett!" he said. "Make it in the bathtub!" The waiter stared back with a face of stone.

Grinning, eyes glistening, swept up by this duet of the great wits, Rale Brigham yelled out, "Bootleg soufflé!" This was so lame, Sherman was pleased to note, that everyone ignored it, even the ray-eyed Mrs. Rawthrote.

"But this *is* a special occasion, all the same," said Leon Bavardage, "because we have a very special friend as our guest during his visit to the United States, Aubrey Buffing." He beamed toward the great man, who turned his gaunt face toward Leon Bavardage with a small tight wary smile. "Now, last year our friend Jacques Prudhomme"—he beamed toward the French Minister of Culture, who was to his right—"told Inez and me he had it on good authority—I hope I'm not speaking out of turn, Jacques—"

"I hope so, too," said the Minister of Culture in his grave voice, shrugging in an exaggerated fashion for humorous effect. Appreciative laughter.

"Well, you *did tell* Inez and me you had it on good authority that Aubrey had won the Nobel Prize. I'm sorry, Jacques, but your intelligence operations are not so hot in Stockholm!"

Another grand shrug, more of the elegant sepulchral voice: "Fortunately, we do not contemplate hostilities with Sweden, Leon." Great laughter.

"But Aubrey was *that close*, anyway," said Leon, putting his forefinger and thumb close together, "and next year may be his year." The old Englishman's small tight smile didn't budge. "But of course, it really doesn't matter, because what Aubrey means to our . . . our *culture* . . . goes way beyond prizes, and I know that what Aubrey means to Inez and me as a *friend* . . . well, it goes beyond prizes and culture . . . and—" He was stumped for a way to finish off his tricolon, and so he said: "—and everything else. Anyway, I want to propose a toast to Aubrey, with best wishes for his visit to America—"

"He just bought himself another month of house guest," Mrs. Rawthrote said to Rale Brigham in a stage whisper.

Leon lifted his glass of sauterne: "Lord Buffing!"

Raised glasses, applause, British-style *hear-hears*.

The Englishman rose slowly to his feet. He was terribly haggard. His nose seemed a mile long. He was not tall, and yet somehow his great hairless skull made him seem imposing.

"You're much too kind, Leon," he said, looking at Leon and then casting his eyes down modestly. "As you may know . . . anyone who entertains the notion of the Nobel Prize is advised to act as if he is oblivious of its very existence, and in any case, I'm far too old to worry about it . . . And so I'm sure I don't know what you're talking about." Light puzzled laughter. "But one can scarcely help being aware of the marvelous friendship and hospitality of you and Inez, and thank goodness I don't have to pretend for a moment to be otherwise." The litotes had now trebled so rapidly, the company was baffled. But they murmured their encouragement. "So much so," he went on, "that I, for one, should be happy to sing for my supper—"

"I should think so," whispered Mrs. Rawthrote.

"—but I don't see how anyone would dare do so after Mr. Shaflett's remarkable allusion to Canio's grief in *Pagliacci*."

As only the English can do it, he pronounced "Mr. Shaflett" very archly, to bring out the ludicrous aspect of giving the dignified title "Mister" to this rustic clown.

Suddenly he stopped and lifted his head and gazed straight ahead, as if looking through the walls of the building and out upon the metropolis beyond. He laughed dryly.

"Forgive me. All at once I was hearing the sound of my own voice, and it occurred to me that I now have the sort of British voice which, had I heard it half a century ago, when I was a young man—a delightfully hotheaded young man, as I recall—would have caused me to leave the room."

People cut glances at one another.

"But I know you won't leave," Buffing continued. "It has always been wonderful to be an Englishman in the United States. Lord *Gutt* may disagree with me"— he pronounced *Gutt* with such a guttural bark, it was as if he were saying Lord *Shithead*—"but I doubt that he will. When I first came to the United States, as a young man, before the Second Great War, and people heard my voice, they would say, 'Oh, you're English!' and I always got my way, because they were so impressed. Nowadays, when I come to the United States and people hear my voice, they say, 'Oh, you're English—you poor thing!'—and I still get my way, because your countrymen never fail to take pity on us."

Much appreciative laughter and relief. The old man was mining the lighter vein. He paused again, as if trying to decide whether he should go on or not. His conclusion, evidently, was yes.

"Why I've never written a poem about the States I really don't know. Well, I take that back. I *do* know, of course. I have lived in a century in which poets are not supposed to write poems *about* anything, at least not anything you can put a geographical name to. But the United States deserve an epic poem. At various times in my career I considered writing an epic, but I didn't do that, either. Poets are also not supposed to write epics any longer, despite the fact that the only poets who have endured and will endure are poets who have written epics. Homer, Virgil, Dante, Shakespeare, Milton, Spenser—where will Mr. Eliot or Mr. Rimbaud"—pronounced like Mr. Shaflett—"be in their light, even twenty-five years from now? In the shadows, I'm afraid, in the footnotes, deep in the *ibid.* thickets . . . along with Aubrey Buffing and a lot of other poets I have thought very highly of from time to time. No, we poets no longer even have the vitality to write epics. We don't even have the courage to make rhymes, and the American epic should have rhymes, rhyme on top of rhyme in a shameless cascade, rhymes of the sort that Edgar Allan Poe gave us . . . Yes . . . Poe, who lived his last years just north of here, I believe, in a part of New York called the Bronx . . . in a little cottage with lilacs and a cherry tree . . . and a wife dying of tuberculosis. A drunk he was, of course, perhaps a psychotic—but with the madness of prophetic vision. He wrote a story that tells all we need to know about the moment we live in now . . . 'The Masque of the Red Death' . . . A mysterious plague, the Red Death, is ravaging the land. Prince Prospero—Prince *Prospero*—even the name is perfect—Prince Prospero assembles all the best people in his castle and lays in two years' provision of food and drink, and shuts the gates against the outside world, against the virulence of all lesser souls, and commences a masked ball that is to last until the plague has burnt itself out beyond the walls. The party is endless and seamless, and it takes place in seven grand salons, and in each the revel becomes more intense than in the one before, and the revelers are drawn on, on, on toward the seventh room, which is appointed entirely in black. One night, in this last room, appears a guest shrouded in the most clever and most hideously beautiful costume this company of luminous masqueraders has ever seen. This guest is dressed as Death, but so convincingly that Prospero is offended and orders him ejected. But none dares touch him, so that the task is left to the Prince himself, and the moment he touches the ghastly shroud, he falls down dead, for the Red Death has entered the house of Prospero . . . *Prospero*, my friends . . . Now, the exquisite part of the story is that somehow the guests have known all along what awaits them in this room, and yet they are drawn irresistibly toward it, because the excitement is so intense and the pleasure is so unbridled and the gowns and the food and the drink and the flesh are so sumptuous— and that is all they have. Families, homes, children, the great chain of being, the eternal tide of chromosomes mean nothing to them any longer. They are bound together, and they whirl about one another, endlessly, particles in a doomed atom —and what else could the Red Death be but some sort of final stimulation, the *ne plus ultra*? So Poe was kind enough to write the ending for us more than a hundred years ago. Knowing that, who can possibly write all the sunnier passages that should come before? Not I, not I. The sickness—the nausea—the pitiless pain—have ceased with the fever that maddened my brain—with the fever called 'Living' that burned in my brain. The fever called 'Living'—those were among the last words he wrote . . . No . . . I cannot be the epic poet you deserve. I am too old and far too tired, too weary of the fever called 'Living,' and I value your company too much, your company and the whirl, the whirl, the whirl. Thank you, Leon. Thank you, Inez."

And with that the spectral Englishman slowly took his seat.

The intruder the Bavardages dreaded most, silence, now commanded the room. The diners looked at one another in embarrassment, three kinds of it. They were embarrassed for this old man, who had committed the gaffe of injecting a

somber note into an evening at the Bavardages'. They were embarrassed because
they felt the need to express their cynical superiority to his solemnity, but they
didn't know how to go about it. Dared they snigger? After all, he was Lord Buffing
of the Nobel Short List and their hosts' house guest. And they were embarrassed
because there was always the possibility that the old man had said something
profound and they had failed to get it. Sally Rawthrote rolled her eyes and pulled
a mock long face and looked about to see if anyone was following her lead. Lord
Gutt put a downcast smile on his great fat face and glanced at Bobby Shaflett,
who was himself looking at Inez Bavardage for a clue. She offered none. She
stared, dumbstruck. Judy was smiling an entirely foolish smile, it seemed to Sherman, as if she thought something very pleasant had just been expressed by the
distinguished gentleman from Great Britain.

Inez Bavardage rose up and said, "We'll have coffee in the other room."

Gradually, without conviction, the hive began to buzz again.

On the ride back home, the six-block ride, costing $123.25, which is to say,
one half of $246.50, with Mayfair Town Car Inc.'s white-haired driver at the
wheel, Judy chattered away. She was bubbling over. Sherman hadn't seen her this
animated for more than two weeks, since the night she caught him in *flagrante
telephone* with Maria. Tonight, obviously, she had not detected a thing concerning
Maria, didn't even know the pretty girl sitting next to her husband at dinner had
been *named* Maria. No, she was in great spirits. She was intoxicated, not by
alcohol—alcohol was fattening—but by Society.

With a pretense of amused detachment she burbled about the shrewdness
with which Inez had chosen her celebrity all-stars: three titles (Baron Hochswald,
Lord Gutt, and Lord Buffing), one ranking politician with a cosmopolitan cachet
(Jacques Prudhomme), four giants of arts and letters (Bobby Shaflett, Nunnally
Voyd, Boris Korolev, and Lord Buffing), two designers (Ronald Vine and Barbara
Cornagglia), three V.I.F.'s—"V.I.F.'s?" asked Sherman—"Very Important Fags,"
said Judy, "that's what everybody calls them" (The only name Sherman caught
was that of the Englishman who had sat to her right, St. John Thomas), and three
business titans (Hochswald, Rale Brigham, and Arthur Ruskin). Then she went
on about Ruskin. The woman on his left, Madame Prudhomme, wouldn't talk to
him, and the woman on his right, Rale Brigham's wife, wasn't interested, and so
Ruskin had leaned over and started telling Baron Hochswald about his air charter
service in the Middle East. "Sherman, have you any idea how that man makes his
money? He takes Arabs to Mecca on airplanes—747s!—by the tens of thousands!
—and he's Jewish!"

It was the first time she had passed on a piece of chitchat to him, in the sunny
vein of yore, since he couldn't remember when. But he was past caring about the
life and times of Arthur Ruskin. He could think only of the gaunt and haunted
Englishman, Aubrey Buffing.

And then Judy said, "What on earth do you suppose got into Lord Buffing?
The whole thing was so . . . so mortifying."

Mortifying, indeed, thought Sherman. He started to tell her that Buffing was
dying of AIDS, but he was long past the joys of gossip also.

"I have no idea," he said.

But of course he did. He knew precisely. That mannered, ghostly English
voice had been the voice of an oracle. Aubrey Buffing had been speaking straight

to him, as if he were a medium dispatched by God Himself. Edgar Allan Poe!— *Poe!*—the ruin of the dissolute!—in the Bronx—*the Bronx!* The meaningless whirl, the unbridled flesh, the obliteration of home and hearth!—and, waiting in the last room, the Red Death.

Eddie had the door open for them by the time they walked from the Mayfair Town Car sedan to the entrance. Judy sang out, "Hello, Eddie!" Sherman barely looked at him and said nothing at all. He felt dizzy. In addition to being consumed by fear, he was drunk. His eyes darted about the lobby . . . The Street of Dreams . . . He half expected to see the shroud.

16

TAWKIN IRISH

Martin's Irish machismo was so icy Kramer couldn't conceive of him as high-spirited, except possibly while drunk. Even then, he figured, he would be a mean and irritable drunk. But this morning he was in high spirits. His sinister Doberman eyes had become big and bright. He was happy as a child.

"So we're standing there in this lobby with these two doormen," he was saying, "and there's a buzz, and this button lights up, and Jesus Christ, one a these guys, he's running out the door like he's got a wire up his ass, and he's blowing a whistle and waving his arms for a cab."

He looked straight at Bernie Fitzgibbon as he told this tale. The four of them, Martin, Fitzgibbon, Goldberg, and himself, were in Fitzgibbon's office. Fitzgibbon, as befitted a Homicide Bureau chief in the District Attorney's Office, was a slender athletic Irishman of the Black Irish stripe with a square jaw, thick black hair, dark eyes, and what Kramer called a Locker Room Grin. A Locker Room Grin was quick but never ingratiating. Fitzgibbon no doubt smiled readily at Martin's story and its boorish details because Martin was a particular type of tough little Harp, and Fitzgibbon understood and valued the breed.

There were two Irishmen in the room, Martin and Fitzgibbon, and two Jews, Goldberg and himself, but to all intents and purposes there were four Irishmen. I'm still Jewish, thought Kramer, but not in this room. All the cops turned Irish, the Jewish cops, like Goldberg, but also the Italian cops, the Latin cops, and the black cops. The black cops even; nobody understood the police commissioners, who were usually black, because their skin hid the fact that they had turned Irish. The same was true of assistant district attorneys in the Homicide Bureau. You were supposed to turn Irish. The Irish were disappearing from New York, so far as the general population was concerned. In politics, the Irish, who twenty years ago still ran the Bronx, Queens, Brooklyn, and much of Manhattan, were down to one seedy little district over on the West Side of Manhattan, over where all the unused piers rusted in the Hudson River. Every Irish policeman Kramer met, including Martin, lived out on Long Island or some place like Dobbs Ferry and commuted to the city. Bernie Fitzgibbon and Jimmy Caughey were dinosaurs. Everybody moving up in the Bronx District Attorney's Office was Jewish or Italian. And yet the Irish stamp was on the Police Department and on the Homicide Bureau of the D.A.'s Office, and it would probably be there forever. Irish machismo—that was the dour madness that gripped them all. They called themselves Harps and Donkeys, the Irish did. Donkeys! They used the word themselves, in pride but also as an admission. They understood the word. Irish bravery was not the bravery of the lion but the bravery of the donkey. As a cop, or as an assistant district attorney in Homicide, no matter what kind of stupid fix you got yourself into, you never backed off. You held your ground. That was what was scary about even the smallest and most insignificant of the breed. Once they took a position, they were ready to fight. To deal with them you had to be willing to fight also, and not that many people on this poor globe were willing to fight. The other side of it was loyalty. When one of them got in a jam, the others never broke ranks. Well, that wasn't completely true, but the game had to be pretty far gone before the Irish started looking out for Number One. The cops were like that, and assistant D.A.'s in Homicide were supposed to be like that. Loyalty was loyalty, and Irish loyalty was a monolith, indivisible. The code of the Donkey! And every Jew, every Italian, every black, every Puerto Rican, internalized that code and became a stone Donkey himself. The Irish liked to entertain one another with Irish war stories, so that when Donkey Fitzgibbon and Donkey Goldberg listened to Donkey Martin, all they lacked was booze so they could complete the picture by getting drunk and sentimental or drunk and in a brutal rage. No, thought Kramer, they don't need alcohol. They're high on what tough, undeluded motherfuckers they are.

"I asked one a the doormen about it," said Martin. "I mean, we had lotsa time. This fucking McCoy makes us wait down in the lobby for fifteen minutes. Anyway, on every floor, beside the elevator, they got two buttons. One is for the elevator, and the other is for cabs. You push the button, and this little shitball runs out in the street blowing his whistle and waving his arms. So anyway, we finally get in the elevator, and it dawns on me I don't know what floor the fucking guy lives on. So I stick my head out the door, and I says to the doorman, 'What button do I push?' And he says, 'We'll send you up there.' *We'll send you up there.* You can push all the buttons you want inside the elevator and it don't mean shit. One a the doormen has to push the button on his panel out by the door. Even if you live in the fucking place and you want to go visit somebody else, you can't just get on the elevator and push somebody else's floor. Not that the place strikes me as the kinda place where they just drop by to shoot the shit. Anyway, this guy McCoy's on the tenth floor. The door opens, and you step out into this little room. It don't open up on a hall, it opens up on this little room, and there's only one door. On that floor the elevator is just for his fucking apartment."

"You've lived a sheltered life, Marty," said Bernie Fitzgibbon.

"Not fucking sheltered enough, if you ask me," said Martin. "We ring the bell, and a maid in a uniform opens the door. She's Puerto Rican or South American or something. This hall you walk into, there's all this marble and wood paneling and one a those big staircases that goes up like this, like something in a fucking movie. So we cool our heels on the marble floor for a while, until the guy figures he's made us wait the proper length a time, and then he comes down the stairs, very slowly, with his fucking chin—I swear to Christ—with his fucking chin up in the air. You catch that, Davey?"

"Yeah," said Goldberg. He snorted with amusement.

"What's he look like?" asked Fitzgibbon.

"He's tall, got the gray suit, got this chin up in the air—your Wall Street asshole. Not a bad-looking guy. About forty."

"How did he react to you guys being there?"

"He was pretty cool about the whole thing at first,' said Martin. "He invited us into this library, I guess it was. It wasn't very big, but you shoulda seen this fucking shit up around the ceiling." He waved his hand in a sweeping motion. "There's all these fucking people, carved outta wood, like crowds a people on the sidewalk, and these shops and shit in the background. You never seen anything like it. So we're sitting there, and I'm telling him how this is a routine check of cars of this make with this license plate and so on, and he's saying yeah, he heard something about the case on television and yeah, he has a Mercedes with a license number that begins with R, and it sure is a fuck ng coincidence, all right —and I mean, I figure, well, this is just another jerk-off name on this fucking jerk-off list they handed us. I mean, if you wanna figure out the least likely character you can think of who would be driving up fucking Bruckner Boulevard in the Bronx at night, this is the guy. I mean, I'm practically *apologizing* to the guy for wasting his fucking time. And then I ask him if we can take a look at it, and he says, 'When?' And I says, 'Now,' and that was all it took. I mean, if he said, 'It's in the shop' or 'My wife's got it' or any goddamned thing, I don't know if I'da even come back to check it out, it all looked so fucking unlikely. But he gets this look on his face, and his lips start trembling, and he starts talking this double-talk about how he *don't know* . . . and what's *the routine* . . . but it's mainly the look on his face. I looked at Davey, and he looked at me, and we both saw the same goddamned thing. Ain't that the truth, Davey?"

"Yeah. Suddenly the bitch comes out in him. You could see it coming out."

"I seen people like this before," said Martin. "He don't like this shit at all. He's not a bad guy. Looks a little stuck-up, but he's probably a nice enough guy. He's got a wife and a kid. He's got this fucking apartment He ain't got the heart for this shit. He ain't got the heart for being on the wrong side a the law. I don't care who you are, sometime in your life you're gonna be on the wrong side a the law, and some people got the heart for it and some don't."

"He don't have the heart for you sitting on his fucking desk," said Goldberg, laughing.

"His desk?" said Fitzgibbon.

"Oh yeah," said Martin, chuckling at the recollection. "Well, the thing is, I see the guy starting to come apart, and I say to myself, 'Well, shit, I ain't read him his fucking rights yet, so I better do that.' So I'm trying to be real casual about it, and I'm telling him how much we appreciate his cooperation and all, but he don't have to say anything if he don't want to, and he's entitled to a lawyer, and so forth, and now I'm thinking ahead. How'm I gonna say, 'If you can't afford an attorney, the state will provide you with one free a charge,' and make that sound casual, when the fucking carvings on the wall cost more than a fucking 18b lawyer makes in a year. So I figure I'll throw in the old 'move over' maneuver for good measure, and I stand right over him—he's sitting down at this big desk—

and I look at him like, 'You're not gonna do a chickenshit thing like keeping your mouth shut, just because I'm reading you your rights, are you?' "

"It was worse than that," said Goldberg. "Marty starts sitting on the edge of the guy's fucking desk!"

"What did he do?" asked Fitzgibbon.

"Nothing at first," said Martin. "He knows something's up. There ain't no way you can just say, 'By the way,' and read somebody his rights like you're just passing the time. But he's confused. I can see his eyes getting bigger and bigger. He's double-talking like a sonofabitch. Then he gets up, and he says he wants to talk to a lawyer. The funny thing is, here he starts coming apart when we ask him about the car, and then we go by and see the car, and it's clean. There's not a mark on it."

"How did you find his car?"

"That was simple. He told us he kept it in a garage. So I figured, if you got as much money as this sonofabitch has, you're gonna keep your car in the nearest garage. So I asked the doorman where's the nearest parking garage. That's all. Didn't even mention McCoy."

"And the garage, they just showed you the car?"

"Yeah, I just flashed the badge, and Davey stood on the other side of him and stared holes in his head. You know, a mean Jew looks a lot meaner than a mean Harp."

Goldberg beamed. He took this as a great compliment.

"The guy says, 'Which car?' " said Goldberg. "Turns out they keep two cars in the garage, the Mercedes and a Mercury station wagon, and it costs $410 a month to keep a car in there. It's posted on the wall. Eight hundred and twenty dollars a month for two cars. That's two hundred dollars more than I pay for my whole fucking house in Dix Hills."

"So the guy shows you the car?" asked Fitzgibbon.

"He tells us where it is and says, 'Help yourself,' " said Goldberg. "I get the idea he's not too crazy about McCoy."

"Well, he don't go outta his way to look out for him," said Martin. "I asked him if the car was used Tuesday a week ago, in the evening, and he says, Oh sure, he remembers it very well. McCoy takes it out about six and comes back about ten, looking like a mess."

"Nice to have people looking out for your interests," said Goldberg.

"Alone?" asked Fitzgibbon.

"That's what he said," said Martin.

"So you feel sure this is the guy."

"Oh yeah."

"Okay," said Fitzgibbon, "then how do we get a case?"

"We got the start a one now," said Martin. "We know he was driving his car that night."

"Give us twenty more minutes with the fucker and we'll get the rest," said Goldberg. "He's got the bitch coming out a him already."

"I wouldn't count on that," said Fitzgibbon, "although you can try. You know, we really ain't got shit. We got no witnesses. The kid himself is out of it. We don't even know where it happened. Not only that, the kid comes into the hospital the night it happens, and he don't say anything about getting hit by a car."

A light began to dawn. Kramer broke in: "Maybe he was already gaga." A radiance emanated from this erstwhile piece a shit. "We know he took a pretty good shot to the head."

"Maybe," said Fitzgibbon, "but that don't give me anything to move with, and I'm telling you, Abe is gonna wanna move. He was not happy about that demonstration yesterday. WEISS JUSTICE IS WHITE JUSTICE. That was all over the newspapers, and it was on TV."

"And it was bullshit," said Goldberg. "We were there. A couple dozen pickets, half a them the usual nutballs, this Reva Whatsis and her elves, and the rest a them were rubberneckers."

"Try telling that to Abe. He saw it on TV, like everybody else."

"Well, you know," said Kramer, "this guy McCoy sounds like somebody we can smoke out maybe."

"Smoke out?"

"Yeah. I'm just thinking out loud now—but maybe by going public with it . . ."

"Going public?" said Fitzgibbon. "Are you kidding? With what? The guy gets squirrelly when two cops come to his apartment to question him, and he was driving his car on the night the kid was hit? You know what that adds up to? Nothing."

"I said I'm just thinking out loud."

"Yeah, well, do me a favor. Don't think out loud that way in front of Abe. He's just liable to take you seriously."

Reade Street was one of those old streets down near the courthouses and City Hall. It was a narrow street, and the buildings on either side, office buildings and light-industry lofts with cast-iron columns and architraves, kept it in a dismal gloaming, even on a bright spring day like this. Gradually the buildings in this area, which was known as TriBeCa, for "triangle below Canal Street," were being renovated as offices and apartments, but the area retained an irreducible grime. On the fourth floor of an old cast-iron building, Sherman walked down a corridor with a dingy tile floor.

Halfway down the corridor was a plastic plate incised with the names DERSHKIN, BELLAVITA, FISHBEIN & SCHLOSSEL. Sherman opened the door and found himself in a tiny and overpoweringly bright glassed-in vestibule tended by a Latin woman who sat behind a glass partition. He gave his name and asked to see Mr. Killian, and the woman pressed a buzzer. A glass door led to a larger, even brighter space with white walls. The lights overhead were so strong Sherman kept his head down. An orange industrial cord carpet covered the floor. Sherman squinted, trying to avoid the ferocious wattage. Just ahead, on the floor, he could make out the base of a couch. The base was made of white Formica. Pale tan leather cushions were on top of it. Sherman sat down, and his tailbone immediately slid forward. The seat seemed to tilt the wrong way. His shoulder blades hit the back cushions, which rested against a slab of Formica set perpendicular to the base. Gingerly he lifted his head. There was another couch across from him. On it were two men and a woman. One man had on a blue-and-white running suit with two big panels of electric-blue leather in front. The other man wore a trench coat made of some dull, dusty, grainy hide, elephant perhaps, with shoulders cut so wide he seemed gigantic. The woman wore a black leather jacket, also cut very large, black leather pants, and black boots that folded down below the knee like a pirate's. All three of them were squinting, just as Sherman was. They also kept sliding forward and then twitching and squirming back up, and their leather clothes rustled and squeaked. The Leather People. Jammed together on the couch, they resembled an elephant tormented by flies.

A man entered the reception area from an inner hallway, a tall thin bald man with bristling eyebrows. He wore a shirt and a tie but no jacket, and he had a revolver in a holster high on his left hip. He gave Sherman the sort of dead smile a doctor might give in a waiting room if he didn't want to be detained. Then he went back inside.

Voices from the inner hallway: a man and a woman. The man appeared to be pushing the woman forward. The woman took little steps and looked back at him over her shoulder. The man was tall and slender, probably in his late thirties. He wore a double-breasted navy-blue suit with a pale blue overplaid and a striped shirt with a stiff white collar. The collar had an exaggerated spread, very much a sharpie's look, to Sherman's way of thinking. He had a lean face, a delicate face, you might have said, had it not been for his nose, which appeared to have been broken. The woman was young, no more than twenty-five, all breasts, bright red lips, raging hair, and sultry makeup, popping out of a black turtleneck sweater. She wore black pants and teetered atop a pair of black spike-heel shoes.

At first their voices were muffled. Then the woman's voice became louder and the man's became lower. It was the classic case. The man wants to confine matters to a quiet private argument, but the woman decides to play one of her trump cards, which is Making a Scene. There is Making a Scene, and there is Tears. This was Making a Scene. The woman's voice became louder and louder, and at last the man's rose, too.

"But you gotta," the woman said.

"But I don't gotta, Irene."

"What am I suppose a do? Rot?"

"You suppose a pay your bills like everybody else," he said, mimicking her. "You already beat me for half my fee. And then you keep asking me to do things that could get me disbarred."

"You dun care."

"It ain't that I dun care, Irene. It's that I dun care anymore. You don't pay your bills. Don't look at me like that. You're on your own."

"But you gotta! What happens if they rearrest me?"

"You shoulda thoughta that, Irene. What did I tell you the first time you walked into this office? I told you two things. I told you, 'Irene, I'm not gonna be your friend. I'm gonna be your lawyer. But I'm gonna do more for you than your friends.' And I said, 'Irene, you know why I do this? I do it for money.' And then I said, 'Irene, remember those two things.' Idd'n'at right? Did'n I say that?"

"I can't go back there," she said. She lowered her heavy Tropical Twilight eyelids and then her whole head. Her lower lip trembled; her head and the raging hair shook, so did her shoulders.

The Tears.

"Oh, for Christ's sake, Irene. Come on!"

The Tears.

"All right. Look . . . I'll find out if they're going after you on a 220–31, and I'll represent you on rearraignment if they are, but that's it."

The Tears!—victorious even after these many millennia. The woman nodded like a penitent child. She walked out through the blazing waiting room. Her bottom bobbed in a glossy black shimmer. One of the Leather Men looked at Sherman and smiled, man to man, and said, "Ay, caramba."

On this alien terrain Sherman felt obliged to smile back.

The sharpie came into the reception room and said, "Mr. McCoy? I'm Tom Killian."

Sherman stood up and shook hands. Killian didn't shake hands very firmly; Sherman thought of the two detectives. He followed Killian down a hallway with more spotlights.

Killian's office was small, modern, and grim. It had no window. But at least it wasn't bright. Sherman looked at the ceiling. Of the nine recessed spotlights, seven had been unscrewed or allowed to burn out.

Sherman said, "The lights out there . . ." He shook his head and didn't bother to finish the sentence.

"Yeah, I know," said Killian. "That's what you get when you fuck your decorator. The guy who leased this place, he brought in this number, and she thought the building was gloomy. She put in, I mean, *lights*. The woman had watt fever. The place is supposed to remind you of Key Biscayne. That's what she said."

Sherman didn't hear anything after "fuck your decorator." As a Master of the Universe, he took a masculine pride in the notion that he could handle all sides of life. But now, like many respectable American males before him, he was discovering that All Sides of Life were colorful mainly when you were in the audience. *Fuck your decorator.* How could he let any decision affecting his life be made by this sort of person in this sort of atmosphere? He had called in sick—that lamest, weakest, most sniveling of life's small lies—to Pierce & Pierce; for this itching slum of the legal world.

Killian motioned toward a chair, a modern chair with a curved chrome frame and Chinese-red upholstery, and Sherman sat down. The back was too low. There was no way to get comfortable. Killian's chair, behind the desk, didn't look much better.

Killian let out a sigh and rolled his eyes again. "You heard me conferring with my client, Miss——" He made a curve in the air with his cupped hand.

"I did. Yes."

"Well, there you had criminal law in its basic form with all the elements." Well, theh you ed crim'nal lawr in its basic fawuhm wit'allee elements. At first Sherman thought the man was talking this way as further mimicry of the woman who had just left. Then he realized it wasn't her accent. It was Killian's own. The starched dandy who sat before him had a New York street accent, full of dropped consonants and tortured vowels. Nevertheless, he had lifted Sherman's spirits a notch or two by indicating that he knew Sherman was new to the world of criminal law and that he existed on a plateau far above it.

"What sort of case?" asked Sherman.

"Drugs. Who else can afford a trial lawyer for eight weeks?" Then, without any transition, he said: "Freddy told me your problem. I also been reading about the case in the tabloids. Freddy's a great man, but he has too much class to read the tabloids. I read 'em. So whyn't you tell me what actually happened."

To his surprise, once he got started, Sherman found it easy to tell his story in this place, to this man. Like a priest, his confessor, this dandy with a fighter's nose, was from another order.

Every now and then a plastic intercom box on Killian's desk would give an electronic beep, and the receptionist's faintly Latin voice would say, "Mr. Killian . . . Mr. Scannesi on 3-0" or "Mr. Rothblatt on 3-1," and Killian would say, "Tell 'im I'll call 'im back," and Sherman would resume. But then the machine beeped, and the voice said, "Mr. Leong on 3-0."

"Tell 'im—I'll take it." Killian gave his hand a deprecating flap in the air, as if to say. "This is nothing compared to what we're talking about, but I'll have to talk to this person for half a second."

"Ayyyyy, Lee," said Killian. "Whaddaya whaddaya? . . . No kiddin'? . . . Hey, Lee, I was just reading a book about you . . . Well, not about you but about you Leongs . . . Would I kid you? Whaddaya think, I want a hatchet in my back?"

Sherman grew increasingly irritated. At the same time, he was impressed. Apparently Killian was representing one of the defendants in the Chinatown voting scandal.

Finally Killian hung up and turned to Sherman and said, "So you took the car back to the garage and you exchanged a few words with the attendant and you walked home." This was no doubt to show that he hadn't been distracted by the interruption.

Sherman kept going, concluding with the visit of the two detectives, Martin and Goldberg, to his apartment.

Killian leaned forward and said, "Awright. The first thing you gotta understand is, from now on, you gotta keep your mouth shut. You understand? You got nothing to gain, *nothing*, by talking about this"—*tawkin*—"to anybody, I don't care who it is. All that's gonna happen is, you're gonna get jerked around some more like you did by these two cops."

"What *should* I have done? They were in the building. They knew I was upstairs. If I refused to talk to them, that would be like a clear indication I had something to hide."

"All you hadda do was tell them, 'Gentlemen, it's nice to meet you, you're conducting an investigation, I have absolutely no experience in this area, so I'm gonna turn you over to my attorney, good evening, don't let the doorknob hit you in the back on your way out.' "

"But even that—"

"It's better'n what happened, right? As a matter of fact, they woulda probably figured, Well, here's this Park Avenue swell who's too busy or too above-it-all to talk to characters like us. He's got people who do things like that for him. It wouldn't've prejudiced your case at all, probably. From now on, it sure as hell won't." He started chuckling. "The guy actually read your rights to you, hunh? I wish I coulda seen it. The dumb fuck probably lives in a two-family in Massapequa, and he's sitting there in an apartment on Park Avenue in the Seventies, and he's gotta inform you that if you are unable to afford a lawyer, the state will provide you one. He's gotta read you the whole thing."

Sherman was chilled by the man's detached amusement. "All right," he said, "but what does it mean?"

"It means they're trying to get evidence for a criminal charge."

"What kind?"

"What kinda evidence or what kinda charge?"

"What kind of charge."

"They have several possibilities. Assuming Lamb don't die"—*don't*—"there's reckless endangerment."

"Is that the same as reckless driving?"

"No, it's a felony. It's a fairly serious felony. Or if they really want to get hard-nosed about it, they could work on a theory of assault with a dangerous weapon, meaning the car. If Lamb dies, that creates two more possibilities. Manslaughter is one, and criminally negligent homicide is the other, although all the time I was in the D.A.'s office up there I never heard a charging anybody with criminally negligent homicide unless there was drunk driving involved. On top a that they got leaving the scene of an accident and failure to report an accident. Both felonies."

"But since I wasn't driving the car at the time this fellow was hit, can they bring any of these charges against *me?*"

"Before we get to that, let me explain something to you. Maybe they can't bring charges against *anybody.*"

"They can't?" Sherman felt his entire nervous system quicken at this first sign of hope.

"You looked your car over pretty carefully, right? No dents? No blood? No tissue? No broken glass? Right?"

"That's right."

"It's pretty obvious the kid wasn't hit very hard. The emergency room treated him for a broken wrist and let him go. Right?"

"Yes."

"The fact of the matter is, you don't even *know* if your car hit him, do you."

"Well, I did hear something."

"With all the shit that was going on at that moment, that coulda been anything. You *heard* something. You didn't see anything. You don't really *know,* do you?"

"Well . . . that's true."

"You beginning to see why I don't want you to talk to anybody?"

"Yes."

"And I mean *anybody.* Okay? Now. Here's another thing. Maybe it wasn't your car that hit him. Did that possibility ever occur to you? Maybe it wasn't *any* car. You don't *know.* And *they* don't know, the cops don't know. These stories in the newspaper are very strange. Here's this big case, supposedly, but nobody knows where this cockamamie hit'n'run's supposed've taken place. *Bruckner Boulevard.* Bruckner Boulevard's five miles long! They got no witnesses. What the kid told his mother is hearsay. It don't"—*don't*—"mean a thing. They have no description of a driver. Even if they could establish that it was your car that hit him —they can't arrest a car. One a the garage attendants coulda loaned it to his sister-in-law's nephew so he could go up to Fordham Road to kiss his girlfriend good night. They don't know. And you don't know. As a matter of fact, stranger things have happened."

"But suppose the other boy comes forward? I swear to you, there was a second boy, a big powerful fellow."

"I believe you. It was a setup. They were gonna take you off. Yeah, he could come forward, but it sounds to me like he has his reasons not to. Judging by this story the mother tells, the kid didn't mention him, either."

"Yes," said Sherman, "but he could. I swear, I'm beginning to feel as if I should preempt the situation and take the initiative and go to the police with Maria—Mrs. Ruskin—and just tell them exactly what happened. I mean, I don't know about the law, but I feel morally certain that I did the right thing and that she did the right thing in the situation we were in."

"Ayyyyyy!" said Killian. "You Wall Street honchos really *are* gamblers! Ayyyyyy!! Whaddaya whaddaya!" Killian was grinning. Sherman stared at him in astonishment. Killian must have detected it, because he put on a perfectly serious face. "You got any idea what the D.A.'d do if you just walked in and said, 'Yeah, it was me and my girlfriend, who lives on Fifth Avenue, in my car'? They'd devour you—*de*-vour you."

"Why?"

"The case is already a political football, and they got *nothing* to go on. Reverend Bacon is yelling about it, it's on TV, *The City Light* has gone bananas over it, and it's putting a lot of pressure on Abe Weiss, who has an election coming up. I know Weiss very well. There is no real world to Abe Weiss. There's only what's on TV and in the newspapers. But I'll tell you something else. They wouldn't give you a break even if no one was watching."

"Why not?"

"You know what you do all day long when you work in the D.A.'s Office? You prosecute people named Tiffany Latour and LeBaron Courtney and Mestaffalah Shabazz and Camilio Rodriguez. You get so you're *dying* to get your hands on somebody with something on the ball. And if somebody gives you a couple like you and your friend Mrs. Ruskin—ayyyyyyyy, Biscuit City!"

The man seemed to have a horrible nostalgic enthusiasm for such a catch.

"What would happen?"

"For a start, there's no way in the world they wouldn't arrest you, and if I know Weiss, he'd make a big show of it. They might not be able to hold you very long, but it would be extremely unpleasant. That's guaranteed."

Sherman tried to imagine it. He couldn't. His spirits hit bottom. He let out a big sigh.

"*Now* you see why I don't want you to talk to anybody? You get the picture?"

"Yes."

"But look, I'm not trying to depress you. My job right now is not to defend you but to keep you from even having to be defended. I mean, that's assuming you decide to have me represent you. I'm not even gonna talk about a fee at this point, because I don't know what this is gonna involve. If you're lucky, I'll find out this is a bullshit case."

"How can you find out that?"

"The head of the Homicide Bureau in the Bronx D.A.'s Office is a guy I started out with up there, Bernie Fitzgibbon."

"And he'll tell you?"

"I think he will. We're friends. He's a Donkey, just like me."

"A donkey?"

"An Irishman."

"But is that wise, letting them know I've hired a lawyer and I'm worried? Won't that put ideas in their heads?"

"Christ, they already"—*awready*—"got ideas in their head, and they know you're worried. If you weren't worried after those two meatballs came to see you, there'd have to be something wrong with you. But I can take care a that. What you oughta start thinking about is your friend Mrs. Ruskin."

"That was what Freddy said."

"Freddy was right. If I'm gonna take this case, I wanna talk to her, and the sooner the better. You think she'd be willing to make a statement?"

"A statement?"

"A sworn statement we could have witnessed."

"Before I talked to Freddy, I would have said yes. Now I don't know. If I try to get her to make a sworn statement, in a legal setting, I don't know what she'll do."

"Well, one way or another, I'll want to talk to her. Can you get hold of her? I don't mind calling her myself, as far as that goes."

"No, it would be better if I did it."

"One thing is, you don't want her going around talking, either." *Tawkin tawkin tawkin*.

"Freddy tells me you went to the Yale Law School. When were you there?"

"The late seventies," said Killian.

"What did you think of it?"

"It was okay. Nobody there knew what the fuck I was talking about." *Tawkin.* "You might as well be from Afghanistan as Sunnyside, Queens. But I liked it. It's a nice place. It's easy, as law schools go. They don't try to bury you in details. They give you the scholarly view, the overview. You get the grand design. They're very good at giving you that. Yale is terrific for anything you wanna do, so long as it don't involve people with sneakers, guns, dope, lust, or sloth."

17

THE FAVOR BANK

OVER THE INTERCOM came the secretary's voice: "I got Irv Stone on the line, from Channel 1." Without a word to Bernie Fitzgibbon, Milt Lubell, or Kramer, Abe Weiss stopped in the middle of a sentence and picked up the telephone. Without a hello or any other preliminary remark, he said into the mouthpiece: "Whadda I gotta do with you guys?" It was the voice of a tired and disappointed parent. "You're supposed to be a news organization in the most important city in the country. Right? And what's the most serious problem in the most important city in the country? Drugs. And what's the worst of the drugs? Crack. Am I right? And we bring in grand-jury indictments against three of the biggest crack dealers in the Bronx, and whadda you guys do? Nothing . . . Lemme finish. We bring all three a them into Central Booking at ten o'clock in the morning, and where are you guys? Nowhere . . . Wait a minute, my ass!" No longer the saddened parent. Now the irate neighbor on the floor below. "You got no excuse, Irv! You guys are lazy. You're afraid you're gonna miss a meal at the Côte Basque. One day you're gonna wake up—what? . . . Don't gimme that, Irv! The only thing wrong with those crack dealers is, they're black and they're from the Bronx! Whaddaya want, Vanderbilt, Astor, and—and—and—and— and Wriston?" He didn't seem too sure about Wriston. "One day you're gonna wake up and realize you're out of it. This is America up here in the Bronx, Irv, modern-day America! And there's black people in modern-day America, whether you know it or not! Manhattan's an offshore boutique! This is America! This is the laboratory of human relations! This is the experiment in urban living! . . . Whaddaya mean, how about the Lamb case? What's'at gotta do with this? Big deal, you covered a story in the Bronx. Whaddaya got, a quota!"

He hung up. No goodbye. He turned to Fitzgibbon, who sat to one side of the district attorney's enormous desk. Kramer and Lubell sat on either side of Fitzgibbon. Weiss put his hands up in the air, as if he were holding a medicine ball over his head.

"They're screaming about crack every night, and we bring in indictments against three major dealers, and he's telling me there's no story in it, it's routine stuff."

Kramer found himself shaking his head, to indicate how saddened he was by the obstinacy of television newsmen. Weiss's press secretary, Milt Lubell, a skinny little man with a grizzly gray beard and big eyes, swiveled his head in a state of advanced disbelief. Only Bernie Fitzgibbon took this news without the slightest locomotor reaction.

"You see?" said Weiss. He jerked his thumb toward the telephone without looking at it. "I try to talk to this guy about drug indictments, and he throws the Lamb case in my face."

The district attorney looked extremely angry. But then, every time Kramer had laid eyes on him he had looked angry. Weiss was about forty-eight. He had a full head of light brown hair, a narrow face, and a strong, lean jaw with a scar on one side. There was nothing wrong with that. Abe Weiss was one of a long line of New York district attorneys whose careers had been based on appearing on television and announcing the latest paralyzing wallop to the solar plexus of crime in the seething metropolis. Weiss, the good Captain Ahab, might be the object of jokes. But he was wired in to the Power, and the Power flowed through him, and his office, with its paneled walls and outsized old wooden furniture and its American flag on a stand, was a command post of the Power, and Kramer tingled with the excitement of being called in on a summit meeting like this.

"Some way," said Weiss, "we gotta get out in fronta this case. Right now I'm stuck in a position where all I can do is react. You musta seen this coming, Bernie, and you didn't warn me. Kramer here talked to Bacon a week ago, it musta been."

"That's just the point, Abe," said Fitzgibbon. "That's—"

Weiss pushed a button on his desk, and Fitzgibbon stopped talking, because obviously the district attorney's mind had departed the immediate vicinity. He was looking at a television screen on the other side of the room. Bulging from the stately paneled wall, like a high-tech goiter, was a bank of four television sets and stacks of steely boxes with steely knobs and black glass dials and green-diode lights in a nest of electrical cords. Rows of videocassettes stretched across the shelves behind the television sets, where books had once been. If Abe Weiss or anything concerning Abe Weiss or anything concerning crime and punishment in the Bronx was on television, Abe Weiss wanted it on tape. One of the sets flared to life. Just the picture; no sound. A cloth banner filled the screen . . . JOHANNE BRONX: WEISS JUSTICE IS APARTHEID JUSTICE . . . Then came a cluster of angry faces, white and black, shot from below so that they looked like an overwhelming mob.

"F'r Chrissake, who the hell's that?" asked Weiss.

"That's Channel 7," said Milt Lubell.

Kramer looked at Lubell. "But they weren't even there, Channel 7. There was only Channel 1." He said it in a low voice, to indicate he was daring to talk only to the district attorney's press secretary. He wasn't presuming to jump into the general conversation.

"You didn't see this?" said Lubell. "This was last night. After I ran it, the rest of them got hot for the story. So they had another demonstration last night."

"You're kidding!" said Kramer.

"Ran on five or six channels. Smart move."

Weiss pushed another button on his desk, and a second screen came on. On the first screen heads continued to flare up and vanish, flare up and vanish. On the second three male musicians with bony faces and huge Adam's apples and one woman . . . in a dark and smoky back alley . . . MTV . . . A whirring sound . . . The musicians split up into vibrating stripes. The videocassette kicks in. A moon-faced young man with a microphone under his chin . . . out in front of the Poe projects . . . The usual pack of teenagers are cutting up in the background.

"Mort Selden, Channel 5," said Weiss.

"Right," said Milt Lubell.

Weiss hit another button. A third screen lit up. The musicians were back on the smoky street. The woman had dark lips . . . like Shelly Thomas's . . . the most exquisite yearning came over Kramer . . . The musicians turned into jittery stripes again. A man with Latin features . . .

"Roberto Olvidado," said Lubell.

The man held a microphone in the face of an angry black woman. In no time there were three sets of heads flaring and vanishing, flaring and vanishing, casting their toxic-wave glow upon the carved wood.

Weiss said to Fitzgibbon: "You realize that's all that was on the news last night, the Lamb case? And all Milt's done all morning is take calls from reporters and these goddamned people wanting to know what we're doing."

"But that's ridiculous, Abe," said Fitzgibbon. "What are we supposed to do? We're prosecutors, and the cops haven't even made an arrest yet."

"Bacon's cute," said Lubell. "He's cute. Oh, he's a cutie. He says the cops have talked to the kid's mother and we've talked to the kid's mother, and for some bullshit reason we're conspiring to do nothing. We don't care about black people in the projects."

All at once Weiss turned a baleful eye upon Kramer, and Kramer braced.

"Kramer, I want you to tell me something. Did you really tell the kid's mother that her information was useless?"

"No, sir, I certainly did not!" Kramer realized that his answer sounded a bit too frantic. "The only thing I said was, I said that what her son said to her was hearsay, in terms of a prosecution, and what we really needed was witnesses, and she should let us know immediately if she heard of anyone who saw what happened. That's all I said. I didn't say what she told me was useless at all. Just the opposite. I thanked her for it. I don't know how anybody could twist it around like that."

And all the while he was thinking: Why did I have to play it so cool with the woman? To impress Martin and Goldberg, so they wouldn't think I was being soft! So they would regard me as properly Irish! Why couldn't I have been a good sympathetic Jew? Now look at the fix I'm in . . . He wondered if Weiss would throw him off the case.

But Weiss just nodded ruefully and said, "Yeah, I know . . . But just remember, you can't always be logical with . . ." He decided not to finish the sentence. He shifted his gaze to Fitzgibbon. "Bacon can say any goddamn thing he wants to, and I have to sit here and say, 'My hands are tied.' "

"I hope you realize, Abe, these demonstrations are pure bullshit. A dozen of Bacon's boys and another coupla dozen of the usual fruitcakes, the Monolithic Socialist Labor Party, whatever. Right, Larry?"

"The night I was there, yeah," said Kramer. But something told him not to play down the importance of the demonstrations. So he motioned toward the television screens and said, "But I tell you, it looks like there was a much bigger crowd last night."

"Well, sure," said Lubell. "It's the old self-fulfilling prophecy. Once it's on TV and all over the newspapers, people figure it's important. They figure they got to get excited about it. The old self-fulfilling prophecy."

"Anyway," said Weiss, "what's the situation? What about this guy McCoy? Whadda we got on him? These two cops—what are their names?"

"Martin and Goldberg," said Fitzgibbon.

"They say this is the guy, right?"

"Yeah."

"They're good men?"

"Martin's got a lot of experience," said Fitzgibbon. "But he's not infallible. Just because this guy got so worked up, that don't necessarily mean he did anything."

"Park Avenue," said Weiss. "His old man ran Dunning Sponget & Leach. Milt found his name in a couple of social columns, and his wife's an interior decorator." Weiss sank back in his chair and smiled, the way one smiles over impossible dreams. "That sure would put an end to this shit about white justice."

"Abe," said the Irish cold shower, Fitzgibbon, "we got zip on the guy so far."

"Is there any way we can bring him in for questioning? We know he was driving his car the night the thing happened."

"He's got a lawyer now, Abe. Tommy Killian, in fact."

"Tommy? I wonder how the hell he found Tommy. How do you know that?"

"Tommy called me up. Said he represented the guy. Wanted to know why the cops were asking him questions."

"What did you tell him?"

"I said the guy's car matches the description of the car they're looking for. So they're trying to check it out."

"What did he say to that?"

"He said they got a bullshit description based on hearsay."

"What did you say?"

"I said we also got a kid in the hospital likely to die, and the cops are investigating with the information they have."

"What's the kid's situation? Any change in his condition?"

"Naw . . . He's still in a coma, in the intensive-care unit. He's living on tubes."

"Any chance he'll regain consciousness?"

"From what they told me, it can happen, but it don't mean anything. They can drift in, but they drift right back out. Besides, he can't talk. He's breathing from a tube down his throat."

"But maybe he can point," said Weiss.

"Point?"

"Yeah. I got an idea." A far-off look; the distant gaze of inspiration. "We take a picture of McCoy over to the hospital. Milt found one in one a these magazines."

Weiss handed Bernie Fitzgibbon a page out of some kind of social weekly called W. The page was mostly pictures of grinning people. The men had on tuxedos. The women were all teeth and gaunt faces. Kramer leaned over to have a look. One picture had been circled by a red marker. A man and a woman, both grinning, in evening dress. Look at them. The Wasps. The man had a narrow pointed nose. His head was thrown back, which brought out his big patrician chin. Such a confident . . . arrogant? . . . smile . . . The woman looked Wasp, too, but in a different way. She had that tight, neat, proper, composed look that immediately makes you wonder what's wrong with what you're wearing or what you just said. The caption said *Sherman and Judy McCoy.* They were at some sort of charity event. Here on floor 6M of the island fortress, when you heard a name like Sherman McCoy, you naturally assumed the person was black. But these were the originals, the Wasps. Kramer hardly ever saw them except in this form, in pictures, and the pictures showed him bland, stiff-necked aliens with pointed noses whom God, in His perversity, had favored with so much. This was no longer a conscious thought, in words, however; by now it was a reflex.

Weiss was saying, "We take this picture of McCoy and three or four other people, three or four other white guys, over there and we put 'em by his bed. He comes to, and he points to McCoy's picture . . . He keeps pointing . . ."

Bernie Fitzgibbon looked at Weiss as if he were waiting for a clue, a tip, that this was only a little joke.

"Maybe it's worth a try," said Weiss.

"Who's gonna witness all this?" said Fitzgibbon.

"A nurse, a doctor, whoever's there. Then we go over and take a proper dying declaration."

Fitzgibbon said, *"Proper?* How? I don't believe what I'm hearing, Abe. Some poor gork with a tube down his throat pointing at a picture? That would never stand up."

"I know that, Bernie. I just wanna bring the guy in. Then we can relax and do the thing right."

"Abe! . . . Jesus Christ! Never mind the legal side of it for a minute. You're gonna put a picture of a Wall Street investment banker and a buncha other white guys on the kid's bedside table while he's fucking *dying?* Suppose he comes to—and he *looks* at the fucking table—and here's half a dozen middle-aged white men in suits and ties staring at him! The fucking kid's gonna stroke out for sure! He's gonna say, 'Holy shit!' and give up the fucking ghost! I mean, have a fucking heart, Abe!"

Weiss let out a great sigh and seemed to deflate before Kramer's eyes. "Yeah. You're right. It's too wild."

Fitzgibbon cut a glance at Kramer.

Kramer didn't bat an eye. He didn't want to cast so much as a twitch of aspersion upon the wisdom of the District Attorney of Bronx County. Captain Ahab was obsessed with the Lamb case, and he, Kramer, still had the case in his hands. He still had a shot at that much-prized, ever-elusive, and, in the Bronx, very nearly mythical creature, the Great White Defendant.

On Fridays the Taliaferro School discharged its students at 12:30 p.m. This was solely because so many of the girls came from families with weekend places in the country who wanted to get out of the city by 2:00 p.m., before the Friday-afternoon rush hour. So, as usual, Judy was going to drive out to Long Island with Campbell, Bonita, and Miss Lyons, the nanny, in the Mercury station wagon. As usual, Sherman would drive out in the Mercedes roadster that evening or the next morning, depending on how late he had to stay at Pierce & Pierce. Very convenient this arrangement had proved to be over the past few months. A leisurely visit with Maria in her little hideaway had become a regular Friday-night custom.

All morning, from his desk at Pierce & Pierce, he tried to reach Maria by telephone, at her apartment on Fifth Avenue and at the hideaway. No one answered at the hideaway. At the apartment a maid professed to know nothing of her whereabouts, not even what state or nation she was in. Finally he became desperate enough to leave his name and telephone number. She didn't call back.

She was avoiding him! At the Bavardages' she had told him to call her last night. He had called repeatedly; no answer at all. She was cutting off all contact! But for precisely what reason? Fear? She wasn't the fearful type . . . The crucial fact that would save him: *she was driving* . . . But if she vanished! That was crazy. She couldn't vanish. Italy! She could vanish in Italy! Awww . . . that was preposterous. He held his breath and opened his mouth. He could actually hear his heart beating . . . *tch, tch, tch, tch* . . . under his sternum. His eyes slid right off the computer terminals. Couldn't just sit here; he had to do something. The hell of it was, there was only one person he could turn to for advice, and that was someone he scarcely even knew, Killian.

About noon he called Killian. The receptionist said he was in court. Twenty minutes later Killian called from a noisy pay telephone and said he would meet him at one o'clock in the main lobby of the Criminal Courts Building at 100 Centre Street.

On the way out, Sherman told Muriel a mere half lie. He said he was going to see a lawyer named Thomas Killian, and he gave her Killian's telephone number. The half lie was in the offhand way he said it, which implied that Thomas Killian, Esq., was involved in Pierce & Pierce business.

On this balmy day in June, 100 Centre Street was an easy walk uptown from Wall Street. In all the years he had lived in New York and worked downtown, Sherman had never noticed the Criminal Courts Building, even though it was one of the biggest and grandest buildings in the City Hall area. An architect named Harvey Wiley Corbett had designed it in the Moderne style, which was now called Art Deco. Corbett, once so famous, had been forgotten except by a handful of architectural historians; likewise, the excitement over the Criminal Courts Building when it was completed in 1933. The patterns of stone and brass and glass at the entrance were still impressive, but when Sherman reached the great lobby within, something put him on red alert. He could not have told you what. In fact, it was the dark faces, the sneakers and the warm-up jackets and the Pimp Rolls. To him it was like the Port Authority bus terminal. It was an alien terrain. Throughout the vast space, which had the soaring ceilings of an old-fashioned railroad station, were huddles of dark people, and their voices created a great nervous rumble, and around the edges of the dark people walked white men in cheap suits or sport jackets, watching them like wolves monitoring the sheep. More dark people, young men, walked through the lobby in twos and threes with a disconcerting pumping gait. Off to one side, in the gloom, a half dozen figures, black and white, leaned into a row of public telephones. On the other side, elevators swallowed up and disgorged more dark people, and the huddles of dark people broke up, and others formed, and the nervous rumble rose and fell and rose and fell, and the sneakers squeaked on the marble floors.

It wasn't hard to pick out Killian. He was near the elevators in another of his sharpie outfits, a pale gray suit with wide chalk stripes and a shirt with a white spread collar and maroon pinstripes. He was talking to a small middle-aged white man in a warm-up jacket. As Sherman walked up, he heard Killian say, "A discount for cash? Gedoudahere, Dennis. Whaddaya whaddaya?" The little man said something. "It's not a big thing, Dennis. Cash is all I get. Halfa my clients ain't been introduced to checking accounts, as it is. Besides, I pay my fucking taxes. That's one less thing to worry about." He saw Sherman walking up, nodded, then said to the little man: "What can I tell you? It's like I said. Get it to me by Monday. Otherwise I can't get started." The little man followed Killian's eyes toward Sherman, said something in a low voice, then walked off, shaking his head.

Killian said to Sherman, "How you doing?"

"Fine."

"You ever been here before?"

"No."

"The biggest law office in New York. You see those two guys over there?" He motioned toward two white men in suits and ties roaming among the huddles of dark people. "They're lawyers. They're looking for clients to represent."

"I don't understand."

"It's simple. They just walk up and say, 'Hey, you need a lawyer?' "

"Isn't that ambulance chasing?"

"That it is. See that guy over there?" He pointed to a short man in a loud, checked sport jacket standing in front of a bank of elevators. "His name is Miguel Escalero. They call him Mickey Elevator. He's a lawyer. He stands there half the morning, and every time somebody who looks Hispanic and miserable walks up, he says, '¿Necesita usted un abogado?' If the guy says, 'I can't afford a lawyer,' he says, 'How much you got in your pocket?' If the guy has fifty dollars, he's got himself a lawyer."

Sherman said, "What do you get for fifty dollars?"

"He'll walk the guy through a plea or an arraignment. If it actually involves working for the client, he don't want to know about it. A specialist. So how you doing?"

Sherman told him of his vain attempts to reach Maria.

"Sounds to me like she's got herself a lawyer," said Killian. As he spoke, he rolled his head around with his eyes half closed, like a boxer loosening up for a fight. Sherman found this rude but said nothing.

"And the lawyer's telling her not to talk to me."

"That's what I'd tell her if she was my client. Don't mind me. I did a buncha wrestler's bridges yesterday. I think I did something to my neck."

Sherman stared at him.

"I used to like to run," said Killian, "but all that pounding up and down screwed up my back. So now I go to the New York Athletic Club and lift weights. I see all these kids doing wrestler's bridges. I guess I'm too old for wrestler's bridges. I'm gonna try to get hold of her myself." He stopped rolling his head.

"How?"

"I'll think a something. Half a my practice consists of talking to people who are not anxious to talk." *Tawk.*

"To tell you the truth," said Sherman, "this really surprises me. Maria—

Maria's not the cautious type. She's an adventuress. She's a gambler. This little Southern girl, from nowhere, who makes it to 962 Fifth Avenue . . . I don't know . . . And this may sound naïve, but I think she genuinely . . . feels something for me. I think she loves me."

"I bet she loves 962 Fifth, too," said Killian. "Maybe she figures it's time to stop gambling."

"Perhaps," said Sherman, "but I just can't believe she would disappear on me. Of course, it's only been two days."

"If it comes to that," said Killian, "we have an investigator works right out of our office. Used to be a detective in Major Cases with the Police Department. But there's no point in running up expenses unless we really need to. And I don't think we gonna need to. Right now they got nothing. I talked to Bernie Fitzgibbon. You remember the fellow I was talking to you about, in the Homicide Bureau of the Bronx D.A.'s Office?"

"You've already talked to him?"

"Yeah. The press has put pressure on them, so they're checking out cars. That's all 'at's happening. They got nothing."

"How can you be sure?"

"Whaddaya mean?"

"How can you be sure he'll tell you the truth?"

"Oh, he might not tell me everything he knows, but he's not gonna lie to me. He's not gonna mislead me."

"Why not?"

Killian looked out over the lobby of 100 Centre Street. Then he turned back to Sherman. "You ever hear of the Favor Bank?"

"The Favor Bank? No."

"Well, everything in this building, everything in the criminal justice system in New York"—*New Yawk*—"operates on favors. Everybody does favors for everybody else. Every chance they get, they make deposits in the Favor Bank. One time when I was just starting out as an assistant D.A., I was trying a case, and I was up against this lawyer, an older guy, and he was just tying me up in knots. The guy was Jewish. I didn't know how to handle him. So I talked it over with my supervisor, who was a Harp, like me. The next thing I know, he's taking me in to see the judge, in his chambers. The judge was a Harp, too, an old guy with white hair. I'll never forget it. We walk in, and he's standing beside his desk playing with one a these indoor putting sets. You hit the golf ball along the carpet, and instead of a hole there's this cup with a rim on it that slopes down. He don't"—*don't*—"even look up. He's lining up this putt. My bureau chief leaves the room, and I'm standing there, and the judge says, 'Tommy . . .' He's still looking at the golf ball. Tommy, he calls me, and I never laid eyes on him except in the courtroom. 'Tommy,' he says, 'you seem like a good lad. I understand there's a certain Jew bastard been giving you a very hard time.' I'm fucking astounded. This is so irregular—you know, fuhgedaboudit. I can't even think a what to say. Then he says, 'I wouldn't worry about it anymore, Tommy.' He still don't look up. So I just said, 'Thank you, Judge,' and left the room. After that, it's the judge who's tying up this lawyer in knots. When I say 'Objection,' I can't get to the second syllable before he says 'Sustained.' All of a sudden I look like a genius. Now this was a pure deposit in the Favor Bank. There was absolutely nothing I could do for that judge—not then. A deposit in the Favor Bank is not *quid pro quo*. It's saving up for a rainy day. In criminal law there's a lotta gray areas, and you gotta operate in 'em, but if you make a mistake, you can be in a whole lotta trouble, and you're gonna need a whole lotta help in a hurry. I mean, look at these guys." He gestured toward the lawyers prowling among the people in the lobby and then toward Mickey Elevator. "They could be arrested. Without the Favor Bank, they'd be finished. But if you've been making your regular deposits in the Favor Bank, then you're in a position to make contracts. That's what they call big favors, contracts. You have to make good on contracts."

"You have to? Why?"

"Because everybody in the courthouse believes in a saying: 'What goes around comes around.' That means if you don't take care a me today, I won't take care a you tomorrow. When you got basically no confidence in your own abilities, that's a frightening idea."

"So you asked your friend Fitzgibbon for a contract? Is that the expression?"

"No, what I got from him was just an everyday favor, just your standard protocol. There's nothing to waste a contract on yet. My strategy is, things shouldn't reach that point. Right now, it seems to me, the loose cannon is your friend Mrs. Ruskin."

"I still think she'll get in touch with me."

"If she does, I tell you what you do. Set up a meeting with her and then call me. I'm never away from my telephone for more than an hour, not even on weekends. I think you ought to go wired."

"Wired?" Sherman sensed what he meant—and was appalled.

"Yeah. You ought to wear a recording device."

"A *recording device?*" Beyond Killian's shoulder Sherman became aware once more of the vast and bilious gloom of the lobby, of the dark shambling forms leaning into the telephone shells, wandering this way and that with their huge sneakers and curious rolling gaits, huddling together in their miserable *tête-à-têtes*, of Mickey Elevator cruising along the edges of this raggedy and miserable herd.

"Nothing to it," said Killian, apparently thinking that Sherman's concern was technological. "We tape the recorder to the small of your back. The microphone goes under your shirt. It's no bigger than the last joint of your little finger."

"Look, Mr. Killian—"

"Call me Tommy. Everybody else does."

Sherman paused and looked at the thin Irish face rising up from out of a British spread collar. All at once he felt as if he were on another planet. He would call him neither Mr. Killian nor Tommy.

"I'm worried about all this," he said, "but I'm not so worried that I would make a surreptitious recording of a conversation with someone I feel close to. So let's just forget about that."

"It's perfectly legal in the State of New York," said Killian, "and it's done all the time. You have every right to record your own conversations. You can do it on the telephone, you can do it in person."

"That's not the point," said Sherman. Involuntarily he thrust his Yale chin upward.

Killian shrugged. "Okay. All I'm saying is, it's kosher, and sometimes it's the only way to hold people to the truth."

"I . . ." Sherman started to enunciate a great principle but was afraid Killian might take it as an insult. So he settled for: "I couldn't do it."

"All right," said Killian. "We'll just see how things go. Try to get hold of her anyhow, and call me if you do. And I'm gonna take a shot at it myself."

As he left the building, Sherman noticed morose huddles of people on the steps. So many young men with stooped shoulders! So many dark faces! For an instant he could see the tall thin boy and the powerful brute. He wondered if it was entirely safe to be in the vicinity of a building that daily, hourly, brought together so many defendants in criminal cases.

Where Albert Vogel found these places Fallow couldn't begin to imagine. The Huan Li was as pompous and stiff-necked as the Regent's Park. Despite the fact that they were in the East Fifties, near Madison Avenue, at the height of the lunch hour, the restaurant was nearly silent. It may or may not have been two-thirds empty. It was difficult to say, because of the darkness and the screens. The restaurant was all booths and pierced screens carved of dark wood with innumerable fishhook shapes. The darkness was such that even Vogel, barely two feet away in the booth, looked like a Rembrandt. A highlit face, a shaft of light turning his old grandmotherly head a brilliant white, a flash of shirtfront bisected by a necktie—and the rest of his form dissolved into the blackness that surrounded it. From time to time Chinese waiters and busboys materialized soundlessly in stewards' jackets and black bow ties. Nevertheless, lunch with Vogel at the Huan Li had one great thing to recommend it. The American would pay for it.

Vogel said, "You sure you won't change your mind, Pete? They have a great Chinese wine here. You ever tried Chinese wine?"

"Chinese wine taste like dead mouse," said Fallow.

"Tastes like what?"

Dead mouse . . . Fallow didn't even know why he said it. He wasn't using that expression anymore. He wasn't even thinking it. He was now marching shoulder to shoulder with Gerald Steiner through the world of tabloid journalism, thanks in part to Albert Vogel, although mainly thanks to his own brilliance. He was already in a mood to forget the contribution of Al Vogel to his Lamb case scoop. He resented the man, with his Pete this and Pete that, and he felt like mocking him. On the other hand, Vogel was his pipeline to Bacon and that crowd. He wouldn't like to have to deal with them entirely on his own.

"Sometimes I prefer beer with Chinese food, Al," said Fallow.

"Yeah . . . I can see that," said Vogel. "Hey, waiter. Waiter! Christ, where are the waiters? I can't see anything in here."

A beer would, in fact, be fine. Beer was practically a health-food drink, like chamomile tea. His hangover today wasn't serious at all, no more than a thick fog. No pain; just the fog. Yesterday, thanks to his enhanced status at The City Light, he had found the moment right to invite the sexiest of the copygirls, a big-eyed blonde named Darcy Lastrega, out to dinner. They went to Leicester's, where he had made his peace with Britt-Withers and even with Caroline Heftshank. They had ended up at the Table with Nick Stopping and Tony and St. John and Billy Cortez and some of the others. The Table had found a perfectly willing fish in no time, a Texan named Ned Perch, who had made an astonishing amount of money at something or other and had bought a lot of old silver in England, as he kept mentioning. Fallow entertained the Table at considerable length with stories about the housing project in the Bronx, by way of acquainting everyone with his recent success. His date, Miss Darcy Lastrega, was not captivated, however. The likes of Nick Stopping and St. John immediately sized her up for what she was, a humorless little American dimwit, and nobody bothered to talk to her, and she began slumping more and more despondently into her chair. To rectify matters, every twenty or thirty minutes Fallow turned toward her and grasped her forearm and put his head close to hers and said in what was supposed to seem only a half-jesting manner: "I don't know what's coming over me. I must be in love. You're not married, are you?" The first time she obliged him with a smile. The second and third times she didn't. The fourth time she wasn't there any longer. She had left the restaurant, and he hadn't even noticed. Billy Cortez and St. John began laughing at him, and he took it badly. A childish little American bird—and yet it was humiliating. After no more than three or four more glasses of wine, he left Leicester's himself without saying goodbye to anyone and went home and, presently, fell asleep.

Vogel had managed to find a waiter and order some beer. He also asked for some chopsticks. The Huan Li was so frankly commercial and unconcerned about authenticity, they set the tables with ordinary hotel silverware. How very American it was to assume that these unsmiling Chinese would be pleased if one showed a preference for their native implements . . . How very American it was to feel somehow guilty unless one struggled over rice noodles and lumps of meat with things that looked like enlarged knitting needles. While chasing some sort of slippery little dumpling around a bowl, Vogel said to Fallow, "Well, Pete, tell the truth. Didn't I tell you? Didn't I tell you this was gonna be a great story?"

That wasn't what Fallow wanted to hear. He didn't want to hear that the story, the Lamb case itself, was great. So he only nodded.

Vogel must have picked up this brain wave, because then he said: "You've really started something. You've got this whole town talking. The stuff you've written—it's dynamite, Pete, dynamite."

Suitably flattered, Fallow now suffered a spasm of gratitude. "I must admit I was skeptical the first time we spoke. But you were correct." He lifted his glass of beer as if making a toast.

Vogel lowered his chin practically into the bowl in order to gobble up the dumpling before it squirted out from between the tips of the chopsticks. "And the great thing, Pete, is that this isn't just one of those passing sensations. This thing gets down to the very structure of the city itself, the class structure, the racial structure, the way the system is put together. That's why it means so much to Reverend Bacon. He's really grateful for what you've done."

Fallow resented these reminders of Bacon's proprietary interest in the story. Like most journalists who have been handed a story, Fallow was eager to persuade himself that he had discovered and breathed life into this clay himself.

"He was telling me," Vogel continued, "he was saying how he was amazed— you're from England, Pete, but you come here and you put your finger right on the central issue, which is how much is a human life worth. Is a black life worth less than a white life? That's what makes this thing important."

Fallow floated in the syrup for a while and then began to wonder where this disquisition was leading.

"But there's one aspect of this thing it seems to me you might hit a little harder, and I was talking to Reverend Bacon about this."

"Oh?" said Fallow. "What's that?"

"The hospital, Pete. So far the hospital has gotten off kind of easy, considering. They say they're 'investigating' how this kid could come in with a subdural concussion and just get treated for a broken wrist, but you know what they're gonna do. They're gonna try to waffle out of it."

"That may very well be," said Fallow, "but they maintain that Lamb never told them he'd been struck by a car."

"The kid was probably already half out of his head, Pete! That's precisely what they shoulda detected—his general condition! That's what I mean about a black life and a white life. No, I think it's time to come down hard on the hospital. And this is a good time to do it. The story has died down a little bit, because the cops haven't found the car and the driver."

Fallow said nothing. He resented being steered like this. Then he said, "I'll think it over. It seems to me they've made a rather complete statement, but I'll think it over."

Vogel said, "Well, now, Pete, I wanna be completely open with you. Bacon has already been in touch with Channel 1 about this angle, but you've been our—our main man, as the saying goes, and we'd like to see you stay out in the lead on this story."

Your main man! What an odious presumption! But he hesitated to let Vogel know how offensive it was. He said, "What is this cozy connection between Bacon and Channel 1?"

"Whaddaya mean?"

"He gave them an exclusive on the first demonstration."

"Well—that's true, Pete. I'm gonna be completely open with you. How did you know about that?"

"Their whatever you call it, anchorman, told me. Corso."

"Ah. Well, the thing is, you gotta work that way. TV news is all PR. Every day the TV news operations wait for PR people to submit menus of things they can film, and then they choose a few. The trick is to know how to appeal to them. They're not very enterprising. They feel a lot better if they've seen something in print first."

"In *The City Light,* just to cite a possible example," said Fallow.

"Well—that's true. I'm gonna be completely out front with you, Pete. You're a real journalist. When these TV channels see a real journalist on to something, they hop to it."

Fallow sat back and took a leisurely draught of beer in the doldrum gloaming of the Huan Li. Yes, his next coup would be a story exposing television news for what it really was. But for now he would forget that. The way the television news people came running in his footsteps on the Lamb case—nothing had ever made him look quite so good.

Within a few minutes he had worked it out in his mind that a story on the hospital's negligence was nothing more than the natural next step. He would have thought of that on his own, inevitably, with or without this ridiculous Yank and his chubby face, pinky-winky as could be.

Today's sandwiches came to Jimmy Caughey, Ray Andriutti, and Larry Kramer from the State of New York, courtesy of the Willie Francisco case. It had taken Judge Meldnick a mere four days to ask around and find out what his opinion was of Willie's petition for a mistrial, and this morning he had given it. He declared a mistrial, based on the fat old Irish juror McGuigan's attack of the doubts. But since the day had begun with the trial technically still in progress, Bernie Fitzgibbon's secretary, Gloria, was entitled duly to order the sandwiches.

Ray was once more lunging across his desk eating a super-sub and drinking his vat of yellow coffee. Kramer was eating a roast beef that tasted like chemicals. Jimmy was scarcely touching his. He was still moaning over the disintegration of such an easy one. He had an outstanding record. The Homicide Bureau kept actual standings, like baseball standings, showing how many guilty pleas and guilty verdicts each assistant district attorney had scored, and Jimmy Caughey hadn't lost a case in two years. His anger had now developed into an intense hatred of Willie Francisco and the vileness of his deed, which to Andriutti and Kramer sounded like just another piece a shit. It was strange to see Jimmy in this state. Ordinarily he had the black Irish coolness of Fitzgibbon himself.

"I've seen this happen before," he said. "You put these germs on trial, and they think they're stars. You see Willie in there jumping up and down and yelling 'Mistrial'?"

Kramer nodded yes.

"Now he's a legal expert. In fact, he's one a the stupidest fucks ever went on trial in Bronx County. I told Bietelberg two days ago that if Meldnick declared a mistrial—and I mean, he *had* to declare a mistrial—we were willing to make a deal. We'd reduce the charge from murder two to manslaughter one, just to avoid another trial. But no. He's too shrewd for that, Willie is. He takes this as an admission of defeat. He thinks he has a power over juries or something. On retrial he's gonna go down like a fucking stone. Twelve and a half to twenty-five he's gonna get himself, instead of three to six or four to eight."

Ray Andriutti gave up whaling down his super-sub long enough to say, "Maybe he's smart, Jimmy. If he takes a plea, he's going to jail for sure. With a fucking Bronx jury, it's a roll of the dice every time. You hear what happened yesterday?"

"What."

"This doctor from out in Montauk?"

"No."

"This doctor, I mean he's some local doctor out in Montauk, probably never laid eyes on the Bronx before. He has a patient with some esoteric tropical disease. The guy's very sick, and the hospital out there don't think they can handle it, but there's this hospital in Westchester with some kind of special unit for this stuff. So the doctor arranges for an ambulance for the guy and gets on the ambulance with him and rides all the way to Westchester with the guy, and the guy dies in the emergency room in Westchester. So the family brings suit against the doctor for malpractice. But where do they bring suit? In Montauk? Westchester? No way. The Bronx."

"How can they bring suit here?" asked Kramer.

"The fucking ambulance had to go up the Major Deegan to get to Westchester. So their lawyer comes up with the theory that the malpractice occurs in the Bronx, and that's where they had the trial. Eight million dollars they were awarded. The jury came in yesterday. Now there's a lawyer who knows his geography."

"Aw hell," said Jimmy Caughey, "I bet you every negligence lawyer in America knows about the Bronx. In a civil case a Bronx jury is a vehicle for redistributing the wealth."

A Bronx jury . . . And all at once Kramer was no longer thinking of the same cluster of dark faces that Ray and Jimmy were thinking of . . . He was thinking of those perfect smiling teeth and those sweet full lips glistening with brown lipstick and those shining eyes across a little table in the very heart of . . . the Life . . . which existed only in Manhattan . . . Jesus . . . He was broke after he paid the bill of Muldowny's . . . but when he hailed her a cab out in front of the place and he held out his hand to thank her and say goodbye, she let her hand stay in his, and he increased the pressure, and she squeezed back, and they stayed that way, locking into each other's eyes, and—God!—that moment was sweeter, sexier, more full of—goddamn it!—*love*, genuine *love*, the love that just *hits* you and . . . *fills up your heart* . . . than any of those slam-bang first-date *scores* he used to pride himself on when he was out prowling like a god-damned cat . . . No, he would forgive Bronx juries a lot. A Bronx jury had brought into his life the woman he had been destined to meet all along . . . Love, Destiny, How Full My Heart . . . Let others shrink from the meaning of those terms . . . Ray whaling down his super-sub, Jimmy grousing morosely about Willie Francisco and Lester McGuigan . . . Larry Kramer existed on a more spiritual plane . . .

Ray's telephone rang. He picked it up and said, "Homicide . . . Unnh-hunnh . . . Bernie's not here . . . The Lamb case? Kramer . . . Larry." Ray looked at Kramer and pulled a face. "He's right here. You wanna speak to him? . . . Okay, just a second." He covered the mouthpiece and said, "It's a guy from Legal Aid named Cecil Hayden."

Kramer got up from his desk and walked over to Andriutti's and took the telephone. "Kramer."

"Larry, this is Cecil Hayden over at Legal Aid." A breezy voice this Cecil Hayden had. "You're handling the Henry Lamb case. Right?"

"That's right."

"Larry, I think the time has come to play Let's Make a Deal." Very breezy.

"What kinda deal?"

"I represent an individual named Roland Auburn, who was indicated two days ago by a grand jury on a charge of criminal possession and sale of drugs. Weiss put out a press release describing him as the Crack King of Evergreen Avenue. My client was immensely flattered. If you ever saw Evergreen Avenue, you'd ask why. The King is unable to make ten thousand dollars bail and is currently on Rikers Island."

"Yeah, well, what's he got to do with the Lamb case?"

"He says he was with Henry Lamb when he was hit by the car. He took him to the hospital. He can give you a description of the driver. He wants to make a deal."

18

SHUHMUN

Daniel Torres, the fat assistant district attorney from the Supreme Court Bureau, arrived at Kramer's office with his ten-year-old son in tow and a ditch down the middle of his forehead. He was furious, in a soft fat way, about having to show up at the island fortress on a Saturday morning. He looked even more of a blob than he had the last time Kramer had seen him, which had been in Kovitsky's courtroom. He wore a plaid sport shirt, a jacket that didn't have a prayer of closing around his great soft belly, and a pair of slacks from the Linebacker Shop, for the stocky man, in Fresh Meadow that made his underbelly protrude beneath his belt like South America. A glandular case, thought Kramer. His son, on the other hand, was slender and dark with fine features, the shy and sensitive type, by the looks of him. He was carrying a paperback book and a baseball glove. After a quick, bored inspection of the office, he sat in Jimmy Caughey's chair and began reading the book.

Torres said, "Wouldn't you know the Yankees'd be on the road"—he motioned toward Yankee Stadium, just down the hill, with his head—"on the Saturday"—*Saddy*—"I gotta come over here? This is my weekend with . . ." Now he motioned his head toward his son. ". . . and I promised him I'd take him to the ball game, and I promised my ex-wife I'd go to Kiel's on Springfield Boulevard and get some shrubs and take them to the house, and how I'm gonna get from here over to Springfield Boulevard and then over to Maspeth and then back to Shea in time for the game, I don't know. Don't even ask me why I said I'd take the shrubs over to the house." He shook his head.

Kramer felt embarrassed for the boy, who appeared to be deep into the book. The title was *Woman in the Dunes*. As best as Kramer could make out from the cover, the author's name was Kobo Abé. Feeling curious and sympathetic, he walked over to the boy and said in the warmest Dutch-uncle manner possible, "Whaddaya reading?"

The boy looked up like a deer caught in a pair of high beams. "It's a story," he said. Or that was what his lips said. His eyes said, "Please, please, let me return to the sanctuary of my book."

Kramer detected that, but he felt obliged to round out his hospitality.

"What's it about?"

"Japan." Pleading.

"Japan? What about Japan?"

"It's about a man who gets trapped in some sand dunes." A very soft voice, pleading, pleading, pleading.

Judging by its abstract cover and dense print, this was not a child's book. Kramer, student of the human heart, got an impression of a bright, withdrawn boy, the product of Torres's Jewish half, who probably looked like his mother and was already estranged from his father. For an instant he thought of his own little son. He tried to imagine having to drag him over here to Gibraltar some Saturday nine or ten years from now. It depressed him profoundly.

"Well, whaddaya know about Mr. Auburn, Danny?" he asked Torres. "What's this Crack King of Evergreen Avenue business?"

"It's a piece a—" Torres stopped short for the boy's sake. "It's a joke, is what it is. Auburn's—you know, just the usual kid from off the block. This is his third drug arrest. The detective who arrested him called him the Crack King of Evergreen Avenue. He was being sarcastic. Evergreen Avenue is about five blocks long. I don't even know how Weiss got hold of it. When I saw that press release, I about—I couldn't believe it. Thank God, nobody paid any attention to it." Torres looked at his watch. "When are they gonna get here?"

"They should be here pretty soon," said Kramer. "Everything's slower over at Rikers Island on Saturday. How did they happen to catch him?"

"Well, that's a screwy thing," said Torres. "They really caught him twice, but this kid has very big—a lotta nerve, or else he's very stupid, I don't know which. About a month ago this undercover cop made a purchase from Auburn and another kid and announced they were under arrest, and so forth, and Auburn told him, 'If you want me, mother—you're gonna have to shoot me,' and he started running. I talked to the cop, Officer Iannucci. He said if the kid hadn't been black, in a black neighborhood, he would've shot him or shot at him, anyhow. A week ago he brought him in, the same cop."

"What's he looking at if he's convicted of a sale?"

"Two to four, maybe."

"You know anything about his lawyer, this Hayden?"

"Yeah. He's a black guy."

"Really?" Kramer started to say, "He didn't sound black," but thought better of it. "You don't see too many black guys in Legal Aid."

"That's not true. There's quite a few. A lot of them need the job. You know, these young black lawyers have a rough time. The law schools graduate them, but there aren't any slots. Downtown—it's pathetic. They're always talking about it, but they don't hire black lawyers, that's the truth of the matter. So they go into Legal Aid or the 18b pool. Some a them scuffle along with a rinky-dink criminal practice. But the big-time black wiseguys, the drug dealers, they don't want a black lawyer representing them. The small-timers don't, either. One time I was in the pens, and this black lawyer from the 18b comes in looking for the client he's been assigned, and he starts yelling out his name. You know the way they yell out the names in the pens. Anyway, the guy he's been assigned is black, and he comes walking over to the bars, and he looks this guy in the eye and he says, 'Get lost, mother—I want a Jew.' I swear! He says, 'Get lost, mother—I want a Jew.' Hayden seems pretty sharp, but I haven't seen a lot of him."

Torres looked at his watch again, and then he looked at the floor in the corner. In no time his thoughts were somewhere out of the room and out of Gibraltar. Kiel's nursery? The Mets? His ex-marriage? His son was off in Japan with the man trapped in the dunes. Only Kramer was right there in the room. He was keyed up. He was aware of the stillness of the island fortress on this sunny Saturday in June. If only this character, Auburn, turned out to be the real goods, if only he wasn't too much of the usual mindless player, trying to get some stupid game over on everybody, trying to trim the world, bawling into the void from behind the wire mesh . . .

Pretty soon Kramer could hear people walking down the hall outside. He opened the door, and there were Martin and Goldberg and, between them, a powerfully built young black man in a turtleneck jersey with his hands behind his back. Bringing up the rear was a short, chunky black man in a pale gray suit. That would be Cecil Hayden.

Even with his hands behind his back Roland Auburn managed to do the Pimp Roll. He was no more than five feet seven or eight, but very muscular. His pectorals, deltoids, and trapezii bulged with mass and sharp definition. Kramer, the atrophied one, felt a jolt of envy. To say that the fellow was aware of his terrific build was putting it mildly. The turtleneck jersey fit him like a skin. He had a gold chain around his neck. He wore tight black pants and white Reebok sneakers that looked as if they had just come out of the box. His brown face was square, hard, and impassive. He had short hair and a narrow mustache lining his upper lip.

Kramer wondered why Martin had cuffed his hands behind his back. It was more humiliating than having them cuffed in front. It made a man feel more helpless and vulnerable. He could *feel* the danger of falling. He would fall like a tree, without being able to protect his head. Since they wanted Roland Auburn's cooperation, Kramer thought Martin would have taken the man on the easy route —or did he think there was actually some danger of this bulked-up rock making a run for it? Or was the Martin way invariably the hard way?

The entourage came crowding into the little office. The introductions were an awkward shuffle. Torres, as the assistant district attorney in charge of the prisoner's drug case, knew Cecil Hayden, but he didn't know Martin, Goldberg, or the prisoner. Hayden didn't know Kramer, and Kramer didn't know the prisoner, and what should they call the prisoner, anyway? His real status was that of punk arrested on a drug charge, but at this moment, technically, he was a citizen who had come forth to assist the authorities in a felony investigation. Martin solved the nomenclature problem by referring to Roland Auburn frequently and in a bored manner as "Roland."

"Okay, Roland, let's see. Where we gonna put you?"

He looked around the office with its clutter of dilapidated furniture. Calling a prisoner by his first name was a standard way of removing any pretensions of dignity and social insulation he might still be clinging to. Martin was going to put the carcass of Roland Auburn wherever he felt like. He paused, stared at Kramer, then cast a dubious glance toward Torres's son. It was clear that he didn't think he should be in the room. The boy was no longer reading his book. He was slouched back in the chair with his head hung low, staring. He had shrunk. There was nothing left but an enormous pair of eyes staring at Roland Auburn.

For everybody else in the room, perhaps even Auburn himself, this was just a routine procedure, a black defendant being brought into an assistant district attorney's office for a negotiation, a little round of plea bargaining. But this sad, sensitive, bookish little boy would never forget what he was now looking at, a black man with his hands shackled behind his back in his daddy's office building on a sunny Saturday before the Mets' game.

Kramer said to Torres, "Dan, I think maybe we're gonna need that chair." He looked toward Torres's son. "Maybe he'd like to sit in there, in Bernie Fitzgibbon's office. There's nobody in there."

"Yeah, Ollie," said Torres, "whyn't you go in there until we get through." Kramer wondered if Torres had really named his son Oliver. Oliver Torres.

Without a word the boy stood up and gathered his book and his baseball glove and headed for the other door, to Bernie Fitzgibbon's office, but he couldn't resist one last look at the manacled black man. Roland Auburn stared back at him with no expression at all. He was closer to the boy's age than to Kramer's. For all of his muscles, he wasn't much more than a boy himself.

"Okay, Roland," said Martin, "I'm gonna take these offa you, and you're gonna sit'n'at chair there and be a good fellow, right?"

Roland Auburn said nothing, just turned his back slightly to present Martin his shackled hands so he could unlock the handcuffs.

"Ayyyyyy, don't worry, Marty," said Cecil Hayden, "my client's here because he wants to *walk* out of this place, without looking over his shoulder."

Kramer couldn't believe it. Hayden was already calling the Irish Doberman by his nickname, Marty, and he had just met him. Hayden was one of those bouncy little fellows whose breeze is so warm and confident you'd have to be in a very bad mood to take offense. He was pulling off the difficult trick of showing his client he was sticking up for his rights and dignity without angering the Irish Cop contingent.

Roland Auburn sat down and started to rub his wrists but then stopped. He didn't want to give Martin and Goldberg the satisfaction of knowing the handcuffs had hurt. Goldberg had walked around behind the chair and was settling his hulk onto the edge of Ray Andriutti's desk. He had a notebook and a ballpoint pen, for taking notes on the interview. Martin moved around to the other side of Jimmy Caughey's desk and sat on the edge over there. The prisoner was now between the two of them and would have to turn to see either one of them head on. Torres sat down in Ray Andriutti's chair, Hayden sat down in Kramer's, and Kramer, who was running the show, remained standing. Roland Auburn was now sitting back in Jimmy Caughey's chair with his knees akimbo and his forearms on the armrests, cracking his knuckles, looking straight at Kramer. His face was a mask. He didn't even blink. Kramer thought of the phrase that kept turning up in the probation reports on these young black male defendants: "lacking in affect." Apparently that meant they were deficient in ordinary feelings. They didn't feel guilt, shame, remorse, fear, or sympathy for others. But whenever it fell to Kramer's lot to talk to these people, he had the feeling it was something else. They pulled down a curtain. They shut him off from what was behind the unblinking surface of their eyes. They didn't let him see so much as an eighth of an inch of what they thought of him and the Power and their own lives. He had wondered before and he wondered now: Who are these people? (These people, whose fates I determine every day . . .)

Kramer looked at Hayden and said, "Counselor . . ." *Counselor.* He didn't know quite what to call the man. Hayden had called him "Larry" on the telephone, from the word go, but he hadn't called him anything in this room, and Kramer didn't want to call him "Cecil," for fear of appearing either too chummy or disrespectful in front of Roland. "Counselor, you've explained to your client what we're doing here, right?"

"Oh, sure," said Hayden. "He understands."

Now Kramer looked at Roland. "Mr. Auburn . . ." *Mr. Auburn.* Kramer figured Martin and Goldberg would forgive him. The usual procedure, when an assistant D.A. was questioning a defendant, was to start off with the respectful Mister, just to set things up, and then switch to the first name after things got going. "Mr. Auburn, I think you already know Mr. Torres here. He's the assistant district attorney handling the case you've been arrested and indicted on, the sale charge. Okay? And I'm handling the Henry Lamb case. Now, we can't promise you anything, but if you help us, then we'll help you. It's as simple as that. But you gotta be truthful. You gotta be completely truthful. Otherwise, you're just jerking everybody around, and it's not gonna be good for you. You understand?"

Roland looked at his lawyer, Cecil Hayden, and Hayden just nodded yes, as if to say, "Don't worry, it's okay."

Roland turned back and looked at Kramer and said, very deadpan: "Unh-hunh."

"Okay," said Kramer. "What I'm interested in is what happened to Henry Lamb the night he was hurt. I want you to tell me what you know."

Still slouched back in Jimmy Caughey's chair, Roland said, "Where you want me to start?"

"Well . . . at the beginning. How'd you happen to be with Henry Lamb that night?"

Roland said, "I was standing on the sidewalk, fixing to go down to 161st Street, down to the takeout, the Texas Fried Chicken, and I see Henry walking by." He stopped.

Kramer said, "Okay, and then what?"

"I say to him, 'Henry, where you going?' And he say, 'I'm going to the takeout,' and I say, 'That's where I'm going.' So we start walking down to the takeout."

"Walking down what street?"

"Bruckner Boulevard."

"Is Henry a good friend of yours?"

For the first time Roland showed an emotion. He seemed faintly amused. A little smile twisted one corner of his mouth, and he lowered his eyes, as if an embarrassing topic had come up. "Naw, I just know him. We live in the same project."

"You hang around together?"

More amusement. "Naw, Henry don't hang around much. He don't come out a lot."

"Anyway," said Kramer, "the two of you are walking down Bruckner Boulevard on the way to the Texas Fried Chicken. Then what happened?"

"Well, we go down to Hunts Point Avenue, and we fixing to cross the street to go over to the Texas Fried Chicken."

"Cross which street, Hunts Point Avenue or Bruckner Boulevard?"

"Bruckner Boulevard."

"Just so we get it straight, you're on which side of Bruckner Boulevard, the east side going over to the west side?"

"That's right. The east side going over to the west side. I was standing out in the street a little ways, waiting for the cars to pass by, and Henry was standing over here." He motioned to his right. "So I can see the cars better than he can, because they be coming up from this way." He motioned to his left. "The cars, mostly they be traveling out in the center lane, in, you know, like a line, and all of a sudden this one car, it pulls out, and it wants to pass all these other cars on the right, and I can see it's coming too close to where I'm standing. So I jump back. But Henry, I guess he don't see anything until he see me jump back, and then I hear this little tap, and I see Henry falling, like this." He made a spinning motion with his forefinger.

"Okay, what happened then?"

"Then I hear this screech. This car, it's putting on the brakes. The first thing I do, I go over to Henry, and he's lying there on the street, by the sidewalk, and he's curled up on one side, kind of hugging one arm, and I say, 'Henry, you hurt?' And he say, 'I think I broke my arm.' "

"Did he say he hurt his head?"

"He told me that later. When I was squatting over him there, he kept on saying his arm hurt. And then I was taking him to the hospital, and he told me when he was falling, he put his arms out and he came down on his arm and then he kept on rolling and hit his head."

"All right, let's get back to right after it happened. You're there beside Henry Lamb in the street, and this car that hit him, it put on its brakes. Did it stop?"

"Yeah. I can see it's stopped up the road."

"How far up the road?"

"I don't know. Maybe a hundred feet. The door opens, and this guy gets out, a white guy. And this guy, he's looking back. He's looking right back at me and Henry."

"What did you do?"

"Well, I figured this guy, he stopped because he hit Henry and was gonna see if he could help. I figured, hey, the guy can take Henry to the hospital. So I got up, and started walking toward him, and I said, 'Yo! Yo! We need some help!' "

"And what did he do?"

"The man looked right at me, and then the door on the other side of the car opens, and there's this woman. She gets kind of, you know, halfway out the car, and she's looking back, too. They both looking back at me, and I say, 'Yo! My friend's hurt!' "

"How far from them were you by this time?"

"Not very far. Fifteen or twenty feet."

"Could you see them clearly?"

"I was looking them right in the face."

"What did they do?"

"This woman, she had this look on her face. She look frightened. She say, 'Shuhmun, look out!' She's talking to the guy."

" 'Shuhmun, watch out'? She said, *'Shuhmun'?*" Kramer cut a glance at Martin. Martin opened his eyes wide and forced a pocket of air up under his upper lip. Goldberg had his head down, taking notes.

"That's what it sound like to me."

"Shuhmun or Sherman?"

"Sound like Shuhmun."

"Okay, what happened then?"

"The woman, she jump back inside the car. The man, he's back behind the car looking at me. Then the woman, she say, 'Shuhmun, get in!' Only now she's sitting in the driver's seat. And the man, he runs around to the other side where she been sitting, and he jumps in the car and slams the door."

"So now they've switched seats. And what did you do? How far away from them were you by this time?"

"Almost as close as I am to you."

"Were you angry? Did you yell at them?"

"All's I said was, 'My friend's hurt.' "

"Did you make a fist? Did you make any threatening gesture?"

"All's I wanted was to get Henry some help. I wasn't angry. I was scared, for Henry."

"Okay, then what happened?"

"I ran around to the front of the car."

"Which side?"

"Which side? The right side, where the guy was. I was looking right through the windshield at them. I'm saying, 'Yo! My friend's hurt!' I'm in the front of the car, looking back down the street, and there's Henry. He's right behind the car. He be walking up, kind of in a daze, you know, holding his arm like this." Roland held his left forearm with his right hand and let his left hand dangle, as if it were afflicted. "So that means, this guy, he could see Henry coming the whole time, holding his arm like this. Ain't no way he don't know Henry was hurt. I'm looking at Henry, and the next thing I know, the woman, she guns the motor and she cuts outta there, laying down rubber. She cuts outta there so fast I can see the man's head snap back. He's looking right at me, and his head snaps back, and they outta there like a rocket. Come that close to me." He brought his thumb and forefinger together. "Like to tore me up worse than Henry."

"You get the license number?"

"Naw. But Henry got it. Or I guess he got part of it."

"Did he tell you what it was?"

"Naw. I guess he told his mother. I saw that on television."

"What kind of car was it?"

"It was a Mercedes."

"What color?"

"Black."

"What model?"

"I don't know what model."

"How many doors?"

"Two. It was, like, you know, built low. It was a sporty car."

Kramer looked at Martin again. Once more he had on his big-eyed *bingo* face.

"Would you recognize the man if you saw him again?"

"I'd recognize him." Roland said this with a bitter conviction that had the ring of truth.

"What about the woman?"

"Her, too. Wasn't nothing but a piece of glass between me and them."

"What did the woman look like? How old was she?"

"I don't know. She was white. I don't know how old she was."

"Well, was she old or young? Was she closer to twenty-five, thirty-five, forty-five, or fifty-five?"

"Twenty-five, most likely."

"Light hair, dark hair, red hair?"

"Dark hair."

"What was she wearing?"

"I think a dress. She was all in blue. I remember because it was a real bright blue, and she had these big shoulders on the dress. I remember that."

"What did the man look like?"

"He was tall. He had on a suit and a necktie."

"What color suit?"

"I don't know. It was a dark suit. That's all I remember."

"How old was he? Would you say he was my age, or was he older? Or younger?"

"A little older."

"And you'd recognize him if you saw him again."

"I'd recognize him."

"Well, Roland, I'm gonna show you some pictures, and I want you to tell me if you recognize anybody in the pictures. Okay?"

"Unh-hunh."

Kramer walked over to his own desk, where Hayden was sitting, and said, "Excuse me a second," and opened a drawer. As he did so, he looked at Hayden for a moment and nodded slightly, as if to say, "It's working out." From the drawer he took the set of pictures Milt Lubell had put together for Weiss. He spread the pictures out on Jimmy Caughey's desk, in front of Roland Auburn.

"You recognize any of these people?"

Roland scanned the pictures, and his forefinger went straight to Sherman McCoy grinning in his tuxedo.

"That's him."

"How do you know it's the same guy?"

"That's *him*. I *recognize* him. That's his chin. The man had this big chin."

Kramer looked at Martin and then at Goldberg. Goldberg was smiling ever so slightly.

"You see the woman in the picture, the woman he's standing beside? Is that the woman who was in the car?"

"Naw. The woman in the car was younger, and she had darker hair, and she was more . . . more foxy."

"Foxy?"

Roland started to smile again but fought it off. "You know, more of a . . . hot ticket."

Kramer allowed himself a smile and a chuckle. It gave him a chance to let out some of the elation he was already feeling. "A hot ticket, hunh? Okay, a hot ticket. All right. So they leave the scene. What did you do then?"

"Wasn't much I could do. Henry was standing there holding his arm. His wrist was all bent outta shape. So I said, 'Henry, you got to go to the hospital,' and he say he don't want to go to no hospital, he want to go home. So we start walking back up Bruckner Boulevard, back to the project."

"Wait a minute," said Kramer. "Did anybody see all this happen? Was there anybody on the sidewalk?"

"I don't know."

"No cars stopped?"

"Naw. I guess Henry, if he be laying there very long, maybe somebody stop. But nobody stopped."

"So now you're walking up Bruckner Boulevard, back toward the project."

"That's right. And Henry, he be moaning and looking like he's fixing to pass out, and I say, 'Henry, you got to go to the hospital.' So I walk him on back down to Hunts Point Avenue, and we go on across to 161st Street, to the subway stop ov'eh, and I see this taxi, belongs to my man Brill."

"Brill?"

"He's a fellow that has two cabs."

"And he drove you to Lincoln Hospital?"

"This fellow Curly Kale, he drove. He's one a Brill's drivers."

"Curly Kale. Is that his real name or is that a nickname?"

"I don't know. That's what they call him, Curly Kale."

"And he drove the two of you to the hospital."

"That's right."

"What did Henry's condition seem to be on the way to the hospital? That's when he told you he'd hit his head?"

"That's right, but mostly he was talking about his arm. His wrist looked *bad.*"

"Was he coherent? Was he in his right mind, the best you could tell?"

"Like I say, he was moaning a lot and saying how his arm hurt. But he knew where he was. He knew what was happening."

"When you reached the hospital, what did you do?"

"Well, we got out, and I walked with Henry to the door, to the emergency room, and he went in there."

"Did you go in with him?"

"No, I got back in the cab with Curly Kale and I left."

"You didn't stay with Henry?"

"I figured I couldn't do no more for him." Roland cut a glance toward Hayden.

"How did Henry get home from the hospital?"

"I don't know."

Kramer paused. "All right, Roland, there's one more thing I want to know. Why haven't you come forth with this information before now? I mean, here you are with your friend, or your neighbor anyhow—he's from the same project—and he's a victim of a hit-and-run accident right in front of your eyes, and the case is on television and all over the newspapers, and we don't hear a peep outta you until now. Whaddaya say to that?"

Roland looked at Hayden, who merely nodded yes, and Roland said, "The cops was looking for me."

Hayden spoke up. "There was a warrant out for criminal sale, criminal possession, resisting arrest, and a couple of other things, the same charges he was just indicted on."

Kramer said to Roland, "So you were protecting yourself. You withheld this information rather than have to talk to the cops."

"That's right."

Kramer was giddy with joy. He could already see it taking shape. This Roland was no sweetheart, but he was entirely credible. Get him out of the bodybuilder jersey and the sneakers! Break his hip so he can't do the Pimp Roll! Bury this business of the Crack King of Evergreen Avenue! Didn't look good to juries if a major criminal came into court offering testimony in exchange for a misdemeanor plea. But just a cleanup and a trim—that's all this case needs! All at once Kramer could see it . . . *the drawing* . . .

He said to Roland, "And you're telling me the complete truth."

"Unh-hunh."

"You're not adding anything or leaving anything out."

"Unh-unh."

Kramer went over to Jimmy Caughey's desk, right beside Roland, and gathered up the pictures. Then he turned to Cecil Hayden.

"Counselor," he said, "I've gotta talk this over with my superiors. But unless I'm mistaken, I think we got a deal."

He saw it before the words were even out of his mouth . . . *the drawing* . . . by the courtroom artist . . . He could see it as if the TV screen were already right in front of him . . . Assistant District Attorney Lawrence N. Kramer . . . on his feet . . . his forefinger raised . . . his massive sternocleidomastoid muscles welling out . . . But how would the artist deal with his skull, where he had lost so much hair? Well, if the drawing did justice to his powerful frame, no one would notice. The courage and the eloquence . . . that's what they would see. The whole city of New York would see it. Miss Shelly Thomas would see it.

19

DONKEY LOYALTY

Fɪʀsᴛ ᴛʜɪɴɢ Monday morning Kramer and Bernie Fitzgibbon were summoned into Abe Weiss's office. Milt Lubell was there, too. Kramer could tell that his status had improved over the weekend. Weiss now called him Larry instead of Kramer and didn't direct every comment about the Lamb case to Bernie, as if he, Kramer, were nothing but Bernie's foot soldier.

But Weiss was looking at Bernie when he said, "I don't wanna have to futz around with this thing if I don't have to. Have we got enough to bring in this guy McCoy or not?"

"We got enough, Abe," said Fitzgibbon, "but I'm not completely happy with it. We got this character Auburn who identifies McCoy as the guy who was driving the car that hit Lamb, and we got the garage attendant who says McCoy had his car out at the time the thing happened, and Martin and Goldberg found the gypsy cab operator, Brill, who verifies that Auburn used one of his cabs that evening. But they haven't found the driver, this Curly Kale"—he rolled his eyes and sucked in his breath, as if to say, "These people and their names"—"and I think we oughta talk to him first."

"Why?" asked Weiss.

"Because there's certain things that don't make sense, and Auburn's a fucking lowlife drug dealer who's out from under his rock. I'd still like to know why Lamb didn't say anything about being hit by a car when he first went to the hospital. I'd like to know what went on in that cab, and I'd like to know if Auburn actually took the kid to the hospital. I'd like to know a little more about Auburn, too. You know, him and Lamb ain't the types who go walking over to the Texas Fried Chicken together. I gather Lamb is a kinda good-doing boy, and Auburn's a player."

Kramer felt an odd passion rising in his breast. He wanted to defend the honor of Roland Auburn. Yes! Defend him!

Weiss waved his hand in a gesture of dismissal. "Loose ends is what that sounds like to me, Bernie. I don't know why we can't bring McCoy in and book him and then tie up the loose ends. Everybody takes this 'we're investigating' business to be a stalling tactic."

"A couple more days ain't gonna matter, Abe. McCoy's not going anywhere, and Auburn certainly ain't going anywhere."

Kramer saw an opening and, buoyed by his new status, plunged in: "We could have a problem there, Bernie. It's true, Auburn"—he started to say *isn't* but switched to *ain't*—"ain't going anywhere, but I think we ought to use him quickly. He probably thinks he's getting out on bail any minute. We oughta get the guy in front of a grand jury as soon as we can, if we're gonna use him."

"Don't worry about that," said Fitzgibbon. "He ain't brilliant, but he knows he's got a choice between three years in jail and no years in jail. He's not gonna shut up on us."

"That's the deal we made?" asked Weiss. "Auburn gets nothing?"

"That's the way it'll wind up. We got to dismiss the indictment and knock the charge down to misdemeanor possession, misdemeanor sale."

"Shit," said Weiss. "I wish we hadn'ta moved so fast with the sonofabitch. I don't like to dismiss grand-jury indictments."

"Abe," said Fitzgibbon, smiling, "*you* said it, *I* didn't! All I'm telling you is, take it a little slower. I'd feel a lot better if we had something else to nail down what he says."

Kramer couldn't hold back. "I don't know—what he says stands up pretty well. He was telling me things he had to be there to know about. He knew the color of the car, the number of doors—he knew it was a sports model. He knew McCoy's first name. He heard it as *Shuhmun*, but I mean, that's pretty close. There's no way he could've dreamed up all that."

"I'm not saying he wasn't there, Larry, and I'm not saying we don't use him. We use him. I'm just saying he's a slimeball and we ought to be careful."

Slimeball? This is *my witness* you're talking about! "I don't know, Bernie," he said. "From what I've been able to find out so far, he's not all that bad a kid. I got hold of a probation report. He's not a genius, but he's never been around anybody who's ever made him use his head. He's third-generation welfare, his mother was fifteen when he was born, and she's had two other kids by different fathers, and now she's living with one of Roland's buddies, a twenty-year-old kid, just a year older than Roland. He's moved right in there to the apartment, along with Roland and one of the other two kids. I mean, Jesus Christ, can you imagine? I think I'd have a worse record than him. I doubt that he's ever known a relative that lived outside the projects."

Bernie Fitzgibbon was now smiling at him. Kramer was startled but plowed on.

"Another thing I found out about him, he has some talent. His probation officer showed me some pictures he's done. They're really interesting. They're these whaddayacall'em . . ."

"Collages?" said Fitzgibbon.

"Yeah!" said Kramer. "Collages, with these sort of silver . . ."

"Crushed aluminum foil for the skies?"

"Yeah! You've seen 'em! Where'd you see 'em?"

"I haven't seen Auburn's, but I've seen a lot like it. It's jail-house art."

"Whaddaya mean?"

"You see it all the time. They do these pictures in jail. These figures, kind of like cartoon figures, right? And then they fill in the background with crushed Reynolds Wrap?"

"Yeah . . ."

"I see that crap all the time. Must be two or three lawyers come in here every year with these tinfoil pictures, telling me I'm keeping Michelangelo behind bars."

"Well, that may be," said Kramer. "But I'd say this kid has some real talent."

Fitzgibbon said nothing. He just smiled. And now Kramer knew what the smile was all about. Bernie thought he was trying to light up his witness. Kramer knew all about that—but this was different! Lighting up the witness was a common psychological phenomenon among prosecutors. In a criminal case, your star witness was likely to be from the same milieu as the defendant and might very well have a record himself. He was not likely to be known as a pillar of probity— and yet he was the only star witness you had. At this point you were likely to feel the urge to light him up with the lamp of truth and credibility. But this was not merely a matter of improving his reputation in the eyes of a judge and jury. You felt the urge to sanitize him *for yourself*. You needed to believe that what you were doing with this person—namely, using him to pack another person off to jail— was not only effective but right. This worm, this germ, this punk, this erstwhile asshole was now your comrade, your point man in the battle of good against evil, and *you yourself* wanted to believe that a light shone round about this . . . organism, this former vermin from under the rock, now a put-upon and misunderstood youth.

He knew all about that—but Roland Auburn was different!

"All right," said Abe Weiss, putting an end to the aesthetic debate with another wave of his hand. "It don't matter. I got to make a decision, and I've made a decision. We got enough. We're bringing McCoy in. We bring him in tomorrow morning, and we make the announcement. Tuesday's a good day?"

He looked at Milt Lubell when he said that. Lubell nodded sagely. "Tuesday and Wednesday are the best. Tuesday and Wednesday." He turned to Bernie Fitzgibbon. "Mondays are lousy. All people do on Mondays is read about sports all day and watch ball games at night."

But Fitzgibbon was looking at Weiss. Finally he shrugged and said, "Okay, Abe. I can live with that. But if we're gonna do it tomorrow, I better call Tommy Killian right now, before he goes into court, to make sure he can produce his man."

Weiss motioned toward the small table and the telephone at the end of the room, beyond the conference table, and Fitzgibbon headed down there. While Fitzgibbon was on the telephone, Weiss said, "Where are those pictures, Milt?"

Milt Lubell dug through a pile of papers in his lap and came up with several pages from a magazine and handed them to Weiss.

"What's the name a this magazine, Milt?"

"Architectural Digest."

"Look at this." The next thing Kramer knew, Weiss was leaning across the desk and handing them to him. He felt tremendously flattered. He studied the pages . . . the creamiest paper imaginable . . . lush photographs in color with detail so sharp it made you blink . . . McCoy's apartment . . . A sea of marble led up to a great curved staircase with a dark wood balustrade . . . Dark wood everywhere and an ornate table with about a truckload of flowers rising up from out of a big vase . . . It was the hall Martin had been talking about. It looked big enough to put three of Kramer's $888-a-month ant colony in, and it was only a hall. He had heard that there were people who lived like this in New York . . . Another room . . . more dark wood . . . Must be the living room . . . So big, there were three or four clumps of heavy furniture in it . . . the kind of room you walk into, and you turn your voice down to a whisper . . . Another picture . . . a close-up of some carved wood, a lustrous reddish-tan wood, all these figures in suits and hats walking this way and that at odd angles in front of buildings . . . And now Weiss was leaning across his desk and pointing at the picture.

"Get a loada that," he said. " 'Wall Street,' it's called, by Wing Wong or some goddamned person, 'Hong Kong's master wood carver.' Iddn'at what it says there? It's on the wall of 'the library.' I like that."

Now Kramer could see what Martin had been talking about. "The library" . . . The Wasps . . . Thirty-eight . . . only six years older than he was . . . They were left all this money by their parents, and they lived in Fairyland. Well, this one was heading for a collision with the real world.

Fitzgibbon returned from the other end of the room.

"You talk to Tommy?" asked Weiss.

"Yeah. He'll have his man ready."

"Take a look at this," said Weiss, motioning toward the magazine pages. Kramer handed them to Fitzgibbon. "McCoy's apartment," said Weiss.

Fitzgibbon took a quick look at the pictures and handed them back to Kramer.

"You ever seen anything like it?" asked Weiss. "His wife was the decorator. Am I right, Milt?"

"Yeah, she's one a these social decorators," said Lubell, "one a these rich women who decorate places for other rich women. They run articles about them in *New York* magazine."

Weiss kept looking at Fitzgibbon, but Fitzgibbon said nothing. Then Weiss opened his eyes wide in a look of revelation. "Can you picture it, Bernie?"

"Picture what?"

"Well, here's the way I see it," said Weiss. "What I think would be a good idea, to stop all this bullshit about white justice and Johannesbronx and all that crap, is we arrest him in his apartment. I think that would be a hell of a thing. You wanna tell the people of this borough that the law is no respecter of persons, you arrest a guy from Park Avenue the same way you arrest José García or Tyrone Smith. You go into their fucking apartment, am I right?"

"Yeah," said Fitzgibbon, "because they ain't coming in any other way."

"That's not the point. We have an obligation to the people of this borough. This office is being held up to them in a very bad light, and this'll put an end to that."

"Isn't that kinda rough, taking a guy in his home to make a point?"

"There's no wonderful way to get arrested, Bernie."

"Well, we can't do that," said Fitzgibbon.

"Why not?"

"Because I just told Tommy we wouldn't do it that way. I told him he could surrender McCoy himself."

"Well, I'm sorry, but you shouldna done that, Bernie. We can't guarantee anybody we'll give his client special treatment. You know that."

"I don't know that, Abe. I gave him my word."

Kramer looked at Weiss. Kramer knew the Donkey had now dug in, but did Weiss? Apparently not.

"Look, Bernie, you just tell Tommy I overruled you, okay? You can blame it on me. I'll take all the heat for it. We'll make it up to Tommy."

"Negative," said Fitzgibbon. "You're not gonna have to take the heat, Abe, because it's not gonna happen. I gave Tommy my word. It's a contract."

"Yeah, well, sometimes you just gotta—"

"Oongots, Abe, it's a contract."

Kramer kept his eyes on Weiss. Bernie's repetition of the word *contract* had gotten to him. Kramer could see it. Weiss had come to a dead stop. Now he knew he was up against that obstinate Irish code of loyalty. Silently Kramer begged Weiss to throw his subordinate aside. Donkey loyalty! It was obscene! Why should he, Kramer, have to suffer for the sake of the fraternal solidarity of the Irish? A highly publicized arrest of this Wall Street investment banker in his apartment—it happened to be a brilliant idea! Demonstrate the evenhandedness of justice in the Bronx—absolutely! Assistant District Attorney Lawrence Kramer —the *Times,* the *News,* the *Post, The City Light,* Channel 1, and the rest of them would know his name by heart soon enough! Why should Abe Weiss cave in to the code of these Harps? And yet he knew he would. He could see it in his face. It wasn't just Bernie Fitzgibbon's black Irish toughness, either. It was also that word *contract.* That cut straight to the soul of every lifer in this business. At the Favor Bank all due bills had to be redeemed. That was the law of the criminal justice system, and Abe Weiss was nothing if not a creature of the system.

"Well, shit, Bernie," said Weiss, "whudja do that for? F'r Chrissake . . ."

The standoff was over.

"Believe me, Abe, you're gonna look better this way. They can't say you gave in to the passions of the crowd."

"Ummmm. Well, next time don't make these commitments without running them by me."

Bernie just looked at him and gave him a tiny smile that as much as said, once more, *"Oongots."*

20

CALLS FROM ABOVE

GENE LOPWITZ didn't receive visitors at his desk. He sat them down in a cluster of huge English Chippendale wing chairs and Irish Chippendale side tables in front of the fireplace. The Chippendale cluster, like the other clusters of furniture in the vast space, was the brainchild of Ronald Vine, the decorator. But the fireplace was Lopwitz's. The fireplace worked. The bond trading room stewards, who were like aged bank guards, could actually build a log fire in it—a fact that had provided several weeks of sniggers for in-house cynics such as Rawlie Thorpe.

Being a modern office tower, the building had no chimney flues. But Lopwitz, after a year of stupendous success, was determined to have a working fireplace with a carved wood mantelpiece in his office. And why? Because Lord Upland, owner of the London *Daily Courier*, had one. The austere peer had given a lunch for Lopwitz in his suite of offices in a grand old brick building on Fleet Street in hopes of having him flog a lot of "creatively structured" *Daily Courier* stock to the Yanks. Lopwitz had never forgotten how a butler had come in from time to time to put a log on the warm and toasty pungent fire in the fireplace. It was so . . . how should one say it? . . . so *baronial*, it was. Lopwitz had felt like a fortunate little boy who had been invited to the home of a great man.

Home. That was the ticket. The British, with that ever sure class instinct of theirs, realized that if a man was at the top in business, he should not have the standard business office, which made one look like an interchangeable part in a large mechanism. No, one should have an office that looked like the home of a nobleman, as much as to declare: "I, personally, am the lord, creator, and master of this great organization." Lopwitz had ended up in a terrific fight with the tower's owners and the management company that ran it for them and the city's Building Department and Fire Department, and the construction of the flues and vents had cost $350,000, but he had finally had his way, and Sherman McCoy now stared reflectively into the mouth of that baronial hearth, fifty floors above Wall Street, off the bond trading floor of Pierce & Pierce. There was no fire in the fireplace, however. There had been none for a long time.

Sherman could feel an electrical trill of tachycardia in his chest. Both of them, Lopwitz and himself, were sitting in the wingback Chippendale monsters. Lopwitz wasn't very good at small talk on even the happiest occasions, and this little meeting was going to be grim. The fireplace . . . the chiggers . . . Christ . . . Well, anything was better than looking like a beaten dog. So Sherman straightened himself up in the chair, lifted his great chin, and even managed to look slightly down his nose at the lord and master of this mighty organization.

"Sherman," said Gene Lopwitz, "I'm not gonna beat around the bush with you. I got too much respect for you to do that."

The electrical trill in his chest! Sherman's mind raced along with his heart, and he found himself wondering, quite idly, whether or not Lopwitz knew where the phrase "beat around the bush" came from. Probably not.

"I had a long talk with Arnold on Friday," Lopwitz was saying. "Now, what I'm gonna say to you—I want to make one thing clear, it's not the money, or it's not any money that was lost—that's not the issue here." This expedition out onto the psychological terrain threw Lopwitz's already sunken cheeks into perplexed creases. He was a jogging zealot (5 a.m. breed). He had the gaunt and haunted athletic look of those who stare daily down the bony gullet of the great god Aerobics.

Now he was into the business of Oscar Suder and the United Fragrance bonds, and Sherman knew he should pay close attention. United Fragrance bonds . . . Oscar Suder . . . and he thought of *The City Light*. What did it mean, "close to a major break in the Henry Lamb Case"? The story, by this same Fallow, was bafflingly vague, except to say that the "break" had been triggered by the *City Light* story about the possible license plate numbers. *Triggered!* That was the word they used! Somehow that word had set off the tachycardia as he sat hidden in the toilet booth. None of the other newspapers carried any such story.

Now Lopwitz was going on about the business of his being AWOL the day the big bond issue came in. Sherman could see Freddy Button's foppish hands fluttering about the cigarette case. Gene Lopwitz's lips were moving. The telephone on the Irish Chippendale table beside Lopwitz's wing chair rang with a discreet murmuring burble. Lopwitz picked it up and said, "Yeah? . . . Okay, good. Is he on the line yet?"

Unaccountably, Lopwitz now beamed at Sherman and said, "Only take a second. I gave Bobby Shaflett a lift on the plane so he could keep a date in Vancouver. They're up over Wisconsin or South Dakota or some goddamned place."

Lopwitz now lowered his eyes and sank back in the wing chair and beamed in anticipation of talking to the famous Golden Hillbilly whose famous buttery bulk and tenor voice were now encased in Lopwitz's own eight-seat jet aircraft with Rolls-Royce engines. Strictly speaking, it was Pierce & Pierce's, but to all practical purposes, it was his, personally, baronially. Lopwitz lowered his head, and great animation came over his face, and he said: "Bobby? Bobby? Can you hear me? . . . What's that? How's it going? . . . They treating you all right up there? . . . What? . . . Hello? Hello? . . . Bobby? You still there? Hello? Can you hear me? Bobby?"

Still holding the telephone, Lopwitz looked at Sherman with a scowl, as if he had just done something far worse than get suckered on the United Fragrance deal or go absent without leave. "Shit," he said. "Lost the connection." He clicked the receiver. "Miss Bayles? . . . Lost the connection. See if you can get the plane again."

He hung up and looked miserable. He had lost the opportunity to have the great artist, the great ball of fat and fame, pay him his thanks and, thereby, homage to the Lopwitz eminence from the skies forty thousand feet over the American heartland.

"Okay, where were we?" asked Lopwitz looking as angry as Sherman had ever seen him. "Oh yeah, the Giscard." Lopwitz began shaking his head, as if something truly dreadful had happened, and Sherman braced, because the debacle of the gold-backed bonds was the worst of it. In the next instant, however, Sherman had the eerie feeling that Lopwitz was really shaking his head over the broken telephone connection.

The telephone rang again. Lopwitz pounced on it. "Yeah? . . . You got the plane? . . . What? . . . Well, all right, put him through."

This time Lopwitz looked at Sherman and shook his head with frustration and bewilderment, as if Sherman was his understanding friend. "It's Ronald Vine. He's calling from England. He's out in Wiltshire. He's found some linenfold paneling for me. They're six hours ahead of us there, so I gotta take it."

His voice asked for understanding and forgiveness. *Linenfold paneling?* Sherman could only stare. But apparently fearful that he might say something at such a critical juncture, Lopwitz held up one finger and closed his eyes for a moment.

"Ronald? Where you calling from? . . . That's what I thought . . . No, I know it very well . . . Whaddaya mean, they won't sell it to you?"

Lopwitz fell into a deep discussion with the decorator, Ronald Vine, about some impediment to the purchase of the linenfold paneling in Wiltshire. Sherman looked at the fireplace again . . . The chiggers . . . Lopwitz had used the fireplace for just about two months and then never again. One day, while sitting at his desk, he had suffered an intense itching and burning sensation on the underside of his left buttock. Fiery red blisters he had . . . *Chigger bites* . . . The only plausible deduction was that somehow chiggers had found their way to the fiftieth floor, to the mighty bond trading floor of Pierce & Pierce, in a load of firewood for the hearth and had bitten the baron on the bottom. On the brass andirons at this moment was a stack of carefully chosen New Hampshire hardwood logs, sculpturally perfect, perfectly clean, utterly antiseptic, buggered with enough insecticide to empty a banana grove of everything that moves, permanently installed, never to be lit.

Lopwitz's voice rose. "Whaddaya mean they won't sell it to 'trade'? . . . Yeah, I know they said it to you, but they know you're getting it for me. What are they talking about, 'trade'? . . . Unnh-hnnh . . . Yeah, well, you tell 'em I got a word for them. *Trayf* . . . Let 'em figure it out for themselves. If I'm 'trade,' they're *trayf* . . . What's it mean? It means, like, 'not kosher,' only it's worse than that. In plain English I guess the word is *shit*. There's an old saying, 'If you look close enough, everything is *trayf*, and that goes for these moth-eaten aristocrats, too, Ronald. Tell 'em to take their linenfold panels and shove 'em."

Lopwitz hung up and looked at Sherman with great irritation.

"All right, Sherman, let's get down to cases." He sounded as if Sherman had been stalling, arguing, evading, double-talking him, and otherwise trying to drive him crazy. "I can't figure out what happened with the Giscard . . . Lemme ask you something." He cocked his head and put on the look that says, "I'm a shrewd observer of human nature."

"I'm not prying," he said, "but I want you to tell me anyway. You having trouble at home or something?"

For a moment Sherman entertained the notion of appealing, man-to-man, for pity and revealing just an inch or two of his infidelity. But a sixth sense told him that "problems at home" would only arouse Lopwitz's contempt and his appetite for gossip, which seemed to be considerable. So he shook his head and smiled slightly, to indicate that the question didn't even trouble him, and said, "No, not at all."

"Well, do you need a vacation or something?"

Sherman didn't know what to say to that. But his spirits rose. At least it didn't sound as if Lopwitz was about to fire him. In fact, he didn't have to say anything, because the telephone rang again. Lopwitz picked up the receiver, although not so rapidly this time.

"Yeah? . . . What's that, Miss Bayles? . . . Sherman?" A big sigh. "Well, he's right here."

Lopwitz looked at Sherman quizzically. "Seems to be for you." He held out the receiver.

Very odd. Sherman got up, took the receiver, and stood beside Lopwitz's chair. "Hello?"

"Mr. McCoy?" It was Miss Bayles, Lopwitz's secretary. "There's a Mr. Killian on the line. He says it's 'imperative' that he speak to you. Do you want to speak to him?"

Sherman felt a thud of palpitation in his chest. Then his heart kicked off into a steady, galloping tachycardia. "Yes. Thank you."

A voice said, "Sherman?" It was Killian. He had never called him by his first name before. "I had to get hold of you." *Hadda gedoldya.*

"I'm in Mr. Lopwitz's office," said Sherman, in a formal voice.

"I know that," said Killian. "But I had to make sure you didn't leave the building or something before I godoldya. I just got a call from Bernie Fitzgibbon. They claim they got a witness who can—make the people who were at the scene. You follow me?"

"Make?"

"Identify 'em."

"I see . . . Let me call you when I get back to my desk." Composed.

"Okay, I'm in my office, but I got to head to court. So make it quick. There's one very important thing you got to know. They're gonna want to see you, officially, tomorrow. Officially, okay? So you call me back immediately." The way Killian said "officially," Sherman could tell it was a code expression, in case someone in Lopwitz's office had access to the conversation.

"All right," he said. Composed. "Thank you." He put the receiver back on the cradle on the Irish Chippendale table and sat back down in the wing chair in a daze.

Lopwitz continued as if the call had never taken place. "As I told you, Sherman, the question is not that you lost money for Pierce & Pierce. That's not what I'm saying. The Giscard was your idea. It was a great strategy, and you thought of it. But I mean, f'r Chrissake, you worked on it for four months, and you're our number one bond salesman out there. So it isn't the money you lost for us, it's that here you are, you're a guy who's supposed to function the best out there, and now we got a situation where we got a whole string of these things that I've been talking to you about—"

Lopwitz stopped talking and stared with astonishment as Sherman, without a word, stood up in front of him. Sherman knew what he was doing, but at the same time he seemed to have no control over it. He couldn't just stand up and walk out on Gene Lopwitz in the middle of a crucial talk about his performance at Pierce & Pierce, and yet he couldn't sit there another second.

"Gene," he said, "you'll have to excuse me. I have to leave." He could hear his own voice as if he were hearing it from outside. "I'm really sorry, but I have to."

Lopwitz remained seated and looked at him as if he'd gone crazy.

"That call," said Sherman. "I'm sorry."

He started walking out of the office. In his peripheral vision he was aware of Lopwitz following him with his eyes.

Out on the floor of the bond trading room, the morning madness had reached its peak. As he headed toward his desk, Sherman felt as if he were swimming through a delirium.

". . . October ninety-twos at the buck . . ."

". . I said we strip the fuckers!"

Ahhhhh, the golden crumbs . . . How pointless it seemed . . .

As he sat down at his desk, Arguello approached and said, "Sherman, do you know anything about 10 million Joshua Tree S&Ls?"

Sherman waved him back, the way you would warn someone away from a fire or the edge of a cliff. He noticed his forefinger shaking as he pressed out Killian's number on the telephone. The receptionist answered, and in his mind Sherman could see the scalding brightness of the reception area in the old building on Reade Street. In a moment Killian was on the line.

"You someplace you can talk?" he asked. *Tawk.*

"Yes. What did you mean, they want to see me officially?"

"They wanna bring you in. It's unethical, it's unnecessary, it's bullshit, but that's what they're gonna do."

"Bring me in?" Even as he said it, he had the dreadful feeling he knew what Killian meant. The question was an involuntary prayer, from his very central nervous system, that he be wrong.

"They're gonna place you under arrest. It's outrageous. They should take whatever they got before a grand jury and get an indictment and then see about an arraignment. Bernie knows that, but Weiss's gotta have a quick arrest to get the press off his back."

Sherman's throat went dry with "place you under arrest." The rest was just words.

"Under arrest?" A croak.

"Weiss is an animal," said Killian, "and he's a whore for the press."

"*Under arrest*—you can't be serious." Please don't let it be true. "What can they—what are they charging me with?"

"Reckless endangerment, leaving the scene of an accident, and failure to report."

"I can't believe it." Please make this unreal. "Reckless endangerment? But from what you said—I mean, how can they? I wasn't even driving!"

"Not according to their witness. Bernie said the witness picked your picture out from a set of photographs."

"But I wasn't driving!"

"I'm only telling you what Bernie told me. He says the witness also knew the color of your car and the model."

Sherman was aware of his own rapid breathing and the roar of the bond trading room.

Killian said, "You there?"

Sherman, hoarsely: "Yes . . . Who *is* this witness?"

"That he wouldn't tell me."

"Is it the other boy?"

"He wouldn't say."

"Or—Christ!—Maria?"

"He's not gonna tell me that."

"Did he say *anything* about a woman in the car?"

"No. They're gonna keep the details to themselves at this point. But look. Lemme tell you something. This is not gonna be as bad as you think. I got a commitment from Bernie. I can bring you up there and surrender you myself. You'll be in there and outta there. *Ba-bing.*"

In and out of *what?* But what he said was "Surrender me?"

"Yeah. If they wanted, they could come downtown and arrest you and take you up there in handcuffs."

"Up where?"

"The Bronx. But that's not gonna happen. I got a commitment from Bernie. And by the time they release it to the press, you'll be outta there. You can be thankful for that."

The press . . . the Bronx . . . surrender . . . reckless endangerment . . . one grotesque abstraction after another. All at once he was desperate to visualize what was about to happen, to picture it, no matter what it was, rather than simply feel the horrible force closing in about him.

Killian said, "You there?"

"Yes."

"You can thank Bernie Fitzgibbon. You remember what I was telling you about contracts? This is a contract, between me and Bernie."

"Look," said Sherman, "I've got to come by and talk to you."

"Right now I got to go over to court. I'm already"—*aweady*—"late. But I should be through by one. Come on over around one. You probably gonna need a couple of hours anyway."

This time Sherman knew exactly what Killian was talking about. "Oh, God," he said in his now husky voice, "I've got to talk to my wife. She doesn't know the first thing about any of this." He was talking as much to himself as to Killian. "And my daughter and my parents . . . and Lopwitz . . . I don't know . . . I can't tell you—this is absolutely incredible."

"It's like the ground's been cut out from under you, right? That's the most natural thing inna world. You're not a criminal. But it's not gonna be as bad as you think. This don't mean they got a case. It just means they think they got enough to make a move. So I'm gonna tell you something. Or I'm gonna tell you something I already told you, again. You're gonna have to tell some people what's happening, but don't get into the details of what happened that night. Your *wife*

—well, what you tell her, that's between you and her, and I can't guide you on that. But anybody else—don't get into it. It can be used against you."

A sad, sad wave of sentiment rolled over Sherman. What could he say to Campbell? And how much would she pick up from what other people said about him? Six years old; so guileless; a little girl who loves flowers and rabbits.

"I understand," he said in an utterly depressed voice. How could Campbell be anything but crushed by it all?

After saying goodbye to Killian, he sat at his desk and let the diode-green letters and numbers on the computer screens skid in front of his eyes. Logically, intellectually, he knew that Campbell, his little girl, would be the first person to believe him totally and the last to lose faith in him, and yet there was no use trying to think logically and intellectually about it. He could see her tender and exquisite little face.

His concern for Campbell had one fortunate effect, at least. It overshadowed the first of his difficult tasks, which was going back in to see Eugene Lopwitz.

When he showed up at Lopwitz's suite again, Miss Bayles gave him a wary look. Obviously Lopwitz had told her that he had gone walking out of the room like a lunatic. She directed him to a bombastic French armchair and kept an eye on him for the fifteen minutes he was kept waiting before Lopwitz summoned him back in.

Lopwitz was standing when Sherman entered the office and didn't offer him a seat. Instead, he intercepted him out in the middle of the room's vast Oriental rug, as if to say, "Okay, I let you back in. Now make it quick."

Sherman raised his chin and tried to look dignified. But he felt giddy at the thought of what he was about to reveal, about to confess.

"Gene," he said, "I didn't mean to walk out of here so abruptly, but I had no choice. That call that came in while we were talking. You asked me if I had any problems. Well, the fact of the matter is, I do. I'm going to be arrested in the morning."

At first Lopwitz just stared at him. Sherman noticed how thick and wrinkled his eyelids were. Then he said, "Let's go over here," and motioned toward the cluster of wingback chairs.

They sat down once more. Sherman felt a twinge of resentment at the look of absorption in Lopwitz's bat face, which had *voyeur* written all over it. Sherman told him of the Lamb case as it had first appeared in the press and then of the visit of the two detectives to his house, although without the humiliating details. All the while he stared at Lopwitz's rapt face and felt the sickening thrill of the hopeless wanton who flings good money after bad and a good life after vile weak sins. The temptation to *tell all*, to be truly wanton, to tell of the sweet loamy loins of Maria Ruskin and the fight in the jungle and his victory over the two brutes— to tell Lopwitz that whatever he had done, he had done it *as a man*—and that as a man he had been blameless—and, more than blameless, perhaps even a hero— the temptation to lay bare the entire drama—*in which I was not a villain!*—was very nearly more than he could withstand. But he held back.

"That was my lawyer who called while I was in here, Gene, and he says I shouldn't go into the details of what happened or didn't happen with anybody right now, but I do want you to know one thing, particularly since I don't know what's going to be said in the press about all this. And that is that I did not hit anybody with my car or drive it recklessly or do anything else that I can't have a completely clear conscience about."

As soon as he said "conscience," he realized that every guilty man talks about his clear conscience.

"Who's your lawyer?" asked Lopwitz.

"His name is Thomas Killian."

"Don't know him. You oughta get Roy Branner. He's the greatest litigator in New York. Fabulous. If I was ever in a jam, I'd get Roy. If you want him, I'll call him."

Nonplussed, Sherman listened as Lopwitz went on about the power of the fabulous Roy Branner and the cases he had won and how he first met him and how close they were and how their wives knew each other and how much Roy would do for him if he, Gene Lopwitz, said the word.

So that was Lopwitz's overpowering instinct upon hearing of this crisis in Sherman's life: to tell him of his inside knowledge and the important people he knew and what a hold he, the magnetic baron, had over the Big Name. The second instinct was more practical. It was set off by the word *press*. Lopwitz proposed, in a way that did not invite debate, that Sherman take a leave of absence until this unfortunate matter was resolved.

This perfectly reasonable suggestion, calmly made, set off a neural alarm. If he took a leave of absence, he might—he wasn't completely sure—he might still draw his base salary of $10,000 a month, which was less than half of what he had to pay each month in loan payments. But he would no longer share in commissions and bond trading division profits. For all practical purposes, he would have no more income.

The telephone on Lopwitz's Irish Chippendale side table rang with its little cooing ring. Lopwitz picked it up.

"Yeah? . . . You do?" Big smile. "Terrific . . . Hello? . . . Hello? . . . Bobby? You hear me all right?" He looked at Sherman and gave him a relaxed smile and mouthed the man's name, *Bobby Shaflett*. Then he looked down and concentrated on the receiver. His face was creased and crinkled with purest joy. "You say it's okay? . . . Wonderful! I'm glad to do it. They've given you something to eat, I assume . . . Good, good. Now listen. You need anything, you just ask them. They're nice fellows. Dja know they both flew in Vietnam? . . . Oh sure. They're terrific fellows. You want a drink or anything, you just ask 'em. I keep some 1934 Armagnac on the plane. I think it's stowed in the back. Ask the smaller one, Tony. He knows where it is . . . Well, when you come back tonight, then. It's great stuff. That's the greatest year there ever was for Armagnac, 1934. It's very smooth. It'll help you relax . . . So it's okay, hunh? . . . Great. Well . . . What? . . . Not at all, Bobby. Glad to do it, glad to do it."

When he hung up, he couldn't have looked happier. The most famous opera singer in America was in his airplane, hitching a ride to Vancouver, Canada, with Lopwitz's own two former Air Force captains, veterans of combat in Vietnam, as chauffeurs and butlers, serving him Armagnac more than half a century old, $1,200 a bottle, and now this wonderful round famous fellow was thanking him, paying his respects, from forty thousand feet above the state of Montana.

Sherman stared at Lopwitz's smiling face and grew frightened. Lopwitz wasn't angry at him. He wasn't perturbed. He wasn't even particularly put out. No, *the fate of Sherman McCoy didn't make all that much difference*. Lopwitz's English

Reproduction life would endure Sherman McCoy's problems, and Pierce & Pierce would endure them. Everybody would enjoy the juicy story for a while, and bonds would go on being sold in vast quantities, and the new chief bond salesman—who?—Rawlie?—or somebody else?—would show up in Lopwitz's Tea-at-the-Connaught conference room to discuss raking Pierce & Pierce's billions to this part of the market or that. Another air-to-ground telephone call from some fat celebrity and Lopwitz wouldn't even remember who he was.

"Bobby Shaflett," said Lopwitz, as if he and Sherman were sitting around having a drink before dinner. "He was over Montana when he called." He shook his head and chuckled, as if to say, "A hell of a guy."

21

THE FABULOUS KOALA

Never in his life had he seen *things*, the things of everyday life, more clearly. And his eyes poisoned every one of them!

In the bank on Nassau Street, which he had entered hundreds of times, where tellers, guards, junior officers, and the manager himself knew him as the estimable Mr. McCoy of Pierce & Pierce and called him by name, where he was so esteemed, in fact, they had given him a personal loan of $1.8 million to buy his apartment—and that loan cost him $21,000 a month!—and where was it going to come from!—*oh God!*—he now noticed the smallest things . . . the egg-and-dart molding around the cornice on the main floor . . . the old bronze shades on the lamps on the check-writing desks in the middle of the lobby . . . the spiral fluting on the posts supporting the railing between the lobby and the section where the officers sat . . . All so solid! so precise! so orderly! . . . and now so specious! such a mockery! . . . so *worthless*, offering no protection at all . . .

Everybody *smiled* at him. Kind respectful unsuspecting souls . . . Today still Mr. McCoy Mr. McCoy Mr. McCoy Mr. McCoy Mr. McCoy . . . How very sad to think that in this solid orderly place . . . tomorrow . . .

Ten thousand in cash . . . Killian said the bail money had to be in cash . . . The teller was a young black woman, no more than twenty-five, wearing a blouse with a high-neck stock and a gold pin . . . a cloud with a face blowing the wind . . . in gold . . . His eyes fastened upon the strange sadness of the wind's face of gold . . . If he presented her with a check for $10,000, would she question it? Would he have to go to a bank officer and explain? What would he say? For *bail?* The estimable Mr. McCoy Mr. McCoy Mr. McCoy Mr. McCoy . . .

In fact all she said was "You know we have to report all transactions of $10,000 or more, don't you, Mr. McCoy?"

Report? To a bank officer!

She must have seen the puzzlement on his face, because she said, "To the government. We have to fill out a form."

Then it dawned on him. It was a regulation designed to foil drug dealers who did business in large amounts of cash.

"How long does it take? Does it involve a lot of paperwork?"

"No, we just fill out the form. We have all the information we need on file, your address and so on."

"Well—all right, that's fine."

"How would you like it? In hundreds?"

"Uh, yes, in hundreds." He didn't have the faintest idea of what $10,000 in hundred-dollar bills would look like.

She left the window and soon returned with what looked like a small paper brick with a band of paper around it. "Here you are. This is a hundred one-hundred-dollar bills."

He smiled nervously. "That's it? Doesn't look like much, does it?"

"Well . . . depends. All bills come in packages of a hundred, the ones same as the hundreds. When you see a hundred on there, it's impressive enough, I guess."

He propped his attaché case up on the marble sill of the window and snapped open the lid and took the paper brick from her and put it inside and snapped the case shut and then glanced at her face again. She knew, didn't she! She knew there was something sordid about having to take out such a desperate amount of cash. There was bound to be!

In fact, her face betrayed neither approval nor disapproval. She smiled, politely, to show her good will—and a wave of fear swept over him. *Good will!* What would she or any other black person who looked into the face of Sherman McCoy think tomorrow—

—of the man who ran down a black honor student and left him to die!

As he walked down Nassau, toward Wall, on his way to Dunning Sponget & Leach, he had an attack of money anxiety. The $10,000 had pretty well wiped out his checking account. He had another $16,000 or so in a so-called money market savings account that could be shifted at any time to the checking account. This was money he kept on hand for—incidentals!—the ordinary bills that came up every month! and would keep on coming up!—like waves at the shore—*and now what?* Very shortly he would have to invade principal—and there wasn't that much principal. Had to stop thinking about it. He thought of his father. He would be there in five minutes . . . He couldn't imagine it. And that would be nothing compared to Judy and Campbell.

As he walked into his father's office, his father rose up from the chair behind his desk . . . but Sherman's poisoned eyes picked out the most insignificant thing . . . the saddest thing . . . Just across from his father's window, in a window of the new glass-and-aluminum building across the street, a young white woman was staring at the street below and probing the intertragian notch of her left ear with a Q-tip . . . a very plain young woman with tight curly hair, staring at the street and cleaning her ears . . . How very sad . . . The street was so narrow he felt as if he could reach out and rap on the plate glass where she stood . . . The new building had cast his father's little office into a perpetual gloom. He had to keep the lights on at all times. At Dunning Sponget & Leach, old partners, such as John Campbell McCoy, were not forced to retire, but they were expected to do the right thing. This meant giving up grand offices and grand views to make way for the rising middle-agelings, lawyers in their forties and early fifties still swollen with ambition and visions of grander views, grander offices.

"Come in, Sherman," said his father . . . the erstwhile Lion . . . with a smile and also a wary note. No doubt he had been able to tell from the tone of Sherman's voice on the telephone that this would not be an ordinary visit. The Lion . . . He was still an impressive figure with his aristocratic chin and his thick white hair combed straight back and his English suit and his heavy watch chain across the belly of his vest. But his skin seemed thin and delicate, as if at any moment his entire leonine hide might crumple inside all the formidable worsted clothes. He motioned toward the armchair by his desk and said, quite pleasantly, "The bond market must be in the doldrums. Suddenly I rate a visit in the middle of the day."

A visit in the middle of the day—the Lion's old office had not only been on the corner, it had commanded a view of New York Harbor. What bliss it had been, as a boy, to go visit Daddy in his office! From the moment he stepped off the elevator on the eighteenth floor he was His Majesty the Child. Everyone, the receptionist, the junior partners, even the porters, knew his name and sang it out as if nothing could bring greater happiness to the loyal subjects of Dunning Sponget than the sight of his little face and budding aristocratic chin. All other traffic seemed to come to a halt as His Majesty the Child was escorted down the hall and deep into the CEO's suite to the office of the Lion himself, on the corner, where the door opened and—glorious!—the sun flooded in from over the harbor, which was spread out for him down below. The Statue of Liberty, the Staten Island ferries, the tugboats, the police boats, the cargo ships coming in through the Narrows in the distance . . . What a show—for him! What bliss!

Several times, in that glorious office, they came close to sitting down and having a real talk. Young as he was, Sherman had perceived that his father was trying to open a door in his formality and beckon him through. And he had never known quite how. Now, in the blink of an eye, Sherman was thirty-eight, and there was no door at all. How could he put it? In his entire life he had never dared embarrass his father with a single confession of weakness, let alone moral decay and abject vulnerability.

"Well, how's it going at Pierce & Pierce?"

Sherman laughed a mirthless laugh. "I don't know. It's going on without *me*. That much I know."

His father leaned forward. "You're not *leaving*?"

"In a manner of speaking." He still didn't know how to put it. So, weakly, guiltily, he fell back on the shock approach, the blunt demand for sympathy, that had worked with Gene Lopwitz. "Dad, I'm going to be arrested in the morning."

His father stared at him for what seemed like a very long time, then opened his mouth and closed it and sighed a little sigh, as if rejecting all of mankind's usual responses of surprise or disbelief when a disaster is announced. What he finally said, while perfectly logical, puzzled Sherman: "By whom?"

"By . . . the police. The New York City police."

"On what charge?" Such bewilderment and pain on his face. Oh, he had stunned him, all right, and probably demolished his capacity to get angry . . . and how contemptible a strategy it was . . .

"Reckless endangerment, leaving the scene of an accident, failure to report an accident."

"Automobile," said his father, as if talking to himself. "And they're going to arrest you tomorrow?"

Sherman nodded and began his sordid story, all the while studying his father's face and noting, with relief and guilt, that he remained stunned. Sherman dealt with the subject of Maria with Victorian delicacy. Scarcely knew her. Had only seen her three or four times, in innocuous situations. Should never have flirted with her, of course. Flirted.

"Who is this woman, Sherman?"

"She's married to a man named Arthur Ruskin."

"Ah. I think I know who you mean. He's Jewish, isn't he?"

What earthly difference does it make? "Yes."

"And who is she?"

"She's from someplace in South Carolina."

"What was her maiden name?"

Her maiden name? "Dean. I don't think she's Colonial Dames material, Dad."

When he got as far as the first appearance of the stories in the newspapers, Sherman could tell his father didn't want to hear any more of the sordid details. He interrupted again.

"Who's representing you, Sherman? I assume you do have a *law*yer."

"Yes. His name is Thomas Killian."

"Never heard of him. Who is he?"

With a heavy heart: "He's with a firm called Dershkin, Bellavita, Fishbein & Schlossel."

The Lion's nostrils quivered, and his jaw muscles bunched up, as if he were trying to keep from retching. "How on earth did you find them?"

"They specialize in criminal law. Freddy Button recommended them."

"Freddy? You let *Freddy* . . ." He shook his head. He couldn't find the words.

"He's my *law*yer!"

"I know, Sherman, but Freddy . . ." The Lion glanced toward the door and then lowered his voice. "Freddy's a perfectly fine person, Sherman, but this is a serious matter!"

"*You* turned me over to Freddy, Dad, a long time ago!"

"I *know!*—but not for anything important!" He shook his head some more. Bewilderment upon bewilderment.

"Well, in any event, I'm represented by a lawyer named Thomas Killian."

"Ah, Sherman." A far-off weariness. The horse is out of the barn. "I wish you had come to me as soon as this thing happened. Now, at this stage—well, but that's where we are, isn't it? So let's try to go from here. One thing I'm quite sure of. You have got to find the very best representation available. You've got to find lawyers you can *trust*, implicitly, because you're putting an awful lot in their hands. You can't just go wandering in to some people named Dershbein—whatever it is. I'm going to call Chester Whitman and Ed LaPrade and sound them out."

Chester Whitman and Ed LaPrade? Two old federal judges who were either retired or close to it. The likelihood of their knowing anything about the machinations of a Bronx district attorney or a Harlem rabble-rouser was so remote . . . And all at once Sherman felt sad, not so much for himself as for this old man before him, clinging to the power of connections that meant something back in the 1950s and early 1960s . . .

"Miss Needleman?" The Lion was already on the telephone. "Would you ring up Judge Chester Whitman for me, please? . . . What? . . . Oh. I see. Well, when you're through, then." He hung up the receiver. As an old partner, he no longer had a secretary of his own. He shared one with half a dozen others, and obviously she, Miss Needleman, did not jump when the Lion opened his mouth. Waiting, the Lion looked out his solitary window and pursed his lips and looked very old.

And in that moment Sherman made the terrible discovery that men make about their fathers sooner or later. For the first time he realized that the man before him was not an aging father but a boy, a boy much like himself, a boy who grew up and had a child of his own and, as best he could, out of a sense of duty and, perhaps, love, adopted a role called Being a Father so that his child would have something mythical and infinitely important: a Protector, who would keep a lid on all the chaotic and catastrophic possibilities of life. And now that boy, that good actor, had grown old and fragile and tired, wearier than ever at the thought of trying to hoist the Protector's armor back onto his shoulders again, now, so far down the line.

The Lion looked away from the window and straight at Sherman and smiled, with what Sherman interpreted as a kindly embarrassment.

"Sherman," he said, "promise me one thing. You won't lose heart. I wish you'd come to me sooner, but that doesn't matter. You're going to have my complete support, and you're going to have Mother's. Whatever we can do for you, we will."

For an instant, Sherman thought he was talking about money. On second thought, he knew he wasn't. By the standards of the rest of the world, the world outside of New York, his parents were rich. In fact, they had just enough to generate the income that would support the house on Seventy-third Street and the house on Long Island and provide them with help a few days each week at both places and take care of the routine expenses that would preserve their gentility. But to cut into their principal would be like cutting a vein. He couldn't do that to this well-meaning gray-haired man who sat before him in this mean little office. And, for that matter, he wasn't at all sure that's what was being offered.

"What about Judy?" asked his father.

"Judy?"

"How has she taken all this?"

"She doesn't know about it yet."

"She *doesn't?*"

"Not the first thing."

Every vestige of an expression left the face of the old gray-haired lad.

When Sherman asked Judy to come with him into the library, he had every intention, every conscious intention, of being completely honest. But from the moment he opened his mouth he was aware of his clumsy secret para-self, the dissembler. It was the dissembler who put that portentous baritone into his voice and who showed Judy to the wing chair the way a funeral director might have done it and who closed the door to the library with lugubrious deliberateness and then turned about and wrapped his eyebrows around his nose so that Judy could see, without hearing the first word, that the situation was grave.

The dissembler didn't sit behind his desk—that would be too corporate a posture—but in the armchair. And then he said:

"Judy, I want you to get a grip on yourself. I—"

"If you're going to tell me about your little whatever it is, don't bother. You can't imagine how uninterested I am."

Astounded: "My little *what?*"

"Your . . . affair . . . if that's what it is. I don't even want to hear about it."

He stared at her with his mouth slightly open, ransacking his mind for something to say: "That's only part of it" . . . "If only that's all it was" . . . "I'm afraid you'll have to hear about it" . . . "It's gone beyond that" . . . All so lame, flat—so he fell back on the bomb. He'd drop the bomb on her.

"Judy—I'm going to be arrested in the morning."

That got her. That knocked the condescending look off her face. Her shoulders dropped. She was just a little woman in a big chair.

"Arrested?"

"You remember the night the two detectives came by here. The thing that happened in the Bronx?"

"That was *you?*"

"It was me."

"I don't believe it!"

"Unfortunately it's true. It was me."

He had her. She was staggered. He felt cheap and guilty all over again. The dimensions of his catastrophe once more hogged the moral terrain.

He started in on his story. Until the very words came out of his mouth, he meant to be completely truthful about Maria. But . . . what good would it do? Why devastate his wife completely? Why leave her with a completely hateful husband? So he told her it had been just a little flirtation. Known the woman barely three weeks.

"I just told her I'd pick her up at the airport. I just all of a sudden told her I'd do that. I probably had—I guess I had something on my mind—won't try to kid you or kid myself—but, Judy, I swear to you, I never even *kissed* the woman, much less had an *affair*. Then this unbelievable *thing* happened, this nightmare, and I haven't seen her since except that one night when all of a sudden there I am sitting next to her at the Bavardages'. Judy, I swear to you, there was no *affair*."

He studied her face to see if by any chance she believed him. A blank. A daze. He plunged on.

"I know I should have told you as soon as the thing happened. But it came right on top of that stupid telephone call I made. And then I *knew* you'd think I was having some kind of affair, which I wasn't. Judy, I've seen the woman maybe five times in my life, always in a public situation. I mean, even picking somebody up at an airport is a public situation."

He halted and tried to size her up again. Nothing. He found her silence overwhelming. He felt compelled to supply all the missing words.

He went on about the newspaper stories, his problems at the office, about Freddy Button, Thomas Killian, Gene Lopwitz. Even as he droned on about one thing, his mind raced ahead to the next. Should he tell her about his conversation with his father? That would win him her sympathy, because she would realize the pain it caused him. No! She might be angry to know he had told his father first . . . But before he reached that point, he realized she was no longer listening. A curious, almost dreamy look had come over her face. Then she started chuckling. The only sound that came out was a little *cluck cluck cluck* in her throat.

Shocked and offended: "This strikes you as funny?"

With just a trace of a smile: "I'm laughing at myself. All weekend I was upset because you were such a . . . dud . . . at the Bavardages'. I was afraid that might hurt my chances of being chairman of the museum benefit."

Despite everything, Sherman was pained to learn that he had been a dud at the Bavardages'.

Judy said, "That's pretty funny, isn't it? Me worrying about the museum benefit?"

With a hiss: "Sorry to be a drag on your ambitions."

"Sherman, now I want you to listen to me." She said it with such a calm maternal kindness, it was eerie. "I'm not responding like a good wife, am I. I want to. But how can I? I want to offer you my love, or if not my love, my . . . what? . . . my sympathy, my closeness, my comfort. But I can't. I can't even pretend. You haven't let me near you. Do you understand that? You haven't let me near you. You have deceived me, Sherman. Do you know what that means, to *deceive* someone?" She said this with the same maternal kindness as the rest.

"Deceive? Good Lord, it was a flirtation, if it was anything. If you . . . make eyes at somebody . . . you can call that deceit if you want, but I wouldn't call it that."

She put on the slight smile again and shook her head. "Sherman, Sherman, Sherman."

"I swear that's the truth."

"Oh, I don't know what you did with your Maria Ruskin, and I don't care. I just don't. That's the least of it, but I don't think you understand that."

"The least of *what?*"

"What you've done to me, and not just to me. To Campbell."

"Campbell!"

"To your family. We *are* a family. This thing, this thing affecting all of us, it happened two weeks ago, and you said nothing about it. You hid it from me. You sat right next to me, in this very room, and watched that news report, the demonstration, and you didn't say a word. Then the police came to our home—the *police!*—to *our home!*—I even asked you why you were in such a state, and you pretended it was a coincidence. And then—that *same night*—you sat next to your . . . your friend . . . your accomplice . . . your sidekick . . . you tell me what to call her . . . and you still said nothing. You let me think nothing was wrong. You let me go on having my foolish dreams, and you let Campbell go on having her childish dreams, of being a normal little girl in a normal family, playing with her little friends, making her little rabbits and turtles and penguins. The night *the world* was learning of *your escapade*, Campbell was showing you a rabbit she made out of clay. Do you remember that? Do you? And you just *looked* at it and said *all the right things!* And now you come home"—all at once her eyes were full of tears—"at the end of the day and you tell me . . . you're . . . gonna . . . be . . . arrested . . . in . . . the . . . morning."

The sentence was gulped down in sobs. Sherman stood up. Should he try to put his arms around her? Or would it only make it worse? He took a step toward her.

She sat up straight and held her hands up before her in a very delicate, tentative way.

"Don't," she said softly. "Just listen to what I'm telling you." Her cheeks were streaked with tears. "I'm going to try to help you, and I'm going to try to help Campbell, in any way I can. But I can't give you my love, and I can't give you tenderness. I'm not that good an actress. I wish I were, because you're going to need love and tenderness, Sherman."

Sherman said, "Can't you forgive me?"

"I suppose I could," she said. "But what would that change?"

He had no answer.

He spoke to Campbell in her bedroom. Just walking in was enough to break his heart. Campbell was sitting at her table (a round table with about eight hundred dollars' worth of flowered cotton fabric from Laura Ashley hanging to the floor and a piece of beveled glass costing $280 covering the top) or, rather, she was halfway on top of it, with her head close to the surface, in an attitude of intense concentration, printing some letters with a big pink pencil. It was the perfect little girl's room. Dolls and stuffed animals were perched everywhere. They were on the white-enameled bookcases with their ribbed pilasters and on the pair of miniature boudoir chairs (more flowered fabric from Laura Ashley). They were perched up against the ribbon-back Chippendale headboard of the bed and the ribbon-back footboard and upon the lacy and carefully thought-out clutter of pillows and on the pair of round bedside tables with another fortune in fabric falling to the floor. Sherman had never begrudged a cent of the stupendous sums of money Judy had put into this one room, and he certainly did not now. His heart was lacerated by the thought that he now had to find the words to tell Campbell that the dream world of this room was finished, many years too soon.

"Hi, sweetheart, what are you doing?"

Without looking up: "I'm writing a book."

"Writing a book! That's wonderful. What's it about?"

Silence; without looking up; hard at work.

"Sweetie, I want to talk to you about something, something very important."

She looked up. "Daddy, can you make a book?"

Make a book? "Make a book? I'm not sure what you mean."

"Make a book!" A bit exasperated by his denseness.

"You mean actually *make* one? No, they do that at a factory."

"MacKenzie's making one. Her dad is helping her. I want to make one."

Garland Reed and his damnable so-called books. Avoiding the issue: "Well, first you have to write your book."

Big smile: "I writed it!" She gestured toward the piece of paper on the table.

"You wrote it?" He never corrected her mistakes in grammar directly.

"Yes! Will you help me make a book?"

Helplessly, sadly: "I'll try."

"You want to read it?"

"Campbell, there's something very important I want to talk to you about. I want you to listen very carefully to what I tell you."

"You want to read it?"

"Campbell—" A sigh; helpless against her single-mindedness. "Yes. I'd love to read it."

Modestly: "It's not very long." She picked up several pieces of paper and handed them to him.

In large, careful letters:

THE KOALA
by Campbell McCoy

There was once a koala. His name was Kelly. He lived in the woods. Kelly had lots of friends. One day someone went on a hike and ate Kelly's food.

He was very sad. He wanted to see the city. Kelly went to the city. He also wanted to see bildings. As soon as he was about to get hold of a nob to open a door, a dog rushed by! But he did not get Kelly. Kelly jumped in a window. And by mistake he pressed the alarm. Then the polees cars were zooming by. Kelly was scared. Kelly finly escaped.

Someone caught Kelly and brought him to the zoo. Now Kelly loves the zoo.

Sherman's skull seemed to fill with steam. It was about himself! For an instant he wondered if in some inexplicable way she had divined . . . picked up the sinister emanations . . . if it were somehow in the very air of their home . . . *By mistake he pressed the alarm. Then the police cars were zooming by!* . . . It couldn't be . . . and yet there it was!

"You like it?"

"Yes, uh . . . I, uh . . ."

"Daddy! You like it?"

"It's wonderful, darling. You're very talented . . . Not many girls your age—not many . . . it's wonderful . . ."

"Now will you help me make the book?"

"I—there's something I have to tell you, Campbell. Okay?"

"Okay. You really like it?"

"Yes, it's wonderful. Campbell, I want you to listen to me. Okay? Now, Campbell, you know that people don't always tell the truth about other people."

"The truth?"

"Sometimes people say bad things, things that aren't true."

"What?"

"Sometimes people say bad things about other people, things they shouldn't say, things that make the other person feel bad. Do you know what I mean?"

"Daddy, should I draw a picture of Kelly for the book?"

Kelly? "Please listen to me, Campbell. This is important."

"Ohhhh-kayyy." Weary sigh.

"Do you remember one time MacKenzie said something that wasn't nice about you, something that wasn't true?"

"MacKenzie?" Now he had her attention.

"Yes. Remember, she said you . . ." For the life of him, he couldn't remember what MacKenzie had said. "I think she said you weren't her friend."

"MacKenzie's my best friend, and I'm her best friend."

"I know. That's just the point. She said something that wasn't true. She didn't mean it, but she said it, and sometimes people do that. They say things that hurt other people, and maybe they don't mean to do it, but they do it, and it hurts the other person, and that's not the right thing to do."

"What?"

Plowing on: "It isn't just children. Sometimes it's grownups. Grownups can be mean like that, too. In fact, they can be worse. Now, Campbell, I want you to listen to me. There are some people who are saying very bad things about me, things that aren't true."

"They are?"

"Yes. They're saying I hit a boy with my car and hurt him badly. Please look at me, Campbell. Now, that isn't true. I didn't do any such thing, but there are bad people who are saying that, and you may hear people say that, but all you have to know is, it isn't true. Even if they say it's true, you know it isn't true."

"Why don't you tell them it isn't true?"

"I will, but these people may not want to believe me. There are bad people who want to believe bad things about other people."

"But why don't you *tell* them?"

"I will. But these bad people are going to put these bad things in the newspaper and on television, and so people are going to believe them, because they will read it in the newspapers and see it on television. But it isn't true. And I don't care what they think, but I do care what you think, because I love you, Campbell, I love you very much, and I want you to know that your daddy is a good person who didn't do what these people are saying."

"You'll be in the newspaper? You'll be on television?"

"I'm afraid so, Campbell. Probably tomorrow. And your friends at school may say something to you about it. But you mustn't pay any attention to them, because you'll know that what's in the newspaper and on television isn't true. Don't you, sweetie?"

"Does that mean you'll be famous?"

"Famous?"

"Will you be in history, Daddy?"

History? "No, I won't be in history, Campbell. But I'll be smeared, vilified, dragged through the mud."

He knew she wouldn't understand a word of it. It just popped out, prodded by the frustration of trying to explain the press to a six-year-old.

Something in his face she understood well enough. With great seriousness and tenderness she looked into his eyes and said:

"Don't worry, Daddy. I love you."

"Campbell—"

He took her in his arms and buried his head on her shoulder to hide his tears.

There was once a koala and a pretty little room where soft sweet creatures lived and slept the trusting sleep of the innocent, and now there was none.

22

STYROFOAM PEANUTS

SHERMAN TURNED OVER onto his left side, but soon his left knee developed an ache, as if the weight of his right leg were cutting off the circulation. His heart was beating a little fast. He turned over onto his right side. Somehow the heel of his right hand ended up under his right cheek. It felt as if he needed it to support his head, because the pillow wasn't enough, but that made no sense, and anyhow, how could he possibly get to sleep with his hand under his head? A little fast, that was all . . . It wasn't running away . . . He turned back onto his left side and then rolled over flat on his stomach, but that put a strain on the small of his back, and so he rolled back over on his right side. He usually slept on his right side. His heart was going faster now. But it was an even beat. He still had it under control.

He resisted the temptation to open his eyes and check out the intensity of the light under the Roman shades. The line gradually brightened toward dawn, so that you could always tell when it was getting on toward 5:30 or 6:00 at this time of year. Suppose it was brightening already! But that couldn't be. It couldn't be more than three o'clock, 3:30 at the worst. But maybe he had slept for an hour or so without knowing it!—and suppose the lines of light—

He could resist no longer. He opened his eyes. Thank God; still dim; so he was still safe.

With that—his heart bolted away from him. It began pounding at a terrific rate and with terrific force, trying to escape from his rib cage. It made his whole body shake. What did it matter whether he had a few more hours to lie here writhing on his bed or whether the heat of the dawn had already cooked up under the shades and the time had come—

I'm going to jail.

With his heart pounding and his eyes open, he was now terribly conscious of being alone in this vast bed. Billows of silk hung down from the ceiling at the four corners of the bed. More than $125 a yard the silk had cost. It was Judy's Decorator approximation of a royal bedchamber from the eighteenth century. *Royal!*

What a mockery it was of himself, a throbbing lump of flesh and fear cowering in bed in the dead of the night!

I'm going to jail.

If Judy had been here next to him, if she hadn't gone to bed in the guest bedroom, he would have put his arms around her and held on for dear life. He wanted to embrace her, longed for it—

And with the next breath: *What good would that do?* None whatsoever. It would make him feel even weaker and more helpless. Was she asleep? What if he walked into the guest room? She often slept flat on her back, like a recumbent statue, like the statue of . . . He couldn't remember whose statue it was. He could see the slightly yellowish marble and the folds in the sheet that covered the body—someone famous, beloved and dead. Well, down the hall Campbell was asleep, for sure. He knew that much. He had looked in her room and watched her for a minute, as if this were the last time he would ever see her. She slept with her lips slightly parted and her body and soul utterly abandoned to the security and peace of her home and family. She had gone to sleep almost at once. Nothing that he had said to her was real . . . *arrest* . . . *newspapers* . . . "You'll be in history?" . . . If only he knew what she was thinking! Supposedly children picked up things in more ways than you knew, from the tone of your voice, the look on your face . . . But Campbell seemed to know only that something sad and exciting was about to happen, and her father was unhappy. Utterly insulated from the world . . . in the bosom of her family . . . her lips slightly parted . . . just down the hall . . . For her sake he had to pull himself together. And for the moment, anyway, he did. His heart slowed down. He began to take command of his body again. He would be strong for her, if for no one else on earth. *I am a man.* When he had to fight, he had fought. He had fought in the jungle, and he had won. The furious moment when he thrust the tire at the . . . brute . . . The brute was sprawled on the pavement . . . *Henry!* . . . If he had to, he would fight again. How bad could it be?

Last night, as long as he was talking to Killian, he had it worked out in his mind. It wasn't going to be so bad. Killian explained every step. It was a formality, not a pleasant formality, but not like really going to jail, either. It would not be like an ordinary arrest. Killian would see to that, Killian and his friend Fitzgibbon. A contract. Not like an ordinary arrest, not like an ordinary arrest; he clung to this phrase, "not like an ordinary arrest." Like what, then? He tried to picture how it was going to be, and before he knew it, his heart was racing, fleeing, panicked, amok with fear.

Killian had arranged it so that the two detectives, Martin and Goldberg, would drive by and pick him up about 7:30 on their way to work on the 8:00 a.m. shift in the Bronx. They both lived on Long Island and they drove to the Bronx every day, and so they would make a detour and drive by and pick him up on Park Avenue. Killian would be here when they arrived, and he would ride up to the Bronx with him and be there when they *arrested* him—and this was *special treatment.*

Lying there in bed, with cascades of $125-a-yard silk at every corner, he closed his eyes and tried to think it through. He would get in the car with the two detectives, the small one and the fat one. Killian would be with him. They would go up the FDR Drive to the Bronx. The detectives would get him to Central Booking first thing, as the new shift began, and he would go through the process first, before the day's buildup of cases. Central Booking—but what was it? Last night it had been a name Killian had used so matter-of-factly. But now, lying here, he realized he had no idea what it would look like. The process—what process? *Being arrested!* Despite everything Killian had tried to explain, it was unimaginable. He would be fingerprinted. *How?* And his fingerprints would be transmitted to Albany by a computer. Why? To make sure there were no warrants for his arrest already outstanding. But surely they knew better! Until the report from Albany came back, via the computer, he would have to wait in the detention pens. Pens! That was the word Killian kept using. *Pens!*—for what sort of animals! As if reading his mind, Killian had told him not to worry about the things you read about concerning jails. The unmentioned term was *homosexual rape*. The pens were temporary cells for people who had been arrested and were awaiting arraignment. Since arrests in the early daylight hours were rare, he might very well have the place to himself. After the report came back, he would go upstairs to appear before a judge. *Upstairs!* But what did that mean? Upstairs from what? He would plead not guilty and be released on $10,000 bail—tomorrow —in a few hours—when the dawn cooks up the light beneath the shade—

I'm going to jail—as the man who ran down a black honor student and left him to die!

His heart was beating violently now. His pajamas were wet with perspiration. He had to stop thinking. He had to close his eyes. He had to sleep. He tried to focus on an imaginary point between his eyes. Behind his eyelids . . . little movies . . . curling forms . . . a pair of puffy sleeves . . . They turned into a shirt, his own white shirt. Nothing too good, Killian said, because the holding pens might be filthy. But a suit and tie, of course, nonetheless, since this was not an ordinary arrest, not an ordinary arrest . . . The old blue-gray tweed suit, the one made in England . . . a white shirt, a solid navy tie or maybe the medium-blue tie with the pin dots . . . No, the navy tie, which would be dignified but not at all showy—*for going to jail in!*

He opened his eyes. The silk billowed down from the ceiling. "Get a grip on yourself!" He said it out loud. Surely this was not actually about to happen. *I'm going to jail.*

About 5:30, with the light turning yellow under the shade, Sherman gave up on the idea of sleep, or even rest, and got up. To his surprise, it made him feel a little better. His heartbeat was rapid, but he had the panic under control. It helped to be doing something, if only taking a shower and putting on the blue-gray tweed suit and the navy necktie . . . *my jail outfit.* The face he saw in the mirror didn't look as tired as he felt. The Yale chin; he *looked* strong.

He wanted to eat breakfast and be out of the apartment before Campbell got up. He wasn't sure he could be brave enough in front of her. He also didn't want to have to talk to Bonita. It would be too awkward. As for Judy, he didn't know what he wanted. He didn't want to see the look in her eye, which was the numb look of someone betrayed but also shocked and frightened. Yet he wanted *his wife* with him. In fact, he had scarcely had a glass of orange juice before Judy arrived in the kitchen, dressed and ready for the day. She hadn't had much more sleep than he had. A moment later Bonita came in from the servants' wing and quietly began fixing them breakfast. Soon enough Sherman was glad Bonita was there. He didn't know what to say to Judy. With Bonita present he obviously wouldn't be able to say much. He could barely eat. He had three cups of coffee in hopes of clearing his head.

At 7:15 the doorman called up to say that Mr. Killian was downstairs. Judy walked with Sherman out into the entry gallery. He stopped and looked at her. She attempted a smile of encouragement, but it gave her face a look of terrible weariness. In a low but firm voice, she said: "Sherman, be brave. Remember who you are." She opened her mouth, as if she was about to say something more; but she didn't.

And that was it! That was the best she could do! I try to see more in you, Sherman, but all that's left is the shell, your dignity!

He nodded. He couldn't get a word out. He turned and went to the elevator.

Killian was standing under the marquee just outside the front door. He was wearing a chalk-striped gray suit, brown suede shoes, a brown fedora. (How dare he be so debonair on the day of my doom?) Park Avenue was an ashy gray. The sky was dark. It looked as if it was about to rain . . . Sherman shook hands with Killian, then moved down the sidewalk about twenty feet, to be out of earshot of the doorman.

"How do you feel?" asked Killian. He asked it the way you ask a sick person.

"Top-notch," said Sherman, with a morose smile.

"It's not gonna be so bad. I talked to Bernie Fitzgibbon again last night, after I talked to you. He's gonna get you through there as fast as possible. Fucking Abe Weiss, he's a wet finger in the wind. All this publicity has him terrified. Otherwise not even an idiot like him would do this."

Sherman just shook his head. He was far beyond speculation on the mentality of Abe Weiss. *I'm going to jail!*

Out of the corner of his eye, Sherman saw a car pull up alongside them, and then he saw the detective, Martin, at the wheel. The car was a two-door Oldsmobile Cutlass, reasonably new, and Martin had on a jacket and tie, and so perhaps the doorman would not figure it out. Oh, they would know soon enough, all the doormen and matrons and money managers and general partners and bond traders and CEO's and all their private-school children and nannies and governesses and housekeepers, all the inhabitants of this social fortress. But that anyone might see he was being *led away by the police* was more than he could bear.

The car had stopped just far enough away from the door of the building that the doorman didn't come out. Martin got out and opened the door and pulled the seat back forward, so that Sherman and Killian could get into the rear. Martin smiled at Sherman. *The smile of the tormentor!*

"Hey, Counselor!" Martin said to Killian. Very cheery about it, too. "Bill Martin," he said, and he held out his hand, and he and Killian shook hands. "Bernie Fitzgibbon tells me you guys worked together."

"Oh yeah," said Killian.

"Bernie's a pistol."

"Worse than that. I could tell ya some stories."

Martin chuckled, and Sherman experienced a small spurt of hope. Killian knew this man Fitzgibbon, who was the chief of the Homicide Bureau of the Bronx District Attorney's Office, and Fitzgibbon knew Martin, and now Martin knew Killian . . . and Killian—Killian was his protector! . . . Just before Sherman bent down to get into the back seat, Martin said, "Watch your clothes back there. There're these fucking—'scuse my French—Styrofoam peanuts back there.

My kid opened up a box, and all these white *pea*nuts they pack things in got all over the place, and they stick to your clothes and every other goddamned thing."

Once he bent down, Sherman saw the fat one with the mustache, Goldberg, sitting in the front passenger seat. He had a bigger smile on.

"Sherman." He said it the way you'd say hello or good morning. Most amiably. And the whole world froze, congealed. *My first name!* A servant . . . a slave . . . a prisoner . . . Sherman said nothing. Martin introduced Killian to Goldberg. More cheery lodge talk.

Sherman was sitting behind Goldberg. There were, indeed, white Styrofoam packing peanuts all over the place. Two had attached themselves to Sherman's pants leg. One was practically on top of his knee. He picked it off and then had trouble getting it off his finger. He could feel another one under his bottom and began fishing around for that.

They had barely started off, heading up Park Avenue toward Ninety-sixth Street and the entrance to the FDR Drive, when Goldberg turned around in his seat and said, "You know, I got a daughter in high school, and she loves to read, and she was reading this book, and this outfit you work for—Pierce & Pierce, right?—they were in it."

"Is that so?" Sherman managed to say. "What was the book?"

"I think it was *Murder Mania.* Something like that."

Murder Mania? The book was called *Merger Mania.* Was he trying to torment him with some hideous joke?

"Murder Mania!" said Martin. "F'r Chrissake, Goldberg, it's *Mer-ger Mania."* Then over his shoulder to Killian and Sherman: "It's great to have a partner who's a intellectual." To his partner: "What shape's a book, Goldberg? A circle or a triangle?"

"I'll show you what shape," said Goldberg, extending the middle finger of his right hand. Then he twisted around toward Sherman again: "Anyway, she really liked that book, and she's only in high school. She says she wants to work on Wall Street when she finishes college. Or that's this week's plan, anyway."

This one, Goldberg, also! The same appalling malapert slavemaster friendliness! Now he was supposed to *like* the two of them! Now that the game was over, and he had lost, and he belonged to them, he should hold nothing against them. He should admire them. They had their hooks in a Wall Street investment banker, and what was he now? Their catch! Their quarry! Their prize pet! In an Oldsmobile Cutlass! *The brutes* from the outer boroughs—the sort of people you saw heading on Fifty-eighth Street or Fifty-ninth Street toward the Queensboro Bridge—fat young men with drooping mustaches, like Goldberg . . . and now he belonged to them.

At Ninety-third Street, a doorman was helping an old woman out the door and onto the sidewalk. She wore a caracal overcoat. It was the sort of very formal black fur coat you never saw anymore. A long happy insulated life on Park Avenue! Heartlessly, Park Avenue, *le tout New York,* would go on living its everyday life.

"All right," Killian said to Martin, "let's get it straight exactly what we're gonna do here. We're going in the 161st Street entrance, right? And then we go downstairs from there, and the Angel takes Sherman—Mr. McCoy—straight into fingerprinting. The Angel's still there?"

"Yeah," said Martin, "he's still there, but we gotta go in around the side, through the outside door to Central Booking."

"What for?"

"That's my orders. The zone captain's gonna be there, and the press is gonna be there."

"The *press!*"

"That's right. And we gotta have cuffs on him by the time we get there."

"Are you shitting me? I talked to Bernie last night. He gave me his word. There's gonna be no bullshit."

"I don't know about Bernie. This is Abe Weiss. This is the way Weiss wants it, and I got my orders straight from the zone captain. This arrest is supposed to be by the book. You're getting a break as it is. You know what they were talking about, don't you? They wanted to bring the fucking press to his apartment and cuff him there."

Killian glowered at Martin. "Who toldja to do this?"

"Captain Crowther."

"When?"

"Last night. He called me at home. Listen, you know Weiss. What can I tell ya?"

"This . . . is . . . not . . . right," said Killian. "I had Bernie's word. This . . . is . . . very . . . wrong. You don't pull this kinda thing. This . . . is . . . not . . . right."

Both Martin and Goldberg turned around and looked at him.

"I'm not gonna forget this," said Killian, "and I'm not happy."

"Ayyyyy . . . whaddaya whaddaya," said Martin. "Don't blame it on us, because it's all the same to us one way or the other. Your beef is with Weiss."

They were now out on the FDR Drive, heading north toward the Bronx. It had begun to rain. The morning traffic was already backing up on the other side of the railing that divided the expressway, but there was nothing holding them back on this side of the road. They approached a footbridge that arched over the river from the Manhattan side to an island out in the middle. The trestle had been painted a hot heliotrope purple in a burst of euphoria in the 1970s. The false hopefulness of it depressed Sherman profoundly.

I'm going to jail!

Goldberg craned around again. "Look," he said, "I'm sorry, but I gotta put on the cuffs. I can't be fucking around with 'em when we get there."

"This is pure bullshit," said Killian. "I hope you know that."

"It's the lawwwr!" said Goldberg plaintively. He put an *r* on the end of *law*. "If you bring somebody in on a felony, you're supposed to put on the cuffs. I'll grant you there's times I ain't done that, but the fucking zone captain is gonna be there."

Goldberg held up his right hand. He held a pair of handcuffs. "Give me your wrists," he said to Sherman. "We can get this over with."

Sherman looked at Killian. The muscles in Killian's jaws were bunched up. "Yeah, go ahead!" he said to Sherman with the sort of high-pitched emphasis that insinuates, "Someone is gonna *pay* for this!"

Martin said, "I tell you what. Why don't you take your jacket off. He'll cuff you in front instead of in back, and you can hold the jacket over your wrists, and you won't even be able to see the fucking cuffs."

The way he said it, it was as if the four of them were friends, all pulling together against an unkind fate. For an instant, that made Sherman feel better. He struggled out of his tweed jacket. Then he leaned forward and put his hands through the gap between the two front seats.

They were crossing a bridge . . . perhaps the Willis Avenue Bridge . . . he didn't really know what bridge it was. All he knew was that it was a bridge, and it went across the Harlem River, away from Manhattan. Goldberg snapped the cuffs onto his wrists. Sherman sank back into the seat and looked down, and there he was, in manacles.

The rain was coming down harder. They reached the other end of the bridge. Well, here it was, the Bronx. It was like an old and decrepit part of Providence, Rhode Island. There were some massive but low buildings, grimy and moldering, and broad weary black streets running up and down slopes. Martin drove down a ramp and onto another expressway.

Sherman reached around to his right to retrieve his jacket and put it over the handcuffs. When he realized that he had to move both hands in order to pick up the coat, and when the effort caused the manacles to cut into his wrists, a flood of humiliation . . . and *shame!* . . . swept over him. This was himself, the very self who existed in a unique and sacrosanct and impenetrable crucible at the center of his mind, who was now in manacles . . . in the Bronx . . . Surely this was a hallucination, a nightmare, a trick of the mind, and he would pull back a translucent layer . . . and . . . The rain came down harder, the windshield wipers were sweeping back and forth in front of the two policemen.

With the handcuffs on, he couldn't drape the jacket over his wrists. It kept balling up. So Killian helped him. There were three or four Styrofoam peanuts on the jacket. There were two more on his pant leg. He couldn't possibly get to them with his fingers. Perhaps Killian . . . But what did it matter?

Up ahead, to the right . . . Yankee Stadium! . . . An anchor! Something to hold on to! He had been to Yankee Stadium! For World Series games, nothing more . . . Nevertheless, he had been there! It was part of a sane and decent world! It was not this . . . Congo!

The car went down a ramp, leaving the expressway. The road went around the base of the huge bowl of the stadium. It wasn't forty feet away. There was a fat man with white hair wearing a New York Yankees warm-up jacket standing outside what looked like a little office door. Sherman had been to the World Series with Gordon Schoenburg, whose company had box seats for the season, and Gordon had served a picnic supper between the fifth and sixth innings from one of those wicker picnic baskets with all the compartments and stainless-steel utensils, and he had served sourdough bread and pâté and caviar to everybody, which had infuriated some drunks, who saw it from the walkway behind and started saying some very abusive things and repeating a word they heard Gordon say. The word was *really*, which they repeated over and over as *rilly*. "Oh, rilly?" they said. "Oh, rilly?" It was the next thing to calling Gordon a faggot, and Sherman always remembered that, even though no one spoke about it afterward. The abuse! The pointless hostility! The resentment! Martin and Goldberg! They were all Martins and Goldbergs.

Then Martin turned onto a very wide street, and they went underneath some elevated subway tracks and headed up a hill. There were mostly dark faces on the sidewalk, hurrying along in the rain. They all looked so dark and sodden. A lot of gray decrepit little shops, like the decaying downtowns of cities all across America, like Chicago's, Akron's, Allentown's . . . The Daffyteria, the Snooker deli, Korn Luggage, the B. & G. Davidoff Travel & Cruise . . .

The windshield wipers swept aside sheets of rain. At the top of the hill there was an imposing limestone building that appeared to take up an entire block, the sort of monumental pile you see in the District of Columbia. Across the way, on the side of a low office building, was a prodigious sign reading, ANGELO COLON, U.S. CONGRESS. They went over the crest of the hill. What he saw down the slope on the other side shocked him. It was not merely decrepit and sodden but ruined, as though in some catastrophe. To the right an entire block was nothing but a great hole in the ground with cyclone fencing around it and raggedy catalpa trees sticking up here and there. At first it appeared to be a junkyard. Then he could see it was a parking lot, a vast pit for cars and trucks, apparently unpaved. Over to the left was a new building, modern in the cheap sense of the word, quite dreary-looking in the rain.

Martin stopped and waited for the traffic coming the other way, so he could turn left.

"What's that?" Sherman asked Killian, motioning toward the building with his head.

"The Criminal Courts Building."

"That's where we're going?"

Killian nodded yes and then stared straight ahead. He looked tense. Sherman could feel his heart going to town. It palpitated every now and then.

Instead of pulling up in front of the building, Martin drove down an incline to one side. There, near a mean little metal door, was a line of men and, behind them, a promiscuous huddle of people, thirty or forty of them, most of them white, all hunched over in the rain wrapped in ponchos, thermal jackets, dirty raincoats. A welfare office, thought Sherman. No, a soup kitchen. They looked like the people he had seen lined up for the soup-kitchen lunches at the church, at Madison Avenue and Seventy-first Street. But then their desperate beaten eyes all turned, as if on a command, toward the car—toward *him*—and all at once he was aware of the cameras.

The mob seemed to shake itself, like a huge filthy sprawling dog, and came bounding toward the car. Some of them were running, and he could see television cameras jouncing up and down.

"Jesus Christ," Martin said to Goldberg "Get out and get that door open or we'll never even get him out of the fucking car."

Goldberg jumped out. Immediately the shaggy sodden people were everywhere. Sherman could no longer see the building. He could only see the mob closing in on the car.

Killian said to Sherman, "Now listen. You don't say anything. You don't show any expression whatsoever. You don't cover your face, you don't hang your head. You don't even know they're there. You can't win with these assholes, so don't even try. Let me get out first."

Bango!—somehow Killian swung both feet over Sherman's knees and rolled over him, all in one motion. His elbows hit Sherman's crossed hands and drove the handcuffs into his lower abdomen. Sherman's tweed jacket was bunched up over his hands. There were five or six Styrofoam peanuts on the jacket, but there was nothing he could do about it. The door was open, and Killian was out of the car. Goldberg and Killian had their hands out toward him. Sherman swung his feet out. Killian, Goldberg, and Martin had created a pocket around the door with their bodies. The mob of reporters, photographers, and cameramen was on top of them. People were shouting. At first he thought it was a melee. They were trying to *get* him! Killian reached in under Sherman's coat and pulled him upright by the handcuffs. Someone stuck a camera over Killian's shoulder and into Sherman's face. He ducked. When he looked down, he could see that five, six, seven, Christ knew how many Styrofoam peanuts were stuck to his pants legs. They were all over his coat and his pants. The rain was streaming down his forehead and his cheeks. He started to wipe his face, but then he realized he would have to raise both hands and his jacket to do it, and he didn't want them to see his handcuffs. So the water just rolled down. He could feel it rolling down his shirt collar. Because of the handcuffs, his shoulders were slumped forward. He tried to throw his shoulders back, but all at once Goldberg yanked him forward by one elbow. He was trying to get him through the mob.

"Sherman!"

"Over here, Sherman!"

"Hey, Sherman!"

They were all yelling *Sherman!* His first name! He was *theirs,* too! The looks on their faces! Such pitiless intensity! They jammed their microphones toward him. Someone came barreling into Goldberg, knocking him back against Sherman. A camera appeared over Goldberg's shoulder. Goldberg swung his elbow and forearm forward with tremendous force.   .d there was a *thumpf,* and the camera fell to the ground. Goldberg still ha   ais other arm hooked inside Sherman's elbow. The force of Goldberg's punch pulled Sherman off balance. Sherman stepped to the side, and his foot landed on the leg of a man who was writhing on the ground. He was a little man with dark curly hair. Goldberg stepped on his abdomen for good measure. The man went *Ooooohahhh.*

"Hey, Sherman! Hey, shitface!"

Startled, Sherman looked to the side. It was a photographer. His camera covered half his face. The other side had a piece of white paper stuck on it. *Toilet paper.* Sherman could see the man's lips moving. "That's it, shitface, look right here!"

Martin was a step in front of Sherman, trying to clear a path. "Coming through! Coming through! Get outta the way!"

Killian took Sherman's other elbow and tried to shield him from that side. But now both of his elbows were being pulled forward, and he was conscious of shambling forward, drenched, with his shoulders stooped. He couldn't keep his head up.

"Sherman!" A woman's voice. A microphone was in his face. "Have you ever been arrested before?"

"Hey, Sherman! How you gonna plead?"

"Sherman! Who's the brunette?"

"Sherman! Did you mean to hit him?"

They were sticking the microphones between Killian and Martin and between Martin and Goldberg. Sherman tried to keep his head up, but one of the microphones hit him in the chin. He kept flinching. Every time he looked down, he could see the white Styrofoam peanuts on his jacket and his pants.

"Hey, Sherman! Fuckhead! How you like this cocktail party!"

Such abuse! It was coming from photographers. Anything to try to make him look their way, but—such abuse! such filth! There was nothing too vile to abuse him with! He was now . . . theirs! Their creature! He had been thrown to them! They could do what they wanted! He hated them—but he felt so *ashamed*. The rain was running into his eyes. He couldn't do anything about it. His shirt was soaked. They were no longer moving forward as before. The little metal door was no more than twenty-five feet away. A line of men was jammed up in front of them. They weren't reporters or photographers or cameramen. Some of them were uniformed policemen. Some of them seemed to be Latins, young men mostly. Then there were some white . . . derelicts . . . winos . . . but, no, they wore badges. They were policemen. They were all standing in the rain. They were soaking wet. Martin and Goldberg were now pressing up against the Latinos and the policemen, with Killian and Sherman in close behind them. Goldberg and Killian still had Sherman's elbows. The reporters and cameramen were still coming at him from the sides and from behind.

"Sherman! Hey! Give us a statement!"

"Just one shot!"

"Hey, Sherman! Why'dja hit him?"

". . . Park Avenue! . . ."

". . . intentionally! . . ."

Martin turned and said to Goldberg, "Jesus Christ, they just busted that social club up on 167th. There's twelve fucking spaced-out carambas in line waiting to get into Central Booking!"

"Beautiful," said Goldberg.

"Look," said Killian, "you gotta get him inside a there. Talk to Crowther, if you have to, but get him in there."

Martin shoved his way out of the mob, and in no time he was back.

"No go," said Martin, with an apologetic shake of the head. "He says this one's gotta be by the book. He's gotta wait on line."

"This is very wrong," said Killian.

Martin arched his eyebrows. (I know, I know, but what can I do?)

"Sherman! How about a statement!"

"Sherman! Hey, cuntface!"

"*All right!*" It was Killian, yelling. "You want a statement? Mr. McCoy's not gonna make a statement. I'm his attorney, and I'm gonna make a statement."

More pushing and jostling. The microphones and cameras now converged on Killian.

Sherman stood just behind him. Killian let go of Sherman's elbow, but Goldberg still had the other one.

Somebody yelled, "What's your name?"

"Thomas Killian."

"Howdaya spell it?"

"K-I-L-L-I-A-N. Okay? This is a *circus arrest!* My client has been ready at all times to appear before a grand jury to confront the charges brought against him. Instead, this circus arrest has been staged in complete violation of an agreement between the district attorney and my client."

"What was he doing in the Bronx?"

"That's the statement, and that's the whole statement."

"Are you saying he's innocent?"

"Mr. McCoy denies these charges completely, and this outrageous circus arrest shoulda never been allowed."

The shoulders of Killian's suit were drenched. The rain had gone through Sherman's shirt, and he could feel the water on his skin.

"¡Mira! ¡Mira!" One of the Latins kept saying this word ¡Mira!

Sherman stood there with his shoulders drenched and bowed. He could feel the sopping jacket weighing down on his wrists. Over Killian's shoulder he could see a thicket of microphones. He could hear the cameras whining away. The horrible fire in their faces! He wanted to die. He had never really wanted to die before, although, like many other souls, he had toyed with the feeling. Now he truly wanted God or Death to deliver him. That was how dreadful the feeling was, and that feeling was, in fact, a scalding shame.

"Sherman!"

"Fuckface!"

"¡Mira! ¡Mira!"

And then he was dead, so dead he couldn't even die. He didn't even possess the willpower to fall down. The reporters and cameramen and photographers—such vile abuse!—still here, not three feet away!—they were the maggots and the flies, and he was the dead beast they had found to crawl over and root into.

Killian's so-called statement had distracted them only for a moment. Killian! —who supposedly had his connections and was going to make sure it was not an ordinary arrest! It was *not* an ordinary arrest. It was *death*. Every bit of honor, respect, dignity, that he, a creature named Sherman McCoy, might ever have possessed had been removed, *just like that*, and it was his dead soul that now stood here in the rain, in handcuffs, in the Bronx, outside a mean little metal door, at the end of a line of a dozen other prisoners. The maggots called him *Sherman*. They were right on top of him.

"Hey, Sherman!"

"How you gonna plead, Sherman!"

Sherman looked straight ahead. Killian and the two detectives, Martin and Goldberg, continued to try to shield Sherman from the maggots. A television cameraman closed in, a fat one. The camera came over his shoulder like a grenade launcher.

Goldberg wheeled toward the man and yelled, "Get that fucking thing outta my face!"

The cameraman retreated. How odd! How completely hopeless! Goldberg was now his protector. He was Goldberg's creature, his animal. Goldberg and Martin had brought their animal in, and now they were determined to see that it was delivered.

Killian said to Martin, "This is not right. You guys gotta do something."

Martin shrugged. Then Killian said in all seriousness, "My shoes are getting fucking ruined."

"Mr. McCoy."

Mr. McCoy. Sherman turned his head. A tall pale man with long blond hair was at the forefront of a pack of reporters and cameramen.

"Peter Fallow of *The City Light*," said the man. He had an English accent, an accent so blimpish it was like a parody of an English accent. Was he taunting him? "I've rung you up several times. I'd very much like to get your side of all this."

Sherman turned away . . . Fallow, his obsessive tormentor in *The City Light* . . . No compunctions at all about walking up and introducing himself . . . of course not . . . his quarry was dead . . . He should have hated him, and yet he couldn't, because he loathed himself so much more. He was dead even to himself.

Finally, all the prisoners arrested in the raid on the social club were inside the door, and Sherman, Killian, Martin, and Goldberg were just outside. "Okay, Counselor," Martin said to Killian, 'we'll take it from here."

Sherman looked beseechingly at Killian. (Surely you're coming inside with me!) Killian said, "I'll be upstairs when they bring you up for arraignment. Don't worry about anything. Just remember, don't make any statements, don't talk about the case, not even to anybody in the pens, *especially* not to anybody in the pens."

In the pens! More shouting from beyond the door.

"How long will it take?" asked Sherman.

"I don't know exactly. They got these guys ahead a you." Then he said to Martin, "Look. Do the right thing. See if you can't get him through fingerprinting ahead a that bunch. I mean, f'r Chrissake."

"I'll try," said Martin, "but I already told you. For some reason they want this one step by step."

"Yeah, but you owe us," said Killian. "You owe us a lot—" He stopped. "Just do the right thing."

All at once Goldberg was pulling Sherman in by the elbow. Martin was right behind him. Sherman turned to keep Killian in sight. Killian's hat was so wet it looked black. His necktie and the shoulders of his suit were soaked.

"Don't worry," said Killian. "It's gonna be all right."

The way Killian said it, Sherman knew his own face must be a picture of pure despair. Then the door closed; no more Killian. Sherman was cut off from the world. He had thought he had no fear left, only despair. But he was afraid all over again. His heart began to pound. The door had closed, and he had disappeared into the world of Martin and Goldberg in the Bronx.

He was in a large low room broken up by cubicles, some of which had plate-glass windows, like the interior windows of a broadcast studio. There were no outside windows. A bright electric haze filled the room. People in uniform were moving about, but they were not all wearing the same sort of uniform. Two men with their hands manacled behind their backs stood in front of a high desk. Two young men in rags were standing beside them. One of the prisoners looked over his shoulder and saw Sherman and nudged the other, and he turned around and looked at Sherman, and they both laughed. Off to the side, Sherman could hear the cry he had heard outside, a man screaming, "¡Mira! ¡Mira!" There were some cackles and then the loud flatulent sound of someone having a bowel movement. A deep voice said, "Yaggh. Filthy."

Another one said, "Okay, get 'em outta there. Hose it down."

The two men in rags were bending over behind the two prisoners. Behind the desk was a huge policeman with an absolutely bald head, a big nose, and a prognathous jaw. He appeared to be sixty years old at least. The men in rags were removing the handcuffs from the two prisoners. One of the young men in rags had on a thermal vest over a torn black T-shirt. He wore sneakers and dirty camouflage pants, tight at the ankles. There was a badge, a police shield, on the thermal vest. Then Sherman could see the other had a badge, too. Another old policeman came up to the desk and said, "Hey, Angel, Albany's down."

"Beautiful," said the man with the bald head. "We got this bunch, and the shift just started."

Goldberg looked at Martin and rolled his eyes and smiled and then looked at Sherman. He still held Sherman by the elbow. Sherman looked down. Styrofoam peanuts! The Styrofoam packing peanuts he had picked up in the back seat of Martin's car were all over the place. They were stuck to the wad of his jacket over his wrists. They were all over his tweed pants. His pants were wet, wrinkled, twisted shapelessly around his knees and his thighs, and the Styrofoam peanuts clung to them like vermin.

Goldberg said to Sherman, "You see that room in there?"

Sherman looked over into a room, through a large plate-glass window. There were filing cabinets and piles of paper. A big beige-and-gray apparatus took up the center of the room. Two policemen were staring at it.

"That's the Fax machine that sends the fingerprints to Albany," said Goldberg. He said it in a pleasant sort of singsong, the way you would say something to a child who is frightened and confused. The very tone terrified Sherman. "About ten years ago," said Goldberg, "some bright fellow got the idea—was it ten years ago, Marty?"

"I don't know," said Martin. "All I know is, it was a stupid fucking idea."

"Anyway, somebody got the idea a putting all the fingerprints, for the whole fucking State a New York, in this one office in Albany . . . see . . . and then every one a the Central Bookings, they're wired into Albany, and you send the prints to Albany on the computer, and you get back your report, and the suspect goes upstairs and gets arraigned . . . see . . . Only it's a freakin' logjam in Albany, especially when the machine goes down, like right now."

Sherman couldn't take in a thing Goldberg was saying, except that something had gone wrong and Goldberg thought he was going out of his way to be nice and explain it.

"Yeah," Martin said to Sherman, "be thankful it's 8:30 in the morning and not 4:30 in the fucking afternoon. If this was the fucking afternoon, you'd probably have to spend the night at the Bronx House of Detention or even Rikers."

"Rikers Island?" asked Sherman. He was hoarse. He barely got the words out.

"Yeah," said Martin, "when Albany goes down in the afternoon, forgedaboudit. You can't spend the night in this place, so they take you over to Rikers. I'm telling you, you're very fortunate."

He was telling him he was very fortunate. Sherman was supposed to like them now! Inside here, they were his only friends! Sherman felt intensely frightened.

Somebody yelled out, "Who *died* in here, f'r Chrissake!"

The smell reached the desk.

"Now *that's* disgusting," said the bald man called Angel. He looked around. "Hose it down!"

Sherman followed his eyes. Off to the side, down a corridor, he could make out two cells. White tiles and bars; they seemed to be constructed of white brick tiles, like a public bathroom. Two policemen stood in front of one of them.

One of them yelled through the bars, "Whatsa matter with you!"

Sherman could feel the pressure of Goldberg's huge hand on his elbow, steering him forward. He was in front of the desk, staring up at the Angel. Martin had a sheaf of papers in his hand.

The Angel said, "Name?"

Sherman tried to speak but couldn't. His mouth was utterly dry. His tongue seemed stuck to the roof of his mouth.

"Name?"

"Sherman McCoy." It was barely a whisper.

"Address?"

"816 Park Avenue. New York." He added "New York" in the interest of being modest and obedient. He didn't want to act as if he just assumed people here in the Bronx knew where Park Avenue was.

"Park Avenue, New York. Your age?"

"Thirty-eight."

"Ever been arrested before?"

"No."

"Hey, Angel," Martin said. "Mr. McCoy here's been very cooperative . . . and uh . . . whyn't you let him sit out here somewheres insteada putting him in there with that buncha bats? The fucking so-called press out there, they gave him a hard enough time."

A wave of profound, sentimental gratitude washed over Sherman. Even as he felt it, he knew it was irrational, but he felt it nonetheless.

The Angel puffed up his cheeks and stared off, as if ruminating. Then he said, "Can't do it, Marty." He closed his eyes and lifted his huge chin upward, as if to say, "The people upstairs."

"Whadda they worrying about? The fucking TV viruses got him standing out there in the rain for a fucking half an hour. Look at him. Looks like he crawled in here through a pipe."

Goldberg chuckled. Then, so as not to offend Sherman, he said to him, "You're not looking your best. You *know* that."

His only friends! Sherman wanted to cry, and all the more so because this horrible, pathetic feeling was genuine.

"Can't do it," said the Angel. "Gotta do the whole routine." He closed his eyes and lifted his chin again. "You can take the cuffs off."

Martin looked at Sherman and twisted his mouth to one side. (Well, friend, we tried.) Goldberg unlocked the handcuffs and took them off Sherman's wrists. There were white rings on his wrists where the metal had been. The veins on top of his hands were engorged with blood. *My blood pressure has gone through the roof.* There were Styrofoam peanuts all over his pants. Martin handed him his soggy jacket. Styrofoam peanuts all over the soggy jacket, too.

"Empty your pockets and hand me the contents," said the Angel.

On the advice of Killian, Sherman hadn't brought much with him. Four $5 bills, about a dollar in change, a key to the apartment, a handkerchief, a ballpoint pen, his driver's license—for some reason he thought he should have identification. As he handed over each item, the Angel described it aloud—"twenty dollars in bills," "one silver ballpoint pen"—and handed it to someone Sherman couldn't see.

Sherman said, "Can I . . . keep the handkerchief?"

"Let me see it."

Sherman held it up. His hand was shaking terribly.

"Yeah, you can keep it. But you gotta give me the watch."

"It's only—it's just a cheap watch," said Sherman. He held up his hand. The watch had a plastic case and a nylon band. "I don't care what happens to it."

"No can do."

Sherman undid the band and surrendered the little watch. A new spasm of panic went through him.

"Please," said Sherman. As soon as the word left his mouth, he knew he shouldn't have said it. He was begging. "How can I figure—can't I keep the watch?"

"You got an appointment or something?" The Angel attempted a smile to show he didn't mean it as much more than a pleasantry. But he didn't return the watch. Then he said, "Okay, and I need your belt and your shoestrings."

Sherman stared at him. He realized his mouth was open. He looked at Martin. Martin was looking at the Angel. Now Martin closed his eyes and lifted his chin, the way the Angel had, and said, "Oh boy." (They really *do* have it in for him.)

Sherman unbuckled the belt and pulled it out of the loops. As soon as he did, the pants fell down around his hips. He hadn't worn the tweed suit in a long time, and the waist was much too big. He pulled the pants up and stuffed his shirt back inside, and they fell down again. He had to hold them up in front. He squatted down to take off the shoelaces. Now he was an abject creature crouched at the feet of Martin and Goldberg. His face was close to the Styrofoam peanuts on his pants. He could see the crinkles on them. Some sort of horrible beetles or parasites! The heat of his body and the woolly funk of the pants gave off an unpleasant odor. He was aware of the humid smell of his armpits under the clammy shirt. A total mess. No two ways about it. He had the feeling that one of them, Martin, Goldberg, the Angel, would just step on him, and, *pop*, that would be the end of that. He pulled out the shoestrings and stood up. Standing up from the crouch made him lightheaded. For an instant he thought he might faint. His pants were falling down again. He pulled them up with one hand and handed the Angel the shoestrings with the other. They were like two little dried dead things.

The voice behind the desk said, "Two brown shoestrings."

"Okay, Angel," said Martin, "all yours."

"Right," said the Angel.

"Well, good luck, Sherman," said Goldberg, smiling in a kindly fashion.

"Thanks," said Sherman. It was horrible. He actually appreciated it.

He heard a cell door slide open. Down the little corridor stood three police officers herding a group of Latins out of one cell and into the one next to it. Sherman recognized several of the men who had been in line ahead of him outside.

"All right, knock it off, and get in there."

"*¡Mira! ¡Mira!*"

One man remained in the corridor. A policeman had him by the arm. He was tall, with a long neck, and his head lolled about. He seemed very drunk. He was muttering to himself. Then he threw his eyes to the heavens and screamed, "*¡Mira!*" He was holding up his pants the same way Sherman was.

"Hey, Angel, whadda I do with this one? It's all over his *pants!*" The policeman said "*pants*" with great disgust.

"Well, shit," said Angel. "Take the pants off him and *bury* 'em, and then wash him off, too, and give him some a those green fatigues."

"I don't even wanna touch him, Sarge. You got any a those things they take the cans off the shelf in the supermarket with?"

"Yeah, I got some," said the Angel, "and I'm gonna take your can off."

The policeman jerked the tall man back toward the first cell. The tall man's legs were like a marionette's.

The Angel said, "Whaddaya got all over your pants?"

Sherman looked down. "I don't know," he said. "They were on the back seat of the car."

"Whose car?"

"Detective Martin's car."

The Angel shook his head as if now he had seen everything. "Okay, Tanooch, take him over to Gabsie."

A young white officer took Sherman by the elbow. Sherman's hand was holding up his pants, and so the elbow came up like a bird's wing. His pants were damp even in the waistband. He carried his wet jacket over his other arm. He started walking. His right foot came out of his shoe, because the strings were gone. He stopped, but the policeman kept walking, jerking his elbow forward in an arc. Sherman put his foot back in the shoe, and the policeman motioned toward the little corridor. Sherman started shuffling, so that his feet wouldn't come out of the shoes. The shoes made a squishing sound because they were so wet.

Sherman was led toward the cubicle with the big windows. Now, just across the corridor, he could see inside the two cells. In one there appeared to be a dozen figures, a dozen hulks of gray and black, up against the walls. The door to the other was open. There was only one person inside, the tall man, slumped on a ledge. There was a brown mess on the floor. The odor of excrement was overpowering.

The policeman steered Sherman into the cubicle with the windows. Inside was a huge freckled policeman with a wide face and blond wavy hair, who looked him up and down. The policeman called Tanooch said, "McCoy," and handed the big one a sheet of paper. The room seemed full of metal stands. One looked like the sort of metal-detection gate you see at airports. There was a camera on a tripod. There was something that looked like a music stand except that it had nothing at the top big enough to hold a page of music.

"Okay, McCoy," said the big policeman, "step through that gate there."

Squish, squish, squish . . . holding his pants up with one hand and holding his wet jacket in the other, Sherman shuffled through the gate. A loud whining beep came from the machine.

"Whoa, whoa," said the policeman. "Okay, give me your coat."

Sherman handed him the jacket. The man went through the pockets and then began kneading the jacket from top to bottom. He threw the jacket over the edge of a table.

"Okay, spread your feet and put your arms straight out to the side, like this."

The policeman put his arms out as if he were doing a swan dive. Sherman stared at the policeman's right hand. He was wearing a translucent rubber surgical glove. It came halfway up his forearm!

Sherman spread his feet. When he spread his arms, his pants fell way down. The man approached him and began patting down his arms, his chest, his ribs, his back and then his hips and his legs. The hand with the rubber glove created an unpleasant dry friction. A new wave of panic . . . He stared at the glove in terror. The man looked at him and grunted, apparently in amusement, and then held up his right hand. The hand and the wrist were enormous. The hideous rubber glove was right in front of Sherman's face.

"Don't worry about the glove," he said. "The thing is, I gotta do your prints, and I gotta pick your fingers up one by one and put 'em on the pad . . . You understand? . . ." His tone was conversational, neighborly, as if there were just the two of them, out by the alley, and he was explaining how the engine in his new Mazda worked. "I do this all day, and I get the ink on my hands, and my skin's rough to begin with, and sometimes I don't get the ink all off, and I go home, and my wife has the whole living room done in white, and I put my hand down on the sofa or someplace, and I get up and you can see three or four fingers on the sofa, and my wife throws a fit." Sherman stared at him. He didn't know what to say. This huge fierce-looking man wanted to be liked. It was all so very odd. Perhaps they all wanted to be liked.

"Okay, walk on back through the gate."

Sherman shuffled back through the gate, and the alarm went off again.

"Shit," said the man. "Try it again."

The alarm went off a third time.

"Beats the hell outta me," said the man. "Wait a minute. Come here. Open your mouth."

Sherman opened his mouth.

"Keep it open . . . Wait a minute, turn it this way. Can't get no light." He wanted to move Sherman's head to a strange angle. Sherman could smell the rubber of the glove. "Sonofabitch. You got a goddamn silver mine in there. I tell you what. Bend over at the waist like this. Try to get way down."

Sherman bent over, holding up his pants with one hand. *Surely he wouldn't—*

"Now back through the gate, but real slow."

Sherman started shuffling backward, bent over at an almost 90-degree angle.

"Okay, real slow, real slow, real slow—that's it . . . whoa!"

Sherman was now mostly through the gate. Only his shoulders and his head remained on the other side.

"Okay, back up . . . a little farther, a little farther, little farther, little farther . . ."

The alarm went off again.

"Whoa! Whoa! Right there! Stay right there!" The alarm remained on.

"Sonofabitch!" said the big man. He began pacing around and sighing. He slapped his legs with his hands. "I had one a these last year. Okay, you can stand up."

Sherman stood up. He looked at the big man, bewildered. The man stuck his head out the door and yelled, "Hey, Tanooch! Come here! Look at this!"

Across the little corridor, a policeman was in the open cell with a hose, washing down the floor. The rush of the water echoed off the tile.

"Hey, Tanooch!"

The policeman who had brought Sherman into the room came from down the corridor.

"Look at this, Tanooch." Then he said to Sherman, "Okay, bend over and do that again. Back through the gate, real slow."

Sherman bent over and did as he was told.

"Okay, whoa, whoa, whoa . . . Now you see that, Tanooch? So far, nothing. Okay, now back up a little more, little more, little more . . ." The alarm went off. The big man was beside himself again. He paced about and sighed and put his hands together. "Dja see that, Tanooch! It's his *head!* Swear to Christ! . . . It's the fellow's head! . . . Okay, stand up. Open your mouth . . . That's it. No, turn it this way." He moved Sherman's head again, to get more light. "Look in there! You wanna see some metal?"

The one called Tanooch said not a word to Sherman. He looked in his mouth, like someone inspecting a crawl space in a cellar.

"Jesus Christ," said Tanooch. "You're right. Set a teeth look like a change maker." Then he said to Sherman, as if noticing him for the first time, "They ever let you on a airplane?"

The big one cracked up over this. "You're not the only one," he said. "I had one like you last year. Drove me outta my mind. I couldn't figure out . . . *what da fuck* . . . you know?" Suddenly it was the casual fellow-out-back-on-Saturday mode of conversation again. "This machine is very sensitive, but you do have a whole head fulla metal, I gotta tell you that."

Sherman was mortified, completely humiliated. But what could he do? Maybe these two, if he played along with them, could keep him out of . . . *the pens!* With *those people!* Sherman just stood there, holding up his pants.

"What's that stuff all over your pants?" asked Tanooch.

"Styrofoam," said Sherman.

"*Styrofoam,*" said Tanooch, nodding his head, but in an uncomprehending fashion. He left the room.

Then the big man stood Sherman in front of a metal stand and took two pictures of him, one from the front and one from the side. It dawned on Sherman that this was what was known as a mug shot. This great huge bear had just taken his mug shot, while Sherman stood there holding up his pants. He led him over to a counter and took Sherman's fingers one by one and pressed them into an ink pad and then rolled them onto a printed form. It was a surprisingly rough operation. He gripped each of Sherman's fingers as if he were picking up a knife or a hammer and plunged it into the ink pad. Then he apologized.

"You have to do all the work yourself," he said to Sherman. "You can't expect nobody comes in here to lift a goddamned finger for you."

From across the corridor came the furious sound of someone retching. Three of the Latins were at the bars of the pen.

"Ayyyyyy!" yelled one of them. "The man puking! He puking plenty!"

Tanooch was the first policeman there.

"Oh, f'r Chrissake. Oh, beautiful. Hey, Angel! This guy's a one-man garbage barge. Whaddaya wanna do?"

"He the same one?" said Angel.

Then the smell of vomit began to spread.

"Ayyyyyyyy, whaddaya whaddaya," said Angel. "Hose it down and leave 'im in there."

They opened the bars, and two policemen stood by outside while a third went inside with the hose. The prisoners hopped this way and that, to keep from getting wet.

"Hey, Sarge," said the policeman. "Guy puked all over his pants."

"The fatigues?"

"Yeah."

"Fuck it. Hose 'em down. This ain't a laundry."

Sherman could see the tall man sitting on the ledge with his head down. His knees were covered in vomit, and his elbows were on his knees.

The big man was watching all this through the window of the fingerprint room. He was shaking his head. Sherman went up to him.

"Look, Officer, isn't there some other place I can wait? I can't go in there. I'm —I just can't do it."

The big man stuck his head out of the fingerprint room and yelled, "Hey, Angel, whaddaya wanna do with my man here, McCoy?"

Angel looked over from his desk and stared at Sherman and rubbed his hand over his bald head.

"Welllll . . ." Then he motioned with his hand toward the cell. "That's it."

Tanooch came in and took Sherman by the arm again. Someone opened up the bars. Tanooch steered Sherman inside, and he went shuffling onto the tile floor, holding up his pants. The bars shut behind him. Sherman stared at the Latins, who were sitting on the ledge. They stared back, all but the tall one, who still had his head down, rolling his elbows in the vomit on his knees.

The entire floor slanted in toward the drain in the middle. It was still wet. Sherman could feel the slant now that he was standing on it. A few driblets of water were still rolling down the drain. That was it. It was a drainpipe, where mankind sought its own level, and the meat spigot was on.

He heard the bars slide shut behind him, and he stood there in the cell holding his pants up with his right hand. He cradled his jacket with his left arm. He didn't know what to do or even where to look and so he picked out an empty space on the wall and tried to take a look at . . . *them* . . . with peripheral vision. Their clothes were a blur of gray and black and brown, except for their sneakers, which created a pattern of stripes and swashes along the floor. He knew they were watching him. He glanced toward the bars. Not a single policeman! Would they even move a muscle if anything . . .

The Latinos had taken every seat on the ledge. He chose a spot about four feet from the end of the ledge and leaned his back up against the wall. The wall hurt his spine. He lifted his right foot, and his shoe fell off. He slipped his foot back into it as casually as he could. Looking down at his foot on the bright tile made him feel as if he was going to keel over with vertigo. The Styrofoam peanuts! They were still all over his pants legs.

He was seized with the terrible fear that they would take him to be a lunatic, the sort of hopeless case they could slaughter at their leisure. He was aware of the smell of vomit . . . vomit and cigarette smoke . . . He lowered his head, as if he were dozing, and cut his eyes toward them. They were staring at him! They were staring at him and smoking their cigarettes. The tall one, the one who had kept saying, "*¡Mira! ¡Mira!*" still sat on the ledge with his head down and his elbows on his knees, which were covered in vomit.

One of the Latinos was rising up from the ledge and walking toward him! He could see him out of the corner of his eye. Now it was starting! They weren't even waiting!

The man was settling up against the wall, right next to him, leaning back the same way Sherman was. He had thin curly hair, a mustache that curved down around his lips, a slightly yellowish complexion, narrow shoulders, a little potbelly, and a crazy look in his eyes. He must have been about thirty-five. He smiled, and that made him look crazier still.

"Hey, man, I see you outside."

See me outside!

"With the TV, man. Why you here?"

"Reckless endangerment," said Sherman. He felt as if he were croaking out his last words on this earth.

"Reckless endangerment?"

"That's . . . hitting somebody with your car."

"With you car? You hit somebody with you car, and the TV come here?"

Sherman shrugged. He didn't want to say anything more, but his fear of appearing aloof got the better of him.

"What are you here for?"

"Oh, man, 220, 265, 225." The fellow threw his hand out, as if to take in the entire world. "Drugs, handguns, gambling paraphernalia—ayyyyyy, every piece a bullshit, you know?"

The man seemed to take a certain pride in this calamity.

"You hit somebody with you car?" he asked once more. He apparently found this trivial and unmanly. Sherman raised his eyebrows and nodded wearily.

The man returned to the seating ledge, and Sherman could see him talking to three or four of his comrades, who looked at Sherman once more and then looked away, as if bored by the news. Sherman had the feeling that he had let them down. Very odd! And yet that was what he felt.

Sherman's fear was rapidly supplanted by tedium. The minutes crawled by. His left hip joint began to hurt. He shifted his weight to the right, and his back hurt. Then his right hip joint hurt. The floor was tile. The walls were tile. He rolled up his jacket to create a cushion. He put it on the floor, next to the wall, and sat down and leaned back. The jacket was damp, and so were his pants. His bladder was beginning to fill, and he could feel little knives of gas in his bowels.

The little man who had come over to talk to him, the little man who knew the numbers, walked to the bars. He had a cigarette in his mouth. He took the cigarette out, and he yelled, "Ayyyyyy! I need a light!" No response from the policeman beyond. "Ayyyyyy, I need a light!"

Finally, the one called Tanooch came up. "What's your problem?"

"Ayyy, I need a light." He held up his cigarette.

Tanooch dug a book of matches out of his pocket and lit one and held it about four feet away from the bars. The little man waited, then put the cigarette between his lips and pressed his face against the bars so that the cigarette protruded outside. Tanooch was motionless, holding the burning match. The match went out.

"Ayyyyyy!" said the little man.

Tanooch shrugged and let the match fall to the floor.

"Ayyyyyy!" The little man turned around toward his comrades and held the cigarette up in the air. (See what he did?) One of the men sitting on the ledge laughed. The little man made a face at this betrayal of sympathies. Then he looked at Sherman. Sherman didn't know whether to commiserate or look the other way. He ended up just staring. The man walked over and squatted down beside him. The unlit cigarette was hanging out of his mouth.

"Dja see that?" he asked.

"Yes," said Sherman.

"You wanna light, they suppose a give you a light. Son a mabitch. Ayyy . . . you got cigarettes?"

"No, they took everything away from me. Even my shoestrings."

"No shit?" He looked at Sherman's shoes. He himself still had on shoelaces, Sherman noticed.

Sherman could hear a woman's voice. She was angry about something. She appeared in the little corridor outside the cell. Tanooch was leading her. She was a tall thin woman with curly brown hair and dark tan skin, wearing black pants and an odd-looking jacket with very big shoulders. Tanooch was escorting her toward the fingerprint room. All at once she wheeled about and said to someone Sherman couldn't see, "You big bag a . . ." She didn't complete the phrase. "Least I don't sit in 'is sewer here all day long, way you do! Think about it, fat boy!"

Much derisive laughter from the policemen in the background.

"Watch it or he'll flush you down, Mabel."

Tanooch prodded her on. "C'mon, Mabel."

She turned on Tanooch. "You talk to me, you call me by my right name! You don't call me Mabel!"

Tanooch said, "I'll call you worse'n that in a minute," and he kept pushing her on toward the fingerprint room.

"Two-twenty–thirty-one," said the little man. "Selling drugs."

"How do you know?" asked Sherman.

The little man just opened his eyes wide and put a knowing look on his face. (Some things go without saying.) Then he shook his head and said, "Focking bus come in."

"Bus?"

It seemed that ordinarily, when people were arrested, they were taken first to a precinct station house and locked up. Periodically a police van made the rounds of the precincts and transported the prisoners to Central Booking for fingerprinting and arraignment. So now a new lot had arrived. They would all end up in this pen, except for the women, who were taken to another pen, down the corridor and around a bend. And nothing was moving, because "Albany was down."

Three more women went by. They were younger than the first one.

"Two-thirty," said the little man. "Prostitutes."

The little man who knew the numbers was right. The bus had come in. The procession began, from the Angel's desk to the fingerprinting room to the cell. Sherman's pang of fear began to heat up all over again. One by one, three tall black youths with shaved heads, windbreakers, and big white sneakers came into the cell. All of the new arrivals were black or Latin. Most were young. Several appeared to be drunk. The little man who knew the numbers got up and went back to join his comrades and secure his place on the ledge. Sherman was determined not to move. He wanted to be invisible. Somehow . . . so long as he didn't move a muscle . . . they wouldn't see him.

Sherman stared at the floor and tried not to think about his aching bowels and bladder. One of the black lines between the tiles on the floor began to move. A cockroach! Then he saw another . . . and a third. Fascinating!—and horrible. Sherman glanced about to see if anyone else noticed. No one seemed to—but he caught the eye of one of the three black youths. All three were staring at him!

Such thin hard malevolent faces! His heart immediately kicked into tachycardia. He could see his foot jerk with the force of his heartbeat pulse. He stared at the cockroaches to try to cool himself down. A cockroach had made its way over to the drunken Latino, who had slumped to the floor. The cockroach began ascending the heel of his shoe. It began walking up his leg. It disappeared up his pant leg. Then it reappeared. It climbed the cuff of his pants. It began climbing toward his knee. When it reached the knee, it settled in amid the cakes of vomit.

Sherman looked up. One of the black youths was heading toward him. He had a little smile on his face. He seemed tremendously tall. His eyes were set close together. He wore black pants with stovepipe legs and big white sneakers that closed in front with Velcro straps rather than shoelaces. He stooped down in front of Sherman. His face had no expression at all. All the more terrifying! He looked right into Sherman's face.

"Hey, man, you got a cigarette?"

Sherman said, "No." But he didn't want him to think he was acting tough or even uncommunicative, and so he added, "Sorry. They took everything away from me."

As soon as he said it, he knew it was a mistake. It was an apology, a signal that he was weak.

"That's okay, man." The youth sounded halfway friendly. "What you in for?"

Sherman hesitated. "Manslaughter," he said. "Reckless endangerment" just wasn't enough.

"Yeah. That's *bad*," said the youth in an approximation of a concerned voice. "What happened?"

"Nothing," said Sherman. "I don't know what they're talking about. What are you here for?"

"A 160-15," said the youth. Then he added, "Armed robbery."

The youth screwed up his lips. Sherman couldn't tell whether that was supposed to say, "Armed robbery is nothing special," or, "It's a bullshit charge."

The youth smiled at Sherman, still looking directly into his face. "Okay, Mr. Manslaughter," he said, and he stood up and turned about and walked back to the other side of the cell.

Mr. Manslaughter! Immediately he knew he could treat me cavalierly! What could they do? Surely they couldn't . . . There had been an incident—where?—in which some of the prisoners in a cell blocked the view through the bars with their bodies while the others . . . But would any of the others in here do such a thing for these three—would the Latinos?

Sherman's mouth was dry, absolutely parched. The urge to urinate was acute. His heart beat nervously, although not as rapidly as before. At that moment, the bars slid open. More policemen. One of them carried two cardboard trays, the sort delicatessens use. He set them down on the floor of the cell. On one was a mound of sandwiches; on the other, rows of plastic cups.

He stood up and said, "Okay, chow time. Share and share alike, and I don't wanna hear any bullshit."

There was no rush toward the food. All the same, Sherman was glad he was not too far away from the two trays. He tucked his filthy jacket under his left arm and shuffled over and picked up a sandwich wrapped in Saran Wrap and a plastic cup containing a clear pinkish liquid. Then he sat down on his coat again and tried the drink. It had a weak sugary taste. He put the plastic cup on the floor beside him and pulled the wrap off the sandwich. He pulled the two pieces of bread apart and peeked inside. There was a slice of lunch meat. It was a sickly yellowish color. In the fluorescent light of the cell it looked almost chartreuse. It had a smooth clammy surface. He raised the sandwich toward his face and sniffed. A dead chemical smell came from the meat. He separated the two pieces of bread and pulled out the piece of meat and wrapped it up in the Saran Wrap and put the crumpled mess on the floor. He would eat the bread by itself. But the bread gave off such an unpleasant smell from the meat he couldn't stand it. Laboriously, he unfolded the Saran Wrap and rolled up the bread into balls and wrapped up the whole mess, the meat and the bread. He was aware of someone standing in front of him. White sneakers with Velcro straps.

He looked up. The black youth was looking down at him with a curious little smile. He sank down on his haunches, until his head was only slightly above Sherman's.

"Hey, man," he said. "I'm kinda thirsty. Gimme your drink."

Gimme your drink! Sherman nodded toward the cardboard trays.

"Ain't none left, man. Gimme yours."

Sherman ransacked his mind for something to say. He shook his head.

"You heard the man. Share and share alike. Thought me and you's buddies."

Such a contemptuous tone of mock disappointment! Sherman knew it was time to draw a line, stop this . . . this . . . Quicker than Sherman's eye could follow it, the youth's arm shot out and seized the plastic cup on the floor beside Sherman. He stood up and threw back his head and ostentatiously drained the drink and held the cup over Sherman and said:

"I asked you politely . . . You understand? . . . In here, you gotta use your head and make *friends.*"

Then he opened his hand, let the cup fall down onto Sherman's lap, and walked away. Sherman was aware the entire room was watching. *I should—I should*—but he was paralyzed with fear and confusion. Across the way, a Latino was pulling the meat out of his sandwich and throwing it on the floor. There were slices of meat everywhere. Here and there were balled-up wads of Saran Wrap and entire sandwiches, unwrapped and thrown on the floor. The Latino had begun to eat the bread by itself—and his eyes were on Sherman. They were looking at him . . . in this human pen . . . yellow lunch meat, bread, Saran Wrap, plastic cups . . . cockroaches! Here . . . over there . . . He looked toward the drunken Latino. He was still collapsed on the floor. There were three cockroaches rooting about in the folds of his left pant leg at the knee. All at once Sherman saw something moving at the mouth of the man's pant pocket. Another roach—no, much too big . . . gray . . . a mouse! . . . a mouse crawling out of the man's pocket . . . The mouse clung to the cloth for a moment, then scampered down to the tile floor and stopped again. Then it darted forward and reached a piece of yellow lunch meat. It stopped again, as if sizing up this bonanza . . .

"¡Mira!" One of the Latinos had seen the mouse.

A foot came flying out from the ledge. The mouse went skidding across the tile floor like a hockey puck. Another leg flew out. The mouse went flying back toward the ledge . . . A laugh, a cackle . . . "¡Mira!" . . . another foot . . . The mouse went skidding on its back, over a wad of lunch meat, which spun it upright again . . . Laughter, shouts . . . "¡Mira! ¡Mira!" . . . another kick . . . The mouse came spinning toward Sherman, on its back. It was just

lying there, two or three inches from his foot, dazed, its legs jerking. Then it
struggled to its feet, barely moving. The little rodent was out of it, finished. Not
even fear was enough to get it moving. It lurched forward a couple of steps . . .
More laughter . . . *Should I kick it as a sign of my solidarity with my cellmates?*
. . . That was what he wondered . . . Without thinking, he stood up. He
reached down and picked up the mouse. He held it in his right hand and walked
toward the bars. The cell grew silent. The mouse twitched feebly in his palm. He
had almost reached the bars . . . *Sonofabitch!* . . . A tremendous pain in his
index finger . . . The mouse had bitten him! . . . Sherman jumped and jerked
his hand up. The mouse held on to his finger with its jaws. Sherman flailed his
finger up and down as if he were shaking down a thermometer. The little beast
wouldn't let go! . . . "¡Mira! ¡Mira!" . . . cackles, laughter . . . It was a terrific show! They were enjoying it immensely! Sherman banged the meaty side of
his hand down on one of the crosspieces of the bars. The mouse went flying off
. . . right in front of Tanooch, who had a sheaf of papers in his hand and was
approaching the cell. Tanooch jumped back.

"Holy shit!" he said. Then he glowered at Sherman. "You gone off the plat-
ter?"

The mouse was lying on the floor. Tanooch stamped on it with the heel of his
shoe. The animal lay flattened on the floor with its mouth open.

Sherman's hand hurt terribly, from where he had hit the bar. He cradled it
with his other hand. *I've broken it!* He could see the teeth marks of the mouse on
his index finger and a single tiny blob of blood. With his left hand, he reached
around behind his back and pulled the handkerchief out of his right hip pocket. It
required a tremendous contortion. They were all watching. Oh, yes . . . all
watching. He swabbed the blood and wrapped the handkerchief around his hand.
He heard Tanooch say to another policeman:

"The guy from Park Avenue. He threw a *mouse.*"

Sherman shuffled back toward where his jacket was balled up on the floor. He
sat back down on the coat. His hand didn't hurt nearly so much any longer.
Maybe I haven't broken it. But my finger may be poisoned from the bite! He pulled the
handkerchief back far enough to look at the finger. It didn't look so bad. The blob
of blood was gone.

The black youth was coming toward him again! Sherman looked up at him
and then looked away. The fellow sat on his haunches in front of him, as before.

"Hey, man," he said, "you know something? I'm cold."

Sherman tried to ignore him. He turned his head. He was conscious of having
a petulant look on his face. *The wrong expression! Weak!*

"Yo! Look at me when I'm talking to you!"

Sherman turned his head toward him. *Pure malevolence!*

"I ask you for a drink, and you wasn't nice, but I'm going to give you a chance
to make up for that . . . see . . . I'm feeling cold, man. I want your coat.
Gimme your coat."

My coat! My clothes!

Sherman's mind raced. He couldn't speak. He shook his head no.

"What'sa matter with you, man? You oughta try and be friendly, Mr. Manslaughter. My buddy, he say he know you. He saw you on TV. You wasted some
ace, and you live on Park Avenue. That's nice, man. But this ain't Park Avenue.
You understand? You best be making some friends, you understand? You been

slicking me some kinda bad, bad, bad, but I'm gonna give you a chance to make up for it. Now gimme the fucking coat."

Sherman stopped thinking. His brain was on fire! He put his hands flat on the floor and lifted his hips and then rocked forward until he was on one knee. Then he jumped up, clutching the jacket in his right hand. He did it so suddenly the black youth was startled.

"Shut up!" he heard himself saying. "You and I got nothing to talk about!"

The black youth stared at him blankly. Then he smiled. "Shut up?" he said. "Shut up!" He grinned and made a snorting noise. "Shut me up."

"Hey! You germs! Knock it off!" It was Tanooch at the bars. He was looking at the two of them. The black youth gave Sherman a big smile and stuck his tongue in his cheek. (Enjoy yourself! You're gonna own your mortal hide for about sixty seconds longer!) He walked back to the ledge and sat down, staring at Sherman the whole time.

Tanooch read from a sheet of paper: "Solinas! Gutiérrez! McCoy!"

McCoy! Sherman hurriedly put on the jacket, lest his nemesis rush forward and snatch it before he could leave the cell. The jacket was wet, greasy, fetid, completely shapeless. His pants fell down around his hips as he put it on. There were Styrofoam peanuts all over the coat and . . . moving! . . . two cockroaches had crawled into the folds. Frantically he swept them off onto the floor. He was still breathing rapidly and loudly.

As Sherman filed out of the cell behind the Latinos, Tanooch said to him in a low voice, "See? We didn't forget you. Your name's actually about six more down the list."

"Thank you," said Sherman. "I appreciate that."

Tanooch shrugged. "I'd rather walk you outta there than sweep you outta there."

The main room was now full of policemen and prisoners. At the desk, the Angel's desk, Sherman was turned over to a Department of Corrections officer, who manacled his hands behind his back and put him in a line with the Latinos. His pants now fell hopelessly around his hips. There was no way he could pull them up. He kept looking over his shoulder, fearful that the black youth might be right behind him. He was the last person in the little line. The Corrections officers led them up a narrow stairway. At the top of the stairs was another windowless room. More Corrections officers sat at some beat-up metal desks. Beyond the desks—more cells! They were smaller, grayer, dingier than the white-tile cells downstairs. Real jail cells, they were. On the first was a peeling sign that said, MEN ONLY—21 AND OVER—8 TO 10 CAP. The 21 AND OVER had been crossed out with some sort of marker. The entire line of prisoners was led into the cell. The handcuffs were left on. Sherman kept his eyes pinned on the doorway they had first entered. If the black youth came in and was put into this small cell with him —he—he—his fear made him crazy. He was sweating profusely. He had lost all track of time. He hung his head down to try to improve his circulation.

Presently they were led out of the cell and toward a door made of steel bars. On the other side of the door Sherman could see a line of prisoners sitting on the floor of a corridor. The corridor was scarcely thirty-six inches wide. One of the prisoners was a young white man with an enormous cast on his right leg. He wore shorts, so that the entire cast was visible. He was sitting on the floor. A pair of crutches leaned against the wall beside him. At the far end of the corridor was a door. An officer stood beside it. He had a huge revolver on his hip. It occurred to Sherman that this was the first gun he had seen since he entered this place. As each prisoner left the detention area and went through the gate, his handcuffs were removed. Sherman slumped against the wall, like all the rest. The corridor was airless. There were no windows. It was filled with a fluorescent haze and the heat and stench of too many bodies. The meat spigot! The chute to the abattoir! Going . . . where?

The door at the end of the corridor opened, and a voice from the other side said, "Lantier." The Corrections officer inside the corridor said, "Okay, Lantier." The young man with the crutches struggled to his feet. The Latino next to him gave him a hand. He bounced on his good foot until he could get the crutches settled under his armpits. *What on earth could he have done in that condition?* The policeman opened the door for him, and Sherman could hear a voice on the other side calling out some numbers and then, "Herbert Lantier? . . . counsel representing Herbert Lantier?"

The courtroom! At the end of the chute was the courtroom!

By the time Sherman's turn came, he felt dazed, groggy, feverish. The voice from the other side said, "Sherman McCoy." The policeman inside said, "Mc-Coy." Sherman shuffled through the door, holding his pants up, sliding his feet so as to keep his shoes on. He was aware of a bright modern room and a great many people going this way and that. The judge's bench, the desks, the seats, were all made of a cheap-looking blond wood. To one side people moved in waves around the judge's elevated blond-wood perch, and on the other side they moved in waves in what appeared to be a spectators' section. So many people . . . such a bright light . . . such confusion . . . such a commotion . . . Between the two sections was a fence, also of blond wood. And at the fence stood Killian . . . He was there! He looked very fresh and dapper in his fancy clothes. He was smiling. It was the reassuring smile you save for invalids. As Sherman shuffled toward him, he became acutely aware of what he himself must look like . . . the filthy sodden jacket and pants . . . the Styrofoam peanuts . . . the wrinkled shirt, the wet shoes with no strings . . . He could smell his own funk of filth, despair, and terror.

Someone was reading out some number, and then he heard his name, and then he heard Killian saying his own name, and the judge said, "How do you plead?" Killian said to Sherman, *sotto voce,* "Say, 'Not guilty.' " Sherman croaked out the words.

There seemed to be a great deal of commotion in the room. The press? How long had he been in this place? Then an argument broke out. There was an intense heavyset balding young man in front of the judge. He seemed to be from the District Attorney's Office. The judge said *buzz buzz buzz buzz* Mr. *Kramer.* Mr. Kramer.

To Sherman, the judge seemed very young. He was a chubby white man with receding curly hair and a set of robes that looked as if they had been rented for a graduation.

Sherman heard Killian mutter, "Sonofabitch."

Kramer was saying, "I realize, Your Honor, that our office agreed to bail of only $10,000 in this case. But subsequent developments, matters that have come to our attention since that time, make it impossible for our office to agree to such a low bail. Your Honor, this case involves a serious injury, very possibly a fatal injury, and we have definite and specific knowledge that there was a witness in this case who has not come forward and that that witness was actually in the car driven by the defendant, Mr. McCoy, and we have every reason to believe that attempts have been or will be made to prevent that witness from coming forth, and we do not believe it will serve the interests of justice—"

Killian said, "Your Honor—"

"—to allow this defendant to go free on a token bail—"

A rumble, a growl, an immense angry mutter rose from the spectators' section, and a single deep voice shouted: "No bail!" Then a mighty mutterers' chorus: "No bail!" . . . "Lock 'im up!" . . . "Bang it shut!"

The judge rapped his gavel. The muttering died down.

Killian said, "Your Honor, Mr. Kramer knows very well—"

The rumble rose again.

Kramer plowed on, right over Killian's words: "Given the emotions in this community, quite justifiably aroused by this case, in which it has appeared that justice is a reed—"

Killian on the counterattack, shouting: "Your Honor, this is patent nonsense!"

A mighty rumble.

The rumble erupted into a roar; the muttering into a great raw yawp. "Awww, man!" . . . "Booooo!" . . . "Yeggggh!" . . . "Shut your filthy mouth and let the man talk!"

The judge banged the gavel again. "Quiet!" The roar subsided. Then to Killian: "Let him finish his statement. You can respond."

"Thank you, Your Honor," said Kramer. "Your Honor, I would call the court's attention to the fact that this case, even in the arraignment stage, on very short notice, has brought out a heavy representation of the community and most specifically of the friends and neighbors of the victim in this case, Henry Lamb, who remains in extremely grave condition in the hospital."

Kramer turned and motioned toward the spectators' section. It was packed. There were people standing. Sherman noticed a group of black men in blue work shirts. One of them was very tall and wore a gold earring.

"I have a petition," said Kramer, and he lifted some sheets of paper and waved them over his head. "This document has been signed by more than a hundred members of the community and delivered to the Bronx District Attorney's Office with an appeal that our office be their representative, to see that justice is done in this case, and of course it is no more than our sworn duty to be their representative."

"Jesus H. Christ," muttered Killian.

"The neighborhood, the community, the people of the Bronx, intend to watch this case, diligently, every step of the judicial process."

Right! . . . *Yegggh!* . . . *Un-hunnnnh!* . . . *Tell 'im!* A terrific yammering started in the spectators' section.

The chubby judge rapped his gavel and called out, "Quiet! This is an arraignment. It's not a rally. Is that all, Mr. Kramer?"

Rumble rumble mutter mutter *booooo!*

"Your Honor," said Kramer, "I have been instructed by my office, by Mr. Weiss himself, to request bail in the amount of $250,000 in this case."

Right! . . . *Yegggh!* . . . *Tell 'im!* . . . Cheers, applause, stamping on the floor.

Sherman looked at Killian. *Tell me—tell me—tell me this can't possibly happen!* But Killian was straining toward the judge. He had his hand in the air. His lips were already moving. The judge was banging the gavel.

"Any more of this and I'll clear the room!"

"Your Honor," said Killian, as the din subsided, "Mr. Kramer is not content to violate an agreement between his office and my client. He wants a circus! This morning my client was subjected to a circus arrest, despite the fact that he has been ready at all times to testify voluntarily before a grand jury. And now Mr. Kramer manufactures a fictitious threat to an unnamed witness and asks the court to set a preposterous bail. My client is a homeowner of long standing in this city, he has a family and deep roots in his community and a bail request has been agreed to, as even Mr. Kramer acknowledges, and nothing has occurred to alter the premise of that agreement."

"A lot has changed, Your Honor!" said Kramer.

"Yeah," said Killian, "the Office of the Bronx District Attorney is what's changed!"

"All right!" said the judge. "Mr. Kramer, if your office has information bearing upon the bail status of this case, I instruct you to gather that information and make a formal application to this court, and the matter will be reviewed at that time. Until then, the court is releasing the defendant, Sherman McCoy, under a bond in the amount of $10,000, pending presentation of this complaint to the grand jury."

Bellows and screams! *Boooo!* . . . *Yegggghh!* . . . *Noooooo!* . . . *Ged'im!* . . . And then a chant began: *"No bail—put 'im in jail!"* . . . *"No bail—put 'im in jail!"*

Killian was leading him away from the bench. To get out of the courtroom they would have to go straight through the spectators' section, straight through a mass of angry people who were now on their feet. Sherman could see fists in the air. Then he saw policemen coming toward him, half a dozen at least. They wore white shirts and bullet belts and colossal holsters with pistol handles showing. In fact, they were court officers. They closed in around him. *They're putting me back in the cell!* Then he realized they were forming a flying wedge to get him through the crowd. So many glowering faces, black and white! *Murderer!* . . . *Motherfucker!* . . . *You gonna get what Henry Lamb got!* . . . *Say your prayers, Park Avenue!* . . . *Tear you a new one!* . . . *McCoy, say—McDead, baby!* . . . He stumbled on, between his white-shirted protectors. He could hear them groaning and straining as they pushed back the crowd. "Coming through! Coming through!" . . . Here and there other faces popped up, lips moving . . . The tall Englishman with the blond hair . . . Fallow . . . The press . . . then more shouts . . . *You mine, Needlenose! Mine!* . . . *Count every breath, baby!* . . . *Geed'um!* . . . *Lights out, sucker!* . . . *Look at 'im—Park Avenue!*

Even in the midst of the storm, Sherman felt strangely unmoved by what was happening. His thoughts told him it was something dreadful, but he didn't feel it. *Since I'm already dead.*

The storm burst out of the courtroom and into a lobby. The lobby was full of people standing about. Sherman could see their expressions change from consternation to fear. They began scurrying to the sides, to make way for the rogue galaxy of bodies that had just burst out of the courtroom. Now Killian and the court officers were steering him onto an escalator. There was a hideous mural on the wall. The escalator was heading down. Pressure from behind—he pitched forward, landing on the back of a court officer on the step below. For a moment it seemed as if an avalanche of bodies—but the court officer caught himself on the rolling railings. Now the screaming galaxy burst through the front doors and out onto the main stairway on 161st Street. A wall of bodies was in the way. Television cameras, six or eight of them, microphones, fifteen or twenty of them, screaming people—the press.

The two masses of humanity met, merged, froze. Killian rose up in front of Sherman. Microphones were in his face, and Killian was declaiming, most oratorically:

"I want you to show the whole city a New York"—*Yawk*— "what you just saw"—*sawwwwr*—"in there"—*in'eh*. With the most curious detachment Sherman found himself aware of every street inflection of the fop's voice. "You saw a circus arrest, and then you saw a circus arraignment, and then you saw the District Attorney's Office prostituting itself and perverting the law"—*the lawwwr* —"for your cameras and for the approval of a partisan mob!"

Booooo! . . . Yegggh! . . . Partisan you, you bent-nose bastard! . . . Somewhere behind him, no more than twenty-four inches away, someone was keening in a singsong falsetto: *"Say your prayers, McCoy . . . Your day is done . . . Say your prayers, McCoy . . . Your day is done . . ."*

Killian said: "We reached an agreement with the district attorney yesterday . . ."

The singsong falsetto said: *"Say your prayers, McCoy . . . Count your breaths . . ."*

Sherman looked up at the sky. The rain had stopped. The sun had broken through. It was a lovely balmy day in June. There was a fluffy blue dome over the Bronx.

He looked at the sky and listened to the sounds, just the sounds, the orotund tropes and sententiae, the falsetto songs, the inquisitory shouts, the hippo mutterings, and he thought: I'm not going back in there, ever. I don't care what it takes to keep me out, even if I have to stick a shotgun in my mouth.

The only shotgun he had was, in fact, double-barreled. It was a big old thing. He stood on 161st Street, a block from the Grand Concourse, in the Bronx, and wondered if he could get both barrels in his mouth.

23

INSIDE THE CAVITY

"WELL, THERE YOU ARE, Larry," said Abe Weiss with a big grin. "They sure gave you a shiny dome."

Since Weiss was now inviting him to do it, Kramer did what he had been wanting to do for the past forty-five seconds, which was to turn completely away from Weiss and look at the bank of television sets on the wall.

And there, indeed, he was.

The videocassette had just reached the part in the Channel 1 broadcast from last night in which the artist's drawing showed the scene in the courtroom. The sound was on low, but Kramer could hear the voice of the announcer, Robert Corso, as if he were right inside his skull: "Assistant District Attorney Lawrence Kramer thrust the petition toward Judge Samuel Auerbach and said, 'Your Honor, the people of the Bronx . . .'" In the drawing, the top of his head was absolutely bald, which was unrealistic and unfair, because he was not bald, he was only balding. Nevertheless, *there he was*. It was not one of Those People We See on TV. It was himself, and if there was ever a powerful warrior for Justice, it was himself on that screen. His neck, his shoulders, his chest, his arms—they were huge, as if he were heaving the 16-pound shot in the Olympics instead of waving a few pieces of paper at Sammy Auerbach. True, one reason he looked so big was that the drawing was a little out of proportion, but that was probably the way the artist had seen him: Larger Than Life. The artist . . . What a juicy Italian girl she had been . . . Lips like nectarines . . . Nice breasts underneath a shiny silky jersey . . . Lucy Dellafloria, her name was . . . If there hadn't been such commotion and confusion, it would have been the easiest thing in the world. After all, she had sat there in the courtroom concentrating on him, at center stage, absorbed in the look of him, in the passion of his presentation, the confidence of his performance on the field of battle. She had been absorbed as an artist and as a woman . . . with full Italian Dirty Girl lips . . . in himself.

All too soon, just like that, the drawing was gone and Weiss was on the screen with a whole forest of microphones sticking up at him. The microphones had been on little metal stands on his desk, for the press conference he gave right after the arraignment. He had given another one this morning. Weiss knew exactly how to keep the focus on himself. Oh yes. The average TV watcher would assume that the show was all Abe Weiss's and that the assistant district attorney who presented the case in the courtroom, this Larry Kramer, was merely the instrument of Abe Weiss's gravel-voiced strategic brilliance. Weiss hadn't actually worked on his feet in a courtroom the whole time he had been in office, which was almost four years. But Kramer didn't resent that; or not very much. That was the given. That was the way it worked. It was thus in every district attorney's office, not just Weiss's. No, on this particular morning Captain Ahab was okay with Kramer. The TV news and the newspapers had featured the name Lawrence Kramer many times, and *she*, luscious Lucy Dellafloria, sexy Lucy Delicate Flower, had done his portrait and captured the mighty Kramer form. No, it was fine. And Weiss had just gone to the trouble of pointing that out to him, by playing the videocassette. The implicit message was: "All right, I make myself the star, because I run this office and I am the one who has to face re-election. But see, I don't leave you out. You get the second billing."

So the two of them watched the rest of the Channel 1 coverage on the television set on the paneled wall. There was Thomas Killian standing outside the Criminal Courts Building with the microphones held up at *his* face.

"Look at those fucking clothes," muttered Weiss. "Looks fucking ridiculous." What crossed Kramer's mind was how much such clothes must cost.

Killian was going on about how this was a "circus arrest" and a "circus arraignment." He appeared to be extremely angry.

"We reached an agreement with the district attorney yesterday that Mr. McCoy would present himself for arraignment here in the Bronx, peacefully, voluntarily, this morning, and the district attorney chose to violate that agreement and bring Mr. McCoy in like a violent felon, like an animal—and for what? For your cameras and for votes."

"Gedoudahere," Weiss said to the screen.

Killian was saying, "Mr. McCoy not only denies these charges, but he is eager for the facts in this case to come out, and when they come out, you will see that the scenario that is being contrived for this case is utterly without foundation."

"Blah blah blah," Weiss said to the screen.

The camera moved to a figure standing just behind Killian. It was McCoy. His tie was loose and pulled to one side. His shirt and jacket were rumpled. His hair was matted. He looked half drowned. His eyes rolled up, toward the sky. He didn't look all there.

Now Robert Corso's face was on the screen, and he was talking about McCoy, McCoy, McCoy. It was no longer the Lamb case. It was the McCoy case. The big Wall Street Wasp with the aristocratic profile had given the case some sex appeal. The press couldn't get enough of it.

Weiss's desk was covered with newspapers. He still had yesterday afternoon's *City Light* right up on top. In enormous letters the front page said:

WALL STREET
SOCIALITE
NABBED IN
HIT-AND-RUN

The words were banked up against a tall narrow picture of McCoy, soaking wet, with his hands in front of him and his suit jacket folded over his hands, obviously to hide his handcuffs. He had his big handsome chin up, and a ferocious scowl beamed straight down his nose at the camera. He looked as if he was saying, "Yeah, and what of it?" Even the *Times* had the case on the front page this morning, but it was *The City Light* that was really going wild. The headline this morning said:

SEEK
"FOXY"
BRUNETTE
MYSTERY
GIRL

A smaller headline up above said, *Team Mercedes: He Hit, She Ran.* The picture was the one from the social magazine *W*, the one Roland Auburn had pointed to, the one of McCoy in his tuxedo, grinning, and of his wife, looking proper and plain. The caption said, *Eyewitness called McCoy's companion younger, more "foxy," a "hotter ticket" than his forty-year-old wife, Judy, shown here with hubby at charity bash.* A line of white letters on a black bar at the bottom of the page said, *Protesters Demand "Jail, Not Bail" for Wall Street Whiz. See page 3.* And: *Chez McCoy and Chez Lamb: A Tale of Two Cities. Pictures, pages 4 and 5.* On pages 4 and 5 were pictures of McCoy's Park Avenue spread, the ones from *Architectural Digest*, on one side and pictures of the Lambs' tiny rooms in the project on the other. A long caption began: *Two vastly different New Yorks collided when Wall Street investment banker Sherman McCoy's $50,000 Mercedes-Benz sports roadster struck honor student Henry Lamb. McCoy lives in a $3 million, 14-room, two-story apartment on Park Avenue. Lamb, in a $247-a-month three-room apartment in a housing project in the South Bronx.*

Weiss loved every square inch of the coverage. It had blown all this talk of "white justice" and "Johannesbronx" right out of the tub. They hadn't managed to jack McCoy's bail up to $250,000, but they had gone after that aggressively. Aggressively? Kramer smiled. Sammy Auerbach's eyes had opened up like a pair of umbrellas when he had waved the petition at him. That had been just a shade outrageous, but it had gotten the point across. The Bronx D.A.'s Office was in touch with the people. And they would keep petitioning for higher bail.

No, Weiss was pleased. That was obvious. This was the first time Kramer had ever been summoned into Weiss's office by himself, without Bernie Fitzgibbon.

Weiss pressed a button, and the television set went blank. He said to Kramer, "Did you see the way McCoy looked standing there? He looked like a fucking mess. Milt said that's the way he looked when he came in the courtroom yesterday. He said he looked like hell. What was that all about?"

"Well," said Kramer, "all it was was, it was raining. He got wet while he was standing in line outside of Central Booking. They made him wait in line like everybody else, which was the whole point. Not to give him special treatment."

"All right," said Weiss, "but f'r Chrissake, here we're bringing Park Avenue into the courtroom, and Milt says the guy looked like he was just fished out of the river. Bernie was giving me a hard time about that, too. He didn't want to take him through Central Booking in the first place."

"He didn't look all that bad, Mr. Weiss," said Kramer.

"Make it Abe."

Kramer nodded, but decided he would wait a decent interval before trying out his first *Abe*. "He didn't look any different from anybody else who comes in from out of the pens."

"And there's Tommy Killian trying to raise a big stink about it, too." He gestured toward the television sets.

Kramer thought, Well, you finally stood up on your hind legs against the two Donkeys. Bernie had been unhappy, to put it mildly, when Weiss overruled him and ordered Kramer to request that McCoy's bail be raised from $10,000 to $250,000 after Bernie had struck a deal at $10,000 with Killian. Weiss told Bernie it was only to placate the angry residents of the community who thought McCoy would get special treatment and that he knew Auerbach wouldn't actually set such a high bail. But to Bernie it was a breach of contract, a violation of Favor Bank regulations, of the sacred code of loyalty of one Harp to another in the criminal justice system.

Kramer could see a cloud passing in front of Weiss's face, and then Weiss said, "Well, let Tommy squawk. You can drive yourself crazy if you try to please everybody. I had to make a decision and I made a decision. Bernie likes Tommy, and that's okay. I like Tommy myself. But Bernie wants to give him the goddamned store! The promises he made Tommy, McCoy was gonna come traipsing through here like Prince Charles. How long was McCoy in the pens?"

"Oh, about four hours."

"Well, hell, that's about normal, isn't it?"

"About. I've seen defendants get shuttled from one precinct lockup to another and then to Central Booking and then to Rikers Island and then back to Central Booking, and then they get arraigned. They get arrested on a Friday evening, they can spend the whole weekend bouncing around. Then you're looking at somebody who's a mess. McCoy didn't even have to start off in a precinct house and get bused over to Central Booking."

"Well then, I don't know what all this goddamned bellyaching is. Did anything happen to him in the pens? What's the big deal?"

"Nothing happened. The computer went down, I think. So there was a delay. But that happens all the time, too. That's normal."

"You wanna know what I think? I think Bernie, without knowing it—don't get me wrong, I like Bernie and I respect Bernie—but I think, without knowing it, he really does think someone like McCoy should get special treatment, because he's white and because he's well known. Now, this is a subtle thing. Bernie's Irish, just like Tommy's Irish, and the Irish have a certain amount of what the English call *deference* built into them, and they don't even know it. They're impressed by these Waspy guys, like McCoy, even though consciously they may act and think like they're members of the IRA. It's not really important, but a guy like Bernie's got this deference thing to deal with, this unconscious Irish thing, and he doesn't even know about it. But we don't represent the Wasps, Larry. I wonder if there's even a Wasp living in the Bronx. There must be one in Riverdale somewhere."

Kramer chuckled.

"No, I'm serious," said Weiss. "This is the Bronx. This is the Laboratory of Human Relations. That's what I call it, the Laboratory of Human Relations."

That was true; he called it the Laboratory of Human Relations. He called it that every day, as if oblivious of the fact that everyone who had ever been in his office had heard him say it before. But Kramer was in the mood to forgive Weiss's fatuous side. More than forgive . . . *to understand* . . . and appreciate the essential truth that underlay his buffoon's way of putting things. Weiss was right. You couldn't run the criminal justice system in the Bronx and pretend you were in some kind of displaced Manhattan.

"Come here," said Weiss. He got up from his great chair and walked over to the window behind him and beckoned to Kramer. From up here on the sixth floor, at the top of the hill, the view was grand. They were up high enough so that all sordid details receded and the Bronx's lovely rolling topology took over. They looked out over Yankee Stadium and John Mullaly Park, which from up here actually looked green and sylvan. In the distance, straight ahead, across the Harlem River, was the skyline of upper Manhattan, up where Columbia-Presbyterian Medical Center was, and from here it looked pastoral, like one of those old landscape paintings in which they put some fuzzy trees in the background and some soft gray clouds.

Weiss said, "Look down there on those streets, Larry. Whaddaya see? Whodaya see?"

All that Kramer could see, in fact, were some tiny figures walking along 161st Street and Walton Avenue. They were so far below they were like insects.

"They're all black and Puerto Rican," said Weiss. "You don't even see any old Jews walking around down there anymore or any Italians, either, and this is the civic center of the Bronx. This is like Montague Street in Brooklyn or City Hall Plaza in Manhattan. In the summertime the Jews used to sit out on the sidewalk at night right over there on the Grand Concourse and just watch the cars go by. You couldn't get Charles Bronson to sit out there now. This is the modern era, and nobody understands it yet. When I was a kid, the Irish ran the Bronx. They ran it for a long time. You remember Charlie Buckley? Charlie Buckley, the congressman? No, you're too young. Charlie Buckley, the Boss of the Bronx, as Irish as they come. Up to about thirty years ago Charlie Buckley was still running the Bronx. And now they're finished, and so who runs it? Jews and Italians. But for how long? There's none down there on the street, and so how long are they gonna be up here in this building? But that's the Bronx, the Laboratory of Human Relations. That's what I call it, the Laboratory of Human Relations. Those are poor people you're looking at down there, Larry, and poverty breeds crime, and the crime in this borough—well, I don't have to tell you. Part of me's an idealist. I want to deal with every case on an individual basis and every person one by one. But with the caseload we got? Ayyyyyyyyyyyyy . . . The other part of me knows that what we're really doing, we're like a little band of cowboys running a herd. With a herd the best you can hope for is to keep the herd *as a whole*"—he made a great round gesture with his hands—"under control and hope you don't lose too many along the way. Oh, the day will come, and maybe pretty soon, when those people down there will have their own leaders and their own organizations, and they'll be the Bronx Democratic Party and everything else, and we won't be in this building any longer. But right now they need us, and we have to do the right thing by them. We have to let them know that we're not removed from them and that they're just as much a part of New York as we are. We have to send them the right signals. We have to let them know that maybe we come down hard on them when they get out of line, but it's not because they're black or Hispanic or poor.

We got to let them know justice really is blind. We got to let them know if you're white and rich, it works out the same way. That's a very important signal. It's more important than any specific point or technicality of the law. That is what this office is all about, Larry. We're not here to handle cases. We're here to create hope. That's what Bernie doesn't understand." The *doesn't*, in preference to the Irish *don't*, signaled the elevation of the D.A.'s thoughts at this moment. "Bernie is still playing Irish politics," said Weiss, "the same way Charlie Buckley used to play it, and that's finished. It's all over. This is the modern era in the Laboratory of Human Relations, and we have a sworn duty to represent those people you're looking at down there."

Kramer peered down diligently at the insects. As for Weiss, the loftiness of his sentiments had filled his voice and his face with emotion. He gave Kramer a sincere look and a tired smile, the sort of look that says, "That's what life is all about, once the petty considerations have been swept away."

"I never thought about it that way before, Abe," said Kramer, "but you're absolutely right." It seemed like a good moment for the first *Abe*.

"I was worried about this McCoy case at the beginning," said Weiss. "It looked like Bacon and those people were forcing the issue, and all we were doing was reacting. But that's okay. It turned out to be a good thing. How *do* we treat some hotshot from Park Avenue? Like anybody else, that's how! He gets arrested, he gets the cuffs, he gets booked, he gets fingerprinted, he waits in the pens, just like anybody down there on those streets! Now, I think that sends a helluva good signal. It lets those people know we represent *them* and they're a part a New York City."

Weiss gazed down upon 161st Street like a shepherd upon his flock. Kramer was glad no one but himself was witnessing this. If more than one witness had been on hand, then cynicism would have reigned. You wouldn't have been able to think about anything other than the fact that Abe Weiss had an election coming up in five months, and 70 percent of the inhabitants of the Bronx were black and Latin. But since there was, in fact, no other witness, Kramer could get to the heart of the matter, which was that the manic creature before him, Captain Ahab, was right.

"You did a great job yesterday, Larry," said Weiss, "and I want you to keep pouring it on. Doesn't it make you *feel good* to use your talents for something that means something? Christ, you know what I make." That Kramer did. It was $82,000 a year. "A dozen times I coulda taken a fork in the road and gone out and made three times, five times that in private practice. But for what? You only pass this way once, Larry. Whaddaya wanna be remembered for? That you had a fucking mansion in Riverdale or Greenwich or Locust Valley? Or that you *made a difference*? I feel *sorry* for Tommy Killian. He was a good assistant D.A., but Tommy wanted to make some money, and so now he's out making some money, · but how? He's holding the hands and wiping the noses of a buncha wise guys, psychotics, and dopers. A guy like McCoy makes him look good. He hasn't seen a guy like that in all the years he's been outta here. No, I'd rather run the Laboratory of Human Relations. That's the way I think of it. I'd rather make a difference."

You did a great job yesterday. And I want you to keep pouring it on.

"Christ, I wonder what time it is," said Weiss. "I'm getting hungry."

Kramer looked at his watch with alacrity. "Almost 12:15."

"Whyn't you stick around and have lunch? Judge Tonneto's coming by, and this guy from the *Times*, Overton Something-or-other—I always forget, they're all named Overton or Clifton or some fucking name like that—and Bobby Vitello and Lew Weintraub. You know Lew Weintraub? No? Stick around. You'll learn something."

"Well, if you're sure . . ."

"Of course!" Weiss motioned toward his gigantic conference table, as if to say there's plenty of room. "Just ordering in some sandwiches."

He said this as if this happened to be one of those spur-of-the-moment lunches where you order in instead of going out, as if he or any other shepherd from the island fortress dared stroll out amid the flock and have lunch in the civic center of the Bronx.

But Kramer banished all cheap cynicism from his thoughts. Lunch with the likes of Judge Tonneto, Bobby Vitello, Lew Weintraub, the real-estate developer, Overton Whichever Wasp of *The New York Times*, and the district attorney himself!

He was emerging from the anonymous ooze.

Thank God for the Great White Defendant. Thank you, God, for Mr. Sherman McCoy.

With a blink of curiosity, he wondered about McCoy. McCoy wasn't much older than he was. How did this little icy dip into the real world feel to a Wasp who had had everything just the way he wanted it all his life? But it was only that, a blink.

The Bororo Indians, a primitive tribe who live along the Vermelho River in the Amazon jungles of Brazil, believe that there is no such thing as a private self. The Bororos regard the mind as an open cavity, like a cave or a tunnel or an arcade, if you will, in which the entire village dwells and the jungle grows. In 1969 José M. R. Delgado, the eminent Spanish brain physiologist, pronounced the Bororos correct. For nearly three millennia, Western philosophers had viewed the self as something unique, something encased inside each person's skull, so to speak. This inner self had to deal with and learn from the outside world, of course, and it might prove incompetent in doing so. Nevertheless, at the core of one's self there was presumed to be something irreducible and inviolate. Not so, said Delgado. "Each person is a transitory composite of materials borrowed from the environment." The important word was *transitory*, and he was talking not about years but about hours. He cited experiments in which healthy college students lying on beds in well-lit but soundproofed chambers, wearing gloves to reduce the sense of touch and translucent goggles to block out specific sights, began to hallucinate *within hours*. Without the entire village, the whole jungle, occupying the cavity, they had no minds left.

He cited no investigations of the opposite case, however. He did not discuss what happens when one's self—or what one takes to be one's self—is not a mere cavity open to the outside world but has suddenly become an amusement park to which everybody, *todo el mundo*, *tout le monde*, comes scampering, skipping and screaming, nerves a-tingle, loins aflame, ready for anything, all you've got, laughs, tears, moans, giddy thrills, gasps, horrors, whatever, the gorier the merrier. Which is to say, he told us nothing of the mind of a person at the center of a scandal in the last quarter of the twentieth century.

At first, in the weeks following the incident in the Bronx, Sherman McCoy had regarded the press as an enemy that was stalking him *out there*. He feared each day's newspapers and news broadcasts the way a man would fear the weapons of any impersonal and unseen enemy, the way he would fear falling bombs or incoming shells. Even yesterday, outside the Central Booking facility, in the rain and the filth, when he saw the whites of their eyes and the yellow of their teeth and they reviled and taunted and baited him, when they did everything short of trampling and spitting upon him, they were still the enemy *out there*. They had closed in for the kill, and they hurt him and humiliated him, but they could not reach his inviolable self, Sherman McCoy, inside the brass crucible of his mind.

They closed in for the kill. And then they killed him.

He couldn't remember whether he had died while he was still standing in line outside, before the door to Central Booking opened, or while he was in the pens. But by the time he left the building and Killian held his impromptu press conference on the steps, he had died and been reborn. In his new incarnation, the press was no longer an enemy and it was no longer *out there*. The press was now a condition, like lupus erythematosus or Wegener's granulomatosis. His entire central nervous system was now wired into the vast, incalculable circuit of radio and television and newspapers, and his body surged and burned and hummed with the energy of the press and the prurience of those it reached, which was everyone, from the closest neighbor to the most bored and distant outlander titillated for the moment by his disgrace. By the thousands, no, the millions, they now came scampering into the cavity of what he had presumed to be his self, Sherman McCoy. He could no more keep them from entering his very own hide than he could keep the air out of his lungs. (Or, better said, he could keep them out only in the same manner that he could deny air to his lungs once and for all. That solution occurred to him more than once during that long day, but he fought against morbidity, he did, he did, he did, he who had already died once.)

It started within minutes after he and Killian managed to disengage themselves from the mob of demonstrators and reporters and photographers and camera crews and get into the car-service sedan Killian had hired. The driver was listening to an Easy Listening station on the car radio, but in no time the every-half-hour news broadcast came on, and right away Sherman heard his name, his name and all the key words that he would hear and see over and over for the rest of the day: Wall Street, socialite, hit-and-run, Bronx honor student, unidentified female companion, and he could see the driver's eyes in the rearview mirror staring into the open cavity known as Sherman McCoy. By the time they reached Killian's office, the midday edition of *The City Light* was already there, and his contorted face was staring back at him from the front page, and everyone in New York was free to walk right in through those horrified eyes of his. Late in the afternoon, when he went home to Park Avenue, he had to run a gauntlet of reporters and television camera crews to get into his own apartment building. They called him "Sherman," as merrily and contemptuously and imperiously as they pleased, and Eddie, the doorman, looked into his eyes and stuck his head way down into the cavity. To make matters worse, he had to ride up on the elevator with the Morrisseys, who lived in the penthouse apartment. They said nothing. They just poked their long noses inside the cavity and sniffed and sniffed at his shame, until their faces stiffened from the stench. He had counted on his unlisted telephone number as a retreat, but the press had already solved that, by the time he got home, and Bonita, kind Bonita, who took only a quick peek inside the cavity, had to screen the calls. Every imaginable news organization called, and there were a few calls for Judy. And for himself? Who would be so deficient in dignity, so immune to embarrassment, as to make a personal telephone call to this great howling public arcade, this shell of shame and funk, which was Sherman McCoy himself? Only his mother and father and Rawlie Thorpe. Well, at least Rawlie had that much in him. Judy—roaming the apartment shocked and distant. Campbell—bewildered but not in tears; not yet. He hadn't thought he would be able to face the television screen, and yet he turned it on. The vilification poured forth from every channel. Prominent Wall Street investment banker, top echelon at Pierce & Pierce, socialite, prep school, Yale, spoiled son of the former general partner of Dunning Sponget & Leach, the Wall Street law firm, in his $60,000 Mercedes sports roadster (now an extra $10,000), with a foxy brunette who was not his wife and not anything like his wife and who makes his wife look dowdy by comparison, runs over an exemplary son of the deserving poor, a young honor student who grew up in the housing projects, and flees in his fancy car without so much as a moment's pity, let alone help, for his victim, who now lies near death. The eerie thing was—and it felt eerie as he had sat there looking at the television set—was that he was not shocked and angered by these gross distortions and manifest untruths. Instead, he was *shamed*. By nightfall they had been repeated so often, on the vast circuit to which his very hide now seemed wired, that they had taken on the weight of truth, in that millions had now *seen* this Sherman McCoy, this Sherman McCoy on the screen, and they knew him to be the man who had committed the heartless act. They were here now, in vast mobs, clucking and fuming and probably contemplating worse than that, inside the public arcade that he had once thought to be the private self of Sherman McCoy. Everyone, every living soul who gazed upon him, with the possible exception of Maria, if she ever gazed upon him again, would know him as this person on the front of two million, three million, four million newspapers and on the screen of God knew how many million television sets. The energy of their accusations, borne over the vast circuit of the press, which was wired into his central nervous system, hummed and burned through his hide and made his adrenaline pump. His pulse was constantly fast, and yet he was no longer in a state of panic. A sad, sad torpor had set in. He could concentrate on . . . nothing, not even long enough to feel sad about it. He thought of what this must be doing to Campbell and to Judy, and yet he no longer felt the terrible pangs he felt before . . . before he died. This alarmed him. He looked at his daughter and tried to feel the pangs, but it was an intellectual exercise. It was all so sad and heavy, heavy, heavy.

The one thing he truly felt was fear. It was the fear of going *back in there*.

Last night, exhausted, he went to bed and thought he would be unable to sleep. In fact, he fell asleep almost at once and had a dream. It was dusk. He was on a bus going up First Avenue. This was odd, because he had not taken a bus in New York for at least ten years. Before he knew it, the bus was up around 110th Street, and it was dark. He had missed his stop, although he couldn't remember what his stop was supposed to be. He was now in a black neighborhood. In fact, it should have been a Latin neighborhood, namely, Spanish Harlem, but it was a black neighborhood. He got off the bus, fearing that if he stayed on, things would only get worse. In doorways, on stoops, on the sidewalks he could see figures in the gloom, but they hadn't seen him yet. He hurried along the streets in the shadows, trying to make his way west. Good sense would have told him to head straight back down First Avenue, but it seemed terribly important to head west. Now he realized the figures were circling. They said nothing, they didn't even come terribly close . . . for the time being. They had all the time in the world. He hurried through the darkness, seeking out the shadows, and gradually the figures closed in; gradually, for they had all the time in the world. He woke up in a dreadful panic, perspiring, his heart leaping out of his chest. He had been asleep for less than two hours.

Early in the morning, as the sun came up, he felt stronger. The humming and burning had ceased, and he began to wonder: Am I free of this dreadful condition? Of course, he hadn't understood. The vast circuit was merely down for the night. The millions of accusing eyes were closed. In any event, he decided: I will be strong. What other choice did he have? He had none, other than to die again, slowly or quickly; and truly. It was in that frame of mind that he decided he would not be a prisoner in his own apartment. He would lead his life as best he could and set his jaw against the mob. He would start by taking Campbell to the bus stop, as always.

At 7:00, Tony, the doorman, called upstairs, with apologies, to say that about a half dozen reporters and photographers were camped outside, on the sidewalk and in cars. Bonita relayed the message, and Sherman squared his jaw and raised his chin and resolved to deal with them the same way you would deal with foul weather. The two of them, Sherman in his most uncompromising nailhead worsted suit from England and Campbell in her Taliaferro school uniform, got off the elevator and approached the door, and Tony said, with genuine feeling, "Good luck. They're a rude lot." Out on the sidewalk the first one was a very young man, babyish in appearance, and he approached with something resembling politeness and said, "Mr. McCoy, I'd like to ask you—"

Sherman took Campbell's hand and raised his Yale chin and said, "I have no comment whatsoever. Now, if you'll just excuse me."

Suddenly five, six, seven of them were all around him and around Campbell, and there was no more "Mr. McCoy."

"Sherman! One minute! Who was the woman?"

"Sherman! Hold it a second! Just one picture!"

"Hey, Sherman! Your lawyer says—"

"Hold it! Hey! Hey! What's your name, Pretty?"

One of them was calling Campbell *Pretty!* Appalled and furious, he turned toward the voice. *The same one*—with the tangles of kinky hair pasted on his skull —and now two pieces of toilet paper on his cheek.

Sherman turned back to Campbell. A confused smile was on her face. The cameras! Picture-taking had always meant a happy occasion.

"What's her name, Sherman!"

"Hi, Pretty, what's your name?"

The filthy one with the toilet paper on his face was bending over his little girl and speaking in an unctuous avuncular voice.

"Leave her alone!" said Sherman. He could see the fear come into Campbell's face with the sharpness of his own voice.

All at once a microphone was in front of his nose, blocking his vision.

A tall sinewy young woman with big jaws: "Henry Lamb lies near death in the hospital, and you're walking down Park Avenue. How do you feel about Henry—"

Sherman swung his forearm up to knock the microphone out of his face. The woman began screaming:

"You big bastard!" To her colleagues: "You saw that! He hit me! The sonofabitch hit me! You saw that! You saw it! I'm having you arrested for assault, you sonofabitch!"

The pack swarmed about them, Sherman and his little girl. He reached down and put his arm around Campbell's shoulders and tried to pull her close to him and walk quickly toward the corner at the same time.

"Come on, Sherman! Just a couple a questions and we'll let you go!"

From behind, the woman was still bellowing and whining: "Hey, you get a picture a that? I wanna see what you got! That's evidence! You gotta show it to me!" Then down the street: "You don't care who you hit, do you, you racist fuck!"

Racist fuck! The woman was white.

Campbell's face was frozen in fear and consternation.

The light changed, and the pack followed the two of them and pigged and hived about them all the way across Park Avenue. Sherman and Campbell, hand in hand, plowed on straight ahead, and the reporters and photographers who surrounded them scampered backward and sideways and crabwise.

"Sherman!"

"Sherman!"

"Look at me, Pretty!"

The parents, nannies, and children waiting at the Taliaferro bus stop shrank back. They wanted no part of the disgusting eruption they saw coming toward them, this noisy swarm of shame, guilt, humiliation, and torment. On the other hand, they also didn't want their little ones to miss the bus, which was approaching. So they shuddered and retreated a few feet into a clump, as if blown together by the wind. For a moment Sherman thought someone might step in to help, not so much for his sake as for Campbell's, but he was mistaken. Some stared, as if they didn't know who he was. Others averted their eyes. Sherman scanned their faces. The lovely little Mrs. Lueger! She had both hands on the shoulders of her little girl, who stared with big, fascinated eyes. Mrs. Lueger looked at him as if he were a vagrant from the Sixty-seventh Street Armory.

Campbell, in her little burgundy uniform, trudged up the steps into the interior of the bus and then cast one last look over her shoulders. Tears streamed down her face, without a sound.

Now a pang tore through Sherman's solar plexus. He had not yet died again. He was not yet dead for a second time; not yet. The photographer with the toilet paper on his cheek was right behind him, not eighteen inches away, with his horrible instrument screwed into his eye socket.

Grab him! Drive it into his brain! "Hey, Pretty!" you dare say to my flesh and blood—

But what was the use? For they weren't the enemy *out there* any longer, were they? They were parasites inside his very hide. The humming and the burning began again for the day.

Fallow sauntered across the city room and let them drink in his imposing figure. He held in his midsection and straightened his back. Tomorrow he would begin a serious exercise regimen. There was no reason why he shouldn't have a heroic physique. On the way downtown he had stopped off at Herzfeld, a haberdashery on Madison Avenue that carried European and British clothes, and he had bought a spotted navy silk-grenadine necktie. The tiny spots were embroidered in white. He had put it on right there in the store, letting the salesman get a load of his detachable collar. He was wearing his best shirt, which was from Bowring, Arundel & Co., Savile Row. It was a sincere shirt, and it was a sincere necktie. If only he could afford a new blazer, with rich belly-cut lapels that didn't shine . . . Ah well, hey ho—soon enough! He stopped by the edge of the desk and picked up a *City Light* from a stack of early editions left there for the use of the staff. SEEK "FOXY" BRUNETTE MYSTERY GIRL. Another page 1 story by Peter Fallow. The rest of the print swam amid the foggy eye trash in front of his face. But he continued to stare at it, so as to give them all a chance to drink in the presence of . . . Peter Fallow . . . Take a look, you poor drudges, humped over your word processors, clattering away and nattering away and grousing about your "one hundred big ones." All at once he felt so grand, he thought about what a superior gesture it would be to walk over to poor Goldman and give him his hundred dollars. Well, he'd put that in the back of his mind.

When he reached his cubicle, there were already six or seven message slips on his desk. He leafed through them, half expecting that one might be from a movie producer.

Sir Gerald Steiner, formerly the Dead Mouse, was heading his way with his coat off and a pair of bright red felt suspenders over his striped shirt and a smile on his face, a charming smile, an ingratiating smile, instead of that malevolent wolf-eyed look of a few weeks back. The canteen of vodka was still hidden in the pocket of the raincoat, which still hung on the plastic coatrack in the corner. He could probably take it out and knock back a fiery jolt right in front of the Mouse, and what would come of it? Nothing but a knowing would-be-comradely Mouse smile, if he knew his Mouse.

"Peter!" said Steiner. *Peter;* no more school proctor's *Fallow.* "Want to see something to brighten your day?"

Steiner slapped the photograph down on Fallow's desk. It showed Sherman McCoy with a terrific scowl on his face giving a backhand swat to the face of a tall woman who was holding some sort of wand, which on close inspection turned out to be a microphone. With his other hand he clutched the hand of a little girl in a school uniform. The little girl looked into the camera in a quizzical daze. In the background was the marquee of an apartment house and a doorman.

Steiner was chuckling. "The woman—dreadful woman, by the way, from some radio station—rings up five times an hour. Says she's going to have McCoy arrested for assault. She wants the picture. She'll have the picture, all right. It's on page 1 of the next edition."

Fallow picked up the picture and studied it. "Hmmm. Pretty little girl. Must be difficult having a father who keeps hitting minorities, black boys, women. Have you ever noticed the way the Yanks refer to women as a minority?"

"The poor mother tongue," said Steiner.

"Marvelous picture," said Fallow, quite sincerely. "Who took it?"

"Silverstein. That chap does have sand. He does, indeed."

"Silverstein's on the death watch?" asked Fallow.

"Oh yes," said Steiner. "He loves that sort of thing. You know, Peter"—*Peter*

—"I have respect, perhaps an inverted respect, but a true respect, for chaps like Silverstein. They're the farmers of journalism. They love the good rich soil itself, *for* itself, not for the pay—they like to plunge their hands into the dirt." Steiner paused, puzzled. He was always nonplussed by his own plays on words.

Oh, how Sir Gerald, baby boy of Old Steiner, would love to be able to wallow in that filth with such Dionysian abandon!—like a chap with sand! His eyes brimmed with a warm emotion: love, perhaps, or nostalgia for the mud.

"The Laughing Vandals," said Steiner, smiling broadly and shaking his head, apropos of the renowned exploits of the sandy photographer. That in turn led him to a broader source of satisfaction.

"I want to tell you something, Peter. I don't know whether you fully appreciate it or not, but you've broken a very important story with this Lamb and McCoy business. Oh, it's sensational, but it's much more than that. It's a morality play. Think of that for a moment. A morality play. You mentioned minorities. I realize you were joking, but we're already hearing from these minorities, from these black organizations and whatnot, the very organizations that have been spreading rumors that we are racist and all the usual sort of rubbish, and now they're congratulating us and looking to us as a sort of . . . *beacon.* That's quite a turnabout in a short time. These Third World Anti-Defamation League people, the very people who were so incensed over the Laughing Vandals, they've just sent me the most *glowing* testimonial. We're the bloody standard-bearers of liberalism and civil rights now! They think you're a genius, by the way. This man, Reverend Bacon, as they call him, seems to run it. He'd give you the Nobel Prize, if it was up to him. I should have Brian show you the letter."

Fallow said nothing. The idiots might be a bit more subtle about it.

"What I'm trying to get across, Peter, is that this is a very significant step in the progress of the newspaper. Our readers don't care about respectability one way or the other. But the advertisers do. I've already set Brian to work on seeing if perhaps we can't get some of these black groups to render their new opinion of *The City Light* formal in some fashion, through citations or awards or—I don't know, but Brian will know how to go about it. I hope you'll be able to take time out to take part in whatever he comes up with. But we'll see how that works out."

"Oh, absolutely," said Fallow. "Of course. I know how strongly these people feel. Did you know that the judge who refused to increase McCoy's bond yesterday has received death threats?"

"Death threats! You're not serious." The Mouse twitched with the horrible excitement of it.

"It's true. And he's taking it quite seriously, too."

"Great God," said Steiner. "This is an amazing country."

Fallow perceived this as a fortunate moment in which to suggest to Sir Gerald a significant step of another sort: a thousand-dollar advance, which in turn might suggest to the eminent Mouse a rise in pay as well.

And he was correct on both counts. As soon as the new blazer was ready, he was going to *burn* this one; with pleasure.

Scarcely a minute after Steiner had left, Fallow's telephone rang. It was Albert Vogel.

"Hey, Pete! Howaya? Things are poppin', things are poppin', things are poppin'. Pete, you got to do me a favor. You got to give me McCoy's telephone number. It's unlisted."

Without knowing precisely why, Fallow found this a startling notion. "Why would you want his telephone number, Al?"

"Well, the thing is, Pete, I've been retained by Annie Lamb, who wants to file a civil suit in behalf of her son. Two suits, actually: one against the hospital, for gross negligence, and one against McCoy."

"And you want his home telephone number? What for?"

"What for? We might have to negotiate."

"I don't see why you don't call his barrister."

"Jesus Christ, Pete." Vogel's voice turned angry. "I didn't call you up for legal advice. All I want's a fucking telephone number. You got his number or not?"

Fallow's better judgment told him to say no. But his vanity wouldn't allow him to tell Vogel that *I, Fallow,* proprietor of the McCoy case, had been unable to procure the McCoy telephone number.

"All right, Al. I propose a barter. You give me the particulars of the civil suits and a one-day head start with the story, and I'll give you the telephone number."

"Look, Pete, I wanna call a press conference about the suits. All I'm asking you for is a lousy telephone number."

"You can still call a press conference. You'll get a larger audience after I write the story."

A pause. "Okay, Pete." Vogel chuckled, but not very heartily. "I think I created a monster when I put you onto Henry Lamb. Who do you think you are, Lincoln Steffens?"

"Lincoln who?"

"Never mind. It wouldn't interest you. Okay, you can have the fucking story. Aren't you getting tired of all these exclusives? So gimme the number."

And so he did.

When one got right down to it, what difference would it make whether he had the number or not?

24

THE INFORMANTS

THE DREADFUL ORANGE CARPET blazed away. Right next to the Formica couch he was slouched upon, it had come loose from the floor where it abutted the wall, and the crinkly metallic fibers frayed out. Sherman stared at the itchy sleaze of it as a way of averting his eyes from the sinister figures on the couch opposite him. He was afraid they would be staring at him and would know who he was. The fact that Killian would make him wait like this sealed it, nailed down the correctness of what he was about to do. This would be his last visit to this place, his last descent into the vulgarity of Favor Banks, contracts lower-crust fops, and cheap gutter philosophies.

But soon curiosity got the better of him, and he looked at their feet . . . Two men . . . One had on a dainty little pair of slip-on shoes with decorative gold chains running across the top. The other wore a pair of snow-white Reebok sneakers. The shoes shuffled a bit as the two men's tails slid down the couch and they pushed themselves back up with their legs and then slid down again and pushed back and slid down and pushed back. Sherman slid down and pushed back. They slid down and pushed back. Sherman slid down and pushed back. Everything about the place, even the obscene downslope of the couches, proclaimed tastelessness, shiftlessness, vulgarity, and, at bottom, sheer ignorance. The two men were talking in what Sherman took to be Spanish. "Oy el meemo," one of them kept saying. "Oy el meemo." He let his eyes creep up as far as their midsections. Both had on knit shirts and leather jackets; more Leather People. "Oy el meemo." He took the big chance: their faces. Immediately he cast his eyes down again. They were staring right at him Such cruel looks! Both appeared to be in their early thirties. They had thick black hair coiffed and trimmed, just so, in vulgar but probably expensive hairdos. Both had their hair parted down the center and teased in such a way that the hair seemed to be gushing up in neat black ceremonial fountains. Such twisted expressions as they stared at him! *Did they know?*

Now he could hear Killian's voice. *Tawk. Lawr. Awright.* He consoled himself with the thought that he wouldn't have to listen to it much longer. The Lion was right. How could he have entrusted his fate to anyone immersed in this sordid milieu? Killian appeared at the doorway from the inner hall. He had his arm around the shoulders of a pudgy and thoroughly dejected little white man who wore a pathetic suit with an especially pathetic vest that popped out in front of his belly.

"What can I tell you, Donald?" Killian was saying. "The law's like anything else. You get what you pay for. All right?" *The lawr's like anything else. Yuh gedwudja pay for.* The little man trudged off without even looking at him. Not once had he been in Killian's presence when the main topic of conversation had not been money—the money due Thomas Killian.

"Ayyyyyy," said Killian, smiling at Sherman, "I didn't mean for you to have to wait." He cast his eyes significantly at the retreating figure of the little man, then shrugged his eyebrows.

As he and Sherman walked down the hallway, beneath the blazing down-lighters, to Killian's office, he said, "Now *that*"—his head nodded back in the general direction of the little man—"is a guy with problems. A fifty-seven-year-old assistant principal, Irish Catholic, wife and family, and he gets picked up on a charge of propositioning a seven-year-old girl. The arresting officer claims he offered her a banana and went on from there."

Sherman said nothing. Did this insensitive wiseguy fop, with his incessant cynicism, actually think that would make him feel better? A chill went through him. It was as if the pudgy little man's fate were his own.

"You check out the two guys across from you?"

Sherman braced. Which hell were they trapped in?

"Twenty-eight, twenty-nine years old, both of them, and they'd be on the Forbes Four Hundred list if their business published annual reports. They got *that much money*. They're Cubans, but they import from Colombia. They're Mike Bellavita's clients."

Sherman's resentment grew with each wiseguy word. Did the fop really think his breezy survey of the local scene, his detachment, his hard-boiled tone would flatter him, would make him feel superior to the detritus caught in the filthy tide that flows through here? I'm not superior, you oh-so-knowing, oh-so-ignorant fool! I'm one of them! My heart goes out to them! An old Irish child molester . . . two young Cuban drug dealers with their sad pompous hair—in short, he was learning for himself the truth of the saying "A liberal is a conservative who has been arrested."

In Killian's office, Sherman took a seat and watched the Irish fop rear back in his desk chair and roll his shoulders about under his double-breasted suit, preen-ing. He resented him even more profoundly. Killian was in excellent spirits. Newspapers were stacked up on his desk. *Team Mercedes: He Hit, She Ran.* But of course! The hottest criminal case in New York was *his*.

Well, he was about to lose it. How should he tell him? He wanted to just *let him have it*. But the words came out with some semblance of tact.

"I hope you realize," said Sherman, "I'm very unhappy about what happened yesterday."

"Ayyyyyy, who wouldn't be? It was outrageous, even for Weiss."

"I don't think you understand. I'm not talking about what I was subjected to, per se, I'm talking about the fact that you—"

He was interrupted by the voice of the receptionist coming over the intercom on Killian's desk: "Neil Flannagan of the *Daily News* on 3-0."

Killian leaned forward in his chair. "Tell him I'll call him back. No, wait a minute. Tell him I'll call him back in thirty minutes. If he's out of the office, then he should call me back in thirty minutes." To Sherman: "Sorry."

Sherman paused, looked balefuly at the fop, and said, "I'm talking about something else. I'm talking about—'

Killian broke in: "I don't mean that we're only gonna be talking for thirty minutes." *Tawkin.* "The whole day is yours if you want it and we need it. But I wanna talk to this guy Flannagan, from the *News*. He's gonna be our antidote . . . to the venom."

"Well, that's fine," said Sherman as flatly as possible, "but we've got a problem. You assured me you had your special 'contacts' in the Bronx District Attorney's Office. You told me you had a 'contract' with this man Fitzgibbon. I seem to recall quite a dissertation on something called the 'Favor Bank.' Now, don't misinterpret what I'm saying. For all I know, you may have as keen a legal mind—"

The voice on the intercom: "Peter Fallow of *The City Light* on 3-0."

"Get his number. Tell him I'll call him back." To Sherman: "Speak of the venom. The head snake checks in."

Sherman's heart shuddered in palpitation, then recovered.

"Go ahead. You were saying."

"I'm not doubting your legal judgment, but you made these assurances to me, and naïvely I went ahead and . . ." He paused to choose the correct word.

Killian jumped in: "You were double-crossed, Sherman. *I* was double-crossed. Bernie Fitzgibbon was double-crossed. What Weiss did was unconscionable. You *do . . . not . . . do . . .* what he did. You *do not do it.*"

"Nevertheless, he did it, and after you told me—"

"I know what it was like. It was like being thrown in a cesspool. But Bernie was not totally unsuccessful. Weiss wanted to do worse. You gotta understand that. The sonofabitch wanted to arrest you *in your home!* He wanted a *Park Avenue arrest!* He's crazy, crazy, crazy! And you know what he woulda done if he had his way? He woulda had the cops put handcuffs on you in your own home, then take you to a precinct house and let you get a whiff of the pens there for a while and then they put you in a van with wire mesh over the windows, with a buncha these animals, and *then* take you to Central Booking and let you go through what you went through. That's what he wanted."

"Nevertheless—"

"Mr. Killian, Irv Stone of Channel 1 on 3-2. This is the third time he's called."

"Get his number and tell him I'll call him back." To Sherman: "Today I gotta talk to these people even though I got nothing to tell them. Just to keep the lines open. Tomorrow we start to turn things around."

"Turn things around," said Sherman in what was meant as bitter irony. The fop didn't notice. The fop's excitement over such attention from the press was written all over his face. *Out of my ignominy, his own cheap glory.*

So he tried it again. "Turn things around, all right," he said.

Killian smiled. "Mr. McCoy, I do believe you doubt me. Well, I got news for you. In fact, I got a lotta news for you." He pressed the intercom button. "Hey,

Nina. Ask Quigley to come in here. Tell him Mr. McCoy is here." To Sherman: "Ed Quigley is our investigator, the guy I told you about, the guy who used to be in Major Cases."

A tall bald man appeared in the doorway. It was the same man Sherman had seen in the blazing reception room on his first visit. He carried a revolver in a holster high on his left hip. He wore a white shirt but no tie. His sleeves were rolled up, revealing a pair of huge wrists and hands. His left hand held a manila envelope. He was the sort of tall angular raw-boned man who looks more powerful and menacing at fifty than he did at twenty-five. His shoulders were wide but had a degenerate slouch. His eyes seemed to have sunk deep into the occipital craters.

"Ed," said Killian, "this is Mr. McCoy."

Sherman nodded morosely.

"Pleased to meet you," said the man. He gave Sherman the same dead smile he had given him the first time.

Killian said, "You got the picture?"

Quigley took a piece of paper out of the envelope and handed it to Killian, and Killian handed it to Sherman.

"This is a Xerox, but it took—I'm not even gonna tell you what it took to get this picture. You recognize him?"

A profile and a head-on picture of a black man, with numbers. Square features, a powerful neck.

Sherman sighed. "It looks like him. The other boy, the big one, the one who said, 'Yo! Need some help?' "

"He's a lowlife named Roland Auburn. Lives in the Poe projects. Right now he's on Rikers Island awaiting disposition of his fourth drug indictment. Obviously he's cutting a deal with the D.A. in return for testimony against you."

"And lying."

"That does not in any way violate the principles that have governed Mr. Roland Auburn's life thus far," said Killian.

"How did you find this out?"

Killian smiled and gestured toward Quigley. "Ed has many friends among our men in blue, and many of our finest owe him favors."

Quigley merely pursed his lips slightly.

Sherman said, "Has he ever been arrested for robbery—or the sort of thing he tried to pull on me?"

"You mean highway robbery?" Killian chuckled at what he had just said. "I never thoughta that before. That's what it is, highway robbery. Right, Ed?"

"I guess so."

"Not that we know of," said Killian, "but we intend to find out a whole lot more about the sonofabitch. Prison inmates are notorious for what they'll testify to—and this is Weiss's whole fucking case! This is what he brought you in on!"

Killian shook his head, with apparent disgust, and kept shaking it. Sherman found himself genuinely grateful. It was the first hint of heartfelt absolution anyone had offered.

"All right, so that's one thing," said Killian. Then to Ed: "Now tell him about Mrs. Ruskin."

Sherman looked up at Quigley, and Quigley said, "She's gone to Italy. I traced her as far as a house she rented on Lake Como. It's some kinda resort in Lombardy."

"That's right," said Sherman. "She'd just come back from there the night all this happened."

"Yeah, well, a couple a days ago," said Quigley, "she left there in a car with some young guy named Filippo. That's all I know, 'Filippo.' You got any idea who that might be? Early or mid-twenties, slender, medium height. Lotta hair. Punk clothes. Nice-looking kid, or so my man told me." `

Sherman sighed. "It's some artist she knows. Filippo Charazza or Charizzi."

"You know of any other place in Italy she might go?"

Sherman shook his head. "How did you find out all this?"

Quigley looked at Killian, and Killian said, "Tell him."

"Wasn't too hard," said Quigley. Proud to be onstage, he couldn't resist a smile. "Most a these people have Globexpress. You know, the credit card. There's a woman—a person I deal with in the accounting office on Duane Street. They got a computer network feeds in from all over the world. I give her a hundred dollars per item. Not too bad for five minutes' work. Sure enough, this Maria Ruskin has two charges three days ago in stores in this town, Como. Clothing stores. So I call up a guy we use in Rome, and he calls up one of the stores and says he's from Globexpress and gives them her account number and says they need to send her a telegram for 'account clarification.' They don't give a shit. They give him the address where they delivered the merchandise, and he goes down to Como and checks it all." Quigley shrugged, as if to say, "Piece a cake for a guy like me."

Noting that Sherman was properly impressed, Killian said, "So now we got a line on both our players. We know who their witness is, and we'll find your friend Mrs. Ruskin. And we'll get her back here, even if Ed has to bring her back in a box with air holes in it. Don't look shocked. I know you give her the benefit of the doubt, but by objective standards she does not exactly qualify as your friend. You're in the biggest jam of your life, and she's your way out, and she's off in Italy with a nice-looking fellow named Filippo. Ayyyyyyyyy, whaddaya whaddaya?"

Sherman smiled in spite of himself. His vanity was such, however, that he immediately assumed that there was an innocuous explanation.

After Quigley had left, Killian said: "Ed Quigley is the best. There is no better private investigator in the business. He . . . will . . . do . . . *anything*. He's your basic hardcore New York Hell's Kitchen Irishman. The kids Ed ran with all became hoodlums or cops. The ones that became cops were the ones that the Church got a hook into, the ones that cooked a little bit from guilt. But they all like the same things. They all like to butt heads and loosen people's teeth. The only difference is, if you are a cop, you can do it legally with the priest nodding over you and looking the other way at the same time. Ed was a hell of a cop. He was a fucking reign of terror."

"How *did* he get this picture?" Sherman was looking at the Xeroxed page. "Was that one of your . . . 'contracts'?"

"A thing like this? Oooooh. Fuhgedaboudit. Getting this information—with *a mug shot?*—this is so far out of bounds—I mean, this goes beyond the Favor Bank. I don't ask, but unless I miss my guess, this is the Favor Bank plus the real bank, like your basic negotiable assets. Fuhgedaboudit. I mean it. For God's sake, don't mention it. Don't even think about it again."

Sherman sat back in his chair and looked at Killian. He had come in here to fire him—and now he wasn't so sure.

As if reading his mind, Killian said: "Let me explain something to you. It's not that Abe Weiss doesn't care about justice." *Doesn't.* He had used the correct third person singular. What exalted notion, wondered Sherman, had wandered into his head? "He probably does. But this case has nothing to do with justice. This is a war. This is Abe Weiss running for re-election, and that job is his fucking life, and when the press gets as hot for a case as they are about this one, he don't know from justice. He's gonna do any goddamned thing he has to do. I don't mean to frighten you, but that's what's going on, a war. I can't just construct a defense for you, I got to wage a campaign. I don't think he'd put a tap on your telephone, but he has that power and he's perfectly capable of doing it. So if I were you, I wouldn't say anything of substance about this case over the telephone. In fact, don't say anything at all about it on the telephone. That way you don't have to worry about what's important and what isn't."

Sherman nodded to show he understood.

"Now I'm gonna be very direct with you, Sherman. This thing is gonna cost a lot of money. You know what Quigley's man in Lombardy costs? Two thousand dollars a week, and that's just one phase of what we got to do. I'm gonna ask you for a big retainer, right up front. This is exclusive of trial work, which I still hope will not be necessary."

"How much?"

"Seventy-five thousand."

"Seventy-five thousand?"

"Sherman, what can I tell you? The lawr is like anything else. Awright? Yuh gedwudja pay for."

"But, good Lord. Seventy-five thousand."

"You force me to be immodest. We are the best. And I'll fight for you. I love a fight. I'm as Irish as Quigley."

So Sherman, he who came to fire his lawyer, wrote out a check for seventy-five thousand dollars.

He handed it to Killian. "You'll have to give me some time to get that much money into my account."

"That's fair enough. What's today? Wednesday? I won't deposit this until Friday morning."

The menu had little black-and-white ads across the bottom, little rectangles with old-fashioned borders and highly stylized logos for things like Nehi chocolate drink and Captain Henry's Canned Herring Roe and Café du Monde Dark Roast Coffee with Chicory and Indian Chief Balloon Tire bicycles and Edgeworth Pipe Tobacco and 666 Cold & Cough Medicine. The ads were sheer decoration, mementos of the old two-lane hardtop days in Louisiana bayou country. A sixth sense made Kramer flinch. This *faux*-Down Home shit was as expensive as the *faux*-Bohemian Casual shit. He didn't even want to think what this was all going to come to, maybe fifty goddamned dollars. But there was no turning back now, was there? Shelly was sitting right across from him in the booth watching his every gesture and expression, and he had spent the past hour and a half projecting the image of a man who takes charge and is in control, and it was *he*, the manly bon vivant, who had suggested that they proceed forthwith to dessert and coffee.

Besides, he felt an acute need for ice cream. His mouth and his gullet were on fire. The Café Alexandria didn't seem to have a single item on any course that wasn't a conflagration. The Creole Gumbo with Bayou Sand—he thought the word *sand* must be a metaphor for some gritty condiment, some ground-up root or something, but there was actual sand in the goddamned soup, apparently drenched in Tabasco. The Cornbread Cayenne—it was like bread with fire ants in it. The Catfish Fillet with Scorched Okra on a Bed of Yellow Rice with Apple Butter and Chinese Mustard Sauce—the Chinese mustard raised a red flag, but he had to order the catfish because it was the only semi-inexpensive entree on the menu, $10.50. And Andriutti had said it was an inexpensive little Creole restaurant on Beach Street, "really terrific." Beach Street was a crummy enough street to have a cheap restaurant, and so he had believed him.

But Shelly kept saying how wonderful it was. She was glowing, a divine radiance with brown lipstick, although he wasn't entirely sure whether it was love, Autumn in the Berkshires makeup, or a fire in the belly he was looking at.

Ice cream, ice cream, ice cream . . . He scanned the swamp-fire prose of the menu, and through the caloric waves he spotted a single ice-cream dish: Hand-Churned Vanilla Ice Cream Topped with Walnut Chili Chutney. *Chili?* Well, he would scrape the topping to one side and stick to the ice cream. He didn't have the nerve to ask the trendy waitress with all the honey curls to leave the topping off. He didn't want to look like an unadventurous wimp in front of Shelly.

Shelly ordered the Key Lime Tart with Relleno Pastry, and they both ordered the Fresh Ground New Orleans Coffee with Chicory, even though something told him the chicory meant more grief for his sizzling innards.

Having placed the dessert and coffee order with a firm voice and manly resolve, he put his forearms on the edge of the table and leaned forward and poured his eyes back into Shelly's, to give her a refill of crime intoxication as well as the last of the bottle of Crockett Sump White Zinfandel wine that was setting him back twelve dollars. That was the next-to-cheapest wine on the wine list. He didn't have the courage to order the cheapest, which was a Chablis for $9.50. Only inexperienced wet smacks ordered Chablis.

"I wish I could take you along and just have you listen to this fellow, this Roland Auburn. I've interviewed him three times now. At first he seems so tough, so hard, so . . . you know . . . menacing. He's a *rock*, with these dead eyes, the kind of teenager that's in everybody's nightmare about a dark street in New York. But if you just listen to him for five minutes—just listen—you start to hear something else. You hear pain. He's a *boy*, for God's sake. He's frightened. These boys grow up in the ghetto without anybody ever caring about them, really. They're terrified. They erect this wall of machismo, thinking it's gonna protect them from harm, when in fact they're ready at any moment to be destroyed. That's what they expect: they're gonna be destroyed. No, I'm not worried about Roland in front of a jury. What I'll do is, I'll lead him through some innocuous questions about his background for the first minute and a half or two minutes, and then he'll start shedding this tough-guy outer skin of his, without even knowing it, and they will *believe him.* He won't come across as a hardened criminal or a hardened anything. He'll come across as a frightened boy who's yearning for just a little of bit of decency and just a little bit of beauty in his life, because that is precisely what he is. I wish I could think of some way to get the jury to see the drawings and collages he does. Shelly, he's brilliant. Brilliant! Well, there's no way that's gonna happen, I suppose. It's gonna be tricky enough just to make sure I lead the real Roland Auburn out of his hard shell. It's gonna be like getting a snail outta one a those shells that goes in a spiral."

Kramer twirled his finger in a spiral and laughed at his own simile. Shelly's shiny lips smiled appreciatively. They glistened. *She* glistened.

"Oh, I'd love to attend the trial," she said. "When will it be?"

"We don't know yet." (Me and the D.A., who happen to be very tight with one another.) "We won't even take it before the grand jury until next week. We could go to trial in two months or six months. It's hard to say in a case that's gotten as much publicity as this one has. When the media go crazy over something, it complicates things." He shook his head, as if to say, "You just have to learn to put up with it."

Shelly fairly beamed. "Larry, when I got home and turned on the television last night, and there you were, that drawing of you—I just started laughing, like a child. I said, 'Larry!' I said it right out loud, as if you'd just stepped into the room. I couldn't get over it."

"It kind of bowled me over, too, to tell you the truth."

"I'd give anything to come to the trial. Could I?"

"Sure."

"I promise I won't do anything silly."

Kramer felt a tingle. He knew *this* was the moment. He moved his hands forward and slid the tips of his fingers under the tips of hers without looking at them. She didn't look down, either, and she didn't pull back. She kept looking into his eyes and pressed the tips of his fingers with hers.

"I don't care if you do something silly," he said. His voice surprised him. It was so hoarse and bashful.

Outside, with practically all his cash left behind in the Colorfully Antiquated non-electric cash register of the Café Alexandria, he took her hand and entwined his thick Pumping Iron fingers among her slender tender fingers, and they began walking along in the decrepit darkness of Beach Street.

"You know, Shelly, you can't imagine what it means to me to have you to talk to about all this. The fellows in my office—you try to get down to the heart of anything with them and they think you're turning soft. And God help you if you turn soft. And my wife—I don't know, she just don't—doesn't want to hear it anymore, no matter what. By now she just thinks she's married to this guy who has this grim task to perform, sending a lot of pathetic people off to jail. But this case is not pathetic. You know what this case is? It's a signal, a very important signal to the people of this city who think they're not part of the social contract. You know? It's about a man who thinks that his exalted station in life relieves him of the obligation to treat the life of someone at the bottom of the scale the way he would treat somebody like himself. I don't doubt for a minute that if he had run down anybody even remotely like himself, McCoy would have done the right thing. He's probably what we all know of as 'a decent sort.' That's what makes it fascinating. He's not an evil person at all—but he did an evil thing. Do you follow me?"

"I guess. The only thing I don't understand is why Henry Lamb didn't say anything about being hit by a car when he went to the hospital. And now that you've told me about your witness, Roland—there hasn't been anything in the papers about him, has there?"

"No, and we won't release anything about him for a while. What I've told you is just between us."

"Well, anyway, now it turns out Roland didn't say anything about his friend being hit by a car for almost two weeks after it happened. Isn't that a little odd?"

"What's odd about it! My God. Shelly, Lamb was suffering from a fatal head injury, or it's probably fatal, and Roland knew he'd be arrested for a major felony if he talked to the cops! I wouldn't call it *odd*.'

Miss Shelly Thomas decided to back out of that avenue. "Odd isn't what I really meant. I guess I meant—I don't envy you, the kind of preparation and research you must have to do to get ready for one of these cases."

"Hah! If I got paid overtime for all the hours I'm gonna have to put into this one—well, I could move to Park Avenue myself. But you know what? That doesn't matter to me. It really doesn't. All I care about is, whatever kind of life I lead, I want to be able to look back and say, 'I made a difference.' This case is *so* important, on every conceivable level, not just in terms of my career. It's just a . . . I don't know how to say it . . . a whole new chapter. I want to *make a difference*, Shelly."

He stopped and, still holding her hand, put it behind her waist and then pulled her to him. She was looking up at him, radiantly. Their lips met. He peeked just once, to see if she was keeping her eyes closed. She was.

Kramer could feel her lower abdomen pressed against his. Was that the knob of her mons veneris? It had come along this far, this fast, so sweetly, so beautifully —and damn! No place to take her!

Imagine! Him! The budding star of the McCoy case—and no place—no place at all!—in the very Babylon of the twentieth century!—to take a lovely willing girl with brown lipstick. He wondered what was going through her mind at this moment.

In fact, she was thinking about the way men are in New York. Every time you go out with one, you have to sit there and listen to two or three hours of My Career first.

It was a triumphant Peter Fallow who entered Leicester's that evening. Everyone at the Table, and scores more among those who packed that noisy bistro, even those who turned up their noses at *The City Light*, knew that it was he who had broken the McCoy case. Even St. John and Billy, who were seldom serious about anything other than one another's infidelities, offered congratulations with apparent sincerity. Sampson Reith, the London *Daily Courier*'s political correspondent, who was out here for a few days, happened by the Table and told of his lunch with Irwin Gubner, deputy managing editor of *The New York Times*, who lamented that *The City Light* had the story practically to itself, which of course meant Peter Fallow, keeper and tender. Alex Britt-Withers sent over a vodka Southside, on the house, and it tasted so good Fallow ordered another. The tidal wave of approval was so great that Caroline smiled the first smile he'd had from her in a very long time. The only sour note was Nick Stopping. His approval was decidedly softspoken and halfhearted. Then Fallow realized that Nick, the Marxist-Leninist, the Oxford Sparticist, the Rousseau of the Third World, was no doubt consumed with jealousy. This was *his* sort of story, not this shallow comedian Fallow's—Fallow could now regard Nick's opinion of him with magnanimous amusement—and yet here was Fallow at the forefront, riding the freight

train of History, while he, Stopping, was writing yet another piece for *House &
Garden* on the latest Mrs. Posh's villa in Hobe Sound, or wherever.

Well, speaking of *posh*, Rachel Lampwick did twit him quite a bit about using
that word so much. "Peter, I do think you might be a bit more *gallant*"—she
pronounced it the French way—"toward this Mrs. McCoy, don't you? I mean, you
do go on about the posh Mr. McCoy and his posh auto and his posh flat and his
posh job and his posh daddy and his posh girlfriend—or what did you call her?—
'foxy'?—I rather like that—and poor Mrs. McCoy is just his 'forty-year-old wife,'
which of course means very plain, doesn't it? *Not* very *gallant*, Peter."

But obviously Rachel had been devouring every word he wrote. So he felt
nothing but a victor's warmth toward her and one and all.

"*The City Light* doesn't consider wives glamorous unless they're unfaithful,"
said Fallow. "We save our enthusiasm for Other Women."

Then everyone began to speculate about the Foxy Brunette, and Billy Cortez,
casting an eye toward St. John, said he had heard of men taking their little tarts
to out-of-the-way places to avoid detection, but, really, *the Bronx* indicated rather
advanced paranoia, and Fallow ordered another vodka Southside.

The hubbub was warm and happy and English, and the orange and ocher
glows of Leicester's were mellow and English, and Caroline was staring at him
quite a lot, sometimes smiling, sometimes looking at him with a smirk, and it did
make him curious, and he had another vodka Southside, and Caroline got up
from her place and walked around the table to where he was and leaned over and
said into his ear, "Come upstairs with me a minute."

Could it be? It was so very unlikely, but—could it be? They went up the spiral
staircase in the back to Britt-Withers's office, and Caroline, suddenly looking
serious, said, "Peter, I probably shouldn't tell you what I'm going to tell you. You
really don't deserve it. You haven't been very nice to me."

"Me!" said Fallow with a jolly laugh. "Caroline! You tried to spread my *snout*
all over New York!"

"What? Your snout?" Caroline smiled through a blush. "Well, not all over
New York. In any event, after the gift I'm about to give you, I think we can call it
even."

"The gift?"

"I think it's a gift. I know who your Foxy Brunette is. I know who was in the
car with McCoy."

"You're joking."

"I'm not joking."

"All right—who?"

"Her name is Maria Ruskin. You met her that night at the Limelight."

"I did?"

"Peter, you get so drunk. She's the wife of a man named Arthur Ruskin, who's
about three times her age. He's a Jewish something-or-other. Very rich."

"How do you know this?"

"Do you remember my friend the artist? The Italian? Filippo? Filippo
Chirazzi?"

"Ah yes. Couldn't very well forget him, could I?"

"Well, he knows her."

"How does he know her?"

"The same way a lot of men know her. She's a slut."

"And she told him?"

"Yes."

"And he told you?"

"Yes."

"My God, Caroline. Where can I find him?"

"I don't know. I can't find him myself. The little bastard."

25

WE THE JURY

"THIS IS NOTHING but the Establishment looking after its own," said Reverend Bacon. He was leaning back in his chair at his desk and talking into the telephone, but his tones were official. For he was talking to the press. "This is the Power Structure manufacturing and disseminating its lies with the willing connivance of its lackeys in the media, and its lies are transparent."

Edward Fiske III, although a young man, recognized the rhetoric of the Movement of the late 1960s and early 1970s. Reverend Bacon stared at the mouthpiece of the telephone with a look of righteous anger. Fiske slumped down a little farther in his chair. His eyes jumped from Reverend Bacon's face to the swamp-yellow sycamores in the yard beyond the window and then back to Reverend Bacon and then back to the sycamores. He didn't know whether eye contact with the man was wise at this point or not, even though the thing that had provoked the anger had nothing to do with Fiske's visit. Bacon was furious over the piece in this morning's *Daily News* suggesting that Sherman McCoy might have been escaping from a robbery attempt when his car hit Henry Lamb. The *Daily News* intimated that Lamb's accomplice was a convicted felon named Roland Auburn and that the district attorney's entire case against Sherman McCoy was based on a story concocted by this individual, who was now seeking a plea bargain in a drug case.

"You doubt that they stoop so low?" Reverend Bacon declaimed into the mouthpiece. "You doubt they can be vile? Now you see them stoop so low, they try to smear young Henry Lamb. Now you see them vilify the victim, who lies mortally wounded and cannot speak for himself. For them to say that Henry Lamb is a robber—*that's* the criminal act . . . see . . . That's the criminal act. But that is the twisted mind of the Power Structure, that is the underlying racist mentality. Since Henry Lamb is a young black male, they think they can brand him as a criminal . . . see . . . They think they can smear him in that way. But they are wrong. Henry Lamb's life refutes their lies. Henry Lamb is everything the Power Structure tells the young black male he is supposed to be, but when the needs of *one a their own* demand it   . . see . . . one a their *own* . . . then they think nothing of turning around and trying to destroy the good name of this young man . . . What? . . . Say, "Who are *they*?" . . . You think Sherman McCoy stands alone? You think he is by himself? He is one a the most powerful men at Pierce & Pierce, and Pierce & Pierce is one a the most powerful forces in Wall Street. I *know* Pierce & Pierce . . . see . . . I *know* what they can do. You heard a capitalists. You heard a plutocrats. You take a look at Sherman McCoy and you're *looking* at a capitalist, you're *looking* at a plutocrat."

Reverend Bacon eviscerated the offending newspaper article. The *Daily News* was a notorious toady of the corporate interests. The reporter who wrote the pack of lies, Neil Flannagan, was a lackey so shameless as to lend his name to such a disgusting campaign. His font of so-called information—referred to coyly as "sources close to the case"—was obviously McCoy and his cabal.

The McCoy case was of no interest to Fiske, except as ordinary gossip, although he did know the Englishman who had first exposed the whole situation, a wonderful witty fellow named Peter Fallow, who was a master of the art of conversation. No, Fiske's only interest was in how much Bacon's involvement in it was going to complicate his task, which was to retrieve the $350,000 or some part of it. In the half hour he had been sitting here, Bacon's secretary had buzzed in with calls from two newspapers, the Associated Press, a Bronx assemblyman, a Bronx congressman, and the executive secretary of the Gay Fist Strike Force, all concerning the McCoy case. And Reverend Bacon was now talking to a man named Irv Stone, from Channel 1. At first Fiske figured his mission was (yet once again) hopeless. But behind Reverend Bacon's baleful orotundity he began to detect a buoyancy, a *joie de combat*. Reverend Bacon loved what was going on. He was leading the crusade. He was in his element. Somewhere in all of this, at last, if he picked the right moment, Edward Fiske III might find an opening through which to retrieve the Episcopal Church's $350,000 from the Heavenly Crusader's promiscuous heap of schemes.

Reverend Bacon was saying, "There's the cause and there's the effect, Irv . . . see . . . And we had a demonstration at the Poe projects, where Henry Lamb lives. That's the effect . . . see . . . What happened to Henry Lamb is the effect. Well, today we gonna take it to the cause. We gonna take it to Park Avenue. To Park Avenue, see, from whence the lies commence . . . from whence they commence . . . What? . . . Right. Henry Lamb cannot speak for himself, but he's gonna have a mighty voice. He's gonna have the voice of his people, and that voice is gonna be heard on Park Avenue."

Fiske had never seen Reverend Bacon's face so animated. He began asking Irv Stone technical questions. Naturally, he couldn't guarantee Channel 1 an exclusive this time, but could he count on live coverage? What was the optimal time? Same as before? And so forth and so on. Finally he hung up. He turned toward Fiske and looked at him with portentous concentration and said:

"The steam."

"The steam?"

"The steam . . . You remember I told you about the steam?"

"Oh yes. I do."

"Well, now you gonna see the steam coming to a head. The whole city's gonna see it. Right on Park Avenue. People think the fire has gone out. They think the rage is a thing of the past. They don't know it's only been bottled up.

It's when the steam is trapped, you find out what it can do . . . see . . . That's when you find out it's Powder Valley for you and your whole gang. Pierce & Pierce only know how to handle one kind of capital. They don't understand the steam. They can't handle the steam."

Fiske spotted a tiny opening.

"As a matter of fact, Reverend Bacon, I was talking to a man from Pierce & Pierce about you just the other day. Linwood Talley, from the underwriting division."

"They know me there," said Reverend Bacon. He smiled, but a trifle sardonically. "They know *me*. They don't know the steam."

"Mr. Talley was telling me about Urban Guaranty Investments. He said it's been highly successful."

"I can't complain."

"Mr. Talley didn't go into any details, but I gather it's been"—he searched for the proper euphemism—"profitable right from the beginning."

"Ummmmmm." Reverend Bacon didn't seem inclined to expand.

Fiske said nothing and tried to hold Reverend Bacon's gaze with his own, in hopes of creating a conversational vacuum the great crusader couldn't resist. The truth about Urban Guaranty Investments, as Fiske had in fact learned from Linwood Talley, was that the federal government had recently given the firm $250,000 as a "minority underwriter" for a $7 billion issue of federally backed municipal bonds. The so-called set-aside law required that there be minority participation in the selling of such bonds, and Urban Guaranty Investments had been created to help satisfy that requirement of the law. There was no requirement that the minority firm actually sell any of the bonds or even receive them. The lawmakers did not want to wrap the task in red tape. It was only necessary for the firm to participate in the issue. Participate was broadly defined. In most cases —Urban Guaranty Investments was but one of many such firms across the country—participation meant receiving a check for the fee from the federal government and depositing it, and not much more. Urban Guaranty Investments had no employees, and no equipment, just an address (Fiske was at it), a telephone number, and a president, Reginald Bacon.

"So it just occurred to me, Reverend Bacon, in terms of our conversations and what the diocese is naturally concerned about and what remains to be worked out, if we are to resolve what I'm sure you want to resolve just as much as the bishop, who, I have to tell you, has been pressing me on this point—" Fiske paused. As often happened in his talks with Reverend Bacon, he couldn't remember how he had begun his sentence. He had no idea what the number and tense of the predicate should be. "—pressing me on this point, and, uh, uh, the thing is, we thought perhaps you might be in a position to shift some funds into the escrow account we mentioned, the escrow account for the Little Shepherd Day Care Center, just until our licensing problems are worked out."

"I don't follow you," said Reverend Bacon.

Fiske had the sinking feeling he was going to have to think of some way to say it again.

But Reverend Bacon bailed him out. "Are you saying we ought to shift money from Urban Guaranty Investments to the Little Shepherd Day Care Center?"

"Not in so many words, Reverend Bacon, but if the funds are available or could be loaned out . . ."

"But that's illegal! You're talking about commingling funds! We can't shift moneys from one corporation to another just because it looks like one of them needs it more."

Fiske looked at the rock of fiscal probity, half expecting a wink, even though he knew Reverend Bacon wasn't a winker. "Well, the diocese has always been willing to go the extra mile with you, Reverend Bacon, in the sense that if there was room to find some flexibility in the strict reading of the regulation, such as the time you and the board of directors of the Inner City Family Restructuring Society made the trip to Paris and the diocese paid for it out of the Missionary Society budget—" Once again he was drowning in the syntactical soup, but it didn't matter.

"No way," said Reverend Bacon.

"Well, if not that, then—"

Reverend Bacon's secretary's voice came over the intercom: "Mr. Vogel is on the line."

Reverend Bacon wheeled about to the telephone on the credenza: "Al? . . . Yeah, I saw it. They'll drag that young man's name through the mud and think nothing of it."

Reverend Bacon and his caller, Vogel, went on for some time about the piece in the *Daily News*. This Mr. Vogel evidently reminded Reverend Bacon that the district attorney, Weiss, had told the *Daily News* there was absolutely no evidence to support the theory of a robbery attempt.

"Can't depend on him," said Reverend Bacon. "He's like the bat. You know the fable of the bat? The birds and the beasts were having a war. As long as the birds were winning, the bat says he's a bird, because he can fly. When the beasts were winning, the bat says he's a beast, because he got teeth. That's why the bat don't come out in the daytime. Don't nobody want to look at his two faces."

Reverend Bacon listened for a bit, then said, "Yes, I do, Al. There's a gentleman from the Episcopal diocese of New York with me right now. You want me to call you back? . . . Unh-hunh . . . Unh-hunh . . . You say his apartment's worth three million dollars?" He shook his head. "I never hearda such a thing. I say it's time Park Avenue heard the voice of the streets . . . Unh-hunh . . . I'll call you back about that. I'll talk to Annie Lamb before I call you. When you thinking about filing? . . . About the same, when I talked to her yesterday. He's on the life-support system. He don't say anything and don't know anybody. When you think about that young man, there's no amount can pay for it, is there? . . . Well, I'll get back to you as soon as I can."

After he hung up, Reverend Bacon shook his head sadly, but then looked up with a gleam in his eye and just a trace of a smile. With an athletic quickness he rose from his chair and came around the desk with his hand out, as if Fiske had just announced he had to leave.

"Always good to see you!"

Reflexively, Fiske shook his hand, at the same time saying, "But, Reverend Bacon, we haven't—"

"We'll talk again. I got an awful lot to do—a demonstration right on Park Avenue, got to help Mr. Lamb file a hundred-million-dollar lawsuit against Sherman McCoy . . ."

"But, Reverend Bacon, I can't leave without an answer. The diocese has really reached the end—that is, they insist that I—"

"You tell the diocese they're doing fine. I told you last time, this is the best investment you people ever made. You tell 'em they're taking an option. They're buying the future at a discount. You tell 'em they'll see what I mean very shortly, no time at all." He put his arm about Fiske's shoulder in a comradely fashion and hastened his exit, all the while saying, "Don't worry about a thing. You're doing fine, see. Doing fine. They're gonna say, 'That young man, he took a risk and hit the jackpot.'"

Utterly befuddled, Fiske was swept outside by a tide of optimism and the pressure of a strong arm across his back.

The noise of the bullhorn and the bellows of rage rose up ten stories from Park Avenue in the heat of June—ten stories!—nothing to it!—they can almost *reach up!*—until the bedlam below seemed to be part of the air he breathed. The bullhorn bellowed his name! The hard C in McCoy cut through the roar of the mob and soared up above the vast sprawl of hatred below. He edged over to the library window and risked looking down. *Suppose they see me!* The demonstrators had spilled out onto the street on both sides of the median strip and had brought traffic to a halt. The police were trying to drive them back onto the sidewalks. Three policemen were chasing another bunch, fifteen or twenty at least, through the yellow tulips on the median strip. As they ran, the demonstrators held a long banner aloft: WAKE UP, PARK AVENUE! YOU CAN'T HIDE FROM THE PEOPLE! The yellow tulips fell before them, and they left a gutter of crushed blossoms behind them, and the three policemen came pounding through the gutter. Sherman stared, horrified. The sight of the perfect yellow spring tulips of Park Avenue falling before the feet of the mob paralyzed him with fear. A television crew lumbered along out in the street, trying to catch up with them. The one carrying the camera on his shoulder stumbled, and down he went, crashing to the pavement, camera and all. The mob's banners and placards bobbed and swayed like sails in a windy harbor. One enormous banner said, inexplicably, GAY FIST AGAINST CLASS JUSTICE. The two s's in CLASS were swastikas. Another one—Christ! Sherman caught his breath. In gigantic letters it said:

SHERMAN McCOY:
WE THE JURY
WANT YOU!

Then there was a crude approximation of a finger pointing straight at you, as in the old UNCLE SAM WANTS YOU posters. They seemed to be holding it at an angle, just so he could read it from up here. He fled the library and sat in the rear part of the living room in an armchair, one of Judy's beloved Louis-Something bergères, or was it a fauteuil? Killian was pacing up and down, still crowing about the article in the *Daily News*, apparently to buck up his spirits, but Sherman was no longer listening. He could hear the deep ugly voice of one of the bodyguards, who was in the library answering the telephone. "Stick it up your face." Every time one of the threats came in over the telephone, the bodyguard, a small swarthy man named Occhioni, said, "Stick it up your face." The way he said it, it sounded worse than any of the classic vulgarities. How had they gotten his private number? Probably from the press—in the open cavity. They were here on Park Avenue *at the door below*. They were coming in over the telephone. How long before they *burst in*, into the entry gallery and came screaming across that solemn green marble floor! The other bodyguard, McCarthy, was in the entry gallery, sitting in one of Judy's beloved Thomas Hope armchairs, and what good would he be? Sherman sat back, his eyes cast downward, fixed upon the slender legs of a Sheraton Pembroke table, a hellishly expensive thing Judy had found in one of those antique shops on Fifty-seventh Street . . . hellishly expensive . . . hellishly . . . Mr. Occhioni, who said "Stick it up your face" to everyone who called threatening his life . . . $200 per eight-hour shift . . . another $200 for the impassive Mr. McCarthy . . . double that for the two bodyguards at his parents' house on East Seventy-third, where Judy, Campbell, Bonita, and Miss Lyons were . . . $800 per eight-hour shift . . . all former New York City policemen from some agency Killian knew about . . . $2,400 a day . . . hemorrhaging money . . . McCOY! . . . McCOY! . . . a tremendous roar from the street below . . . And presently he wasn't thinking about the Pembroke table or the bodyguards anymore . . . He was staring catatonically and wondering about the barrel. How big was it? He had used it so many times, most recently on the Leash Club hunt last fall, but he couldn't remember how big it was! It was big, being a double-barrel 12-gauge. Was it too big to get in his mouth? No, it couldn't be *that* big, but what would it feel like? What would it feel like, touching the roof of his mouth? What would it *taste* like? Would he have trouble breathing long enough to . . . to . . . How would he pull the trigger? Let's see, he'd hold the barrel steady in his mouth with one hand, his left hand—but how long was the barrel? It was long . . . Could he reach the trigger with his right hand? Maybe not! His toe . . . He'd read somewhere about someone who took off his shoe and pressed the trigger with his toe . . . Where would he do it? The gun was at the house on Long Island . . . assuming he could get to Long Island, get out of this building, escape from besieged Park Avenue, get away alive from . . . WE THE JURY . . . .The flower bed out beyond the tool house . . . Judy always called it the cutting bed . . . He'd sit down out there . . . If it made a mess, it wouldn't matter . . . *Suppose Campbell was the one who found him!* . . . The thought didn't reduce him to tears the way he thought it might . . . *hoped* it might . . . She wouldn't be finding her father . . . He wasn't her father anymore . . . wasn't anything anyone had ever known as Sherman McCoy . . . He was only a cavity fast filling with hot vile hate . . .

The telephone rang in the library. Sherman braced. *Stick it up your face?* But all he heard was the rumble of Occhioni's normal voice. Presently the little man stuck his head into the living room and said, "Hey, Mr. McCoy, it's somebody named Sally Rawthrote. You wanna talk to her or not?"

Sally Rawthrote? She was the woman he had sat next to at the Bavardages', the woman who had lost interest in him immediately and then froze him out for the rest of the dinner. Why would she want to talk to him now? Why should he want to talk to her at all? He didn't, but a tiny spark of curiosity was lit within the cavity, and he stood up and looked at Killian and shrugged and went into the library and sat at his desk and picked up the telephone.

"Hello?"

"Sherman! Sally Rawthrote." *Sherman.* Oldest friend in the world. "I hope this isn't a bad time?"

A *bad time?* From below a tremendous roar welled up, and the bullhorn screamed and bellowed, and he heard his name. McCOY! . . . McCOY!

"Well, of course it's a bad time," said Sally Rawthrote. "What am I saying? But I just thought I'd take a chance and call and see if there's any way I might help."

Help? As she spoke, her face came back to him, that dreadful tense near-sighted face that focused about four and a half inches from the bridge of your nose.

"Well, thank you," said Sherman.

"You know, I live just a few blocks down from you. Same side of the street."

"Oh, yes."

"I'm on the northwest corner. If you're going to live on Park, I think there's nothing quite like the northwest corner. You get so much *sun!* Of course, where you are is nice, too. Your building's got some of the most beautiful apartments in New York. I haven't been in yours since the McLeods had it. They had it before the Kittredges. Anyway, from my bedroom, which is on the corner, I can look right down Park to where you are. I'm looking down there right now, and *that* mob—it's absolutely outrageous! I feel so badly for you and Judy—I just had to call and see if there's anything I can do. I hope I'm not being out of place?"

"No, you're very kind. By the way, how did you get my number?"

"I called Inez Bavardage. Was that all right?"

"To tell you the truth, it doesn't make a hell of a lot of difference at this point, Mrs. Rawthrote."

"Sally."

"Anyway, thank you."

"As I say, if I can be of any help, let me know. With the apartment, is what I mean."

"With the apartment?"

Another rumble . . . a roar . . . MCCOY! MCCOY!

"If you should decide you want to do anything with the apartment. I'm with Benning Sturtevant, as you probably know, and I know that often in situations like this people sometimes find it advantageous to become as liquid as they can. Hah hah, I could stand a bit of that myself! Anyway, it's a consideration, and I assure you—*assure* you—I can get you three and a half for your apartment. Just like that. I can guarantee it."

The woman's gall was astounding. It was beyond good and bad form, beyond . . . taste . . . It was astounding. It made Sherman smile, and he didn't think he could smile.

"Well, well, well, well, Sally. I do admire foresightedness. You looked out your northwest window and you saw an apartment for sale."

"Not at all! I just thought—"

"Well, you're just one step too late, Sally. You'll have to talk to a man named Albert Vogel."

"Who's that?"

"He's the lawyer for Henry Lamb. He's filed a hundred-million-dollar lawsuit against me, and I'm not sure if I'm free to sell a rug at this point. Well, maybe I could sell a rug. You want to sell a rug for me?"

"Hah hah, no. Rugs I don't know anything about. I don't see how they can freeze your assets. That seems totally unfair. I mean, you were the *victim*, after all, weren't you? I read the story in the *Daily News* today. Ordinarily I only read Bess Hill and Bill Hatcher, but I was turning the pages—and there was your picture. I said, 'My God, it's Sherman!' So I read the story—and you were only avoiding a robbery attempt. It's so unfair!" She chattered on. She was fireproof. She couldn't be mocked.

After hanging up, Sherman returned to the living room.

Killian said, "Who was that?"

Sherman said, "A real-estate broker I met at dinner. She wanted to sell my apartment for me."

"She say how much she could get you?"

"Three and a half million dollars."

"Well, let's see," said Killian. "If she gets her 6 percent commission, that's . . . ummmm . . . $210,000. That's worth sounding stone-cold opportunistic over, I guess. But I'll say one thing for her."

"What's that?"

"She made you smile. So she ain't all bad."

Another roar, the loudest yet . . . MCCOY! . . . MCCOY! . . . The two of them stood in the middle of the living room and listened for a moment.

"Jesus, Tommy," said Sherman. It was the first time he had called him by his first name, but he didn't stop to think about that. "I can't believe I'm standing here and all this is happening. I'm holed up in my apartment and Park Avenue is occupied by a mob waiting to kill me. *Kill* me!"

"Awwwwww, f'r Chrissake, that's the *last* thing they wanna do. You ain't worth a goddamned thing to Bacon dead, and he thinks you're gonna be worth a lot to him alive."

"To Bacon? What does he get out of it?"

"Millions is what he thinks he's gonna get out of it. I can't prove it, but I say this whole thing is over the civil suits."

"But Henry Lamb is the one who's suing. Or his mother, I guess it is, in his behalf. How does Bacon get anything out of it?"

"All right." *Awright.* "Who is the lawyer representing Henry Lamb? Albert Vogel. And how does Henry Lamb's mother get to Albert Vogel? Because she admired his brilliant defense of the Utica Four and the Waxahachie Eight in 1969? Fuhgedaboudit. Bacon steers her to Vogel, because the two a them are tight. Whatever the Lambs get in a lawsuit, Vogel gets at least a third a that, and you can be sure he splits that with Bacon, or he's gonna have a mob coming after him that means business. One thing in this world I know from A to Z, and that's lawyers and where their money comes from and where it goes."

"But Bacon had his campaign going about Henry Lamb before he even knew I was involved."

"Oh, at the beginning they were just going after the hospital, on the grounds of malpractice. They were gonna sue the city. If Bacon could get it built up into a big deal in the press, then a jury might give 'em what they wanted. A jury in a civil case . . . with a racial angle? They had a good shot."

"So the same goes for me," said Sherman.

"I won't try to kid you. That's very true. But if you beat the felony case, then there's no civil case."

"And if I don't win the felony case, I won't care about the civil case," said Sherman, looking very glum.

"Well, you gotta admit one thing," said Killian in a cheer-up voice, "this thing has made you a giant on Wall Street. One freakin' *giant*, bro. Juh see what

Flannagan called you in the *Daily News?* 'Pierce & Pierce's fabled chief bond salesman.' *Fabled.* A legend in your own time. You're the son of 'the aristocratic John Campbell McCoy,' former head of Dunning Sponget & Leach. You're the fabled investment banking genius aristocrat. Bacon probably thinks you got half the money in the world."

"If you want to know the truth," said Sherman, "I don't even know where I'm gonna get the money to pay . . ." He motioned toward the library, where Occhioni was. "This civil suit mentions *everything.* They're even after the quarterly share of profits I was supposed to get at the end of this month. I can't imagine how they knew about it. They even referred to it by the in-company name, which is the 'Pie B.' They'd have to know someone at Pierce & Pierce."

"Pierce & Pierce'll look after you, won't they?"

"Hah. I don't exist at Pierce & Pierce anymore. There's no such thing as loyalty on Wall Street. Maybe there once was—my father always talked as if there was—but there isn't now. I've gotten one telephone call from Pierce & Pierce, and that wasn't from Lopwitz. It was from Arnold Parch. He wanted to know if there was anything they could do, and then he couldn't get off the telephone fast enough, for fear I'd think of something. Although I don't know why I single out Pierce & Pierce. Our own friends have all been the same way. My wife can't even make play dates for our daughter. She's six years old . . ."

He stopped. He suddenly felt uncomfortable parading his personal woes before Killian. Goddamned Garland Reed and his wife! They wouldn't even let Campbell come play with MacKenzie! Some utterly lame excuse . . . Garland hadn't even called once, and he'd known him all his life. At least Rawlie had had the guts to call. He'd called three times. He'd probably even have the guts to come see him . . . if WE THE JURY ever vacated Park Avenue . . . Maybe he would . . .

"It's damned sobering, how fast it goes when it goes," he said to Killian. He didn't want to say this much, but he couldn't help himself. "All these ties you have, all these people you went to school with and to college, the people who are in your clubs, the people you go out to dinner with—it's all a thread, Tommy, all these ties that make up your life, and when it breaks . . . that's it! . . . That's it . . . I feel so sorry for my daughter, my little girl. She'll mourn me, she'll mourn her daddy, the daddy she remembers, without knowing he's already dead."

"What the hell you talking about?" said Killian.

"You've never been through anything like this. I don't doubt you've seen a lot of it, but you've never been through it. I can't explain the feeling. All I can tell you is that I'm already dead, or the Sherman McCoy of the McCoy family and Yale and Park Avenue and Wall Street is dead. Your *self*—I don't know how to explain it, but if, God forbid, anything like this ever happens to you, you'll know what I mean. Your *self* . . . is *other people*, all the people you're tied to, and it's only a thread."

"Ayyyyy, Sherman," said Killian. "Gimme a break. It don't do any good to philosophize in the middle of a war."

"Some war."

"F'r Chrissake, whaddaya whaddaya? This story in the *Daily News* is very important for you. Weiss must be going crazy. We've blown the cover on this lowlife smokehead he's got for a witness. Auburn. Now we've got another theory out there for the whole business. Now there's a basis for people to support you.

We've gotten across the idea that you were the intended victim of a setup, a robbery. That changes the whole picture for you, and we haven't compromised you in the slightest."

"It's too late."

"Whaddaya mean, too late? Give it a little time, f'r Chrissake. This guy Flannagan at the *The City Light*, been beating his brains out with this story. So he'll take whatever I give him. This fucking story he just wrote couldn'tta come out any better if I dictated it to him. He not only identifies Auburn, he uses the mug shot Quigley got!" Killian was hugely delighted. "And he got in the fact that two weeks ago Weiss was calling Auburn the Crack King of Evergreen Avenue."

"What difference does that make?"

"It don't look good. If you got a guy in jail on a major felony and he suddenly comes forward to give evidence in return for dropping the charge or knocking it down, it don't look good. It don't look good to a jury, and it don't look good to the press. If he's in on a misdemeanor or an E felony or something, it don't make so much difference, because the presumption is, it don't matter that much to him, the time he's facing."

Sherman said, "One thing I've always wondered about, Tommy. Why did Auburn, when he made up his story—why did he have me driving the car? Why not Maria, who was actually driving the car when Lamb got hit? What difference did it make to Auburn?"

"He had to do it that way. He didn't know what witnesses might have seen your car just before Lamb got hit and just after he got hit, and he has to have some explanation for why you were driving up to the point where the thing happened and she was the one who drove away from there. If he says you stopped, and then you and her changed places and she drove off and hit Lamb, then the logical question is 'Why did they stop?' and the logical answer is 'Because some lowlife like Roland Auburn put up a barricade and tried to take them off.' "

"What's his name?—Flannagan—doesn't get into any of that."

"That's right. You'll notice I didn't give him anything about a woman being in the car one way or the other. When the time comes, we want Maria on our side. You'll also notice that Flannagan wrote the whole fucking story without even making any big deal about the 'mystery woman.' "

"Very obliging fellow. Why is that?"

"Oh, I know the guy. He's another Donkey, same as me, just trying to make his way in America. He makes his deposits in the Favor Bank. America is a wonderful country."

For a moment Sherman's spirits rose a calibration or two, but then they sank lower than ever. It was Killian's obvious elation that did it. Killian was crowing over his strategic genius in "the war." He had conducted a successful sortie of some kind. To Killian this was a game. If he won, terrific. If he lost . . . well, on to the next war. For him, Sherman, there was nothing to be won. He had already lost almost everything, irretrievably. At best, he could only keep from losing all.

The telephone rang in the library. Sherman braced once more, but soon Occhioni was at the doorway again.

"It's some guy named Pollard Browning, Mr. McCoy."

"Who's he?" asked Killian.

"He lives here in the building. He's the president of the co-op board."

He went into the library and picked up the telephone. From the street below, another roar, more bellowing on the bullhorn . . . McCOY! . . . McCOY! . . . No doubt it was just as audible *chez* Browning. He could imagine what Pollard thought.

But his voice was friendly enough. "How you bearing up, Sherman?"

"Oh, all right, Pollard, I suppose."

"I'd like to drop up and see you, if that wouldn't be too much of an imposition."

"You're home?" asked Sherman.

"Just got here. It wasn't easy, getting into the building, but I made it. Would that be all right?"

"Sure. Come on up."

"I'll just walk on up the fire stairs, if that's okay. Eddie's got his hands full down at the front door. I don't know if he can even hear the buzzer."

"I'll meet you back there."

He told Killian he was going back to the kitchen to let Browning in.

"Ayyyy," said Killian. "See? They haven't forgotten you."

"We'll see," said Sherman. "You're about to meet Wall Street in its pure form."

Back in the big silent kitchen, with the door open, Sherman could hear Pollard clanging up the metal treads of the fire stairs. Soon he came into view, puffing, from his climb of all of two flights, but impeccable. Pollard was the sort of plump forty-year-old who looks tonier than any athlete the same age. His smooth jowls welled up from out of a white shirt of a lustrous Sea Island cotton. A beautifully made gray worsted suit lay upon every square inch of his buttery body without a ripple. He wore a navy tie with the Yacht Club insignia and a pair of black shoes so well cut they made his feet look tiny. He was as sleek as a beaver.

Sherman led him out of the kitchen and into the entry gallery, where the Irishman, McCarthy, sat in the Thomas Hope chair. The door to the library was open and Occhioni was plainly visible in there.

"Bodyguards," Sherman felt compelled to say to Pollard, in a low voice. "I bet you never thought you'd know anybody who had bodyguards."

"One of my clients—you know Cleve Joyner of United Carborundum?"

"I don't know him."

"He's had bodyguards for six or seven years now. Go with him everywhere."

In the living room, Pollard gave Killian's fancy clothes a quick once-over, and a pained, pinched look came over his face. Pollard said, "How do you do?" which came out as "Howja do?" and Killian said, "How are you?" which came out as "Hehwaya?" Pollard's nostrils twitched slightly, the same way Sherman's father's had when he mentioned the name Dershkin, Bellavita, Fishbein & Schlossel.

Sherman and Pollard sat down in one of the clusters of furniture Judy had arranged in order to fill up the vast room. Killian went off into the library to talk to Occhioni.

"Well, Sherman," said Pollard, "I've been in touch with all the members of the executive committee, except for Jack Morrissey, and I want you to know you have our support, and we'll do anything we can. I know this must be a terrible situation for you and Judy and Campbell." He shook his smooth round head.

"Well, thank you, Pollard. It hasn't been too terrific."

"Now, I've been in touch with the inspector at the Nineteenth Precinct myself, and they'll provide protection for the front door, so that we can get in and out, but he says he can't keep the demonstrators away from the building alto-gether. I thought they could make them stay back five hundred feet, but he maintains they can't do that. I think it's outrageous, frankly. That bunch of . . ." Sherman could see Pollard ransacking his smooth round head for some courtly way to express a racial epithet. He abandoned the effort: ". . that mob." He shook his head a great deal more.

"It's a political football, Pollard. I'm a political football. That's what you've got living up over your head." Sherman tried a smile. Against all his better instincts, he wanted Pollard to like him and sympathize with him. "I hope you read the *Daily News* today, Pollard."

"No, I hardly ever see the *Daily News*. I did read the *Times*."

"Well, read the story in the *Daily News*, if you can. It's the first piece that gives any idea of what's really going on."

Pollard shook his head more woefully still. "The press is as bad as the demon-strators, Sherman. They're downright abusive. They waylay you. They waylay anybody who tries to come in here. I had to walk a goddamned gauntlet just now to get in my own building. And then they were all over my driver! They're insolent! They're a bunch of filthy little wogs." *Wogs?* "And of course the police won't do anything about it. It's as if you're fair game just because you're fortunate enough to be living in a building like this."

"I don't know what to say. I'm sorry about everything, Pollard."

"Well, unfortunately . . ." He dropped that. "There's never been anything like this on Park Avenue, Sherman. I mean, a demonstration aimed *at Park Avenue* as a residential area. It's intolerable. It's as if because this *is* Park Avenue, we're denied the sanctity of our homes. And *our* building is the focus of it."

Sherman experienced a neural alert as to what might be coming, but he couldn't be sure. He began shaking his head in time with Pollard's, to show his heart was in the right place.

Pollard said, "Apparently they intend to come here every day or stay around the clock, until—until I don't know what." His head was really going now.

Sherman picked up the tempo of his own head. "Who told you that?"

"Eddie."

"Eddie, the doorman?"

"Yes. Also Tony, who was on duty until Eddie came on at four. He told Eddie the same thing."

"I can't believe they'll do that, Pollard."

"Until today you couldn't have believed a bunch of—that they'd hold a demonstration in front of our building on Park Avenue, could you? I mean, there you are."

"That's true."

"Sherman, we've been friends a long time. We went to Buckley together. That was an innocent era, wasn't it?" He smiled a small brittle smile. "My father knew your father. So I'm talking to you as an old friend who wants to do what he can for you. But I'm also president of the board for all the tenants of the building, and I have a responsibility to them that has to take precedence over my personal preferences."

Sherman could feel his face getting hot. "Which means what, Pollard?"

"Well, just this. I can't imagine this is in any way a comfortable situation for you, being held virtual prisoner in this building. Have you considered . . . changing residence? Until things quiet down a bit?"

"Oh, I've thought about it. Judy and Campbell and our housekeeper and the nanny are staying over at my parents' now. Frankly, I'm already terrified that those bastards out there are going to find out and go over *there* and do something, and a town house is *completely* exposed. I've thought about going out to Long Island, but you've seen our house. It's wide open. French doors everywhere. It wouldn't keep a chipmunk out. I've thought of a hotel, but there's no such thing as security in a hotel. I've thought of staying at the Leash, but that's a town house, too. Pollard, I'm getting death threats. *Death* threats. There've been at least a dozen calls today."

Pollard's little eyes swiveled swiftly about the room, as if *They* might be coming in the windows. "Well, frankly . . . all the more reason, Sherman."

"Reason for what?"

"Well, that you should consider . . . making some arrangements. You know, it's not just yourself who is at risk. Everyone in this building is at risk, Sherman. I realize it's not your fault, not directly, certainly, but that doesn't alter the facts."

Sherman knew his face was blazing red. "Alter the facts! The facts are that my life is being threatened, and this is the most secure place available to me, and it also happens to be my home, if I may remind you of *that fact.*"

"Well, let me remind you—and again, I'm only doing this because I have a higher responsibility—let me remind you that you have a home here because you are a shareholder in a *cooperative* residential venture. It's called a cooperative for a reason, and certain obligations, on your part and the board's part, proceed from the contract you executed when you purchased your shares. There's no way I can alter *those* facts."

"I'm at the most critical juncture in my life—and you're spouting contract law?"

"Sherman . . ." Pollard cast his eyes down and threw his hands up, most sadly. "I have to think not only of you and your family but of thirteen other families in this building. And we're not asking you to do anything of a permanent nature."

We! We the Jury—*inside* the walls!

"Well, why don't *you* move out, Pollard, if you're so fucking terrified? Why don't you and the entire executive committee move out? I'm sure your shining example will inspire the others, and they'll move out, and no one will be at risk in your beloved building except the damnable McCoys, who created all the problems in the first place, right!"

Occhioni and Killian were peering in from the doorway to the library, and McCarthy was looking in from out in the entry gallery. But he couldn't rein himself in.

"Sherman—"

"*Move . . . out?* Have you any idea what a pompous preposterous *jerk* you are? Coming in here, scared to death, and telling me the board in its wisdom deems it proper for me to . . . *move out?*"

"Sherman, I know you're excited—"

"*Move . . . out?* The only one who's moving out, Pollard, is you! You're moving out of this apartment—right now! And you're going out the way you came—out the kitchen door!" He pointed a ramrod arm and forefinger in the direction of the kitchen.

"Sherman, I came up here in good faith."

"Awwwwww, Pollard . . . You were a ridiculous fat blowhard at Buckley and you're a ridiculous fat blowhard now. I've got enough on my mind without your *good faith*. Goodbye, Pollard." He took him by the elbow and tried to turn him toward the kitchen.

"Don't you put a hand on me!"

Sherman took his hand away. Seething: "Then get out."

"Sherman, you're not leaving us any choice but to enforce the provision concerning Unacceptable Situations."

The ramrod pointed to the kitchen and said softly: "March, Pollard. If I hear one more word from you between here and those fire stairs, there's gonna be an unacceptable situation sure enough."

Pollard's head seemed to swell up apoplectically. Then he turned and strode rapidly through the entry gallery and into the kitchen. Sherman followed him, as noisily as he could.

When Pollard reached the sanctuary of the fire stairs, he turned and, furious, said: "Just remember, Sherman. *You* called the tune."

" 'Called the tune.' Terrific. You're a real phrasemaker, Pollard!" He slammed the kitchen's old metal fire door.

Almost immediately he regretted the whole thing. As he walked back to the living room, his heart was beating violently. He was trembling. The three men, Killian, Occhioni, and McCarthy, were standing about with a mime-show nonchalance.

Sherman made himself smile, just to show everything was all right.

"Friend a yours?" said Killian.

"Yes, an old friend. I went to school with him. He wants to throw me out of the building."

"Fat chance," said Killian. "We can fucking tie him up in knots for the next ten years."

"You know, I have a confession to make," said Sherman. He made himself smile again. "Until that sonofabitch came up here, I was thinking of blowing my brains out. Now I wouldn't dream of it. That would solve all his problems, and he'd dine out on it for a month and be damned sanctimonious while he was at it. He'd tell everybody how we grew up together, and he'd shake that big round bubble head of his. I think I'll invite those bastards"—he motioned toward the streets—"on up here and let 'em dance the mazurka right over his big bubble head."

"Ayyyyyy," said Killian. "That's better. Now you're turning fucking *Irish*. The Irish been living the last twelve hundred years on dreams of revenge. Now you're *talking*, bro."

Another roar rose from Park Avenue in the heat of June . . . McCOY! . . . McCOY! . . . McCOY!

26

DEATH NEW YORK STYLE

IT WAS the Dead Mouse himself, Sir Gerald Steiner, who got the bright idea. Steiner, Brian Highridge, and Fallow were meeting in Steiner's office. Just being here, breathing the Mouse's own eminent air, gave Fallow a warm feeling. Thanks to his triumphs with the McCoy case, the upper rooms and inner circles of *The City Light* were open to him. Steiner's office was a big corner room overlooking the Hudson River. There was a large wooden desk, a Mission-style worktable, six armchairs, and that necessary proof of high corporate position, a couch. Otherwise the decor was Working Newspaperman. Steiner kept promiscuous heaps of newspapers, reference books, and copy paper on his desk and the worktable. A computer terminal and a manual typewriter stood on workmanlike metal stands near his swivel chair. A Reuters wire-service machine chattered away in a corner. A police radio was in another. It was now silent, but he had kept the thing on for a year before its yawps and bursts of static finally wore him out. The plate-glass windows, which offered a sweeping view of the river and the clam-gray Hoboken shore, had no curtains, only Venetian blinds. The Venetian blinds gave the vista a Light Industry, Working Newspaperman aspect.

The purpose of this summit meeting was to figure out how to proceed with Fallow's smoking-hot tip: namely, that Maria Ruskin was the mystery woman, the foxy brunette who took the wheel of McCoy's Mercedes roadster after McCoy ran down Henry Lamb. Four reporters—including, Fallow was happy to see, Robert Goldman—had been assigned to do legwork on the story. Legwork *for him;* they were his drudges. So far they had established only that Maria Ruskin was out of the country, probably in Italy. As for the young artist, Filippo Chirazzi, they had been unable to find any trace of him at all.

Steiner was sitting at his desk with his jacket off, his tie pulled down, and his red felt suspenders blazing away on his striped shirt, when it came to him, his bright idea. *The City Light*'s business section was currently running a series on "The New Tycoons." Steiner's scheme was to approach Arthur Ruskin as a subject for the series. This would not be entirely devious, since Ruskin was in fact typical of the "new tycoon" of latter-day New York, the man of immense, new, inexplicable wealth. The interviewer of the new tycoon would be Fallow. If he could get close to the old man, he would play it by ear. At the very least, he might find out where Maria Ruskin was.

"But do you think he'll go for it, Jerry?" asked Brian Highridge.

"Oh, I know these chaps," said Steiner, "and the old ones are the worst. They've made their fifty million or their hundred million—that's what the Texans call a unit. Did you know that? They call a hundred million dollars a unit. I think that's delightful. A unit, of course, is a *starting* point. In any case, this sort of chap makes his great colossal pile, and he goes to a dinner party, and he's sitting next to some pretty young thing, and he's getting a bit of the old tingle—but she hasn't the faintest notion who he is. A hundred million dollars!—and she's never even heard his name, and she isn't interested in who he is when he tries to tell her. What can he do? He can't very well go about with a sign around his neck saying FINANCIAL GIANT. At that point, believe me, they begin to lose some of their purported scruples concerning publicity."

Fallow believed him. It was not for nothing that Steiner had founded *The City Light* and kept it going at an operating loss of about ten million dollars a year. No longer was he merely another financier. He was the dread buccaneer of the dread *City Light*.

The Mouse proved to be an able psychologist of the newly and anonymously rich. Two telephone calls from Brian Highridge and it was all set. Ruskin said he generally avoided publicity, but in this case he would make an exception. He told Highridge he would like for the writer—what was his name? Mr. Fallow?—to be his guest for dinner at La Boue d'Argent.

When Fallow and Arthur Ruskin reached the restaurant, Fallow pushed the brass revolving door for the old man. Ruskin lowered his chin slightly, and then he lowered his eyes, and the most profoundly sincere smile spread over his face. For an instant Fallow marveled that this gruff barrel-chested seventy-one-year-old man could be so grateful for a gesture of such innocuous politeness. In the next instant he realized it had nothing to do with him and his courtesy at all. Ruskin was merely feeling the first ambrosial radiations of the greeting that awaited him beyond the threshold.

As soon as Ruskin entered the vestibule and the light of the restaurant's famous sculpture, *The Silver Boar*, shone upon him, the fawning began in earnest. The maître d', Raphael, fairly leaped from behind his desk and his daybook. Not one but two captains came forward. They beamed, they bowed, they filled the air with *Monsieur Ruskins*. The great financier lowered his chin still further, until it floated on a cushion of jowl, and he mumbled his replies, and his grin became broader and broader and, curiously, more and more diffident. It was the smile of a boy at his own birthday party, the lad who is both humbled and wondrously elated by the realization that he is in a room full of people who are happy, abnormally happy, one might say, to see him alive and in their presence.

To Fallow, Raphael and the two captains gave a few quick *Hello, sirs* and returned to sprinkling Ruskin with the sweet nothings of their calling. Fallow noticed two odd characters in the vestibule, two men in their mid-thirties, wearing dark suits that seemed to be mere screens for bodies of pure prole brawn. One appeared to be American, the other Asian. The latter was so large and had such a huge head, with such wide flat menacing features, Fallow wondered if he was Samoan. Ruskin noticed him, too, and Raphael said, with a smug smile, "Secret service. *Two* secret services, the American and the Indonesian. Madame Tacaya will be dining here this evening." After imparting this bit of news, he smiled again.

Ruskin turned to Fallow and made a face, without smiling, perhaps fearing that he could not compete with the wife of the Indonesian dictator for the restaurant's attentions and homage. The big Asian eyed them both. Fallow noticed that he had a cord coming out of his ear.

Raphael smiled again at Ruskin and gestured toward the dining room, and a procession began, led by Raphael himself, followed by Ruskin and Fallow, with a captain and a waiter at the rear. They turned right at the spotlit form of *The Silver Boar* and headed into the dining room. Ruskin had a grin on his mug. He loved this. Only the fact that he kept his eyes downcast prevented him from looking like a complete fool.

At night the dining room was well lit and seemed much more garish than at lunchtime. The dinner crowd seldom had the social cachet of the lunch crowd, but the place was packed nonetheless and was roaring with conversation. Fallow could see cluster after cluster of men with bald heads and women with pineapple-colored hair.

The procession stopped beside a round table that was far bigger than any other but was as yet unoccupied. A captain, two waiters, and two busboys were buzzing about, arranging stemware and silverware in front of every place. This was evidently Madame Tacaya's table. Immediately opposite it was a banquette under the front windows. Fallow and Ruskin were seated side by side on the banquette. They had a view of the entire front section, which was all that any true aspirant for the high ground of La Boue d'Argent required.

Ruskin said, "You wanna know why I like this restaurant?"

"Why?" asked Fallow.

"Because it's got the best food in New York and the best service." Ruskin turned and looked Fallow squarely in the face. Fallow could think of no adequate response to this revelation.

"Oh, people talk about this social stuff," said Ruskin, "and sure, a lot of well-known people come here. But why? Because it's got great food and great service." He shrugged. (No mystery to it.)

Raphael reappeared and asked Ruskin if he cared for a drink.

"Oh, Christ," said Ruskin, smiling. "I'm not supposed to, but I feel like a drink. You got any Courvoisier V.S.O.P.?"

"Oh yes."

"Then gimme a sidecar with the V.S.O.P."

Fallow ordered a glass of white wine. Tonight he intended to remain sober. Presently, a waiter arrived with the glass of wine and Ruskin's sidecar. Ruskin lifted his glass.

"To Fortune," he said. "I'm glad my wife's not here."

"Why?" asked Fallow, all ears.

"I'm not supposed to drink, especially not a little bomb like this." He held the drink up to the light. "But tonight I feel like a drink. It was Willi Nordhoff who introduced me to sidecars. He used to order them all the time, over at the old

King Cole Bar of the St. Regis. 'Zitecar,' he'd say. 'Mit Fay, Es, Oh, Pay,' he'd say. You ever run into Willi?"

"No, I don't think so," said Fallow.

"But you know who he is."

"Of course," said Fallow, who had never heard the name in his life.

"Jesus," said Ruskin. "I never thought I'd ever become such a great pal of a Kraut, but I love the guy."

This thought launched Ruskin on a long soliloquy about the many roads he had traveled in his career and about the many forks in those roads and how America was a wonderful country and who would have ever given a little Jew from Cleveland, Ohio, one chance in a thousand to get where he was today. He began to paint Fallow the view from the top of the mountain, ordering a second sidecar as he did. He painted with vigorous but vague strokes. Fallow was glad they were sitting side by side. It would be difficult for Ruskin to read the boredom on his face. Every now and then he ventured a question. He fished about for information as to where Maria Ruskin might stay when she visited Italy, such as at this moment, but Ruskin was vague about that, too. He was eager to return to the story of his life.

The first course arrived. Fallow had ordered a vegetable pâté. The pâté was a small pinkish semicircle with stalks of rhubarb arranged around it like rays. It was perched in the upper left-hand quadrant of a large plate. The plate seemed to be glazed with an odd Art Nouveau painting of a Spanish galleon on a reddish sea sailing toward the . . . sunset . . . but the setting sun was, in fact, the pâté, with its rhubarb rays, and the Spanish ship was not done in glaze at all but in different colors of sauce. It was a painting in sauce. Ruskin's plate contained a bed of flat green noodles carefully intertwined to create a basket weave, superimposed upon which was a flock of butterflies fashioned from pairs of mushroom slices, for the wings; pimientos, onion slices, shallots, and capers, for the bodies, eyes, and antennae. Ruskin took no note of the exotic collage before him. He had ordered a bottle of wine and was becoming increasingly expansive about the peaks and valleys of his career. Valleys, yes; oh, he had had to overcome many disappointments. The main thing was to be decisive. Decisive men made great decisions not because they were smarter than other people, necessarily, but because they made *more* decisions, and by the law of averages some of them would be great. Did Fallow get it? Fallow nodded. Ruskin paused only to stare gloomily at the fuss Raphael and his boys were making over the big round table in front of them. *Madame Tacaya is coming.* Ruskin seemed to feel upstaged.

"They all want to come to New York," he said dismally, without mentioning whom he was talking about, although it was clear enough. "This city is what Paris used to be. No matter what they are in their own country, it starts eating at them, the idea that in New York people might not give a damn who they are. You know what she is, don't you? She's an empress, and Tacaya's the emperor. He calls himself president, but they all do that. They all pay lip service to democracy. You ever notice that? If Genghis Khan was around today, he'd be President Genghis, or president-for-life, like Duvalier used to be. Oh, it's a great world. There's ten or twenty million poor devils flinching on their dirt floors every time the empress wiggles a finger, but she can't sleep nights thinking that the people at La Boue d'Argent in New York might not know who the hell she is."

Madame Tacaya's secret-service man stuck his huge Asian head into the dining room and scanned the house. Ruskin gave him a baleful glance.

"But even in Paris," he said, "they didn't come all the way from the goddamned South Pacific. You ever been to the Middle East?"

"Mmmm-n-n-n-n-n-n-no," said Fallow, who for half a second thought of faking it.

"You oughta go. You can't understand what's going on in the world unless you go to these places. Jidda, Kuwait, Dubai . . . You know what they wanna do there? They wanna build glass skyscrapers, to be like New York. The architects tell them they're crazy. A glass building in a climate like that, they'll have to run the air conditioning twenty-four hours a day. It'll cost a fortune. They just shrug. So what? They're sitting on top of all the fuel in the world."

Ruskin chuckled. "I'll tell you what I mean about making decisions. You remember the Energy Crisis, back in the early 1970s? That was what they called it, the Energy Crisis. That was the best thing that ever happened to me. All of a sudden everybody was talking about the Middle East and the Arabs. One night I was having dinner with Willi Nordhoff, and he gets on the subject of the Muslim religion, Islam, and how every Muslim wants to go to Mecca before he dies. "Efry focking Muslim vants to go dere." He always threw a lot of *fockings* in, because he thought that made him sound fluent in English. Well, as soon as he said that, a light bulb went on over my head. Just like that. Now I was almost sixty years old, and I was absolutely broke. The stock market had gone to hell about then, and that was all I had done for twenty years, buy and sell securities. I had an apartment on Park Avenue, a house on Eaton Square in London, and a farm in Amenia, New York, but I was broke, and I was desperate, and this light bulb went on over my head.

"So I says to Willi, 'Willi,' I says, 'how many Muslims are there?' And he says, 'I dunt know. Dere's millions, tense of millions, hundruts of millions.' So I made my decision right then and there. 'I'm going in the air-charter business. Efry focking Arab who wants to go to Mecca, I'm gonna take him there.' So I sold the house in London and I sold the farm in Amenia, to raise some cash, and I leased my first airplanes, three worn-out Electras. All my goddamned wife could think of —I'm talking about my former wife—was where were we gonna go in the summer, if we couldn't go to Amenia and we couldn't go to London. That was her entire comment on the whole goddamned situation."

Ruskin swelled up to his story. He ordered some red wine, a heavy wine that started a delicious fire in Fallow's stomach. Fallow ordered a dish called veal Boogie Woogie, which turned out to be rectangles of veal, small squares of spiced red apples, and lines of puréed walnuts arranged to look like Piet Mondrian's painting *Broadway Boogie Woogie*. Ruskin ordered *médaillons de selle d'agneau Mikado*, which was perfectly pink ovals of leg of lamb with tiny leaves of spinach and sticks of braised celery arranged to resemble a Japanese fan. Ruskin managed to down two glasses of the fiery red wine with a rapidity that was startling, given the fact that he did not stop talking.

It seemed that Ruskin had taken many of the early flights to Mecca himself, posing as a crewman. Arab travel agents had roamed the remotest villages, inveigling the natives to squeeze the price of an airplane ticket out of their pitiful possessions in order to make the magical pilgrimage to Mecca that took a few hours rather than thirty or forty days. Many of them had never laid eyes on an airplane. They arrived at the airports with live lambs, sheep, goats, and chickens. No power on earth could make them part with their animals before boarding the aircraft. They realized the flights were short, but what were they supposed to do for food once they got to Mecca? So the livestock went right into the cabins with their owners, bleating, cackling, urinating, defecating at will. Sheets of plastic were put in the cabins, covering the seats and the floors. So man and beast traveled to Mecca shank to flank, flying nomads on a plastic desert. Some of the passengers immediately set about arranging sticks and brush in the aisles to build fires to prepare dinner. One of the most urgent tasks of the crewmen was discouraging this practice.

"But what I wanna tell you about is the time we went off the runway at Mecca," said Ruskin. "It's nighttime and we come in for a landing, and the pilot lands long and the goddamned ship goes off the runway and we hit the sand with a helluva jolt and the right wing tip digs into the sand and the plane skids around practically 360 degrees before we come to a stop. Well, Jesus Christ, we figure there's gonna be wholesale panic with all these Arabs and the sheep and the goats and the chickens. We figure it's gonna be bloody murder. Instead, they're all talking in normal voices and staring out the window at the wing and the little fire that's started on the tip. Well, I mean, we're the ones who are panicked. Then they're getting up, taking their sweet time about it, and gathering up all their bags and sacks and animals and whatnot and just waiting for us to open the doors. They're so cool—and we're scared to death! Then it dawns on us. They think it's normal. Yeah! They think that's the way you stop an airplane! You stick a wing in the sand and spin around, and that brings the thing to a stop, and you get off! The thing is, they never rode in an airplane before, and so whadda they know from landing an airplane! They think it's normal! They think that's the way you do it!"

The thought threw Ruskin into a great phlegmy laugh, deep in his throat, and then the laugh turned into a coughing spasm, and his face became very red. He pushed himself back from the table with his hands until he seemed to be pressed back against the banquette, and he said, "Unnnh! Hmmmm! Hmmmmm, hmmmmm, hmmmm," as if he were reflecting in an amused way on the scene he had just described. His head fell forward, as if he were deep in thought about it all. Then his head fell sideways, and a snoring sound came from his mouth, and he leaned his shoulder against Fallow's. For an instant, Fallow thought the old man had fallen asleep. Fallow turned, in order to look into Ruskin's face, and when he did, Ruskin's body fell toward him. Startled, Fallow twisted about in his seat, and Ruskin's head ended up on his lap. The old man's face was no longer red. Now it was a ghastly gray. The mouth was slightly open. The breath was coming out in rapid little heaves. Without thinking, Fallow tried to sit him back up on the banquette. It was like trying to lift a sack of fertilizer. As he grappled and tugged, Fallow could see the two women and two men at the next table, along the banquette, staring with the contemptuous curiosity of people watching something distasteful. No one lifted a finger, of course. Fallow now had Ruskin propped up against the banquette and was looking around the room for help. Raphael, a waiter, two captains, and a busboy were fussing with the big round table that awaited Madame Tacaya and her party.

Fallow called out, "Excuse me!" Nobody heard him. He was conscious of how silly it sounded, this British *Excuse me*, when what he meant was *Help!* So he said,

"Waiter!" He said it as belligerently as he could. One of the captains by Madame Tacaya's table looked up and frowned, then walked over.

With one arm Fallow kept Ruskin upright. With the other hand he gestured toward his face. Ruskin's mouth was half open, and his eyes were half closed.

"Mr. Ruskin's suffered some sort of—I don't know what!" Fallow said to the captain.

The captain looked at Ruskin the way he might have looked at a pigeon that had unaccountably walked into the restaurant and taken the best seat in the house. He turned around and fetched Raphael, and Raphael peered at Ruskin.

"What happened?" he asked Fallow.

"He's suffered some sort of attack!" said Fallow. "Is there anyone here who's a doctor?"

Raphael scanned the room. But you could tell he wasn't looking for anyone in particular. He was trying to calculate what would happen if he tried to quiet the room and appeal for medical assistance. He looked at his watch and swore under his breath.

"For God's sake, get a doctor!" said Fallow. "Call the police!" He gestured with both his hands, and when he took the one hand off Ruskin, the old man pitched face forward into his plate, into the *selle d'agneau Mikado*. The woman at the next table went, "Aaaaoooooooh!" Almost a yelp it was, and she lifted her napkin to her face. The space between the two tables was no more than six inches, and somehow Ruskin's arm had become wedged in.

Raphael barked at the captain and the two waiters at Madame Tacaya's table. The waiters began pulling the table away from the banquette. Ruskin's weight was on the table, however, and his body began to slide forward. Fallow grabbed him around the waist to try to keep him from hitting the floor. But Ruskin's massive body was a dead weight. His face was slipping off the plate. Fallow couldn't hold him back. The old man slid off the table and took a header onto the carpet underneath. Now he was lying on the floor on his side, with his legs jackknifed. The waiters pulled the table out farther, until it blocked the aisle between the tables at the banquette and Madame Tacaya's table. Raphael was yelling to everybody at once. Fallow knew some French, but he couldn't make out a word Raphael was saying. Two waiters carrying trays full of food stood there looking down and then at Raphael. It was a traffic jam. Taking charge, Raphael squatted down and tried to pick Ruskin up by the shoulders. He couldn't budge him. Fallow stood up. Ruskin's body prevented him from getting out from behind the table. One look at Ruskin's face and it was obvious he was a goner. His face was an ashy gray, smeared with a French sauce and pieces of spinach and celery. The flesh around his nose and mouth was turning blue. His still-open eyes were like two pieces of milk glass. People were craning this way and that, but the joint was still roaring with conversation. Raphael kept looking toward the door.

"For God's sake," said Fallow, "call a doctor."

Raphael gave him a furious look and then a dismissing wave of the hand. Fallow was startled. Then he was angry. He didn't want to be stuck with this dying old man, either, but now he had been insulted by this arrogant little maître d'. So now he was Ruskin's ally. He knelt down on the floor, straddling Ruskin's legs. He loosened Ruskin's necktie and tore open his shirt, popping off the top button. He unbuckled his belt and unzipped the trousers and tried to pull

Ruskin's shirt away from his body, but it was wrapped around it tightly, apparently from the way he had fallen.

"What's wrong with him? 'S'e choking? 'S'e choking? Lemme g'im the Heimlich maneuver!"

Fallow looked up. A big florid man, a great Percheron Yank, was standing over him. He was apparently another diner.

"I think he's had a heart attack," said Fallow.

" 'S'what it looks like when they're choking! ' said the man. "Good God, g'im the Heimlich maneuver!"

Raphael had his hands up, trying to steer the man away. The man brushed him aside and knelt down beside Ruskin.

"The Heimlich maneuver, damn it!" he said to Fallow. "Heimlich maneuver!" It sounded like a military command. He put his hands under Ruskin's arms and managed to lift him to a sitting position, whereupon he slipped his arms around Ruskin's chest, from behind. He squeezed Ruskin's body, then lost his balance, and both he and Ruskin keeled over onto the floor. It looked as if they were wrestling. Fallow was still on his knees. The Heimlich Maneuverer stood up, holding his nose, which was bleeding, and staggered away. His struggling had succeeded mainly in pulling Ruskin's shirt and undershirt loose from his body, so that now a large expanse of the old man's ponderous gut was exposed to the view of one and all.

Fallow started to stand up, when he felt a heavy pressure on his shoulder. It was the woman on the banquette trying to squeeze past. He looked up at her face. It was a picture of frozen panic. She was shoving Fallow as if she were trying to catch the last train out of Barcelona. She accidentally stepped on Ruskin's arm. She looked down. "Aaaaaaoooh!" Another yelp. She took two steps beyond. Then she looked up at the ceiling. She began turning slowly. There was a blur of action in front of Fallow's eyes. It was Raphael. He lunged toward Madame Tacaya's table, grabbed a chair, and slipped it under the woman at the precise moment she fainted and collapsed. All at once she was sitting down, comatose, with one arm hanging over the back of the chair.

Fallow stood up and stepped over Ruskin's body and stood between Ruskin and the table that awaited Madame Tacaya. Ruskin's body was stretched out across the aisle, like some enormous beached white whale. Raphael stood two feet away, talking to the Asian bodyguard with the cord in his ear. Both looked toward the door. Fallow could hear them saying *Madame Tacaya Madame Tacaya Madame Tacaya*.

The little bastard! "What are you going to do?" Fallow demanded.

"Monsieur," said Raphael angrily, "we have call the police. The ambulance will arrive. There is nothing more I can do. There is nothing more *you* can do."

He gestured to a waiter, who stepped over the body, carrying a huge tray, and began serving a table a few feet away. Fallow looked at the faces at the tables all around. They stared at the appalling spectacle, but they did nothing. A large old man was lying on the floor in very bad condition. Perhaps he was dying. Certainly any of them who managed to get a lock at his face could tell that much. At first they had been curious. Is he going to die right in front of us? At first there had been the titillation of Someone Else's Disaster. But now the drama was dragging on too long. The conversational roar had died down. The old man looked repulsive, with his pants unzipped and his big gross bare belly bulging out. He had become a problem of protocol. If an old man was dying on the carpet a few feet from your table, what was the proper thing to do? Offer your services? But there was already a traffic jam there in the aisle between the rows of tables. Clear the area and give him air and come back later to complete the meal? But how would empty tables help the man? Stop eating until the drama had played itself out and the old man was out of sight? But the orders were in, and the food had begun to arrive, and there was no sign of any halt—and this meal was costing about $150 per person, once you added in the cost of the wine, and it was no mean trick getting a seat in a restaurant like this in the first place. Avert your eyes? Well, perhaps that was the only solution. So they averted their eyes and returned to their picturesque dishes . . . but there was something damned depressing about it all, because it was hard for your eyes not to wander every few seconds to see if, f'r Chrissake, they hadn't moved the stricken hulk. A man dying! O mortality! Probably a heart attack, too! That deep fear lodged in the bosom of practically every man in the room. The old arteries were clogging up micromillimeter by micromillimeter, day by day, month by month, from all the succulent meats and sauces and fluffy breads and wines and soufflés and coffee . . . And was that the way it would look? Would you be lying on the floor in some public place with a blue circle around your mouth and cloudy eyes that were half open and a hundred percent dead? It was a damned unappetizing spectacle. It made you queasy. It prevented you from relishing these expensive morsels arranged in such pretty pictures on your plate. So curiosity had turned to discomfort, which now turned to resentment—an emotion that had been picked up by the restaurateurs and doubled and then doubled again.

Raphael put his hands on his hips and looked down at the old man with a frustration bordering on anger. Fallow had the impression that had Ruskin so much as fluttered an eyelid, the little maître d' would have launched into a lecture laced with the bitter-cold courtesy in which the breed couched its insults. The roar was building up again. The diners finally were managing to forget the corpse. But not Raphael. *Madame Tacaya was coming.* The waiters were now skipping over the corpse mindlessly, as if they did it every night, as if every night there were one corpse or another lying in that spot, until the rhythm of the leap was built into one's nervous system. But how could the Empress of Indonesia be ushered in over this hulk? Or even be seated in its presence? What was keeping the police?

Gruesome bloody childish Yanks, thought Fallow. Not one of them, other than the ridiculous Heimlich Maneuverer, had moved a muscle to help this poor old bastard. Finally, a policeman and two crewmen from an emergency squad arrived. The noise dipped once more as everyone inspected the crewmen, one of whom was black and the other Latin, and their equipment, which consisted of a folding stretcher and an oxygen tank. They put an oxygen mask over Ruskin's mouth. Fallow could tell from the way the crewmen were talking to each other that they were getting no response from Ruskin. They unfolded the stretcher and slipped it under Ruskin's body and strapped him on.

When they took the stretcher to the front door, a disturbing problem arose. There was no way they could get the stretcher through the revolving door. Now that the stretcher was no longer folded but was extended with a body on it, it was too long. They began trying to fold back one of the wings of the door, but no one seemed to know how to do it. Raphael kept saying, "Stand it up! Stand it up!

Walk it through!" But apparently this was a grave breach of medical procedure, tilting the body vertically, in the case of a heart-attack victim, and the crewmen had their own necks to look after. So they all stood there in the vestibule, before the statue of *The Silver Boar*, having a discussion.

Raphael began throwing his hands up in the air and stamping his feet. "Do you think I allow *this*"—he gestured at Ruskin's body, paused, then gave up on supplying an appropriate noun—"to remain here in the restaurant, before *tout le monde?* Please! See for yourself! This is the main entrance! This is a business! People are coming here! Madame Tacaya will be here at any moment!"

The policeman said, "Okay, take it easy. Is there any other way out?"

Much discussion. A waiter mentioned the ladies' room, which had a window onto the street. The policeman and Raphael went back into the dining room to check out that possibility. Soon they returned, and the policeman said, "Okay, I think we can make it." So now Raphael, his captain, the policeman, the stretcher-bearers, a waiter, Fallow, and the inert hulk of Arthur Ruskin re-entered the dining room. They headed along the very same aisle, between the banquette tables and Madame Tacaya's table, where Ruskin had trod triumphantly barely an hour before. He was still the cynosure of the procession, although he was now laid out cold. The roar in the room dropped off sharply. The diners couldn't believe what they were seeing. Ruskin's stricken face and white gut were now being paraded by their very tables . . . the grim remains of the joys of the flesh. It was as if some plague, which they all thought had been eradicated at last, had sprung back up in their midst, more virulent than ever.

The procession entered a little door on the far side of the dining room. The door led into a small vestibule, off which were two more doors, to the men's room and the ladies' room. The ladies' room had a small lounge area, and in it was the window to the street. After a considerable struggle, a waiter and the policeman managed to open the window. Raphael produced a set of keys and unlocked the hinged bars that protected the window from the street. A cool sooty draft blew in. It was welcome. The pileup of human beings, the quick and the dead, had made the little room unbearable.

The policeman and one of the crewmen climbed through the window out onto the sidewalk. The other crewman and the waiter passed one end of the stretcher, the end where Ruskin's face lay, growing grimmer and grayer by the minute, through the window to the two men outside. The last Fallow saw of the mortal remains of Arthur Ruskin, ferry captain to Mecca for the Arabs, were the soles of his bench-made English shoes disappearing through the window of the ladies' room of La Boue d'Argent.

In the next instant Raphael bolted past Fallow, out of the ladies' room and back into the dining room. Fallow followed. Halfway across the dining room, Fallow was intercepted by the captain who had been in charge of his table. He gave Fallow the sort of solemn smile you give someone in the hour of bereavement. "Monsieur," he said, still smiling in this sad but kindly way, and he gave Fallow a slip of paper. It looked like a bill.

"What's this?"

"*L'addition*, monsieur. The check."

"The *check?*"

"*Oui, naturellement*. You ordered dinner, monsieur, and it was prepared and served. We are very sorry about your friend's misfortune . . ." Then he shrugged and tucked his chin down and pulled a face. (But it has nothing to do with us, and life goes on, and we must make a living all the same.)

Fallow was shocked by the crassness of the demand. Far more shocking, however, was the thought of having to pay a check in a restaurant like this.

"If you're so bloody keen on *l'addition,*" he said, "I expect you ought to talk it over with Mr. Ruskin." He brushed by the captain and headed for the door.

"No, you don't!" said the captain. It was no longer the oily voice of a restaurant captain. "Raphael!" he yelled, and then he said something in French. In the vestibule, Raphael wheeled about and confronted Fallow. He had a very stern look on his face.

"Just a moment, monsieur!"

Fallow was speechless. But at that moment Raphael turned back toward the door and broke into a professional smile. A big glum flat-faced Asian in a business suit came in through the revolving door, his eyes darting this way and that. Behind him appeared a small olive-skinned woman, about fifty, with dark red lips and a huge carapace of black hair and a long red silk mandarin-collared coat with a floor-length red silk gown beneath it. She wore enough jewelry to light up the night.

"Madame Tacaya!" said Raphael. He held up both hands, as if catching a bouquet.

The next day the front page of *The City Light* consisted mainly of four gigantic words, in the biggest type Fallow had ever seen on a newspaper:

DEATH
NEW YORK
STYLE

And above that, in smaller letters: SOCIETY RESTAURANT TO TYCOON: "KINDLY FINISH DYING BEFORE MADAME TACAYA ARRIVES."

And at the bottom of the page: A CITY LIGHT *Exclusive by our man at the table: Peter Fallow.*

In addition to the main story, which recounted the evening in lavish detail, down to the waiters skipping busily over the body of Arthur Ruskin, there was a side story that attracted almost as much attention. The headline read:

DEAD TYCOON'S SECRET:
KOSHER 747s TO MECCA

By noon the fury of the Muslim world was chattering in over the Reuters wire in the corner of the Mouse's office. The Mouse smiled and rubbed his hands. The interview with Ruskin had been *his idea.*

He hummed to himself with a joy that all the money in the world couldn't have brought him: "Oh, *I* am a member of the working press, *I* am a member of the working press, *I* am a member of the worrrrrking press."

27

HERO OF THE HIVE

THE DEMONSTRATORS vanished as rapidly as they had arrived. The death threats ceased. *But for how long?* Sherman now had to balance the fear of death against the horror of going broke. He compromised. Two days after the demonstration he cut the number of bodyguards down to two, one for the apartment and one for his parents' house.

Nevertheless—*hemorrhaging money!* Two bodyguards on duty around the clock, at twenty-five dollars per hour per man, a total of $1,200 a day—$438,000 per year—*bleeding to death!*

Two days after that, he got up the nerve to keep an engagement Judy had made almost a month before: dinner at the di Duccis'.

True to her word, Judy had been doing what she could to help him. Equally true to her word, this did not include being affectionate. She was like one asphalt contractor forced into an alliance with another by some sordid turn of fate . . . Better than nothing perhaps . . . It was in that spirit that the two of them planned their return to Society.

Their thinking (McCoy & McCoy Associates') was that the long story in the *Daily News* by Killian's man Flannagan offered a blameless explanation of the McCoy Case. Therefore, why should they hide? Shouldn't they go through the motions of a normal life, and the more publicly the better?

But would *le monde*—and, more specifically, the very social di Duccis—see it that way? With the di Duccis they at least had a fighting chance. Silvio di Ducci, who had lived in New York since he was twenty-one, was the son of an Italian brake shoe manufacturer. His wife, Kate, had been born and reared in San Marino, California; he was her third wealthy husband. Judy was the decorator who had *done* their apartment. She now took the precaution of ringing up and offering to back out of the dinner party. "Don't you dare!" said Kate di Ducci. "I'm counting on your coming!" This gave Judy a terrific lift. Sherman could read it in her face. It did nothing for him, however. His depression and skepticism were too

profound for a polite boost from the likes of Kate di Ducci. All he could manage
to say to Judy was, "We'll see, won't we."

The bodyguard at the apartment, Occhioni, drove the Mercury station wagon
over to his parents' house, picked up Judy, returned to Park Avenue, and picked
up Sherman. They headed for the di Duccis' on Fifth Avenue. Sherman pulled
the revolver of his Resentment out of his waistband and braced for the worst. The
di Duccis and the Bavardages ran with precisely the same crowd (the same vulgar
non-Knickerbocker crowd). At the Bavardages' they had frozen him out even
when his respectability was intact. With their combination of rudeness, crude-
ness, cleverness, and chic, what would they inflict upon him now? He told himself
that he was long past caring whether they approved of him or not. His intention
—their intention (McCoy & McCoy's)—was to show the world that, being without sin, they could proceed with their lives. His great fear was of the sort of
outcome that would prove them wrong: namely, an ugly scene.

The di Duccis' entry gallery had none of the dazzle of the Bavardages'. Instead
of Ronald Vine's clever combinations of materials, of silk and hemp and gilt wood
and upholsterer's webbing, the di Duccis' betrayed Judy's weakness for the solemn
and grand: marble, fluted pilasters, huge classical cornices. Yet it was every bit as
much from another century (the eighteenth), and it was filled with the same
clusters of social X rays, Lemon Tarts, and men with dark neckties; the same grins,
the same laughter, the same 300-watt eyes, the same sublime burble and ecstatic
rat-tat-tat-tat chatter. In short, the hive. The hive!—the hive!—the familiar buzz
closed in about Sherman, but it no longer resonated in his bones. He listened to
it, wondering if his tainted presence would stop the hive's very hum in mid-
sentence, mid-grin, mid-guffaw.

An emaciated woman emerged from the clusters and came toward them,
smiling . . . Emaciated but absolutely beautiful . . . He had never seen a more
beautiful face . . . Her pale golden hair was swept back. She had a high forehead and a face as white and smooth as china, and yet with large, lively eyes and
a mouth with a sensual—no, more than that—a *provocative* smile. Very provocative! When she grasped his forearm, he felt a tingle in his loins.

"Judy! Sherman!"

Judy embraced the woman. In all sincerity she said, "Oh, Kate, you're so kind.
You're so wonderful." Kate di Ducci hooked her arm inside Sherman's and drew
him toward her, so that the three of them formed a sandwich, Kate di Ducci
between the two McCoys.

"You're more than kind," said Sherman. "You're brave." All at once he realized he was using the sort of intimate baritone he used when he wanted to get the
old game going.

"Don't be silly!" said Kate di Ducci. "If you hadn't come, both of you, I'd have
been very, very cross! Come over here, I want you to meet some people."

Sherman noticed with trepidation that she was leading them toward a conversational bouquet dominated by the tall patrician figure of Nunnally Voyd, the
novelist who had been at the Bavardages'. An X ray and two men with navy suits,
white shirts, and navy ties were beaming great social grins at the great author.
Kate di Ducci made the introductions, then led Judy out of the entry gallery, into
the grand salon.

Sherman held his breath, ready for an affront or, at best, ostracism. Instead,
all four kept smiling mightily.

"Well, Mr. McCoy," said Nunnally Voyd with a mid-Atlantic accent, "I must tell you, I've thought about you more than once over the past few days. Welcome to the legion of the damned . . . now that you've been properly devoured by the fruit flies."

"The fruit flies?"

"The press. I'm amused by all the soul-searching these . . . *insects* do. 'Are we too aggressive, too cold-blooded, too heartless?'—as if the press were a rapacious beast, a tiger. I think they'd like to be thought of as bloodthirsty. That's what I call praise by faint damnation. They've got the wrong animal. In fact, they're fruit flies. Once they get the scent, they hover, they swarm. If you swing your hand at them, they don't *bite* it, they dart for cover, and as soon as your head is turned, they're back again. They're fruit flies. But I'm sure I don't have to tell *you* that."

Despite the fact that this grand literatus was using his predicament as a pedestal upon which to place this entomological conceit, this set piece that came out a bit shopworn in the delivery, Sherman was grateful. In some way Voyd was, indeed, a brother, a fellow legionnaire. He seemed to recall—he had never paid much attention to literary gossip—that Voyd had been stigmatized as homosexual or bisexual. There had been some sort of highly publicized squabble . . . How very unjust! How dare these . . . *insects* pester this man who, while perhaps a bit affected, had such largeness of spirit, such sensitivity to the human condition? What if he *was* . . . gay? The very word *gay* popped into Sherman's head spontaneously. (Yes, it is true. A liberal is a conservative who has been arrested.)

Emboldened by his new brother, Sherman told of how the horse-faced woman had shoved a microphone in his face as he and Campbell left the apartment building and how he had swung his arm, purely to get the device out of his face— and the woman was now suing him! She was crying, pouting, whimpering—and filing a civil suit for $500,000!

Everyone in the bouquet, even Voyd himself, was looking directly at him, absorbed, beaming a social grin.

"Sherman! Sherman! Goddamn!" A booming voice . . . He looked around . . . A huge young man coming toward him . . . Bobby Shaflett . . . He had broken off from another bouquet and was coming toward him with a big barnyard grin on his face. He held out his hand, and Sherman shook it, and the Golden Hillbilly sang out, "You sure have been making the feathers fly since the last time I saw you! You sure as hell have, godalmighty dog!"

Sherman didn't know what to say. As it turned out, he didn't have to say a thing.

"I got arrested in Montreal last year," said the Towheaded Tenor with evident satisfaction. "You probably saw something about that."

"Well, no . . . I didn't."

"You *didn't?*"

"No—why on earth—what were you arrested for?"

"PEEING ON A TREE!" *Haw haw haw haw haw haw haw haw haw haw!* "They don't cotton to it when you pee on their trees at midnight in Montreal, leastways not right outside the hotel!" *Haw haw haw haw haw haw haw haw haw haw!*

Sherman stared at his beaming face with consternation.

"They threw me in jail! *Indecent exposure!* PEEING ON A TREE!" *Haw haw haw*

haw haw haw haw haw! He calmed down a bit. "You know," he said, "I never was in jail before. What'd *you* think a jail?"

"Not much," said Sherman.

"I know what you mean," said Shaflett, "but it wudd'n so awful. I'd heard all this stuff about what the other prisoners do to you in jail?" He enunciated this as if it were a question. Sherman nodded. "You wanna know what they did to me?"

"What?"

"They gave me *apples!*"

"Apples?"

"Sure did. The first meal I got in'eh, it was so bad I couldn't eat it—and I like to *eat!* All's I could eat was this apple that came with it. So you know what? The word got out that all's I'd eat was the apple, and they all sent me their apples, all the other prisoners. They passed 'em along, hand over hand, through the bars, till they got to me. By the time I got outta there, there was just my head stickin' out of a pile of apples!" *Haw haw haw haw haw haw haw haw haw haw haw haw!*

Encouraged by this favorable gloss put upon jail time, Sherman told of the Puerto Rican in the holding pen who had seen the television crews filming him in handcuffs and wanted to know what he had been arrested for. He told of how his answer, "Reckless endangerment," had obviously disappointed the man and how, therefore, he told the next questioner, "Manslaughter." (The black youth with the shaved head . . . He felt a twinge of the original terror . . . This he did not mention.) Eagerly they stared at him, the entire bouquet—*his* bouquet—the renowned Bobby Shaflett and the renowned Nunnally Voyd, as well as the other three social souls. Their expressions were so rapt, so deliriously expectant! Sherman felt an irresistible urge to improve upon his war story. So he invented a third cellmate. And when this cellmate asked him what he was in for, he said, "Second-degree murder."

"I was running out of felonies," said the adventurer, Sherman McCoy.

Haw haw haw haw haw haw haw haw, went Bobby Shaflett.

Ho ho ho ho ho ho ho ho ho ho, went Nunnally Voyd.

Hah hah hah hah hah hah hah, went the X ray and the two men in navy suits.

Heh heh heh heh heh heh heh heh heh, went Sherman McCoy, as if his time in the holding pen had amounted to nothing more than a war story in the life of a man.

The di Duccis' dining room, like the Bavardages', featured a pair of round tables, and at the center of each table was a creation by Huck Thigg, the florist. For this night he had created a pair of miniature trees, no more than fifteen inches high, out of hardened wisteria vines. Glued to the branches of the trees were scores of brilliant blue dried cornflowers. Each tree was set in a meadow, about a foot square, of living buttercups sown so thick they touched. Around each meadow was a miniature split-rail fence made of yew wood. This time, however, Sherman had no opportunity to study the artistry of the celebrated young Mr. Thigg. Far from being stumped for a conversational mate, he now commanded an entire section of the table. To his immediate left was a renowned social Xray named Red Pitt, known *sotto voce* as the Bottomless Pitt, because she was so superbly starved that her glutei maximi and the surrounding tissue—in the vulgate, her ass—appeared to have vanished altogether. You could have dropped a plumb line from the small of her back to the floor. To her left was Nunnally Voyd, and to his left was a Real-Estate X ray named Lily Bradshaw. Sitting on

Sherman's right was a Lemon Tart named Jacqueline Balch, the blond third wife
of Knobby Balch, heir to the Colonaid indigestion-remedy fortune. To her right
was none other than Baron Hochswald, and to his right was Kate di Ducci.
During much of the dinner all six of these men and women were tuned in solely
to Mr. Sherman McCoy. Crime, Economics, God, Freedom, Immortality—whatever McCoy of the McCoy Case cared to talk about, the table listened, even such
an accomplished, egotistical, and ceaseless talker as Nunnally Voyd.

Voyd said he had been surprised to learn that such vast amounts of money
could be made in bonds—and Sherman realized that Killian was right: the press
had created the impression that he was a titan of finance.

"Frankly," said Voyd, "I've always thought of the bond business as . . .
ummmmm . . . rather *poky stuff.*"

Sherman found himself smiling the wry smile of those who know a big luscious secret. "Ten years ago," he said, "you'd have been right. They used to call us
'the bond bores.' " He smiled again. "I haven't heard that for a long time. Today I
suppose there's five times as much money changing hands in bonds as in stocks."
He turned toward Hochswald, who was leaning forward to follow the conversation. "Wouldn't you say so, Baron?"

"Oh, yes, yes," said the old man, "I expect that's so." And then the baron
shut up—in order to hear what Mr. McCoy had to say.

"All the takeovers, buy-outs, mergers—all done with bonds," said Sherman.
"The national debt? A trillion dollars? What do you think that is? All bonds.
Every time interest rates fluctuate—up or down, it doesn't matter—little crumbs
fall off all the bonds and lodge in the cracks in the sidewalk." He paused and
smiled confidently . . . and wondered . . . Why had he used this hateful
phrase of Judy's? . . . He chuckled and said, "The important thing is not to stick
your nose up at those crumbs, because there are billions and billions and billions
of them. At Pierce & Pierce, believe me, we sweep them up very diligently." *We!*
—at *Pierce & Pierce!* Even the little Tart on his right, Jacqueline Balch, nodded at
all this as if she understood.

Red Pitt, who prided herself on her bluntness, said, "Tell me, Mr. McCoy, tell
me—well, I'm going to come right out and ask you: What *did* happen up there in
the Bronx?"

Now they all leaned forward and stared, enthralled, at Sherman.

Sherman smiled. "My lawyer says I mustn't say a word about what happened."
Then he leaned forward himself and looked to his right and then to his left and
said, "But, strictly *entre nous,* it was a robbery attempt. It was literally highway
robbery."

They were now all leaning forward so far it became a huddle around Huck
Thigg's wisteria tree in the buttercup meadow.

Kate di Ducci said, "Why can't you come out and say so, Sherman?"

"That I can't go into, Kate. But I will tell you one other thing: I didn't hit
*any*body with my car."

None of them said a word. They were spellbound. Sherman glanced at Judy
at the other table. Four people, two on either side, including their vulpine little
host, Silvio di Ducci, were honed in on her. McCoy & McCoy. Sherman
pressed on:

"I can offer you some very sound advice. Don't *ever* . . . get *caught up* . . .
in the *criminal-justice system* . . . in this city. As soon as you're caught in the

machinery, just the ma*chinery*, you've lost. The only question remaining is *how much* you're going to lose. Once you enter a cell—even before you've had a chance to declare your innocence—you become a cipher. There *is* no more you."

Silence all around him . . . The *look* in their *eyes!* . . . Begging for war stories!

So he told them about the little Puerto Rican who knew all the numbers. He told them about the game of hockey with the live mouse and of how he (the hero) rescued the mouse and threw it out of the cell, whereupon a cop crushed it with his heel. Confidently he turned to Nunnally Voyd and said, "I think that falls under the heading of a metaphor, Mr. Voyd." He smiled wisely. "A metaphor for the whole thing."

Then he looked to his right. The lovely Lemon Tart was drinking in his every word. He felt the tingle in his loins again.

After dinner quite a cluster it was that gathered around Sherman McCoy in the di Duccis' library. He entertained them with the story of the cop who kept making him go through the metal detector.

Silvio di Ducci spoke up: "They can *force* you to do that?"

Sherman realized the story made him sound a bit too compliant and was undercutting his new status as one who had braved the fires of hell.

"I made a deal," he said. "I said, 'Okay, I'll let you show your buddy how I set off the alarm, but you've got to do something for me. You've got to get me out of that fucking' "—he said *fucking* very softly, to indicate that, yes, he knew it was in poor taste but that under the circumstances the verbatim quote was called for— " 'hog pen.' " He pointed his finger in a knowing way, as if he were pointing toward the holding pen in Central Booking in the Bronx. "And it paid off. They brought me out early. Otherwise I would have had to spend the night on Rikers Island, and that, I gather, is *not . . . too . . . terrific.*"

Every Tart in the cluster was his for the asking.

As the bodyguard, Occhioni, drove them to his parents' house, to drop Judy off, it was Sherman who was enjoying a social high. At the same time, he was confused. Just who *were* these people?

"It's ironic," he said to Judy. "I've never liked these friends of yours. I guess you've deduced that."

"It didn't require much in the way of deduction," said Judy. She wasn't smiling.

"And yet they're the only people who've been decent to me since this whole thing started. My so-called old friends obviously wish I'd do the right thing and disappear. These people, these people I don't even know, they treated me like a living human being."

In the same guarded voice Judy said, "You're famous. In the newspapers, you're a rich aristocrat. You're a tycoon."

"Only in the newspapers?"

"Oh, are you feeling rich all of a sudden?"

"Yes, I'm a rich aristocrat with a fabulous apartment by a famous designer." He wanted to get on her good side.

"Hah." Quietly, bitterly.

"It's perverse, isn't it? Two weeks ago, when we were at the Bavardages', these same people froze me out. Now I'm smeared—*smeared!*—across every newspaper and they can't get enough of me."

She looked away from him, out the window. "You're easily pleased." Her voice was as far off as her gaze.

McCoy & McCoy shut down for the night.

"Whadda we got this morning, Sheldon?"

As soon as the words left his mouth, the Mayor regretted them. He *knew* what his tiny assistant would say. It was inevitable, and so he braced himself for the vile phrase, and sure enough, here it came.

"Mainly plaques for blacks," said Sheldon. "Bishop Bottomley is here, waiting to see you, and there's been a dozen or so requests for you to comment on the McCoy case."

The Mayor wanted to remonstrate, as he had several times before, but instead he turned away and looked out the window, toward Broadway. The Mayor's office was at ground level, a small but elegant room on the corner with a high ceiling and grand Palladian windows. The view across the little park around City Hall was sullied by the presence, in the immediate foreground, right outside the window, of rows of blue police barricades. They were stored there, permanently, on the grass—or rather on bare patches where grass had once been—for use whenever demonstrations erupted. They erupted all the time. When they did, the police created a big blue fence with the barricades, and he could look out at the broad beams of the cops as they faced whatever raggedy horde of demonstrators was yammering away on the other side. What an amazing array of stuff the cops carried on their backsides! Billies, blackjacks, flashlights, handcuffs, bullets, citation books, walkie-talkies. He continually found himself gazing upon the hulking cluttered backsides of cops, while various malcontents shouted and growled, all for television, of course.

Plaques for blacks plaques for blacks plaques for blacks plaques for blacks. Now the vile phrase was running through his mind. *Plaques for blacks* was a small way of fighting fire with fire. Every morning he went from his office across to the Blue Room, and amid the portraits of bald-headed politicians of years gone by, he handed out plaques and citations to civic groups and teachers and prize-winning students and brave citizens and noble volunteer workers and various other tillers and toilers of the urban terrain. In these troubled times, with the surveys going the way they were going, it was wise, and probably good, to single out as many black recipients of these trophies and rhetorical flourishes as possible, but it was not wise and it was not good for Sheldon Lennert, this homunculus with his absurdly tiny head and his mismatched checked shirts, jackets, and pants, to call the process "plaques for blacks." Already the Mayor had heard a couple of people in the press office use the expression. What if some of the black members of the staff overheard it? They might even laugh. But they wouldn't be laughing inside.

But no . . . Sheldon continued to say "plaques for blacks." He knew the Mayor hated it. Sheldon had the malicious streak of a court jester. Outwardly he was as loyal as a dog. Inwardly he seemed to be mocking him half the time. The Mayor's anger rose.

"Sheldon, I told you I don't want to hear that expression in this office again!"

"Awright, awright," said Sheldon. "Now whaddaya gonna say when they ask you about the McCoy case?"

Sheldon always knew exactly how to distract him. He would bring up whatever he knew confused the Mayor most profoundly, whatever made him most dependent on Sheldon's small but amazingly facile mind.

"I don't know," said the Mayor. "At first it looked pretty clear-cut. We got this Wall Street guy who runs over a black honor student and takes off. But now it turns out there was a second black kid, and he's a crack dealer, and maybe it was a robbery attempt. I guess I take the judicial approach. I call for a full investigation and a careful weighing of the evidence. Right?"

"Negative," said Sheldon.

"Negative?" It was bewildering, the number of times Sheldon challenged the obvious—and turned out to be absolutely right.

"Negative," said Sheldon. "The McCoy case has become one of those touch-stone issues in the black community. It's like divestiture and South Africa. There *are* no two sides to the question. You suggest there might be two sides, and you're not even-handed, you're biased. Same thing here. The only question is, is a black life worth as much as a white life? And the only answer is, white guys like this McCoy, from Wall Street, driving their Mercedes-Benzes, can't go around running over black honor students and taking off because it's inconvenient to stop."

"But that's bullshit, Sheldon," said the Mayor. "We don't even know for sure what happened yet."

Sheldon shrugged. "So what else is new? That's the only version Abe Weiss is even willing to talk about. He's running with this case like he's Abe Fucking Lincoln."

"Weiss started all this?" The thought troubled the Mayor, because he knew Weiss had always entertained the notion of making a bid for mayor himself.

"No, Bacon started it," said Sheldon. "Somehow he got to this drunk on *The City Light,* this Brit, Fallow. That's how it started. But now it's caught on. It's gone way beyond Bacon and his gang. Like I say, it's a touchstone issue. Weiss's got an election coming up. So do you."

The Mayor thought for a moment. "What kind of name is McCoy? Irish?"

"No, he's a Wasp."

"What kind of person is he?"

"Rich Wasp. All the way. All the right schools, Park Avenue, Wall Street, Pierce & Pierce. His old man used to be the head of Dunning Sponget & Leach."

"Did he support me? Or do you know?"

"Not that I know of. You know these characters. They don't even think about local elections, because in an election in New York City voting Republican don't mean shit. They vote for President. They vote for senator. They talk about the Federal Reserve and supply side and all that shit."

"Unnnh-hunnnh. Well, what *do* I say?"

"You call for a complete and thorough investigation of McCoy's role in this tragedy and the appointment, if necessary, of a special prosecutor. By the gover-nor. 'If necessary,' you say, 'if all the facts are not forthcoming.' That way you give a little jab to Abe, without mentioning his name. You say the law must be no respecter of persons. You say McCoy's wealth and position cannot be allowed to keep this case from being treated the same way it would be if Henry Lamb had run over Sherman McCoy. Then you pledge the kid's mother—Annie, I think, is her name—you pledge the kid's mother your full support and backing in bringing to justice the perpetrator of the foul deed. There's no way you can lay it on too thick."

"Kind of rough on this guy McCoy, isn't it?"

"That's not your fault," said Sheldon. "The guy hit the wrong kind of kid in the wrong part of town driving the wrong brand of car with the wrong woman, not his wife, in the bucket seat next to him. He doesn't come away looking so wonderful."

The whole thing made the Mayor feel uneasy, but Sheldon's instincts were always correct in these can-of-worms situations. He thought some more. "Okay," he said, "I'll grant you all that. But aren't we making Bacon look awfully good? I hate that son of a bitch."

"Yeah, but he's already hit a home run with this thing. You can't change that. All you can do is go with the flow. It isn't long until November, and if you make a wrong move on the McCoy case, Bacon can really give you some grief."

The Mayor shook his head. "I guess you're right. We put the Wasp to the wall." He shook his head again, and a cloud came over his face. "The stupid bastard . . . What the hell *was* he doing tooling around on Bruckner Boulevard at night in a Mercedes-Benz? Some people are just determined to bring the roof down on themselves, aren't they? He was asking for it. I still don't like it—but you're right. Whatever he gets, he was asking for it. Okay. So much for McCoy. Now, what's Bishop What's-his-name want?"

"Bottomley. It's about that Episcopal church, St. Timothy's. The bishop is black, incidentally."

"The Episcopalians have a black bishop?"

"Oh, they're very liberal," said Sheldon, rolling his eyes. "It coulda just as easy been a woman or a Sandinista. Or a lesbian. Or a lesbian Sandinista."

The Mayor shook his head some more. He found the Christian churches baffling. When he was growing up, the *goyim* were all Catholics, unless you counted the *shvartzer*, which nobody did. They didn't even rate being called *goyim*. The Catholics were two types, the Irish and the Italians. The Irish were stupid and liked to fight and inflict pain. The Italians were stupid and slob-like. Both were unpleasant, but the lineup was easy enough to comprehend. He was in college before he realized there was this whole other set of *goyim*, the Protestants. He never saw any. There were only Jews, Irishmen, and Italians in college, but he heard about them, and he learned that some of the most famous people in New York were this type of *goyim*, the Protestants, people like the Rockefellers, the Vanderbilts, the Roosevelts, the Astors, the Morgans. The term *Wasp* was invented much later. The Protestants were split up into such a crazy bunch of sects nobody could even keep track of them all. It was all very pagan and spooky, when it wasn't ridiculous. They were all worshipping some obscure Jew from halfway around the world. The Rockefellers were! The Roosevelts even! Very spooky it was, and yet these Protestants ran the biggest law firms, the banks, the investment houses, the big corporations. He never saw such people in the flesh, except at ceremonies. Otherwise they didn't exist in New York. They barely even showed up in the voting surveys. In sheer numbers they were a nullity—and yet there they were. And now one of these sects, the Episcopalians, had a black bishop. You could joke about the Wasps, and he often did so with his friends, and yet they weren't so much funny as creepy.

"And this church," said the Mayor, "something about Landmarks?"

"Right," said Sheldon. "The bishop wants to sell St. Timothy's to a developer, on the grounds that the membership is declining and the church is losing a lot of money, which is true. But the community groups are putting a lot of pressure on the Landmarks Commission to landmark it so that nobody can alter the building even if they buy it."

"Is this guy honest?" asked the Mayor. "Who gets the money if they sell the church?"

"I never heard he wasn't honest," said Sheldon. "He's a learned gentleman of the cloth. He went to Harvard. He could still be greedy, I suppose, but I have no reason to think he is."

"Unnh-hunh." The Mayor suddenly had an idea. "Well, send him in."

Bishop Warren Bottomley turned out to be one of those well-educated, urbane black people who immediately create the Halo Effect in the eyes of white people who hadn't known what to expect. For a moment or two the Mayor was even intimidated, so dynamic was Bishop Bottomley. He was handsome, slender, about forty-five, athletic in build. He had a ready smile, a glittering eye, a firm handshake, and he wore a clerical outfit that was similar to a Catholic priest's but had an expensive look. And he was tall, much taller than the Mayor, who was touchy about his small size. Once they sat down, the Mayor got his perspective back and thought about his idea. Yes, Bishop Warren Bottomley would be perfection itself.

After a few well-delivered pleasantries about the Mayor's illustrious political career, the bishop began laying out the financial plight of St. Timothy's.

"Of course, I can understand the concerns of the people of the community," said the bishop. "They don't want to see a larger building or a different sort of building."

No black accent at all, thought the Mayor. He seemed to run into black people with no accent all the time now. The fact that he noticed it made him feel mildly guilty, but he noticed it all the same.

"But very few of these people are members of St. Timothy's Church," the bishop continued, "which of course is precisely the problem. There are fewer than seventy-five regular members in a very large building, which incidentally has no architectural distinction. The architect was a man named Samuel D. Wiggins, a contemporary of Cass Gilbert who has left not a single footprint in the sands of architectural history, so far as I can determine."

This casual reference intimidated the Mayor still further. Art and architecture were not his strong suits.

"Frankly, St. Timothy's Church is no longer serving its community, Mr. Mayor, because it is no longer in a position to do so, and we feel it would be of far greater benefit, not only to the Episcopal Church and its more vital manifestations in our city, but to the city itself—since a large taxable entity could be erected on that site, and even the community would benefit, indirectly, in the sense that the whole city would gain through the increase in tax revenues. That's why we would like to sell the present structure, and we request your consideration . . . so that the building will not be landmarked, as the Landmarks Commission wants to do."

Thank God! The Mayor was relieved to see that the bishop had gotten tangled up in his grammar and had left an incomplete sentence in the road behind him. Without saying a word, the Mayor smiled at the bishop and put his finger beside his nose, like Santa Claus in "The Night before Christmas." Then he pointed his finger straight up in the air, as if to say "Hark!" or "Watch this!" He beamed at the bishop and pushed a button on the intercom box on the credenza by his desk and said, "Get me the Landmarks Commissioner." Presently, there was a low *beep-beep* sound, and the Mayor picked up his telephone.

"Mort? . . . You know St. Timothy's Church? . . . Right. Exactly . . . Mort—lay off!"

The Mayor hung up and leaned back in his chair and smiled once more at the bishop.

"You mean—that's it?" The bishop seemed genuinely startled and delighted. "That's . . . the commission . . . they won't . . ."

The Mayor nodded and smiled.

"Mr. Mayor, I scarcely know how to thank you. Believe·me—I've been told you have a way of getting things done, but—well! I'm very grateful! and I can assure you that I will see to it that everyone in the diocese and all of our friends are aware of what a great service you have done for us. Yes indeed, I will!"

"That's not necessary, Bishop," said the Mayor. "There's no need to regard it as a favor or even as a service. The facts you so ably presented to me were very persuasive, and I think the entire city is going to benefit. I'm happy to do something for yoooou that's good for yoooou and for the city of New York."

"You certainly have! And I'm most appreciative."

"Now, in the same spirit," said the Mayor, adopting his best schoolteacherly tone, which had served him so well so often, "I want yo-o-o-ou to do something for me-e-e . . . that is *like*wise good for yo-o-o-ou and for the city of New York."

The Mayor cocked his head and smiled more broadly than ever. He looked like a robin eyeing a worm.

"Bishop, I want you to serve on a special blue-ribbon commission on crime in New York that I will be forming shortly. I'd like to announce your appointment the same time that I announce the formation of the commission. I don't have to tell you what a crucial issue this is, and one of our biggest problems is all the racial overtones, all the perceptions and misperceptions about who commits crimes and how our police officers deal with crimes. There's not a more important service you could render the city of New York at this time than to serve on this commission. How about it?"

The Mayor could see the dismay in the bishop's face immediately.

"I feel highly flattered, Mr. Mayor," said the bishop. He didn't look highly flattered, however. No more smiles. "And I agree with you, of course. But I must explain to you that insofar as my activities as bishop of this diocese interact with the public or, let me say, the official sector, my hands are somewhat tied, and . . ."

But his hands were not tied at this moment. He began twisting them as if trying to open a jar of pickled peaches, as he attempted to explain to the Mayor the structure of the Episcopal Church and the theology underlying the structure and the teleology of the theology and what could or could not be rendered unto Caesar.

The Mayor tuned out after ten or twelve seconds but let the bishop ramble on, taking a bitter pleasure in the man's distress. Oh, it was quite clear. The bastard was filling the air with bullshit to cover up the fact that no Rising Black Leader such as himself could afford to affiliate with the Mayor in any way, not even to the extent of serving on a fucking commission on fucking crime. And it had been such a brilliant idea! A biracial commission on crime, with a half dozen good-looking dynamic black leaders such as the bishop. Bishop Warren Bottomley would resonate with the heartbeats of every decent black person in New York, the very constituency the Mayor had to have if he was to win in November. And this smooth Harvard-educated snake was already wiggling out of his grasp! Long before the bishop had completed his exegeses and apologies, the Mayor had abandoned the idea of a special blue-ribbon commission on crime in New York City.

"I'm truly sorry," said the bishop, "but church policy leaves me no choice."

"Oh, I understand," said the Mayor. "What you can't do, you can't do. I can't think of anyone I'd rather see serve on the commission, but I understand your situation completely."

"I'm doubly sorry, Mr. Mayor, in view of what you've just done for our church." The bishop was wondering if the deal was still on.

"Oh, don't worry about that," said the Mayor. "Don't worry about that at all. As I said, I didn't do it for you, and I didn't do it for your church. I did it because I think it's in the best interests of the city. It's as simple as that."

"Well, I *am* grateful, nonetheless," said the bishop, getting up, "and you can be sure that the entire diocese will be grateful. I'll see to that."

"That's not necessary," said the Mayor. "Every now and then it's nice to come across a proposition that has an irresistible logic all its own."

The Mayor gave the bishop his broadest smile and looked him squarely in the face and shook his hand and kept smiling until the bishop left the room. When the Mayor returned to his desk, he pressed a button and said, "Get me the Landmarks Commissioner."

Presently there was a low *beep-beep*, and the Mayor picked up his telephone and said, "Mort? You know that church, St. Timothy's? . . . Right . . . LANDMARK THE SON OF A BITCH!"

28

OFF TO A BETTER PLACE

"Listen, Sherman. Do you think she honestly cares whether you're a gentleman or anything else at this point? Do you think she's gonna voluntarily jeopardize her interests to help you out? She don't even tawk to you, f'r Chrissake."

"I don't know."

"I *do* know. You don't get the picture yet? She *married* Ruskin, f'r Chrissake, and whaddaya think she felt for him? I bet she studied the actuarial tables. Awright? I bet you she actually studied the fucking actuarial tables."

"You may be right. But that doesn't excuse anything I do. This is a *funeral* we're talking about, her husband's *funeral!*"

Killian laughed. "You can call it a funeral if you want. To her it's Christmas."

"But to do this to a *widow* on the day of her husband's funeral, practically on top of the corpse!"

"Awright. Let me put it to you another way. Whaddaya want, a gold star for ethics . . . or your own funeral?"

Killian had his elbows on the arms of his desk chair. He leaned forward and cocked his head, as if to say, "What's that, Sherman? I don't hear you."

And in that instant, Sherman had a vision of *that place* and *them*. If he had to go to jail, even for a few months—let alone *years*—

"This is the one time you *know* you're gonna see her" said Killian. "She's *got* to turn up for the guy's fucking funeral. She'll face you and ten like you for the payoff at the end of that one."

Sherman lowered his eyes and said, "Okay. I'll do it."

"Believe me," said Killian, "it's perfectly legal, and under the circumstances it's perfectly fair. You're not doing anything to Maria Ruskin. You're protecting yourself. You have every right."

Sherman looked up at Killian and nodded yes, as if he were assenting to the end of the world.

"We better get started," said Killian, "before Quigley goes out to lunch. He does all our wiring."

"You do that much of it?"

"I'm telling you, this is a standard procedure now. We don't exactly advertise it, but we do it all the time. I'm gonna get Quigley."

Killian got up and went down the corridor. Sherman's eyes drifted over the dreadful blind interior of the little office. How inexpressibly grim! And yet here he was. This was his last redoubt. He was sitting here, of his own free will, waiting to be *wired* in order to steal, through the most indecent sort of deception, testimony from someone he had loved. He nodded, as if someone else were in the room, and that nod said, "Yes, but that's what I'm going to do."

Killian returned with Quigley. High on Quigley's waistband, on the left side, was a .38-caliber revolver, in a holster, with the handle facing forward. He came in carrying some sort of attaché case. He smiled at Sherman in an abrupt businesslike fashion.

"Okay," Quigley said to Sherman, "you'll have to take off your shirt."

Sherman did as he was told. The bodily vanity of the male knows no bounds. Sherman's immediate concern was that the definition of his pectoral, abdominal, and triceps muscles stand out sufficiently for these two men to be impressed by his physique. For a moment this cut through everything else. He knew that if he extended his arms straight down as if he were simply holding them at his sides, the triceps muscles would flex.

Quigley said, "I'm gonna put the recorder in the small of your back. You're gonna wear a jacket over there, right?"

"Yes."

"Okay. That'll be no problem then."

Quigley got down on one knee, opened his attaché case, took out the wires and the recorder, which was about the size of a deck of cards. The microphone was a gray cylinder the size of the eraser and metal band on the top of an ordinary pencil. First he taped the recorder onto Sherman's back. Then he taped the wire around his waist from back to front and up his abdomen to the hollow between his pectoral muscles, just above the sternum, where he taped the microphone.

"That's good," he said. "It's down deep. It won't show at all, especially if you wear a necktie."

Sherman took that as a compliment. *Down deep . . . between the massive hillocks of my manly chest muscles.*

"Okay," said Quigley, "you can put your shirt on, and we'll test it."

Sherman put his shirt and tie and jacket back on. Well . . . he was now *wired.* Cold spots of metal in the small of his back and over his sternum . . . He had become that loathsome animal . . . the . . . the . . . But *loathsome* was only a word, wasn't it? Now that he had actually become that creature, he no longer actually *felt* even a twinge of guilt. Fear had remapped the moral geography very quickly.

"Awright," said Killian. "Now we're gonna go over what you're gonna say. You're only gonna need a couple of statements out of her, but you gotta know exactly how you're gonna get 'em. Awright? So let's get started."

He motioned toward the white plastic chair, and Sherman sat down to learn the manly art of entrapment. "Not entrapment," he said to himself. "Truth."

Harold A. Burns's, on Madison Avenue, had been the most fashionable funeral parlor in New York for many years, but Peter Fallow had never set foot in the place before. The dark green double doors on Madison were framed by a formal set of pilasters. The vestibule within was no more than twelve by twelve feet. Yet from the moment he entered, Fallow was aware of an overpowering sensation. The light in the little space was intensely bright, so bright he didn't even want to seek out the source, for fear it would blind him. A bald-headed man in a dark gray suit stood in the vestibule. He handed Fallow a program and said, "Please sign the register." There was a podium, upon which was a large date book and a ballpoint pen tethered by a brass chain. Fallow added his name to the roster.

As his eyes began to adjust to the light, he became aware that there was a large doorway beyond the vestibule and that someone was staring at him. Not someone, however, but several people . . . not several, but . . . scores of them! The doorway led to a short flight of stairs. So many eyes bearing down upon him! The mourners were seated in what looked like the sanctuary of a small church, and they were all staring at him. The pews faced a stage, upon which the service would take place and in front of which rested the coffin of the recently departed. The vestibule was a second stage, off to one side, and by turning their heads the mourners could see each person who arrived. And everyone turned his head. But of course! This was Manhattan. The Upper East Side! The dear deceased, who reposeth in that box up front? Alas, the poor devil is done for, dead and gone. But the quick and the living—ah!—there you have something. They still burn with the lovely social wattage of the city. Not who leaveth, but who cometh in! Let us by all means illuminate them and measure their radiance!

They kept coming, Baron Hochswald, Nunnally Voyd, Bobby Shaflett, Red Pitt, Jackie Balch, the Bavardages, one and all, the whole bold-faced population of the gossip columns, stepping into the blazing light of the vestibule with faces so suitably grim that it made Fallow want to laugh. Solemnly they entered their names in the register. He would want to take a good look at that list of autographs before he left.

Soon the place was packed. A rustle ran through the crowd. A door to the side of the stage opened. People began to rise up in their seats to get a better look. Fallow rose to a crouch.

Well, there she was—or Fallow assumed it was she. At the head of a procession was . . . the Mystery Brunette, the Widow Ruskin. She was a trim woman wearing a long-sleeved black silk suit with huge shoulders and a black silk blouse and a black fez-style hat, from which issued a voluminous black veil. That outfit was going to cost the estate a few Mecca ticket receipts. With her were half a dozen people. Two of them were Ruskin's sons by his first marriage, a pair of middle-aged men, each old enough to be Maria Ruskin's father. There was a fortyish woman who Fallow assumed was Ruskin's daughter by his second wife. There was an old woman, perhaps Ruskin's sister, plus two more women and two men Fallow couldn't figure out at all. They sat down in the front row, near the coffin.

Fallow was on the opposite side of the room from the door from which Maria Ruskin had come and through which she might disappear at the end of the service. Some rude journalistic aggressiveness might be called for. He wondered if the Widow Ruskin had hired any sort of bodyguards for the occasion.

A tall slender very dapper figure ascended the four or five steps to the stage in front and went to the podium. He was fashionably dressed for mourning, with his navy double-breasted suit, black tie, white shirt, and narrow-toed black shoes. Fallow looked at his program. This was apparently a man named B. Monte Griswold, director of the Metropolitan Museum of Art. He fished a pair of half spectacles out of his breast pocket, spread some sheets of paper out before him, looked down, looked up, took off the half spectacles, paused, and said, in a rather fluty voice:

"We are here not to mourn Arthur Ruskin but to celebrate his very full . . . and very generous life."

It made Fallow's flesh crawl, this American penchant for the personal and the sentimental. The Yanks couldn't even let the dead depart with dignity. Everyone in the hall would be in for it now. He could feel it coming, the pointless bathos, the dripping spoonfuls of soul. It was enough to drive an Englishman back into the bosom of the Church of England, wherein death and all the major junctures of life were dealt with upon the high ground of the Divine, an invariable and admirably formal eminence.

Ruskin's eulogizers were every bit as witless and tasteless as Fallow had imagined they would be. The first was a United States senator from New York, Sidney Greenspan, whose accent was exceptionally vulgar, even by American standards. He stressed Arthur Ruskin's generosity toward the United Jewish Appeal, an unfortunate note in view of the just-revealed fact that his financial empire was founded upon the ferrying of Muslims to Mecca. The senator was followed by one of Ruskin's partners, Raymond Radosz. He started off pleasantly enough with an anecdote about a period when the two of them were close to bankruptcy, but then trailed off on an embarrassing tangent about the glories of their holding company, Rayart Equities, which would keep Artie's—he called him Artie—Artie's spirit alive, so long as loans floated and debentures were convertible. Then came a jazz pianist, "Arthur's favorite," named Manny Leerman, to play a medley of "Arthur's favorite songs." Manny Leerman was a fat red-haired man who wore a robin's-egg-blue double-breasted suit, which he laboriously unbuttoned after sitting down at the piano, so that the collar of the suit wouldn't ride up above his shirt collar. Arthur's favorite songs turned out to be "September in the Rain," "The Day Isn't Long Enough (When I'm with You)," and "The Flight of the Bumblebee." This last the florid little pianist played in a rousing but not flawless manner. He wound up his performance by spinning around 180 degrees on the piano stool, before it dawned on him that this was not a club date and he was not supposed to take a bow. He buttoned up his double-breasted jacket before he left the stage.

Then came the main speaker, Hubert Birnley, the movie actor, who had decided that what was needed was the light touch and the human side of Arthur the great financier and ferry captain to the Arab world. He became mired in an anecdote that hinged largely upon one's comprehension of the problems people have with swimming-pool-filtration systems in Palm Springs, California. He left the stage dabbing a handkerchief at the corners of his eyes.

Last on the program was Cantor Myron Branoskowitz, of Congregation Schlomoch'om, Bayside, Queens. He was a huge young man, a three-hundred-pounder, who began singing in Hebrew in a strong clear tenor voice. His lamentations began to swell in volume. They were unending and irrepressible. His voice took on throbs and vibratos. If there was a choice between ending a phrase in a high octave or a low one, he invariably went high, like an opera singer in concert, indulging his virtuosity. He put tears into his voice that would have embarrassed the worst hambone Pagliacci. At first the mourners were impressed. Then they were startled as the voice grew in volume. Then they became concerned as the young man appeared to swell like a frog. And now they were beginning to look at one another, each wondering if his neighbor was thinking the same thing: "This kid is out to lunch." The voice rose, rose, then peaked with a note just this side of a yodel before plunging to a lower range with a teary cascade of vibrato and coming to an abrupt halt.

The service was over. The audience paused, but Fallow did not. He slipped out into the aisle and, crouching slightly, began hurrying down toward the front. He was ten or twelve rows from the front when a figure ahead of him did the same thing.

It was a man wearing a navy-blue suit, a snap-brim hat, and dark glasses. Fallow caught only the briefest glimpse of the side of his head . . . the chin . . . It was Sherman McCoy. He had no doubt worn the hat and the glasses in order to enter the funeral home without being recognized. He rounded the bend at the first pew and fell in behind the family's little entourage. Fallow did the same. Now he could get a glimpse of the profile. It was McCoy all right.

The crowd was already in the hubbub of departing a funeral service and letting off the steam of thirty or forty minutes of obligatory respectfulness toward a rich man who, while alive, had not been particularly warm or likable. A funeral-parlor functionary was holding open the little side door for the Widow Ruskin. McCoy stayed close on the heels of a tall man who was in fact, as Fallow could now see, Monte Griswold, the master of ceremonies. The eulogizers were joining the family backstage. McCoy and Fallow were merely part of a mournful troop of dark blue suits and black dresses. Fallow folded his arms over his chest to hide the brass buttons on his blazer, for fear they would look out of place.

There was no problem. The funeral-home doorman was intent only on herding inside everyone who was going inside. The little door led to a short flight of stairs, at the top of which was a suite of rooms, like a little apartment. Everyone gathered in a small reception room decorated with balloon shades and panels of fabric framed in gilded wood, in the nineteenth-century French manner. Everyone was paying his condolences to the widow, who could scarcely be seen behind the wall of blue suits. McCoy hung about the edges, still wearing his dark glasses. Fallow stayed behind McCoy.

He could hear the baritone burble of Hubert Birnley talking to the widow and no doubt saying perfectly proper and fatuous things with a sad but charming Birnley smile on his face. Now it was Senator Greenspan's turn, and his nasal voice could be heard saying no doubt several wrong things along with the right ones. And then Monte Griswold had his turn, uttering impeccable things, one could be sure, and waiting to receive the widow's compliments for his skills as emcee. Monte Griswold said goodbye to the Widow Ruskin, and—bango!—McCoy confronted her. Fallow was right behind him. He could see Maria Ruskin's features through the black veil. Young and beautiful! Nothing quite like it! Her dress accentuated her breasts and brought out the conformation of her lower abdomen. She was looking straight at McCoy. McCoy leaned so close to her face Fallow thought at first he was going to kiss her. But he was whispering. The Widow Ruskin was saying something in a low voice. Fallow leaned in closer. He crouched right behind McCoy.

He couldn't make it out . . . A word here and there . . . "straight" . . . "essential" . . . "both" . . . "car"—

Car. As soon as he heard the word, Fallow experienced a feeling that journalists live for. Before the mind can digest what the ears have just heard, an alarm puts the nervous system on red alert. A *story!* It is a neural event, a feeling as palpable as any recorded by the five senses. A *story!*

Damn. McCoy was mumbling again. Fallow leaned in still closer . . . "other one" . . . "ramp" . . . "skidded"—

Ramp! Skidded!

The widow's voice rose. "Shuhmun"—she seemed to be calling him *Shuhmun.* "Kint we tuk about it letter?"

"Letter?" wondered Fallow. "Something about a letter?" Then he realized she was saying *later.*

Now McCoy's voice rose: ". . . *time,* Maria!" . . . "right there with me— you're my only witness!"

"Uh kint make myself think about all that now, Shuhmun." The same strained voice, ending with a little throb in the throat. "Kintchuh understand? Duntchuh know where you uh? My husband's dead, Shuhmun."

She cast her eyes down and began shaking with soft sobs. Immediately a wide squat man was by her side. It was Raymond Radosz, who had spoken during the service.

More sobs. McCoy walked away quickly, heading out of the room. For an instant Fallow started to follow him, then wheeled about. The Widow Ruskin was the story now.

Radosz was now hugging the widow so hard the enormous shoulders of her mourning outfit were buckling. She looked lopsided. "It's okay, honey," he said. "You're a brave kid, and I know exactly how you feel, because me and Artie went through a lot together. We go back a long, long way, back before you weren't even born, I guess. And I can tell you one thing. *Artie woulda liked the service.* I can tell you that. He woulda liked it, with the senator and everybody."

He waited for a compliment.

The Widow Ruskin pulled her grief together. It was the only way to disengage from her ardent mourner. "But you most especially, Ray," she said. "You knew him best, and you knew just how to put it. I know Arthur rests easier, for what you said."

"Awwww, well, thank you, Maria. You know, I could kinda see Artie in front of me while I was talking. I didn't have to think what I was gonna say. It just came out."

Presently he departed, and Fallow stepped forward. The widow smiled at him, just the least bit disconcerted because she didn't know who he was.

"I'm Peter Fallow," he said. "As you may know, I was with your husband when he died."

"Oh yes," she said, giving him a quizzical look.

"I just wanted you to know," said Fallow, "that he didn't suffer. He simply lost consciousness. It happened"—Fallow brought his hands up in a gesture of help-lessness—"like *that.* I wanted you to know that everything that could have been done was done, or so it seems to me. I attempted artificial respiration, and the police responded very rapidly. I know how one can wonder about these things, and I wanted you to know. We had just had an excellent dinner and an excellent conversation. The last thing I remember was your husband's wonderful laugh. In all honesty I must tell you, there are worse ways—it's a terrible loss, but it was not a terrible ending."

"Thank you," she said. "You're awfully kind to tell me this. I've reproached myself for being away from him when . . ."

"You shouldn't," said Fallow.

The Widow Ruskin looked up at him and smiled. He was aware of the sparkle in her eyes and the curious curl of her lips. She was able to put a coquettish edge even on a widow's thanks.

Without changing his tone of voice, Fallow said, "I couldn't help but notice Mr. McCoy speaking to you."

The widow was smiling with her lips parted slightly. First the smile shrank away. Then the lips closed.

"In fact, I couldn't help but overhear your conversation," said Fallow. Then, with a bright and amiable look on his face and a full-blown English Country Weekend accent, as if he were asking about the guest list at a dinner party: "I gather you were in the car with Mr. McCoy when he had his unfortunate accident in the Bronx."

The widow's eyes turned into a pair of cinders.

"I was hoping that perhaps you might tell me exactly what happened that night."

Maria Ruskin stared at him a moment longer and then said, between tight lips: "Look, Mr.—Mr.—"

"Fallow."

"—Peckerhead. This is my husband's funeral, and I don't want you here. You understand? So get out—and disintegrate."

She turned and walked off toward Radosz and a group of blue suits and black dresses.

As he left the Harold A. Burns funeral home, Fallow was giddy with the knowledge of what he had. The story existed not only in his mind but in his skin and his solar plexus. It surged like a current in every axon and dendrite of his body. As soon as he got near the word processor, the story would pour out of his fingers—pre-formed. He wouldn't have to say, allege, imply, speculate that the beautiful and now fabulously wealthy merry young Widow Ruskin was the Mystery Brunette. McCoy had said it for him. "Right there with me—my only witness!" The Widow Ruskin had remained tight-lipped—but she hadn't denied it. Nor had she denied it when the journalist, the great Fallow, when I—when I—when I—that was it. He would write it in the first person. Another first-person exclusive, like DEATH NEW YORK STYLE. I, Fallow—dear God, he hungered, lusted, for the word processor! The story vibrated in his mind, his heart, his very groin.

But he made himself stop by the register in the vestibule and copy down the names of all the celebrated souls who had been on hand to pay their respects to the lovely widow of Mecca's Kosher Ferry Captain without dreaming of the drama unfolding beneath their prurient noses. They would know soon enough. I, Fallow!

Out on the sidewalk, just beyond the vestibule, were clusters of these very same luminous personages, most of them having the sort of exuberant grinning conversations people in New York somehow can't help having at events that dramatize their exalted status. Funerals were no exception. The huge young cantor, Myron Branoskowitz, was talking with—or talking to—a severe-looking older man whose name Fallow had just copied from the register: Jonathan Buchman, the chief executive officer of Columbia Records. The cantor spoke with great animation. His hands made little flights in the air. Buchman's expression was rigid, paralyzed by the sonorous logorrhea that spewed so ceaselessly into his face.

"No problem!" said the cantor. It was almost a shout. "No problem at all! I've already made the cassettes! I've done every one of the Caruso standards! I can have them over to your office tomorrow! You got a card?"

The last thing Fallow saw, before he left, was Buchman fishing a card out of a trim little lizard-skin card wallet, while Cantor Branoskowitz added, in the same declamatory tenor:

"Mario Lanza, too! I've done Mario Lanza! I want you to have them, too!"

"Well—"

"No problem!"

29

THE RENDEZVOUS

The NEXT MORNING Kramer and Bernie Fitzgibbon and the two detectives, Martin and Goldberg, were in Abe Weiss's office. It was like a board meeting. Weiss sat at the head of the big walnut conference table. Fitzgibbon and Goldberg sat to his left; Kramer and Martin, to his right. The subject was how to proceed with a grand-jury hearing on the Sherman McCoy case. Weiss did not like what he was now hearing from Martin. Neither did Kramer. From time to time Kramer took a look at Bernie Fitzgibbon. All he could make out was a mask of black Irish impassivity, but it emitted short waves that said, "I told you so."

"Wait a minute," said Weiss. He was talking to Martin. "Tell me again how you picked up these two characters."

"It was in a crack sweep," said Martin.

"A crack sweep?" said Weiss. "What the hell's a crack sweep?"

"A crack sweep's a—that's what we do now. Some blocks up there, there's so many crack dealers on the block it's like a flea market. A lot of the buildings are abandoned, and the others, the people that live there, they're afraid to come out the front door, because there's nothing on the street but people selling crack, people buying crack, and people smoking crack. So we make these sweeps. We move in and we pick up everything that's loose."

"Does it work?"

"Sure. You do it a couple of times and they'll move to another block. It's got to the point where as soon as the first cruiser comes around the corner, they start running from the buildings. It's like these construction sites when they set off the dynamite and the rats start running down the street. Somebody oughta take along a movie camera one time. Here's all these people running down the fucking street."

"Okay," said Weiss. "So these two guys you picked up, they know Roland Auburn?"

"Yeah. They all know Roland."

"Okay. So what you're telling us—this is something Roland told them personally or this is something they heard?"

"No, this is the word that's going around."

"In Bronx crack circles," said Weiss.

"Yeah, I guess," said Martin.

"Okay, go ahead."

"Well, the word is that Roland happens to see this kid, Henry Lamb, walking
up to the Texas Fried Chicken place, and he tags along. Roland enjoys giving this
kid a hard time. Lamb's what they call a 'good-doing boy,' a mama's boy, a boy
who don't 'come out.' He don't come out of the house and get into the street life.
He goes to school, he goes to church, he wants to go to college, he don't get into
trouble—he don't even belong in the projects. His mother's trying to save up
money for a down payment on a house in Springfield Gardens, or they wouldn't
even be living there."

"These two guys didn't tell you that."

"No, that's what we already found out about the kid and his mother."

"Well, let's stick to these two smokeheads and what they said."

"I was trying to give you the background."

"Good. Now give me the foreground."

"Awright. So anyway, Roland's walking down Bruckner Boulevard with
Lamb. They're walking past the ramp at Hunts Point Avenue, and Roland sees
this shit on the ramp, these tires or trash cans or something, and he knows
somebody's been up there trying to take off cars. So he says to Lamb, 'Come on,
I'll show you how to take off a car.' Lamb don't want any part of that, and so
Roland says, 'I'm not gonna do it, I'm just gonna show you how you do it.
Whaddayou afraid of?' He's, you know, taunting the kid, because he's such a
mama's boy. So the kid walks up on the ramp with him, and the next thing he
knows, Roland throws a tire or a can or something in front of this car, this
terrific-looking Mercedes, and it turns out to be McCoy and some broad. This
poor fucker, Lamb, is just standing there. He's probably scared shitless to be there,
and he's scared shitless about running, too, because of Roland, who's only doing
this whole number to let him know what a faggot he is in the first place. Then
something goes wrong, because McCoy and the woman manage to get the hell
outta there, and Lamb gets sideswiped. Anyway, that's what's going around out on
the street."

"Well, that's some theory. But have you found anybody who says they actually
heard Roland say any a that?"

Bernie Fitzgibbon broke in. "That theory would explain why Lamb don't say
anything about being hit by a car when he goes to the hospital. He don't want
anybody to think he was involved in trying to take off a car. He just wants to get
his wrist fixed up and go home."

"Yeah," said Weiss, "but all we got here is a theory presented by two
smokeheads. Those people don't know the difference between what they're hearing and what they're *hearing*." He twirled his forefinger up around his temple in
the Looney Tunes mode.

"Well, I think it's worth checking out, Abe," said Bernie. "I think we oughta
spend a little time on it, anyhow."

Kramer felt alarmed and resentful and protective, protective of Roland

Auburn. None of them had bothered to get to know Roland the way he had. Roland was not a saint, but he had goodness in him, and he was telling the truth.

He said to Bernie, "There's no harm in checking it out, but I can think of ways a theory like this actually gets started. I mean, it's really the McCoy theory. It's what McCoy fed the *Daily News*, and it's on TV. I mean, this theory is already out on the street, and this is what it grows into. It answers one question, but it raises ten more. I mean, why would Roland try to take off a car with this kid along who he knows is a wimp, a lame? And if McCoy is the victim of a robbery attempt and he hits one of his assailants, why would he hesitate to report it to the cops? He'd do it *like that*." Kramer snapped his fingers and realized an argumentative tone had taken over his voice.

"I agree, it raises a lot of questions," said Bernie. "All the more reason not to rush this thing through the grand jury."

"We got to rush it," said Weiss.

Kramer caught Bernie looking at him in a certain way. He could see accusations in his black Irish eyes.

Just then the telephone on Weiss's desk gave three low beeps. He got up, walked over to the desk, and answered it.

"Yeah? . . . Okay, put him on . . . No, I haven't seen *The City Light* . . . What? You gotta be kidding . . ."

He turned toward the conference table and said to Bernie, "It's Milt. I don't think we gotta worry about any smokehead theories for a while."

In no time Milt Lubell, wide-eyed, slightly out of breath, was walking into the room with a copy of *The City Light*. He laid it on the conference table. The front page jumped up at them.

City Light EXCLUSIVE:

FINANCIER'S

WIDOW IS

MCCOY CASE

MYSTERY GIRL

McCoy at Funeral: "Help Me!"

Across the bottom of the page ran a line saying: *Peter Fallow's Eyewitness Report, Pictures, pages 3, 4, 5, 14, 15.*

All six of them stood up and leaned over with their palms on the walnut table to support themselves. Their heads converging over the epicenter, which was the headline.

Weiss straightened up. On his face was the look of the man who knows that it falls to his lot to be the leader.

"All right, here's what we're gonna do. Milt, call up Irv Stone at Channel 4." He then reeled off the names of the news producers of five other channels. "And call Fallow. And that fellow Flannagan at the *News*. And here's what you tell them. We're gonna question this woman as soon as possible. That's for the record. Not for attribution, tell 'em if she is the woman who was with McCoy, then she faces felony charges, because she was the one who drove off after McCoy hit the kid. That's leaving the scene and failure to report. Hit-and-run. He hit, she ran. Okay?"

Then to Bernie: "And you guys . . ." He let his eyes pan quickly over Kramer, Martin, and Goldberg, to show them they were included. "You guys get hold of this woman, and you tell her the exact same thing. "We're sorry your husband is dead, et cetera, et cetera, et cetera, but we need some answers very fast, and if you're the one who was in the car with McCoy, then you're in a whole lotta freakin' trouble." But if she's willing to come clean about McCoy, we'll grant her immunity before the grand jury." To Kramer: "Don't get too specific about that at first. Well, hell, you know how to do it."

By the time Kramer, Martin, and Goldberg pulled up in front of 962 Fifth Avenue, the sidewalk looked like a refugee camp. Television crewmen, radio broadcasters, reporters, and photographers sat, milled, and lollygagged about in the jeans, knit shirts, zipper jackets and Trapper Dan shoes their trade currently affected, and the idle gawkers who looked on weren't dressed much better. The cops from the 19th Precinct had set up a double row of blue police line sawhorses to create an alley to the front door for the benefit of the people who lived in the building. A uniformed patrolman stood by. For such a building, fourteen stories high and half a block wide, the front entrance was not particularly grand. Nevertheless, it bespoke money. There was a single plate-glass door framed in heavy brass, highly polished, and protected by an ornate brass grillwork, which also gleamed. A canopy stretched from the door to the edge of the sidewalk. The canopy was supported by brass poles with brass guy rods, likewise polished until they looked like white gold. As much as anything else, it was the eternity of mule's work represented by all the hand-polished brass that said money. Behind the plate glass, Kramer could see the figures of a pair of uniformed doormen, and he thought of Martin and his soliloquy on the *shitballs* at McCoy's building.

Well . . . here he was. He had looked up at these apartment buildings on Fifth Avenue, facing Central Park, a thousand times at least, most recently on Sunday afternoon. He had been out in the park with Rhoda, who was pushing Joshua in the baby carriage, and the afternoon sun had lit up the great limestone façades to the point where the phrase itself had crossed his mind: *the gold coast*. But it was merely an observation, devoid of emotion, except perhaps for a mild feeling of satisfaction at being able to stroll amid such golden surroundings. It was well known that the richest people in New York lived in those buildings. But their life, whatever it was, was as remote as another planet. Such people were merely types, far outside the range of any conceivable envy. They were The Rich. He couldn't have told you the name of a single one of them.

Now he could.

Kramer, Martin, and Goldberg got out of the car, and Martin said something to the cop in the uniform. The raggedy pack of journalists bestirred themselves. Their itchy clothes flopped about. They looked the three of them up and down and sniffed for the scent of the McCoy case.

Would they recognize him? The car was unmarked, and even Martin and Goldberg were wearing coats and ties, and so they might pass for three men who just happened to be coming to this building. On the other hand . . . was he any longer just an anonymous functionary of the criminal-justice system? Hardly. His picture (by luscious Lucy Dellafloria) had appeared on television. His name had appeared in every newspaper. They started walking up the alley between the police barricades. Halfway there—Kramer felt let down. Not a tumble from this huge twitching assembly of the New York press.

Then: "Hey, Kramer!" A voice over to his right. His heart leapt. "Kramer!" His impulse was to turn and smile, but he fought it. Should he just keep on walking and ignore it? No, he shouldn't high-hat them, should he? . . . So he turned toward the voice with a look of high seriousness on his face.

Two voices at once:

"Hey, Kramer, you gonna—"

"What are the charges—"

"—talk to her?"

"—against her?"

He heard someone else saying: "Who is that?" And someone answering: "That's Larry Kramer. He's the D.A. on this case."

Kramer kept his lips set grimly and said, "I got nothing for you right now, fellows."

Fellows! They were *his* now, this bunch—*the press*, which was formerly merely an abstraction so far he was concerned. Now he was looking the whole itchy mob of them in the face, and they hung on his every word, his every step. One, two, three photographers were in position. He could hear the whine of the rewind mechanisms of their cameras. A television crew was lumbering over. A video-camera protruded from the skull of one of them like a horn. Kramer walked a bit slower and stared at one of the reporters, as if considering a reply, to give the fellows a few more seconds of this solemn mug of his. (They were only doing their job.)

When he and Martin and Goldberg reached the front door, Kramer said to the two doormen, with guttural authority: "Larry Kramer, Bronx District Attorney's Office. They're expecting us."

The doormen hopped to it.

Upstairs, the door to the apartment was opened by a little man in uniform who appeared to be Indonesian or Korean. Kramer stepped inside—and the sight dazzled him. This was to be expected, since it was designed to dazzle people far more inured to luxury than Larry Kramer. He glanced at Martin and Goldberg. The three of them were straight-out sightseers . . . the two-story ceiling, the enormous chandelier, the marble staircase, the fluted pilasters, the silver, the balcony, the huge paintings, the sumptuous frames, any one of which, just the frame, cost about half a cop's annual pay. Their eyes were gobbling it all up.

Kramer could hear a vacuum cleaner going somewhere upstairs. A maid in a black uniform with a white apron appeared on the marble floor of the entry gallery and then disappeared. The Oriental butler led them across the gallery. Through a doorway they got an eyeful of a vast room flooded with light from the tallest windows Kramer had ever seen in a private home. They were as big as the windows in the courtrooms of the island fortress. They looked out over the tops of the trees of Central Park. The butler took them to a smaller, darker room next to it. Or it was darker by comparison; in fact, a single tall window facing the park admitted so much light that at first the two men and the woman who waited inside were visible only as silhouettes. The two men were standing. The woman sat in a chair. There was a set of rolling library stairs, a large desk with gilded decorations on its curved legs, and antique knickknacks on top of it, plus two small couches with a large burled-wood coffee table between them, several arm-chairs and side tables and . . . and this *stuff*.

One of the silhouettes stepped forward from out of the glare and said, "Mr. Kramer? I'm Tucker Trigg."

Tucker Trigg; that was the guy's actual name. He was her lawyer, from Curry, Goad & Pesterall. Kramer had set up this meeting through him. Tucker Trigg had a nasal honk Wasp voice that really put Kramer off, but now that Kramer could see him, he didn't look like his idea of a Wasp. He was big, round, pudgy, like a football player gone to fat. They shook hands, and Tucker Trigg said in his honk voice:

"Mr. Kramer, this is Mrs. Ruskin."

She was seated in a high-backed armchair that made Kramer think of one of those series on Masterpiece Theatre. There was a tall gray-haired guy standing beside her. The *widow*—how young and bouncy she looked! *Foxy,* Roland had said. Arthur Ruskin had had a lot on his hands, seventy-one years old, with his second pacemaker ticking away. She wore a plain black silk dress. The fact that the wide shoulders and cadet collar treatment were currently quite chic was lost on Larry Kramer, but her legs weren't. Her legs were crossed. Kramer tried to keep his eyes from running up the highlit curve of the top of her foot and the glisten-ing curve of her calves and the shimmering curve of her thighs under the black silk. He tried his best. She had the most wonderful long ivory neck, and her lips were parted slightly, and her dark eyes seemed to be drinking his right up. He was flustered.

"I'm sorry to intrude under these circumstances," he stammered. He immedi-ately felt he had said something foolish. Was she supposed to conclude that under other circumstances he would be happy to intrude?

"Oh, I understand, Mr. Kramer," she said softly, with a brave smile. *Oh, I unnerstin, Mr. Krimmuh.* Or was it *merely* a brave smile? God almighty, the way she *looked* at him!

He couldn't imagine what to say to her next. Tucker Trigg spared him the task by introducing the man who stood next to the chair. He was a tall, older man. His gray hair was combed back smartly. He had the sort of military posture seldom seen in New York. His name was Clifford Priddy, and he was well known for defending prominent people in federal criminal cases. This one had Wasp written all over him. He looked at you straight down his long, thin nose. His clothes were subdued and rich, as only these bastards knew how to do it. His shiny black shoes were oh-so-sweetly fitted in the instep and trim in the toe. The man made Kramer feel clumsy. His own shoes were heavy brown sloggers, with soles that stuck out like rock ledges. Well, this case wasn't in federal court, where the old Ivy League network still looked out for its own. No, they were dealing with the basic Bronx now.

"How do you do, Mr. Kramer," said Mr. Clifford Priddy, affably.

"Fine," said Kramer, shaking hands and thinking, Let's see how smug you look when we get you up to Gibraltar.

Then he introduced Martin and Goldberg, and everyone sat down. Martin and Goldberg and Tucker Trigg and Clifford Priddy; there was a quartet for you. Goldberg sat hunched over, a bit subdued, but Martin was still the Tourist Un-fazed. His eyes were dancing all over the room.

The young widow in black pressed a button on the table beside her chair. She recrossed her legs. The curved sheens flew apart and reassembled, and Kramer tried to avert his eyes. She looked toward the doorway. A maid, a Filipino, if Kramer had to guess, was standing there.

Maria Ruskin looked at Kramer and then Goldberg and Martin and said, "Would you gentlemen care for some coffee?"

No one cared for coffee. She said, "Nora, I'd like some coffee, and—"

"*Cora,*" the woman said tonelessly. Every head turned toward her, as if she had just produced a revolver.

"—and bring some extra cups, please," said the widow, ignoring the correction, "in case any of the gentlemen change their mind."

Not perfect with the grammar, thought Kramer. He tried to figure out exactly what was wrong with what she had said—and then realized that everyone was quiet and looking at him. Now it was his show. The widow's lips were parted in the same strange little smile. Was it bravery? Mockery?

"Mrs. Ruskin," he began, "as I say, I'm sorry to have to come to you at this particular time, and I'm very grateful for your cooperation. I'm sure Mr. Trigg and Mr. Priddy have explained to you the purpose of this meeting, and I just, uh, want to—" She stirred her legs under her dress, and Kramer tried not to notice the way her thighs welled up under the shiny black silk. "—uh, emphasize that this case, which involves a very serious injury, possibly fatal, to a young man, Henry Lamb —this case is highly important to our office, because it's highly important to the people of Bronx County and to all the people of this city." He paused. He realized he was sounding pompous, but he didn't know how to get back down off his high horse. The presence of these Wasp lawyers and the scale of this palace had made him get up here.

"I understand," said the widow, possibly to help him out. Her head was slightly cocked, and she smiled the smile of an intimate friend. Kramer had rogue stirrings. His mind leapt ahead to the trial. Sometimes you ended up working very closely with a cooperative witness.

"That's why your cooperation would be of such great value to us." He threw his head back, to emphasize the grandeur of his sternocleidomastoid muscles. "Now, all I want to do right now is to try to explain to you what's going to be involved if you do cooperate or if for any reason you decide not to cooperate, because I think we have to be completely clear on that. Certain things are gonna naturally flow from either decision. Now, before we start, I should remind you that—" He paused again. He had started the sentence off wrong and was going to get tangled up in his syntax. Nothing to do but plow on. "—you're represented by eminent counsel, so I don't have to remind you of your rights in that respect." *In that respect.* Why these pompous, pointless block phrases? "But I am obliged to remind you of your right to remain silent, should you want to for any reason."

He looked at her and nodded, as if to say, 'Is that clear?" She nodded back, and he noticed the swell of her breasts moving under the black silk.

From beside the chair he lifted his attaché case up to his lap and immediately wished he didn't have to. The case's scuffed corners and edges were an exposé of his lowly status. (A $36,000-a-year assistant D.A. from the Bronx.) Look at the goddamned case! All dried out, cracked, and scuffed! He felt humiliated. What was going through these fucking Wasps' minds at this moment? Were they just holding back their smirks for tactical reasons, or out of some condescending Wasp politeness?

From the case he took two pages of notes on yellow legal paper and a folder full of Xeroxed material, including some newspaper clippings. Then he closed up the telltale luggage and put it back on the floor.

He looked down at his notes. He looked up at Maria Ruskin. "There are four persons known to have intimate knowledge of this case," he said. "One is the victim, Henry Lamb, who is in an apparently irreversible coma. One is Mr. Sherman McCoy, who is charged with reckless endangerment, leaving the scene of an accident, and failure to report an accident. He denies these charges. One is an individual who was present when the incident occurred and who has come forth and has positively identified Mr. McCoy as the driver of the car that struck Mr. Lamb. This witness has told us that Mr. McCoy was accompanied in that car by another person, a white female in her twenties, and the information provided makes her his accomplice in one or more of the felonies that Mr. McCoy is charged with." He paused, for what he hoped would be maximum effect. "That witness has positively identified that woman as . . . yourself."

Kramer now stopped and looked the widow squarely in the face. At first she was perfection. She didn't blink. Her lovely brave little smile never wavered. But then her Adam's apple, almost imperceptibly, went up and down just once.

She swallowed!

An excellent feeling came over Kramer, in every cell and every neural fiber. In that instant, the instant of that little swallow, his scuffed attaché case meant nothing, nor did his clodhopper shoes nor his cheap suit nor his measly salary nor his New York accent nor his barbarisms and solecisms of speech. For in that moment he had something that these Wasp counselors, these immaculate Wall Street partners from the universe of the Currys & Goads & Pesteralls & Dunnings & Spongets & Leaches would never know and never feel the inexpressible pleasure of possessing. And they would remain silent and polite in the face of it, as they were right now, and they would swallow with fear when and if their time came. And he now understood what it was that gave him a momentary lift each morning as he saw the island fortress rise at the crest of the Grand Concourse from the gloom of the Bronx. For it was nothing less than the Power, the same Power to which Abe Weiss himself was totally given over. It was the power of the government over the freedom of its subjects. To think of it in the abstract made it seem so theoretical and academic, but to *feel* it—to see the *looks on their faces*—as they stare back at you, courier and conduit of the Power—Arthur Rivera, Jimmy Dollard, Herbert 92X, and the guy called Pimp—even them—and now to see *that little swallow of fright* in a perfect neck worth millions—well, the poet has never sung of that ecstasy or even dreamed of it, and no prosecutor, no judge, no cop, no income-tax auditor will ever enlighten him, for we dare not even mention it to one another, do we?—and yet we *feel* it and we *know* it every time they look at us with those eyes that beg for mercy or, if not mercy, Lord, dumb luck or capricious generosity. (Just one break!) What are all the limestone façades of Fifth Avenue and all the marble halls and stuffed-leather libraries and all the riches of Wall Street in the face of *my* control of *your* destiny and your helplessness in the face of the Power?

Kramer stretched that moment out for as long as the bounds of logic and minimal decency would allow and then just a little bit longer. None of them, not the two immaculate Wasp lawyers from Wall Street and not the beautiful young widow with her new millions, dared make a peep.

Then he said softly, paternally, "All right. Now let's see what that means."

When Sherman entered Killian's office, Killian said, "Ayyyyyy, whaddaya whaddaya? What's the long face for? You won't mind coming all the way down here when I tell you why. Dja think I brought you down here to show you this?"

He tossed The City Light over to the edge of the desk. FINANCIER'S WIDOW . . . Sherman barely glanced at it. It had already come humming and sizzling into the arcade.

"He was right there in the room at Burns's. This Peter Fallow. I never saw him."

"It don't matter," said Killian, who was in a jolly mood. "This is old news. We awready knew this. Am I right? I brought you down here for the news."

The truth was, Sherman didn't mind these trips down to Reade Street at all. Sitting in the apartment . . . waiting for the next telephoned threat . . . The very grandeur of the apartment mocked what he had now been reduced to. He sat there and waited for the next blow. Doing anything was preferable. Riding in a car to Reade Street, moving horizontally without resistance—swell! Terrific!

Sherman sat down, and Killian said, "I didn't want to even mention this over the telephone, but I got a very interesting telephone call. The jackpot, in fact."

Sherman just looked at him.

"Maria Ruskin," said Killian.

"You're kidding."

"That I wouldn't kid you about."

"Maria called you?"

" 'Mistuh Killyun, muh nim is Muhreeuh Ruskin. Uhm a frin uvuh client uh yuhs, Mistuh Shuhmun McCoy.' Does that sound like the correct party?"

"My God! What did she say? What did she want?"

"She wants to see you."

"I'll be damned . . ."

"She wants to see you this afternoon at four-thirty. She said you'd know where."

"I'll . . . be . . . damned . . . You know, she told me yesterday, at Burns's, she was going to call me. But I didn't believe that for a second. Did she say why?"

"No, and I didn't ask her. I didn't want to say one word that might make her change her mind. All I said was, I was sure you'd be there. And I'm sure you will be, bro."

"Didn't I tell you she'd call me?"

"You did? You just said you didn't believe she would."

"I know. Yesterday I didn't, because she's been avoiding me. But didn't I say she wasn't the cautious type? She's a gambler. She's not the type to play it safe. She likes to mix it up, and her game is—well, it's men. Your game is the law, mine is investments, hers is men."

Killian started chuckling, more at the change in Sherman's spirits than anything else. "Okay," he said, "terrific. Let's you and her play. Let's get started. I had another reason for bringing you down here instead of me coming up to your place. We got to get you wired."

He pressed a button and said into the intercom: "Nina? Tell Ed Quigley to come in here."

At precisely 4:30, with his heart pumping away at a good clip, Sherman pressed the bell marked "4B Boll." She must have been waiting by the intercom box—the intercom itself no longer worked—because right away he could hear a buzz in the door and the heavy *click-click-click* of the electric lock opening, and he entered the town house. The smell was instantly familiar, the dead air, the filthy carpet on the stairs. There was the same old lugubrious paint and battered door-ways and the dismal light—familiar and at the same time new and dreadful, as if he had never taken the trouble to notice what was really here. The wonderful bohemian spell of the place was broken. He now had the misfortune to gaze at an erotic dream with the eyes of a realist. How could he ever have found it enchanting?

The creak of the stairs reminded him of things he wanted to forget. He could still see the dachshund hauling his fat tube up the risers . . . "You're a wet little piece a salami, Muhshull" . . . And he had been sweating . . . Sweating, he had made three trips up this decrepit staircase carrying Maria's luggage . . . And now he carried the heaviest burden of all. *I'm wired.* He could feel the tape deck in the small of his back, the microphone over his sternum; he could feel, or he imagined he felt, the grip of the tape that held the wire to his body. Each of these artful, stealthy, miniaturized elements seemed to grow with each step he took. His skin magnified them, like a tongue feeling a broken tooth. Surely they were obvious! How much of it showed on his face? How much deceit? How much dishonor?

He sighed and discovered he was already sweating and panting, from the climb or from adrenaline or from funk. The heat of his body made the tape prickly—or was it his imagination?

By the time he reached the door, that sad painted door, he was breathing hard. He paused, sighed again, then rapped on the door with the signal they had always used, *tap tappa tap tap—tap tap.*

The door opened slowly, but there was no one there. Then—

"Boo!" Her head popped out from behind the door, and she was grinning at him. "Scare yuh?"

"Not really," said Sherman. "Lately I've been scared by experts."

She laughed, and it seemed to be a genuine laugh. "You, too? We're a pair, aren't we, Sherman?" With that she held out her arms to him, the way you would for a welcoming embrace.

Sherman stared at her, astonished, confused, paralyzed. The calculations running through his mind faster than he could deal with them. There she was, in a black silk dress, her widow's weeds, fitted closely at the waist, so that her gorgeous body welled out above and below. Her eyes were large and brilliant. Her dark hair was perfection itself, with a luxurious sheen. Her coyly curved lips, which had always driven him crazy, were full and parted and smiling. But it added up to nothing but a certain arrangement of clothes and flesh and hair. There was a slight furze of dark hair on her forearms. He should slip between those arms and embrace her, if that's what she wanted! It was a delicate moment! He needed her on his side, in his confidence, for however long it took to get certain matters of fact into the microphone over his sternum and onto the tape in the small of his back! A delicate moment—and a dreadful dilemma! Suppose he embraced her—and she felt the microphone—or ran her hands down his back! He had never considered such a thing, not for a moment. (Who would even *want* to embrace a man who was *wired?*) Nevertheless—do something!

So, he moved toward her, thrusting his shoulders forward and humping his back, so that she couldn't possibly flatten herself against his chest. Thus they embraced, a voluptuous supple young thing and a mysterious cripple.

Quickly he disengaged, trying to smile, and she looked at him, as if to see if he was all right.

"You're right, Maria. We are a pair, we're on the front page." He smiled philosophically. (So let's get down to cases!) Nervously he looked about the room. "Come on," she said, "sit down." She gestured toward the oak pedestal table. "I'll get you a drink. What would you like?"

Fine; let's sit down and talk. "Any scotch?"

She went into the kitchen, and he looked down at his chest to make sure the microphone didn't show. He tried to run over the questions in his mind. He wondered if the tape was still running.

Presently she returned with his drink and one for herself, a clear drink, gin or vodka. She sat down in the other bentwood chair and crossed her legs, her glistening legs, and smiled.

She raised her glass as if in a toast. He did the same.

"So here we are, Sherman, the couple all New York is talking about. There's a lotta people'd like to hear *this* conversation."

Sherman's heart jumped. He was dying to peek downward to see if his microphone was showing. Was she insinuating something? He studied her face. He couldn't make out a thing.

"Yes, here we are," he said. "To tell you the truth, I thought you'd decided to vanish on me. I haven't had a very pleasant time since you left."

"Sherman, I swear to you I didn't know anything about it until I got back."

"But you didn't even tell me you were going."

"I know, but that had nothing to do with you, Sherman. I was—I was half crazy."

"What did it have to do with?" He tilted his head and smiled, to show he wasn't bitter.

"With Arthur."

"Ah. With Arthur."

"Yes, with Arthur. You think I had a very free-and-easy arrangement with Arthur, and in a way I did, but I also had to live with him, and nothing was really free with Arthur. He took it out one way or the other. I told you how he'd started swearing at me."

"You mentioned it."

"Calling me a whore and a bitch, right in front of the servants or anybody else, if he felt like it. Such *resentment*, Sherman! Arthur wanted a young wife, and then he turned around and hated me because I was young and he was an old man. He wanted exciting people around, because he thought with all his money, he deserved exciting people, and then he turned around and he hated them and he hated me, because they were my friends or else they were more interested in me than they were in him. The only people interested in Arthur were those old yids, like Ray Radosz. I hope you saw what a fool he made of himself at the funeral.

Then he came in the back there and started trying to *hug* me. I thought he was gonna pull my *dress* off me. Did you see that? You were *so excited!* I kept trying to tell you to *calm down!* I never saw you like that. And that big-nosed bastard from *The City Light,* that horrible hypocritical Brit, was standing right behind you. He *heard* you!"

"I *know* I was excited," he said. "I thought you were ducking me. I was afraid it was the last chance I was going to have to talk to you."

"I wasn't ducking you, Sherman. I'm trying to explain. The only person I was ducking was Arthur. I just left, I just—I didn't think. I just left. I went to Como, but I knew he could find me there. So I went to visit Isabel di Nodino. She has a place in the mountains, in a little town outside of Como. It's like a castle in a book. It was wonderful. No telephone calls. I didn't even see a newspaper."

All alone, except for Filippo Chirazzi. But that didn't matter, either. As calmly as he could, he said, "It's nice that you could get away, Maria. But you knew I was worried. You knew about the piece in the newspaper, because I showed it to you." He couldn't get the agitation out of his voice. "The night that big maniac was here—I know you remember that."

"Come on, Sherman. You're getting all worked up again."

"Have you ever been arrested?" he said.

"No."

"Well, I have. That was one of the things I did while you were away. I . . . ." He stopped, suddenly realizing he was doing something very foolish. To get her frightened about the prospects of being arrested was the last thing he needed to do right now. So he shrugged and smiled and said, "Well, it's an experience," as if to say, "But not as bad as you might think."

"But I've been threatened with it," she said.

"What do you mean?"

"A man from the Bronx District Attorney's Office came around to see me today, with two detectives."

This hit Sherman like a jolt. "He did?"

"A pompous little bastard. He thought he was being so tough. He kept throwing his head back and doing something weird with his neck, like this, and looking at me through these little slits for eyes. What a creep."

"What did you tell him?" Very nervous now.

"Nothing. He was too busy telling me what he could do to me."

"What do you mean?" A riff of panic.

"He told me about this witness he has. He was so pompous and official about it. He wouldn't even say who it was, but it was obviously that other kid, the big one. I can't tell you what a jerk this man was."

"Was his name Kramer?"

"Yeah. That was it."

"He was the same one who was in court when I was arraigned."

"He made it real simple, Sherman. He said if I would testify against you and corroborate the other witness, he'd give me immunity. If I didn't, then I'd be treated as an accomplice, and they'd charge me with these . . . felonies. I can't even remember what they were."

"But surely—"

"He even gave me these Xeroxes of stories in the newspapers. He practically drew me a map. These were the correct stories, and these were the ones you concocted. I'm supposed to agree with the correct stories. If I say what actually happened, I go to prison."

"But surely you told him what actually happened!"

"I didn't tell him anything. I wanted to talk to you first."

He was sitting on the edge of the chair. "But, Maria, certain things are so *clear-cut* about this thing, and they don't even know them yet. They've only heard lies from this kid who was trying to rob us! For example, it didn't happen on a *street*, it happened on a *ramp*, right? And we stopped because the *road* was blocked, before we even *saw* anybody. Right? Isn't that right?" He realized his voice had risen.

A warm, sad smile, the sort of smile you give people who are in pain, came over Maria's face, and she stood up and put her hands on her hips and said, "Sherman, Sherman, Sherman, what are we gonna do with you?"

She slewed her right foot out in a certain way she had and let it pivot for a moment on the heel of her black high-heeled shoe. She gave him a look with her big brown eyes and held out her hands toward him, palms up.

"Come here, Sherman."

"Maria—this is important!"

"I know it is. Just come here."

Christ! She wanted to embrace him again! Well—embrace her, you idiot! It's a sign she wants to be on your side! Embrace her within an inch of your life! Yes! —but how? *I'm wired up!* A cartridge of shame on my chest! A bomb of dishonor in the small of my back! What'll she want to do next? Flop on the bed? What then? Well—good God, man! The look on her face says, "I'm yours!" She's your ticket out! Don't blow this chance! *Do something! Act!*

So he rose from the chair. He lurched toward the best of both worlds. He got into a crouch, so that her chest wouldn't touch his so the small of his back would be beyond the reach of her hands. He embraced her like an old man leaning over a fence to touch a flagpole. This brought his head down low. His chin was practically on her clavicle.

"Sherman," she said, "what's wrong? What's wrong with your back?"

"Nothing."

"You're all hunched over."

"I'm sorry." He turned sideways, with his arms still around her shoulders. He tried to embrace her sideways.

"Sherman!" She stepped back for a moment. "You're all bent sideways. What's the matter? You don't want me to touch you?"

"No! No . . . I guess I'm just tense. You don't know what I've been through." He decided to improve on that. "You don't know how much I've missed you, how much I've needed you."

She studied him, then gave him the warmest, wettest, most labial look imaginable. "Well," she said, "here I am."

She stepped toward him. He was in for it now. No more crouching, you dolt! No more sidewinding! He'd have to take a chance! Maybe the microphone was down deep enough so that she wouldn't feel it, especially if he kissed her—kissed her feverishly! Her arms would be around his neck. So long as she kept them there, she'd never get to the small of his back. They were just inches apart. He slipped his arms under hers, in order to force hers up around his neck. He embraced her around her shoulder blades, to keep them forced up high. Awkward, but it would have to do.

"Oh, Maria." This kind of passionate moan wasn't typical of him, but it would have to do also.

He kissed her. He closed his eyes in the interest of sincerity and concentrated on bracing his arms up high on her torso. He was conscious of flesh slightly caked with lipstick and warm saliva and the smell of her breath, which bore the recycled vegetable smell of gin.

Wait a minute. What the hell was she doing? She was sliding her arms down outside of his arms, down toward his hips! He raised his elbows and tensed the muscles of his upper arms to try to force her arms away from his body without making an obvious point of it. Too late! She had her hands on his hips, trying to press his hips against hers. But her arms weren't long enough! Suppose her hands then edged up to the small of his back. He jutted his tail out. If her fingers lost contact with his hips, maybe she'd give up. Her fingers—where were they? For a moment he felt nothing. Then—something on his waist, on the side. Shit! Confuse her—that was his only chance. Her lips remained pressed against his. She squirmed rhythmically and passionately amid the high vegetable funk. He squirmed back and jiggled his hips a bit, to throw her off. Her fingers—he'd lost them again. Every nerve fiber was on red alert, seeking to detect their presence. All at once her lips stopped squirming. Their lips were still together, but the motor had cut out. She disengaged her mouth and pulled her head back a few inches, so that he saw three eyes swimming in front of his face. But her arms were still around him. He didn't like the way those three eyes swam.

"Sherman . . . What's this on your back?"

"My back?" He tried to move, but she stayed with him. Her arms were still around him.

"There's a lump, a piece a metal or something—this thing, on your back."

Now he could feel the pressure of her hand. It was right on top of the tape deck! He tried a little turn this way and a little turn that way, but she still had her hand on it. He tried a real shimmy. No use! Now she had a grip on it!

"Sherman, what is this?"

"I don't know. My belt—my belt buckle—I don't know."

"You don't have a belt buckle in the back!"

Now she pulled loose from him in front, but she still had her hand on the deck.

"Maria! What the hell!"

He swung to the side in an arc, but she swung around behind him like a college wrestler looking for a takedown. He got a glimpse of her face. Half a smile —half a furious scowl—an ugly dawn breaking.

He spun and broke free. She confronted him head on.

"Sherman!" *Shuhmun.* A quizzical smile, waiting for the right instant to break into a howl of accusation. Slowly: "I want to know . . . what's'at on your back."

"For God's sake, Maria. What's gotten into you? It's nothing. My suspender buttons maybe—I don't know."

"I want to see, Sherman."

"What do you mean, see?"

"Take off your jacket."

"What do you mean?"

"Take it off. I want to see."

"That's crazy."

"You've taken off a lot more than that in here, Sherman."

"Come on, Maria, you're being silly."

"Then humor me. Let me see what's on your back."

A plea: "Maria, come on. It's too late in the day to play games."

She came toward him, the terrible smile still on her face. She was going to see for herself! He jumped to one side. She came after him. He dodged again.

A would-be game-like giggle: "What are you doing, Maria!"

Beginning to breathe heavily: "We'll see!" She charged at him. He couldn't get out of the way. Her hands were on his chest—trying to get at his shirt! He covered himself like a maiden.

"Maria!"

The howl began: "You're *hiding something*, aren't you!"

"Now just hold on . . ."

"You're *hiding something!* Whaddaya got under your shirt!"

She lunged at him again. He dodged, but before he knew it, she was behind him. She had her hands under his jacket. She had a grip on the tape deck, although it was still under his shirt, and his shirt was still tucked into his pants. He could feel it coming away from his back.

"And a *wire*, Sherman!"

He clamped down on her hand with his own, to keep her from pulling it out. But her hand was under his jacket, and his hand was on top of the jacket. He began hopping around, holding on to this writhing red-angry mass under his jacket.

"It's—on—a—*wire*—you—bastard!"

The words were squirting out in awful grunts as the two of them hopped about. Only the exertion kept her from screaming bloody murder.

Now he had her hand by the wrist. He had to make her let go. He squeezed harder and harder.

"You're—hurting me!"

He squeezed harder.

She gave a little shriek and let go. For a moment he was paralyzed by the fury in her face.

"Sherman—you rotten, dishonest bastard!"

"Maria, I swear—"

"You—*swear*, do yuh!" She lunged again. He bolted for the door. She grabbed one sleeve and the back of his jacket. He tried to wrench free. The sleeve began tearing away from the body. He plowed on toward the door. He could feel the tape deck bouncing on his buttocks. It was hanging out of his pants by now, out from under the shirt and hanging off his body by the wire.

Then there was a blur of black silk and a thud. Maria was on the floor. One of her high heels had buckled and her legs went out from under her. Sherman ran to the door. It was all he could do to open it, because his jacket was pulled down over his arms.

Now he was out into the hallway. He heard Maria sobbing, and then she yelled out:

"That's right, run! Drag your tail between your legs!"

It was true. He was hobbling down the stairs with the tape deck dangling ignominiously down his backside. He felt more shameful than any dog.

By the time he reached the front door, the truth had hit him. Through stupidity, incompetence, and funk he had now managed to lose his one last hope.

Oh, Master of the Universe.

30

AN ABLE PUPIL

THE GRAND-JURY ROOMS in the island fortress were not like regular courtrooms. They were like small amphitheaters. The members of the grand jury looked down on the table and chair where the witnesses sat. Off to one side was the clerk's table. There was no judge in a grand-jury proceeding. The prosecutor sat his witnesses down in the chair and questioned them, and the grand jury decided either that the case was strong enough to put the defendant on trial or that it wasn't and threw the case out. The concept, which had originated in England in 1681, was that the grand jury would protect the citizenry against unscrupulous prosecutors. That was the concept, and the concept had become a joke. If a defendant wanted to testify before the grand jury, he could bring his lawyer into the grand-jury room. If he was (a) perplexed or (b) petrified or (c) grievously abused by the prosecutor's questions, he could leave the room and confer with a lawyer outside in the hall—and thereby look like someone who was (b) petrified, a defendant with something to hide. Not many defendants took the chance. Grand-jury hearings had become a show run by the prosecutor. With rare exceptions, a grand jury did whatever a prosecutor indicated he wanted them to do. Ninety-nine percent of the time he wanted them to indict the defendant, and they obliged without a blink. They were generally law-and-order folk anyway. They were chosen from long-time residents of the community. Every now and then, when political considerations demanded it, a prosecutor wanted to have a charge thrown out. No problem; he merely had to couch his presentation in a certain way, give a few verbal winks, as it were, and the grand jury would catch on immediately. But mainly you used the grand jury to indict people, and in the famous phrase of Sol Wachtler, chief judge of the State Court of Appeals, a grand jury would "indict a ham sandwich," if that's what you wanted.

You presided over the proceedings, you presented the evidence, questioned the witnesses, gave the summations. You stood up while the witnesses sat. You orated, gestured, walked about, spun on your heels, shook your head in disbelief or smiled in paternal approbation, while the witnesses sat properly in their seats and looked up at you for direction. You were both the director and the star of this little amphitheater production. The stage was all yours.

And Larry Kramer had rehearsed his actors well.

The Roland Auburn who came walking into the grand-jury room this morning neither looked nor walked like the hard case who had popped up in Kramer's office two weeks ago. He wore a button-down shirt, albeit with no necktie; it had been enough of a struggle to get him into the lame Brooks Brothers button-down shirt. He wore a blue-gray tweed sport jacket, of which his opinion was roughly the same, and a pair of black pants, which he already owned and weren't too bad. The whole ensemble had nearly come apart over the issue of the shoes. Roland had an obsession with Reebok sneakers, which had to be new-right-out-of-the-box snow white. At Rikers Island he managed to get *two new pairs per week*. This showed the world that he was a hard case worthy of respect inside the walls and a shrewd player with connections outside. To ask him to walk out of Rikers without his white Reeboks was like asking a singer to cut off his hair. So Kramer finally let him leave Rikers with the Reeboks on, with the understanding that he would change into a pair of leather shoes in the car before they arrived at the courthouse. The shoes were loafers, which Roland found contemptible. He demanded assurances that no one he knew or might know be allowed to see him in this lame condition. The final problem was the Pimp Roll. Roland was like a runner who's been running marathons too long; very hard to change the stride. Finally Kramer had a brainstorm. He had Roland walk with his hands clasped behind his back, the way he had seen Prince Philip and Prince Charles walk on television while inspecting an artifacts museum in New Guinea. It worked! The clasped hands locked his shoulders, and the locked shoulders threw his hip rhythm off. So now, as Roland came walking into the grand-jury room, toward the table at center stage, in his preppy clothes, he could have passed for a student at Lawrenceville ruminating over the Lake poets.

Roland took his seat on the witness chair the way Kramer had told him to; that is, without rearing back and spreading his legs as if he owned the joint and without popping his knuckles.

Kramer looked at Roland and then turned and faced the grand jury and took a few steps this way and a few steps that way and gave them a thoughtful smile, in such a way as to announce, without saying a word: "This is a sympathetic and believable individual sitting before you."

Kramer asked Roland to state his occupation, and Roland said softly, modestly, "I'm an artist." Kramer asked him if he was currently employed. No, he was not, said Roland. Kramer nodded for a few moments, then began a line of questioning that brought out precisely why this young man of talent, this young man eager to find an outlet for his creativity, had not found the proper outlet and was, in fact, currently facing a minor drug charge. (The Crack King of Evergreen Avenue had abdicated and become a mere serf of the environment.) Like his friend Henry Lamb, but without Henry Lamb's advantages in terms of a stable home life, Roland had challenged the crushing odds against young men in the projects and emerged with his dreams intact. There was just this matter of keeping body and soul together, and Roland had drifted into a pernicious commerce but one not at all uncommon in the ghetto. Neither he, the prosecutor, nor Roland, the witness, was attempting to hide or minimize his petty crimes; but given the environment in which he had lived, they should not impair his credibility among fair-minded people in a matter as grave as the fate of Henry Lamb.

Charles Dickens, he who explained the career of Oliver Twist, couldn't have done it any better, at least not on his feet in a grand-jury room in the Bronx.

Then Kramer led Roland through the narrative of the hit-and-run accident. He lingered lovingly on one particular moment. It was the moment at which the foxy-looking brunette yelled at the tall man who'd been driving the car.

"And what did she say to him, Mr. Auburn?"

"She say, 'Shuhmun, watch out.'"

"She said *Shuhmun?*"

"That's what it sound like to me."

"Would you say that name again, Mr. Auburn, exactly the way you heard it that night?"

"Shuhman."

"'Shuhmun, watch out?'"

"That's right, 'Shuhmun, watch out.'"

"Thank you." Kramer turned toward the jurors, and let *Shuhmun* float there in the air.

The individual sitting in that witness chair was a young man of those mean streets whose bravest and best efforts had not been enough to save Henry Lamb from the criminal negligence and irresponsibility of a Park Avenue investment banker. Carl Brill, the gypsy-cab operator, came into the room and told how Roland Auburn had indeed hired one of his cabs to rescue Henry Lamb. Edgar (Curly Kale) Tubb told of driving Mr. Auburn and Mr. Lamb to the hospital. He could remember nothing of what Mr. Lamb said except that he was in pain.

Officers William Martin and David Goldberg told of their dogged police work in tracing part of a license number to an investment banker on Park Avenue who became flustered and evasive. They told how Roland Auburn, without hesitation, identified Sherman McCoy from a lineup of photographs. A parking-garage attendant named Daniel Podernli told of how Sherman McCoy had taken his Mercedes-Benz roadster out on the night in question, during the hours in question, and had returned in a state of dishevelment and agitation.

They all came in and sat down at the table and looked up at the forceful but patient young assistant district attorney, whose every gesture, every pause, every stride said, "We have but to let them tell their story their own way, and the truth makes itself manifest."

And then he brought *her* in. Maria Ruskin came into the amphitheater from an antechamber, where a court officer manned the door. She was superb. She had struck just the right note in her wardrobe, a black dress with a matching jacket edged in black velvet. She had not dressed up, and she had not dressed down. She was the perfect widow in mourning who had business to attend to. And yet her youth, her voluptuousness, her erotic presence, her sensual self seemed ready to burst forth from those clothes, from that stunning but composed face, from that full flawless head of dark hair ready to be tousled with mad abandon—at any moment!—on any pretext!—with the next tickle!—the merest wink! Kramer could hear the jurors rustling and buzzing. They had read the newspapers. They had watched television. The Foxy Brunette, the Mystery Girl, the Financier's Widow—it was *her*.

Involuntarily Kramer pulled in his midsection and flattened his abdomen and

threw back his shoulders and his head. He wanted her to see his powerful chest
and neck, not his unlucky pate. Too bad he couldn't tell the jury the whole story.
They would enjoy it. They would view him with renewed respect. The very fact
that she had walked through that door and was now sitting at this table, right on
cue, had been a triumph, *his* triumph, and not merely of his words but of his
particular presence. But of course he couldn't tell them about his visit to the Foxy
Brunette's apartment, to her containerized palace.

Had she decided to support McCoy in the story he had concocted about a
robbery on a ramp, it would have been very much a problem. The whole case
would have been thrown back on the credibility of Roland Auburn, the erstwhile
Crack King who was now trying to leverage himself out of a jail term. Roland's
testimony provided the foundation for a case, but not a very solid one, and
Roland was capable of blowing it at any moment, not by what he said—Kramer
had no doubt that he was telling the truth—but through his demeanor. But now
he had her, too. He had gone to her apartment and looked her in the eye, her and
her Wasp retainers, too, and he had put her in a box, a box of irrefutable logic
and dread of the Power. He had put her in that box so quickly and securely she
hadn't even known what was happening. She had swallowed—gulped—gulped
her multimillion-dollar gulp—and it was all over. By nightfall Messrs. Tucker
Trigg and Clifford Priddy—Trigg and Priddy, Priddy and Trigg—oh, ye Wasps!—
had been on the telephone to make the deal.

Now she was seated before him, and he looked down at her and let his eyes
fasten upon hers, seriously at first and then with (or so he imagined it) a twinkle.

"Would you please state your full name and address."

"Maria Teresa Ruskin, 962 Fifth Avenue."

Very good, Maria Teresa! It was he himself, Kramer, who had discovered her
middle name was Teresa. He had figured there would be a few older Italian and
Puerto Rican women on the grand jury, and sure enough there were. *Maria Teresa*
would bring her closer to them. A touchy matter, her beauty and her money. The
jurors were staring ropes. They couldn't get enough of her. She was the most
glamorous human being they had ever seen in the flesh. How long had it been
since anybody had sat in a witness chair in this room and given an address on
Fifth Avenue in the Seventies? She was everything they were not and (Kramer
was sure) wanted to be: young, gorgeous, chic, and unfaithful. And yet that could
be a positive advantage, so long as she behaved in a certain fashion, so long as she
was humble and modest and seemed slightly abashed by the scale of her own
advantages, so long as she was little Maria Teresa from a small town in South
Carolina. So long as she took pains to be *one of us* at heart, they would feel
flattered by their association with her in this excursion into criminal justice, by
her success and celebrity, by the very aura of her money.

He asked her to state her occupation. She hesitated and stared at him with
her lips parted slightly, then said, "Umm . . . I'm a" . . . *Um-uh* . . . "uh
guess um-uh housewife."

A rush of laughter ran through the jurors, and Maria cast her eyes down and
smiled modestly and shook her head slightly, as if to say, "I know it sounds
ridiculous, but I don't know what else to say." Kramer could tell by the way the
jurors smiled in return that so far they were on her side. They were already
captivated by this rare and beautiful bird who now fluttered before them in the
Bronx.

Kramer took this moment to say, "I think the jurors should be made aware that Mrs. Ruskin's husband, Mr. Arthur Ruskin passed away just five days ago. Under these circumstances, we are indebted to her for her willingness to come forward at this time and cooperate with this jury in these deliberations."

The jurors stared at Maria all over again. *Brave, brave girl!*

Maria lowered her eyes again, quite becomingly.

Good girl, Maria! "Maria Teresa" . . . "Housewife" . . . If only he could give these worthy jurors a little exegesis of how he had coached her in these small but telling points. All true and honest—but even truth, and honesty can disappear without a light. So far she had been a bit cool toward him, but she followed directions and thereby signaled her respect. Well, there would be many sessions to come, when they went to trial—and even at this moment, in this room, under these austere circumstances, at this plain dock of justice, there was something about her—ready to burst forth! A crook of the finger . . . a single wink . . .

Calmly, quietly, to show how difficult he knew this must be for her, he began to lead her through the events of the fateful evening Mr. McCoy had picked her up at Kennedy Airport. (No need, for the purposes of these proceedings, to say why.) They get lost in the Bronx. They're a bit anxious. Mr. McCoy is driving in the left lane of a wide avenue. She sees a sign over on the right indicating a way back to an expressway. He suddenly veers right at a high speed. He's heading straight for two boys standing on the edge of the pavement. He sees them too late. He grazes one, nearly hits the other. She tells him to stop. He does.

"Now, Mrs. Ruskin, would you please tell us . . . At this point, when Mr. McCoy stopped, was the car on the ramp to the expressway or on the avenue itself?"

"It was on the avenue."

"The avenue."

"Yes."

"And was there any obstruction or barricade or any kind of obstacle that caused Mr. McCoy to stop the car where he did?"

"No."

"All right, tell us what happened then."

Mr. McCoy got out to see what had happened, and she opened the door and looked back. They could see both youths heading toward the car.

"And would you please tell us your reaction when you observed them coming toward you?"

"I was frightened. I thought they were going to attack us—because of what had happened."

"Because Mr. McCoy had hit one of them?"

"Yes." Eyes downcast, perhaps in shame.

"Did they threaten you verbally or through any sort of gesture?"

"No, they did not." More shame.

"But you thought they might attack you."

"Yes." A humble tone.

A kindly voice: "Could you explain why?"

"Because we were in the Bronx, and it was at night."

A gentle, paternal voice: "Is it also possible that it was because these two young men were black?"

A pause. "Yes."

"Do you think Mr. McCoy felt the same way?"

"Yes."

"Did he at any time, verbally, indicate that he felt that way?"

"Yes, he did."

"What did he say?"

"I don't remember exactly, but we talked about it later, and he said it was like being in a fight in the jungle."

"A *fight in the jungle?* These two young men walking toward you, after one of them has been struck by Mr. McCoy's car—this was like a fight in the jungle?"

"That was what he said. Yes."

Kramer paused to let that sink in. "All right. The two young men are approaching Mr. McCoy's car. What did you do then?"

"What did I do?"

"What did you do—or say?"

"I said, 'Sherman, watch out.' " *Shuhmun.* One of the jurors giggled.

Kramer said, "Would you repeat that, please, Mrs. Ruskin? Repeat what you said to Mr. McCoy?"

"I said, 'Shuhmun, watch out.' "

"Now, Mrs. Ruskin . . . if you'll permit me . . . You have a distinctive accent. You give Mr. McCoy's first name a soft pronunciation. *Shuhmun.* Isn't that correct?"

A regretful but becoming little smile crossed her face. "I guess so. You're a better judge than I am."

"Well, would you pronounce it in your own way for us, just once more? Mr. McCoy's first name."

"Shuhmun."

Kramer turned toward the jurors and just looked at them. *Shuhmun.*

"All right, Mrs. Ruskin, what happened next?"

She told how she slid behind the wheel and Mr. McCoy got in the passenger seat, and she sped off, very nearly hitting the young man who had escaped injury when Mr. McCoy was driving. Once they were safely back on the expressway, she had wanted to report the incident to the police. But Mr. McCoy would have none of it.

"Why was he reluctant to report what had happened?"

"He said he was driving when it happened, and so it was his decision to make, and he wasn't going to report it."

"Yes, but he must have offered a reason."

"He said it was just an incident in the jungle, and it wouldn't do any good to report it anyway, and he didn't want word to get back to his employer and his wife. I think he was more worried about his wife."

"Knowing that he had hit someone with his car?"

"Knowing that he had picked me up at the airport." Eyes downcast.

"And that was reason enough not to report that a young man had been struck and, as it turns out, gravely injured?"

"Well—I don't know. I don't know everything that was on his mind." Softly; sadly.

Very good, Maria Teresa! An able pupil! Most becoming, to confess the limits of your knowledge!

And thus the lovely Widow Ruskin sank Mr. Sherman McCoy like a stone.

Kramer left the grand-jury room in the state of bliss known chiefly to athletes who have just won a great victory. He tried hard to suppress a smile.

"Hey, Larry!"

Bernie Fitzgibbon was hurrying toward him down the hall. Good! Now he had a war story and a half for the black Irishman.

But before he could get out the first word about his triumph, Bernie said, "Larry, have you seen this?"

He thrust a copy of The City Light toward him.

Quigley, who had just come in picked up The City Light from Killian's desk and read it for himself. Sherman sat beside the desk in the miserable fiberglass armchair and averted his eyes, but he could still see it, the front page.

A band across the top read: EXCLUSIVE! NEW MCCOY CASE SHOCKER!

On the upper left-hand side of the page was a picture of Maria in a low-cut dress with the tops of her breasts welling up and her lips parted. The picture was set into a headline of enormous black type that read:

COME
INTO MY
RENT-CONTROLLED
LOVE NEST!

Below, a band of smaller type:

MILLIONAIRESS MARIA ENTERTAINED
MCCOY IN $331-A-MONTH TRYST
PAD   By Peter Fallow.

Killian was behind the desk, leaning back in his swivel chair and studying Sherman's gloomy face.

"Look," said Killian, "don't worryboudit. It's a sleazy story, but it don't hurt our case any. Maybe it helps. It tends to undermine her credibility. She comes off looking like a hooker."

"That's very true," said Quigley, in a voice that was supposed to be encouraging. "We already know where she was when her husband was dying. She was in Italy shacked up with some kid named Filippo. And now here's this guy Winter saying she had guys up there all the time. This Winter's a prince, ain't he, Tommy?"

"A real lovable landlord," said Killian. Then to Sherman: "If Maria rats you out, then this can only help. Not a lot, but some."

"I'm not thinking about the case," said Sherman. He sighed and let his great chin sink down to his collarbone. "I'm thinking about my wife. This will do it. I think she'd halfway forgiven me, or at least she was going to be with me, she was going to keep our family together. But this will do it."

"You got involved with a high-class hooker," said Killian. "It happens all the time. It's not that big a deal."

Hooker? To his own surprise, Sherman felt an urge to defend Maria. But what he said was: "Unfortunately, I swore to my wife that I'd never . . . never done anything but flirt with her once or twice."

"You really think she believed that?" said Killian.

"It doesn't matter," said Sherman. "I swore that was the truth, and then I asked her to forgive me. I made a big point of it. And now she learns with the rest of New York, with the rest of the world, from the front page of a tabloid, that I was . . . I don't know . . ." He shook his head.

"Well, it wasn't as if it was anything serious," said Quigley. "The woman's a high-class hooker, like Tommy says."

"Don't call her that," said Sherman in a low, melancholy voice, without looking at Quigley. "She's the only decent person in this whole mess."

Killian said, "She's so decent she's gonna rat you out, if she ain't already done it."

"She was prepared to do the right thing," said Sherman. "I'm convinced of that, and I shoved her good instincts right back in her face."

"Gedoudahere. I don't believe I'm listening to this."

"She didn't call me up and ask me to meet her in that apartment in order to do *me* in. I went there *wired* . . . to do *her* in. What did she have to gain by seeing me? Nothing. Her lawyers probably told her to have nothing to do with me."

Killian nodded. "That's true."

"But that isn't the way Maria's mind works. She isn't cautious. She isn't going to turn legalistic, just because she's in a tight corner. I once told you her medium was men, and that's the truth, just the way a . . . a . . . a dolphin's medium is the sea."

"Would you settle for a shark?" said Killian.

"No."

"Okay, have it your way. She's a mermaid."

"You can call her what you want. But I'm convinced that whatever she was going to do in this case concerning me, a man she'd been involved with, she wasn't going to do it behind a screen of lawyers—and she wasn't going to come *wired* . . . .for *evidence*. Whatever was going to happen, she wanted to see me, be next to me, have a real talk with me, an *honest* talk, not some game with words —and go to bed with me. You may think I'm crazy, but that's exactly what she wanted to do."

Killian just raised his eyebrows.

"I also believe she didn't go to Italy to duck out of this case. I think she went for exactly the reason she said. To get away from her husband . . . and from me . . . and I don't blame her . . . and to go have fun with a good-looking boy. You can call that being a hooker if you want, but she's the only one in this whole thing who's walked in a straight line."

"That's a neat trick, walking on your back," said Killian. "What's C. S. Lewis's emergency night-line number? We got a whole new concept of morality going here."

Sherman drove his fist into his hand. "I can't believe what I've done. If I had only played it straight with her! Me!—with my pretensions of respectability and propriety! And now look at this."

He picked up *The City Light*, more than ready to drown himself in his public shame. " 'Love nest' . . . 'tryst pad' . . . a picture of the very bed where 'the millionairess Maria entertained McCoy' . . . This is what my wife picks up, she and a couple of million other people . . . and my daughter . . . My little girl's almost seven. Her little friends will be perfectly capable of filling her in on what all this means . . . and ready and eager . .   You can be sure of that . . . Imagine. That sonofabitch, Winter, he's so slimy he takes the press in to take a picture of *the bed!*"

Quigley said, "They're wild men, Mr. McCoy, these landlords in the rent-controlled buildings. They're maniacs. They got one thing on their minds from morning to night, and that's getting tenants out. Ain't no Sicilian hates anybody worse than a rent-control landlord hates his tenants. They think the tenants are stealing their life's blood. They go crazy. This guy sees Maria Ruskin's picture in the paper, and she's got a twenty-room apartment on Fifth Avenue, and he flips out and goes running to the newspaper."

Sherman opened the newspaper to page 3, where the full story began. There was a picture of the front of the brownstone. Another picture of Maria, looking young and sexy. A picture of Judy looking old and haggard. Another picture of himself . . . and his aristocratic chin . . . and a big grin . . .

"That'll do it," he said to himself, but loud enough for Killian and Quigley to hear. Sinking, sinking, *diving* down into his shame . . . Reading aloud:

" 'Winter said he had information that Mrs. Ruskin was paying $750 a month under the table to the actual leaseholder, Germaine Boll, who then paid the $331 controlled rent.' That's true," said Sherman, "but I wonder how he knew it? Maria didn't tell him, and I'm sure Germaine didn't tell him. Maria mentioned it to me once, but I never mentioned it to a soul."

"Where?" asked Quigley.

"Where what?"

"Where were you when she told you about it?"

"I was . . . It was the last time I was in the apartment. It was the day the first story came out in *The City Light*. It was the day that big lunatic, that Hasidic monster, came barging in."

"Ayyyy," said Quigley. A smile spread over his face. "You see it, Tommy?"

"No," said Killian.

"Well, I do," said Quigley. "I could be wrong, but I think I see it."

"See what?"

"That sneaky sonofabitch," said Quigley.

"Whaddaya talking about?"

"I'll tell you later," said Quigley, still grinning. "Right now I'm going over there."

He left the room and went walking down the corridor at a good clip.

"What's he doing?" asked Sherman.

"I'm not sure," said Killian.

"Where's he going?"

"I don't know. I let him do what he wants. Quigley is a force of nature."

Killian's telephone rang, and the receptionist's voice came over the intercom. "It's Mr. Fitzgibbon on 3-0."

"I'll take it," said Killian, and he picked up the telephone. "Yeah, Bernie?"

Killian listened, with his eyes looking down, but every now and then they turned up and picked out Sherman. He took some notes. Sherman could feel his heart starting to bang away.

"On what theory?" said Killian. He listened a bit more. "That's bullshit, and you know it . . . Yeah, well, I'm . . . I'm . . . What? . . . Whose part's it

going into? . . . Unh hunh . . ." After a while he said, "Yeah, he'll be there."
He looked up at Sherman when he said that. "Okay. Thanks, Bernie."

He hung up and said to Sherman, "Well . . . the grand jury has returned an
indictment against you. She ratted you out."

"He told you that?"

"No. He can't talk about what goes on inside the grand jury. But he put it
there between the lines."

"What does this mean? What happens now?"

"The first thing that happens is, tomorrow morning the D.A. petitions the
court to set higher bail."

"Higher bail? How can they do that?"

"The theory is that now that you've been indicted, you'll have an increased
motivation to flee the jurisdiction of the court."

"But that's absurd!"

"Of course it is, but that's what they're doing, and you got to be there for it."

A terrible realization was beginning to come over Sherman. "How much will
they ask for?"

"Bernie don't know, but it'll be a lot. Half a million. A quarter of a million,
anyway. Some bullshit figure. It's just Weiss playing for the headlines, playing for
the black vote."

"But—can they actually put it that high?"

"It all depends on the judge. The hearing's before Kovitsky, who's also the
supervising judge of the grand jury. He's got a pair a stones. With him, at least
you got a fighting chance."

"But if they do it—how long do I have to raise the money?"

"How long? As soon as you post the bond, you're out."

"I'm *out?*" Terrible realization—"What do you mean, *out?*"

"Out of custody."

"But why would I be *in* custody?"

"Well, as soon as a new bail is set, you're in custody until you post bond,
unless you post it immediately."

"Wait a minute, Tommy. You don't mean that if they raise my bail tomorrow
morning, they put me in custody immediately, right there, as soon as the bail is
set?"

"Well, yeah. But don't jump to conclusions."

"You mean they take me right there in the courtroom?"

"Yeah, *if*—but don't—"

"Take me and put me *where?*"

"Well, the Bronx House of Detention, probably. But the point is—"

Sherman began shaking his head. He felt as if the lining of his skull were
inflamed. "I can't do that, Tommy."

"Don't immediately assume the worst! There's things we can do."

Still shaking his head: "There's no way I can get half a million dollars this
afternoon and put it in a bag."

"I'm not talking"—*tawkin*—"about anything like that, f'r Chrissake. It's a bail
hearing. The judge has to hear the arguments. We got a good argument."

"Oh sure," said Sherman. "You said yourself the thing's a political football."
He hung his head and shook it some more. "Jesus Christ, Tommy, I can't do it."

* * *

Ray Andriutti was whaling down his pepperoni and his coffee swill, and Jimmy Caughey held half a roast-beef hero up in the air like a baton while he talked to somebody on the telephone about some piece a shit he'd been assigned to. Kramer wasn't hungry. He kept reading the story in *The City Light*. He was fascinated. Rent-controlled love nest, $331 a month. The revelation didn't really affect the case much one way or the other. Maria Ruskin wouldn't come off as quite the sympathetic little lovely who had wowed them in the grand-jury room, but she'd make a good witness all the same. And when she did her "Shuhmun" duet with Roland Auburn, he'd have Sherman McCoy cocked and locked. Rent-controlled love nest, $331 a month. Did he dare call Mr. Hiellig Winter? Why not? He should interview him in any case . . . see if he can amplify the relationship of Maria Ruskin and Sherman McCoy as it pertains to . . . to . . . to rent-controlled love nest, $331 a month.

Sherman walked out of the living room and into the entry gallery and listened to the sound of his shoes on the solemn green marble. Then he turned and listened to himself walking across the marble to the library. In the library there was still one lamp, by a chair, that he hadn't turned on. So he turned it on. The entire apartment, both floors, was blazing with light and throbbing with stillness. His heart was working away at a good clip. In custody—tomorrow they would put him back *in there!* He wanted to cry out, but there was no one in this vast apartment to cry out to; nor anyone outside it.

He thought of a knife. In the abstract, it was so steely efficient, a long kitchen knife. But then he tried to enact it in his mind. Where would he thrust it in? Could he stand it? What if he made a bloody mess of it? Throw himself out a window. How long before he hit the pavement from this height? Seconds . . . interminable seconds . . . in which he would think of what? Of what it would do to Campbell, of how he was taking the coward's way out. Was he even serious about it? Or was this just superstitious speculation, in which he presumed if he thought of the worst he could bear . . . the actual . . . *back in there?* No, he couldn't bear it.

He picked up the telephone and called the number in Southampton again. No answer; there had been no answer all evening, despite the fact that, according to his mother, Judy and Campbell, Bonita, Miss Lyons, and the dachshund had left the house on East Seventy-third Street for Southampton before noon. Had his mother seen the newspaper article? Yes. Had Judy seen it? Yes. His mother hadn't even been able to bring herself to comment on it. It was too sordid to discuss. Then how much worse it had been for Judy! She hadn't gone to Southampton at all! She had decided to disappear, taking Campbell with her . . . to the Midwest . . . back to Wisconsin . . . A flash of memory . . . the bleak plains punctuated only by silvery aluminum water towers, in the shape of modernistic mushrooms, and clumps of wispy trees . . . A sigh . . . Campbell would be better off there than in New York living with the degraded memory of a father who in fact no longer existed . . . a father cut off from everything that defined a human being, except his name, which was now that of a villainous cartoon that newspapers, television, and slanderers of every sort were free to make sport of as they saw fit . . . Sinking, sinking, sinking, he gave himself up to ignominy and self-pity . . . until on about the twelfth ring someone picked up the telephone.
"Hello?"

"Judy?"

A pause. "I thought it might be you," said Judy.

"I suppose you saw the story," Sherman said.

"Yes."

"Well, look—"

"Unless you want me to hang up right now, don't even talk about it. Don't even begin."

He hesitated. "How is Campbell?"

"She's doing all right."

"How much does she know?"

"She understands that there's trouble. She knows something's up. I don't think she knows what. Fortunately, school is over, although it'll be bad enough out here."

"Let me explain—"

"Don't. I don't want to listen to your explanations. I'm sorry, Sherman, but I don't feel like having my intelligence insulted. Not any more than it already has been."

"All right, but I ought to at least tell you what's going to happen. I'm going back into custody tomorrow. Back into jail."

Softly: "Why?"

Why? It doesn't matter why! I cry out to you—to hold me! But I no longer have the right! So he merely explained to her the problem of the increased bail.

"I see," she said.

He waited a moment, but that was it. "Judy, I just don't know if I can do it."

"What do you mean?"

"It was horrible the first time, and I was only inside for a few hours in a temporary detention pen. This time it'll be in the Bronx House of Detention."

"But only until you post bail."

"But I don't know if I can even take a day of it, Judy. After all this publicity, it'll be full of people . . . who *have it in for me* . . . I mean, it's bad enough even when they don't know who you are. You can't imagine what it's like—" He stopped. *I want to cry out to you!* But he had lost the right.

She picked up the agony in his voice. "I don't know what to say to you, Sherman. If I could be with you in some way, I would. But you keep cutting the ground out from under me. We've had this same conversation before. What do I have left to give you? I just . . . feel so sorry for you, Sherman. I don't know what else to tell you."

"Judy?"

"Yes?"

"Tell Campbell I love her very much. Tell her . . . tell her to think of her father as the person who was here before all this happened. Tell her that all this does something to you and that you can never be the same person again."

Desperately he wanted Judy to ask him what he meant. At even the most tentative invitation he was ready to pour out everything he felt. But all she said was:

"I'm sure she'll always love you, no matter what."

"Judy?"

"Yes?"

"Do you remember when we used to live in the Village, the way I used to go off to work?"

"The way you used to go off to work?"

"When I first started working for Pierce & Pierce? The way I used to give you the raised left fist when I left the apartment, the Black Power salute?"

"Yes, I remember."

"You remember why?"

"I guess so."

"It was supposed to say that yes, I was going to work on Wall Street, but my heart and soul would never belong to it. I would use it and rebel and break with it. You remember all that?"

Judy said nothing.

"I know it didn't work out that way," he went on, "but I remember what a lovely feeling it was. Don't you?"

Again silence.

"Well, now I've broken with Wall Street. Or Wall Street's broken with me. I know it's not the same thing, but in an odd way I feel liberated." He stopped, hoping to coax a comment.

Finally Judy said, "Sherman?"

"Yes?"

"That's a memory, Sherman, but it's not alive." Her voice broke. "All our memories of that time have been terribly abused. I know you want me to tell you something else, but I've been betrayed and I've been humiliated. I wish I could be something I was a long time ago and help you, but I just can't." *Snuffling back tears.*

"It would help if you could forgive me—if you would give me one last chance."

"You asked me that once before, Sherman. All right, I forgive you. And I'll ask you again: What does that change?" She was crying softly.

He had no answer, and that was that.

Afterward, he sat in the brilliant blazing stillness of the library. He sank back into the swivel chair at his desk. He was aware of the pressure of the edge of the seat on the underside of his thighs. Ox-blood Moroccan leather; $1,100 just to cover the back and the seat of this one chair. The library door was open. He looked out into the entry gallery. There on the marble floor he could see the extravagantly curved legs of one of the Thomas Hope armchairs. Not a mahogany reproduction but one of the rosewood originals. Rosewood! The childish joy with which Judy had discovered her rosewood originals!

The telephone rang. *She was calling back!* He picked up the receiver at once.

"Hello?"

"Ayyyyy, Sherman." His heart sank again. It was Killian. "I want you to come on back down here. Got something to show you."

"You're still at your office?"

"Quigley's here, too. We got something to show you."

"What is it?"

"Just as soon not talk about it"—*tawkaboudit*—"on the telephone. I want you to come on down here."

"All right . . . I'll leave right now."

He wasn't sure he could have remained in the apartment another minute, in any case.

At the old building on Reade Street, the night watchman, who appeared to be Cypriot or Armenian, was listening to a country-music station on a huge portable radio. Sherman had to stop and write down his name and the time on a ledger. In a thick accent the watchman kept joining in the chorus of the song:

> My *chin's up*,
> My *smile's on*,
> My *heart's fee-*
> > *lin'*
> > > *down* . . .

Which came out:

> My *cheen's op*,
> Mice *a mile's on*,
> My *hut's fee-*
> > *leen*
> > > *doan* . . .

Sherman took the elevator up, walked through the dingy stillness of the corridor, and came to the door with the incised plastic sign that read DERSHKIN, BELLAVITA, FISHBEIN & SCHLOSSEL. For an instant he thought of his father. The door was locked. He rapped on it, and after five or ten seconds Ed Quigley opened it.

"Ayyyyy! Come on in!" said Quigley. His dour face was all lit up. *Beaming* is the word. All of a sudden he was Sherman's warmest pal. Half a chuckle bubbled out of him as he led Sherman toward Killian's office.

Killian was standing inside with the smile of the cat that ate the canary. On his desk was a large tape machine that was obviously from the higher and more sophisticated reaches of the Audio-Visual Kingdom.

"Ayyyyyyyyyy!" said Killian. "Have a seat. Get a good grip on yourself. Wait'll you hear this."

Sherman sat down beside the desk. "What is it?"

"You tell me," said Killian. Quigley stood next to Killian, looking at the machine and fidgeting like a schoolboy onstage to receive a prize. "I don't want to get your hopes up too high over this thing," said Killian, "because there's a couple very serious problems with it, but you'll find it interesting."

He pushed something on the machine, and a stream of low static began. Then a man's voice:

"I knew it. I knew it at the time. We should have reported it immediately." For the first second or so he didn't recognize it. Then it sank in. *My own voice!* It continued: "I can't believe I'm—I can't believe we're in this situation."

A woman's voice: "Well, it's too late now, Sherman." *Shuhmun.* "That's spilt milk."

The entire scene—the fear, the tension, the very atmosphere of it—flooded through Sherman's nervous system . . . In her hideaway the evening the first article about Henry Lamb appeared in *The City Light* . . . HONOR STUDENT'S MOM:

COPS SIT ON HIT'N'RUN . . . He could see the headline itself on top of the oak pedestal table . . .

His voice: "Just . . . tell what actually happened."

Her voice: "That'll sound wonderful. Two boys stopped us and tried to rob us, but you threw a tire at one of them, and I drove outta there like a . . . a . . . hot-rodder, but I didn't know I hit anybody."

"Well, that's exactly what happened, Maria."

"And who's gonna believe it? . . ."

Sherman looked at Killian. Killian had a tight little smile on his face. He raised his right hand as if to caution Sherman to keep listening and not speak yet. Quigley kept his eyes fixed on the magical machine. His lips were pursed to hold back the broad grin he felt he was due.

Soon the Giant arrived. "You live here?"

His own voice: "I said we don't have time for this." He sounded terribly snooty and precious. All over again he felt the humiliation of that moment, the dreadful feeling that he was about to be forced into a masculine duel, very likely physical, that he could not possibly win.

"You don't live here, and she don't live here. What you doing here?"

The snooty fellow: "That's not your concern! Now, be a good fellow and leave!"

"You don't belong here. Okay? We got a real problem."

Then Maria's voice . . . the squabbling . . . a tremendous crack, as the chair breaks and the Giant hits the floor . . . his ignominious retreat . . . Maria's whoops of laughter . . .

Finally her voice saying: "Germaine pays only $331 a month, and I pay her $750. It's rent-controlled. They'd love to get her out of here."

Soon the voices stopped . . . and Sherman remembered, felt, the fitful session on the bed . . .

When the tape had played out, Sherman said to Killian, "My God, that's astounding. Where did that come from?"

Killian looked at Sherman but pointed his right index finger at Quigley. So Sherman looked at Quigley. It was the moment Quigley had been waiting for.

"As soon as you told me where she told you about her rent scam, I knew it. I just fucking knew it. Those lunatics. This Hiellig Winter ain't the first one. The voice-activated tapes. So I went straight over there. This character has microphones hidden in the intercom boxes inside the apartments. The recorder's down in the cellar in a locked closet."

Sherman stared at the man's suddenly radiant face. "But why would he even bother?"

"To get the tenants out!" said Quigley. "Half the people in these rent-controlled apartments ain't in there legally. Halfa them are scamming, just like your friend there. But proving it in court is another thing. So this lunatic's taping every conversation in the joint with the voice-activated tape. Believe me, he ain't the first one, either."

"But . . . isn't that illegal?"

"Illegal," said Quigley with great joy, "it's so fucking illegal it ain't even funny! It's so fucking illegal, if he walked in that door right now, I'd say, 'Hi, I took your fucking tape. Whaddaya thinka that?' And he'd say, 'I don't know what you're talking about,' and walk away like a nice boy. But I'm telling you, these maniacs are *crazed.*"

"And you just took it? How did you even get in there?"

Quigley shrugged with consummate smugness. "That's no big deal."

Sherman looked at Killian. "Christ . . . then maybe . . . if that's on tape, then maybe . . . Right after the thing happened, Maria and I went back to her apartment and we talked the whole thing over, everything that happened. If that's on tape—that would be . . . fantastic!"

"It ain't there," said Quigley. "I listened to miles a this stuff. It don't go back that far. He must erase it every now and then and record right over it, so he don't have to keep buying new tape."

His spirits soaring, Sherman said to Killian, "Well, maybe this is enough!"

Quigley said, "Incidentally, you ain't the only visitor she receives in that joint."

Killian broke in: "Yeah, well, that's of historical interest at this point. Now, here's the thing, Sherman. I don't want you to get your hopes up too high over this. We got two serious problems. The first one is that she don't come right out and say she hit the kid and you didn't. What she says is indirect. Half the time, it sounds like she might be going along with what you're saying. Nevertheless, it's a good weapon. It's certainly enough to create doubt in a jury. She certainly seems to be concurring with your theory that this was a robbery attempt. But we got another problem, and to be honest with you, I don't know what the hell we can do about it. There's no way I can get this tape into evidence."

"You can't? Why not?"

"Like Ed says, this is a totally illegal tape. This crazy guy Winter could go to jail for doing this. There is absolutely no way that a surreptitious, illegal tape can be used as evidence in a court of law."

"Well then, why did you wire *me?* That's a surreptitious tape. How could that be used?"

"It's surreptitious but not illegal. You're entitled to record your own conversations, secretly or not. But if it's somebody else's conversation, it's illegal. If this lunatic landlord Winter was recording his own conversations, there'd be no problem."

Sherman stared at Killian with his mouth open his just-hatched hopes already crushed. "But that's not *right!* Here's . . . *vital evidence!* They can't suppress vital evidence on a technicality!"

"I got news for you, bro. They can. They would. What we gotta do is think of some way to use this tape to get somebody to give us some legitimate testimony. Like if there's some way we can use this to make your friend Maria come clean. You got any bright ideas?"

Sherman thought for a moment. Then he sighed and looked off past the two men. It was all too preposterous. "I don't know how you'd even get her to listen to the goddamned thing."

Killian looked at Quigley. Quigley shook his head. The three of them were quiet.

"Wait a minute," said Sherman. "Let me see that tape."

"See it?" said Killian.

"Yes. Give it to me."

"Take it off the machine?"

"Yes." Sherman held out his hand.

Quigley rewound it and took it off the machine very gingerly, as if it were a precious piece of hand-blown glass. He gave it to Sherman.

Sherman held it in both hands and stared at it. "I'll be damned," he said, looking up at Killian. "It's mine."

"Whaddaya mean, it's yours?"

"This is my tape. I made it."

Killian looked at him quizzically, as if searching out a joke. "Whaddaya mean, you made it?"

"I wired myself up that night, because this article in *The City Light* had just come out and I figured I might need some verification of what actually happened. What we just listened to—that's the tape I made that night. This is my tape."

Killian's mouth was open. "What are you saying?"

"I'm saying I made this tape. Who's going to say I didn't? This tape is in my possession. Right? Here it is. I made this tape in order to have an accurate record of my own conversation. Tell me, Counselor, would you say this tape is admissible in a court of law?"

Killian looked at Quigley. "Jesus H. Fucking Christ." Then he looked at Sherman. "Let me get this straight, Mr. McCoy. You're telling me you wired yourself and made this tape of your conversation with Mrs. Ruskin?"

"Exactly. Is it admissible?"

Killian looked at Quigley, smiled, then looked back. "It's entirely possible, Mr. McCoy, entirely possible. But you gotta tell me something. Just how did you make this tape? What kind of equipment did you use? How did you tape yourself? I think if you want the court to admit this evidence, you better be able to account for everything you did, from A to Z."

"Well," said Sherman, "I'd like to hear Mr. Quigley here *guess* how I did it. He seems knowledgeable in this area. I'd like to hear him *guess*."

Quigley looked at Killian.

"Go ahead, Ed," said Killian, "take a guess."

"Well," said Quigley, "if it was me, I'd get me a Nagra 2600, voice-activated, and I'd . . ." He proceeded to outline in great detail just how he would use the fabled Nagra machine and wire himself and make sure he secured the highest-quality recording of such a conversation.

When he was through, Sherman said, "Mr. Quigley, you are truly knowledgeable in this area. Because you know what? That is exactly what I did. You didn't leave out a single step." Then he looked at Killian. "There you have it. What do you think?"

"I'll tell you what I think," Killian said slowly. "You surprise the hell outta me. I didn't think you had it in you."

"I didn't, either," said Sherman. "But something's gradually dawned on me over the past few days. I'm not Sherman McCoy anymore. I'm somebody else without a proper name. I've been that other person ever since the day I was arrested. I knew something . . . something fundamental had happened that day, but I didn't know what it was at first. At first I thought I was still Sherman McCoy, and Sherman McCoy was going though a period of very bad luck. Over the last couple of days, though, I've begun to face up to the truth. I'm somebody else. I have nothing to do with Wall Street or Park Avenue or Yale or St. Paul's or Buckley or the Lion of Dunning Sponget."

"The Lion of Dunning Sponget?" asked Killian.

"That's the way I've always thought of my father. He was a ruler, an aristocrat. And maybe he was, but I'm not related to him anymore. I'm not the person my wife married or the father my daughter knows. I'm a different human being. I exist *down here* now, if you won't be offended by me putting it that way. I'm not an exceptional client of Dershkin, Bellavita, Fishbein & Schlossel. I'm standard issue. Every creature has its habitat, and I'm in mine right now. Reade Street and 161st Street and the pens—if I think I'm above it, I'm only kidding myself, and I've stopped kidding myself."

"Ayyyyy, wait a minute," said Killian. "It ain't that bad yet."

"It's that bad," said Sherman. "But I swear to you, I feel better about it now. You know the way they can take a dog, a house pet, like a police dog that's been fed and pampered all its life, and train it to be a vicious watchdog?"

"I've heard of it," said Killian.

"I've seen it done," said Quigley. "I saw it done when I was on the force."

"Well, then you know the principle," said Sherman. "They don't alter that dog's personality with dog biscuits or pills. They chain it up, and they beat it, and they bait it, and they taunt it, and they beat it some more, until it turns and bares its fangs and is ready for the final fight every time it hears a sound."

"That's true," said Quigley.

"Well, in that situation dogs are smarter than humans," said Sherman. "The dog doesn't cling to the notion that he's a fabulous house pet in some terrific dog show, the way the man does. The dog gets the idea. The dog knows when it's time to turn into an animal and fight."

31

INTO THE SOLAR PLEXUS

It WAS A SUNNY DAY this time, a balmy day in June. The air was so light it seemed pure and refreshing, even here in the Bronx. A perfect day, in short; Sherman took it badly. He took it personally. How very heartless! How could Nature, Fate —God—contrive such a sublime production for his hour of misery? Heartlessness on all sides. A spasm of fear reached down to the very bottom of his descending colon.

He was in the back seat of a Buick with Killian. Ed Quigley was in the front seat, next to the chauffeur, who had dark skin, thick straight black hair, and fine, exquisite, almost pretty features. An Asian? They came down the ramp from the expressway right past the bowl of Yankee Stadium, and a big sign said, TONIGHT 7 PM YANKEES VS. KANSAS CITY. How very heartless! Tens of thousands of people would come to this place tonight *anyway*—to drink beer and watch a white ball hop and pop around for two hours—and he would be *back in there*, in a darkness he couldn't imagine. *And it would begin.* The poor fools! They didn't know what the real thing was like! Tens of thousands of them in Yankee Stadium, watching a *game*, a mere *charade* of war, while he was *in* a war. And it would begin . . . the elemental physical violence . . .

Now the Buick was going up the long hill, up 161st Street. They would be there in no time.

"It's not the same courthouse," said Killian. "It's the building up on the top of the hill, on the right."

Sherman could see an immense limestone structure. It looked quite majestic sitting up there on the crest of the Grand Concourse in the sunlight of a perfect day; majestic and stupendously heavy.

Sherman could see the driver's eyes seeking him out in the rearview mirror, and then they locked in an embarrassing contact and jumped away. Quigley, up front next to the driver, was wearing a tie and a jacket, but just barely. The jacket, a curious Meat Gone High teal-green tweed, was riding up away from the pitted skin of his neck. He looked like the kind of fidgety Hard Case who is spoiling for an opportunity to peel off the jacket and tie and start fighting and cultivating hematomas or, better still, intimidate some funk-ridden weakling who isn't ready to meet the challenge to fight.

As the car ascended the hill, Sherman could see a crowd in the street near the top, out in front of the limestone building. Cars were squeezing over in order to get by.

"What's going on?" he said.

"Looks like a demonstration," said Quigley.

Killian said, "Well, at least they aren't in front of your apartment house this time."

"A de-mon-strrra-tion? Hahahaha," said the chauffeur. He had a singsong accent and a polite and thoroughly nervous laugh. "What it is about? Hahahaha."

"It's about us," said Quigley in his dead voice.

The chauffeur looked at Quigley. "About yooouuu? Hahahaha."

"You know the gentleman who hired this car? Mr. McCoy?" Quigley motioned with his head toward the back seat.

In the mirror the chauffeur's eyes searched and locked on again. "Hahahaha." Then he became quiet.

"Don't worry," said Quigley. "It's always safer in the middle of a riot than out on the edge. That's a well-known fact."

The chauffeur looked at Quigley again and said, "Hahahaha." Then he became *very* quiet, no doubt trying to figure out which to be more afraid of, the demonstrators he was approaching on the street or the Hard Case who was inside and merely inches away from his as yet unwrung neck. Then he sought out Sherman again with his eyes and locked on and then jumped inside the cavity and flailed away, bug-eyed with panic.

"Nothing's gonna happen," Killian said to Sherman. "There'll be cops up there. They'll be ready for 'em. It's the same bunch every time, Bacon and that crowd. Do you think the people of the Bronx give a damn one way or the other? Don't flatter yourself. This is the same bunch, doing their same weird number. It's a show. Just keep your mouth shut and look straight ahead. This time we have a surprise for them."

As the car neared Walton Avenue, Sherman could see the crowd out in the street. They were all around the base of the huge limestone building at the top of the hill. He could hear a voice coming over a microphone. People were answering the voice with a chant. Whoever was screaming over the microphone seemed to be up on the terrace of the stairway on the 161st Street side. There were camera crews with their equipment sticking up out of the sea of faces.

The driver said, "You waaaant me to stop? Hahahahaha."

"Just keep moving," said Quigley. "I'll tell you when to stop."

"Hahahaha."

Killian said to Sherman, "We're going in through the side." Then to the driver: "Take the next right!"

"All the peeeoooople! Hahahaha."

"Just take the next right," said Quigley, "and don't worry about it."

Killian said to Sherman, "Duck down. Tie your shoe or something."

The car turned onto the street that ran along the lower edge of the great limestone building. But Sherman sat up straight in his seat. It no longer mattered. *When would it begin?* He could see blue-and-orange vans with wire mesh over their windows. The crowd had spilled off the sidewalk. They were looking up toward the 161st Street side. The voice harangued them, and the chants arose from the mob on the stairs.

"Hook a left," said Killian. "Right in there. See that red cone? That's it."

The car was heading in at a ninety-degree angle toward the curbing at the base of the building. Some sort of policeman was out there lifting up a Day-Glo rubber cone from the middle of a parking place. Quigley was holding a card up in the windshield with his left hand, apparently for the benefit of the policeman. There were four or five other policemen on the sidewalk. They wore short-sleeved white shirts and had tremendous revolvers on their hips.

"When I open the door," said Killian, "you get in between me and Ed and make tracks."

The door opened, and they scrambled out. Quigley was on Sherman's right; Killian on his left. People on the sidewalk stared at them but didn't seem to know who they were. Three of the policemen in white shirts sidled between the crowd and Sherman, Killian, and Quigley. Killian took hold of Sherman's elbow and steered him toward a door. Quigley was carrying a heavy case. A policeman in a white shirt stood in the doorway, then stepped aside to let them through into a lobby lit by dim fluorescent bulbs. On the right was a doorway to what looked like a utility room. Sherman could make out the black and gray hulks of people slumped on benches.

"They did us a favor by having their demonstration on the steps," said Killian. His voice was high-pitched and tense. Two officers led them toward an elevator, which another officer was holding open for them.

They entered the elevator, and the officer stepped inside with them. The officer pressed the button for the ninth floor, and they began their ascent.

"Thanks, Brucie," Killian said to the officer.

"It's okay. You got Bernie to thank, though." Killian looked at Sherman, as if to say, "What did I tell you?"

On the ninth floor, outside a room marked Part 60, there was a noisy crowd in the corridor. A line of court officers was holding them back.

Yo! . . . There he is!

Sherman looked straight ahead. *When does it begin?* A man jumped out in front of him—a white man, tall, with blond hair swept back from a sharp widow's peak. He wore a navy blazer and a navy tie, and a shirt with a striped front and a stiff white collar. It was the reporter, Fallow. Sherman had last seen him when he was about to enter Central Booking . . . *that place . . .*

"Mr. McCoy!!" *That voice.*

With Killian on one side and Quigley on the other and the court officer, Brucie, leading the way, they were like a flying wedge. They brushed the Englishman aside and went through a door. They were in the courtroom. A crowd of people to Sherman's left . . . in the spectator seats . . . Black faces . . . some white faces . . . In the foreground was a tall black man with a gold earring in one lobe. He rose up from his seat in a crouch and pointed a long, thin arm at Sherman and said in a loud guttural whisper: "That's him!" Then in a louder voice: "Jail! No bail!"

The deep voice of a woman: "Lock him up!"

Yegggh! . . . That's the one! . . . Look at him! . . . Jail! No bail!

Now? Not yet. Killian held his elbow and whispered in his ear, "Ignore it!"

A falsetto croon: "Sherrrr-maannnn . . . Sherrrr-maannnn."

"SHUT UP! SIT DOWN!"

It was the loudest voice Sherman had ever heard. At first he thought it was directed at himself. He felt terribly guilty, even though he hadn't uttered a sound.

"ANY MORE OUTBURSTS—I CLEAR THE COURT! DO I MAKE MYSELF CLEAR?"

Up at the judge's bench, beneath the inscription IN GOD WE TRUST, a thin bald hawk-nosed man in black robes stood with his fists on top of his desk and his arms straight, as if he were a runner about to spring from the starting position. Sherman could see the white beneath the irises as the judge's blazing eyes swept the crowd before him. The demonstrators grumbled but grew still.

The judge, Myron Kovitsky, continued to stare at them with his furious gaze. "In this courtroom you speak when the court asks you to speak. You pass judgment on your fellow man when you are selected for a jury and the court asks you to pass judgment. You stand up and render your obiter dicta when the court asks you to stand up and render your obiter dicta. Until then—YOU SHUT UP AND SIT DOWN! AND I . . . AM THE COURT! DO I MAKE MYSELF CLEAR? Is there anyone who disputes what I have just said and holds this court in such contempt that he would like to spend some time as a guest of the state of New York contemplating what I have just said? DO—I—MAKE—MYSELF—CLEAR?"

His eyes panned the crowd from left to right and right to left and left to right again.

"All right. Now that you understand that, perhaps you can observe these proceedings as responsible members of the community. So long as you do so, you are welcome in this courtroom. And the moment you don't—you'll wish you hadda stood in bed! Do—I—make—myself—clear?"

His voice rose again so suddenly and to such an intensity the crowd seemed to recoil, startled at the thought that the wrath of this furious little man might descend upon them again.

Kovitsky sat down and spread his arms. His robes billowed out like wings. He lowered his head. The whites still showed beneath his irises. The room was now still. Sherman, Killian, and Quigley stood near the fence—the bar—that separated the spectators' section from the court proper. Kovitsky's eyes settled on Sherman and Killian. He appeared to be angry at them, too. He breathed what seemed to be a sigh of disgust.

Then he turned to the clerk of the court, who sat at a large conference table to one side. Sherman followed Kovitsky's gaze, and there, standing beside the table, he saw the assistant district attorney, Kramer.

Kovitsky said to the clerk, "Call the case."

The clerk called out: "Indictment number 4-7-2-6, the People *versus* Sherman McCoy. Who is representing Mr. McCoy?"

Killian stepped up to the bar and said, "I am."

The clerk said, "Please give your appearance."

"Thomas Killian, 86 Reade Street."

Kovitsky said, "Mr. Kramer, you have a motion to make at this time?"

This man, Kramer, took a few steps toward the bench. He walked like a football player. He stopped, threw his head back, tensed his neck, for some reason, and said, "Your Honor, the defendant, Mr. McCoy, is currently free on ten thousand dollars' bail, an insignificant sum for a person with his particular advantages and resources in the financial community."

Yegggh! . . . Jail! No bail! . . . Make him pay!

Kovitsky, his head down low, glowered. The voices died down to a rumble.

"As Your Honor knows," Kramer continued, "the grand jury has now brought in an indictment against the defendant on serious charges: reckless endangerment, leaving the scene of an accident, and failure to report an accident. Now, Your Honor, inasmuch as the grand jury has already found sufficient evidence of the defendant's abandonment of his responsibilities to indict him, the People feel there also exists the substantial possibility that the defendant might ignore and abandon his bond, given the small amount of that bond."

Yeah . . . That's right . . . Unh-hunh . .

"So, Your Honor," said Kramer, "the People feel it is incumbent upon the court to send a clear signal not only to the defendant but to the community that what is at issue here is in fact regarded with the utmost seriousness. At the heart of this case, Your Honor, is a young man, an exemplary young man, Mr. Henry Lamb, who has become a symbol to the people of the Bronx of both the hopes they have for their sons and daughters and the callous and deadly obstacles that they face. Your Honor is already aware of the passion with which the community is following every step of this case. Were this courtroom larger, the people of this community would be here at this moment by the hundreds, possibly the thousands, just as they are even now in the corridors and on the streets outside."

Right on! . . . Jail! No bail! . . . You tell him!

KAPOW!

Kovitsky brought his gavel down with a tremendous explosion.

"QUIET!"

The rumble of the crowd sank back to a low boil.

His head down low, his irises floating on a sea of white, Kovitsky said, "Get to the point, Mr. Kramer. This isn't a pep rally. It's a hearing in a court of law."

Kramer knew he was staring at all the usual signs. The irises were floating on that foaming sea. The head was down. The beak was out. It wasn't going to take much more to set Kovitsky off. On the other hand, he thought, I can't back down. Can't give in. Kovitsky's attitude so far—even though it was nothing but standard Kovitsky, the usual yelling, the usual belligerent insistence on his authority—Kovitsky's attitude so far established him as an adversary of the demonstrators. The Office of the District Attorney of Bronx County was their friend. Abe Weiss was their friend. Larry Kramer was their friend. The People were . . . truly *the People.* That was what he was here for. He would just have to take his chance with Kovitsky—with those furious Masada eyes that now bore down on him.

His own voice sounded funny to him as he said, "I'm mindful of that, Your Honor, but I must also be mindful of the importance of this case to the People, to all the Henry Lambs, present and future, in this county and in this city—"

Tell him, bro! . . . Right on! . . . That's right!

Kramer hastened to continue, in an even louder voice, before Kovitsky detonated: "—and therefore the People petition the court to increase the defendant to a significant and credible amount—to one million dollars—in order to—"

Jail! No bail! . . . Jail! No bail! . . . Jail! No bail! The demonstrators erupted into a chant.

That's right! . . . Million dollars! . . . Yaggghh! . . . The voice of the crowd rose in a cheer laced with exultant laughter and then crested with a chant: *Jail! No bail! . . . Jail! No bail! . . . Jail! No bail! . . . Jail! No bail!*

Kovitsky's gavel rose a full foot above his head and Kramer flinched inwardly before it hit.

KAPOW!

Kovitsky gave Kramer a furious glance, then leaned forward and fastened upon the crowd.

"ORDER IN THE COURT! . . . SHUDDUP! . . . DO YOU DOUBT MY WORD?" His irises surfed this way and that on the furious boiling sea.

The chanting stopped, and the cries lowered to a rumble. But little riffs of laughter indicated they were just waiting for the next opening.

"THE COURT OFFICERS WILL—"

"Your Honor! Your Honor!" It was McCoy's lawyer, Killian.

"What is it, Mr. Killian?"

The interruption threw the crowd off stride. They quieted down.

"Your Honor, may I approach the bench?"

"All right, Mr. Killian." Kovitsky beckoned him forward. "Mr. Kramer?" Kramer headed for the bench also.

Now he was standing next to Killian, Killian in his fancy clothes, before the bench, beneath the glowering brow of Judge Kovitsky.

"Okay, Mr. Killian," said Kovitsky, "what's up?"

"Judge," said Killian, "if I'm not mistaken, you're the supervising judge of the grand jury in this case?"

"That's correct," he said to Killian, but then he turned his attention to Kramer. "You hard of hearing Mr. Kramer?"

Kramer said nothing. He didn't have to answer a question like that.

"You intoxicated by the sound of this bunch"—Kovitsky nodded toward the spectators—"cheering you on?"

"No, Judge, but there's no way this case can be treated like an ordinary case."

"In this courtroom, Mr. Kramer, it's gonna be treated any fucking way I say it's gonna be treated. Do I make myself clear?"

"You always make yourself clear, Judge."

Kovitsky eyed him, apparently trying to decide if there was any insolence in the remark. "All right, then you know that if you pull any more of that arrant bullshit in this courtroom, you're gonna wish you never laid eyes on Mike Kovitsky!"

He couldn't just *take* this, with Killian standing right there, and so he said, "Look, Judge, I have every right—"

Kovitsky broke in: "Every right to do what? Run Abe Weiss's re-election campaign for him in my courtroom? Bullshit, Mr. Kramer! Tell him to hire a hall, call a press conference. Tell him to go on a talk show, f'r Chrissake."

Kramer was so angry he couldn't speak. His face was flaming red. Between his teeth he said, "Is that all, Judge?" Without waiting for an answer, he turned on his heels and started away.

"Mr. Kramer!"

He stopped and turned around. Glowering, Kovitsky motioned him back to the bench. "Mr. Killian has a question, I believe. Or do you want me to listen to him by myself?"

Kramer just clenched his teeth and stared.

"All right, Mr. Killian, go ahead."

Killian said, "Judge, I am in possession of important evidence that bears not only upon Mr. Kramer's application concerning bail but upon the validity of the indictment itself."

"What kind of evidence?"

"I have tapes of conversations between my client and a principal in this case that make it appear highly likely that tainted testimony was presented to the grand jury."

What the hell was this? Kramer broke in: "Judge, this is nonsense. We have a valid indictment from the grand jury. If Mr. Killian has any quarrel—"

"Just hold it, Mr. Kramer," said Kovitsky.

"—if he has any quarrel with the grand-jury proceedings, he has the customary avenues—"

"Just hold it. Mr. Killian says he has some evidence—"

"Evidence! This isn't an evidentiary hearing, Judge! He can't come walking in here and dispute the grand-jury process, *ex post facto.* And you can't—"

"MR. KRAMER!"

The sound of Kovitsky raising his voice sent a growl through the demonstrators, who were all at once rumbling again.

Eyes surfing on the turbulent sea: "Mr. Kramer, you know your problem? You don't fucking listen, do you! You can't fucking *hear!*"

"Judge—"

"SHUDDUP! The court is gonna listen to Mr. Killian's evidence."

"Judge—"

"We're gonna do this in camera."

"In camera? Why?"

"Mr. Killian says he has some tapes. First we're gonna listen to 'em in camera."

"Look, Judge—"

"You don't wanna go in camera, Mr. Kramer? You afraid you gonna miss your audience?"

Seething, Kramer looked down and shook his head.

Sherman was stranded back at the fence, the bar. Quigley was somewhere behind him, holding the heavy case. But mainly . . . *they* were behind him. *When would it begin?* He kept his eyes fixed on the three figures at the judge's bench. He didn't dare let his eyes wander. Then the voices began. They came from behind him in menacing singsongs.

"Your last mile, McCoy!"

"Last *supper.*"

Then a soft falsetto: "Last breath."

Somewhere, on either side, were court officers. They were doing nothing to stop it. *They're as frightened as I am!*

The same falsetto: "Yo, Sherman, why you squirmin'?"

Squirming. Evidently the others liked that. They began piping up in falsetto, too.

"Sherrr-maaannnn . . ."

"Squirmin' Sherman!"

Sniggers and laughter.

Sherman stared at the bench, wherein seemed to reside his only hope. As if in answer to his supplication, the judge now looked toward him and said, "Mr. McCoy, would you step up here a minute?"

A rumble and a chorus of falsettos as he started walking. As he drew near the bench, he heard the assistant district attorney, Kramer, say, "I don't understand, Judge. What purpose is served by the presence of the defendant?"

The judge said, "It's his motion and his evidence. Besides, I don't want him rattling around out here. That okay with you, Mr. Kramer?"

Kramer said nothing. He glared at the judge and then at Sherman.

The judge said, "Mr. McCoy, you're gonna come with me and Mr. Killian and Mr. Kramer into my chambers."

Then he gave three loud raps with his gavel and said to the room, "The court will now convene with the attorney for the People and the counsel for the defense in camera. In my absence the proper decorum WILL BE MAINTAINED in this room. Do I make myself clear?"

The rumble of the demonstrators rose to a low angry boil, but Kovitsky chose to ignore it and got up and descended the stairs of the dais. The clerk got up from his table to join him. Killian gave Sherman a wink, then headed back toward the spectator section. The judge, the clerk, the judge's law secretary, and Kramer headed toward a door in the paneled wall to one side of the dais. Killian returned, carrying the heavy case. He paused and motioned for Sherman to follow Kovitsky. The court officer, with a huge tube of fat rolling over his gun belt, brought up the rear.

The door led into a room that belied everything that the courtroom itself and the swell term *chambers* had suggested to Sherman. The "chambers" were, in fact, a single room, a single very sad room. It was small, dirty, bare, run-down, painted Good Enough for Government Work cream, except that the paint was missing in splotches here and there and peeling off in miserable curls in other places. The only generous notes were the extraordinarily high ceiling and a window eight or nine feet high that flooded the room with light. The judge sat down at a beat-up metal desk. The clerk sat at another one. Kramer, Killian, and Sherman sat in some heavy and ancient round-backed wooden chairs, the sort known as banker's chairs. Kovitsky's law secretary and the fat court officer stood up against the wall. A tall man came in carrying the portable stenotype machine that court stenographers use. How odd!—the man was so well dressed. He wore a lovat tweed jacket, a white button-down shirt, as flawless as Rawlie's, an ancient madder necktie, black flannel trousers, and half-brogue shoes. He looked like a Yale professor with an independent income and tenure.

"Mr. Sullivan," said Kovitsky, "you better bring your chair in here, too."

Mr. Sullivan went out, then returned with a small wooden chair, sat down, fiddled with his machine, looked at Kovitsky, and nodded.

Then Kovitsky said, "Now, Mr. Killian, you state that you are in possession of information having a material and substantial bearing on the grand-jury proceedings in this case."

"That's correct, Judge," said Killian.

"All right," said Kovitsky. "I want to hear what you have to say, but I must warn you, this motion better not be frivolous."

"It's not frivolous, Judge."

"Because if it is, I'm gonna take a very dim view of it, as dim a view as I've ever taken of anything in my years on the bench, and that would be very dim, indeed. Do I make myself clear?"

"You certainly do, Judge."

"All right. Now, you're prepared to submit your information at this time?"

"I am."

"Then go ahead."

"Three days ago, Judge, I received a telephone call from Maria Ruskin, the widow of Mr. Arthur Ruskin, asking if she could talk to Mr. McCoy here. According to my best information—and according to news reports—Mrs. Ruskin has testified before the grand jury in the case."

Kovitsky said to Kramer, "Is that correct?"

Kramer said, "She gave testimony yesterday."

The judge said to Killian, "All right, go ahead."

"So I set up a meeting between Mrs. Ruskin and Mr. McCoy, and at my urging Mr. McCoy wore a concealed recording device to this meeting in order to have a verifiable record of that conversation. The meeting was in an apartment on East Seventy-seventh Street that Mrs. Ruskin apparently keeps for . . . uh, private meetings . . . and a taped recording of that meeting was obtained. I have that tape with me, and I think the court should be aware of what's on that tape."

"Wait a minute, Judge," said Kramer. "Is he saying that his client went to see Mrs. Ruskin *wired?*"

"I take it that's the case," said the judge. "Is that right, Mr. Killian?"

"That's correct, Judge," said Killian.

"Well, I want to register an objection, Judge," said Kramer, "and I would like for the record to so state. This isn't the time to consider this motion, and besides that, there's no way of checking on the authenticity of this tape Mr. Killian purports to have."

"First we're gonna listen to the tape, Mr. Kramer, and see what's on it. We'll see if it warrants further consideration, *prima facie*, and then we'll worry about the other questions. That meet with your approval?"

"No, Judge, I don't see how you can—"

The judge, testily: "Play the tape, Counselor."

Killian reached into the case and took out the big tape machine and placed it on Kovitsky's desk. Then he inserted a cassette. The cassette was exceedingly small. Somehow this secret miniature cartridge seemed as devious and sordid as the enterprise itself.

"How many voices are on this tape?" asked Kovitsky.

"Just two, Judge," said Killian. "Mr. McCoy's and Mrs. Ruskin's."

"So it'll be clear enough to Mr. Sullivan what we're hearing?"

"It should be," said Killian. "No, I'm sorry, Judge, I forgot. At the beginning of the tape you're gonna hear Mr. McCoy talking to the driver of the car that took him to the building where he met Mrs. Ruskin. And at the end you'll hear him talking to the driver again."

"Who is this driver?"

"He's a driver for the car service that Mr. McCoy hired. I didn't want to edit the tape in any way."

"Unh-hunh. Well, go ahead and play it."

Killian turned on the machine, and all you could hear at first was background noise, a low steamy rush of sound with occasional traffic noises, including the braying horn of a fire engine. Then a half-mumbled exchange with the driver. It was all so devious, wasn't it? A wave of shame rolled over him. They would play it to the end! The stenographer would record it all, every last sniveling word as he tried to dance away from Maria and deny the obvious, which was that he was a deceitful bastard who had come to her apartment wired up. How much of it would come through in the words alone? Enough; he was vile.

Now the muffled deceitful tape recorder broadcast the sound of the buzzer in the door of the town house, the *click-click-click* of the electric lock and—or was it his imagination?—the groan of the stairs as he trudged up. Then a door opening . . . and Maria's gay, unsuspecting voice: "Boo! . . . Scare yuh?" And the perfidious actor's casual response in a voice he scarcely recognized: "Not really. Lately I've been scared by experts." He cut a glance this way and that. The other men in the room had their heads down, staring at the floor or at the machine on the judge's desk. Then he caught the fat court officer looking straight at him. What must he be thinking? And what about the others, with their eyes averted? But of course! They didn't have to look at him, because they were already deep inside the cavity, rooting about as they pleased, all straining to hear the words of his deceitful bad acting. The long fingers of the stenographer danced about on his delicate little machine. Sherman felt a paralyzing sadness. So heavy . . . couldn't move. In this sad moldering little room were seven other men, seven other organisms, hundreds of pounds of tissue and bone, breathing, pumping blood, burning calories, processing nutrients, filtering out contaminants and toxins, transmitting neural impulses, seven warm grisly unpleasant animals rooting about, for pay, in the entirely public cavity he used to think of as his soul.

Kramer was dying to look at McCoy, but decided to be cool and professional. What does a rat look like when he's listening to himself being a rat in a room full of people who know he's a rat—going wired to see his girlfriend? Unconsciously, but profoundly, Kramer was relieved. Sherman McCoy, this Wasp, this Wall Street aristocrat, this socialite, this Yale man, was as much a rat as any of the drug dealers he had wired up to go rat out their species. No, McCoy was more of a rat. One doper didn't expect much from another. But in these upper reaches, upon these pinnacles of propriety and moralism, up in this stratosphere ruled by the pale thin-lipped Wasps, honor, presumably, was not a word to be trifled with. Yet backed to the wall, they turned rat just as quickly as any lowlife. This was a relief, because he had been troubled by what Bernie Fitzgibbon had said. Suppose the case had not, in fact, been investigated carefully enough? Maria Ruskin had corroborated Roland's story before the grand jury, but in his heart he knew he had pushed her pretty hard. He had put her in a small tight box so fast she might have—

He preferred not to finish the thought.

The knowledge that McCoy was at bottom nothing but a rat with a better résumé put his mind at rest. McCoy was caught in this particular mess because it was his natural milieu, the filthy nest of his defective character.

Having reassured himself of the rightness of his cause, Kramer treated himself to some positive resentment of this big pseudo-aristocrat who now sat only a few feet from him filling up the room with his rat aroma. As he listened to the two voices on the tape, the aristocratic honk of McCoy, the Southern Girl drawl of Maria Ruskin, it didn't take too much imagination to figure out what was going

on. The pauses, the breathing, the rustling about—McCoy, the rat, had taken this
gorgeous foxy creature into his arms . . . And this apartment on East Seventy-
seventh Street where they were meeting—these people on the Upper East Side
had apartments just for *their pleasures!*—while he still searched his brain (and his
pockets) for some place to accommodate the yearnings of Miss Shelly Thomas.
The Beauty and the Rat talked on. . . . There was a pause while she left the
room to fix him a drink and a scraping noise as he apparently touched his hidden
microphone. The Rat. The voices resumed, and then she said, "There's a lotta
people'd like to hear *this* conversation."

Not even Kovitsky could resist looking up and around the room at that one,
but Kramer refused to oblige him with a smile.

Maria Ruskin's voice droned on. Now she was whining about her marriage.
Where the hell was this tape supposed to be leading? The woman's complaints
were boring. She had married an old man. What the hell did she expect? Idly he
wondered—he could see her, as if she were right here in the room. The languor-
ous way she crossed her legs, the little smile, the way she looked at you sometimes—

All at once he was jerked alert: "A man from the Bronx District Attorney's
Office came around to see me today, with two detectives." Then: "A pompous
little bastard."

Whuh—he was stunned. A scalding tide rose up in his neck and face. Somehow it was the *little* that wounded him most. Such a contemptuous dismissal—and
him with his mighty sternocleidomastoids—he lifted his eyes to search out the
faces of the others, ready to laugh defensively if anyone else happened to look up
and smile at such outrageousness. But no one looked up, least of all McCoy,
whom he would have gladly throttled.

"He kept throwing his head back and doing something weird with his neck,
like this, and looking at me through these little slits for eyes. What a creep."

His face was now scarlet, aflame, boiling with anger and, worse than anger,
dismay. Someone in the room made a sound that might be a cough and might be
a laugh. He didn't have enough heart to investigate. *Bitch!* said his mind, consciously. But his nervous system said, *Wanton destroyer of my fondest hopes!* In this
little room full of people he was suffering the pangs of men whose egos lose their
virginity—as happens when they overhear for the first time a beautiful woman's
undiluted, full-strength opinion of their masculine selves.

What came next was worse.

"He made it real simple, Sherman," said the voice on the tape. "He said if I
would testify against you and corroborate the other witness, he'd give me immunity. If I didn't, then I'd be treated as an accomplice, and they'd charge me with
these . . . felonies."

And then:

"He even gave me these Xeroxes of stories in the newspapers. He practically
drew me a map. These were the correct stories, and these were the ones you
concocted. I'm supposed to agree with the correct stories. If I say what actually
happened, I go to prison."

The lying bitch! He had put her in the box, of course—but he hadn't drawn her
any map!—hadn't *instructed* her as to what to say—hadn't warned her away from
the truth—

He blurted out: "Judge!"

Kovitsky held up his hand, palm outward, and the tape wound on.

Sherman was startled by the assistant district attorney's voice. The judge immediately shut him up. Sherman was braced for what he knew was coming next.

Maria's voice: "Just come here."

He could *feel* that moment all over again, that moment and that horrible wrestling match . . . "Sherman, what's wrong? What's wrong with your back?" . . . But that was just the start . . . His own voice, his own cheap lying voice: "You don't know how much I've missed you, how much I've needed you." And Maria: "Well . . . here I am." Then the dreadful telltale rustling—and he could smell her breath all over again and feel her hands on his back.

"Sherman . . . What's this on your back?"

The words filled the room in a gush of shame. He wanted to drop through the floor. He slumped back into his chair and let his chin fall onto his chest. "Sherman, what is this?" . . . Her rising voice, his wretched denials, the thrashing about, her breathless gasps and shrieks . . . "And a *wire*, Sherman!" . . . "You're—hurting me!" . . . "Sherman—you rotten, dishonest bastard!"

Too true, Maria! Too horribly true!

Kramer listened to it in a red haze of mortification. The Bitch and the Rat—their *tête-à-tête* had degenerated into some sort of sordid rat-bitch fight. *Pompous little bastard. Creep. Something weird with his neck.* She had scorned him, humiliated him, undercut him, slandered him—opening him up to a charge of subornation to perjury.

Sherman was astonished by the sound of his own desperate gulps for air, which came heaving out of the little black machine on the judge's desk. It was a mortifying sound. Pain, panic, cowardice, weakness, deceit, shame, indignity—all of those things at once, followed by an ungainly clumping. That was the sound of himself fleeing down the town-house stairs. Somehow he knew everyone in the room could see him running away with the tape deck and *the wire* between his legs.

By the time the tape had petered out, Kramer had managed to crawl out from under his wounded vanity and collect his thoughts. "Judge," he said, "I don't know what—"

Kovitsky broke in: "Just a second. Mr. Killian, can you rewind that tape? I want to hear the exchange between Mr. McCoy and Mrs. Ruskin concerning her testimony."

"But, Judge—"

"We're gonna listen to it again, Mr. Kramer."

They listened to it again.

The words sailed by Sherman. He was still drowning in ignominy. How could he look any of them in the face?

The judge said, "All right, Mr. Killian. What conclusion are you proposing that the court should draw from this?"

"Judge," said Killian, "this woman, Mrs. Ruskin, was either instructed to give certain testimony and omit certain other testimony or suffer severe consequences, or she thought she was, which amounts to the same thing. And—"

"That's absurd!" said the assistant district attorney, Kramer. He was leaning forward in his chair with a big meaty forefinger pointed at Killian and a red-mad look on his face.

"Let him finish," said the judge.

"And furthermore," said Killian, "as we've just heard, she had ample motivation to testify falsely, not only to protect herself, but to injure Mr. McCoy, whom she calls a 'rotten, dishonest bastard.'"

The rotten, dishonest bastard was mortified all over again. What could be more mortifying than the plain truth? A shouting match broke out between the assistant district attorney and Killian. What were they saying? It meant nothing in the face of the obvious, miserable truth.

The judge roared, "SHUDDUP!" They shut up. "The question of subornation is not one that interests me at this time, if that's what you're worried about, Mr. Kramer. But I do think there exists the possibility of tainted testimony before the grand jury."

"That's preposterous!" said Kramer. "The woman had two lawyers by her side at all times. Ask them what I said!"

"If it comes to that, they'll be asked. But I'm less concerned with what you said than with what was on her mind when she testified before the grand jury. You understand, Mr. Kramer?"

"No, I don't, Judge, and—"

Killian broke in: "Judge, I have a second tape."

Kovitsky said, "All right. What's the nature of that tape?"

"Judge—"

"Don't interrupt, Mr. Kramer. You'll have a chance to be heard. Go ahead, Mr. Killian. What's the nature of that tape?"

This is a conversation with Mrs. Ruskin that Mr. McCoy informs me he recorded twenty-two days ago, after the first newspaper article concerning the injuries to Henry Lamb was printed."

"Where did this conversation take place?"

"Same place as the first one, Judge. Mrs. Ruskin's apartment."

"Likewise without her knowledge?"

"That's correct."

"And what is the bearing of the tape on this hearing?"

"It gives Mrs. Ruskin's account of the incident involving Henry Lamb when she is talking candidly, of her own volition, with Mr. McCoy. It raises the question of whether or not she might have altered her honest account when she testified before the grand jury."

"Judge, this is crazy! Now we're being told the defendant *lives* with a *wire* on! We already know that he's a rat, in the parlance of the street, so why should we believe—"

"Calm down, Mr. Kramer. First, we're gonna listen to the tape. Then we'll evaluate it. Nothing's engraved in the record yet. Go ahead, Mr. Killian. Wait a minute, Mr. Killian. First I want to swear Mr. McCoy in."

When Kovitsky's eyes met his, it was all Sherman could do to hold his gaze. To his surprise, he felt terribly guilty about what he was about to do. He was about to commit perjury.

Kovitsky had the clerk, Bruzzielli, put him under oath, then asked him if he had made the two tapes in the way and at the times Killian had said he had. Sherman said yes, forced himself to keep looking at Kovitsky, and wondered if the lie showed up somehow on his face.

The tape began: "I knew it. I knew it at the time. We should have reported it immediately . . ."

Sherman could barely listen to it. I'm doing something illegal! Yes . . . but in the name of the truth . . . This is the subterranean path to the light . . . This is the actual conversation we had . . . Every word, every sound, is truth . . . For this to be suppressed . . . that would be the greater dishonesty . . . Wouldn't it? . . . Yes—but I'm doing something illegal! Around and around it went in his mind as the tape rolled on . . . And Sherman McCoy, he who had now vowed to be his animal self, discovered what many had discovered before him. In well-reared girls and boys, guilt and the instinct to obey the rules are reflexes, ineradicable ghosts in the machine.

Even before the Hasidic giant had lumbered down the stairs and Maria's whoops of laughter had ceased in this moldering chamber in the Bronx, the prosecutor, Kramer, was protesting furiously.

"Judge, you can't allow this—"

"I'll give you an opportunity to speak."

"—cheap trick—"

"Mr. Kramer!"

"—influence—"

"MR. KRAMER!"

Kramer shut up.

"Now, Mr. Kramer," said Kovitsky, "I'm sure you know Mrs. Ruskin's voice. Do you agree that that was her voice?"

"Probably, but that's not the point. The point is—"

"Just a minute. Assuming that to be the case, did what you just heard on that tape differ from Mrs. Ruskin's testimony before the grand jury?"

"Judge . . . this is preposterous! It's hard to tell *what's* going on on that tape!"

"Does it *differ*, Mr. Kramer?"

"It varies."

"Is 'varies' the same as 'differs'?"

"Judge, there's no way to tell the conditions under which this thing was made!"

"*Prima facie*, Mr. Kramer, does it differ?"

"*Prima facie* it differs. But you can't let this cheap trick"—he swung his hand contemptuously in the direction of McCoy—"influence your—"

"Mr. Kramer—"

"—judgment!" Kramer could see that Kovitsky's head was gradually lowering. The white was beginning to appear below his irises. The sea was beginning to foam. But Kramer couldn't restrain himself. "The simple fact is, the grand jury has handed down a valid indictment! You have—this hearing has no jurisdiction over—"

"Mr. Kramer—"

"—the duly completed deliberations of a grand jury!"

"THANK YOU FOR YOUR ADVICE AND COUNSEL, MR. KRAMER!"

Kramer froze, his mouth still open.

"Let me remind you," Kovitsky said, "that I am the presiding judge for the grand jury, and I am not enchanted by the possibility that testimony by a key witness in this case might be tainted."

Fuming, Kramer shook his head. "Nothing that these two . . . *individuals*"—he flung his hand toward McCoy again—"say in their little love nest . . ." He shook his head again, too angry to find the words to finish the sentence.

"Sometimes that's when the truth comes out, Mr. Kramer."

"The *truth!* Two spoiled rich people, one of them wired up like a rat—try telling that to the people in that courtroom, Judge!—"

As soon as the words popped out, Kramer knew he had made a mistake, but he couldn't hold back.

"—and to the thousands outside that room hanging on every word of this case! Try telling them—"

He stopped. Kovitsky's irises again surfed the turbulent sea. He expected him to explode once more, but instead he did something more unnerving. He smiled. The head was down, the beak was out, the irises hydroplaned over the ocean, and he smiled.

"Thank you, Mr. Kramer. I will."

By the time Judge Kovitsky returned to the courtroom, the demonstrators were having a merry time for themselves, talking at the top of their voices, cackling, walking around, and pulling faces and otherwise showing the platoon of white-shirted court officers who was boss. They quieted down a bit when they saw Kovitsky, but as much out of curiosity as anything else. They were wound up.

Sherman and Killian headed for the defendant's desk, a table out in front of the judge's bench, and the falsetto singsong started up again.

"Sherrrr-maaannnn . . ."

Kramer was over by the clerk's table, talking to a tall white man in a cheap gabardine suit.

"That's the aforesaid Bernie Fitzgibbon, in whom you have no faith," said Killian. He was grinning. Then he said, indicating Kramer, "Keep your eye on that sucker's face."

Sherman stared without comprehending.

Kovitsky still had not ascended to the bench. He stood about ten feet away, talking to his secretary, the redheaded man. The noise in the spectators' section grew louder. Kovitsky walked slowly up the steps to the bench without looking in their direction. He stood at the bench with his eyes down, as if he were looking at something on the floor.

All at once—KAPOW! *The gavel*—it was like a cherry bomb.

"YOU! SHUT UP AND SIT DOWN!"

The demonstrators froze for a moment, shocked by the furious volume of this little man's voice.

"SO YOU INSI-I-I-IST . . . ON TESTING . . . THE WI-I-I-ILL . . . OF THIS COURT?"

They grew silent and began to take their places.

"Very well. Now, in the case of the People *versus* Sherman McCoy, the grand jury has returned an indictment. Pursuant to my authority to supervise the grand jury's proceedings, I am ordering that indictment dismissed in the interests of justice, without prejudice and with leave to re-present by the district attorney."

"Your Honor!" Kramer was on his feet, his hand in the air.

"Mr. Kramer—"

"Your action will do irreparable damage not only to the People's case—"

"Mr. Kramer—"

"—but to the cause of the People as well. Your Honor, in this courtroom today"—he gestured toward the spectators' section and the demonstrators—"are many members of the community so vitally affected by this case, and it ill behooves the criminal-justice system of this county—"

"MR. KRAMER! KINDLY BEHOOVE ME NO ILL-BEHOOVES!"

"Your Honor—"

"MR. KRAMER! THE COURT DIRECTS YOU TO SHUT UP!"

Kramer looked up at Kovitsky with his mouth wide open, as if the wind had been knocked out of him.

"Now, Mr. Kramer—"

But Kramer had gotten his breath back. "Your Honor, I want the record to show that the court raised its voice. Shouted, to be precise."

"Mr. Kramer . . . the court is going to raise . . . MORE THAN ITS VOICE! What makes you think you can come before the bench waving the banner of community pressure? The law is not a creature of the few or of the many. The court is not swayed by your threats. The court is aware of your conduct before Judge Auerbach in the criminal court. You waved a petition, Mr. Kramer! You waved it in the air, like a banner!" Kovitsky raised his right hand and waved it about. "You were on TELEVISION, Mr. Kramer! An artist drew a picture of you brandishing your petition like Robespierre or Danton, and you were on TELEVISION! You played to the mob, didn't you—and perhaps there are those in this courtroom RIGHT NOW who ENJOYED that performance, Mr. Kramer. Well, I got NEWS for you! Those who come into THIS courtroom waving banners . . . LOSE THEIR ARMS! . . . DO I MAKE MYSELF CLEAR?"

"Your Honor, I was merely—"

"DO I MAKE MYSELF CLEAR?"

"Yes, Your Honor."

"All right. Now, I am dismissing the indictment in the case of the People *versus* McCoy, with leave to re-present."

"Your Honor! I must repeat—such an action would irreparably damage the People's case!" Kramer blurted the words out so that Kovitsky couldn't overpower him with his tremendous voice. Kovitsky seemed surprised by the brashness of his declaration and by his vehemence. He froze, and that gave the demonstrators just enough courage to erupt.

"Yagggghhh! . . . No more Park Avenue Justice!" One popped up out of his seat, and then another and another. The tall one with the earring was in the front row with his fist in the air. "Whitewash!" he yelled. "Whitewash!"

KAPOW! The gavel exploded again. Kovitsky stood up and put his fists on his desktop and leaned forward. "The officers will . . . REMOVE THAT MAN!" With that, Kovitsky's right arm shot out and pointed toward the tall demonstrator with the earring. Two court officers in short-sleeved white shirts, with .38s on their hips, moved toward him.

"You can't remove the People!" he shouted. "You can't remove the People!"

"Yeah," said Kovitsky, "but YOU will be removed!"

The officers closed in on either side of the man and began pushing him toward the exit. He looked back at his confreres, but they seemed confused. They were yammering, but they didn't have the heart to take on Kovitsky en masse.

KAPOW!

"SILENCE!" said Kovitsky. As soon as the crowd was reasonably quiet, Kovitsky looked toward Fitzgibbon and Kramer. "Court is adjourned."

The spectators stood up, and their yammering now grew into an angry rumble as they headed toward the door, glowering at Kovitsky as they went. Nine court officers created a line between the spectators and the bar. Two of them had their hands resting on the handles of their revolvers. There were muffled shouts, but Sherman couldn't make them out. Killian got up and started walking toward Kovitsky. Sherman followed him.

A tremendous commotion from behind. Sherman spun around. A tall black man had burst through the line of court officers. It was the one with the gold earring, the one Kovitsky had ordered out of the court. Apparently the court officers had deposited him out in the hallway, and now he had returned, in a rage. He was already past the bar. He headed toward Kovitsky, his eyes blazing.

"You bald-headed old pussy! You bald-headed old pussy!"

Three officers left the line that was trying to herd the demonstrators out of the courtroom. One of them grabbed the tall man by the arm, but he spun away.

"Park Avenue justice!"

Demonstrators now began surging through the breach in the line of officers, rumbling and growling and trying to figure out just how fierce they wanted to be. Sherman stared at them, paralyzed by the sight. *Now it begins!* A feeling of fear . . . *anticipation!* . . . *Now it begins!* The court officers are falling back, trying to stay between the mob and the judge and the court personnel. The demonstrators are milling about, growling, baying, building up steam, trying to figure out just how powerful they are and how brave.

Booooo! . . . *Yeggghhh!* . . . *Yaaaggghhh!* . . . *Yo! Goldberg!* . . . *You bald-headed old pussy!*

All at once, just to his left, Sherman sees the wild rawboned form of Quigley. He's joined the court officers. He's trying to herd the mob back. He has a crazy look on his face.

"Okay, Jack, that's enough. It's all over. Everybody's going home now, Jack." He calls them all Jack. He's armed, but the revolver remains somewhere under his teal-green sport jacket. The court officers are edging slowly backward. They keep moving their hands toward the holsters on their hips. They touch the butts of the revolvers, then pull their hands away, as if terrified of what would happen in this room if they unsheathed the weapons and started firing away.

Pushing and shoving . . . a terrific thrashing about . . . Quigley! . . . Quigley grabs a demonstrator by the wrist and twists his arms behind his back and jerks it up—Aaaagggh!—and kicks his legs out from under him. Two of the court officers, the one called Brucie and the big one with the tire of fat around his waist, come backing past Sherman, crouched over, hands on the guns in their holsters. Brucie starts yelling over his shoulder to Kovitsky: "Get on your elevator, Judge! F'r Chrissake, get on your elevator!" But Kovitsky doesn't budge. He's glowering at the mob.

The tall one, the one with the gold earring, is barely a foot from the two officers. He doesn't try to get past them. He has his head stuck way up in the air on his long neck, yelling at Kovitsky: "You bald-headed old pussy!"

"Sherman!" It's Killian, by his side. "Come on! We're going down in the judge's elevator!" Feels Killian tugging at his elbow, but he's rooted to the spot. *Now it begins! Why postpone it?*

A blur. He looks up. A furious figure in a blue work shirt charging toward him. A contorted face. An enormous bony finger. "Time's up, Park Avenue!"

Sherman braces. Suddenly—Quigley. Quigley steps between the two of them and with an utterly crazy smile sticks his face in the man's and says, "Hi!"

Startled, the man stares at him, and in that moment, still looking straight into his eyes and smiling, Quigley raises his left foot and smashes it down on the man's toe. A terrific yelp.

That sets the mob off. *Yagggghhhh!* . . . *Ged'im!* . . . *Ged'im!* . . . Shoving past the court officers. Brucie pushes the tall black man with the earring. He goes reeling to one side. All at once he's directly in front of Sherman. He stares. He's amazed. Face to face! And now what? He just stares. Sherman's transfixed . . . terrified . . . *Now!* He ducks, pivots on his hip, and turns his back—*now!*—*it begins now!* He wheels about and drives his fist into the man's solar plexus.

"Ooooo!"

The big sonofabitch is sinking, with his mouth open and his eyes bugged out and his Adam's apple convulsing. He hits the floor.

"Sherman! Come on!" Killian is pulling on his arm. But Sherman is frozen. He can't take his eyes off the man with the gold earring. He's on the floor, doubled up on his side, gasping. The earring dangles off his earlobe at a crazy angle.

Sherman is knocked backward by two thrashing forms. *Quigley*. Quigley has a tall white boy around the neck with one arm and appears to be trying to drive his nose back up into his skull with the heel of the other hand. The white boy is going *Aaaaaah, aaaaaah* and bleeding terribly. The nose is a bloody pudding. Quigley is grunting *Unnnnh unnnh unnnh*. He lets the white boy fall to the floor, then smashes the heel of his shoe into his arm. A dreadful *Aaaaah*. Quigley takes Sherman by the arm and pushes him backward.

"Come on, Sherm!" *Sherm*. "Let's get the fuck outta here!"

I drove my forearm into his belly—and he went Ooooooo! *and hit the floor*. One last look at the dangling earring—

Now Quigley is pushing him backward and Killian is pulling him.

"Come on!" yells Killian. "You outta your fucking mind?"

There was only a little semicircle of court officers, plus Quigley, between the mob and Sherman and Killian and the judge, his secretary, and the clerk, who squeezed back through the door into the judge's chamber, shoulder to shoulder, jostling about. The demonstrators—plenty for them to be furious about now! One of them is trying to push through the door . . . Brucie can't hold him back . . . *Quigley* . . . He's pulled his revolver out. He holds it up in the air. He thrusts his face toward the demonstrator in the doorway.

"Okay, faggot! You want a new hole in your fucking nose?"

The man freezes—freezes like a statue. It's not the revolver. It's the look on Quigley's face that gets him.

One beat . . . two beats . . . That's all they need. The court officer with the big tire of flab has the door to the judge's elevator open. They're herding everybody on—Kovitsky, his secretary, the big clerk, Killian. Sherman backs in with Quigley, Brucie and Quigley right on top of him. Three court officers remain in the chamber, ready to draw their guns. But the mob has lost steam, lost heart. *Quigley. The look on his face. Okay, faggot. You want a new hole in your fucking nose?*

The elevator starts down. It's overpoweringly hot inside. All jammed to-gether. *Aaah, aaaahh, aaaaaah, aaaaahhhh.* Sherman realizes it's himself, gulping for air, himself and Quigley, too, and Brucie and the other court officer, the fat one. *Aaaaaah, aaaahhhh, aaaaahhhhh, aaaahhhhh, aacaahhhhhhhh.*

"Sherm!" It's Quigley, talking between gasps, "You cold-cocked . . . that cocksucker . . . Sherm! You . . . cold-cocked him."

Sank to the floor. Doubled up. The earring dangled. Now!—and I triumphed. He's consumed with cold fear—*they'll get me!*—and soaring anticipation. *Again! I want to do it again!*

"Don't congratulate yourselves." It was Kovitsky, in a low stern voice. "The whole thing was a fucking fiasco. You don't even know how bad it was. I shouldn't have adjourned the court so fast. I should've talked to them. They . . . *don't know.* They don't even know what they've done."

"Judge," said Brucie, "it ain't over yet. We got demonstrators in the halls and outside the building."

"Where outside?"

"It's mainly on the front steps, on 161st Street, but some a them are around on Walton Avenue, too. Where's your car, Judge?"

"The usual place. The pit."

"Maybe one a us oughta drive it around to the Concourse entrance."

Kovitsky thought for a moment. "Fuck it. I won't give 'em the satisfaction."

"They won't even know about it, Judge. I don't mean to alarm you, but they're already out there . . . talking about you . . . They got a sound system and everything."

"Oh, yeah?" said Kovitsky. "They ever heard of obstructing governmental administration?"

"I don't think they ever hearda nothing except raising hell, but they know how to do that."

"Well, thanks, Brucie." Kovitsky began to smile. He turned to Killian. "Remember the time I ordered you off the judge's elevator? I can't even remember how you got on."

Killian smiled and nodded.

"And you wouldn't get off, and I said I was holding you in contempt? And you said, 'Contempt of what? Contempt of elevator?' You remember that?"

"Oh, you better believe I remember that, Judge, but I always hoped *you* wouldn't."

"You know what burned me up? You were right. That was what burned me up."

Even before the elevator reached the first floor, they could hear the tremen-dous BRAAANNNNNGG! of the alarm.

"Christ. What jerk set that off?" said Brucie. "Who the hell they think's gonna respond? Every officer in the building's already at a station."

Kovitsky was somber again. He was shaking his head. He looked so small, a bony little bald-headed man in voluminous black robes squeezed into this swelter-ing elevator. "They don't know how bad this is. They just don't fucking know . . . I'm their only friend, their only friend . . ."

When the elevator door opened, the noise of the alarm—BRAAANNNNNGGGGG! —was overpowering. They emerged into a little vestibule. One door led to the street. Another led to the ground-floor hallway of the island fortress. Brucie shouted to Sherman, "How you figuring on getting outta here?"

Quigley answered, "We got a car, but Christ knows where it is. The fucking driver was terrified just fucking driving up to the building."

Brucie said, "Where's he supposed to be?"

Quigley said, "The Walton Avenue door, but if I know that faggot, he's halfway to fucking Candy."

"Candy?"

"It's the fucking town he comes from, in Ceylon, Candy. The closer we get to this fucking building, the more he starts talking about this fucking town he comes from, Candy. The fucking town is called Candy."

Brucie's eyes opened wide, and he yelled, "Hey, Judge!"

Kovitsky was heading through the door that led into the interior hallway of the building.

"Judge! Don't go in there! They're all over the halls!"

Now! Again! Sherman bolted for the door and ran after the little figure in black.

Killian's voice: "Sherman! What the hell you doing!"

Quigley's voice: "Sherm! Jesus Christ!"

Sherman found himself in a vast marble hall filled with the stupendous sound of the alarm. Kovitsky was up ahead of him, walking so fast that his robes were billowing out. He looked like a crow trying to gain altitude. Sherman broke into a trot to try to catch up. A figure came running past him. Brucie.

"Judge! Judge!"

Brucie caught up with Kovitsky and tried to grab his left arm. Sherman was now right behind them. With a furious gesture Kovitsky forced the court officer's hand away.

"Judge, where you going! What you doing!"

"Gotta tell 'em!" said Kovitsky.

"Judge—they'll kill you!"

"Gotta tell 'em!"

Sherman was now aware that the others were pulling up on either side, running . . . the fat court officer . . . Killian . . . Quigley . . . All the faces in the hallway stopped and stared, trying to figure out what in the name of God they were looking at . . . this furious little judge in his black robes with his outriders running along beside him yelling: "Judge! Don't do it!"

Shouts in the corridor . . . *That's him!* . . . *Yo! That's that fucker!* . . . BRAAANNNNGGGG! . . . The alarm battered one and all with its shock waves.

Brucie tried again to restrain Kovitsky. "Leggo my FUCKING ARM!" screamed Kovitsky. "That's a FUCKING ORDER, BRUCIE!"

Sherman broke into a trot to keep up. He was only a half step behind the judge. He searched out the faces in the hallway. *Now!—again!* They went around a bend in the hallway. They were in the great Moderne lobby that led out onto the terrace overlooking 161st Street. Fifty or sixty onlookers, fifty or sixty rapt faces, were inside the lobby, looking out at the terrace. Through the glass doors Sherman could see the silhouette of a mass of figures.

Kovitsky reached the front doors and pushed one open and paused. BR-RAAAANNNGGGG! Brucie yelled: "Don't go out there, Judge! I'm begging you!"

At the center of the terrace was a microphone on a stanchion, such as you might see on a bandstand. At the microphone was a tall black man in a black suit and a white shirt. Black people and white people were crowded in on either side of him. A white woman with wiry gray-blond hair was next to him. A whole mob, black and white, was up on the terrace and on the stairs that led up to the terrace from either side. Judging by the noise, hundreds more, possibly thousands, were on the grand staircase and the sidewalk down below on 161st Street. Then Sherman realized who the tall man at the microphone was. Reverend Bacon.

He spoke to the crowd in a steady, controlled baritone, as if each word were one more resolute footstep of fate.

"We have put our trust in this society . . . and in this power structure . . . and what've we got?" Much yammering and many angry shouts from the crowd. "We have believed their promises . . . and what've we got?" Groans, moans, yelps. "We believed in their justice. They told us Justice was blind. They told us Justice was a blind woman . . . an *impartial* woman . . . see? . . . And this woman did not know the color of your skin . . . And who does that blind woman turn out to be? What's her *name?* When she plays her lying racist games, what's the face she wears?" Shouts, boos, howls, cries for blood. "We *know* that face, we *know* that name . . . MY-RON KO-VIT-SKY!" Boos, yowls, cackles, shouts, a colossal baying noise rose up from the mob. 'MY-RON KO-VIT-SKY!" The noise welled up into a roar. "But we can wait, brothers and sisters . . . we can wait . . . We waited *this* long, and we got no place more to go. WE CAN WAIT! . . . We can wait for the power structure's henchmen to show their faces. He's in there. He's in there!" Bacon kept his face turned toward the microphone and the crowd, but he flung his arm and his pointed finger behind him in the direction of the building. "And he knows the people are here, for . . . *he* . . . is . . . not . . . blind . . . He lives in fear on this island, in the mighty sea of people, for he knows that the people—and justice!—wait for him. And there is no escape!" The crowd roared, and Bacon leaned to one side for a moment while the woman with wiry gray-blond hair whispered something in his ear.

At that moment Kovitsky threw open both the glass doors in front of him. His robes billowed out like enormous black wings.

"Judge! For God's sake!"

Kovitsky stopped in the doorway, arms outstretched. The moment lengthened . . . lengthened . . . The arms dropped. The billowing wings collapsed against his frail body. He turned around and walked back inside the lobby. His eyes were down, and he was muttering.

"Their only friend, their only fucking friend." He looked at the court officer. "Okay, Brucie, let's go."

No! Now! Sherman yelled out: "No, Judge! Do it! I'll go with you!"

Kovitsky spun about and looked at Sherman. Obviously he hadn't even known he was there. A furious scowl. "What the hell—"

"Do it!" said Sherman. "Do it, Judge!"

Kovitsky just looked at him. At Brucie's urging they were now all heading back down the hallway at a good clip. The corridors were much more crowded . . . an ugly mob . . .

That's Kovitsky! That's the one! Shouts . . . a tremendous rumble . . . BRRAAAANNNGGG!—the alarm battered and battered and ricocheted off the marble, doubling, trebling . . . An older man, not a demonstrator, came up from the side, as if to confront Kovitsky, pointing and shouting, *"You . . ."* Sherman lunged at him and screamed: "Get your fucking face outta the way!" The man jumped back, his mouth hanging open. His *expression*—frightened! *Now!*—*again!*—drive a fist into his belly, mash his nose into a pulp, ram a heel into his eye!—Sherman turned to look at Kovitsky.

Kovitsky was staring at him the way you'd stare at a lunatic. So was Killian. So were the two court officers.

"You outta your mind?" yelled Kovitsky. "You wanna get killed?"

"Judge," said Sherman, "it don't matter! It don't matter!"

He smiled. He could feel his upper lip stretching across his teeth. He let out a short harsh red laugh. Leaderless, the mob in the corridor held back, not sure what they were dealing with. Sherman sought out their faces, as if to obliterate them with his very eyes. He was terrified—and quite ready—*again!*

The little band beat a retreat down the marble halls.

EPILOGUE

A year later, to the day, the following article appeared on page B1 of the Metropolitan News section of *The New York Times*:

Financier Is Arraigned In Honor Student's Death

By OVERTON HOLMES, JR.

Former Wall Street financier Sherman McCoy was brought in handcuffs to the Bronx yesterday and arraigned on a charge of manslaughter in the death of Henry Lamb, a 19-year-old black honor student who had been the pride of a South Bronx housing project.

Mr. Lamb died Monday night at Lincoln Hospital as a result of cerebral injuries suffered when he was struck by Mr. McCoy's Mercedes-Benz sports car on Bruckner Boulevard in the Bronx thirteen months ago. He had never regained consciousness.

Demonstrators from the All People's Solidarity and other organiza-

tions chanted "Wall Street murderer," "Capitalist killer," and "Justice at last," as detectives led Mr. McCoy toward the Bronx Criminal Courts Building on East 161st St. Mr. McCoy's alleged role in Mr. Lamb's injuries became the center of a political storm last year.

A Patrician Figure

Asked by reporters to comment on the contrast between his Wall Street and Park Avenue background and his current situation, Mr. McCoy yelled out, "I have nothing to do with Wall Street and Park Avenue. I'm a professional defendant. I've undergone a year of legal harassment, and I'll undergo another—or perhaps another 8¹/₃ to 25."

This was an apparent reference to the prison sentence he will face if convicted of the new charge. Bronx District Attorney Richard A. Weiss is said to have prepared a 50-page indictment to present to a grand jury. Mr. Weiss's tenacious prosecution of the case was widely regarded as the key to his successful bid for re-election in November.

A tall, patrician figure, son of the eminent Wall Street lawyer John Campbell McCoy and a product of St. Paul's School and Yale, Mr. McCoy, 39, was dressed in an open-necked sport shirt, khaki pants, and hiking shoes. This was in sharp contrast to the $2,000 custom-tailored English suits he was famous for as the legendary $1,000,000-a-year "king of the bond market" for Pierce & Pierce.

As he was ushered through a basement door of the courthouse into the Bronx Central Booking facility, Mr. McCoy said in response to a reporter's query, "I told you, I'm a career defendant. I now dress for jail, even though I haven't been convicted of any crime."

Diminished Life-Style

At his arraignment six hours later, Mr. McCoy appeared before Judge Samuel Auerbach with a slightly swollen left jaw and abrasions on the knuckles of both hands. Questioned about it by Judge Auerbach, he said, clenching his fists, "Don't worry, Judge. It's something I'll take care of myself."

Police officials said Mr. McCoy had become involved in a "dispute" with two other prisoners in a communal detention cell, resulting in a scuffle, but had declined offers of medical treatment.

When the judge asked him how he pleaded, Mr. McCoy said in a loud voice, "Absolutely innocent." Against the judge's advice, he insisted on representing himself at the arraignment and indicated he will do likewise during his forthcoming trial.

Sources close to Mr. McCoy, whose worth was once estimated as more than $8,000,000, said that a year of extraordinary legal expenses and entanglements has left him "barely able to pay the rent." Formerly the owner of a $3,200,000 cooperative apartment at 816 Park Avenue, he now rents two modest rooms in a postwar high-rise building on East 34th Street near First Avenue.

The original charge against Mr. McCoy, reckless endangerment, was thrown out last June during a turbulent hearing in the courtroom of former Supreme Court Justice Myron Kovitsky. Amid the ensuing storm of protest in the black community, Mr. Weiss brought the charge before a second grand jury and obtained a new indictment.

The Bronx Democratic organization, responding to community demands, refused to renominate Judge Kovitsky, and he was soundly defeated in his November re-election attempt. He was replaced by veteran Justice Jerome Meldnick. Mr. McCoy's trial, in February, ended in a hung jury, with all three white jurors and one Hispanic juror holding out for acquittal.

Two months ago a Bronx jury awarded Mr. Lamb $12,000,000 in a civil action against Mr. McCoy, who has appealed. Recently, Attorney Albert Vogel, acting for Mr. Lamb, charged that Mr. McCoy was hiding assets in order to evade the judgment. The assets in dispute are the proceeds of the sale of his Park Avenue apartment and his house in Southampton, L.I., which he attempted to give outright to his estranged wife, Judy, and their seven-year-old daughter, Campbell. The court has frozen these funds, along with the remainder of Mr. McCoy's securities and salable personal belongings, pending the outcome of his appeal of his civil damages.

Mrs. McCoy and her daughter reportedly have moved to the Midwest, but Mrs. McCoy was in the spectator section of the courtroom yesterday, apparently unrecognized by the noisy group of demonstrators, black and white, who occupied most of the seats. At one point, Mr. McCoy looked toward his wife, smiled slightly, and raised his left hand in a clenched-fist salute. The meaning of this gesture was unclear. Mrs. McCoy refused to speak to reporters.

"Rent-Controlled Love Nest"

Mr. McCoy's marriage was rocked by the revelation that Maria Ruskin Chirazzi, heiress of the Ruskin air-charter fortune, was in the automobile with Mr. McCoy at the time Mr. Lamb was struck. The couple, it developed, had been conducting an affair in a secret apartment later dubbed the "rent-controlled love nest." Mrs. Chirazzi's then-husband, Arthur Ruskin, died of a heart attack shortly before her involvement in the case was made known.

District Attorney Weiss had been prepared to begin a new trial on the reckless endangerment charge when Mr. Lamb died, exposing Mr. McCoy to the more serious charge of manslaughter. Mr. Weiss had already announced that Assistant District Attorney Raymond I. Andriutti would head the prosecution. In an unusual development, Mr. Weiss was forced to remove the prosecutor of the first trial, Lawrence N. Kramer, from the case when it was disclosed that Mr.

Kramer had interceded with a landlord to secure the so-called rent-controlled love nest apartment for a friend, Shelly Thomas, an advertising copywriter. Mr. Kramer, who is married, met Ms. Thomas when she served as a juror in an unrelated case which he prosecuted. The defendant in that case, Herbert (Herbert 92X) Cantrell, has obtained a reversal of his first-degree manslaughter conviction on the grounds of "prosecutorial misconduct."

Mr. Andriutti said yesterday that he would call Mrs. Chirazzi as a prosecution witness in Mr. McCoy's new trial despite the fact that it was a controversy over her testimony before a grand jury that led to the dismissal of the first indictment by Judge Kovitsky. She did not testify at the first trial.

Fashionable Estate

Mr. McCoy's legal problems were multiplied yesterday when a real-estate-firm employee, Sally Rawthrote, filed suit against him in Manhattan Civil Court for $500,000. Ms. Rawthrote had received a $192,000 commission for the $3,200,000 sale of Mr. McCoy's Park Avenue apartment. But Mr. Lamb, via Mr. Vogel, sued her for the $192,000 on the grounds that the money should go toward the payment of Mr. Lamb's $12,000,000 judgment against Mr. McCoy. Mrs. Rawthrote's suit yesterday accused Mr. McCoy of "deceptively proffering encumbered property for sale." In a statement she said she was "merely hedging against the possible loss of my rightful commission" and in fact wishes Mr. McCoy well.

Just how Mr. McCoy might deal with this and other complex legal matters growing out of the case was uncertain. Reached at his home on Long Island, Mr. McCoy's former attorney, Thomas Killian, said that he was no longer able to represent Mr. McCoy due to Mr. McCoy's lack of sufficient funds to mount a defense.

Mr. Killian himself currently has his hands full with a barrage of lawsuits brought by his new neighbors in the fashionable North Shore community of Lattingtown. He recently purchased the 20-acre Phipps estate and commissioned the noted Neo-Shingle architect, Hudnall Stallworth, to design a large addition to the main house, which is listed by the National Historic Registry. Local preservationists object to any alteration of the stately Georgian structure.

Mr. Killian is heated in his support of Mr. McCoy, however. In a speech before a private luncheon group yesterday, he reportedly referred to the manslaughter indictment with a common tauro-scatological expletive and was quoted as saying, "If this case was being tried in foro conscientiae [in the court of the conscience], the defendants would be Abe Weiss, Reginald Bacon, and Peter Fallow of The City Light."

Milton Lubell, spokesman for Mr.

Weiss, said the District Attorney would not respond to "kibbitzing" by "someone no longer involved in the case." He added: "Only preferential treatment by certain elements of the judicial system has kept Mr. McCoy aloof from the law so far. It is tragic that it has required the death of Henry Lamb, who represented the highest ideals of our city, to see to it that justice will at last be served in his case."

Buck Jones, a spokesman for the Reverend Mr. Bacon's All People's Solidarity, dismissed Mr. Killian's charge as "the usual racist double-talk by a racist mouthpiece for a well-known capitalist racist" who seeks to "avoid paying what he owes for the racist destruction of a fine young man."

Mr. Fallow, winner of a Pulitzer Prize for his coverage of the McCoy case, could not be reached for comment. He was reportedly on a sailing vessel in the Aegean Sea with his bride of two weeks, Lady Evelyn, daughter of Sir Gerald Steiner, the publisher and financier.

THE
RIGHT STUFF

For Kailey Wong

FOREWORD

This book grew out of some ordinary curiosity. What is it, I wondered, that makes a man willing to sit up on top of an enormous Roman candle, such as a Redstone, Atlas, Titan, or Saturn rocket, and wait for someone to light the fuse? I decided on the simplest approach possible. I would ask a few astronauts and find out. So I asked a few in December of 1972 when they gathered at Cape Canaveral to watch the last mission to the moon, Apollo 17. I discovered quickly enough that none of them, no matter how talkative otherwise, was about to answer the question or even linger for more than a few seconds on the subject at the heart of it, which is to say, courage.

But I did sense that the answer was not to be found in any set of traits specific to the task of flying into space. The great majority of the astronauts who had flown the rockets had come from the ranks of test pilots. All but a few had been military test pilots, and even those few, such as Neil Armstrong, had been trained in the military. And it was this that led me to a rich and fabulous terrain that, in a literary sense, had remained as dark as the far side of the moon for more than half a century: military flying and the modern American officer corps.

Immediately following the First World War a certain fashion set in among writers in Europe and soon spread to their obedient colonial counterparts in the United States. War was looked upon as inherently monstrous, and those who waged it—namely, military officers—were looked upon as brutes and philistines. The tone was set by some brilliant novels; among them, *All Quiet on the Western Front*, *The Journey to the End of the Night*, and *The Good Soldier Schweik*. The only proper protagonist for a tale of war was an enlisted man, and he was to be presented not as a hero but as Everyman, as much a victim of war as any civilian. Any officer above the rank of second lieutenant was to be presented as a martinet or a fool if not an outright villain, no matter whom he fought for. The old-fashioned tale of prowess and heroism was relegated to second- and third-rate forms of literature, ghost-written autobiographies and stories in pulp magazines on the order of *Argosy* and *Bluebook*.

Even as late as the 1930s the favorite war stories in the pulps concerned World War I pilots. One of the few scientific treatises ever written on the subject of bravery is *The Anatomy of Courage* by Charles Moran, who served as a doctor in the trenches for the British in World War I (and who was better known later as Lord Moran, personal physician to Winston Churchill). Writing in the 1920s, Moran predicted that in the wars of the future adventurous young men who sought glory in war would tend to seek it as pilots. In the twentieth century, he said, they would regard the military pilot as the quintessence of manly daring that the cavalryman had been in the nineteenth.

Serious treatment of the drama and psychology of this new pursuit, flying high-performance aircraft in battle, was left to the occasional pilot who could write, the most notable of them being Antoine de Saint-Exupéry. The literary world remained oblivious. Nevertheless, young men did exactly what Moran predicted. They became military officers so that they could fly, and they flew against astonishingly deadly odds. As late as 1970, I was to discover in an article by a military doctor in a medical journal, a career Navy pilot faced a 23 percent likelihood of dying in an accident. This did not even include deaths in combat, which at that time, with the war in Vietnam in progress, were catastrophically high for Navy pilots. *The Right Stuff* became the story of why men were willing— willing?—*delighted!*—to take on such odds in this, an era literary people had long since characterized as the age of the anti-hero. Such was the psychological mystery that antimated me in the writing of this book. And if there were those readers who were not interested in the exploration of space per se but who were interested in *The Right Stuff* nonetheless, perhaps it might have been because the mystery caught their imagination, as well as mine.

Since this book was first published in 1979 I have enjoyed corresponding with many pilots and with many widows of pilots. Not all have written to pat me on the back, but almost all seemed grateful that someone had tried—and it had to be an outsider—to put into words certain matters that the very code of the pilot rules off-limites in conversation. These . . . matters . . . add up to one of the most extraordinary and most secret dramas of the twentieth century.

T.W.
August 1983

CONTENTS

1

THE ANGELS

WITHIN FIVE MINUTES, or ten minutes, no more than that, three of the others had called her on the telephone to ask her if she had heard that something had happened out there.

"Jane, this is Alice. Listen, I just got a call from Betty, and she said she heard something's happened out there. Have you heard anything?" That was the way they phrased it, call after call. She picked up the telephone and began relaying this same message to some of the others.

"Connie, this is Jane Conrad. Alice just called me, and she says something's happened . . ."

Something was part of the official Wife Lingo for tiptoeing blindfolded around the subject. Being barely twenty-one years old and new around here, Jane Conrad knew very little about this particular subject, since nobody ever talked about it. But the day was young! And what a setting she had for her imminent enlightenment! And what a picture she herself presented! Jane was tall and slender and had rich brown hair and high cheekbones and wide brown eyes. She looked a little like the actress Jean Simmons. Her father was a rancher in southwestern Texas. She had gone East to college, to Bryn Mawr, and had met her husband, Pete, at a debutante's party at the Gulph Mills Club in Philadelphia, when he was a senior at Princeton. Pete was a short, wiry, blond boy who joked around a lot. At any moment his face was likely to break into a wild grin revealing the gap between his front teeth. The Hickory Kid sort, he was; a Hickory Kid on the deb circuit, however. He had an air of energy, self-confidence, ambition, *joie de vivre*. Jane and Pete were married two days after he graduated from Princeton. Last year Jane gave birth to their first child, Peter. And today, here in Florida, in Jacksonville, in the peaceful year 1955, the sun shines through the pines outside, and the very air takes on the sparkle of the ocean. The ocean and a great mica-white beach are less than a mile away. Anyone driving by will see Jane's little house gleaming like a dream house in the pines. It is a brick house, but Jane and Pete painted the bricks white, so that it gleams in the sun against a great green screen of pine trees with a thousand little places where the sun peeks through. They painted the shutters black, which makes the white walls look even more brilliant. The house has only eleven hundred square feet of floor space, but Jane and Pete designed it themselves and that more than makes up for the size. A friend of theirs was the builder and gave them every possible break, so that it cost only eleven thousand dollars. Outside, the sun shines, and inside, the fever rises by the minute as five, ten, fifteen, and, finally, nearly all twenty of the wives join the circuit, trying to find out what has happened, which, in fact, means: to whose husband.

After thirty minutes on such a circuit—this is not an unusual morning around here—a wife begins to feel that the telephone is no longer located on a table or on the kitchen wall. It is exploding in her solar plexus. Yet it would be far worse right now to hear the front doorbell. The protocol is strict on that point, although written down nowhere. No woman is supposed to deliver the final news, and certainly not on the telephone. The matter mustn't be bungled!—that's the idea. No, a man should bring the news when the time comes, a man with some official or moral authority, a clergyman or a comrade of the newly deceased. Furthermore, he should bring the bad news in person. He should turn up at the front door and ring the bell and be standing there like a pillar of coolness and competence, bearing the bad news on ice, like a fish. Therefore, all the telephone calls from the wives were the frantic and portentous beating of the wings of the death angels, as it were. When the final news came, there would be a ring at the front door—a wife in this situation finds herself staring at the front door as if she no longer owns it or controls it—and outside the door would be a man . . . come to inform her that unfortunately something has happened out there, and her husband's body now lies incinerated in the swamps or the pines or the palmetto grass, "burned beyond recognition," which anyone who had been around an air base for very long (fortunately Jane had not) realized was quite an artful euphemism to describe a human body that now looked like an enormous fowl that has burned up in a stove, burned a blackish brown all over, greasy and blistered, fried, in a word, with not only the entire face and all the hair and the ears burned off, not to mention all the clothing, but also the *hands* and *feet*, with what remains of the arms and legs bent at the knees and elbows and burned into absolutely rigid angles, burned a greasy blackish brown like the bursting body itself, so that this husband, father, officer, gentleman, this *ornamentum* of some mother's eye, His Majesty the Baby of just twenty-odd years back, has been reduced to a charred hulk with wings and shanks sticking out of it.

My own husband—how could this be what they were talking about? Jane had heard the young men, Pete among them, talk about other young men who had "bought it" or "augered in" or "crunched," but it had never been anyone they knew, no one in the squadron. And in any event, the way they talked about it, with such breezy, slangy terminology, was the same way they talked about sports. It was as if they were saying, "He was thrown out stealing second base." And that was all! Not one word, not in print, not in conversation—not in this amputated language!—about an incinerated corpse from which a young man's spirit has vanished in an instant, from which all smiles, gestures, moods, worries, laughter, wiles, shrugs, tenderness, and loving looks—*you, my love!*—have disappeared like a sigh, while the terror consumes a cottage in the woods, and a young woman, sizzling with the fever, awaits her confirmation as the new widow of the day.

The next series of calls greatly increased the possibility that it was Pete to whom something had happened. There were only twenty men in the squadron, and soon nine or ten had been accounted for . . . by the fluttering reports of the death angels. Knowing that the word was out that an accident had occurred, husbands who could get to a telephone were calling home to say *it didn't happen to me*. This news, of course, was immediately fed to the fever. Jane's telephone would ring once more, and one of the wives would be saying:

"Nancy just got a call from Jack. He's at the squadron and he says something's happened, but he doesn't know what. He said he saw Frank D—take off about ten minutes ago with Greg in back, so they're all right. What have you heard?"

But Jane has heard nothing except that other husbands, and not hers, are safe and accounted for. And thus, on a sunny day in Florida, outside of the Jacksonville Naval Air Station, in a little white cottage, a veritable dream house, another beautiful young woman was about to be apprised of the *quid pro quo* of her husband's line of work, of the tradeoff, as one might say, the subparagraphs of a contract written in no visible form. Just as surely as if she had the entire roster in front of her, Jane now realized that only two men in the squadron were unaccounted for. One was a pilot named Bud Jennings; the other was Pete. She picked up the telephone and did something that was much frowned on in a time of emergency. She called the squadron office. The duty officer answered.

"I want to speak to Lieutenant Conrad," said Jane. "This is Mrs. Conrad."

"I'm sorry," the duty officer said—and then his voice cracked. "I'm sorry . . . I . . ." He couldn't find the words! He was about to cry! "I'm—that's—I mean . . . he can't come to the phone!"

He can't come to the phone!

"It's very important!" said Jane.

"I'm sorry—it's impossible—" The duty officer could hardly get the words out because he was so busy gulping back sobs. *Sobs!* "He can't come to the phone."

"Why not? Where is he?"

"I'm sorry—" More sighs, wheezes, snuffling gasps. "I can't tell you that. I—I have to hang up now!"

And the duty officer's voice disappeared in a great surf of emotion and he hung up.

The duty officer! *The very sound of her voice was more than he could take!*

The world froze, congealed, in that moment. Jane could no longer calculate the interval before the front doorbell would ring and some competent long-faced figure would appear, some Friend of Widows and Orphans, who would inform her, officially, that Pete was dead.

Even out in the middle of the swamp, in this rot-bog of pine trunks, scum slicks, dead dodder vines, and mosquito eggs, even out in this great overripe sump, the smell of "burned beyond recognition" obliterated everything else. When airplane fuel exploded, it created a heat so intense that everything but the hardest metals not only *burned*—everything of rubber, plastic, celluloid, wood, leather, cloth, flesh, gristle, calcium, horn, hair, blood, and protoplasm—it not only burned, it gave up the ghost in the form of every stricken putrid gas known to chemistry. One could smell the horror. It came in through the nostrils and burned the rhinal cavities raw and penetrated the liver and permeated the bowels like a black gas until there was nothing in the universe, inside or out, except the stench of the char. As the helicopter came down between the pine trees and settled onto the bogs, the smell hit Pete Conrad even before the hatch was completely open, and they were not even close enough to see the wreckage yet. The rest of the way Conrad and the crewmen had to travel on foot. After a few steps the water was up to their knees, and then it was up to their armpits, and they kept wading through the water and the scum and the vines and the pine trunks, but it was nothing compared to the smell. Conrad, a twenty-five-year-old lieutenant junior grade, happened to be on duty as squadron safety officer that day and was supposed to make the on-site investigation of the crash. The fact was, however, that this squadron was the first duty assignment of his career, and he had never been at a crash site before and had never smelled any such revolting stench or seen anything like what awaited him.

When Conrad finally reached the plane, which was an SNJ, he found the fuselage burned and blistered and dug into the swamp with one wing sheared off and the cockpit canopy smashed. In the front seat was all that was left of his friend Bud Jennings. Bud Jennings, an amiable fellow, a promising young fighter pilot, was now a horrible roasted hulk—with no head. His head was completely gone, apparently torn off the spinal column like a pineapple off a stalk, except that it was nowhere to be found.

Conrad stood there soaking wet in the swamp bog, wondering what the hell to do. It was a struggle to move twenty feet in this freaking muck. Every time he looked up, he was looking into a delirium of limbs, vines, dappled shadows, and a chopped-up white light that came through the treetops—the ubiquitous screen of trees with a thousand little places where the sun peeked through. Nevertheless, he started wading back out into the muck and the scum, and the others followed. He kept looking up. Gradually he could make it out. Up in the treetops there was a pattern of broken limbs where the SNJ had come crashing through. It was like a tunnel through the treetops. Conrad and the others began splashing through the swamp, following the strange path ninety or a hundred feet above them. It took a sharp turn. That must have been where the wing broke off. The trail veered to one side and started downward. They kept looking up and wading through the muck. Then they stopped. There was a great green sap wound up there in the middle of a tree trunk. It was odd. Near the huge gash was . . . tree disease . . . some sort of brownish lumpy sac up in the branches, such as you see in trees infested by bagworms, and there were yellowish curds on the branches around it, as if the disease had caused the sap to ooze out and fester and congeal—except that it couldn't be sap because it was streaked with blood. In the next instant— Conrad didn't have to say a word. Each man could see it all. The lumpy sac was the cloth liner of a flight helmet, with the earphones attached to it. The curds were Bud Jennings's brains. The tree trunk had smashed through the cockpit canopy of the SNJ and knocked Bud Jennings's head to pieces like a melon.

In keeping with the protocol, the squadron commander was not going to release Bud Jennings's name until his widow, Loretta, had been located and a competent male death messenger had been dispatched to tell her. But Loretta Jennings was not at home and could not be found. Hence, a delay—and more than enough time for the other wives, the death angels, to burn with panic over the telephone lines. All the pilots were accounted for except the two who were in the woods, Bud Jennings and Pete Conrad. One chance in two, acey-deucy, one finger-two finger, and this was not an unusual day around here.

Loretta Jennings had been out at a shopping center. When she returned home, a certain figure was waiting outside, a man, a solemn Friend of Widows and Orphans, and it was Loretta Jennings who lost the game of odd and even, acey-deucey, and it was Loretta whose child (she was pregnant with a second) would have no father. It was this young woman who went through all the final horrors that Jane Conrad had imagined—*assumed!*—would be hers to endure forever. Yet this grim stroke of fortune brought Jane little relief.

On the day of Bud Jennings's funeral, Pete went into the back of the closet and brought out his bridge coat, per regulations. This was the most stylish item in the Navy officer's wardrobe. Pete had never had occasion to wear his before. It was a double-breasted coat made of navy-blue melton cloth and came down almost to the ankles. It must have weighed ten pounds. It had a double row of gold buttons down the front and loops for shoulder boards, big beautiful belly-cut collar and lapels, deep turnbacks on the sleeves, a tailored waist, and a center vent in back that ran from the waistline to the bottom of the coat. Never would Pete, or for that matter many other American males in the mid-twentieth century, have an article of clothing quite so impressive and aristocratic as that bridge coat. At the funeral the nineteen little Indians who were left—Navy boys!—lined up manfully in their bridge coats. They looked so young. Their pink, lineless faces with their absolutely clear, lean jawlines popped up bravely, correctly, out of the enormous belly-cut collars of the bridge coats. They sang an old Navy hymn, which slipped into a strange and lugubrious minor key here and there, and included a stanza added especially for aviators. It ended with: "O hear us when we lift our prayer for those in peril in the air."

THREE MONTHS LATER another member of the squadron crashed and was burned beyond recognition and Pete hauled out the bridge coat again and Jane saw eighteen little Indians bravely going through the motions at the funeral. Not long after that, Pete was transferred from Jacksonville to the Patuxent River Naval Air Station in Maryland. Pete and Jane had barely settled in there when they got word that another member of the Jacksonville squadron, a close friend of theirs, someone they had had over to dinner many times, had died trying to take off from the deck of a carrier in a routine practice session a few miles out in the Atlantic. The catapult that propelled aircraft off the deck lost pressure, and his ship just dribbled off the end of the deck, with its engine roaring vainly, and fell sixty feet into the ocean and sank like a brick, and he vanished, *just like that.*

Pete had been transferred to Patuxent River, which was known in Navy vernacular as Pax River, to enter the Navy's new test-pilot school. This was considered a major step up in the career of a young Navy aviator. Now that the Korean War was over and there was no combat flying, all the hot young pilots aimed for flight test. In the military they always said "flight test" and not "test flying." Jet aircraft had been in use for barely ten years at the time, and the Navy was testing new jet fighters continually. Pax River was the Navy's prime test center.

Jane liked the house they bought at Pax River. She didn't like it as much as the little house in Jacksonville, but then she and Pete hadn't designed this one. They lived in a community called North Town Creek, six miles from the base. North Town Creek, like the base, was on a scrub-pine peninsula that stuck out into Chesapeake Bay. They were tucked in amid the pine trees. (Once more!) All around were rhododendron bushes. Pete's classwork and his flying duties were very demanding. Everyone in his flight test class, Group 20, talked about how difficult it was—and obviously loved it, because in Navy flying this was the big league. The young men in Group 20 and their wives were Pete's and Jane's entire social world. They associated with no one else. They constantly invited each other to dinner during the week; there was a Group party at someone's house practically every weekend; and they would go off on outings to fish or waterski in Chesapeake Bay. In a way they could not have associated with anyone else, at least not easily, because the boys could talk only about one thing: their flying. One of the phrases that kept running through the conversation was "pushing the outside of the envelope." The "envelope" was a flight-test term referring to the limits of a particular aircraft's performance, how tight a turn it could make at such-and-such a speed, and so on. "Pushing the outside," probing the outer limits, of the envelope seemed to be the great challenge and satisfaction of flight test. At first "pushing the outside of the envelope" was not a particularly terrifying phrase to hear. It sounded once more as if the boys were just talking about sports.

Then one sunny day a member of the Group, one of the happy lads they always had dinner with and drank with and went waterskiing with, was coming in for a landing at the base in an A3J fighter plane. He came in too low before lowering his flaps, and the ship stalled out, and he crashed and was burned beyond recognition. And they brought out the bridge coats and sang about those in peril in the air and put the bridge coats away, and the Indians who were left talked about the accident after dinner one night. They shook their heads and said it was a damned shame, but he should have known better than to wait so long before lowering the flaps.

Barely a week had gone by before another member of the Group was coming in for a landing in the same type of aircraft, the A3J, trying to make a ninety-degree landing, which involves a sharp turn, and something went wrong with the controls, and he ended up with one rear stabilizer wing up and the other one down, and his ship rolled in like a corkscrew from 800 feet up and crashed, and he was burned beyond recognition. And the bridge coats came out and they sang about those in peril in the air and then they put the bridge coats away and after dinner one night they mentioned that the departed had been a good man but was inexperienced, and when the malfunction in the controls put him in that bad corner, he didn't know how to get out of it.

Every wife wanted to cry out: "Well, my God! The *machine* broke! What makes *any* of you think you would have come out of it any better!" Yet intuitively Jane and the rest of them knew it wasn't right even to suggest that. Pete never indicated for a moment that he thought any such thing could possibly happen to him. It seemed not only wrong but dangerous to challenge a young pilot's confidence by posing the question. And that, too, was part of the unofficial protocol for the Officer's Wife. From now on every time Pete was late coming in from the flight line, she would worry. She began to wonder if—no! *assume!*—he had found his way into one of those corners they all talked about so spiritedly, one of those little dead ends that so enlivened conversation around here.

Not long after that, another good friend of theirs went up in an F-4, the Navy's newest and hottest fighter plane, known as the Phantom. He reached twenty thousand feet and then nosed over and dove straight into Chesapeake Bay. It turned out that a hose connection was missing in his oxygen system and he had suffered hypoxia and passed out at the high altitude. And the bridge coats came out and they lifted a prayer about those in peril in the air and the bridge coats were put away and the little Indians were incredulous. How could anybody fail to check his hose connections? And how could anybody be in such poor condition as to pass out *that quickly* from hypoxia?

A couple of days later Jane was standing at the window of her house in North Town Creek. She saw some smoke rise above the pines from over in the direction of the flight line. Just that, a column of smoke; no explosion or sirens or any other sound. She went to another room, so as not to have to think about it but there was no explanation for the smoke. She went back to the window. In the yard of a house across the street she saw a group of people . . . standing there and looking at her house, as if trying to decide what to do. Jane looked away—but she couldn't keep from looking out again. She caught a glimpse of *a certain figure* coming up the walkway toward her front door. She knew exactly who it was. She had had nightmares like this. And yet this was no dream. She was wide awake and alert. Never more alert in her entire life! Frozen, completely defeated by the sight, she simply waited for the bell to ring. She waited, but there was not a sound. Finally she could stand it no more. In real life, unlike her dream life, Jane was both too self-possessed and too polite to scream through the door: "Go away!" So she opened it. There was no one there, no one at all. There was no group of people on the lawn across the way and no one to be seen for a hundred yards in any direction along the lawns and leafy rhododendron roads of North Town Creek.

Then began a cycle in which she had both the nightmares and the hallucinations, continually. Anything could touch off an hallucination: a ball of smoke, a telephone ring that stopped before she could answer it, the sound of a siren, even the sound of trucks starting up (crash trucks!). Then she would glance out the window, and a certain figure would be coming up the walk, and she would wait for the bell. The only difference between the dreams and the hallucinations was that the scene of the dreams was always the little white house in Jacksonville. In both cases, the feeling that *this time it has happened* was quite real.

The star pilot in the class behind Pete's, a young man who was the main rival of their good friend Al Bean, went up in a fighter to do some power-dive tests. One of the most demanding disciplines in flight test was to accustom yourself to making precise readings from the control panel in the same moment that you were pushing the outside of the envelope. This young man put his ship into the test dive and was still reading out the figures, with diligence and precision and great discipline, when he augered straight into the oyster flats and was burned beyond recognition. And the bridge coats came out and they sang about those in peril in the air and the bridge coats were put away, and the little Indians remarked that the departed was a swell guy and a brilliant student of flying; a little too *much* of a student, in fact; he hadn't bothered to look out the window at the real world soon enough. Beano—Al Bean—wasn't quite so brilliant; on the other hand, he was still here.

Like many other wives in Group 20 Jane wanted to talk about the whole situation, the incredible series of fatal accidents, with her husband and the other members of the Group, to find out how they were taking it. But somehow the unwritten protocol forbade discussions of this subject, which was the fear of death. Nor could Jane or any of the rest of them talk, really *have a talk*, with anyone around the base. You could talk to another wife about being worried. But what good did it do? Who *wasn't* worried? You were likely to get a look that said: *"Why dwell on it?"* Jane might have gotten away with divulging the matter of the nightmares. But *hallucinations?* There was no room in Navy life for any such anomalous tendency as that.

By now the bad string had reached ten in all, and almost all of the dead had been close friends of Pete and Jane, young men who had been in their house many times, young men who had sat across from Jane and chattered like the rest of them about the grand adventure of military flying. And the survivors still sat around *as before*—with the same inexplicable exhilaration! Jane kept watching Pete for some sign that his spirit was cracking, but she saw none. He talked a mile a minute, kidded and joked, laughed with his Hickory Kid cackle. He always had. He still enjoyed the company of members of the group like Wally Schirra and Jim Lovell. Many young pilots were taciturn and cut loose with the strange fervor of this business only in the air. But Pete and Wally and Jim were not reticent; not in any situation. They loved to kid around. Pete called Jim Lovell "Shaky," because it was the last thing a pilot would want to be called. Wally Schirra was outgoing to the point of hearty; he loved practical jokes and dreadful puns, and so on. The three of them—*even in the midst of this bad string!*—would love to get on a subject such as accident-prone Mitch Johnson. Accident-prone Mitch Johnson, it seemed, was a Navy pilot whose life was in the hands of two angels, one of them bad and the other one good. The bad angel would put him into accidents that would have annihilated any ordinary pilot, and the good angel would bring him out of them without a scratch. Just the other day—this was the sort of story Jane would hear them tell—Mitch Johnson was coming in to land on a carrier. But he came in short, missed the flight deck, and crashed into the fantail, below the deck. There was a tremendous explosion, and the rear half of the plane fell into the water in flames. Everyone on the flight deck said, "Poor Johnson. The good angel was off duty." They were still debating how to remove the debris and his mortal remains when a phone rang on the bridge. A somewhat dopey voice said, "This is Johnson. Say, listen, I'm down here in the supply hold and the hatch is locked and I can't find the lights and I can't see a goddamned thing and I tripped over a cable and I think I hurt my leg." The officer on the bridge slammed the phone down, then vowed to find out what morbid sonofabitch could pull a phone prank at a time like this. Then the phone rang again, and the man with the dopey voice managed to establish the fact that he was, indeed, Mitch Johnson. The good angel had not left his side. When he smashed into the fantail, he hit some empty ammunition drums, and they cushioned the impact, leaving him groggy but not seriously hurt. The fuselage had blown to pieces; so he just stepped out onto the fantail and opened a hatch that led into the supply hold. It was pitch black in there, and there were cables all across the floor, holding down spare aircraft engines. Accident-prone Mitch Johnson kept tripping over these cables until he found a telephone. Sure enough, the one injury he had was a bruised shin from tripping over a cable. The man was accident-prone! Pete and Wally and Jim absolutely cracked up over stories like this. It was amazing. Great sports yarns! Nothing more than that.

A few days later Jane was out shopping at the Pax River commissary on Saunders Road, near the main gate to the base. She heard the sirens go off at the field, and then she heard the engines of the crash trucks start up. This time Jane was determined to keep calm. Every instinct made her want to rush home, but she forced herself to stay in the commissary and continue shopping. For thirty minutes she went through the motions of completing her shopping list. Then she drove home to North Town Creek. As she reached the house, she saw a figure going up the sidewalk. It was a man. Even from the back there was no question as to who he was. He had on a black suit, and there was a white band around his neck. It was her minister, from the Episcopal Church. She stared, and this vision did not come and go. The figure kept on walking up the front walk. She was not asleep now, and she was not inside her house glancing out the front window. She was outside in her car in front of her house. She was not dreaming, and she was not hallucinating, and the figure kept walking up toward her front door.

THE COMMOTION AT THE FIELD was over one of the most extraordinary things that even veteran pilots had ever seen at Pax River. And they had all seen it, because practically the entire flight line had gathered out on the field for it, as if it had been an air show.

Conrad's friend Ted Whelan had taken a fighter up, and on takeoff there had been a structural failure that caused a hydraulic leak. A red warning light showed up on Whelan's panel, and he had a talk with the ground. It was obvious that the leak would cripple the controls before he could get the ship back down to the field for a landing. He would have to bail out; the only question was where and when, and so they had a talk about that. They decided that he should jump at 8,100 feet at such-and-such a speed, directly over the field. The plane would crash into the Chesapeake Bay, and he would float down to the field. Just as coolly as anyone could have asked for it, Ted Whelan lined the ship up to come across the field at 8,100 feet precisely and he punched out, ejected.

Down on the field they all had their faces turned up to the sky. They saw Whelan pop out of the cockpit. With his Martin-Baker seat-parachute rig strapped on, he looked like a little black geometric lump a mile and a half up in the blue. They watched him as he started dropping. Everyone waited for the parachute to open. They waited a few more seconds, and then they waited some more. The little shape was getting bigger and bigger and picking up tremendous speed. Then there came an unspeakable instant at which everyone on the field who knew anything about parachute jumps knew what was going to happen. Yet even for them it was an unearthly feeling, for no one had ever seen any such thing happen so close up, from start to finish, from what amounted to a grandstand seat. Now the shape was going so fast and coming so close it began to play tricks on the eyes. It seemed to stretch out. It became much bigger and hurtled toward them at a terrific speed, until they couldn't make out its actual outlines at all. Finally there was just a streaking black blur before their eyes, followed by what seemed like an explosion. Except that it was not an explosion; it was the tremendous *crack* of Ted Whelan, his helmet, his pressure suit, and his seat-parachute rig smashing into the center of the runway, precisely on target, right in front of the crowd; an absolute bull's-eye. Ted Whelan had no doubt been alive until the instant of impact. He had had about thirty seconds to watch the Pax River base and the peninsula and Baltimore County and continental America and the entire comprehensible world rise up to smash him. When they lifted his body up off the concrete, it was like a sack of fertilizer.

Pete took out the bridge coat again and he and Jane and all the little Indians went to the funeral for Ted Whelan. That it hadn't been Pete was not solace enough for Jane. That the preacher had not, in fact, come to her front door as the Solemn Friend of Widows and Orphans, but merely for a church call . . . had not brought peace and relief. That Pete still didn't show the slightest indication of thinking that any unkind fate awaited him no longer lent her even a moment's courage. The next dream and the next hallucination, and the next and the next, merely seemed more real. For she now *knew*. She now knew the subject and the essence of this enterprise, even though not a word of it had passed anybody's lips. She even knew why Pete—the Princeton boy she met at a deb party at the Gulph Mills Club!—would never quit, never withdraw from this grim business, unless in a coffin. And God knew, and she knew, there was a coffin waiting for each little Indian.

Seven years later, when a reporter and a photographer from *Life* magazine actually stood near her in her living room and watched her face, while outside, on the lawn, a crowd of television crewmen and newspaper reporters waited for a word, an indication, anything—perhaps a glimpse through a part in a curtain!—waited for some sign of what she felt—when one and all asked with their ravenous eyes and, occasionally, in so many words: "How do you feel?" and "Are you scared?"—America wants to know!—it made Jane want to laugh, but in fact she couldn't even manage a smile.

"Why ask *now?*" she wanted to say. But they wouldn't have had the faintest notion of what she was talking about.

2

THE RIGHT STUFF

W HAT AN EXTRAORDINARY grim stretch that had been . . . and yet thereafter Pete and Jane would keep running into pilots from other Navy bases, from the Air Force, from the Marines, who had been through their own extraordinary grim stretches. There was an Air Force pilot named Mike Collins, a nephew of former Army Chief of Staff J. Lawton Collins. Mike Collins had undergone eleven weeks of combat training at Nellis Air Force Base, near Las Vegas, and in that eleven weeks twenty-two of his fellow trainees had died in accidents, which was an extraordinary rate of two per week. Then there was a test pilot, Bill Bridgeman. In 1952, when Bridgeman was flying at Edwards Air Force Base, sixty-two Air Force pilots died in the course of thirty-six weeks of training, an extraordinary rate of 1.7 per week. Those figures were for fighter-pilot trainees only; they did not include the test pilots, Bridgeman's own confreres, who were dying quite regularly enough.

Extraordinary, to be sure; except that every veteran of flying small high-performance jets seemed to have experienced these bad strings.

In time, the Navy would compile statistics showing that for a career Navy pilot, i.e., one who intended to keep flying for twenty years as Conrad did, there was a 23 percent probability that he would die in an aircraft accident. This did not even include combat deaths, since the military did not classify death in combat as accidental. Furthermore, there was a better than even chance, a 56 percent probability, to be exact, that at some point a career Navy pilot would have to eject from his aircraft and attempt to come down by parachute. In the era of jet fighters, ejection meant being exploded out of the cockpit by a nitroglycerine charge, like a human cannonball. The ejection itself was so hazardous—men lost knees, arms, and their lives on the rim of the cockpit or had the skin torn off their faces when they hit the "wall" of air outside—that many pilots chose to wrestle their aircraft to the ground rather than try it . . . and died that way instead.

The statistics were not secret, but neither were they widely known, having been eased into print rather obliquely in a medical journal. No pilot, and certainly no pilot's wife, had any need of the statistics in order to know the truth, however. The funerals took care of that in the most dramatic way possible. Sometimes, when the young wife of a fighter pilot would have a little reunion with the girls she went to school with, an odd fact would dawn on her: *they* have not been going to funerals. And then Jane Conrad would look at Pete . . . Princeton, Class of 1953 . . . Pete had already worn his great dark sepulchral bridge coat more than most boys of the Class of '53 had worn their tuxedos. How many of those happy young men had buried more than a dozen friends, comrades, and coworkers? (Lost through violent death in the execution of everyday duties.) At the time, the 1950's, students from Princeton took great pride in going into what they considered highly competitive, aggressive pursuits, jobs on Wall Street, on Madison Avenue, and at magazines such as *Time* and *Newsweek*. There was much fashionably brutish talk of what "dog-eat-dog" and "cutthroat" competition they found there; but in the rare instances when one of these young men died on the job, it was likely to be from choking on a chunk of Chateaubriand, while otherwise blissfully boiled, in an expense-account restaurant in Manhattan. How many would have gone to work, or stayed at work, on cutthroat Madison Avenue if there had been a 23 percent chance, nearly one chance in four, of dying from it? Gentlemen, we're having this little problem with chronic violent death . . .

And yet was there any basic way in which Pete (or Wally Schirra or Jim Lovell or any of the rest of them) was different from other college boys his age? There didn't seem to be, other than his love of flying. Pete's father was a Philadelphia stockbroker who in Pete's earliest years had a house in the Main Line suburbs, a limousine, and a chauffeur. The Depression eliminated the terrific brokerage business, the house, the car, and the servants; and by and by his parents were divorced and his father moved to Florida. Perhaps because his father had been an observation balloonist in the First World War—an adventurous business, since the balloons were prized targets of enemy aircraft—Pete was fascinated by flying. He went to Princeton on the Holloway Plan, a scholarship program left over from the Second World War in which a student trained with midshipmen from the Naval Academy during the summers and graduated with a commission in the Regular Navy. So Pete graduated, received his commission, married Jane, and headed off to Pensacola, Florida, for flight training.

Then came the difference, looking back on it.

A YOUNG MAN MIGHT go into military flight training believing that he was entering some sort of technical school in which he was simply going to acquire a certain set of skills. Instead, he found himself all at once enclosed in a fraternity. And in this fraternity, even though it was military, men were not rated by their outward rank as ensigns, lieutenants, commanders, or whatever. No, herein the world was divided into those who had it and those who did not. This quality, this *it*, was never named, however, nor was it talked about in any way.

As to just what this ineffable quality was . . . well, it obviously involved bravery. But it was not bravery in the simple sense of being willing to risk your life. The idea seemed to be that any fool could do that, if that was all that was required, just as any fool could throw away his life in the process. No, the idea here (in the all-enclosing fraternity) seemed to be that a man should have the ability to go up in a hurtling piece of machinery and put his hide on the line and then have the moxie, the reflexes, the experience, the coolness, to pull it back in the last yawning moment—and then to go up again *the next day*, and the next day, and every next day, even if the series should prove infinite—and, ultimately, in its best expression, do so in a cause that means something to thousands, to a people, a nation, to humanity, to God. Nor was there *a test* to show whether or not a pilot had this righteous quality. There was, instead, a seemingly infinite series of tests. A career in flying was like climbing one of those ancient Babylonian pyramids made up of a dizzy progression of steps and ledges, a zig-gurat, a pyramid extraordinarily high and steep; and the idea was to prove at every foot of the way up that pyramid that you were one of the elected and anointed ones who had *the right stuff* and could move higher and higher and even—ultimately, God willing, one day—that you might be able to join that special few at the very top, that elite who had the capacity to bring tears to men's eyes, the very Brotherhood of the Right Stuff itself.

None of this was to be mentioned, and yet it was acted out in a way that a young man could not fail to understand. When a new flight (i.e., a class) of trainees arrived at Pensacola, they were brought into an auditorium for a little lecture. An officer would tell them: "Take a look at the man on either side of you." Quite a few actually swiveled their heads this way and that, in the interest of appearing diligent. Then the officer would say: "One of the three of you is not going to make it!"—meaning, not get his wings. That was the opening theme, the *motif* of primary training. We already know that one-third of you do not have the right stuff—it only remains to find out who.

Furthermore, that was the way it turned out. At every level in one's progress up that staggeringly high pyramid, the world was once more divided into those men who had the right stuff to continue the climb and those who had to be *left behind* in the most obvious way. Some were eliminated in the course of the opening classroom work, as either not smart enough or not hardworking enough, and were left behind. Then came the basic flight instruction, in single-engine, propeller-driven trainers, and a few more—even though the military tried to make this stage easy—were washed out and left behind. Then came more demanding levels, one after the other, formation flying, instrument flying, jet training, all-weather flying, gunnery, and at each level more were washed out and left behind. By this point easily a third of the original candidates had been, indeed, eliminated . . . from the ranks of those who might prove to have the right stuff.

In the Navy, in addition to the stages that Air Force trainees went through, the neophyte always had waiting for him, out in the ocean, a certain grim gray slab; namely, the deck of an aircraft carrier; and with it perhaps the most difficult routine in military flying, carrier landings. He was shown films about it, he heard lectures about it, and he knew that carrier landings were hazardous. He first practiced touching down on the shape of a flight deck painted on an airfield. He was instructed to touch down and gun right off. This was safe enough—the shape didn't move, at least—but it could do terrible things to, let us say, the gyroscope of the soul. *That shape!—it's so damned small!* And more candidates were washed out and left behind. Then came the day, without warning, when those who remained were sent out over the ocean for the first of many days of reckoning with the slab. The first day was always a clear day with little wind and a calm sea. The carrier was so steady that it seemed, from up there in the air, to be resting on pilings, and the candidate usually made his first carrier landing successfully, with relief and even *élan*. Many young candidates looked like terrific aviators up to that very point—and it was not until they were actually standing on the carrier deck that they first began to wonder if they had the proper stuff, after all. In the training film the flight deck was a grand piece of gray geometry, perilous, to be sure, but an amazing abstract shape as one looks down upon it on the screen. And yet once the newcomer's two feet were on it . . . *Geometry*—my God, man, this is a . . . skillet! It *heaved*, it moved up and down underneath his feet, it pitched up, it pitched down, it rolled to port (this great beast *rolled!*) and it rolled to starboard, as the ship moved into the wind and, therefore, into the waves, and the wind kept sweeping across, sixty feet up in the air out in the open sea, and there were no railings whatsoever. This was a *skillet!*—a frying pan!—a short-order grill! —not gray but black, smeared with skid marks from one end to the other and glistening with pools of hydraulic fluid and the occasional jet-fuel slick, all of it still hot, sticky, greasy, runny, virulent from God knows what traumas—still ablaze!—consumed in detonations, explosions, flames, combustion, roars, shrieks, whines, blasts, horrible shudders, fracturing impacts, as little men in screaming red and yellow and purple and green shirts with black Mickey Mouse helmets over their ears skittered about on the surface as if for their very lives (you've said it now!), hooking fighter planes onto the catapult shuttles so that they can explode their afterburners and be slung off the deck in a red-mad fury with a *kaboom!* that pounds through the entire deck—a procedure that seems absolutely controlled, orderly, sublime, however, compared to what he is about to watch as aircraft return to the ship for what is known in the engineering stoicisms of the military as "recovery and arrest." To say that an F-4 was coming back onto this heaving barbecue from out of the sky at a speed of 135 knots . . . that might have been the truth in the training lecture, but it did not begin to get across the idea of what the newcomer saw from the deck itself, because it created the notion that perhaps the plane was gliding in. On the deck one knew differently! As the aircraft came closer and the carrier heaved on into the waves and the plane's speed did not diminish and the deck did not grow steady—indeed, it pitched up and down five or ten feet per greasy heave—one experienced a neural alarm that no lecture could have prepared him for: This is not an *airplane* coming toward me, it is a brick with some poor sonofabitch riding it (*someone much like myself!*), and it is not *gliding*, it is *falling*, a fifty-thousand-pound brick, headed not for a stripe on the deck but for *me*—and with a horrible *smash!* it hits the skillet, and with a blur of momentum as big as a freight train's it hurtles toward the far end of the deck—another blinding storm!—another roar as the pilot pushes the throttle up to full military power and another smear of rubber screams out over the skillet— and this is nominal!—quite okay!—for a wire stretched across the deck has grabbed the hook on the end of the plane as it hit the deck tail down, and the smash was the rest of the fifteen-ton brute slamming onto the deck, as it tripped up, so that it is now straining against the wire at full throttle, in case it hadn't held and the plane had "boltered" off the end of the deck and had to struggle up into the air again. And already the Mickey Mouse helmets are running toward the fiery monster . . .

And the candidate, looking on, begins to *feel* that great heaving sun-blazing deathboard of a deck wallowing in his own vestibular system—and suddenly he finds himself backed up against his own limits. He ends up going to the flight surgeon with so-called conversion symptoms. Overnight he develops blurred vision or numbness in his hands and feet or sinusitis so severe that he cannot tolerate changes in altitude. On one level the symptom is real. He really cannot see too well or use his fingers or stand the pain. But somewhere in his subconscious he knows it is a plea and a beg-off; he shows not the slightest concern (the flight surgeon notes) that the condition might be permanent and affect him in whatever life awaits him outside the arena of the right stuff.

Those who remained, those who qualified for carrier duty—and even more so those who later on qualified for *night* carrier duty—began to feel a bit like Gideon's warriors. *So many have been left behind!* The young warriors were now treated to a deathly sweet and quite unmentionable sight. They could gaze at length upon the crushed and wilted pariahs who had washed out. They could inspect those who did not have that righteous stuff.

The military did not have very merciful instincts. Rather than packing up these poor souls and sending them home, the Navy, like the Air Force and the Marines, would try to make use of them in some other role, such as flight controller. So the washout has to keep taking classes with the rest of his group, even though he can no longer touch an airplane. He sits there in the classes staring at sheets of paper with cataracts of sheer human mortification over his eyes while the rest steal looks at him . . . this man reduced to an ant, this untouchable, this poor sonofabitch. And in what test had he been found wanting? Why, it seemed to be nothing less than *manhood* itself. Naturally, this was never mentioned, either. Yet there it was. *Manliness, manhood, manly courage . . .* there was something ancient, primordial, irresistible about the challenge of this stuff, no matter what a sophisticated and rational age one might think he lived in.

Perhaps because it could not be talked about, the subject began to take on superstitious and even mystical outlines. A man either had it or he didn't! There was no such thing as having *most* of it. Moreover, it could blow at any seam. One day a man would be ascending the pyramid at a terrific clip, and the next—bingo! —he would reach his own limits in the most unexpected way. Conrad and Schirra met an Air Force pilot who had had a great pal at Tyndall Air Force Base in Florida. This man had been the budding ace of the training class; he had flown the hottest fighter-style trainer, the T-38, like a dream; and then he began the routine step of being checked out in the T-33. The T-33 was not nearly as hot an aircraft as the T-38; it was essentially the old P-80 jet fighter. It had an exceedingly small cockpit. The pilot could barely move his shoulders. It was the sort of airplane of which everybody said, "You don't get into it, you *wear* it." Once inside a T-33 cockpit this man, this budding ace, developed claustrophobia of the most paralyzing sort. He tried everything to overcome it. He even went to a psychiatrist, which was a serious mistake for a military officer if his superiors learned of it. But nothing worked. He was shifted over to flying jet transports, such as the C-135. Very demanding and necessary aircraft they were, too, and he was still spoken of as an excellent pilot. But as everyone knew—and, again, it was never explained in so many words—only those who were assigned to fighter squadrons, the "fighter jocks," as they called each other with a self-satisfied irony, remained in the true fraternity. Those assigned to transports were not humiliated like washouts—*somebody* had to fly those planes—nevertheless, they, too, had been *left behind* for lack of the right stuff.

Or a man could go for a routine physical one fine day, feeling like a million dollars, and be grounded for *fallen arches*. It happened!—just like that! (And try raising them.) Or for breaking his wrist and losing only *part* of its mobility. Or for a minor deterioration of eyesight, or for any of hundreds of reasons that would make no difference to a man in an ordinary occupation. As a result all fighter jocks began looking upon doctors as their natural enemies. Going to see a flight surgeon was a no-gain proposition; a pilot could only hold his own or lose in the doctor's office. To be grounded for a medical reason was no humiliation, looked at objectively. But it was a humiliation, nonetheless!—for it meant you no longer had that indefinable, unutterable, integral stuff. (It could blow at *any* seam.)

All the hot young fighter jocks began trying to test the limits themselves in a superstitious way. They were like believing Presbyterians of a century before who used to probe their own experience to see if they were truly among *the elect*. When a fighter pilot was in training, whether in the Navy or the Air Force, his superiors were continually spelling out strict rules for him, about the use of the aircraft and conduct in the sky. They repeatedly forbade so-called hotdog stunts, such as outside loops, buzzing, flat-hatting, hedgehopping and flying under bridges. But somehow one got the message that the man who truly *had* it could ignore those rules—not that he should make a point of it, but that he *could*—and that after all there was only one way to find out—and that in some strange unofficial way, peeking through his fingers, his instructor halfway expected him to challenge all the limits. They would give a lecture about how a pilot should never fly without a good solid breakfast—eggs, bacon, toast, and so forth—because if he tried to fly with his blood-sugar level too low, it could impair his alertness. Naturally, the next day every hot dog in the unit would get up and have a breakfast consisting of one cup of black coffee and take off and go up into a vertical climb until the weight of the ship exactly canceled out the upward pull of the engine and his air speed was zero, and he would hang there for one thick adrenal instant—and then fall like a rock, until one of three things happened: he keeled over nose first and regained his aerodynamics and all was well, he went into a spin and fought his way out of it, or he went into a spin and had to eject or crunch it, which was always supremely possible.

Likewise, "hassling"—mock dogfighting—was strictly forbidden, and so naturally young fighter jocks could hardly wait to go up in, say, a pair of F-100s and start the duel by making a pass at each other at 800 miles an hour, the winner being the pilot who could slip in behind the other one and get locked in on his tail ("wax his tail"), and it was not uncommon for some eager jock to try too tight an outside turn and have his engine flame out, whereupon, unable to restart it, he has to eject . . . and he shakes his fist at the victor as he floats down by parachute and his half-a-million-dollar aircraft goes *kaboom!* on the palmetto grass or the desert floor, and he starts thinking about how he can get together with the other guy back at the base in time for the two of them to get their stories straight before the investigation: "I don't know what happened, sir. I was pulling up after a target run, and it just flamed out on me." Hassling was forbidden, and hassling that led to the destruction of an aircraft was a serious court-martial offense, and the man's superiors knew that the engine hadn't *just flamed out*, but every unofficial impulse on the base seemed to be saying: "Hell, we wouldn't give you a nickel for a pilot who hasn't done some crazy rat-racing like that. It's all part of the right stuff."

The other side of this impulse showed up in the reluctance of the young jocks to admit it when they had maneuvered themselves into a bad corner they couldn't get out of. There were two reasons why a fighter pilot hated to declare an emergency. First, it triggered a complex and very public chain of events at the field: all other incoming flights were held up, including many of one's comrades who were probably low on fuel; the fire trucks came trundling out to the runway like yellow toys (as seen from way up there), the better to illustrate one's hapless state; and the bureaucracy began to crank up the paper monster for the investigation that always followed. And second, to declare an emergency, one first had to reach that conclusion in his own mind, which to the young pilot was the same as saying: "A minute ago I still *had* it—now I need your help!" To have a bunch of young fighter pilots up in the air thinking this way used to drive flight controllers crazy. They would see a ship beginning to drift off the radar, and they couldn't rouse the pilot on the microphone for anything other than a few meaningless mumbles, and they would know he was probably out there with engine failure at a low altitude, trying to reignite by lowering his auxiliary generator rig, which had a little propeller that was supposed to spin in the slipstream like a child's pinwheel.

"Whiskey Kilo Two Eight, do you want to declare an emergency?"

This would rouse him!—to say: "Negative, negative, Whiskey Kilo Two Eight is not declaring an emergency."

Kaboom. Believers in the right stuff would rather crash and burn.

ONE FINE DAY, after he had joined a fighter squadron, it would dawn on the young pilot exactly how the losers in the great fraternal competition were now being left behind. Which is to say, not by instructors or other superiors or by failures at prescribed levels of competence, but by death. At this point the essence of the enterprise would begin to dawn on him. Slowly, step by step, the ante had been raised until he was now involved in what was surely the grimmest and grandest gamble of manhood. Being a fighter pilot—for that matter, simply taking off in a single-engine jet fighter of the Century series, such as an F-102, or any of the military's other marvelous bricks with fins on them—presented a man, on a perfectly sunny day, with more ways to get himself killed than his wife and children could imagine in their wildest fears. If he was barreling down the runway at two hundred miles an hour, completing the takeoff run, and the board started lighting up red, should he (a) abort the takeoff (and try to wrestle with the monster, which was gorged with jet fuel, out in the sand beyond the end of the runway) or (b) eject (and hope that the goddamned human cannonball trick works at zero altitude and he doesn't shatter an elbow or a kneecap on the way out) or (c) continue the takeoff and deal with the problem aloft (knowing full well that the ship may be on fire and therefore seconds away from exploding)? He would have one second to sort out the options and act, and this kind of little workaday decision came up all the time. Occasionally a man would look coldly at the binary problem he was now confronting every day—Right Stuff/Death—and decide it wasn't worth it and voluntarily shift over to transports or reconnaissance or whatever. And his comrades would wonder, for a day or so, what evil virus had invaded his soul . . . as they left him behind. More often, however, the reverse would happen. Some college graduate would enter Navy aviation through the Reserves, simply as an alternative to the Army draft, fully intending to return to civilian life, to some waiting profession or family business; would become involved in the obsessive business of ascending the ziggurat pyramid of flying; and, at the end of his enlistment, would astound everyone back home and very likely himself as well by signing up for another one. What on earth got into him? He couldn't explain it. After all, the very words for it had been amputated. A Navy study showed that two-thirds of the fighter pilots who were rated in the top rungs of their groups—i.e., the hottest young pilots—reenlisted when the time came, and practically all were college graduates. By this point, a young fighter jock was like the preacher in *Moby Dick* who climbs up into the pulpit on a rope ladder and then pulls the ladder up behind him; except the pilot could not use the words necessary to express the vital lessons. Civilian life, and even home and hearth, now seemed not only far away but far *below*, back down many levels of the pyramid of the right stuff.

A fighter pilot soon found he wanted to associate only with other fighter pilots. Who else could understand the nature of the little proposition (right stuff/death) they were all dealing with? And what other subject could compare with it? It was riveting! To talk about it in so many words was forbidden, of course. The very words *death, danger, bravery, fear* were not to be uttered except in the occasional specific instance or for ironic effect. Nevertheless, the subject could be adumbrated in *code* or *by example*. Hence the endless evenings of pilots huddled together talking about flying. On these long and drunken evenings (the bane of their family life) certain theorems would be propounded and demonstrated—and all by *code* and *example*. One theorem was: There are no *accidents* and no fatal flaws in the machines; there are only pilots with the wrong stuff. (I.e., blind Fate can't kill me.) When Bud Jennings crashed and burned in the swamps at Jacksonville, the other pilots in Pete Conrad's squadron said: *How could he have been so stupid?* It turned out that Jennings had gone up in the SNJ with his cockpit canopy opened in a way that was expressly forbidden in the manual, and carbon monoxide had been sucked in from the exhaust, and he passed out and crashed. All agreed that Bud Jennings was a good guy and a good pilot, but his epitaph on the ziggurat was: *How could he have been so stupid?* This seemed shocking at first, but by the time Conrad had reached the end of that bad string at Pax River, he was capable of his own corollary to the theorem: viz., no single factor ever killed a pilot; there was always a chain of mistakes. But what about Ted Whelan, who fell like a rock from 8,100 feet when his parachute failed? Well, the parachute was merely part of the chain: first, someone should have caught the structural defect that resulted in the hydraulic leak that triggered the emergency; second, Whelan did not check out his seat-parachute rig, and the drogue failed to separate the main parachute from the seat; but even after those two mistakes, Whelan had fifteen or twenty seconds, as he fell, to disengage himself from the seat and open the parachute manually. Why just stare at the scenery coming up to smack you in the face! And everyone nodded. (He failed—but I wouldn't have!) Once the theorem and the corollary were understood, the Navy's statistics about one in every four Navy aviators dying meant nothing. The figures were averages, and averages applied to those with average stuff.

A riveting subject, especially if it were one's own hide that was on the line. Every evening at bases all over America, there were military pilots huddled in officers clubs eagerly cutting the right stuff up in coded slices so they could talk about it. What more compelling topic of conversation was there in the world? In the Air Force there were even pilots who would ask the tower for priority landing clearance so that they could make the beer call on time, at 4 p.m. sharp, at the Officers Club. They would come right out and state the reason. The drunken rambles began at four and sometimes went on for ten or twelve hours. Such conversations! They diced that righteous stuff up into little bits, bowed ironically to it, stumbled blindfolded around it, groped, lurched, belched, staggered, bawled, sang, roared, and feinted at it with self-deprecating humor. Nevertheless!—they never mentioned it by name. No, they used the approved codes, such as: "Like a jerk I got myself into a hell of a corner today." They told of how they "lucked out of it." To get across the extreme peril of his exploit, one would use certain oblique cues. He would say, "I looked over at Robinson"—who would be known to the listeners as a non-com who sometimes rode backseat to read radar—"and he wasn't talking any more, he was just staring at the radar, like this, giving it that *zombie* look. Then I *knew* I was in trouble!" Beautiful! Just right! For it would also be known to the listeners that the non-coms advised one another: "*Never* fly with a lieutenant. *Avoid* captains and majors. Hell, man, do yourself a favor: don't fly with anybody below colonel." Which in turn said: "Those young bucks shoot dice with death!" And yet once in the air the non-com had his own standards. He was determined to remain as outwardly cool as the pilot, so that when the pilot did something that truly petrified him, he would say nothing; instead, he would turn silent, catatonic, like a zombie. Perfect! *Zombie.* There you had it, compressed into a single word all of the foregoing. I'm a hell of a pilot! I shoot dice with death! And now all you fellows know it! And I haven't spoken of that unspoken stuff even once!

The talking and drinking began at the beer call, and then the boys would break for dinner and come back afterward and get more wasted and more garrulous or else more quietly fried, drinking good cheap PX booze until 2 a.m. The night was young! Why not get the cars and go out for a little proficiency run? It seemed that every fighter jock thought himself an ace driver, and he would do anything to obtain a hot car, especially a sports car, and the drunker he was, the more convinced he would be about his driving skills, as if the right stuff, being indivisible, carried over into any enterprise whatsoever, under any conditions. A little proficiency run, boys! (There's only one way to find out!) And they would roar off in close formation from, say, Nellis Air Force Base, down Route 15, into Las Vegas, barreling down the highway, rat-racing, sometimes four abreast, jockeying for position, piling into the most listless curve in the desert flats as if they were trying to root each other out of the groove at the Rebel 500—and then bursting into downtown Las Vegas with a rude fraternal roar like the Hell's Angels—and the natives chalked it up to youth and drink and the bad element that the Air Force attracted. They knew nothing about the right stuff, of course.

More fighter pilots died in automobiles than in airplanes. Fortunately, there was always some kindly soul up the chain to certify the papers "line of duty," so that the widow could get a better break on the insurance. That was okay and only proper because somehow the system itself had long ago said *Skol!* and *Quite right!* to the military cycle of Flying & Drinking and Drinking & Driving, as if there were no other way. Every young fighter jock knew the feeling of getting two or three hours' sleep and then waking up at 5:30 a.m. and having a few cups of coffee, a few cigarettes, and then carting his poor quivering liver out to the field for another day of flying. There were those who arrived not merely hungover but still drunk, slapping oxygen tank cones over their faces and trying to burn the alcohol out of their systems, and then going up, remarking later: "I don't *advise* it, you understand, but it *can* be done." (Provided you have the right stuff, you miserable pudknocker.)

AIR FORCE AND NAVY airfields were usually on barren or marginal stretches of land and would have looked especially bleak and Low Rent to an ordinary individual in the chilly light of dawn. But to a young pilot there was an inexplicable bliss to coming out to the flight line while the sun was just beginning to cook up behind the rim of the horizon, so that the whole field was still in shadow and the ridges in the distance were in silhouette and the flight line was a monochrome of Exhaust Fume Blue, and every little red light on top of the water towers or power stanchions looked dull, shriveled, congealed, and the runway lights, which were still on, looked faded, and even the landing lights on a fighter that had just landed and was taxiing in were no longer dazzling, as they would be at night, and looked instead like shriveled gobs of candlepower out there—and yet it was beautiful, exhilarating!—for he was revved up with adrenalin, anxious to take off before the day broke, to burst up into the sunlight over the ridges before all those thousands of comatose souls down there, still dead to the world, snug in home and hearth, even came to their senses. To take off in an F-100F at dawn and cut on the afterburner and hurtle twenty-five thousand feet up into the sky in thirty seconds, so suddenly that you felt not like a bird but like a trajectory, yet with full control, full control of *four tons* of thrust, all of which flowed from your will and through your fingertips, with the huge engine right beneath you, so close that it was as if you were riding it bareback, until all at once you were supersonic, an event registered on earth by a tremendous cracking boom that shook windows, but up here only by the fact that you now felt utterly free of the earth—to describe it, even to wife, child, near ones and dear ones, seemed impossible. So the pilot kept it to himself, along with an even more indescribable . . . an even more sinfully inconfessable . . . feeling of superiority, appropriate to him and to his kind, lone bearers of the right stuff.

From *up here* at dawn the pilot looked down upon poor hopeless Las Vegas (or Yuma, Corpus Christi, Meridian, San Bernardino, or Dayton) and began to wonder: How can all of them down there, those poor souls who will soon be waking up and trudging out of their minute rectangles and inching along their little noodle highways toward whatever slots and grooves make up their everyday lives —how could they live like that, with such earnestness, if they had the faintest idea of what it was like up here in this righteous zone?

But of course! Not only the washed-out, grounded, and dead pilots had been left behind—but also all of those millions of sleepwalking souls who never even attempted the great gamble. The entire world below . . . *left behind*. Only at this point can one begin to understand just how big, how titanic, the ego of the military pilot could be. The world was used to enormous egos in artists, actors, entertainers of all sorts, in politicians, sports figures, and even journalists, because they had such familiar and convenient ways to show them off. But that slim young man over there in uniform, with the enormous watch on his wrist and the withdrawn look on his face, that young officer who is so shy that he can't even open his mouth unless the subject is flying—that young pilot—well, my friends, his ego is even *bigger!*—so big, it's *breathtaking!* Even in the 1950's it was difficult for civilians to comprehend such a thing, but *all* military officers and many enlisted men tended to feel superior to civilians. It was really quite ironic, given the fact that for a good thirty years the rising business classes in the cities had been steering their sons away from the military, as if from a bad smell, and the officer corps had never been held in lower esteem. Well, career officers returned the contempt in trumps. They looked upon themselves as men who lived by higher standards of behavior than civilians, as men who were the bearers and protectors of the most important values of American life, who maintained a sense of discipline while civilians abandoned themselves to hedonism, who maintained a sense of honor while civilians lived by opportunism and greed. Opportunism and greed: there you had your much-vaunted corporate business world. Khrushchev was right about one thing: when it came time to hang the capitalist West, an American businessman would sell him the rope. When the showdown came—and the showdowns always came—not all the wealth in the world or all the sophisticated nuclear weapons and radar and missile systems it could buy would take the place of those who had the uncritical willingness to face danger, those who, in short, had the right stuff.

In fact, the feeling was so righteous, so exalted, it could become religious. Civilians seldom understood this, either. There was no one to teach them. It was no longer the fashion for serious writers to describe the glories of war. Instead, they dwelt upon its horrors, often with cynicism or disgust. It was left to the occasional pilot with a literary flair to provide a glimpse of the pilot's self-conception in its heavenly or spiritual aspect. When a pilot named Robert Scott flew his P-43 over Mount Everest, quite a feat at the time, he brought his hand up and snapped a salute to his fallen adversary. He thought he had *defeated* the mountain, surmounting all the forces of nature that had made it formidable. And why not? "God is my co-pilot," he said—that became the title of his book—and he meant it. So did the most gifted of all the pilot authors, the Frenchman Antoine de Saint-Exupéry. As he gazed down upon the world . . . from up there . . . during transcontinental flights, the good Saint-Ex saw civilization as a series of tiny fragile patches clinging to the otherwise barren rock of Earth. He felt like a lonely sentinel, a protector of those vulnerable little cases, ready to lay down his life in their behalf, if necessary; a saint, in short, true to his name, flying up here at the right hand of God. The good Saint-Ex! And he was not the only one. He was merely the one who put it into words most beautifully and anointed himself before the altar of the right stuff.

THERE WERE MANY pilots in their thirties who, to the consternation of their wives, children, mothers, fathers, and employers, volunteered to go active in the reserves and fly in combat in the Korean War. In godforsaken frozen Chosen! But it was simple enough. Half of them were fliers who had trained during the Second World War and had never seen combat. It was well understood—and never said, of course—that no one could reach the top of the pyramid without going into combat.

The morale of foot soldiers in the Korean War was so bad it actually reached the point where officers were prodding men forward with gun barrels and bayonets. But in the air—it was Fighter Jock Heaven! Using F-86s mainly, the Air Force was producing aces, pilots who had shot down five planes or more, as fast as the Koreans and Chinese could get their Soviet MiG-15s up to fight them. By the time the fighting was stopped, there were thirty-eight Air Force aces, and they had accounted for a total of 299.5 kills. Only fifty-six F-86s were lost. High spirits these lads had. They chronicled their adventures with a good creamy romanticism such as nobody in flying had treated himself to since the days of Lufbery, Frank Luke, and von Richthofen in the First World War. Colonel Harrison R. Thyng, who shot down five MiGs in Korea (and eight German and Japanese planes in the Second World War), glowed like Excalibur when he described his Fourth Fighter-Interceptor Wing: "Like olden knights the F-86 pilots ride up over North Korea to the Yalu River, the sun glinting off silver aircraft, contrails streaming behind, as they challenge the numerically superior enemy to come on up and fight." Lances and plumes! *I'm a knight!* Come on up and fight! Why hold back! Knights of the Right Stuff!

When a pilot named Gus Grissom (whom Conrad, Schirra, Lovell, and the others would meet later on) first went to Korea, the Air Force used to take the F-86 jocks out to the field before dawn, in the dark, in buses, and the pilots who had not been shot at by a MiG in air-to-air combat had to stand up. At first Grissom couldn't believe it and then he couldn't bear it—those bastards sitting down were *the only ones with the right stuff!* The next morning, as they rumbled out there in the dark, he was sitting down. He had gone up north toward the Yalu on the first day and had it out with some howling supersonic Chinee just so he could have a seat on the bus. Even at the level of combat, the main thing was not to be *left behind.*

Combat had its own infinite series of tests, and one of the greatest sins was "chattering" or "jabbering" on the radio. The combat frequency was to be kept clear of all but strategically essential messages, and all unenlightening comments were regarded as evidence of funk, of the wrong stuff. A Navy pilot (in legend, at any rate) began shouting, "I've got a MiG at zero! A MiG at zero!"—meaning that it had maneuvered in behind him and was locked in on his tail. An irritated voice cut in and said, "Shut up and die like an aviator." One had to be a Navy pilot to appreciate the final nuance. A good Navy pilot was a real *aviator*; in the Air Force they merely had pilots and not precisely the proper stuff.

No, the tests were never-ending. And in the periods between wars a man's past successes in combat did not necessarily keep him at the top of the heavenly pyramid. By the late 1950's there was yet another plateau to strive for. On that plateau were men who had flown in combat in the Second World War or Korea and had then gone on to become test pilots in the new age of jet and rocket engines. Not every combat pilot could make the climb. Two of the great aces of the Second World War, Richard I. Bong and Don Gentile, tried it but didn't have the patience for the job. They only wanted to light the afterburner and poke holes in the sky; and presently they were just part of combat history. Of course, by now, thanks to the accident of age, you began to find young men who had reached the exalted level of test pilot without ever having had a chance to fight in combat. One was Pete Conrad, who was just graduating, with the survivors of Group 20, to the status of full-fledged test pilot at Pax River. Like every Navy test pilot, Conrad was proud of Pax River and its reputation. Out loud every true Navy aviator insisted that Pax River was the place . . . and inwardly knew it really wasn't. For every military pilot knew where the apex of the great ziggurat was located. You could point it out on a map. The place was Edwards Air Force

Base in the high desert 150 miles northeast of Los Angeles. Everyone knew who resided there, too, although their actual status was never put into words. Not only that, everyone knew the name of the individual who ranked foremost in the Olympus, the ace of all the aces, as it were, among the true brothers of the right stuff.

3

≡

YEAGER

Anyone who travels very much on airlines in the United States soon gets to know the voice of *the airline pilot* . . . coming over the intercom . . . with a particular drawl, a particular folksiness, a particular down-home calmness that is so exaggerated it begins to parody itself (nevertheless!—it's reassuring) . . . the voice that tells you, as the airliner is caught in thunderheads and goes bolting up and down a thousand feet at a single gulp, to check your seat belts because "it might get a little choppy" . . . the voice that tells you (on a flight from Phoenix preparing for its final approach into Kennedy Airport, New York, just after dawn): "Now, folks, uh . . . this is the captain . . . ummmm . . . We've got a little ol' red light up here on the control panel that's tryin' to tell us that the *landin'* gears're not . . . uh . . . *lock*in' into position when we lower 'em . . . Now . . . *I* don't believe that little ol' red light knows what it's *talk*in' about—I believe it's that little ol' red *light* that iddn' workin' right" . . . faint chuckle, long pause, as if to say, *I'm not even sure all this is really worth going into—still, it may amuse you* . . . "But . . . I guess to play it by the rules, we oughta *humor* that little ol' light . . . so we're gonna take her down to about, oh, two or three hundred feet over the runway at Kennedy, and the folks down there on the ground are gonna see if they caint give us a *visual* inspection of those ol' landin' gears"—with which he is obviously on intimate ol'-buddy terms, as with every other working part of this mighty ship—"and if I'm right . . . they're gonna tell us everything is copacetic all the way aroun' an' we'll jes take her on in" . . . and, after a couple of low passes over the field, the voice returns: "Well, folks, those folks down there on the ground—it must be too early for 'em or somethin' —I 'spect they still got the *sleep*ers in their eyes . . . 'cause they say they caint tell if those ol' landin' gears are all the way down or not . . . But, you know, up here in the cockpit we're convinced they're all the way down, so we're jes gonna take her on in . . . And oh" . . . *(I almost forgot)* . . . "while we take a little swing out over the ocean an' empty some of that surplus fuel we're not gonna be needin' anymore—that's what you might be seein' comin' out of the wings—our lovely little ladies . . . if they'll be so kind . . . they're gonna go up and down the aisles and show you how we do what we call 'assumin' the position' " . . . another faint chuckle (*We do this so often, and it's so much fun, we even have a funny little name for it*) . . . and the stewardesses, a bit grimmer, by the looks of them, than *that voice*, start telling the passengers to take their glasses off and take the ballpoint pens and other sharp objects out of their pockets, and they show them *the position*, with the head lowered . . . while down on the field at Kennedy the little yellow emergency trucks start roaring across the field—and even though in your pounding heart and your sweating palms and your broiling brainpan you *know* this is a critical moment in your life, you still can't quite bring yourself to *believe* it, because if it were . . . how could *the captain*, the man who knows the actual situation most intimately . . . how could he keep on drawlin' and chucklin' and driftin' and lollygaggin' in that particular voice of his—

Well!—who doesn't know that voice! And who can forget it!—even after he is proved right and the emergency is over.

That particular voice may sound vaguely Southern or Southwestern, but it is specifically Appalachian in origin. It originated in the mountains of West Virginia, in the coal country, in Lincoln County, so far up in the hollows that, as the saying went, "they had to pipe in daylight." In the late 1940's and early 1950's this up-hollow voice drifted down from on high, from over the high desert of California, down, down, down, from the upper reaches of the Brotherhood into all phases of American aviation. It was amazing. It was *Pygmalion* in reverse. Military pilots and then, soon, airline pilots, pilots from Maine and Massachusetts and the Dakotas and Oregon and everywhere else, began to talk in that poker-hollow West Virginia drawl, or as close to it as they could bend their native accents. It was the drawl of the most righteous of all the possessors of the right stuff: Chuck Yeager.

Yeager had started out as the equivalent, in the Second World War, of the legendary Frank Luke of the 27th Aero Squadron in the First. Which is to say, he was the boondocker, the boy from the back country, with only a high-school education, no credentials, no cachet or polish of any sort, who took off the feed-store overalls and put on a uniform and climbed into an airplane and lit up the skies over Europe.

Yeager grew up in Hamlin, West Virginia, a town on the Mud River not far from Nitro, Hurricane Whirlwind, Salt Rock, Mud, Sod, Crum, Leet, Dollie, Ruth, and Alum Creek. His father was a gas driller (drilling for natural gas in the coalfields), his older brother was a gas driller, and he would have been a gas driller had he not enlisted in the Army Air Force in 1941 at the age of eighteen. In 1943, at twenty, he became a flight officer, i.e., a non-com who was allowed to fly, and went to England to fly fighter planes over France and Germany. Even in the tumult of the war Yeager was somewhat puzzling to a lot of other pilots. He was a short, wiry, but muscular little guy with dark curly hair and a tough-looking face that seemed (to strangers) to be saying: "You best not be lookin' me in the eye, you peckerwood, or I'll put four more holes in your nose." But that wasn't what was puzzling. What was puzzling was the way Yeager talked. He seemed to talk with some older forms of English elocution, syntax, and conjugation that had been preserved uphollow in the Appalachians. There were people up there who never said they disapproved of anything, they said: "I don't hold with it." In the present tense they were willing to *help* out, like anyone else; but in the past tense they only *holped*. "H'it weren't nothin' I hold with, but I holped him out with it, anyways."

In his first eight missions, at the age of twenty, Yeager shot down two German fighters. On his ninth he was shot down over German-occupied French territory, suffering flak wounds; he bailed out, was picked up by the French underground, which smuggled him across the Pyrenees into Spain disguised as a peasant. In Spain he was jailed briefly, then released, whereupon he made it back to England and returned to combat during the Allied invasion of France. On October 12, 1944, Yeager took on and shot down five German fighter planes in succession. On November 6, flying a propeller-driven P-51 Mustang, he shot down one of the new jet fighters the Germans had developed, the Messerschmitt-262, and damaged two more, and on November 20 he shot down four FW-190s. It was a true Frank Lukestyle display of warrior fury and personal prowess. By the end of the war he had thirteen and a half kills. He was twenty-two years old.

In 1946 and 1947 Yeager was trained as a test pilot at Wright Field in Dayton. He amazed his instructors with his ability at stunt-team flying, not to mention the unofficial business of hassling. That plus his up-hollow drawl had everybody saying, "He's a natural-born stick 'n' rudder man." Nevertheless, there was something extraordinary about it when a man so young, with so little experience in flight test, was selected to go to Muroc Field in California for the X-1 project.

Muroc was up in the high elevations of the Mojave Desert. It looked like some fossil landscape that had long since been left behind by the rest of terrestrial evolution. It was full of huge dry lake beds, the biggest being Rogers Lake. Other than sagebrush the only vegetation was Joshua trees, twisted freaks of the plant world that looked like a cross between cactus and Japanese bonsai. They had a dark petrified green color and horribly crippled branches. At dusk the Joshua trees stood out in silhouette on the fossil wasteland like some arthritic nightmare. In the summer the temperature went up to 110 degrees as a matter of course, and the dry lake beds were covered in sand, and there would be windstorms and sandstorms right out of a Foreign Legion movie. At night it would drop to near freezing, and in December it would start raining, and the dry lakes would fill up with a few inches of water, and some sort of putrid prehistoric shrimps would work their way up from out of the ooze, and sea gulls would come flying in a hundred miles or more from the ocean, over the mountains, to gobble up these squirming little throwbacks. A person had to see it to believe it: flocks of sea gulls wheeling around in the air out in the middle of the high desert in the dead of winter and grazing on antediluvian crustaceans in the primordial ooze.

When the wind blew the few inches of water back and forth across the lake beds, they became absolutely smooth and level. And when the water evaporated in the spring, and the sun baked the ground hard, the lake beds became the greatest natural landing fields ever discovered, and also the biggest, with miles of room for error. That was highly desirable, given the nature of the enterprise at Muroc.

Besides the wind, sand, tumbleweed, and Joshua trees, there was nothing at Muroc except for two quonset-style hangars, side by side, a couple of gasoline pumps, a single concrete runway, a few tarpaper shacks, and some tents. The officers stayed in the shacks marked "barracks," and lesser souls stayed in the tents and froze all night and fried all day. Every road into the property had a guardhouse on it manned by soldiers. The enterprise the Army had undertaken in this godforsaken place was the development of supersonic jet and rocket planes.

At the end of the war the Army had discovered that the Germans not only had the world's first jet fighter but also a rocket plane that had gone 596 miles an hour in tests. Just after the war a British jet, the Gloster Meteor, jumped the official world speed record from 469 to 606 in a single day. The next great plateau would be Mach 1, the speed of sound, and the Army Air Force considered it crucial to achieve it first.

The speed of sound, Mach 1, was known (thanks to the work of the physicist Ernst Mach) to vary at different altitudes, temperatures, and wind speeds. On a calm 60-degree day at sea level it was about 760 miles an hour, while at 40,000 feet, where the temperature would be at least sixty below, it was about 660 miles an hour. Evil and baffling things happened in the transonic zone, which began at about .7 Mach. Wind tunnels choked out at such velocities. Pilots who approached the speed of sound in dives reported that the controls would lock or "freeze" or even alter their normal functions. Pilots had crashed and died because they couldn't budge the stick. Just last year Geoffrey de Havilland, son of the famous British aircraft designer and builder, had tried to take one of his father's DH 108s to Mach 1. The ship started buffeting and then disintegrated, and he was killed. This led engineers to speculate that the g-forces became infinite at Mach 1, causing the aircraft to implode. They started talking about "the sonic wall" and "the sound barrier."

So this was the task that a handful of pilots, engineers, and mechanics had at Muroc. The place was utterly primitive, nothing but bare bones, bleached tarpaulins, and corrugated tin rippling in the heat with caloric waves; and for an ambitious young pilot it was perfect. Muroc seemed like an outpost on the dome of the world, open only to a righteous few, closed off to the rest of humanity, including even the Army Air Force brass of command control, which was at Wright Field. The commanding officer at Muroc was only a colonel, and his superiors at Wright did not relish junkets to the Muroc rat shacks in the first place. But to pilots this prehistoric throwback of an airfield became . . . shrimp heaven! the rat-shack plains of Olympus!

Low Rent Septic Tank Perfection . . . yes; and not excluding those traditional essentials for the blissful hot young pilot: Flying & Drinking and Drinking & Driving.

Just beyond the base, to the southwest, there was a rickety wind-blown 1930's-style establishment called Pancho's Fly Inn, owned, run, and bartended by a woman named Pancho Barnes. Pancho Barnes wore tight white sweaters and tight pants, after the mode of Barbara Stanwyck in *Double Indemnity*. She was only forty-one when Yeager arrived at Muroc, but her face was so weatherbeaten, had so many hard miles on it, that she looked older, especially to the young pilots at the base. She also shocked the pants off them with her vulcanized tongue. Everybody she didn't like was an old bastard or a sonofabitch. People she liked were old bastards and sonsabitches, too. "I tol' 'at ol' bastard to get 'is ass on over here and I'd g'im a drink." But Pancho Barnes was anything but Low Rent. She was the granddaughter of the man who designed the old Mount Lowe cable-car system, Thaddeus S. C. Lowe. Her maiden name was Florence Leontine Lowe. She was brought up in San Marino, which adjoined Pasadena and was one of Los Angeles' wealthiest suburbs, and her first husband—she was married four times—

was the pastor of the Pasadena Episcopal Church, the Rev. C. Rankin Barnes. Mrs. Barnes seemed to have few of the conventional community interests of a Pasadena matron. In the late 1920's, by boat and plane, she ran guns for Mexican revolutionaries and picked up the nickname Pancho. In 1930 she broke Amelia Earhart's airspeed record for women. Then she barnstormed around the country as the featured performer of "Pancho Barnes's Mystery Circus of the Air." She always greeted her public in jodhpurs and riding boots, a flight jacket, a white scarf, and a white sweater that showed off her terrific Barbara Stanwyck chest. Pancho's desert Fly Inn had an airstrip, a swimming pool, a dude ranch corral, plenty of acreage for horseback riding, a big old guest house for the lodgers, and a connecting building that was the bar and restaurant. In the barroom the floors, the tables, the chairs, the walls, the beams, the bar were of the sort known as extremely weatherbeaten, and the screen doors kept banging. Nobody putting together such a place for a movie about flying in the old days would ever dare make it as dilapidated and generally go-to-hell as it actually was. Behind the bar were many pictures of airplanes and pilots, lavishly autographed and inscribed, badly framed and crookedly hung. There was an old piano that had been dried out and cracked to the point of hopeless desiccation. On a good night a huddle of drunken aviators could be heard trying to bang, slosh, and navigate their way through old Cole Porter tunes. On average nights the tunes were not that good to start with. When the screen door banged and a man walked through the door into the saloon, every eye in the place checked him out. If he wasn't known as somebody who had something to do with flying at Muroc, he would be eyed like some lame goddamned mouseshit sheepherder from *Shane*.

The plane the Air Force wanted to break the sound barrier with was called the X-1. The Bell Aircraft Corporation had built it under an Army contract. The core of the ship was a rocket of the type first developed by a young Navy inventor, Robert Truax, during the war. The fuselage was shaped like a 50-caliber bullet— an object that was known to go supersonic smoothly. Military pilots seldom drew major test assignments; they went to highly paid civilians working for the aircraft corporations. The prime pilot for the X-1 was a man whom Bell regarded as the best of the breed. This man looked like a movie star. He looked like a pilot from out of *Hell's Angels*. And on top of everything else there was his name: Slick Goodlin.

The idea in testing the X-1 was to nurse it carefully into the transonic zone, up to seven-tenths, eight-tenths, nine-tenths the speed of sound (.7 Mach, .8 Mach, .9 Mach) before attempting the speed of sound itself, Mach 1, even though Bell and the Army already knew the X-1 had the rocket power to go to Mach 1 and beyond, if there *was* any *beyond*. The consensus of aviators and engineers, after Geoffrey de Havilland's death, was that the speed of sound was an absolute, like the firmness of the earth. The sound barrier was a farm you could buy in the sky. So Slick Goodlin began to probe the transonic zone in the X-1, going up to .8 Mach. Every time he came down he'd have a riveting tale to tell. The buffeting, it was so fierce—and the listeners, their imaginations aflame, could practically see poor Geoffrey de Havilland disintegrating in midair. And the goddamned aerodynamics—and the listeners got a picture of a man in ballroom pumps skidding across a sheet of ice, pursued by bears. A controversy arose over just how much bonus Slick Goodlin should receive for assaulting the dread Mach 1 itself. Bonuses for contract test pilots were not unusual; but the figure of

$150,000 was now bruited about. The Army balked, and Yeager got the job. He took it for $283 a month, or $3,396 a year; which is to say, his regular Army captain's pay.

The only trouble they had with Yeager was in holding him back. On his first powered flight in the X-1 he immediately executed an unauthorized zero-g roll with a full load of rocket fuel, then stood the ship on its tail and went up to .85 Mach in a vertical climb, also unauthorized. On subsequent flights, at speeds between .85 Mach and .9 Mach, Yeager ran into most known airfoil problems— loss of elevator, aileron, and rudder control, heavy trim pressures, Dutch rolls, pitching and buffeting, the lot—yet was convinced, after edging over .9 Mach, that this would all get better, not worse, as you reached Mach 1. The attempt to push beyond Mach 1—"breaking the sound barrier"—was set for October 14, 1947. Not being an engineer, Yeager didn't believe the "barrier" existed.

O CTOBER 14 WAS A TUESDAY. On Sunday evening, October 12, Chuck Yeager dropped in at Pancho's, along with his wife. She was a brunette named Glennis, whom he had met in California while he was in training, and she was such a number, so striking, he had the inscription "Glamorous Glennis" written on the nose of his P-51 in Europe and, just a few weeks back, on the X-1 itself. Yeager didn't go to Pancho's and knock back a few because two days later the big test was coming up. Nor did he knock back a few because it was the weekend. No, he knocked back a few because night had come and he was a pilot at Muroc. In keeping with the military tradition of Flying & Drinking, that was what you did, for no other reason than that the sun had gone down. You went to Pancho's and knocked back a few and listened to the screen doors banging and to other aviators torturing the piano and the nation's repertoire of Familiar Favorites and to lone-some mouse-turd strangers wandering in through the banging doors and to Pancho classifying the whole bunch of them as old bastards and miserable peck-erwoods. That was what you did if you were a pilot at Muroc and the sun went down.

So about eleven Yeager got the idea that it would be a hell of a kick if he and Glennis saddled up a couple of Pancho's dude-ranch horses and went for a romp, a little rat race, in the moonlight. This was in keeping with the military tradition of Flying & Drinking and Drinking & Driving, except that this was prehistoric Muroc and you rode horses. So Yeager and his wife set off on a little proficiency run at full gallop through the desert in the moonlight amid the arthritic silhou-ettes of the Joshua trees. Then they start racing back to the corral, with Yeager in the lead and heading for the gateway. Given the prevailing conditions, it being nighttime, at Pancho's, and his head being filled with a black sandstorm of many badly bawled songs and vulcanized oaths, he sees too late that the gate has been closed. Like many a hard-driving midnight pilot before him, he does not realize that he is not equally gifted in the control of all forms of locomotion. He and the horse hit the gate, and he goes flying off and lands on his right side. His side hurts like hell.

The next day, Monday, his side still hurts like hell. It hurts every time he moves. It hurts every time he breathes deep. It hurts every time he moves his right arm. He knows that if he goes to a doctor at Muroc or says anything to anybody even remotely connected with his superiors, he will be scrubbed from the flight on Tuesday. They might even go so far as to put some other miserable peckerwood in his place. So he gets on his motorcycle, an old junker that Pancho had given him, and rides over to see a doctor in the town of Rosamond, near where he lives. Every time the goddamned motorcycle hits a pebble in the road, his side hurts like a sonofabitch. The doctor in Rosamond informs him he has two broken ribs and he tapes them up and tells him that if he'll just keep his right arm immobilized for a couple of weeks and avoid any physical exertion or sudden movements, he should be all right.

Yeager gets up before daybreak on Tuesday morning—which is supposed to be the day he tries to break the sound barrier—and his ribs still hurt like a sonofabitch. He gets his wife to drive him over to the field, and he has to keep his right arm pinned down to his side to keep his ribs from hurting so much. At dawn, on the day of a flight, you could hear the X-1 screaming long before you got there. The fuel for the X-1 was alcohol and liquid oxygen, oxygen converted from a gas to a liquid by lowering its temperature to 297 degrees below zero. And when the lox, as it was called, rolled out of the hoses and into the belly of the X-1, it started boiling off and the X-1 started steaming and screaming like a teakettle. There's quite a crowd on hand, by Muroc standards . . . perhaps nine or ten souls. They're still fueling the X-1 with the lox, and the beast is wailing.

The X-1 looked like a fat orange swallow with white markings. But it was really just a length of pipe with four rocket chambers in it. It had a tiny cockpit and a needle nose, two little straight blades (only three and a half inches thick at the thickest part) for wings, and a tail assembly set up high to avoid the "sonic wash" from the wings. Even though his side was throbbing and his right arm felt practically useless, Yeager figured he could grit his teeth and get through the flight —except for one specific move he had to make. In the rocket launches, the X-1, which held only two and a half minutes' worth of fuel, was carried up to twenty-six thousand feet underneath the wings of a B-29. At seven thousand feet, Yeager was to climb down a ladder from the bomb bay of the B-29 to the open doorway of the X-1, hook up to the oxygen system and the radio microphone and earphones, and put his crash helmet on and prepare for the launch, which would come at twenty-five thousand feet. This helmet was a homemade number. There had never been any such thing as a crash helmet before. Throughout the war pilots had used the old skin-tight leather helmet-and-goggles. But the X-1 had a way of throwing the pilot around so violently that there was danger of getting knocked out against the walls of the cockpit. So Yeager had bought a big leather football helmet—there were no plastic ones at the time—and he butchered it with a hunting knife until he carved the right kind of holes in it, so that it would fit down over his regular flying helmet and the earphones and the oxygen rig. Anyway, then his flight engineer, Jack Ridley, would climb down the ladder, out in the breeze, and shove into place the cockpit door, which had to be lowered out of the belly of the B-29 on a chain. Then Yeager had to push a handle to lock the door airtight. Since the X-1's cockpit was minute, you had to push the handle with your right hand. It took quite a shove. There was no way you could move into position to get enough leverage with your left hand.

Out in the hangar Yeager makes a few test shoves on the sly, and the pain is so incredible he realizes that there is no way a man with two broken ribs is going to get the door closed. It is time to confide in somebody, and the logical man is Jack Ridley. Ridley is not only the flight engineer but a pilot himself and a good old boy from Oklahoma to boot. He will understand about Flying & Drinking and Drinking & Driving through the goddamned Joshua trees. So Yeager takes Ridley off to the side in the tin hangar and says: Jack, I got me a little ol' problem here. Over at Pancho's the other night I sorta . . . dinged my goddamned ribs. Ridley says, Whattya mean . . . *dinged?* Yeager says, Well, I guess you might say I damned near like to . . . *broke* a coupla the sonsabitches. Whereupon Yeager sketches out the problem he foresees.

Not for nothing is Ridley the engineer on this project. He has an inspiration. He tells a janitor named Sam to cut him about nine inches off a broom handle. When nobody's looking, he slips the broomstick into the cockpit of the X-1 and gives Yeager a little advice and counsel.

So with that added bit of supersonic flight gear Yeager went aloft.

At seven thousand feet he climbed down the ladder into the X-1's cockpit, clipped on his hoses and lines, and managed to pull the pumpkin football helmet over his head. Then Ridley came down the ladder and lowered the door into place. As Ridley had instructed, Yeager now took the nine inches of broomstick and slipped it between the handle and the door. This gave him just enough mechanical advantage to reach over with his left hand and whang the thing shut. So he whanged the door shut with Ridley's broomstick and was ready to fly.

At 26,000 feet the B-29 went into a shallow dive, then pulled up and released Yeager and the X-1 as if it were a bomb. Like a bomb it dropped and shot forward (at the speed of the mother ship) at the same time. Yeager had been launched straight into the sun. It seemed to be no more than six feet in front of him, filling up the sky and blinding him. But he managed to get his bearings and set off the four rocket chambers one after the other. He then experienced something that became known as the ultimate sensation in flying: "booming and zooming." The surge of the rockets was so tremendous, forced him back into his seat so violently, he could hardly move his hands forward the few inches necessary to reach the controls. The X-1 seemed to shoot straight up in an absolutely perpendicular trajectory, as if determined to snap the hold of gravity via the most direct route possible. In fact, he was only climbing at the 45-degree angle called for in the flight plan. At about .87 Mach the buffeting started.

On the ground the engineers could no longer see Yeager. They could only hear . . . that poker-hollow West Virginia drawl.

"Had a mild buffet there . . . jes the usual instability . . ."

Jes the usual instability?

Then the X-1 reached the speed of .96 Mach, and that incredible caint-hardlyin' aw-shuckin' drawl said:

"Say, Ridley . . . make a note here, will ya?" (*if you ain't got nothin' better to do*) ". . . elevator effectiveness *re*-gained."

Just as Yeager had predicted, as the X-1 approached Mach 1, the stability improved. Yeager had his eyes pinned on the machometer. The needle reached .96, fluctuated, and went off the scale.

And on the ground they heard . . . that voice:

"Say, Ridley . . . make another note, will ya?" (*if you ain't too bored yet*) ". . . there's somethin' wrong with this ol' machometer . . ." (faint chuckle) ". . . it's gone kinda screwy on me . . ."

And in that moment, on the ground, they heard a boom rock over the desert floor—just as the physicist Theodore von Kármán had predicted many years before.

Then they heard Ridley back in the B-29: "If it is, Chuck, we'll fix it. Personally I think you're seeing things."

Then they heard Yeager's poker-hollow drawl again:

"Well, I guess I am, Jack . . . And I'm still goin' upstairs like a bat."

The X-1 had gone through "the sonic wall" without so much as a bump. As the speed topped out at Mach 1.05, Yeager had the sensation of shooting straight through the top of the sky. The sky turned a deep purple and all at once the stars and the moon came out—and the sun shone at the same time. He had reached a layer of the upper atmosphere where the air was too thin to contain reflecting dust particles. He was simply looking out into space. As the X-1 nosed over at the top of the climb, Yeager now had seven minutes of . . . Pilot Heaven . . . ahead of him. He was going faster than any man in history, and it was almost silent up here, since he had exhausted his rocket fuel, and he was so high in such a vast space that there was no sensation of motion. He was master of the sky. His was a king's solitude, unique and inviolate, above the dome of the world. It would take him seven minutes to glide back down and land at Muroc. He spent the time doing victory rolls and wing-over-wing aerobatics while Rogers Lake and the High Sierras spun around below.

On THE GROUND THEY had understood the code as soon as they heard Yeager's little exchange with Ridley. The project was secret, but the radio exchanges could be picked up by anyone within range. The business of the "screwy machometer" was Yeager's deadpan way of announcing that the X-1's instruments indicated Mach 1. As soon as he landed, they checked out the X-1's automatic recording instruments. Without any doubt the ship had gone supersonic. They immediately called the brass at Wright Field to break the tremendous news. Within two hours Wright Field called back and gave some firm orders. A top security lid was being put on the morning's events. That the press was not to be informed went without saying. But neither was anyone else, anyone at all, to be told. Word of the flight was not to go beyond the flight line. And even among the people directly involved—who were there and knew about it, anyway—there was to be no celebrating. Just what was on the minds of the brass at Wright is hard to say. Much of it, no doubt, was a simple holdover from wartime, when every breakthrough of possible strategic importance was kept under wraps. That was what you did—you shut up about them. Another possibility was that the chiefs at Wright had never quite known what to make of Muroc. There was some sort of weird ribald aerial tarpaper mad-monk squadron up on the roof of the desert out there . . .

In any case, by mid-afternoon Yeager's tremendous feat had become a piece of thunder with no reverberation. A strange and implausible stillness settled over the event. Well . . . there was not supposed to be any celebration, but come nightfall . . . Yeager and Ridley and some of the others ambled over to Pancho's. After all, it was the end of the day, and they were pilots. So they knocked back a few. And they had to let Pancho in on the secret, because Pancho had said she'd serve a free steak dinner to any pilot who could fly supersonic and walk in here to tell about it, and they had to see the look on *her* face. So Pancho served Yeager a big steak dinner and said they were a buncha miserable peckerwoods all the same, and the desert cooled off and the wind came up and the screen doors banged and they drank some more and bawled some songs over the cackling dry piano and the stars and the moon came out and Pancho screamed oaths no one had ever heard before and Yeager and Ridley roared and the old weatherbeaten bar boomed and the autographed pictures of a hundred dead pilots shook and clattered on the frame wires and the faces of the living fell apart in the reflections, and by and by they all left and stumbled and staggered and yelped and bayed for glory before the arthritic silhouettes of the Joshua trees. Shit!—there was no one to tell except for Pancho and the god-damned Joshua trees!

O VER THE NEXT FIVE MONTHS Yeager flew supersonic in the X-1 more than a dozen times, but still the Air Force insisted on keeping the story secret. *Aviation Week* published a report of the flights late in December (without mentioning Yeager's name) provoking a minor debate in the press over whether or not *Aviation Week* had violated national security—and *still* the Air Force refused to publicize the achievement until June of 1948. Only then was Yeager's name released. He received only a fraction of the publicity that would have been his had he been presented to the world immediately, on October 14, 1947, as the man who "broke the sound barrier." This dragged-out process had curious effects.

In 1952 a British movie called *Breaking the Sound Barrier*, starring Ralph Richardson, was released in the United States, and its promoters got the bright idea of inviting the man who had actually done it, Major Charles E. Yeager of the U.S. Air Force, to the American premiere. So the Air Force goes along with it and Yeager turns up for the festivities. When he watches the movie, he's stunned. He can't believe what he's seeing. Far from being based on the exploits of Charles E. Yeager, *Breaking the Sound Barrier* was inspired by the death of Geoffrey de Havilland in his father's DH 108. At the end of the movie a British pilot solves the mystery of "the barrier" by *reversing the controls* at the critical moment during a power dive. The buffeting is tearing his ship to pieces, and every rational process in his head is telling him to *pull back* on the stick to keep from crashing— and he *pushes it down* instead . . . and zips right through Mach 1 as smooth as a bird, regaining full control!

Breaking the Sound Barrier happened to be one of the most engrossing movies about flying ever made. It seemed superbly realistic, and people came away from it sure of two things: it was an Englishman who had broken the sound barrier, and he had done it by reversing the controls in the transonic zone.

Well, after the showing they bring out Yeager to meet the press, and he doesn't know where in the hell to start. To him the whole goddamned picture is outrageous. He doesn't want to get mad, because this thing has been set up by Air Force P.R. But he is not happy. In as calm a way as he can word it on the spur of the moment, he informs one and all that the picture is an utter shuck from start to finish. The promoters respond, a bit huffily, that this picture is not, after all, a documentary. Yeager figures, well, anyway, that settles that. But as the weeks go by, he discovers an incredible thing happening. He keeps running into people who think he's the first *American* to break the sound barrier . . . and that he learned how to *reverse the controls* and zip through from the Englishman who did it first. The last straw comes when he gets a call from the Secretary of the Air Force.

"Chuck," he says, "do you mind if I ask you something? Is it true that you broke the sound barrier by reversing the controls?"

Yeager is stunned by this. The Secretary—*the Secretary!*—of the U.S. Air Force!

"No, sir," he says, "that is . . . not correct. Anyone who reversed the controls going transonic would be dead."

Yeager and the rocket pilots who soon joined him at Muroc had a hard time dealing with publicity. On the one hand, they hated the process. It meant talking to reporters and other fruit flies who always hovered, eager for the juice . . . and invariably got the facts screwed up . . . *But that wasn't really the problem, was it!* The real problem was that reporters violated the invisible walls of the fraternity. They blurted out questions and spoke boorish words about . . . all the unspoken things!—about fear and bravery (they would say the words!) and how you *felt* at such-and-such a moment! It was obscene! They presumed a knowledge and an intimacy they did not have and had no right to. Some aviation writer would sidle up and say, "I hear Jenkins augered in. That's too bad." *Augered in!*—a phrase that belonged exclusively to the fraternity!—coming from the lips of this *ant* who was *left behind* the moment Jenkins made his first step up the pyramid long, long ago. It was repulsive! But on the other hand . . . one's healthy pilot ego loved the glory—wallowed in it!—lapped it up!—no doubt about it! The Pilot Ego—ego didn't come any bigger! The boys wouldn't have minded the following. They wouldn't have minded appearing once a year on a balcony over a huge square in which half the world is assembled. They wave. The world roars its approval, its applause, and breaks into a sustained thirty-minute storm of cheers and tears (moved by my righteous stuff!). And then it's over. All that remains is for the wife to paste the clippings in the scrapbook.

A little adulation on the order of the Pope's; that's all the True Brothers at the top of the pyramid really wanted.

YEAGER RECEIVED JUST about every major decoration and trophy that was available to test pilots, but the Yeager legend grew not in the press, not in public, but within the fraternity. As of 1948, after Yeager's flight was made public, every hot pilot in the country knew that Muroc was what you aimed for if you wanted to reach the top. In 1947 the National Security Act, Title 10, turned the Army Air Force into the U.S. Air Force, and three years later Muroc Army Air Base became Edwards Air Force Base, named for a test pilot, Glenn Edwards, who had died testing a ship with no tail called the Flying Wing. So now the magic word became *Edwards*. You couldn't keep a really hot, competitive pilot away from Edwards. Civilian pilots (almost all of whom had been trained in the military) could fly for the National Advisory Committee for Aeronautics (NACA) High Speed Center at Edwards, and some of the rocket pilots did that: Scott Crossfield, Joe Walker, Howard Lilly, Herb Hoover, and Bill Bridgeman, among them. Pete Everest, Kit Murray, Iven Kincheloe, and Mel Apt joined Yeager as Air Force rocket pilots. There was a constant rivalry between NACA and the Air Force to push the rocket planes to their outer limits. On November 20, 1953, Crossfield, in the D-558-2, raised the speed record to Mach 2. Three weeks later Yeager flew the X-1A to Mach 2.4. The rocket program was quickly running out of frontiers within the atmosphere; so NACA and the Air Force began planning a new project, with a new rocket plane, the X-15, to probe altitudes as high as fifty miles, which was well beyond anything that could still be called "air."

My God!—to be a part of Edwards in the late forties and early fifties!—even to be on the ground and hear one of those incredible explosions from 35,000 feet somewhere up there in the blue over the desert and know that some True Brother had commenced his rocket launch . . . in the X-1, the X-1A, the X-2, the D-558-1, the horrible XF-92A, the beautiful D-558-2 . . . and to know that he would soon be at an altitude, in the thin air at the edge of space, where the stars and the moon came out at noon, in an atmosphere so thin that the ordinary laws of aerodynamics no longer applied and a plane could skid into a flat spin like a cereal bowl on a waxed Formica counter and then start tumbling, not spinning and not diving, but tumbling, end over end like a brick . . . In those planes, which were like chimneys with little razor-blade wings on them, you had to be "afraid to panic," and that phrase was no joke. In the skids, the tumbles, the spins, there was, truly, as Saint-Exupéry had said, only one thing you could let yourself think about: *What do I do next?* Sometimes at Edwards they used to play the tapes of pilots going into the final dive, the one that killed them, and the man would be tumbling, going end over end in a fifteen-ton length of pipe, with all aerodynamics long gone, and not one prayer left, and he knew it, and he would be screaming into the microphone, but not for Mother or for God or the nameless spirit of Ahor, but for one last hopeless crumb of information about the loop: "I've tried A! I've tried B! I've tried C! I've tried D! Tell me what else I can try!" And then that truly spooky click on the machine. *What do I do next?* (In this moment when the Halusian Gulp is opening!) And everybody around the table would look at one another and nod ever so slightly, and the unspoken message was: Too bad! There was a man with the right stuff. There was no national mourning in such cases, of course. Nobody outside of Edwards knew the man's name. If he were well liked, he might get one of those dusty stretches of road named for him on the base. He was probably a junior officer doing all this for four or five thousand a year. He owned perhaps two suits, only one of which he dared wear around people he didn't know. But none of that mattered!—not at Edwards —not in the Brotherhood.

What made it truly beautiful (for a True Brother!) was that for a good five years Edwards remained primitive and Low Rent, with nothing out there but the bleached prehistoric shrimp terrain and the rat shacks and the blazing sun and the thin blue sky and the rockets sitting there moaning and squealing before dawn. Not even Pancho's changed—except to become more gloriously Low Rent. By 1949 *the girls* had begun turning up at Pancho's in amazing numbers. They were young, lovely, juicy, frisky—and there were so many of them, at all hours, every day of the week! And they were not prostitutes, despite the accusations made later. They were just . . . well, just young juicy girls in their twenties with terrific young conformations and sweet cupcakes and loamy loins. They were sometimes described with a broad sweep as "stewardesses," but only a fraction of them really were. No, they were lovely young things who arrived as mysteriously as the sea gulls who sought the squirming shrimp. They were moist labial piping little birds who had somehow learned that at this strange place in the high Mojave lived the hottest young pilots in the world and that this was *where things were happening.* They came skipping and screaming in through the banging screen doors at Pancho's—and it completed the picture of Pilot Heaven. There was no other way to say it. Flying & Drinking and Drinking & Driving and Driving & Balling. The pilots began calling the old Fly Inn dude ranch "Pancho's Happy Bottom Riding Club," and there you had it.

All of this was fraternal bliss. No pilot was shut off from it because he was "in the public eye." Not even the rocket aces were isolated like stars. Most of them also performed the routine flight-test chores. Some of Yeager's legendary exploits came when he was merely a supporting player, flying "chase" in a fighter plane while another pilot flew the test aircraft. One day Yeager was flying chase for another test pilot at 20,000 feet when he noticed the man veering off in erratic maneuvers. As soon as he reached him on the radio, he realized the man was suffering from hypoxia, probably because an oxygen hose connection had come loose. Some pilots in that state became like belligerent drunks—prior to losing consciousness. Yeager would tell the man to check his oxygen system, he'd tell him to go to a lower altitude, and the man kept suggesting quaint anatomical impossibilities for Yeager to perform on himself. So Yeager hit upon a ruse that only he could have pulled off. "Hey," he said, "I got me a problem here, boy. I caint keep this thing running even on the emergency system. She just flamed out. Follow me down." He started descending, but his man stayed above him, still meandering. So Yeager did a very un-Yeager-like thing. He *yelled* into the microphone! He yelled: "Look, my dedicated young scientist—*follow me down!*" The change in tone—*Yeager yelling!*—penetrated the man's impacted hypoxic skull. *My God! The fabled Yeager! He's yelling—Yeager's yelling!—to me for help! Jesus H. Christ!* And he started following him down. Yeager knew that if he could get the man down to 12,000 feet, the oxygen content of the air would bring him around, which it did. *Hey! What happened?* After he landed, he realized he had been no more than a minute or two from passing out and punching a hole in the desert. As he got out of the cockpit, an F-86 flew overhead and did a slow roll sixty feet off the deck and then disappeared across Rogers Lake. That was Yeager's signature.

Yeager was flying chase one day for Bill Bridgeman, the prime pilot for one of the greatest rocket planes, the Douglas Skyrocket, when the ship went into a flat spin followed by a violent tumble. Bridgeman fought his way out of it and regained stability, only to have his windows ice up. This was another common danger in rocket flights. He was out of fuel, so that he was now faced with the task of landing the ship both deadstick and blind. At this point Yeager drew alongside in his F-86 and became his eyes. He told Bridgeman every move to make every foot of the way down . . . as if he knew that ol' Skyrocket like the back of his hand . . . and this was jes a little ol' fishin' trip on the Mud River . . . and there was jes the two of 'em havin' a little poker-hollow fun in the sun . . . and that lazy lollygaggin' chucklin' driftin' voice was still purrin' away . . . the very moment Bridgeman touched down safely. You could almost hear Yeager saying to Bridgeman, as he liked to do:

"How d'ye hold with rockets now, son?"

That was what you thought of when you saw the F-86 do a slow roll sixty feet off the deck and disappear across Rogers Lake.

Yeager had just turned thirty. Bridgeman was thirty-seven. It didn't dawn on him until later that Yeager always called him *son.* At the time it had seemed perfectly natural. Somehow Yeager was like the big daddy of the skies over the dome of the world. In keeping with the eternal code, of course, for anyone to have suggested any such thing would have been to invite hideous ridicule. There were even other pilots with enough Pilot Ego to believe that *they* were actually better than this drawlin' hot dog. But no one would contest the fact that as of that time, the 1950's, Chuck Yeager was at the top of the pyramid, number one among all the True Brothers.

And *that voice* . . . started drifting down from on high. At first the tower at Edwards began to notice that all of a sudden there were an awful lot of test pilots up there with West Virginia drawls. And pretty soon there were an awful lot of fighter pilots up there with West Virginia drawls. The air space over Edwards was getting so caint-hardly supercool day by day, it was terrible. And then that lolly-gaggin' poker-hollow air space began to spread, because the test pilots and fighter pilots from Edwards were considered the pick of the litter and had a cachet all their own, wherever they went, and other towers and other controllers began to notice that it was getting awfully drawly and down-home up there, although they didn't know exactly why. And then, because the military is the training ground for practically all airline pilots, it spread further, until airline passengers all over America began to hear that awshuckin' driftin' gone-fishin' Mud River voice coming from the cockpit . . . "Now, folks, uh . . . this is the captain . . . ummmm . . . We've got a little ol' red light up here on the control panel that's tryin' to tell us that the *land*in' gears're not . . . uh . . . *lock*in' into position . . ."

But so what! What could possibly go wrong! We've obviously got a man up there in the cockpit who doesn't have a nerve in his body! He's a block of ice! He's made of 100 percent righteous victory-rolling True Brotherly stuff.

Y EAGER QUIT TESTING rocket planes in 1954 and returned to strictly military flying. First he went to Okinawa to test a Soviet MiG-15 that a North Korean defector, a pilot named Kim Sok No, had arrived in, giving the Air Force its first opportunity to study this fabled craft. American pilots used to come back from the Yalu River saying that the MiG-15 was so hot you could put your F-86 in a power dive and the MiG would fly outside loops around you all the way down. Yeager took the MiG-15 up to 50,000 feet and then down to 12,000 feet in a power dive without even so much as an instruction manual to go by. He found that it would outclimb and outaccelerate the F-86, but that the F-86 had a higher top speed in both level flight and in dives. The MiG-15 was good but not exactly a superfighter that should strike terror in the heart of the West. Yeager had to chuckle. Some things never changed. You let any fighter jock talk about the enemy aircraft and he'll tell you it's the hottest thing that ever left the ground. After all, it made him look just that much better when he waxed the bandit's tail. Then Yeager went to Germany to fly F-86s and to train the American combat squadrons there in a special air-alert system. By October 4, 1957, he was back in the United States, at George Air Force Base, about fifty miles southeast of Edwards, commanding a squadron of F-100s, when the Soviet Union launched the rocket that put a hundred-pound artificial satellite called Sputnik I into orbit around the earth.

Yeager was not terribly impressed. The thing was so goddamned small. The idea of an artificial earth satellite was not novel to anyone who had been involved in the rocket program at Edwards. By now, ten years after Yeager had first flown a rocket faster than Mach 1, rocket development had reached the point where the idea of unmanned satellites such as Sputnik I was taken for granted. Two years ago, 1955, the government had published a detailed description of the rockets that would be used to launch a small satellite in late 1957 or early 1958 as part of the United States' contribution to the International Geophysical Year. Engineers for NACA and the Air Force and several aircraft companies were already designing manned spacecraft as the logical extension of the X series. The preliminary design section of North American Aviation had working drawings and most of the specifications for a fifteen-ton ship called the X-15B, a winged craft that would be launched by three enormous rockets, each with 415,000 pounds of thrust, whereupon the ship's two pilots would take over with the X-15B's own 75,000-pound engine, make three or more orbits of the earth, reenter the atmosphere, and land on a dry lake bed at Edwards like any other pilots in the X series. This was no mere dream. North American was already manufacturing a ship almost as ambitious: namely the X-15. Scott Crossfield was in training to fly it. The X-15 was designed to achieve an altitude of 280,000 feet, just above fifty miles, which was generally regarded as the boundary where all trace of atmosphere ended and "space" began. Within a month after the launching of Sputnik I, North American's chief engineer, Harrison Storms, was in Washington with a completely detailed proposal for the X-15B project. His turned out to be one among 421 proposals for manned spacecraft that had been submitted to NACA and the Defense Department. The Air Force was interested in a rocket-glider craft, similar to the X-15B, that would be called the X-20 or Dyna-Soar, for "dynamic soaring"; an Air Force rocket, the Titan, which was under development, would provide the 500,000 pounds of thrust that would be required. Naturally the pilots of the X-15B or the X-20 or whatever—the first Americans and possibly the first men in the world to go into space—would come from Edwards. At Edwards you had men like Crossfield, Iven Kincheloe, and Joe Walker, who had already flown rockets many times.

So what was the big deal about Sputnik I? The problem was already on the way to being solved.

That was the way it looked to Yeager and to everybody involved in the X series at Edwards. It was hard to realize how Sputnik I looked to the rest of the country and particularly to politicians and the press . . . and other technological illiterates with influence . . . It was hard to realize that Sputnik I, if not the MiG-15, would strike terror in the heart of the West.

After two weeks, however, the situation was obvious: a colossal panic was underway, with congressmen and newspapermen leading a huge pack that was baying at the sky where the hundred-pound Soviet satellite kept beeping around the world. In their eyes Sputnik I had become the second momentous event of the Cold War. The first had been the Soviet development of the atomic bomb in 1953. From a purely strategic standpoint, the fact that the Soviets had the rocket power to launch Sputnik I meant that they now also had the capacity to deliver the bomb on an intercontinental ballistic missile. The panic reached far beyond the relatively sane concern for tactical weaponry, however. Sputnik I took on a magical dimension—among highly placed persons especially, judging by opinion surveys. It seemed to dredge up primordial superstitions about the influence of heavenly bodies. It gave birth to a modern, i.e., technological, astrology. Nothing less than *control of the heavens* was at stake. It was Armageddon, the final and decisive battle of the forces of good and evil. Lyndon Johnson, who was the Senate majority leader, said that whoever controlled "the high ground" of space would control the world. This phrase, "the high ground," somehow caught hold. "The Roman Empire," said Johnson, "controlled the world because it could build roads. Later—when it moved to sea—the British Empire was dominant because it had ships. In the air age we were powerful because we had airplanes. Now the Communists have established a foothold in outer space." *The New York Times*, in an editorial, said the United States was now in a "race for survival." The panic became more and more apocalyptic. Nothing short of doom awaited the loser, now that the battle had begun. When the Soviets shot a Sputnik called *Mechta* into a heliocentric orbit, the House Select Committee on Astronautics, headed by House Speaker John McCormack, said that the United States faced the prospect of "national extinction" if it did not catch up with the Soviet space program. "It cannot be overemphasized that the survival of the free world—indeed, all the world—is caught up in the stakes." The public, according to the Gallup poll, was not all that alarmed. But McCormack, like a great many powerful people, genuinely believed in the notion of "controlling the high ground." He was genuinely convinced that the Soviets would send up space platforms from which they could drop nuclear bombs at will, like rocks from a highway overpass.

The Soviet program gave off an aura of sorcery. The Soviets released practically no figures, pictures, or diagrams. And no names; it was revealed only that the Soviet program was guided by a mysterious individual known as "the Chief Designer." But his powers were indisputable! Every time the United States announced a great space experiment, the Chief Designer accomplished it first, in the most startling fashion. In 1955 the United States announces plans to launch an artificial earth satellite by early 1958. The Chief Designer startles the world by doing it in October 1957. The United States announces plans to send a satellite into orbit around the sun in March of 1959. The Chief Designer does it in January 1959. The fact that the United States went ahead and successfully conducted such experiments on schedule, as announced, impressed no one—and Americans least of all. In a marvelously morose novel of the future called *We*, completed in 1921, the Russian writer Evgeny Zamyatin describes a gigantic "fire-breathing, electric" rocket ship that is poised to "soar into cosmic space" in order to "subjugate the unknown beings on other planets, who may still be living in the primitive condition of freedom"—all this in the name of "the Benefactor," ruler of "the One State." This omnipotent spaceship is called the Integral, and its designer is known only as "D-503, Builder of the Integral." In 1958 and early 1959, as magical success followed magical success, that was the way Americans, the leaders even more so than the followers, began to look on the Soviet space program. It was a thing of misty but stupendous dimensions . . . the mighty Integral . . . with an anonymous but omnipotent Chief Designer . . . Builder of the Integral. Within the federal government and throughout the education bureaucracies rose a cry for a complete overhauling of American education in order to catch up with the new generation, the new dawn, of socialist scientists, out of which had come geniuses like the Chief Designer (Builder of the Integral!) and his assistants.

The panic was greatly exacerbated by the figure of Nikita Khrushchev, who now emerged as the new Stalin in terms of his autocratic rule of the Soviet Union. Khrushchev was a type whom Americans could readily understand and fear. He was the burly, hearty, crude but shrewd farmboy capable of grinning with barnyard humor one moment and of tormenting small animals the next. After Sputnik I Khrushchev became the wicked master of mocking the United States for its incompetence. Two months after Sputnik I the Navy tried to launch the first American satellite with a Vanguard rocket. The first nationally televised *countdown* began . . . "Ten, nine, eight . . ." Then . . . "Ignition!" A mighty surge of noise and flames. The rocket lifts—some six inches. The first stage, bloated with fuel, explodes, and the rest of the rocket sinks into the sand beside the launch platform. It appears to sink very slowly, like a fat old man collapsing into a Barcalounger. The sight is absolutely ludicrous, if one is in the mood for a practical joke. Oh, Khrushchev had fun with that, all right! This picture—the big buildup, the dramatic countdown, followed by the exploding cigar—was unforgettable. It became *the* image of the American space program. The press broke into a hideous cackle of national self-loathing, with the headline KAPUTNIK! being the most inspired rendition of the mood.

The rocket pilots at Edwards simply could not understand what sort of madness possessed everybody. They watched in consternation as a war effort mentality took over. Catch up! On all fronts! That was the imperative. They could scarcely believe the outcome of a meeting held in Los Angeles in March of 1958. This was an emergency meeting (*what* emergency?) of government, military, and aircraft industry leaders to discuss the possibility of getting a man into space before the Russians. Suddenly there was no longer time for orderly progress. To put an X-15B or an X-20 into orbit, with an Edwards rocket pilot aboard, would require rockets that were still three or four years away from delivery. So a so-called quick and dirty approach was seized upon. Using available rockets such as the Redstone (70,000 pounds) and the just-developed Atlas (367,000 pounds), they would try to launch not a flying ship but a pod, a container, a *capsule*, with a man in it. The man would not be a pilot; he would be a human cannonball. He would not be able to alter the course of the capsule in the slightest. The capsule would go up like a cannonball and come down like a cannonball, splashing into the ocean, with a parachute to slow it down and spare the life of the human specimen inside. The job was assigned to NACA, the National Advisory Committee for Aeronautics, which was converted into NASA, the National Aeronautics and Space Administration. The project was called Project Mercury.

The capsule approach was the brainchild of a highly regarded Air Force research physician, Brigadier General Don Flickinger. The Air Force named it the MISS project, for "man in space soonest." The man in the MISS capsule would be an aero-medical test subject and little more. In fact, in the first flights, as Flickinger envisioned it, the capsule would contain a chimpanzee. Mercury was a slightly modified version of MISS, and so naturally enough Flickinger became one of the five men in charge of selecting Project Mercury's astronauts, as they would be called. The fact that NASA would soon be choosing men to go into space had not been made public, but Scott Crossfield was aware of it. Shortly after the Sputnik I launching, Crossfield, Flickinger, and seven others had been named to an emergency committee on "human factors and training" for space flight. Crossfield had also worked closely with Flickinger when he was testing pressure suits at Wright-Patterson Air Force Base in preparation for the X-15 project. Now

Crossfield approached Flickinger and told him he was interested in becoming an astronaut. Flickinger liked Crossfield and admired him. And he told him: "Scotty, don't even bother applying, because you'll only be turned down. You're too independent." Crossfield was the most prominent of the rocket pilots, now that Yeager was no longer at Edwards, and he had as well developed an ego as any of Edwards' fabled jocks, and he was one of the most brilliant of all the pilots when it came to engineering. Flickinger seemed to be telling him that Project Mercury just wasn't suited for the righteous brethren of yore, the veterans of those high desert rat-shack broomstick days when there were no chiefs and no Indians and the pilot huddled in the hangar with the engineer and then went out and took the beast up and lit the candle and reached for the stars and rode his chimney and landed it on the lake bed and made it to Pancho's in time for beer call. When Flickinger explained to him that the first flight of the Mercury system would be made by a chimpanzee . . . well, Crossfield wasn't even particularly interested any more. Nor were most of the other pilots who were in line to fly the X-15. A *monkey's gonna make the first flight.* That was what you started hearing. Astronaut meant "star voyager," but in fact the poor devil would be a guinea pig for the study of the effects of weightlessness on the body and the central nervous system. As the brethren knew, NASA's original civil-service job specifications for Mercury astronaut did not even require that the star voyager be a pilot of any description whatsoever. Just about any young male college graduate with experience in a physically dangerous pursuit would do, so long as he was under five feet eleven and could fit into the Mercury capsule. The announcement calling for volunteers did mention test pilots as being among the types of men who might qualify, but it also mentioned submarine crew members, parachute jumpers, arctic explorers, mountain climbers, deep sea divers, even scuba divers, combat veterans, and, for that matter, mere veterans of combat training, and men who had served as test subjects for acceleration and atmospheric pressure tests, such as the Air Force and Navy had been running. The astronaut would not be expected to *do* anything; he only had to be able to take it.

NASA was ready to issue the call when the President himself, Eisenhower, stepped in. He foresaw bedlam. Every lunatic in the U.S.A. would volunteer for this thing. Every dingaling in the U.S. Congress would be touting a favorite son. It would be chaos. The selection process might take months, and the inevitable business of security clearances would take a few more. Late in December Eisenhower directed that NASA select the astronauts from among the 540 military test pilots already on duty, even though they were rather overqualified for the job. The main thing was that their records were immediately available, they already had security clearances, and they could be ordered to Washington at a moment's notice. The specifications were that they be under five feet eleven and no older than thirty-nine and that they be graduates of test-pilot schools, with at least 1,500 hours of flying time and experience in jets, and that they have bachelor's degrees "or the equivalent." One hundred and ten of the pilots fit the profile. There were men on the NASA selection committee who wondered if the pool was big enough. They figured that they would be lucky if one test pilot in ten volunteered. Even that wouldn't be quite enough, because they were looking for twelve astronaut candidates. They only needed six for the flights themselves, but they assumed that at least half the candidates would drop out because of the frustration of training to become passive guinea pigs in an automated capsule.

After all, they already knew how the leading test pilots at Edwards felt. North American had rolled out the first X-15 in the fall of 1958, and Crossfield and his colleagues, Joe Walker and Iven Kincheloe, had become absorbed in the assignment. Joe Walker was NASA's prime pilot for the project, and Kincheloe was prime pilot for the Air Force. Kincheloe had set the world altitude record of 126,000 feet in the X-2, and the Air Force envisioned him as the new Yeager . . . and then some. Kincheloe was a combat hero and test pilot from out of a dream, blond, handsome, powerful, bright, supremely ambitious and yet popular with all who worked with him, including other pilots. There was absolutely no ceiling on his future in the Air Force. Then one perfectly sunny day he was making a routine takeoff in an F-104 and the panel lit up red and he had *that one second* in which to decide whether or not to punch out at an altitude of about fifty feet . . . a choice complicated by the fact that the F-104's seat ejected straight down, out of the belly . . . and so he tried to roll the ship over and eject upside down, but he went out sideways and was killed. His backup, Major Robert White, took his place in the X-15 project. Joe Walker's backup was a former Navy fighter pilot named Neil Armstrong. Crossfield, White, Walker, Armstrong—they no longer had time to even think about Project Mercury. Project Mercury did not mean the end of the X-15 program. Not at all. The testing of the X-15 would proceed, in order to develop a true spacecraft, a ship that a pilot could fly into space and fly back down through the atmosphere for a landing. Much was made of the fact that the X-15 would "land with dignity" rather than splash down in the water like the proposed Mercury capsule. Press interest in the X-15 had become tremendous, because it was the country's sole existing "spaceship." Reporters had started writing about Kincheloe as "Mr. Space," since he was the one who held the altitude record. After his death they hung the title on Crossfield. It was a bother . . . but a fellow could learn to live with it . . . In any case, Project Mercury, the human cannonball approach, looked like a Larry Lightbulb scheme, and it gave off the funk of panic. Any pilot who went into it would no longer be a pilot. He would be a laboratory animal wired up from skull to rectum with medical sensors. The rocket pilots had fought this medical crap every foot of the way. Scott Crossfield had reluctantly allowed them to wire him for heartbeat and respiration in rocket flights but had refused to let them insert a rectal thermometer. The pilots who signed up to crawl into the Mercury capsule—the *capsule*, everybody noted, not the *ship*—would be called "astronauts." But, in fact, they would be lab rabbits with wires up the tail and everywhere else. Nobody in his right mind would hang his hide out over the edge for ten or fifteen years and ascend the pyramid and finally reach the dome of the world, Edwards . . . only to end up like that: a lab rabbit curled up motionless in a *capsule* with his little heart pitter-patting and a wire up the kazoo.

Some of the most righteous of the brethren weren't even eligible for the preliminary screening for Project Mercury. Yeager was young enough—still only thirty-five—but had never attended college. Crossfield and Joe Walker were civilians. Not that any of them gave a damn . . . at the time. The commanding officer at Edwards passed the word around that he wanted his top boys, the test pilots in Fighter Ops, to avoid Project Mercury because it would be a ridiculous waste of talent; they would just become "Spam in a can." This phrase "Spam in a can" became very popular at Edwards as the nickname for Project Mercury.

4

THE LAB RAT

Pᴇᴛᴇ Cᴏɴʀᴀᴅ, being an alumnus of Princeton and the Philadelphia Main Line, had the standard E.S.A. charm and command of the proprieties. E.S.A. was 1950's Princeton club code for "Eastern Socially Attractive." E.S.A. qualities served a man well in the Navy, where refinement in the officer ranks was still valued. Yet Conrad remained, at bottom, the Hickory Kid. He had the same combination of party manners and Our Gang scrappiness that his wife, Jane, had found attractive when she met him six years before. Now, in 1959, at the age of twenty-eight, Conrad was still just as wirily built, five feet six and barely 140 pounds, still practically towheaded, and he had the same high-pitched nasal voice, the same collegiate cackle when he laughed, and the same Big Weekend grin that revealed the gap between his two front teeth. Nevertheless, people gave him room. There was an old-fashioned Huck Finn hickory-stick don't-cross-that-line-or-I'll-crawl-you streak in him. Unlike a lot of pilots, he tended to say exactly what was on his mind when aroused. He couldn't stand being trifled with. Consequently he seldom was.

That was Conrad. Add the normal self-esteem of the healthy young fighter jock making his way up the mighty ziggurat . . . and the lab rat's revolt was probably in the cards from the beginning.

The survivors of Group 20's *bad string* had just completed their flight-test training when the orders arrived. Conrad received them, and so did Wally Schirra and Jim Lovell. "Shaky" Lovell—he was stuck with the nickname Conrad had given him—had finished first in the training class. The orders were marked "top secret." That already had half the base talking, of course. There was nothing like issuing top-secret orders for a whole batch of officers in the same outfit to make the grapevine start lunging about like a live wire. They were supposed to report to a certain room at the Pentagon disguised as civilians.

So on the appointed Monday morning, February 2, Conrad, along with Schirra and Lovell, arrives at the Pentagon and presents his orders and files into a room with thirty-four other young men, most of them with crew cuts and all of them with lean lineless faces and suntans and the unmistakable cocky rolling gait of fighter jocks, not to mention the pathetic-looking civilian suits and the enormous wristwatches. The wristwatches had about two thousand calibrations on them and dials for recording everything short of the sound of enemy guns. These terrific wristwatches were practically fraternal insignia among the pilots. Thirty-odd young souls wearing Robert Hall clothes that cost about a fourth as much as their watches: in the year 1959 this just had to be a bunch of military pilots trying to disguise themselves as civilians.

Once inside the room, the boys realized that they were part of a secret gathering of military test pilots from all over the country. That was rather righteous stuff. Two of the highest ranking engineers of the National Aeronautics and Space Administration, Abe Silverstein and George Low, started briefing them. They had been brought to Washington, they were told, because NASA needed volunteers for suborbital and orbital flights above the earth's atmosphere in Project Mercury. The project had the highest national priority, comparable to that of a crash program in wartime. NASA intended to put astronauts into space by mid-1960, fifteen months from now.

A pilot could tell, if he listened carefully to the briefing, that an astronaut on a Project Mercury flight would do none of the things that comprised *flying* a ship: he would not take it aloft, control its flight, or land it. In short, he would be a passenger. The propulsion, guidance, and landing would all be determined automatically, by the ground. Yet the slender engineer, Low, went out of his way to show that the astronaut would exercise some forms of control. He would have "attitude control," for example. In fact, this meant only that the astronaut could make the capsule yaw, pitch, or roll by means of little hydrogen-peroxide thrusters, just as you could rock a seat on a Ferris wheel but couldn't change its orbit or direction in the slightest. But when a capsule was put into earth orbit, said Low, controlling the attitude would be essential for bringing the capsule back in through the atmosphere. Otherwise, the vehicle would burn up, and the astronaut with it. If the automatic control system malfunctioned, then the astronaut would have to take over on the manual or the fly-by-wire. In the fly-by-wire system the apparatus of the automatic system could be commandeered by the astronaut for manual control. The astronaut might also have to override the automatic system, in the case of a malfunction, to fire the retrorockets to reduce the capsule's speed and bring it out of orbit. *Retrofire! Fly-by-wire!* It was as if you really would be flying the thing. The stocky engineer, Silverstein, told them that obviously the Mercury flights might be hazardous. The first men to go into space would be running considerable risk. Therefore, the astronauts would be chosen on a strictly volunteer basis; and if a man did not volunteer, that fact would not be entered on his record or held against him in any way.

The message had a particular ring to it; but coming, as it did, from a civilian, it took a while for it to register.

Conrad and the rest of the Pax River contingent were staying at the Marriott motel near the Pentagon, and after dinner they got together in one of the rooms and had a long discussion. Schirra was there, and Lovell, and Alan Shepard, a veteran test pilot who had recently been reassigned from Pax River to a staff position in Norfolk, and a few others. What they talked about was not space travel, the future of the galaxy, or even the problems of riding a rocket into earth orbit. No, they talked about a rather more urgent matter: what this Project Mercury might do to your Navy career.

Wally Schirra had a lot of reservations about the thing, and Conrad and everybody else listened. Schirra was farther up the pyramid than anybody else in the room. Alan Shepard had more flight test experience, but he had never been in combat. Schirra, at thirty-five, had an outstanding combat record and was the sort of man who was obviously going places in the Navy. He had graduated from the Naval Academy, and his wife, Jo, was the stepdaughter of Admiral James Holloway, former commander of the Pacific Theater in the Second World War. Wally had been on ninety combat missions in Korea and shot down two MiGs. He had been chosen for the initial testing of the Sidewinder air-to-air missile out at China Lake, California, he had tested the F-4H for the Navy at Edwards itself —all this before joining Group 20 to complete his flight test training. Wally was quite popular. He was a stocky fellow with a big wide open face who was given to pranks, cosmic winks, fast cars, and all other ways of "maintaining an even strain," to use a Schirraism. He was a practical joker of the amiable sort. He would call up and say, "Hey, you gotta come over here! You'll never guess what I caught in the woods . . . A mongoose! I'm not kidding—a mongoose! You gotta see this thing!" And it would sound so incredible, you'd go over and take a look. Up on a table Wally would have a box that looked as if it had been converted into a cage, and he'd say: "Here, I'll open the top a little, so you can see him. But don't put your hand in, because he'll take it off for you. This baby is vicious." You'd lean down to take a look and—bango!—the lid flies open and this huge gray streak springs toward your face—and, well, my God, veteran aviators would recoil in terror, dive for the deck—and only then realize that the gray streak was some sort of fox-tail rig and the whole thing was a jack-in-the-box, Schirra-style. It was a broad joke, strictly speaking, but the delight Wally took in such things came in a wave, a wave so big that it swept you along in spite of yourself. A smile about a foot wide would spread over his face and his cheekbones would well up into a pair of cherub bellies, St. Nicholas-style, and an incredible rocking-druid laugh would come shaking and rumbling up from his rib cage, and he'd say: "Gotcha!" Schirra's "got-chas" were famous. Wally was one of those people who didn't mind showing their emotions, happiness, rage, frustration, whatever. But in the air he was as cool as they made them. His father had been an ace in the First World War, shooting down five German planes, and both his father and his mother had done barnstorm stunt flying after the war. For all his cutting up, Wally was absolutely serious about his career. And that was his mood now that this "astronaut" business confronted them.

There were some obvious problems. One, Project Mercury was a civilian program; two, NASA had not yet developed the rockets or the capsule to carry it out; three, it involved no flying, at least not in the sense a pilot used that word. The Mercury capsule was not a ship but a can. Not only did it involve no flying, there wasn't even a window to look out of. There wasn't even a hatch you could egress from like a man; it would take a crew of swabbos with lug wrenches to get you out of the thing. It was a can. Suppose you volunteered and got tied up in the project for two or three years, and then the whole thing fizzled? That was entirely possible, because this rocket-and-capsule system was novel and had a lot of Rube Goldberg stuff in it. Any test pilot who had ever been to the Society of Experimental Test Pilots convention, to one of those sessions where they show movies of Great Ideas that never made it out of the test stage, would know what he meant . . . the Sea Dart, a ten-ton jet fighter that was supposed to take off and land on water skis (up on the screen it keeps hopping up out of the waves, like a rock skipping across a pond, and the audience roars with laughter) . . . the single-engine plane, with a 25-foot propeller, that was propped up on its tail to take off vertically, like a hummingbird (it hangs in the air, suspended at forty feet, tail down, its engine churning furiously, not realizing that it has turned from an airplane into a cockeyed helicopter, and the audience roars with laughter) . . . In the history of flight these well-meant farces took place all the time. And where would you be then? You would be three years behind in flight test. You would be three years off the line in the general jockeying for promotion. You would be giving up whatever brownie points you had built up over the past four or five years. For somebody like Wally this was no joke. He was at the point in his career where you really start to climb—or you go off on some ill-advised tangent. He was in line to command his own fighter squadron. That was the route to the top, to admiral rank, for a Navy flier.

They talked for a long time. Someone Schirra's age had more to lose than Conrad, who was only twenty-eight. But as every officer knew, it was never too early to screw up your career in the Navy by getting involved in what was known, with some sarcasm, as "innovative duty."

From the beginning George Low and others in the NASA hierarchy had been afraid that the pilots would react in precisely this way. As a result, they were amazed. They had briefed thirty-five test pilots on Monday, February 2, Conrad, Schirra, Lovell, and Alan Shepard among them, and another thirty-four the following Monday; and of the total of sixty-nine, fifty-six volunteered to become astronauts. They now had so many volunteers they didn't even call in the remaining forty-one men who fit the profile. Why bother? They already had fifty-six grossly overqualified volunteers. Not only that, the men seemed so gung-ho about the project, they figured they could get by with seven astronauts instead of twelve.

Pete Conrad had ended up volunteering, and so had Jim Lovell. In fact, every man who had been in that room at the motel had volunteered, including Wally Schirra, who had been the most dubious of all. And why? That was a good question. Despite all the pondering, all the discussions, all the career-wrestling, all the toting up of pros and cons, none of them could give you a very clear-cut answer. The matter had not been decided by sheer logic. Somehow, in that briefing in the inner room at the Pentagon, Silverstein and Low had hit every button just right. It was as if they possessed a blueprint of the way the fighter jock was wired.

"The highest national priority" . . . "hazardous undertaking" . . . "strictly volunteer" . . . so hazardous that "if you don't volunteer, it won't be held against you" . . . And they had all gotten the signal, subliminally, in the solar plexus. They were being presented with the Cold War version of *the dangerous mission*. One of the maxims that was drilled into all career officers went: *Never refuse a combat assignment*. Moreover, there was the business of "the first men to go into space." *The first men to go into space*. Well . . . suppose it happened just that way? The rocket aces at Edwards, from their eminence, might be able to look down upon the whole scheme. But within the souls of the rest of the fighter jocks who came to the Pentagon was triggered a motivation that overrode all strictly logical career considerations: I must not get . . *left behind.*

That feeling was magnified by the public reaction. No sooner had the first group of men been briefed than the news that NASA was looking for Mercury astronauts made its way into the press. From the beginning the reporters and broadcasters dealt with the subject in tones of awe. It was the awe that one has of an impending death-defying stunt. The question of whether an astronaut was a pilot or a mere guinea pig never entered into it for a moment, so far as the press was concerned. "Are they really looking for somebody to go into space on top of a rocket?" That was the question and the only one that seemed to matter. To almost anyone who had followed NASA's efforts on television, the odds against the successful launch of an American into space seemed absolutely dreadful. For fourteen months now the Eisenhower Administration had adopted the strategy of openly publicizing its attempts to catch up with the Russians—and so people were being treated to the sight of the rockets at Cape Canaveral either blowing up on the launch pad in the most ignominious, if briefly hilarious, fashion or else heading off on crazy trajectories, toward downtown Orlando instead of outer space, in which case they had to be blown up by remote control. Well, not all of them, of course, for the United States had succeeded in putting up some small satellites, mere "oranges," as Nikita Khrushchev liked to put it, in his cruel colorful farmboy way, as compared to the 1,000-pound Sputniks the mighty Integral was sending around the earth loaded with dogs and other experimental animals. But the only obvious American talent was for blowing up. They had many names, these rockets, Atlas, Navaho, Little Joe, Jupiter, but they all blew up.

Conrad, like Schirra or any other test pilot, did not look at the TV footage in the same light, however. What people were seeing on television were, in fact, ordinary test events. Blown engines were par for the course in testing aircraft prototypes and were inevitable in testing an entirely new propulsion system, such as jet or rocket engines. It had happened at Muroc in testing the engine of the second American jet fighter, the XP-80. Obviously you didn't send a man up with an engine until it had attained a certain level of reliability. The only thing unusual about the testing of big rocket engines like the Navaho and the Atlas was that so much of it was televised and that these normal test events came across as colossal "failures." They were not even radical engines. The rocket engines that had been used in the X-1 project and all of the X projects that followed employed the same basic power plants as the Atlas, the Jupiter, and the other rockets NASA was working with. They used the same fuel, a mixture of liquid oxygen and alcohol. The X-project rockets, inevitably, had *blown* in the testing stage, but had been made reliable in the end. No rocket pilot had ever had an engine blow up under him in flight, although one, Skip Ziegler, had died when an X-2 had exploded while it was still attached to the B-29 that was supposed to launch it. To pilots who had been through *bad strings* at Pax River or Edwards, it was hard to see how the risk would be any greater than in testing the Century series of jet fighters. Just think of a beast like the F-102 . . . or the F-104 . . . or the F-105 . . .

When Pete talked to Jane about Project Mercury, she was all for it! If he wanted to volunteer, then he should by all means do so. The thought of Pete riding a NASA rocket did not fill her with horror. On the contrary. Although she never quite put it this way to Pete, she felt that anything would be better, safer, saner than for him to continue flying high-performance jet fighters for the Navy. At the very least, astronaut training would take him away from that. As for rocket flights themselves, how could they possibly be any more dangerous than flying every day at Pax River? What rocket pilot's wife had ever been to more funerals than the wives of Group 20?

ALBUQUERQUE, home of the Lovelace Clinic, was a dirty red sod-hut tortilla highway desert city that was remarkably short on charm, despite the Mexican touch here and there. But career officers were used to dreary real estate. That was what they inhabited in America, especially if they were fliers. No, it was Lovelace itself that began to get everybody's back up. Lovelace was a fairly new private diagnostic clinic, somewhat like the Mayo Clinic, doing "aerospace-medical" work for the government, among other things. Lovelace had been founded by Randy Lovelace—W. Randolph Lovelace II—who had served along with Cross-field and Flickinger on the committee on "human factors" in space flight. The chief of the medical staff at Lovelace was a recently retired general of the Air Force medical corps, Dr. A. H. Schwichtenberg. He was General Schwichtenberg to everybody at Lovelace. The operation took itself very seriously. The candidates for astronaut would be given their physical testing here. Then they would go to Wright-Patterson Air Force Base in Dayton for psychological and stress testing. It was all very hush-hush. Conrad went to Lovelace in a group of only six men, once more in their ill-fitting mufti and terrific watches, apparently so that they would blend in with the clinic's civilian patients. They had been warned that the tests at Lovelace and Wright-Patterson would be more exacting and strenuous than any they had ever taken. It was not the tests *per se*, however, that made every self-respecting fighter jock, early in the game, begin to hate Lovelace.

Military pilots were veterans of physical examinations, but in addition to all the usual components of "the complete physical," the Lovelace doctors had de-vised a series of novel tests involving straps, tubes, hoses, and needles. They would put a strap around your head, clamp some sort of instrument over your eyes —and then stick a hose in your ear and pump cold water into your ear canal. It would make your eyeballs flutter. It was an unpleasant, disorienting sensation, although not painful. If you wanted to know what it was all about, the Lovelace doctors and technicians, in their uncompromising white smocks, indicated that you really didn't need to know, and that was that.

What really made Conrad feel that something *eccentric* was going on here, however, was the business of the electrode in the thumb muscle. They brought him into a room and strapped his hand down to a table, palm up. Then they brought out an ugly-looking needle attached to an electrical wire. Conrad didn't like needles in the first place, and this one looked like a monster. *Hannh?*—they drove the needle into the big muscle at the base of his thumb. It hurt like a bastard. Conrad looked up as if to say, "What the hell's going on?" But they weren't even looking at him. They were looking—at the meter. The wire from the needle led to what looked like a doorbell. They pushed the buzzer. Conrad looked down, and his hand—his own goddamned hand!—was balling up into a fist and springing open and balling up into a fist and springing open and balling up into a fist and springing open and balling up into a fist and springing open at an absolutely furious rate, faster than he could have ever made it do so on its own, and there seemed to be nothing that he, with his own mind and his own central nervous system, could do to stop his own hand or even slow it down. The Lovelace doctors in their white smocks, with their reflectors on their heads, were having a hell of a time for themselves . . . with his hand . . . They were reading the meter and scribbling away on their clipboards at a jolly rate.

Afterward Conrad said, "What was that for?"

A doctor looked up, distractedly, as if Conrad were interrupting an important train of thought.

"I'm afraid there's no simple way to explain it to you," he said. "There's nothing for you to worry about."

It was then that it began to dawn on Conrad, first as a feeling rather than as a fully formed thought: "Lab rats."

It went on like that. The White Smocks gave each of them a test tube and said they wanted a sperm count. *What do you mean?* Place your sperm in the tube. *How?* Through ejaculation. *Just like that?* Masturbation is the customary procedure. *What!* The best results seem to be obtained through fantasization, accompanied by masturbation, followed by ejaculation. *Where, f'r chrissake?* Use the bathroom. A couple of the boys said things such as, "Well, okay, I'll do it if you'll send a nurse in with me—to help me along if I get stuck." The White Smocks looked at them as if they were schoolboys making obscene noises. This got the pilots' back up, and a couple of them refused, flat out. But by and by they gave in, and so now you had the ennobling prospect of half a dozen test pilots padding off one by one to the head in their skivvies to jack off for the Lovelace Clinic, Project Mercury, and America's battle for the heavens. Sperm counts were supposed to determine the density and motility of the sperm. What this had to do with a man's fitness to fly on top of a rocket or anywhere else was incomprehensible. Conrad began to get the feeling that it wasn't just him and his brother lab rats who didn't know what was going on. He now had the suspicion that the Reflector Heads didn't know, either. They had somehow gotten *carte blanche* to try out any goddamned thing they could think up—and that was what they were doing, whether there was any logic to it or not.

Each candidate was to deliver two stool specimens to the Lovelace laboratory in Dixie cups, and days were going by and Conrad had been unable to egest even one, and the staff kept getting after him about it. Finally he managed to produce a single bolus, a mean hard little ball no more than an inch in diameter and shot through with some kind of seeds, whole seeds, undigested. Then he remembered. The first night in Albuquerque he had gone to a Mexican restaurant and eaten a lot of jalapeño peppers. They were jalapeño seeds. Even in the turd world this was a pretty miserable-looking *objet*. So Conrad tied a red ribbon around the goddamned thing, with a bow and all, and put it in the Dixie cup and delivered it to the lab. Curious about the ribbons that flopped out over the lip of the cup, the technicians all peered in. Conrad broke into his full cackle of mirth, much the way Wally might have. No one was swept up in the joke, however. The Lovelace staffers looked at the beribboned bolus, and then they looked at Conrad . . . as if he were a bug on the windshield of the pace car of medical progress.

One of the tests at Lovelace was an examination of the prostate gland. There was nothing exotic about this, of course; it was a standard part of the complete physical for men. The doctor puts a rubber sleeve on a finger and slips the finger up the subject's rectum and presses the prostate, looking for signs of swelling, infection, and so on. But several men in Conrad's group had come back from the prostate examination gasping with pain and calling the doctor a sadistic little pervert and worse. He had prodded the prostate with such force a couple of them had passed blood.

Conrad goes into the room, and sure enough, the man reams him so hard the pain brings him to his knees.

"What the hell!—"

Conrad comes up swinging, but an orderly, a huge monster, immediately grabs him, and Conrad can't move. The doctor looks at him blankly, as if he's a vet and Conrad's a barking dog.

The probings of the bowels seemed to be endless, full proctosigmoidoscope examinations, the works. These things were never pleasant; in fact, they were a bit humiliating, involving, as they did, various things being shoved up your tail. The Lovelace Clinic specialty seemed to be the exacting of maximum indignity from each procedure. The pilots had never run into anything like this before. Not only that, before each ream-out you had to report to the clinic at seven o'clock in the morning and give yourself an enema. *Up yours!* seemed to be the motto of the Lovelace Clinic—and they even made you do it to yourself. So Conrad reports at seven one morning and gives himself the enema. He's supposed to undergo a lower gastrointestinal tract examination that morning. In the so-called lower G.I. examination, barium is pumped into the subject's bowels; then a little hose with a balloon on the end of it is inserted in the rectum, and the balloon is inflated, blocking the canal to keep the barium from forcing its way out before the radiologist can complete his examination. After the examination, like everyone who has ever been through the procedure, Conrad now feels as if there are eighty-five pounds of barium in his intestines and they are about to explode. The Smocks inform him that there is no john on this floor. He's supposed to pick up the tube that is coming out of his rectum and follow an orderly, who will lead him to a john two floors below. On the tube there is a clamp, and he can release the clamp, deflating the balloon, at the proper time. *It's unbelievable!* To try to walk, with this explosive load sloshing about in your pelvic saddle, is agony. Nevertheless, Conrad picks up the tube and follows the orderly. Conrad has on only the standard bed patient's tunic, the angel robes, open up the back. The tube leading out of his tail to the balloon gizmo is so short that he has to hunch over to about two feet off the floor to carry it in front of him. His tail is now, as the saying goes, flapping in the breeze, with a tube coming out of it. The orderly has on red cowboy boots. Conrad is intensely aware of that fact, because he is now hunched over so far that his eyes hit the orderly at about calf level. He's hunched over, with his tail in the breeze, scuttling like a crab after a pair of red cowboy boots. Out into a corridor they go, an ordinary public corridor, the full-moon hunchback and the red cowboy boots, amid men, women, children, nurses, nuns, the lot. The red cowboy boots are beginning to trot along like mad. The orderly is no fool. He's been through this before. He's been through the whole disaster. He's seen the explosions. Time is of the essence. There's a hunchback stick of dynamite behind him. To Conrad it becomes more incredible every step of the way. They actually have to go down an elevator—full of sane people—and do their crazy tango through another public hallway—agog with normal human beings—before finally reaching the goddamned john.

Later that day Conrad received, once more, instructions to report to the clinic at seven the next morning to give himself an enema. The next thing the people in the administrative office of the clinic knew, a small but enraged young man was storming into the office of General Schwichtenberg himself, waving a great flaccid flamingo-pink enema bag and hose like some sort of obese whip. As he waved it, it gurgled.

The enema bag came slamming down on the general's desk. It landed with a tremendous *plop* and then began gurgling and sighing.

"General Schwichtenberg," said Conrad, "you're looking at a man who has given himself his last enema. If you want enemas from me, from now on you can come get 'em yourself. You can take this bag and give it to a nurse and send her over—"

Just you—

"—and let her do the honors. I've given myself my last enema. Either things shape up around here, or I ship out."

The general stared at the great flamingo bag, which lay there heaving and wheezing on his desk, and then he stared at Conrad. The general seemed appalled . . . All the same it wouldn't do anybody any good, least of all the Lovelace Clinic, if one of the candidates pulled out, firing broadsides at the operation. The general started trying to mollify this vision of enema rage.

"Now, Lieutenant," he said, "I know this hasn't been pleasant. This is probably the toughest examination you'll ever have to go through in your life, but as you know, it's for a project of utmost importance. The project needs men like yourself. You have a compact build, and every pound saved in Project Mercury can be critical."

And so forth and so on. He kept spraying Conrad's fire.

"All the same, General, I've given myself my last enema."

Word of the Enema Bag Showdown spread rapidly among the other candidates, and they were delighted to hear about it. Practically all of them had wanted to do something of the sort. It wasn't just that the testing procedures were unpleasant; the entire atmosphere of the testing constituted an affront. There was something . . . decidedly *out of joint* about it. Pilots and doctors were natural enemies, of course, at least as pilots saw it. The flight surgeon was pretty much kept *in his place* in the service. His only real purpose was to tend to pilots and keep 'em flying. He was an attendant to the pilots' vital stuff. In fact, flight surgeons were encouraged to fly backseat with fighter pilots from time to time, so as to understand what stresses and righteous stuff the job entailed. Regardless of how much he thought of himself, no flight surgeon dared position himself *above* the pilots in his squadron in the way he conducted himself before them: i.e., it was hard for him to be a consummate panjandrum, the way the typical civilian doctor was.

But at Lovelace, in the testing for Project Mercury, the natural order was turned upside down. These people not only did not treat them as righteous pilots, they did not treat them as pilots of any sort. They never even alluded to the fact that they were pilots. An irksome thought was beginning to intrude. In the competition for *astronaut* the kind of stuff you were made of as a *pilot* didn't count for a goddamned thing. They were looking for a certain type of animal who registered bingo on the meter. You wouldn't win this competition in the air. If you won it, it would be right here on the examination table in the land of the rubber tubes.

Yes, the boys were delighted when Conrad finally told off General Schwichtenberg. Attaboy, Pete! At the same time, they were quite content to let the credit for the Lab Rat Revolt fall to Conrad and to him alone.

At Wright-Patterson Air Force Base, where they went for the psychological and stress testing, the air of secrecy was even more pronounced than at Lovelace. At Wright-Patterson they went through the testing in groups of eight. They were billeted off to themselves at the BOQ, the Bachelor Officers Quarters. If they had to call for anything on the base, they were not to refer to themselves by name. Instead, each of them had a number. Conrad was "Number 7." If he needed a car to take him from one place to another, to keep an appointment, he was supposed to ring up the car pool and say only: "This is Number Seven. I need a car . . ."

The testing, on the other hand, seemed—at first—more like what a self-respecting fighter jock might expect. They gave the candidate an oxygen mask and a partial-pressure suit and put him in an air-pressure chamber and reduced the pressure until an altitude of 65,000 feet was simulated. It made one feel as if his entire body were being squeezed by thongs, and he had to force his breath out in order to bring new oxygen into his lungs. Part of the stress was in the fact that they didn't tell him how long he had to stay there. They put each man in a small, pitch-black, windowless, soundproofed room—a "sensory deprivation chamber" —and locked the door, again without telling him how long he would have to stay there. It turned out to be three hours. They strapped each man into a huge human milkshake apparatus that vibrated the body at tremendous amplitudes and bombarded it with high-energy sound, some of it at excruciating frequencies. They put each man at the console of a machine called "the idiot box." It was like a simulator or a trainer. There were fourteen different signals that the candidate was supposed to respond to in different ways by pressing buttons or throwing switches; but the lights began lighting up so fast no human being could possibly keep up with them. This appeared to be not only a test of reaction times but of perseverance or ability to cope with frustration.

No, there was nothing wrong with tests of this sort. Nevertheless, the atmosphere around them was a bit . . . off. Psychiatrists were running the show at Wright-Patterson. Every inch of the way there were psychiatrists and psychologists standing over you taking notes and giving you little jot'em'n'dot'em tests. Before they put you in the Human Milkshake, some functionary in a white smock would present you with a series of numbered dots on a piece of paper on a clipboard and you were supposed to take a pencil and connect the dots so that the numbers beside them added up to certain sums. Then when you got out of the machine, the White Smock character would give you the same test again, presumably to see if the physical experience had impaired your ability to calculate. And that was all right, too. But they also had people staring at the candidate the whole time and taking notes. They took notes in little spiral notebooks. Every gesture you made, every tic, twitch, smile, stare, frown, every time you rubbed your nose—there was some White Smock standing by jotting it down in a notebook.

One of the most assiduous of the monitors was a psychologist, a woman named Dr. Gladys J. Loring—as Conrad could tell from the nameplate on her smock. Gladys J. Loring was beginning to annoy him intensely. Every time he turned around she seemed to be standing there staring at him, without a word, staring at him with utter White Smock detachment, as if he were a frog, a rabbit, a rat, a gerbil, a guinea pig, or some other lab animal, scribbling furiously in her notebook. For days she had been watching him, and they had never even been introduced. One day Conrad suddenly looked her straight in the eye and said: "Gladys! What . . . are . . . you . . . writing . . . in . . . your . . . notebook!"

Dr. Gladys J. Loring looked at him as if he were a flatworm. All she did was make another notation of the specimen's behavior in her notebook.

To fighter jocks it was bad enough to have doctors of any sort as your final judges. To find psychologists and psychiatrists positioned above you in this manner was irritating in the extreme. Military pilots, almost to a man, perceived psychiatry as a pseudo-science. They regarded the military psychiatrist as the modern and unusually bat-brained version of the chaplain. But the shrink could be dealt with. You just turned on the charm—lit up the halo of the right stuff—and did some prudent lying.

In the interviews for this job of "astronaut," as in other situations, the psychiatrists would get on the subject of the hazards of the assignment, the unknowns, the potentially high risk, and then gauge the candidate's reaction. As all heads-up pilots knew, this called for "second-convolution" thinking. It was a mistake to say anything along the lines of: *Oh, I rather enjoy risks, I enjoy hanging my hide out over the edge, day in and day out, for that is what makes me superior to other men.* The psychiatrists always interpreted that as a reckless love of danger, an irrational impulse associated with the late-Freudian concept of "the death wish." The proper response—heard more than once during that week at Wright-Patterson—was to say: "Oh, I don't regard Project Mercury as a particularly high-risk proposition, certainly not compared to the routine test work I've been doing for [the Air Force, the Navy, the Marines]. Since this project has a high national priority, I'm sure that the safety precautions will be far more thorough and reliable than they were on something like the [F-100F, F-102, F-104, F-4B], when I had *that one* in the test stage." (Very slight smile and roll of the eyeballs.) Beautiful stuff! This showed that you were a rational test pilot, as concerned about safety as any sensible professional . . . while at the same time getting across the idea that you had been routinely risking your life and were so used to it, had such righteous stuff, that riding a rocket seemed like a vacation by comparison. That created the Halo Effect. Offhand allusions to derring-do would have the psychiatrists looking at you with big wide eyes, like little boys.

Conrad knew all this as well as the rest of them. He knew exactly how the prudent officer should deal with these people. It was hard not to know. Every night the boys got together in the BOQ and regaled each other with stories of how they had lied their heads off or otherwise diligently subverted the inquiries of the shrinks. Conrad's problem was that somewhere along the way the Hickory Kid always took over and had to add *a wink or two* for good measure.

In one test the interviewer gave each candidate a blank sheet of paper and asked him to study it and describe what he saw in it. There was no one right response in this sort of test, because it was designed to force the candidate to free-associate in order to see where his mind wandered. The test-wise pilot knew that the main thing was to stay on dry land and not go swimming. As they described with some relish later on in the BOQ, quite a few studied the sheet of paper and then looked the interviewer in the eye and said, "All I see is a blank sheet of paper." This was not a "correct" answer, since the shrinks probably made note of "inhibited imaginative capacity" or some goddamned thing, but neither did it get you in trouble. One man said, "I see a field of snow." Well, you might get away with that, as long as you didn't go any further . . . as long as you did not thereupon start ruminating about freezing to death or getting lost in the snow and running into bears or something of that sort. But Conrad . . . well, the man is sitting across the table from Conrad and gives him the sheet of paper and asks him to study it and tell him what he sees. Conrad stares at the piece of paper and then looks up at the man and says in a wary tone, as if he fears a trick: "But it's upside down."

This so startles the man, he actually leans across the table and looks at this absolutely blank sheet of paper to see if it's true—and only after he is draped across the table does he realize that he has been had. He looks at Conrad and smiles a smile of about 33 degrees Fahrenheit.

This was *not* the way to produce the Halo Effect.

In another test they showed the candidates pictures of people in various situations and asked them to make up stories about them. One of the pictures they showed Conrad was a piece of American Scene Okie Realism, apparently from the Depression years. You could see a poor sunken hookwormy sharecropper in bib overalls trying to push a rusty plow through some eroded ground that was more gully than topsoil, aided by a mule with all his ribs showing, while off to one side the man's sallow hollow-socketed pellagra-ravaged wife with a swollen eight-month belly covered by a dress made from a fertilizer sack leans up against their shack to catch her breath or else to prop up the side wall. Conrad looks at the picture and says, "Well, you can tell that this man is a nature lover. He not only tills the soil, he appreciates the scenery, as you can tell by the way he is looking off toward the mountains, the better to observe the way the pale blue of the range in the distance harmonizes with the purple haze of the hills near his beloved homestead"—and on and on in this fashion until, at long last, it draws on the interviewer that this wiry wiseacre who chatters away with a gap between his front teeth . . . is sending him up, him and his whole test.

This did not create the Halo Effect, either.

Oh, Conrad was rolling now. He was beginning to have a good time. But he had one piece of unfinished business. That night he called up the car pool.

"This is Number Seven," he said. "Number Seven needs a car to go to the PX."

The next day, after the heat-chamber test, in which he spent three hours shut up in a cubicle heated to 130 degrees, Conrad was rubbing the sweat off the end of his nose when he looked up—and sure enough, Dr. Gladys J. Loring was right there, making note of the event in her spiral notebook with a ballpoint pen. Conrad reached into the pocket of his pants . . . and came up with a spiral notebook and a ballpoint pen just like hers.

"Gladys!" he said. She looked up. She was startled. Conrad started scribbling in his notebook and then looked at her again. "Aha! You touched your ear, Gladys! We call that inhibition of the exhibitionism!" More scribbling in the notebook. "Oh-oh! Lowering of the eyes, Gladys! Repressed hypertrophy of the latency! I'm sorry, but it has to go in the report!"

Word of how the flatworm turned . . . how the lab rat had risen up . . .

how Pavlov's dog rang Pavlov's bell and took notes on it . . . oh, word of all this circulated quickly, too, and everyone, from Number 1 to Number 8, was quite delighted. There was no indication, however, then or later, that Dr. Gladys Loring was amused in the slightest.

W HEN SCOTT CARPENTER called home to California from Wright-Patterson in the evenings—and he was always careful to take advantage of the lower evening rates—his wife, Rene, was usually in the living room. They had a house in Garden Grove, a town near Disneyland. The focal point of the living room was a three-piece sectional sofa that had a great teardrop-shaped monkeypod coffee table in front of it and a monkeypod end table at this end and another monkeypod end table at the other end. A great deal was summed up by those three great showy slabs of monkeypod wood with the yellow-brown grain streaks curling this way and that. Every officer and his wife in the U.S. Navy in the year 1959 understood the Monkeypod Life.

Scott was a lieutenant, which meant that his pay, including subsistence and housing allowance, was only about $7,200 a year, plus some extra flight pay. Young officers and their wives realized from the outset, of course, that abysmal pay was one of the realities of a service career. There were other forms of compensation: the opportunity to fly, which Scott loved; the status of a Naval officer; the community of the squadron (when one was in the mood for it); a certain sense of mission (if you were feeling good about yourself) that civilians lacked—extras, such as flight pay and a housing allowance, and *the goodies*. Given the dreadfully low pay, the goodies, which were usually trivial by ordinary standards, tended to take on an overblown importance. That was why so many young military couples in the late 1950's had living rooms dominated, ruled, oppressed, enslaved by the most bizarre furniture imaginable: Chinese k'ang tables with entire village scenes carved into the tops of them in deep relief, squads of high-backed Turkish chairs that could have swallowed a ballroom, Korean divans with wood frames so ornately inlaid with mother-of-pearl that the entire room seemed to be grinning hideously, Spanish armoires so gross, so gloomy, so overbearing that the mere sight of them brought conversation to a halt . . . and the flamboyant monkeypod. For one of the goodies was the opportunity to buy hand-carved wooden furniture cheaply when you were assigned to the far ends of the earth. That was your opportunity to furnish the living room at last!—and the military would ship it back to the States free of charge. Of course, your choice was limited by the local taste. In Korea you settled for mother-of-pearl or Chinese baroque. And in Hawaii, where Scott and Rene had been assigned, there was always the monkeypod.

In a department store in Hawaii a first-rate finished monkeypod coffee table cost about $150. A modest sum, one might say; but if your base pay was only $7,200 a year, that meant you had only forty-eight such sums to last you for an entire year. And Scott and Rene had four children! But unfinished slabs of this amazing wood with its flaming yellow grain were available for as little as nine dollars. If you were willing to spend twenty-four hours sanding, rubbing, oiling, and polishing them, and another ten or twenty constructing legs or frames, you could save $140. Fortunately, Rene had a good sense of design and was even able to use the monkeypod with finesse—a rare accomplishment in the Monkeypod Life.

Both Scott and Rene had been brought up in Boulder, Colorado. Scott was top drawer by Boulder social standards, such as they were. He was descended from the first white settlers in the state. His mother's father, Victor Noxon, owned and edited a newspaper, the Boulder *Miner-Journal*. Scott's parents had separated when he was only three, and his mother contracted tuberculosis and was confined to a sanitarium for long stretches, so that Scott lived in Victor Noxon's house and was, as it turned out, raised by him. Rene met Scott at the University of Colorado and dropped out in her sophomore year to marry him. They spent practically that entire first year on the ski slopes. They were an extraordinarily good-looking couple, both blond, trim, athletic, high-spirited, outgoing, the sort of couple you seldom actually saw outside the Lucky Strike ads. Many wives of fighter pilots would end up looking on helplessly as their husbands grew more and more distant, a fact they would acknowledge in what were meant as lighthearted remarks, such as: "I'm only his mistress—he's married to an airplane." Often she would be overstating their intimacy; the actual mistress would be someone she didn't know about. Scott, on the contrary, was completely devoted to Rene and their two sons and two daughters. Many nights, during the testing for Project Mercury, Scott wrote Rene long letters, some of them ten or fifteen pages, rather than run up more telephone bills. He kept trying to reassure her that he wasn't getting involved in anything reckless. One night he wrote: "Most of all, don't worry. You know what is uppermost in my mind and that I wouldn't needlessly jeopardize what we have together." He was determined, he said, to live long enough "to make love to you as a grandmother."

All along, his feelings on this score had been so profound that he had done an extraordinary thing eight years before. After finishing his basic flight training at Pensacola and his advanced training at Corpus Christi, he had voluntarily chosen to fly multi-engine PBY-4 patrol planes rather than fighter planes. He didn't even like PBY-4s. He could barely stand to fly them. Who could? They were big slow awkward trucks. Yet he had stepped down off the great ziggurat pyramid here at the first major plateau. If the subject ever came up, he would say: "I did it out of allegiance to my family," meaning that patrol planes didn't leave as many widows behind. The Korean War was just beginning, and Scott ended up flying P2V patrol planes up and down the Pacific mainland. Naturally this was completely outside the big league for Navy pilots in the war. Any truly righteous aviator wanted to be assigned, on loan, to an Air Force fighter squadron for aerial combat over North Korea. But reconnaissance had its own hazards and trials, and Scott was considered extremely proficient at it; so much so that after the war he was brought to Patuxent River and trained as a test pilot.

Nevertheless, Scott had forsaken the righteous competition. Of his own accord! Out of allegiance to his family! Perhaps it had to do with his memories of how his own family had been disrupted during his early childhood. Well, that was something for psychiatrists to speculate about, and no doubt they were doing so. In his first psychiatric interview at Wright-Patterson, Scott himself had opened the session. He asked the first question. He said to the man: "How many children do you have? I have four."

Scott was surprised when he found himself among the thirty-two finalists in the competition for astronaut. He had bowed out of the big-league competition long ago. He had only two hundred hours of flying time in jets; and most of that he had accumulated in the course of flight test training. The other candidates all seemed to have fifteen hundred to twenty-five hundred. Yet here he was. Not only that, as the days had gone by, first at Lovelace and now at Wright-Pat, his prospects had begun to look promising. It was amazing.

One thing Scott had going for him was his superb physical condition, although at the outset he would have never believed that sheer physical condition could be of any vital importance. He had been a gymnast at the University of Colorado and had terrific shoulders with the deltoid muscles bulging out in high relief, a thick strong neck, an absolutely lean and perfectly formed chest, like a South Sea pearl diver's—and, in fact, he had done a great deal of scuba diving—and his torso tapered down like Captain America's in the comic strip. Others complained the whole time, but the tests at Lovelace and Wright-Patterson didn't bother Scott in the slightest. Each one was a moment of triumph for him.

One night Scott called, and Rene could tell that he was exceptionally pleased over how things were going. It seemed that there was a test of lung capacity. The candidate sat at a table and blew into a tube. The tube led into an instrument with a column of mercury. The idea was to see how long you could hold the column of mercury up to a designated level with the pressure of your breath. The record, they were informed, was ninety-one seconds. Scott—as he excitedly told Rene that night—knew from years of undersea swimming that after your lungs feel completely out of air and every signal in your central nervous system predicts disaster if you hold your breath an instant longer, you actually have a substantial reserve supply of oxygen in your system. It is the buildup of carbon dioxide in the lungs, not the absolute depletion of oxygen, that signals the emergency. Scott forced himself to hold his breath, through all the early signals, while he counted slowly to one hundred, with the idea of surpassing the mark of ninety-one seconds. He counted very slowly, as it turned out, and held the column of mercury up for 171 seconds, almost doubling the record.

Another candidate in Scott's group also broke the old record by holding the mercury up 150 seconds. He was a Marine pilot named John Glenn. Scott had known Glenn slightly when both were at Pax River during Scott's flight test training. Glenn had set a cross-country speed record, Los Angeles to New York, of three hours and twenty-three minutes in an F8U fighter plane in July 1957. The two of them had hit it off immediately at Wright-Pat, partly, perhaps, because they appeared to be the two pacesetters in the testing. Scott had broken five records in all, and Glenn was usually his runner-up. One day they overheard one of the doctors saying to another: "Let's call Washington and tell them about these two guys."

Dr. Gladys J. Loring and the others were astounded by Scott's performance, and not merely by such matters as his lung capacity, either; for many of the tests were not physical tests in the ordinary sense but, rather, tests of perseverance and one's willingness to push oneself beyond the usual limits of human endurance.

Scott Carpenter did not mind the note-taking of Dr. Gladys J. Loring in the slightest. Scribble away! Scott was in his element.

CONRAD WAS BACK HOME in North Town Creek, back at Pax River, when the letter from NASA arrived. He knew he had not played it very smoothly during the testing. He had compared notes with Wally Schirra, and it turned out that when Wally's group had gone through Lovelace, they had been just as ticked off at the way the place was run as Conrad and his group had been. Wally had even led his own little rebellion when they wanted their goddamned stool samples. One afternoon they had told Wally and the boys to avoid all highly seasoned food that evening, because they wanted to take stool samples the next day. So the whole group headed off to the Mexican section of Albuquerque, and they had picked out the rankest-looking restaurant they could find and fired up their innards with every red-mad dish they had ever heard of and hosed it down with plenty of good cheap rank Mexican beer. The jalapeño peppers had even gotten into the act! One of the boys had discovered a bowl of jalapeño pepper sauce on the table, a fiery reddish-brown concoction, and had poured it into a Dixie cup and presented it to the lab technicians as if he had a ferocious case of diarrhea— and had laughed his head off when the first sultry cloud of jalapeño aroma nearly wiped them out. But that was as far as he went—the lab technician level. He let the good General Schwichtenberg remain reserved and serene. That was the way Wally himself would have done it. He always knew where the outside of the envelope was, even when it came to pranks.

No, Conrad knew he had poked a few unfortunate holes in the old envelope . . . Still, he had spoken his mind before and it had never hurt him. His career in the Navy had gone up on a steady curve. He had never been left behind. So he opened the letter.

From the very first line he knew the rest. The letter noted that he had been among the finalists in the selection process and said he was to be commended for that. Alas, it went on, he had not been one of the seven chosen for the assignment, but NASA and one & all were grateful to him for volunteering and so forth and so on.

Well, there it was, your classic Dear John letter. Even though in his detached moments he realized that he had perhaps screwed the pooch here and there, it was hard to believe. He had been left behind. This was something that had never happened to him in the nearly six years he had been moving up the great invisible ziggurat.

A couple of days later he found out that Wally had made it. Wally was one of the seven. So was Alan Shepard, who had also been in that room at the Marriott.

Well, what the hell. Wally himself had given them all a lot of pretty sound reasons why a man shouldn't feel too goddamned unlucky if he *didn't* get involved in this Rube Goldberg *capsule* business. It was probably all for the best. Project Mercury was a civilian enterprise and slightly wacky when you got right down to it. They hadn't even chosen *pilots*, f'r chrissake. Jim Lovell had been ranked number one in Group 20 at Pax River, and he hadn't been chosen, either. They had all been lab rats from beginning to end. It was a good thing someone had set the record straight . . .

Still! It was incredible! He had been . . . *left behind!*

Not too long afterward, Conrad was told that across the master sheet on top of his file at Wright-Patterson had been written: "Not suitable for long-duration flight."

5

IN SINGLE COMBAT

T HEY BUBBLE, THEY BOIL, they steam and scream, they rumble, and then they boil some more in the most excited way. This sound of boiling voices was exactly like the sound an actor hears backstage before the curtain goes up on a play that everyone—*tout le monde*—must attend. Once there, everyone starts chattering away, out of the sheer excitement of being there at all, of being *where things are happening*, until everybody's beaming face is boiling away with words and grins and laughs that burst out whether or not anything the least bit funny has been said.

As he was not much of an actor, however, this was the sort of sound that terrified Gus Grissom. He was only moments away from the part he was likely to be worst at, and these people were all waiting on the other side of the curtain. At 2 p.m. the curtain was pulled back, and he had to walk onto the stage.

A sheet of light hit Gus and the others, and the boiling voices dropped down to a rumble, or a buzz, and then you could make them out. There appeared to be hundreds of them, packed in shank to flank, sitting, standing, squatting. Some of them were up on a ladder that was propped against the wall under one of the huge lights. Some of them had cameras with the most protuberant lenses, and they had a way of squatting and crawling at the same time, like the hunkered-down beggars you saw all over the Far East. The lights were on for television crews. This building was the Dolley Madison House, at the northeast corner of Lafayette Square, just a few hundred yards from the White House. It had been converted into NASA's Washington headquarters, and this room was the ballroom, which they used for press conferences, and it was not nearly big enough for all these people. The little beggar figures were crawling all over it.

The NASA people steered Gus and the other six to seats at a long table on the stage. The table had a felt cloth over it. They put Gus in a seat at the middle of the table, and sticking up over the felt right in front of him was the needle nose of a miniature escape tower on top of a model of the Mercury capsule mounted on an Atlas rocket. The model was evidently propped up against the other side of the table so that the press could see it. A man from NASA named Walter Bonney got up, a man with a jolly-sounding voice, and he said: "Ladies and gentlemen, may I have your attention, please. The rules of this briefing are very simple. In about sixty seconds we will give you the announcement that you have all been waiting for: the names of the seven volunteers who will become the Mercury astronaut team. Following the distribution of the kit—and this will be done as speedily as possible—those of you who have p.m. deadline problems had better dash for your phones. We will have about a ten- or twelve-minute break during which the gentlemen will be available for picture taking."

Some men from over on the sides appeared and began handing out folders, and people were rushing up and grabbing these kits and bolting from the room. Bonney pointed to the seven of them sitting there at the table and said: "Gentlemen, these are the astronaut volunteers. Take your pictures as you will, gentlemen."

And now began a very odd business. Without another word, all these grim little crawling beggar figures began advancing toward them, elbowing and hipping one another out of the way, growling and muttering, but never looking at each other, since they had their cameras screwed into their eye sockets and remained concentrated on Gus and the six other pilots at the table in the most obsessive way, like a swarm of root weevils which, no matter how much energy they might expend in all directions trying to muscle one another out of the way, keep their craving beaks homed in on the juicy stuff that the whole swarm has sensed—until they were all over them, within inches of their faces in some cases, poking their mechanical beaks into everything but their belly buttons. Yet this by itself was not what made the moment so strange. It was something else on top of it. There was such frantic excitement—and their names had not even been mentioned! Yet it didn't matter in the slightest! They didn't care whether he was Gus Grissom or Joe Blow! They were ravenous for his picture all the same! They were crawling all over him and the other six as if they were creatures of tremendous value and excitement, real prizes.

Ravenous they were!—these swarming photographers who could grunt but not speak, who crawled over them for a full fifteen minutes. Nevertheless, who was dying for the press conference to start? Anytime Gus had to tell total strangers how he felt about anything, it made him uncomfortable; and the thought of doing so publicly, in this room, in front of several hundred people, made him extremely uncomfortable. Gus came from the sort of background where, to put it mildly, glibness was not encouraged. Back in Mitchell, Indiana, his father had been a railroad worker. His mother used to take the family to the Church of Christ, a Protestant denomination that was so fundamentalist no musical instruments were allowed in the church, not even a piano. The human voice raising thanks to God was music enough. Not that Gus was much of a singer, either, however. His public incantations consisted mainly of Hoosier gus gruffisms. He was a short man with sloping shoulders, a compact build, black crew-cut hair, and black bushy eyebrows, a broad nose, and a face given to very dour looks. The only time Gus felt like talking was when he was with other pilots, particularly at beer call. Then he became another human being. His sleepy eyes lit up to about 200 watts. A crazy confident grin took over his mouth. He would start talking a streak and drinking a lake and, when the midnight madness struck, getting into his hot rod and sucking the surrounding countryside up his two exhaust pipes. Flying &

Drinking and Drinking & Driving, of course. Gus was one of those young men, quite common in the United States, actually, who would fight you down to the last unbroken bone over an insult to the gray little town they came from or the grim little church they fidgeted in all those years—while at the same time, in some hidden corner of the soul, they prostrated themselves daily in thanksgiving to the things that had gotten them the hell out of there. In Gus's case those things had been hot rods and, now, airplanes.

Gus had flown a hundred missions in combat in Korea and had won the Distinguished Flying Cross, after breaking formation to chase away a MiG-15 that was about to jump one of his outfit's reconnaissance planes, although somehow, during that great duck shoot over Korea, to his regret, he had never succeeded in downing an enemy plane. After the war he had done all-weather testing of fighter planes at Wright-Patterson and was highly thought of there. So far he had not reached the big league, which was being prime pilot for testing a new fighter, preferably at Edwards. But Gus had every confidence in himself; which is to say, he was a typical fighter jock heading up the pyramid. He already sensed that winning out in the competition for Project Mercury was a tremendous achievement for him, even if it remained to be seen just how far this advanced a man up the ziggurat.

There was just one odd thing about the situation. Last night, at Langley Field, near Newport News, Virginia, Gus had met the other six pilots who had won out. Two of the Air Force pilots were from Edwards. That was to be expected; Edwards was the big league. But one of them, Gordon Cooper, was a man Gus had known at Wright-Pat at one point, and Cooper was not in Fighter Ops at Edwards. The very hottest pilots at Edwards, of course, were in the rocket-plane projects, the X-series. The best line-test pilots were in Fighter Ops as prime pilots in the testing of aircraft such as the Century series of jet fighters. That was what the other Edwards pilot, Deke Slayton, had been involved in. But Cooper—Cooper had graduated from Test Pilot School and was officially a test pilot, but he had been involved mainly in engineering. Not only that, there was this fellow from the Navy, Scott Carpenter. He seemed to be a likable sort—but he had never been in a fighter squadron. He had been flying multi-engine propeller planes and had only two hundred hours in jets. What did this say about the business of being selected as a Mercury astronaut?

Finally, the NASA people were shooing the photographers away from the table, and the head of NASA, a man with big smooth jowls named T. Keith Glennan, got up and said: "Ladies and gentlemen, today we are introducing to you and to the world these seven men who have been selected to begin training for orbital space flight. These men, the nation's Project Mercury astronauts, are here after a long and perhaps unprecedented series of evaluations which told our medical consultants and scientists of their superb adaptability to their upcoming flight."

And it was probably noticed by no one other than the seven pilots themselves that he mentioned only their *adaptability*. He had nothing to say, not a word, about their prowess or standing as pilots.

"It is my pleasure," said Glennan, "to introduce to you—and I consider it a very real honor, gentlemen—Malcolm S. Carpenter, Leroy G. Cooper, John H. Glenn, Jr., Virgil I. Grissom, Walter M. Schirra, Jr., Alan B. Shepard, Jr., and Donald K. Slayton . . . the nation's Mercury Astronauts!"

With that, applause erupted, applause of the most fervent sort, amazing applause. Reporters rose to their feet, applauding as if they had come for no other reason. Smiles of weepy and grateful sympathy washed across their faces. They gulped, they cheered, as if this were one of the most inspiring moments of their lives. Even some of the photographers straightened up from out of their beggar's crouches and let their cameras dangle from their straps, so that they could use their hands for clapping.

But for what?

Once the reporters and photographers got hold of themselves again, men from NASA, the Air Force, and the Navy got up and testified to how terrifically the seven of them had done on all the tests at Lovelace and Wright-Patterson—yet *not one word* was uttered about any ability or experience they might have had *as pilots*. The tone of the thing, the angle, didn't improve with the questions from the reporters. The first reporter who raised his hand wanted to know from each of them whether his wife and children had "had anything to say about this."

Wife and children?

Most of them, Gus included, dealt with this question in typical military-pilot fashion. Which is to say, they managed to get out something brief, obvious, abstract, and above all safe and impersonal. But when it becomes the turn of the guy sitting on Gus's left, John Glenn, the only Marine in the group—it's hard to believe. This guy starts *turning on the charm!* He has a regular little speech on the subject.

"I don't think any of us could really go on with something like this," he says, "if we didn't have pretty good backing at home, really. My wife's attitude toward this has been the same as it has been all along through my flying. If it is what I want to do, she is behind it, and the kids are, too, a hundred percent."

What the hell was he talking about? *I don't think any of us could really go on with something like this . . . What* possible difference could a *wife's attitude* make about an opportunity for a giant step up the great ziggurat? What was with this guy? It kept on in that fashion. Some reporter gets up and asks them all to tell about their religious affiliations (religious affiliations?)—and Glenn tees off again.

"I am a Presbyterian," he says, "a Protestant Presbyterian, and I take my religion very seriously, as a matter of fact." He starts telling them about all the Sunday schools he has taught at and the church boards he has served on and all the church work that he and his wife and his children have done. "I was brought up believing that you are placed on earth here more or less with sort of a fifty-fifty proposition, and this is what I still believe. We are placed here with certain talents and capabilities. It is up to each of us to use those talents and capabilities as best you can. If you do that, I think there is a power greater than any of us that will place the opportunities in our way, and if we use our talents properly, we will be living the kind of life we should live."

Jesus Christ—share it, brother. You can see the boys cutting glances from either end of the table up at this flying churchman Gus is sitting next to. They're seated in alphabetical order, with Scott Carpenter at one end and Deke Slayton at the other and Glenn in the middle. What can anybody say as a follow-up to this man and his speeches about the Wife and the Children and the Family and Sunday School and God? What can you do, say that as a matter of fact you can get along just as well without any of them as long as they'll let you fly? That didn't seem very prudent. (Turn on the halo—and lie!) You could see these pilots struggling to put up enough chips to stay in the God & Family game with this pious Marine named Glenn.

When it was Gus's turn, he said: "I consider myself religious. I am a Protestant and belong to the Church of Christ. I am not real active in church, as Mr. Glenn is"—*Mister* Glenn, he calls him—"but I consider myself a good Christian still." Deke Slayton says: "As far as my religious faith is concerned, I am a Lutheran, and I go to church periodically." One of the Navy pilots, Alan Shepard, says: "I am not a member of any church. I attend the Christian Science Church regularly." And so it went. It was a struggle.

God . . . Family . . . the only thing that Glenn hadn't wrapped them all up in was Country, and so he took care of that, too. He gave a nice little speech that started with Orville and Wilbur Wright standing on a hill at Kitty Hawk, North Carolina, tossing a coin to see which one would take the first airplane flight, and then he tied that in with the first space flight. "I think we are very fortunate," he said, "that we have, should we say, been blessed with the talents that have been picked for something like this.' (No one had said a word about *talents*, however.) "I think we would be most remiss in our duty," he went on, "if we didn't make the fullest use of our talents in volunteering for something that is as important as this is to our country and to the world in general right now. This can mean an awful lot to this country, of course."

This guy had the halo turned on at all times! Glenn had all the verbal skills that Gus lacked, and yet he didn't seem glib or smooth about it. He looked like a balding and slightly tougher version of the cutest-looking freckle-faced country boy you ever saw. He had a snub nose, light-hazel eyes, reddish-blond hair, a terrific smile, and thousands of freckles. He had the sunniest face in ten counties. He was also one of the best-known pilots in the Marines. He had flown in combat in both the Second World War and the Korean War and had won many medals, including five DFC's, and two years ago, in 1957, he had made the first coast-to-coast non-stop supersonic flight. On the basis of that accomplishment, he had been invited onto a TV show, *Name That Tune*, with a child singer, Eddie Hodges, as his partner, and he had beamed the freckled smile on TV and just charmed the hell out of everybody. The two of them were on the show several weeks.

Well . . . hell . . . maybe he was sincere, after all. God knew that for any pilot to get involved in that much Sunday school and that many church boards and good works, he'd have to be a true believer and a half. Perhaps he even meant it about Wife & Family . . . which would make him an even rarer breed of fighter pilot. If anybody asked Gus—like right now—if he were religious, a family man, and a patriot, he would say yes, he was religious, and yes, he was a family man, and yes, he was a patriot. But the firmest conviction of the three was about being a patriot. When Gus said he would gladly ride a Mercury rocket for the sake of his country, he meant it. Alan Shepard said the same thing and there was not the slightest doubt that he meant it. And there was no doubt that Glenn meant it, no matter how he went on about it. That was one of the inexpressible things about being a military flying officer. You *meant* it! You were among the few who had "the uncritical willingness to face danger"! There was an exhilaration to this that few civilians could possibly comprehend! No, Gus was a patriot, and he had his hundred combat missions and his DFC to attest to that simple, beautiful fact. Now, as for being a family man . . . aw, hell . . . he meant to be a family man, but somehow his career, or something, always got in the way. He and his wife, Betty, had gotten married as soon as they finished high school in Mitchell. Right from the very first he found himself in situations where he became separated from her. He didn't plan it that way, but it kept happening. Right after they got married, he was due to start his freshman year at Purdue, and so he went off to Purdue to find some place for them to live. Well . . . somehow the only place he could find was a basement room. She said that was okay, she didn't mind, they'd live in a basement room. He said, well, the problem was, he was going to have to share the room with another guy—it was the only way he could afford it—so he would get back to Mitchell as often as he could, on weekends. So that was the way they started out, with him on the campus at Purdue and Betty living with her parents in Mitchell. Military flying was hard on home life, too. Gus graduated and started his Air Force training at Randolph Field in Texas. Betty was pregnant, and he was in training and was making only $100 a month anyway, and so why didn't she stay in Seymour, Indiana, with her sister Mary Lou, and Gus would visit her when he could. The only trouble was, he couldn't visit her very often, it being so expensive to travel from Texas to Indiana. When Betty gave birth to their first child, Scott, Gus was at an important part in his flight training and couldn't get to Indiana for that, either. He gets on the phone and says to her: "Well, you tell me what you really want me to do" . . . and she says, "Well, I guess you ought not to interrupt your training." In fact, he didn't quite manage to see his first child until six months later. Now, that sort of thing could happen in the service, because a fellow could get sent overseas at a moment's notice. But he, Gus, hadn't been sent anywhere except down the road to Arizona, to Williams Air Force Base, for advanced training. At the time . . . well, it just seemed damned hard to get all the way from the Southwestern U.S.A. to Indiana when you were in the thick of flight training. Then the Air Force *did* send him overseas, to Korea, and Betty went back to Indiana again. Korea! He *loved* it! He liked combat missions so much that when he completed a hundred missions, he volunteered for twenty-five more. He wanted to *stay* there! But the bastards made him come back. Somehow he and Betty managed to get by through all this. He gruffed a lot of Hoosier gus gruffisms at her and she gruffed some back at him. They didn't get in many fights. Most weekends he could manage it, he would fly cross-country, piling up flight time. But how different was he from the other pilots at this table, if the truth were known—except for this unbelievable Marine, Glenn, who was sitting here next to him painting some goddamned amazing picture of the Perfect Pilot wrapped up in a cocoon of Home & Hearth and God & Flag!

Neither he nor any of the others set about altering that picture, however. At first it was hard to figure out what was happening. Glenn could have never gone off on these fantastic outside loops of his if it were not for the fact that practically every question had to do with families and faith and motivation and patriotism and so on. There had not been a single question about their achievements or experience as pilots. Then one of the reporters gets up and says:

"Could I ask for a show of hands of how many are confident that they will come back from outer space?"

Gus and the others started looking down the table at each other, and then they all started hoisting their hands in the air. It really made you feel like an idiot, raising your hand this way. If you didn't think you were "coming back," then you would really have to be a fool or a nut to have volunteered at all. As the seven of them looked at each other sitting there with their hands up in the air like school-children, they began grinning in embarrassment, and then the heart of the matter dawned on them. This question about "coming back" was nothing other than a euphemistic way of asking: Aren't you afraid you're going to die? That was the question these people had been circling around the whole time. That was what they really wanted to know, all these wide-eyed reporters and their grunting crawling beggar photographers. They didn't care whether the seven Mercury astronauts were pilots or not. Infantrymen or acrobats would have done just as well. The main thing was: they had volunteered to sit on top of the rockets—which *always blew up!* They were brave lads who had volunteered for a suicide mission! They were kamikazes going forth to vie with the Russians! And all the questions about wives and children and faith and God and motivation and the Flag . . . they were really questions about widows and orphans . . . and how a warrior talks himself into going on a mission in which he is bound to die.

And this man, John Glenn, had given them an answer as sentimental as the question itself, and Gus and the rest had gone along with it. Henceforth, they would be served up inside the biggest slice of Mom's Pie you could imagine. And it had all happened in just about an hour. The seven of them sat there like fools with their hands hung up in the air, grinning with embarrassment. But that was all right; they would get over the embarrassment soon enough. Glenn, one couldn't help noticing, had *both* hands up in the air.

B<small>Y THE NEXT MORNING</small> the seven Mercury astronauts were national heroes. It happened just like that. Even though so far they had done nothing more than show up for a press conference, they were known as the seven bravest men in America. They woke up to find astonishing acclaim all over the press. There it was, in the more sophisticated columns as well as in the tabloids and on television. Even James Reston of *The New York Times* had been so profoundly moved by the press conference and the sight of the seven brave men that his heart, he confessed, now beat a little faster. "What made them so exciting," he wrote, "was not that they said anything new but that they said all the old things with such fierce convictions . . . They spoke of 'duty' and 'faith' and 'country' like Walt Whitman's pioneers . . . This is a pretty cynical town, but nobody went away from these young men scoffing at their courage and idealism." Manly courage, the right stuff—the Halo Effect, with Deacon Glenn leading the hallelujah chorus, had practically wiped the man out. If Gus and some of the others had been worried that they weren't being regarded as hot pilots, their worries were over when they saw the press coverage. Without exception, the newspapers and wire services picked out the highlights of their careers and carefully massed them to create a single blaze of glory. This took true journalistic skill. It meant citing a great deal from John Glenn's career, his combat flying in two wars, his five Distinguished Flying Crosses with eighteen clusters, and his recent speed record, plus the combat that Gus and Wally Schirra had seen in Korea and the medals they had won, one DFC apiece, and the bombing missions Slayton had flown in the Second World War and a bit about the jet fighters he had helped test at Edwards and the ones Shepard had tested at Pax River—and going easy on the subject of Scott Carpenter and Gordon Cooper, who had not flown in combat (Shepard had not, either) or done any extraordinary testing. John Glenn came out of it as tops among seven very fair-haired boys. He had the hottest record as a pilot, he was the most quotable, the most photogenic, and the lone Marine. But all seven, collectively, emerged in a golden haze as the seven finest pilots and bravest men in the United States. A blazing aura was upon them all.

It was as if the press in America, for all its vaunted independence, were a great colonial animal, an animal made up of countless clustered organisms responding to a single nervous system. In the late 1950's (as in the late 1970's) the animal seemed determined that in all matters of national importance the *proper emotion*, the *seemly sentiment*, the *fitting moral tone* should be established and should prevail; and all information that muddied the tone and weakened the feeling should simply be thrown down the memory hole. In a later period this impulse of the animal would take the form of blazing indignation about corruption, abuses of power, and even minor ethical lapses, among public officials; here, in April of 1959, it took the form of a blazing patriotic passion for the seven test pilots who had volunteered to go into space. In either case, the animal's fundamental concern remained the same: the public, the populace, the citizenry, must be provided with *the correct feelings!* One might regard this animal as the consummate hypocritical Victorian gent. Sentiments that one scarcely gives a second thought to in one's private life are nevertheless insisted upon in all public utterances. (And this grave gent lives on in excellent health.)

Even so, why was the press aroused to create *instant* heroes out of these seven men? This was a question that not James Reston or the pilots themselves or anyone at NASA could have answered at the time, because the very language of the proposition had long since been abandoned and forgotten. The forgotten term, left behind in the superstitious past, was *single combat*.

Just as the Soviet success in putting Sputniks into orbit around the earth revived long-buried superstitions about the power of heavenly bodies and the fear of hostile control of the heavens, so did the creation of astronauts and a "manned space program" bring back to life one of the ancient superstitions of warfare. Single combat had been common throughout the world in the pre-Christian era and endured in some places through the Middle Ages. In single combat the mightiest soldier of one army would fight the mightiest soldier of the other army as a substitute for a pitched battle between the entire forces. In some cases the combat would pit small teams of warriors against one another. Single combat was not seen as a humanitarian substitute for wholesale slaughter until late in its history. That was a Christian reinterpretation of the practice. Originally it had a magical meaning. In ancient China, first the champion warriors would fight to the death as a "testing of fate," and then the entire armies would fight, emboldened or demoralized by the outcome of the single combat. Before Mohammed's first battle as the warrior-prophet, the Battle of Badr, three of Mohammed's men challenged the Meccans to pick out any three of their soldiers to fight in single combat, proceeded to destroy them with all due ceremony, whereupon Mohammed's entire force routed the entire Meccan force. In other cases, however, the single combat settled the affair, and there was no full-scale battle, as when the Vandal and Aleman Armies confronted each other in Spain in the fifth century A.D. They believed that the gods determined the outcome of single combat; therefore, it was useless for the losing side to engage in a full-scale battle. The Old Testament story of David and Goliath is precisely that: a story of single combat that demoralizes the losing side. The gigantic Goliath, with his brass helmet, coat of mail, and ornate greaves, is described as the Philistine "champion" who comes forth to challenge the Israelites to send forth a man to fight him; the proposition being that whoever loses, his people will become the slaves of the other side. Before going out to meet Goliath, David—an unknown volunteer commoner—is given King Saul's own decorative armor, although he declines to wear it. When he kills Goliath, the Philistines regard this as such a terrible sign that they flee and are pursued and slaughtered.

Naturally the brave lads chosen for single combat enjoyed a very special status in the army and among their people (David was installed in the royal household and eventually superseded Saul's own sons and became king). They were revered and extolled, songs and poems were written about them, every reasonable comfort and honor was given them, and women and children and even grown men were moved to tears in their presence. Part of this outpouring of emotion and attention was the simple response of a grateful people to men who were willing to risk their lives to protect them. But there was also a certain calculation behind it. The steady pressure of fame and honor tended to embolden the lads still further by constantly reminding them that the fate of the entire people was involved in their performance in battle. At the same time—and this was no small thing in such a high-risk occupation—the honor and glory were in many cases rewards *before the fact*; on account, as it were. Archaic cultures were quite willing to elevate their single-combat fighters to heroic status even *before* their blood was let, because it was such an effective incentive. Any young man who entered the corps would get his rewards here on earth, "up front," to use the current phrase, come what may.

With the decline of archaic magic, the belief in single combat began to die out. The development of the modern, highly organized army and the concept of "total war" seemed to bury it forever. But then an extraordinary thing happened: the atomic bomb was invented, with the result that the concept of total war was nullified. The incalculable power of the A-bomb and the bombs that followed also encouraged the growth of a new form of superstition founded upon awe not of nature, as archaic magic had been, but of technology. During the Cold War period small-scale competitions once again took on the magical aura of a "testing of fate," of a fateful prediction of what would inevitably happen if total nuclear war did take place. This, of course, was precisely the impact of Sputnik I, launched around the earth by the Soviets' mighty and mysterious Integral in October of 1957. The "space race" became a fateful test and presage of the entire Cold War conflict between the "superpowers," the Soviet Union and the United States. Surveys showed that people throughout the world looked upon the competition in launching space vehicles in that fashion, i.e., as a preliminary contest proving final and irresistible power to destroy. The ability to launch Sputniks dramatized the ability to launch nuclear warheads on ICBMs. But in these neo-superstitious times it came to dramatize much more than that. It dramatized the entire technological and intellectual capability of the two nations and the strength of the national wills and spirits. Hence . . . John McCormack rising in the House of Representatives to say that the United States faced "national extinction" if she did not overtake the Soviet Union in the space race.

The next great achievement would be the successful launching of the first man into space. In the United States—no one could say what was taking place in the land of the mighty Integral—the men chosen for this historic mission took on the archaic mantles of the single-combat warriors of a long-since-forgotten time. They would not be going into space to do actual combat; or not immediately, although it was assumed that something of the sort might take place in a few years. But they were entering into a deadly duel in the heavens, in any event. (*Our rockets always blow up.*) The space war was on. They were risking their lives for their country, for their people, in "the fateful testing" versus the powerful Soviet Integral. And even though the archaic term itself had disappeared from memory, they would receive all the homage, all the fame, all the honor and heroic status . . . *before the fact* . . . of the single-combat warrior.

Thus beat the mighty drum of martial superstition in the mid-twentieth century.

It was glorious! It was crazy! The following month, May, the House Committee on Science and Astronautics, of which McCormack was a member, called the seven astronauts before them in closed session. So the brave lads went to the Capitol for the secret proceedings. It was a strange and marvelous time. It became immediately apparent that from the committee chairman, Representative Overton Brooks, on down, no one had anything pertinent to ask them and nothing to tell them. The congressmen kept saying things like "As you men know, you are an outstanding group in our country and in our country's history." Or they would ask them questions that elicited choral responses. Brooks himself said, "All of you gentlemen have been in this type of work—that is, handling experimental planes —in the past, haven't you? You know what this is. You know that in handling any new experimental flying machine there is a certain type of risk. You understand that, isn't that right?" Then he peered beseechingly at the seven of them until they began chiming in, all at once: "Yes, sir!" "Right, sir!" "Certainly, sir!" "That's correct, sir!" There was something gloriously goofy about it. The congressmen in the room just wanted to see them, to use their position to arrange a personal audience, to gaze upon them with their own eyes across the committee table, no more than four feet away, to shake hands with them, occupy the same space on this earth with them for an hour or so, fawn over them, pay homage to them, bathe in their magical aura, feel the radiation of their righteous stuff, salute them, wish upon them the smile of God . . . and do their bit in bestowing honor upon them *before the fact* . . . upon our little Davids . . . before they got up on top of the rockets to face the Russians, death, flames, and fragmentation. (*Ours all blow up!*)

C͟HUCK YEAGER was in Phoenix to make one of his many public appearances on behalf of the Air Force. By now the Air Force couldn't publicize Yeager, breaker of the sound barrier, enough. Like the other branches of the service, the Air Force now saw that there was nothing like heroes and record holders for getting good press and winning appropriations. The only problem was that, in terms of publicity, every other form of flier was now overshadowed by the Mercury astronauts. As a matter of fact, today, in Phoenix, what was it the local reporters wanted to ask Chuck Yeager about? Correct: the astronauts. One of them got the bright idea of asking Yeager if he had any regrets about not being selected as an astronaut.

Yeager smiled and said, "No, they gave me the opportunity of a lifetime, to fly the X-1 and the X-1A, and that's more than a man could ask for, right there.

They gave this new opportunity to some new fellows coming along, and that's what they ought to do."

"Besides," he added, "I've been a pilot all my life, and there won't be any flying to do in Project Mercury."

No flying?—

That was all it took. The reporters looked stunned. In some way they couldn't comprehend immediately, Yeager was casting doubt on two undisputable facts: one, that the seven Mercury astronauts were chosen because they were the seven finest pilots in America, and two, that they would be pilots on the most daring flights in American history.

The thing was, he said, the Mercury system was completely automated. Once they put you in the capsule, that was the last you got to say about the subject.

Whuh!—

"Well," said Yeager, "a monkey's gonna make the first flight."

A monkey?—

The reporters were shocked. It happened to be true that the plans called for sending up chimpanzees in both suborbital and orbital flights, identical to the flights the astronauts would make, before risking the men. But to just *say* it like that! . . . Was this national heresy? What the hell was it?

Fortunately for Yeager, the story didn't blow up into anything. The press, the eternal Victorian Gent, just couldn't deal with what he had said. The wire services wouldn't touch the remark. It ran in one of the local newspapers, and that was that.

But f'r chrissake . . . Yeager was only saying what was obvious to all the rocket pilots who had flown at Edwards. Here was everybody talking as if the Mercury astronauts would be the first men to ride rockets. Yeager had done precisely that more than forty times. Fifteen other pilots had done it also, and they had reached speeds greater than three times the speed of sound and an altitude of 126,000 feet, nearly twenty-five miles, and that was just the beginning. This very next month, June 1959, Scott Crossfield would begin the first testing of the X-15, designed for a pilot (a *pilot*, not a passenger) to take up to more than fifty miles, into space, at speeds approaching Mach 7.

All of this should have been absolutely obvious to anyone, even people who knew nothing about flying—and surely it would become clear that anybody in Project Mercury was more of a test subject than a pilot. Two of the people they chose weren't even in Fighter Ops. They had one excellent test pilot from Edwards, Deke Slayton, but he had never been high on the list of those considered for something like the X series. The other Air Force pilot, Grissom, was assigned to Wright-Pat and was doing more secondary testing than prime work. Two of the Navy guys, Shepard and Schirra, were good experienced test pilots, solid men, even though neither had done anything to make anybody's mouth fall open at Edwards. Glenn had made a name for himself by setting the speed record in the F8U, but he had not done much major flight test work, at least not by Edwards standards. Well, hell, what did anybody expect? *Naturally* they hadn't picked the seven hottest pilots they could find. They wouldn't be doing any flying!

Surely all this would become obvious in time . . . and yet it wasn't becoming obvious. Here at mighty Edwards itself the boys could feel the earth trembling. A great sliding of the templates was taking place inside the invisible pyramid. You could feel the old terrain crumbling, and . . . seven rookies were somehow being installed as the hottest numbers in flying—and they hadn't done a goddamned thing yet but turn up at a press conference!

6

ON THE BALCONY

FROM THE VERY BEGINNING this "astronaut" business was just an unbelievable good
deal. It was such a good deal that it seemed like tempting fate for an astronaut to
call himself an astronaut, even though that was the official job description. You
didn't even refer to the others as astronauts. You'd never say something such as
"I'll take that up with the other astronauts." You'd say, "I'll take that up with the
other fellows" or "the other pilots." Somehow calling yourself an "astronaut" was
like a combat ace going around describing his occupation as "combat ace." This
thing was such an unbelievable good deal, it was as if "astronaut" were an honor-
ific, like "champion" or "superstar," as if the word itself were one of the infinite
variety of *goodies* that Project Mercury was bringing your way.

And not just *goodies* in the crass sense, either. It had *all* the things that made
you feel good, including the things that were good for the soul. For long stretches
you'd bury yourself in training, in blissful isolation, good rugged bareboned isolation, in Low Rent surroundings, in settings that even resembled hallowed Edwards in the old X-1 days, and with that same pioneer spirit, which money cannot
buy, and with everybody pitching in and working endless hours, so that rank
meant nothing, and people didn't even have the inclination, much less the time,
to sit around and make the usual complaints about government work.

And then, just about the time you were entering a good healthy state of
exhaustion from the work, they would take you out of your isolation and lead you
up to that balcony that all fighter jocks secretly dreamed of, the one where you
walked out before the multitudes like the Pope, and . . . it actually happened!
The people of America cheered their brains out for thirty minutes or so, and then
you went back into your noble isolation for more work . . . or for a few proficiency runs at nailing down the holy coordinates of the fighter jock's life, which
were, of course, Flying & Drinking and Drinking & Driving and the rest of it.
These things you could plot on the great graph of Project Mercury in the most
spectacular way, with the exception of the first: Flying. The lack of flying time
was troubling, but the other items existed in such extraordinary dimensions that

it was hard to concentrate on it at first. Any man who wasn't above a little regrouping now and then, to keep the highly trained mechanism from being wound up too tight, to "maintain an even strain," in the Schirra parlance, found himself in absolute Fighter Jock Heaven. But even the rare pilot who was aloof from such cheap thrills, such as the deacon, John Glenn, found plenty of *goodies* to even out the strain of hard work and mass adoration.

Each of them had an eye on Glenn, all right. Glenn's own personal conduct was a constant reminder of what the game was really all about. To all but Scott Carpenter, and perhaps one other, the way Glenn was going about this thing was irritating.

The seven of them were stationed at Langley Air Force Base in the Tidewater section of Virginia on the James River, about 150 miles due south of Washington. Langley had been the experimental facility of the old National Advisory Committee for Aeronautics and was now the headquarters of NASA's Space Task Group for Project Mercury. Every morning they could count on seeing John Glenn up early, out on the grounds, in the middle of everything, where nobody could miss him, doing his roadwork. He'd be out there in full view, on the circular driveway of the Bachelor Officers Quarters, togged out in his sweatsuit, his great freckled face flaming red and shining with sweat, going around and around, running a mile, two miles, three miles, there was no end to it, in front of everybody. It was irritating, because it was so unnecessary. There had been a vague medical directive to the effect that each of them would engage in at least four hours of "unsupervised exercise" per week, but that was the last that was heard of. The medical staff assigned to Project Mercury were mainly young military doctors, a bit dazzled by the mission, some of them, and they were not about to call an astronaut on the carpet and demand an accounting of his four hours. Fighter jocks, as a breed, put physical exercise very low on the list of things that made up the right stuff. They enjoyed the rude animal health of youth. They put their bodies through dreadful abuses, often in the form of drinking bouts followed by lack of sleep and mortal hangovers, and they still performed like champions. ("I don't advise it, you understand, but it *can* be done"—provided you have the right stuff, you miserable pudknocker.) Most agreed with Wally Schirra, who felt that any form of exercise that wasn't fun, such as waterskiing or handball, was bad for your nervous system. But here was Glenn, pounding through everybody's field of vision with his morning roadwork, as if he were preparing for the championship fight.

The good Marine didn't just do his roadwork and leave it at that, either. Oh, no. The rest of them had their families installed at Langley Air Force Base or at least in the Langley vicinity. Gordon Cooper and Scott Carpenter and their families were packed into apartments on the base, the usual sort of worn-out base housing that junior officers rated. Wally Schirra, Gus Grissom, and Deke Slayton lived in a rather sad-looking housing development on the other side of the Newport News airport. Around the development was a stucco wall of the color known as glum ocher. Alan Shepard and his family lived a little farther away in Virginia Beach, where they happened to be living when he was chosen for Project Mercury. But Glenn . . . Glenn has his family housed 120 miles away in Arlington, Virginia, outside of Washington, and at Langley he stays in the Bachelor Officers Quarters, the BOQ, and does his running out front in the driveway. If this had been some devilishly clever scheme for him to get away from home and hearth and indulge in Drinking & Driving & so forth, that would have been one thing. But he wasn't the type. He was living in a bare room with nothing but a narrow bed and an upholstered chair and a little desk and a lamp and a lineup of books on astronomy, physics, and engineering, plus a Bible. On the weekends he would faithfully make his way home to his wife, Annie, and the children in an ancient Peugeot, a real beat-up junker that was about four feet long and had perhaps forty horsepower, the sorriest-looking and most underpowered automobile still legally registered to any fighter pilot in America. A jock with any natural instincts at all, with any true devotion to the holy coordinates, either possessed or was eating his heart out for the sort of car that Alan Shepard had, which was a Corvette, or that Wally Schirra had, which was a Triumph, i.e., a sports car, or some kind of hot car, anyway, something that would enable you to hang your hide out over the edge with a little class when you reached the Driving juncture on the coordinates several times a week, as was inevitable for everyone but someone like John Glenn. This guy was putting on an incredible show! He was praying in public. He was presenting himself in their very midst as the flying monk or whatever the Presbyterian version of a monk was. A saint, maybe; or an ascetic; or maybe just the village scone crusher.

Being a good Presbyterian, John Glenn knew that praying in public was no violation of the faith. The faith even encouraged it: it set a salubrious example for the public. Nor did John Glenn feel the slightest discomfort because now, in post-World War II America, virtue was out of style. Sometimes he seemed to enjoy shocking people with his clean living. Even when he was no more than nine years old, he had been the kind of boy who would halt a football game to read the riot act to some other nine-year-old who said "Goddamn it" or "Aw shit" when a play didn't go right. This was an unusual gesture even where he grew up, which was New Concord, Ohio, but not so extraordinary as it might have been a lot of other places. New Concord was a sort of town, once common in America, whose peculiar origins have tended to disappear in the collective amnesia as *tout le monde* strives to be urbane. Which is to say, it began as a religious community. A hundred years ago any man in New Concord with ambitions that reached as high as feedstore proprietor or better joined the Presbyterian Church, and some of the awesome voltage of live Presbyterianism still existed when Glenn was growing up in the 1920's and 1930's. His father was a fireman for the B&O Railroad and a good churchgoing man and his mother was a hardworking churchgoing woman, and Glenn went to Sunday school and church and sat through hundreds of interminable Presbyterian prayers, and the church and the faith and the clean living served him well. There was no contradiction whatsoever between the Presbyterian faith and ambition, even soaring ambition, even ambition grand enough to suit the invisible ego of the fighter jock. A good Presbyterian demonstrated his *election* by the Lord and the heavenly hosts through his success in this life. In a way, Presbyterianism was tailor-made for people who intended to make it in this world, as well as on the Plains of Heaven; which was a good thing, because John Glenn, with his sunny round freckled country-boy face, was as ambitious as any pilot who had ever hauled his happy burden of self-esteem up the pyramid.

So Glenn went pounding around the driveway of the BOQ of Langley Air Force Base in his sweatsuit, doing his roadwork, and he frankly didn't care if most of the others didn't like it. The running was good for him on several levels. At thirty-seven he was the oldest of the fellows, and there was a little more pressure on him to demonstrate that he was in good condition. Besides that, he had a tendency to put on weight. From the waist up he was of only average size and musculature and, in fact, had surprisingly small hands. But his legs were huge, real kegs, muscular and fleshy at the same time, and he tended to pack on weight in the thighs. He was pushing 185 when he was selected for this thing, and he could well afford to get down to 170 or even less. As for living in the BOQ . . . why not? He and his wife, Annie, had bought their house in Arlington because the children would be in excellent public schools there. Why transplant them again when he would be on the road half the time and probably wouldn't see them except on weekends, anyway?

If it looked to the others as if he were living a monastic life . . . that wouldn't hurt too much . . . Competition was competition, and there was no use pretending it didn't exist. He already had an advantage over the other six because of his Marine flying record and the way he tended to dominate the publicity. He was ready to give a 110 percent on all fronts. If they wanted four hours of unsupervised exercise per week—well, give them eight or twelve. Other people could think what they wanted; he happened to be completely sincere in the way he was going about this thing.

The goal in Project Mercury, as in every important new flight project, was to be the pilot assigned to make the first flight. In flight test that meant your superiors looked upon you as *the* man who had the right stuff to challenge the unknowns. In Project Mercury the first flight would also be the most historic flight. They had been told that the first flight would be suborbital. There might be as many as ten or eleven suborbital flights, going to an altitude of about one hundred miles, fifty miles above the commonly accepted boundary line between the earth's atmosphere and space. These flights would not go into orbit, because the rocket they would be using, the Redstone, could not generate enough power to overcome the pull of gravity. The capsule would go up and come down in a big arc, like an artillery shell's. As it came over the top of the arc, the astronaut would experience about five minutes of weightlessness. These suborbital flights were scheduled to begin in mid-1960, and all seven pilots would get a crack at them.

Other men would no doubt go farther into space, into earth orbit and beyond. But they, in turn, would be chosen from the first men to fly suborbitally; so the first astronaut would be the one the world remembered. When a man realized something like that, there was no use being shy about the opportunity he had. Glenn had not gotten this far in his career by standing still in a saintly fashion and waiting for his halo to be noticed. When he reached Korea, flying strafing and bombing missions in support of Marine ground troops, he realized that the biggest accolade was being assigned to Air Force fighter squadrons, on loan (like Schirra), for air-to-air combat up at the Yalu River. So he had gone after that assignment and had gotten it and had shot down three MiGs during the last few days of the war. As soon as the war ended, he realized that flight test was the hot new arena and had gone straight to his superiors and asked to be assigned to the Navy's Patuxent River Test Pilot School, and they sent him there. He had been in flight test barely three years when he dreamed up the F8U transcontinental run. He dreamed it up himself, as a major in the Marines! Although everyone knew it was possible, no one had ever made a sustained coast-to-coast flight at an average speed of greater than Mach 1. Glenn developed the whole scheme, the aerial rendezvous with three different AJ1 refueling tankers, the way he would dive down to 22,000 feet to meet them, the whole thing. He pulled it off on July 16, 1957, flying from Los Angeles to Floyd Bennett Field near New York, in three hours and twenty-three minutes. The word was that there were some test pilots who were put out because he got the assignment. They seemed to think they had done the major test work on the F8U, and so forth and so on. But it was his idea! He got it launched! If he hadn't put himself forward, it wouldn't have happened at all. Last year, 1958, it was obvious to him that all the services were working on the problems of manned space flight. There was no Project Mercury yet, and no one knew who would be running the show when a manned program began. All he knew was that it was not likely to be the Marines but he wanted to play a part in it. So he had himself assigned to the Navy Bureau of Aeronautics. He volunteered for runs on the Navy's human centrifuge machine at Johnsville, Pennsylvania, exploring the high g-forces associated with rocket flight. By March of this year, 1959, just a month before the seven of them were selected as astronauts, he had been at the McDonnell Aircraft plant in St. Louis as a representative of the Bureau of Aeronautics on a NASA Mockup Review Board, reviewing progress of the manufacture of the Mercury capsule. He didn't know just how the seven of them were selected . . . but obviously all that hadn't hurt his chances.

And now the ante had been raised once more, and he was after nothing short of being the first man to go into space. NASA would have to beat the Russians to it, of course, for him or any other American to be first. But that was one of the things that made it exhilarating, exhilarating enough even to endure this sweaty pounding over a salty pine-tag circular driveway in Tidewater, Virginia. There was the same sort of *esprit*—usually called patriotism but better described as *joie de combat*—that had existed during the Second World War and, among pilots (and practically no one else), during the Korean War. Project Mercury was officially a civilian undertaking. But it struck Glenn as being like a new branch of the armed services. All seven of them were still in the military, drawing military pay, even though they wore civilian clothes. There was a warlike urgency and priority about the whole enterprise. And in this new branch of the military *no one outranked you*. It was almost too good to be true.

On the organization chart the seven of them had superiors. They reported to Robert Gilruth, the head of the new Space Task Group, who was a subordinate of Hugh Dryden, the deputy administrator of NASA. Gilruth was a superb engineer and a fine man; he had literally *written the book* on the handling characteristics of aircraft, the first scientific treatise on the subject, "Requirements for Satisfactory Flying Qualities of Airplanes," NACA Report No. 755, 1937, which had become a classic. He was a big, bald, shy man with a reedy voice. Most recently he had been head of the NACA Pilotless Aircraft Research Division, which had experimented with unmanned rockets. Gilruth was not used to marching the troops and certainly not a group of ambitious pilots. He was no Vince Lombardi. He was a genius among engineers, but he was not the type to take seven colossal stars who were suddenly the most famous pilots in America and mold them into Bob Gilruth's Astroteam.

They were so famous, so revered, so lavishly fussed and worried over at all times that they were without peers in this new branch of the military. Everywhere they went in their travels people stopped what they were doing and gave them a certain look of awe and sympathy. Sympathy . . . because *our rockets all blow up.* It was a nice, friendly, warm look, all right, and yet it was strange. It was a sort of glistening smile with tears and joy suffusing it; both tears and joy. In fact, it was an ancient look, from the primordial past, never seen in America before. It was the smile of homage and astonishment—at such bravery!—that had been given to single-combat warriors, in advance, on account, before the fact, since time was.

Well . . . Glenn was ready; he was ready for *election;* he was ready to be the first to go into the heavens when that debt of homage and honor and glistening faces came due.

O NE OF THE PEOPLE who beamed that look at them with a sincere devotion was a Washington lawyer named Leo DeOrsey. Walter Bonney, the NASA public affairs officer who had run the press conference, had seen the frenzy of publicity building up around the seven men and concluded that they needed some expert help in their new role as celebrities. He approached DeOrsey. DeOrsey was a tax lawyer. Harry Truman had once considered making him head of the Internal Revenue Service. He had represented many show-business celebrities, including President Eisenhower's friend Arthur Godfrey. So the seven of them wound up having dinner with DeOrsey in a private room at the Columbia Country Club outside of Washington. DeOrsey was an affable gentleman with a little round pot belly. He had terrific clothes. He put on a long face and related how he had been approached by Bonney. He said he was willing to represent them.

"I insist on only two conditions," he said.

Glenn thought to himself, "Well, here it comes."

"One," said DeOrsey, "I will accept no fee. Two, I will not be reimbursed for expenses."

He kept the grave look on his face for a moment. And then he smiled. There were no catches and no angles. He was obviously sincere. He thought they were terrific and felt tickled pink to be involved with them at all. He couldn't do enough for them. And that was the way it went with Leo DeOrsey from that evening onward. He couldn't have been straighter or more generous.

DeOrsey proposed that the book and magazine rights to their personal stories be put up for sale to the highest bidder. Bonney was sure the President and NASA would allow it, because several military men had made such an arrangement since the Second World War, most notably Eisenhower himself. The selling point for NASA would be that if the seven of them sold exclusive rights to one organization, then they would have a natural shield against the endless requests and intrusions by the rest of the press and would be better able to concentrate on their training.

Sure enough, NASA approved the idea, the White House approved it, and DeOrsey started getting in touch with magazines, setting $500,000 as the floor for bids. The one solid offer—$500,000—came from *Life,* and DeOrsey closed the deal. *Life* had an excellent precedent for the decision. Few people remembered, but *The New York Times* had bought the rights to Charles Lindbergh's personal story before his famous transatlantic flight in 1927. It worked out splendidly for both parties. Having bought an exclusive, the *Times* devoted its first five pages to Lindbergh the day after his flight and the first *sixteen* the day after he returned from Paris, and all other major newspapers tried their best to keep up. In return for *Life*'s exclusive rights to their personal stories and their wives', the astronauts would share the $500,000 evenly; the sum amounted to just under $24,000 a year for each man over the three years Project Mercury was scheduled to run, about $70,000 in all.

For junior officers with wives and children, used to struggling along on $5,500 to $8,000 a year in base pay, plus another $2,000 in housing and subsistence allowances and perhaps $1,750 in extra flight pay, the sum was barely even imaginable at first. It wasn't real. They wouldn't see any of it for months, in any case . . . Nevertheless, the *goodies* were the *goodies*. A career military officer denied himself and his family many things . . . with the understanding that when the *goodies* came along, they would be accepted and shared. It was part of the unwritten contract. The *Life* deal even provided them with foolproof protection against the possibility that their personal stories might become all-too-personal. Although written by *Life*, the stories would appear in the first person under their own by-lines . . . "by Gus Grissom" . . . "by Betty Grissom" . . . and they would have the right to eliminate any material they objected to. NASA, moreover, would have the same right. So there was nothing to keep the boys from continuing to come across as what they had looked like at the first press conference: seven patriotic God-fearing small-town Protestant family men with excellent backing on the home front.

Here in the summer of 1959 that was fine with *Life* and with the rest of the press, for that matter. Americans seemed to be deriving profound satisfaction from the fact that the astronauts turned the conventional notions of Glamour upside down. It was assumed—and the Genteel Beast kept underlining the point —that the seven astronauts were the greatest pilots and bravest men in America *precisely because of* the wholesome circumstances of their backgrounds: small towns, Protestant values, strong families, the simple life. Henry Luce, *Life*'s founder and boss of bosses, had not played a major role, other than parting with the money, in making the astronaut deal, but eventually he came to look upon them as *his boys*. Luce was a great Presbyterian, and the Mercury astronauts looked like seven incarnations of Presbyterianism. This was no rural-American miracle, however. It was John Glenn who had set the moral tone of the Astronaut at the first press conference. The others had diplomatically kept their mouths shut ever since. From the Luces and Restons on down, the Press, that ever-seemly Victorian Gent, saw the astronauts as seven slices of the same pie, and it was mom's pie, John Glenn's mom's pie, from the sturdy villages of the American heartland. The Gent thought he was looking at seven John Glenns.

AMONG THE SEVEN instant heroes John Glenn's light shone brightest. Probably the least conspicuous, using that same measure, was Gordon Cooper. Cooper was a thin, apparently guileless soul, handsome in a down-home manner. He was from Shawnee, Oklahoma. He had a real Oklahoma drawl. He was also the youngest of the seven, being thirty-two years old. He had never flown in combat, nor had his test work at Edwards been of the sort that attracted much notice. Scott Carpenter was no further up the great ziggurat of flying, of course, but Carpenter was not at all reluctant to talk about his own relative lack of experience in jets, and so on. What seemed to annoy some of the boys was that none of the foregoing, obvious as it surely was, fazed Gordon Cooper in the slightest.

Two people who sometimes seemed to get impatient with Cooper were his Air
Force comrades Gus Grissom and Deke Slayton. Grissom and Slayton had become great pals practically from the day they were selected as astronauts. They
were from out of the same grim clay. Slayton was raised on a farm in western
Wisconsin, up near the town of Sparta and the Elroy Sparta State Park Trail. He
was taller than Grissom, more rugged, rather handsome, in fact, and quite intelligent, once you penetrated the tundra. When the subject was flying, his expression
lit up, and he radiated confidence and had all the wit and charm and insights you
could ask for. In other situations, however, he had Grissom's lack of patience for
party manners and small talk and Grissom's way of lapsing into impenetrable
blank stares, as if some grim wintertime north-country Lutheran cloud of Original
Sin were passing in front of his face. Deke had started flying in the Second World
War, when the Air Force was still part of the Army. In the Army one was
continually around people who spoke Army Creole, a language in which there
were about ten nouns, five verbs, and one adjective, or participle, or whatever it
was called. There always seemed to be a couple of good buddies from Valdosta or
Oilville or some place sitting around saying:

"I tol'im iffie tried to fuck me over, I was gonna kick'is fuckin' ass, iddnat
right?"

"Fuckin' A."

"Soey kep'on fuckin' me over and I kicked'is fuckin' ass in fo'im, iddnat
right?"

"Fuckin' A."

"An' so now they tellin' me they gon' th'ow my fuckin' ass inna fuckin' *stockade*! You know what? They some kinda fuckin' me over!"

"Fuckin' A well tol', Bubba."

Now that Deke was all of a sudden a celebrity, there were people who knew
him who cringed every time he got near a microphone. They were afraid he was
going to Army Creole the nationwide TV and scorch the brains of half the people
of the U.S.A. The truth was, Deke was far too sharp for that. He was okay in
Gus's book. They lived just two doors away from each other at Langley, and if
they were both at home on the weekend, they usually did something together,
such as go hunting or wangle a T-33 from Langley Air Force Base and fly cross-
country, taking turns at the controls. Sometimes they would fly all the way to
California and back, and it was likely that if they exchanged a total of forty
sentences, transcontinental, they would come back feeling like they'd had a hell
of an animated conversation and a deep talk.

Just a couple of years ago, at Wright-Patterson, it was Gus and Gordo—as
Gordon Cooper was known—who had been the great weekend flying buddies.
Then Gordo had been transferred to Edwards, where Deke Slayton happened to
be. And now that all three of them were in the same corps, this extraordinary
new corps of astronauts, there were nights when the others would hear Cooper's
Oklahoma drawl getting cranked up . . . and the gorge would rise . . . They
would all be knocking back a few at somebody's house, some Saturday night, and
they would hear Cooper starting to talk about something extraordinary that happened when he was testing the F-106B or whatever at Edwards . . . and the
blood would come into somebody's baleful eyes, and he'd say, "I'll tell you what
Gordo did at Edwards. He was in *engineering*." The way *engineering* was

pronounced, you would have thought Gordo had been a quartermaster or a drum major or a chaplain.

Deke Slayton took pride in the fact that he was in the hot branch of flight test at Edwards, which was Fighter Operations. The pilots in Fighter Ops at Edwards pushed the outsides of the envelopes of the hottest new airplanes made, the most recent examples being the Century series, of which Gordo's F-106B was one. But to be in engineering was to be an also-ran. Gus and Gordo remained friends and even did some rat-racing in their cars together and, later on, in speedboats. He was so friendly and easygoing, it was hard not to like the man. But sometimes Gus would cluck and fume over Gordo's yarns, too.

And none of this fazed Gordo in the slightest! He seemed to be oblivious of it all! He just went on drawling and lollygagging along as if he were sitting in the catbird seat the whole time! He was also given to sounding off now and then in ways the rest of them just couldn't comprehend. Like that business of the flight pay!

The truth was that none of them, not even Gus, who knew him fairly well, understood Cooper's particular makeup. Cooper may have had his blind spots, but if so, it was the blindness of the fighter jock resolutely making his way up the mighty ziggurat. So what if, by outward standards, he had not had the most brilliant career of all the seven astronauts? The day was young! He was only thirty-two! Cooper's fighter jock self-esteem seemed to be like a PAR lamp. It was as if wherever he landed, the light shone 'round about him, and that was the place to be. Cooper knew as well as anyone else that it was more prestigious to be in Fighter Ops than in engineering at Edwards. But once he was in engineering, the light shone 'round about him, and the picture of him in that place was good. As a pilot in engineering you saw the project from both sides, from the design and administrative side as well as from the test pilot's side. It was like being a project manager who also flew . . . that was what it was like . . . Much of Cooper's fireproof confidence was based on the fact that he was "a natural-born stick-and-rudder man," as the phrase went. When it came to sheer aplomb in controlling a winged aircraft, there was probably no other astronaut who could outdo him. His father had been a colonel in the old Army Air Force, a career officer, and Cooper had started flying before he was sixteen. He had met his wife, Trudy, at Hickam Field after he had enrolled in the University of Hawaii. She was also a pilot. Flying was like breathing to Cooper. He seemed to feel absolutely immune to the ordinary dangers of flight; in any event, he was absolutely cool when it came to dealing with them. As far as his career went, he was never troubled by doubts. It was only a matter of time before everything would go his way. Of that he seemed to be convinced.

When the tests for selection of astronauts began at Lovelace and Wright-Patterson . . . well, it was obvious, wasn't it? Everything was now going his way. He never had the slightest doubt that he would be chosen. His relative lack of credentials didn't trouble him at all. He would be chosen! He could tell! When it came to things like the rigors of the physical tests at Lovelace, he went through it all with a knowing wink. Things like scuttling down a corridor with barium exploding out of your tail—he figured it was intentionally set up as part of the stress testing. Nothing to it, once you understood the drill. Stress? He was so relaxed, the psychologists giving the stress tests at Wright-Patterson could hardly believe it. As soon as the tests at Wright-Pat were completed, Cooper told his commanding officer at Edwards that he had better look for a replacement for him. He was going to be chosen as an astronaut. This was more than a month before the choices were actually made.

Cooper turned out to be neither so naive nor so guileless as some thought. From the beginning, in the interview sessions, the NASA psychologists had asked the candidates for astronaut many questions about their family lives. Quite aside from any possible public-relations considerations, there was a well-known theory in the psychology of flight to the effect that marital discord was a major cause of erratic behavior among pilots and often led to fatal accidents. The sound instincts of the career officer led Cooper to respond that his family life, with Trudy and the children, was real fine, terrific; regulation issue. This wasn't likely to bear much checking into, however, inasmuch as Cooper and Trudy were not living in the same house or even in the same latitude. They had separated; Trudy and the children were living down near San Diego, while he remained at Edwards. Clearly it was time for a reconciliation. Cooper took a quick trip to San Diego . . . he talked a whole rope . . . a veritable lasso . . . the separation, his prospects with NASA, and so on . . . In any case, Trudy and their two daughters returned to Edwards, and Cooper had the American dream back intact, under one roof, before the final round of the selection process, and nobody at NASA was the wiser.

After Cooper was selected, one of the *Life* writers brought up the point that he had less experience than most of the other astronauts. Cooper was not fazed for a moment. He said that he was also younger than the others and would probably be the only one of them to fly to Mars.

The only side of the whole deal that appeared to shake Cooper's confidence was the p.r. side of it, the publicity routine, the trips here and there, where various local worthies put you at the head table and whacked you on the back and asked you to get up and "just say a few words." Most of the trips were to cities where components of the Mercury system were being manufactured, such as St. Louis, where the capsule was being built at the McDonnell factory, or San Diego, where the Atlas rocket was being built at Convair. St. Louis, San Diego, Akron, Dayton, Los Angeles—somebody was always suggesting that you "just say a few words."

It was on such occasions that a man realized most acutely that America's seven astronauts were not by any means identical. Glenn seemed to eat this stuff up. He couldn't get enough grins or handshakes, and he had a few words filed away in every pocket. He would even come back to Langley and write cards to workers he had met on the assembly line, giving them little "attaboys," as if they were all in this thing together, partners in the great adventure, and he, the astronaut, would never forget his, the welding inspector's, beaming mug. The idea, much encouraged by NASA, was that the personal interest of the astronaut would infuse everyone working for the contractors with a greater concern for safety, reliability, efficiency.

Oddly enough, it seemed to work. Gus Grissom was out in San Diego in the Convair plant, where they were working on the Atlas rocket, and Gus was as uneasy at this stuff as Cooper was. Asking Gus to "just say a few words" was like handing him a knife and asking him to open a main vein. But hundreds of workers are gathered in the main auditorium of the Convair plant to see Gus and the other six, and they're beaming at them, and the Convair brass say a few words and then the astronauts are supposed to say a few words, and all at once Gus realizes it's his turn to say something, and he is petrified. He opens his mouth and out come the words: "Well . . . do good work!" It's an ironic remark, implying: ". . . because it's my ass that'll be sitting on your freaking rocket." But the workers started cheering like mad. They started cheering as if they had just heard the most moving and inspiring message of their lives: *Do good work!* After all, it's Little Gus's ass on top of our rocket! They stood there for an eternity and cheered their brains out while Gus gazed blankly upon them from the Pope's balcony. Not only that, the workers—the workers, not the management but the workers!—had a flag company make up a huge banner, and they strung it up high in the main work bay, and it said: DO GOOD WORK.

All these people with their smiles of sympathy didn't ask for much. A few words here and there would do fine. *Do good work.* Nevertheless, that didn't make these public appearances any better for Cooper. He was in the same boat with Gus and Deke, who was also no Franklin D. Roosevelt when it came to public appearances. Everybody latched on to you during these trips, congressmen and businessmen and directors and presidents of this and that. Every hotshot in town wanted to be next to *the astronaut.* For the first ten or fifteen minutes it was enough for them to breathe the same air you breathed and occupy the same space as your famous body. But then they began looking at you . . . and waiting . . . Waiting for what? Well, dummy!—waiting for you to say a few words! They wanted something hot! If you were one of the seven greatest pilots and seven bravest men in America, then obviously you must be fascinating to listen to. *Riveting*—that was what you were supposed to be. A few war stories, man! And you would sit there with the clutch in, furiously trying to think of something, anything, and it would make you gloomier and gloomier. Your light no longer shone 'round about you.

It was on such occasions that the three Air Force men, Cooper and Gus and Deke, wouldn't have minded being like Alan Shepard. Shepard was all right. He didn't go for these public appearance stints any more than they did. But Al could shift gears anytime he had to. Al was a Naval Academy man, and if he had to glad-hand and shoot the breeze and trade the small talk with all these congressmen and realty board chairmen and rye distillers and get up and make extemporaneous remarks when called upon, then he could do it. Wally Schirra was another Naval Academy man, and he could play it any way he wanted to, also. Wally was a regular guy, a fighter jock through and through, but he also had the knack of turning on the old Academy charm around strangers. As for the other Navy guy, Carpenter, he wasn't an Academy man, but he was Mr. Charm himself, all the same. He knew how to turn on the party manners.

There was damned little social crap in the Air Force, and that was probably one reason why Cooper liked the blue suit. The "officers and gentlemen" business was kept at a minimum. At most bases the only well-to-do locals who invited Air Force officers to parties were the automobile dealers. They just loved the way those crazy blue-suit sombitches bought those cars and racked them up and then came back and bought some more. In the Air Force there was a nice piece of built-in democracy. Until an officer had reached the level of lieutenant colonel, there was only one way for him to make his mark and advance, and that was by proving himself as a pilot. If he could demonstrate that he had the right stuff in the air, there was nothing, short of gross character defects, that could keep him from rising through the middle ranks. In the Navy Air Force an officer also had to prove himself in the air, but at the test-pilot level the Navy began to insist on "leadership qualities" as well, meaning polish and the rest of it.

There you had a man like Al Shepard, who had come from out of what was sometimes called "the service aristocracy." Which was to say, Al was the son of a career officer. By now you ran into these fellows, the second-generation officers, all over the service. They seemed to make up half the graduates of West Point or Annapolis, like Al and Wally Schirra. Al's father was a retired Army colonel. Wally Schirra's was in effect a service family. His father had been a pilot in the First World War, had then left the service, but then became a civil engineer for the Air Force after the Second World War, helping to rebuild Japanese airfields. You very seldom ran into career officers who were the sons of businessmen, doctors, or lawyers. They steered their sons away from the service. They looked down on it. So what you found were the second-generation officers on the one hand, like Shepard and Schirra, and the sons of workingmen and farmers on the other, fellows like Gus and Deke and John Glenn. Fellows like Shepard and Schirra (and Carpenter) might come from small towns, strictly speaking, but it was a mistake to call them "small-town boys," the way you could apply that term to Gus or Deke, and it showed in the way they could handle themselves in public.

It wasn't long before Cooper began to miss flying, the stick 'n' rudder life, in the worst kind of way. He began to miss it the way another man might have missed food. The daily business of taking a high-performance aircraft aloft and hanging it out over the edge—this was at the heart of the fighter jock's life, even though its importance was never expressed except in the term "proficiency." Pilots devoutly believed that it was necessary to fly out to the edge with regularity in order to maintain proficiency or "decision-making ability." On one level it was a logical enough equivalent to an athlete's concern with staying in shape; but on another it had to do with the mysteries of the right stuff and the ineffable joys of showing the world, and yourself, that you had it. It was damned strange to be in flight training, as America's first astronauts, and yet to be doing no flying themselves, except as passengers.

There was no flying whatsoever on their training agenda! As the weeks went by, all seven men began to be bothered by this, but it was Cooper who voiced the complaint publicly. The early months included a heavy schedule of lectures, on astronomy, rocket propulsion, flight operations, capsule systems, and the trips to the contractors, and to the subcontractors, and to Cape Canaveral, where the rockets would be launched, to Huntsville, Alabama, where Wernher von Braun and his Germans were developing the rockets, to Johnsville, Pennsylvania, where the human centrifuge was located. There was no end to it. On all these trips Cooper, like the others, had to travel by commercial airline. It seemed as if he spent half of every day standing around airports waiting for luggage or going through his pockets to see how much money he had. Here he was, flying half the month—as a passenger! On top of everything else, he was losing flight pay! It was no laughing matter! DeOrsey was negotiating the *Life* deal but had not yet closed it. If an Air Force captain kept up his proficiency flying, he stood to receive an extra $145 a month in flight pay, and there was not a sane blue-suiter alive who did not go out and get that flight pay each month unless bedridden or grounded. The extras—my God, it was impossible to explain to an outsider, but these things were built into the psyche of the career officer like first principles! Besides, your family always needed the money. Cooper, like the other six, was being paid by the military, and so he was losing a significant percentage of his income, which hadn't been much to begin with. Not only that, an officer in the military received a mere nine dollars a day in expenses for day trips and twelve dollars a day for overnight trips. To stay in hotels, to eat in restaurants—it was a losing proposition. Especially when they were supposed to be some sort of celebrities. They all felt like the biggest deadbeat celebrities in America. Say you were having lunch with five or six hotshots in Akron, where you went for pressure-suit fittings at B. F. Goodrich. You didn't dare reach for the check. Suppose through delayed psychomotor response or some other dreadful accident they let you *have* it! The damned thing might be for thirty-five dollars—and there went your family's food money for two weeks . . . And yet the flight pay itself was the least of it. It was more evidence of the curious *non-pilot* status of the astronaut. Cooper figured he was spending forty hours a month on commercial airliners in order to go through all this. What he wouldn't have given to have access to a supersonic fighter plane like the F-104B . . . Gus and Deke were managing to cadge rides on the weekends in T-33's at Langley. But the T-33 was pretty tame stuff, a subsonic trainer. The F-104B was something you could cut loose with. Langley Air Force Base wasn't even equipped to maintain such an aircraft, however. So Cooper was going all the way to McGhee-Tyson in Knoxville, where he had a buddy who could get him signed up for the occasional workout in the F-104B. With a ship like that he could *live and breathe* . . . and maintain proficiency and keep in touch with that righteous stuff . . .

Such thoughts were once more running through his mind as he sat down to lunch one day at Langley, when a reporter for the *Washington Star* named William Hines joined him and said hello. Well, they talked a little bit and one thing led to another, and pretty soon Cooper was painting the entire picture. When the story appeared in the *Star*—depicting Cooper's complaint, accurately, as a complaint common to practically all the astronauts—NASA officials were dumbfounded. Overton Brooks's House Committee on Science and Astronautics was dumbfounded. Gordo's fellow deservers of perks and goodies were dumbfounded, even though most of them agreed with him completely. They all looked a trifle petty. Here they were, seven heroes, warriors of the heavens, patriots, and they're all over the press complaining about flight pay and airplane rides . . .

Overton Brooks sent a committee investigator to Langley to see what the hell was going on. The report he brought back was a masterpiece, a veritable model performance, in the tactful handling of the grousing of his country's first single-combat warriors. "The astronauts," he wrote, "are fully aware of their responsibilities to the project and the American public, particularly with regard to the heroic role they are beginning to assume with the young people of the country. They have imposed upon themselves strict rules of conduct and behavior, which credits them with constructive and mature evaluation of their position as a cynosure of all eyes." The only thing is, they still want their goddamned flight pay and some hot airplanes.

LIKE MOST OF THE OTHER WIVES, Betty Grissom was stuck at Langley with small children to take care of. At first she had thought she and Gus were at last going to be able to settle in for some ordinary home life, but somehow Gus was away as much as ever. Even when he had the weekends off, he would somehow wander over to Deke's house, and before she knew it, the two of them would be heading off to the base for some "proficiency" flying, and there went another weekend.

If Gus was home for the weekend, he was apt to get in some fast flurries of fatherhood for the benefit of their two boys, Mark and Scott. This might take the form of some good gruff-gus obedience lectures about obeying their mother when he wasn't there. Or it might take the form of something like the floating dock. The development they lived in backed up on a little lake. One weekend Gus set about building a floating dock so that the boys could use the lake as a proper swimming hole. The problem was that the older of the boys, Scott, was only eight, and Betty was afraid they were going to drown back there. She had nothing to worry about, as it turned out. The boys never took to the old swimming hole. They much preferred the swimming pool across the street at the community club. It had a diving board and a concrete apron and clear water and other children to play with. The floating dock remained out back moldering in the lake like a reminder of the kind of fatherhood that the astronaut life began imposing on all seven families.

Betty was not as upset about her husband's protracted absences as a lot of other wives would have been. When they had been stationed at Williams Air Force base, other wives had even put pressure on her not to let Gus have so many weekends off, because it was giving their husbands ideas. But few wives seemed to believe as firmly as Betty did in the unofficial Military Wife's Compact. It was a compact not so much between husband and wife as between the two of them and the military. It was because of the compact that a military wife was likely to say "We were reassigned to Langley" . . . we, as if both of them were in the military. Under the terms of the unwritten compact, they were. The wife began her marriage—to her husband and to the military—by making certain heavy sacrifices. She knew the pay would be miserably low. They would have to move frequently and live in depressing, exhausted houses. Her husband might be gone for long stretches, especially in the event of war. And on top of all that, if her husband happened to be a fighter pilot, she would have to live with the fact that any day, in peace or war, there was an astonishingly good chance that her husband might be killed, *just like that*. In which case, the code added: *Please omit tears, for the sake of those still living.* In return for these concessions, the wife was guaranteed the following: a place in the military community's big family, a welfare state in the best sense, which would see to it that all basic needs, from health care to babysitting, were taken care of. And a flying squadron tended to be the most tightly knit of all military families. She was also guaranteed a permanent marriage, if she wanted it, at least for as long as they were in the service. Divorce —still, as of 1960—was a fatal step for a career military officer; it led to damaging efficiency reports by one's superiors, reports that could ruin chances of advancement. And she was guaranteed one thing more, something that was seldom talked about except in comical terms. Underneath, however, it was no joke. In the service, when the husband moved up, the wife moved up. If he advanced from lieutenant to captain, then she became Mrs. Captain and now outranked all the Mrs. Lieutenants and received all the social homage the military protocol provided. And if her husband received a military honor, then she became the Honorable Mrs. Captain—all this regardless of her own social adeptness. Of course, it was well known that a gracious, well-spoken, small-talking, competent, sophisticated wife was a great asset to her husband's career, precisely because they were a team and *both* were in the service. At all the teas and socials and ceremonies and obligatory parties at the C.O.'s and all the horrible Officers Wives Club functions, Betty always felt at a loss, despite her good looks and intelligence. She always wondered if she was holding Gus back in his career because she couldn't be the Smilin' & Small-Talkin' Whiz that was required.

Now that Gus had been elevated to this extraordinary new rank—astronaut—Betty was not loath to receive her share, per the compact. It was as if . . . well, precisely because she had endured and felt out of place at so many teas and other small-talk tests, precisely because she had sat at home near the telephone throughout the Korean War and God knew how many hundreds of test flights wondering if the fluttering angels would be ringing up, precisely because her houses all that time had been typical of the sacrificial lot of the junior officer's wife, precisely because her husband had been away so much—it was as if precisely because that was the way things were, she fully intended to be the honorable Mrs. Captain Astronaut and to accept all the honors and privileges attendant thereupon.

Betty thought the *Life* deal was terrific. She didn't have to wrestle with the angels over that one for a second. They would be getting just under $25,000 a year from it, a sum almost beyond her imagining after all these glum ocher years. But that was only part of the beauty of this goodie. On the day it had been announced that Gus had been chosen as an astronaut. Betty had been even more terrified than Gus. Gus had only a NASA-controlled press conference to deal with. Betty, with practically no warning, had been mobbed, overrun, at their house in Dayton by the press. They came crawling in through the windows like ravenous termites, like fruit flies, taking pictures and yelling questions. She felt as if she had been engulfed in the monster Small-Talk Tea of all times, and merely the entire country would see her as an unsophisticated Hoosier grit. To her great relief, whatever answers she had come up with emerged as coherent whole sentences, and not at all foolish, in the newspapers the next day, and she looked splendid in the pictures. (Naturally she did not know that the press was an anachronistic colonial animal, a Victorian Gent who was determined to give to all important moments the proper tone.) Still, she wouldn't want to have to go through that sort of thing again. And now she wouldn't! She would only have to talk to *Life* reporters, and they turned out to be marvelous. They were polite, well-educated, well-dressed, friendly, kind, real ladies and gentlemen. They had no desire whatsoever to make her look bad. Betty and the other wives came bursting forth like great blossoms before the ten million readers of *Life* in a cover story in the September 21, 1959, issue. Their faces, smooth round white things with coronas of hair, were arranged on the cover like a corsage of flowers with Rene Carpenter's face in the middle—no doubt because the editors regarded her as prettiest. But who is that? Oh, that's Trudy Cooper. And who is *that*? Oh, that's Jo Schirra. And who is *that*? Oh, that's . . . They hardly recognized each other! Then they saw why. *Life* had retouched the faces of all of them practically down to the bone. Every suggestion of a wen, a hickie, an electrolysis line, a furze of mustache, a bag, a bump, a crack in the lipstick, a rogue cilia of hair, an uneven set of the lips . . . had disappeared in the magic of photo retouching. Their pictures all looked like the pictures girls can remember from their high-school yearbooks in which so many zits, hickies, whiteheads, blackheads, goopheads, goobers, pips, acne trenches, boil volcanoes, candy-bar pustules, rash marks, tooth-brace lumps, and other blemishes have been scraped off by the photography studio, you looked like you had just healed over from plastic surgery. The headline said: SEVEN BRAVE WOMEN BEHIND THE ASTRONAUTS.

Whether by design or not, *Life* had seized upon the idea that Luce's fellow Presbyterian John Glenn had put forth at the first press conference: "I don't think any of us could really go on with something like this if we didn't have pretty good backing at home." Pretty good backing? Perfect backing they were going to have: seven flawless cameo-faced dolls sitting in the family room with their pageboy bobs in place, ready to offer any and all aid to the brave lads. There was something crazy about it, but it was marvelous. The week before, in the September 14, 1959, issue, *Life* had ushered Gus and the other fellows out onto the Pope's balcony with a cover story headlined READY TO MAKE HISTORY that left no doubt whatsoever that these were the seven bravest men and the seven greatest pilots in American history, even if it was necessary to go easy on the details. Now *Life* was leading Betty and the other wives out onto that balcony.

Betty, for one, did not object to that at all.

They had to let the *Life* writers and photographers come into their houses and follow them around pretty much anywhere they wanted to, but that turned out to be no particular problem. Pretty soon they all realized they didn't even have to keep their guard up. The *Life* people were very sympathetic. The men among them obviously had a kind of male awe of Gus and the others; you could even detect a tinge of envy every now and then, because the *Life* reporters and the fellows were about the same age. But they were loyal. In any case, they were hamstrung, since Gus and Betty and the rest of the men and their wives had the right to censor anything that was going to appear under their names. And don't think they were bashful about it, either! Not for a minute! You'd hear one of the fellows on the telephone going over a manuscript with a *Life* writer line by line, telling him, in just so many words, what could stay in and what was coming out. Oh, the *Life* writers sometimes had their own notions of what was candid and colorful and "good copy." They liked to get on such subjects as the rivalries between the boys and such "colorful" matters as Driving & Drinking and the unspoken intrafraternal business of fear and courage . . . Well, the hell with that! It was not so much that the men wanted to come out sounding like the Hardy Boys in Outer Space—it was just that you'd have to be an idiot to let your personal story actually get personal. Every career military officer, and especially every junior officer, knew that when it came to publicity, there was only one way to play it: with a salute stapled to your forehead. To let yourself be turned into a *personality*, to become *colorful*, to be portrayed as an egotist or a rake-hell, was only asking for grief, as many people, including General George Patton, had learned. Scott Carpenter was a case in point. He was open and forthright by nature, and he happened to tell one of the *Life* writers how his teenage years had been anything but standard-issue astronaut-corps mom's-pie material, especially after his grandfather had died and he had drifted around Boulder raising hell when he felt like it—and some of this stuff came out in *Life*, without NASA being sent a draft of it, and Scott caught flak for weeks . . . on the grounds that he had put the program in a bad light.

As far as the wives were concerned, their outlook was the same as that of officers' wives generally, only more so. The main thing was not to say or do anything that reflected badly upon your husband. There wasn't much to worry about with *Life* on this score. If Betty or any of the others did happen to say anything wrong, she could always remove it before it saw print. As time went by, the *Life* writers must have despaired of getting any personal stuff at all into their personal stories.

Deke Slayton's wife, Marge, had been divorced, which was a matter of record, but that wasn't about to be printed in *Life* magazine. A *once-divorced astronaut's wife* was by now an unthinkable concatenation of words. When the selection process for astronaut had begun, Trudy Cooper, Gordon Cooper's wife, had been living by herself down at San Diego. The writers from *Life* may have known about it and they may not have. It was a moot point, because in any event there were not going to be any astronauts with washed-up marriages in the pages of *Life* magazine on the eve of the battle in the heavens with the Russians. The exclusive rights to the "personal stories" of the astronauts and their families that *Life* had purchased did not encompass any such tangled terrain as that.

And it didn't have to be that personal for them to wave the wand and make it disappear. Look at what they did with John Glenn's wife, Annie. Annie was a good-looking and highly capable woman, but she also had what was referred to as a "slight speech impediment" or "a hesitation in her speech." The truth was that she had a terrific stutter, the classic kind, the kind in which you get hung up on a syllable until you either force it out or run out of breath. Annie was game about it, and she would hang in there until she said what she wanted to say, but it was a real disability—everywhere except in *Life* magazine. In *Life* magazine there were going to be no ferocious stammering jackhammer stutters on the home front.

As for Betty, she came out in *Life* as the thoughtful, articulate, competent, much respected Honorable Mrs. Captain Astronaut. She didn't ask for much more than that. If it pleased them, the people at *Life* could sit around removing dour grim grit and zits until they earned a place beside the angels in Retouch Heaven.

7

THE CAPE

CAPE CANAVERAL WAS IN FLORIDA, but not any part of Florida you would write home about, except on one of those old Tichnor Brothers postcards on which there is a drawing of two grinning dogs positioned in front of a lamp post, each with a hind leg hoisted, and a caption that says: THIS IS A WONDERFUL PLACE . . . JUST BETWEEN YOU AND ME AND THE LAMP POST! No, Cape Canaveral was not Miami Beach or Palm Beach or even Key West. Cape Canaveral was Cocoa Beach. That was the resort town at the Cape. Cocoa Beach was the resort town for all the Low Rent folk who couldn't afford the beach towns farther south. Cocoa Beach was so Low Rent that nothing on this earth could ever change it. The vacation houses at Cocoa Beach were little boxes with front porches or "verandas" nailed onto them and a 1952 De Soto coupe with venetian blinds in the rear window rusting in the salt air out back by the septic tank.

Even the beach at Cocoa Beach was Low Rent. It was about three hundred feet wide at high tide and hard as a brick. It was so hard that the youth of postwar Florida used to go to the stock-car races at Daytona Beach, and then, their brains inflamed with dreams of racing glory, they would head for Cocoa Beach and drive their cars right out on that hardtack strand and race their gourds off, while the poor sods who were vacationing there gathered up their children and their Scotch-plaid picnic coolers, and ran for cover. At night some sort of prehistoric chiggers or fire ants—it was hard to say, since you could never see them—rose up from out of the sand and the palmetto grass and went for the ankles with a bite more vicious than a mink's. There was no such thing as "first-class accommodations" or "red-carpet treatment" in Cocoa Beach. The red carpet, had anyone ever tried to lay one down, would have been devoured in midair by the No See'um bugs, as they were called, before it ever touched the implacable hard-cracker ground.

And that was one reason why the boys loved it! Even Glenn—even Glenn, who did not partake of all of its Low Rent glories.

The place reminded them of what they had heard Edwards, or Muroc, was like in the legendary days of the late 1940's and early 1950's. It was one of those bleached, sandy, bare-boned stretches where the land that any sane man wants runs out . . . and the government takes it over for the testing of hot and dangerous machines, and the kings of the resulting rat-shack kingdom are those who test them. Just south of Cocoa Beach was Patrick Air Force Base, site of the headquarters of the Atlantic Missile Range, for the testing of the weaponry of the Cold War: guided missiles, intermediate-range ballistic missiles, and intercontinental ballistic missiles. North of Cocoa Beach, on the very tip of the Cape itself, was the huge new secret launching facility from which all these rockets and pilotless aircraft were fired, a stone boondock dune plain with the Atlantic Ocean on one side and the Banana River on the other, with soil so sandy that the scrub pines had trouble growing fifteen feet high, and yet malarial and so marshy that the cottonmouth moccasins stood their ground and stared you down, the sort of hopeless stone boondock spit where the vertebrates give up and the slugs and the No See'um bugs take over. The few buildings on the base were of the World War II Beaverboard Temporary variety. And like Edwards of old, the Cape, this poor godforsaken afterthought in the march of terrestrial evolution, turned out to be a paradise of Flying & Drinking and Drinking & Driving and Driving & the rest, for those who cared about such things. Or of Drinking & Driving & the rest, in any event. There was still no flying.

Langley remained the astronauts' headquarters, but the Cape would be their launching site, eventually, and they went there increasingly for training. They would fly in by commercial airliner, landing in Melbourne or Orlando. Most of them would rent convertibles and head for the Holiday Inn on Route A1A just north of Cocoa Beach, a motel run by a man named Henry Landiwirth, who soon found himself becoming innkeeper to the astronauts. Quite a little 1960's-style American Rat-Shack Strip was beginning to develop on Route A1A near the Holiday Inn: hamburger restaurants with plate-glass walls and hot magenta lights, night spots with Kontiki roofs, and little shopping slabs by the side of the highway, slabs of concrete with one-story cinderblock sheds on them broken up into store fronts with SPACE AVAILABLE signs posted.

Military units had always been great ones for creating "traditions" instantly, on the spot, and this unofficial corps of astronauts was no exception. The tradition was: the Cape is off limits to wives. This came about rather naturally. The Cape was not a good place for wives and children, because there were no kitchen facilities in the motels and there were none of the usual beach resort amenities, and none of them could afford the plane fares for family trips to Florida in the first place. Besides that, the boys' training hours were very long, sometimes ten or twelve hours a day. They did nothing at the Cape but work their butts off all day and then fall into bed, albeit this was a matter open to interpretation.

The boys' training at the Cape was not so much arduous as tedious. It was sedentary, even. It involved no flying. Some days they would be briefed on launch procedures. Or they would drive out to the launching base and go inside an old converted rat-shack hangar, Hangar S, and sit all day in a simulator known as the "procedures trainer," which on the inside was a replica of the capsule they would ride in during flight. Or technically they sat in there all day; in fact, they were lying down. It was as if you took a chair and pushed it over backward, so that its back was on the floor, and then sat in it. That was the position the astronaut would be in during his launch atop the rocket and the position he would be in as he came down toward the water inside the capsule at the end of the flight.

It was hard for Glenn or anyone else to explain exactly what you did for ten or twelve hours inside this thing. But clearly, once a man had had a day full of this tedious regimen, he was ready to limber up a little, get the blood flowing again, wiggle his fanny a bit. For Glenn it was enough to go out to that hardtack strand at Cocoa Beach and run two or three miles. It was the greatest long-distance running track you could possibly ask for, with pure ocean air to help your pump get going efficiently. And there would be John Glenn, the very picture of astronaut dedication, pounding along the same shore from which he would one day be hurled into the heavens. John Glenn Running for the Big One at Cocoa Beach was an even better picture than the one he had put on display at Langley. Glenn noticed that some of his confreres were loosening up in quite another way, however. Which is to say, they were checking in at the holy coordinates. After a long day of make-believe flying in the simulator . . . a little Drinking & Driving & the rest of the real pilot's life.

The *driving* eventually took on an extraordinary dimension here at the Cape. Gus Grissom and Gordon Cooper, and then Al Shepard and Wally Schirra, would discover Jim Rathmann. Rathmann was a big rugged character who had one of the largest automobile dealerships in the area, a General Motors agency about twenty miles south of Cocoa Beach near Melbourne. It was typical Air Force stuff that Gus and some of the others should become great pals of his. Rathmann was no ordinary auto dealer, however. He turned out to be a racing driver; the best, in fact. In 1960 he won the Indianapolis 500 after having finished second three times. Rathmann was a great friend of Ed Cole, the president of Chevrolet. Cole had helped Rathmann set up his agency. When he found out that Rathmann knew the Mercury astronauts, he became the astrobuff of all astrobuffs. America seemed to be full of businessmen like Cole who exercised considerable power and were strong leaders but who had never exercised power and leadership in its primal form: manly courage in the face of physical danger. When they met someone who *had it*, they wanted to establish a relationship with that righteous stuff. After meeting the astronauts, Cole, who had just turned fifty, was determined to learn to fly. Meantime, Rathmann set up a leasing arrangement whereby the boys could lease any type of Chevrolet they wanted for practically nothing per year. Eventually, Gus and Gordo had Corvettes like Al Shepard's; Wally moved up from an Austin-Healy to a Maserati; and Scott Carpenter got a Shelby Cobra, a true racing vehicle. Al was continually coming by Rathmann's to have his gear ratios changed. Gus wanted flared fenders and magnesium wheels. The fever gripped them all, but Gus and Gordo especially. They were determined to show the champ, Rathmann, and each other that they could handle these things. Gus would go out rat-racing at night at the Cape, racing full-bore for the next curve, dealing with the oncoming headlights by psychokinesis, spinning off the shoulders and then scrambling back up on the highway for more of it. It made you cover up your eyes and chuckle at the same time. The boys were fearless in an automobile, they were determined to hang their hides right out over the edge—and they had no idea what mediocre drivers they actually were, at least by the standards of professional racing. Which is to say, they were like every group of pilot trainees at every base in America who ever reached that crazed hour of the night when it came time to prove that the right stuff works in all areas of life.

Cocoa Beach had begun to take on the raw excitement of a boom town and the manic and motley cast of characters that goes with it. In boom towns of the oil-gush or gold-rush variety the excitement had always come from simple greed. But Cocoa Beach was more like a Second World War boom town. There was enough greed in the air to make things spicy, but the true fervor was the *joie de combat*. People coming to work at the Cape, for NASA, private contractors, or whomever, felt like part of the mad rush to battle the Soviets for dominion over the heavens. At Edwards, or Muroc, in the old days, the worthy warriors used to repair in the evening to Pancho's, which, though theoretically a public place, was like a club for the adventurers over the high desert. At the Cape, by 1960, the warriors had the motels on the rat-shack strip along Route A1A. At night the pool areas of the motels became like the roaring fraternity house lounge of Project Mercury. Very few people, no matter what their rank in the project, had a place big enough, much less attractive enough, to entertain in. But every night the fraternal lounge was open, under the skies, in the salt air, out near the beach, and the party was on, and one and all braved the palmetto bugs and the No See'um bugs and celebrated the fact that they were on the scene where this great Cold War adventure was taking place. Naturally nothing gave the party quite so much magic as the presence of an astronaut.

And Glenn could see that after eight, ten, twelve hours of lying cooped up in the procedures trainer out in Hangar S, most of his brethren were ready to provide the magic. No matter what time it was, it was beer-call time, as they said in the Air Force, and they would get in their cars and go barreling into Cocoa Beach for the endless, seamless party. And what lively cries and laughter would be rising up on all sides as the silvery moon reflected drunkenly on the chlorine blue of the motel pools! And what animated revelers were to be found! There were NASA people and the contractors and their people, and there were the Germans. Although they scrupulously avoided publicity, many of Wernher von Braun's team of V-2 experts had important jobs at the Cape and were happy to find a fraternal atmosphere in which they could take off their official long faces and let the funny bone out for a tap dance or two. And many were the mid-summer nights in Cocoa Beach, nights so hot and salty that the No See'um bugs were sluggish, when sizzling *glühwein* materialized as if from out of a time warp and drunken Germans could be heard pummeling the piano in the cocktail lounge and singing the "Horst Wessel Song"! It was like some improbable echo of Pancho's along the hardtack Florida littoral. Oh, yes, it was! As at Pancho's, the most marvelous lively young cookies were materializing also, and they were just *there*, waiting beside the motel pools, when one arrived, young juicy girls with stand-up jugs and full-sprung thighs and conformations so taut and silky that the very sight of them practically pulled a man into the delta of priapic delirium. Some of them had come to work for the contractors, some to work for NASA, some to work for this or that business that was starting up in the little boom town—and some simply *got there, materialized*. And when an astronaut arrived, it was as if they dropped out of the sky or rose up from out of the Bermuda grass. In any event, they were always there and ready.

As even Glenn could tell, it was enough just to *be* an astronaut, whether a handsome devil like Scott Carpenter or a gruff little fellow like Gus Grissom. As soon as Gus arrived at the Cape, he would put on clothes that were Low Rent even by Cocoa Beach standards. Gus and Deke both wore these outfits. You could see them tooling around the Strip in Cocoa Beach in their Ban-Lon shirts and baggy pants. The atmosphere was casual at Cocoa Beach, but Gus and Deke knew how to squeeze casual until it screamed for mercy. They reminded you, in a way, of those fellows whom everyone growing up in America had seen at one time or another, those fellows from the neighborhood who wear sport shirts designed in weird blooms and streaks of tubercular blue and runny-egg yellow hanging out over pants the color of a fifteen-cent cigar, with balloon seats and pleats and narrow cuffs that stop three or four inches above the ground, the better to reveal their olive-green GI socks and black bulb-toed bluchers, as they head off to the Republic Auto Parts store for a set of shock-absorber pads so they can prop up the 1953 Hudson Hornet on some cinderblocks and spend Saturday and Sunday underneath it beefing up the suspension. Gus and Deke made a perfect pair, even down to their names. Not even the sight of the boys in their Mechanics & Tradesmen's Ban-Lon could turn off the girls to the presence of the astronauts.

There were juicy little girls going around saying, "Well, four down, three to go!" or whatever—the figures varied—and laughing like mad. Everybody knew what they meant but only halfway believed them. There was no question but that the temptations for the Fighter Jock Away from Home were enormous. It was all so easy and casual on these mid-summer nights. Before the missiles came to the Cape, Cocoa Beach was a hard-shelled Baptist stronghold with more churches than gasoline stations, and practically all of them were of the pietistic or Dissenting Protestant variety. But the new Cocoa Beach, the Project Mercury boom town, was part of the new face of the 1960's: the little town whose life was completely keyed to the automobile. Naturally, nobody built hotels in Cocoa Beach, only motels; and when they built apartment houses, they built them like motels, so that you could drive up to your own door. At neither the motels nor the apartment houses did you have to go through a public lobby to get to your room. A minor architectural note, one might say—and yet in Cocoa Beach, like so many towns of the new era, this one fact did more than *the pill* to encourage what would later be rather primly named "the sexual revolution."

There had always been a part of the Military Wife's Compact that tacitly granted an officer a little latitude in this area. Naturally, there would be times when a military man would be sent far from home, perhaps for extended periods, and he might find it necessary to satisfy his healthy manly urges on these far-off terrains. There was even the implication that such urges were a good sign of a fighting man's virility. So the wife and the military itself would avert their eyes and stand mute—so long as the officer caused no scandal and did nothing to shake the solidity of his marriage and his family. This tradition had originated, of course, long before the airplane made it possible for an officer to reach the distant terrain in two or three hours for a long weekend or an overnight stand. Traditions often began on a moment's notice in the military; but they took a long time to die, and this one was in no danger of dying at Cocoa Beach.

That much John Glenn could discern also . . . and such was the background of the Konakai Séance.

* * *

Every now and then the seven pilots would shut the door of their office at Langley, and not even the secretary could come in. If anybody wanted to know what was going on in there, they were told that the astronauts were having a séance. A *séance?* Oh, it's just a name they thought up for a meeting in which they try to come up with a common position, a consensus, concerning certain problems. The implication was that the problems were mostly technical in nature. Wally Schirra would mention that they had had a séance before going to the engineers and insisting on changes in the design of the instrument panel of the Mercury capsule. The idea was to give the corps of astronauts some of the solidity of a squadron. The seven of them might have their rivalries, their differences in backgrounds and temperaments and approaches to the job at hand, but they should be able to arrive at firm decisions as a group, no matter how acrimonious the debate might be, and then close ranks and pull together, one for all, all for one. Whether or not the session at the Konakai qualified as a séance by the usual standards was hard to say. But God knows it dealt with a recurrent problem . . . and the debate was acrimonious . . .

One day all seven of them were out in San Diego for a tour of the Convair plant and a look at the latest progress on the Atlas rocket. Convair wanted to do it up right and had treated them all to their own rooms at the Konakai, a rather high-toned hotel built in a Polynesian motif on Shelter Island, overlooking the Pacific. It so happened that Scott Carpenter had drawn a room with a double bed. That evening one of the boys approached him in a comradely fashion and said that his room had two twin beds, whereas in fact he was going to require a double bed for the evening. Would Scott mind switching rooms? It was all the same to Scott, and so they switched rooms. Scott mentioned it to his buddy John Glenn with a smile, as an amusing local note, and thought no more about it.

The next day the seven of them were in the living room of a suite that had been set aside for their use, when Glenn launched into a lecture, along the following lines: the playing around with the girls, the cookies, had gotten out of hand. He knew, and they knew, that it could blow up into something very unfortunate. They were all squarely in the public eye. They had the opportunity of a lifetime, and he was sorry but he just wasn't going to stand by and let other people compromise the whole thing because they couldn't keep their pants zipped.

There was no doubt whatsoever that Glenn meant every word of it. When he got his back up, he was formidable. He was not to be trifled with. In his eyes burned four centuries of Dissenting Protestant fervor, nailed down by two million laps that his legs had pounded around the BOQ driveway.

But there was more than one hard customer in the room. Staring straight back at Glenn, volt for volt, was Al Shepard. The others, Glenn included, understood Shepard least of all, because there seemed to be two Al Shepards, and no one ever knew for sure which one he was dealing with. Back home at Langley you saw one Alan Shepard, the utterly, and if necessary, icily correct career Navy officer. Shepard's father, Colonel Alan Shepard, Sr., was an impressive figure whom few people cared to challenge. Shepard was always a good son. The colonel sent him to private schools, and in due course he followed the colonel's model of a military career, graduated from the Naval Academy, and became a pilot; and although he had never served in combat, he was considered one of the Navy's best test pilots, drawing important assignments in testing the F3H, the F8U, the F4D Skyray, the

F11F Tigercat, the F2H3 Banshee, and the F5D Skylancer, including the tricky business of proving out some of these monsters in their first landings on the then-new angled carrier decks. He was regarded as a topnotch Navy aviator, tough, quick-witted, and a leader. He had married a good-looking woman of great charm and poise—"a real lady," people always said—named Louise Brewer. She was a Christian Scientist. Shepard was from New Hampshire, and in New England the Christian Scientists had considerable social cachet, since they were on the average the wealthiest church members in the United States and had an intellectual tradition somewhat similar to the Unitarians'. Although this side of Christian Scientist life was not generally known in America, it was not lost upon the Navy, where the brass traditionally kept tabs on religious affiliations. Being an Academy man was the most important thing, but belonging to a socially correct Protestant denomination was the next best thing. The Episcopal Church ranked first, unofficially, throughout the military (both Schirra and Carpenter were Episcopalians). Well, the Christian Scientists, although smaller in numbers, were even tonier. Such were the general contours of the correct life of Commander Shepard, the icy career officer. But inside his locker he kept . . . Smilin' Al of the Cape! In point of fact, Shepard himself had never joined the Christian Scientist Church or even come close to it. In his secret heart he was probably stone atheist. At the original press conference he had rather adroitly finessed the point by saying that he belonged to no church but attended the Christian Science Church regularly. Somehow the impression was left that Shepard was a Christian Scientist who had done everything but sign on the dotted line. (The press, the ever-proper Gent, was happy enough to see it that way.) As long as he was at home, however, Shepard could have passed for a model Christian Scientist husband, had he chosen to. He did go to church with Louise regularly. He did not drink, smoke, swear, or let his lips—his eyes and lips were his most pronounced features—spread into a warm and winning fighter jock grin when a pretty girl came by.

No, he didn't flash that famous Smilin' Al Shepard look until he stepped out of his airplane Away from Home—and most especially at the Cape. Then Al looked like a different human being, as if he had removed his ice mask. He would come out of the airplane with his eyes dancing. A great goomba-goomba grin would take over his face. You halfway expected to see him start snapping his fingers, because everything about him seemed to be asking the question: "Where's the action?" If he then stepped into his Corvette—well, then, there you had it: the picture of the perfect Fighter Jock Away from Home.

But now, in this room at the Konakai Hotel, it was the Icy Commander who stared back at Glenn. Commander Al, the colonel's son, knew how to put on all the armor of military correctness, in the stern old-fashioned way. He informed Glenn that he was way out of line. He told him not to try to foist his view of morality on anybody else in the group. In the succeeding weeks the Glenn position and the Fighter Jock position began to form, with various hands adding their own amendments. As for the Fighter Jock position: The seven of them had volunteered to do a job and they were devoting long hours of training to prepare for it and were doing many things above and beyond the strict call of duty, such as the morale tours of the factories, and forgoing flight pay and vacations and any semblance of an orderly family life—and that therefore what one did with what little time he had to himself was his own business, so long as he used good sense.

Shepard had struck the tone of the by-the-book commander. He sounded as utterly convinced and correct in his own fashion as Glenn did in his. Commander Al was capable of a rather formal rhetoric in discussions of this sort, complete with a little litotes.

There was no reason why one should have an aversion to the company of women, so long as one's acquaintanceships did not impair one's performance in the program or reflect adversely upon it.

John Glenn, however, was buying none of that. He stared back at Smilin' Al of the Cape and the Icy Commander, both of them, with John Calvin's own eyes. As time went by, the Glenn position became: Look, whether we like it or not, we're public figures. Whether we deserve it or not, people look up to us. So we have a terrific responsibility. It's not enough not to get caught. It's not even enough to know to your own satisfaction that you've done nothing wrong. We've got to be like Caesar's wife. We've got to be above even the appearance of doing wrong.

It went on like that, with neither giving an inch. That line about "Caesar's wife" would not be forgotten. Everybody knew there was something to what the fellow was saying . . . Nevertheless . . . Could you believe it? Could you believe that the day would come when you would actually see a pilot, an equal among equals, give his comrades a little sermon about keeping their hands clean and their peckers stowed? Where did he get off setting himself above them this way, and what was his real game?

Glenn knew he was making no friends with this approach. Yet there were key moments in a military career when a man had to assume leadership. That was the essence of leadership caliber, and surely that fact would be appreciated—if not by the pilots themselves, then surely by . . . others who would hear about it. The competition for the first flight was not a popularity contest among the troops, after all. Bob Gilruth and his deputies in the Space Task Group would make the choice. Glenn had never been afraid to alienate his peers when he knew he was right; perhaps this, too, had always impressed his superiors—and he had *never* been left behind. His faith in what was right was part of his righteous stuff.

Glenn had one great ally among the other six, and that was Scott Carpenter. Carpenter looked up to him and backed him in the debate. Wally Schirra and Gordon Cooper tended to back Shepard, arguing that when you were on duty you should be a model of correctness, but that when you were off duty your personal life was your own lookout. Schirra was finding Glenn more and more irritating. Who the hell did he think he was? After a while, they barely spoke to each other unless the job forced them to.

Grissom and Slayton somewhat dourly sided with Glenn on this particular point. Since he was making such a federal case out of it, they would acknowledge the soundness of his logic. But this didn't mean they idolized him any more than Schirra or Shepard did. A basic division was building up in the group. It was the other five against the pious fair-haired boy and his sidekick, Carpenter. Some of them seemed to derive some satisfaction from lumping Carpenter with Glenn. What was Carpenter even doing here! They couldn't get over the fact that Scott and his wife, Rene, had flamboyant cushions on the floor of their living room and they actually sat there while Scott played the guitar and Rene sang. The fact that she had a trained voice made no difference. It was beatnik stuff. Not only that, Carpenter was a great pal of the doctors. He and Glenn were both like that. They went out of their way to cooperate with the Life Sciences people, too.

Glenn and Carpenter were even willing guinea pigs for the two psychiatrists who had just come on board, Sheldon Korchin from the University of California and George Ruff, who had been in charge of the psychiatric testing at Wright-Pat. Both men were likable enough as individuals, but this thing of submitting to psychiatric study seemed dispensable to some of the boys, particularly Schirra and Cooper. The two psychiatrists were continually having you urinate into bottles so that they could analyze your urine for corticosteroid levels, which supposedly were an index of stress. But Carpenter thought this was terrific stuff, too. He even *talked* to them about it!

What some of the other five found eccentric in Carpenter was what Glenn (and the doctors) found interesting. Scott was about the only one you could sit down with and talk about the broader and more philosophical sides of Project Mercury and space exploration. Scott was the only one with a touch of the poet about him, in the sense that the idea of going into space stirred his imagination. He would even go out at night and prop a telescope up on top of his car on a tripod and just stargaze and let himself drift into the most profound speculation of astronomy: *What is my place in the cosmos?*

Just try to imagine Grissom doing that! If Gus had a telescope, he might use the small end of it to try to whack a turkey joint out of the maw of the Disposall if the thing was stuck, but that would be the end of that. Gus and Deke were the duo at the other end of the spectrum. The main thing was to ride the bird up there into space and get the job done and get back, and let's hold the Mickey Mouse down to a minimum.

Shepard and Wally Schirra were paired somewhere in between. It was not that they were inseparable pals or even buddies, however. Shepard had no intimates, so far as anyone knew, and Schirra probably spent as much time wondering what made Shepard tick as the rest of them did. It was just that they came into the astronaut corps with similar backgrounds. There was no particular advantage to forming a clique in this seven-man corps, because only one man could win the competition, i.e., get the first flight, and it wasn't a voting situation, in any case. Nevertheless, if any such situation came up, Al and Wally would probably tend to side with Deke and Gus . . . As for Gordon Cooper, he seemed to be regarded as the odd man out. One got the impression that he was not in the running. As far as Gordo himself was concerned, however, he sided with Gus and Deke and Al and Wally on most of the pertinent questions, from the business of medical experiments to life after hours.

They were all beginning to realize that the stakes were tremendous. With the first flight into space, the holy first flight, one of them would become not only the pre-eminent *astronaut* . . . but also the True Brother at the top of the entire pyramid. The first American into space—who might very well be the first human being to go into space—would have an eminence that not even Chuck Yeager had ever enjoyed, because he would belong not just to the history of aviation but to world history.

And who would this one man be? Well . . . who else would it be but John Glenn! Glenn was just pouring it on. He was even assuming the role of natural group leader—giving them a little moral lecture at the séances!

The begrudging consensus that had developed from the Konakai séance was that, yeah, Glenn was right; they ought to watch themselves a little more carefully. But Al Shepard, for one, was not the type to let Glenn get away with it unmarked. Al kept putting the needle in. If there was anyone else around to enjoy it, Al would say to Glenn: "John, I think you need to loosen up a little bit, boy. What you need is a sports car. Why don't you get rid of that junk heap you're driving and do a little rat-racing. It'll do you good, John."

Al never missed an opportunity to stick it to Glenn about his terrible-looking underpowered Peugeot and his need to get a car with a little more juice and loosen up. It became a refrain. Glenn knew how to roll with this kind of ribbing and grin through it. At the same time, you could tell it was getting under his skin. You couldn't help but get the feeling that the piece of equipment Al was really saying Glenn should loosen up and turn on the juice with was not an automobile.

One morning, when they came into the Astronaut Office, there was a big inscription up on the blackboard:

THE SPORTS CAR IS A SYMPTOM OF THE MALE MENOPAUSE.

8

THE THRONES

In the eyes of the engineers assigned to Project Mercury the training of the astronauts would be the easy task on the list. Naturally you needed a man with the courage to ride on top of a rocket, and you were grateful that such men existed. Nevertheless, their training was not a very complicated business. The astronaut would have little to do in a Mercury flight except stand the strain, and the engineers had devised what psychologists referred to as "a graded series of exposures" to take care of that. No, the difficult, the challenging, the dramatic, the pioneering part of space flight, as the engineers saw it, was the technology.

It was only thanks to a recent invention, the high-speed electronic computer, that Project Mercury was feasible at all. There was an analogy here with the great Admiral of the Uncharted Seas himself, Columbus. It was only thanks to a recent invention of his day, the magnetic compass, that Columbus had dared to sail across the Atlantic. Until then ships had stayed close to the great land masses for even the longest voyages. Likewise, putting a man into space the quick and dirty way without high-speed computers was unthinkable. Such computers had not been in production before 1951, and yet here it was, 1960, and engineers were already devising systems for guiding rockets into space, through the use of computers built into the engines and connected to accelerometers, for monitoring the temperature, pressure, oxygen supply, and other vital conditions of the Mercury capsule and for triggering safety procedures automatically—meaning they were creating, with computers, systems in which machines could communicate with one another, make decisions, take action, all with tremendous speed and accuracy . . .

Oh, genius-engineers!

Ah, yes, there was such a thing as self-esteem among engineers. It may not have been as grandiose as that of fighter jocks . . . nevertheless, many was the steaming encephalitic summertime Saturday night at Langley when some NASA engineer would start knocking back that good sweet Virginia A.B.C. store bourbon on the patio and letting his ego out for a little romp, like a growling red dog.

The glorification of the astronauts had really gotten out of control! In the world of science—and Project Mercury was supposed to be a scientific enterprise—pure scientists ranked first and engineers ranked second and the test subjects of experiments ranked so low that one seldom thought about them. But here the test subjects . . . were national heroes! They created a zone of awe and reverence wherever they set foot! Everyone else, whether physicist, biologist, doctor, psychiatrist, or engineer, was a mere attendant.

At the outset it had been understood—it didn't even require comment—that the astronauts would be just that: test subjects in an experiment. Mercury was an adaptation of the Air Force's Man in Space Soonest concept, in which you would attach biosensors to your human subject, seal him up in a capsule, propel him into space ballistically—i.e., like an artillery shell—and bring him back to earth with completely automatic guidance and see how he made out. In November 1959, six months after the seven astronauts were chosen, Randy Lovelace and Scott Crossfield presented a paper at an aerospace medical symposium in which they said that biomedical research was "the sole purpose of the ride," so far as having an astronaut on board was concerned. They added that an aerodynamic space vehicle, such as the proposed X-15B or X-20, would require "a much more highly trained pilot." Since he was involved in the X-15 project, Crossfield had his own ax to grind, but what he and Lovelace were saying was perfectly obvious to any engineer who knew the difference between ballistic and aerodynamic space vehicles. In short, the astronaut in Project Mercury would not be a pilot under any conventional definition.

Even as late as the summer of 1960, at an Armed Forces-National Research Council conference at Woods Hole, Massachusetts, on "the training of astronauts," various engineers and scientists from outside NASA thought nothing of describing the Mercury rocket-capsule vehicle as a fully automated system in which "the astronaut does not need to turn a hand." They would say, "The astronaut has been added to the system as a redundant component." (A *redundant component!*) If the automatic system broke down, he might step in as a repairman or manual conductor. Above all, of course, he would be wired with biosensors and a microphone to see how a human being responded to the stress of the flight. That would be his main function. There were psychologists who advised against using pilots at all—and this was more than a year after the famous Mercury Seven had been chosen. The pilot's, particularly the hot pilot's, main psychological bulwark under stress was his knowledge that he controlled the ship and could always *do something* ("I've tried A! I've tried B! I've tried C!" . . .) This obsession with active control, it was argued, would only tend to cause problems on Mercury flights. What was required was a man whose main talent was for *doing nothing* under stress. Some suggested using a new breed of military flier, the radar man, the Air Force Strategic Air Command radar observer or the Navy radar intercept officer, a man who had experience riding in the rear in high-performance aircraft under combat conditions and doing nothing but reading the radar, come what may, abandoning all control of the craft (and protection of his own life) to someone else, the pilot ("I looked over at Robinson—and he was staring at the radar like a *zombie!*"). An experienced zombie would do fine. In fact, considerable attention had been given to a plan to anesthetize or tranquillize the astronauts, not to keep them from panicking, but just to make sure they would lie there peacefully with their sensors on and not *do something* that would ruin the flight.

The scientists and engineers took it for granted that the training of the astronauts would be unlike anything ordinarily thought of as flight training. Flight training consisted of teaching a man how to take certain actions. He was taught how to control an unfamiliar craft or how to put a familiar craft through unfamiliar maneuvers, such as bombing runs or carrier landings. On the other hand, the only actions the astronauts would have to learn how to take would be to initiate the emergency procedures in the case of a bad rocket launch or a bad landing and to step in as a backup (redundant component) if the automatic control system failed to hold the heatshield in the correct position prior to re-entry through the earth's atmosphere. The astronaut would not be able to control the path or the speed of the capsule at all. A considerable part of his training would be what was known as de-conditioning, de-sensitizing, or adapting out fears. There was a principle in psychology that maintained that "bad habits, including overstrong emotionality, can be eliminated by a graded series of exposures to the anxiety-arousing stimulus." That was what much of astronaut training was to be. The rocket launch was regarded as a novel and possibly disorienting event, in part *because* the astronaut would have no control over it whatsoever. So they had devised "a graded series of exposures." They took the seven men to the Navy's human centrifuge facility in Johnsville, Pennsylvania. The centrifuge looked like a Wild Bolo ride; it had a fifty-foot arm with a cockpit, or gondola, on the end of it, and the arm could be whirled around at astonishing speeds, great enough to put up to 40 g's of pressure on the rider inside the gondola, one g being equal to the force of gravity. The high g-forces generated by combat aircraft in dives and turns during the Second World War had sometimes caused blackouts, red-outs, gray-outs, or made it impossible for pilots to lift their hands to the controls; the giant centrifuge at Johnsville had been built to explore this new problem of high-speed flight. By 1959 the machine had been computerized and turned into a simulator capable of duplicating the g-forces and accelerations of any form of flight, even rocket flight. The astronaut was helped into his full pressure suit, with his biosensors attached and his rectal thermometer inserted, and then placed into the gondola, in a contoured seat molded for his body, whereupon all the wires, hoses, and microphones he would have in actual flight were hooked up, and the gondola was depressurized to five pounds per square inch, as it would be in space flight. The interior of the gondola had been converted into a replica of the Mercury capsule's interior, with all the switches and console displays. The taped noise of an actual Redstone rocket firing was played over the astronaut's headset, and the ride began. Using the computers, the engineers would put the man through an entire Mercury flight profile. The centrifuge built up the g-forces at precisely the same rate they would build up in flight, up to six or seven g's, whereupon the g-forces would suddenly drop off, as they would in flight as the capsule went over the top of its arc, and the astronaut experienced a tumbling sensation, as he would, presumably, in flight. All the while the astronaut would be required to push a few switches, as he would in actual flight, and talk to a mock flight controller, forcing his words out into the microphone, no matter how great the pressure of the g-forces on his chest. The centrifuge could also duplicate the pressures of deceleration a man would experience during the return through the earth's atmosphere.

To get the seven men used to weightlessness, they took them on parabolic rides in the cargo holds of C-131 transports and backseat in F-100Fs. When the jet came up over the top of the arc of the parabola, the subject would experience from fifteen to forty-five seconds of weightlessness. This was the only flying scheduled for the astronauts' entire training program; and they were, of course, merely passengers on board, as they would be in the Mercury flights.

The only way the astronaut would be able to move the capsule in the slightest would be to fire hydrogen-peroxide thrusters during the interval of weightlessness, tipping or swinging the capsule this way or that, in order to get a particular view out the portholes, for example. NASA built a machine, the ALFA trainer, to accustom each trainee to the sensation. He sat in a seat resting on air bearings and used a hand controller to make it pitch up and down or yaw back and forth. On a screen in front of him, where the capsule's periscope screen would be, aerial photographs and films of the Cape, the Atlantic Ocean, Cuba, Grand Bahama Island, Abaco, all the landmarks, rolled by . . . and veered off as the astronaut pitched or yawed, just as they would in actual flight. The ALFA even made a whooshing sound like that of hydrogen-peroxide thrusters when the astronaut pushed the stick.

By mid-1960 the engineers had developed the "procedures trainer," which was in fact a simulator. There were identical procedures trainers at the Cape and at Langley. At the Cape the trainer was in Hangar S. It was there that the astronaut spent his long day's training. He climbed into a cubicle and sat in a seat that was aimed straight up at the roof. The back of the seat was flat on the floor of the cubicle, so that the astronaut rested on his back. He looked up at a replica of a console that would be used in the Mercury capsule. It was as if he were on top of the rocket, with his face aimed at the sky. The console was wired to a bank of computers. About twenty feet behind the astronaut, on the floor of Hangar S, sat a technician at another console, feeding simulated problems into the system.

The technician would start off saying, "Count is at T minus fifty seconds and counting."

From inside the trainer, over his microphone, the astronaut would answer: "Roger."

"Check your periscope—fully retracted?"

"Periscope retracted."

"Ready switch on?"

"Ready switch on."

"T minus ten seconds. Minus eight . . . seven . . . six . . . five . . . four . . . three . . . two . . . one . . . Fire!"

Inside the trainer the dials in front of the astronaut would start indicating that he was on his way, and he was supposed to start reading the gauges and reporting to the ground. He would say, "Clock is operating . . . okay, twenty seconds . . . one thousand feet [altitude] . . . one-point-five g's . . . Trajectory is good . . . Twelve thousand feet, one-point-nine g's . . . Inner cabin pressure is five p.s.i. . . . . Altitude forty-four thousand, g-level two-point-seven . . . one hundred thousand feet at two minutes and five seconds . . ." The instructor might pick this point to hit a button on his console marked "oxygen." A red warning light marked O_2EMERG would light up, and the astronaut would say: "Cabin pressure decreasing! . . . Oxygen is apparently leaking! . . . It's still leaking . . . Switching to emergency reserve . . ." The astronaut could throw a switch that brought more oxygen into the simulator system—i.e., into its computer calculations—but the instructor could hit his "oxygen" button again, and that meant that the leak was continuing, and the astronaut would say: "Still leaking . . . It's approaching zero-flow rate . . . Abort because of oxygen leak! Abort! Abort!" Then the astronaut would hit a button, and a button marked MAYDAY would light up red on the instructor's console. In actual flight the escape tower was supposed to fire at this point, pulling the capsule free of the rocket and bringing it down by parachute.

The astronauts spent so much time hitting the abort handle in the procedures trainer that it got to the point where it seemed as if they were training for an abort rather than for a launch. There was very little action that an astronaut could take in a Mercury capsule, other than to abort the flight and save his own life. So he was not being trained to *fly* the capsule. He was being trained to ride in it. In a "graded series of exposures" he was being introduced to all sights, sounds, and sensations he might conceivably experience. Then he was reintroduced to them, day after day, until the Mercury capsule and all its hums, g-forces, window views, panel displays, lights, buttons, switches, and peroxide squirts became as familiar, as routine, as workaday as an office. All flight training had a certain amount of desensitizing built into it. When a Navy pilot practiced carrier landings on the outline of a flight deck painted on an airfield, it was hoped that the maneuver might also desensitize his normal fear of landing a hurtling machine in such a small space. Nevertheless, he was there chiefly in order to learn to land the machine. Not until Project Mercury had there been a flight training program so long and detailed, so sophisticated, and yet so heavily devoted to desensitizing the trainee, to adapting out man's ordinary fears, and enabling one to think and use his hands normally in a novel environment.

Oh, all of this had been well known at the outset! . . . so much so that the original NASA selection committee had been afraid that the military test pilots they were interviewing would regard the job as boring or distasteful. Since they figured they needed six astronauts for Mercury, they had considered training twelve—on the assumption that half of them would resign once they fully understood how passive their role would be. And now, in 1960, they began to realize that they had been correct; or halfway, in any case. The boys were, indeed, finding the role of biomedical passenger in an automated pod, i.e., the role of human guinea pig, distasteful. That much had proved to be true. The boys' response, however, had not been resignation or anything close to it. No, the engineers now looked on, eyebrows arched, as the guinea pigs set about . . . *altering the experiment*.

THE DIFFERENCE BETWEEN pilot and passenger in any flying craft came down to one point: control. The boys were able to present some practical, workmanlike arguments on this score. Even if an astronaut were to be a redundant component, an observer and repairman, he should be able to *override* any of the Mercury vehicle's automatic systems *manually*, if only to correct malfunctions. So went the argument. But there was another argument that could not be put into so many words, since one was forbidden to state the premise itself: the right stuff.

After all, the right stuff was not bravery in the simple sense of being willing to risk your life (by riding on top of a Redstone or Atlas rocket). Any fool could do that (and many fools would no doubt volunteer, given the opportunity), just as any fool could throw his life away in the process. No, the idea (as all *pilots* understood) was that a man should have the ability to go up in a hurtling piece of machinery and put his hide on the line and have the moxie, the reflexes, the experience, the coolness, to pull it back at the last yawning moment—but how in the name of God could you either hang it out or haul it back if you were a lab animal sealed in a pod?

Every signal they received told the boys that the true brethren at Edwards looked upon them as glorified "klutzes," to use Wally Schirra's phrase. Schirra knew the Edwards outlook in such matters well enough. He had done some major testing of the F-4H at Edwards for the Navy in 1956. But it was Deke Slayton who felt the condescension of the brethren most of all. He had come into Project Mercury straight from Fighter Ops at Edwards, and his pals there kidded him unmercifully. "A monkey's gonna make the first flight." That was the typical refrain. When the boys went to Edwards for their briefings on the X-15 program and their weightless parabolas—riding backseat with Edwards pilots—they picked up a whiff of . . . contempt . . . It hadn't helped any that Scott Carpenter and a couple of the others had taken over the controls on the F-100Fs and tried to fly the weightless parabolas from the front seat . . . and had failed. They hadn't been able to fly the correct profile and produce the weightless interval. Of course, with a little practice they could have no doubt mastered it . . . Nevertheless! . . . Rightly or wrongly, some of the boys felt that rocket pilots like Crossfield were high-hatting them. And what about the Society of Experimental Test Pilots? The SETP was the main organization within the fraternity. Several of the boys didn't even qualify for membership. The SETP required that a member have at least twelve months' experience in the first flights of new aircraft, probing the outer limits of the envelope. The SETP was not about to accept astronauts until they had done a hell of a lot more than volunteer for Mercury and sign a contract with *Life*. On the upper elevations of the pyramid the brave lads—they could sense it—were viewed as seven green rookies; and all the while there was the infuriating question: "Are astronauts even *pilots?*"

Deke Slayton, who was a member of the Society of Experimental Test Pilots, had been invited to address the annual conference in Los Angeles in September 1959 on that very subject: the role of the astronaut in Project Mercury. The meeting happened to come just two weeks after *Life* had started its sunburst of stories categorizing the seven astronauts as the best and bravest pilots in American history. No reader of *Life* would have recognized the Deke Slayton who went to the podium in a hotel convention hall to speak to the brotherhood. From the start his tone was defensive. He said he had some "stubborn, frank" comments on the role of *the pilot* in Project Mercury. There were people in the military, he said, who wondered "whether a college-trained chimpanzee or the village idiot might not do as well in space as an experienced test pilot." (*A monkey's gonna make the first flight!*) He knew there was that kind of talk going around, and it annoyed him. These people were confusing Mercury "with the Air Force Man in Space Soonest or Army Adam programs, which were essentially man-in-a-barrel approaches." His audience looked at him blankly, since such had been precisely the origin of the Mercury program. "I hate to hear anyone contend that present-day pilots have no place in the space age and that non-pilots can perform the space mission effectively," he said. "If this were true, the aircraft driver could count himself among the dinosaurs not too many years hence." That was hardly likely, he went on. A non-pilot might be able to do part of the job. But in those critical moments when it was necessary to keep your head and make observations and record data while cantilevered out over the bottomless Gulp . . . who else could cope with it but someone made of the stuff of the professional test pilot?

Slayton possessed a forcefulness that people often failed to detect at first. His remarks may not have convinced many skeptics within the Society of Experimental Test Pilots. Nevertheless, they became, in effect, the keynote address of the campaign that began inside NASA.

By now, September 1959, Slayton and the rest of them realized that, as Glenn had first divined, the astronaut corps was like a new branch of the service and that in this new branch no one outranked them. Certainly Robert Voas didn't outrank them. Voas was a Navy lieutenant who had been designated as the astronauts' training officer. Voas was neither a flight instructor nor an aeronautical engineer but an industrial psychologist who had been chosen precisely because the training of astronauts was regarded not as a form of pilot training but as a form of psychological adaptation. Voas was no older than they and ranked below them even in the regular military; so one of the boys' first moves was to see that Voas, as training officer, functioned more like a trainer on a sports team and, in any case, not like the coach. *They* began telling *him* what their training schedule was going to be. Voas became a coordinator and spokesman for the astronauts in matters of training.

Gordon Cooper had been frowned upon a few months before when he complained about the lack of supersonic fighter planes for "proficiency" flying, but now the boys took up his complaint within the corridors of NASA, with Slayton and Schirra leading the way and Voas arguing their case for them. Soon they had two F-102s on loan from the Air Force. The ships were somewhat the worse for wear, however—absolute junkers, in fact, in the eyes of the seven pilots. The Air Force had sloughed these wrecks off on them like hand-me-downs. The poor condition of the F-102s wasn't the worst of it, however. The galling thing was that the F-102, which had been one of the first in the Century series, was by now a back number. It would go supersonic but just barely, Mach 1.25 being about top speed. Wally Schirra knew how to formulate the argument on this score. Wally was not merely an expert prankster; he could also turn stern and bang the table and conjure up the aura of the right stuff and its privileges and prerequisites without once uttering the unspoken things. Wally would say to the brass: You're presenting us to the American people as the seven best test pilots in America, and we are *among* the best, all the p.r. aside, and yet you're not even giving us the opportunity to keep up our proficiency! Before I joined this program I was flying fighter aircraft capable of Mach 2 or better. And now we're supposed to keep up our proficiency with a couple of old clunkers that will hardly go Mach 1 even when they're in half-decent shape. It doesn't make any sense! It's as if you decided to prepare a major-league ball club for World Series competition by having them take a year off to play against a bunch of old crocks in a Parks & Recreation league in south Jersey. Wally was terrific in moments like this; and by and by, the boys would get a couple of F-106s, which were second-generation F-102s and capable of mach 2.3. In the meantime, they tried to make do with the F-102s. But, hell, even flying F-102s was a big step beyond the original training agenda— which assumed that proficiency flights of whatever sort would be of no use for the astronaut in Project Mercury. Nor had this assumption yet died, Wally and Deke or no Wally and Deke.

At the Woods Hole conference Voas described the advantages of the F-102 flights in sustaining the astronauts' "decision-making abilities," and an aviation psychologist from the University of Illinois, Jack A. Adams, could scarcely believe what he was hearing.

"Frankly," he said, "I cannot see how decision making, or any other type of response, for that matter, in the F-102 can transfer significantly to the comparatively unique responding required of the astronaut in the Mercury vehicle." Then he added: "The astronaut's task is actually more like a radar observer's job than a pilot's." Another aviation psychologist, Judson Brown of the University of Florida, was just as baffled: "It has been frequently mentioned that skilled pilots must be used for Mercury, for the X-15, and the Dyna-Soar projects. Clearly, the use of skilled pilots seems to be of much less importance for Mercury than for the other two. There is a serious question whether positive transfer will occur from pilot training to Mercury capsule operation."

Inside NASA, however, this position was no longer tenable. From a sheerly political or public relations standpoint, *the astronaut* was NASA's prize possession, and the seven Mercury astronauts had been presented to the public and the Congress as great pilots, not as test subjects. If they now insisted on *being* pilots, great or otherwise—who was going to step in and say no? The boys sensed this; or as Wally Schirra put it, they realized they had "a fair amount of prestige around the country." So next they began whittling down the number of medical and scientific experiments they were expected to take part in—the guinea-pig stuff— simply by characterizing them as useless or stupid and cutting them out of their schedules. Here they tended to have the support of Gilruth's chief of operations, Walt Williams. Williams was a big hearty powerful-looking engineer who had been one of the true geniuses of the X series at Edwards, the man who had turned supersonic flight test into a precise and rational science. Williams was a flight-line engineer; he didn't have much patience with matters of flight test that were not *operational*. The one engineer who didn't mind letting it be known that Astro-power, as it came to be called, was getting out of hand was one of Williams's lieutenants, Christopher Columbus Kraft, Jr. Chris Kraft was a hard-driving young man, thirty-six years old, urbane and sharp-witted, as aeronautical engineers went, and he was scheduled to be flight director for Mercury; but he didn't yet have the clout to do much of anything where the astronauts were concerned. The seven men pressed on. They were tired of the designation of "capsule" for the Mercury vehicle. The term as much as declared that the man inside was not a pilot but an experimental animal in a pod. Gradually, everybody began trying to work the term "spacecraft" into NASA publications and syllabuses. Next the men raised the question of a cockpit window for the spacecraft. As it was now designed, the Mercury capsule had no window, just a small porthole on either side of the astronaut's head. His main way of seeing the outside world would be through a periscope. A window had been regarded as an unnecessary way of inviting rupture due to changes in pressure. Now the astronauts insisted on a window. So the engineers went to work designing a window. Next the men insisted on a hatch they could open by themselves. The hatch, as currently designed, would be bolted shut by the ground crew. In order to leave the capsule after splashing down, the astronaut would either have to slither out through the neck, as if he were coming out of a bottle, or wait for another crew to unbolt the hatch from the outside. So the engineers went to work designing a hatch with explosive bolts so that the astronaut could blow it off by hitting a detonator. It was too late to incorporate the new items into the capsule—the *spacecraft*—that would be used for the first Mercury flight. That vehicle was already badly behind schedule as it was. But they would be in each craft thereafter . . .

And why? Because *pilots* had windows in their cockpits and hatches they could open on their own. That was what it was all about: being a *pilot* as opposed to a guinea pig. The men hadn't stopped with the window and the hatch, either. Not for a moment. Now they wanted . . . *manual control of the rocket!* They weren't kidding! This was to take the form of an override system: if the astronaut believed, in his judgment, as captain of the ship (not *capsule*), that the booster rocket engine was malfunctioning, he could take over and guide it himself—like any proper pilot.

How could they be serious!—the engineers would say. Any chance of a man being able to guide a rocket from inside a ballistic vehicle, a projectile, was so remote as to be laughable. This proposal was so radical the engineers knew they would be able to block it. It was no laughing matter to the seven pilots, however. They also wanted complete control of the re-entry procedure. They wanted to establish the capsule's angle of attack manually and fire the retro-rockets them- selves without any help from the automatic control system. This suggestion made the engineers wince. Slayton even wanted to redesign the hand controller that would activate the hydrogen peroxide thrusters to make the capsule pitch, roll, or yaw. He wanted the hand controller to operate the pitch and roll thrusters only; yaw would be controlled by pedals which the astronaut would operate with his feet. That was the conventional setup on aircraft: a two-axis stick plus pedals. That was the way *pilots* established attitude control.

Life magazine and the worshipful public and the worshipful politicians and all the others who had already exalted the seven astronauts did not care in the slightest whether they functioned like pilots or not. It was enough that they were willing to climb atop the rocket at all, in the name of the battle with the Soviets for the high ground, and be exploded into space or to the harp farm. It was not enough for the men themselves, however. All of them were veteran military pilots, and five of them had already reached the higher elevations of the invisible ziggurat when Project Mercury began, and they were determined to go into space as pilots and as nothing else.

Control—in the form of overrides at the very least—was the one thing that would neutralize the recurring taunt within the fraternity: *A monkey's gonna make the first flight.* In his speech before the brotherhood Slayton had brought that out into the open with his crack about the "college-trained chimpanzee." That had seemed like a Slayton sortie into sarcasm and hyperbole. He made no reference to the fact that such a college actually existed.

Bᴜᴛ ɪɴ ᴛʜᴇ ᴅᴇsᴇʀᴛs of New Mexico, about eighty miles north of El Paso and the Mexican border, at Holloman Air Force Base, which was part of the White Sands missile-range complex, NASA had set up a Project Mercury chimpanzee colony. There was nothing secret about it, but it attracted little notice. The chimpanzee program had been devised mainly to satisfy "the medical Cassandras." From the

moment a Joint Armed Forces-National Research Council Committee on Bioas-
tronautics had visited the new NASA facility at Langley in January 1959, there
had been doctors warning that the weightless state or high g-forces, or both, could
be devastating and that animal flights should be mandatory. So NASA had
twenty veterinarians training forty chimpanzees in a compound at the Aeromedical Research Laboratory at Holloman. Eventually one of the beasts would be
chosen for what amounted to a dress rehearsal of the first manned flight. The idea
would be not only to see if the chimpanzee could stand the strain but also to see if
he could use his brain and his hands normally throughout the ride.

Chimpanzees were chosen as much for their intelligence as their physiological
similarity to humans. They could be trained to do fairly complex manual tasks, on
cue, particularly if one got hold of them when they were young. Once they were
trained to do the tasks on the ground, it would be possible to give them the cues
to do the same tasks during a space flight and see if the weightless condition
impeded them. Early in the game the vets decided that rewards, mere positive
reinforcement, would not be sufficient for the job at hand. The only sure-fire
training technique was *operant conditioning*. The principle here was the avoidance
of pain. Or, to put it another way, if the ape didn't do the job right, he was
punished with electric shocks in the soles of his feet.

The Holloman veterinarians, like most veterinarians, were compassionate
men who were interested in relieving pain in animals and not in inflicting it upon
them. But this was war! The chimpanzee program was an essential part of the
battle for the high ground! It was no time for halfway measures! As congressmen
told you every day, national survival was at stake! The veterinarians' brief was to
get the job done with the utmost speed and efficacy. There were several ways of
training animals, but only *operant conditioning*, based on concepts developed by
B. F. Skinner, seemed anywhere near foolproof. In any case, the "psychomotor
stimulus plates" were attached to the beasts' feet and they were strapped into
chairs, and the process began . . . And when the apes did well, you gave them
hugs and nuzzles, to be sure, first taking the precaution of making certain they
weren't in a mood to bite your goddamned nose off.

Oh, the apes knew a thing or two! Their intelligence was only just below that
of man. They had memories; they could figure out the situation. At an early age
they had been seized in West Africa and separated from their mothers by this new
species, the humans, and removed from all familiar surroundings and put in cages
and shipped to this godforsaken alien landscape, the New Mexico desert, where
they remained in cages . . . when they weren't in the hands of a bunch of
human ballbreakers in white smocks who strapped them down and zapped them
and put them through insane exercises and routines. The beasts tried everything
they could think of to escape. They snapped, snarled, spit, bit, thrashed at the
straps, and made runs for it. Or they bided their time and used their heads. They
would go along with a training task, seeming to cooperate, until the white
smocker seemed to let his guard down—then they'd make a break for it. But the
resistance and the wiles were of no avail. All they got for their struggles was more
zaps and blue bolts. Some of the brightest apes were also the most intractable and
resourceful; they would take the electric shocks and then seem to give up and
submit to fate—and *then* try to tear the white smockers a new asshole or two
and make a run for it. With these implacable little bastards it was sometimes
necessary to give them a tap or two with a rubber hose, or whatever.

Then, at last, the sophisticated part of the training could begin. It took two main forms: the desensitizing or adapting out of the fears that a rocket flight would ordinarily hold for the animal (just confining an untrained chimpanzee in a Mercury capsule would have driven him berserk with fear); and placing the animal in a procedures trainer, a replica of the capsule he would be inside in flight, and teaching him to respond to lights and buzzers and throw the proper switches on cue—and having him do this day after day until it became a thoroughly familiar environment, as familiar, routine, and workaday as an office.

The vets took the chimpanzees by airplane to Wright-Patterson for rides on the centrifuge the Air Force had there. They would strap each ape into the gondola, close the hatch, and pipe in the sound of a Redstone rocket launch and start him spinning, gradually introducing him to higher g-forces. They took them for parabolic rides backseat in fighter planes to familiarize them with the feeling of weightlessness. They put them in the simulator for endless hours and endless days of on-cue manual-task training. Since the chimpanzee would not be wearing a pressure suit in flight, he was put inside a pressurized cubicle, which in turn would be placed in the Mercury capsule. The monkey's instrument panel was inside the inner cubicle. Therein, day by day, month by month, the monkey learned to operate certain switches in different sequences when cued by flashing lights. If he did the job incorrectly, he received an electric shock. If he did it correctly, he received banana-flavored pellets, plus some attaboys and nuzzles from the vets. Gradually the beasts were worn down. They were tractable now. The *operant conditioning* was taking place. A life of avoiding the blue bolts and gratefully accepting the attaboys and pellets had become the better part of valor. Rebellion had proved to be a dead end.

The apes had begun their training at the same time as the astronauts, i.e., in the late spring of 1959. By now, 1960, they had been through almost every phase of astronaut training, other than abort and re-entry emergency sequences and attitude control.

Some of the apes could operate their procedures trainer like a breeze, almost as rapidly as a man. The vets had every reason to be proud of what they had accomplished. On the outside the animals were as mild, tractable, smart, and lovable as the best little boy on the block, although inside . . . something was building up like Code Blue in the boiler room.

ABOUT EIGHT HUNDRED miles west of Holloman Air Force Base, in the same latitude of the great American desert, was Edwards. The X-15 program had begun to pick up some momentum. There were even journalists coming to Edwards—in the midst of this, the Era of the Astronaut—and talking about the X-15 as "America's first spaceship." There were two men on hand at the base writing books about the project; one of them was Richard Tregaskis, who had written the best seller *Guadalcanal Diary*. The X-15, *America's first spaceship* . . . could it be? A year ago it would have seemed impossible. But now the Mercury program was beginning to lag. NASA had talked of making the first manned flight in mid-1960; well, it was now mid-1960, and they didn't even have the capsule ready for unmanned testing.

NASA's prime pilot for the X-15 project was Joe Walker. He looked like a young towheaded version of Chuck Yeager, the country boy who loved to fly. He

talked like Yeager. Well, hell, who didn't around here? But with Walker it came
naturally. Just as Yeager was from the coal country of West Virginia, Walker was
from the coal country of Pennsylvania, and Walker liked to do that Yeager thing
where you mixed up a lot of up-hollow talk—"The mother liked to blowed up on
me"—with postwar engineerese about parameters, inputs, and extrapolations. As
a matter of fact, Yeager had let it be known that he thought Walker was the pick
of the litter at Edwards now.

Yes, Walker looked and sounded like a younger version of Yeager—but in fact
he was two years older. Yeager was still only thirty-seven, and Walker was thirty-
nine. Walker was seven months older than Scott Crossfield. So aside from everything else, Walker didn't have time to cool his heels. If the X-15 and X-20
programs at Edwards got stalled while all the money and attention went to Project Mercury, it would be bad news.

Edwards had grown until it was about twenty times the size it was during the
heyday of Yeager. Pancho Barnes's Happy Bottom Riding Club was long gone.
The Air Force had taken her property by eminent domain for the building of a
new runway. There had been a bitter fight in court, during which a base commander had accused Pancho of running a whorehouse, and Pancho had told the
court that she had it on good authority that the old peckerwood had instructed
his pilots to accidentally-on-purpose napalm her ranch. Pancho had gone into
retirement, with her fourth husband, her erstwhile ranch foreman, over in the
town of Boron, to the northeast of the base.

There were now about three thousand Air Force personnel at Edwards and
about seven thousand civilians, some with NASA, including Walker himself. Yet
the high desert was so vast and so open that it swallowed up all ten thousand of
them with no trouble at all, and the place didn't look terribly different except
during the afternoon traffic jam, when all the civil servants got off work and sped
toward the air conditioners that awaited them in their tract homes. Walker and
his wife and two children lived in Lancaster, a desert town about a half hour's
drive west of Edwards. Walker had built a house in a tract that some inspired
developer—inspiration was the choicest item in the real-estate boom of the period—had named White Fence Farms. You had to build a white fence around
your house in order to live there. That he did. As for the Farm part—here you
had yourself a problem, unless you farmed Joshua trees. The developer's idea, in
his sales pitch, was that you could build chicken coops at the rear end of your lot
and have a second income.

At that, Walker's place looked like a little bit of heaven compared to Bob
White's. But then, on the surface, Walker and White were different in every
respect. White, who was a major, was the Air Force's prime pilot for the X-15
project. He was the eternally correct and reserved Air Force blue-suiter. He didn't
drink. He exercised like a college athlete in training. He was religious. He was an
usher in the Roman Catholic chapel of the base and never, but never, missed
Mass. He was slender, black-haired, handsome, intelligent—even cultivated, if
the truth were known. And he was terribly serious. He was not a beer-call fighter
jock. Not many people picked out Bob White to just shoot the breeze with.
White and his family lived on the base itself at 116 Thirteenth Street in a
miserable grid of military housing plots known as the Wherry housing section. Or
it had been known as Wherry at the outset. By 1960 it was usually referred to as
Weary housing. Children grew up there thinking that Weary housing was the real

name. Parked out front of White's place was an unpainted Model A Ford. The Air Force, being the newest branch of the service, was strong on instant tradition. This old junker, the Ford, was bestowed, as an ironic sculpture of the Right Stuff, upon whomever was the number-one Air Force test pilot at Edwards. Scott Crossfield, the prime pilot for the manufacturer, North American, had completed the first phase of testing the X-15, checking out the power system and basic aerodynamics. White and Walker had been chosen to push the rocket plane to its outer limits, which were envisioned as speeds in excess of Mach 6, or about 4,000 miles per hour, and, more important, an altitude of 280,000 feet. Just where "space" began was a matter of definition that had never been fully resolved. But fifty miles up was generally accepted as the boundary line. There was no atmosphere, no air, left at that altitude; in fact, once a ship reached 100,000 feet, there was not enough air remaining to provide aerodynamics. The X-15's target of 280,000 feet was 53 miles up.

White and Walker had begun to fly the X-15 with the so-called Little Engine. This was, in fact, two X-1 engines built into a single fuselage. They provided 16,000 pounds of thrust. The X-15 was the most evil-looking beast ever put into the air. It was a 7.5-ton black chimney with little fins on it and an enormous blocky tail. The black paint had been created to withstand the heat generated by friction when the ship went up above 100,000 feet and re-entered the denser atmosphere below. Everyone was waiting for the delivery of the Big Engine, the XLR-99. This was a rocket with 57,000 pounds of thrust, or four times the base weight of the ship. Once the XLR-99 was installed . . . well, Walker just might become the first man to cross the boundary into space. The engine's 57,000 pounds of thrust were only 21,000 pounds less than that of the Redstone rocket, which—eventually—was supposed to take the astronauts on their first flights. As a matter of fact, it was the development of the Redstone as an intercontinental ballistic missile that had first given NASA engineers like Walt Williams the idea for the X-15, back in the early 1950's.

How, then, could there be so much excitement over Project Mercury and so little over the X-15? Here was the thing that got to the boys after a while, no matter how nonchalant they tried to appear: the Mercury astronauts were national heroes without ever having left the ground—all because they had volunteered to ride on top of rockets. Well . . . Walker and White and Crossfield, like Yeager before them, had *already* ridden rockets, from the X-1 to the X-15. And they had ridden them as *pilots*. Your own brain was the guidance system for the X-15, and your own hand maneuvered the ship. In the Mercury-Redstone system, a bank of computers was the pilot, and the astronaut was a passenger. Why couldn't everyone comprehend such a simple fact? Was it because the astronauts were seen as America's front runners in the race with the Russians? Well, if so, that was pretty ironic. By now, mid-1960, the astronauts were supposed to have gone up in their first ballistic flights. That was the whole point of choosing the Mercury system. It was dirty—but it was quick; supposedly. But the Mercury capsule wasn't even ready yet. There had been one delay after another. It was beginning to look unlikely that there would be a manned launch before 1961. The X-15 project was now actually *ahead* of Project Mercury in the attempt to reach space.

On May 7 Walker had cut loose the X-15 on its first real speed run with the Little Engine and reached Mach 3.19 or 2,111 miles an hour, just a shade faster than Mel Apt's world record of 2,094 miles an hour in the X-2. On May 19 Bob

White took the X-15 on its first bid for maximum altitude with the Little Engine and reached 109,000 feet, which was 17,000 feet under Iven Kincheloe's record in the X-2. And that was another point that everybody should have known about . . . and didn't. Kinch and Mel were now dead. Mel Apt died just a few minutes after he set his world speed record, the victim of a demon that was waiting especially for rocket ships reaching speeds of Mach 2 or more in the thin air up around 70,000 feet: instability in the yaw or roll axis . . . followed by an uncontrollable tumble. Sometimes it took the form of "inertia coupling," which usually occurred when a pilot tried to bank a rocket ship and it snapped into a full roll and then began pitching and yawing—*and* rolling violently. This would throw it end over end. Some pilots felt that the formal term "inertia coupling" added damned little to your understanding of the phenomenon. The ship simply "uncorked" (as Crossfield liked to put it) and lost all semblance of aerodynamics and fell out of the sky like a bottle or a length of pipe. There was no way to maneuver out of a hypersonic tumble. The pilot took a furious beating from the g-forces and from being thrown about the cockpit. The more he experimented with the controls, the worse fix he was in. Yeager had been the first rocket pilot to go through this particular hole in the hypersonic envelope, and it was during the flight in the X-1A in which he set a speed record of Mach 2.42. He was battered unconscious and fell seven miles before hitting the denser atmosphere at 25,000 feet and coming to and managing to put the ship into a spin. That was good; a mere spin he knew how to get out of, and he survived. Kinch went into a hypersonic tumble, during his record flight, and came out of it at low altitude, as Yeager had done. That was just twenty days before Mel Apt augered in. Mel went into the wild tumble and tried to eject, but wasn't able to complete the sequence in the X-2. Yeager had always figured it was useless to try to punch out of a rocket plane. Crossfield called it "committing suicide to keep from getting killed." Inertia coupling nearly killed Kit Murray in 1954, when he set an altitude record of 94,000 feet in the X-1A, and it had hit Joe Walker twice, once in the XF-102 and again in the X-3.

When he talked about it, Joe Walker would say he got out of it each time through "the J.C. maneuver." He'd say: "In the J.C. maneuver you take your hands off the controls and put the mother in the lap of a su-per-na-tu-ral power." And, in fact, that was the only choice you had.

The way Walker talked about it, with his big mountainboy grin on, it was . . . just like talking about sports . . . But every prospective X-15 pilot had seen the on-board film from Mel Apt's flight, and it was not a droll experience to watch that film. The camera had been mounted just behind Apt in the cockpit. It was a stop-frame camera that took one picture per second. In one frame Apt and his white helmet would be upright in the cockpit. In the next you would see his head, body, and helmet keeled over, crashing into the wall of the cockpit. In the first you saw a mountain ridge framed in the cockpit window, as if he were headed down in a dive, and in the next you saw empty sky: he was going end over end like an extra-point kick. The film seemed to go on forever. It was eerie looking at it, because you knew that at the end that little figure bouncing around in the white helmet would be dead.

Life magazine was writing about how Deke Slayton had once been in an inverted spin in an F-105. No picnic, to be sure, and yet the rocket pilots looked at inverted spins as their friends on the way out of hypersonic instability. People were impressed because the seven Mercury astronauts were willing to risk having Redstone rockets blow up under them. Christ! Rockets had already blown up under good men! Skip Ziegler's X-2 exploded while still attached to the mother ship, a B-29, killing Skip and a B-29 crewman. The same thing had very nearly happened to Pete Everest in the X-1D—and to Walker himself in the X-1A. Walker was strapped into the X-1A, under the bomb bay of a B-29, at 35,000 feet, seventy seconds from launch, when a fuel tank exploded in the rear of the rocket plane. Walker got out, climbed back up into the B-29, passed out from lack of oxygen, was revived by a "walk-around" oxygen bottle, went back down into the burning X-1A, and tried to jettison the rest of the fuel so as to prevent both ships, the X-1A and the B-29, from burning up. The rocket plane was finally dropped, like a bomb, over the desert. Walker received the Distinguished Service Medal for his trip back into the burning ship.

That was back in August of 1955, and the newspapers talked about it for a little while, but now no one remembered, or comprehended, that all of these things had been adventures in *manned rocket flight*. With the Big Engine already on the way, the XLR-99—well, it was likely that if NASA would just pour the money and personnel and emphasis into the X-15 project and the X-20 project, the United States could have orbiting spacecraft in reasonably short order. *Ships*, vehicles with a pilot who took them aloft and brought them back through the atmosphere with his own hand and then landed them . . . on the dome of the world, at Edwards. It wasn't merely that the Mercury plan of a man in a pod splashing down in the middle of the ocean under a parachute was "dirty," primitive, and an embarrassing way for a pilot to come down, as the Edwards pilots saw it. It was also needlessly dangerous. A slight error in trajectory or timing, and he might hit the water scores or hundreds of miles off target; and any man who had ever flown a search plane knew how hopeless it could be to spot a small object in the open sea, particularly in bad weather.

It could even be argued that the X-15 pilots were a year or so ahead of the astronauts when it came to training for space flight. The Mercury training program had borrowed a lot of X-15 training—without flying. Each X-15 flight was so expensive—about $100,000 if you figured in the time and wages of all the support personnel—it was impractical to have a pilot use the X-15 itself for his basic training. Using the new piece of engineering technology, the computer, NASA built the first full-scale flight simulator. The realism of it was uncanny. Of course, they couldn't simulate the g-forces of rocket flight—so they had dreamed up the idea of using the Navy's human centrifuge at Johnsville.

Up above the centrifuge arm there was a balcony, and this balcony was known as the Throne Room, because arrayed upon it was a lineup of green plastic seats with high backs. Each had been custom-made, molded to the contours of the torsos and legs of a rocket pilot. Each had his name on it: "A. Crossfield" (Scott Crossfield's first name was Albert), "J. Walker," "R. White," "R. Rushworth," "F. Petersen," "N. Armstrong," and so forth. They looked like royal mummies when they were lined up like that, and they were already there in the Throne Room when the shells of "J. Glenn," "A. Shepard," "W. Schirra," and the four others joined the tableau. The astronauts took centrifuge training that had first been worked out for Walker and the X-15 pilots. The astronauts' procedures trainer was a modified version of the X-15 simulator. NASA even rigged up an inertia-coupling trainer for the astronauts, a device called the Wild Mastiff that spun you in all three axes, pitch, roll, and yaw, at once; but the ride was so horrendous it wasn't used much. Joe Walker & Co. had taken that ride in real time . . . at altitude . . . And where did the astronauts go for their parabolic rides in the F-100Fs, to experience weightlessness? To Edwards. Chuck Yeager himself had flown the first weightless parabolas for the Air Force, and then Crossfield had flown them for NASA. Edwards pilots took the astronauts up in the back seat.

For the most part, the men involved in the X-15 program were realistic about the situation. Technically there was no reason why the X-15 should not lead to the X-15B or the X-20 or some other aerodynamic spaceship. Politically, however, the chances were not good and hadn't been good since October 1957, when Sputnik I went up. The politics of the space race demanded a small manned vehicle that could be launched as soon as possible with existing rocket power. And as the Edwards brethren knew, there was no use trying to wish the politics of the situation away.

But now, in mid-1960, the political reality itself had begun to change. The first signs had come in May. This was the same month it so happened, in which Walker and White had begun to unlimber the X-15 and the Little Engine. But the change was being caused by events quite outside of their control.

THE STARTING POINT was the so-called U-2 incident. A Soviet surface-to-air missile—no one even knew the Soviets had created such a weapon—shot down an American CIA "spy plane," the U-2, flown by a former Air Force pilot named Francis Gary Powers. Khrushchev used the incident to humiliate President Eisenhower at a summit conference in Paris. This was an election year, of course, and both of the main Democratic contenders, Lyndon Johnson and John F. Kennedy, began citing the Soviets' superiority in rockets as a means of attacking the Eisenhower Administration. Meanwhile, the Soviets and their mighty Integral began pouring it on in earnest. They sent up a series of huge, five-ton Korabl ("Cosmic") Sputniks, carrying dummy cosmonauts or dogs or both; they obviously had a system powerful enough and sophisticated enough to put a man into orbit. NASA was not only unable to keep up with its original schedule of a manned ballistic flight in 1960, it couldn't even deliver a finished capsule—and its test rocket launches, all public events, went from bad to worse.

On July 29, NASA brought the seven astronauts and hundreds of VIPs to Cape Canaveral for a highly publicized first test of the Mercury-Atlas vehicle, a Mercury capsule atop an Atlas rocket. The Atlas, with its 367,000 pounds of thrust, would be used for manned orbital flights; the first Mercury flights, which would be suborbital, would use the smaller Redstone. July 29 was a dark rainy day, which only made the lift-off of the mighty rocket all the more spectacular. The earth rumbled underfoot, and the rocket rose slowly on three columns of flame. It was a terrific show. After sixty seconds it seemed to be directly overhead and gradually nosing over on its long arc toward the horizon, and the astronauts and everybody else had their necks up and their heads bent back, watching the Ahura-Mazda surge, when—*kabcom!*—it blew up. Just like that, right over their heads. For a moment it seemed as if it was going to come down in a few thousand enormous flaming pieces, right on everybody's bean. There was no danger, in fact; the rocket's momentum carried the debris away from the launch site. It was damned sobering, however, with your gullet stuck up in the air like a bird's . . . And it was very bad news for Project Mercury.

It was not the ultimate fiasco, however. The ultimate fiasco came later in the year when NASA put on a test at Cape Canaveral designed to show all the politicians that the Mercury capsule-and-rocket system was now almost ready for manned flight. They flew five hundred VIPs, including many congressmen and prominent Democrats, down to the Cape for the big event. The rocket, the Redstone, was not powerful enough to place the capsule into orbit, but it was supposed to take it up more than one hundred miles, fifty miles above the earth's atmosphere, and then it would reenter the atmosphere and splash down in the Atlantic by parachute about three hundred miles from the Cape, near Bermuda. Everything except an astronaut was on the launch pad. The dignitaries were all seated in grandstands, and the countdown was intoned over the public-address system: "Nine . . . eight . . . seven . . . six . . ." and so forth, and then: "We have ignition!" . . . and the mighty belch of flames bursts out of the rocket in a tremendous show of power . . . The mighty white shaft rumbles and seems to bestir itself—and then seems to change its mind, its computerized central nervous system, about the whole thing, because the flames suddenly cut off, and the rocket settles back down on the pad, and there's a little *pop*. A cap on the tip of the rocket comes off. It goes shooting up in the air, a tiny little thing with a needle nose. In fact, it's the capsule's escape tower. As the great crowd watches, stone silent and befuddled, it goes up to about 4,000 feet and descends under a parachute. It looks like a little party favor. It lands about four hundred yards away from the rocket on the torpid banks of the Banana River. Five hundred VIPs had come all the way to Florida, to this goddamned Low Rent sandspit, where bugs you couldn't even see invaded your motel room and bit your ankles until they ran red onto the acrylic shag carpet—all the way to this rock-beach boondock they had come, to see the fires of Armageddon and hear the earth shake with the thunder—and instead they get this . . . this *pop* . . . and a cork pops out of a bottle of Spumante. It was the original Project Vanguard fiasco all over again, except that it was worse in a way. At least with Vanguard, back in December of 1957, the folks got lots of flames and explosion. It at least looked halfway like a catastrophe. Besides that, it was very early in the game, in the contest for the heavens. But this—it was ridiculous! It was pathetic!

Kennedy had won the election, and during the campaign he had made such a point of attacking NASA's ineptness that it was a foregone conclusion that NASA's chief, T. Keith Glennan, who was a Republican in any case, would be replaced. The question now was how many other heads would roll. What about Bob Gilruth? After all, he was in charge of Project Mercury, which was going nowhere. Or von Braun, the alleged German rocket genius? Much sarcasm was creeping into the debate, and even von Braun was being attacked. For that matter, what about the seven brave lads . . .

As this sort of talk began to circulate, people at Edwards began to beam up the radar . . . For months the word within NASA had been that the X-15 project would be the last hurrah for "the flyboys." Now that was all changing. No one was saying it publicly yet, but the unthinkable was now possible: for the first time, Project Mercury itself was regarded as expendable. Kennedy's advisor in scientific areas was Jerome Wiesner of M.I.T. He had drawn up a report for Kennedy that said the following, in effect:

Project Mercury had been sold to the Eisenhower Administration during the original Sputnik panic as the "quick and dirty" solution to getting a man into space ahead of the Russians. It had merely proved to be dirty, or hopeless, as in the Popped Cork business, which demonstrated that NASA did not even have the primitive Mercury-Redstone system ready. Even if the system worked, the Redstone could put a man into only a suborbital trajectory, with just fifteen minutes in space. The mighty Soviet Integral had already launched a series of huge Korabls and was probably on the verge of putting a man not only into space but into earth orbit. But in one area, Wiesner was telling Kennedy, the United States was ahead of the Soviets, and this was in unmanned scientific satellites. Why not concentrate on that program for the time being and play down—in effect, forfeit—the losing race to put a man into space? Why not abandon all these frantic attempts to convert the underpowered Redstone and Atlas missiles into space rockets and instead develop a careful, solid, long-range program using bigger rockets, such as the Titan, which might be ready in eighteen months?

And there you had it! As Joe Walker and everyone at Edwards knew, the "solid, long-range program" using the Titan was the X-20 or Dyna-Soar program, which would begin at Edwards as soon as the X-15 project was completed. The Air Force, which was in charge of the X-20 project, had never abandoned its hopes of running the entire manned space program. All along it had seemed unjust that NASA had been able to appropriate all the research and planning that had gone into Flickinger's Man-in-Space-Soonest program and convert it into Project Mercury. Perhaps with the change in administrations the situation could be corrected.

Joe Walker was feeling good. In August he had pushed the X-15 just about as fast as the Little Engine could take it, to a new world speed record of Mach 3.31, or 2,196 miles per hour. After he landed it on Rogers Lake, he cut loose with a cowboy yell that startled everyone on the radio circuit: "Yippeeeee!" That was Joe Walker. A week later Bob White went up in the X-15 and set a new altitude record of 136,500 feet, or slightly more than twenty-five miles. It had been a perfect flight. It was as much as you could expect from the Little Engine. The conditions had been almost precisely the conditions of space flight. He took the ship up in a ballistic arc, the same sort of arc the Mercury-Redstone vehicle was supposed to go on . . . someday . . . He experienced five g's during the rocket thrust on the way up. An astronaut in Mercury was supposed to experience six. He was weightless for two minutes as he came up over the top of the arc. An astronaut was supposed to be weightless for five minutes. At 136,500 feet the air was so thin, White had no aerodynamic control at all. It was absolutely silent up there. He could see for hundreds of miles, from Los Angeles to San Francisco.

It was much like the Mercury flights were supposed to be—except that Bob White was *a pilot* from beginning to end! He was in control! He took the ship up and he brought it back down through the heavy atmosphere and he landed it at Edwards! He didn't splash down in the water like a monkey in a bucket! Bob White's picture wound up on the cover of *Life*. There was Justice, there was Logic, in the universe, after all. Bob White on the cover of *Life*! For a solid year *Life* had been the fraternity bulletin for the Mercury astronauts. But now even Henry Luce and that bunch had woken up to the truth. Perhaps they had been betting on the wrong horses! Right? Walker and White and Crossfield could afford a little jealousy now . . . toward one another for a change. People from the TV show *This Is Your Life* had turned up at Edwards and were talking to everybody they could find who knew Joe Walker. This was one of the most popular shows on television, and it was run like a surprise party; the subject, in this case Walker, didn't learn about it until the moment of the show itself, after a biography of him had been put together on film. Scott Crossfield had a book contract, to write his autobiography, and Time-Life was talking to Bob White about a contract like the astronauts'.

Bob White was all right. You could read the cover story they had already written about him in *Life*, and you could see that White had not unbent so much as one inch for the occasion. You could see them straining to manufacture one of those "personality profiles" about White, and all he would give them was the Blue Suit and a straight arrow. That was Bob White.

A True Brother!

9

THE VOTE

EVEN THE SCENERY was depressing. There was nothing to see but the snow blowing over the road and the stunted countryside rolling by in slow motion. Between Langley and Arlington even the woods looked stunted. There had been a blizzard the day before, but the landscape was all so raggedy it didn't even look good in the snow. Over the car radio he could hear John F. Kennedy delivering his inaugural address. The reception was poor, and the broadcast kept fading in and out through the static. The announcer, who spoke in hushed tones as if he were describing a tennis match, had said that it was seventeen degrees in Washington and a wind was blowing on Capitol Hill and Kennedy was bareheaded and wore no overcoat. Kennedy had his voice set at a strangely high pitch. He seemed to be screaming to keep warm. He was screaming a great many sonorous rhetorical figures. The words merely drifted by John Glenn, as he drove, like the snow and the stunted scrub pines outside.

That was ironic, because at first Loudon Wainwright thought that Glenn was totally absorbed in the new President's inaugural address. He kept fiddling with the dial, battling the static, trying to make the broadcast come in better. When Wainwright made the occasional comment, Glenn had no response at all. Wainwright was one of the *Life* writers assigned to the personal stories of the astronauts, and he had come to know Glenn fairly well. As this very moment Glenn was giving him a lift to National Airport before heading home. If John had been determined to digest every single word and nuance of Kennedy's address, it would not have been terribly surprising. John was one of those rare celebrities who came pretty much as advertised. He really was serious about God, country, home, and hearth. He probably even had it in him to take a Presidential inaugural address seriously. But then Wainwright noticed that John not only wasn't reacting to what he said, he wasn't reacting to what Kennedy said, either. He was a thousand miles away, as the saying goes, and not particularly happy to be there.

The curious thing, in light of what happened yesterday, was that for about three months the intense competitive feeling among the seven of them had died down. The entire Mercury project, the astronauts included, had been in serious—no, *horrendous*—trouble. After the MA-1 fiasco and the Popped Cork fiasco, it had no longer been a question of which one of them was going to get the first flight, but whether any of them would go into space at all, or even continue to bear the title *astronaut.*

Naturally it would have been crushing to Bob Gilruth, Hugh Dryden, Walt Williams, Christopher Kraft, and all of the NASA brass to have Mercury canceled for delays or ineptness or whatever. But not so crushing as it would have been to the Mercury astronauts! Oh, no! To be pronounced the seven bravest lads in America, the fearless pioneers of space, to be on the cover of *Life*, to have factory workers in San Diego agonize over your hide and every sweet little Konakai cookie on both shores lust over it . . . and then to be told, "Thanks a lot, but we've called the whole thing off" . . . They would become factory seconds! They would be back in uniform, in the Air Force, the Navy, and the Marines, saluting and flapping in the breeze as the seven most laughable duds in the service!

One had only to imagine it . . . and it was easy to imagine by late 1960. All of them, astronauts, administrators, engineers, technicians, were suddenly in such trouble that a wagon-train phase began. Everyone, from top to bottom, began pulling together like pioneers besieged in the pass. It was now of supreme importance to push the Mercury-Redstone program forward before the new President and his science advisor, Wiesner, had time to go to work on NASA. The frantic hope was to complete some tests that would bring the program so close to the first manned flight that Kennedy could hardly afford to dismantle Project Mercury without letting them have at least one try. So everyone rode hell-for-leather for the top of the next hill, and never mind the ordinary precautions. The number of unmanned tests was cut down drastically. Tests were scheduled one on top of the other, so that the first manned flight might be scheduled within three months. They were ready to try things they would never have thought of doing before. Rather than prepare a new rocket for the next test, they used the one that had been left on the pad after the Popped Cork fiasco. After all, it hadn't blown up; it had merely refused to leave the ground.

That was the spirit of the hour—ride! *más allá!* over the next hill! don't look back!—when Bob Gilruth called in Glenn and the other six for a meeting at the office at Langley just before Christmas. Gilruth had always been a sympathetic soul around the seven of them; and now that the cowboy rush was on, his concern for them was written all over his face. The message seemed to be: "It's terrible, but I may have to send one of you boys up without all the precautions that I would like to take." When they assembled in his office, he told them he wanted them to take a little "peer vote," along the following lines: "If you can't make the first flight yourself, which man do you think should make it?" Peer votes were not unknown in the military. They had been used among seniors at West Point and Annapolis for some time. For that matter, during the selection process for astronaut, the groups of finalists at Lovelace and Wright-Patterson took peer votes. But peer votes had never amounted to anything more than what they were *prima facie:* an indication of how men at the same level regarded one another, whether for reasons of professionalism or friendship or jealousy or whatever. Pilots regarded peer votes as a waste of time, because a man either had the right stuff in the air or he didn't, and a military career, particularly among those with "the uncritical willingness to face danger," was not a personality contest. But there was something about Bob Gilruth's deep concern . . . They were to think the whole thing over and put their choices down on paper and drop them off at Gilruth's office. The look on Bob Gilruth's face set off a neural alarm.

Even so, the esprit throughout NASA was tremendous over that Christmas holiday. Everyone was working like a zealot. Christmas itself was a mere syncopation in the mad cowboy rush. Bureaucratic lines no longer meant anything. Anyone in Project Mercury could immediately get in to see anybody else about any problem that came up. At Langley, if some GS-14 wanted to get hold of Gilruth face to face, all he had to do was wait around in the cafeteria at lunchtime and walk up to him while he waited in line, edging his tray along the stainless-steel tubing. There weren't enough hours in the day to do all the things that had to be done.

On January 19, the day before Kennedy's inauguration, Gilruth again convened the seven of them in the astronaut office. He said that what he was about to tell them must be kept in strictest confidence. As they all knew, he said, the original plan had been to select the pilot for the first flight on the very eve of the flight itself. But he had thought better of that, because it now seemed clear that the prime pilot should have maximum access to the procedures trainer and other training facilities during the final weeks before the flight. So a decision had been made as to who was to be the prime pilot and as to which two men would be the backup pilots for the first flight. In due course, the press would be given the names of all three men, but the fact that the prime pilot had already been chosen would not be revealed. The press and the public would be told only that it would be one of these three men. All three men would go through the same training, and it would seem that the original plan was being adhered to, and the prime pilot would be spared the public pressure that would otherwise bear down on him.

This had been a very difficult decision, he said, because all seven of them had worked with such dedication, and he knew that any of them would make a capable pilot for the first flight. But it had been necessary to come to a decision. And the decision was that the prime pilot would be . . . Alan Shepard. The backup pilots would be John Glenn and Gus Grissom.

The words hit Glenn like a ray. The cause, effect, and outrageous results thereof came to him in a flash, and he was stunned. Al was staring at the floor. Then Al looked up at him and the rest of them with his eyes gleaming, resisting the temptation to break into a grin of triumph. Yet Al had triumphed! It was unbelievable, and yet it was really happening. Glenn knew what he had to do and he made himself do it. He made himself smile the earnest-looking smile of the runner-up and congratulate Al and shake his hand. Now the other five were doing the same thing, coming up to Al and smiling earnest smiles and shaking his hand. It was a shocking thing, and yet it had happened—Glenn was absolutely sure of it. To get around the agony of having to *designate* someone to sit up on top of the first rocket—*a peer vote!* After he, Glenn, had spent twenty-one months doing everything humanly possible to impress Gilruth and the rest of the brass, it had been turned into a popularity contest among the boys.

A peer vote!—it was unbelievable! Every move Glenn had made undoubtedly worked against him like a captured weapon in the peer vote. In the peer vote he was the prig who had risen at the séance like John Calvin himself and told them all to keep their pants zipped and their wicks dry. He was the Eddie Attaboy who had gotten up every morning at dawn and done all that ostentatious running and tried to make the rest of them look bad. He was the Harry Hairshirt who lived like an Early Christian martyr in the BOQ. He was the Willie Workadaddy who drove around in a broken-down Peugeot, like a lonely beacon of restraint and self-sacrifice in a squall of car crazies.

But Smilin' Al Shepard—Smilin' Al was the fighter jock's fighter jock, if all you were doing was taking a peer vote. He was His Lordship of Langley and the King of the Cape. He gave off the *aura* of the hot pilot. Since they had done practically no flying for twenty-one months, there had been no way for Glenn or anyone else to impress the others in the air—and so it came down to a question of which one other than he, Glenn, the Offending Saint, *looked* the most like a hot pilot. It was not only a popularity contest, it was a *cosmetic* popularity contest. How else was he to regard it? It was as if the past twenty-one months of training had never happened.

And so now Glenn was driving back home, through the stunted Virginia countryside and the raggedy snowflakes, to tell Annie the secret bad news. And the new President was screaming over the car radio: "Together let us explore the stars . . ." Shepard would be first! It was incredible. Shepard would be . . . *the first man to go into space!* He would be famous throughout eternity! And here was something even more unbelievable: he, John Glenn, for the first time in his career, would be one of those who were *left behind.*

THE ASTRONAUT HEADQUARTERS on the base at the Cape were in the building known as Hangar S. The hangar had been rebuilt inside to house the procedures trainer, a pressure chamber, and most of the other facilities an astronaut would need in the final preparations for a flight. There was a suite of rooms for living quarters, a dining room, a medical examination room, a ready room in which the astronaut would put on his pressure suit, a special doorway where the astronaut would get into a van to be driven out to the launch pad, and so forth. The boys seldom stayed there overnight, however, much preferring the motels in Cocoa Beach—and of course they had yet to use Hangar S for an actual flight. In fact, the first creatures to use Hangar S fully, from procedures trainer to rocket launch, were the chimpanzees. The chimpanzees were already at Hangar S on the morning before the inauguration, when Gilruth told the seven men that Alan Shepard had won the competition for the first flight. The chimpanzees had been there, ready for the first flight for almost three weeks. The veterinarians at Holloman Air Force Base had cut the original field of forty chimpanzees down to eighteen and, finally, to six, two males and four females, and had flown them to the Cape and installed them out back of Hangar S in a fenced-in compound. In the middle were two long, narrow trailer units, each made up of two eight-foot-wide trailers hooked up end to end. Around them was an assortment of other trailers and vans, including a special transfer van for carrying a chimpanzee from Hangar S to the rocket launch pad. The press was not invited into the little trailer park, nor would the good Gent have been interested. The chimpanzee test seemed to be merely one more tedious preliminary to the main event. Not even people at the base had much of an idea what was going on out back of Hangar S. The apes spent most of the day inside the two double-trailer units. The trailers were home and office, cage and *operant conditioning* cubicle, for the beasts. Inside each unit were three cages, two procedures trainers, and a mockup of the Mercury capsule. The veterinarians in their white smocks and the attendants in their white T-shirts and white ducks had a trailer unit of their own; they were on hand, in shifts, twenty-four hours a day. Within those long skinny trailers the biggest countdown in the brief history of Project Mercury was underway. Every day for twenty-nine days, at the heart of the American space facility, out back of a great moldering hangar, on a stone boondock scrub-pine spit on the point of Cape Canaveral, a tribe of six scrawny apes and twenty humans in white were up in the early morning, on the move, restless, earnest, driven, scratching, flapping, ricocheting through the trailers' innards, yammering at fate and each other. The humans were giving the apes physical examinations and wiring them from top to bottom, sticking eight-inch thermometers up their rectums, imbedding sensors in their thoracic cages, clamping the psychomotor stimulus plates on the soles of their feet, threading them into their restraint harnesses, strapping them into their procedures-trainer cubicles, closing the hatches, pressurizing the cubicles with pure oxygen, inserting the cubicles in the mock Mercury capsules, and then flashing the lights. The apes had to throw their switches on cue or get the dread dose of volts in the soles of the feet. How their scrawny fingers did fly! All six apes were stringy-looking, like those overtrained fleaweight college wrestlers who have run so many laps and taken so many B-12s and diuretics at the training table that they appear to be little dried-up lengths of gristle, nodes, and nerve ganglia. But out back of Hangar S the little bastards could play their Mercury consoles like a dream.

The white-smock humans zapped the apes through their workouts right up to the last. On January 30, on the eve of the flight, they made the final selection. Originally the first astronaut was to have been chosen at this same stage. They chose a male chimpanzee as the prime flier and a female as the backup. The Air Force had bought the male from a supplier in the Cameroons, West Africa, eighteen months ago, when he was about two years old. All this time the animals had been known by numbers. He was test subject Number 61. On the day of the flight, however, his name was announced to the press as Ham. Ham was an acronym for Holloman Aerospace Medical Center.

Before dawn on January 31 they woke Number 61 up and led him out of his cage and fed him and gave him a medical examination and attached his biosensors—and put the zap plates on his feet—and put him in his cubicle and closed the hatch and depressurized it. Another goddamned day with these earnest hard-zapping ballbreaking white-smock humans. The vets put the cubicle in the transfer van, and the chimpanzee was taken to the launch pad, out by the sea. The sun was up now, and a white rocket with a Mercury capsule and an escape tower on top of it stood gleaming, and they took Number 61 in his cubicle up an elevator on a gantry beside the rocket and then put the cubicle in the capsule. There were more than a hundred NASA engineers and technicians nearby, working on the flight, monitoring consoles, and an entire team of veterinarians was monitoring the dials that read the ape's heartbeat, respiration, and temperature. Hundreds more NASA and Navy personnel were strung out across the Atlantic, toward Bermuda, in a communications and recovery network. This was the most crucial test in the entire history of the space program and they were giving it everything they had.

It was four hours before they were able to fire the rocket. The biggest problem was an inverter, a device that was supposed to prevent rogue surges of power in the Mercury capsule's control system. The inverter kept overheating. All the while, during the "hold," as they called the delay, Chris Kraft, director for the first ape flight, just as he would be for the first human flight, kept asking how the ape was doing, apparently on the presumption that the long confinement would make the beast anxious. The doctors checked their dials. The ape didn't seem to have a nerve in his body. He was lying up there in his cubicle as if he lived there. And why not? For the ape every hour of the delay was like a holiday. No lights! No zaps! Peace . . . bliss! They gave him two fifteen-minute workouts with the lights, just to keep him alert. Otherwise it was terrific. "Hold" for an eternity! Don't let anything stop you!

When they fired the rocket, shortly before noon, it climbed at a slightly higher angle than it was supposed to, driving Number 61 back into his couch with a force of seventeen g's, i.e., seventeen times his own weight, five g's more than anticipated. His heart rate shot up as he strained against the force, but he didn't panic for a moment. He had been through this same sensation many times on the centrifuge. As long as he just took it and didn't struggle, they wouldn't zap all those goddamned blue bolts into the soles of his feet. There were a lot worse things in this world than g-forces . . . He was weightless now, hurtling toward Bermuda, and they flashed the lights in his cubicle, and the ape's pulse returned to normal, to no more than what it was on the ground. The usual shit was flowing. The main thing was to keep ahead of those blue bolts in the feet! . . . He started pushing the buttons and throwing the switches like the greatest electric Wurlitzer organist who ever lived, never missing a signal . . . Then the Mercury retro-rockets were fired, automatically, and the capsule came down through the atmosphere at the same angle at which it had gone up. Another 14.6 g's hit Number 61 on the way down, making him feel as if his eyeballs were coming out of his head. He had been through so-called eyeballs-out g's, too, many times, on the centrifuge. It could get a lot worse. There were worse things than feeling as if his eyeballs were coming out . . . The goddamned zap plates on his feet, for a start . . . So far as mere space flight was concerned, Number 61 was fearless. The beast had been operantly conditioned, aerospatially desensitized.

The high angle of the launch also caused the capsule to overshoot the planned splashdown area by 132 miles. So it took two hours for a Navy helicopter crew to find the capsule out in the Atlantic and bring it aboard a recovery ship. The capsule and the ape were riding up and down in seven-foot swells. Water had begun to seep in where the landing bag had torn loose in the heavy seas. The capsule was wheezing and gurgling with water and pitching up and down like a ball in the waves. It wouldn't have stayed afloat too much longer. Eight hundred pounds of water had seeped in. For the ordinary prudent human being it would have been two hours of freaking terror. They brought the capsule to a recovery ship, the Donner, and opened it and brought out the ape's cubicle and opened the hatch. The ape was lying there with his arms crossed. They offered him an apple and he took it and ate it with considerable deliberation, as if gloriously bored. Those two hours of being slung up and down in the open sea in seven-foot gulps inside a closed coffin-like cubicle had been . . . perhaps the best time ever in this miserable land of the white smocks! No voices! No zaps! No bolts, no lengths of hose, no more breaking of his bloody balls . . .

There was great elation among the astronauts and almost everyone involved in Project Mercury. There seemed to be no way that Kennedy and Wiesner could intervene and keep them from trying at least one manned flight. The pall of the Day the Cork Popped had been removed.

Late the next day they flew Number 61 back to the Cape and Hangar S, where a great mob of reporters and photographers were now waiting out in the compound by the Mercury capsule that had been used for the training. The vets led the ape out of a van. As the mob closed in and the flashbulbs began exploding, the animal—brave little Ham, as he was now known—became furious. He bared his teeth. He began snapping at the bastards. It was all the vets could do to restrain him. This was immediately—on the spot!—interpreted by the press, the seemly Gent, as an understandable response to the grueling experience he had just been through. The vets took the ape back inside the van until he calmed down. Then they led him out again, trying to get him near a mockup of a Mercury capsule, where the television networks had set up cameras and tremendous lights. The reporters and photographers surged forward again, yammering, yelling, exploding more camera lights, shoving, groaning, cursing—the usual ya-hoo sprawl, in short—and the animal came unglued again, ready to twist the noodle off anybody he could get his hands on. This was interpreted by the Gent as a manifestation of Ham's natural fear upon laying eyes once again on the capsule, which looked precisely like the one that had propelled him into space and subjected him to such severe physical stresses.

The stresses the ape was reacting to were probably of quite another sort. Here he was, back in the compound where they had zapped him through his drills for a solid month. Just two years ago he had been captured in the jungles of Africa, separated from his mother, shipped in a cage to a goddamned desert in New Mexico, kept prisoner, prodded and shocked by a bunch of humans in white smocks, and here he was, back in a compound where they had been zapping him through their fucking drills for a solid month, and suddenly there was a whole new mob of humans on hand! Even worse than the white smocks! Louder! Crazier! Totally out of their gourds! Yammering, roaring, brawling, exploding lights beside their bug-eyed skulls! Suppose they threw him to these assholes! *Fuck this*—

At some point in the madhouse scene out back of Hangar S, a photograph was taken in which Ham was either grinning or had on a grimace that looked like a grin in the picture. Naturally, this was the picture that went out over the wire services and was printed in newspapers throughout America. Such was the response of the happy chimpanzee to being the first ape in outer space . . . A fat happy grin . . . Such was the perfection with which the Proper Gent observed the proprieties.

W ELL, THERE WERE SOME BIG GRINS, all right, up in the high desert, at Edwards, among the brethren. Here were some men who had something to smile about. Now the whole business of Project Mercury was no doubt clear to everyone. No one, not even in the general public, could possibly miss the point now. It was that obvious. The first flight—the coveted *first flight of the new bird*—that full-bore first flight that every test pilot strove for—had just been made in Project Mercury. *And the test pilot was an ape!* An ape made the first flight! "A college-trained chimpanzee"!—to use the very words that they had heard Astronaut Deke Slayton himself use before the Society of Experimental Test Pilots. And the ape had performed flawlessly, done as well as any man could possibly have done—for there was nothing for a man to do in the Mercury system except push a few perfunctory buttons and switches. This any college-trained chimpanzee could do also! He hadn't missed a beat! Give him a signal and he'll toggle you a switch! To see the point—and surely all the world now saw the point—you only had to imagine sending an ape up for the first flight of the X-15. You would have a twenty-million-dollar hole in the ground and a pulverized ape. But in Project Mercury an ape was fine! First-rate! In fact . . . the ape *was* an astronaut! He was the first one! Perhaps the female ape who backed him up deserved the next flight. Let *her* fly, goddamn it! She has earned it as much as the seven human ones—she's been through the same training! . . . and so forth and so on . . . The brethren let their beer-call brains soar. Perhaps the ape would go to the White House and get a medal. (Why not!) Perhaps the ape would address the September meeting of the Society of Experimental Test Pilots in Los Angeles. (Why not!—another *astronaut* had done it, Deke Slayton, without flying at all!) Oh, it was a laugh and a half, the whole thing. For now the truth was out—it was obvious in a way that no one in the world could miss.

And in the days that followed, the first days of February 1961, the True Brothers waited for this revelation to sweep across the press and the public and the Kennedy Administration and the military brass. But, strange to say, there was not even one such sign anywhere. In fact, they could begin to see signs of something quite the opposite. It was incredible, but the world was now full of people who were saying:

"My God, do you mean there are *men* brave enough to try what the ape has just gone through?"

J OHN GLENN FOUND himself in a ridiculous situation. It was nothing less than a charade. He had to pretend to be in the running for the first flight—and then he would read in the newspapers that he was the front runner. Since he had always been the fair-haired boy of the seven, that was the way it kept coming out. He and Gus Grissom had to tag along with Shepard through the training grind to keep up the fiction that the decision had not yet been made. In fact, Shepard was now the king—and Al knew how to *act* like the king. His Majesty the Prime Pilot —and Glenn was just a spear carrier.

Yet the charade, which Gilruth himself insisted on, also offered Glenn one last chance. No more than a handful of people knew that Shepard had been chosen for the first flight. Therefore, it was not too late to change the decision, to rectify what Glenn viewed as the incredible and outrageous business of the peer vote. But if this meant going over someone's head in one way or another . . . well, in the military it was a grave error, a serious breach of all that was holy, to go over the head of a superior unless (1) it was a critical situation and you were in the right and (2) your brash move worked (i.e., those at the top backed you up). On the other hand, there was nothing in the Presbyterian faith, another code Glenn knew very well, that said you had to stand around shy and obedient while the Pharisees waffled and oscillated, making imaginary snowballs. And was not NASA a civilian agency? (God knew it was not run like the Marines.) Glenn seemed to favor the Presbyterian course. He began talking to people in the hierarchy, asking what they thought of the decision.

He did not argue that he should be the one who was chosen, or not in so many words. He argued that the choice could not be made from a narrow perspective. America's first astronaut would not be merely a test pilot with a mission to carry out; he would be a historic representative of America, and his character would be viewed in that light. If he did not measure up to that test, it would be unfortunate not only for the space program but for the nation.

The new administrator of NASA, appointed by Kennedy to replace T. Keith Glennan, was James E. Webb, a former oil company executive and a political grand master in the Democratic Party. Webb was of a valuable breed well known in Washington: the off-the-ballot politician. The off-the-ballot politician usually looked like a politician, talked like a politician, walked like a politician, loved to mix with politicians, moved and shook with politicians, winked with politicians, sighed ruefully with them. He was the sort of man of whom a congressman or a senator was likely to say: "He speaks my language." The ablest and most distinguished of the off-the-ballot politicians, like Webb, were likely to end up with high-level appointments. Webb had been Director of the Bureau of the Budget and Undersecretary of State under Truman. He was also a great friend of Lyndon Johnson and Senator Robert Kerr of Oklahoma, who was chairman of the Senate Committee on Aeronautical and Space Sciences. For six years Webb had been head of a subsidiary of the Kerr family's oil empire. Webb was the sort of man whom corporations doing work for the government, such as McDonnell Aircraft and Sperry Gyroscope, liked to have on their boards of directors. He looked the part. He had big smooth jowls like Glennan's and even better hair, wavy, thick, as if every strand were nailed in, and dark, but graying smartly, and combed straight back in the manner favored by all serious men of the day. He had the sort of record that made him an ideal appointee to commissions like the Municipal Manpower Commission, which had occupied much of his time since 1959. He was known as a man who could make bureaucracies run. He was used to corner offices with terrific views. He was no fool. What would he have made of this business of Astronaut Glenn's dissatisfaction with the selection of Astronaut Shepard for the first Mercury flight? Gilruth said he had made the decision himself; and it was based on a wide range of criteria, many of them quite objective. Shepard had performed best on the procedures trainer, for example. When Gilruth considered all criteria, and not just the peer vote, Shepard ranked first and Glenn ranked second. So what was Glenn objecting to? It was a bit baffling. But one thing was sure: Webb was not likely to start his tenure as administrator of NASA by taking a flying leap into some incomprehensible dogfight among the seven bravest lads in the history of the United States. Astronaut Glenn's objections—and his last chance to become the world's first man in space—simply sank without a bubble one day, and that was that.

B‌Y NOW, LATE FEBRUARY of 1961, Glenn was not the only supremely miffed astronaut. Gilruth had finally published the names of the men who would make the first three flights—Glenn, Grissom, and Shepard, always in alphabetical order —implying that no decision had been made as to which of them would make the first flight, due to take place within ninety days. So Life ran a big story with pictures of Glenn, Grissom, and Shepard on the cover with the headline: THE FIRST THREE. Life was really excited about the whole thing. They tried to get

NASA to label the first three "the Gold Team" and the rest of them "the Red Team." The Gold Team and the Red Team. Jesus! The picture possibilities alone were fabulous.

This being the fraternal bulletin, *Life*, the notion of "the first three" struck Slayton, Wally Schirra, Scott Carpenter, and Gordon Cooper as a humiliation. In their minds they were now labeled "the Other Four." There were now the First Three and the Other Four. They had been . . . *left behind!* In some hard-to-define way, it was the equivalent of washing out.

Life really did it up in the best *Life* style. They flew the First Three and the First Three Wives and the First Three Children down to the Cape and took a lot of Inseparable Astronaut Family pictures on Cocoa Beach. The results were bizarre evidence of the determination of the Proper Gent to make everything come out in a seemly fashion. For a start, the travel schedules of the astronauts had made an absolute hash of ordinary home life. To show three astronauts having an outing with their families at the same time, even in different locations, would have been stretching the truth considerably. To present such a spectacle at the Cape—which was, in effect, off limits to wives—was an absolute howler. On top of that, if you were going to put astronaut families together for a frolic on the beach, you could scarcely come up with a less likely combination than the Glenns, the Grissoms, and the Shepards—the clans of the Deacon, the Hoosier Grit, and the Icy Commander. They would have passed like ships in the night in even the calmest of times, and these were not the calmest of times. Not even *Life* with all its powers of orchestration (and they were great) could make it come out right. They ran a big double-truck picture of the First Three and their wives and broods, the glorious First Three tribe, out on the hardtack sands of Cocoa Beach, engrossed (the caption would have one believe) in the sight of an exploratory rocket rising from the base several miles away. In fact, they looked like three families from warring parts of our restless globe who had never laid eyes on each other until they were washed up upon this godforsaken shore together after a shipwreck, shivering morosely in their leisure togs, staring off into the distance, desperately scanning the horizon for rescue vessels, preferably three of them, flying different flags.

As for the Other Four, they might as well have dropped through a crack in the earth.

GLENN WORKED AT BEING backup astronaut and charade master as if these were the roles the Presbyterian God had elected him to play. He gave it "a hundred percent," to use one of his favorite phrases. Besides . . . if, in the Lord's mysterious workings . . . it so happened that Shepard was not able to make the first flight, for some reason or another, he would be a hundred percent ready to step in. As a matter of fact, by April it had become blessedly, healingly possible for a fighter jock like Glenn to swallow his personal ambitions and lose himself in the mission itself. A true *sense of mission* had taken over Project Mercury. The mighty Soviet Integral had just sent two more huge Korabls into orbit with dummy cosmonauts and dogs aboard, and both flights had been successful from beginning to end. The race was coming down to the wire. Gilruth had even considered sending Shepard up in March, but Wernher von Braun had insisted on one last test of the Redstone rocket. The test went perfectly and everyone now wondered, in hindsight, if valuable time had been lost. Shepard's flight was scheduled for May 2, although it was not referred to publicly as Shepard's flight. The charade continued in full force, with Glenn still reading about himself in the newspapers as the likely choice. Around Hangar S there were NASA people who were talking about bringing all three, Glenn, Grissom, and Shepard, out to the launch pad on May 2 in their pressure suits with hoods over their heads, so that no one would know who was taking the first flight until he was inside the capsule. The reason why it should even matter had been long since forgotten.

NASA engineers and technicians at the Cape were pushing themselves so hard in the final weeks people had to be ordered home to rest. It was a grueling time and yet the sort of interlude of adrenal exhilaration that men remember all their lives. It was an interlude of the dedication of body and soul to a cause such as men usually experience only during war. Well . . . this *was* war, even though no one had spelled it out in just that way. Without knowing it, they were caught up in the primordial spirit of single combat. Just days from now one of the lads would be up on top of the rocket for real. Everyone felt he had the life of the astronaut, whichever was chosen (only a few knew), in his hands. The MA-1 explosion here at the Cape nine months ago had been a chilling experience, even for veterans of flight test. The seven astronauts had been assembled for the event, partly to give them confidence in the new system. And their gullets had been stuck up toward the sky like everybody else's, when the whole assembly blew to bits over their heads. In a few days one of those very lads would be lying on top of a rocket (albeit a Redstone, not an Atlas) when the candle was lit. Just about everybody here in NASA had seen the boys close up. NASA was like a family that way. Ever since the end of the Second World War the phrase "government bureaucracy" had invariably provoked sniggers. But a bureaucracy was nothing more than a machine for communal work, after all, and in those grueling and gorgeous weeks of the spring of 1961 the men and women of NASA's Space Task Group for Project Mercury knew that bureaucracy, when coupled with a spiritual motivation, in this case true patriotism and profound concern for the life of the single-combat warrior himself—bureaucracy, poor gross hideously ridiculed twentieth-century bureaucracy, could take on the aura, even the ecstasy, of communion. The passion that now animated NASA spread out even into the surrounding community of Cocoa Beach. The grisliest down-home alligator-poaching crackers manning the gasoline pumps on Route A1A would say to the tourists, as the No-Knock flowed, "Well, that Atlas ve-hicle's given us more fits than a June bug on a porch bulb, but we got real confidence in that Redstone, and I think we're gonna make it." Everyone who felt the spirit of NASA at that time wanted to be part of it. It took on a religious dimension that engineers, no less than pilots, would resist putting into words. But all felt it.

Whoever had possessed any doubts about Gilruth's powers of leadership dismissed them now. He had all phases of Project Mercury coming together in a coda. His calmness was all at once like a seer's. Wiesner, who had become Kennedy's Cabinet-level science advisor, had ordered a full-scale review of the space program and its progress, meaning of course its lack of progress, and he and a special committee under his jurisdiction kept sending queries and memoranda to NASA about careless planning, disregard of precautions, and the need for an entire series of chimpanzee flights before risking the life of one of the astronauts. At Langley and at the Cape they treated Wiesner and all his minions as if they were aliens. They ignored their paperwork and didn't return their telephone calls. Finally, Gilruth told them that if they wanted that many more chimpanzee flights, they ought to move NASA to Africa. Gilruth seldom said anything cutting or even ironic. But when he did, it stopped people in their tracks.

The launch procedures were now rehearsed endlessly and with great fidelity. The three of them, Shepard, Glenn, and Grissom, were staying in motels in Cocoa Beach, but they would get up early in the morning, before dawn, drive to the base, to Hangar S, have breakfast in the same dining room where Shepard would eat on the morning of the flight, go to the same ready rooms he would use on that morning for the physical exams and for putting on the pressure suit, have the biosensors attached and the suit pressurized, get into the van at the door and ride out to the launch pad, go up in the gantry elevator, get into the capsule on top of the rocket, and go through the procedures training—"Abort! Abort!"—the whole thing—using the actual instrument panel that would be used in flight and the actual radio hookups. All of this was done over and over. They were now using the capsule itself for simulation—just as the chimpanzees had. The idea was to decondition the beast completely, so that there would not be a single novel sensation on the day of the flight itself.

All three of them were taking part, but naturally Shepard, as prime pilot (no other word was used now), had precedence. And he *took* precedence. The little group in Hangar S now saw Al in both his varieties . . . and both were king, both the Icy Commander and Smilin' Al. Usually he left the Icy Commander back in Langley and brought only Smilin' Al to the Cape. But now he had both installed at the Cape. As the pressure built up, Al set a standard of coolness and competence that would be hard to top. In the medical examinations, in the heat-chamber sessions, in the altitude-chamber runs, he was as calm as ever. By now the White House had become extremely jittery—fearing what the debacle of a Dead Astronaut would do to American prestige—and so some dress rehearsals were conducted on the centrifuge at Johnsville, with Al and his two charade hands, Glenn and Grissom, taking part, and Al was imperturbable. Likewise, in the eleventh-hour simulations atop the rocket at the Cape. Al showed only one sign of stress: the cycles—Smilin' Al/Icy Commander—now came one on top of the other, in the same place, and alternated so suddenly that the people around him couldn't keep track. They learned a little more about the mysterious Al Shepard here in the eleventh hour. Smilin' Al was a man who wanted very much to be liked, even loved, by those around him. He wanted not just their respect but also their affection. Now, in April, on the eve of the great adventure, Smilin' Al was more jovial and convivial than ever. He did his José Jiménez routine. His great grin spread wider and his great beer-call eyes beamed brighter than ever before. Smilin' Al was crazy about a comedy routine that had been developed by a comedian named Bill Dana. It concerned the Cowardly Astronaut and was a great hit. Dana portrayed the Cowardly Astronaut as a stupid immigrant Mexican named José Jiménez, whose tongue wrapped around the English language like a taco. The idea was to interview Astronaut Jiménez like a news broadcaster.

You'd say things like: "What has been the most difficult part of astronaut training, José?"

"Obtaining de maw-ney, señor."

"The money? What for?"

"For de bus back to Mejico, you betcha, reel queeck, señor."

"I see. Well, now, José, what do you plan to do once you're in space?"

"Gonna cry a lot, I theeeenk."

Smilin' Al used to crack up over this routine. He liked to do the José Jiménez part; and if he could get someone to feed him the straight lines, he was in Seventh Heaven, Smilin' Al version. Feed him the lines for his José Jiménez knock-off, and he'd treat you like the best beer-call good buddy you ever had. Of course, the Cowardly Astronaut routine was also a perfectly acceptable way for bringing up, on the oblique, as it were, the subject of the righteous stuff that the first flight into space would require. But that was probably unconscious on Al's part. The main thing seemed to be the good fun, the camaraderie, the closeness and blustery affection of the squadron on the eve of battle. In these moments you saw Smilin' Al supreme. And in the next moment—

—some poor Air Force lieutenant, thinking this was the same Smilin' Al he had been joking and carrying on with last night, would sing out, "Hey, Al! Somebody wants you on the phone!"—and all at once there would be Al, seething with an icy white fury, hissing out: "If you have something to tell me, Lieutenant . . . you will call me 'Sir'!" And the poor devil wouldn't know what hit him. Where the hell did that freaking arctic avalanche come from? And then he would realize that . . . all at once the Icy Commander was back in town.

Of course those few who knew he was the man who was going up first were in a mood to forgive him all . . . well, save for an astronaut or two . . . As for the NASA technicians and the military personnel assigned to the mission, they were in a mood of utter adoration of the *single-combat warriors*, all three of them, for one of them would be placing his hide on top of the rocket. (And our rockets always blow up.) Toward the end the three of them would enter a room for some sort of test . . . and the technicians and workmen would stop what they were doing and break into applause and beam at them that warm moist smile of sympathy. Without knowing it, they were bestowing homage and applause in the classic manner: before the fact. These little scenes pressed Glenn's powers as charade master to the limit. More of these warm beams would be aimed at him than at either of the other two. He was the one mentioned in the press as the most likely choice. Not only that, he was the warmest of the three, the most consistently friendly toward one and all when he ran into them. It was just about too much. He had to keep smiling and aw-shucking and playing Mr. Modest, just as if it might, in fact, be he who was going up on top of the rocket on May 2 as the first man in the world to risk the mighty shot into space.

AND THEN THE OMNIPOTENT Integral intervened . . . a practical joker to the end! Early on the morning of April 12, the fabulous but anonymous Builder of the Integral, Chief Designer of the Sputniks, struck another of his cruel but dramatic blows. Just twenty days before the first scheduled Mercury flight he sent a five-ton Sputnik called *Vostok 1* into orbit around the earth with a man aboard, the first cosmonaut, a twenty-seven-year-old test pilot named Yuri Gagarin. *Vostok 1* completed one orbit, then brought Gagarin down safely, on land, near the Soviet village of Smelovka.

The omnipotent Integral! NASA had really believed—and the astronauts had really believed—that somehow, in the religious surge of *the mission*, Shepard's flight would be the first. But there was no putting one over on the Integral, was there! It was as if the Soviets' Chief Designer, that invisible genius, was toying with them. Back in October 1957, just four months before the United States was supposed to launch the world's first artificial earth satellite, the Chief Designer had launched Sputnik I. In January 1959, just two months before NASA was scheduled to put the first artificial satellite into orbit around the sun, the Chief Designer launched *Mechta I* and did just that. But this one, *Vostok I*, in April 1961, had been his *pièce de résistance*. Given the huge booster rockets at his disposal, he seemed to be able to play these little games with his adversaries at will. There was the eerie feeling that he would continue to let NASA struggle furiously to catch up—and then launch some startling new demonstration of just how far ahead he really was.

The Soviets persisted in offering no information as to the Chief Designer's identity. For that matter, they identified no one involved in Gagarin's flight other than Gagarin himself. Nor did they offer any pictures of the rocket or even such elementary data as its length and its rocket thrust. Far from casting any doubt as to the capabilities of the Soviet program, this policy seemed only to inflame the imagination. The Integral! Secrecy was by now accepted as "the Russian way." Whatever the CIA might have been able to do in other parts of the world, in the Soviet Union they drew a blank. Intelligence about the Soviet space program remained nonexistent. Only two things were known: the Soviets were capable of launching a vehicle of tremendous weight, five tons; and whatever goal NASA set for itself, the Soviet Union reached it first. Using those two pieces of information, everyone in the government, from President Kennedy to Bob Gilruth, seemed to experience an involuntary leap of the imagination similar to that of the ancients . . . who used to look into the sky and see a clump of stars, sparks in the night, and deduce therefrom the contours of . . . an enormous bear! . . . the constellation Ursa Major! . . . On the evening of Gagarin's flight, April 12, 1961, President Kennedy summoned James E. Webb and Hugh Dryden, Webb's deputy administrator and NASA's highest-ranking engineer, to the White House; they met in the Cabinet room and they all stared into the polished walnut surface of the great conference table and saw . . . the mighty Integral! . . . and the Builder!—the Chief Designer! . . . who was laughing at them . . . and it was awesome!

In Washington, at Langley, and at the Cape, NASA was deluged with telephone calls from newspapers, wire services, magazines, radio stations—and most callers wanted to know what the astronauts' reaction was to Gagarin's flight. So the First Three, Glenn, Grissom, and Shepard, all prepared statements. Shepard cranked out something that said next to nothing at all; standard government issue. Privately he was put out with Gilruth and von Braun and everyone else for not sending him up in March, as it now appeared they could have.

As usual, it was Glenn whom the press quoted most. He as much as said: "Well, they just beat the pants off us, that's all, and there's no use kidding ourselves about that. But now that the space age has begun, there's going to be plenty of work for everybody." Glenn was considered especially forthright, gracious, and magnanimous. He was big about the thing, as the saying goes—and that seemed especially commendable, since he was still considered the American front runner for the flight that would have made him "the first man in space." He had swallowed his own disappointment like a man.

10

RIGHTEOUS PRAYER

ALAN SHEPARD FINALLY got his turn on May 5. He was inserted in the capsule, on top of a Redstone rocket, about an hour before dawn, with an eye toward a launch shortly after daybreak. But as in the case of the ape, there was a four-hour hold in the countdown, caused mainly by an overheating inverter. Now the sun was up, and all across the eastern half of the country people were doing the usual, turning on their radios and television sets, rolling the knobs in search of something to give the nerve endings a little tingle—and what suspense awaited them! An astronaut sat on the tip of a rocket, preparing to get himself blown to pieces.

Even in California, where it was very early, highway patrolmen reported a strange and troubling sight. For no apparent reason drivers, hordes of them, were pulling off the highways and stopping on the shoulders, as if controlled by Mars. The patrolmen were slow in figuring it out, because they did not have AM radios. But the citizenry did, and they had become so excited as the countdown progressed at Cape Canaveral, so ravenously curious as to what would happen to the mortal hide of Alan Shepard when they fired the rocket, it was too much. Even the simple act of driving overloaded the nervous system. They stopped; they turned up the volume; they were transfixed by the prospect of the lonely volunteer about to be exploded into hash.

This tiny lad, up on the tip of that enormous white bullet, appeared to have about one chance in ten of living through it. Over the three weeks since the great Soviet triumph of Gagarin's flight, one terrible event had followed another. The United States had sent in a puppet army of Cuban exiles to conquer the Soviets' puppet regime in Cuba, and instead suffered the humiliation that became known as the Bay of Pigs. This had nothing directly to do with the space flight, of course, but it heightened the feeling that this was not the time to be trying brave and desperate deeds in the contest with the Soviets. The sad truth was, *our boys always botch it*. Eight days after that, on April 25, NASA had another big test of an Atlas rocket. It was supposed to carry a dummy astronaut into orbit, but it went off course and had to be blown up by remote control after forty seconds. The explosion nearly wiped out Gus Grissom, who was following the rocket's ascent as chase pilot in an F-106. Three days after that, April 28, a so-called Little Joe rocket with a Mercury capsule on top of it went off on another crazy trajectory and had to be aborted after thirty-three seconds. Both of these were tests of the Mercury-Atlas system, which would be used for orbital flights, and they had nothing to do with the Mercury-Redstone system, which Shepard would be riding —but it was far too late to make fine points. *Our rockets always blow up and our boys always botch it.*

And so now, on the morning of May 5, thousands, millions, stopped by the side of the road, paralyzed by the drama. This was the greatest death-defying hell-driver stunt ever broadcast, a patriotic stunt, a hash-mad stunt bound up with the fate of the country. People were beside themselves.

What must be going through the man's mind? Him and his poor wife . . . Then the radio announcer would tell how Shepard's wife, Louise, was following the countdown over television inside their home in Virginia Beach, Virginia. What a state the poor woman must be in! And so forth and so on. Brave lad! He hasn't resigned yet!

As for Shepard, what was going through his mind at that moment, and through much of his body, from his brain to his pelvic saddle, was a steadily increasing desire to urinate. It was no joke. He had been through 120 complete simulations of his flight, simulations that included the smallest details anyone could imagine: the early-morning wakeup by the official astronaut physician, Dr. William Douglas, the physical exam, the attaching of all the biosensors, the slipping of the thermometer tube up the rectum, the putting on of the suit, the hooking up of the oxygen tube and the communications lead, the ride out to the launch pad, the insertion, as it was known, into the capsule, the closing of the hatch, the works. They even went through the process of sucking the air out of the capsule with a hose and pressurizing the interior with pure oxygen. Then Shepard would go through yet more simulated rides and aborts, using the capsule itself as if it was a procedures trainer.

Three days ago, it turned out, even *the mental atmosphere* of the real thing was simulated. It was three days ago, May 2, that Shepard was originally scheduled to be launched. The weather made it a doubtful proposition, but they went ahead with the countdown, and Shepard had dinner in crew quarters the night before the flight, with much comradely banter, and Dr. Douglas tiptoed into his room the next morning and woke him up, and then he had the pre-launch breakfast, steak wrapped in bacon, plus eggs—in fact, Shepard went through everything, right up to the point where he would have climbed into the van and ridden out to the rocket, in the belief that this just might be it. Then the launch was postponed because of bad weather. Only at this point did NASA finally reveal that it was Shepard who had been assigned to the flight and was suited up and waiting behind the door in Hangar S. So Shepard had even been through the actual feeling of . . . *this is the day.* But no one had ever seriously envisioned the problem he now faced.

There was no easy way out when one's bladder kept getting larger and the capsule kept getting smaller. The dimensions of this little pod had been kept as tight as possible in order to hold down the weight. Once the various tanks, tubes, electrical circuits, instrument panels, radio hookups, and so on, were crammed in, along with the astronaut's emergency parachute, the space left over was not much more than a holster you could slip two legs and a torso into, with a tiny bit of room remaining for arms. The word they used, *insertion*, was not far off. The seat was literally a mold of Shepard's back and legs. They had packed the plaster right onto his body up at Langley Field. He was now in his seat, but resting on his back. It was as if a man were sitting in a very small sports car that had been upended so that it pointed straight up at the sky. In the rehearsals Shepard had reached the point where he could slip into his slot with one continuous series of moves. But this time, for the real thing, he had on a new pair of white boots, and the boot slipped on the armrest of the couch when he was snaking his right leg up into the capsule. That threw him off, and he wound up with everything inside except his left arm. The capsule was so small that getting his left arm inside became a terrific operation, with him wrenching this way and that and crewmen out on the gantry offering advice. Now he was so jammed in that the cuff on his right wrist, where his glove joined the sleeve of the pressure suit, kept catching on the parachute. He looked at the parachute and all of a sudden wondered what good it was. Technicians were craning in and fastening him to the couch with knee straps and a lap belt and a chest strap and screwing hoses to his pressure suit to maintain the pressure and control the temperature and wiring up leads for the biomedical sensors and the radio hookup and attaching and sealing a hose to the face plate of his helmet, for oxygen. In all likelihood, if he ever needed the parachute, he'd be a hole in the ground before he could get all these rigs undone. Then they closed the hatch, and he could feel his heartbeat quicken. But it soon subsided, and he was stuffed into this little thimble, lying on his back, practically immobile, with his legs jackknifed.

It was like being a china Cossack packed in a box full of styrofoam. His face was pointed straight up toward the sky, but he couldn't see it because he had no window. All he had were two little portholes, one on either side, above his head. The *true pilot's* window and hatch wouldn't be ready until the second Mercury flight. He might as well have been inside a box. A greenish fluorescent light filled the capsule. He could see outside only through the periscope window on the panel in front of him. The window was round, about a foot in diameter, in the middle of the panel. Outside, in the dark, the launch crewmen on the gantry could see the lens of the periscope if he pointed it their way. They kept walking in front of it and giving him big grins. Their faces filled the window. There was a wide-angle distortion, so that their noses protruded about eight feet out in front of their ears. When they grinned, they seemed to have more teeth than a perch. Once the dawn broke he could look out of the periscope and turn it this way and that, and see the Atlantic over here . . . and some people down on the ground . . . although the perspectives were a bit strange, because he was lying on his back and the periscope window was not terribly big and the angles were unusual. But then the sun grew brighter and brighter and he kept getting bursts of sunlight in the periscope window, lying on his back like this and looking up, and so he reached up with his left hand and clicked a gray filter into place. That helped a great deal, even though it neutralized most colors. Now that the hatch had been bolted shut, Shepard could hear practically nothing from the outside world except the voices that came over the headset inside his helmet. He spent part of the time, as before any test flight, going over the checklist. Over the headset came the voice of the leader of the launch pad team, saying:

"Auto retro jettison switch. Arm?"

And Shepard would say, "Roger. Auto retro jettison switch. Arm."

"Retro heater switch. Off?"

And Shepard would say, "Retro heater switch. Off."

"Landing bag switch. Auto?"

"Landing bag switch. Auto."

And on down the line. After a while, however, as the holds dragged on, people were coming onto the circuit to keep him company and find out how he was bearing up. He could hear Gordon Cooper, who was serving as the "capcom," the capsule communicator, in the blockhouse near the launch pad, and Deke Slayton, who would be the capcom in the flight control center during the launch itself. Cooper had a telephone hookup with the capsule, and every now and then Bill Douglas or another of the doctors would come on the line, apparently as much to assess his spirits as anything else. Wernher von Braun talked to him at one point. The countdown progressed very slowly. Shepard asked Slayton to have someone call his wife to make sure she understood the reasons for the delay. And then he was back in the tight little world of the capsule. There was an irritating tone, very high up in the audible range, coming over the headset the whole time, some sort of feedback sound, apparently. He could hear the hum of the cabin fans and the pressure-suit fans, both used for cooling, and he could hear the inverters moaning up and down. So here he was, stuffed into this little blind thimble, spliced into the loop by every conceivable sort of wire and hose, leading from his body, his helmet, and his suit, listening to the hums, moans, overtones . . . and the minutes and the *hours* began to go by . . . and he'd swivel his knee and ankle joints a few centimeters this way and that to keep his circulation up . . . and two annoying little pressure points began to build up where his shoulders pressed back into the couch . . . and then the tide began to build up in his bladder.

The problem was, there was nothing to urinate into. Since the flight would last only fifteen minutes, it had never occurred to anybody to include a urine receptacle. Some of the simulations had dragged on for so long the astronauts had ended up urinating in their pressure suits. It had been the only thing to do, short of spending hours removing the man from all his hookups and the capsule and the suit itself. The chief danger in introducing liquid into a pure-oxygen environment, such as that of the capsule and the pressure suit, was of causing an electrical short circuit that might start a fire. Luckily, the only wires that urine was likely to come in contact with inside the pressure suit were the low-voltage leads to the biomedical sensors, and the procedure had seemed safe enough. There was even a sponge mechanism inside the suit for removing excess moisture, which ordinarily would come in the form of perspiration. Nevertheless, no one had seriously studied the possibility that on *the day* itself, the day of the first American manned space flight, the astronaut might end up on top of the rocket and stuffed into the capsule with his legs practically immobile for more than four hours . . . with his bladder to answer to. There was no way the astronaut could simply urinate into the lining of the pressure suit and have it go unnoticed. The suit had its own cooling system, and the temperature was monitored by interior thermometers, which led to consoles, and in front of these consoles were some by now highly keyed-up technicians whose sole mission was to stare at the dials and account for every fluctuation. If a nice steaming subdermal river of 98.6 degrees was introduced into the system with no warning, the Freon flow would suddenly increase— Freon was the gas used to cool the suit—and, well, God knew what would result. Would they hold up the whole production? Terrific. Then the No. 1 astronaut could explain, over a radio transmitter, while the nation waited, while the Russians girded themselves for round 2 of the battle of the heavens, that he had just peed in his pressure suit.

Compared to the prospect of such a flap, no matter how minor, in the final phase of the countdown, any possible danger of blowing up on the launch pad was far down an astronaut's list of worries. For a test pilot the right stuff in the prayer department was not "Please, God, don't let me blow up." No, the supplication at such a moment was "Please, dear God, don't let me fuck up."

To come this far . . . and *fuck up* . . .

All along the constant fear of the righteous pilot was not of death but of ending up where John Glenn was this morning: standing by as a mere spear carrier in the drama. You had to hand it to Glenn, however. He had really buckled down and worked like a Trojan as backup pilot during the last month of the training. He had really proved helpful. He had even come up with a little Dawn Patrol camaraderie this morning. Shepard was in a mood for that. Ever since he got up, he had been in his Smilin' Al of the Cape cycle. On the way out in the van he had gotten Gus Grissom to play straight man for the José Jiménez routine. Shepard liked to do the Mexican accent the way Dana did it. "Eef you osk me what make de good astronaut, I tail you dat you got to have de courage and de good blood pressure and de four legs." "Four legs?" Gus asked dutifully. "Weh-ayl, eet ees a dog dey want to send, bot dey theenk dot ees too croo-el." Yes, they would remember him as having been loose as a goose on the way to the top of the rocket. When he came up the gantry elevator and stepped out, to enter the capsule, Glenn was already up there, dressed in white like the technicians. He was smiling. When Shepard finally squeezed himself into the capsule and looked at the instrument panel, there was a little sign on it saying NO HANDBALL PLAYING IN THIS AREA. That was Glenn's little joke, and he grinned and reached in and took the sign out. Actually, it was funny enough . . .

Too late, John! Shepard wasn't going to get run over or break a leg or be struck down by an angry God. He was in the capsule and they were bolting the hatch, and all the others were . . . *left behind* . . . out there . . . beyond the portal . . . There was no way a righteous pilot could have explained to anyone but another pilot what this feeling was, and of course he would not have dared to try to explain it even to a pilot. The holy *first flight!*—and he would be up there at the apex of the entire pyramid if he survived it.

And if he didn't? This would have been even more difficult to explain: the evil odds were essential to the enterprise. That unmentionable *stuff*, after all, involved a man hanging his hide out over the edge in a hurtling piece of machinery. And such unmentionable payoffs it brought you! One, which he had started receiving even *before* this morning, was a look. It was a look of fraternal awe, of awe in the presence of *manly honor*, that came over the faces of other men at a base when a test pilot or combat pilot headed for the aircraft for a mission when the odds were known to be evil. Shepard had rated that look before, particularly when testing overpowered, overweight jet fighters in their first carrier landings. It was the look that came over another man when one's own righteous stuff triggered *his* adrenalin. And this morning, every step of the way, from the crew quarters in Hangar S to the gantry deck outside the capsule, where Glenn and the technicians had been waiting to help him inside, men had beamed that look straight at him—and then they had *broken into applause*. Just as he was getting ready to go onto the gantry and take the elevator up to the capsule, the entire ground crew had started applauding. They had that warm and humid smile on their face and tears glistened in their eyes and they were banging their hands together and yelling things to him. Shepard had his helmet on, with the visor sealed, and he was carrying his own portable oxygen unit, which was pumping away, and so it was all happening in a muffled pantomime, but there was no mistaking what was going on. They were giving him the applause and homage . . . *up front* . . . come what may! . . . payable in advance!

From a sheerly analytical standpoint one knew that the odds in this flight, while bad enough, were no worse than the odds he had faced before in testing winged aircraft. Wernher von Braun had said repeatedly that the Redstone rocket's record of reliability was 98 percent, which was better than that of some of the Century series of supersonic jet fighters during the test stage. But the truth was that by now Shepard would have accepted far worse odds. He had accepted a great many rewards up front. He and his confreres had already been lionized, such as few pilots in history. The very top pilots, with the most righteous stuff, were content to receive that unmentionable glistening look from aviators and support personnel at their own base. Shepard had already had it beamed upon him by every sort of congressman, canned-food distributor, Associated Florists board chairman, and urban-renewal speculator, not to mention the anonymous little cookies with their trembling little custards who simply materialized around you at the Cape. He had already accepted the payment . . . *up front!*—and millions of wide-open humid eyes were now upon him. The ancient instinct of a people, their so-called folk wisdom, in the matter of the care, preparation, and recompense of single-combat warriors was indeed sound. Like his predecessors in the ancient past, he had reached the blessed state where one was far more afraid of not delivering on his end of the bargain—having been paid up front—than he was of getting killed. *Please, dear Lord, don't let me fuck up.* He was now where he belonged and had striven to be: atop the very thrust point of the danger. He was now precisely at that critical elevation that separated the great pilots, bearing their gigantic albeit invisible pictures of themselves, from the mere mortals on the terrain below. No one would ever know whether or not another type of human being would have handled this day with the same aplomb—this day when one became the first human being ever to sit up on top of an eight-story-high bullet and have a 66,000-pound Redstone rocket lit under his tail. All the racing drivers, mountain climbers, scuba divers, bobsledders, and Seabees they once considered using—what would have been the state of their souls at this moment? Well, by now it was pointless to ask. One could only say this: for the typical competitive military pilot, possessing the regulation-issue heroic self-esteem of the breed, throbbing with rude animal health, convinced of his utterly righteous stuff, and ravenous for glory—which is to say, for a man like Alan Shepard—being where he was right now was his vocation, his calling, his holy *Beruf*. He was home, upon the right stuff's highest elevations.

On top of everything else, the organism's deconditioning was very nearly complete. After all the full-dress rehearsals and simulations of this flight, complete with the sounds, the g-forces, and even the wires protruding from his body, after more than a hundred *pre-creations* of this moment, after riding up the gantry elevator over and over and fitting himself into the human holster and having them close the hatch and start the countdown, after lying in this very capsule, day after day, with the capsule communicator's voice coming over his headset and the signals of flight flashing on the instrument panel, until every inch and every second of the experience was familiar and the capsule had become more like an office than a vehicle . . . it was hard for a man to sense any difference this time in his own nervous system, even though intellectually he knew that this was *that day*. Now and then he could feel the adrenalin building up and his pulse rate increasing and his breathing speeding up and his heart palpitating slightly, and he would force himself to concentrate on the checklist, the console, the equipment connections, the radio hookup, and the rush would pass, and he would be back once more in his workshop, in his procedures trainer.

No, the one thing he had experienced all morning that was not second nature was his aching bladder. That had become the first terra incognita. *Please, dear Lord, don't let me fuck up.*

Shepard waited for another step in the countdown—this time it was to wait for some clouds to pass over the launch area—and he announced his problem over the closed radio circuit. He said he wanted to relieve his bladder. Finally they told him to go ahead and "do it in the suit." And he did. Because his seat, or couch, was angled back slightly, the flood headed north, toward his head, carrying consternation with it. The flood set off a suit thermometer, and the freon flow jumped from 30 to 45. On swept the flood until it hit his left lower chest sensor, which was being used to record his electrocardiogram, and it knocked that sensor out partially, and the doctors were nonplused. The news of the flood rushed through the worlds of the Life Science specialists and the suit technicians, like the destruction of Krakatoa, west of Java. There was no stopping it now. The wave rolled on, over rubber, wire, rib, flesh, and ten thousand baffled nerve endings, finally pooling in the valley up the middle of Shepard's back. Gradually it cooled, and he could feel a cool lake of urine in the valley. In any case, the discomfort in his bladder was gone and everything was still. They had not scratched the flight because of the dam break. He had not fucked up.

The next thing the medical team knew, a voice was coming over the closed loop, their private radio linkup with the Mercury capsule:

"Weh-ayl . . . I'm a wetback now."

The man was beautiful!

Imperturbable at every juncture!

Fifteen minutes, in the countdown, before they fire a seven-story bullet full of liquid oxygen underneath him, and he remains:

Smilin' Al!

The hold had now dragged on for four hours, and each engineer monitoring the panels showing the status of the various flight systems was agonizing over whether to declare, finally, that his system was "go"—after which it would be his responsibility if the system malfunctioned. By now there was agony on all sides. It was transmitted into the capsule in a thousand unspoken ways and sometimes in so many words. It was as if Shepard, lying here on his back, inserted, wired, strapped, and screwed into this tiny holster, were the ganglion, the agony junction, for a thousand tense and tortured souls on the gantry outside and on the ground below. Through it all he had remained Smilin' Al of the Cape. At T minus 6—six minutes before the completion of the sequence that would lead to the launching—there was yet another hold, and one of the doctors came on the closed telephone circuit and said to Shepard:

"Are you *really* ready?"

It was hard to figure out whether the question was addressed to the body or the soul. It wandered into the unmentionable terrain of the most righteous stuff itself, and it was Smilin' Al who handled it.

He laughed and said: "Go!"

"Good luck, old friend," said the doctor.

Farewell . . . from the valley of the woeful abyss . . .

At T minus 2 minutes and 40 seconds there was another hold. Now Shepard could hear engineers in the blockhouse agonizing over the fuel pressure in the Redstone, which was running high. He could sense what would be coming next. They were going to talk themselves into resetting the pressure valve inside the booster engine manually. That would mean postponing the launch for another two days at least. He could see it coming! They were going to scrub the whole thing, lest *they* hold themselves accountable for *his hide* if something went wrong! This was not a job for Smilin' Al. It was time for the Icy Commander to arrive and take charge. So he got on the circuit and put the glacial edge on his voice, as only he could do it, and he said:

"All right, I'm cooler than you are. Why don't you fix your little problem . . . and *light this candle.*"

Light the candle! he says. The words of Chuck Yeager himself! The voice of the rocket ace! Oddly enough, it seemed to do the trick. Realizing the astronaut's irritation, they began wrapping up the process and declaring their systems "go." It was nearly 9:30 a.m. by the time the countdown entered its last minute. Shepard's periscope began automatically retracting inside the capsule, and he remembered that he had put in the gray filter to cut out the sunlight. If he didn't remove it, he wouldn't be able to see any colors in flight. So he started moving his left hand toward the periscope, but his left forearm hit the abort handle. Shit! That was all he needed now! Fortunately, he had barely brushed it. The abort handle was the equivalent of the ejection seat cinch ring in an airplane. If the astronaut sensed some catastrophe that the automatic system had not picked up, he could turn the handle and the escape tower rocket would fire and pull the capsule free of the Redstone rocket and bring it down by parachute. That was all he needed—the world waits for the first American spaceman, and Shepard gives them an exhibition of a little man popping up a few thousand feet in a thimble and floating down by parachute . . . He could see it all in a flash . . . Another Popped Cork fiasco . . . The hell with changing the filter. He would look at the world in black and white. Who cared? *Don't fuck up.* That was the main thing.

Time seemed to speed up tremendously in the final thirty seconds of the countdown. In thirty seconds the rocket would ignite right underneath his back. In those last moments his entire life did not pass before his eyes. He did not have a poignant vision of his mother or his wife or his children. No, he thought about abort procedures and the checklist and about not fucking up. He only half paid attention to Deke Slayton's voice over his headset as he read out the final "ten . . . nine . . . eight . . . seven . . . six . . ." and the rest of it. The only word that counted, here in this little blind stuffed pod, was the last word. Then he heard Deke Slayton say it: "Fire! . . . You're on your way, José!"

L OUISE SHEPARD WAS NOT in the valley of the woeful abyss. She was here in her house in Virginia Beach—but beyond that it was hard to chart the locus of her soul at that moment. Never in the history of flight test had the wife of a pilot been put in any such bizarre position as this. Naturally all the wives had been aware that there might be some "press interest" in the reactions of the wife and family of the first astronaut—but Louise hadn't bargained for anything like what was now going on in her front yard. Every now and then Louise's daughters would peek out the window, and the yard looked like the clay flats three hours after the Marx Midway Carnival pulls in. Mobs of reporters and cameramen and other Big Timers were out there wearing bush jackets with leather straps running this way and that and knocking back their Pepsi-Colas and Nehis and yelling to each other and mainly just milling about, crazy with the excitement of being *on the scene*, bawling for news of the anguished soul of Louise Shepard. They wanted a moan, a tear, some twisted features, a few inside words from friends, any god-damned thing. They were getting desperate. Give us a sign! Give us anything! Give us the diaper-service man! The diaper-service man comes down the street with his big plastic bags, smoking a cigar to provide an aromatic screen for his daily task—and they're all over him and his steamy bag. Maybe he knows the Shepards! Maybe he knows Louise! Maybe he's been in there! Maybe he knows the layout of *chez* Shepard! He locks himself in the front seat, choking on cigar smoke, and they're banging on his panel truck. "Let us in! We want to see!" They're on their knees. They're slithering in the ooze. They're interviewing the dog, the cat, the rhododendrons . . .

These incredible maniacs were all out there tearing up the lawn and yearning for their pieces of Louise's emotional wreckage. The truth was, however, that Louise Shepard could hardly be said to be experiencing the feelings that all these people were so eager to wolf down. Louise had had her chances to become a nervous wreck over Al's flying many times, most recently at Pax River. In 1955 and 1956 Al had tested one hot new fighter plane after another. Their names were a delirium of sharp teeth, cold steel, cosmic warlords, and evil spirits: the Banshee, the Demon, the Tigercat, the Skylancer, and so on, and Al took them through not only maximum performance runs but also high-altitude tests, in-flight refueling tests, and "carrier suitability tests"—a stolid phrase that covered a multitude of ways for a test pilot to expire. Louise knew the entire world of the test pilot's wife . . . the calls from other wives saying that "something" has happened out there . . . the wait, in a little house with small children, to see if the Friend of Widows and Orphans is coming to make his duty call . . . Day after day she tries to be stoic, she tries not to think about the subject, not to pay attention to the clock when he doesn't return from the flight line on time—

Well, my God—what an improvement Project Mercury was over the daily lot of the test pilot's wife! No question about it! The worst part of the Pax River days had been the constant wondering and worrying, alone or with uncomprehending little faces around you. This morning Louise knew exactly where Al was every minute. He was hard to miss. He was on nationwide television. There he was. She had merely to look at the screen. On nationwide television they were talking about no one else. You could hear the laconic baritone voice of Shorty Powers, the NASA public affairs officer, in the Mercury Control room at the Cape periodically reporting the astronaut's status as the countdown proceeded. Then the telephone rings—and she hears that same voice, calling to speak to her, Louise. Al had spoken to Deke, and Deke had spoken to Shorty, and now Shorty— possessor of the voice that the entire nation was listening to—was talking to her personally, explaining the reasons for the delays, as Al had requested. Nor was she alone in this house. Hardly! It was getting crowded in here. In addition to the children, there were her parents, who had come from Ohio and had been here for days. A few of the other wives had arrived. Al had been stationed nearby in Norfolk when the program began, and so they had many Navy friends and neighbors whom they knew well, and quite a few of them had come by. There was quite a burble of voices building up in the living room. It didn't sound very tense in there. And of course she had merely half the newspapers in America in the front yard, plus the usual rabble of gawkers who materialize for car wrecks or roof jumps or traffic arguments, and the whole lot would have liked nothing better than to charge in and gather round if she had opened the front door to them so much as a crack. *Life* had wanted to have two writers and a photographer on the premises to record her reactions from start to finish, but she had held out against that. So they were waiting in a hotel on the beach, and it was agreed they could come inside as soon as the flight was completed. Louise hadn't even had all that much opportunity to sit in front of the television set and let the tension build. She had gotten up before dawn, in the dark, to fix breakfast for everybody who was staying in the house, and then there was the whole business of fixing coffee and whatnot for the other good folks as they arrived . . . until before she knew it she was caught up in the same psychology that works at a *wake*. She was suddenly the central figure in a Wake for My Husband—in his hour of danger, however, rather than his hour of death. The secret of the wake for the dead was that it put the widow on stage, whether she liked it or not. In the very moment in which, if left alone, she might be crushed by grief, she was suddenly thrust into the role of hostess and star of the show. It's free! It's *open house!* Anybody can come on in and gawk! Of course, the widow can still turn on the waterworks—but it takes more nerve to do that in front of a great gawking mob than it does to be the brave little lady, serving the coffee and the cakes. For someone as dignified and strong as Louise Shepard, there was no question as to how it was going to come out. As hostess and main character in this scene, what else was there for the pilot's wife to do but set about pulling everybody together? The press, the ravenous but genteel Beast out there upon the lawn, did not know it but he was covering not the Anguished Wife at Lift-off . . . but the Honorable Mrs. Commander Astronaut at Home . . . in the first wake, not for the dead, but for the Gravely Endangered . . . Louise didn't even have *time* to collapse in neurasthenic paralysis over the possible fate of her husband. It was all that the star and hostess could do to get back to the TV room in time for the final minutes of the countdown, to watch the flames roaring out of the Redstone's nozzles.

Hmmmm . . . with all the world wondering about the state of her soul at this moment . . . what kind of face should she have on?

OVER HIS HEADSET Shepard heard Deke Slayton, from inside the Mercury Control Center, as it was called, saying, "We have lift-off!" And as he had done hundreds of times on the centrifuge and on the procedures trainer, he reached up and turned on the onboard clock—which would tell him when to do this and that on his flight schedule—and he said over his microphone: "Roger, lift-off, and the clock is started" . . . as he had said hundreds of times on the centrifuge and the procedures trainer. And then, with the automatic anticipation of someone who has heard the same phonograph record over and over again and is now hearing it yet once again and senses every chord and phrase before it sounds, he waited for the gradual buildup of the g-forces and for the beating noise as the rocket lifted off . . . which he had felt and which he had heard hundreds of times on the centrifuge—

Hundreds of times! Even if he had been ordered at that point to broadcast to the American people a detailed description of precisely what it felt like to be the first American riding a rocket into space, and even if he had had the leisure to do it, he could not possibly have expressed what he was feeling. For he was introducing the era of precreated experience. His launching was an utterly novel event in American history, and yet he could feel none of its novelty. He could not feel "the awesome power" of the rocket beneath him, as the broadcasters kept referring to it. He could only compare it to the hundreds of rides he had taken on the centrifuge at Johnsville. The memory of all those rides was imbedded in his nervous system. Scores of times he had sat in the gondola on the wheel, as he sat here now, in his pressure suit, with the Mercury instrument panel in front of him and the noise of a Redstone launch piped into his headset. And compared to that —what was happening at this moment was not awesome. Quite the opposite. He was braced for it, but . . . *It didn't throw you around like the centrifuge* . . . The centrifugal force of the centrifuge threw you around inside the capsule as well as increasing the speed and the g-forces . . . The rocket was smoother and easier . . . *It wasn't as noisy as the centrifuge* . . . On the wheel the recorded sound of the Redstone rocket was piped directly into the capsule. But now, since he was the figurine in the packing box, it came from outside, through layer after layer. By the time it penetrated the escape-tower cover and the capsule wall and the contoured seat behind his head and the helmet and his headset, it was no louder than the engine noises a commercial airline pilot hears on takeoff. In fact, he was far more conscious of the noises inside the capsule . . . The camera . . . There was a camera set up to record his facial expressions and eye and hand movements, and he could hear that whirring about a foot from his head . . . There was a tape recorder set up to record all the sounds inside the capsule, and he could hear its little motor running . . . And the fans and the gyros and inverters . . . It was like an extremely compact modern kitchen in here . . . with all the gadgets running at once . . . And of course the radio . . . He thought he would have to turn the volume up to maximum, as he had on the centrifuge, but he didn't have to touch it. All he had to do was talk into his voice mike and say the exact same things he had said a thousand times on the procedures trainer . . . "Altitude one thousand . . . one-point-nine g's . . ." and so on . . . and they would answer back, "Roger, we copy, you're looking good . . ." and it even *sounded* the same way over the headset.

He could still see nothing. The periscope was still retracted. He had no way to judge his speed except by the needle on the instrument panel that showed his rising altitude and the buildup of the g-forces on his body. But this was gradual. It was a very familiar feeling. He had felt it hundreds of times on the centrifuge. It was much easier than pulling four g's in a supersonic aircraft, because he didn't have to struggle to push his hands forward against the weight of the g-forces to control the trajectory of the aircraft. He didn't have to lift a finger if he didn't want to. The computers guided the rocket automatically by swiveling the nozzles. He had very little feeling of motion, just the g-forces driving him deeper and deeper into the seat he was lying on.

The rocket rose so gradually it took forty-five seconds to reach Mach 1. An F-104 fighter plane could have done it faster. When the rocket reached transonic speed, .8 Mach, a vibration started building up—just as it had for the X series of rocket planes at Edwards years before. Shepard was quite prepared for it . . . He had been through it on the centrifuge . . . so many times . . . But it was a different vibration. It didn't shake his head about as violently, but the amplitudes were more rapid. His vision began to blur. He couldn't read the instrument panel any longer. He started to report the phenomenon over his headset but thought better of it. *Some bastard would panic and abort the mission.* Christ, the vibrations, no matter how bad, were preferable to an abort. Within another thirty seconds all the vibrations were gone, and he knew he was going supersonic. With the vibration gone, he once again had no sensation of motion. He was still blind to the world outside. He was still lying on his back, looking at the instrument panel, no more than eighteen inches from his eyes, in the greenish light of the capsule. The g-forces reached six times the force of gravity, then began to tail off as the rocket and the capsule approached the weightless phase of the arc of flight. *It was different from the centrifuge—It was easier!* On the centrifuge the only way to reduce the g-load as you simulated the approach to the weightless phase was to reduce the speed of the centrifuge arm, and this always threw you forward against your straps. When the simulated moment of zero-g arrived, you were thrown against the straps quite hard. On a rocket ride, however—as all the rocket pilots at Edwards knew—your speed did not abruptly decrease as the rocket ran out of fuel. It kept sailing. Shepard was eased into weightlessness so smoothly it was as if the weight of the g-forces had simply slid off his body. Now he could feel his heart pounding. The most critical part of the flight, next to the launch itself, was only a moment away . . . the separation of the capsule from the rocket . . . He heard a muffled explosion from above . . . *just the way it sounded in the simulations* . . . and the escape rocket blew off and the capsule was now free of the rocket. The force of the rocket pulling away accelerated his speed, and he felt as if he had had a kick from below. A three-inch-long rectangular light lit up green on the instrument panel. On it were the letters JETT TOWER, for Jettison Tower. With the tower gone, the periscope would start operating, and he could look out, but he had his eyes pinned on the green light. It was beautiful. It meant everything was going perfectly. He could forget about the abort handle now. The launch phase was over. The most treacherous part of the entire ride was now behind him. All that endless training in the procedures trainer . . . "Abort! . . . Abort! . . . Abort!" . . . he could put that behind him and forget about it. Small portholes were on either side, above his head, and he could see only the sky through them. He was now slightly more than a hundred miles up. The sky was almost navy blue. It was not the much-talked-of "blackness of space." It was the same dark-blue sky that pilots begin to see at 40,000 feet. It looked no different. The capsule was now automatically turning so that its blunt end, the end beneath his back, which had a heat shield for the re-entry into the earth's atmosphere, was aimed toward the target area. He was facing back toward Florida, toward the Cape. He could not see the earth out of the high portholes at all, however. He wasn't even particularly interested in looking. He kept his eyes pinned on the instrument panel. The gauges told him he was weightless. After reaching this point so many times on the procedures trainer, he knew he must be weightless. But he felt nothing. He was so tightly strapped and stuffed into this little human holster there was no way he could float as he had in the cargo bays of the big C-131s. He didn't even experience the tumbling sensation he felt when riding backseat in the F-100s at Edwards. *It was all milder!—easier!* No doubt he should say something to the ground about the sensation of weightlessness. It was the great unknown in space flight. *But he didn't feel anything at all!* He noticed a washer floating in front of his eye. The washer must have been left in there by a workman. It was just floating there in front of his left eye. That was the only evidence his five senses had to show that he was weightless. He tried to grab the washer with his left hand, with his glove, but he missed it. It floated away, and he couldn't move his hand far enough to get it. He had no sensation of speed at all, even though he knew he was going Mach 7, or about 5,180 miles an hour. There was nothing to judge speed by. There were no vibrations at all in the capsule. Since he was now completely beyond the earth's atmosphere and was no longer attached to the rocket, there was no rushing sound whatsoever. It was as if he were standing still, parked in the sky. The sounds of the interior of the capsule, the rising and falling and whirring and moaning of the inverters and the gyros . . . the cameras, the fans . . . the busy little kitchen—they were exactly the same sounds he had heard over and over in the simulations inside the capsule on the ground at the Cape . . . The same busy little kitchen in operation, whirring and buzzing and humming along . . . There was nothing new going on! . . . He knew he was in space, but there was no way to tell it! . . . He looked out the periscope, the only way he had of looking at the earth. *The goddamned gray filter!* He couldn't see any colors at all! He had never changed the filter! The first American to ever fly this high above the earth—and it was a black-and-white movie. Nevertheless, they'll want to know about it—

"What a beautiful view!" he said.

He could hear Slayton say: "I bet it is."

In fact, there was a cloud cover over most of the East Coast and much of the ocean. He was able to see the Cape. He could see the west coast of Florida . . . Lake Okeechobee . . . He was up so high he seemed to be moving away from Florida ever so slowly . . . And the inverters moaned up and the gyros moaned down and the fans whirred and the cameras hummed . . . He tried to find Cuba. Was that Cuba or wasn't that Cuba? Over there, through the clouds . . . Everything was black and white and there were clouds all over . . . There's Bimini Island and the shoals around Bimini. He could see that. *But everything looked so small!* It had all been bigger and clearer in the ALFA trainer, when they flashed the still photos on the screen . . . The real thing didn't measure up. It was *not realistic*. He couldn't see anything but a medium-gray ocean and light-gray beaches and dark-gray vegetation . . . There were the Bahamas, Grand Bahama Island, Abaco Island . . . or were they? The pale-gray cloud cover and the medium-gray water and the pale-gray beaches and the medium-gray . . . the grays ran together like goulash . . . He didn't have time to fool with it. He had a long checklist. He was supposed to try out the roll, yaw, and pitch controls. They were all operating automatically up to now. He switched over to manual one at a time and tried using the hand controller.

"Okay," he said into his microphone, "switching to manual pitch."

And the capsule nosed up and then down.

"Pitch is okay," he said. "Switching to manual yaw."

All this he seemed to have said a hundred, a thousand times before, in the procedures trainer. And the capsule yawed from side to side, and he had *felt* it a thousand times before—on the ALFA trainer. Only the sound was different. Every time he turned the manual control handles, hydrogen-peroxide jets discharged outside the capsule. He knew it was happening, because the capsule would pitch, roll, yaw, just as it was supposed to, but he couldn't hear the jets. On the ALFA trainer he had always been able to hear the jets. The real thing was not nearly so realistic as that. The capsule pitched and yawed just like the ALFA . . . *no difference* . . . but he couldn't hear the jets at all because of the humming, moaning, and whining of the inverters and gyros and fans . . . the busy little kitchen.

Whuh?—before he knew it the ride was practically over. It was time to prepare himself for re-entry into the earth's atmosphere. He was descending the arc . . . just like a mortar shell on the way down . . . The ground was starting the countdown for the firing of the retro-rockets that would slow the capsule down for re-entry through the atmosphere. There was no need for them on this flight, because the capsule was going to come back down in any event like a cannonball, but they would be essential in orbital flights, and this flight was supposed to test the system. The retro-rockets fired automatically. He didn't have to move a finger. There was another muffled rocket firing, not a loud noise at all . . . The little kitchen kept humming and whining away . . . He was riding backward, still facing Florida. The rocket firing drove him backward into his seat with a force of about five g's. It was much more sudden than the transition from six g's to zero-g on the way up. *Man, that wasn't like the centrifuge.* The centrifuge jerked you around at this point. In the next instant he was weightless again, as he knew he would be. The retrofire was like pumping the brakes once. But it had slowed down the capsule, and soon the g-forces would start building up. They would build up gradually, however. He knew the interval exactly . . . At this point an explosive device was supposed to go off and jettison the rigs that held the retro-rockets. He heard the little dull explosions outside the capsule and then he saw one of the straps of the rig go by his window. He could feel the twist from the torque of the retro-rocket nozzles, but it corrected itself automatically. Now he was supposed to practice controlling the attitude of the capsule while it was slowing down. So he swung it this way and that way . . . like a Ferris-wheel seat . . . Oh, shit! The dial showed the g-forces were building up slightly . . . One-half g . . . This meant he had about forty-five seconds to check out the *stars* . . . He was supposed to look at the stars and the horizon and see if he could get a fix on particular constellations. Eventually this would have some bearing on space navigation. But mainly there would be millions down there wanting to know that the first American in space had been up there in the neighborhood of the stars . . . Oh, they would all want to know how the stars looked from outside the earth's atmosphere. They weren't supposed to twinkle when you looked at them from up here. They would just be little shining balls in the blackness of space . . . Except that it wasn't black, it was blue . . . The *stars*, man! . . . He kept staring out the windows trying to make out the stars . . . He couldn't see a damned thing, not one goddamned star. If the capsule were pitched up this way or rolled over that way, he would get zaps of sunlight in his face. If he pitched it or rolled it this way—he still couldn't see a damned thing. The light in the interior of the capsule was too bright. All he could make out was the navy-blue sky. He couldn't even see the horizon. There were supposed to be spectacular color bands at the horizon when viewed from above the atmosphere. But he couldn't see them out the portholes. He could see them through the periscope—but the periscope was a black-and-white movie.

What inna namea—the g-forces were building up too fast! This wasn't the way it happened on the centrifuge! The g-forces were coming up so fast, driving him back so deep into his seat, he knew he couldn't complete the maneuvers he was supposed to make on the fly-by-wire system. Whether he did them or not on this flight would make no difference as far as his own safety was concerned. This was practice for orbital flights. In orbital flights the one thing the astronaut would be able to *do* would be to hold the capsule at the proper attitude, the proper angles, if the automatic system malfunctioned. Nevertheless—he was behind on the checklist! *Falling behind* put you on the threshold of *fucking up* . . . Soon he wouldn't be able to control the capsule's attitude with the manual controls or the fly-by-wire. The g-forces would be too severe for him to use his arms. So he switched back to automatic, forgetting to shut off one of the manual buttons when he did so . . . He was behind on the checklist! The simulation had crossed him up! He was supposed to have more time than this! He was in no danger whatsoever—but how could real life vary this much from the simulation! Looking for those motherless *stars* and *color bands* had thrown him off!—eaten up time! But even so, the buildup of the g-forces came smoothly. The capsule began to swing from side to side as it came through the denser and denser layers of atmosphere, but it was not nearly as rough a ride as the same interval in the centrifuge. He was lying on his back again. If he looked up, he looked straight toward the sky. He tensed his calves and the muscles of his abdomen to counter-act the g-forces . . . just as he had a thousand times on the centrifuge . . . He forced his breath out in grunts as the g's pressed down on his chest . . . He grunted out the g readings as they rose on the dial . . . "Uhhsix . . . uh seven . . . uhh eight . . . unhh nine . . ." Then he kept repeating, kept grunting out the word "Ohhkay . . . Ohhkay . . . Ohhkay . . . Ohhkay . . . Ohhkay . . . Ohhkay . . . Ohhkay" . . . to let the ground know that the g-forces were on top of him but that he was all right. He could see nothing except indigo out the portholes. He didn't even bother looking. He kept staring at the instrument panel at the big lights that would show the parachutes were coming out. They would come out automatically. The first green light came on. The drogue chute, the parachute that pulled the main chute out, had deployed. Now Shepard could see it through the periscope. He could see the needle pass 20,000 on his altimeter. *Why doesn't it*—At 10,000 feet the main chute came out, as he could see through the periscope. Then it filled and the jolt slammed him back into his seat once more. *A kick in the butt! For reassurance!* He knew he had it made. The capsule swayed from side to side under the parachute, but there was nothing to it. He was lying on his back. The landing bag was right underneath his back. He started undoing his knee straps. Get out of all these goddamned straps, hoses, and wires. That was the main thing. He took his face seal hose and oxygen exhaust hoses off his helmet. Through the periscope he could see he was coming closer and closer to the water. It was sunny out there. He was near Bermuda. The ships were all nearby. He could hear them clearly on the radio. Then the blunt end of the capsule hit the water. It was right under his back. The impact drove him back into his seat yet again. *It was just like they said it would be!* It was about the same jolt you get when you land on the deck of an aircraft carrier. No more than that. The capsule keeled over to the right. The right-hand window was underwater. But he could look out the other one and see his yellow dye marker on the surface of the water. It was released automatically. It made a big yellow stain, so that the rescue helicopters could spot the capsule better. Shepard was busy trying to get himself out of the rest of the rig. *Get free!* He broke the neck ring seal off his helmet so that he could get the helmet off. He kept looking at the window that was underwater. The capsule was supposed to right itself. The goddamned window stayed underwater. Gurgling! He kept looking all around it for signs of water seeping in. He couldn't see any but he could hear it. It had finally started seeping in on the ape's flight. The goddamned capsule was not made for the water. What a way to blow the whole thing this would be. Bobbing around in the goddamned water in a bucket. The capsule slowly came up vertical. The helicopter was already overhead radioing for instructions. He had it made as long as he didn't fuck it up getting out of the capsule. He opened the door at the top of the capsule, the neck, with a cable device and pulled himself up. A tremendous burst of sunlight hit him, sunlight on the open sea. It was barely quarter of ten in the morning. He was forty miles from Bermuda on a sunny day out in the Atlantic. The noise of the helicopter overhead obliterated every other sound. The crewmen were lowering a rescue sling, which looked like an old-fashioned horse collar, the kind they used to put on dray horses. It was a big helicopter, an industrial type. It had already hooked onto the capsule and pulled it up out of the water. There were some Marine Corps crewmen inside the helicopter. The noise was overwhelming. They kept staring at him and smiling. It was that glistening look.

It took only seven minutes to reach the helicopter's mother ship, the aircraft carrier *Lake Champlain*. The capsule swayed back and forth below the helicopter. It was very sunny. It was a perfect day in May out near Bermuda. The helicopter began descending to the flight deck of the carrier. Shepard looked down and he could see hundreds of faces. They were all looking up toward the helicopter. The entire crew of the ship seemed to be on the deck. Their faces were all turned up toward him in the sunlight. Hundreds of faces turned up in the sun. They covered the whole aft section of the deck. They were massed in between the moored airplanes. They were all looking up toward the helicopter and moving, surging toward the spot where the helicopter would come down. He could make out a whole force of masters-at-arms down there trying to hold them back behind the ropes. As the helicopter came close to the deck, he could see the faces more clearly, and they had that look. Hundreds of faces already had that glistening look.

11

THE UNSCREWABLE POOCH

GLENN AND THE OTHERS now watched from the sidelines as Al Shepard was hoisted out of their midst and installed as a national hero on the order of a Lindbergh. That was the way it looked. As soon as his technical debriefings had been completed, Shepard was flown straight from Grand Bahama Island to Washington. The next day the six also-rans joined him there. They stood by as President Kennedy gave Al the Distinguished Service Medal in a ceremony in the Rose Garden of the White House. Then they followed in his wake as Al sat up on the back of an open limousine waving to the crowds along Constitution Avenue. Tens of thousands of people had turned out to watch the motorcade, even though it had been arranged with barely twenty-four hours' notice. They were screaming to Al, reaching out, crying, awash with awe and gratitude. It took the motorcade half an hour to travel the one mile from the White House to the Capitol. Al sometimes seemed to have transistors in his solar plexus. But not now; now he seemed truly moved. They adored him. He was on . . . the Pope's balcony . . . Thirty minutes of it . . . The next day New York City gave Al a ticker-tape parade up Broadway. There was Al on the back ledge of the limousine, with all that paper snow and confetti coming down, just the way you used to see it in the Movietone News in the theaters. Al's hometown, Derry, New Hampshire, which was not much more than a village, gave Al a parade, and it drew the biggest crowd the state had ever seen. Army, Navy, Marine, Air Force, and National Guard troops from all over New England marched down Main Street, and aerobatic teams of jet fighters flew overhead. The politicians thought New Hampshire was entering Metro Heaven and came close to renaming Derry "Spacetown U.S.A." before they got hold of themselves. In the town of Deerfield, Illinois, a new school was named for Al, overnight, just like that. Then Al started getting tons of greeting cards in the mail, cards saying "Congratulations to Alan Shepard, Our First Man in Space!" That was already printed on the cards, along with NASA's address. All the buyers had to do was sign them and mail them. The card companies were cranking these things out. Al was that much of a hero.

Next to Gagarin's orbital flight, Shepard's little mortar lob to Bermuda, with its mere five minutes of weightlessness, was no great accomplishment. But that didn't matter. The flight had unfolded like a drama, the first drama of *single combat* in American history. Shepard had been the tiny underdog, sitting on top of an American rocket—*and our rockets always blow up*—challenging the omnipotent Soviet Integral. The fact that the entire thing had been televised, starting a good two hours before the lift-off, had generated the most feverish suspense. And then he had gone through with it. He let them light the fuse. *He hadn't resigned.* He hadn't even panicked. He handled himself perfectly. He was as great a daredevil as Lindbergh, and he was purer: he did it all for his country. Here was a man . . . with the right stuff. No one spoke the phrase—but every man could feel the rays from that righteous aura and that primal force, the power of physical courage and manly honor.

Even Shorty Powers became famous. "The voice of Mercury Control," he was called; that, and "the eighth astronaut." Powers was a light colonel in the Air Force, a onetime bomber pilot, and all during Shepard's flight he had come on the air from the flight control center at the Cape saying, "This is Mercury Control . . ." and reporting the astronaut's progress with a baritone coolness of the combat pilot's righteous sort, and people loved it. After the capsule splashed down, Powers had quoted, or seemed to have quoted, Shepard as saying everything was "A-Okay." In fact, this was a Shorty Powers paraphrase borrowed from NASA engineers who used to say it during radio transmission tests because the sharper sound of A cut through the static better than O. Nevertheless, "A-Okay" became shorthand for Shepard's triumph over the odds and for astronaut coolness under stress, and Shorty Powers was looked up to as the medium who communicated across the gulf between ordinary people and star voyagers with the right stuff.

Bob Gilruth's status rose sharply, too. After a solid year of flak and grief, Gilruth had finally earned the eminence of riding in one of the limousines in Shepard's triumphal motorcade through Washington. James E. Webb was sitting next to him, and they were looking out at the thousands of people who were smiling and crying and waving and cheering and taking pictures. "If it hadn't worked," said Webb, "they'd be asking for your head." As it was, Gilruth and Mercury and NASA were, all at once, names that stood for American technological competence. *(Our boys no longer botch it and our rockets don't blow up.)*

None of this was lost on the President. His opinion of NASA had now swung around 180 degrees. Webb was aware of that. Three weeks before, after Gagarin's flight, when Kennedy had summoned Webb and Dryden to the White House, the President had been in a funk. He was convinced that the entire world was judging the United States and his leadership in terms of the space race with the Soviets. He was muttering, "If somebody can just tell me how to catch up. Let's find somebody—anybody . . . There's nothing more important." He kept saying, "We've got to catch up." *Catching up* became an obsession. Finally, Dryden told him that it looked hopeless to try to catch up with the mighty Integral in anything that involved flights in earth orbit. The one possibility was to start a program to put a man on the moon within the next ten years. It would require a crash effort on the scale of the Manhattan Project of the Second World War and would cost anywhere from twenty to forty billion dollars. Kennedy found the figure appalling. Less than a week later, of course, the Bay of Pigs debacle had occurred, and now his "new frontier" looked more like a retreat on all fronts. Shepard's successful flight was the first hopeful note Kennedy had enjoyed since then. For the first time he had some confidence in NASA. And the tremendous public response to Shepard as the patriotic daredevil, challenging the Soviets in the heavens, gave Kennedy an inspiration.

One morning Kennedy asked Dryden, Webb, and Gilruth to come to the White House. They sat down in the Oval Office, and Kennedy said: "All over the world we're judged by how well we do in space. Therefore, we've got to be first. That's all there is to it." After this buildup Gilruth figured Kennedy was going to tell them to cut the Redstone suborbital flights short and move straight to the series of orbital flights using the Atlas rocket. They were still considering six and possibly ten more suborbital flights, like Shepard's, using the Redstone rocket. Gilruth had thought of moving straight to the orbital flights, although it was a daring proposition, given the problems they had been having on tests of the Mercury-Atlas system. So they were all absolutely startled when Kennedy said: "I want you to start on the moon program. I'm going to ask Congress for the money. I'm going to tell them you're going to put a man on the moon by 1970."

On May 25, twenty days after Shepard's flight, Kennedy appeared before Congress to deliver a message on "urgent national needs." This was, in fact, the beginning of his political comeback from the Bay of Pigs disaster. It was as if he were starting his administration over and delivering a new inaugural address.

"Now is the time to take longer strides," he said, "time for a great new American enterprise, time for this nation to take a clearly leading role in space achievement, which in many ways may hold the key to our future on earth." He said that the Russians, thanks to "their large rocket engines," would continue to dominate the competition for some time, but that this should only make the United States step up its efforts. "For while we cannot guarantee that we shall one day be first, we can guarantee that any failure to make this effort will make us last. We take an additional risk by making it in full view of the world; but as shown by the feat of Astronaut Shepard, this very risk enhances our stature when we are successful." Then he said: "I believe this nation should commit itself to achieving the goal, before this decade is out, of landing a man on the moon and returning him safely to the earth. No single space project in this period will be more impressive to mankind or more important for the long-range exploration of space; and none will be so difficult or expensive to accomplish."

Congress was not about to quibble over expenses. NASA was given a $1.7 billion budget for the next year, and that was merely the start. It was made clear that NASA could have practically as much as it wanted. Shepard's flight had made quite a hit. An amazing period of "budgetless financing" began. It was astonishing. Suddenly money was in the air. Businessmen of all sorts were trying to bestow it directly upon Shepard. Within a few months Leo DeOrsey, who was still the boys' unpaid business manager, had counted up half a million dollars' worth of proposals from companies who wanted Shepard to endorse products. One congressman, Frank Boykin of Alabama, wanted the government to give Shepard a house. Shepard turned it all down, but it did make one stop and think.

If Smilin' Al's experience was any indication, then this astronaut business was becoming even more of a Fighter Jock Heaven than it had been in the first year of Project Mercury. Eisenhower had never paid much attention to the astronauts personally. He had looked upon them as military volunteers for an experiment,

and that was that. But Kennedy now made them an integral part of his Administration and included them in its social as well as its official life.

The other fellows had gone along for Al's trip to the White House, but the
wives had remained at the Cape. When they flew back down to Patrick, the wives
were out at the field to meet their plane. And they all had a single question:
"What's Jackie like?"

Jackie Kennedy's exotic face and Sixth Floor Designer Collection clothes
were in every magazine . . . They all had a curious sensation. In one corner of
their souls they were still junior-level military officers & wives who saw people
like Jackie Kennedy only on the pages of magazines and newspapers. And at the
same time they were beginning to realize that they were part of the strange world
where Those People, the people who do things and run things, actually exist.

"What's Jackie like?"

Soon enough they would all meet her. They would go to private lunches at
the White House, where there were so many servants there seemed to be one
behind every chair. They played you like man-to-man basketball. Jack Kennedy
was very warm toward the fellows. He courted them. That glistening look would
come over his face from time to time. The business of *manly honor* cut through
everything at last, and even the President would become merely another awed
male in the presence of the right stuff. As for Jackie, she had a certain Southern
smile, which she had perhaps picked up at Foxcroft School, in Virginia, and her
quiet voice, which came through her teeth, as revealed by the smile. She barely
moved her lower jaw when she talked. The words seemed to slip between her
teeth like exceedingly small slippery pearls. Her excitement, if any, over the
prospect of lunch with seven pilots and their fraus may not have been great. But
she couldn't have been kinder or more attentive. At one point she invited Rene
Carpenter back for a private visit, and they talked like any two friends, about all
sorts of things, including the problems of raising children in the modern age. One
had only to think of any other seven pilots' wives in a squadron . . . All of a
sudden the Honorable Mrs. Astronaut existed on a plateau, upon the upper
reaches of American protocol, where the perquisites included *Jackie Kennedy*.

And for the fellows, it was pure heaven. None of this altered the Edwards-
style perfection of their lives. It merely added something new and marvelous to
the ineffable contrasts of this astronaut business. Within hours after lunch at the
White House or waterskiing in Hyannis Port you could be back at the Cape, back
Drinking & Driving in that marvelous Low Rent rat-shack terrain, back in your
Corvette spinning out on the shoulders of those hardtrack Baptist roadways and
pulling into the all-night diner for a little coffee to stabilize the system for the
proficiency runs ahead. And if you had switched to your Ban-Lon shirts and your
go-to-hell pants, they might not even recognize you in there, which would be all
the better, and you could just sit there and drink coffee and have a couple of
cigarettes and listen to the two policemen in the next booth with the Dawn
Patrol radio sets in their pockets, and a little voice packed in static would be
coming out of the radios saying, "Thirty-one, thirty-one [garble, garble] . . .
man named Virgil Wiley refuses to return to his room at the Rio Banana," and
the policemen would look at each other as if to say, "Well, shit, is that anything
to have to rise up from over a plate of french fries and death balls for?"—and then
they'd sigh and start getting up and buckling on their gunbelts, and about the
time they would head out the door, in would come the Hardiest Cracker, the

Aboriginal Grit, an old guy drunk as a monkey and ricocheting off the doorframe and sliding in bowlegged over a counter stool and saying to the waitress:

"How you doing?"

And she says: "So-so, how you doing?"

"I ain't doing any more," he says. "It's dragging in the mud and it won't come up"—and since this doesn't get a rise out of her, he says it again: "It's dragging in the mud and it won't come up," and she just clamps a burglar-proof look of aloofness across her face—and all this was bound to make you smile, because here you were, listening to the merry midnight small talk of the hardiest hardtack crackers of the most Low Rent stretch of the Cape, and just twelve hours ago you were leaning across a table in the White House, straining to catch the tiny shiny pearls of tinytalk from the most famous small talker in the world—and somehow you belonged and thrived in both worlds. Oh, yes, it was the perfect balance of the legendary Edwards, the fabled Muroc, in the original Chuck Yeager and Pancho Barnes days . . . now brought forward into the billion-volt limitless-budget future.

THE TRUTH WAS that the fellows had now become the personal symbols not only of America's Cold War struggle with the Soviets but also of Kennedy's own political comeback. They had become *the* pioneers of the New Frontier, recycled version. They were the intrepid scouts in Jack Kennedy's race to beat the mighty Integral to the moon. There was no way they could be regarded as ordinary test pilots, much less test subjects, ever again.

For Gus Grissom that was a very fortunate thing.

Gus was assigned to the second Mercury-Redstone flight, scheduled for July. He would be in a newer capsule, one in which certain changes had been made— all of them in response to the astronauts' insistence that the astronaut function more like a pilot. It had been too late to renovate the capsule Shepard used, but Grissom's had a window, not just portholes, and a new set of hand controllers designed to let the astronaut control the capsule's attitude in a manner that was more like an aircraft pilot's, and a hatch with a set of explosive bolts that the astronaut could blow in order to get out of the capsule after the splashdown. Nevertheless, the flight would be a repetition of Shepard's, a suborbital lob three hundred miles out into the Atlantic. Gus himself encouraged certain changes in the flight plan. Since he would be taking the next flight, he had sat in on Shepard's debriefing sessions on Grand Bahama Island. Nobody, not even within NASA, was about to criticize Al openly for anything he did, but there was implied criticism of what he did toward the end of the flight when the g-forces built up faster than he expected them to and he was desperately staring out of his two portholes trying to find some stars. Some character from the Flight Systems Division kept asking him if he hadn't left a manual control button on after he shifted over to automatic control. This would have wasted hydrogen peroxide, the fuel that operated the attitude-control jets. It didn't particularly matter on a fifteen-minute suborbital flight, but it could have made a difference if it had been an orbital flight. Al kept saying he didn't think he had left the button on but he really couldn't say for sure. And this character kept coming back in and asking the question all over again. This was the first indication that the fellows had about a major truth concerning space flights. You didn't "take" the capsule off the ground, you didn't bring it up to altitude, you didn't alter its course, and you didn't land it; i.e., you didn't *fly* it—and so your performance was not going to be rated on how well you *flew* the craft, as it would be in flight test or combat. You could be rated only on how well you covered the items on your checklist. Therefore, the fewer items you had on your checklist, the better shot you had at a "perfect" flight. Each flight was so expensive there would always be people on the ground—engineers, doctors, and scientists—who wanted to load up your checklist with all sorts of things to try, their little "experiments." The way you handled this problem was to allow "operational" items on your list and growl, gruff, and otherwise balk over the rest. Testing the attitude-control system was acceptable, because that had "operational" written all over it. That was *like* flying an airplane. By the time he took off, Gus's checklist had been pared down to the point where he could concentrate on the new hand controller that had been installed.

G US STAYED AT THE HOLIDAY INN until practically the day before his flight, maintaining an even strain. He cut down a little on the waterskiing, which was his main form of exercise, and on the nocturnal proficiency runs on the highways, in order to avoid getting banged up on the eve of the flight, but otherwise life went on pretty much as usual at the Cape, here in Fighter Jock Heaven.

One night just before the flight, when he was in the cocktail lounge evening out the strain a bit, who should Gus run into but Joe Walker. NASA had given Joe a few days off from Edwards to attend the launch, and so here he was. By this time, July of 1961, Walker and Bob White had been flying up a storm in the X-15. In April, White had set a new speed record of Mach 4.62, which was just over 3,000 miles an hour, and in May Joe Walker had topped that by going Mach 4.95, and White had come right back in June and flown Mach 5.27. The X-15 now had the Big Engine, the XLR-99, with its 57,000 pounds of thrust. The True Brothers were ready to go all-out toward their goal of exceeding Mach 6 and an altitude of more than fifty miles . . . in *piloted* flight. *Piloted!* These developments could be found in the press . . . if one cared to look for them . . . but they were obscured by Gagarin's flight, followed by Shepard's flight . . . the single combat for the heavens. As a matter of fact, Joe Walker had taken the X-15 to Mach 4.95, the highest speed in the history of aviation, on the same day that Kennedy addressed Congress to propose the race for the moon . . . Next to the notion of a moon voyage Walker's Mach 4.95 was pretty pedestrian stuff. But surely the truth would dawn on them eventually! It was with that in mind . . . the simple truth! . . . that Joe Walker happened to run into Gus Grissom at the Holiday Inn's cocktail lounge.

Both Gus and Joe had knocked back a few, it being after dark, after all, and Joe starts in with a little Yeager-style country-boy banter about how Gus and his pals had better hurry up or him and his boys would pass them on the way up. Oh, yeah, says Gus, how's that? Well, says Joe Walker, we've got a 57,000-pound rocket engine now, and the Redstone that shoots your little peapod up there only puts out 78,000, so we're almost up with you—and we *fly* the damn thing. We actually *fly* it and we *land* it. Joe Walker meant to keep it light and just rag Grissom a little bit, but he couldn't hold back a note in his voice concerning where things actually stood in the true scheme of things, on the *real* pyramid of flying competition. Everybody is looking at Grissom, the astronaut, to see what he's going to say. Grissom, who is a tough little nut when he wants to be, stares at Walker . . . and then he breaks into a grin and starts a kind of gruff-gus chuckle. Oh, I'll be looking over my shoulder the whole time, Joe, and if you come by, I swear I'll wave.

And so much for Joe Walker and the True Brothers! It was all right there in that scene, the *new* simple truth. Grissom didn't even *feel* angry. There was nothing that Joe Walker could say or do—and nothing that even Chuck Yeager himself could say or do—that would change the new order. The astronaut was now at the apex of the pyramid. The rocket pilots were already . . . the old guys, the eternal remember-whens . . . Oh, it didn't even have to be *said!* It was in the air, and everyone knew it. Hell, when they started flying jets and rocket planes at Muroc, somewhere there must have been the old guys, the bitter old bastards, the remember-whens, who could just fly the hell out of a propeller plane and were still insisting that that was what it was all about. Flying wasn't a competition like baseball or football. No, in flying any major advance in technology could change the rules. The Mercury rocket-capsule system—the word "system" was now on everybody's lips—was the new cutting edge. No, Gus had no need to get excited any more over Joe Walker or anybody else at Edwards.

Gus seemed like a pretty relaxed man all the way around. He would get a little irritated at the engineering sessions he sat in on during the last couple of weeks before the flight and would give them a few gus-gruff growls if they seemed to want to tinker with this and that at the last minute, but that seemed to be sheer eagerness to get on with the flight. There was even a bit of the old boondock Edwards broomstick-and-baling wire spirit about the whole thing. Just two nights before the flight it dawned on one of the doctors that they had never made provisions for a urine receptacle for Gus, to avoid the sort of thing Shepard had experienced. That was a hell of a note. They figured they could make do with an ordinary rubber condom for the receptacle. But what would hold it in place and keep it from coming off? Dee O'Hara, the nurse, helped out. She drove into Cocoa Beach and bought a panty girdle, and they rigged that up with the condom. The goddamned girdle gave you a hell of a tight grip on the groin, but Gus figured he could get by with it. All in all, he seemed pretty loose, a test pilot of the old school. He even had a foretaste of the mental atmosphere of the real thing, just as Shepard had. On July 19 he was inserted into the capsule, and the hatch was sealed, when the flight was canceled because of bad weather. The flight finally took place on July 21. Judging by his pulse rate and respiration, which was transmitted via his body sensors, Gus was more nervous than Shepard during the countdown. These rates, taken by themselves, didn't mean a great deal, however, and no one would have thought twice about it except for what happened at the end of the flight. The flight itself was very nearly a duplicate of Shepard's, except that Grissom's capsule had a window, not just a periscope, giving him a much better view of the world, and he had a more sophisticated hand controller. His pulse stayed up around 150 throughout the five minutes he was weightless— Shepard's pulse had never reached 140, not even during lift-off—and went up to 171 during the firing of the retro-rockets before the re-entry through the earth's atmosphere. The informal consensus among the program's doctors was that if an astronaut's pulse rate went above 180, the mission should be aborted. The capsule splashed down almost precisely on target, just as Shepard's had, within three miles of the recovery ship, the carrier *Randolph*. The capsule hit the water, then keeled over on one side, just as Shepard's had, and took its own sweet time righting itself. Grissom thought he heard a gurgling noise inside the capsule—as had Shepard—and began looking for water seeping in, but didn't see any. The recovery helicopter, designated Hunt Club 1, was over the capsule within less than two minutes. Grissom was still in the seat, resting on his back, as he had been at the outset of the flight, and the capsule was bobbing around in the water.

Over his microphone Grissom said, "Okay, give me how much longer it'll be before you get here."

The helicopter pilot, a Navy lieutenant named James Lewis, said: "This is Hunt Club 1. We are in orbit now at this time, around the capsule."

Grissom said, "Roger, give me about another five minutes here, to mark these switch positions here, before I give you a call to come in and hook on. Are you ready to come in and hook on any time?"

Lewis said, "Hunt Club 1, roger, we are ready any time you are."

There was a chart on which the astronaut was supposed to record the switch positions (on or off) with a grease pencil.

Five and a half minutes later Grissom radioed Lewis in the helicopter again: "Okay, Hunt Club, this is Liberty Bell. Are you ready for the pickup?"

Lewis said, "This is Hunt Club 1, this is affirmative."

Grissom said, "Okay, latch on, then give me a call and I'll power down and blow the hatch, okay?"

"This is Hunt Club 1, roger, will give you a call when we're ready for you to blow."

Grissom said, "Roger, I've unplugged my suit so I'm kinda warm now . . . so . . ."

Lewis said, "One, roger."

"One, roger."

"Now if you tell me to, ah, you're ready for me to blow, I'll have to take my helmet off, power down, and then blow the hatch."

"One, roger, and when you blow the hatch, the collar will already be down there waiting for you, and we're turning base at this time."

"Ah, roger."

As the helicopter pilot, Lewis, looked down on the capsule, it shaped up as a routine retrieval, such as he and his co-pilot, Lieutenant John Reinhard, had practiced many times. Reinhard had a pole with a hook on it, like a shepherd's crook, that he was going to slip through a loop at the neck of the capsule. The crook was attached to a cable. The helicopter could hoist up to 4,000 pounds in this fashion; the capsule weighed about 2,400 pounds. Lewis had swung out and was making a low pass toward the capsule when suddenly he saw the capsule's side hatch go flying off into the water. But Grissom wasn't supposed to blow the hatch until he told him he had hooked on! And Grissom—there was Grissom scrambling out of the hatch and plopping into the water without even looking up at him. Grissom was swimming like mad. Water was pouring into the capsule through the hatch and the damned thing was sinking! Lewis wasn't worried about Grissom, because he had practiced water egress with the astronauts many times and he knew their pressure suits were more buoyant than any life preserver. They even seemed to enjoy playing around in the water in the suits. So he gunned the helicopter down to the level of the water to try to snare the capsule. By now only the neck of the thing is visible above the water. Reinhard goes to work with the shepherd's crook, leaning out of the helicopter, desperately trying to hook on. He finally hooks on, as the capsule disappears under the water and starts sinking like a brick. Lewis is now down so low all three wheels of the helicopter are in the water. The helicopter is like a fat man squatting over a tree stump, trying to pull it out of the ground. Full of water, as it is, the capsule weighs 5,000 pounds, 1,000 over the helicopter's capacity. Lewis already has a red-light warning of impending engine failure—so he signals for a second helicopter, which is already nearby, to pick up Grissom. He finally pulls the capsule up out of the water, but he can't make the helicopter move forward toward the carrier. He's just hanging there in the air like a hummingbird. Red lights are lighting up all over the panel. He's about to lose the ship as well as the capsule. So he cuts the capsule loose. It drops and disappears forever. The water is three miles deep at that point.

They turn away finally. Grissom is still in the water. He's waving. He seems to be saying, "I'm okay." The second helicopter is moving in to lower the horse collar.

In fact, Gus's waves were saying, "I'm drowning!—you bastards—I'm drowning!"

As soon as Gus scrambled out of the hatch, he had begun swimming for his life. The goddamned capsule's going under! His suit caught momentarily on some sort of strap outside the capsule, probably leading to the dye canister. It was like a parachute!—it would pull him under!—He'd drown! The drowning man . . . No question about it . . . By this point he was neither an astronaut nor a pilot. He was the drowning man. Get away from the death capsule!—that was the idea. Then he calmed down a little. He was swimming around in the ocean under the roar of the helicopter blades. He wasn't sinking, after all. The pressure suit kept him bobbing in the water, as high as his armpits. He looked up. The horse collar was hanging out of the helicopter. The horse collar that gets him out of this! But they were pulling away from him!—they were going to the capsule! He could see the man named Reinhard leaning out of the helicopter trying to snag the loop of the capsule. Only the neck of the capsule was out of the water. He started swimming back to the capsule. It was hard swimming in the pressure suit, but it kept him up. He bobbed right up to his armpits when he stopped swimming. Little swells kept breaking over his head and he swallowed some water. He felt out of control. He was floundering around in the middle of the ocean. He looked up again and there was another helicopter. He kept waving and waving, but nobody seemed to pay any attention. And now he wasn't bobbing up so high any more. The pressure suit was losing its buoyancy. It was getting heavier . . . starting to drag him down . . . The suit had a rubber diaphragm that rolled up around his neck like a turtleneck sweater to keep the water from seeping down inside the suit. It didn't fit tight enough . . . air was escaping . . . No!—it was the oxygen inlet valve! He had completely forgotten! The valve allowed oxygen into his suit while he was in flight. He had unhooked the tube but forgotten to close the valve. The oxygen was bubbling out down there somewhere . . . the suit was becoming dead weight, pulling him down . . . He reached down and closed the valve underwater . . . But now his head kept going under and he had to fight to get to the surface and then the swells broke over his head and he swallowed more water and he'd look up at the helicopters and wave and they'd just wave back—the bastards!—how could they not know! In the window of one of the helicopters was a man with a camera, merrily taking pictures of him—they were waving and taking snapshots! The stupid bastards! They were going crazy over the goddamned capsule and he was drowning before their very eyes . . . He kept going under. He'd fight his way back up and swallow some more water and wave. But that drove him back under. The suit—he seemed to be packed in two hundred pounds of wet clay . . . The *dimes!*—and all that other shit! Christ, the dimes and those goddamned trinkets! Down there in his knee pocket . . . He'd had the bright idea of carrying a hundred one-dollar bills on the flight as souvenirs, but he didn't have a spare hundred dollars to his name—so he decided on two rolls of fifty dimes each—and he had put in three one-dollar bills for good measure and a whole bunch of little models of the capsule—and now this big junkheap of travel sentiment stuffed in his knee pocket was taking him under . . . *Dimes!* . . . *Silver deadweight!*

Deke! . . . Where was Deke! . . . Surely Deke would be here! . . . He had done as much for Deke. Somehow Deke would materialize and save him. Deke and Wally and him had been down at Pensacola practicing water egress, and somehow Deke, in his whole pressure suit, with his helmet on, had fallen off his raft and was going under and couldn't do a goddamn thing about it, but he and Wally had been nearby with their swimming flippers on, and they had swum straight to him and held him up until one of the Navy swabbos could reach them with the raft, and it was no sweat, because they had been by his side, and surely . . . *Deke!* . . . *Or somebody! Deke!*

Cox . . . That face up there!—it's Cox . . . Deke wasn't here and wasn't going to be here. But Cox!—Cox, whom he hardly knew, was his sole redeemer now. Cox was a Navy man in the second helicopter. Gus knew that face. Cox wasn't a stupid bastard. Cox had picked up Al Shepard! Cox had picked up the goddamned chimpanzee! Cox knew how to get people out of here! . . . *Cox!* . . . He could see Cox leaning out of the helicopter lowering the horse collar. There was a hell of a roar everywhere from the two helicopters. But Cox! Cox and his helicopter were just suspended there. They weren't coming any closer, and Gus's head kept going under. The wash from the helicopter propellers was driving him back. The closer his redeemer came in the helicopter, the farther he was driven back. *The sharks—they can smell panic!* And he was sheer panic, 160 pounds of it, plus a hundred pounds of death dimes! Lost at last at 2,800 fathoms in the middle of the Atlantic Ocean! But helicopters can drive off sharks with their prop wash! Cox would rout the sharks and save him—but Cox got no closer, even though the horse collar was now touching the water. He was still about ninety feet away, across the billows. Now he could see it, now he couldn't. The swells kept washing over him. But it was the only thing left. He swam for it. He couldn't get his legs to come up. So he fought toward the horse collar with his arms. He had no strength left. Everything pulled him down. He couldn't get enough breath. There was nothing but furious noise . . . blazing water . . . The water kept getting in his mouth. He would never make it. But the horse collar! Cox was up there! There was the horse collar. It was in front of him. He grabbed it and hung on. He was supposed to sit in it as if he were sitting on a swing. The hell with that. He flopped through the hole like a dead flounder landing on the fish-market scales. He hung on with his arms. He felt as if he weighed a ton. The suit was full of water. And it had already dawned on him: *I lost the capsule.*

As soon as Cox and his co-pilot pulled Grissom up into the helicopter, they could see that he was in a bad way. He looked funny. He was gasping for breath and he was shaking. His eyes kept darting around. He found what he was looking for: a Mae West, a life preserver. He grabbed it and started trying to strap it on. He was having a hell of a time with it because he was shaking so. His arms would fly one way and the straps would fly the other. The engines made a terrific noise. They were heading back to the carrier. Grissom was still struggling with the straps. He obviously thought they were going to crash at any moment. He thought he was going to drown. He gasped. He battled the Mae West all the way back to the carrier. What the hell had happened to the man? First he had blown the hatch before the lead helicopter could hook on and then he had floundered around out in the ocean and now he was preparing to abandon ship in a god-damned helicopter on a perfectly calm sunny morning out near Bermuda.

Once they got over the carrier *Randolph*, Grissom calmed down a bit. The same sort of awed faces that had welcomed Alan Shepard were craning up at the helicopter. But Grissom hardly noticed them. His head was in a very dark cloud.

When he went below deck, he was still shaking. He kept saying, "I didn't do anything. The damned thing just blew."

Within an hour they had started the preliminary debriefing, and Grissom kept saying, "I didn't do anything, I was just lying there—and it just blew."

A couple of hours later, at the formal debriefing on Grand Bahama Island, Grissom was much calmer, although he looked exhausted and drawn. He was grim. He was a very unhappy man. His pulse was still up to 90. Normally, at rest, it was 68 or 69. He kept saying, "I didn't touch it, I was just lying there—and it blew."

According to Gus, here was what happened. Once he knew the helicopters were nearby, he felt secure in the capsule and therefore asked for five minutes to finish getting unhooked and record his switch positions. While the capsule was still descending under the parachute, he had opened his face plate and disconnected the visor seal hose. Once the capsule was in the water, he disconnected the oxygen hose to his helmet, unfastened the helmet from the pressure suit, undid his chest strap, lap belt, shoulder harness, and knee straps, disconnected the wire leading to the biomedical sensors, and rolled the rubber neck dam up around his neck. His pressure suit was still attached to the capsule by the oxygen inlet hose, which he needed for cooling the suit, and his helmet still had its radio wiring leads hooked up; but all he had to do was take the helmet off and he would be free of the wires. Then—all in keeping with the checklist—he removed the emergency knife that was clamped onto the hatch and put it in the survival kit, which was a canvas bag about two feet long containing an inflatable life raft, shark repellant, a desalinization rig, food, a signal light, and so on. Before leaving the capsule via the hatch, as Gus recounted it, he had one more chore to perform. He was supposed to take out a chart and a grease pencil and mark the positions of all the switches on the instrument panel. Since he still had on his pressure-suit gloves, making it hard to grip the grease pencil, this took him three or four minutes. Then he armed the explosive hatch by removing the cover from the detonator, which was a button about three inches in diameter, and removed the safety pin, which was like the safety catch on a revolver. Once the cover and pin were removed, five pounds of pressure on the detonator button would blow the bolts and propel the hatch out into the water. Now he radioed Lewis in the helicopter to come in and hook on. He unhooked the oxygen hose to his pressure suit and settled back on the seat and waited for Lewis to tell him he had hooked on to the capsule. Once he got the word from Lewis, he would blow the hatch. While he was lying there, he said, he started wondering if there were some way he could retrieve the knife from the survival kit before he blew the hatch and left the capsule. He figured it would make a terrific souvenir. This thought was running idly through his mind, he said, when he heard a dull thud. He knew immediately that it was the hatch blowing. In the next instant he was looking straight out the hatchway at the brilliant blue sky over the ocean, and water was pouring in. There was not even time to grapple for the survival kit. He took his helmet off and grabbed the right side of the instrument panel and thrust his head through the hatchway and wriggled out.

"I had the cap off and the safety pin out," Gus said, "but I don't think that I hit the button. The capsule was rocking around a little, but there weren't any loose items in the capsule, so I don't see how I could have hit it, but possibly I did."

As the day wore on, and the formal debriefing got underway, Gus discounted even the possibility that he had hit the button. "I was lying there, flat on my back —and it just blew."

Nobody was about to *accuse* Gus of anything, but the engineers kept rolling their eyes at each other. The explosive hatch was new to the Mercury capsule, but explosive hatches had been in use on jet fighters since the early 1950s. When a pilot pulled his cinch ring and ejected, the hatch blew and a TNT charge rocketed the pilot and his seat-parachute rig through the opening. The pilot and anyone who might be riding backseat routinely armed their hatches and the TNT charges out on the runway before takeoff. This was the equivalent of Gus's removing the detonator cover and the safety pin. No one had ever heard of a hatch "just blowing," even though the fighter planes went through violent maneuvers, pulled tremendous g-loads, flew weightless for brief intervals, and vibrated until you had nothing but shotgun vision left. The damned things had been wrung inside out, but never, so far as anyone could recall, had a single hatch ever "just blown."

Of course, any apparatus rigged up with explosive charges had the potential of exploding at the wrong time. Later on, NASA put a hatch assembly through every test the engineers could dream up to try to make the hatch blow without hitting the detonator button. They subjected it to trial by water, trial by heat; they shook it, pounded it, dropped it on concrete from a height of one hundred feet—and it never *just blew*.

There were many conjectures uttered very quietly, very privately.

And at Edwards . . . the True Brothers . . . well, my God, as you can imagine, they were . . . *laughing!* Naturally they couldn't say anything. But now —surely!—it was so obvious! Grissom had just screwed the pooch!

In flight test, if you did something that stupid, if you destroyed a major prototype through some lame-brain mistake such as hitting the wrong button— you were through! You'd be lucky to end up in Flight Engineering. Oh, it was obvious to everybody at Edwards that Grissom had just *fucked it,* screwed the pooch, that was all. It was doubtful that he had hit the detonator on purpose, because even if he were feeling a little panicky in the water (you have to be *afraid* to panic, old buddy), he wasn't likely to ask for trouble by blowing the hatch before the helicopter hooked on and was overhead with the horse collar. But if a man is beginning to panic, logic goes first. Maybe the poor bastard just wanted out, and—bango!—he punched the button. But what about the business of the knife? He said he wanted to take the knife as a souvenir. So he may have been trying to fish the knife out of the survival kit. The capsule is rocking in the swells . . . he bangs into the detonator—that's all it would have taken. Oh, there was no question that he had hit the damn button some way. The only thing they liked about his entire performance was the way he said, "I was lying there—and it just blew," and the way he stuck to it. There, Gus old boy, you showed the instincts of the true fighter jock! Oh, you learned many of the lessons well! After you've done some forbidden hassling and your ship flames out and you have to eject and your F-100F goes *kaboom!* on the desert floor . . . naturally you come back to base and say: "I don't know what happened, sir—it just flamed out on me!" I was minding my own business! The demons did it! And go easy on the details. A broad stroke of vagueness—that's the ticket.

"I was lying there—and it just blew" . . . oh, that was rich. And then the brethren sat back and waited for the Mercury astronaut to *get his*, the way any one of them would have *gotten his*, had a comparable *fuckup* occurred at Edwards.

And . . . nothing happened.

From first to last the publicity that came out of NASA, out of the White House, from wherever, told of what a severe disappointment it had been to brave little Gus to lose the capsule through a malfunction after so successful a flight. *Little* Gus he became. The sympathy that welled up was terrific. Only five feet six with a round face. It was amazing that so much courage could be packed into sixty-six inches. And we almost lost him through drowning.

The True Brothers were incredulous . . . the Mercury astronauts had an official immunity to three-fourths of the things by which test pilots were ordinarily judged. They were by now ablaze with the superstitious aura of the single-combat warrior. They were the heroes of Kennedy's political comeback, the updated new frontier whose symbol was a voyage to the moon. To announce that the second one, Gus Grissom, had prayed to the Lord: "Please, dear God, don't let me fuck up"—but that his prayer had not been answered, and the Lord let him *screw the pooch*—well, this was an interpretation of that event that was to be avoided at all cost. NASA was no more anxious to have to call Grissom on the carpet than Kennedy was. NASA had just been handed a *carte blanche* for a moon project. Just six months before, the organization had been in live danger of losing the space program altogether. So nothing about this flight was going to be called a failure. It was possible to argue that Grissom's flight had been a great success . . . There had just been a small problem immediately afterward. As for public opinion, the loss of the capsule didn't really matter very much. The fact that the engineers needed the capsule to study the effects of heat and stress and to retrieve various types of automatically recorded data—this certainly created no national gloom. Get the man up and bring him down alive; that, not engineering, was at the heart of the single combat. So the possibility that Gus might have blundered was never brought up again. Far from having a tarnished record, he was a hero. He had endured and overcome so much. He was back solidly in the rotation for whatever great flights might come up in the future . . . as if by magic.

In THE DAYS AFTER the flight Gus looked gloomier and gruffer than ever. He could manage an official smile when he had to and an official hero's wave, but the black cloud would not pass. Betty Grissom looked the same way after she and the two boys, Mark and Scott, joined Gus in Florida for the celebration. Some celebration . . . It was as if the event had been poisoned by the gus-grim little secret. Betty also had the sneaking suspicion that everyone was saying, just out of earshot: "Gus blew it." But her displeasure was a bit more subtle than Gus's. They . . . NASA, the White House, the Air Force, the other fellows, 'Gus himself . . . were not keeping their side of the compact! Nobody could have looked at Betty at that time . . . this pretty, shy, ever-silent, ever-proper Honorable Mrs. Astronaut . . . and guessed at her anger.

They were violating the Military Wife's Compact!

By now Betty knew what to expect from Gus personally; which is to say, she seldom saw him. In one 365-day period he had been with her a total of sixty days. About six months before, Betty had had to go into the hospital near Langley for exploratory surgery. There was a good chance that she would require a hysterectomy.

Betty had a real siege in the hospital. She was there for twenty-one days. She was there for so long she had to get some of her relatives to fly in from Indiana to look after the boys. Gus managed to make it to see her in the hospital exactly once and he didn't quite make it through the entire visiting hour. He got a call right there in the hospital asking him to return to the base, and he left.

Betty seldom speculated, even to herself, on what Gus did during the 80 percent of the year that he was not with her. She had worked that out in her mind. The compact took care of it. If Gus was occasionally the Complete Fighter Jock Away from Home, that did not violate the compact . . . And now it was time for the other part of the compact to take effect. It was her time to be the Honorable Mrs. Captain Second American in Space. They *owed her* every bit of it.

Louise Shepard, over in Virginia Beach, hadn't known what was going to happen when Al went up, and so her place was invaded by reporters and sightseers. They practically tore the yard to pieces just by milling around and tramping through the shrubbery to press their noses up against the window. Gus was not having any of that. Gus saw to it that the local police were out patrolling in front of the house early in the morning, before dawn. Betty was inside the house in front of the TV set with Rene Carpenter, Jo Schirra, Marge Slayton, the children. Outside slavered the Animal. There were a lot of reporters on the sidewalk and back in the driveway of the house next door, but the palace guard kept them all under control. Betty actually felt pretty good. It was the Danger Wake business again. She was the hostess and star of the drama. She almost missed the final countdown. She was in the kitchen turning off the flame under some soft-boiled eggs for somebody.

After the flight all sorts of neighbors and NASA people at Langley came rushing in, congratulating her and bringing more food and making a fuss over her. But Betty knew enough about flight tests to know that the loss of the capsule could have some grim results. A call came in from Gus on Grand Bahama Island. There were a lot of people still in the house, but she had to ask the question, anyway.

"You didn't do anything wrong, did you . . ."

"I did not do anything wrong," he said very slowly. You could almost see the black gus gruff look over the telephone. "That hatch just blew."

"I'm glad."

She started telling him about all the people who were telephoning congratulations.

"That's good," said Gus. "Say, by the way, the motel lost two pairs of my slacks in the laundry, and I need shirts. Will you bring me some when you come down to the Cape?"

The laundry? He wanted her to remember to bring the laundry.

Betty and the boys arrived at the Cape on one of those blinding hot July days that made all of Cocoa Beach feel like a fried concrete parking lot. They were led out to a runway at Patrick Air Force Base along with a lot of NASA and military dignitaries to meet Gus's plane as it came in from Grand Bahama Island. There was a big canopy set up nearby. Under the canopy there would be a press conference. Betty stood out there on the slab with James Webb and some other NASA brass, and she slowly began to realize that . . . *they were reneging!*

This was going to be it!—a reception out on this brainfrying slab! There was going to be no trip to the White House. Webb—not John Kennedy—was going to give Gus the Distinguished Service Medal . . . under a dreadful Low Rent tent here on the slab. There was going to be no parade in Washington, no ticker-tape parade in New York—not even a parade in Mitchell, Indiana. *That* . . . Betty would have loved. To come back to Mitchell and parade down Main Street . . . But Gus would be getting nothing, just a medal from James E. Webb. They couldn't do this to her!—they were reneging.

But they did, and it was even worse than she feared. The plane comes in, taxis up to the ramp, a big cheer goes up, Gus steps out—and some NASA functionaries take her and the children by the elbows and thrust them forward at Gus like religious objects . . . Behold, the Wife, the Children . . . and Gus can hardly even look at Betty as someone he knows. She's merely the ceremonial Solid Backing on the Home Front trundled forward on the concrete slab. Gus mutters hello, hugs the two boys, and they trundle the Wife and the Children back, and then Gus is marched over to the canopy, where they have the press conference. The reporters keep harping on the blown hatch and the lost capsule. The dismal bastards—they haven't gotten the message yet. They haven't picked up the proper moral tone. But being part of the great colonial animal, the Victorian Gent, they would get it all straight in a few days and never mention the damnable hatch again . . . But for now they gave the event another shot of the poisonous secret . . . Was that what was responsible for this wretched, shabby, mean little ceremony? Gus struggled with the questions and sweated under the canopy. He kept saying, "I was just lying there minding my own business when the hatch blew. It just blew." Betty could see he was getting angrier and angrier, gruffer and grimmer and darker about the eyes. He hated talking to reporters, as it was. Her heart went out. They were making him squirm. And *this* was the Big Parade! This was what she got out of the compact after all this! It was a travesty. She was . . . the Honorable Mrs. Squirming Hatch Blower!

The day only got hotter. After the little ceremony, with Webb waxing sonorous, they drove Gus and Betty and the boys to the VIP guesthouse at Patrick Air Force Base. This was supposed to be a big deal. They were told that these were secret quarters where they would be completely screened off from the press and the gawkers. The VIP guesthouse . . . Betty looked around. Even the military VIP quarters here at Cocoa Beach were Low Rent. This VIP guesthouse was like some musty cabin court from the late 1930's. She looked out the window. Over there was the beach, that amazing hot-brick Cocoa Beach. But between the guesthouse and the beach was Route A1A, with cars roaring back and forth in the screaming heat of mid-July. She would never even make it across the highway to the beach with the children. Well, they could watch TV—but there was no TV; and no pool. Then she looked in the kitchen and opened the refrigerator. It was stuffed with food, everything you could imagine. For some reason this made her furious. She could see the afternoon shaping up and the rest of the day and tomorrow, too. She would stay here with the children, cooking and risking her life dragging them to the worst beach in Florida . . . and Gus would no doubt go to the space center or into town . . .

Town meant the Holiday Inn, where the other fellows and their wives would be. That's where they would be celebrating and having the good times.

Listen, while you're getting settled, I think I'll—

Suddenly Betty was furious: *She was not staying in this place!* Gus didn't know what had gotten into her.

She said she wanted to go to the Holiday Inn. That was where everybody would be. She told Gus to call the Holiday Inn and get a room.

She gruffed it out with such fury that Gus called the Holiday and pulled the strings and got them a room. If Gus had managed to park her here in this faded VIP mausoleum and vanish, so that she could sit here in the heat of the slab watching the hours go by while he tooled around the pool at the Holiday as the big shot—she would have slit a wrist. That was how grim it was. That was how shabbily they had treated her. That was how grossly they had welshed on the compact. Now . . . they *truly owed her*.

12

THE TEARS

Since the pooch proved to be unscrewable, officially, and Gus Grissom's flight was therefore on the record as a success, NASA was suddenly in great shape. John Kennedy was happy. "We have started our long voyage to the moon." That was the idea. Neither Shepard's nor Grissom's suborbital flight measured up to Yuri Gagarin's orbit of the earth, but the fact that NASA had completed two successful manned flights seemed to mean that the United States was battling back successfully in the competition for the heavens.

Naturally, true to form, that was the moment the anonymous and uncanny Chief Designer, D-503, Builder of the Integral, chose to show the world who actually ruled the heavens.

Just sixteen days after Grissom's flight, which is to say, on August 6, 1961, the Soviets sent *Vostok 2* into orbit with a cosmonaut named Gherman Titov aboard. Titov circled the earth for an entire day, completing seventeen full orbits, and landing where he had started, on Soviet soil. Three times he came over the United States, 125 miles overhead. Once again, all over the country, politicians and the press seemed profoundly alarmed, and the awful vision was presented: suppose the cosmonaut were armed with hydrogen bombs and flung them as he came over, like Thor flinging thunderbolts . . . one here, one there . . . Toledo disappears off the face of the earth . . . Kansas City . . . Lubbock . . . Titov's flight seemed so awesome it made the Shepard and Grissom flights look terribly insignificant. The Integral and its Chief Designer could apparently do anything they wanted, and at any time.

Seven days later, August 13, 1961, Nikita Khrushchev began the steps that led to the building of a wall, precisely like a penitentiary wall, through the middle of an entire city, Berlin, to prevent the population of East Berlin from crossing over to the West. But the world was still blinking at the radiance of the day-long space flight. "They're a bit brutal—but you have to admit they're geniuses. Imagine keeping a man in space for twenty-four hours!"

So far as NASA was concerned, the Titov flight put an end to the Mercury-

Redstone program then and there. The next astronaut in line to ride on top of the Redstone, John Glenn, was now assigned to attempt an orbital flight, using the Atlas rocket, which had done so poorly in unmanned tests. Later there were those who speculated that NASA had been "saving Glenn for the big one" all along. But Glenn did not have that kind of status within NASA. He had learned that to his bitter regret. No, he had only the invisible Chief Designer, Builder of the Integral, to thank for the fact that he was assigned to be the first American to orbit the earth.

After Titov's flight the phrase *the space gap* began to be repeated throughout the American press. *Space gap* was a superstitious condition. It began to seem of urgent importance for NASA to put a man into space before the sands stopped flowing in the hourglass on the last day of the year 1961. The great cowboy rush of the winter of 1960–61 started all over again. The hell with fastidious precautions . . . For example, the Soviets revealed that Titov had suffered from nausea throughout his flight. Later they changed that to say that he had suffered nausea after "prolonged" flight. They would have probably not revealed even that much, except that they decided to participate in international scientific conferences in order to publicize their space feats. It also came out—although few specifics were given—that the Soviet manned space-flight program, from selection of their cosmonauts (from among military pilots) and their training (centrifuge rides, parabolic rides in jet fighters, and so forth) to capsule design and launching and retrorocket systems, was remarkably similar to NASA's. Everyone at NASA regarded this as vastly reassuring. *We're on the right track, anyway!* Of course, the Soviet rockets were far more powerful. That was the given. How else could the Soviet cosmonauts land safely on earth? The capsules apparently were equipped with an additional set of retro-rockets large enough to counteract the forces of gravity, once the capsule had re-entered the earth's atmosphere. And if a cosmonaut of the Integral had suffered nausea in orbit, then astronauts probably would, too. But there was no time to worry about that now. Find out about it the way Titov did: *up there. Más allá!* Over the next hill!

In September NASA successfully launched a Mercury-Atlas capsule with a dummy astronaut aboard and brought it back on target into the Atlantic, near Bermuda, after one orbit of the earth. The press speculated that Kennedy would pressure NASA to put an astronaut on the next flight, but Hugh Dryden and Bob Gilruth managed to hold out for an additional test. They wanted to send a chimpanzee into orbit with the Atlas rocket first.

This time, out at Edwards, the True Brothers didn't even derive a chilly smile from the fact that once more in the exalted Project Mercury an ape would be taking *the first flight*. An ape would make the first orbit of the earth for the U.S.A. The prestige of Project Mercury had by now rendered such considerations meaningless. On October 11, at Edwards, Bob White had made an extraordinary flight in the X-15—and the country hardly noticed. White took the X-15 up to 217,000 feet with the Big Engine—and the press merely nodded perfunctorily. So a man had just flown very high in an airplane; how interesting; and that was that. The fact that White was on top of a rocket, the same sort of rocket as the Redstone or the Atlas, the fact that his flight to 217,000 feet was in effect *piloted space flight*— none of this was likely to impress Kennedy or the public amid the panic over Titov and the *space gap*. White had gone forty miles up, ten miles short of the arbitrarily set boundary of "space." The XLR-99, the Big Engine, had delivered

57,000 pounds of thrust, just 21,000 short of the thrust of the Redstones that took Shepard and Grissom aloft. White's speed reached Mach 5.21, or 3,647 miles an hour; Shepard's and Grissom's rocket velocities were only slightly greater, about 5,180 miles per hour. White was weightless for three minutes during his tremendous arc over the top, as compared to Shepard's and Grissom's five minutes. White saw all the things that Shepard and Grissom saw (and Shepard, only barely) . . . including the entire blue band of atmosphere at the horizon of the earth. Above all, White was a *pilot*. He controlled his plane's ascent. He used hydrogen-peroxide thrusters to control his attitude once the air became too thin for aileron control—the same system of hydrogen-peroxide thrusters that Shepard and Grissom had used—and he did it all without benefit of any automatic backup. And he brought the ship back down through the earth's atmosphere himself . . . and *landed* it himself on the holy plateau of Edwards . . . on the dome of the world. A rocket *pilot* (quoth the brethren), but the national press barely noticed.

So it was with a mainly academic fascination that the boys at Edwards followed the second Project Mercury chimpanzee flight. For nine months the veterinarians at Holloman Air Force Base had been putting their colony of chimpanzees through the operant conditioning regimen in preparation for an orbital flight. The training included all the things that had gone into the training for the first suborbital flight, the centrifuge runs, the weightless parabolas, the procedures-trainer sessions, the heat-chamber and altitude-chamber sessions, plus some intelligence tests. In one test the ape had to be able to judge time intervals. The signal light would go on, and he had to wait twenty seconds before pulling the lever or he would receive the ever-cocked electrical shock. In another the animal was required to *read* the instrument panel and throw a switch. Three symbols would flash on the panel, two of which would be identical, such as two triangles and one square, and the animal had to pull the lever under the odd one or receive the shock in the soles of his feet.

By the beginning of November, twenty veterinarians had moved into Hangar S at the Cape with five chimpanzees. One of them was Ham, thinner and more strung out than ever but still an ace in the procedures trainer, his life dedicated to the avoidance of the invisible volts. Ham was not regarded as the pick of the lot, however. The brightest and quickest member of the colony was a male who had been brought from Africa to Holloman Air Force Base in April of 1960, when he was about two and a half years old. He was known as Number 85. Number 85 had fought the veterinarians and the process of operant conditioning like a Turkish prisoner of war. He fought them with his hands, his feet, his teeth, his saliva, and his cunning. He would shake off each jolt of electricity and give them a hideous grin. When he couldn't take the shocks any more, he would cooperate temporarily, and his hands would fly across the procedures trainer console like E. Power Biggs's at the organ—and *then* he would turn on the vets, making another desperate thrash toward freedom. He was like the slave who wouldn't break. Finally, they shut him up inside a metal box and let him thrash about in there for a week with his feces and urine for company. When they let him out, he was, at last, a different ape. He had had enough. He didn't want any more of the box. His operant conditioning could now begin in earnest. The box was certainly not the course that the good vets of Holloman would have chosen, had the times been normal. No, they had chosen this course in the name of the battle for the heavens and under the pressure of national urgency; Number 85 was the ape that the

MA-5 mission (the fifth test of the Mercury-Atlas vehicle) required. He was the quickest study in the universe of the Simia satyrus. They took him up in jet fighters to get him used to the accelerations, the noise, and the disorienting sensations of high-speed flight. They put him in the gondola of the human centrifuge at the University of Southern California and ran him through entire profiles of the proposed first American orbital mission, until he was used to the seven or eight g's he would experience on ascent and on re-entry. Under high g's or low g's Number 85 could operate a Mercury console like no ape that had ever lived. He was so good they used him as the test subject for a laboratory experiment that simulated a fourteen-day orbital mission. For fourteen days Number 85 was on the procedures trainer performing the same tasks he would perform in the 4½-hour MA-5 mission. For MA-5 they had added rewards as well as the punishment of the shocks in the feet. Number 85 had two tubes positioned near his mouth. Out of one came banana-flavored pellets, if he did his tasks correctly, and from the other he could take sips of water. Number 85 could do the tasks so handily, including reading the odd-symbol panel, he could have kept the tubes popping banana pellets and water until he was sated or bilious. He was outstanding.

By now, November of 1962, he had been through 1,263 hours of training—the equivalent of 158 eight-hour days. For the equivalent of 43 days he had been strapped in one simulator or conditioning apparatus or another, whether the centrifuge, the jets, or the procedures trainer. He was a marvel. The only problem was his blood pressure. Back in June of 1960, two months after his training began, they had put a blood-pressure cuff on him and obtained a reading of from 140 to 160 systolic. This was certainly high, but it was hard to tell with Number 85. He had fought every medical examination as if it were an assault. It took two or three people just to restrain him. Three months later they were getting readings from 140 to 210; by now they were running from 190 to 210. The blood pressures of all five chimpanzees out back of Hangar S had mounted steadily over the past two years, although none was so elevated as Number 85's. Well, maybe it was the pressure cuff, which he didn't see very often and which probably struck him as a big black restraining mechanism. After all, Number 85 was excitable. Perhaps they would find out more during the flight. There had been no way to read the blood pressure of the other ape, Number 61, during his Mercury-Redstone flight. But for this one they put catheters in a main artery and a main vein of Number 85's legs to provide pressure readings before the launch and throughout the flight. They also put a catheter in his urethra to collect urine.

Number 85 went through procedures trainer drills out in the vans behind Hangar S right up to the eve of the flight. He was still the pick of the litter. He must have been wound up tighter than a window-shade spring, judging by the systolic readings.

Just before the flight his name was announced to the press as Enos. Enos meant *man* in Greek.

The flight did not attract much interest. The public, like the President, was impatient with the tests, especially since it was already November 29 when the ape was launched and it was becoming clear that there would be no manned launch before the year was over. The year would end without a manned flight. Number 85 was supposed to make three orbits of the earth. The launch went perfectly, with Number 85 pulling his levers a mile a minute. The Atlas rocket delivered 367,000 pounds of thrust, nearly five times what Shepard and Grissom had experienced, but neither the noise nor the vibrations fazed Number 85 in the slightest. He had heard and felt worse in the centrifuge runs with their piped-in sound. And since he had no window, he did not know he was leaving the earth, and for that matter the noise, the vibrations, or departure from this globe, was preferable to the box. He kept working his levers as fast as they could light up the panel. The capsule went into a perfect orbit. Throughout the first orbit Number 85 performed like a dream, not only hitting the levers on cue and in complicated sequences, but also taking six-minute rest periods when signaled to . . . or at least lying motionless, the better to avoid the juice.

During the second orbit the wiring went haywire. When Number 85 did the odd-symbol exercise, he started getting electrical shocks in his left foot even when he pulled the correct lever. He kept pulling the correct levers, nonetheless. He was unstoppable. His suit started overheating. He didn't even slow down. Now the automatic attitude controls began malfunctioning, so that the capsule kept rolling over forty-five degrees before the thrusters on either side would correct it. It kept rolling back and forth. Didn't throw Number 85 out of his routine for a second. He kept reading the lights and flipping the levers. It would have to get a whole lot worse than this before it was as bad as the box.

Because the rolling was using up too much hydrogen peroxide—they had to be sure there was enough left to position the capsule correctly, blunt end down, for re-entry—they brought the capsule down after two orbits, into the Pacific, off Point Arguello, California. Number 85 bobbed around and the capsule bobbed around in the ocean for an hour and fifteen minutes before a ship arrived to retrieve them. The capsule had an explosive hatch, but it did not "just blow." Nor had Number 85 thrown up (like Titov) because of weightlessness or erratic motion. He had been weightless for a full three hours during the flight. He was calm when they removed him from the capsule. There was evidence, however, that he had had a merry old time for himself cut there in the water. He hadn't just cooled his heels. The little bastard had ripped through the belly panel of his restraint suit and removed most of the biomedical sensors from his body and damaged the rest, including those that had been inserted under the skin. He had also yanked the urinary catheter out of his penis. To just pull it out like that must have hurt like hell. What came over him?

The flight had been a great success, all things considered. But one thing bothered the NASA Life Sciences people. The animal's blood pressure had been badly elevated. It had run from 160 to 200 throughout—even when his pulse rate was normal and he was watching his lights and pulling his levers with great efficiency. Was this some sort of morbid and unforeseen effect of prolonged weightlessness? Were astronauts in earth orbit going to be candidates for apoplexy? The Holloman veterinarians hastened to reassure them that Number 85— er, Enos—had registered high-blood-pressure readings for two years now. It seemed to be the nature of the beast. The NASA folk nodded . . . although 200, systolic, was awfully goddamned high . . .

Privately, the situation had the Holloman scientists thinking, and not about space flight, either. The readings they had gotten from Number 85 in the past with the cuff may or may not have been reliable. But there was no mistaking the readings of the catheters during the flight and just before it. Once they were inserted, Number 85 wasn't even aware of them. They were giving true readings. His blood pressure had not gone up because of the stresses of the flight. He took the flight with the utmost aplomb; his heart and respiratory rates and body temperatures were actually below the readings obtained during the centrifuge runs. In fact, his blood pressure had not *gone up* at all. It had been up there all along. A theory with implications for man-on-earth, not man-in-space, was beginning to form . . . Number 85, smartest of the Simia satyrus, prince of the lower primates, had swallowed so much rage over the past two years, thanks to the operant-conditioning process, it had begun pumping out through his arteries . . . until every heartbeat was about to blow his eardrums out for him . . .

There was even a press conference at which the chimpanzee appeared. "Enos" he was, of course. At the press conference Bob Gilruth announced that John Glenn would be the pilot for the first manned orbital flight, with Scott Carpenter as the backup pilot. Deke Slayton would take the second flight, with Wally Schirra as the backup pilot. All the while the astronaut who took *the first flight* was sitting right there at the table (quoth the brethren, sotto voce). Number 85 stole the show, which was only just. He took the flashbulbs and all the talk and hubbub without blinking or even fidgeting, as if he had been waiting all along for his moment in the spotlight. Of course, the ape had been, as it were, overtrained for such a moment and was long past being able to let such things alter his behavior. Number 85 had been in rooms full of bright lights and large numbers of human beings before. Noise, vibrations, oscillations, weightlessness, space flight, fame—what earthly difference did it make compared to the shocks and the box?

At the outset neither Glenn nor his wife, Annie, foresaw the sort of excitement that was going to build up over his flight. Glenn regarded Shepard as the winner of the competition, since he looked at it the way pilots had always looked at it on the great ziggurat of flying. Al had been picked for *the first flight*, and there was no getting around that. He had been the first American to go into space. It was as if he were the project pilot for Mercury. The best Glenn could hope for was to play Scott Crossfield to Shepard's Chuck Yeager. Yeager had broken the sound barrier and become the True Brother of all the True Brothers, but at least Crossfield had gone on to become the first man to fly Mach 2 and, later on, the first man to fly the X-15.

Not even when reporters began arriving in New Concord, Ohio, his old hometown, and pushing his parents' doorbell and roaming and foaming over the town like gangs of strays, looking for anything, scraps, morsels of information about John Glenn—not even then did Glenn fully realize just what was about to happen. The deal with *Life* kept all but *Life* reporters away from him, and so the other fellows were out trying to root up whatever they could. That seemed to be the explanation. The Cape hadn't turned into a madhouse yet. As late as December, Glenn could go out to the strip on Route A1A in Cocoa Beach with Scott Carpenter, who was training with him as backup man, out to that little Kontiki Village joint, whatever the name of it was, and listen to the combo play "Beyond the Reef." John got a kick out of "Beyond the Reef." By early January, however, it was madness to try to go to the Kontiki joint or anywhere else in Cocoa Beach. There were now reporters all over the place, all of them rabid for a glimpse of John Glenn. They would even pile into the little Presbyterian church when John went there on Sunday and turn the service into a sort of muffled melee, with the photographers trying to keep quiet and muscle their way into position at the same time. They were really terrible. So John and Scott now stuck pretty much to the base, working out on the procedures trainer and the capsule itself. At night, in Hangar S, John would try to answer the fan mail. But it was like trying to beat back the ocean with a hammer. The amount of mail he was getting was incredible.

Nevertheless, the training regimen created a curtain around John, and he didn't really have as clear an idea of the storm of publicity . . . and the *passion* of it all . . . as his wife did. At their house in Arlington, Virginia, Annie was getting the whole storm, and she had practically no protection from it and few happy distractions. John's flight was first scheduled for December 20, 1961, but bad weather over the Cape kept forcing postponements. He was finally set to go on January 27. He was inserted into the capsule before dawn. Annie was in a state. She was petrified. This had little to do with fear for John's life, however. Annie could take that kind of pressure. She had been through the whole course of worrying over a pilot. John had flown in combat in the Pacific Theater in the Second World War and then in Korea. In Korea he was hit seven times by flak. Annie had also been through just about everything that Pax River had to inflict upon a pilot's wife, short of the visit of the Friend of Widows and Orphans at her own door. But one thing she had never done. She had never had to step outside after one of John's flights and say a few words on television. She knew that would be coming up when John flew, and she was already dreading the moment. Some of the other wives were at her house for the Danger Wake, and she asked them to bring some tranquilizers. She wouldn't need them for the flight. She would take them before she had to step outside for the ordeal with the TV people. With her ferocious stutter . . . the thought of millions of people, or even hundreds, or even five . . . seeing her struggling on television . . . She had been in front of microphones with John before, and John always knew how to step in and save the day. She had certain phrases she had no trouble with—"Of course," "Certainly," "Not at all," "Wonderful," "I hope not," "That's right," "I don't think so," "Fine, thank you," and so on—and most of the questions from the television reporters were so simpleminded she could handle them with those eight phrases, plus "yes" and "no"—and John or one of the children would chime in if any amplification was called for. They were a great team that way. But today she would have to solo.

Annie could see the impending catastrophe easily enough. All she had to do was look at the television screen. Any channel . . . it didn't matter . . . she could count on seeing some woman holding a microphone covered in black foam rubber and giving a declamation on the order of:

"Inside this trim, modest suburban home is Annie Glenn, wife of Astronaut John Glenn, sharing the anxiety and pride of the entire world at this tense moment but in a very private and very crucial way that only she can understand. One thing has prepared Annie Glenn for this test of her own courage and will sustain her through this test, and that one thing is her faith: her faith in the ability of her husband, her faith in the efficiency and dedication of the thousands of engineers and other personnel who provide his guidance system . . . and her faith in Almighty God . . ."

In the picture on the screen all you could see was the one TV woman, with the microphone in her hand, standing all by herself in front of Annie's house. The curtains were pulled, somewhat unaccountably, inasmuch as it was nine o'clock in the morning, but it all looked very cozy. In point of fact, the lawn, or what was left of it, looked like Nut City. There were three or four mobile units from the television networks with cables running through the grass. It looked as if Arlington had been invaded by giant toasters. The television people, with all their gaffers and go-fers and groupies and cameramen and couriers and technicians and electricians, were blazing with 200-watt eyeballs and ricocheting off each other and the assembled rabble of reporters, radio stringers, tourists, lollygaggers, policemen, and freelance gawkers. They were all craning and writhing and rolling their eyes and gesturing and jabbering away with the excitement of the event. A public execution wouldn't have drawn a crazier mob. It was the kind of crowd that would have made the Fool Killer lower his club and shake his head and walk away, frustrated by the magnitude of the opportunity.

Meanwhile, John is up on top of the rocket, the Atlas, a squat brute, twice the diameter of the Redstone. He's lying on his back in the human holster of the Mercury capsule. The count keeps dragging on. There's hold after hold because of the weather. The clouds are so heavy they will make it impossible to monitor the launch properly. Every day for five days Glenn has psyched himself up for the big event, only to have a cancellation because of the weather. Now he has been up there for four hours, four and a half, five hours—he has been stuffed into the capsule, lying on his back, for five hours, and the engineers decide to scrub the flight because of the heavy cloud cover.

He's drained. He makes his way back to Hangar S, and they start taking the suit off and unwiring him. John is sitting there in the ready room with just the outer covering of the suit off—he still has on the mesh lining underneath and all the sensors attached to his sternum and his rib cage and his arms—and a delegation from NASA comes trooping in to confront him with the following message from on high:

John, we hate to trouble you with this, but we're having a problem with your wife.

My wife?

Yes, she won't cooperate, John. Perhaps you can give her a call. There's a phone hookup right here.

A call?

Absolutely befuddled, John calls Annie. Annie is inside their house in Arlington with a few of the wives, a few friends, and Loudon Wainwright, the writer from Life, watching the countdown and, finally, the cancellation on television. Outside is the bedlam of the reporters baying for scraps of information about the ordeal of Annie Glenn—and resenting the fact that Life has exclusive access to the poignant drama. A few blocks away, on a quaint Arlington side street, in a limousine, waits Lyndon Johnson, Vice-President of the United States. Kennedy had appointed Johnson his special overseer for the space program. It was the sort of meaningless job that Presidents give Vice-Presidents, but it had a symbolic significance now that Kennedy was presenting manned space flight as the very vanguard of his New Frontier (version number two). Johnson, like many men who have had the job of Vice-President before him, has begun suffering from publicity deprivation. He decides he wants to go inside the Glenn household and console Annie Glenn over the ordeal, the excruciating pressure of the five-hour wait and the frustrating cancellation. To make this sympathy call all the more memorable, Johnson decides it would be nice if he brought in NBC-TV, CBS-

TV, and ABC-TV along with him, in the form of a pool crew that will feed the touching scene to all three networks and out to the millions. The only rub—the only rub, to Johnson's way of thinking—is that he wants the *Life* reporter, Wainwright, to get out of the house, because his presence will antagonize the rest of the print reporters who can't get in, and they will not think kindly of the Vice-President.

What he does not realize is that the only ordeal that Annie Glenn has been going through has been over the possibility that she was going to have to step outside at some point and spend sixty seconds or so stammering a few phrases. And now . . . various functionaries and secret-service personnel are calling on the telephone and banging on the door to inform her that the Vice-President is already in Arlington, in a White House limousine, waiting to pull up and charge in and pour ten minutes of hideous Texas soul all over her on nationwide TV. Short of the rocket blowing up under John, this is the worst thing she can imagine occurring in the entire American space program. At first Annie is trying to deal with it gracefully by saying that she can't possibly ask *Life* to leave, not only because of the contract, but because of their good personal relationship. Wainwright, being no fool, doesn't particularly care to get caught in the middle like this and so he offers to bow out, to leave. But Annie is not about to give up her *Life* shield at this point. Her mind is made up. She's getting angry. She tells Wainwright: "You're *not leaving* this house!" Her anger does wonders for her stutter. It flattens it right out temporarily. She's practically ordering him to stay. Annie's stutter often makes people underestimate her, and Johnson's people didn't realize that she was a Presbyterian pioneer wife living in full vitality in the twentieth century. She could deal with any five of them with just a few amps from the wrath of God when she was angry. Finally, they're getting the picture. She's too much for them. So they start trying to bend arms at NASA to get someone to *order* her to play ball. But it has to be done very rapidly. Johnson is sitting out there a few blocks away in his limousine, fuming and swearing and making life hell for everyone within earshot, wondering, in so many words, why the fuck there isn't anybody on his staff who can deal with a *housewife*, f'r chrissake, and his staff is leaning on NASA, and NASA is bucking the problem up the chain, until in a matter of minutes it's at the top, and the delegation is trooping into Hangar S to confront the astronaut himself.

So there's John, with half his mesh underlining hanging off his body and biosensor wires sprouting from out of his thoracic cage . . . there's John, covered with sweat, drawn, deflated, beginning to feel very tired after waiting for five hours for 367,000 pounds of liquid oxygen to explode under his back . . . and the hierarchy of NASA has one thing on its mind: keeping Lyndon Johnson happy. So John puts in the call to Annie, and he tells her: "Look, if you don't want the Vice-President or the TV networks or anybody else to come into the house, then that's it as far as I'm concerned, they are *not* coming in—and I will back you up all the way, one hundred percent, and you tell them that. I don't want Johnson or any of the rest of them to put so much as *one toe* inside our house!"

That was all that Annie needed, and she simply became a wall. She wouldn't even discuss the matter any further, and there was no question any longer about Johnson getting in. Johnson, of course, was furious. You could hear him bellowing and yelling over half of Arlington, Virginia. He was talking about his aides.

Pansies! Cows! Gladiolas! Webb could scarcely believe what was going on. The astronaut and his wife had shut the door in the Vice-President's face. Webb had a few words with Glenn. Glenn wouldn't back down an inch. He indicated that Webb was *way out of line*.

Way out of line! What the hell was this? Webb couldn't figure out what was happening. How could the number-one man, himself, the administrator of NASA, be *way out of line*? Webb called in some of his top deputies and described the situation. He said he was considering changing the order of the flight assignments—i.e., putting another astronaut in Glenn's place. This flight required a man who could comprehend the broader interests of the program better. His deputies looked at him as if he were crazy. He'd never get away with it! *The astronauts* wouldn't stand for it! . . . They had their differences, but on something like this the seven would stand together like an army . . . Webb was beginning to see something he had never quite figured out before. The astronauts were not *his* men. They were in a category new to American life. They were single-combat warriors. If anything, *he* was *their* man.

One could imagine what would happen if Webb tried to exercise his authority nonetheless . . . Here comes the showdown . . . the seven Mercury astronauts on the TV . . . explaining that in the very moments when their lives are on the line, he, Webb, is meddling, trying to curry favor with Lyndon Johnson, being vindictive because John Glenn's wife, Annie, would not let the hideous hand-wringing Texan into her living room to emote all over her on nationwide television . . . He sits in his office suite in Washington while their hides are up on the tip of the rocket . . . One could see the lines drawn in just that way. Webb would be issuing denials, furiously . . . Kennedy would be the umpire—and it wasn't too hard to figure out which way the decision would go. The changing of the assignments was never mentioned again.

Not long thereafter an old friend visited Webb in his corner office, and Webb unburdened himself.

"Look at this office," he said, making a grand gesture across a room with all the trappings of Cabinet-level rank known to the General Services Administration syllabus. "And I . . . *cannot* . . . *get* . . . *a* . . . *simple* . . . *order* . . . *carried out!*"

But in the next moment his mood changed. "All the same," he said, "I love those guys. They're putting their lives on the line for their country."

Dryden and Gilruth decided to postpone the launch for at least two weeks, to the middle of February. Glenn made a statement to the press about the delays. He said that anybody who knew the first thing about "the flight test business" expected delays; they were all part of it; the main thing was not to involve people who became "panicky" when everything didn't go just right . . . Glenn went home to Arlington for a three-day weekend. While he was there, President Kennedy invited him to the White House for a private get-together. He did not invite Webb or Johnson to join them.

O<small>N</small> F<small>EBRUARY</small> 20 Glenn was once again squeezed inside the Mercury capsule on top of the Atlas rocket, lying on his back, whiling away the holds in the countdown by going over his checklist and looking at the scenery through the periscope. If he closed his eyes it felt as if he were lying on his back on the deck of an old ship. The rocket kept creaking and twisting, shaking the capsule this way and that. The Atlas had 4.3 times as much fuel as the Redstone, including 80 tons of liquid oxygen. The liquid oxygen, the "lox," had a temperature of 293 degrees below zero, so that the shell and tubing of the rocket, which were thin, kept contracting and twisting and creaking. Glenn was at the equivalent of nine stories up in the air. The enormous rocket seemed curiously fragile, the way it moved and creaked and whined. The contractions created high-frequency vibrations and the lox hissed in the pipes, and it all ran up through the capsule like a metallic wail. It was the same rocket lox wail they used to hear at dawn at Edwards when they fueled the D-558-2 many years before.

Through the periscope Glenn could see for miles down the Banana River and the Indian River. He could just barely make out the thousands of people along the beaches. Some of them had been camping out along there in trailers since January 23, when the flight was first scheduled. They had elected camp mayors. They were having a terrific time. A month in a Banana River trailer camp was not too long to wait to make sure you were here when an event of this magnitude occurred.

There they were, thousands of them, off on the periphery as Glenn looked out. He could only see them through the periscope. They looked very small and far away and far below. And they were all wondering with a delicious shudder what it must be like to be in his place now. How frightened is he! *Tell us! That's all we want to know!* The fear and the gamble. Never mind the rest. Lying on his back like this, with his legs jackknifed up above him, stuffed blind into the holster, with the hatch closed, he couldn't help but be aware of his own heartbeat from time to time. Glenn could tell that his pulse was slow. Out loud, if the subject ever came up, everyone said that pulse rates didn't matter; it was a very subjective thing; many variables; and so on. It had only been within the past five years that biosensors had ever been put on pilots. They resented them and didn't care to attach any importance to them. Nevertheless, without saying so, everyone knew that they provided a rough gauge of a man's emotional state. Without saying so—not a word!—everyone knew that Gus Grissom's pulse rate had been *somewhat panicky*. It kept jumping over 100 during the countdown and then spurted up to 150 during the lift-off and stayed that high throughout his weightless flight, then jumped again, all the way to 171, just before the retro-rockets went off. No one—certainly not out loud—no one was going to draw any conclusions from it, but . . . it was not a sign of the right stuff. Add to that his performance in the water . . . In his statement about people who get panicky over the flight test business, Glenn had said you had to know how to control your emotions. Well, he was as good as his word. Did any yogi ever control his heartbeat and perspiration better! (And, as the biomedical panels in the Mission Control room showed, his pulse never went over 80 and was holding around 70, no more than that of any normal healthy bored man having breakfast in the kitchen.) Occasionally he could feel his heart skip a beat or beat with an odd electrical sensation, and he knew that he was feeling the tension. (And at the biomedical panels the young doctors looked at each other in consternation—and then shrugged.) Nevertheless, he was aware that he was feeling no fear. He truly was not. He was more like an actor who is going out to perform in the same play yet once again—the only difference being that the audience this time is enormous and highly prestigious. He knew every sensation he would feel once the event began. The main thing was not to . . . "foul up." Please, dear God, don't let me foul up. In fact, there was little chance that he would forget so much as a word or a single move. Glenn had been the backup pilot—everyone said *pilot* now —for both Shepard and Grissom. During the charade before the first flight, he had gone through all of Shepard's simulations, and he had repeated most of Grissom's. And the simulations he had gone through as prime pilot for the first orbital flight had surpassed any simulations ever done before. They had even put him in the capsule on top of the rocket and *moved the gantry* away from the rocket, because Grissom had reported the odd sensation of perceiving the gantry as *falling over*, as he witnessed the event through his periscope, just before lift-off. Therefore, this feeling would be *adapted out* of Glenn. They put him in the capsule on top of the rocket and instructed him to watch the gantry move away through his periscope. *Nothing* must be novel about the experience! On top of all that, he had Shepard's and Grissom's descriptions of variations from the simulations. "On the centrifuge you feel thus-and-such. Well, during the actual flight it feels like that but with this-and-that difference." No man had ever lived an event so completely ahead of time. He was socketed into the capsule, lying on his back, getting ready to do precisely what his enormous Presbyterian Pilot self-esteem had been dying to do for fifteen years: demonstrate to the world his righteous stuff.

Exactly that! The Presbyterian Pilot! Here he is!—within twenty seconds of lift-off, and the only strange thing is how little adrenalin is pumping when the moment comes . . . He can hear the rumble of the Atlas engines building up down there below his back. All the same, it isn't terribly loud. The huge squat rocket shakes a bit and struggles to overcome its own weight. It all happens very slowly in the first few seconds, like an extremely heavy elevator rising. They've lit the candle and there's no turning back, and yet there's no surge inside him. His pulse rises only to 110, no more than the minimum rate you should have if you have to deal with a sudden emergency. How strange that it should be this way! He has been more wound up for a takeoff in an F-102.

"The clock is operating," he said. "We're underway."

It was all very smooth, much smoother than the centrifuge . . . just as Shepard and Grissom said it would be. He had gone through the same g-forces so many times . . . he hardly noticed them as they built up. It would have bothered him much more if they had been less. Nothing novel! No excitement, please! It took thirteen seconds for the huge rocket to reach transonic speed. The vibrations started. It was just as Shepard and Grissom said: it was much gentler than the centrifuge. He was still lying flat on his back, and the g-forces drove him deeper and deeper into the seat, but it all felt so familiar. He barely noticed it. He kept his eyes on the instrument panel the whole time . . . All quite normal, every little needle and switch in the right place . . . No malevolent instructor feeding *Abort* problems into the loop . . . As the rocket entered the transonic zone, the vibration became intense. The vibrations all but obliterated the roar of the engines. He was entering the area of "max q," maximum aerodynamic pressure, in which the pressure of the shaft of the Atlas forcing its way through the atmosphere at supersonic speed would reach almost a thousand pounds per square foot. Through the cockpit window he could see the sky turning black. Almost 5 g's were driving him back into his seat. And yet . . . *easier than the centrifuge* . . . All at once he was through *max q*, as if through a turbulent strait, and the trajectory was smooth and he was supersonic and the rumble of the rocket engines was more muffled than ever and he could hear all the little fans and recorders and the busy little kitchen, the humming little shop . . . The pressure on his chest reached 6 g's. The rocket pitched down. For the first time he could see clouds and the horizon. In a moment —*there it was*—the Atlas rocket's two booster engines shut down and were jettisoned from the side of the shaft and his body was slammed forward, as if he were screeching to a halt, and the g-forces suddenly dropped to 1.25, almost as if he were on earth and not accelerating at all, but the central sustainer engine and two smaller engines were still driving him up through the atmosphere . . . A flash of white smoke went up past the window . . . *No! The escape tower was firing early—but the* JETTISON TOWER *light wasn't on!* . . . He didn't see the tower go . . . Wait a minute . . . There went the tower, on schedule . . . The JETTISON TOWER light came on green . . . The smoke must have been from the booster rockets as they left the shaft . . . The rocket pitched back up . . . going straight up . . . The sky was very black now . . . The g-forces began pushing him back into his seat again . . . 3 g's . . . 4 g's . . . 5 g's . . . Soon he would be forty miles up . . . the last critical moment of powered flight, as the capsule separated from the rocket and went into its orbital trajectory . . . or didn't . . . *Hey!* . . . All at once the whole capsule was whipping up and down, as if it were tied to the end of a diving board, a springboard. The g-forces built up and the capsule whipped up and down. Yet no sooner had it begun than Glenn knew what it was. The weight of the rocket on the launch pad had been 260,000 pounds, practically all of it rocket fuel, the liquid oxygen. This was being consumed at such a furious rate, about one ton per second, that the rocket was becoming merely a skeleton with a thin skin of metal stretched over it, a tube so long and light that it was flexing. The g-forces reached six and then he was weightless, just like that. The sudden release made him feel as if he were tumbling head over heels, as if he had been catapulted off the end of that same springboard and was falling through the air doing forward rolls. But he had felt this same thing on the centrifuge when they ran the g-forces up to seven and then suddenly cut the speed. At the same moment, right on schedule . . . a loud report . . . the posigrade rockets fired, throwing the capsule free of the rocket shaft . . . the capsule began its automatic turnabout, and all the proper green lights went on in front of him, and he knew he was "through the gate," as they said.

"Zero-g and I feel fine," he said. "Capsule is turning around . . ."

Glenn knew he was weightless. From the instrument readings and through sheer logic he knew it, but he couldn't feel it, just as Shepard and Grissom had never felt it. The turnaround brought him up to a sitting position, vertical to the earth, and that was the way he felt. He was sitting in a chair, upright, in a very tiny cramped quiet little cubicle 125 miles above the earth, a little metal closet, silent except for the humming of its electrical system, the inverters, the gyros, the cameras, the radio . . . *the radio* . . . He had been specifically instructed to violate the Fighter Jock code of No Chatter. He was supposed to radio back every sight, every sensation, and otherwise give the taxpayers the juicy stuff they wanted to hear. Glenn, more than any of the others, was fully capable of doing the job. Yet it was an awkward thing. It seemed unnatural.

"Oh!" he said. "That view is tremendous!"

Well, it was a start. In fact, the view was not particularly extraordinary. It was extraordinary that he was up here in orbit about the earth. He could see the exhausted Atlas rocket following him. It was tumbling end over end from the force of the small rockets throwing the capsule free of it.

He could hear Alan Shepard, who was serving as capcom in the Mercury Control Center at the Cape. His voice came in very clearly. He was saying, "You have a go, at least seven orbits."

"Roger," said Glenn. "Understand Go for at least seven orbits . . . This is *Friendship 7*. Can see clear back, a big cloud pattern way back across toward the Cape. Beautiful sight."

He was riding backward, looking back toward the Cape. It must be tremendous, it must be beautiful—what else could it be? And yet it didn't look terribly different from what he had seen at 50,000 feet in fighter planes. He had no greater sense of having left the bonds of earth. The earth was not just a little ball beneath him. It still filled his field of consciousness. It slid by slowly underneath him, just the way it did when you were in an airplane at forty or fifty thousand feet. He had no sense of being a *star voyager*. He couldn't see any stars at all. He could see the Atlas booster tumbling behind him and beginning to grow smaller, because it was in a slightly lower orbit. It just kept tumbling. There was nothing to stop it. Somehow the sight of this colossal great tumbling cylinder, which had weighed more than the average freighter while it was on the ground and which now weighed nothing and had been discarded like a candy wrapper—somehow it was more extraordinary than the view of earth. It shouldn't have been, but it was. The earth looked the way it had looked to Gus Grissom. Shepard had seen a low-grade black-and-white movie. Through his window Glenn could see what Grissom saw, the brilliant blue band at the horizon, a somewhat wider band of deeper blues leading into the absolutely black dome of the sky. Most of the earth was covered in clouds. The clouds looked very bright, set against the blackness of the sky. The capsule was heading east, over Africa. But, because he was riding backward, he was looking west. He saw everything after he had passed over it. He could make out the Canary Islands, but they were partly obscured by clouds. He could see a long stretch of the African coast . . . huge dust storms over the African desert . . . but there was no sense of taking in the whole earth at a glance. The earth was eight thousand miles in diameter and he was only a hundred miles above it. He knew what it was going to look like in any case. He had seen it all in photographs taken from the satellites. It had all been flashed on the screens for him. Even the view had been simulated. *Yes . . . that's the way they said it would look . . .* Awe seemed to be demanded, but how could he express awe honestly? He had lived it all before the event. How could he explain that to anybody? The view wasn't the main thing, in any case. The main thing . . . was *the checklist!* And just try explaining that! He had to report all his switch and dial readings. He had to put a special blood-pressure rig on the arm of his pressure suit and pump it up. (His blood pressure was absolutely normal, 120 over 80—*perfect stuff!*) He had to check the manual attitude-control system, swing the capsule up and down, side to side, roll to the right, roll to the left . . . and there was nothing novel about it, not even in orbit, a hundred miles above the earth. *How could you explain that!* When he swung the capsule, it felt the same as it did in a one-g state on earth. He still didn't feel weightless. He merely felt less cramped, because there were no longer any pressure points on his body. He was sitting straight up in a chair drifting slowly and quietly around the earth. Just the hum of his little shop, the background noises in his headset, and the occasional spurt of the hydrogen-peroxide jets.

"This is *Friendship 7*," he said. "Working just like clockwork on the control check, and it went through just about like the procedures-trainer runs."

Well, that was it. The procedures trainer and the ALFA trainer and the centrifuge . . . He noticed that, in fact, he seemed to be moving a little faster than he had been on the ALFA trainer. When you sat in the trainer, cranking your simulated hydrogen-peroxide thrusters, they ran films on the screen of the earth rolling by below you, just the way it would be in orbital flight. "They didn't roll it by fast enough," he said to himself. Not that it mattered particularly . . . The sensation of speed was no more than that of being in an airliner and watching a cloud bank slide by far below . . . The world demanded awe, because this was a voyage through the stars. But he couldn't feel it. The backdrop of the event, the stage, the environment, the true orbit . . . was not the vast reaches of the universe. It was the simulators. *Who could possibly understand this?* Weightless he was, in the vacuum of space, humming around the earth . . . but his center of gravity was still back in that Baptist hardtack Low Rent stretch of sand and palmetto grass in Florida.

Ahhhh—but now this was truly something. Forty minutes into the flight, as he neared the Indian Ocean, off the east coast of Africa, he began sailing into the night. Since he was traveling east, he was going away from the sun at a speed of 17,500 miles an hour. But because he was riding backward, he could see the sun out the window. It was sinking the way the moon sinks out of sight as seen on earth. The edge of the sun began to touch the edge of the horizon. He couldn't tell what part of the earth it was. There were clouds everywhere. They created a haze at the horizon. The brilliant light over the earth began to dim. It was like turning down a rheostat. It took five or six minutes. Very slowly the lights were dimming. Then he couldn't see the sun at all, but there was a tremendous band of orange light that stretched from one side of the horizon to the other, as if the sun were a molten liquid that had emptied into a tube along the horizon. Where there had been a bright-blue band before, there was now the orange band; and above it a wider dimmer band of oranges and reds shading off into the blackness of the sky. Then all the reds and oranges disappeared, and he was on the night side of the earth. The bright-blue band reappeared at the horizon. Above it, stretching up about eight degrees, was what looked like a band of haze, created by the earth's atmosphere. And above that . . . for the first time he could make out the stars. Down below, the clouds picked up a faint light from the moon, which was coming up behind him. Now he was over Australia. He could hear Gordon Cooper's voice. Cooper was serving as the capcom at the tracking station in the town of Muchea, out in the kangaroo boondocks of western Australia. He could hear Cooper's Oklahoma drawl.

"That sure was a short day," said Glenn.

"Say again, *Friendship 7*," said Cooper.

"That was about the shortest day I've ever run into," said Glenn. Somehow that was the sort of thing to say to old Oklahoma Gordo sitting down there in the middle of nowhere.

"Kinda passes rapidly, huh?" said Gordo.

"Yessir," said Glenn.

The clouds began to break up over Australia. He could make out nothing in the darkness except for electric lights. Off to one side he could make out the lights of an entire city, just as you could at 40,000 feet in an airplane, but the concentration of lights was terrific. It was an absolute mass of electric lights, and south of it there was another one, a smaller one. The big mass was the city of Perth and the smaller one was a town called Rockingham. It was midnight in Perth and Rockingham, but practically every living soul in both places had stayed up to turn on every light they had for the American sailing over in the satellite.

"The lights show up very well," said Glenn, "and thank everybody for turning them on, will you?"

"We sure will, John," said Gordo.

And he went sailing on past Australia with the lights of Perth and Rockingham sliding into the distance.

He was over the middle of the Pacific, about halfway between Australia and Mexico, when the sun began to come up behind him. This was just thirty-five minutes after the sun went down. Since he was traveling backward, he couldn't see the sunrise through the window. He had to use the periscope. First he could see the blue band at the horizon becoming brighter and brighter. Then the sun itself began to slide up over the edge. It was a brilliant red—not terribly different from what he had seen at sunrise on earth, except that it was rising faster and its outlines were sharper.

"It's blinding through the scope on clear," said Glenn. "I'm going to the dark filter to watch it come on up."

And then—*needles!* A tremendous layer of them—Air Force communications experiment that went amok . . . Thousands of tiny needles gleaming in the sun outside the capsule . . . But they couldn't be needles, because they were luminescent—they were like snowflakes—

"This is *Friendship 7*," he said. "I'll try to describe what I'm in here. I am in a big mass of some very small particles that are brilliantly lit up like they're luminescent. I never saw anything like it. They're round, a little. They're coming by the capsule, and they look like little stars. A whole shower of them coming by. They swirl around the capsule and go in front of the window and they're all brilliantly lighted. They probably average maybe seven or eight feet apart, but I can see them all down below me also."

"Roger, *Friendship 7*." This was the capcom on Canton Island out in the Pacific. "Can you hear any impact with the capsule? Over."

"Negative, negative. They're very slow. They're not going away from me more than maybe three or four miles per hour."

They swirled about his capsule like tiny weightless diamonds, little bijoux—no, they were more like fireflies. They had that lazy but erratic motion, and when he focused on one it would seem to be lit up, but the light would go out and he would lose track of it, and then it would light up again. That was like fireflies, too. There used to be thousands of fireflies in the summers, when he was growing up. These things were like fireflies, but they obviously couldn't be any sort of organism . . . unless all the astronomers and all the satellite recording mechanisms had been fundamentally wrong . . . They were undoubtedly particles of some sort, particles that caught the sunlight at a certain angle. They were beautiful, but were they coming from the capsule? That could mean trouble. They must have been coming from the capsule, because they traveled along with him, in the same trajectory, at the same speed. But wait a minute. Some of them were far off, far below . . . there might be an entire field of them . . . a minute cosmos . . . something never seen before! And yet the capcom on Canton Island didn't seem particularly interested. And then he sailed out of range of Canton and would have to wait to be picked up by the capcom at Guaymas, on the west coast of Mexico. And when the Guaymas capcom picked him up, he didn't seem to know what he was talking about.

"This is *Friendship 7*," said Glenn. "Just as the sun came up, there were some brilliantly lighted particles that looked luminous that were swirling around the capsule. I don't have any in sight right now. I did have a couple just a moment ago, when I made the transmission over to you. Over."

"Roger, *Friendship 7*."

And that was it. "Roger, *Friendship 7*." Silence. They didn't particularly care.

Glenn kept talking about his fireflies. He was fascinated. It was the first true unknown anyone had encountered out here in the cosmos. At the same time he was faintly apprehensive. *Roger, Friendship 7*. The capcom finally asked a polite question or two, about the size of the particles and so on. They obviously were not carried away by this celestial discovery.

All of a sudden the capsule swung out to the right in a yaw, out about twenty degrees. Then it was as if it hit a little wall. It bounced back. Then it swung out again in the yaw and hit the little wall and bounced back. Something had gone out in the automatic attitude control. Never mind the celestial fireflies. He was sailing over California, heading for Florida. Now all the capcoms were coming alive, all right.

President Kennedy was supposed to come on the radio as Glenn came over the United States. He was going to bless his single-combat warrior as he came over the continental U.S.A. He was going to tell him the hearts of all his fellow citizens were with him. But that all went by the boards in view of the problem with the automatic controls.

Glenn went sailing over Florida, over the Cape, starting his second orbit. He couldn't see much of anything down below, because of the clouds. He no longer cared particularly. The attitude control was the main thing. One of the small thrusters seemed to have gone out, so that the capsule would drift to the right, like a car slowly skidding on ice. Then a bigger thruster would correct the motion and bounce it back. That was only the start. Pretty soon other thrusters began acting up when he was on automatic. Then the gyros started going. The dials that showed the angle of the capsule with respect to the earth and the horizon were giving obviously wrong readings. He had to line it up visually with the horizon. Fly by wire! Manual control! It was no emergency, however, at least not yet. As long as he was in orbit, the attitude control of the capsule didn't particularly matter, so far as his safety was concerned. He could be going forward or backward or could have his head pointed straight at the earth or could be drifting around in circles or pitching head over heels, for that matter, and it wouldn't change his altitude or trajectory in the slightest. The only critical point was the re-entry. If the capsule were not lined up at the correct angle, with the blunt end and the heat shield down, it might burn up. To line it up correctly, fuel was required, the hydrogen peroxide, no matter whether it was lined up automatically or by the astronaut. If too much fuel was used keeping the capsule stable while it sailed around in orbit, there might not be enough left to line it up before the re-entry. That had been the problem in the ape's flight. The automatic attitude control had started malfunctioning and was using up so much fuel they brought him down after two orbits.

Every five minutes he had to shift his radio communications to a new capcom. You couldn't receive and send at the same time, either. It wasn't like a telephone hookup. So you spent half the time just making sure you could hear each other.

"*Friendship 7, Friendship 7,* this is CYI." That was the Canary Islands capcom. "The time is now 16:32:26. We are reading you loud and clear; we are reading you loud and clear. CYI."

Glenn said: "This is *Friendship 7* on UHF. As I went over recovery area that time, I could see a wake, what appeared to be a long wake in the water. I imagine that's the ships in our recovery area."

"*Friendship 7* . . . We do not read you, do not read you. Over."

"*Friendship 7,* this is Kano. At G.M.T. 16:33:00. We do not . . . This is Kano. Out."

"*Friendship 7, Friendship 7,* this is CYI Com Tech. Over."

Glenn said: "Hello, Canary. *Friendship 7.* Receive you loud and a little garbled. Do you receive me? Over."

"*Friendship 7, Friendship 7,* this is CYI Com Tech. Over."

"Hello, Canary, *Friendship 7.* I read you loud and clear. How me? Over."

"*Friendship 7, Friendship 7,* this is CYI Com Tech. Over."

"Hello, CYI Com Tech. *Friendship 7.* How do you read me? Over."

"*Friendship 7, Friendship 7,* this is CYI, CYI Com Tech. Do you read? Over."

"Roger. This is *Friendship 7,* CYI. I read you loud and clear. Over."

"*Friendship 7, Friendship 7,* this is CYI Com Tech, CYI Com Tech. Do you read? Over."

"Hello, CYI Com Tech. Roger, read you loud and clear."

"*Friendship 7,* this is CYI Com Tech. Read you loud and clear also, on UHF, on UHF. Standby."

"Roger. *Friendship 7.*"

"*Friendship 7, Friendship 7, Friendship 7,* this is Canary capcom. How do you read? Over."

"Hello, Canary capcom. *Friendship 7.* I read you loud and clear. How me?"

Finally, the Canary Islands capcom said: "I read you loud and clear. I am instructed to ask you to correlate the actions of the particles surrounding your spacecraft with the actions of your control jets. Do you read? Over."

"This is *Friendship 7.* I did not read you clear. I read you loud but very garbled. Over."

"Roger. Cap asks you to correlate the actions of the particles surrounding the vehicle with the reaction of one of your control jets. Do you understand? Over."

"This is *Friendship 7.* I do not think they were from my control jets, negative. Over."

There—exactly five minutes to get one question out and one answer. Well, at least they finally showed an interest in the fireflies. They wondered if they might have something to do with the malfunctioning thrusters. Oh, but it was a struggle.

In any case, he was not particularly worried. He could control the attitude manually if he had to. The fuel seemed to be holding out. Everything hummed and whined and buzzed as usual inside the capsule. The same high background tones came over the radio. He could hear the oxygen coursing through his pressure suit and his helmet. There was no "sensation" of motion speed at all, unless he looked down at the earth. Even then it slid by very slowly. When the thrusters spurted hydrogen peroxide, he could feel the capsule swing this way and that. But it was like the ALFA trainer on earth. He still didn't feel weightless. He was still sitting straight up in his chair. On the other hand, the camera—when he wanted to reload it, he just parked it in the empty space in front of his eyes. It just floated there in front of him. Way down there were little flashes all over the place. It was lightning in the clouds over the Atlantic. Somehow it was more fascinating than the sunset. Sometimes the lightning was inside the clouds and looked like flashlights going on and off underneath a blanket. Sometimes it was on top of the clouds, and it looked like firecrackers going off. It was extraordinary, and yet there was nothing new about the sight. An Air Force colonel, David Simons, had gone up in a balloon, alone, to 102,000 feet, for thirty-two hours and had seen the same thing.

Glenn was now over Africa, riding over the dark side of the earth, sailing backward toward Australia. The Indian Ocean capcom said: "We have message from MCC for you to keep your landing-bag switch in off position. Landing-bag switch in off position. Over."

"Roger," said Glenn. "This is *Friendship 7*.'

He wanted to ask why. But that was against the code, except in an emergency situation. That fell under the heading of nervous chatter.

Over Australia old Gordo, Gordo Cooper, got on the same subject: "Will you confirm the landing-bag switch is in the off position? Over."

"That is affirmative," said Glenn. "Landing-bag switch is in the center off position."

"You haven't had any banging noises or anything of this type at higher rates?"

"Negative."

"They wanted this answer."

They still didn't say why, and Glenn entered into no nervous chatter. He now had two red lights on the panel. One was the warning light for the automatic fuel supply. All the little amok action of the yaw thrusters had used it up. Well, it was up to the Pilot now . . . to aim the capsule correctly for re-entry . . . The other was a warning about excess cabin water. It built up as a by-product of the oxygen system. Nevertheless, he pressed on with the checklist. He was supposed to exercise by pulling on the bungee cord and then take his blood pressure. The Presbyterian Pilot! He did it without a peep. He was pulling on the bungee and watching the red lights when he began sailing backward into the sunrise again. Two hours and forty-three minutes into the flight, his second sunrise over the Pacific . . . seen from behind through a periscope. But he hardly watched it. He was looking for the fireflies to light up again. The great rheostat came up, the earth lit up, and now there were thousands of them swirling about the capsule. Some of them seemed to be miles away. A huge field of them, a galaxy, a microuniverse. No question about it, they weren't coming from the capsule, they were part of the cosmos. He took out the camera again. He had to photograph them while the light was just right.

"*Friendship 7*." The Canton Island capcom was coming in. "This is Canton. We also have no indication that your landing bag might be deployed. Over."

Glenn's first reaction was that this must have something to do with the fireflies. He's telling them about the fireflies and they come in with something about the landing bag. But who said anything about the landing bag being deployed?

"Roger," he said. "Did someone report landing bag could be down? Over."

"Negative," said the capcom. "We had a request to monitor this and to ask you if you heard any flapping, when you had high capsule rates."

"Well," said Glenn, "I think they probably thought these particles I saw might have come from that, but these are . . . there are thousands of these things, and they go out for it looks like miles in each direction from me, and they move by here very slowly. I saw them at the same spot on the first orbit. Over."

And so he thought that explained all the business about the landing bag.

They gave him the go-ahead for his third and final orbit as he sailed over the United States. He couldn't see a thing for the clouds. He pitched the capsule down sixty degrees, so he could look straight down. All he could see was the cloud deck. It was just like flying at high altitudes in an airplane. He was really no longer in the mood for sightseeing. He was starting to think about the sequence of events that would lead to the retrofiring over the Atlantic after he had been around the world one more time. He had to fight both the thrusters and the gyros now. He kept releasing and resetting the gyros to see if the automatic attitude control would start functioning again. It was all out of whack. He would have to position the capsule by using the horizon as a reference. He was sailing backward over America. The clouds began to break. He began to see the Mississippi delta. It was like looking at the world from the tail-gun perch of the bombers they used in the Second World War. Then Florida started to slide by. Suddenly he realized he could see the whole state. It was laid out just like it is on a map. He had been around the world twice in three hours and eleven minutes and this was the first sense he had had of how high up he was. He was about 550,000 feet up. He could make out the Cape. By the time he could see the Cape he was already over Bermuda.

"This is *Friendship 7*," he said. "I have the Cape in sight down there. It looks real fine from up here."

"Rog. Rog." That was Gus Grissom on Bermuda.

"As you know," said Glenn.

"Yea, verily, sonny," said Grissom.

Oh, it all sounded very fraternal. Glenn was modestly acknowledging that his loyal comrade Grissom was one of the only three Americans ever to see such a sight . . . and Grissom was calling him "sonny."

Twenty minutes later he was sailing backward over Africa again and the sun was going down again, for the third time, and the rheostat was dimming and he . . . saw *blood*. It was all over one of the windows. He knew it couldn't be blood, and yet it was blood. He had never noticed it before. At this particular angle of the setting rheostat sun he could see it. Blood and dirt, a real mess. The dirt must have come from the firing of the escape tower. And the blood . . . *bugs*, perhaps . . . The capsule must have smashed into bugs as it rose from the launch pad . . . or *birds* . . . but he would have heard the thump. It must have been bugs, but bugs didn't have blood. Or the blood red of the sun going down in front of him diffusing . . . And then he refused to think about it any more. He just turned the subject off. Another sunset, another orange band streaking across the rim of the horizon, more yellow bands, blue bands, blackness, thunderstorms, lightning making little sparkles under the blanket. It hardly mattered any more.

The whole thing of lining the capsule up for retrofire kept building up in his mind. In slightly less than an hour the retro-rockets would go off. The capsule kept slipping its angles, swinging this way and that way, drifting. The gyros didn't seem to mean a thing any more.

And he went sailing backward through the night over the Pacific. When he reached the Canton Island tracking point, he swung the capsule around again so that he could see his last sunrise while riding forward, out the window, with his own eyes. The first two he had watched through the periscope because he was going backward. The fireflies were all over the place as the sun came up. It was like watching the sunrise from inside a storm of the things. He began expounding upon them again, about how they couldn't possibly come from the capsule, because some of them seemed to be miles away. Once again nobody on the ground was interested. They weren't interested on Canton Island, and pretty soon he was in range of the station on Hawaii, and they weren't interested, either. They were all wrapped up in something else. They had a little surprise for him. They backed into it, however. It took him a while to catch on.

He was now four hours and twenty-one minutes into the flight. In twelve minutes the retro-rockets were supposed to fire, to slow him down for re-entry. It took him another minute and forty-five seconds to go through all the "do you reads" and "how me's" and "overs" and establish contact with the capcom on Hawaii. Then they sprang their surprise.

"*Friendship 7,*" said the capcom. "We have been reading an indication on the ground of segment 5-1, which is Landing Bag Deploy. We suspect this is an erroneous signal. However, Cape would like you to check this by putting the landing-bag switch in auto position, and seeing if you get a light. Do you concur with this? Over."

It slowly dawned on him . . . *Have been reading* . . . For how long? . . . Quite a little surprise. And they hadn't told him! They'd held it back! *I am a pilot and they refuse to tell me things they know about the condition of the craft!* The insult was worse than the danger! If the landing bag had deployed—and there was no way he could look out and see it, not even with the periscope, because it would be directly behind him—if it had deployed, then the heat shield must be loose and might come off during the re-entry. If the heat shield came off, he would burn up inside the capsule like a steak. If he put the landing-bag switch in the automatic control position, then a green light should come on if the bag was deployed. Then he would know. Slowly it dawned! . . . That was why they kept asking him if the switch were in the off position!—they didn't want him to learn the awful truth too quickly! Might as well let him complete his three orbits—then we'll let him find out about the bad news!

On top of that, they now wanted him to fool around with the switch. *That's stupid!* It might very well be that the bag had not deployed but there was an electrical malfunction somewhere in the circuit and fooling with the automatic switch might then cause it to deploy. But he stopped short of saying anything. Presumably they had taken all that into account. There was no way he could say it without falling into the dread nervous chatter.

"Okay," said Glenn. "If that's what they recommend, we'll go ahead and try it. Are you ready for it now?"

"Yes, when you're ready."

"Roger."

He reached forward and flipped the switch. Well . . . this was it—

No light. He immediately switched it back to off.

"Negative," he said. "In automatic position did not get a light and I'm back in off position now. Over."

"Roger, that's fine. In this case, we'll go ahead, and the re-entry sequence will be normal."

The retro-rockets would be fired over California, and by the time the retro-rockets brought him down out of his orbit and through the atmosphere, he would be over the Atlantic near Bermuda. That was the plan. Wally Schirra was the capcom in California. Less than a minute before he was supposed to fire the retro-rockets, by pushing a switch, he heard Wally saying: "John, leave your retropack on through your pass over Texas. Do you read?"

"Roger."

But why? The retropack wrapped around the edges of the heat shield and held the retro-rockets. Once the rockets were fired, the retropack was supposed to be jettisoned. They were back to the heat shield again, with no explanation. But he had to concentrate on firing the retro-rockets.

Next to the launch this was the most dangerous part of the flight. If the capsule's angle of attack was too shallow, you might skip off the top of the earth's atmosphere and stay in orbit for days, until long after your oxygen had run out. You wouldn't have any more rockets to slow you down. If the angle were too steep, the heat from the friction of going through the atmosphere would be so intense you would burn up inside the capsule, and a couple of minutes later the whole thing would disintegrate, heat shield or no heat shield. But the main thing was not to think about it in quite those terms. The field of consciousness is very small, said Saint-Exupéry. *What do I do next?* It was the moment of the test pilot at last. Oh, yes! *I've been here before! And I am immune! I don't get into corners I can't get out of!* One thing at a time! He could be a true flight test hero and try to line the capsule up all by himself by using the manual controls with the horizon as his reference—or he could make one more attempt to use the automatic controls. Please, dear God . . . don't let me foul up! What would the Lord answer? (Try the automatic, you ninny.) He released and reset the gyros. He put the controls on automatic. The answer to your prayers, John! Now the dials gibed with what he saw out the window and through the periscope. The automatic controls worked perfectly in pitch and roll. The yaw was still off, so he corrected that with the manual controls. The capsule kept pivoting to the right and he kept nudging it back. The ALFA trainer! One thing at a time! It was just like the ALFA trainer . . . no sense of forward motion at all . . . As long as he concentrated on the instrument panel and didn't look at the earth sliding by beneath him, he had no sense at all of going 17,500 miles an hour . . . or even five miles an hour . . . The humming little kitchen . . . He sat up in his chair squirting his hand thruster, with his eyes pinned on the dials . . . Real life, a crucial moment— against the eternal good beige setting of the simulation. One thing at a time!

Schirra began giving him the countdown for firing the rockets. "Five, four—"

He nudged it back once more with the yaw thruster.

"—three, two, one, fire."

He pushed the retro-rocket switch with his hand.

The rockets started firing in sequence, the first one, the second one, the third one. The sound seemed terribly muffled—but in that very moment, the jolt! Pure gold! One instant, as Schirra counted down, he felt absolutely motionless. The next . . . *thud thud thud* . . . the jolt in his back. He felt as if the capsule had been knocked backward. He felt as if he were sailing back toward Hawaii. All as it should be! Pure gold! The retro-light was lit up green. It was all going perfectly. He was merely slowing down. In eleven minutes he would be entering the earth's atmosphere.

He could hear Schirra saying: "Keep your retropack on until you pass Texas."

Still no reason given! He couldn't see the pattern yet. There was only the dim sense that in some fashion they were jerking him around. But all he said was: "That's affirmative."

"It looked like your attitude held pretty well," said Schirra. "Did you have to back it up at all?"

"Oh, yes, quite a bit. Yeah, I had a lot of trouble with it."

"Good enough for government work from down here," said Schirra. That was one of Schirra's favorite lines.

"Do you have a time for going to Jettison Retro?" said Glenn. This was an indirect way of asking for some explanation for the mystery of keeping the retropack on.

"Texas will give you that message," said Schirra. "Over."

They weren't going to tell him! Not so much the thought . . . as the *feeling* . . . of the insult began to build up.

Three minutes later the Texas capcom tracking station came in: "This is Texas capcom, *Friendship 7*. We are recommending that you leave the retropackage on through the entire re-entry. This means that you will have to override the zero-point-oh-five-g switch, which is expected to occur at 04:43:53. This also means that you will have to manually retract the scope. Do you read?"

That did it.

"This is *Friendship 7*," said Glenn. "What is the reason for this? Do you have any reason? Over."

"Not at this time," said the Texas capcom. "This is the judgment of Cape Flight . . . Cape Flight will give you the reason for this action when you are in view."

"Roger. Roger. *Friendship 7*."

It was really unbelievable. It was beginning to fit—

Twenty-seven seconds later he was over the Cape itself and the Cape capcom, with the voice of Alan Shepard on the radio was telling him to retract his periscope manually and to get ready for re-entry into the atmosphere.

It was beginning to fit together, he could see the pattern, the whole business of the landing bag and the retropack. This had been going on for a couple of hours now—and they were telling him nothing! Merely giving him the bits and pieces! But if he was going to re-enter with the retropack on, then they wanted the straps in place for some reason. And there was only one possible reason— something was wrong with the heat shield. And this they would not tell him! *Him!*—the pilot! It was quite unbelievable! It was—

He could hear Shepard's voice.

He was winding in the periscope, and he could hear Shepard's voice: "While you're doing that . . . we are not sure whether or not your landing bag has deployed. We feel it is possible to re-enter with the retropackage on. We see no difficulty at this time in that type of re-entry."

Glenn said, "Roger, understand."

Oh, yes, he understood now! If the landing bag was deployed, that meant the heat shield was loose. If the heat shield was loose, then it might come off during the re-entry, unless the retropack straps held it in place long enough for the capsule to establish its angle of re-entry. And the straps would soon burn off. If the heat shield came off, then he would fry. If they didn't want him—*the pilot!*—to know all this, then it meant they were afraid he might panic. And if he didn't even *need* to know the whole pattern—just the pieces, so he could follow orders—*then he wasn't really a pilot!* The whole sequence of logic clicked through Glenn's mind faster than he could have put it into words, even if he had dared utter it all at that moment. He was being treated like a passenger—a redundant component, a backup engineer, a boiler-room attendant—in an automatic system!—like someone who did not have that rare and unutterably righteous stuff! —as if the right stuff itself did not even matter! It was a transgression against all that was holy—all this in a single limbic flash of righteous indignation as John Glenn re-entered the earth's atmosphere.

"*Seven*, this is Cape," said Al Shepard. "Over."

"Go ahead, Cape," said Glenn. "You're ground . . . you are going out."

"We recommend that you . . ."

That was the last he could hear from the ground. He had entered the atmosphere. He couldn't feel the g-forces yet, but the friction and the ionization had built up, and the radios were now useless. The capsule was beginning to buffet and he was fighting it with the controls. The fuel for the automatic system, the hydrogen peroxide, was so low he could no longer be sure which system worked. He was descending backward. The heat shield was on the outside of the capsule, directly behind his back. If he glanced out the window he could see only the blackness of the sky. The periscope was retracted, so he saw nothing on the scope screen. He heard a *thump* above him, on the outside of the capsule. He looked up. Through the window he could see a strap. *From the retropack. The straps broke! And now what!* Next the heat shield! The black sky out the window began to turn a pale orange. The strap flat against the window started burning—and then it was gone. The universe turned a flaming orange. That was the heat shield beginning to burn up from the tremendous speed of the re-entry. This was something Shepard and Grissom had not seen. They had not re-entered the atmosphere at such speed. Nevertheless, Glenn knew it was coming. Five hundred, a thousand times he had been told how the heat shield would *ablate*, burn off layer by layer, vaporize, dissipate the heat into the atmosphere, send off a corona of flames. All he could see now through the window were the flames. He was inside of a ball of fire. But!—a huge flaming chunk went by the window, a great chunk of something burning. Then another . . . another . . . The capsule started buffeting . . . The heat shield was breaking up! It was crumbling—flying away in huge flaming chunks . . . He fought to steady the capsule with the hand controller. *Fly-by-wire!* But the rolls and yaws were too fast for him . . . The ALFA trainer gone amok, inside a fireball . . . The heat! . . . It was as if his entire central nervous system were now centered in his back. If the capsule was disintegrating and he was about to burn up, the heat pulse would reach his back first. His backbone would become like a length of red-hot metal. He already knew what the feeling would be like . . . and when . . . *Now!* . . . But it didn't come. There was no tremendous heat and no more flaming debris . . . Not the heat shield, after all. The burning chunks had come from what remained of the retropack. First the straps had gone and then the rest of it. The capsule kept rocking, and the g-forces built up. He knew the g-forces by heart. A thousand times he had felt them on the centrifuge. They drove him back into the seat. It was harder and harder to move the hand controller. He kept trying to damp out the rocking motion by firing the yaw thrusters and the roll thrusters, but it was all too fast for him. They didn't seem to do much good, at any rate.

No more red glow . . . he must be out of the fireball . . . seven g's were driving him back into the seat . . . He could hear the Cape capcom:

". . . How do you read? Over."

That meant he had passed through the ionosphere and was entering the lower atmosphere.

"Loud and clear; how me?"

"Roger, reading you loud and clear. How are you doing?"

"Oh, pretty good."

"Roger. Your impact point is within one mile of the uprange destroyer."

Oh, pretty good. It wasn't Yeager, but it wasn't bad. He was inside of one and a half tons of non-aerodynamic metal. He was a hundred thousand feet up, dropping toward the ocean like an enormous cannonball. The capsule had no aerodynamic qualities whatsoever at this altitude. It was rocking terribly. Out the window he could see a wild white contrail snaked out against the blackness of the sky. He was dropping at a thousand feet per second. The last critical moment of the flight was coming up. Either the parachute deployed and took hold or it didn't. The rocking had intensified. The retropack! Part of the retropack must still be attached and the drag of it is trying to flip the capsule . . . He couldn't wait any longer. The parachute was supposed to deploy automatically, but he couldn't wait any longer. Rocking . . . He reached up to fire the parachute manually—but it fired on its own, automatically, first the drogue and then the main parachute. He swung under it in a huge arc. The heat was ferocious, but the chute held. It snapped him back into the seat. Through the window the sky was blue. It was the same day all over again. It was early in the afternoon on a sunny day out in the Atlantic near Bermuda. Even the landing-bag light was green. There was nothing even wrong with the landing bag. There had been nothing wrong with the heat shield. There was nothing wrong with his rate of descent, forty feet per second. He could hear the rescue ship chattering away over the radio. They were only twenty minutes away from where he would hit, only six miles. He was once again lying on his back in the human holster. Out the window the sky was no longer black. The capsule swayed under the parachute, and over this way he looked up and saw clouds and over that way blue sky. He was very, very hot. But he knew the feeling. All those endless hours in the heat chambers —it wouldn't kill you. He was coming down into the water only 300 miles from where he started. It was the same day, merely five hours later. A balmy day out in the Atlantic near Bermuda. The sun had moved just seventy-five degrees in the sky. It was 2:45 in the afternoon. Nothing to do but get all these wires and hoses disconnected. *He had done it.* He began to let the thought loose in his mind. He must be very close to the water. The capsule hit the water. It drove him down into his seat again, on his back. It was quite a jolt. It was hot in here. Even with the suit fans still running, the heat was terrific. Over the radio they kept telling him not to try to leave the capsule. The rescue ship was almost there. They weren't going to try the helicopter deal again, except in an emergency. He wasn't about to attempt a water egress. He wasn't about to hit the hatch detonator. The Presbyterian Pilot was not about to foul up. His pipeline to the dear Lord could not be clearer. He had done it.

Annie Glenn had already had a taste of what it was going to be like. But the other six and their wives were not ready for it. It was as if some enormous tidal wave were heading for the Cape and the entire U.S.A. from out in the Atlantic, from the vicinity of Grand Bahama Island, where John was being debriefed. Riding the crest, like Triton, was the Freckled Face God, John himself. Word got back that the sailors on the *Noa,* the ship that hauled the capsule, with John in it, out of the water, had painted white lines around his footprints on the deck after he walked from the capsule to a hatchway. They didn't want his footprints on their deck to ever disappear! Well, it just seemed like some sort of goony swabbo sentimentality. But that was only the beginning.

Al Shepard and Gus Grissom didn't know what the hell was happening. Poor Gus—all he had gotten after his flight was a medal, a handshake, a gust of rhetoric from James Webb, out on a brain-frying strip of asphalt at Patrick Air Force Base, plus a few attaboys from a crowd of about thirty. For John—well, the mobs that had showed up for the launch, for the fireworks, barely seemed to have thinned out at all. Cocoa Beach was still full of the crazy adrenalin of the event. Out-of-towners were still tooling around all over the place in their automobiles and asking where the astronauts hung out. They didn't want to miss a thing. They knew that John would be flying back to the Cape after the debriefing. The next thing they knew, Lyndon Johnson was in town. He was going to meet John at the landing strip at Patrick. Underlings like Webb would just be part of the scenery. Then they learned that the President was coming, John F. Kennedy himself. Glenn wasn't going to him, in Washington—he was coming to Glenn.

Something quite extraordinary was building up. It was a wave and a half, and the other six and their wives were more surprised than anybody else. It was ironic. They had all assumed that Al Shepard was the big winner. Al had won out in the competition for the first flight. Al had been invited to the White House to receive a medal, whereas Gus had gotten his about eight steps from the palmetto grass, because Al was the certified number-one man in this thing and had taken the first flight. But even before John got back to the Cape from Grand Bahama Island, there was a note of worshipful swooning in the air that indicated that Al had not made the first flight, after all. He had merely made the first suborbital flight, which now looked like nothing at all. He was now more like Slick Goodlin to John's Chuck Yeager. Slick Goodlin had, technically, made the first flight of the X-1. But it was Yeager who made the flight that counted, the flight in which they first tried to push the bird supersonic. As Slick Goodlin to John's Chuck Yeager—what was Al supposed to do, cheer about it? And Betty Grissom—who never even got a parade down the poor dim dowdy main street of Mitchell, Indiana—was she supposed to be tickled pink about the Glenns, who were going to be paraded up and down every high road in the United States? But there was precious little time to brood. Once John's plane touched down at Patrick on February 23, the wave became so big it simply carried everyone along with it. The fellows and the wives and the children were all out at Patrick, waiting for John's plane, and the Vice-President was on hand, along with about two hundred reporters. Johnson was right up there at the head of the mob with Annie and the two children. He had gotten next to her at last. Johnson was right beside her now, out at Patrick, oozing protocol all over her and craning and straining his huge swollen head around, straining to get at John and pour Texas all over him. The plane arrives and John disembarks, a tremendous cheer goes up, a cry from the throat, from the diaphragm, from the solar plexus, and they bring Annie and the two children forward . . . the holy icons . . . the Wife and the Children . . . the Solid Backing on the Home Front . . . and John is too much! He reaches into his pocket and pulls out a handkerchief and dabs his eye, wipes away a tear! And some little guy from NASA stretched out his hand and took the used handkerchief . . . so that it could be preserved in the Smithsonian! (With this handkerchief Astronaut John H. Glenn, Jr., wiped away a tear upon being reunited with his wife after his historic earth-orbital flight.) From that moment on, Al and Gus were also-rans, minor leaguers. And they didn't even have time to fume! The events, day by day, were becoming like something elemental, like a huge change in the weather, a shift in the templates, the Flood, the Last Day, the True Brother Entering Heaven . . .

John did not merely get a parade through Washington and a trip to the White House and the medal from the President. Oh, he got those things, all right. But he also addressed a special joint session of Congress—the Senate and the House met together to hear John, the way they had for presidents, prime ministers, kings. There was John standing up there at the podium, with Lyndon Johnson and John McCormack seated behind him, and the rest of them looking up at him from their seats. In absolute adoration, too! That was where the tears started! The tears —they couldn't hold them back. John's great round freckled face was shining with glory. He knew just what he was doing. He was the Presbyterian Pilot addressing the world. He said some things that nobody else in the world could have gotten away with, even in 1962. He said, "I still get a lump in my throat when I see the American flag passing by." But he pulled it off! And then he lifted his hand up toward the gallery—this was in the House side of the Capitol—and five hundred pairs of congressional eyes swung up with his hand toward the gallery, and he introduced his mom and dad from New Concord, Ohio, and a few aunts and uncles for good measure, and then his children and, finally, ". . . above all, I want you to meet my wife, Annie . . . Annie . . . the Rock!" Well, that did it. That turned on the waterworks. Senators and representatives were trying to clap and reach for their handkerchiefs at the same time. They were dabbing their eyes and cheering through the fluttering ends of their handkerchiefs. Their faces glistened. Some fought back the tears and a couple let go. They applauded, cheered, snuffled, wheezed . . . A couple of them said, "Amen!" They said it out loud; it just came popping out of their good hardtack cracker evangelical dissenting Protestant hearts as the Presbyterian Pilot lifted up his eyes and his hand to the Rock and the eternal Mother of us all . . .

And that was just the start. In a way that was nothing compared to the ticker-tape parade in New York. After all, a ceremonial joint session of Congress is a tailor-made event, a command performance. But the parade in New York was an amazing event, so amazing that anyone, even Al or Gus could only blink and shake his head and ride the wave. John had the good sense to invite Al and Gus and "the Other Four," Wally, Scott, Deke, and Gordo, and their families to join

him and Annie and the children in the parade. John could have called the shot
any way he wanted it. There was nobody in NASA or in the U.S. government,
with the exception of Kennedy himself, who could have arranged it any way John
didn't want it. So everybody came along for the show, the whole gang.

Despite the tide of cheers and tears that had already started in Washington,
none of them knew what to expect in New York. Like most military people,
including those in the Brooklyn Navy Yard, they didn't really consider New York
part of the United States. It was like a free port, a stateless city, an international
protectorate, Danzig in the Polish corridor, Beirut the crossroads of the Middle
East, Trieste, Zurich, Macao, Hong Kong. Whatever ideals the military stood for,
New York City did not. It was a foreign city full of a strange race of curiously tiny
malformed gray people. And so forth and so on. What they saw when they got
there bowled them over. The crowds were not only waiting in the airport, which
was not surprising—a little publicity was all it took to get a mob of gawkers to an
airport—but they were also lining the godforsaken highway into the city, through
the borough of Queens, or whatever it was, out in the freezing cold in the most
rancid broken-down industrial terrain you have ever seen, a decaying landscape
that seemed to belong to another century—they were out there *along the highway*,
anywhere they could squeeze in, and . . . they were crying!—crying as the black
cars roared by!

People were crying, right out in the open, as soon as they laid eyes on John,
and perhaps the rest of them, too. They were all swept up in the wave now. The
wave was too enormous for fine distinctions. When they reached the city proper,
Manhattan, and came in off the expressway, the FDR Drive, there were people
hanging over the railings, twenty or thirty feet up above the ramp, and they were
crying and waving little flags and pouring their hearts out.

And that was just the beginning. The parade started in lower Manhattan and
headed up Broadway. Each astronaut was in an open limousine. John led the
lineup, of course, with Lyndon Johnson, Vice-President, in the seat beside him. It
was cold as hell, seventeen degrees, but the streets were mobbed. There must
have been millions of people out there, packed from the curbings clear back to
the storefronts, and there were people hanging out of all the windows, particularly
along lower Broadway, where the buildings were older and they could open the
windows, and they were filling the air with shreds of paper, every piece of paper
they could get their hands on.

Sometimes the pieces of paper would flutter right in front of your face—and
you could see that they were tearing up their telephone books, just ripping the
pages out and tearing them to bits and throwing them out the window as homage,
as garlands, rose petals—and it was so touching! This horrible rat-gray city was
suddenly touching, warm! You wanted to protect these poor souls who loved you
so much! Huge waves of emotion rolled over you. You couldn't hear yourself talk,
but there was nothing you could have said, anyway. All you could do was let these
incredible waves roll over you. Out in the middle of the intersections were the
policemen, the policemen they had all heard about or read about, New York's
Finest, big tough-looking men in blue greatcoats—and they were crying! They
were right out in the intersections in front of everybody, bawling away—tears
streaming down their faces, saluting, then cupping their hands and yelling amazing things to John and the rest of them—"We love you, Johnny!"—and then
bawling some more, just letting it pour out. The New York cops!

And what was it that had moved them all so deeply? It was not a subject that you could discuss, but the seven of them knew what it was, and so did most of their wives. Or they knew about part of it. They knew it had to do with the presence, the aura, the radiation of *the right stuff*, the same vital force of manhood that had made millions vibrate and resonate thirty-five years before to Lindbergh —except that in this case it was heightened by Cold War patriotism, the greatest surge of patriotism since the Second World War. Neither the term nor the concept of the single-combat warrior did they know about, but the sheer patriotism of that moment—even in New York, the Danzig corridor!—was impossible to miss. We pay homage to you! You have fought back against the Russians in the heavens! There was something pure and rare about it. Patriotism! Oh, yes! Here you saw it in a million-footed form, before your very eyes! Most of the seven had been around the Kennedys at one time or another, with Jack or with Bobby, and knew the way a crowd reacted to them—but it was something different from this. Around the Kennedys you saw a fan's hysteria, involving a lot of shrieking and clutching, with people reaching out to grab souvenirs and swooning and squealing, as if the Kennedys were movie stars who happened to be in power. But what the multitudes showed John Glenn and the rest of them on that day was something else. They anointed them with the primordial tears that the right stuff commanded.

The seven righteous families were put up in suites at the Waldorf-Astoria, which as far as they knew was still the grandest hotel in America. Suites!—two bedrooms and a living room! For junior officers in the military it was an experience from a fable. They were still soaring on what they had just been through, but they were afraid to try to put the right name on it, afraid of what it might reveal about what was going through their minds. They were beginning to ask themselves the question "What, precisely, have we become?"

Henry Luce gave a dinner for them at the Tower Suite, the restaurant at the top of the Time-Life Building. After dinner on the spur of the moment, the whole bunch of them went to see a play, *How to Succeed in Business Without Really Trying*, which was a big hit at the time. John and Annie and the children, all of the other fellows and their wives and children, plus the bodyguards and some NASA people and some Time-Life people, quite an entourage—and all of it arranged at the last minute. The start of the play was held up for them. People in the audience gave up their seats, so the astronauts and their party could have the best seats in the house, a whole bloc. Just like that they gave up their seats. When John and the others walked into the theater, everybody else was already seated, because by now the play was a good thirty minutes late starting—and the audience rose and cheered until John sat down. Then a member of the cast came out in front of the curtain and welcomed them and congratulated John and praised the fellows as great human beings and humbly hoped that the little diversion about to be offered would please them. "And now the play will commence!"

Then the lights went down and the curtain went up, and you had to be pretty dense not to realize what this was: a command performance! Royal treatment, point for point, right down the line, and they were the royal families. And it didn't stop there. They had rewritten some of the lines, rewritten them in an hour or so—to make the jokes contain references to space and John's flight and putting a man on the moon and so on. When they left the theater, there were still other people outside, waiting, hundreds more people, waiting in the cold, and they started yelling in those horrible twisted rat-gray New York street voices, but everything they said, even the wisecracks, was full of warmth and admiration. Christ, if they owned even New York, even this free port, this Hong Kong, this Polish corridor—what was not theirs now in America?

Somehow, extraordinary as it was, it was . . . right! The way it should be! The unutterable aura of the right stuff had been brought onto the terrain *where things were happening!* Perhaps that was what New York existed for, to celebrate those who *had it,* whatever it was, and there was nothing like the right stuff, for all responded to it, and all wanted to be near it and to feel the sizzle and to blink in the light.

Oh, it was a primitive and profound thing! Only pilots truly had it, but the entire world responded, and no one knew its name!

NOT LONG AFTER THAT, Kennedy brought the seven astronauts to the White House for a smaller, more personal visit. Kennedy's father was there, Joseph Kennedy. The old man had had a stroke, and half his body was paralyzed, and he was sitting in a wheelchair. The President took the seven astronauts in to meet his father, and the first one he introduced him to was John. John Glenn!—the first American to orbit the earth and challenge the Russians in the heavens. The old man, Joe Kennedy, reaches up with his one good hand to shake hands with John, and suddenly he starts crying. But the thing is, only half his face is crying, because of the stroke. One half of his face isn't moving a muscle. It's set, absolutely impassive. But the other half—well, it's blubbering, that's the word for it. His eyebrow is curling down over his eye, the way it does when you're really bawling, and the tears are streaming out of the crevice where his eyebrow and his eye and his nose come together, and one of his nostrils is quivering and his lips are writhing and contorting on that side, and his chin is all pulled up and pitted and trembling—but just on the one side! The other side is just staring at John, as if he saw right through him, as if he were just another Marine colonel whose career had somehow led him briefly into the White House.

The President would lean down and put his arm around the old man's shoulders and say: "Now, now, Dad, it's all right, it's okay." But Joe Kennedy was still crying when they left the room.

Obviously if the man hadn't had a stroke, he wouldn't have burst out crying. Until his stroke he had been a bear. Nevertheless, the emotion was there, and it would have been there whether he had had a stroke or not. That was what the sight of John Glenn did to Americans at that time. It primed them for the tears. And those tears ran like a river all over America. It was an extraordinary thing, being the sort of mortal who brought tears to other men's eyes.

13

===

THE OPERATIONAL STUFF

JULY 4 WAS NOT the time of year for anyone to be introduced to Houston, Texas, although just what the right time would be was hard to say. For eight months Houston was an unbelievably torrid effluvial sump with a mass of mushy asphalt, known as Downtown, set in the middle. Then for two months, starting in November, the most amazing winds came sweeping down from Canada, as if down a pipe, and the humid torpor turned into a wet chill. The remaining two months were the moderate ones, although not exactly what you would call spring. The clouds closed in like a lid, and the oil refineries over by Galveston Bay saturated the air, the nose, the lungs, the heart, and the soul with the gassy smell of oil funk. There were bays, canals, lakes, lagoons, bayous everywhere, all of them so greasy and toxic that if you trailed your hand in the water off the back of your rowboat you would lose a knuckle. The fishermen used to like to tell the weekenders: "Don't smoke out there or you'll set the bay on fire." All the poisonous snakes known to North America were in residence there: rattlers, copperheads, cottonmouths, and corals.

No, there was no best time to be introduced to Houston, Texas, but July 4 was the worst. And it was on July 4, 1962, that the seven Mercury astronauts moved to Houston. For the prodigious effort that Kennedy's moon program would require, NASA was building a Manned Spacecraft Center on a thousand acres of cattle pasture south of Houston near Clear Lake, which was not a lake but an inlet and was about as clear as the eyeballs of a poisoned bass. The astronauts, Gilruth, most of the Langley and the Cape personnel would move to Houston, although the Cape would continue to be the launching center. The small scale and modest appearance of Langley and the Cape had somehow been perfect for the hell-for-leather *más allá* phase that Project Mercury had just been through. They all knew Houston would be bigger. The rest they could never have guessed.

They stepped out of the airplane at the Houston airport and started gulping in the molten air. It was 96 degrees. Not that it mattered particularly; they had been assured that their entry into Houston would be easygoing and casual, Texas-style.

There would be a zippy little motorcade through Downtown, just to give the good folks a look-see . . . and then there would be a cocktail party with a few prominent local figures, during which they could let their hair down and knock back a couple of long cool ones, or whatever, and relax.

Waiting there at the airport is a lineup of convertibles, one for each astronaut and his family with his name on a big paper banner taped to the side. So off they go in a motorcade, all seven of them and their wives and children, except for Jo Schirra, who was still at Langley recovering from some minor surgery. Pretty soon they're moving through the streets of Houston at a good clip, and it seems painless enough, but then all seven cars head down a ramp, into the bowels of an arena called the Houston Coliseum.

A bone-splitting chill hits them. They shudder and shake their heads. They are down inside some vast underground parking lot. The place is air-conditioned Houston-style, which is to say, within an inch of your life. There is a whole army of frozen people waiting down there in the gloaming, endless rows of marching bands in uniform, standing there like ice sculpture, politicians waiting in yet more convertibles, too cold to open their mouths, policemen, firemen, National Guard troops, stiff and still as lead, and more bands. Then they turn right around and head out of the underground parking lot, up the ramp, and back out into the blast of sunlight, a hundred degrees of heat, and the asphalt, which was lying there heaving and rippling in the caloric waves. All at once they are at the head of a big parade through the streets of Houston. Well, not quite in the lead. In the lead convertible now is a Texas congressman, a rubicund fellow named Albert P. Thomas, an influential member of the House Appropriations Committee, waving a ten-gallon hat, as if to say, "Look what I brought you!"

It began to dawn on the boys and their wives that these people, the businessmen and the politicians, looked upon the opening of the Manned Spacecraft Center and the arrival of the astronauts as about the biggest thing in Houston history. Neiman-Marcus and all the other high-tone stores, the great banks and museums and other grand institutions, all the class, all the Culture, were in Dallas. By Houston lights Dallas was Paris, once you set your watch to Central Standard, and Houston was nothing but oil and hard grabbers. The space program and the seven Mercury astronauts were going to make Boom Town respectable, legitimate, a part of America's soul. So the big parade began with Representative Albert Thomas's waving ten-gallon hat signaling the start of the redemption of Houston.

The seven pilots and their wives thought they had seen every sort of parade there was, but this one was *sui generis*. There were thousands of people lining the streets. They did not make a sound, however. They stood there four and five deep at the curbs, sweating and staring. They sweated a river and they stared ropes. They just stared and sweated. The seven lads, each in his emblazoned convertible, were standing up grinning and waving, and the wives were smiling and waving, and the children were smiling and looking around—everyone was doing the usual —and the crowds just stared back. They didn't even smile. They looked at them with a morose curiosity, as if they were prisoners of war or had come from Alpha Centauri and no one was sure whether or not they comprehended the local lingo. Every now and then some very old person would wave and yell something hearty and encouraging, but the rest were just planted there in the sun like tarbabies. Of course, anyone fool enough to stand around in the asphalt mush of Downtown at noon watching a parade was obviously defective to begin with. The parade plowed on, however, through wave after wave of catatonia and rippling lassitude.

After about an hour of this, the fellows and their families noticed with considerable misgiving that the parade was heading back into that hole in the ground underneath the Coliseum. The air conditioning hit them like a wall. Everybody's bone marrow congealed. It made you feel like your teeth were loose. It turned out that this was where the little cocktail party was going to take place: in the Houston Coliseum. They led them up to the floor of the Coliseum, which was like a great indoor bowl. There were thousands of people milling around and some sort of incredible smell and a storm of voices and the occasional insane cackle. There were five thousand extremely loud people on the floor eager to tear into roast cow with both hands and wash it down with bourbon whiskey. The air was filled with the stench of burning cattle. They had set up about ten barbecue pits in there, and they were roasting thirty animals. Five thousand businessmen and politicians and their better halves, fresh from the 100-degree horrors of Downtown in July, couldn't wait to sink their faces in it. It was a Texas barbecue, Houston-style.

First they took the seven brave lads and their wives and children up onto a stage that had been set up at one end of the arena, and there was a little welcoming ceremony in which they introduced them one by one, and a great many politicians and businessmen made speeches. All the while the great cow carcasses sizzled and popped and the smoke of the burning meat was wafted here and there in the chilly currents of the air conditioning. Only the extreme cold kept you from throwing up. The ganglia of the solar plexus were frozen. The wives tried to be polite, but it was a losing game. The children were squirming up on the stage and the wives were getting up and whispering to any locals they could get close to. The children were *in extremis*. They hadn't been near a bathroom for hours. The wives were frantically trying to find out where the johns were in this place.

Unfortunately, now came the part where they were just supposed to relax, eat a side of beef and a peck of kidney beans sinking in gravy, drink a little whiskey, and shake hands with the good folks and make themselves at home. So they led them back out onto the floor of the arena, cleared out a space, got some folding chairs for them and some paper plates loaded with huge joints of Texas steer, and then put a lineup of folding chairs around the whole group of them, in a circle, on the order of a stockade, and around the stockade they put a ring of Texas Rangers, facing outward, toward the crowd. The crowd was now lining up, by the hundreds, at the barbecue pits, getting great lubricated hunks of beef on paper plates . . . and more whiskey. Then they took seats in the stands, thousands of them, and looked down at the stockade floor. This was the main event, the reception, the Big Howdy: five thousand people, VIPs one and all, sitting up in the stands of the Houston Coliseum amid the burning cattle . . . watching the astronauts *eat*.

Certain VIPs with clout, however, were allowed to enter the stockade through the ring of Rangers and greet the lads and their wives personally as they juggled the great maroon hunks of meat. It was always someone such as Herb Snout from Kar Kastle, and he would come up and say: "Hi, there! Herb Snout! Kar Kastle! Listen! We're damned glad to have you folks here, just damned glad, goddamn it!" And then he would turn to one of the wives, whose hands were so full of cow meat she couldn't budge, and he would bend down and turn on a huge Karo-syrup grin, to show his deference to the ladies, and say in a suddenly huge voice that would make the poor startled woman drop the reeking maroon all over her lap: "Hi, there, little lady! Just *damned* glad to see *you*, too!" And then he'd give a huge horrible wink that would practically implode his eye, and he'd say, "We've heard a lot of good things about you gals, a *lot* of good things"—all with this eye-wrenching wink.

After a while, there were Herb Snouts and Gurney Frinks all over the place and the huge Hereford joints were sliding down every leg and splashing in the puddles of whiskey on the floor, and five thousand spectators watched their struggling jaws, and the smoke and the babble filled the air and the children screamed for mercy and relief. Just then, when the madness seemed to have outdone itself once and for all, a band struck up and the houselights dimmed and a spotlight searched out the stage and a show began and a mighty hearty voice boomed out over the p.a. system: "Ladies and gentlemen . . . in honor of our mighty special guests and mighty fine new neighbors, we are proud to present . . . Miss Sally Rand!"

The band struck up "Sugar Blues" . . . much raunchy high-hatting of the trumpets . . . *Oh, owwwwwwwww wahwahwah* . . . and out into the spotlight pranced an ancient woman with yellow hair and a white mask of a face . . . Her flesh looked like the meat of a casaba melon in the winter . . . She carried some enormous plumed fans . . . She began her famous striptease act . . . Sally Rand! . . . who had been an aging but still famous stripper when the seven brave lads were in their teens, during the Depression . . . *Oh-owwwwwwwww wahwahwah* . . . and she winked and minced about and took off a little here and covered up a little there and shook her ancient haunches at the seven single-combat warriors. It was electrifying. It was quite beyond sex, show business, and either the sins or rigors of the flesh. It was two o'clock in the afternoon on the Fourth of July, and the cows burned on, and the whiskey roared *goddamned glad to see you* and the Venus de Houston shook her fanny in an utterly baffling blessing over it all.

J UST THREE YEARS ago Rene had still been in that dogged military wife's frame of mind in which you gladly spent three days sanding a slab of monkeypod, until your hands were raw, to save the fabulous sum of ninety-five dollars. When Scott had run up a fifty-dollar telephone bill calling her from Washington, Albuquerque, and Dayton during the testing back in 1959, it had seemed like the end of the world. Fifty dollars! That was the food budget for *a month!* That was three years ago. Now she was in the living room of her own house—custom-made, not a tract home—on a lake, underneath the live oak and the pines. She and Annie Glenn had flown down to Houston one weekend from Washington and picked out lots, just like that, but they turned out to be in the best spot in the vicinity of the Space Center, a development called Timber Cove. The Schirras and Grissoms had moved into the same neighborhood. With admirable foresight, as it turned out, they had built their houses so that they opened up in the back to look out on the water and the trees, while on the side facing the street they were practically blank walls of brick. They had barely moved the first stick of furniture in when the tour buses started arriving, plus the freelance tourists in cars. They were extraordinary, these people. Sometimes you could hear the loudspeaker inside the bus. You could hear the tour guide saying, "This is the home of Scott Carpenter,

the second Mercury astronaut to fly in earth orbit in outer space." Sometimes
people would get out and grab handfuls of grass from your lawn. They'd get back
on the bus with the miserable little green sprouts sticking out of their fingers.
They believed in magic. Sometimes people would drive up, get out, stare at the
house as if waiting for something to happen, and then walk up to the door and
ring the bell and say: "We hate to bother you, but do you suppose you could send
one of your children out so we could have our pictures taken with him?" And yet
they weren't like the fans of movie stars. There was no frenzy. They thought they
were really being considerate by not asking you to come out for the snapshot
session yourself. They really meant it. They had more of the attitude of being at a
living shrine.

This was the first house that Rene and Scott had ever built, the first house
that had really seemed theirs. They had turned the page, all right. Things happened so fast now. At one point it looked as if they were going to be *given* houses
completely furnished! The best that $60,000 could buy in 1962, at wholesale! A
month after John Glenn's flight, a Houston man named Frank Sharp presented to
Leo DeOrsey, as the fellows' business advisor, the following proposition: To show
their pride in the astronauts and the new Manned Space Center, the builders,
developers, furniture dealers, and others involved in the suburban home business
would give each of the seven brave lads one of the homes being built for the 1962
Parade of Homes in Sharpstown. Sharpstown was a housing tract that Frank
Sharp himself had been the impresario for. The Parade of Homes was a row of
model houses that contractors who expected to do business in Sharpstown were
putting up by way of advertising their wares. Sharp would contribute the land, a
$10,000 lot to each astronaut; the contractors would contribute the houses; and
the furniture and department stores would furnish them from top to bottom. The
seven astronauts and their families would live right there on Rowan Drive in the
Country Club Terrace section of Sharpstown, between Richmond Road and Bel-
laire Boulevard, in $60,000 worth of home and hearth each. Since Sharpstown at
this point was nothing but maps, signs, bunting, Englishy thatchy tweedy-sound-
ing street names and thousands of acres of wind-swept boondocker gumbo scrub-
land, Astronauts Row wouldn't be a bad way to start filling in the spaces. Sharp
was the Big Howdy through and through, a self-made man and already quite a
prominent citizen, close to the mayor, Representative Albert Thomas, Governor
John Connally, and Vice-President Lyndon Johnson. He underwrote annual golf
trophies and things of that sort. He had the right credentials, or the Houston
version thereof, and so DeOrsey had talked it over with the boys, and they all
decided the deal was okay. It had nothing to do with the space program and
didn't obligate them to anything. It was just an unencumbered *goodie*, pure and
simple. None of them actually wanted to live in Sharpstown, from what they had
heard about the area. It was too far from the NASA facility, for a start. So they
figured they would accept the houses, shake hands with one and all, and then
. . . *sell them.* John Glenn was as agreeable to this type of goodie as anybody
else. It was that age-old concern of the military officer with the extras. John had
been in the Marines for nearly twenty years now. He was too far down that road,
had been through too many measly paychecks, to decondition himself anytime
soon when it came to the perks, the extras, the irresistible and perfectly honorable and authorized goodies. Therefore, not even John, for all his quite sincere
sense of morality, could comprehend the furor that was erupting. Gilruth and

Webb and everybody else in the NASA hierarchy were blowing fuses over Frank Sharp's Parade of the Homes of the Astronauts. And that was only the start. It had touched off a true emergency: the *Life* deal was under review! From what Scott and the others had picked up, the President himself was considering putting an end to *all* commercial exploitation of astronaut status. The rest of the press had resented the *Life* deal from the beginning and had argued that it cast a venal shadow on the astronauts' patriotic service. Sharpstown showed you where the exploitation route could lead . . .

Sharpstown was one thing . . . but a threat to the *Life* deal—now, there you had something serious! *Unthinkable* was the word. The seven pilots, steeped in the honorable goodies tradition of the military, had begun to look upon the *Life* deal in the same way they looked upon the military pension that you rated after twenty years. It was an immutable condition of the service! It was part of the drill! Regulation issue! Covered in the manual! All holes in the argument were immediately vulcanized by the heat of the emotion. This was no time to sit around waiting for the orders to be posted on the bulletin board. It was only three weeks before Scott's flight, and he was in the thick of training, but on May 3 most of the others went to see Lyndon Johnson at his ranch in Texas to try to straighten the matter out. Webb was there, too. They had quite a conclave. Lyndon Johnson gave them some fatherly discourses on private lives and public responsibility, twisting his great hands around in the air in front of him, as if making imaginary snowballs. This pained him as much as it did them, and so on. The hell of it was that neither Johnson nor Webb would miss a minute's sleep if the *Life* deal was canceled forthwith. They had both been burned by the astronaut-*Life* connection during the incident at the Glenns' house in January. In fact, if it hadn't been for Glenn—

Fortunately, there was no getting around John. By now, three months after his flight, John had ascended to a status that only a Biblical scholar could fully appreciate. John was the triumphant single-combat warrior. He had risked his life to challenge the mighty Soviet Integral on the high ground. Through his skill and courage he had neutralized the enemy's advantage, and the tears of joy and gratitude and awe still flowed. In the Bible, first Book of Samuel, eighteenth chapter, it is written that after David slew Goliath and the Philistines fled in terror and the Israelites achieved a mighty victory, King Saul took David into the royal household and gave him the status of an adopted son. It is also written that wherever Saul and David went, people thronged the streets, and the women sang of the thousands Saul had slain and the tens of thousands David had slain. "And Saul was very wroth, and the saying displeased him; and he said, They have ascribed unto David ten thousands, and to me they have ascribed *but* thousands: and *what* can he have more but the kingdom? And Saul eyed David from that day forward." And President Kennedy eyed John Glenn. The President had begun to regale John and bring him into the Kennedy family orbit. John was the sort of man a president needed to keep squarely within his camp. A vice-president, too, for that matter. Johnson had gone out of his way to be friendly to John and Annie, and they had genuinely begun to like the man. They wound up inviting Johnson and his wife, Lady Bird, for dinner at their house in Arlington, on John's fortieth birthday. And the Johnsons accepted, just like that. Rene and Scott were also invited. "What on earth are you going to serve?" Rene said to Annie.

"My ham loaf," said Annie.

"Ham loaf!"

"Why not? Everybody likes it. I bet you Lady Bird asks for the recipe, too."

The Johnsons stayed until almost midnight. Lyndon had his coat off and his sleeves rolled up and was having a rare old time for himself. As they left, Rene heard Lady Bird ask Annie for the recipe for her ham loaf.

One day John was out on the Atlantic Ocean, beyond the Hyannis Port, Massachusetts, harbor, aboard the President's yacht, the *Honey Fitz,* when the subject of the *Life* contract came up. The President wanted to know what John thought of one particular argument against the *Life* arrangement that was frequently presented; namely, that a soldier in battle—a Marine at Iwo Jima, for example—ran just as great a risk of death as any astronaut and yet did not expect recompense from Time, Inc. John said yes, that was so, but suppose that soldier's or Marine's private life, his children, his thoughts, his hopes, his dreams, became of such intense interest that the press camped on his doorstep and he had to live under glass, as it were. Then he should have the right to receive compensation. The President nodded sagaciously, and the *Life* contract was saved, right there on the *Honey Fitz.*

Well, thanks to the *Life* deal, Scott and Rene could now get mortgage money and afford to build a new house in a nice area like Timber Cove. Or thanks to that and the panting eagerness of the developers to have astronauts in their new developments. It was the best advertisement they could have. They gave the boys close to at-cost deals on the land and the houses, and they let them have the mortgage money at 4 percent, with very little down payment. And for astronauts like John and Scott, who had now flown, they couldn't do enough.

The contractors and developers and the public generally thought Scott and his flight were terrific . . . but within NASA something . . . was going on. Scott and Rene had both begun to detect it, although no one ever said anything openly. Scott had gotten all the medals and all the parades and the trip to the White House, but something was up, and not even the other wives would tell Rene what it was.

Scott had flown on May 24, three months after John. Deke Slayton had been scheduled to take the flight, but then NASA made it known that Deke had a medical problem: idiopathic atrial fibrillation. This was a condition in which the electrical firing sequence of the heart went out of sync occasionally, causing an irregular pulse and a slight lowering of the pumping capacity of the organ. *Idiopathic* meant that the causes were unknown. The condition had been discovered, said NASA, during centrifuge runs in August 1959. Slayton had been examined at the Philadelphia Navy Hospital and the Air Force's School of Aviation Medicine at San Antonio, where the verdict—or so Slayton was told—was that the condition was a minor anomaly and not serious enough to cost him his job as astronaut. But, in fact, one of the Air Force doctors at San Antonio, a highly regarded cardiologist, had written a letter to Webb recommending that Slayton not be assigned to a flight, since atrial fibrillation, idiopathic or not, did reduce the efficiency of the heart to some degree.

Webb just kept the letter on file. Slayton was assigned, in November 1961, to the second orbital flight. Early in January Webb ordered a complete reassessment of the man's heart condition. His argument was that Slayton was an Air Force pilot on loan to NASA, and an Air Force cardiologist had recommended that he not be used for flights. Therefore, the case should be reviewed. Slayton's case now went before two boards, one made up of high-ranking NASA doctors and the other made up of eight doctors convened by the Air Force Surgeon General. Both approved Slayton for the approaching Mercury flight. Nevertheless, Webb bucked the case up to three Washington cardiologists, including Eugene Braunwall of the National Institutes of Health, as a sort of blue-ribbon panel. He also requested an opinion from Paul Dudley White, who had become famous as Eisenhower's cardiologist. Why this was happening so late in the game, three months after Deke had been assigned to the flight, no one could figure. All four doctors came to the same conclusion, apparently out of sheer common sense as much as anything else. Here was a case concerning a pilot with a minor heart defect. He could probably make a space flight or any other flight with no problems. Nevertheless, from the administrator on down, the entire space agency seemed to be agonizing and oscillating and spinning its wheels over the matter, which by now had accumulated a file as thick as your arm. So if Project Mercury had plenty of ready and willing astronauts with no cardiovascular anomalies at all, why not use one of them and have done with it? That was it, so far as Webb was concerned. It was now the middle of March. Two months ago, in his set-to with Glenn, James E. Webb had run up against *astropower* and had lost. This time he had his way. Slayton was off the flight.

The great Victorian Animal was utterly baffled. The Animal had been dutifully cranking out human-interest stories about Slayton. How could NASA decide now that he was a washout with a bad heart? There was no . . . proper emotion . . . for the event.

According to the official NASA wording, Slayton was "keenly disappointed" about the decision. That was putting it somewhat delicately. The man was furious. Slayton tried to keep a rein on himself in public statements, however, because he didn't want to jeopardize his chances of reinstatement. He was convinced that the whole thing had somehow been blown up into a specious issue and that they would all come to their senses by and by. Privately he was tying knots in the flagpole. He kept saying that Paul Dudley White had made an *operational* decision. His argument was that White and the other doctors had first delivered their medical opinion—he was fit to fly—and then they had delivered their operational opinion, which was: "Even so, why not choose somebody else?" They were entitled to their medical opinion; period. But they had made an *operational* decision! This word, *operational*, was a holy word to Slayton. He was the King of Operational. *Operational* referred to action, the real thing, piloting, the right stuff. *Medical* referred to one of the many accessories to the business at hand. You didn't call in doctors to make an operational decision. The *Life* reporters knew very well how angry Slayton was, and other reporters had strong hints of it. But the Genteel Beast could find no appropriate . . . tone . . . for it. So after a short time they just dropped it. They stuck with the NASA version: "Keenly disappointed." Few of them realized that it went beyond anger. Deke Slayton was crushed. He had not merely lost his ride on the next flight; he had lost everything. NASA had just announced that he no longer had . . . the right stuff. It could blow at any seam!—and his had blown. Idiopathic atrial fibrillation —it didn't matter! *Any* seam! His whole career, his ascension from the dour grim tundra of Wisconsin was based upon his indisputable possession of that righteous stuff. That was the most important thing he had ever possessed in this Trough of Mortal Error, and it was plenty. It was the ultimate. And it had *blown,* just like that! He felt humiliated. This thing would now be rubbed in his face everywhere he turned. He couldn't go back to Edwards now, even if he wanted to. The Air Force was not going to use a NASA reject for major flight test work. Flight test? Hell, he couldn't even fly a fighter plane by himself any more! It was true. He could go up only in two-seaters with another pilot—someone who was still intact, with no ruptured seams from which his vital stuff had leaked. There was even the possibility that the Air Force might ground him altogether, notwithstanding the fact that the Surgeon General's board had pronounced him "fully qualified as an Air Force pilot and as an astronaut." Air Force pride was at stake. The Air Force's Chief of Staff himself, General Curtis LeMay, was taking the position that if he wasn't qualified to fly for NASA, how could he be qualified to fly for the Air Force? All this was being said about *him*, Deke Slayton, who had fought hardest of all to have *the astronaut* be treated as *a pilot*, even to the extent of insisting on airplane-style controls for the capsule, or, rather, damn it, *spacecraft*.

It wasn't likely to make him any happier, either, to know that Scott Carpenter had taken his place. Carpenter had the least flight test experience of any of them, and yet he was replacing Deke Slayton—Deke Slayton, who had stood up before the Society of Experimental Test Pilots and insisted that only an experienced test pilot could do this job correctly. Wally Schirra, a man with real flight test credentials, had been training as Deke's backup. Why had he been passed over in favor of Carpenter? The two buddies, Glenn and Carpenter, were getting the first two orbital flights . . . and Deke Slayton was being *left behind* . . . to hitch airplane rides with other pilots.

Gilruth's opinion, backed up by Walt Williams, was that Carpenter had logged far more flight training, as Glenn's backup, than Schirra could possibly hope to cram in during the ten weeks remaining before the flight. Scott was not exactly ecstatic over having been handed Deke's flight on such short notice. He had trained for six months with John, but the second orbital flight was to be quite a different proposition. NASA's experimental scientists would finally have an inning. The astronaut was supposed to deploy a multicolored balloon outside the capsule in order to study the perception of light in space and the amount of drag, if any, in the presumed vacuum of space. He was supposed to observe how water in a glass bottle behaved in a weightless state and whether or not capillary action was altered. There would be a small glass sphere for that experiment. He would have a densitometer, as it was known, to measure the visibility of a ground flare. He would be trained in the use of a hand-held camera to take weather photographs and pictures of the daylight horizon and the atmospheric band above the horizon and of various land masses, particularly North America and Africa. They had the right man. Scott was intrigued by the experiments. But the addition of all these things to the checklist, which was already undergoing last-minute changes of the operational sort, put him under increasing pressure. In making all of these sightings, for the use of the camera, the densitometer, or whatever, he would be using an entirely new manual control apparatus. It was a system in which you created one pound of thrust if you pushed the hand controller slightly and twenty-five more if you pushed it beyond a small angle. It would be either/or; there would be no turning the capsule gradually like an airplane or an automobile.

The flight went off on schedule on May 24. For the first two orbits Scott had a picnic. He was more relaxed and in higher spirits than any of the three men who had preceded him. He was enjoying himself. His pulse rate, before lift-off, during the launch, and in orbit, was even lower than Glenn's. He talked more, ate more, drank more water, and did more with the capsule than any of them ever had. He obviously loved all the experiments. He was swinging the capsule this way and that way, taking photographs a mile a minute, making detailed observations of the sunrises and horizon, releasing balloons, tending his bottles, taking readings with the densitometer, having a grand time. The only problem was that the new control system used up fuel at a terrific rate. You wanted to pitch or yaw the capsule just ever so slightly, and—*bango!*—you were over the invisible line and another outsized geyser of hydrogen peroxide squirted out of the tanks.

During the second orbit he was warned by several capcoms to start conserving fuel, so that he would have enough for re-entry, but it was not until the third and last orbit that he himself seemed to realize just how low the fuel was. For most of the final orbit he just let the capsule drift and turn in any attitude it wanted to, so as not to have to use any of the thrusters, high or low, automatic or manual. It presented no problems at all. Even when you were upside down in relation to the earth, with your head pointed straight down, there was no feeling of disorientation, no feeling of up or down. Floating in a weightless state was even more enjoyable than swimming underwater, which Scott loved.

The diminished fuel supply was very much on his mind. Still, he couldn't resist the opportunity to experiment. He reached for the densitometer, and his hand hit the hatch of the capsule, and a cloud of John Glenn's "fireflies" appeared outside the window. So he swung the capsule over in a yaw to have a look at the fireflies. To him they looked more like frost or snowflakes, so he banged on the hatch and another cloud flew up and he swung around some more to take a look and used up some more fuel. Whatever they were, they were attached to the hull of the capsule and no doubt emanated from or were created by the capsule and were not some sort of micro-galaxy, all of which aroused his curiosity, and so he banged away and pitched and yawed and tooled around some more, the better to unravel the mystery. All of a sudden it was time to prepare for re-entry, and Scott was already behind in the retro-sequence, as that part of the checklist was known. Also, the fuel situation was beginning to get a little dicey. On top of that, the automatic control system would no longer hold the capsule at the proper angle for re-entry. So he switched to fly-by-wire . . . but at the same time forgot to throw the switch that cut off the manual system. For ten minutes he was eating up fuel out of both systems. He would have to fire the retro-rockets manually, as Alan Shepard, the capcom in Arguello, California, sounded off the countdown. When Shepard called "Fire one!" the capsule's angle was off about nine degrees and Scott was late in hitting the switch. He had practically no fuel left for controlling the capsule's oscillations during re-entry. By the time he hit the denser atmosphere and the radio blackout began, Chris Kraft and the other flight control engineers feared the worst. Long after radio communication should have resumed —nothing. It looked as if Carpenter had consumed all his fuel up there playing around—and had burned up. They all looked at each other and were already thinking one step ahead: "This disaster is going to set the program back a year— or do worse than that."

*   *   *

Rene was following Scott's re-entry over television inside a rented house in Cocoa Beach. For two days she had been involved in a hide-and-seek operation that had finally became absolutely loony. Bridge dragnets . . . amok helicopters . . . Rene had decided that since *Life*'s accounts of the brave wives bravely enduring the ordeal of their husbands' flights were written in the first person, she was actually going to write hers. Loudon Wainwright could edit what she wrote and rewrite the rough spots, but she was going to write the whole thing herself. That being the case, she wasn't going to let herself be imprisoned inside her house at Langley by the television crews and all the rest of that madness. She had seen Annie being driven far crazier from having to play quavering pigeon for the press —and the likes of Lyndon Johnson—than by any fears she had for John. It was an undignified position to be in. Despite the attention lavished on you, you were not treated as an individual but as the anxious loyal mate of the male up on top of the rocket. After a while Rene didn't know whether it was her modest literary ambitions or her resentment of the pat role of Astronaut Wife that made her do it. *Life* rented a "safe house" for her in Cocoa Beach. *Life* did things right. They rented a backup safe house as well, in case Rene's presence in the first one was discovered. Rene called up Shorty Powers, who was NASA's official press officer in matters concerning the astronauts, and told him that she was going to the Cape for the launch but wanted privacy and was telling no one where she would be, including him. Powers was not happy. The astronauts' *Life* contract had already made his job difficult enough. He was cut off from all "personal" material about the men and their families, since that was supposed to go to *Life* exclusively. And yet when a flight was on, 90 percent of the reporters Powers had to deal with were really interested in only two questions: (1) What is the astronaut doing now and how does he feel? (Is he afraid?); and (2) What is his wife doing now and how does she feel? (Is she dying from anxiety?) One of Powers's main roles was serving the television networks—and telling them where *the wife* would be during the flight, so that they could congregate for the death-watch campout. And this time all he could tell them was that *the wife* would be at the Cape . . . somewhere . . . That did it. The networks took the situation as an insult and a challenge. Before Rene left for the Cape, a correspondent for one of the networks called her and told her they were *going to find out* where she was staying . . . They could do it the hard way, if they had to, but they'd rather do it the easy way. So she'd better just tell them. It was like something out of a gangster movie. But sure enough, when she reached the Cape, the networks had people watching every bridge and causeway into Cocoa Beach. Rene knew they would be looking for a car with a woman with four children. So she had the children lie on the floor, and they slipped through. The networks were not going to be foiled that easily. After all, how could they camp on her front lawn and film her drawn shades if they didn't even know where she was? So they hired helicopters and began scouring Cocoa Beach. They went up and down the hardtack beach, looking for congregations of four small children. They would swoop right down on children on the beach until they could read the terror in their eyes. People were running for cover, abandoning their Scotch coolers and telescopes and cameras and tripods, trying to save their children from the amok helicopters. It was crazy, utterly bananas, but by now not knowing where *the wife* was—it was like not knowing where the rocket was. Finally, Rene was sending her children over to the beach two by two, in order to foil the insane people in the network helicopters.

Came time for the launch, and now Rene and the children watched the countdown on the TV in the safe house, with Wainwright and a *Life* photographer in attendance. Then the children rushed out and watched part of the rocket's slow ascent through a telescope mounted on a garage roof. The children didn't seem at all apprehensive. Flying was what their father *did*. They were in high spirits. . . . And now they were following the re-entry, as best they could, on television. They had CBS turned on. There was Walter Cronkite. Rene knew him. Cronkite had become an astrobuff. He had more than the usual reasons to like the astronauts. It was his coverage of John Glenn's flight that, in the strange workings of the television news business, had led to his current eminence among the network anchormen. Cronkite had been explaining Scott's fuel problem as he entered the atmosphere. Then Cronkite's voice began to take on more and more concern. They didn't know where Scott was. They weren't sure he had begun his re-entry at the proper angle. All at once Cronkite's voice broke. Tears came into his eyes. "I'm afraid that . . ." There was a catch in his voice. His eyes glistened. He had the waterworks turned on. "I'm afraid . . . we may have . . . *lost an astronaut* . . ." What instincts the man had! There was the Press, the Genteel Gent, coming up with the appropriate emotion . . . *live* . . . with no prompting whatsoever! Rene's children were very quiet, staring at the screen. Yet Rene herself did not believe for a moment that Scott had perished. She was like every military pilot's wife in that respect. If he were merely missing—if no dead body had been found—then he was alive and would come through it all right. There were no two ways about it. Rene had known of a case in which a cargo plane had crash-landed in the Pacific and broken in two on impact, the rear half sinking like a brick. Some men were rescued from the front half, which stayed afloat a few minutes. And yet the wives of the men who had been in the rear of the craft refused to believe that they were lost. They were out there somewhere; it was only a matter of time. Rene had marveled at how long it had taken them to accept the obvious. But her reaction was precisely the same. Scott was all right, because there was no real proof that he wasn't. Cronkite gulped on the television screen. No tears came to her eyes at all. Scott was all right. He would turn up . . . No two ways about it.

AS A MATTER OF FACT, she was correct. Scott had come through the atmosphere in good shape. The capsule began rocking violently in the dense atmosphere below 50,000 feet, and he had to release his parachute early and by hand, the automatic system being out of fuel. The capsule had overshot the target area by some 250 miles. A reconnaissance plane found him in about forty minutes, but throughout that period the impression created on television was that he might be dead. When a rescue aircraft reached Scott, they found him bobbing contentedly on a life raft beside the capsule. He was very pleased with the whole adventure. When he reached the aircraft carrier *Intrepid*, he was in terrific spirits. He talked and talked into the night. He wanted to stay up and keep talking about the grand adventure he had been through. He was really pleased about all the experiments he had been able to do, despite the overcrowded checklist he had, and about solving, or at least greatly narrowing down, the mystery of the "fireflies." He hadn't determined precisely what they were, but he had proved that they were produced by the spacecraft itself; they were not some extraterrestrial material, and so on . . . He could have gone on all night . . . He was content . . . a job well done . . . He felt that he had helped create one of the most important roles in astronautics: man as scientist in space . . .

Over the next two weeks Scott received a hero's homage. It was not on the scale of John's, which was understandable, but it was sweet enough. There were parades in the East and parades in the West. He rode in a motorcade through Boulder, his old hometown, and through Denver, which was just down the highway. It was a great day. The sun was out and it was a light fluffy Rocky Mountain day in May, and Rene was beside him, sitting up on the ridge of the seat back in the convertible, wearing white gloves, like a proper Navy wife, and smiling and looking absolutely beautiful and radiant. Well, Scott thought he had just shot the moon.

Back at the Cape, Chris Kraft was telling his colleagues: "That sonofabitch will never fly for me again."

Kraft was furious. The truth was, he had been quietly put out before . . . about the seven brave lads. As he saw it, Carpenter had ignored repeated warnings from capcoms all around the world about wasting fuel, and this had almost resulted in a disaster, one that might have done irreparable damage to the program. As it was, Carpenter's performance had cast doubt on the capability of the Mercury system to carry out a long flight such as Titov's seventeen orbits. And why had this catastrophe nearly occurred? Because Carpenter had insisted on comporting himself like an Omnipotent and Omniscient Mercury Astronaut. He didn't have to pay attention to suggestions and warnings from mere groundlings. He apparently believed that the astronaut, the passenger in the capsule, was the heart and soul of the space program. All of the resentment that the engineers had about the top-lofty status of the astronauts now crept out of its cage . . . at least within NASA. Outside of NASA, publicly, nothing was to change. Carpenter, like Grissom before him, was an exemplary brave lad; just a little dicey scrape at the end of the flight, that was all. Very successful flight; go ahead, let him have his medals and his receiving lines.

And now that the wound had been opened, there were those who were only too pleased to see the following line develop concerning the Carpenter flight: Carpenter had not merely wasted fuel while up there playing with the capsule's attitude controls, doing his beloved "experiments." No, he had also become . . . rattled . . . when he finally realized he was getting low on fuel. The evidence for this was that he forgot to turn off the manual system when he switched to fly-by-wire and thereby really blew his fuel supply. And then he . . . panicked! . . . That was why he couldn't line the capsule up at the right angle and that was why he couldn't fire the retro-rockets right on the button . . . and that was why he hit the atmosphere at such a shallow angle. He nearly skipped off it instead of going through it . . . he nearly skipped off into eternity . . . because . . . he panicked! There! We've said it! That was the worst charge that could be brought against a pilot on the great ziggurat of flying. It said that a man had lost whatever stuff he had in the most awful manner. He had funked it. It was a sin for which there was no redemption. Damned eternally! Once such a verdict had been pronounced, no judgment was too vile. Did you hear his voice on the tape just before the blackout? You could hear the panic! In fact, they could hear no such thing. Carpenter sounded very much the way Glenn had sounded and a good deal less excited than Grissom. But if one wanted to hear panic, especially in the words that a man had to force out after the g-forces built up, if that was what one was after . . . then you could hear panic. But, then, Carpenter never had the right stuff to begin with! That much was obvious. He had given up long ago. He had opted for multi-engine planes! (Now we know why!) He had only two hundred hours in jets. He was here only through a fluke of the selection process. And so forth and so on. Certain objective data had to be ignored, of course. Carpenter's pulse rate remained lower, *during the re-entry* as well as during the launch and orbital flight, than any other astronaut's, including Glenn's. It never rose above 105, even during the most critical point of the re-entry. One could argue that pulse rate was not a dependable indication of a pilot's coolness. Scott Crossfield had a chronically rapid pulse rate, and he was in the league with Yeager. Nevertheless, it was inconceivable that a man in *a state of panic*—in a *life-or-death* emergency—in a crisis that did not last for a matter of seconds but for *twenty minutes*—it was inconceivable that such a man would maintain a heart rate of less than 105 throughout. Even a pilot's heart rate could jump to more than 105 for nothing more than the fact that some cocky bastard had cut into line ahead of him at the PX. One might argue that Carpenter had mishandled the re-entry, but to accuse him of *panic* made no sense in light of the telemetered data concerning his heart rate and his respiratory rate. Therefore, the objective data would be ignored. Once it had begun, the denigration of Carpenter had to proceed at any cost.

It served many purposes at once. It made the rest of them seem like *real pilots* after all and not mere riders in a pod. A man either *had it* or he didn't . . . in space as in the air. As every pilot knew in his secret heart—deny it, if you wish! —it required washouts to make your own righteous stuff stand out. So was Carpenter, by implication, to be designated *the washout?* Logic no longer mattered— especially since none of this could be talked of openly in any case: publicly there were to be no flaws in the manned space program whatsoever. Sheer logic would have raised the question: why pick Carpenter and not Grissom? Grissom had *lost the capsule* and had then come back with the classic pilot's response to gross error: "I don't know what happened—the machine malfunctioned." The telemetry showed that Grissom's heart was on the edge of tachycardia at times. Just before re-entry his heart rate had reached 171 beats per minute. Even after Grissom was safe and sound on the carrier *Lake Champlain*, his heart rate was 160 beats a minute, his breathing was rapid, his skin was warm and moist; he didn't want to talk about it, he wanted to go to sleep. Here was the clinical picture of a man who had abandoned himself to panic. Then why was not Grissom designated *the washout*—if anybody cared to find one? But logic had nothing to do with it. One was in the area of magical beliefs now. In his everyday life doughty little Gus *lived* the life of the right stuff. He was a staunch bearer of the Operational banner. Here Gus's fate and Deke's fate came together. Deke had said all along: You need a proven operational test pilot up there. Gus and Deke were great pals. For three years they had flown together, hunted together, drunk together; their children had played together. They were both committed to the holy word: *operational*. Schirra was with them on this particular commitment, and Shepard threw his weight toward them, too, as did Cooper.

Deke had plenty to be thankful to Shepard for. One day Al had gotten the other boys together and said, "Listen, we've got to do something for Deke. We've got to do something to give him back his pride." Shepard's suggestion was that

Deke be made a sort of chief of the astronauts, with an office and a title and
official duties. They all went for the idea and took it to Gilruth, and in no time
Deke had the title "Coordinator of Astronaut Activities." There may have been
people at NASA who figured this would be a supernumerary make-work job for
the fallen astronaut; if so, they underestimated Deke. He was a far shrewder and
more determined individual than his Wisconsin tundra manner let on. The job
gave him something to channel his tremendous thwarted energy into. The
NASA hierarchy was still a political vacuum, and Deke set about filling it . . .
with a vengeance, as it were. Soon Deke was a power within NASA, a man to be
reckoned with, and his motivation never varied: the more powerful he became,
the better his chances of reversing the decision that prevented him from flying.
Justice, simple operational justice . . . in the name of the right stuff.

   Operational; the word had new clout now, and a corollary to the theory of the
Carpenter flight began to develop. Carpenter's flight agenda had been loaded
with Larry Lightbulb experiments. The scientists, lowest men in the NASA peck-
ing order up to now, had been given their heads on this flight . . . and the
results were there for your inspection. Carpenter had taken all this Mad Professor
stuff seriously, and that was what led to his problems. He became so wrapped up
in his various "observations" that he fell behind in the checklist and became
rattled and then blew it. All this science nonsense could wait. Just now, in the
critical operational phase of the program, the crucial period of real *flight test*, it
wasn't just ding-a-ling stuff, it was dangerous. There were too many goddamned
doctors involved in this thing, too. (Look what they did to Deke!) On top of that,
they had the two psychiatrists to contend with. They were nice enough men
personally, Ruff and Korchin were, but they were . . . *in the way!* What the hell
was all this pissing into bags and hitting little circles with a pencil . . . after
you've just hung your hide out over the edge in a space flight? They hadn't even
picked up the fact that Carpenter had *panicked*. They found him exhilarated,
alert, full of energy, ready to take off and do it all over again . . . The two men
were not invited to continue with the program after the move from Langley to
Houston. Thanks a lot, gentlemen, and don't let the doorknob hit you in the
butt.

   Here the outlook of Grissom, Slayton, and Schirra coincided with that of
Kraft and Walt Williams. Kraft and Williams also felt that non-operational experiments should be kept to a minimum at this stage of the space program. From now
on, whenever anyone said otherwise. one had only to roll his eyeballs and turn his
palms up and say: You want another Carpenter flight?

O N AUGUST 11 and 12 the mighty Integral struck again, and now there was
absolutely no stopping the *operational* theory. On August 11 the Soviets launched
Vostok 3 on what at first looked as if it would be a repetition of Titov's day-long
flight. But no! Exactly twenty-four hours later the Chief Designer sent up *Vostok
4*, and the two craft flew together, in tandem, within three miles of each other.
Within three miles of one another in the infinity of space! The Soviets spoke of a
"group flight," as if the two cosmonauts, Nikolayev and Popovich, were flying in
formation. In fact, neither could change his flight path in the slightest, and their
proximity was due solely to the precision with which the second *Vostok* was
launched as the first came orbiting overhead—but even this seemed to be a feat of

incalculable sophistication. The Genteel Beast and many congressmen seemed to be on the edge of hysteria. Entire *formations* of Soviet space warriors, hurling thunderbolts at Schenectady . . . Grand Forks . . . Oklahoma City . . . Once again the Chief Designer was toying with them! God knew what his next surprise would be . . . (It would be a big one.) Well, that settled it. No more densitometers and varicolored balloons and other White Smock accessories. (No more pilots with non-operational stuff!) Which explained the singular nature of Wally Schirra's flight on October 3.

Schirra named his capsule *Sigma 7*, and there you had it. Scott Carpenter had named his *Aurora 7* . . . *Aurora* . . . the rosy dawn . . . the dawn of the intergalactic age . . . the unknowns, the mystery of the universe . . . the music of the spheres . . . Petrarch on the mountain top . . . and all that. Whereas *Sigma* . . . *Sigma* was a purely engineering symbol. It stood for the summation, the solution of the problem. Unless he had come right out and named the capsule *Operational*, he couldn't have chosen a better name. For the purpose of Schirra's flight was to prove that Carpenter's need not have happened. Schirra would make six orbits—twice as many as Carpenter—and yet use half as much fuel and land right on target. Whatever did not have to do with that goal tended to be eliminated from the flight. The flight of *Sigma 7* was designed to be Armageddon . . . the final and decisive rout of the forces of experimental science in the manned space program. And that it was.

Schirra cut the jolly fun-loving figure so well that people sometimes failed to notice how formidable he could be. But his emphasis, after all, was on maintaining an *even* strain. His pranksterish, rib-shaking, wild-driving gotcha intervals gave him plenty of slack when the time came to wind things up tight and get tough. Every bit as much as Shepard, Wally had the instincts of an Academy man, a leader of men, the commander, the captain of the ship. He merely operated in a different fashion. He was cool; he had "the uncritical willingness to face danger," but he wasn't afraid to show his feelings when strategy seemed to dictate it. If it was going to be his show, he insisted on running it; and he was shrewd enough to recognize the political outlines of a situation. Having seen four flights from up close, Wally couldn't help but have noticed that the secret of a successful mission lay in a simplified checklist with white space between tasks. The fewer tasks you had, the better chance you had for a one hundred percent performance. Not only that, if you could control the checklist, then you could give your flight a theme, a clear-cut goal that everyone could immediately appreciate and respond to. Wally's theme for this flight was Operational Precision, which, being translated, meant conserving fuel and landing on target. Now that the operational forces were lined up shoulder to shoulder, it was possible to keep offboard most novel items that engineers or scientists had dreamed up for the flight.

It was decided that one of Wally's major operational tests would consist of powering down all of the attitude-control systems, automatic as well as manual, and just drifting in any attitude the capsule's inertia took it, upside down (in relation to the earth), head over heels, canted this way and that, whatever. Scott heard about it and told Wally that he didn't really think it was necessary. He had drifted for most of his last orbit, in an attempt to conserve fuel for the re-entry, and had proved to his own satisfaction that you could stand the capsule right up on its aerial or let it revolve or put yourself in any other attitude and it was not the least bit disorienting or uncomfortable. Why didn't Wally put the proposed drifting time to other uses? Wally said no, he was going to devote his flight to experimenting with drifting flight and to conserving fuel, in order to prepare the way for missions of long duration.

Scott would learn that planning sessions had been held—and he had not been informed of them. It was not that Scott was supposed to take any official part in the planning for Wally's flight, and it was not unusual in flight test for a pilot to have his own particular circle of colleagues and ground crew he preferred to consult with. But be that as it may, anyone could recall how much Scott had valued John Glenn's counsel before his flight. In fact, one of Scott's concerns had been that John wasn't available more. The demands on John's time in his role as NASA's number-one hero had become enormous. But anytime John was around, Scott —and the engineers, too—wanted John at the meetings. Wally also complained that John wasn't around. He caused quite a flap when he told Walter Cronkite, in a taped interview, that John was off on the banquet circuit so much, he was lost to the program. He didn't complain about the absence of Scott, however. Scott began to conclude that Kraft and Williams were overreacting to the fact that he had overshot the target by 250 miles. The possibility that there were people—*pilots*—going around saying that he had *panicked* never even crossed his mind.

Given the goal of the flight—which was to prove that a *cool* pilot could travel twice as far as Carpenter with half as much fuel consumption and ten times the accuracy—Schirra was terrific. From the moment he got up that morning, he was about as cool and relaxed a human being who ever went out to sit on top of a rocket shaft. A few days ago Wally had played one of his patented *gotchas* on Dee O'Hara, the nurse. One of her tasks was to collect urine samples. She gives him the usual little bottle and asks him to bring in a sample and leave it on her desk. She comes into her office, and on top of her desk is not a little bottle but a huge beaker holding about five gallons of an amber liquid with a head of foam on top. It couldn't possibly be—but *could* it possibly be—and so she puts her hands on the sides of the beaker to see if it's warm, and—

"Gotcha!"

—she wheels about, and there's Wally peeking in the doorway, him and his beaming face and a couple of the boys. He had concocted it of water, tincture of iodine, and detergent. The next day Dee O'Hara presents Wally with a clear plastic bag, a big thing, about four feet long, telling him that it's the urine receptacle for his flight, replacing the little condom device that Grissom, Glenn, and Carpenter had worn. *Gotcha!* So today, the morning of his flight, here comes Wally down the hallway in Hangar S in his bathrobe, heading for the medical room. Flopping out below the robe and dragging along the floor between his legs is the huge plastic bag. He parades right past Dee O'Hara, as if he were going to suit up that way. *Gotcha!* And he kept it up. That whole day he was the jolly Wally from beginning to end. He was amazing. He never sounded for a moment like someone under the stress of a novel form of flight test. It was like listening to a good buddy at beer call, recollecting in tranquillity. He practically out-yeagered Yeager. As soon as the escape tower blew off, marking the successful completion of the fully powered part of his ascent, Schirra saw it streaking through the sky and said: "This tower is a real sayonara."

Chris Kraft, the flight director, gave his approval for the first orbit, and Deke

Slayton, the capcom at the Cape, told Schirra: "You have a go from Control Center."

Schirra said: "You have a go from me. It's real fat."

Then Slayton said: "Are you a turtle today?"

"Going to VOX recorder only," said Wally. Then he spoke into the tape recorder, whose microphone was not hooked into the open radio circuit.

"You bet your sweet ass I am," he said.

The Turtle Club was one of Wally's gotcha games. If one good buddy who played the turtle game met another good buddy in public—preferably in the company of very proper folk—and challenged him with the question "Are you a turtle?" that good buddy had to answer, "You bet your sweet ass I am," in a loud voice or else treat everybody else to a round of drinks. This was three minutes and forty-one seconds into the flight. Wally was already maintaining an even strain.

He buckled down to the task of conserving hydrogen peroxide. Ordinarily, when the booster rocket separated from the capsule, the capsule was then turned around by the automatic control system, but this consumed considerable fuel. This time Schirra nudged it around manually, using only the low thrusters, the five-pound thrusters, of the fly-by-wire system. Soon he was telling Deke at the Cape: "I'm in chimp mode right now and she's flying beautifully." He started using this phrase *chimp mode*. On the chimpanzee flights the attitude of the capsule had been controlled automatically throughout. *The chimp mode* was a little zinger for the benefit of all those on the mighty ziggurat, whether astronauts or X-15 "dream pilots," who were aware of the taunt: "A monkey's gonna make the first flight." Schirra's continual reference to *the chimp mode* as much as said: "Who cares! Here—I'll wave the bloody monkey in your face." As soon as he could, however, he went into what he called *the drifting mode*. He just let the capsule twist into any attitude it wanted, as Scott had on his final orbit.

"I'm having a ball up here drifting," said Wally. "Enjoying it so much I haven't eaten yet."

When he came over California during the fourth orbit, John Glenn, acting as capcom at Point Arguello, was instructed to have Wally say something for live broadcast over television and radio.

"Ha, ha," said Wally. "I suppose an old song, 'Drifting and Dreaming,' would be apropos at this point, but at this point I don't have a chance to dream. I'm enjoying it too much." When he was over South America, he was asked to say something in Spanish for live broadcast.

"*Buenos días*, you all," said Wally. (And the Latins loved it.)

After nearly four orbits, drifting and yakking and yukking it up, cool, relaxed, a turtle to the last, Wally had used up barely 10 percent of his hydrogen peroxide. He had already traveled one orbit farther than Carpenter or Glenn. He had floated every which way, and (as Scott had told him) there was nothing to it. There was no sensation of up or down in weightless flight. It was obvious that you could send a Mercury capsule on a seventeen-orbit flight, like Titov's, if you wanted. As Schirra came over the Cape, Deke Slayton said, "Flight would like to talk to you now."

"Flight" meant the flight director, Kraft himself, was coming onto the circuit.

"Been a real good show up there," said Kraft. "I think we are proving our point, old buddy!"

Glenn was sitting in front of a microphone in the tracking station at Point

Arguello. Scott was sitting in front of a microphone in the tracking station at Guaymas. Kraft had never come on the circuit to say any such thing to either of them. Scott was beginning to see what the point, *our point*, was.

As he neared the completion of his sixth and last orbit, Wally announced that he had 78 percent of the fuel left in both the automatic and manual systems. He had flown twice as far as Glenn or Carpenter, and he could have gotten through another fifteen orbits or so if he had to. One of Kraft's lieutenants, an engineer named Gene Kranz, came on the circuit and said to Wally: "Now *that's* what I call a real engineering test flight!"

Scott picked up the message in his central nervous system even before his mind analyzed it. *Unlike the last one*, the man was saying. There was even a hint of . . . *unlike the last two*.

To complete an operational triumph Schirra now had only to land on target. Carpenter had landed 250 miles off the mark. As he began his descent toward the atmosphere, Wally told Al Shepard, the capcom on Bermuda, near the target area, "I think they're gonna put me on the number-three elevator." He was talking about the number-three elevator used for moving aircraft up to the flight deck on the carrier *Kearsage*. This was a bit of the Schirra metonymy for "squarely on target." Oh, yes! And in fact he landed just 4.5 miles from the carrier. The swabbos crowding the flight deck could see him coming down under his big parachute. Carpenter had found the capsule uncomfortably hot once he splashed down and had crawled out through the neck of the capsule and waited on his life raft for the rescue planes. Glenn had also complained of the heat. Schirra's suit had an improved cooling system, and he was willing to stay in the capsule indefinitely. He refused a helicopter's offer of a lift to the carrier. What was the rush? He stayed in the capsule while a crew of swabbos in a motor-driven whaling boat towed him back to the carrier. Once he was on the *Kearsage* he told the doctors: "I feel fine. It was a textbook flight. The flight went just the way I wanted it to."

That became the verdict on Schirra's performance: "A textbook flight." He had done everything on the checklist. He had turned in a hundred percent performance. He had successfully proved that a man could ride around the earth six times and barely turn a hand or move a muscle and hardly use an ounce of fuel or expend an extra heartbeat and never, not for a moment, surrender to psychological stress, and ride the ship down to a designated drop in the vastness of the ocean. Sigma, summa, Q.E.D.: *Operational!*

Wally came back to celebrations in Houston and Florida and a big Wally Schirra day in his hometown of Oradell, New Jersey. The next day he went to the White House for congratulations by President Kennedy, and the President presented him with the Distinguished Service Medal. It all turned out to be rather brief and unceremonious, however, and something of a disappointment. A little chat, a few grins, a few photographs with the Chief Executive in the Oval Office, and that was it. The date was October 16. In time Wally would learn that Kennedy had just seen photographic evidence, from U-2 flights, that the Soviets had set up missile bases in Cuba. The President had kept his appointment with the astronaut only to maintain appearances, to prevent word from getting out about the critical situation that was developing.

14

THE CLUB

B Y AND BY Conrad started carrying Glenn's bag, as well as his own, and facing up to the role. It was the only sensible thing to do. Otherwise, the two of them would arrive at some airport, St. Louis, Akron, Los Angeles, wherever, and it would take them five minutes to walk forty feet. The autograph seekers came in waves. Every few steps Glenn would have to put his bag down and sign some more autographs and shake some more hands. Actually he was great at it. That big sunny freckle-faced smile of his lit up the place. People came up to him as if they knew him personally and loved him. *He is my protector. He risked his life and challenged the Russians in the heavens for me.* They adored him so much it would have been hard for him to brush past them, even had he been of that sort of disposition. So he would put his bag down and sign some more autographs, and the two of them would have to stop.

If Conrad carried both bags, they could keep moving. Glenn could wave and sign autographs and shake hands and chat and beam that terrific smile at everybody in transit without seeming rude. As for Conrad, he was in absolutely no danger of having to stop and put down the bags. He was now an astronaut, officially, but not to the mobs of autograph seekers. They couldn't have cared less. He looked like some little guy who carried bags for John Glenn. What was more, that was what he felt like. That was about all the second group of astronauts was doing: chores for the first, for the one, the only, the Original Seven. Conrad, as part of his training, had been accompanying Glenn in his travels. Now that Project Mercury was drawing to a close, Glenn was supposed to make Project Apollo, the moon program, his "area of specialization." He was visiting the factories of the major contractors, just as he had in the early days of Mercury. Conrad's area of specialization, officially, was "cockpit layout and systems integration"; but mainly he was . . . with John Glenn. John Glenn visiting the factory took on the aura of the general coming to inspect the troops. He was a magnet for every sort of VIP who could get next to him, particularly congressmen and senators. There were times when senators actually pushed—elbowed! hipped! bellied!—

secretaries, stenographers, and other mere gawkers out of the way to get next to Glenn's fabled hide and speak to him and grin a great deal. Standing by, all the while, would be an unknown young man, the single-combat hero's valet, apparently, his batman, as the British Army called military servants. Namely, the anonymous Lieutenant Conrad, Group II Astronaut.

Nevertheless, Conrad had made it this time, and that was the main thing. That was all that any really competitive military pilot upon the great ziggurat could focus on any more: becoming an astronaut. By now, only three years later, any such session as he and Wally Schirra and Alan Shepard and Jim Lovell and the others had gone through at the Marriott motel in February of 1959 . . . it was hard to believe it could have ever taken place. Remember Wally that night? Wally! . . . adding up the pros and cons and agonizing over what the space program might do to his chances of commanding a squadron of F-4Hs! And now Wally—the same Wally with whom they had gone waterskiing on Chesapeake Bay, with whom they had weathered that bad string at Pax River, the old affable prankster himself—now Wally stood at the very apex of the great invisible pyramid of flying. For the seven Mercury astronauts had *become* the True Brotherhood. They were so dazzling you couldn't even *see* the erstwhile True Brethren of Edwards Air Force Base any longer.

In April, when NASA announced it was accepting applications for a second group of astronauts, both Conrad and Jim Lovell had looked like good bets this time around, since they had been among the thirty-one finalists in the original selection process. Conrad was stationed at Miramar, California, requalifying for a phase of the Navy fighter jock's training he had already been through, which was night carrier landings. There was a good reason why night carrier landings required requalifying time; even, as in Conrad's case, after training as a test pilot at Patuxent. Night landings were a routine part of carrier operations—and perhaps the best of all examples of how a man's accumulated good works did him no good whatsoever at each new step up the great pyramid, of how each new step was an absolute test, and of how each bright new day's absolutes—chosen or damned—were built into the routine. By 1962 the Navy had already shifted over to light-beam systems using angled mirrors and Fresnel lenses at the end of the flight deck. Conrad and the rest of them going through night carrier training at Miramar did not have to depend on a landing-signal officer standing at the end of the deck in a luminescent orange suit waving a pair of luminescent orange wigwag flags. At night—to the pilot way up there in the dark—there was now a blob of light, known as the *meatball*, rising and falling on a dimly perceived little slab in the middle of the ocean. The shining blob, the motherless meatball, was rising and falling because the heaving greasy skillet did not stop wallowing in the waves simply out of respect for the night. The carrier was plowing on away from you, into the wind, and therefore into the waves, and therefore was pitching up and down—five, eight, even ten feet at a gulp. On a night when the clouds were low and the moon was obscured, when the sky was black, the ocean was black, and the deck was black, the little meatball (no more than an inch high from up there) and the lights on the ship were like a single low-wattage comet, dim and lurching through the vast blackness of the universe, and the pilot was expected to have the will, the moxie, the illustrious, the all-illuminating stuff to bring a five- or ten-ton jet fighter onto that dim drunken astral plate at 125 knots. In training he had a limited number of passes down the invisible glide path. If he couldn't bring himself to make contact with the deck for so long that his fuel ran low, then the word *bingo!* sounded over his earphones, and he had to return to land, to the training base, where the landing strip didn't move when you approached it . . . and where everybody on the flight line would know that another poor sad *bingo* was coming into a safe haven, having funked it in the business of night carrier landings. A persistent case of the bingos was enough to wash a man out of night carrier landings. That did not mean you were finished as a Navy pilot. It merely meant that you were finished so far as carrier ops were concerned, which meant that you were finished so far as combat was concerned, which meant you were no longer in *the competition,* no longer ascending the pyramid, no longer qualified for the company of those with the right stuff. To have every recommendation in the book as a test pilot, to have survived bad strings·galore, meant nothing when such a thing happened. Chosen or damned! (It could blow at any seam.) There were nights when that little meatball way down yonder on the deck was jumping around like the silver BBs in those maddening games you hold in the palm of your hand, and a pilot would have to drive his F-4, a big fifteen-ton brute, down onto the deck through sheer willpower, drive it down practically like *a nail.* Anything —even the Great Kaboom!—was better than hearing *bingo* over your earphones. To bingo out of a carrier landing after eight years of military flying, after completing test-pilot school at Pax River, after becoming the top of the breed . . . now, there you had something unthinkable.

Conrad had just requalified for night carrier landings, for "all-weather carrier operations," meaning that he was now fully qualified for Navy air combat, when he received his invitation to apply for astronaut. The fact that there was nothing in the role of *astronaut* that would require one-tenth the *piloting* skill of night carrier landings did not deter Conrad, Lovell, or anyone else for a second this time around. This time Conrad went through the selection process like Lt. Straight Arrow. As before, there were thirty-odd finalists. They did not have to go through the Lovelace Clinic or the Wright-Patterson Aeromedical Center, however. Instead, they were sent to Brooks Air Force Base in San Antonio, the Air Force's medical center, for a set of physicals that were time-consuming but on the whole conventional. After five Mercury flights it was obvious that no extraordinary physical hardiness was required for the job.

For the last phase of the testing they took you straight to Olympus, which was now Houston. Part of the testing was a formal interview, across a table, with NASA engineers, plus Deke Slayton, John Glenn, and Al Shepard, concerning technical matters. But part of it seemed to be social. You were expected to go to a cocktail party and a dinner in a private dining room in the Rice Hotel in Houston, with the Mercury astronauts in attendance. Al Shepard was there for a while, and Gus Grissom, Scott Carpenter . . . and here was Wally. You kept your brain dialed up in all sectors, trying to strike the perfect middle ground between being a good righteous beer-call buddy and showing a good sober respect for the eminence of those already in the club. *Maybe I better hold it down to just one drink.* It was like a rush party in a fraternity you desperately wanted to belong to.

Naturally Wally talked to Conrad and Jim Lovell as if he were the same old Wally, comrade-in-arms, good old Wally of Group 20. Nevertheless, the difference in their ranks existed in that room like a ray of light which beamed straight upon Walter Schirra, outstandingly successful single-combat warrior; for there were now the seven Mercury astronauts up there at the apex . . . and all the rest of the pilots in America far below.

Not that the Original Seven's national eminence altered the *true and secret* nature of things, however. The self-esteem of the fighter jock knew no limits, and the members of Group II were no exceptions to this rule. As soon as they were selected, the boys began looking around and comparing themselves—the Next Nine—with the Original Seven. Here was Neil Armstrong, who had flown the X-15. (What Mercury astronaut had done anything like that?) Here was John Young, who held two world speed-to-climb records. (What Mercury astronaut, other than Glenn, could claim any such distinction?) Here were Frank Borman, Tom Stafford, and Jim McDivitt, who had been flight test instructors at Edwards. (What Mercury astronaut had ever qualified for that, except for Slayton?) The Next Nine were really rolling now. The Original Seven were chosen to withstand stress, period. Look at Carpenter! Look at Cooper! Oh, the Next Nine felt very good about themselves. Nevertheless, the exalted *status* of the Original Seven was a fact. Once the initial euphoria of being chosen as an astronaut had subsided, Conrad and the others realized that now, for all their righteous stuff, they occupied a somewhat humiliating position in the corps of astronauts. They were like plebes, rookies, fraternity pledges. Gus Grissom had a nice grim ingratiating gruff gus way of telling them—if their paths had to cross here and there—not to get big ideas, not to go around calling themselves *astronauts*. "You're not an astronaut," he would say, "you're a trainee. You're not an astronaut until you go up." He said it without a trace of a smile. The Next Nine spent their time going to classes, like nine freshmen, like nine primary flight training candidates at Pensacola, which was bad enough, and doing scutwork for the Holy Seven, which was worse.

That was how Conrad had ended up being John Glenn's go-fer and carrying his bags. It could get cold as hell here on Olympus. There were levels upon levels, even here at the top. At the very apex there was John Glenn, and there were others among the Original Seven themselves who could not get over that fact. At the very first press conference, the one introducing the Next Nine to the public, the Original Seven were on hand, and Shorty Powers happened to introduce them in the reverse order of their flights. When he got to Shepard, he said: "And finally, this is Alan Shepard, the man who's been saying for years, 'But I was first!'" Well, that just cracked the place up. Everyone was laughing, with the single and obvious exception of Smilin' Al. He didn't even move a lip. If slow burns gave off needle rays, Shorty Powers would have had two small green holes through his frontal lobes. And you realized all at once that after Glenn's great orbital triumph Shepard—the prime pilot, the first American in space—must have felt like a forgotten man. Nobody ranked with Glenn, however, not even Webb, the administrator of NASA.

One day Glenn dropped by Webb's office in Washington and informed him that there was going to be a change in his personal agenda. He was going to make no more trips for NASA at the request of this or that congressman or senator. He was no longer going to fly halfway across the country, nor would he walk across the street, to stand on a platform to please some congressman who was looking for votes or whatever else. Glenn didn't put it as a request. He was letting Webb know how it was going to be from now on. He was just laying down the law. There was no way for Webb to take it except as a direct contradiction of his authority. Webb answered in a reasonable, if somewhat aroused, manner. Now, listen, John, we don't send you anywhere because some congressman wants you to be there. We send you because NASA wants you to be there. Congressional support is absolutely essential at this point, and this is one of the most important things you could possibly do for the program. To which Glenn says that nevertheless, he is taking no more such trips. Webb's color begins to rise, and he says that if he is instructed to carry out such duties, then he will be obliged to carry them out. To which Glenn says that Webb happens to be mistaken; he will do no such thing. All at once it's practically a shouting match.

Webb didn't push the situation to the brink. He just let the storm wear itself out; and when it was over, it was obvious that the Administrator of NASA was not a chief so long as John Glenn was in the room. Glenn did not back down or apologize. Far from it; he made it obvious who held the cards around here, and that was that.

I T WAS JOHN GLENN who had realized from the first that Project Mercury was like a new branch of the armed services, despite its civilian coloration. It would have simplified matters tremendously if NASA had given everybody formal rankings and had done with it. That way people such as Webb would have known where they actually stood. The seven Mercury astronauts could have been designated Single-Combat General, a category with the honors and privileges of five-star general but with none of the duties and obligations of command. After his flight John Glenn, then, would have been promoted to Galactic Single-Combat General, a category ranking slightly above the Chiefs of Staff of the Armed Services and slightly below the Commander-in-Chief. Webb, as NASA administrator, would have been a two-star general and would have known the protocol for dealing with GSC General Glenn. Newly inducted astronauts, such as Conrad, Lovell, and Young, could have been ranked as majors, with rapid promotion promised in the event of the successful completion of flights.

It would have greatly simplified matters for the wives as well. For as much as they would have denied it, had anyone confronted them with the topic, many of the wives of the Original Seven reacted to the arrival of the Next Nine and their wives . . . precisely like service wives since time was. The classic and often-told story of service wives concerned the wives of a group of Navy pilots who had just been transferred to a new base. A commander designated to give the wives an orientation lecture says: "First, would you ladies please rearrange yourselves by rank, with the highest-ranking wives sitting in the first row and so on back to the rear." It takes about fifteen minutes for the women to sort themselves out and change their seats, since very few of them know one another. Once the process has been completed, the commander fixes a stern glare upon them and says: "Ladies, I want you to know that I have just witnessed the most ridiculous performance I have ever seen in my entire military career. Allow me to inform you that no matter who your husbands are, *you* have *no* rank whatsoever. You are all equals, and you should kindly remember to conduct yourselves as such in all dealings with one another." That was not the end of the story, however. The wives stared back at their instructor with looks of utter bemusement and, as if with a single mind, said to themselves: "Who is this idiot and what planet has he been stationed on?" For the inexpressible provisions of the Military Wife's Compact were well known to all. A military officer's wife rose in rank with her husband and immediately took on all the honors and perquisites pertaining thereto, and only a fool or the sort of simpleminded jerk who was assigned to give orientation lectures to wives could fail to comprehend this.

Further, said the code, the wise wife of a junior officer was careful not to make her family's style of living so ostentatious that it outdazzled that of higher-ranking families. It was on just this point that the Next Nine began to rankle some of the wives of the Original Seven and, for that matter, some of the seven astronauts, as well. They were irritated to notice what *terrific houses* many of the Next Nine immediately bought. Just like that—in Timber Cove even!—they began gobbling up *the goodies!* For the Original Seven the ascension from the drab life of the junior officer had seemed like a glorious pioneer struggle and part of the prize for winning the contest, for being chosen as the Original Seven. They found something distasteful about the attitude of the new crowd—this notion that as soon as a man was designated an astronaut, he and his family were entitled to stride out upon the golden boulevards of the Celestial City as if they owned the place.

The Group II astronauts immediately produced an agent, their version of Leo DeOrsey, and sat down to negotiate and cut up the *Life* pie. He was Harry Batten, president of the N. W. Ayer advertising agency in Philadelphia. He was as much of a big leaguer as DeOrsey, and like DeOrsey he agreed to serve as agent without pay. It was a bit too much! People were already treating the Next Nine like the Original Seven! The developers in Timber Cove and Nassau Bay, the second-best development, offered them big houses for small down payments and huge mortgages at low interest—a mortgage of forty to fifty thousand dollars seemed enormous in 1962—and the Next Nine took it all on without even blinking. They were *not behaving like junior officers* in the presence of the Single-Combat Generals. For, as everyone understood, tacitly, this was no mere civilian agency; this was a new branch of the service.

It was in that spirit that the "A.W.C." was started. Without anyone coming out and saying so, it was understood that Marge Slayton was the C.O.'s wife in this outfit. By now Deke had taken on his job as Coordinator of Astronaut Activities with such determination that he was about to be put in charge of crew selection—meaning that he would be the one man who had the most to say about who flew, and in what order, particularly when it came to the Next Nine. He was about to be made Assistant Director of Flight Crew Operations. He became the equivalent of a commanding officer, making Marge the C.O.'s wife. Marge organized a couple of coffee hours for all the wives, the First Seven and the Next Nine, so they could all get to know each other. By the second time they met, they all realized, without a word—nobody had to say it—what this was. This was . . . the Officers Wives Club, such as existed at every base in the land. One of the newcomers who seemed absolutely tickled to death about the coffee hours was Sue Borman, the wife of one of the Next Nine, Frank Borman. Borman had been one of the first instructors at the Air Force's new Experimental Test Pilot School at Edwards. He was a short, compact West Point man from Arizona, and his wife, Sue, was the perfect superefficient officer's wife. She had a fireproof cheeriness about her and a determination to get things organized. They were a great team. "This is fun," she said, speaking of Marge's coffee hours for the wives. "Let's start doing this on an organized basis." So the A.W.C. began. The initials stood for Astronauts Wives Club, of course, but the full name was never used. It was a gaffe for an astronaut or an astronaut's wife to use the word *astronaut*. Marge herself was always talking about "the fellows." Besides, the full name would make the military analogy too pointed.

The A.W.C. was no great delight to most of the wives of the Original Seven, however. Some of the newcomers, such as Sue Borman, were too gung-ho about it all. That was what they would tell themselves. In fact, the newcomers acted too *equal* about it all. There was no protocol for showing the deference due Single-Combat Generals' wives. The wives of the Original Seven began attending the monthly A.W.C. hours less and less. Betty Grissom almost never showed up; but then Betty had hated teatime functions from the very beginning. If one was going to feel ill at ease in the cheery chitchat game *and* not be treated as the Honorable Mrs. Single-Combat General . . . why bother?

For both the wives and the men there was at first an Oaken Bucket nostalgia for the early days, the Langley era, the pioneer period, the period of youth and idealism and spartan courage and yahoo cowboy disregard for the bureaucratic proprieties. You would even see engineers and support personnel who had moved from Langley and the Cape here to Houston getting misty about those old days . . . three years ago . . . The new facility, the Manned Spacecraft Center, was taking shape out in the middle of a thousand acres of absolutely flat gumbo pasture. The buildings were great squat beige cubes set at grandiose intervals from one another and connected by wide roads, veritable highways, lined with aluminum light poles. The place looked like one of those "industrial parks" that were always being touted in the real-estate sections of the Sunday newspapers.

Nevertheless, it was obvious that something of vast proportions was underway; and given a rosy enough picture of what lies down the road, a man could get over a case of homesickness soon enough. Perhaps Houston, the boom town of boom towns, was just the place for the expansion occurring in the space program. After a while you could begin to appreciate Houston's energy and its sense of the grand sweep, the risk-all plunge. And Timber Cove and Nassau Bay and the other new housing developments out by Clear Lake weren't half bad, it turned out. In fact, they were luxury itself compared to what you found around most air bases, and the locals, out here in this erstwhile farming country, were really good folks. Two-thirds of NASA was already geared up for Projects Gemini and Apollo and the great race to beat the Soviets to the moon. Just imagine what waited, here on earth, for the first man to walk on the moon . . . and the boys could imagine it. You had only to look at John Glenn. Glenn had not been the first man to fly in earth orbit or even the second, merely the first American. Yet he had ascended to a status so extraordinary it had no precedent. Some of the boys were convinced that Glenn had his eyes set on becoming President. (Nor was the notion far-fetched; after all, it was David who had succeeded to the throne of Saul.) Glenn now moved in a world full of the Kennedys, the Johnsons, senators, congressmen, foreign dignitaries, heads of corporations, VIPs of every description. Next to John Kennedy himself, John Glenn was probably the best-known and most admired American in the world. Oh, the boys were aware of all that! Just ask Al Shepard! —although of course no one did.

Al was now in training as backup for Gordon Cooper's flight, which would be in May 1963. Gordo, the last in line, had drawn what was shaping up as the final flight in the Mercury series, thirty-four hours, twenty-two orbits, designed to put the United States into the game with the Soviets, who had now achieved flights of seventeen, sixty-four, and forty-eight orbits. The original planning had called for four long-duration flights, with the second one lasting three days. Shepard had been counting on that. He was desperate for an orbital flight. His suborbital flight, as well as Grissom's, now seemed terribly insignificant. As for Gus, he was already getting revved up for the Gemini program, spending a lot of time in St. Louis, where McDonnell was building the Gemini spacecraft. Gus had put the gloom of his flight behind him and was looking ahead to Gemini and Apollo. His friend Deke was in charge of crew selection for the two new programs and was throwing himself heart and soul into the job, and not just because he enjoyed the exercise of his newly found power. The main thing was that he would be on top of every flight from beginning to end, familiar with every detail of every mission. It seemed to be Deke's fervent belief that it would be only a matter of time—following the next physical or the one after that, or the one next year—before he was back on full flight status and into the rotation. And Wally—Wally was riding high. Wally's flight was still the shining example of what an *operational space flight* should be. It had taken Wally's performance to show that Cooper's twenty-two-orbit flight would be possible. Wally couldn't have been in better shape in the program. He had been as efficient and as cool as they made them.

Wally had come back from his flight and landed in the middle of the Cuban missile crisis. For a week Kennedy and Khrushchev had their showdown, which appeared to bring the world to the brink of a nuclear war, but then Khrushchev backed off and withdrew all Soviet missiles from Cuba. After that things cooled down considerably. Like everyone else, the boys noticed that negotiations for a nuclear test ban and for "cooperation in space," whatever that might prove to be, were in the news a lot. But to tell the truth, it didn't seem like much more than the usual drizzle of words. For that matter, on May 11, four days before Cooper was to go up, Lyndon Johnson drew the lines the same way they had been drawn ever since October of 1957, when the first Sputnik went up. He made a speech answering charges that some congressmen were making about the high cost of the new programs, Gemini and Apollo, and he said: "I, for one, don't want to go to bed by the light of a Communist moon." Christ, that was *worse* than Sputnik: every night, overhead, sails the silvery moon, occupied by the Russians.

As for Gordo himself, he was already on top of the world. There were those among his brethren who had their doubts about the man, but he never had a moment's doubt about himself. Once more his light shone 'round about him. Was he the last of the seven to be assigned a flight? Well, so what . . . it wasn't a contest . . . the press had dreamed up all that crap . . . Shepard, Glenn, and the others had paved the way for his endurance test. The potential hazards? They didn't bother him in the slightest. They hadn't from the beginning.

Confronted with any feasible form of manned flight, Gordo was a picture of righteous aplomb. This was a side of Cooper that Jim Rathmann understood better than any of his confreres in the corps. Gordo had been in Florida for a long stretch, preparing for his flight, and he saw Rathmann a lot. Thanks to Rathmann, he, like Gus and Wally and Al, had become crazy about automobile racing. Rathmann, in turn, had decided to learn to fly. Cooper took him up in a Beechcraft one day and told him: "Never fly under a sea gull—they'll shit on your airplane." Rathmann made the mistake of laughing, as if he thought Gordo was kidding, whereupon Gordo said, "I'll show you," and headed for a flock of sea gulls flying low over the Everglades. The first thing Rathmann knew, Cooper was down so low he could hear a sound that went *whup whup whup whup whup whup whup whup*. It was the propellers cutting the marsh grass. For more than a mile old Gordo mowed the marsh grass to make sure he stayed under the sea gulls. Rathmann could hear it the whole time: *whup whup whup whup whup whup*. By the time they landed, Rathmann was Jell-O. But Cooper just popped open the cockpit door and stood up on the lower frame and pointed triumphantly at the roof and yelled to Rathmann: "Look here—I *told* you!"

So far as a Mercury flight was concerned, he seemed to regard it as easy enough. He had lobbied as hard as Deke Slayton himself for more *pilot* control of the spacecraft. But since you didn't have it, why get excited? Why get your bowels in an uproar? Just take the ride and relax.

Early in the morning of May 15, while it was still dark, Gordo was inserted into the little human holster atop the rocket. As usual there was a long hold before the lift-off. The doctors monitoring the biomedical telemetry began noticing something very odd. In fact, they couldn't believe it. Every objective reading of the calibrations and printouts indicated . . . the astronaut had gone to sleep! The man was up there stacking Z's on top of a rocket loaded with 200,000 pounds of liquid oxygen!

Well, why the hell not? Gordo had had plenty of opportunity to see how the launch days always went. You hit the sack in Hangar S about ten or eleven the night before, and then they woke you up about three in the morning, in the dark, and they took you out to the rocket and they laid you down on a contoured couch for two, three, four hours while they tuned in all the systems for the lift-off. You didn't have a damned thing to do, really, during most of this; so why not catch up on all the sleep you'd missed?

Throughout America, throughout the world, untold millions were by their radios and in front of television sets, waiting for the moment of lift-off, wondering, as always: *My God, what goes through a man's mind at a moment like this!* Scarcely able to believe it themselves, NASA never supplied the answer.

BY THE MOMENT of lift-off there was quite a circus in progress out front of Gordo's house in Timber Cove. The Genteel Beast was outdoing itself in the death-watch department. One of the television networks had erected a stupendous aerial on the lawn of a house across the way, a gigantic thing, about eight stories high, the better to beam to the world live pictures of the house inside which Astronaut Cooper's wife, Trudy, was maintaining her anxious vigil in front of the TV set. Milling around underneath the aerial and in the street and on the sidewalks was the biggest mob of reporters and camera crewmen you could imagine. Slovenly but nevertheless seemly they were. They treated Trudy Cooper, in their coverage, as if she had stepped right out of *Life* magazine, as if she were wearing a pageboy bob and playing "Moonlight in Vermont" on the old upright in the family room to keep up the spirits of herself and the children while Gordon's life was on the line in the longest American mission yet.

That was rich. By now the very presence of the Beast itself had made any such private and personal response to the event impossible, even in households where the marriage was a lot more solid than Gordo and Trudy's. For the astronaut's wife the days of the lonely vigil by the telephone with the little ones tugging at her skirt, Edwards- or Pax River-style, were over. First had come the Danger Wake, as Louise Shepard had experienced it, with a big crowd in the house and a bigger one—the Genteel Animal—out on the front lawn. Since then the Astronaut's Wife had been converted from an individual to a performer, at least for the duration of the flight—ready or willing or good at it or not. It had become an immutable part of the drill: at the completion of the flight the astronaut's wife had to leave the house and confront the Beast and all his cameras and micro- phones and submit to a press conference and answer questions and be the Perfect Astronaut's Wife with merely the entire world watching. It was this grim prospect that truly lacerated one's heart while Mr. Wonderful was aloft. It was *this* that gave the test pilot's wife a royal case of nerves in the space age. For the astronaut the flight consisted of riding the rocket and, God willing, not fucking up. For the wife the flight consisted of . . . the Press Conference.

The questions they asked you were unbelievably simpleminded, and yet there was no smooth way to field them. As soon as you touched one, it popped all over your face like bubble gum.

"What is in your heart?"

"What advice do you have for other women whose husbands have to go through dangerous situations?"

"What's the first meal you plan to cook for [Al, Gus, John, Scott, Wally, Gordon]?"

"Did you feel you were with him while he was in orbit?"

Pick out one! Try answering it!

Problems of protocol had arisen. Sometimes the Genteel Animal besieged the Mother's house as well as the Wife's. John Glenn's mother had been a great hit on television. She looked and sounded like about as ideal a mother as an astro- naut could possibly have. She had white hair and a marvelous smile, and when Walter Cronkite, on CBS, cut from the Cape to New Concord, Ohio, to say a few words to her, she said, "Well, Wal-ter Cron-kite!"—as if she were saying hello to a cousin she hadn't heard from in years. But whom should the networks interview first after a flight, the Wife, the Mother, or the President? Opinions varied, and this added to the tension. Regardless of the order, however, there seemed to be no way for the wife to get out of it. Even Rene, after hiding throughout Scott's flight, had dutifully turned up at the press tent on the base at the Cape for the Wife's Press Conference. By now, when the other wives came around to the house of the Wife during a flight, they were not there to hold her hand over the dangers her husband was facing. They were there to hold her hand over the television cam- eras she would be facing. They were there to try to buck her up for a *true ordeal*. They liked to do the Squarely Stable routine. One of the wives—Rene Carpenter was good at it—would take the role of Nancy Whoever, TV correspondent, and hold her fist up to her mouth, as if she were holding a microphone and say:

"We're here in front of the trim, modest suburban home of Squarely Stable, the famous astronaut who has just completed his historic mission, and we have with us his attractive wife, Primly Stable. Primly Stable, you must be happy, proud, and thankful at this moment."

And then she would shift her fist over underneath the chin of another wife, and she would say:

"Yes, Nancy, that's true. I'm happy, proud, and thankful at this moment."

"Tell us, Primly Stable—may I call you Primly?"

"Certainly, Nancy, Primly."

"Tell us, Primly, tell us what you felt during the blast-off, at the very moment when your husband's rocket began to rise from the earth and take him on this historic journey."

"To tell you the truth, Nancy, I missed that part of it. I'd sort of dozed off, because I got up so early this morning and I'd been rushing around a lot taping the shades shut, so the TV people wouldn't come in the windows."

"Well, would you say you had a lump in your throat as big as a tennis ball?"

"That's about the size of it, Nancy, I had a lump in my throat as big as a tennis ball."

"And finally, Primly, I know that the most important prayer of your life had already been answered: Squarely has returned safely from outer space. But if you could have one other wish at this moment and have it come true, what would that one wish be?"

"Well, Nancy, I'd wish for an Electrolux vacuum cleaner with all the attachments—"

—and they'd all crack up at the thought of what a dim lummox the Genteel Beast really was. Still . . . that didn't make it any easier when your time came.

Gordo's flight was to last thirty-four hours, meaning that Trudy would undergo the longest siege by the Beast and have the most protracted danger wake yet. Two sets of wives came by. Louise Shepard brought most of the other Original Seven wives in her convertible. Later on, some of the Other Nine wives came by—Jim Lovell's wife Marilyn, Ed White's wife Pat, Neil Armstrong's wife Jan, and John Young's wife Barbara. Everybody tried to listen to Gordo's transmissions from the capsule over a high-frequency radio receiver Wally Schirra had loaned Trudy. It was the receiver that had been in Wally's capsule during his flight. But about all you could get out of it was static. So they went out on the patio in the back, out of sight of the Animal, and watched the television coverage of the flight, off and on, and ate devil's-food cake. In the true spirit of the wake, friends and neighbors had brought over food. During his ninth orbit, which began about 7:30 p.m., Gordo was supposed to try to go to sleep for a few hours, and Trudy decided that she and their two daughters, Jan and Cam, should try to get some rest, too. In the morning Gordo was still up there, twenty-four hours into the flight, and the Beast was still outside the door, and the danger wake was going strong. About noon, as Gordo began his last four orbits, you could tell from the television reports that his capsule was beginning to develop electrical problems. During the next-to-last orbit they became worse. It now appeared as if Gordo would have to line up the capsule for re-entry manually, without any assistance from the automatic control system at all. Trudy received a telephone call from Deke Slayton. He told her that she and the children shouldn't worry, because Gordo had practiced completely manual re-entries many times on the procedures trainer. "This is what we wanted to do anyway," he said.

Well, Gordo was going to have his hands full. Nevertheless, Trudy couldn't help but jump yet one more step forward in the retro sequence. If Gordo was beginning his re-entry, then very soon . . . she would have to step out the front door and face the Beast and his cameras and microphones and go through the press conference . . .

* * *

Meantime, ALOFT, Gordo was having a hell of a time for himself. Right after the lift-off he said to Wally Schirra, who was serving as the capcom, "Feels good, buddy . . . All systems go." He kept adding things such as "Working just like advertised." The Life Sciences people, who had finally been allowed a few experiments since the flight was so long, were interested in determining the limits of adaptability to weightlessness. They hoped to see what sleep would be like, although they were not sure they could learn anything about this during a thirty-four-hour flight, given the naturally high adrenal excitement of the astronaut. They needn't have worried. Ol' Gordo obliged by falling asleep during his second orbit, even though his suit was overheating and he had to adjust the temperature settings continually. One of his tasks was to provide urine samples at specified intervals. This he dutifully did. Since in a weightless condition it would be impossible to pour the sample from the urine receptacle—it would have floated about the cockpit as globules—Gordo was provided with a syringe to transfer it from the receptacle to a container. But the syringe leaked all over the place, and Gordo had the reeking amber globules floating around, anyway. So he just tried to herd them together into one big blob periodically and went on with his tasks, which included light and photographic experiments, somewhat like Carpenter's. Gordo was really something. He seemed even cooler about the whole thing than Schirra, and nobody had believed that possible. Every now and then he would look out the window and give the folks on the ground a little travelogue, Gordo-style.

"Down there's the Himalayas," he said. He seemed to like the sound of the word. "Ay-yuh . . . the Himalayas." In Oklahoma lingo Gordo it came out "Himmuh-lay-yuz."

On the nineteenth orbit, with three more to go, Gordo started getting readings of g-force buildups, as if the capsule had begun its re-entry. Sure enough, the capsule started rolling, just as it would have during a re-entry in order to increase stability. The automatic control system had begun the re-entry sequence, even though the capsule was still in orbit and hadn't slowed down in the slightest. The electrical system was shorting out. On the next orbit, the twentieth, the capsule lost all attitude readings. This meant Cooper would have to line it up manually for the re-entry. On the next-to-last orbit, the twenty-first, the automatic control system went out completely. For re-entry Cooper would not only have to establish the capsule's angle of attack by hand, using the horizon as his point of reference, he would also have to hold the capsule steady on all three axes, pitch, roll, and yaw, with the hand controller and fire the retro-rockets by hand. Meantime, the electrical malfunction had done something to the oxygen balance. Carbon dioxide started building up in the capsule and inside Cooper's suit and helmet as well.

"Well . . . things are beginning to stack up a little," said Gordo. It was the same old sod-hut drawl. He sounded like the airline pilot who, having just slipped two seemingly certain mid-air collisions and finding himself in the midst of a radar fuse-out and control-tower dysarthria, says over the intercom: "Well, ladies and gentlemen, we'll be busy up here in the cockpit making our final approach into Pittsburgh, and so we want to take this opportunity to thank you for flying American and we hope we'll see you again real soon." It was second-generation Yeager, now coming from earth orbit. Cooper was having a good time. He knew everybody was in a sweat down below. But this was what he and the boys had wanted all along, wasn't it? They had wanted to take over the complete re-entry process—become *true pilots* in this damned thing, bring her in manually—and the engineers had always shuddered at the thought. Well, now they had no other choice, and he had the controls. On top of that, during his final orbit he would have to keep the capsule at the proper angle, by eye, on the night side of the earth and then be ready to fire the retro-rockets soon after he entered daylight over the Pacific. No sweat. Just made it a little more of a sporty course, that was all—and Gordo lined up the capsule, hit the button for the retro-rockets, and splashed down even closer to the carrier *Kearsage* than Schirra had.

No one could deny it . . . no brethren, old or new, could fail to see it . . . when the evil wind was up, Ol' Gordo had shown the world the pure and righteous stuff.

Over the next week Gordo became the most celebrated of all the astronauts aside from John Glenn himself. Ol' Gordo!—whose confreres had pictured him as forever bringing up the rear . . . There he was, sitting on the back of the open limousine, in parade after parade . . . Honolulu, Cocoa Beach, Washington, New York . . . And such parades! The ticker-tape parade in New York was one of the biggest ever, Glenn-scale, with signs along the way, saying things such as GORDO COOPER—YOU'RE SUPER-DUPER! in letters three or four feet high. Not only that, he addressed a joint session of Congress, just as Glenn had. A "textbook flight" like Schirra's was all well and good, but there was nothing like a hair-raiser to capture the imagination and stir the gourds. Gordo was also the first American to spend an entire day in space, of course, and he had put the United States back in the ball game with the Soviets. The role of single-combat warrior seemed more glorious than ever.

15

THE HIGH DESERT

B Y THE TIME of Gordon Cooper's flight, Chuck Yeager had returned to Edwards Air Force Base. He was only thirty-nine, the same age, it so happened, as Wally Schirra and Alan Shepard and two years younger than John Glenn. Yeager no longer had quite the head of dark curly hair that everybody at Edwards saw in the framed photographs of him stepping out of the X-1 in October 1947. And God knows, his face had more mileage on it. This was typical of military pilots by that age and came not so much from the rigors of the job as from taking the sun rays head-on twelve months every year out on the concrete of the flight lines. Yeager had the same trim muscular build as always. He had been flying supersonic fighter aircraft as regularly, day in and day out, as any colonel in the Air Force. So in the ten years since he had made his last record-setting flight here at Edwards, that wild ride to Mach, 2.4 in the X-1A, he really hadn't changed too much. You couldn't say the same about Edwards itself.

When Yeager had departed in 1954, Pancho's had still been standing. Today the base was loaded with military and civil-service personnel, every GS-type in the manual, working for the Air Force, for NASA, even for the Navy, which had a small piece of the X-15 program. At four o'clock it was worth your life to be heading upstream during the mad rush from the air conditioners in the office buildings to the air conditioners in the tract homes in Lancaster.

This much Yeager already knew about; this was the part that was easy to take. He had been commanding a squadron of F-100s at George Air Force Base, which was only about fifty miles southeast of Edwards in the same stretch of prehistoric dry-lake terrain. Yeager and Glennis and their four children had lived at Victorville in the same sort of housing development you found in Lancaster; just a bit more barren, if anything, a little grid of Contractor Suburbans lined up alongside Interstate Highway 15. The same old arthritic Joshua trees dared you to grow a blade of grass, much less a real tree, and the cars heading from Los Angeles to Las Vegas hurtled by without so much as a flick of the eye. Not that any of this weighed upon Yeager, however. As commander of a squadron of supersonic fighters he had led training operations and readiness maneuvers over half the world and as far away as Japan. Besides, nobody stayed in the Air Force because of the glories of the domestic architecture. Where he was living was standard issue for a colonel such as himself who after twenty years was making just a little over two hundred dollars a week, including extra flight pay and living allowance . . . and without magazine contracts or any other unorthodox goodies . . .

The Air Force had brought Yeager back to Edwards two years ago to be director of flight test operations. Last year, 1962, they created the new Aerospace Research Pilot School and made him commandant. ARPS, as the school became known, was part of big plans the Air Force had for a manned space program of its own. As a matter of fact, the Air Force had envisioned a major role in space ever since the first Sputnik went up, only to be thwarted by Eisenhower's decision to put the space effort in civilian hands. They now wanted to create a military program, quite apart from NASA's, using fleets of ships such as the X-20 and various "lifting body" craft, wingless ships whose hulls would be shaped to give them aerodynamic control when they re-entered the earth's atmosphere, and the Manned Orbiting Laboratory, which would be a space station. Boeing was building the first X-20 at its plant in Seattle. The Titan 3C rocket booster it would require was almost ready. Six pilots had already been chosen to train to take it into orbit.

The X-20 and the MOL were not yet operational, of course. In the meantime, it seemed to be highly important that Air Force pilots be chosen as NASA astronauts. The prestige of the Astronaut absolutely dominated flying, and the Air Force was determined to be the prime supplier of the breed. Four of the nine new astronauts selected in 1962, before ARPS was instituted, had been from the Air Force; that was not considered good enough.

To tell the truth, the brass had gone slightly bananas over this business of producing astronauts. They had even set up a "charm school" in Washington for the leading candidates. The best of the young test pilots from Edwards and Wright-Patterson flew to Washington and were given a course in how to impress the NASA selection panels in Houston. And it was dead serious! They listened to pep talks by Air Force generals, including General Curtis LeMay himself. They went through drills on how to talk on their feet—and that was the more sensible, credible part of the course. From there it got right down to the level of cotillion etiquette. They were told what to wear to the interviews with the engineers and the astronauts. They were to wear knee-length socks, so that when they sat down and crossed their legs no bare flesh would show between the top of the socks and bottom of the pant cuffs. They were told what to drink at the social get-togethers in Houston: they should drink alcohol, in keeping with the pilot code of Flying & Drinking, but in the form of a tall highball, either bourbon or Scotch, and only one. They were told how to put their hands on their hips (if they must). The thumbs should be to the rear and the fingers forward. Only women and interior decorators put the thumbs forward and the fingers back.

And the men went through it all willingly! Without a snigger! The brass's passion for the astronaut business was nothing compared to that of the young pilots themselves. Edwards had always been the precise location on the map of the apex of the pyramid of the right stuff itself. And now it was just another step on the way up. These boys were coming through Chuck Yeager's prep school so they could get a ticket to Houston.

The glamour of the space program was such that there was no longer any arguing against it. In addition to the chances for honor, glory, fame, and the celebrity treatment, all the new hot dogs could see something else. It practically glowed in the sky. They talked about it at beer call at every Officers Club at every air base in the land. Namely, the Astronaut Life. The youngsters knew about that, all right. It existed just over the rainbow, in Houston, Texas . . . the *Life* contract . . . $25,000 per year over and above your salary . . . veritable *mansions* in the suburbs, custom-designed . . . No more poor sad dried-up asbestos-shingle-roof clapboard shacks rattling in the sandstorms . . . free Corvettes . . . an enormous free lunch from one side of America to the other, for that matter . . . and the tastiest young cookies imaginable! One had only to reach for them! . . . The vision of all the little sugarplums danced above the mighty ziggurat . . . You bet! A veritable Fighter Jock's Forbidden Dream of *the goodies* had been brought to life, and all these young hot dogs looked upon it like people who believed in miracles . . .

It really made some of the older pilots shake their heads. If a man got a piece of tail every now and then, the world wasn't going to come to an end. But to dream of a goddamned aerial nookie circus . . . What was worse, however, was the *Life* contract. The way any true Blue-Suiter saw it, to let an experimental test pilot exploit his job commercially was only asking for trouble. If a man had the opportunity to fly machines with incalculable millions of dollars' worth of resources and facilities and man hours built into them, if they put him in a position to make history—that was more than enough compensation.

Yeager had flown the X-1 at straight pay, $283 a month. The Blue Suit!—that was enough for him. The Blue Suit had brought him everything he had in this world, and he asked for nothing else.

And what would all of that mean to these boys, even if someone said it? Not a hell of a lot, probably. Not even the fact that the X-15 project was in its finest hour, right here, for all to see, affected the new order of things. In June the X-15, with Joe Walker at the controls, had achieved Mach 5.92, or 4,104 miles per hour, which brought the project close to the optimum speed—"in excess of Mach 6"—it had been aiming for. In July Bob White had flown to 314,750 feet, or 59.6 miles, 9.6 miles into space (50 miles was now officially regarded as the boundary line) and well above the project's goal of 280,000 feet. These and many less spectacular flights of the X-15 were bringing back data concerning heat buildup (from air friction) and stability upon which the design of all the supersonic and hypersonic aircraft of the future, commercial and military, would be based. The X-15's XLR-99 rocket had 57,000 pounds of thrust. The Mercury-Redstone had 78,000; the Mercury-Atlas had 367,000 pounds; but soon there would be the X-20, and the X-20 would have a Titan 3 rocket's 2.5 million pounds of thrust, and it would be the first ship to go into orbit with a pilot at the controls from beginning to end, a pilot who could land it anywhere he wanted, eliminating the tremendous expense and risk of the Mercury ocean-rescue operations, which involved carriers, spotter planes, helicopters, frogmen, and backup vessels strung halfway around the world.

Yeager's students had a chance to experience something close to what such space piloting would be like. They went "booming and zooming" in the F-104. The F-104 was a fighter-interceptor that had been built to counter the MiG-21, which the Russians were known to be developing. The F-104 was fifty feet long and had two razor-thin wings, each only seven feet long, set far back on the fuselage, close to the tail assembly. The pilot and his guy-in-back were in two seats way up in the nose. The F-104 was built for speed in combat, period. It could climb at speeds in excess of Mach 1 and it could achieve Mach 2.2 in level flight. The faster it went, the steadier it was; it was unstable at low speeds, however, and oversensitive to the controls, with an evil tendency to pitch up and then snap into rolls and spins. At glide speed it seemed to want to fall like a length of pipe. After practicing on an F-104 simulator, Yeager's students would take the ship up to 35,000 feet and open her up to Mach 2 (the boom), then aim her up at about forty-five degrees and try to poke a hole in the sky (the zoom). The g-forces slammed them back in their seats and they shot up like shells, and the pale-blue desert sky turned blue-black and the g-forces slid off and they came sailing over the top of the arc, about 75,000 feet up, silent and weightless—an experience like unto what the brethren themselves had known!—

—and these boys thought that was neat. Maybe it would be nice to fly the X-15 or the X-20, if you didn't make astronaut . . .

Yeager liked to take the ARPS students up for mock dog-fights, hassling, just to . . . keep the proficiency up . . . Few of the lads had ever been in combat and they knew little about the critical tolerances of fighter aircraft during violent maneuvers. They knew where the outside of the envelope was, but they didn't know about the part where you reached the outside and then *stretched* her a little . . . without breaking through . . . Yeager waxed their tails with regularity, but they took that in stride. These days the way to the top—meaning the road to test-pilot astronaut—involved being very good at a lot of things without necessarily being "shit-hot," to use the beer-call expression, at anything. A balance of pilot skills and engineering; that was the ticket. Joe Walker's backup pilot in the X-15 project, Neil Armstrong, was typical of the new breed. A lot of people couldn't figure out Armstrong. He had a close blond crew cut and small pale-blue eyes and scarcely a line or a feature in his face that you could remember. His expression hardly ever changed. You'd ask him a question, and he would just stare at you with those pale-blue eyes of his, and you'd start to ask the question again, figuring he hadn't understood, and—*click*—out of his mouth would come forth a sequence of long, quiet, perfectly formed, precisely thought-out sentences, full of aniso-tropic functions and multiple-encounter trajectories, or whatever else was called for. It was as if his hesitations were just data punch-in intervals for his computer. Armstrong had been preparing for an X-15 launch from the Smith's Ranch dry-lake bed last year when Yeager, who was director of flight test operations, told him the lake bed was still too muddy from the rains. Armstrong said the meteorologi-cal data, considering the wind and temperature factors, indicated the surface would be satisfactory. Yeager received a call from NASA asking him if he would take a small plane over to the lake bed and make a ground inspection. "Hell, no," said Yeager. "I've been flying over these lakes for fifteen years, and I know it's muddy. I'm not going to be responsible for disabling an Air Force plane." Well, would he fly a NASA plane up there? Hell, no, said Yeager; he didn't want that on his record, either. It was finally arranged that he would fly up there backseat, with Armstrong at the controls and therefore responsible for the mission. As soon as they touched down, Yeager could tell that the mud was going to suck up the landing gears like a couple of fence posts, which it did. Now they were hopelessly mired in the muck, and a range of hills blocked radio contact with the base.

"Well, Neil," said Yeager, "in a few hours it'll be dark, and the temperature's going down to zero, and we're two guys standing out here in the mud wearing windbreakers. Got any good ideas?" Armstrong stared at him, and the computer interval began, and it ended, and nothing came out. A rescue team from the base, alerted by the loss of radio contact, retrieved them before nightfall—and brought back the story, which entertained the old-timers for a few days.

Nevertheless, the new breed had their share of the proper righteous stuff, same as the stick'n'rudder tigers of yore. Armstrong himself had flown more than a hundred missions off carriers during the Korean War, and had done good work in the X-15. Then you had men like Dave Scott and Mike Adams, who were two of Yeager's ARPS students. They were practicing low lift-over-drag landings one day in the F-104. In this maneuver, which simulated an X-15 landing, you gunned the afterburner for speed (and stability) and flared the flaps and tried to grease the ship onto the runway at 200 knots. As Scott and Adams neared the ground, the "eyelids" on the afterburner malfunctioned, opening too wide, cutting the thrust down to 20 or 30 percent of maximum. Visually they could tell the ship was sinking too fast. Scott, who had the controls, gunned it but got very little response. They were dropping like a brick. Adams, in back, knew that the tail would hit the runway first, due to the angle of attack they were in, if Scott couldn't regain power. He told Scott over the radio circuit that if the tail hit he was ejecting. The tail hit, and in that moment he pulled his cinch ring and ejected at zero altitude. Scott elected to stay with the ship. The belly smashed onto the runway and the ship went careening down it and off into the mesquite. When the beast finally came to a halt, Scott looked back, and the engine was jammed up into the space where Adams used to be. Both men had made the right decision. Adams had been exploded up into the air and had come down safely by parachute. Scott's ejection mechanism had been broken in the torque of the initial impact and he would have been killed had he pulled the cinch ring, either by the nitroglycerine explosion or by a partial ejection.

Yeager was tremendously impressed by those two decisions by two men in the very mouth of the Gulp. There you had it, with the ante doubled: the right stuff. And when NASA had announced several months ago that a third group of astronauts would be chosen both men immediately applied, although Adams also seemed to have a sincere interest in the X-15 project. The X-15 pilots themselves had their eyes on Houston, for that matter. Armstrong had applied as soon as civilians had been eligible and was now a Group II astronaut. He had Joe Walker's blessing, too. Walker himself had considered applying but figured that his age—he was forty-two—pretty well ruled him out.

That was the way the pyramid was now constructed. The old argument—namely, that an astronaut would be a mere passenger monitoring an automated system—didn't have much sock to it any more. The truth was that there you had a picture of the pilot in practically all the hypersonic vehicles of the future, whether in space or in the atmosphere. The Mercury vehicle had merely been one of the first. Way back in April of 1953, Yeager had made a speech in which he said, "Some of the proposed fighters of tomorrow will be able to find and destroy a target and even return to their home stations and land by themselves. The only reason a pilot will be needed is to take over and decide what to do if anything goes wrong with the electronic equipment." Talking about the Ships of Tomorrow had made it all seem far off. But now, ten years later, they were already bringing such systems into the hardware stage. They were even working on a system to land F-4s automatically on aircraft carriers; the pilot would take his hands off the controls and let the computers bring him down onto that heaving slab. The supersonic transports and airliners would be so automated they would give the pilot an override stick just so he could push on it every now and then and feel *like a pilot;* it would be a goddamned right-stuff security blanket. They were even developing an automatic guidance system to bring the X-15 back through the atmosphere at a precise angle of attack. Maybe the age of "the flyboys," the stick'n'rudder fighter jocks, was about finished.

All of that Yeager could accept. On the great pyramid there was no steady state. Sixteen years ago, when he came to Muroc, he was only twenty-four, and few other test pilots had ever heard of him, and most people in aviation thought "the sound barrier" was as solid as a wall. Once he flew Mach 1, however, it was a whole new ball game. And now there were cosmonauts and astronauts, and it was a whole new ball game once again. A man could do a pretty good job of being philosophical about it. What finally got to Yeager, however, was the Ed Dwight case.

It had been early this year that Yeager got word from the brass that the President, John F. Kennedy, was determined that NASA have at least one Negro astronaut in their lineup. The whole process was to take place organically, however, as if in the natural order of things. Kennedy was leaning on the Defense Department, Defense was leaning on the Air Force brass, and they tossed the potato to Yeager. The pilot who had been singled out was an Air Force captain named Ed Dwight. He was to go through ARPS and be selected by NASA. The clouds developed soon enough. Dwight was enrolled in the basic flight test course along with twenty-five other candidates. Only the top eleven students could enter ARPS's six-month space-flight course, which had limited facilities, and Dwight did not rank among the top eleven. Yeager didn't see how he could jump him over other young tigers, all of them desperate to become astronauts. Every week, it seemed like, a detachment of Civil Rights Division lawyers would turn up from Washington, from the Justice Department, which was headed by the President's brother Bobby. The lawyers squinted in the desert sunlight and asked a great many questions about the progress and treatment of Ed Dwight and took notes. Yeager kept saying he didn't see how he could simply jump Dwight over these other men. And the lawyers would come back the next week and squint some more and take some more notes. There were days when ARPS seemed like the Ed Dwight case with a few classrooms and some military hardware appended. A compromise was finally struck in which Dwight would be admitted to the space-flight course, but only if every man who ranked above him was also admitted. That was how it came to pass that the next class had fourteen students instead of eleven and included Captain Dwight. Meantime, the White House, apparently, was signaling to the Negro press that Dwight was going to be "the first Negro astronaut," and he was being invited to make public appearances. He was being set up for a fall, because the chances of NASA accepting him as an astronaut appeared remote in any event.

The whole thing was baffling. On the upper reaches of the great ziggurat the subject of race had never been introduced before. The unspoken premise was that you either had the right stuff or you didn't, and no other variables mattered. When the seven Mercury astronauts had been chosen in 1959, the fact that they were all white and all Protestant seemed to be interpreted as wholly benign evidence of their Small-Town American virtues. But by now, four years later, Kennedy, who had been supported by a coalition of minority groups in the 1960 election, had begun to raise the question of race as a matter of public policy in many areas. The phrase "white Protestant" took on a different meaning, so that it was now possible to regard the astronauts as some sort of cadre of whites of northern European racial background. In fact, this had nothing to do, *per se*, with their being astronauts. It was typical of career military officers generally. Throughout the world, for that matter, career officers came from "native" or "old settler" stock. Even in Israel, which had existed for barely a generation as an independent nation and was dominated politically by immigrants from Eastern Europe, the officer corps was made up overwhelmingly of "real Israelis"—men born or raised from an early age in the pre-war Jewish settlements of the old Palestine. The other common denominator of the astronauts was that they were all first or only sons; yet not even this had any special significance, for studies soon showed that first or only sons dominated many occupations, including scholarly ones. (In an age when the average number of children per family was barely more than two, the odds were two out of three that *any* male would be a first or only son.) None of which was going to mollify the White House, however, because the astronaut, the single-combat warrior, had become a creature with greater political significance than any other type of pilot in history.

The squinting and hassling was still going on the day the NF-104 arrived. Perhaps that was one reason the monster looked so good to Yeager. All of the world's accumulated political cunning, from Machiavelli to John McCormack, wouldn't be worth a dogscratch in the NF-104 at 65,000 feet. Two extraordinary pieces of equipment were being developed specifically for ARPS. One was a space mission simulator, a device more realistic and sophisticated than the Mercury procedures trainer or any simulator NASA had on the boards. The other was the NF-104, which was an F-104 with a rocket engine mounted over the tailpipe. The rocket engine used hydrogen peroxide and JP4 fuel and would deliver 6,000 pounds of thrust. It was like a super-afterburner. The main engine plus the regular afterburner would take you to about 60,000 feet, and then you cut in the rocket, and that would take you somewhere between 120,000 and 140,000 feet. At least that was what the engineers confidently assumed. The plan was that the ARPS students would run profiles on the space mission simulator, then put on silver pressure suits, space-flight-style, and take the NF-104 up to 120,000 feet or more in a tremendous arc, affording up to two minutes of weightlessness. During this interval they could master the use of the reaction controls, which were hydrogen-peroxide thrusters of the sort used in all vehicles above 100,000 feet, whether the X-15, the Mercury capsule, or the X-20.

The only problem was, nobody had ever wrung out the NF-104. Just how it would handle in the weak molecular structure of the atmosphere above 100,000 feet, what the limits of its performance envelope would be, nobody knew. The F-104 had been built as a high-speed interceptor, and when you tried to do other things with it, it became very "unforgiving," as the expression went. Pilots were already beginning to crunch it with the F-104 simply because the engine flamed out and they fell to the ground with about as much glide as a set of car keys. But Yeager loved the damned ship. It went like a bat. As the commandant of ARPS, he seized the opportunity to test the NF-104 as if it had his name on it.

The main reason he would be testing it would be for use in the school, but there was an extra dividend. Whoever was first to push the NF-104 to optimum performance was certain to set a new world record for altitude achieved by a ship taking off under its own power. The Soviets had set the current record, 113,890 feet, in 1961 with the E-66A, a delta-winged fighter plane. The X-2 and the X-15 had flown higher, but they had to be hauled aloft by a larger ship before their rockets were ignited. The Mercury and Vostok space vehicles were lifted to altitude by automated booster rockets, which were then disengaged and jettisoned. Of course, all aircraft records were losing their dazzle now that space flight had begun. It was getting to be like setting some sort of new record for railroad trains. Yeager hadn't tried to break a record in the skies over Edwards since December 1953, ten years ago, when he had set a new speed mark of Mach 2.4 in the X-1A and had come down the far side of the arc in the most horrendous bout with high-speed instability any man had ever survived. Now Yeager was back on the flight line again to go for broke, out by the shimmering mirage surface of Rogers Lake, under that pale-blue desert sky, and the righteous energy was flowing again. And if the good lads of the prep school could sense through him . . . and through that wild unbroken beast . . . a few volts of that righteous old-time religion . . . well, that would be all right, too.

Yeager had taken the NF-104 up for three checkout flights, edging it up gradually toward 100,000 feet, where the limits of the envelope, whatever they were, would begin to reveal themselves. And now he was out on the flight line for the second of two major preliminary flights. Tomorrow he would let it all out and go for the record. It was another of those absolutely clear brilliant afternoons on the dome of the world. In the morning flight everything had gone exactly according to plan. He had taken the ship up to 108,000 feet after cutting in the rocket engine at 60,000. The rocket had propelled the ship up at a 50-degree angle of attack. One of the disagreeable sides of the ship was her dislike of extreme angles. At any angle greater than 30 degrees, her nose would pitch up, which was the move she made just before going into spins. But at 108,000 feet it was no problem. The air was so thin at that altitude, so close to being pure "space," that the reaction controls, the hydrogen-peroxide thrusters, worked beautifully. Yeager had only to nudge the sidearm hand controller by his lap and a thruster on top of the nose of the plane pushed the nose right down again, and he was in perfect position to re-enter the dense atmosphere below. Now he was going up for one final exploration of that same region before going for broke tomorrow.

At 40,000 feet Yeager began his speed run. He cut in the afterburner and it slammed him back in his seat, and he was now riding an engine with nearly 16,000 pounds of thrust. As soon as the Machmeter hit 2.2, he pulled back on the stick and started the climb. The afterburner would carry him to 60,000 feet before exhausting its fuel. At precisely that moment he threw the switch for the rocket engine . . . terrific jolt . . . He's slammed back in his seat again. The nose pitches up to 70 degrees. The g-forces start rising. The desert sky starts falling away. He's going straight up into the indigo. At 78,000 feet a light on the console . . . as usual . . . the main engine overheating from the tremendous exertion of the climb. He throws the switch, and shuts it down, but the rocket is still accelerating. Who doesn't know this feeling if he doesn't! The bastards are fantastic! . . . One hundred thousand feet . . . He shuts down the rocket engine. He's still climbing. The g-forces slide off . . . makes you feel like you're pitching

forward . . . He's weightless, coming over the top of the arc . . . 104,000 feet
. . . It's absolutely silent . . . Twenty miles up . . . The sky is almost black.
He's looking straight up into it, because the nose of the ship is pitched up. His
angle of attack is still about 50 degrees. He's over the top of the arc and coming
down. He pushes the sidearm control to bring down the nose of the ship. Nothing
happens . . . He can hear the thruster working but the nose isn't budging. It's
still pitched up. He hits the thruster again . . . Shit! . . . She won't go down!
. . . Now he can see it, the whole diagram . . . This morning at 108,000 feet
the air was so thin it offered no resistance and you could easily push the nose
down with the thrusters. At 104,000 feet the air remains just thick enough to
exert aerodynamic pressure. The thrusters aren't strong enough to overcome it
. . . He keeps hitting the reaction controls . . . The hydrogen peroxide squirts
out of the jet on the nose of the ship and doesn't do a goddamned thing . . .
He's dropping and the nose is still pitched up . . . The outside of the envelope!
. . . well, here it is, the sonofabitch . . . It doesn't want to stretch . . . and
here we go! . . . The ship snaps into a flat spin. It's spinning right over its
center of gravity, like a pinwheel on a stick. Yeager's head is on the outer edge of
the circle, spinning around. He pushes the sidearm control again. The hydrogen
peroxide is finished. He has 600 pounds of fuel left in the main engine but there's
no way to start it up. To relight the engine you have to put the ship nose down
into a dive and force air through the intake duct and start the engine windmilling
to build up the rpms. Without rpms there's no hydraulic pressure and without
hydraulic pressure you can't move the stabilizer wings on the tail and without the
stabilizer wings you can't control this bastard at the lower altitudes . . . He's in
a steady-state flat spin and dropping . . . He's whirling around at a terrific rate
. . . He makes himself keep his eyes pinned on the instruments . . . A little
sightseeing at this point and it's vertigo and you're finished . . . He's down to
80,000 feet and the rpms are at dead zero . . . He's falling 150 feet a second
. . . 9,000 feet a minute . . . And what do I do next? . . . here in the jaws of
the Gulp . . . I've tried A!—I've tried B!—The damned beast isn't making a
sound . . . just spinning around like a length of pipe in the sky . . . He has
one last shot . . . the speed brakes, a parachute rig in the tail for slowing the
ship down after a high-speed landing . . . The altimeter keeps winding down
. . . Twenty-five thousand feet . . . but the altimeter is based on sea level . . .
He's only 21,000 feet above the high desert . . . The slack's running out . . .
He pops the speed brake . . . Bango!—the chute catches with a jolt . . . It
pulls the tail up . . . He pitches down . . . The spin stops. The nose is pointed
down. Now he only has to jettison the chute and let her dive and pick up the
rpms. He jettisons the chute . . . and the beast heaves up again! The nose goes
back up in the air! . . . It's the rear stabilizer wing . . . The leading edge is
locked, frozen into the position of the climb to altitude. With no rpms and no
hydraulic controls he can't move the tail . . . The nose is pitched way above 30
degrees . . . Here she goes again . . . She's back into the spin . . . He's spinning out on the rim again . . . He has no rpms, no power, no more speed chute,
and only 180 knots airspeed . . . He's down to 12,000 feet . . . 8,000 feet
above the farm . . . There's not a goddamned thing left in the manual or the
bag of tricks or the righteousness of twenty years of military flying . . . Chosen
or damned! . . . It blows at any seam! Yeager hasn't bailed out of an airplane
since the day he was shot down over Germany when he was twenty . . . I've

tried A!—I've tried B!—I've tried C! . . . 11,000 feet, 7,000 from the farm . . .
He hunches himself into a ball, just as it says in the manual, and reaches under
the seat for the cinch ring and pulls . . . He's exploded out of the cockpit with
such force it's like a concussion . . . He can't see . . . *Wham* . . . a jolt in
the back . . . It's the seat separating from him and the parachute rig . . . His
head begins to clear . . . He's in midair, in his pressure suit, looking out through
the visor of his helmet . . . Every second seems enormously elongated . . . infinite . . . such slow motion . . . He's suspended in midair . . . weightless
. . . The ship had been falling at about 100 miles an hour and the ejection
rocket had propelled him up at 90 miles an hour. For one thick adrenal moment
he's weightless in midair, 7,000 feet above the desert . . . The seat floats nearby,
as if the two of them are parked in the atmosphere . . . The butt of the seat, the
underside, is facing him . . . a red hole . . . the socket where the ejection
mechanism had been attached . . . It's dribbling a charcoal red . . . lava . . .
the remains of the rocket propellant . . . It's glowing . . . it's oozing out of the
socket . . . In the next moment they're both falling, him and the seat . . . His
parachute rig has a quarter bag over it and on the bag is a drogue chute that pulls
the bag off so the parachute will stream out gradually and not break the chute or
the pilot's back when the canopy pops open during a high-speed ejection. It's
designed for an ejection at 400 or 500 miles an hour, but he's only going about
175. In this infinitely expanded few seconds the lines stream out and Yeager and
the rocket seat and the glowing red socket sail through the air together . . . and
now the seat is drifting above him . . . into the chute lines! . . . The seat is
nestled in the chute lines . . . dribbling lava out of the socket . . . eating
through the lines . . . An infinite second . . . He's jerked up by the shoulders
. . . it's the chute opening and the canopy filling . . . in that very instant *the
lava*—it smashes into the visor of his helmet . . . Something slices through his
left eye . . . He's knocked silly . . . He can't see a goddamned thing . . . The
burning snaps him to . . . His left eye is gushing blood . . . It's pouring down
inside the lid and down his face and his face is on fire . . . Jesus Christ! . . .
the seat rig . . . The jerk of the parachute had suddenly slowed his speed, but
the seat kept falling . . . It had fallen out of the chute lines and the butt end
crashed into his visor . . . 180 pounds of metal . . . a double visor . . . the
goddamned thing has smashed through both layers . . . He's burning! . . .
There's rocket lava inside the helmet . . . The seat has fallen away . . . He
can't see . . . blood pouring out of his left eye and there's smoke inside the
helmet . . . Rubber! . . . It's the seal between the helmet and the pressure suit
. . . It's burning up . . . The propellant won't quit . . . A tremendous *whoosh*
. . . He can feel the rush . . . He can even hear it . . . The whole left side of
the helmet is full of flames . . . A sheet of flame goes up his neck and the side of
his face . . . The oxygen! . . . The propellant has burned through the rubber
seal, setting off the pressure suit's automatic oxygen system . . . The integrity of
the circuit has been violated and it rushes oxygen to the helmet, to the pilot's
face . . . A hundred percent oxygen! Christ! . . . It turns the lava into an
inferno . . . Everything that can burn is on fire . . . everything else is melting
. . . Even with the hole smashed in the visor the helmet is full of smoke . . .
He's choking . . . blinded . . . The left side of his head is on fire . . . He's
suffocating . . . He brings up his left hand . . . He has on pressure-suit gloves
locked and taped to the sleeve . . . He jams his hand in through the hole in the

visor and tries to create an air scoop with it to bring air to his mouth . . . The flames . . . They're all over it . . . They go to work on the glove where it touches his face . . . They devour it . . . His index finger is burning up . . . His goddamned finger is burning! . . . But he doesn't move it . . . Get some air! . . . Nothing else matters . . . He's gulping smoke . . . He has to get the visor open . . . It's twisted . . . He's encased in a little broken globe dying in a cloud of his own fried flesh . . . The stench of it! . . . rubber and a human hide . . . He has to get the visor open . . . It's that or nothing, no two ways about it . . . It's smashed all to hell . . . He jams both hands underneath . . . It's a tremendous effort . . . It lifts . . . Salvation! . . . Like a sea the air carries it all away, the smoke, the flames . . . The fire is out. He can breathe. He can see out of his right eye. The desert, the mesquite, the motherless Joshua trees are rising slowly toward him . . . He can't open his left eye . . . Now he can feel the pain . . . Half his head is broiled . .   That isn't the worst of it . . . The damned finger! . . . Jesus! . . . He can make out the terrain, he's been over it a million times . . . Over there's the highway, 466, and there's Route 6 crossing it . . . His left glove is practically burned off . . . The glove and his left index finger . . . he can't tell them apart . . . they look as if they exploded in an oven . . . He's not far from base . . . Whatever it is with the finger, it's very bad . . . Nearly down . . . He gets ready . . . Right out of the manual . . . A terrific wallop . . . He's down on the mesquite, looking across the desert, one-eyed . . . He stands up . . . Hell! He's in one piece! . . . He can hardly use his left hand. The goddamn finger is killing him. The whole side of his head . . . He starts taking off the parachute harness . . . It's all in the manual! Regulation issue! . . . He starts rolling up the parachute, just like it says . . . Some of the cords are almost melted through, from the lava . . . His head feels like it's still on fire . . . The pain comes from way down deep . . . But he's got to get the helmet off . . . It's a hell of an operation . . . He doesn't dare touch his head . . . It feels enormous . . . Somebody's running toward him . . . It's a kid, a guy in his twenties . . . He's come from the highway . . . He comes up close and his mouth falls open and he gives Yeager a look of stone horror . . .

"Are you all right!"

The look on the kid's face! Christalmighty!

"I was in my car! I saw you coming down!'

"Listen," says Yeager. The pain in his finger is terrific. "Listen . . . you got a knife?"

The kid digs into his pocket and pulls out a penknife. Yeager starts cutting the glove off his left hand. He can't bear it any more. The kid stands there hypnotized and horrified. From the look on the kid's face Yeager can begin to see himself. His neck, the whole left side of his head, his ear, his cheek, his eye must be burned up. His eye socket is slashed, swollen, caked shut, and covered with a crust of burned blood, and half his hair is burned away. The whole mess and the rest of his face and his nostrils and his lips are smeared with the sludge of the burning rubber. And he's standing there in the middle of the desert in a pressure suit with his head cocked, squinting out of one eye, working on his left glove with a penknife . . . The knife cuts through the glove and it cuts through the meat of his finger . . . You can't tell any longer . . . It's all run together . . . The goddamn finger looks like it's melted . . . He's got to get the glove off. That's all there is to it. It hurts too goddamned much. He pulls off the glove and a big hunk of melted meat from the finger comes off with it . . . It's like fried suet . . .

"Arrggghhh . . ." It's the kid. He's retching. It's too much for him, the poor bastard. He looks up at Yeager. His eyes open and his mouth opens. All the glue has come undone. He can't hold it together any longer.

"God," he says, "you . . . look *awful!"* The Good Samaritan, A.A.D.! Also a Doctor! And he just gave his diagnosis! That's all a man needs . . . to be forty years old and to fall one hundred goddamned thousand feet in a flat spin and punch out and make a million-dollar hole in the ground and get half his head and his hand burned up and have his eye practically ripped out of his skull . . . and have the Good Samaritan, A.A.D., arrive as if sent by the spirit of Pancho Barnes herself to render a midnight verdict among the motherless Joshua trees while the screen doors bang and the pictures of a hundred dead pilots rattle in their frames: "My God! . . . you look awful."

A FEW MINUTES LATER the rescue helicopter arrived. The medics found Yeager standing out in the mesquite, him and some kid who had been passing by. Yeager was standing erect with his parachute rolled up and his helmet in the crook of his arm, right out of the manual, and staring at them quite levelly out of what was left of his face, as if they had had an appointment and he was on time.

At the hospital they discovered one stroke of good luck. The blood over Yeager's left eye had been baked into a crustlike shield. Otherwise he might have lost it. He had suffered third- and second-degree burns on his head and neck. The burns required a month of treatment in the hospital, but he was able to heal without disfigurement. He even regained full use of his left index finger.

It so happened that on the day of Yeager's flight, at just about the time he headed down the runway on takeoff, the Secretary of Defense, Robert McNamara, announced that the X-20 program had been canceled. Although the Manned Orbiting Laboratory scheme remained alive officially, it was pretty obvious that there would be no American military space voyagers. The boys in Houston had the only ticket; the top of the pyramid was theirs to extend to the stars, if they were able.

Yeager was returned to flight status and resumed his duties at ARPS. In time he would go on to fly more than a hundred missions in Southeast Asia in B-57 tactical bombers.

No one ever broke the Russian mark with the NF-104 or even tried to. Up above 100,000 feet the plane's envelope was goddamned full of holes. And Yeager never again sought to set a record in the sky over the high desert.

EPILOGUE

W ELL, THE LORD GIVETH, and the Lord taketh away. After Gordon Cooper's triumph, Alan Shepard had launched a campaign for one more Mercury flight, a three-day mission, which it would be his turn to fly. He had the backing of Walt Williams and most of the astronauts. James Webb headed them off easily, however, with President Kennedy's tacit blessing, and announced that Project Mercury had been completed. NASA and the Administration were having a hard enough time keeping the Congress in line to support the $40 billion Gemini and Apollo lunar-landing programs without prolonging the Mercury series. The spirit of two years before, when Kennedy had raised his arms toward the moon and congressmen cheered and issued forth a limitless budget, had evaporated. The space race was a . . . "race for survival"? The United States faced . . . "national extinction"? Whoever controlled outer space . . . controlled the earth? The Russians were going to . . . put a red spot on the moon? It was impossible to recall the emotion of those days. In mid-June 1963 the Chief Designer (still the anonymous genius!) put *Vostok 5* into orbit with Cosmonaut Valery Bykovsky aboard, and two days later he sent the first woman into space, Cosmonaut Valentina Tereshkova, aboard *Vostok 6*, and they remained in orbit for three days, flying within three miles of each other at one point and landing on Soviet soil on the same day—and not even then did the old sense of warlike urgency revive in the Congress.

In July, Shepard began to be bothered by a ringing in his left ear and occasional dizziness, symptoms of Meunière's syndrome, a disease of the inner ear. Like Slayton, he had to go on inactive status as an astronaut and could only fly an aircraft with a co-pilot aboard. Slayton, meantime, had made a decision that would have been unthinkable to most military officers. He had resigned from the Air Force after nineteen years—one year short of qualifying for the twenty-year-man's pension, that golden reward that blazed out there beyond the horizon throughout the career officer's years of financial hardship. Slayton's problem was that the Air Force had decided to ground him altogether because of his heart condition. As a civilian working for NASA, he could continue to fly high-performance aircraft, so long as he was accompanied by a co-pilot. He could keep up his proficiency, he could remain on flight status, he could keep alive his hopes of proving, somewhere down the line, that he had the right stuff to go aloft as an astronaut, after all. Next to that consideration the pension didn't amount to much.

On July 19 Joe Walker flew the X-15 to 347,800 feet, which was sixty-six miles up, surpassing the record of 314,750 feet set by Bob White the year before; and on August 22 Walker reached 354,200 feet, or sixty-seven miles, which was seventeen miles into space. In addition to White and Walker, one other man had flown the X-15 above fifty miles. That was White's backup, Bob Rushworth, who had achieved 285,000 feet, fifty-four miles, in June. The Air Force had instituted the practice of awarding *Air Force Astronaut* wings to any Air Force pilot who flew above fifty miles. They used the term itself: *astronaut*. As a result, White and Rushworth, the Air Force's prime and backup pilots for the X-15, now had their astronaut wings. Joe Walker, being a civilian flying the X-15 for NASA, did not qualify. So some of Walker's good buddies at Edwards took him out to a restaurant for dinner, and they all knocked back a few, and they pinned some cardboard wings on his chest. The inscription read: "Asstronaut."

On September 28 the seven Mercury astronauts went to Los Angeles for the awards banquet of the Society of Experimental Test Pilots. Iven Kincheloe's widow, Dorothy, presented them with the Iven C. Kincheloe Award for outstanding professional performance in the conduct of flight test. The wire services devoted scarcely more than a paragraph to the occasion, and that they took from the handout. After all the Distinguished Service Medals and the parades and the appearances before Congress, after every sort of tribute that politicians, private institutions, and the Genteel Beast could devise, the Iven C. Kincheloe Award didn't seem like very much. But for the seven astronauts it was an important night. The radiant Kinch, the great blond movie-star picture of a pilot, was the most famous of the dead rocket pilots and could have cut his own orders in the Air Force, had he lived. He would have had Bob White's job as prime pilot of the X-15 and God knows what else. There were aviation awards and aviation awards, but the Kincheloe Award—for "professional performance"—was the big one within the flight test fraternity. The seven men had finally closed the circle and brought together the scattered glories of their celebrity. They had fought for a true pilot's role in Project Mercury, they had won it, step by step, and Cooper's flight, on top of the others, had shown they could handle it in the classic way, out on the edge. Now they had the one thing that had been denied them for years while the rest of the nation worshipped them so unquestioningly: acceptance by their peers, their true brethren, as *test pilots* of the space age, deserving occupants of the top of the pyramid of the right stuff.

During the summer Kennedy had gone on television to tell the nation that a nuclear test ban agreement with the Russians had been reached. Thereupon the Soviet foreign minister, Andrei Gromyko, had proposed a corollary that would ban even the placing of nuclear weapons in earth orbit. The Soviets themselves were extinguishing the notion of the thunderbolts from space. On August 30 there had gone into service the piece of equipment by which the entire interlude would be remembered: the hotline, a telephone hookup between the White House and the Kremlin, the better to avoid misunderstandings that might result in nuclear war. When Kennedy was assassinated on November 22 by a man with

Russian and Cuban ties, there was no anti-Soviet or anti-Cuban clamor in the Congress or in the press. The Cold War, as anyone could plainly see, was over.

No one, and certainly not the men themselves, could comprehend the meaning of this for the role of *the astronaut*, however. The new President, Lyndon Johnson, proved to be even more of a proponent of the space program than his predecessor. Due partly to the political genius of James E. Webb, who now came into his own, the Congress swung about and gave NASA a blank check for the missions to the moon. Nevertheless, the fact remained: the Cold War was over.

No more manned spaceflights were scheduled until the start of the Gemini program in 1965. By then the seven Mercury astronauts would begin to feel a change in the public attitude toward them and, for that matter, toward the Next Nine and the groups of astronauts that were to follow. They would *feel* the change, but they would not be able to put it into words. What *was* that feeling? Why, it was the gentle slither of the mantle of soldierly glory sliding off one's shoulders!—and the cooling effect of oceans of tears drying up! The single-combat warriors' war had been removed. They would continue to be honored, and men would continue to be awed by their courage: but the day when an astronaut could parade up Broadway while traffic policemen wept in the intersections was no more. Never again would an astronaut be perceived as a protector of the people, risking his life to do battle in the heavens. Not even the first American to walk on the moon would ever know the outpouring of a people's most primal emotions that Shepard, Cooper, and, above all, Glenn had known. The era of America's first single-combat warriors had come, and it had gone, perhaps never to be relived.

The Lord giveth, and the Lord taketh away. The mantle of Cold Warrior of the Heavens had been placed on their shoulders one April day in 1959 without their asking for it or having anything to do with it or even knowing it. And now it would be taken away, without their knowing that, either, and because of nothing they ever did or desired. John Glenn had made up his mind to run for the Senate in Ohio in 1964. He could not have foreseen that the voters of Ohio would no longer regard him as a man with a protector's aura. But at least he would be remembered. It would have been still more impossible for his confreres to realize that the day might come when Americans would hear their names and say, "Oh, yes—now, which one was he?"

AUTHOR'S NOTE

The writing of this book would have been impossible without the personal recollections of many people, pilots and non-pilots, who were intimately involved in the beginning of the era of manned rocket flight in America. I wish there were some way to thank them properly for their generosity and for the time and effort it took them to review events that go back twenty years or more in some cases.

The NASA history office at the Johnson Space Center in Houston was unfailingly helpful, especially in giving me access to transcriptions of the post-flight debriefings of the astronauts. I should mention in particular NASA historian James M. Grimwood, the author, with his colleagues, Loyd S. Swenson, Jr., and Charles C. Alexander, of *This New Ocean: a History of Project Mercury*. Other books I would like to acknowledge are *Always Another Dawn*, by A. Scott Crossfield with Clay Blair, Jr.; *Starfall*, by Betty Grissom and Henry Still; *Across the High Frontier*, by Charles E. Yeager and William Lundgren; *The Lonely Sky*, by William Bridgeman and Jacqueline Hazard; *X-15 Diary*, by Richard Tregaskis; and *We Seven*, by the seven Mercury astronauts.

The names of four figures appearing briefly in the narrative have been changed: Bud and Loretta Jennings, Mitch Johnson, and Gladys Loring.

ABOUT THE AUTHOR

Since he burst upon the literary scene as one of the founders of New Journalism in the mid-1960s, **Tom Wolfe** has produced eleven highly praised bestsellers, including *The Electric Kool-Aid Acid Test*, *The Pump House Gang* and *The Painted Word*. Tom Wolfe grew up in Richmond, Virginia, received a bachelor's degree from Washington and Lee University and a doctorate in American Studies from Yale University, and now lives in New York City.